ASP 3.0 Programmer's Reference

Richard Anderson, Dan Denault, Brian Francis,
Matthew Gibbs, Marco Gregorini, Alex Homer, Craig McQueen,
Simon Robinson, John Schenken, Kevin Williams

Wrox Press Ltd. ®

ASP 3.0 Programmer's Reference

Reprinted   June 2000

Published by Wrox Press Ltd
Arden House, 1102 Warwick Road, Acock's Green, Birmingham B27 6BH, UK
Printed in USA
ISBN 1-861003-23-4

Trademark Acknowledgements

Credits

Authors
Richard Anderson
Dan Denault
Brian Francis
Matthew Gibbs
Marco Gregorini
Alex Homer
Craig McQueen
John Schenken
Simon Robinson
Kevin Williams

Technical Reviewers
Duncan Godwin
Kevin Trojanowski
Gerry O'Brien
Jeff Johnson
Kevin Spencer
Joseph Bustos
John Timney

Additional Material
Bud Berrett
David Sussman

Design / Layout
Tom Bartlett
Mark Burdett
William Fallon
Jonathan Jones
Laurent Lafon

Editors
Julian Skinner
Jenny Watson
Chanoch Wiggers

Illustrations
William Fallon

Index
Martin Brooks

Cover Design
Chris Morris

Development Editor
Liz Toy

Project Manager
Sophie Edwards

Managing Editor
Joanna Mason

About the Authors

Richard Anderson

Richard Anderson is an established software developer who has worked with Microsoft technologies for nearly 10 years. He works for a small yet globally known software house in Peterborough (England), where he currently holds the position of "Research and Development Manager". What that means is that he plays with lots of great new technologies, and then tells people how they work, ensuring they are correctly understood and adopted correctly and successfully in new applications. He also writes applications, and is responsible for mentoring and managing C++ and VB developers. Richard can be contacted via his private email account rja@arpsolutions.demon.co.uk.

Daniel Denault

Daniel Denault is a developer and network administrator developing Internet applications and doing high security network configuration designs and installations in the behavioral healthcare industry. Dan Denault is also an independent consultant. These applications are developed using the following technologies customized ActiveX controls, ActiveX DLL's, Active Server Pages, Word and Excel OLE automation, JavaScript, VBScript, DHTML, IIS 4.0, and SQL Server 7.0. Daniel can be contacted at admin@csopgh.com.

Brian Francis

Brian Francis is the technical evangelist for NCR's Web Kiosk Solutions. Brian is responsible for enlightening NCR and their customers in the technologies and tools used for Web Kiosk Applications. Brian also uses the tools he evangelizes in developing solutions for NCR's customers. He has worked extensively with Wrox Press as a technical reviewer and has also co-authored on a number of projects including IE5 Programmer's Reference, Professional ASP 3.0 and Beginning ASP 3.0.

Matthew Gibbs

Matthew Gibbs is a software developer at Microsoft. He has spent the past several years as part of the Internet Information Services development team and is currently working on a new internet-based product. He continues to focus on improving performance and reliability for web technologies. Matthew is also pursuing a graduate degree from the University of Washington in Seattle where he resides with his wife, son and dog.

Marco Gregorini

Marco Gregorini is an independent software consultant and designer specialising in Component Object Model, C++ and server-side Web programming. He gives his technical advice as a free-lance, mostly in the telecommunications industry and industrial automation field. His favourite commitments have to do with the Net, focusing on the intersection between COM and Internet technologies. Feel free to get in touch with Marco at marcogregorini@msn.com.

Alex Homer

Alex Homer came to writing computer books through an unusual route, including tractor driver, warehouse manager, garden products buyer, glue sales specialist, and double-glazing salesman. With this wide-ranging commercial and practical background, and a love of anything that could be taken to pieces, computers were a natural progression. Now, when not writing books for Wrox, he spends his spare time sticking together bits of code for his wife's software company (Stonebroom Software - http://www.stonebroom.com) or just looking out of the window at the delightfully idyllic and rural surroundings of the Peak District in Derbyshire, England.

Craig McQueen

Craig McQueen is a Principal Consultant at Sage Information Consultants, Inc. His role at Sage is to guide clients in their adoption of Internet technologies into their existing businesses. Recently, he led an e-commerce implementation of Site Server at a major consumer electronics company. Previous to consulting, Craig led the development of two small retail Internet products: InContext WebAnalyzer and InContent FlashSite.
Craig has a Master of Science degree from the University of Toronto where he specialized in Human-Computer Interaction.

Simon Robinson

Simon Robinson lives in Lancaster, in the UK, where he shares a house with some students. He first encountered serious programming when he was doing his PhD in physics, modeling all sorts of weird things to do with superconductors and quantum mechanics. The experience of programming was nearly enough to put him off computers for life (though oddly, he seems to have survived all the quantum mechanics), and he tried for a while being a sports massage therapist instead. But then he realized how much money was in computers and wasn't in sports massage and rapidly got a job as a C++ programmer/researcher instead. (Simon is clearly the charitable, deep, spiritual type, who understands the true meaning of life). His programming work eventually lead him into writing, and he now makes a living mostly writing great books for programmers. He is also an honorary research associate at Lancaster University, where he does research in computational fluid dynamics with the environmental science department. You can visit Simon's web site at http://www.SimonRobinson.com.

John Schenken

John Schenken is a Software Test Lead on the Visual Basic Product Team. He has worked at Microsoft in software testing for three years. During that time he has worked on Visual Interdev, Microsoft Script Debugger, and Visual Basic. He has application development experience with BackOffice, Windows 2000 Component Services, Exchange, Active Server Pages, and ADO. He graduated from Texas A&M University with a computer science degree.

Kevin Williams

Kevin's first experience with computers was at the age of 10 (in 1980) when he took a BASIC class at a local community college on their PDP-9, and by the time he was 12, he stayed up for four days straight hand-assembling 6502 code on his Atari 400. His professional career has been focused on Windows development – first client-server, then on to Internet work. He's done a little bit of everything, from VB to Powerbuilder to Delphi to C/C++ to MASM to ISAPI, CGI, ASP, HTML, XML, and any other acronym you might care to name, but these days, he's focusing on XML work. Kevin is currently working with the Mortgage Bankers' Association of America to help them put together an XML standard for the mortgage industry.

Table of Contents

Table of Contents

The ASP Intrinsic Objects   59

Table of Contents

Table of Contents

Table of Contents

Table of Contents

Table of Contents

ActiveX Data Objects   373

Table of Contents

Table of Contents

Table of Contents

Performance and Security — 1007

Table of Contents

Miscellaneous Reference   1079

Table of Contents

Introduction

This book provides a reference to the ASP 3.0 Object Model and the surrounding technologies. It covers all the basic technologies and includes examples throughout.

The increasing integration between the Windows operating system, database services and other aspects including web services, have had a great impact on ASP 3.0. Many more packages, applications and services expose interfaces that enable ASP to utilize them. This increasing complexity, and increased opportunities, means that the distinctions between resources on the local system or network and the Internet are blurring and we, as Developers, must be aware of it. This increased access to resources means that much of the infrastructure has been built and debugged and if we choose to we can use this to our advantage.

In fact everywhere we look, much of the hard work has been done and we are left to concentrate on the business specific implementation of our applications. The popularity of ASP has placed at our disposal a great wealth of expertise. We are also not dependent on Microsoft – the prevalence of systems and companies which use ASP as the core technology means that we can rest assured that any problems will be resolved quickly, and in fact many of them already have.

What Is This Book About?

This book provides a reference to **Active Server Pages 3.0**, as included with **Windows 2000** and because ASP is now a core part of so many Web-oriented features within Windows, this book covers a far wider area than just how ASP works. ASP is maturing all the time to integrate with other Windows services and software, and so there are many other areas that impinge directly on the use and performance of ASP.

We will examine the core features of ASP 3.0, laying down a foundation on which you can start to build or enhance your applications. The book contains handy examples in both VBScript and JScript, and a coordinated reference to the methods and properties most useful to the developer.

We will look in particular at the new security features of Windows 2000 through Active Directory, and the Internet server software that comes with Windows 2000 – Internet Information Server (IIS). This provides us with exciting additions including messaging and transaction services through COM+.

The integration with COM and ActiveX means that ASP can effectively access anything on the web server, or a connected network (and this includes the Internet), which provides a suitable interface. From this alone, a huge market has grown for components and objects that implement or encapsulate specific functions. Furthermore, almost all installed software and services in Windows either include a set of service-specific ActiveX components, or directly expose a COM interface, which allows ASP to access it.

One of the most essential parts of any business-aware application is the maintenance of, and access to, data sources. Without these we have no customer base, no control over resource access and no guide as to the effectiveness of our application. One of the most obvious of these is access to data in a relational database or other type of data store (such as Active Directory), and you'll see several chapters devoted to these topics. To add to this we have also investigated access to content within the directory of the local and networked drives.

We'll also look at the development of COM to give us COM+ and see how this affects the way our applications are designed and built.

There are also some fundamental changes in the IIS/COM(+) relationship, which it's important that you grasp. If you didn't really do much with COM and MTS in version 2.0 of ASP (a lot of people managed to ignore them), then now is the time to get to grips with them and start building pages and components to integrate with it.

Who Is This Book For?

Version 3.0 of ASP heralds a level of stability in ASP. There have not been many significant changes made from version 2.0 except the addition of services. This book is designed to be useful to several groups of people. Firstly it is aimed at the experienced, practicing developer who needs comprehensive reference to the functionality and scope of ASP, where key information is easy to find. Secondly it is aimed at those who are coming from other web development backgrounds and who are looking to expand their skills, transfer their applications to or provide additional functionality to the sites. If you need to find out what ASP is capable of then this book will give you a good overview.

We will cover what changes have been made both to ASP and to it's supporting languages JScript and VBScript. We cover in details the new technologies available for us to exploit.

For newcomers to web applications and dynamic web page creation, we recommend you look at *Beginning Active Server Pages 3.0* (ISBN 1-861003-38-2) first.

What Does This Book Cover?

Conceptually, this book is divided into several sections. This allows us to cover widely differing ASP-related topics in an orderly sequence, and helps you to grasp the basics of the way that ASP works before going on to learn about higher-level features that depend on these core topics. Each chapter provides a concise reference to a specific element of ASP or associated technology.

❑ We first quickly cover the basics of ASP and its relationship with Windows 2000. We will also look at the implications of Windows DNA for ASP and ASP applications.

❑ Section I covers ASP's intrinsic objects. We examine the Application object, cover the use of sessions and the Session object, and discuss the Request and Response objects – the backbone of ASP. We also cover the ASPError object.

❑ Section II introduces the Scripting objects. We look at access to our system, the variables defined on our server and the level of control we can exert over the system's associated drives through the Scripting objects.

❑ Section III covers Active Server Components. A set of components is provided with IIS to cover the basic functionality required by the majority of Internet applications. We examine the Ad Rotator's ability to manage advertising on the site, and discuss the Browser capabilities component. We also cover content management with the Content Linking and the Content Rotator components and other essential services.

❑ Section IV covers **ActiveX Data Objects (ADO)**, the de-facto communication technology for all Microsoft applications, plus a look at **data shaping**.

❑ Section V covers Transactions and Message Queuing, XML, and the associated XSLT and XPath technologies. We also examine Active Directory Service Interfaces (ADSI), CDO and Indexing Services and how they impact on ASP.

❑ Section VI will cover Performance and Security and discusses how our choices affect the server's ability to service our client request.

❑ Section VII contains further useful **reference material** in the form of **appendices** including the constants you will need and a section of certificate services. Language references for JScript and VBScript are available for download from the Wrox Web site, with the other sample files for this book. This section also contains details of discussion forums and support provided by Wrox for this book.

What Do I Need To Use This Book?

You always know when you get to this point in a book what it's going to say. Yes, you need to have Active Server Pages installed to be able to use this book to the full. However, let's take a slightly more scientific approach than that. The requirements are:

Hardware

A machine with Windows 2000 installed to act as a Web server. Preferably this should be Windows 2000 Server or better. However, Internet Information Server and most of the associated services (with some exceptions) are included with Windows 2000 Professional (which replaces Windows NT Workstation) as options. For Windows 2000 Server, you should aim for a machine with at least a 233MHz processor, and at least 128MB of RAM (256MB is better). For Windows 2000 Professional, you can get away with 64MB of RAM, though 128MB makes it smoother and more relaxing to use. You can run Internet Information Server 5.0 with ASP 3.0 on a Windows 9x machine, however we are concentrating in this book only on Windows 2000.

A client machine connected to the Windows 2000 machine via TCP/IP. While you can develop directly on the web server, it's usually better to use a separate client machine, although you will still need access to the web server in order to transfer your ASP scripts across to it. All you need for the client is something capable of running a web browser. The browser we are using predominantly is Internet Explorer 5.0 (IE5), though you can use another if you prefer. However, some examples that take advantage of IE5-specific features will probably fail to work on other browsers. The network between the machines should include TCP/IP amongst the active protocols. In fact, you only need TCP/IP—the rest can be disabled or uninstalled when working with ASP.

> If you are working on a corporate network, be sure to check with your system administrator before changing the network protocol installation or setup.

Non-Microsoft Platforms

As Active Server Pages has gained popularity within the Web-development community, the limitation of running only on a Windows platform has been seen as a problem. Two companies have moved to spread the coverage of ASP to enable ASP scripts to run on other platforms and operating systems:

- ❑ The best known of these it **Chili!ASP**© (http://www.chilisoft.com) which is functionally equivalent to ASP. It utilizes the same development tools and functionality as ASP but runs on Netscape, Lotus Go, as well as NT 4.0-based Web servers.

- ❑ The second ASP look-alike is Halcyon Software's **Instant ASP**™ (http://www.halcyonsoft.com), which runs on a whole range of Web server, application server, and operating system platforms. These include Windows NT, Sun, Novell, AIX, AS/400, S/390, Apple, OS/2, Linux, Apache, Netscape, Websphere, and more.

We aren't covering these environments directly in this book, as we are concentrating on ASP 3.0 running on Internet Information Server version 5 and Windows 2000

Server. However, the knowledge you gain will apply to the other ASP-like environments as well, though you will need to confirm the actual range of coverage and compatibility on your chosen platform and operating system from the relevant supplier.

Software

Almost all of the software you'll need is included in a full installation of Windows 2000 Server. After the main OS installation has completed, and you reboot the server, Internet Explorer fires up with a page entitled Windows 2000 Configure Your Server:

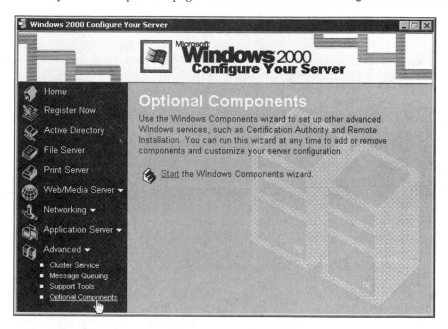

You can use this page to install the extra services and applications that you want to run on the server. You'll need to select the Advanced option and then Optional Components in the left-hand menu, then Start the Windows Components Wizard in the right-hand window to install IIS and the other web-related software such as the Indexing Services, Clustering Services, Message Queuing Services, etc. If you want to install Active Directory, you must also first install and set up DNS from this page, then select the Active Directory option. There are Wizards that will step you through each of the processes, and they generally make the whole task very simple.

There are other items of software that you may like to install as you use this book. There are several server components that we include with the sample files, or which we provide links to so that you can download them from the original source. The sample files you'll see used in this book can all be downloaded from our own web sites at:

```
http://webdev.wrox.co.uk/books/3234
http://www.wrox.com/Store/Details.asp?Code=3234
```

Development Tools

Probably the most obvious development tool for working with ASP is Microsoft's own **Visual Studio** package, or even just **Visual InterDev** (one of the components of Visual Studio) on its own. Visual InterDev, especially in the latest version, provides a whole range of editing, debugging and code building tools. There are also many Wizards to help you get the job done more quickly.

As well as Visual InterDev, Visual Studio contains **Visual Basic** and **Visual C++**, both of which are good for building your own Active Server Components for use in your Web applications. You can also build Active Server Components using any other COM-enabled language such as other C++ development environments, Delphi, J++, PowerBuilder, etc.

Other companies also provide tools to build ASP pages and complete web applications, including Drumbeat© (http://www.elementalsw.com), Fusion© 3.0 (http://www.netobjects.com), HAHTSite© (http://www.haht.com), Cold Fusion© (http://www.allaire.com), XBuilder© (http://www.signmeup.com) and many others.

If you are a hardened keyboard hacker, and don't like anything to get in the way of writing code your way, you might prefer to use a simple text editor to create ASP pages instead. You can even build them using a pure HTML page creation tool (such as Microsoft FrontPage), and then insert your ASP script afterwards. The old favorite ASP tool, Windows **NotePad**, will do quite nicely, though something that includes line numbers (to help in locating errors) is more useful. We've been using **TextPad**© (http://www.textpad.com) for some time, and find it a great improvement over **NotePad**. Not only do you get a multiple document interface with line numbers and macros, but may other useful options and add-ins as well.

There are other tools and add-ins that we use for specific tasks, particularly load testing and performance measurement, and you'll find these described in several places throughout the book. For a useful list of the various tools that are available, take a look at the Tools page at the 15 Seconds Web site (http://www.15seconds.com/tool/default.htm).

Conventions

We use a number of different styles of text and layout in the book to help differentiate between the different kinds of information. Here are examples of the styles we use and an explanation of what they mean.

Bullets appear indented, with each new bullet marked as follows:

- ❑ **Important Words** are in a bold type font.
- ❑ Words that appear on the screen, such as menu options, are in a similar font to the one used on screen, for example the File | New... menu. The levels of a cascading menu are separated by a pipe character (|).
- ❑ Keys that you press on the keyboard, like *Ctrl* and *Enter*, are in italics.

Code has several styles. If it's a word that we're talking about in the text, such as a `For...Next` loop or a file name like `Default.asp`, we'll use `this font`. If it's a block of code that is new, important or relevant to the current discussion, it will be presented like this:

```
<%
    Response.Write "Professional ASP 3.0"
%>
```

Sometimes, you'll see code in a mixture of styles, like this:

```
<%
    Response.Write "Professional ASP 3.0"
    Response.Write "...enjoy the book"
%>
```

The code with a white background is code we've already looked at, or that has little to do with the matter at hand.

> *Advice, hints, background information, references and extra details appear in an italicized, indented font like this.*

These boxes hold important, not-to-be forgotten, mission-critical details that are directly relevant to the surrounding text.

1

What is ASP?

Since its introduction, the use of Microsoft's **Active Server Pages**, or ASP, has grown rapidly. Many programmers consider it *the* tool for dynamic, easily maintainable web content. The real power of ASP derives firstly from the fact that the HTML for the page is only generated when the specific page is requested by the user, and secondly from the fact that it is browser-independent, since what is sent to the browser is usually purely HTML (although it can also include client-side code), rather than relying on the browser to support a particular language or application.

ASP enables us to tailor our web pages to the specific requirements of our users and their browser type, as well as our own needs. It allows us to interact with the user, which helps to keep our site interesting and up-to-date. Although it is not the first technology to offer dynamic page creation, it is one of the fastest and most powerful. It is indicative of the impact that ASP has made that it has now got its own imitators.

This book is for primarily intended for developers who need a reference to the many ways in which ASP contributes to the running of web sites and the resources we can utilize to achieve that goal. In order to get the maximum benefit from this book you will need to have some understanding of both ASP and the Web in general. Some knowledge of a scripting language such as VBScript or JScript is assumed.

This is the book for you if you need easy access to the methods and properties which the different components and objects expose, you are looking to expand the scope and functionality of your site, or you are fairly new to ASP and need an overview of what it has to offer. We hope that you benefit from and enjoy this book.

Firstly in this chapter we explore where ASP is derived from, look at some of the essential building blocks of ASP and briefly explore what is new to ASP 3.0. We look at:

❑   The origins of ASP

❑   ASP, HTTP, HTML and IIS

❑   Managing state on the Web

❑   The role of `global.asa`

- ❑ ASP directives
- ❑ Virtual applications
- ❑ What's new in ASP version 3.0
- ❑ What's new in JScript 5.0
- ❑ What's new in VBScript 5.0

The Origins of ASP

At the same time that the huge business potential of the Web was being realised, the limitations of HTML and HTTP were also becoming very apparent to developers. The static, stateless nature of HTML pages means that, although they are great for 'on-line brochure' web sites, they do not meet the specific needs and requirements of fast-moving business, building customer loyalty and selling goods and services. Various technologies, including ASP, grew out of the need to create pages with content specific to an individual user.

A simple type of customer interaction is processing information entered by a user on an HTML form. This normally involves either a user searching for information, or alternatively the customer entering personal information that needs to be stored by a business for further processing. In either case, we probably want to communicate with a database, which cannot be done purely using HTML. The initial solution to these, and other applications that are equally problematic with HTML and HTTP, involved reading the user input and programmatically creating a response. The interface which the server exposed to connect HTML and other applications became known as the Common Gateway Interface (CGI), and can be implemented in any language (the most popular being Perl). This approach, however, requires developers to have extensive programming knowledge and is restricted by the need to compile the code. Although Perl and CGI are still valuable tools, several alternatives are now also available, including ASP. This enables sections of script to be embedded in HTML pages. ASP-embedded code can contain logic which inserts content, formats data and carries out actions depending on decisions relating to how a page is requested.

ASP, HTTP, HTML and IIS

HyperText Transfer Protocol (HTTP) is the protocol that handles requests and responses sent between a web server and browser. The HTTP Request is the format of any message sent from the client to a server. It includes the URL of the required resource and information about the client and the platform they are using. The HTTP Response can contain a resource, a redirection to another page or site, an error message, etc.

ASP provides its own `Request` and `Response` objects, which enable us to access the information stored in the HTTP Request message and Response headers respectively. Using these objects we can check for certificates, read and write cookies, and get access to browser information and forms data. We can insert data into the body of the page to be sent to the client, redirect the browser, check if the client is connected, and manage the sending of content so that the client does not wait for too long for long sections of content.

The relationship between ASP and HTML can be described as follows:

> **Active Server Pages is a technology that allows for the programmatic construction of HTML pages for delivery to the browser.**

In other words, with ASP we can write a set of instructions that can be used to generate HTML and other content just before it is delivered. This makes it a good tool for HTML developers, because of its power and flexibility to generate fresher HTML, and ultimately produce more spectacular, interactive, personalized and up-to-date web sites.

But what actually *is* ASP? It's not a conventional programming language in the sense that Pascal and C++ are, although it does make use of existing scripting languages such as VBScript or JScript. It's also not an application in the sense that FrontPage and Word are. The best way to think of ASP is as a technology for building dynamic and interactive web pages.

An alternative way to create dynamic pages is to use client-side scripting. This must be written in a language interpreted by the client browser and hence code generally consists of sections of Javascript embedded in an HTML page. This can programmatically control the layout of the page, how the page reacts to user actions and what is shown on the page. This is all useful but has its limitations. Typical uses for client-side code are, for example, to respond to user actions like clicking their mouse on the page, passing it over certain hotspots, and also checking forms prior to sending them.

Client-side code depends on the browser supporting the scripting language, and can fall over if the language is not supported, or includes code which differs between implementations and language versions. A second limitation is that the code is accessible to the user, which makes it unsuitable for passing, for example, passwords and connection strings.

The alternative then, and this is what ASP relies on, is to include scripts which are processed by the server. These server-side scripts do not depend on the browser or the user's platform executing, as the result returned to the browser is typically in plain HTML (or text, XML etc). However, server-side script is often used in conjunction with client-side code – there's no reason why an ASP page can't contain <SCRIPT> sections.

IIS (previously called Internet Information Server, but renamed with IIS5 to **Internet Information Services**) was Microsoft's answer to dynamic page creation by servers. Originally IIS 1.0 consisted of a fairly standard setup with CGI support and an interface to allow more efficient execution of compiled applications written in languages like C and C++. It provided additional features to access the input and output streams. This interface is called the **Internet Server Application Programming Interface**, or **ISAPI**.

The ASP scripting engine still uses ISAPI to connect to IIS5. It runs in-process with the server. This means that it shares the same memory space with the server and can get direct access to values in that memory. This does mean that if the application fails it can cause the server to fail, but makes for a very efficient and fast process and generally gives ASP the edge over other technologies.

What does ASP Code Look Like?

When a web author writes an ASP page, it is likely to be composed of a combination of three types of syntax – some ASP, some HTML tags, and some pure text. The following table summarizes these ingredients, their purpose, and their appearance:

Type	Purpose	Interpreter	Hallmarks
Text	This is hard-coded information to be shown to the user	The viewer's browser shows the text	Simple ASCII text.
HTML tags	This consists of instructions to the browser about how to format text and display images	The viewer's browser interprets the tags to format the text	Each tag within < > delimiters. Most HTML tags come in pairs (an open tag and a close tag), e.g. `<TABLE>`, `</TABLE>`.
ASP statements	This consists of instructions to the web server running ASP about how to create portions of the page to be sent out	The web server's DLL `asp.dll` performs the ASP commands	Each ASP section contained within `<%` `%>` delimiters. ASP statements support features such as variables, decision trees, cyclical repetitions etc.

The file containing these constituent parts of the ASP page is saved with an `.asp` extension.

It's not too hard to distinguish the different elements of the ASP page. Anything that falls between the `<%` and `%>` markers is **ASP script**, and will be processed on the web server by the ASP script engine.

Lets take a look at an example and at the same time demonstrate one of the keys to ASP's success – how easy it is to get started. For example, consider the few lines of code below:

```
<HTML>
<P>This date/time is now : <%= Now() %> </P>
</HTML>
```

The content of the resulting web page depends on the HTML that is generated by the ASP code. In this particular example, the effect of the script code is to generate HTML for the time and date that the page is requested, and then to make a decision (based on the situation) on what text will be sent to the browser as part of the HTML stream.

How does ASP Work

ASP works with a single DLL called `asp.dll` (or alternatively the ASP scripting engine). This is installed by default into your `WinNT\System32\Inetsrv` directory. This DLL is responsible for taking an ASP page (indicated by the `.asp` file extension) and parsing it for any server-side script content. The script is passed to the appropriate scripting engine, to interpret for example the VBScript or JScript. The results of executing the script are combined with any text and HTML in the ASP page and the completed page is then sent back the client browser via the web server.

To see this, open the Internet Services Manager from the Administrative Tools section of your Start menu (for Windows 2000 Server version – or go to it via Administrative Tools in your Control Panel with Windows 2000 Professional). This runs the Microsoft Management Console (MMC) to display the entire Internet Information Services tree for IIS, which looks something like this:

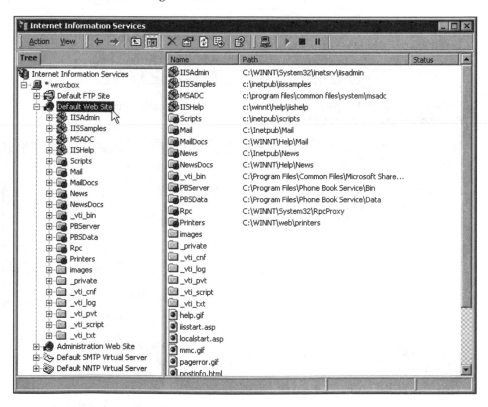

Right-click on the Default Web Site entry and select Properties, then the Home Directory page:

In the lower half of the page there is a name for the application and the Execute Permissions and Application Protection settings.

Then, click the Configuration button to open the Application Configuration dialog. In the App Mappings tab, you can see the way that IIS links each type of file (using the file extension) with a specific DLL:

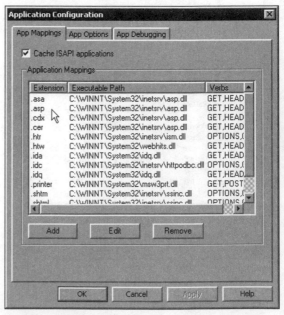

Any pages that have the `.asp` file extension are sent to the `asp.dll` for processing; you can see our `global.asa` page (which we discuss later in this chapter) is also mapped to the asp DLL, as well as several others. Pages with file extensions that are *not* mapped to a DLL, for example `.html` and `.htm` for HTML pages, and `.xml` for XML files, are simply loaded from disk and sent directly to the client.

You might like to have a look at the other file types in this page. Pages with
`.ida`, `.idc`, *and* `.idq` *file extensions are sent to the DLL*
`httpodbc.dll` *for processing. As you can guess from its name, it uses*
ODBC (discussed later in this book) to execute a SQL statement that returns a
set of records for inclusion in the page. Likewise, the `.shtm`, `.shtml` *and*
`.stm` *file extensions are mapped to a DLL named* `ssinc.dll`*. These file*
*types are traditionally used for files that require **server-side include (SSI)***
processing.

While you have the Application Configuration and Properties dialogs open, you might
want to briefly explore it (just don't change any settings for the moment, unless you're
sure that you know what you're doing, the defaults usually suffice!).

Processing an ASP File

When `asp.dll` receives an ASP page, it converts it to an output suitable for the server
to send to the client. It deals with any script marked for its attention, evaluating it, and
sending the result on to the server. It does this by first checking the page to see if
contains any ASP code. If it does not find any, it informs IIS to send the page to the
client. A new feature of Windows 2000 means that this is done with no marked
performance penalty.

When ASP receives a page that does contain server-side scripting, it parses it line by
line and each section of script is passed to the approroate scripting engine for
compiling and execution. The result of this is inserted into any content which does not
require server intervention by ASP and the whole is passed on to the client.

To make this more efficient, ASP caches the compiled code so that it does not need to be
compiled again unless the source is changed. The result of this is that subsequent
requests for the specific page are returned more quickly as the compilation stage is
bypassed.

Including Separate Script Files

An additional feature is the ability to include separate files that contain script code. This
allows us to write generic functions and both encourages and greatly simplifies code reuse. It also allows us to encapsulate processes which depend on the setup of our system
and our server, and so may change.

Scripting Performance Issues

Web servers generally have plenty of spare processor cycles available (except on the
busiest of sites) because the main task they have is loading pages from disk and sending
them to the client. Therefore, each page request results in the processor waiting for the
disk to respond. These spare cycles mean that ASP scripts can usually be executed with
very little overall hit on performance. To add to this, as most page requests will be for
pages where a compiled version of the script code is available, only the execution of this
script needs to take place.

Of course, as the number of requests, and hence the server load, increases, the effect of
having to parse and execute each ASP page takes its toll. It's wise, therefore, to squeeze
as much performance as possible from the ASP interpreter. Here are some useful tips:

Avoid Mixing Scripting Languages on the Same Page

Using both scripting languages on any one page has an effect on the execution order of the code. This will mean both scripting engines will be loaded by the ASP DLL, increasing memory usage and the time taken to process the request.

Avoid Excessive Context Switching Between Script and Other Content

Having sections of ASP interspersed within other content can have a significant effect on the time it takes to process the page request. Every time a section of script ends, control is passed back to IIS (and vice versa) and this will have an impact on performance. An alternative to this is to use the Response.Write method (rather than using <% = ...%>) and this is recommended for any but small sections of code.

Build a Separate Component

For any complex processes, consider building a separate componant to install on the server. This will be far more efficient than instantiating and interpreting ASP script code. This will become even more important with the next version of ASP (currently called ASP+) in which almost everything is done using COM+.

Managing State on the Web

In a normal single-user program, such as when we build an executable application (an .exe file for example) using C++, Delphi etc., we take for granted the fact that we can declare a global (or Public) variable and then access it from anywhere in our code. All the time the application is running, the value remains valid and accessible.

The ability to hold values in memory, and relate specific values to specific users, provides **state**. You can think of it as representing the values and context of the applications' and users' internal variables throughout the life of the application.

When we create web-based **applications**, we often need be able to provide an individual *state* for each user. This might be as simple as remembering their name, or as complex as storing object references or recordsets that are different for each user. If we can't do that, we can't reasonably expect to do anything that requires more than *one* ASP page, as the variables and other references in that page are all destroyed when the page is finished executing. When the user requests the next page, we've lost all the information that they've already provided.

It is also useful to be able to store values that are global to *all* users. An obvious example is a web-style visitor counter. There's not much point in giving each user their own counter, because they usually want to see the total number of visitors, not just the number of times that they have visited. The number of visitors needs to be stored with **application-level state**, rather than **user-level state**.

With ASP we need a way of storing state information, otherwise variables and references within a page are destroyed when that page has finished execution. One of the ways of providing state between page requests and site visits is through **cookies**, which are sent along with each page request to the domain for which the cookie is valid. ASP uses a cookie to provide the concept of a user **session**, which we interact with through the ASP Session object.

A new and separate `Session` object is created for each individual visitor when they first access an ASP page on the server. A session identifier number is allocated to the session, and a cookie containing a specially encrypted version of the session identifier is sent to the client. The `Path` of the cookie (see the previous chapter for a description of cookie properties) is set to the path of the root of the ASP application running on our server. This will be the root of the Default Web site (i.e. "/") or the root directory of the ASP application containing the page they request. No `Expires` value is provided in the cookie, so it will expire when the browser is closed.

Every time that this user accesses an ASP page, ASP looks for this cookie, named `ASPSESSIONIDxxxxxxxx`, where each *x* is an alphabetic character. If found, it can be used to connect the visitor with their current `Session`, which is held in memory on the server.

This cookie doesn't appear in the `Request.Cookies` or `Response.Cookies` collections. ASP hides it from us, but it's still there on the browser and ASP looks for it with each ASP page request.

If the client browser doesn't accept or support cookies, each new page request forces a new session to be created, thus state cannot be maintained without cookies.

As a warning you might note that if the browser does not support, or is set to reject, cookies this function will not be available. What do we do then? An alternative is to have server-side cookies. The information is stored on the server and matched to each user. We can then persistently store information on that user for a length of time determined by ourselves. This just leaves matching the user to their information and this can be done with the use of logins. Each time that a user enters the domain of our server they can be asked to log in with their name and password. We can then make our site available to them according to their specific needs and preferences.

In addition we can restrict access to resources so that we can expose varying levels of access to the general public, clients of the company or subscribers, staff or site administrators. Now we are starting to have a level of control over our site which in any other application we might take for granted.

The Role of global.asa

All ASP applications can contain a file named `global.asa`, placed in the root directory of the application and which applies to all sub-directories of this. The `global.asa` file in the root directory of the entire web site (`Inetpub\wwwroot`) defines the whole site as being part of the **Default ASP application**.

The `global.asa` file can contain code that instantiates objects and creates and sets the values of variables that will be available in either **Application-level** or **Session-level** scope. Object instances can be created using the `Server.CreateObject` method or an `<OBJECT>` element.

Creating Object Instances

If an `<OBJECT>` element is used, the `SCOPE` attribute can be set to `"Application"` or `"Session"`, and the object is then created in the appropriate context:

```
<!-- Declare ASPCounter component with application-level scope -->
<OBJECT ID="ASPCounter" RUNAT="Server" SCOPE="Application"
       PROGID="MSWC.Counters">
</OBJECT>

<!-- Declare ASPContentLink component with session-level scope -->
<OBJECT ID="ASPContentLink" RUNAT="Server" SCOPE="Session"
       PROGID="MSWC.NextLink">
</OBJECT>
...
```

The remainder of the `global.asa` file can contain ASP script that defines event handlers that run when the application or a user session starts or ends. Using VBScript this looks like:

```
...
<SCRIPT LANGUAGE="VBScript" RUNAT="Server">

Sub Application_OnStart()
   'Code here is executed when the application starts
End Sub

Sub Application_OnEnd()
   'Code here is executed when the application ends
End Sub

Sub Session OnStart()
   'Code here is executed when a user session starts
End Sub

Sub Session_OnEnd()
   'Code here is executed when a user session ends
End Sub

</SCRIPT>
```

Or using JScript:

```
...
<SCRIPT LANGUAGE=JScript RUNAT=Server>

function Application_OnStart() {
   // Code here is executed when the application starts
}

function Application_OnEnd() {
   // Code here is executed when the application ends
}

function Session OnStart() {
   // Code here is executed when a user session starts
}

function Session_OnEnd() {
   // Code here is executed when a user session ends
}

</SCRIPT>
```

Within the `OnStart` event handlers, script code can be used to instantiate objects with the `Server.CreateObject` method. This code creates an instance of the Ad Rotator component (see Chapter 15):

```
Set Session("ASPAdRotator") = Server.CreateObject("MSWC.AdRotator")
```

If placed in the `Application_OnStart` event handler, the object will have application-level scope. If placed in the `Session_OnStart` event handler, the object will have session-level scope, i.e. each visitor will have a separate instance of the object. The `Server.CreateObject` method is covered in detail in Chapter 7.

Referencing Object Type Libraries

Many objects and components provide enumerated and other constants which the various methods take as their paramters. This allows us to use the constant's name in place of its value. These constants can be referenced through the `METADATA` directive. Using the `METADATA` directive we can specify a type-library which ASP will then load when the page is executed. The syntax for this is shown below:

```
<!-- METADATA TYPE="TypeLib"
          FILE="path_and_name_of_file" | UUID="type_library_uuid"
          [VERSION="major_version_number.minor_version_number"]
          LCID="locale_id" -->
```

where:

❑ `path_and_name_of_file` is the absolute physical path to a type library file (`.tlb`) or ActiveX DLL. If this is not provided the `type_library_uuid` must be specified.

❑ `type_library_uuid` is the unique identifier for the type library. Either this or the `path_and_name_of_file` parameter must be provided.

❑ `major_version_number.minor_version_number` (optional) defines the version of the component required. If this version is not found the most recent version is used.

❑ `locale_id` (optional) is the locale identifier to be used. If a type library with this locale is not found the default locale for the machine (defined during setup) will be used.

For example, this code makes the intrinsic ADO pre-defined constants available in an ASP page:

```
<!-- METADATA TYPE="TypeLib"
          FILE="c:\Program Files\Common Files\System\ado\msado15.dll"
-->
```

In order to maintain backward compatibility the file name `msado15.dll` is used for later (i.e. ADO 2.5) versions of the ADO component.

If ASP is unable to load the type library, it will return an error and halt execution of the page. The possible error values are:

Error	Description
ASP 0222	'Invalid type library specification'.
ASP 0223	'Type library not found'.
ASP 0224	'Type library cannot be loaded'.
ASP 0225	'Type library cannot be wrapped' (i.e. ASP cannot create a type library wrapper object from the type library specified).

Web Applications

We have used the term web application a number of times rather loosely, to indicate something that isn't really a web site, but isn't a 'traditional' application (an .exe file for example) either. We can think of a web application as a set of web pages and other resources, such as COM+ objects, that are designed to carry out some task.

A COM object is an instance of a COM component, which should be thought of as a compiled piece of code that can provide a service to the system, not just a single application. (COM objects are discussed further in Chapter 2, ASP, Windows 2000 and Windows DNA.)

When IIS and ASP are installed in Windows 2000, a **Default Web Site** is created. This is configured as an ASP application, which involves several settings in the **Properties** dialog, that we looked at earlier. The global.asa is used to determine the way that this default application behaves.

Virtual Applications

In addition to the default web application, ASP virtual applications can be created in any subdirectory of the web site. All sub-directories will then be part of this virtual application. Now, because the directory is itself within the default application for the site, this means that it will share the global space created by the default Application object. Any variables stored in the default application are available within the application; however, if an ASP page in the virtual application overwites a global value, the original value is maintained for the root application. This offers some protection to the server and other applications running alongside.

Creating ASP Virtual Applications

In **Internet Services Manager**, right-click on the directory in which you wish to create the new virtual application, select **New**, then **Virtual Directory**. This starts the **New Virtual Directory Wizard**, which steps through the settings required. This includes the name (or **alias**) for the new virtual application. Combined with the path of the directory selected in **Internet Services Manager**, this will become the URL of the application. To convert an existing directory into an application with the same name as the directory, select the directory containing the one you want to convert and use the directory name in the **Virtual Directory Alias** page of the wizard.

The wizard also allows you to specify the path that contains the content (pages) for the application. You can click **Browse** to select an existing directory. This is the directory that the new virtual application will point to. The final step allows you to select the access permissions, with the default being **Read** and **Run Scripts**. These settings can be changed later if required. The wizard then creates the new application, and marks it in **Internet Services Manager** with an 'open box' icon:

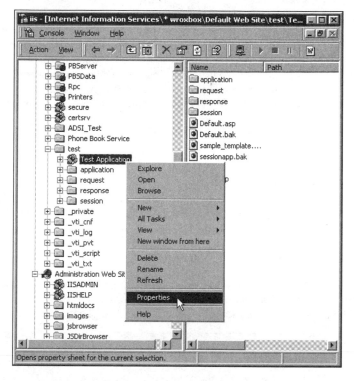

Right-click the new application and select Properties to see the settings that the wizard has chosen. The Local Path, access permissions, and Application Settings can be changed here if required. You'll also see a Remove button, which we can use to remove the virtual application:

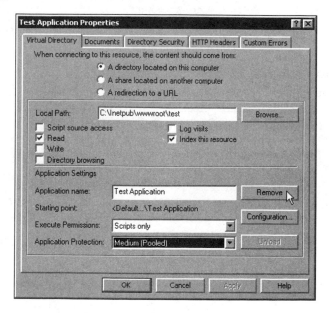

Clicking the Remove button doesn't actually remove the entry in Internet Services Manager. Instead, it converts the existing virtual application into a **virtual directory**. It will have a 'folder' icon with a 'globe' on it, indicating that this is a *redirection* to another folder on disk. It is accessed in the same way as the virtual application from which it was created (i.e. using the same URL), but does not act as an application. In other words, it doesn't support its own Application object but inherits the one for the default web site, or for another application within this directory's parent directories.

To delete a virtual application, select Delete from the right-click shortcut menu for the application in Internet Services Manager.

Virtual Application Configuration

Virtual applications provide control and management of objects and components that are instantiated in pages within that application's directories. The settings for a virtual application provide control over whether objects are created in the memory space of the web server, or separately in shared or individual out-of-process instances of DLLHost.dll.

The Properties dialog in Internet Services Manager provides these settings. At the bottom of the Home Directory page of the Properties dialog for a virtual application are two combo boxes marked Execute Permissions and Application Protection:

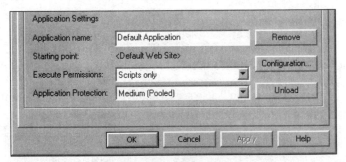

Application Protection and Execution Settings

The Execute Permissions options are:

Execute Permission	Description
None	No scripts or executables can be run in this virtual application. In effect, this provides a quick and easy way to disable an application if required.
Scripts Only	Allows only script files, such as ASP, IDC or others to run in this virtual application. Executables cannot be run.
Scripts and Executables	Allows any script or executable to run within this virtual application.

While the Execute Permissions options control the type of execution that can take place in the virtual application, the Application Protection options affect the way that executables and components are run. The available options are:

Application Protection	Description
Low (IIS Process)	All application executables and components for ASP virtual applications with this setting are run in the process (i.e. the memory space) of the web server executable (Inetinfo.exe). Hence the web server is at risk if any one of the executables or components should fail. This provides the fastest and least resource-intensive application execution option.
Medium (Pooled)	(Default) All application executables and components from all ASP virtual applications with this setting are run in the process (i.e. the memory space) of a single shared instance of DLLHost.exe. This protects the web server executable (Inetinfo.exe) from the risk of any one of the executables or components failing. However, one failed executable or component can cause the DLLHost.exe process to fail, and with it all the other hosted executables and components.
High (Isolated)	All application executables and components for an ASP virtual application with this setting are run in the process (i.e. the memory space) of a single instance of DLLHost.exe, but each ASP application has its own instance of DLLHost.exe that is exclusive to that application. This protects the web server executable (Inetinfo.exe) from the risk of any one of the executables or components failing, and protects the virtual application from risk if an executable or component from another virtual application should fail. Microsoft suggests that a maximum of ten isolated virtual applications should be hosted on any one web server.

Microsoft recommends a configuration where mission-critical applications run in their own processes, i.e. **High (Isolated)**, and all remaining applications in a shared, pooled process, i.e. **Medium (Pooled)**.

Threading Issues and Object Scope

One other factor that affects the performance of instantiated objects and components is the threading model that they use. This also controls the scope in which they will perform successfully. There are five different threading models:

❑ **Single-threaded** components allow only one process to access the component at a time, and so each must wait in turn for the component to become available. Single-threaded components should **never** be used in ASP.

- **Apartment-threaded** components allow multiple instances of an object to be created, with each user getting their own instance. Object instances cannot be shared amongst processes, however. Apartment-threaded components are suitable for use in ASP with certain limitations as described in the table below.

- **Free-threaded** components allow multiple processes to access them concurrently, so a single instance can service more than one process. However, access is slower than with apartment-threaded objects as each access has to cross a process boundary. Free-threaded objects are suitable for use in ASP pages.

- **Both-threaded** components can act as though they are either apartment-threaded or free-threaded, depending on the context of the calling application. Both-threaded objects are suitable for use in ASP pages.

- **Neutral-threaded** components (new in Windows 2000 with COM+) allow multiple instances of the object to be created like apartment-threaded components. However, they do not limit each instance to always working in the same process, and so can be shared amongst requests. Neutral-threaded components are the best choice for ASP applications, although few tools are currently able to create this type of component.

> This is only an overview of the different component types. Threading issues are covered further in Chapter 41, Optimizing ASP Performance. For an exhaustive technical discussion of threading issues see Beginning ASP Components from Wrox (ISBN 1-861002-88-2).

Object instances can be created in three different levels of scope:

- **Application-level** scope means that the object will be available to all pages within that virtual application (or the default web site). One instance of the object will service all requests from all users. For this reason, only both-threaded or neutral-threaded components should be used in application-level scope. However, if possible, avoid using any components at application-level scope at all as this always risks becoming a performance limitation.

- **Session-level** scope means that one object instance will service all requests from a single user within their ASP session. Both-threaded or neutral-threaded components work well at session-level scope, because they do not tie the session to a single process thread, as do apartment-threaded objects. Again, if possible, avoid using any components at session-level scope unless it is absolutely necessary.

- **Page-level** scope means that the object is created and destroyed within a single ASP page. While this seems to be inefficient, the COM+ Component Services within Windows 2000 are specially designed to make this fast and provide minimum use of resources. Objects can be pooled and/or recreated very quickly. With the exception of single-threaded components, any threading model is acceptable at page-level scope. However, apartment-threaded objects generally provide the best performance here.

ASP Directives

For each page that we put together we have several options which we can set which affect the way that the server processes it. A processing **directive** is always the first line of the ASP Page and is delimited by `<%@...%>`. The outside section you may recognize as the standard way of informing `asp.dll` that inside it there is content pertinent to it. The additional @ sign denotes that it is the processing directive. This may contain all or any of the following keywords; if none are required this line can be omitted:

Processing Directives	Description
`CODEPAGE-"code-page"`	This defines the character set for this page. The code page is the numeric value of the character set. This value may differ between locales and languages to support both additional and alternative characters.
`ENABLESESSIONSTATE="True |False"`	This value can be set to `False` in which case no session cookie is set to the browser, this effectively disables sessions. The default is `True`. The main reason for doing this is to improve efficiency for pages that do not require state information.
`LANGUAGE="language-name"`	This sets the default language for the page. This does not preclude use of other languages within that page. The default language if this is not specified is VBScript, unless the default for the entire application has been changed.
`LCID="locale-identifier"`	An integer value which uniquely identifies the locale from which the page has been sent. This may affect such things as the currency symbol used.
`TRANSACTION="transaction_type"`	This directive specifies that the page will run under a transaction context. See Chapter 34, Transactions and Message Queuing.

What's New in ASP Version 3.0

If you're already familiar with ASP 2.0, and are looking for a concise list of what has actually changed in version 3.0, you'll find the information below:

Summary of New Features in ASP 3.0

These are the new, or substantially changed and improved, features which have been added to ASP in version 3.0. (Also see Chapter 2, ASP, Windows 2000 and Windows DNA for details of how Windows 2000 improves ASP 3.0.)

Scriptless ASP

ASP is now much faster at processing .asp pages that don't contain any script. If you are creating a site or Web application where the files may eventually use ASP, you can assign these files the .asp file extensions, regardless of whether they contain server-side script or only static (HTML and text) content.

New Flow Control Capabilities

A new feature to ASP 3.0 is an alternative to the Response.Redirect statement. Effectively this sent an instruction to the client browser to load an alternative page. Unfortunately, this is both error-prone and a slow process. In ASP 3.0, two new methods to the server object allow page transfers without browser intervention.

Server.Transfer transfers execution to another page, while Server.Execute will execute another page then return control to the original one. Inside the new page you can access the original page's context, including all the ASP objects like Response and Request, but you lose access to page scope variables. If the original page indicates that it is a transaction type in the processor directive (the opening <%@...%> element), the transaction context is passed to the new page. If this happens and the second ASP file's transaction flag indicates that transactions are supported or required, then an existing transaction will be used and a new transaction will not be started.

Error Handling and the New ASPError Object

Configurable error handling is now available, by providing a single custom ASP page that is automatically called if an error occurs with the Server.Transfer method. In that page, Server.GetLastError can be used to return an instance of the new ASPError object, which contains more details about the error including the error description and the relevant line number.

Encoded ASP Scripts

ASP script and client-side script can now be encoded using Base64 encryption, and higher levels of encryption are planned for future releases of ASP. (Note that this feature is implemented by the VBScript 5.0 and JScript 5.0 scripting engines, and so requires them.) Encoded scripts are decoded at run time by the script engine, so there's no need for a separate utility. Although not a secure encryption method, it does prevent casual users from browsing or copying scripts.

A New Way to Include Script Files

Rather than using the <!-- #include ... --> element to force IIS to server-side include a file containing script code, ASP 3.0 can do the 'including' itself. The <SCRIPT> element can be used with RUNAT="SERVER" and SRC="file_path_and_name" attributes to include files containing script code. The full and relative physical path or virtual path of the file can be used in the SRC attribute:

```
<SCRIPT LANGUAGE="language" RUNAT="SERVER" SRC="path_and_filename">
</SCRIPT>
```

Server Scriptlets

ASP 3.0 supports a powerful new scripting technology called **server scriptlets**. These are XML-format text files that are hosted on the server and become available to ASP as normal COM objects (i.e. Active Server Components). This makes it much easier to implement (or just prototype) your web application's business logic script procedures as reusable components, as well as using them in other COM-compliant programs.

Performance-Enhanced Active Server Components

Many of the Active Server Components that come with ASP have been improved to provide better performance or extra functionality. One example is the new Browser Capabilities component. In addition, there are some new components, such as the XML Parser that allows applications to handle XML formatted data on the server. Closer integration between ADO and XML is also provided (through the new version 2.5 of ADO that ships with Windows 2000), which opens up new opportunities for storing and retrieving data from a data store in XML format.

Performance

A great deal of work has been done to improve performance and scalability of ASP and IIS. This includes self-tuning features in ASP, which detect blocking situations and automatically increase the number of available process threads. ASP now senses when requests that are currently executing are blocked by external resources, and automatically provides more threads to simultaneously execute additional requests and to continue normal processing. If the CPU becomes overloaded, however, ASP reduces the number of available threads, to minimize the thread switching that occurs when too many non-blocking requests are executing simultaneously.

Changes from ASP Version 2.0

These are the features that have been changed or updated from version 2.0.

Buffering is On by Default

ASP has offered optional output buffering for some time. Since IIS 4.0, this has provided much faster script execution, as well as the ability to control the output that is streamed to the browser. In ASP 3.0, this improved performance has been reflected by changing the default setting of the Response.Buffer property to True, so that buffering is on by default. This means that the final output will be sent to the client only at the completion of processing, or when the script calls the Response.Flush or Response.End method.

> Note that you should turn buffering off by setting the Response.Buffer property to False when sending XML-formatted output to the client to allow the XML parser to start work on it as it is received. You may also want to use Response.Flush to send sections of very large pages, so that the user sees some output arrive quickly.

27

Changes to Response.IsClientConnected

The `Response.IsClientConnected` property can now be read before any content is sent to the client. In ASP 2.0, this only returned accurate information after at least some content had been sent. This resolves the problem of IIS responding to every client request, even though the client might have moved to another page or site. Also, if the client is no longer connected after three seconds, the complete output that has been created on the server is dumped.

Query Strings with Default Documents

When a user accesses a site without providing the name of the page they require, the default document is sent back to them. However, if a query string is appended to that URL this is now passed to the default page. In previous versions this information was lost. For example, if the default page in a directory that has the URL `http://www.wrox.com/store/` is `default.asp`, then both the following will send the name/value pair `code=1274` to the `default.asp` page:

```
http://www.wrox.com/store/?code=1274
http://www.wrox.com/store/default.asp?code=1274
```

Server-side Include File Security

Server-side include files are often used for sensitive information, such as database connection strings or other access details. In ASP 2.0 specifying the virtual path of a file in a server side include to specify a file bypassed the security checking for the file. In other words the authenticated or anonymous account was not compared with the access control list entries for the file.

In ASP 3.0 on IIS 5.0, these credentials are now checked, and can be used to prevent unauthorized access.

Configurable Entries Moved to the Metabase

In IIS 5.0, the registry entries for `ProcessorThreadMax` and `ErrorsToNTLog` have been moved into the metabase. All configurable parameters for ASP can be modified in the metabase via Active Directory and the Active Directory Service Interface (ADSI).

Behavior of Both-Threaded Objects in Applications

For best performance in ASP, where there are often multiple concurrent requests, components should be **Both-Threaded** (Single Threaded Apartment (STA) and Multi-Threaded Apartment (MTA)) *and* support the COM Free-Threaded Marshaller (FTM). Both-Threaded COM objects that do not support the Free-Threaded Marshaller will fail if stored in the ASP `Application` state object.

Earlier Release of COM Objects

In IIS 5.0, instantiated objects or components are now released earlier. In IIS 4.0, COM objects were only released when ASP finished processing a page. In IIS 5.0, if a COM object does not use the `OnEndPage` method, and the reference count for the object reaches zero, then the object is released before processing completes.

COM Object Security

IIS uses the new **cloaking** feature provided by COM+ so that local server applications instantiated from ASP can run in the security context of the originating client. In previous versions, the security context assigned to the local server COM object depended on the identity of the user who created the instance.

Components Run Out-of-Process By Default

In earlier versions of ASP, all components created within the context of an ASP page ran **in-process** by default, i.e. within the memory space of the web server. In IIS 4.0, the ability to create a virtual application allowed components to be run **out-of-process**. In IIS 5.0 and ASP 3.0, components are now instantiated **out-of-process** by default. This is controlled by the metabase property `AspAllowOutOfProcComponents`, which now has a default value of 1. Setting it to zero changes the default back to that of IIS 4.0.

To better fine-tune the component performance to Web server protection trade-off, you can now choose from the three options for Application Protection in the Properties dialog for a virtual application; see earlier in this chapter. The recommended configuration is to run mission-critical applications in their own processes – i.e. **High (Isolated)** – and all remaining applications in a shared, pooled process – i.e. **Medium (Pooled)**. It is also possible to set the **Execute Permissions** for the scripts and components that make up each virtual application. The three options are: None, Scripts only, or Scripts and Executables.

What's New in JScript 5.0

The only change to JScript is the long-awaited introduction of proper error handling.

Exception Handling

The Java-style `try` and `catch` constructs are now supported in JScript 5.0. For example:

```
function GetSomeKindOfIndexThingy() {

  try {
    // If an exception occurs during the execution of this
    // block of code, processing of this entire block will
    // be aborted and will resume with the first statement in its
    // associated catch block.
    var objSomething = Server.CreateObject("SomeComponent");
    var intIndex = objSomething.getSomeIndex();
    return intIndex;
  }

  catch (exception) {
    // This code will execute when *any* exception occurs during
    // the execution of this function
    alert('Oh dear, the object didn't expect you to do that');
  }

}
```

The built-in JScript Error object has three properties that define the last run-time error. We can use these in a catch block to get more information about the error:

```
alert(Error.number);  // Gives the numeric value of the error number
// AND the result with 0xFFFF to get a 'normal' error number in ASP

alert(Error.description);  // Gives an error desciption as a string
```

If you want to throw your own errors, you can raise an error (or **exception**) with a custom **exception object**. However there is no built-in exception object, so you have to define a constructor for one yourself:

```
// Define our own Exception object
function MyException(intNumber, strDescription, strInfo) {
  this.Number = intNumber;             // Set the Number property
  this.Description = strDescription;   // Set the Description property
  this.CustomInfo = strInfo;           // Set some 'information' property
}
```

An object like this can then be used to raise custom exceptions within our pages, by using the throw keyword and then examining the type of exception in the catch block:

```
function GetSomeKindOfIndexThingy() {
  try {
    var objSomething = Server.CreateObject("SomeComponent");
    var intIndex = objSomething.getSomeIndex();
    if (intIndex == 0) {
      // Create a new MyException object
      theException = new MyException(0x6F1, "Zero index not " +
                                    "permitted", "Index_Err");
      throw theException;
    }
    return intIndex;
  }

  catch (objException) {
    if (objException instanceof MyException) {
      // This is one of our custom exception objects
      if (objException.Category == "Index_Err") {
        alert('Index Error: ' + objException.Description);
      else
        alert('Undefined custom error:' + objException.Description);
      }
      else
        // Not "our" exception, display & raise to next high routine
        alert(Error.Description + ' (' + Error.Number + ')');
        throw exception;
    }
  }
}
```

What's New in VBScript 5.0

The features that are available in ASP include those provided by the scripting engines, which means that improvements there are also available in ASP. The changes to VBScript are as follows.

Using Classes in Script

The full Visual Basic Class model is implemented, with the obvious exception of events in ASP server-side scripting. You can create classes within your script, which make their properties and methods available to the remainder of the code in your page. For example:

```
Class MyClass

  'local variable to hold value of HalfValue
  Private m_HalfValue

  'executed to set the HalfValue property
  Public Property Let HalfValue(vData)
    If vData > 0 Then m_HalfValue = vData
  End Property

  'executed to return the HalfValue property
  Public Property Get HalfValue()
    HalfValue = m_HalfValue
  End Property

  'implements the GetResult method
  Public Function GetResult()
    GetResult = m_HalfValue * 2
  End Function

End Class

Set objThis = New MyClass

objThis.HalfValue = 21

Response.Write "Value of HalfValue property is " & _
               objThis.HalfValue & "<BR>"
Response.Write "Result of GetResult method is " & _
               objThis.GetResult & "<BR>"
. . .
```

This produces the result:

```
Value of HalfValue property is 21
Result of GetResult method is 42
```

The With Construct

The With construct is now supported, allowing more compact scripts to be written where the code accesses several properties or methods of one object:

```
. . .
Set objThis = Server.CreateObject("This.Object")

With objThis
  .Property1 = "This value"
  .Property2 = "Another value"
  TheResult = .SomeMethod
End With
. . .
```

String Evaluation

The Eval function (long available in JavaScript and JScript) is now supported in VBScript 5.0. This allows you to build a string containing script code that evaluates to True or False, and then execute it to obtain a result:

```
...
datYourBirthday = Request.Form("Birthday")
strScript = "datYourBirthday = Date()"

If Eval(strScript) Then
   Response.Write "Happy Birthday!"
Else
   Response.Write "Have a nice day!"
End If
...
```

Statement Execution

The new Execute function allows script code in a string to be executed in much the same way as the Eval function, but without returning a result as is usually the case with the Eval statement. It can be used to dynamically create procedures that are executed later in the code. For example:

```
...
strCheckBirthday = "Sub CheckBirthday(datYourBirthday)" & vbCrlf _
            & "  If Eval(datYourBirthday = Date()) Then" & vbCrlf _
            & "    Response.Write ""Happy Birthday!""" & vbCrlf _
            & "  Else" & vbCrlf _
            & "    Response.Write ""Have a nice day!""" & vbCrlf _
            & "  End If" & vbCrlf _
            & "End Sub" & vbCrlf
Execute strCheckBirthday
CheckBirthday(Date())
...
```

Either a carriage return (as shown) or a colon character ':' can be used to delimit the individual statements within the string.

Setting Locales

The new SetLocale method can be used to change the current locale of the script engine. This enables it to properly display special locale-specific characters, such as those with accents or from a different character set:

```
strCurrentLocale = GetLocale
SetLocale("en-gb")
```

Regular Expressions

VBScript 5.0 now supports regular expressions (again, long available in JavaScript, JScript and other languages). The RegExp object is used to create and execute a regular expression. For example:

```
strTarget = "test testing tested attest late start"
Set objRegExp = New RegExp        'create a regular expression

objRegExp.Pattern = "test*"       'set the search pattern
objRegExp.IgnoreCase = False      'set the case sensitivity
objRegExp.Global = True           'set the scope

Set colMatches = objRegExp.Execute(strTarget)  'execute the search

For Each Match in colMatches      'iterate the colMatches collection
  Response.Write "Match found at position " & Match.FirstIndex & "."
  Response.Write "Matched value is '" & Match.Value & "'.<BR>"
Next
```

This produces the result:

```
Match found at position 0. Matched value is 'test'.
Match found at position 5. Matched value is 'test'.
Match found at position 13. Matched value is 'test'.
Match found at position 22. Matched value is 'test'.
```

Setting Event Handlers in Client-side VBScript

While not applying directly to ASP scripting techniques, this new feature is useful when writing client-side VBScript. You can now assign a reference to a function or subroutine to an event dynamically. For example, given a function named MyFunction(), you can assign it to a button's ONCLICK event using:

```
Function MyFunction()
   ...
   'Function implementation code here
   ...
End Function
...
Set objCmdButton = document.all("cmdButton")
Set objCmdButton.onClick = GetRef("MyFunction")
```

This provides similar functionality to that existing in JavaScript and JScript, where functions can be assigned as properties of an object dynamically.

On Error Goto 0 in VBScript

Although this technique was not documented previously, it does in fact work in existing versions of VBScript (as those of you with a VB background and an inquisitive mind will have already discovered). It is now documented, and can be used to 'turn off' custom error handling in a page after an On Error Resume Next has been executed. The result is that any subsequent errors will raise a browser-level or server-level error and the appropriate dialog/response.

Other New Features

A couple of other features have been made available in IIS 5.0.

Distributed Authoring and Versioning (DAV)

This standard, created by the Internet Engineering Task Force (IETF) and now in version 1.0, allows authors in several locations to concurrently build and maintain Web pages and other documents. It is designed to provide upload and download access, and control versions so that the process can be properly managed. Internet Explorer contains features that integrate with DAV in IIS 5.0. However, in the IETF standard, and in the current release of IIS 5.0, the versioning capabilities are not yet implemented.

Referencing Type Libraries

In the past, it has been common practice to use a server-side include file to add constants from a type library (such as scripting objects, ADO, or MSMQ) to an ASP page. This is necessary, as ASP does not create a reference to the type library or component DLL as does, for example, Visual Basic. In IIS 5.0, you no longer need to use include files for constants. Instead, you can access the type library of a component directly using a new HTML comment-style element, placed in the <HEAD> section of the page:

```
<!-- METADATA TYPE="typelib" FILE="c:\WinNT\System32\scrrun.dll" -->
```

This makes all the constants in the specified file available within the current ASP page. (Although this is slated as being new in IIS 5.0, it was working but undocumented in IIS 4.)

FTP Download Restarts

The FTP service now (at last, some would say) provides a restart facility for downloads. If a file download stops part way through – perhaps because of a dropped connection at the user end – it can be resumed from that point. This means that failed file downloads do not require the client to download the entire file all over again.

HTTP Compression

IIS now automatically implements compression of the HTTP data stream for static and dynamically generated files, and caches compressed static files as well. This gives faster response and reduces network loading when communicating with suitably equipped clients.

New versions of the scripting engines, JScript 5.5 and VBScript 5.5 are currently available in beta. A description of the key new features of these can be downloaded from our web site.

Summary

In this chapter, we've very briefly looked at many of the major topics that you need to be aware of when working with ASP 3.0. We've purposely taken the point of view of the experienced web developer, assuming that either you have previous experience of ASP through using an earlier version, or at least you know how the Web works when clients and servers interact.

By now, you should have a good overall view of what ASP 3.0 offers – both in terms of the existing features in earlier versions, and the new features that are available in version 3.0. If you feel that you don't fully understand the concepts of the ASP object model, or the way that context is used to allow access to this object model from other sources, don't worry. Providing you have a broad understanding of the topics we've covered here, you will easily be able to follow the next chapter and the following section, which cover it all in more detail.

2

ASP, Windows 2000 and Windows DNA

In this chapter we focus on Windows 2000, and Windows DNA, and look at how they affect the way we use ASP.

First let's take a look at Windows 2000. This latest release provides us with many exciting new technologies such as Active Directory, along with enhancements to products like IIS and ASP, substantial improvements to core technologies such as COM+, and enhancements to supporting techologies like ADO, where a common theme is improved XML support.

A major change over former Windows operating systems is that all these technologies are more tightly integrated into the Windows 2000 operating system. Some are installable components, but many are fundamental to the Windows 2000 operating system and are ready for us also to use on any Windows 2000 installation. Many of these features have the potential to *dramatically* enhance the functionality, stability, integration, and performance of our web applications.

For the ASP developer, two obvious changes to Windows 2000 are that it ships with ASP 3.0 and IIS 5.0 as standard. These provide some great new functionality, especially in the area of performance. The new versions represent an evolution in each of these technologies, with no new programming paradigms to learn and many of the improvements being internal. This makes the task of upgrading while continuing to get the best out of our applications, much less onerous.

There are no major new changes to the ASP object model (a new ASPError object and a few methods and attributes here and there), so our existing IIS4 applications should continue to work fine in IIS5. You'll also find that the base functionality of IIS isn't radically different from before, although a few names have been changed and some of the dialogs have been streamlined. The fact that, at least on the surface, IIS5 doesn't appear much different from IIS4 is deceptive, however. It is much faster and has many new features such as server-side page redirection, nested ASP page execution and many new and improved add-on components and user friendly dialogs. These are listed in Chapter 1, What is ASP?

Windows 2000 itself, however, is *significantly* different to Windows NT, and ASP and IIS are able to take advantage of many major changes and improvements in the underlying operating system. Whilst these benefits may not be immediately apparent, the net result is that the web server is now a fundamental service of the OS rather than just an add-on. This is reflected by a new name – **Internet Information Services** (it was previously called Internet Information Server).

IIS 5.0 takes advantage of all the native services provided by Windows 2000 such as transaction services, object pooling, queued components, role-based security, cloaking etc., which now work in a more tightly integrated way. While some of these services were available with Windows NT and with add-ons like MTS, they were not integrated to the OS or COM and so incurred an overhead in terms of performance and programmer sanity. (If you've ever used MTS and forgotten to call `SafeRef` you know what I'm talking about.)

> MTS is still part of Windows 2000: Now it is an integral part of component services, rather than a separate add-on, and the name MTS has been dropped (although we still refer to it this way in Chapter 34 for convenience).

I guess it's an obvious statement, but ASP *is* now a pivotal technology used by hundreds of thousands of web sites worldwide today. Based upon the technique of combining HTML with server-side scripting to create web pages dynamically, IIS and ASP provide a significant amount of infrastructure and functionality that is needed to create both simple and advanced intranet/internet/extranet applications. In conjuction with ADO and other proximate techologies, rich user interfaces and functional web applications can easily be created.

We can create a dynamic page with only a few lines of code. Since ASP script has the ability to create and access COM objects, our ASP pages can have staggering power and flexibility to scale, adapt, and develop.

COM is *the* most important feature of Windows 2000 for ASP programmers (now called COM+ to reflect enhancements such as the addition of MTS). COM enables ASP to use ADO and therefore access databases. It also enables our ASP pages to access numerous other components such as the Ad Rotator, and to use features such as transaction support. Even ASP's own object model is a set of COM objects. Moreover, not only is it fundamental to Windows 2000, IIS5 and ASP, but also the forthcoming ASP+ uses COM for just about everything.

Windows 2000

Windows 2000 is a functionally rich operating system that comes with numerous ready-built services and applications. This frees us, as developers, to focus on our application rather than devoting time to the core infrastructures needed to make our applications work.

Windows 2000 allows us to use IIS5 as our web server, Active Directory to share enterprise information, Message Queueing Services and Transaction support. Microsoft's intention is clearly to provide an attractive, all-encompasing operating system, hosting and supporting all types of applications, ranging from those suited to small businesses, up to enterprise-level applications.

OK, by using Microsoft's built-in services and applications, we may be giving up a degree of control (like waiting until the first service pack if we find a serious bug), but typically the tradeoff with the amount of time saved not having to write, develop, and maintain these components ourselves is worthwhile.

So far, Windows 2000 has proved to be a very stable operating system. I would recommend installing it sooner rather than later given my experience of it. (Of course, don't put it on your production servers before testing your required configuration on a test server first!) Microsoft is also already well underway with major updates to IIS and ASP which should be released within 12-18 months. These will extend Windows 2000 with more operating systems services in the shape of COM+, and some very exciting features in ASP 4.0 (ASP+).

Windows DNA

In 1997 Microsoft announced **Microsoft Windows Distributed interNet Architecture (Windows DNA)**, its framework for designing and implementating web-enabled n-tier applications that utilize the power and capabilities of the Windows platform. Windows DNA is a programming model or blueprint for designing and developing distributed component-based applications that use a broad set of products and services.

Microsoft Windows Distributed interNet Architecture 2000 (Windows DNA 2000) is a revised version of Windows DNA which uses the functionality of Windows 2000 and related Microsoft products such as BizTalk Server 2000 (an e-commerce server primarily aimed at business-to-business XML document exchange). Another key extension to Windows DNA 2000 is its use of non-Microsoft-specific technologies such as XML and SOAP (Simple Object Access Protocol). The adoption of such technologies demonstrates Microsoft's acknowledgment of the importance of having Windows applications achieve a good level of interoperability with other platforms.

> **SOAP is an open standard that defines how simple remote procedure calls can be made using XML as the payload, and HTTP as the transport mechanisms.** For more information about SOAP see
> `http://www.develop.com/soap`.

The Structure of a DNA 2000 Application

The basic premise of Windows DNA 2000 is that applications consist of a number of logical tiers. Focussing on each tier of this model helps us factor the overall architecture of our applications, making it easier to extend and understand it, as shown here:

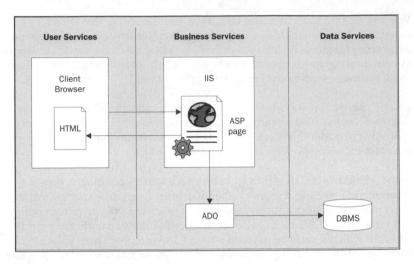

The three tiers shown in this diagram are:

❑ **User Services** – This tier is responsible for user interfaces and interactions. As ASP programmers, our user interfaces are typically HTML or DHTML (XML, XSLT, and XPath are covered in Chapter 35 and 36) pages and communicate with the business services tier using HTTP. Alternatively, the user services tier could consist of regular WIN32 applications using DCOM to connect to the business services tier. Windows DNA defines four types of application that exist in this tier depending how they interact with the Internet. These are:

   ❑ **internet-enhanced** applications (WIN32 applications, such as Microsoft Money, that can be used with or without the Internet).

   ❑ **internet-reliant** applications (traditional WIN32 applications that require an internet connection to function).

   ❑ **browser-enhanced** applications (HTML/DHTML-based but typically requiring a specific browser such as IE4/5).

   ❑ **browser-neutral** applications (HTML 3.2 based and therefore suitable for most Netscape or IE users).

❑ **Business Services** – This tier contains components for carrying out the core processing in our applications, abiding by any business rules or constraints. Typically the business logic is either written into ASP pages for simple applications, or preferably held in COM components that are instantiated and used by our ASP pages (and/or a regular WIN32 application). This use of COM components for our business logic is also good preparation for the forthcoming ASP+, which uses this model.

❑ **Data Services** – The data services tier contains the data for an application, residing in one or more data sources such as SQL Server or Oracle.

Each logical tier interacts with its neighbouring tiers. It isn't good practice to bypass tiers, for example accessing a data source directly from the user interface, since this sacrifices benefits of n-tier design such as encapsulation and scalability. In this example our HTML pages would need to have intimate knowledge of the data source structure (and probably the data store type) and hence we'd have to update every single HTML page if we wanted to change our database structure or store. Alternatively if our HTML pages made use of a COM object to interact with the database, we'd only need to update that single point of knowledge, and all our HTML pages referencing it would continue to work. The same rationale applies for scalability: if an additional layer of indirection exists between the user interface and the database, that middle layer (the mediator) could potentially reside on many different machines and possibly cache the database state, therefore reducing hits upon a database server if that's a hot spot in a busy system.

DNA applications can consist of more than just three tiers. We can add additional tiers, maybe sub-dividing tiers into several sub-tiers. For example, the business services tier could be sub-divided into three tiers: one containing ASP pages, one containing COM components that hold our business logic, and one for COM components that encapsulate data access.

> **Each tier in an n-tier web application provides a layer of indirection that affords us flexibility at the potential cost of some performance.**

In addition to the logical tiers which are conceptually important, we also need to think about the **physical tiers** across which our application is deployed in practice. A physical tier is a machine on which the elements defined in a logical tier execute. We can either have a different physical tier (machine) for each of our various logical tiers, or they can co-exist on the same machine. For a large system each tier typically is on a different machine, for load and performance reasons:

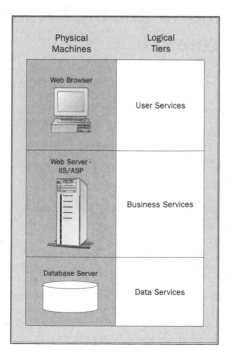

For medium sized applications several logical tiers execute on the same physical tier:

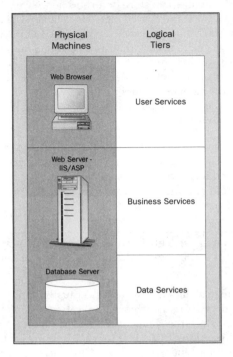

Using Windows 2000 DNA for an N-tier Infrastructure

Windows DNA 2000 presumes you are going to use the technologies, tools, and products provided with Windows 2000. The key elements of Windows DNA 2000 are:

- ❑ Components Services – COM/COM+
- ❑ IIS & Active Server Pages
- ❑ Data access (ADO, ADSI)
- ❑ Transactions
- ❑ Messaging
- ❑ XML/Web Services

Component Services – COM/COM+

Component Services are the foundations upon which Windows DNA 2000, Windows 2000, IIS and ASP are built. Microsoft has made it clear that our web applications should be using components if we want them to be usable in the future and in order to make the most ASP+, the next generation of ASP. With ASP+ you'll be able to write your ASP pages using VB or C/C++. To use these new features without major rewriting of your pages you will need to use components.

> **If you're unfamiliar with using COM and MTS we recommend reading an ASP-centric introduction to COM, such as *'Beginning ASP Components'* published by Wrox Press** (ISBN 1-861002-88-2).

Put simply, COM is a mechanism by which software components (such as ADO) can be written in one programming language, packaged up into a DLL or EXE file, and then used by any another programming language or environment that supports COM (such as ASP). COM is based on a binary specification which means that it is language neutral, as long as the component compiles into an agreed format, it can interact with and be used by, any COM-aware language or application. It's specification defines how a client can consume the functionality of the object, and on the flip side, how an object exposes it's functionality to a client. It is also object-based and builds upon the three object-oriented principals of identity, state and behavior.

COM+ extends COM by integrating the functionality of MTS into the COM runtime. To be more precise, it uses interception and a runtime environment to provide services to our COM+ components dynamically at creation time. MTS did this to provide transaction support, Just-In-Time activation and As-Soon-As-Possible deactivation. COM+ uses the same technique in a far more generic fashion, and provides a far greater number of services.

If we look at the Microsoft Management Console (MMC) snap-in for component services (the administration tool for COM+ which can be found under comexp.msc) we can see the integration between COM+ and IIS5:

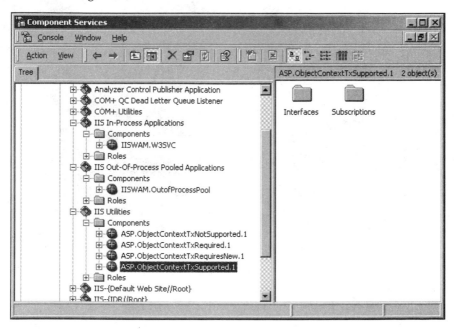

Under the COM+ Applications folder we can see the sub-folders IIS In-Process Applications, IIS Out-Of-Process Pooled Applications, and IIS Utilities. IIS has created these folders so it can utilitize transaction support, process isolation and other features such as fail-safe restart from COM+, rather than implementing them itself. Given these features are also probably going to be needed in non-IIS applications too, it makes sense that Component Services works this way.

Each COM+ application uses **declarative attributes** to specify the services it uses. In English, declarative attributes mean check boxes in the GUI, that when clicked define additional runtime behavior and functionality the component should inherit when used. When an instance of any component within a COM+ application is created, COM+ uses interception to ensure that services you specified using declarative attributes are correctly injected and used at runtime.

To create a COM+ application, we can change the Application Protection attribute of a web site to be High (Isolated):

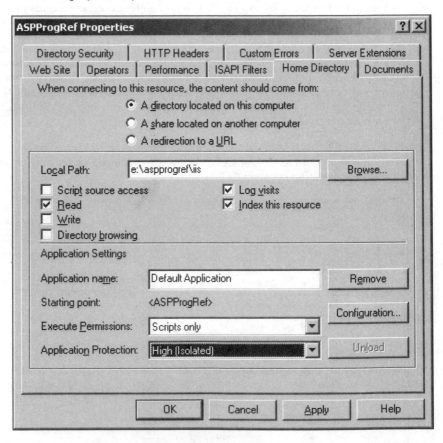

We'll see that IIS5 creates a COM+ application by means of which the process isolation for that web site is provided:

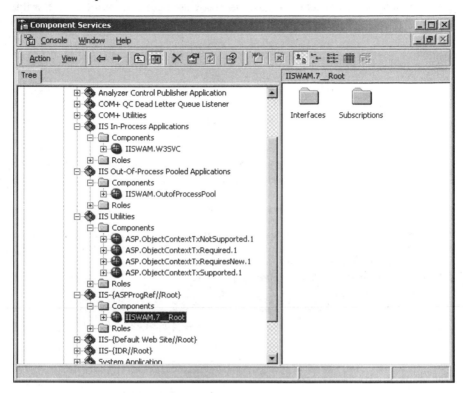

At runtime you'll see an instance of dllhost.exe for each highly isolated web site and one instance for pooled web sites (medium isolation).

If you've used IIS4 and have a good understanding of IIS/COM/MTS relationships, you'll see that this isn't very different. The name of MTS has changed due to being a COM+ application. However, the key difference is that transactions are now an integrated part of the operating system. This integration applies all the way down to the context object (see more later), which is the recommended way for ASP intrinsic objects to be accessed.

Contexts and Interception

The most important feature that MTS brings to COM is the notion of the **context**. This information container enables MTS to make a stand-alone object form part of a distributed application, with synchronized concurrency, distributed transactions, and role-based security. You've probably seen this when accessing the ASP intrinsic objects with code like this:

```
Set objContext = GetObjectContext
objContext.Response.Write "ASP Rules OK!"
```

At first sight this looks like the object context is an IIS intrisic object, but it's not; the object context is transparently created by COM+ and is basically used to track and service objects. COM+ makes it possible to add services to a component after it is compiled, using **declarative attributes**. We don't have to write additional code to use transactions, queuing, security etc., it is done by the COM+ runtime automatically. It does this by inserting code before and after each method call pertaining to each requested service. This technique is referred to as **interception**.

Every COM+ object is associated with a single context when it is first created, or pulled from an object pool. For example, when IIS processes an ASP file, it creates a COM+ object to interpret the contents of the page and execute any ASP script statements. Once activated, the context associated with an object such as the ASP interpreter remains static throughout the object's lifetime, until the object is returned to a pool, or destroyed. The context is being used by COM+ to associate **out-of-band** information with an object throughout its lifetime, data needed to apply services to a component. The term 'out-of-band' simply means that the data is managed by COM+ behind the scenes. Without the context you would have to maintain such information yourself.

Several objects can share a context if their runtime requirements are compatible. The algorithm COM+ uses for its context compatibly test is not currently documented. If you do need to ensure objects are activated within the same context, you can use the 'Must be activated in caller's context' check box:

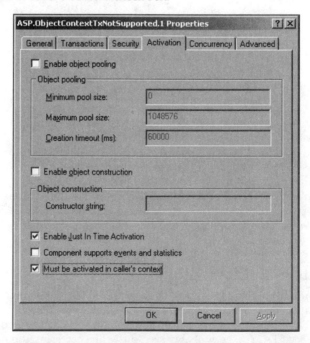

If two objects cannot be created in the same context, the creation will fail with the error CO_E_ATTEMPT_TO_CREATE_OUTSIDE_CLIENT_CONTEXT.

Within an object, you can obtain a reference to the context object by calling the GetObjectContext API. This returns a COM object called the **ObjectContext**. The default interface returned and used on this object is IObjectContext.

Activation

The process of getting an object into a state in which a client can use it is known as **activation**. The object creating the object is called the **activator**, and the activation process occurs when you call `CreateObject` in an ASP script. A context is associated with an object during its activation.

Objects and Contexts

The relationship between an object, the object context, and the context is shown here, and remains static once an object has been activated:

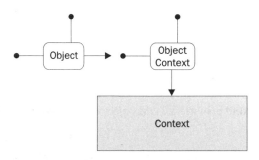

> The name 'object context' is somewhat confusing, and don't be surprised if you find people using the terms 'object context' and 'context object' interchangeably.

Context Negotiation

When a COM+ object is created, the COM+ catalog is used to determine the services a component uses. If an existing context matches the newly-created object's requirements it will be used, if not, a new context is created:

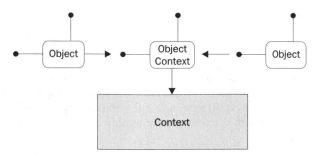

If the services required by the component mean that the context of the activator is incompatible with what it needs, a different context (and therefore object context) is used for the object.

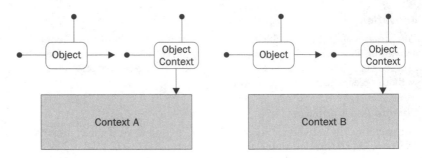

COM+ uses interception (sometimes also referred to as a lightweight proxy) to ensure that the differences between the contexts of the activator and the object it creates are transparently managed at runtime by the COM+ runtime, so we don't have to worry about that in our code – client or component.

IIS and the Context

IIS uses the context to provide a COM object with access to the ASP intrinsic objects:

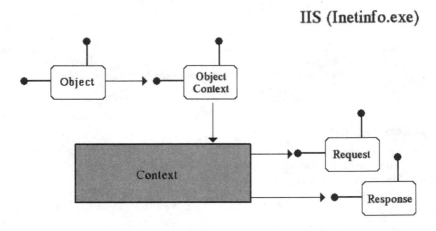

References to all of the ASP intrinsic objects (such as Request and Response objects) are held with the context as properties, put there by IIS. Any COM object that is associated with that context can access those properties through the object context associated with the context. Remembering the object context is a COM object that provides an interface into the context from within an object, we can access the IIS objects and use them:

```
Set objContext = GetObjectContext
objContext.Response.Write "ASP Really Does Rule OK!"
```

What this means is that a COM object can access the functionality of IIS (or any other application that uses the context to expose functionality) even though there is no **explicit** link or association between IIS and the object.

Using COM+, we can build **COM+ applications** out of components, leveraging foundation **services** and code from the operating system. These services give us a jump-start when developing n-tier applications based upon the Windows DNA framework. The applications we create can take advantage of the services and infrastructure that COM+ provides, which a typical enterprise application needs, such as transaction processing, component management, security and object pooling. A lot of Windows DNA 2000 is provided by COM+.

Each COM+ service is non-trivial to implement and would typically require many years of development and testing, but as they are provided as part of Windows 2000, all we have to do to make use of them is to use the **Component Services Explorer** to define our applications – a tool to manage and administer our COM+ applications and associated components in a very easy-to-use environment.

> *Component Services is the umbrella name Microsoft uses to encompass COM, COM+, and the related technologies like Microsoft Message Queue (MSMQ).*

IIS and Active Server Pages

The role of IIS and ASP within Windows DNA should be fairly clear: they connect the user services tier with the business services tier. Using the HTTP protocol, web pages and any others type of document can be sent between the two tiers. One of the enhancements in IIS5 is that the ASP Request and Response objects now support streaming of data in-memory. This means that a file (such as an XML document) can be saved directly to the Response object, or loaded directly from the Request object without having to go via file or some other medium. For example, the XML object model in IE5 can be used to create an XML document and save it to the Response object. In VBScript this looks like:

```
<%
Response.ContentType = "text/xml"
Set objResponse = Server.CreateObject("Microsoft.XMLDOM")

Dim objDocElement
Set objPI = objResponse.createProcessingInstruction("xml", _
                "version='1.0' encoding='UTF-8' standalone='yes'")

Set objDocElement = objResponse.createElement("GREETING")
objDocElement.text = "hello"

objResponse.appendChild objPI
objResponse.appendChild objDocElement

objResponse.save response
%>
```

Or in JScript:

```
<%@ LANGUAGE=JScript %>

<%
Response.ContentType = 'text/xml';
var objResponse = Server.CreateObject('Microsoft.XMLDOM');
```

```
var objPI = objResponse.createProcessingInstruction('xml',
         "version='1.0' encoding='UTF-8' standalone='yes' ");

var objDocElement = objResponse.createElement('GREETING');
objDocElement.text = 'hello';

objResponse.appendChild (objPI);
objResponse.appendChild (objDocElement);

objResponse.save (Response);
%>
```

If we view this page under a Windows 2000 client (and therefore IE5) the browser will render the XML:

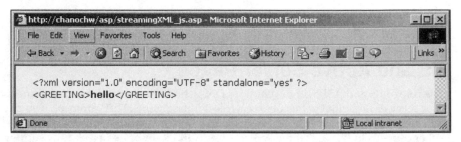

Even if you don't know much about the XML object model (which is covered in Chapter 35) you can appreciate the benefits of in-memory streaming as the document didn't have to be saved to disk. As it turns out, this code is also the only way in which we can send XML documents in UTF-8 format via ASP. If we tried writing code like this:

```
objResponse.save objResponse.xml
```

you'd find the XML document sent back to the client would be invalid if it contained characters that were outside of the range 0-126. Characters > 126 (such as Umlauts – Ü) require special encoding.

That is because the XML property returns a Unicode string which doesn't match the UTF-8 encoding we specified in the XML declaration.

Transactions

A transaction is any set of operations which must be performed as a single unit and any changes by which must be undone if any one operation fails. There is no intermediate state or partial completion; either they all succeed in which case the changes are saved or no changes occur. Transactions have the following properties, known as ACID:

- ❑ Atomicity – the set of operations must be completed as a whole or all will fail,

- ❑ Consistency – the end result is that which we were trying to achieve,

- ❑ Isolation – from other transactions; any one transaction can complete its tasks without needing to know about other such transactions

- ❑ Durability – which means that only when the transaction has completed should it report succesful completion.

For more information see Chapter 34, Transactions and Message Queueing.

Transaction support is available to an ASP script in two ways. The first way uses the @TRANSACTION directive inside of an ASP page to cause a transaction to be started when the page is first processed, which then completes when the page has been completely processed. This looks like:

```
<%@ TRANSACTION=Required %>

<%
    ' Some work here
    ' and here ...
%>
```

The second way of using transactions is within a page using one or more components. These need to be installed into Component Services using the MMC (since with Windows 2000, MTS is now just another part of Component Services (COM+) known as **Transaction Services**) and marked as transactional. In this scenario the transaction starts when an instance of the component is first created, and completes when all references to that component are released.

If we select the properties of a component from within the MMC and select the Transactions tab, we see:

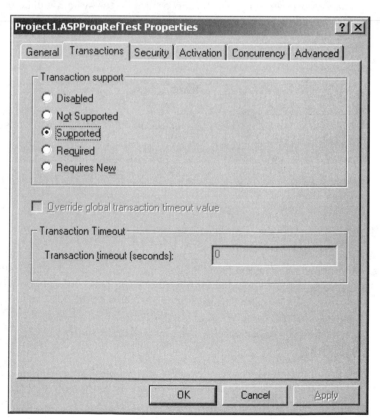

When MTS was a layer on top of COM in NT 4.0, COM didn't actually know about it, so there was a degree of trickery and overhead in terms of performance and programming. With MTS you couldn't pass a reference to a COM object installed inside of an MTS package directly. Instead you had to call `SafeRef` to return a special context wrapper (not context object!) that you could pass safely. The context wrapper would ensure that the runtime environment for an MTS component was setup before a method was invoked. Because transaction services are now an integral part of COM+, both of these overheads have been removed.

A new feature of IIS5 in transactions is that ASP pages can now invoke other ASP pages much like subroutines:

```
<%@ TRANSACTION=Required %>

<%
    ' Some work here
    Server.Execute "somepage.asp"
    ' Some more work here
%>
```

If the second page has a compatible transaction attribute, the same transaction is used to encompass the work of *both* pages and so actions can be rolled back across several pages; that is, any changes made will not be saved unless all the operations within each page have processed successfully, and otherwise the system will be returned to the state it was in when we began:

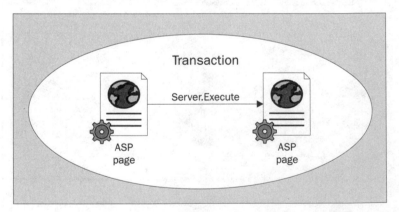

Although not as efficient as using components, this technique of being able to nest pages is an interesting way of reusing ASP scripts. Common code that has to be transactional can easily be included within other files. This could not be achieved using the include directive, as page attributes such as @TRANSACTION are not valid for them.

Messaging

Messaging is an integral part of Windows 2000. It enables asynchronous messages to be sent between two parties. If the two systems are disconnected, messages are queued until the recipient is accessible.

Allowing disconnected operations is important for modern applications as more and more people have laptops and need to work on the move. In this situation they need to be able to use their applications whether or not they are connected to their company's network. They therefore may or may not have access to the data sources that an application typically depends upon. The application must be willing to take an order for a salesman even if they are in a plane over the Atlantic and may not be connected to a network.

Another example: Imagine a Wrox salesman who is at a customer site. He sells 20,000 copies of "Professional XML" and 10,000 copies of "Beginning ASP Components". He enters the order into his laptop (which is not connected to any network), thanks the customer for the order, and then heads off back to the office thinking about his bonus. The operation was performed in a disconnected mode. The order can't be entered into the main order processing database back at Wrox, until he gets back to base, so the application has created a **message** and placed it in a **queue** for later processing. Assuming the journey back to the office goes well, when the laptop is connected to the Wrox network, the queue can be processed and the message forwarded to the ordering processing system.

Messaging is also important from a web perspective to allow our applications to work in a disconnected mode and may be useful for resource management. For example, we might want to be able to still accept orders, even when our database is down for maintenance work. We can achieve this by sending all orders via a message queue. An interesting application of such messaging is for controlled resource throttling on a busy system. Rather than processing every single request (such as an order) completely as they are received, we can partially process each one. We can then create a message describing the rest of the work to be carried out, and place it in a queue for further processing. By using a queue you can decide how many messages are processed at once. So, rather than your server trying to process thousands of simultaneous orders requests SSLLOOWWLLYY, driving your customers away, you can do the initial processing, give the user the initial confirmation quickly, then forward the requests for complete processing at your leisure.

Windows 2000 uses **Microsoft Message Queue Server** (MSMQ) to provide messaging. A layer on top of this known as **queued components** provides the messaging service that most *component*-based Windows 2000 DNA applications will use. This additional layer allows you to asynchronously invoke methods on COM objects. The way this works is simple but very clever. When you create a COM object you actually get returned a reference to a **recorder** object, and not the actual object. You invoke the methods of the COM object as usual, and the queued components layer creates a message that records all the methods you called along with all the parameters etc. The message is forwarded to a **player** object that then creates the real COM object and invokes the various methods just as if you'd directly called them. This eliminates the need for you to implement the recorder/player infrastructure yourself. This is good news because it is difficult and time consuming to do, and it requires knowledge of fairly low-level C/C++ programming.

MSMQ supports and works together with Transaction Services. Using a salesman example, when a new order is taken we could log it against the value of sales, then create a message to process the sale later (check availablity, arrange delivery, charge the client) and place it in the new orders queue. Transaction services would ensure that, if the order was cancelled for any reason, the log entry would be deleted.

Last but not least, an important aspect of messaging is reliability. Window 2000 messaging ensures that once a message is placed in a queue it will be delivered once and only once.

Universal Data Access

Most applications today are centered around data in some way. Data is kept in spreadsheets, e-mail folders, databases and Mainframes etc. The business services tier of our Windows DNA application will need access to much of this data.

In order to access data from many diverse data stores, Microsoft has devised a strategy known as **Universal Data Access**. UDA describes how we can access structured and unstructured data in heterogeneous data sources. It is important to note that UDA isn't a database or data source API, but rather a strategy for data access. From an ASP perspective the key technologies for implementing UDA are: ADO, OLE DB, and ODBC.

Typically, data access is performed by an ASP page or data-access component within the business services tier using ActiveX Data Objects (ADO). This is very simple to use in ASP, as shown by this small VBScript example that simply opens a connection to an Access database:

```
<%
'Create a connection object.
Set objConn = Server.CreateObject("ADODB.Connection")
objConn.Open "Provider=Microsoft.Jet.OLEDB.4.0;Data Source=" & _
        "C:\aspprogref\rja.mdb"
%>
```

Or in JScript:

```
<%@ LANGUAGE=JScript%>
<%
//Create a connection object
var objConn = Server.CreateObject("ADODB.Connection");
objConn.Open ('Provider=Microsoft.Jet.OLEDB.4.0;Data Source=' +
        'C:\\aspprogref\\rja.mdb');
%>
```

> **ADO is described in more detail in Section IV of this book (Chapters 26 to 33).**

ADO is a layer on top of OLE DB, that consists of a set of low-level COM interfaces and components that define how a data source can be accessed and manipulated. OLE DB cannot be directly used in ASP script or VB. This limitation exists because VB and ASP script are not 100% COM capable, and cannot access COM interfaces that do not use automation-compatible data types, a subset of the full COM data types that can be used in C/C++.

OLE DB 2.5 (the version shipped with Windows 2000) is not defined as an API for relational databases like older APIs such as ODBC. Instead it is defined as an API for accessing data sources, and is therefore far more flexible. A data source can be just about anything, a text file, your e-mail folders or the afore-mentioned relational database. OLE DB was originally geared towards structured data in the form of columns and rows, but OLE DB 2.5 makes accessing unstructured data, such as ASP files from your web site a lot easier, thanks to some new interfaces and components.

XML

Over the past year or two we've all heard a lot about the promise of XML: the new markup language of the Web. It differs from HTML is that it does not have predefined tags and it is primarily concerned with describing the data rather than how it should be displayed.

For example, an HTML page containing information about a book might look like this:

```
<H1>ASP Prog Ref 3.0</H1>
<P>The aim of this book is to provide a comprehensive reference to
both the ASP technology itself as well as the ways that ASP can be
used within the Microsoft environment.</P>
```

Whilst a browser understands how to display this, and as humans, we can guess that it is information about a book, HTML does not explicitly say that the text within the H1 tags is the title of a book, and that the paragraph text is the abstract for the book. Here lies the biggest and most important different; with XML you can define your own tags, which will describe the content within them:

```
<Book>
   <Title>ASP Prog Ref 3.0</Title>
   <Abstract>The aim of this book is to provide a comprehensive
   reference to both the ASP technology itself as well as the
   ways that ASP can be used within the Microsoft environment.
   </Abstract>
</Book>
```

XML allows us to define our own tags that give semantic meaning to our data. Book, Title, and Abstract are far more evident and allow us more control over the data.

We can therefore use XML in many different ways within our DNA applications. We could pass XML between tiers, maybe to describe orders to be added to a database, or we could use XML as a simple client-side caching mechanism to reduce round trips. Microsoft is investing heavily in XML and this is reflected in Windows 2000 shipping with native support for XML in the form of MSXML. Originally released as an XML add-on component for IE4, MSXML version 2.0 is part of IE5, the native browser for Windows 2000.

In the next few months IE 5.5 will be released. This will ship by default with MSXML 2.6. This version of MSXML implements the latest W3C working drafts, and is significantly more scalable on multiple CPU boxes.

> **XML, XSLT, and XPath are covered in chapters 35 and 36.**

Web Services – The Next Generation of Web Development

Currently, information that a company exposes on the Web is mostly only available in HTML format. When we have found it we can remember it, save it to disk, print it out, or write it down, but all of these involve interpretation and are time consuming. We can develop a parser to extract the information but this is dependant on the structure of that site's pages.

For example, Amazon.com lists most of the Wrox Press books including this one. As an author I like to go to Amazon and see how the books I've been involved with are selling. To do this I have to manually go to each page and view the ranking and reviews. This is a real pain as I'm not interested in the flashy graphics and plugs for other books; I want to see only the two elements of information I'm interested in, the ranking of my book and the reviews. In SQL terms, I'd like to write something like this:

```
SELECT ranking, reviews FROM WWW.AMAZON.COM
WHERE PUBLISHER = 'Wrox Press' and Author = 'ME'
```

It would be very useful for me if Amazon would expose function for getting this information. It's safe to assume that the data access infrastructure is there, so all we need is a simple access method which bypasses the adding of all that HTML noise.

Any solution must take into account platform compatibility issues, it must be fairly easy, and it must be secure. This brings us to XML, or XML over HTTP. If Amazon were to use XML pages, we could have access to the information in either HTML or XML. While I could surf to the page traditionally is which a fairly simple .asp file could convert it to HTML, if I were to specifically ask for it in XML format, the page would be returned in the following form:

```
<Books>
  <Book>
    <Title>ProXML</Title>
    <Ranking>81</Ranking>
    <Reviews>
        <Review>I am new to XML and ...</Review>
        <Review>This book is ...</Review>
        <Review>Another review of this book</Review>
    <Reviews>
  </Book>
  ..
</Books>
```

The URL for this request might look something like:

```
http://www.amazon.com/querybooks.asp?publisher=wrox&author=me
```

This output can be generated just like any other HTML page, by using ASP and ADO. We've used HTTP, and all we've done is returned an XML document rather than HTML. XML is easy to parse, in fact made to parse, so I could easily write an application to load this file and process it. The page is not design-specific, that is it would be contained in the ASP file, so it wouldn't change if Amazon redesigned its site. What we've achieved is the creation of a web service. Using this simple technique sites like Amazon can expose all sorts of function to clients. Furthermore, other sites can easily consume this data and expose it on their sites. For example, Wrox Press could automatically display the Amazon ranking and reviews of their books on wrox.com.

What I've defined as a web service here is what I call a first generation web service. XML is returned from the server to client, but the client doesn't use XML to talk to the server. In a second generation web service XML is used by the client to the talk to the server. This gives the client more flexibility because the input data base to the web service can be arbitrarily complex. This model also means that more advanced services, potentially object-based, can be implemented. This second generation web service is what SOAP addresses.

> More details on SOAP can be found at `http://www.develop.com/soap`.

Summary

This introductory chapter contains:

- ❏ An overview of Windows 2000.
- ❏ An overview of Windows DNA.
- ❏ An overview of Component Services and COM+.
- ❏ An introduction to the topics covered in the rest of the book .

The ASP Intrinsic Objects

The ASP Intrinsic Objects

In this section we look at each of the ASP intrinsic objects. The two main intrinsic objects, the Request and Response objects map directly to the request and the response which the HTTP protocol uses to transfer information between the client and the web server. The other four objects provide a number of functions that are useful in scripting our ASP applications.

Each intrinsic object provides a range of methods, properties and collections.

❑ The **Application object** is created in response to the first request for an ASP page. It provides a repository for storing variables and object references that are available to all visitors accessing our site for the entire duration of our ASP application.

❑ The **ASPError object** is a new object in ASP 3.0. It provides a range of detailed information about the last error that occurred in ASP. It is used within custom error pages.

❑ The **Request object** exposes all the information provided by the client when requesting a page or submitting a form. This includes the HTTP variables identifying the client, the cookies stored for our site, and any values appended to the URL as a query string or in HTML controls from a form. It also enables us to access certificates used to identify a client through **Secure Sockets Layer (SSL)** or other encryption protocols, and provides properties for managing the connection.

❑ The **Response object** is used to create the response sent back to the client. It enables our scripts or components to use the HTTP variables for the server, information about the content we're sending to the browser, and any new cookies we're going to be store the browser. In addition, it provides methods for creating output, such as the Response.Write method.

❑ The **Server object** provides methods and properties that are useful in scripting with ASP, for example the Server.CreateObject method, for properly instantiating other COM objects on the server within the context of the current page or session. There are also methods for translating strings into the correct format for use in URLs and in HTML, by converting non-legal characters to the correct legal equivalent.

❑ The **Session object** is created for each visitor when they first request an ASP page. It provides a repository for storing variables and object references (although that should generally be avoided) that are available only to the pages that this visitor opens during the lifetime of the session. This is a very important way to maintain state.

Note that the ObjectContext object is not an ASP intrinsic object. It is an object created by COM+ used by IIS to expose these objects to our ASP pages and ASP components. We can think of these objects as forming a hierarchy based on the context object, though it is perhaps more useful to visualize them in relation to the process of receiving and responding to a client request.

The following diagram illustrates the relationship between ASP and the process of creating and serving ASP pages:

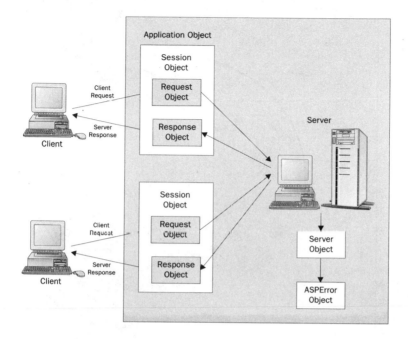

3

The Application Object

The ability to maintain state by remembering the values of particular variables between one page and the next is likely to be a fundamental requirement of a web application. ASP provides two objects which allow us to do this. As well as providing individual user sessions (which we can manage through the Session object, discussed in Chapter 8), ASP maintains a global Application object that can share values between *all* users of that application. An Application object is created when the first request is received for a page from the default web site application or a virtual application. Immediately afterwards, a user session is started for this user, and their individual Session object is created.

The single Application object then remains in scope (i.e. instantiated and available) as more sessions are started. The application ends, and the Application object is destroyed, only when the web server is stopped or the application is explicitly unloaded from the server. A single Application object is available to all multiple users and provides a repository for storing variables and object references that are available to all the pages that all visitors open.

The Application object has the following methods, properties, collections and events:

Methods	Properties	Events	Collections
Lock	Value	onStart	Contents
UnLock		onEnd	StaticObjects

As mentioned above, one of the features of an application is that information can be stored that is available to all clients accessing the web application. This information is stored in variables with what are called **application-level scope**.

Using Application-Scoped Objects and Variables

Our `global.asa` file can contain code that instantiates objects as well as code that creates and sets the values of variables that will be available in either application-level or session-level scope.

Creating and Storing Application-Level Objects

Application-level objects can be instantiated in the `global.asa` file using either the `Server.CreateObject` method, placed in the `Application_OnStart` event handler, or using an `<OBJECT>` HTML element. It is essential with applications that you *explicitly* declare application- and session-level objects and variables before they are used.

An instance of an application-level object can be created in our `global.asa` file by using the `<OBJECT>` element with either the Prog ID or Class ID of the object:

```
<OBJECT ID="ID" RUNAT="Server" SCOPE="Application" PROGID="progID"></OBJECT>
```

Or, if we are using the Class ID:

```
<OBJECT ID="ID" RUNAT="Server" SCOPE="Application" CLASSID="classID">
</OBJECT>
```

For example:

```
<!-- To declare an instance of the ASPCounter component
     with application-level scope -->

<OBJECT ID="MyCounter" RUNAT="Server" SCOPE="Application"
        PROGID="MSWC.Counters">
</OBJECT>
```

Alternatively, the `Server.CreateObject` method (described in detail in Chapter 7) can be used in the `Application_OnStart` event handler of `global.asa` to create an instance. For example, using VBScript to instantiate the Counters component:

```
Sub Application_OnStart()
   Dim MyCounter
   Set Application("MyCounter")=Server.CreateObject("MSWC.Counters")
   Application("MyCounter").Set "mycount",0
   ' and more stuff here ...
End Sub
```

Or using JScript:

```
function Application_OnStart() {
   var MyCounter
   Application("MyCounter") = Server.CreateObject("MSWC.Counters");
   Application("MyCounter").Set("mycount",0);
   // and more stuff here ...
}
```

> **Warning:** You should refrain from creating object instances at application- (and session-) level scope wherever possible due to performance implications. However, if you do require application-scoped objects, they should be agile components – both-threaded components that aggregate the Free Threaded Marshaler or neutral-threaded components. Apartment-threaded components should be avoided, and single-threaded objects should *never* be instantiated with application- (and session-) level scope. See Chapter 41 for more details.

When setting values in the `Application` object from another page, or from within the `Session_OnStart` event handler, the `Application.Lock` and `Application.UnLock` methods should be used to prevent concurrent updates from different users causing corruption of the values.

Creating and Storing Application-Level Variables

Application-level variables can be created, accessed and modified from any ASP page in the application. They are useful, for example, for creating log files or maintaining an application-specific connection *string* for accessing a database connection (note that maintaining the open connection is *not* a good use of application-scope variables). However, as with the use of global variables in traditional stand-alone applications, application-scoped variables in ASP should be used with care.

To store and retrieve application-level variables or arrays, we need to reference the variable name in the `Application` object: The syntax for creating or setting the value of application variables or arrays is:

```
Application("variable_name") = variable_value_or_variable_array
Application("variable_name") = object_reference
```

To retrieve the values of application-scoped variables or arrays:

```
variable_value_or_variable_array = Application("variable_name")
object_reference = Application("variable_name")
```

For example in VBScript:

```
' Store a starting Date as a string
Application("Start_Date") = CStr(Now)
' Retrieve the starting value
datStartDate = Application("Start_Date")
Response.write "Application Start Date = " & datStartDate
```

Or in JScript:

```
Application("Start_Date") = Date();
AppStartDate = Application("Start_Date");
Response.write("Application Start Date = " + AppStartDate);
```

Variant arrays can also be stored in an Application object, for example in VBScript:

```
' Create a Variant array and fill it
Dim varArray(2)
varArray(0) = "This is a Variant array "
varArray(1) = "stored in the "
varArray(2) = "Application object."
' Store it in the Application
Application("Variant_Array") = varArray
```

Because of the performance hit involved with storing apartment-threaded objects in the Application object, an error will be raised if we attempt to do this (although we can create apartment-threaded objects with application scope in the HTML <OBJECT> tag). JScript Array objects are apartment-threaded, so we are not allowed to store these in the Application; however, we can store a JScript VBArray object with application scope.

> You should be wary of placing too much information in application-
> (or session-) scoped objects. For example, if you stored recordsets in
> an application-scoped variant array, a large number of simultaneous
> visitors to your site could cause the server to run out of memory
> resources.

Application Object Methods

The Application object's methods allow us to control concurrent accesses to application-scoped variables.

Lock Method

The Lock method locks the Application object so that only the current ASP page has access to the contents. This ensures that concurrency issues do not corrupt the contents by allowing two users to read and update the values simultaneously.

```
Application.Lock()
```

To unlock the Application object variables, the ASP page should explicitly call the UnLock method, described below. If we do not call the UnLock method, the server will unlock the Application object when the page times out.

For example, this VBScript code can be used in Application_OnStart in global.asa or in any ASP page:

```
Response.Write "Number of Visitors = " & _
            Application("Visit_Count") & "<BR>"
Application.Lock
intVisits = Application("Visit_Count") + 1
Application("Visit_Count") = intVisits
Application.UnLock
Response.Write "New Count = " & Application("Visit_Count")
```

Or in JScript:

```
Response.Write ("Number of Visitors = " +
               Application("Visit_Count") + "<BR>");
Application.Lock()
Application("Visit_Count")++
Application.UnLock();
Response.Write("New Count = " + Application("Visit_Count"));
```

UnLock Method

The UnLock method releases this ASP page's lock on the Application object.

```
Application.UnLock()
```

This method should be called explicitly as soon as possible after the Lock method was called. When the page has locked the Application object, no other client accessing the web application can access any part of the Application object. This means that all the other clients will sit and wait for it to be released. If the Application object is locked for any longer than is necessary, our site will appear to be very slow, and its usability will decrease.

For an example of this method, see under the Lock method.

Application Object Properties

The only property of the Application object is the very rarely used Value property.

Value Property

The Value property (normally omitted) sets or returns the value of a variable stored in the Application object.

```
Application.Value(variable_name) = Variant
Variant = Application.Value(variable_name)
```

For example:

```
Application.Value("FirstName") = "John"
FirstName = Application.Value("FirstName")
```

Application Object Events

The Application object exposes two events that occur when the application starts and ends. The code for the handlers for these events is placed in the global.asa file.

An application *starts* when the first user requests an ASP page that is within the application scope, i.e. the default root directory of the web site or a user-defined virtual application within a subdirectory of the site. This occurs before any user sessions start. An application *ends* only when the web server is stopped or the application is explicitly unloaded from the server.

OnEnd Event

The OnEnd event is fired when the ASP application ends. This happens when the web server is stopped or the application is explicitly unloaded from the server. All variables existing in the application are destroyed when it ends; however, it is good practice to destroy explicitly any variables used.

For example in VBScript:

```
Sub Application_OnEnd()
    Set Application("ADOConnection") = Nothing
End Sub
```

Or in JScript:

```
function Application_OnEnd() {
    delete Application("ADOConnection");
}
```

OnStart Event

The OnStart event is raised when the ASP application starts, before the page that the user has requested is executed, and before any Session objects are created. The handler can be used to initialize variables, create objects, or run other code.

For example, this code can be placed in global.asa to create an instance of an ADO Connection object, a variant array, and two other variables – all with application-level scope:

```
Sub Application_OnStart()

    'Create an instance of an ADO Recordset with application scope
    Set Application("ADOConnection") = _
                            Server.CreateObject("ADODB.Connection")

    'Create a Variant array and fill it
    Dim varArray(2)
    varArray(0) = "This is a Variant array "
    varArray(1) = "stored in the "
    varArray(2) = "Application object."

    'Store it in the Application
    Application("Variant_Array") = varArray

    'Store the date/time as a string
    Application("Start_Time") = CStr(Now)

    'Set counter variable to zero
    Application("Visit_Count") = 0

End Sub
```

While we can't store a JScript Array in the Application (as we saw above), we can store objects and other variables:

```
function Application_OnStart() {
   Application("ADOConnection") =
                       Server.CreateObject("ADODB.Connection");
   Application("Start_Time") = String(Date());
   Application("Visit_Count") = 0;

}
```

> Note that this is only an example of the code that you use to create
> object instances. In general, you should refrain from creating object
> instances with application scope where possible. If you do require
> application-scoped objects, they should be agile objects: both-
> threaded components that aggregate the Free Threaded Marshaler or
> neutral-threaded components. Apartment-threaded and single-
> threaded objects should never be instantiated with application-level
> scope. See Chapter 41 for more details.

Application Object

Application Object Collections

The `Application` object has two collections – the `Contents` collection and the `StaticObject` collection.

The Contents Collection

The `Contents` collection is a collection of all variables and their values that are stored in the `Application` object, and are *not* defined using an <OBJECT> element (i.e., which have been added through script code). This includes variant arrays and variant-type object instance references.

```
Variant = Application.Contents(objItem)
```

The `Contents` collection exposes the following methods and properties:

Methods	Properties
Remove	Count
RemoveAll	Item
	Key

Although the `Contents` collection can be used to set and retrieve application-scoped variables, normally it is only used to obtain lists of variables that are available. The `Application` object is typically accessed directly to set or retrieve the contents of each variable:

```
Application("variable_name") = Variant
Variant = Application("variable_name")
```

We can iterate through the `Contents` collection using VBScript's `For Each...Next` construct:

```
For Each objItem in Application.Contents
   If IsObject(Application.Contents(objItem)) Then
      Response.Write "Object reference: '" & objItem & "'<BR>"
   ElseIf IsArray(Application.Contents(objItem)) Then
      Response.Write "Array: '" & objItem & "' contents are:<BR>"
      varArray = Application.Contents(objItem)
      'Note: the following only works with a one-dimensional array
      For intLoop = 0 To UBound(varArray)
         Response.Write "  Index(" & intLoop & ") = " &
varArray(intLoop) & "<BR>"
      Next
   Else
      Response.Write "Variable: '" & objItem & "' = " &
Application.Contents(objItem) & "<BR>"
   End If
Next
```

Or in JScript, using an Enumerator object:

```
var objEnum = new Enumerator(Application.Contents)
for (;!objEnum.atEnd();objEnum.moveNext()) {
   var objItem = objEnum.item();
   Response.Write('Application("' + objItem + '") = ' +
Application.Contents(objItem) + '<BR>');
}
```

Contents Collection Methods

The Contents collection provides two methods for removing variables from the Application object.

Remove Method

The Remove method removes a named variable from the Contents collection.

```
Application.Contents.Remove(variable_name)
```

Parameter	Data Type	Description
variable_name	Variant	The name of the variable to be removed from the Application.Contents collection.

For example, to remove a variable named Visit_Count from the Application object:

```
' VBScript
Application.Contents.Remove "Visit_Count"
```

```
Application.Contents.Remove('Visit_Count');
```

RemoveAll Method

The RemoveAll method removes all variables from the Contents collection.

```
Application.Contents.RemoveAll()
```

Contents Collection Properties

The Contents collection has three properties, which we can use to access the information in the collection.

Count

The Count property returns the number of items in the collection.

```
Integer = Application.Contents.Count
```

Item

The Item property sets or returns the value of a specific member of the collection.

```
Application.Contents.Item(Index) = Variant
Variant = Application.Contents.Item(Index)
```

Item is the default property of the Contents collection, so this is equivalent to:

```
Application.Contents(Index) = Variant
Variant = Application.Contents(Index)
```

The Index we use to specify the item can be either its ordinal position in the collection, or its name (key):

```
' VBScript
Application.Contents.Item("FirstName") = "John"
FirstName = Application.Contents.Item(1)
Response.Write "First Name = " &  FirstName
```

```
// JScript
Application.Contents.Item("FirstName") = "John";
FirstName = Application.Contents.Item(1);
Response.Write ("First Name = " +  FirstName);
```

Key

The Key property allows us to access the key of a specific member of the collection using its (one-based) ordinal position in the collection.

```
Index = Application.Contents.Key(Index)
```

For example, to find the key for the first item:

```
' VBScript
str_key = Application.Contents.Key(1)
str_item = Application.Contents.Item(str_key)
Response.Write "str_item = " & str_item
```

```
// JScript
var strkey = Application.Contents.Key(1);
var stritem = Application.Contents.Item(strkey);
Response.Write ('stritem = ' + stritem);
```

Application Object

The StaticObjects Collection

The StaticObjects collection is a collection of all of the variables that are stored in an application-scoped object that is created by using an <OBJECT> element in the global.asa file. For example, the StaticObjects collection would contain the ASPADRotator object created as follows:

```
<OBJECT ID="ASPADRotator" RUNAT="Server" SCOPE="Application"
        PROGID="MSWC.AdRotator">
</OBJECT>
```

The StaticObjects collection has the following methods and properties:

Methods	Properties
Remove	Count
RemoveAll	Item
	Key

Each member of the StaticObjects collection is read-only. Normally the StaticObjects collection is used only to obtain lists of variables that are available, whereas the Application object is accessed directly to retrieve the contents of each variable:

```
Variant = Application("variable_name")
```

For example:

```
' VBScript
objADRot = Application("ASPADRotator")
intBorder = Application.StaticObjects("ASPADRotator").Border
Response.Write "Border Integer = " & intBorder
```

```
// JScript
objADRot = Application('ASPADRotator');
var intBorder = Application.StaticObjects('ASPADRotator').Border;
Response.Write ("Border Integer = " + intBorder);
```

We can iterate through the StaticObjects collection using VBScript's For Each...Next construct:

```
For Each objItem in Application.StaticObjects
   If IsObject(Application.StaticObjects(objItem)) Then
      Response.Write "OBJECT element ID = " & objItem & "<BR>"
   End if
Next
```

Or in JScript, using an Enumerator object:

```
var objEnum = new Enumerator(Application.StaticObjects);
for (; !objEnum.atEnd(); objEnum.moveNext()) {
   var objItem = objEnum.item();
   Response.Write("OBJECT element ID = " + objItem + "<BR>");
}
```

StaticObjects Collection Methods

Remove Method

The Remove method removes a named variable from the StaticObjects collection.

```
Application.StaticObjects.Remove(Variable_name)
```

Parameter	Data Type	Description
Variable_name	Variant	The name of the variable to be removed from the Application.StaticObjects collection.

Note that objects cannot be removed from the Application.StaticObjects collection at run-time.

RemoveAll Method

The RemoveAll method removes all variables from the StaticObjects collection.

```
Application.StaticObjects.RemoveAll()
```

Note that variables cannot be removed from the Application.StaticObjects collection at run-time.

StaticObjects Collection Properties

The StaticObjects collection has three properties, which we can use to access the information in the collection.

Count

The Count property returns the number of items in the StaticObjects collection:

```
Integer = Application.StaticObjects.Count
```

Item

The Item property returns a specific member of the StaticObjects collection.

```
Application.StaticObjects.Item.(object_name) = Variant
Variant = Application.StaticObjects.Item(object_name)
```

This is equivalent to:

```
Application.StaticObjects(variant_name) = Variant
Variant = Application.StaticObjects(variant_name)
```

We can specify the item to be accessed using its ordinal position in the collection, or using its name (key).

Key

The Key property allows us to access the key of a specific member of the StaticObjects collection using its (one-based) ordinal position in the collection.

```
Variant = Application.StaticObjects.Key(Index)
```

Summary

In this chapter, we've looked at the Application object, which represents an ASP application. ASP applications allow us to allocate special properties to a set of pages that define how IIS and ASP will manage these pages, and any other components that they use.

However, the main reason for using ASP applications (and sessions) is often to maintain **state** automatically. In other words, the ability to store information and variable references that are either global and available to all pages loaded by users (i.e. in an application), or available to all pages for just a specific user (in a session). This makes it much easier to build web applications that can behave like traditional compiled applications to achieve specific tasks.

Application Object

4

The ASPError Object

ASP 3.0 introduces a number of features which enable us to better control the execution of pages, particularly when errors occur. The new ASPError object provides much better information for managing errors than previous versions of ASP.

The ASPError object – new in ASP 3.0 – is used to retrieve details of the last error that occurred in an ASP page. It is returned by the Server.GetLastError method described in Chapter 7. For example:

```
' VBScript
Set objASPError = Server.GetLastError()
```

```
// JScript
objASPError = Server.GetLastError();
```

IIS allows us the ability to create our own error pages: we can specify the page which will be displayed whenever an error occurs in a specific directory or even a specific page. The ASPError object is designed to be accessed within such a custom error page. We will look at how to set up a custom error page in the section on 'Configuring Custom Error Pages' later in this chapter.

The ASPError object provides nine properties that describe the error that occurred, the nature and source of the error, and (where possible) returns the actual code that caused it:

ASPError Object Properties

The ASPError object provides the following nine properties:

Properties		
ASPCode	Column	Line
ASPDescription	Description	Number
Category	File	Source

ASPCode Property

The ASPCode property returns a string which contains the error number that was generated by ASP or IIS.

```
String = ASPError.ASPCode
```

The ASPCode property value is generated by IIS, and will be empty for most script errors. It is more likely to appear for errors involving the use of external components.

The table below shows some common ASP error codes with the corresponding messages and extended information:

Error Code	Error Message	Extended Information
ASP 0100	Out of memory	Unable to allocate the required memory.
ASP 0101	Unexpected error	The function returned *exception_name*.
ASP 0102	Expecting string input	
ASP 0103	Expecting numeric input	
ASP 0104	Operation not allowed	
ASP 0105	Index out of range	An array index is out of range.
ASP 0106	Type Mismatch	A data type was encountered that cannot be handled.
ASP 0107	Stack Overflow	The quantity of data being processed is above the permitted limit.
ASP 0115	Unexpected error	A trappable error *exception_name* occurred in an external object. The script cannot continue running.
ASP 0177	Server.CreateObject Failed	Invalid ProgID.
ASP 0190	Unexpected error	A trappable error occurred while releasing an external object.
ASP 0191	Unexpected error	A trappable error occurred in the OnStartPage method of an external object.

Error Code	Error Message	Extended Information
ASP 0192	Unexpected error	A trappable error occurred in the OnEndPage method of an external object.
ASP 0193	OnStartPage Failed	An error occurred in the OnStartPage method of an external object.
ASP 0194	OnEndPage Failed	An error occurred in the OnEndPage method of an external object.
ASP 0240	Script Engine Exception	A script engine threw exception *exception_name* in *object_name* from *object_name*.
ASP 0241	CreateObject Exception	The CreateObject of *object_name* caused exception *exception_name*.
ASP 0242	Query OnStartPage Interface Exception	The querying object *object_name*'s OnStartPage or OnEndPage method caused exception *exception_name*.

ASPError Object

ASPDescription Property

The ASPDescription property returns a string containing the detailed description of the error, if it is ASP-related.

```
String = ASPError.ASPDescription
```

The ASPDescription property value is generated by the ASP pre-processor (rather than the script engine currently in use), and again will be empty for most script errors.

Category Property

The Category property is a string that indicates the source of the error – whether it was generated by ASP, by the scripting language, or by an external object.

```
String = ASPError.Category
```

There will always be a value for this property when an error has occurred.

Column Property

The Column property is a long integer value indicating the character position within a line of the file that generated the error.

```
Long = ASPError.Column
```

The Column property is only set if the details are available when the error occurs; this will usually be the case for syntax errors raised during compilation. For runtime errors, the File and Line properties are usually valid, but the Column property often returns -1.

Description Property

The Description property returns a short text description of the error.

```
String = ASPError.Description
```

There will always be a value for this property when an error has occurred.

File Property

The File property returns the name of the file that was being processed when the error occurred.

```
String = ASPError.File
```

Line Property

The Line property returns the number of the line within the file where the error was detected.

```
Long = ASPError.Line
```

The Line property is only set if the details are available when the error occurs. For a run-time error, the File and Line properties are usually valid, but the Column property often returns -1.

Number Property

The Number property returns the standard COM error code for the error that occurred.

```
Long = ASPError.Number
```

There will always be a value for the Number property, even if no error has occurred (if you call GetLastError and query this property in your ASP page, it will be zero if no error has occurred). Generally, for ASP script runtime errors, the Number property returns the hexadecimal value 0x800A0000 plus the standard scripting engine error code. For example, VBScript error code for a Subscript out of range error is 9, so ASPError.Number will return 0x800A0009 (-2146828279 decimal) for this error.

Source Property

The Source property returns the actual source code of the line where the error was detected, where available.

```
String = ASPError.Source
```

The source code which produced the error is only returned when the error is a syntax error that prevents the page being *processed* by ASP (rather than a runtime error that prevents it being *executed*). Generally in these cases, the Line and Column properties will be valid as well. If you write the value of the Source property into the page, it's wise to use the Server.HTMLEncode method in case it contains any characters which are illegal in HTML.

A Generic Custom Error Page

The ASPError object provides a way to display more details of any error that occurs when processing an ASP page. The following code demonstrates how to obtain a reference to an ASPError object and use its properties to display an informative error message. This page will be used as a custom error page that is executed automatically by ASP when an error occurs. We will see in the next section how we can configure IIS to load this page rather than the one supplied with IIS when an error is raised.

```
<HTML>
<HEAD>
<TITLE>ASP Error</TITLE>
</HEAD>
<BODY>
<%
Set objASPError = Server.GetLastError()

intNumber = objASPError.Number
strDesc = objASPError.Description
strSource = Server.HTMLEncode(objASPError.Source)
strFile = objASPError.File
intLine = objASPError.Line
intColumn= objASPError.Column
strCategory = objASPError.Category
strASPCode = objASPError.ASPCode
strASPDesc = objASPError.ASPDescription

strMsg = "<H2>" & strCategory & " error " & intNumber & "</H2>"
strMsg = strMsg & strDesc & "<BR><B>"
strMsg = strMsg & strFile & "</B>"

If intLine > 0 Then
   strMsg = strMsg & ", line " & intLine
End If

' If it's not a syntax error, the column will be -1
If intColumn > 0 Then
   strMsg = strMsg & ", column " & intColumn
End if
strMsg = strMsg & "<BR>"

' The source is only returned for compilation errors
If strSource <> "" Then
   strMsg = strMsg & "<BR><FONT FACE='courier'>" & strSource & "<BR>"
   For intCount = 1 To intColumn
      strMsg = strMsg & "-"
   Next
   strMsg = strMsg & "^</FONT><BR>"
End If
```

```
strMsg = strMsg & "<BR>"

' ASP-specific errors provide additional information in the
' ASPCode and ASPDescription properties
If strASPCode <> "" Then
   strMsg = strMsg & "ASP Error: " & strASPCode & ". " & strASPDesc
End If

Response.Write strMsg
Set objASPError = Nothing
%>
</BODY>
</HTML>
```

The JScript version of this page is:

```
<HTML>
<HEAD>
<TITLE>ASP Error</TITLE>
</HEAD>
<BODY>
<%
var objASPError = Server.GetLastError();
var intNumber = objASPError.Number;
var strDesc = objASPError.Description;
var strSource = Server.HTMLEncode(objASPError.Source);
var strFile = objASPError.File;
var intLine = objASPError.Line;
var intColumn= objASPError.Column;
var strCategory = objASPError.Category;
var strASPCode = objASPError.ASPCode;
var strASPDesc = objASPError.ASPDescription;

var strMsg = "<H2>" + strCategory + " error " + intNumber + "</H2>";
strMsg += strDesc + "<BR><B>";
strMsg += strFile + "</B>";

if (intLine > 0) {
   strMsg += ", line " + intLine;
}

// If it's not a syntax error, the column will be -1
if (intColumn > 0) {
   strMsg += ", column " + intColumn;
}
strMsg += "<BR>";

// The source is only returned for compilation errors
if (strSource != "") {
   strMsg += "<BR><FONT FACE='courier'>" + strSource + "<BR>";
   for (i = 0; i < intColumn; i++) {
      strMsg += "-";
   }
   strMsg += "^</FONT><BR>";
}
strMsg += "<BR>";

// ASP-specific errors provide additional information in the
```

```
// ASPCode and ASPDescription properties
if (strASPCode != "") {
    strMsg += "ASP Error: " + strASPCode + ". " + strASPDesc;
}
Response.Write(strMsg);
delete objASPError;
%>
</BODY>
</HTML>
```

This page simply gets a reference to the ASPError object using the Server.GetLastError method, and displays all its available properties in a format similar to the intrinsic error message supplied by Microsoft with IIS.

For a page that contains a syntax error, this produces an error message in the format:

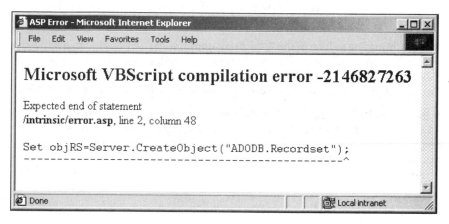

For a runtime scripting error, the message will not contain the line of source code which generated the error, but may contain additional information provided by ASP (the ASPCode and ASPDescription properties):

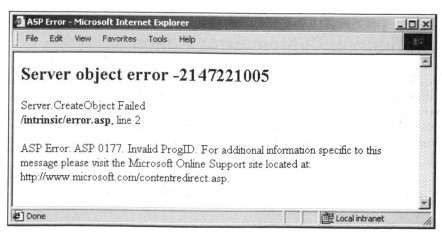

Code Inside a Custom Error Page

Remember that the full context of the page that contained the error is passed to the custom error page. This means that you can still use the values stored in any of the intrinsic ASP object collections or properties. For example if you retrieve the HTTP_REFERER value from the Request.ServerVariables collection, it will reflect the URL of the page that called the original page (i.e. the page before the one where the error occurred). It doesn't change when the server transfers execution to the error page, and so will not contain the URL of the page that was executing when the error occurred.

Likewise, the SCRIPT_NAME value will be the name of the page that contained the error, and not the error page URL. You can confirm this by checking the URL in the **Address** bar of your browser when an error page has been loaded. However, the values stored in script variables within the original page are *not* available in the custom error page.

By examining the values in the ASPError object, it is also possible to make a decision on what to do next. You may decide to ignore some kinds of errors, or use Server.Execute to go to different pages depending on what kind of error occurred. You might also want to store the error details in a log file or database for review later.

If the original ASP page is likely to be running within a transaction, i.e. it contains an <%@ TRANSACTION="..." %> directive at the top of the page, you should also consider whether you need to take some action within the page to abort the transaction. For example you may need to call the SetAbort method of the intrinsic ObjectContext object:

```
ObjectContext.SetAbort    'fail the transaction if an ASP error occurs
```

Or in JScript:

```
ObjectContext.setAbort();  //fail the transaction if an ASP error occurs
```

We'll be looking at the whole topic of transactions later in the book (in Chapter 34), and examine the role that ASP plays within them.

Configuring Custom Error Pages

When an error occurs on an ASP page and the page itself cannot be sent to the browser, IIS sends a page containing information about the error instead. This can be either an ASP page or a normal HTML page. IIS is installed with a number of default error pages – the standard ASP error messages you've probably encountered all too often during debugging – but we can actually instruct IIS to load any other page instead, these error pages are usually referred to as **custom error pages**.

The default error pages supplied with IIS can be found in the WinNT\Help\iishelp\common directory. These pages can be opened in a browser just like any other web pages, or the source code can be viewed in a text editor.

Error Page Mapping in IIS

When IIS detects an error, it sends an error page back to the client. Because different errors can result in different error pages, IIS maps individual error types to specific pages. We can alter these mappings on a directory-by-directory or a file-by-file basis. To change the error page for a particular directory or web page, open up the Custom Errors page of the directory's or file's Properties dialog by right-clicking on the directory or file in the Internet Services Manager and selecting Properties, and then selecting the Custom Errors tab:

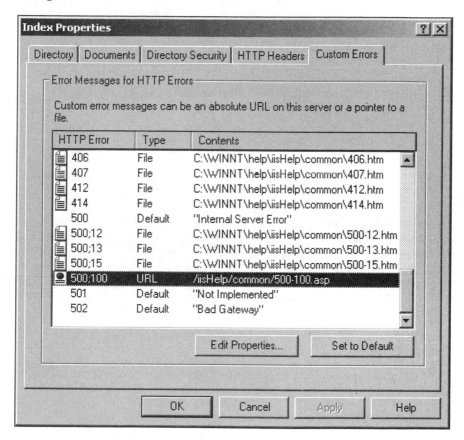

This displays a list of the HTTP errors to which we can map error pages, together with either the absolute URL or the physical path of the page to which the error is currently mapped. Errors generated by ASP are of type 500, and as you can see, some of these errors are already mapped to specific pages; these are generic errors such as Invalid Application and Server Shutting Down.

When ASP loads a page that contains a syntax error or in which a runtime error occurs, the error raised is of type 500;100. As the screenshot above shows, this error is by default mapped to an ASP page named 500-100.asp which resides in the /iishelp/common/ directory. We can, of course, edit this page if we want, but we can also change this setting to point to an entirely different page.

Specifying a Custom Error Page

Select the entry for the 500;100 error and click on the Edit Properties button. This will open the Error Mapping Properties dialog:

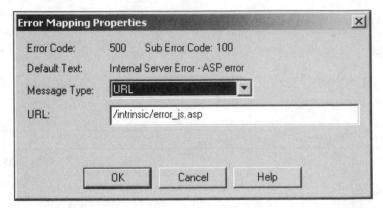

Because our custom error page is an ASP page rather than a normal HTML page, we have to map the error to a URL rather than a physical file path. So select URL in the Message Type drop-down box, and type the full virtual path (minus domain name, but including preceding forward slash) to your own custom error page. The generic error page example described earlier in this chapter can be used, or you can create your own. Now this custom error page will be opened whenever an error of type 500:100 occurs.

Summary

In this chapter, we examined the ASPError object, which is a new intrinsic object in ASP 3.0. It provides better error handling for our scripts. We can now provide 'proper' script error handling on a directory-by-directory or even file-by-file basis, and get better information about what went wrong. So in this chapter, we saw:

- ❑ How to get an instance of the ASPError object.
- ❑ How to use the properties of the ASPError object to retrieve information about an error.
- ❑ How to create a generic ASP error page.
- ❑ How to configure IIS to load custom error pages when an ASP error occurs.

The Request Object

The Request object makes available to our script all the information contained in the HTTP request; that is, the information provided by the client when it requests a page or submits a form. This includes the HTTP variables that identify the browser and the user; the cookies stored on the browser for this domain; and any values appended to the URL as a query string or in HTML controls in a <FORM> section of the page. It also provides us with access to the data in any client-side digital certificate if the connection is through a secure channel such as **Secure Sockets Layer (SSL)**.

The Request object has the following methods, properties and collections:

Methods	Properties	Collections
BinaryRead	TotalBytes	ClientCertificate
		Cookies
		Form
		QueryString
		ServerVariables

Request Object Methods

The Request object has a single method – the BinaryRead method.

BinaryRead Method

The BinaryRead method enables us to access the raw, unparsed content of the user's request that is POSTed to the server from a <FORM> on a web page.

```
Variant = Request.BinaryRead(number_of_bytes)
```

Parameter	Data Type	Description
number_of_bytes	Variant	The number of bytes to be read from the client when execution of this method is invoked

The `BinaryRead` method returns a read-only safe array of bytes (a safe array is an array that specifies the number of dimensions and the bounds of its dimensions). When the execution of the method is complete, `intCount` returns the number of bytes actually read from the client. This is usually less than or equal to the value returned by the `TotalBytes` property.

For example:

```
lngNumBytes = Request.TotalBytes                    'the size of the request
varPostedData = Request.BinaryRead(lngNumBytes)     'the raw data
```

Because scripting languages are usually able to deal only with variants and safe arrays of variants, you may find that you have limited use for this method. `BinaryRead` is typically used when uploading files; see the article at `http://www.15seconds.com/Issue/981121.htm`. It *cannot* be used successfully if you have already referenced the `Form` collection. Likewise, the `Form` collection cannot be successfully accessed if the `BinaryRead` method has already been called.

Request Object Properties

The `Request` object also has only one property, `TotalBytes`.

TotalBytes Property

The `TotalBytes` property allows us to determine the total number of bytes in the body of a request from the client. It is relatively rarely used in ASP pages, since we are normally more concerned with the specific values than the entire request string.

```
Long = Request.TotalBytes
```

The `TotalBytes` property returns the total number of bytes in the body of the request sent by the client. The property is read-only:

For example:

```
lngNumBytes = Request.TotalBytes
```

Request Object Collections

As well as giving us access to the raw data from the HTTP request through the `BinaryRead` method, the `Request` object has five collections which provide access to individual parts of the request.

ClientCertificate Collection

When the client makes contact with a web server over a secured channel, either end can gain high levels of assurance over the identity of the other by inspecting their **digital certificate**. A digital certificate contains a number of items of information about an individual or an organization and this is generated by a trusted third party called a **Certificate Authority** (CA). The CA is responsible for checking the credentials of the certificate owner.

> *A secured channel is a communications protocol that provides strong levels of security by providing encryption, message tampering detection and end-point authentication. The common secured channel protocol used by web servers and web browsers is the **Secure Sockets Layer (SSL)** – this is a variation of the HTTP protocol used when a web application required high levels of security.*
>
> *An SSL connection is instantiated by the client specifying a URL with an* https:// *protocol prefix. In fact, HTTPS is simply SSL underlying HTTP. This protocol defines how servers request certifications and browsers send the appropriate certification fields.*

The format of a digital certificate is defined by the X.509 specification. You can find this at http://www.ietf.cnri.reston.va.us/html.charters/pkix-charter.html, and there's an explanation of X.509 at http://poetry-server.cc.columbia.edu/acis/rad/columbiaca/more-info-cert.html. Secured channels and digital certificates rely on complex cryptographic algorithms that are far beyond the scope of this book. All an ASP developer really needs to know is that a client-side digital certificate contains various items of information about the certificate holder, such as the holder's key, name and address, the length of time the certificate is valid for.

By setting up a secure web site or a secure section of a site, IIS can force browsers to provide a client certificate to the server. If we want to configure IIS to require client certificates, we first need to obtain a server-side certificate for our web site and configure IIS to be able to recognize client certificates which are sent from the browser. We can do this by installing Certificate Services and issuing our own client certficates; we show how to do this in Appendix C.

The client's details are digitally encrypted into this certificate as a set of **fields**, and each time that client requests a secure page, the values from the certificate are exposed through the ClientCertificate collection. The data from this collection can be accessed using the syntax:

> *String* = Request.ClientCertificate(*field_name[sub_field]*)

Name	Data Type	Description
field_name	String	The name of the field in the ClientCertificate collection (see the table below).
sub_field	String	Optional. Used to extract individual items in place of the whole Issuer or Subject field.

91

Accessing the ClientCertificate collection and passing in the name of a specific field (and optionally also a subfield) returns the value of that field in the client certificate that the browser presents to the server when it accesses a page or resource. This is read-only.

For example, in VBScript:

```
strExpires = Request.ClientCertificate("ValidUntil")
Response.Write "The certificate is valid until " & strExpires
```

And in JScript:

```
var strExpires = Request.ClientCertificate('ValidUntil');
Response.Write('The certifiate is valid until ' + strExpires);
```

You should always check that a certificate is available before accessing the certificate's fields. This can be done, for example, using:

```
If Len(Request.ClientCertificate("Subject"))=0 Then
   Response.Write "Error - There is no client certificate available."
End if
```

The easiest way to do this in JScript is to check the collection's Count property (discussed below):

```
if (Request.ClientCertificate.Count==0) {
   Response.Write('Error - There is no client certificate available.');
}
```

Users can obtain digital certificates from a variety of sources, such as Verisign (http://www.verisign.com) or Thawte Consulting (http://www.thawte.com).

ClientCertificate Fields

As we have seen, the data in the certificate is exposed as a set of fields which are available through the ClientCertificate collection. These fields are not identical for every certificate, but will include:

Name	Data Type	Description
Certificate	String	The certificate content in its entirety, in ASN.1 format (Abstract Syntax Notation One – a notation for describing abstract types and values – see http://auchentoshan.cs.ucl.ac.uk: 8877/htm/pkcs/layman.htm).

Name	Data Type	Description
Flags	Variant	Additional information about the certificate. This can be ceCertPresent (or 1) (meaning that a client certificate is present), or ceUnrecognizedIssuer (2) (meaning that the last certification in this chain is from an unknown issuer). These constants are defined in the server-side include file cervbs.inc.
Issuer	Comma-delimited list of strings	Contains information relating to the trusted third party that is the issuer of the certificate. Consists of a number of separate sub-fields that can be extracted individually (see below).
SerialNumber	String	Contains the certification serial number that is allocated by the trusted third party that issued the certificate. It is formatted as an ASCII representation of hexadecimal bytes separated by hyphens, for example "04-67-F3-02".
Subject	Comma-delimited list of strings	Contains information on the visitor that is presenting the certificate. Consists of a number of separate sub-fields that can be extracted individually (see below).
ValidFrom	Date	The date that the certificate becomes valid. The format depends on the international settings of the browser.
ValidUntil	Date	The date that the certificate expires. The format depends on the international settings of the browser.

The Subject and Issuer fields can also accept a sub-field name. This usually consists of one or two letters that identify the sub-field value that is required. If no sub-field identifier is specified, then the entire field is returned with all the sub-field values concatenated into a single string:

```
String = Request.ClientCertificate(field_name_and_subfield_letters)
```

For example in VBScript:

```
strOrgName = Request.ClientCertificate("SubjectO")
Response.Write "The user's organizaion is " & strOrgName
```

And in JScript:

```
var strOrgName = Request.ClientCertificate('SubjectO');
Response.Write('The user\'s organizaion is ' + strOrgName);
```

Request Object

The most common sub-fields for the Subject and Issuer fields are:

Sub-field ID	Description
C	The user's country name
CN	The common name of the user (only used with the Subject field)
GN	The user's given name or first name
I	The user's initials
L	The user's locality
O	The user's company or organization name
OU	The user's organizational unit name
S	The user's state or province name
T	The user's title or the organization type

Properties of the ClientCertificate Collection

The ClientCertificate collection has three properties, which we can use to access the information in the collection.

ClientCertificate Properties
Count
Item
Key

Count

The Count property returns the number of fields in the certificate.

```
Integer = Request.ClientCertificate.Count
```

If this property returns zero, no client certificate has been sent, so we can use this property to check that a client certificate is present before accessing its fields.

Item

The Item property allows us to access a specific member of the collection.

```
Variant = Request.ClientCertificate.Item(Index)
```

We can specify the item to be accessed using either its index in the collection or its name:

```
' VBScript
Response.Write "Serial number = " &
Request.ClientCertificate.Item("SerialNumber")
' Or:
Response.Write "Serial number = " & Request.ClientCertificate.Item(20)
```

```
// JScript
Response.Write("Serial number = " +
Request.ClientCertificate("SerialNumber"));
// Or:
Response.Write("Serial number = " + Request.ClientCertificate(20));
```

Since this property is the default, it can also be omitted:

```
' VBScript
Response.Write "Serial number = " & Request.ClientCertificate("SerialNumber")
```

```
// JScript
Response.Write("Serial number = " +
Request.ClientCertificate("SerialNumber"));
```

Key

The Key property allows us to retrieve the name of a specific field.

```
Variant = Request.ClientCertificate.Key(Index)
```

We can use this property to iterate through the collection:

```
' VBScript
For intCount = 1 To Request.ClientCertificate.Count
    strKey = Request.ClientCertificate.Key(intCount)
    strValue = Request.ClientCertificate(intCount)
    If Len(strValue) > 60
        strValue = Left(strValue, 60) & ".. etc."
    End If
    Response.Write strKey & " = " & strValue & "<BR>"
Next
```

Or in JScript:

```
// JScript
for (i=1; i<Request.ClientCertificate.Count; i++) {
    strKey = Request.ClientCertificate.Key(i);
    strValue = String(Request.ClientCertificate(i));
    if (strValue.length > 60) {
        strValue = strValue.slice(0, 60) + ".. etc."
    }
    Response.Write(strKey + " = " + strValue + "<BR>");
}
```

The output from this code will be something like this:

Cookies Collection

The cookies mechanism enables a web server to store a small packet of information – a **cookie** – in a file on the client's hard drive for later access and use. Cookies are a popular way of getting round the problem that HTTP is a stateless protocol: that is, every time a page is requested, the server just produces a response and returns it. When another request is received from the same user, the server has no idea whether there was a previous request. Because information stored in a cookie on the client will be sent to the server whenever that user requests a page from our domain, cookies provide a way of tracking users or retaining the values of variables. A cookie can contain information that was sent from the client to the server, or information that was created by the server without client intervention. For example, a cookie may contain a CustomerID number that's generated by the server and used exclusively by the server for admin purposes. Our ASP script can use this CustomerID to identify individual users and personalize the pages which are served to them.

> *See the Response.Cookies collection in the following chapter for more information on creating cookies.*

The cookie is written to the client by including the cookie name and its value (and optionally a domain/path name and expiry date) within an HTTP response. With ASP this is done using the Response.Cookies collection (see the next chapter). When the server wants to access the information contained within a cookie, it does so through the Request.Cookies collection.

If you're curious about this distinction, you might be interested to note that behind the scenes ASP implements two different interfaces for the cookie objects. Each member of the Request.Cookies *collection exposes the* IReadCookie *interface, whereas the objects in the* Response.Cookies *collection expose the* IWriteCookie *interface. This is why these objects are able to have different sets of properties.*

Cookies contain information that can be structured in two ways: **single value** cookies and **multiple value** cookies. In the former case, the cookie stores only a single value, for example the date the web site was last visited. Multiple value cookies however, store data organized into key/item pairs. for example if the cookie is used to store details captured from a form. In key/item pairs (also commonly called name/value pairs) each item or value is associated with a unique key that is used to distinguish that item. For example the key "firstName" might be associated with the item "John" and another key "familyName" might be associated with the item "Smith".

Key/item pairs are discussed in relation to the Dictionary *object in Chapter 9.*

The syntax for retrieving a value from a cookie in the Request.Cookies collection is:

```
String = Request.Cookies(index, [subfield])
```

Name	Data Type	Description
index	Variant	Either a string containing the name of the cookie to be retrieved, or a number indicating the position of the cookie in the collection.
subfield	Variant	Optional. Used to retrieve individual items from a cookie that contains multiple values. Again, this can be either a string containing the key for the item, or a number representing its position.

Accessing the Request.Cookies collection only returns values for the cookies that are valid for the domain containing the resource to the server. If a single value cookie is used then using the Cookies collection returns the value of the cookie as a read-only string. For a multiple value cookie the read only string returned can either contain all the key/item pairs or, if a sub field is specified, the specified individual item from the cookie.

An example of using a single value cookie in VBScript:

```
strSingleValue = Request.Cookies("LastVisit")
```

Or in JScript:

```
var strSingleValue = Request.Cookies('LastVisit');
```

And an example of using a multiple value cookie in VBScript:

```
strSubItemValue = Request.Cookies("Preferences")("BGColor")
```

Or in JScript:

```
var strSubItemValue = Request.Cookies('Preferences')('BGColor');
```

Properties of the Cookies Collection

The `Request.Cookies` collection, in common with other collections provides the properties `Count`, `Item` and `Key`. To create, modify and send cookies back to the client, the `Response.Cookies` collection is used.

Request.Cookies Properties
Count
Item
Key

Count

The `Count` property returns the number of cookies which are sent by the browser in the request. Note that cookies will only be sent to servers in the same domain as the server which originally created the cookie. When a cookie is created, we can further limit the pages to which it will be sent by setting its `Path` property or by stipulating that it can only be sent over secure channels: see the `Response.Cookies` collection in Chapter 6.

```
Integer = Request.Cookies.Count
```

As with other collections, the `Count` property can be used to loop through all the members of the collection:

```
' VBScript
For intCount = 1 To Request.Cookies.Count
    Response.Write Request.Cookies(intCount) & "<BR>"
Next
```

```
// JScript
for (i=1; i<Request.Cookies.Count; i++) {
    Response.Write(Request.Cookies(intCount) + "<BR>");
}
```

Item

The `Item` property retrieves the value of the item for a specified key or index number.

```
Variant = Request.Cookies.Item(Index)
```

This property returns either an object representing an individual cookie (for a multiple-valued cookie), or a string containing the value stored in the cookie (for a single-valued cookie).

For example, we can represent a specific cookie in the cookie collection, by using `Request.Cookie.Item("myCookie");` this is equivalent to `Request.Cookie("myCookie")`.

Key

The read-only `Key` property returns the name of a specific cookie based on its position.

```
Cookie = Request.Cookies.Key(Index)
```

The *Index* can actually be either an integer representing the cookie's position in the collection, or a string containing the name of the cookie. Since this is the same as the value returned by the property, this syntax isn't very useful.

The `Key` can be used when the name of a specific key is unknown, or when iterating through the cookies in the collection:

```
' VBScript
For intCount = 1 To Request.Cookies.Count
    Response.Write Request.Cookies.Key(intCount) & " = " & _
                   Request.Cookies.Item(intCount) & "<BR>"
Next
```

```
// JScript
for (i = 1; i <= Request.Cookies.Count; i++) {
    Response.Write(Request.Cookies.Key(i) + " = " +
                   Request.Cookies.Item(i) + "<BR>");
}
```

Properties of Individual Cookies

Each item in the `Cookies` collection is itself an object, representing a cookie stored on the client. Since cookie objects can themselves contain more than one item of data, stored in key/item pairs, the cookie object exposes four properties to allow us to access this data:

Cookie Properties
Count
HasKeys
Item
Key

Count

The `Count` property returns the number of key/item pairs stored in the cookie.

```
Integer = Request.Cookies(Cookiename).Count
```

HasKeys

The `HasKeys` property indicates whether a cookie is a multiple-value or single-value cookie.

```
Boolean = Request.Cookies(Cookiename).HasKeys
```

If the cookie has sub-items (that is, if it is a dictionary cookie), this will return `true`. If the cookie is single-valued, `HasKeys` will return `false`.

It is a good idea to check this property before accessing the data in the cookie, since the structure of the data will vary, depending on whether the cookie is single- or multiple-valued. For example in VBScript:

```
For Each objItem In Request.Cookies
    If Request.Cookies(objItem).HasKeys Then
        'Use another For Each to iterate all subkeys
        For Each objItemKey in Request.Cookies(objItem)
            Response.Write objItem & "(" & objItemKey & ") = " & _
                            Request.Cookies(objItem)(objItemKey) & "<BR>"
        Next
    Else
        'Print out the cookie string as normal
        Response.Write objItem & " = " & Request.Cookies(objItem) & "<BR>"
    End If
Next
```

Or in JScript (using an `Enumerator` object to iterate through the collection):

```
var enumCookies = new Enumerator(Request.Cookies)
for (;!enumCookies.atEnd();enumCookies.moveNext()) {
    var objCookie = enumCookies.item();
    if (Request.Cookies(objCookie).HasKeys) {
        // Use another Enumerator to iterate all subkeys
        var enumTheCookie = new Enumerator(Request.Cookies(objCookie));
        for (;!enumTheCookie.atEnd();enumTheCookie.moveNext()) {
            var objSubItem = enumTheCookie.item();
            Response.Write(objCookie + '(' + objSubItem + ') = ' +
                            Request.Cookies(objCookie)(objSubItem) + '<BR>');
        }
    } else {
        // Print out the cookie string as normal
        Response.Write(objCookie + ' = ' + Request.Cookies(objCookie) +
'<BR>');
    }
}
```

Item

The `Item` property returns a specific value from a dictionary cookie.

```
Variant = Request.Cookies(Cookiename).Item(Index)
```

The `Index` can be either a string containing the key for the item This is the default property for a cookie, and is usually omitted. For example:

```
strFirst = Request.Cookies("name").Item("first")
```

This is identical to:

```
strFirst = Request.Cookies("name")("first")
```

Key

The Key property returns a specific key from a multiple-valued cookie.

```
Variant = Request.Cookies(Cookiename).Key(Index)
```

Again the *Index* can either be a string containing the value of the key, or a number representing its position in the cookie, but using a string value doesn't make much sense.

Form Collection

Let's briefly take a look at the familiar **HTML form** where we enter the information into text boxes or select boxes and then click on the SUBMIT button. Each element of a form is named, and the name (or key) is paired with the data item given in that form element. These key/item pairs (also commonly called name/value pairs) are sent back to the server in the form of a string, which is accessed either by the Form collection or by the QueryString collection. When the form is submitted, the web browser initiates an HTTP request for the URL specified in the form's ACTION attribute (see the examples below).

The METHOD attribute of the <FORM> tag specifies how the elements in the form are to be packaged within the HTTP Request message when they are sent to the server. Also, if the page specified in the form's ACTION attribute is an .asp page, the form's METHOD attribute determines the appropriate Request object collection to be populated with the HTML form data. The METHOD attribute takes one of the following values:

METHOD attribute	How are the form elements sent?	Request collection used to read data
POST	Inside HTTP request body (the free format area of the HTTP request).	Form
GET	Tagged onto the end of the URL.	QueryString

The default if omitted is the GET method. Here's an example of a <FORM> tag for a form sent using the GET method.

```
<FORM NAME="CureAmnesia" ACTION="memory.asp" METHOD="GET">
```

Here, the URL (specified by the ACTION attribute) is suffixed with a question mark delimiter, followed by the key/item pairs from the HTML form.

```
http://testserver.com/memory.asp?FirstName=Abraham&LastName=Lincoln
```

The section of the URL that follows the ? is called the **query string**. The HTML form information (in this case, the values FirstName and LastName) are then accessible in the Request.QueryString collection. The GET method has the disadvantage that there are limits imposed by the browser and server on the length of URL strings and also the query string is exposed in the **Address** bar of the browser, which is not only ugly but may expose values you may not want visible in the HTTP request that is passed over the Web.

For these reasons you should generally use the POST method for a form. An example of an HTML <FORM> tag for a form sent using the POST method:

```
<FORM NAME="BirthdayCard" ACTION="InMailbox.asp" METHOD="POST">
```

Here, the key/item pairs are sent in the body of the HTTP request that requests InMailbox.asp. The HTML form information is then accessible via the Request.Form collection.

The Form collection enables us to retrieve the values the user has submitted into web page forms. It is a collection of the values of all the HTML control elements in the <FORM> section that was submitted as the request, where the value of the METHOD attribute is POST. The key/item pairs used to store data in forms are similar to those used in the Dictionary object – see Chapter 9.

```
String = Request.Form(control_name)
```

Name	Data Type	Description
control_name	String	Specifies the name of the element

The Form collection returns the values of the items submitted to the form as a read-only string.

For example in VBScript:

```
strName = Request.Form("txtName")
Response.Write "The control value is " & strName
```

Or in JScript:

```
var strName = Request.Form('txtName');
Response.Write('The control value is ' + strName);
```

To retrieve the complete list of key/item pairs as a string, omit the control name:

```
strAllValues = Request.Form
```

If there are two controls on the <FORM> that has METHOD="POST", named Text1 and Text2 with values Value1 and Value2, this returns:

```
Text1=Value1&Text2=Value2
```

Values from HTML controls in a <FORM> section of a page arrive at the server in the Form collection only when the value of the METHOD attribute for the <FORM> is POST. If it is GET (or omitted), the values arrive in the QueryString collection instead. See the section on 'HTML Control Values' for information on how the different types of controls provide values to this collection.

Properties of the Form Collection

The Form collection provides the properties Count, Item and Key, which are illustrated in the examples following example using simple forms and dealing with multi-selection controls:

Request.Form Properties
Count
Item
Key

Count

The Count property returns an integer giving the number of items in the collection.

```
Integer = Request.Form.Count
```

We can use this to iterate through the collection with VBScript by using an integer index:

```
For intLoop = 1 To Request.Form.Count
   Response.Write Request.Form.Item(intLoop) & "<BR>"
Next
```

An alternative is to use of the For Each...Next construct:

```
For Each objItem In Request.Form
   Response.Write objItem & " = " & Request.Form(objItem) & "<BR>"
Next
```

The equivalent for construct in JScript is:

```
for (intLoop = 1; intLoop <= Request.Form.Count; intLoop++)
   Response.Write(Request.Form(intLoop) + '<BR>');
```

A JScript `Enumerator` object can also be used as the equivalent of the VBScript `For...Next` construct:

```
var objEnum = new Enumerator(Request.Form);
for (; !objEnum.atEnd(); objEnum.moveNext()) {
   var objItem = objEnum.item();
   Response.Write(objItem + ' = ' + Request.Form(objItem) + '<BR>');
}
```

Item

The `Item` property retrieves the value of the item for a specified key or index number.

```
Variant = Request.Form.Item(Index)
```

This is equivalent to:

```
Variant = Request.Form(Index)
```

Key

The `Key` property retrieves the name of an object in the Form collection as a read-only variant.

```
Variant = Request.Form.Key(Index)
```

This property can be used when the name of a specific key is unknown, although this is not recommended since it makes your code less clear and means you may have to change a considerable amount of code if a small change is made to a form.

HTML Control Values

The different HTML controls on a `<FORM>` behave in different ways as to how their values are submitted to the server. This is reflected in the values that appear in the `Form` and `QueryString` collections.

HTML Control Type:	Form or QueryString Collection Contains:
INPUT TYPE="TEXT"	The text string in the control, as set by the user or the VALUE attribute.
INPUT TYPE="HIDDEN"	The text string in the control, as set by the VALUE attribute.
INPUT TYPE="CHECKBOX"	When checked, the value of the HTML VALUE attribute or "on" if it has no VALUE attribute. When not checked, no value is returned.
INPUT TYPE="RADIO"	When checked, the value of the HTML VALUE attribute or "on" if it has no VALUE attribute. When not checked, no value is returned.
INPUT TYPE="SUBMIT"	When clicked to submit the form, the value of the HTML VALUE attribute if one exists.

HTML Control Type:	Form or QueryString Collection Contains:
INPUT TYPE="IMAGE"	When clicked to submit the form, the value of the HTML VALUE attribute if one exists.
SELECT	The value of the HTML VALUE attribute from the selected item's OPTION element, or the text string displayed in the list for that OPTION element if it has no VALUE attribute.
SELECT MULTIPLE	A comma-delimited string containing values of the HTML VALUE attributes from all selected OPTION elements, or the text string displayed in the list for these OPTION elements if they have no VALUE attributes.

If there is more than one INPUT TYPE="TEXT" or INPUT TYPE="HIDDEN" control on the <FORM> that has the same value for the NAME attribute, the value that is returned for that control name is a comma-delimited string of all the values.

If more than one INPUT TYPE="RADIO" control on the <FORM> has the same value for the NAME attribute, the value that is returned for that control name is the value of the selected control's VALUE attribute if present, or "on" if no VALUE is specified for the selected control. If there are more than one form field with the same name, the values appear as a comma-delimited list of values.

Working with Simple Forms

Here's the HTML code that makes a form, handled using the POST method:

```
<FORM NAME="SimpleForm" ACTION="DealWithForm.asp" METHOD="POST">
    Type your name here: <INPUT TYPE="TEXT" NAME="USERNAME"> <BR>
    Type your phone number here: <INPUT TYPE="TEXT" NAME="PHONENO"> <P>
    <INPUT TYPE=RESET  VALUE="Clear">
    <INPUT TYPE=SUBMIT VALUE="Submit">
</FORM>
```

As you can see, we have two input lines implemented with <INPUT> HTML elements of the type "TEXT", and two buttons with default actions – RESET and SUBMIT. In this form. we use the POST method to send data from the client browser to an ASP application; so the data is placed in the Form collection.

Now it's up to the ASP script logic to process the data sent from the client. Because we've used the POST method on the client side, we extract the data from the Form collection. As with other collections, we can simply iterate through the items as shown below:

```
<% ' VBScript
    For Each Item in Request.Form
        Response.Write "For element '" & Item & _
                        "' you've entered the value '" & _
                        Request.Form(Item) & "'<BR>"
    Next
%>
```

```
<% // JScript
    enmForm = new Enumerator(Request.Form);
    for (; !enmForm.atEnd(); enmForm.moveNext()) {
        item = enmForm.item();
        Response.Write("For element '" + item +
                        "' you've entered the value '" +
                        Request.Form(item) + "'<BR>");
    }
%>
```

The generated HTML will produce this output for our simple form, which displays the name of each element (set using the NAME attribute of the appropriate HTML tag), and the value of that element:

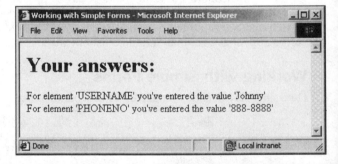

Alternatively, rather than dumping the entire contents of the form onto the browser display, we can access the values of individual elements. Assuming we know the names of the elements in the form, we can simply use names to access their values:

```
Response.Write "Hello, <I>" & Request.Form("USERNAME") & "</I>!<BR>"
```

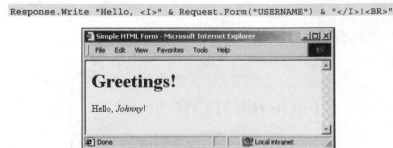

Dealing with Multi-Selection Controls

There are some controls that allow users to choose more than one value from a list of options. We can see this in action by looking at the <SELECT> control. Consider the following example:

```
<FORM NAME="MultiChoice" ACTION="DealWithForm3.asp" METHOD="POST">
   <H2>Which continents have you visited? </H2><BR>
   <INPUT NAME="Cnent" TYPE=CHECKBOX VALUE="Africa"> Africa <BR>
   <INPUT NAME="Cnent" TYPE=CHECKBOX
                       VALUE="North America"> North America <BR>
   <INPUT NAME="Cnent" TYPE=CHECKBOX
                       VALUE="South America"> South America <BR>
   <INPUT NAME="Cnent" TYPE=CHECKBOX VALUE="Asia"> Asia <BR>
   <INPUT NAME="Cnent" TYPE=CHECKBOX
                       VALUE="Australasia"> Australasia <BR>
   <INPUT NAME="Cnent" TYPE=CHECKBOX VALUE="Europe"> Europe <P>
   <INPUT TYPE=RESET  VALUE="Clear">
   <INPUT TYPE=SUBMIT VALUE="Submit">
</FORM>
```

The user is permitted to choose any number of options in the list. When the form is submitted, we can use the `Request.Form` collection's `Count` property to determine the number of selected element items:

```
<%
   If Request.Form("Cnent").Count<=1 Then
      Response.Write("Not too well-traveled, huh?")
   Else
      Response.Write("You've really been to all these places?" & "<BR>")
      For i = 1 To Request.Form("Cnent").Count
         Response.Write (Request.Form("Cnent")(i) & "<BR>")
      Next
      Response.Write("<BR>" & "Impressive...")
   End If
%>
```

Or in JScript:

```
<%
   if (Request.Form("Cnent").Count<=1) {
      Response.Write("Not too well-traveled, huh?");
   } else {
      Response.Write("You've really been to all these places?" + "<BR>");
```

```
    for (i = 1; i <= Request.Form("Cnent").Count; i++) {
        Response.Write (Request.Form("Cnent")(i) + "<BR>");
    }
    Response.Write("<BR>" + "Impressive...");
}
%>
```

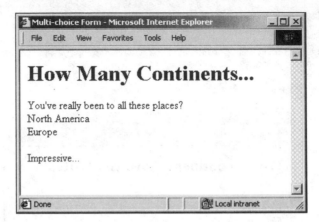

QueryString Collection

The QueryString collection enables us to retrieve the values of query strings – the key/item pairs (also commonly called name/value pairs) appended to the URL in the user's request. Such query strings result for example when an HTML form is submitted using the GET method, or where the attribute is omitted. You can see examples of query strings in the address bar of the browser, say, after an internet search.

```
http://www.wrox.com/Consumer/Store/ListTitles.asp?By=104
http://search.yahoo.com/bin/search?p=socks+football
```

The syntax for accessing an item in the QueryString collection is:

```
String = Request.QueryString(Name)
```

Name	Data Type	Description
Name	String	Specifies the name of the variable in the HTTP query string to be retrieved

The QueryString collection returns the items associated with the key values if a key is specified, or the complete query string if the method is used without specifying a value or control name.

For example, if the requested URL is:

```
http://yourserver.com/yourpage.asp?FirstName=John&FamilyName=Jones
```

then the following VBScript example:

```
strName = Request.QueryString("FirstName")
strSurname = Request.QueryString("FamilyName")
Response.Write "'" & strName & "' has the Family Name '" & strSurname & "'."
```

will give:

```
'John' has the Family Name 'Jones'.
```

To retrieve the complete list of key/item pairs as a string, omit the value or the control name:

```
strAllValues = Request.QueryString
Response.Write strAllValues
```

For the URL above, this returns:

```
FirstName=John&FamilyName=Jones
```

A query string is attached to a URL when GET is specified as the value of the METHOD attribute for the <FORM> (or when the METHOD is omitted). If METHOD="POST", the values arrive in the Form collection instead. See the section on 'HTML Control Values' for information on how the different types of controls provide values to this collection.

For example, the following form has two controls:

```
<FORM NAME="MainStories" ACTION="news.asp" METHOD="GET">
    <P>Which main story do you want to read more details about?</P>
    <SELECT NAME="NewsItem">
       <OPTION VALUE="Story1">World Cup News</OPTION>
       <OPTION VALUE="Story2">Hurricane</OPTION>
       <OPTION VALUE="Story3">Politician's Downfall</OPTION>
    </SELECT>
    <P>What coverage do you want?<BR>
    <INPUT TYPE="RADIO" NAME="Coverage"
                        VALUE="Short">Short (single page)<BR>
    <INPUT TYPE="RADIO" NAME="Coverage" VALUE="Long">2-3 Pages</P>
    <INPUT TYPE=RESET  VALUE="Clear">
    <INPUT TYPE=SUBMIT VALUE="Submit">
</FORM>
```

This leads to a requested URL such as:

```
news.asp?NewsItem=Story1&Coverage=Short
```

Query strings can also be generated explicitly by using the <A> anchor tag in an HTML page: For example the following generates a query string when the user answers the question:

```
<H2>Question 2 </H2><BR>
What planet is closest to the sun? <BR>
<A HREF="q2answer.asp?answer=Mercury&rw=right">Mercury</A><BR>
<A HREF="q2answer.asp?answer=Venus&rw=wrong">Venus</A><BR>
<A HREF="q2answer.asp?answer=Mars&rw=wrong">Mars</A><BR>
```

Request Object

When the user clicks on a link, the <A> tag sends a query string that consists of the two variables – answer and rw. The ASP code that handles the query string looks like this:

```
<%
   Response.Write("Your answer was " & Request.QueryString("answer") &
"...<BR>")
   If Request.QueryString("rw")="right" Then
      Response.Write("That's the correct answer!")
   Else
      Response.Write("No, that's the wrong answer.")
   End If
%>
```

The JScript equivalent of this would be:

```
<%
   Response.Write("Your answer was " + Request.QueryString("answer") +
"...<BR>");
   if (Request.QueryString("rw")=="right") {
      Response.Write("That's the correct answer!");
   } else {
      Response.Write("No, that's the wrong answer.");
   }
%>
```

Note that this example illustrates some of the shortcomings of query strings: firstly the correct answer to the question is viewable in the source code; and secondly the query string's data appears in the address box – which affirms that this isn't a secure way to send information:

Another way that query strings can be generated is to add them manually to the URL that you type into the address box of your web browser.

Properties of the QueryString Collection

The Querystring collection has three properties: Count, Item and Key.

Request.QueryString Properties
Count
Item
Key

Count

The Count property returns the number of key/item pairs in the query string.

```
Integer = Request.QueryString.Count([Variable])
```

This gives the number of key/item pairs that have been submitted in the query string, including empty ones (with no value), or, if an optional *Variable* parameter is specified, the number of values associated with that variable. For example, if the requested URL is:

```
http://yourserver.com/yourpage.asp?FirstName=John&FamilyName=Jones
```

Then Request.QueryString.Count will return 2.

Another example of using the Count property is if a parameter can hold multiple values, when we use it to count the number of values. Let's briefly return to the "How many continents..." example (used earlier in this chapter to demonstrate the forms collection). This time, we'll pass the information using the GET method:

```
<FORM NAME="MultiChoiceQS" ACTION="DealWithQS.asp" METHOD="GET">
    <H2>Which continents have you visited? </H2><BR>
    <INPUT NAME="Cnent" TYPE=CHECKBOX VALUE="Africa"> Africa <BR>
<!-- ...snip... -->
    <INPUT NAME="Cnent" TYPE=CHECKBOX VALUE="Europe"> Europe  <P>
    <INPUT TYPE=RESET  VALUE="Clear">
    <INPUT TYPE=SUBMIT VALUE="Submit">
</FORM>
```

The only change from the Form collection version is in the values for the ACTION and METHOD attributes of the <FORM> tag. To the user, the form looks identical, however when it is submitted, the information is sent appended to the URL (DealWithQS.asp) as follows:

```
http://johns/DealWithQS.asp?Cnent=North+America&Cnent=Asia
```

The code that we use to handle this info is:

```
<%
    If Request.QueryString("Cnent").Count<=1 Then
        Response.Write("Not too well-traveled, huh?")
    Else
        Response.Write("You've really been to all these places?" & "<BR>")
        For i = 1 To Request.QueryString("Cnent").Count
            Response.Write (Request.QueryString("Cnent")(i) & "<BR>")
        Next
        Response.Write("<BR>" & "Impressive...")
    End If
%>
```

Item

The Item property of the QueryString collection returns a value for an item when the key is specified.

```
Variant = Request.QueryString.Item(variant)
```

For example, if the page URL is:

```
http://yourserver.com/yourpage.asp?FirstName=John&FamilyName=Jones
```

Then `Request.QueryString("FirstName")` will give `"John"` and
`Request.QueryString.Item(2)` will give `"Jones"`.

Key

Using the `Key` property of the `QueryString` returns the key in the key/item pair.

```
Variant = Request.QueryString.Key(variant)
```

This is useful for processing query strings where the key values are unknown. For example, with the URL:

```
http://yourserver.com/yourpage.asp?FirstName=John&FamilyName=Jones
```

then:

```
Response.Write (Request.QueryString.Key(2))
```

will give:

```
FamilyName
```

Query String URL Encoding

Some browsers cannot handle illegal characters or spaces in URL/query string combinations. Illegal characters such as /, :, ?, % and &, are those used to delimit parts of the URL and query string. The `Server` object's `URLEncode` method should be used to convert spaces into plus signs (+), and other illegal characters into a character string consisting of the percent sign (%) followed by the ANSI character code in hexadecimal.

For example if we want to a append some text to a URL where say `Text1` can have a value `"More books from Wrox Press!"`, the value of `QueryString` should be:

```
Text1=More+books+from+Wrox+Press%21
```

We can achieve this using, say:

```
<A HREF="myURL.asp?<%= Server.URLEncode(Text1) %> "> </A>
```

*For more information, see the section in Chapter 7 on the ASP `Server`
object's `URLEncode` method.*

ServerVariables Collection

When an ASP application is executed, lots of information is passed across concerning the environment in which the application is running. This includes, for example, who is running the application, the server name, details of the port to which the request was sent, etc. This list of variables, which is predefined by the server are called the **environment variables**. These variables are available to our ASP script through the `ServerVariables` collection.

The `ServerVariables` collection contains all the HTTP header values sent from the client with their request, plus the values of several environment variables for the web server. Each member is read-only.

```
String = Request.ServerVariables(HTTP_variable_name)
```

Name	Data Type	Description
`HTTP_variable_name`	String	The name of the server variable to be retrieved.

For example, to determine the name of the server and the script being executed, we can access the `"SERVER_NAME"` and `"SCRIPT_NAME"` variables:

```
strServerName = Request.ServerVariables("SERVER_NAME")
strScriptName = Request.ServerVariables("SCRIPT_NAME")
Response.Write "Executing the page " & strScriptName & _
          " on the server " & strServerName
```

And in JScript:

```
var strServerName = Request.ServerVariables('SERVER_NAME');
var strScriptName = Request.ServerVariables('SCRIPT_NAME');
Response.Write('Executing the page ' + strScriptName +
          ' on the server ' + strServerName);
```

Any HTTP header that is sent by a client browser is available in this collection. HTTP headers are used to exchange information between the client and the server, such as the identity of the client, type of client, type of connection, and so on. The standard HTTP headers are automatically defined as members of the `ServerVariables` collection. Most of the names of the items in the `ServerVariables` collection are the standard HTTP header name with any hyphens replaced by underscores.

For example, we can determine how the form data was sent to the server by checking the `REQUEST_METHOD` member of the `ServerVariables` collection:

```
strSendMethod = Request.ServerVariables("REQUEST_METHOD")
```

This will set the value of the `strSendMethod` variable to either `"GET"` or `"POST"`, depending on how the data was sent from the client browser.

HTTP Header Variables

The following table shows the standard HTTP server variables:

HTTP Variable Name	Description
`ALL_HTTP`	All the HTTP headers sent by the client as a string, with the header names capitalized, prefixed by "HTTP_", and with hyphens replaced by underscores.
`ALL_RAW`	All the HTTP headers in raw format so that the values appear exactly as sent by the client.

Table Continued on Following Page

Request Object

HTTP Variable Name	Description
APPL_MD_PATH	The metabase path for the application, for example /LM/W3SVC/1/ROOT.
APPL_PHYSICAL_PATH	The physical path corresponding to the metabase path, for example C:\Inetpub\wwwroot\.
AUTH_PASSWORD	The password entered by the user when **Basic** authentication is enabled and **Anonymous** is disabled.
AUTH_TYPE	The authentication method used to validate the user, for example NTLM or BASIC.
AUTH_USER	The user name entered by the user when **Anonymous** authentication is disabled.
CERT_COOKIE	The unique ID for a client certificate if one is provided, returned as a string.
CERT_FLAGS	A flag value with bit 0 is set to 1 if a client certificate is present. Bit 1 is set to 1 if the certification authority of the certificate is invalid or is not in the list of recognized CAs (Certificate Authorities) on the server.
CERT_ISSUER	The issuer field of the client certificate if presented, as returned in the ClientCertificate collection.
CERT_KEYSIZE	The number of bits in the Secure Sockets Layer connection key if one is in use.
CERT_SECRETKEYSIZE	The number of bits in the server certificate's private key.
CERT_SERIALNUMBER	The serial number field of the client certificate if presented.
CERT_SERVER_ISSUER	The issuer field of the server certificate if presented.
CERT_SERVER_SUBJECT	The subject field of the server certificate if presented.
CERT_SUBJECT	The subject field of the client certificate if presented.
CONTENT_LENGTH	The length of the client request content.
CONTENT_TYPE	The data type of the client request content, for example "application/x-www-form-urlencoded" for the contents of a <FORM>.
GATEWAY_INTERFACE	The revision of the CGI specification used by the server. The format is CGI/*revision*.

HTTP Variable Name	Description
HTTP_ACCEPT	A comma-delimited list of document types that the client can support, for example: `"image/gif, image/x-xbitmap, image/jpeg, image/pjpeg, application/x-comet, */*"`. The asterisk wildcards indicate that all other types can be accepted as well as those specified.
HTTP_ACCEPT_LANGUAGE	A language identifier indicating the language in use, for example `"en-gb"`.
HTTP_USER_AGENT	A string that describes the browser type that sent the request.
HTTP_COOKIE	All the cookies that were sent from the client presented as a single string.
HTTP_REFERER	The URL of the page containing the link followed to arrive at this page, if this is how the client loaded the page.
HTTPS	Returns `"ON"` if the request came in through a secure channel (i.e. SSL) or `"OFF"` if not.
HTTPS_KEYSIZE	The number of bits in the Secure Sockets Layer connection key when this method is in use.
HTTPS_SECRETKEYSIZE	The number of bits in the server certificate private key when in use.
HTTPS_SERVER_ISSUER	The entire issuer field of the server certificate.
HTTPS_SERVER_SUBJECT	The entire subject field of the server certificate.
INSTANCE_ID	The numeric ID of the current IIS instance as defined in the Metabase, presented as a string.
INSTANCE_META_PATH	The metabase path of the current IIS instance.
LOCAL_ADDR	The IP address on the server to which the request came in. There can be multiple IP addresses bound to the server.
LOGON_USER	The username of the Windows account that the user logged on to.
PATH_INFO	The virtual path of the script being executed, for example `/Chapter02/show_request.asp`.
PATH_TRANSLATED	The physical path of the script being executed, for example `C:\Inetpub\wwwroot\Chapter02\show_request.asp`.

Table Continued on Following Page

Request Object

HTTP Variable Name	Description
QUERY_STRING	The entire query string that follows the '?' character in the URL of the request.
REMOTE_ADDR	The IP address of the remote machine hosting the client that made the request.
REMOTE_HOST	The name of the remote machine hosting the client that made the request if available.
REMOTE_USER	The original unmapped user-name string sent when **Anonymous** authentication is disabled, before modified by any authentication filter installed on the server.
REQUEST_METHOD	The method used to make the request, for example GET, HEAD, POST, etc.
SCRIPT_NAME	The virtual path of the script being executed. Useful for creating pages that are self-referencing, i.e. which are reloaded in response to a form being submitted.
SERVER_NAME	The server's host name, DNS alias, or IP address.
SERVER_PORT	The number of the port to which the request was sent.
SERVER_PORT_SECURE	If the request is being handled on the secure port, returns "1". Otherwise returns "0".
SERVER_PROTOCOL	The name and revision of the request information protocol. The format is protocol/revision, for example "HTTP/1.1".
SERVER_SOFTWARE	The name and version of the server software that answers the request. The format is name/version.
URL	The URL of the currently executing page, without the server name or DNS name.

For other header variables not listed (for example those created using the Response.AddHeader method), the value can be retrieved by using "HTTP_*HeaderName*", where *HeaderName* is the name of the HTTP header required, with any hyphens converted to underscores. If the header is not found, an empty string is returned. This technique can be used to retrieve custom headers. For example, if the client sends an ExtraInfo header, then we can retrieve this using:

```
strExtraInfo = Request.ServerVariables("HTTP_ExtraInfo")
```

Properties of the ServerVariables Collection

Like other collections, the ServerVariables collection has three properties: Count, Item and Key.

Request.ServerVariables Properties
Count
Item
Key

Count

This enables the number of elements in the collection to be determined.

```
Integer = Request.ServerVariables.Count
```

Item

This gives the value of a specific item in the ServerVariables collection.

```
Variant = Request.ServerVariables.Item(Variant)
```

For example:

```
strServerName = Request.ServerVariables.Item("SERVER_NAME")
```

Alternatively, to iterate through the entire collection:

```
' VBScript
For Each Item in Request.ServerVariables
   Response.Write("For element '" & Item & "' you've entered the value '" & _
                Request.ServerVariables(Item) & "'<BR>")
Next
```

The following example retrieves the values of all HTTP server variables:

```
<%@ LANGUAGE="JScript" %>
<HTML>
<HEAD><TITLE>HTTP Server Variables</TITLE>
</HEAD>
<BODY>
   <P ALIGN=CENTER><FONT SIZE=5><B>HTTP Server Variables</B></FONT></P>
   <TABLE BORDER>
   <TR><TH>Variable</TH><TH>Value</TH></TR>
   <%
      // create new Enumerator object
      http = new Enumerator(Request.ServerVariables)

      // iterate through collection
      while (!http.atEnd(http)) {
         // get one item
         i = http.item();
         // show it and its value
         Response.Write('<TR><TD>' + i + '</TD><TD>' +
Request.ServerVariables(i) +
                      '</TD></TR>');
         // get next item
         http.moveNext();
      }
   %>
   </TABLE>
</BODY>
</HTML>
```

Key

This gives the key of the specific item in the `ServerVariables` collection.

```
Variant = Request.ServerVariables.Key(Index)
```

This can be useful, for example, when you do not kow the name of the key, but want to find both this and its value.

```
strServerName = Request.ServerVariables.Key(2)
```

Using the ServerVariables Collection

There are many ways that the `ServerVariables` collection can be used; we'll look at two examples here.

Using the HTTP_USER_AGENT Header Variable

The `HTTP_USER_AGENT` variable enables us to check the type of the client browser or the operating system they are running and hence to perform appropriate actions based on this information. By establishing the type and version of the user agent (i.e. the web browser), we can redirect the user to the page that is designed to work for that particular web browser.

We can easily retrieve the value of this variable using the `"HTTP_USER_AGENT"` member of the `ServerVariables` collection:

```
String = Request.ServerVariables("HTTP_USER_AGENT")
```

For example, to establish quickly the client's platform type (Windows, Macintosh or other):

```
' VBScript
strUA = Request.ServerVariables("HTTP_USER_AGENT")
If InStr(strUA, "Win") Then
   Response.Write "This machine is running a Windows operating system."
ElseIf InStr(strUA, "Mac") Then
   Response.Write "This machine is running a Macintosh operating system."
Else
   Response.Write "This platform isn't running either a Windows or a" & _
"Macintosh operating system."
End If
```

```
// JScript
strUA = String(Request.ServerVariables("HTTP_USER_AGENT"));
if (strUA.indexOf("Win") > 0) {
   Response.Write("This machine is running a Windows operating system.");
} else {
   if (strUA.indexOf("Mac") > 0) {
      Response.Write("This machine is running a Macintosh operating
system.");
   } else {
      Response.Write("This platform isn't running either a Windows or a " +
"Macintosh "operating system.");
   }
}
```

Using the HTTP_ACCEPT_LANGUAGE Header Variable

HTTP_ACCEPT_LANGUAGE allows us to determine which human language is supported by the client's browser and software. For example, if the client supports the Russian language (this can be set in the browser by selecting Tools | Internet Options... and then selecting Languages... on the General tab), the HTTP_ACCEPT_LANGUAGE member returns the string "ru". We can use this information to redirect users to localized pages and sites that contain local information.

Using the AUTH_TYPE Header Variable

If you're using a CDO site (see Chapter 38) then, ideally, it should be contained in its own virtual directory with IIS Anonymous Access turned off – this forces users to log on. However, if Anonymous Access is switched on, we can write a line to query AUTH_TYPE from the Request.ServerVariables collection for _BasicNTLM – either Basic or Challenge/Response authentification – and force a log on box to appear if necessary.

Using the SCRIPT_NAME Header Variable

The SCRIPT_NAME header can be used to create a self-referencing <FORM>:

```
<FORM ACTION="<%= Request.ServerVariables("SCRIPT_NAME") %>" METHOD="POST">
```

Using the Request Collections Efficiently

Accessing an ASP collection to retrieve values is an expensive process in terms of computing resources, because the operation involves a search through the relevant collection. This is far slower than accessing a normal local variable. Therefore, if you intend to refer to a value from a collection more than once in your page, you should consider storing it in a local variable. Furthermore, since the Request collection is read-only, if you intend to manipulate the data in any way prior to using it, you should do so when you assign the value from the Request collection to the local variable. For example in VBScript

```
strTitle = Trim(Server.HTMLEncode(Request.Form("Title"))).
```

Searching through all the Request Collections

In some cases, you may know the key name of a value that will arrive in the Request collections, but not exactly which collection it will arrive in. For example, if you have more than one page (or different sections of a page) that sends a value to the same ASP script, it might appear in either the Form or the QueryString collection.

To access the value when you don't know which collection it will be in, we can omit the collection name:

```
Request (page)
```

Request Object

This searches through all the Request collections in the following order: QueryString, Form, Cookies, ClientCertificate, ServerVariables, until it finds the first matching value name (or a blank if no matching variable is found). However, this technique is far less efficient than accessing the appropriate collection directly and should be avoided where possible.

Unlike the other Request collections, the ServerVariables collection is not populated automatically when an ASP page is loaded and executed. However, the first call to read a value from the collection causes IIS to populate the collection.

Summary

In this chapter we looked at the Request object and its collections, properties and methods. We saw that the Request object has five collections (all read-only), which hold different kinds of information that the client sends to the server in the HTTP request:

❑ The ClientCertificate collection holds client certificate values

❑ The Cookies collection holds the values of cookies on the browser machine

❑ The Form collection holds the values of any of HTML <FORM> elements sent to the server

❑ The QueryString collection holds any variables sent in the HTTP query string (i.e. appended to the URL by a form or ASP request)

❑ The ServerVariables collection holds values of the HTTP headers and environment variables

We discussed retrieving information sent to the server through a client request, how to access data sent from HTML forms, how to read data store cookies, how to check for client certificate and we looked at examples using colletions in conjunction with both VBScript and JScript.

In the next chapter we will take a look at the Response object, which plays its own crucial part in the client-server conversation.

The Response Object

The ASP Response object is used to access the HTTP response which is sent back to the client after the client has made a request. It makes available to our script the HTTP variables that identify the server and its capabilities, information about the content being sent to the client, and any new cookies that will be stored on the client browser for this domain. It also provides a series of methods that can be used to create output.

Viewing Response Headers

Since the Response object is designed to be sent to the client, not to be read on the server, much of the information it provides is write-only. In particular, the Response object provides an AddHeader method but not a GetHeader method. This isn't likely to be a problem in live code, but can be inconvenient when debugging. Fortunately, there is an object which we can use in a client-side script to check the headers that are sent. The XMLHTTPRequest object can send a request for a given URL, receive the response and provide information on it. So, in order to access the headers which are sent to the client, we need to set up an HTML page with a client-side script which instantiates this object, sends a request to the desired page and displays the headers which are sent in the response:

```
<SCRIPT>
    // Instantiate the object
    var objHttpRequest=new ActiveXObject("Microsoft.XMLHTTP");

    // Open the request specifying the GET method, the URL of the ASP page
    // and synchronous loading of the page
    objHttpRequest.open("GET", "http://domain_name/response.asp", false);

    // Send the request
    objHttpRequest.send();

    // Display all header information
    document.write(objHttpRequest.getAllResponseHeaders());
</SCRIPT>
```

This page will display all the response headers sent by the requested page:

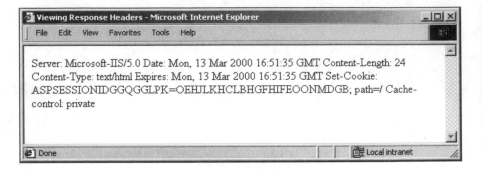

As well as displaying all headers, we can select one using the getResponseHeader method. See Chapter 35 for more information on the XMLHTTPRequest object.

Response Object Members

The Response object has the following collections, properties and methods:

Methods	Properties	Collections
AddHeader	Buffer	Cookies
AppendToLog	CacheControl	
BinaryWrite	Charset	
Clear	ContentType	
End	Expires	
Flush	ExpiresAbsolute	
PICS	IsClientConnected	
Redirect	Status	
Write		

Response Object Methods

The following sections describe the methods of the Response object. The AddHeader, PICS and Redirect methods affect the HTTP headers for the returned page and therefore must be called before any other output is sent to the client. When buffering is enabled (Buffer = True is now the default in ASP 3.0) the page output is not sent to the client until the Flush or End methods are called or *all* the scripts in the page have been processed. If the output is not buffered, the server sends it to the client as it is processed.

AddHeader Method

The AddHeader method is used to create or modify a custom HTTP header using specified *name* and *content* values and to add to the response.

```
Response.AddHeader(header_name, content)
```

Parameter	Data Type	Description
header_name	String	The name of the new header variable
content	String	The value stored in the new header variable

For example, we can add a new custom HTTP header "WWW-Authenticate" with the value "BASIC" with the following VBScript code:

```
<%
Response.AddHeader "WWW-Authenticate", "BASIC"
%>
<HTML>
... Your HTML code here
</HTML>
```

Or in JScript:

```
<%
Response.AddHeader('WWW-Authenticate', 'BASIC');
%>
<HTML>
... Your HTML code here
</HTML>
```

Custom headers such as this, which are not standard HTTP header variables, can be retrieved using the Request.ServerVariables collection as described in the previous chapter. For example in VBScript:

```
Request.ServerVariables("HTTP_WWW_Authenticate")
```

Using the AddHeader method as above is equivalent to the client-side <META> element:

```
<META HTTP-EQUIV="WWW-Authenticate" CONTENT="BASIC">
```

Note that once a header has been added, it cannot be removed. Sending a second header with the same name will *not* replace an existing header. The AddHeader method must be used before any output is sent to the client, i.e. before any HTML and text page content or any calls to the Flush or End methods. The header name must not contain any underscore (_) characters, since these are detected and incorrectly interpreted as dashes.

AppendToLog Method

The `AppendToLog` method adds a text string to the end of the web server log entry for this request.

```
Response.AppendToLog(string)
```

Parameter	Data Type	Description
string	String	Text that is to be appended to the log file

The text that is appended to the log file must not contain commas and mustn't exceed 80 characters in length. This method can be called multiple times within the same script and each time it will append the string to the end of the existing one. An example of using the `AppendToLog` method in VBScript is:

```
<%
strToAppend = "String appended to log file entry"
Response.AppendToLog strToAppend
Response.Write "Done ..." & strToAppend
%>
```

Or in JScript:

```
<%
var strToAppend = 'String appended to log file entry';
Response.AppendToLog(strToAppend);
Response.Write("Done ..." + strToAppend);
%>
```

This will add an entry like the following to the current log file for your site:

```
18:11:41 192.168.0.163 GET /appendtolog.asp
String+appended+to+log+file+entry 200
```

IIS web site log files are saved by default in the
WINNT\system32\LogFiles\W3SVCn directory (one such directory
will be created for each web site on your server), but this can be changed in the
Internet Services MMC.

The `AppendToLog` method requires W3C Extended Log File Format to be in use. It also requires the URI Query box to be checked in the Extended Properties dialog for the site that contains the page. This dialog is opened by selecting Properties on the right-click menu of a web site opened in Internet Services Manager, choosing the Web Site page and selecting the Properties button when W3C Extended Log File Format is selected for the logging type:

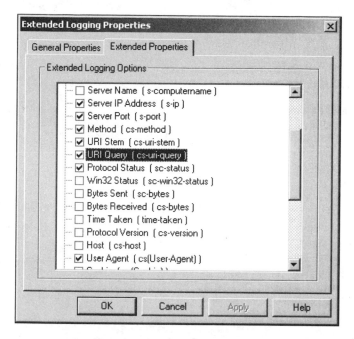

Response Object

Note that this method has implications for the log file size and may be undesirable with a busy web site.

BinaryWrite Method

The BinaryWrite method writes the content of a Variant-type array (or SafeArray) to the current HTTP output stream without any character conversion. It is useful for writing non-string information such as the bytes to make up an image file, or the binary data required by a custom application and is the default method for handling database BLOBS (binary large objects).

```
Response.BinaryWrite(variant_array)
```

Parameter	Data Type	Description
variant_array	Variant	Data to be written to the client

For example using the BinaryWrite method in VBScript:

```
Response.BinaryWrite varBinaryValueArray
```

Or in JScript:

```
Response.BinaryWrite(varBinaryValueArray);
```

Note that no HTML or other output can be made prior to using the BinaryWrite method.

The following example shows how to output graphics stored on the server in a database:

```
<%
  ' Clear out the existing HTTP header information
  Response.Expires = 0
  Response.Buffer = True
  Response.Clear

  ' Change the HTTP header to reflect that an image is being passed
  Response.ContentType = "image/gif"

  ' Open a database
  Set objConn = Server.CreateObject("ADODB.Connection")

  ' Here we assume that we have System Data Source by the name of GRAPH
  objConn.Open "GRAPH", "", ""
  Set objRS = objConn.Execute("SELECT bookcover FROM logos WHERE book_id =
'3234'").
  Response.BinaryWrite objRS("bookcover")
  Response.End
%>
```

Or in JScript:

```
<%
  // Clear out the existing HTTP header information
  Response.Expires = 0;
  Response.Buffer = true;
  Response.Clear();

  // Change the HTTP header to reflect that an image is being passed
  Response.ContentType = "image/bmp";

  // Open a database
  var objConn = Server.CreateObject("ADODB.Connection");

  // Here we assume that we have System Data Source by the name of GRAPH
  objConn.Open("NWind", "", "");
  var objRS = objConn.Execute("SELECT photo FROM Employees WHERE employeeID
= 1");
  Response.BinaryWrite(objRS("photo"));
  Response.End();
%>
```

Clear Method

The Clear method erases any page content stored in the IIS response buffer when Buffer is True, without sending it to the client. It can be used to abort partly completed pages.

```
Response.Clear()
```

It is good practice to use the Clear method along with the End method to clear any data left in the buffer at the end of your ASP script and hence prevent it being written to the client. For example, in VBScript:

```
Response.Clear
Response.End
```

Or in JScript:

```
Response.Clear();
Response.End();
```

If the Response.Buffer is not set to True, the Clear method will generate a run-time error. Also note that the Clear method does *not* erase HTTP response headers, and will only erase information that has been added to the HTML since the last Flush method.

End Method

The End method stops ASP from processing the page script and returns the currently created content, then aborts any further processing of this page.

```
Response.End()
```

If the Response.Buffer is set to True (the default for ASP 3.0), then End will flush the buffer and return any contents to the client. It is therefore commonly used along with the Clear method to prevent the remaining contents in the page being written to the browser. For example in VBScript:

```
Response.Clear
Response.End
```

Or in JScript:

```
Response.Clear();
Response.End();
```

Flush Method

The Flush method sends all currently buffered page content in the IIS buffer immediately to the client when Buffer is True (the default for ASP 3.0). The Flush method can be used to send sections of output to the browser individually for very large pages, or ones that take a while to be built by ASP or other server-side code and components:

```
Response.Flush()
```

If the Response.Buffer is not set to True, the Flush method will generate a run-time error.

PICS Method

To restrict the distribution of certain kinds of materials over the Internet, a set of technical specifications (called PICS – Platform for Internet Control Selection) was proposed in 1995. PICS provides a way to implement client-side control over Internet content. The idea behind PICS is that every site has an associated label – the PICS label. The PICS label is the digital equivalent to the film classification labels found on video tapes and in the cinema, in the USA and other countries.

Response Object

You can obtain a label from one of the two self-rating authorities that give them out (RSACi and SafeSurf), by going to their web sites (http://www.rsac.org/ratingsv01.html and http://www.classify.org/safesurf/) and filling out a questionnaire about the type of material contained on your site. They'll send you a label for each page you completed a questionnaire for (or if every page has the same sort of content, you'll just get a single label for your site). PICS labels are then placed in the META tag.

When a client browser requests your web page, it examines the PICS label and decides (according to rules set by the parent or administrator) whether to allow the user to see the content.

In Internet Explorer, the user can set ratings via View | Internet Options, selecting the Content tab and clicking the Enable button in the Content Advisor section. Content can be rated according to four categories – language, nudity, sex and violence – and each category can be rated from level 0 to level 4.

The PICS method is used to create a PICS label and add it to the HTTP headers sent to the client in the HTTP response.

```
Response.PICS(PICS_label)
```

Parameter	Data Type	Description
PICS_label	String	The text of the PICS label which defines the content of the web page or site

We can use the PICS method if we need to set a PICS label for a page dynamically. For example:

```
' VBScript
QUOT = Chr(34) 'double-quote character
strPicsLabel = "(PICS-1.0 " & QUOT & "http://www.rsac.org/ratingsv01.html" & _
               QUOT & " 1 gen true comment " & QUOT & _
               "RSACi North America Server" & QUOT & " for " & QUOT & _
               "http://yoursite.com" & QUOT & " on " & QUOT & _
               "1999.08.01T03:04-0500" & QUOT & " r (n 0 s 0 v 2 1 3))"
Response.Pics(strPicsLabel)
```

```
// JScript
var strPicsLabel = '(PICS-1.0 "http://www.rsac.org/ratingsv01.html"' +
                   ' 1 gen true comment "RSACi North America Server"' +
                   ' for "http://yoursite.com" on ' +
                   '"1999.08.01T03:04-0500" r (n 0 s 0 v 2 1 3))';
Response.Pics(strPicsLabel);
```

This code adds a PICS label that looks like the following:

```
(PICS-1.0 "http://www.rsac.org/ratingsv01.html" 1 gen true comment "RSACi
North America Server" for "http://yoursite.com" on "1999.08.01T03:04-0500"
r (n 0 s 0 v 2 1 3))
```

*For more information about PICS, and the way you define the content of your
page in regard to its suitability for young people and other visitors, check out
`http://www.rsac.org/`.*

Redirect Method

The `Redirect` method instructs the browser to load the page specified in the string
`url` parameter by sending a `"302 Object Moved"` HTTP header in the response. It is
commonly used in situations where you carry out some form of authenication, for
example forcing visitors to present a client certificate, or comparison and want to
redirect different types of visitors to appropriate pages.

```
Response.Redirect(url)
```

Parameter	Data Type	Description
url	String	The URL of the web page

For example in VBScript:

```
Response.Redirect "http://www.wrox.com"
```

Or in JScript:

```
Response.Redirect('http://www.wrox.com');
```

The `Redirect` method can't be used after sending any page content such as HTML or
text since the page would then be both executing the requested page and redirecting
the browser to a different page.

> **The `Server.Transfer` and `Server.Execute` methods (described in
> the next chapter) also transfer control to another page, but without a
> server round trip, and hence provide similar functionality with
> potentially less performance hit. They cannot, however, be used with
> the server-side include #exec directive.**

Write Method

The `Write` method writes the specified text to the current HTTP response stream and
IIS buffer so that it becomes part of the returned page.

```
Response.Write(text)
```

There is also a shorthand form of this method:

```
<%= text %>
```

Parameter	Data Type	Description
text	Variant	The data to be sent to the browser

The *text* parameter can be any data type supported by the scripting language, including strings, characters and integers. The only restriction is that it cannot contain the %> character combination. You will need to use the escape sequence %\> for this. As well as plain text, we can also send HTML content to the browser using the Response.Write method (or, if we set Response.ContentType to the appropriate value, any other text format, such as XML).

For example in VBScript:

```
Response.Write "This text will be written to the page. <BR>"
```

Or in JScript:

```
Response.Write('This text will be written to the page. <BR>');
```

The notation <%= %> can be used in place of the Response.Write syntax as a shortcut, where a single-line ASP statement is needed. For example:

```
<%= "This text will also be written to the page. <BR>" %>
```

Although this is much quicker to type than the full Response.Write syntax, it should not be used for multiple calls to this method, since it involves context-switching. Every time the context changes (from ASP to HTML or vice versa), there is a performance cost. So, while it is much quicker to *type* something like this:

```
<%= "This text is written " %>
<%= "using the shortcut tags, " %>
<%= "and therefore isn't efficient." %>
```

This actually takes longer to execute than the equivalent Response.Write written out in full. A neat alternative is to use the VBScript With construct, which actually improves performance slightly:

```
With Response
    .Write "This text is written "
    .Write "using the With construct, "
    .Write "and is therefore more efficient."
End With
```

There is also a similar with statement in JScript:

```
with (Response) {
    Write("This text is written ");
    Write("using the JScript ");
    Write("with statement.");
}
```

Response Object Properties

The following sections list and describe all the properties of the Response object. With the exception of the IsClientConnected property, setting the property values affects the HTTP headers for the returned page. This must be done before any other output is sent to the client.

Buffer Property

The ASP Scripting Host's task is to process an .asp file's HTML statements and script logic and dynamically generate the HTML page to send to the browser. Before it can do this, an empty HTML output stream is created. The HTML output stream is essentially a receptacle or **buffer** where the web server can create the HTML pages dynamically. Each line of HTML in order is added to the end of the buffer; and if the ASP script logic generates HTML statements, they too are appended to the end of the buffer. When the page is sent to the browser, the HTML headers are written first, followed by the contents of the page, in the HTML output stream.

If the output is buffered, as described above, the buffered page output is not sent to the client until *all* of the ASP scripts have been processed, or the Flush method or the End method is called. If the output is not buffered, the server sends output to the client as it is processed.

The read/write Buffer property allows us to set or determine whether this buffering should take place. Buffering is on (True) by default in ASP 3.0, whereas it was off (False) by default in earlier versions.

```
Response.Buffer = Boolean
Boolean = Response.Buffer
```

The Buffer property must be set before any output is sent to IIS, including HTTP header information, so it should be the first line of the .asp file after any <%@...%> directives such as the <%@ LANGUAGE=...%> statement.

Setting the Buffer property to True normally provides much more efficient page delivery than with Buffer=False. It enables very large pages, or those that take a while to be built by ASP or other server-side code and components, to be sent to the browser in sections.

Setting the Buffer property to false can, be useful when debugging your ASP code to display any debugging output created by Response.Write statements. Note that if the Buffer is set to False, any calls to the Flush or End methods lead to a runtime error.

CacheControl Property

The CacheControl property is a read/write string value that determines whether a proxy server can cache the output generated by ASP.

```
Response.CacheControl = "Public" | "Private"
String = Response.CacheControl
```

Many organizations use proxy servers as a gateway between users' machines and the Internet, responsible for separating the enterprise network from outside networks via a firewall, while being transparent to users. They can be used to control security, administration and (sometimes) caching (storing a local copy of a web page).

The default value for the CacheControl property is "Private" for ASP pages, which prevents proxy caching taking place. This is important when the pages served are personalized to individual users or groups of users: if a page is cached on a proxy server, the same page will be delivered to all users who go through that server.

Setting the CacheControl property to "Public" allows proxy servers to cache the page. If you have a large page which doesn't change very often, allowing proxy servers to cache it enables client browsers to download it much more quickly.

For example, to set CacheControl to "Public":

```
' VBScript
Response.CacheControl = "Public"
```

```
// JScript
Response.CacheControl = 'Public';
```

Charset Property

The Charset property is a read/write string value that appends the name of the character set (e.g. ISO-LATIN-7) to the HTTP Content-Type header created by the server for each response. This enables the browser to display the page correctly (or inform the user if the specified character set is not available).

```
Response.Charset = String
String = Response.Charset
```

If the ASP page does not include the Charset property the content-type header will be:

```
content-type:text/html
```

The default Charset property is "ISO-LATIN-1" for PCs. On the Apple Macintosh, the default U.S. character set is not "ISO-LATIN-1"; however, when serving documents where no Charset is specified, PWS for Macintosh automatically convert content to "ISO-LATIN-1".

The Charset property is important when the data will need to be translated to a readable character set. A list of the character sets known by a system, can be found in the Windows Registry under HKEY_CLASSES_ROOT\MIME\Database\Charset.

If, for example, our ASP page contains the VBScript statement:

```
Response.Charset = "ISO-LATIN-7"
```

Or the JScript statement:

```
Response.Charset = 'ISO-LATIN-7';
```

Then the content-type header will be:

```
content-type:text/html; charset=ISO-LATIN-7
```

When multiple characters sets are specified, the last one listed will take priority and be used.

ContentType Property

The ContentType property is a read/write String value that specifies a standard MIME type (such as "text/xml" or "image/gif") for the HTTP content type for the response, i.e. the type of media sent to the client browser – such as text, graphics, Word documents, Excel spreadsheets etc. MIME stands for either **Multi-purpose Internet Multimedia Extension** or **Multi-purpose Internet Mail Extension** – usually depending on the context in which it's used.

```
Response.ContentType = String
String = Response.ContentType
```

Where the String is a MIME type describing the content. This is in the format "type/subtype" where type is the general content type (such as application, audio, image, message, multipart, text, or video) and subtype is the specific content type. The default value is "text/html". A table of other common MIME types is given later in this section.

For example in VBScript:

```
Response.ContentType = "image/jpeg"        'JPEG images file
```

Or:

```
Response.ContentType = "text/xml"          'XML document stream
```

Or in JScript:

```
Response.ContentType = 'text/xml';         //XML document stream
```

Some Common MIME Types and File Extensions

ASP script logic can generate and return web content *other* than the normal HTML documents, by setting the Response object's ContentType property to a string that identifies the type of information. This string is known as the **Multipurpose Internet Mail Extensions type** (or **MIME type**) and is sent in the HTTP Response Headers along with the web content.

Alternatively, if the web user navigates directly to a web resource (not via ASP), the web server will determine the MIME type to include in the HTTP response; this is achieved by using a table that maps file extensions to an associated MIME type.

The web browser uses this information to identify the type of web content and to determine how to process the information; this might involve handling it within the browser or invoking another helper application to handle the task. The web browser uses the MIME type/file extension mapping to determine the application that is associated with the web content.

The set of common MIME types and their associated file extensions are given in the table:

MIME Type	Description	File Extension
application/acad	AutoCAD Drawing Files	.dwg
application/clariscad	ClarisCAD Files	.ccad
application/dxf	DXF (AutoCAD)	.dxf
application/msaccess	Microsoft Access File	.mdb
application/msword	Microsoft Word File	.doc
application/octet-stream	Uninterpreted Binary	.bin
application/pdf	PDF (Adobe Acrobat)	.pdf
application/postscript	PostScript, encapsulated PostScript, Adobe Illustrator	.ai, .ps, .eps
application/rtf	Rich Text Format	.rtf
application/vnd.ms-excel	Microsoft Excel File	.xls
application/vnd.ms-powerpoint	Microsoft Power Point File	.ppt
application/x-cdf	Channel Definition File	.cdf
application/x-csh	C-shell script	.csh
application/x-dvi	TeX	.dvi
application/x-javascript	JavaScript Source File	.js
application/x-latex	LaTeX Source	.latex
application/x-mif	FrameMaker MIF format	.mif
application/x-msexcel	Microsoft Excel File	.xls
application/x-mspowerpoint	Microsoft Power Point File	.ppt
application/x-tcl	TCL Script	.tcl
application/x-tex	TeX Source	.tex
application/x-texinfo	Texinfo (emacs)	.texinfo, .texi
application/x-troff	troff	.t, .tr, .roff
application/x-troff-man	troff with MAN macros	.man
application/x-troff-me	troff with ME macros	.me

MIME Type	Description	File Extension
application/x-troff-ms	troff with MS macros	.ms
application/x-wais-source	WAIS Source	.src
application/zip	ZIP Archive	.zip
audio/basic	Basic Audio (usually m-law)	.au, .snd
audio/x-aiff	AIFF Audio	.aif, .aiff, .aifc
audio/x-wav	Windows WAVE Audio	.wav
image/gif	GIF Image	.gif
image/ief	Image Exchange Format	.ief
image/jpeg	JPEG Image	.jpeg, .jpg, .jpe
image/tiff	TIFF Image	.tiff, .tif
image/x-cmu-raster	CMU Raster	.ras
image/x-portable-anymap	PBM Anymap Format	.pnm
image/x-portable-bitmap	PBM Bitmap Format	.pbm
image/x-portable-graymap	PBM Graymap Format	.pgm
image/x-portable-pixmap	PBM Pixmap Format	.ppm
image/x-rgb	RGB Image	.rgb
image/x-xbitmap	X Bitmap	.xbm
image/x-xpixmap	X Pixmap	.xpm
image/x-xwindowdump	X Windows Dump (xwd) Format	.xwd
multipart/x-gzip	GNU ZIP Archive	.gzip
multipart/x-zip	PKZIP Archive	.zip
text/css	Cascading Style Sheet Source	.css
text/html	HTML File	.html, .htm
text/plain	Plain Text	.txt
text/richtext	MIME Rich Text	.rtx

MIME Type	Description	File Extension
text/tab-separated-values	Text with Tab-Separated Values	.tsv
text/x-setext	Struct-Enhanced Text	.etx
text/xml	Text in XML Format	.xml
video/mpeg	MPEG Video	.mpeg, .mpg, .mpe
video/quicktime	QuickTime Video	.qt, .mov
video/x-msvideo	Microsoft Windows Video	.avi
video/x-sgi-movie	SGI Movieplayer Format	.movie

> **For more information on MIME types, see**
> `http://www.rad.com/networks/1995/mime/mime.htm`. **See also the list of MIME types at** `ftp://ftp.isi.edu/in-notes/iana/assignments/media-types`.

Expires Property

If you've permitted a page to be cached (e.g. using `CacheControl`), the read/write `Expires` property contains the number of minutes for which a page is valid. If the user returns to the same page before it expires, the cached version is displayed. After that period, the page expires, and should not be held in a private (user) or public (proxy) cache.

```
Response.Expires = Long
Long = Response.Expires
```

For example, the following to set the page to expire in 20 minutes, by setting the `Expires` header in the HTTP header:

```
' VBScript
Response.Expires = 20      'value in minutes
```

```
// JScript
Response.Expires = 20;     //value in minutes
```

If you want your pages to expire immediately, set the `Expires` property to a large negative number such as `-10,000`. This value allows for the local time on the server and client being different, i.e. when the machines are located in different time zones.

If the `Expires` property is set more than once on the same page, the earliest time/date will be used as the expiry time.

ExpiresAbsolute Property

As well as setting a relative expiry date using the Expires property, we can set an absolute expiry date. The ExpiresAbsolute property is a read/write Date/Time value that specifies an absolute date and time when a page will expire and no longer be valid. If the user returns to the same page before it expires, the cached version is displayed. After that time it expires, and should not be held in a private (user) or public (proxy) cache.

```
Response.ExpiresAbsolute = Date
Date = Response.ExpiresAbsolute
```

For example:

```
' VBScript
Response.ExpiresAbsolute = #Dec 31, 2003 12:00:00#
```

```
// JScript
Response.ExpiresAbsolute = new Date("Dec 31, 2003 12:00:00").getVarDate();
```

Note that if we're using JScript, we have to convert the JScript Date object into the VT_DATE format used by ActiveX objects (including ASP), by calling its getVarDate method.

IsClientConnected Property

The IsClientConnected property is a read-only Boolean value returning True or False depending whether the client is still connected to and loading the page from the server.

```
Boolean - Response.IsClientConnected
```

It can, for example, be used to stop processing (with the End method) if a user moves to another page before the current page has finished executing. For example in VBScript:

```
If Not Response.IsClientConnected Then
    Response.End
End If
```

Or in JScript:

```
if (!Response.IsClientConnected) {
    Response.End();
}
```

Status Property

The Status property is a read/write String value that specifies the status value and message that will be sent to the browser in the HTTP headers of the response to indicate an error or successful processing of the page.

```
Response.Status = String
String = Response.Status
```

For example in VBScript:

```
Response.Status = "200 OK"
Response.Status = "404 Not Found"
```

Or in JScript:

```
Response.Status = '200 OK';
Response.Status = '404 Not Found';
```

Response Object Collections

Cookies Collection

In the previous chapter we discussed cookies and the Request.Cookies collection which is used to retrieve the values of cookies stored on the client machine. The Response object also provides a Cookies collection, that is used to *set* the values of cookies that will be sent to the browser. When the client machine receives the HTTP response it creates and stores cookies according to the values in the Response.Cookies collection. If a cookie of the same name already exists on the client machine the new value overwrites the existing one.

```
Response.Cookies(item_name)[(sub_item_name)] = item_value
```

Name	Data Type	Description
item_name	String	The name of the cookie to be set
sub_item_name	String	Optional. Used to set individual items in a multiple value cookie.

Cookies must be created before any other output is sent to the client because they are part of the HTTP headers for the page. Since buffered output is true as default in ASP 3.0, there is no output before the end of the script is reached or the Flush or End method is called. This means that code to create cookies can come anywhere in the page as long as it is *executed* before any HTML or text output is flushed out of the buffer to the client.

As discussed in the previous chapter, two types of cookie exist: **single value** cookies (storing only a single value) and **multiple-value** cookies (storing data organized into key/item pairs, also commonly called name/value pairs). For example, a multiple value cookie could have the key "firstName" associated with the item "John" and another key "familyName" associated with the item "Smith". It's up to the Request object's code to check whether it's dealing with a single value or a multiple value cookie using the HasKeys property.

Single-value cookies are created with:

```
Response.Cookies(item-name) = item-value
```

For example the single value cookie called `"UserName"` can be set to contain the value `"JSmith"`:

```
' VBScript
Response.Cookies("UserName") = "JSmith"
```

```
// JScript
Response.Cookies('UserName') = 'JSmith';
```

Multiple-value cookies are created using the syntax:

```
Response.Cookies(item-name)(sub-item-name) = sub-item-value
```

For example in VBScript:

The values in the `Response.Cookies` collection are write-only. However, the item names (or **keys**) can be read from the `Cookies` collection.

Properties of the Cookies Collection

The `Response.Cookies` collection is used to create, modify and send cookies back to the client. In common with other ASP collections, it provides the properties `Count`, `Item` and `Key`.

Response.Cookies Properties
Count
Item
Key

Count

The `Count` property returns the number of cookies in the collection.

```
Integer = Response.Cookies.Count
```

Item

The `Item` property returns the value of the item with the specified key or at the specified ordinal position.

```
Variant = Response.Cookies.Item(index)
```

This is the default property, so can be omitted. If the first cookie in the `Response.Cookies` collection is called `"myCookie"` we can therefore access it in any of four ways:

❑   `Response.Cookies.Item(0)`

❑   `Response.Cookies.Item("myCookie")`

❑   `Response.Cookies(0)`

❑   `Response.Cookies("myCookie")`

141

Key

The Key property returns the value of a specific key in the collection. This can be used when the name of the key is unknown.

```
Variant = Response.Cookies.Key(index)
```

The *index* can actually be either an integer representing the cookie's position in the collection, or a string containing the name of the cookie. Since this is the same as the value returned by the property, this syntax isn't very useful.

Properties of Individual Cookies

The individual cookies in the Response.Cookies collection also have Domain, Expires, HasKeys, Item, Path, and Secure properties.

Cookie Object Properties
Domain
Expires
HasKeys
Item
Path
Secure

We can iterate through the cookies to set the properties of all the individual cookies. For example, to set all of the cookies to expire on a particular date, use the following in VBScript.

```
For Each cookie In Response.Cookies
    Response.Cookies(cookie).Expires = #January 1, 2001#
Next
```

Or in JScript:

```
var enmCookies = new Enumerator(Response.Cookies);
for (; !enmCookies.atEnd(); enmCookies.moveNext()) {
    cookie = enmCookies.item();
    Response.Cookies(cookie).Expires = new Date("Jan 1, 2001").getVarDate();
}
```

Domain

The Domain property indicates whether the cookie is only returned to the pages within the domain from which it was created. The default value is the current domain of the page – you should change this if you want to specify the scope of the cookie "visibility". This property is write-only.

```
Response.Cookies(cookie_name).Domain = strDomain
```

The following code sets the domain of the cookie to the Wrox web site, the path to the root of this site (which then applies to all subdirectories):

```
' VBScript
Response.Cookies("UserName").Domain = "http://www.wrox.com"
```

```
// JScript
Response.Cookies("UserName").Domain = 'http://www.wrox.com';
```

Expires

The Expires property sets the expiration date of the cookie. Be sure to distingush this property from the Response.Expires property discussed earlier. Also note that this property takes an absolute, not a relative value (unlike Response.Expires).

```
Response.Cookies(cookie_name).Expires = Date
```

If the Expires property is not set, the cookie will be destroyed when the user closes the current browser instance. The Expires property is write-only. For example:

```
' VBScript
Response.Cookies("UserName").Expires = DateAdd("m", 3, Now)
'Cookie set to expire in 3 months
```

```
// JScript
var objDate = new Date();
objDate.setMonth(objDate.getMonth()+3);
Response.Cookies("UserName").Expires = objDate.getVarDate();
```

> As with the Response.ExpiresAbsolute property, if we're using JScript, we have to call the getVarDate method to convert the JScript Date object into the VT_DATE format used by ASP.

HasKeys

The HasKeys property is a boolean that specifies whether the cookie has multiple values. It is read-only

```
blnHasSubItems = Response.Cookies(cookie_name).HasKeys
```

If True then all the existing keys and their values can be read from the Request.Cookies collection and re-written using the Response.Cookies collection.

> Note that writing a new sub-item value to an existing cookie will destroy the existing values in all other sub-items.

In the following example, we check whether a cookie is multiple- or single-value. The value associated with each key in multiple-value cookies is set to blank. Or if the cookie is single-value, its value is also set to blank:

```
' VBScript
Set cookie=Response.Cookies("myCookie")
If cookie.HasKeys Then
    'Set the value for each key in a multiple value cookie to blank
    For Each key in cookie
```

```
        cookie(key) = ""
    Next
Else
    Response.Cookies("myCookie") = ""        'Set single value cookies to blank
End If
```

```
//
cookie = Response.Cookies("myCookie");
if (cookie.HasKeys) {
    //Set the value for each key in a multiple value cookie to blank
    var enmCookie = new Enumerator(cookie);
    for (; !enmCookie.atEnd(); enmCookie.moveNext()) {
        cookie(enmCookie.item()) = "";
    }
} else {
    Response.Cookies("myCookie") = "";       //Set single value cookies to blank
}
```

Item

The Item property returns the value of the item for a specified key or index number.

```
Response.Cookies.Item(cookie_name).Item(index)
```

Path

Setting the Path property means that the cookie is *only* sent in response to requests for pages within this path. The default value is the root directory of the current ASP application. It is write-only.

```
Response.Cookies(cookie_name).Path = String
```

For example in VBScript:

```
Response.Cookies("UserName").Path = "/"    'Apply to Entire Site
```

Or in JScript:

```
Response.Cookies("UserName").Path = "/";          //Apply to Entire Site
```

Secure

The Secure property specifies whether the cookie is 'secure'. A secure cookie is sent only if the HTTPS protocol (HTTP over Secure Sockets Layer, SSL) is being used. 'Insecure' cookies can be sent via either the HTTP or HTTPS protocols. In both cases, the cookie itself is stored as is: i.e., there is no encryption provided. The Secure property is write-only.

```
Response.Cookies(cookie_name).Secure = Boolean
```

For example using VBScript:

```
Response.Cookies("UserName").Secure = True
```

or in JScript:

```
Response.Cookies("UserName").Secure = true;
```

Accessing Cookies on the Client Side

While this book is about ASP (server-side scripting), it is worth mentioning how to access cookies through client-side code.

Cookies are available to the client-side JavaScript or VBScript as the property of the Document object. Here's some code to illustrate this:

```
<HTML>
<HEAD><TITLE>Cookies</TITLE>
    <SCRIPT LANGUAGE="JavaScript">
        function doCookie() {
            var strName = "Name=";
            if (document.cookie.indexOf(strName) != -1) {
                intStart = document.cookie.indexOf(strName);
                intEnd   = document.cookie.length;
                intLen   = intStart + strName.length;
                strValue = document.cookie.substring(intLen, intEnd);
                alert("Welcome, " + unescape(strValue));
            } else {
                name = prompt("Enter your name please...", "...in this box");
                document.cookie = strName + escape(name) + ";";
                document.location.reload();
            }
        }
    </SCRIPT>
</HEAD>
<BODY onLoad=doCookie()>
</BODY>
</HTML>
```

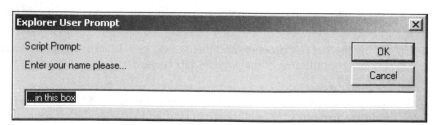

This HTML page tries to find the cookie called Name. If the cookie is found, it produces the greeting such as **Welcome, Jack** – the name of the user is taken from the cookie. If the cookie is not found, user receives a prompt to supply his name – this information is then stored in the cookie.

Handling cookies on the client side requires a lot of code – particularly if you're trying to set a cookie. Bill Dortch has implemented a set of cookie functions that can be found at `http://www.hidaho.com/cookies/cookie.txt`.

If your browser doesn't support cookies, or refuses to accept them, you might like to look at a filter supplied by Microsoft, called Cookie Munger. This filter detects any browsers that can't (or won't) use cookies. It checks for a cookie called `ASPSESSIONID` *(this is a cookie that ASP sends with each request). If* `ASPSESSIONID` *is not found, then it rewrites the HTTP header, 'munges' any URLs embedded in the page and appends them to the HTTP header. You can find more information about Cookie Munger from* `http://msdn.microsoft.com/workshop/server/toolbox/cookie.asp.`

Summary

In this chapter, we looked at the `Response` object and its collections, properties and methods, which allow us to create and modify the response that our server sends to the client browser. The `Response` object has one collection – the `Cookies` collection (write-only) – along with some eight properties and nine methods:

- ❑ The `Cookies` collection enables you to write cookies on the browser machine and set various properties of these such as expiry date.

- ❑ Using the `Buffer` property and the `Clear`, `End`, `Flush` methods we can control the buffering of the page and its content.

- ❑ Several properties of the `Response` object, namely `CacheControl`, `Charset`, `ContentType`, `Expires`, `ExpiresAbsolute` and `Status`, along with the `AddHeader` and `PICS` methods, can be used to change the values of the HTTP header.

- ❑ The `Redirect` method can be used to instruct the browser to connect to a different URL (also see `Server.Transfer` and `Server.Execute` methods).

- ❑ The `Write` and `BinaryWrite` methods allow us to insert textual and non-textual information into a page.

- ❑ The `IsClientConnected` method can be used to check whether the client is still connected to the server.

- ❑ The `AppendToLog` method is used to write to the server's log file.

Response Object

The Server Object

The Server object is designed for carrying out specific tasks on the server, in particular those that relate to the server's environment and processing activities. It provides what many would say is *the* main reason for ASP's popularity - the ability to extend the capabilities of ASP script by allowing it to instantiate and use other external objects and components. This ability matches well with the overall aims of Microsoft's Windows 2000 DNA strategy, where we build applications made up of individual components.

The ASP 3.0 Server object has some new features that allow us to control the execution of pages, particularly when errors occur.

The methods and properties of the Server object are:

Methods	Properties
CreateObject	ScriptTimeout
Execute	
GetLastError	
HTMLEncode	
MapPath	
Transfer	
URLEncode	

Server Object Methods

The Server object has seven methods that can be used to format data in server-specific ways, manage execution of other pages, manage execution of external objects and components, and assist in handling errors.

CreateObject Method

The CreateObject method of the Server object creates an instance of the object (i.e. a component, application or scripting object) and returns a reference to the object.

The CreateObject method can be used in an ASP page to create objects with page-level scope, or in the global.asa page of a virtual application to create objects with session-level or application-level scope. The object can be identified by its Class ID which uniquely identifies the component such as "{clsid:BD96C556-65A3...37A9}", or by a programmatic identifier (ProgID), e.g. for the ADO Connection object with the string "ADODB.Connection".

```
Object = Server.CreateObject(identifier)
```

Parameter	Data Type	Description
identifier	String	The Prog ID or Class ID of the component to be instantiated.

The CreateObject method returns an object reference that can be used in our code.

> The Server.CreateObject method should not be confused with the generic VBScript CreateObject function.

For example, to instantiate the Ad Rotator component:

```
' VBScript
Set objADRotator = Server.CreateObject("MSWC.AdRotator")   ' in VBScript
```

```
// JScript
var objADRotator = Server.CreateObject('MSWC.AdRotator'); // in JScript
```

Object and component instances can also be created using the HTML <OBJECT> element as described below.

Creating Object and Component Instances

When an object instance is created within an ASP page, it needs to be instantiated within the context of the currently executing page. If not, it will not be able to access the page's ObjectContext object. The ObjectContext object provides access to the intrinsic ASP objects that exist within the page, i.e. the Request, Response, Application or Session objects that ASP exposes. It is also used to interact with any existing transactions that may be current within the context. The ObjectContext provides methods that can be used to commit or abort a transaction.

For more information on using transactions within ASP pages, see Chapter 34.

Even if the component does not need to interact with the context of the page, the CreateObject method of the Server object should still be used (as opposed to the VBScript CreateObject function or the ActiveXObject constructor in JScript). IIS automatically instantiates objects within a special COM+ run-time wrapper called DLLHost.dll, which enables the object to be properly pooled and reused within the current **virtual application** (remember that the default web site is itself a virtual application).

For more information on virtual applications see Chapter 1.

Creating Objects with the Correct Scope

The CreateObject method of an <OBJECT> element can be used to create instances of objects and components at different levels of scope. The scope of an object defines the lifetime of the object and the pages from which it will be accessible.

Objects with **application scope** are accessible to every page in the web application. They are created when the application starts and destroyed when the application ends. There will be only one instance of an application-level object, which is accessible to all users. To create an object instance with application scope, use Server.CreateObject within the Application_OnStart event handler in global.asa, or place an <OBJECT> element in global.asa with the SCOPE attribute set to "Application". The global.asa file is discussed in Chapter 2.

```
<OBJECT ID="ASPCounter" RUNAT="Server" SCOPE="Application"
        PROGID="MSWC.Counters">
</OBJECT>
```

If we want one instance of an object to be available to each user for their entire session (over a number of pages), we can instantiate the object with **session scope**. To create an object instance with session scope, use Server.CreateObject within the Session_OnStart event handler in global.asa, or place an <OBJECT> element in global.asa with the SCOPE attribute set to "Session":

```
<OBJECT ID="ASPCounter" RUNAT="Server" SCOPE="Session"
        PROGID="MSWC.Counters">
</OBJECT>
```

Creating object instances with session- or application-level scope for single-, apartment- or both-threaded components can have serious performance implications (see Chapter 41). For this reason, only neutral-threaded objects, or both-/free-threaded objects that aggregate the FTM (Free-Threaded Marshaler), should be created with session or application scope. For more information, see 'Beginning Components for ASP', ISBN 1-861002-88-2, also from Wrox Press.

Objects with **page-level scope** are destroyed when the page on which they are instantiated ends. A new instance will be created each time the page is executed. To create an object instance with **page-level** scope use CreateObject or an <OBJECT> element within the ASP page that requires access to the object. The SCOPE attribute of the <OBJECT> element can be set to "Page" or omitted ("Page" is the default).

```
<OBJECT ID="ASPCounter" RUNAT="Server" SCOPE="Page"
        PROGID="MSWC.Counters">
</OBJECT>
```

The main difference between the Server.CreateObject method and the <OBJECT> element is that the component instance is created immediately with CreateObject, but it is not created until first referenced when an <OBJECT> element is used.

Execute Method

The Execute method stops execution of the current page and transfers control to the page specified by the URL passed in as a parameter. The user's current environment (i.e. the session state and any current transaction state) is carried over to the new page. Any output from the original page will be displayed up to the point where the server transfer occurs. After that page has finished execution, control passes back to the original page and execution resumes at the statement after the Execute method call. This feature is new in ASP 3.0.

```
Server.Execute(url)
```

Parameter	Data Type	Description
url	String	The relative URL of the page to which control is transferred

For example in VBScript:

```
Server.Execute "/books/reference.asp"        ' in VBScript
```

Or in JScript:

```
Server.Execute('/books/reference.asp');       // in JScript
```

The introduction of the Execute method provides programmable **server-side redirection**, with the advantage over using the Response.Redirect method that it does not involve a round-trip from server to client and back, causing the client to request the new page. Unfortunately the Execute and Transfer methods cannot be used with the server side include #exec directive, and Response.Redirect should be used.

The Execute method causes control to be passed immediately to another page, which can be an ASP script page or any other resource such as an HTML page, zip file, or other type of file. It 'calls' the other page, much like calling a subroutine or function in our script code.

When the other page or resource has completed execution or streaming to the client, control passes back to the statement following the call to the `Execute` method in the original page, and execution continues from there. See also the `Server.Transfer` method.

What Gets Transferred to the New Page?

The current page's **context** is also passed to the target page or resource. This includes the values of all the variables in all the intrinsic ASP objects, such as the collections of the `Request`, `Response` and `Session` objects, and all their properties. The `Application` object context is also transferred, even if the page is within a different virtual application. The current **transaction context** is also passed to the new page, allowing it to take part seamlessly in any current transaction.

Meanwhile, the browser's address bar still shows the original URL, and the Back, Forward and Refresh buttons work normally. When we use client-side redirection, especially with an HTML meta tag, this isn't usually the case.

However, the values of any script variables or object references that were created or set within the first page are **not** available within the new page.

GetLastError Method

The `GetLastError` method enables details of the last error that occurred within the ASP programming of the page to be found. This feature is new in ASP 3.0.

```
ASPError = Server.GetLastError()
```

The `GetLastError` method returns a reference to an `ASPError` object that includes the file name, line number, error code, etc., for the last error that occurred within the ASP processing of the page. For example:

```
Set objASPError = Server.GetLastError()       ' in VBScript
```

```
var objASPError = Server. GetLastError();      // in JScript
```

This can only be used successfully when single-page error handling is set up, within a custom error page. See Chapter 4 for more details.

Calling the `GetLastError` method after executing an `On Error Resume Next` statement in VBScript returns an `ASPError` object that does not contain any error information. Instead, in this situation, the existing VBScript `Err` object must be used. The equivalent to the `Err` object in JScript is the new `Exception` object, which is used together with the `try ... catch` construction.

HTMLEncode Method

The HTMLEncode method enables illegal HTML characters to be displayed in the web page rather than interpreted by the browser.

```
String = Server.HTMLEncode(unencoded_string)
```

Parameter	Data Type	Description
unencoded_string	String	The string containing non-legal HTML characters.

The HTMLEncode method returns a string that is a copy of the input value "string" but with all non-legal HTML characters, such as '<', '>', '&' and double quotes, converted into the equivalent HTML entity – i.e. <, >, &, ", etc. This enables these special characters to be displayed in the web page rather than interpreted by the browser.

For example:

```
strResult = Server.HTMLEncode("<?xml version=""1.0""?>")          ' in VBScript
```

Or in JScript:

```
var strResult = Server.HTMLEncode('<?xml version="1.0"?>');   // in JScript
```

In this case, the returned string will contain:

```
&lt;?xml version=&quot;1.0&quot;?&gt;
```

The Server.HTMLEncode method is mainly used when inserting values into a page where they will be used as the VALUE attribute for an HTML control element, or when displaying examples of HTML code in an HTML page. It prevents the browser interpreting and rendering the text as HTML. Suppose we want to display a string such as the following in the browser:

```
<%
strValue = "<B>This is some ""HTML formatted"" text</B>"
%>
```

What the string actually contains is this:

```
<B>This is some "HTML formatted" text</B>
```

If the string is not HTML-encoded, the double-quote before HTML will cause the string to be truncated in the VALUE attribute of a text box:

```
<INPUT TYPE="TEXT" VALUE="<%= Server.HTMLEncode("strValue") %>">
```

When the browser sends the value of a control that has been HTML-encoded to our server, however, it automatically reverses the encoding. This means that the value is available in the original format within the Request collections.

If the string were written to the page without being HTML-encoded, the angle brackets would be treated as HTML element delimiters, `<B>` and `</B>` would not be visible, and the rest of the text would be displayed in bold font.

HTML-Encoded Character Equivalents

During HTML-encoding, all characters that are not legal or valid in HTML are converted into the equivalent HTML **character entity**. The more common HTML character entities include:

Character	HTML	Character	HTML
"	"	Î	Î
&	&	Ï	Ï
<	<	Ð	Ð
>	>	Ñ	Ñ
		Ò	Ò
¡	¡	Ó	Ó
¢	¢	Ô	Ô
£	£	Õ	Õ
¤	¤	Ö	Ö
¥	¥	×	×
¦	¦	Ø	Ø
§	§	Ù	Ù
¨	¨	Ú	Ú
©	©	Û	Û
ª	ª	Ü	Ü
«	«	Ý	Ý
¬	¬	Þ	Þ
	­	ß	ß
®	®	à	à
¯	¯	á	á
°	°	â	â
±	±	ã	ã
²	²	ä	ä

Character	HTML	Character	HTML
³	&sup3;	å	&aring;
´	&acute;	æ	&aelig;
µ	&micro;	ç	&ccedil;
¶	&para;	è	&egrave;
·	&middot;	é	&eacute;
¸	&cedil;	ê	&ecirc;
¹	&sup1;	ë	&euml;
º	&ordm;	ì	&igrave;
»	&raquo;	í	&iacute;
¼	&frac14;	î	&icirc;
½	&frac12;	ï	&iuml;
¾	&frac34;	ð	&eth;
¿	&iquest;	ñ	&ntilde;
À	&Agrave;	ò	&ograve;
Á	&Aacute;	ó	&oacute;
Â	&Acirc;	ô	&ocirc;
Ã	&Atilde;	õ	&otilde;
Ä	&Auml;	ö	&ouml;
Å	&Aring;	÷	&divide;
Æ	&AElig;	ø	&oslash;
Ç	&Ccedil;	ù	&ugrave;
È	&Egrave;	ú	&uacute;
É	&Eacute;	û	&ucirc;
Ê	&Ecirc;	ü	&uuml;
Ë	&Euml;	ý	&yacute;
Ì	&Igrave;	þ	&thorn;
Í	&Iacute;	ÿ	&yuml;

All characters with an ANSI code value greater than 126 can be represented in HTML as the ANSI code of the character in decimal prefixed with &# and suffixed with a semi-colon. For example the ½ (one half) character has an entity equivalent of ½.

MapPath Method

The MapPath method allows us to determine the physical path corresponding to a given URL.

```
String = Server.MapPath(url)
```

Parameter	Data Type	Description
url	String	The string containing the URL.

The MapPath method returns a string giving the full physical path and filename of the file or resource specified in the url parameter.

For example in VBScript:

```
strResult = Server.MapPath("/books/reference.asp")          ' in VBScript
```

Or in JScript:

```
var strResult = Server.MapPath('/books/reference.asp');     // in JScript
```

Often when we work with files stored in our web site, we need to be able to get the actual physical path for those files, rather than using the virtual path or URL by which they are normally referenced within other pages. An example is when we use the FileSystemObject (which we'll meet in Chapter 12) to read and write files that are outside the InetPub\WWWRoot folder of the web site. Alternatively, when we are creating our own custom components, or using commercial components that have to access the file system, we often need to provide them with a physical path to a file.

For example, the code:

```
Response.Write Server.MapPath("/iishelp/default.htm")
```

returns "c:\winnt\help\default.htm" on our server.

Transfer Method

The Transfer method stops execution of the current page and transfers control to the page specified in the supplied URL. The user's current environment (i.e. session state and any current transaction state) is carried over to the new page. This is similar to the Execute method described previously, but unlike that method, execution *does not* resume in the original page, but ends when the new page has completed executing. This feature is new in ASP 3.0.

```
Server.Transfer(url)
```

Parameter	Data Type	Description
url	String	The string containing the URL.

For example in VBScript:

```
Server.Transfer "/books/reference.asp"        ' in VBScript
```

Or in JScript:

```
Server.Transfer('/books/reference.asp');      // in JScript
```

See the section on 'What Gets Transferred to the New Page?' under the Execute method for details of the context that is available within the new page.

URLEncode Method

The URLEncode method converts any illegal characters in a URL string into their equivalent HTTP/URL entities.

```
String = Server.URLEncode(unencoded_string)
```

Parameter	Data Type	Description
unencoded_string	String	The URL string containing illegal characters.

The URLEncode method returns a string that is a copy of the argument "string" but all the characters that are not valid in a URL, such as '?', '&' and spaces, are converted into the equivalent URL entity – i.e. '%3F', '%26', and '+'.

To send values to a server as members of the QueryString collection, they are appended to the end of the URL after a question mark character '?'. This might occur for the values entered into controls on a <FORM> that has its METHOD set to "GET", or which has the METHOD attribute omitted altogether. Alternatively, it may be values that are appended directly to the URL (possibly for use in an <A> element):

```
<%
strURL = "http://myserver.com/mypage.asp?title=ASP 3.0 (Prog Ref)"
%>
<A HREF="<%= strURL %>">ASP 3.0 (Prog Ref)</A>
```

To work properly in all browsers, the values in the query string must not contain any illegal characters such as spaces or brackets (as in the code above). Some browsers (such as Internet Explorer) can cope with this, as they automatically perform the conversion necessary before they send the HTTP request to the server.

However, most other browsers don't do this, and the result is that the URL is usually truncated at the first space or non-legal character. So, in Netscape Navigator for example, the link shown above would request the page http://myserver.com/mypage.asp?title=ASP. On the server, the missing part of the title name/value pair could cause the code to fail.

The correct technique is to use the URLEncode method:

```
<A HREF="<%= Server.URLEncode(strURL) %>">ASP 3.0 (Prog Ref)</A>
```

This converts our string to the valid URL:

```
http://myserver.com/mypage.asp?title=ASP+3%2E0+%28Prog+Ref%29
```

To stay within the limitations of the HTTP protocol definition, we have to make sure that certain characters are removed from any string that is used as a URL in an HTTP request. The non-legal characters are all those with an ANSI code above 126 and certain others with ANSI codes below this.

Characters with an ANSI code above 126 must be replaced by a percent sign (%), followed by the ANSI code in hexadecimal. For example, the copyright character (©) becomes %A9. The characters with ANSI codes below 126 that are not legal in a URL, together with their legal replacements, are:

Character	HTTP/URL Replacement	Character	HTTP/URL Replacement
space	+	\	%5C
'	%27	]	%5D
!	%21	^	%5E
#	%23	`	%60
$	%24	{	%7B
%	%25	|	%7C
&	%26	}	%7D
(	%28	+	%2B
)	%29	<	%3C
/	%2F	=	%3D
:	%3A	>	%3E
;	%3B	Chr(10)	ignored
[	%5B	Chr(13)	%0D

Server Object

Server Object Properties

The Server object has a single property – the ScriptTimeout property.

ScriptTimeout Property

The ScriptTimeout property is a read/write Integer that determines the number of seconds that script in the page runs for before the server aborts page execution and reports an error. It prevents the server becoming overloaded with badly behaved pages, by automatically halting and removing from memory, pages that contain errors that may lock execution into a loop or that stall while waiting for a resource to become available.

```
Server.ScriptTimeout = Integer
Integer = Server.ScriptTimeout
```

The default is 90 seconds, but you may need to increase this value for pages that take a long time to run. This default is set in the Metabase, and if the timeout value is shorter than this, the default metabase setting of 90 seconds will be used.

For example:

```
Server.ScriptTimeout = 240
intTimeout = Server.ScriptTimeout
```

Summary

The Server object doesn't have a large number of methods or properties, and has no collections, but it does provide a few very useful utility methods. In this chapter we saw how to:

- ❑ Instantiate objects using the Server's CreateObject method.

- ❑ Transfer control to another page using the Execute and Transfer methods.

- ❑ HTML- and URL-encode strings to avoid illegal characters.

- ❑ Obtain an ASPError object.

- ❑ Map URLs to physical paths on the server.

Server Object

The Session Object

In Chapter 3, we looked at the Application object, which allows us to maintain state throughout an entire ASP application. In this chapter, we will consider the Session object, which allows us to retain variable values for a specific client between pages in our application. A Session object is created for each visitor when they first request an ASP page from the site, and it remains available until the client's connection times out or is explicitly ended. It provides a repository for storing variables and object references that are available to the pages executed by this client during the lifetime of the session. The Session object can be used to maintain state between different pages requested by the user.

The Session object has the following methods, properties, events and collections:

Methods	Properties	Events	Collections
Abandon	CodePage	OnStart	Contents
	LCID	OnEnd	StaticObjects
	SessionID		
	Timeout		
	Value		

One of the ways of providing state between page requests and site visits is through **cookies**, which are sent along with each page request to the domain for which the cookie is valid. ASP uses a cookie to provide the concept of a user session, with which we interact through the ASP Session object.

A new and separate Session object is created for each individual visitor when they first access an ASP page on the server. A session identifier number is allocated to the session, and a cookie containing a specially encrypted version of the session identifier is sent to the client. The Path of the cookie (see the previous chapter for a description of cookie properties) is set to the path of the root of the ASP application running on our server. This will be the root of the Default Web Site (i.e. "/") or the root directory of the ASP application containing the page requested. No Expires value is provided in the cookie, so it will expire when the browser is closed.

Every time this user accesses an ASP page, ASP looks for this cookie, named ASPSESSIONID*xxxxxxxx*, where each *x* is an alphabetic character. If found, it is sent to the server, where the `SessionID` variable can be used to connect the visitor with their current `Session` held in memory on the server.

This cookie doesn't appear in the `Request.Cookies` or `Response.Cookies` collections. ASP hides it from us, but it's still there in the header, and ASP looks for it with each ASP page request.

If the client browser doesn't accept or support cookies, each new page request forces a new session to be created, so state cannot be maintained.

Using Session-Scoped Objects and Variables

The `global.asa` file can contain code that instantiates objects, as well as code that creates and sets the values of variables that will be available in either session-level or application-level scope.

Creating Session-Level Objects

Session-level scope object instances can be created in the `global.asa` file either using the `Server.CreateObject` method, placed in the `Session_OnStart` event handler, or using an `<OBJECT>` element.

An instance of a session-scoped object can also be created in our `global.asa` file by using the `<OBJECT>` element with `RUNAT="SERVER"` and `SCOPE="SESSION"` attributes. We can specify the object using either its Programmatic ID (Prog ID) or Class ID:

```
<OBJECT ID=ID RUNAT="SERVER" SCOPE="SESSION" PROGID=ProgID></OBJECT>
```

Or, using the Class ID of the object:

```
<OBJECT ID=ID RUNAT="SERVER" SCOPE="SESSION" CLASSID=ClassID>
</OBJECT>
```

For example, to instantiate the Counters component with session scope:

```
<OBJECT RUNAT=Server SCOPE=Session ID=MyCounter
        PROGID="MSWC.Counters">
</OBJECT>
```

Alternatively, the `Server.CreateObject` method (described in detail in Chapter 7) can be used in the `Session_OnStart` event handler of `global.asa` to create an instance. For example, to instantiate the Ad Rotator component:

```
' VBScript
Sub Session_OnStart()
    Dim MyCounter
    Set Session("MyCounter") = Server.CreateObject("MSWC.Counters")
    Session("MyCounter").Set "mycount",0
    ' and more stuff here ...
End Sub
```

```
// JScript
function Session_OnStart() {
    var MyCounter
    Session("MyCounter") = Server.CreateObject("MSWC.Counters");
    Session("MyCounter").Set("mycount", 0);
    // and more stuff here ...
}
```

> **Warning:** you should refrain from creating object instances at session-
> (and application-) level scope wherever possible due to performance
> implications. However, if you do require session- (or application-)
> scoped objects, they should be agile objects; that is, neutral-threaded
> components or both-threaded components that aggregate the Free
> Threaded Marshaler. Apartment-threaded components should be
> avoided in high-volume sites. Single-threaded objects should *never*
> be instantiated with session- or application-level scope. See Chapter
> 41 for more details.

Creating and Storing Session-Level Variables

Session-level variables can be created, accessed and modified from any ASP page
where they are in scope. However, as with the use of global variables in traditional
stand-alone sessions, session-scoped variables in ASP should be used with care.

To store and retrieve session-scoped variables or arrays, we need to reference the
variable name in the Session object: The syntax for creating or setting the value of
session variables or arrays is:

```
Session(variable_name) = variable_value_or_variable_array
Session(variable_name) = object_reference
```

To retrieve the values of session-scoped variables or arrays:

```
variable_value_or_variable_array = Session(variable_name)
object_reference = Session(variable_name)
```

For example in VBScript:

```
' Store the session start time as a string
Session("Start_Time") = CStr(Now)

' Retrieve the starting value
datStartTime = Session("Start_Time")
Response.write "Session Start Time = " & datStartTime
```

Or in JScript:

```
// Store the session start time as a string
Session("Start_Time") = Date();

// Retrieve the starting value
var datStartTime = Session("Start_Time");
Response.Write ("Session Start Time = " + datStartTime);
```

Variant arrays can also be stored in a session object:

```
' Create a Variant array and fill it
Dim varArray(2)
varArray(0) = "This is a Variant array "
varArray(1) = "stored in the "
varArray(2) = "Session object."

' Store it in the Session
Session("Variant_Array") = varArray
Response.Write varArray(0) & varArray(1) & varArray(2)
```

Because of the performance hit involved with storing apartment-threaded objects in the Session object, an error will be raised if we attempt to do this (although we can create apartment-threaded objects with session scope in the HTML <OBJECT> tag). JScript Array objects are apartment-threaded, so we are not allowed to store these in the Session; however, we can store a JScript VBArray object with session scope.

> You should be wary of placing too much information in session-scoped objects. For example, if you store a recordset in a session-scoped variant array, a large number of simultaneous visitors to your site could cause the server to run out of memory resources.

Session Object Methods

The Session methods allow us to remove values from the user-level session space, and terminate sessions on demand.

Abandon Method

The Abandon method ends the current user session and destroys the current Session object once execution of this page is complete. You can still access the current session's variables in this page, even after calling the Abandon method. However, the next ASP page that is requested by this user will start a new session, and create a new Session object with only the default values defined in global.asa (if any exist).

```
Session.Abandon()
```

If, when a user finishes browsing a certain page, you know that they don't need any more session variables, you can call the Abandon method to release server memory resources associated with that session. Bear in mind that if you set certain useful session variable values, like UserName, these values will be lost. On the other hand, if you are programming web games, which use server memory resources heavily, you might be better off explicitly ending the session and having the user log in for another game.

Session Object Properties

The `Session` object provides four properties: `CodePage`, `LCID`, `SessionID` and `Timeout`.

CodePage Property

The read/write `CodePage` property contains a number that defines the code page used to display the web page content in the browser. The code page is the numeric value of the character set, and different languages and locales may use different code pages. For example, ANSI code page `1252` is used for American English and most European languages, while code page `932` is used for Japanese Kanji.

```
Session.CodePage = Long
Long = Session.CodePage
```

For example, to set the code page to `1252`:

```
Session.CodePage = 1252
```

The specific code page for an individual ASP page can also be set in the opening `<%@..%>` ASP processing directive, and this overrides the setting in the `CodePage` property of the session:

```
<%@ LANGUAGE="VBScript" CODEPAGE="1252" %>
```

For the most commonly-used code pages, a list of character encoding schemes, and the associated code page numbers, is given in the table below:

Code page	Name	Alias
1200	Universal Alphabet	unicode
1201	Universal Alphabet (Big-Endian)	unicodeFEFF
1250	Central European Alphabet (Windows)	windows-1250
1251	Cyrillic Alphabet (Windows)	windows-1251
1252	Western Alphabet	iso-8859-1
1253	Greek Alphabet (Windows)	windows-1253
1254	Turkish Alphabet	iso-8859-9
1255	Hebrew Alphabet (Windows)	iso-8859-8
1256	Arabic Alphabet (Windows)	windows-1256
1257	Baltic Alphabet (Windows)	windows-1257
1258	Vietnamese Alphabet (Windows)	windows-1258
20866	Cyrillic Alphabet (KOI8-R)	koi8-r

Code page	Name	Alias
21866	Ukrainian Alphabet (KOI8-RU)	koi8-ru
28592	Central European Alphabet (ISO)	iso-8859-2
28593	Latin 3 Alphabet (ISO)	iso-8859-3
28594	Baltic Alphabet (ISO)	iso-8859-4
28595	Cyrillic Alphabet (ISO)	iso-8859-5
28596	Arabic Alphabet (ISO)	iso-8859-6
28597	Greek Alphabet (ISO)	iso-8859-7
50220	Japanese (JIS)	iso-2022-jp
50221	Japanese (JIS-Allow 1 byte Kana)	csISO2022JP
50222	Japanese (JIS-Allow 1 byte Kana)	iso-2022-jp
50225	Korean (ISO)	iso-2022-kr
50932	Japanese (Auto Select)	none
50949	Korean (Auto Select)	none
51932	Japanese (EUC)	euc-jp
51949	Korean (EUC)	euc-kr
52936	Chinese Simplified (HZ)	hz-gb-2312
65000	Universal Alphabet (UTF-7)	utf-7
65001	Universal Alphabet (UTF-8)	utf-8
852	Central European (DOS)	ibm852
866	Cyrillic Alphabet (DOS)	cp866
874	Thai (Windows)	windows-874
932	Japanese (Shift-JIS)	shift_jis
936	Chinese Simplified (GB2312)	gb2312
949	Korean	ks_c_5601-1987
950	Chinese Traditional (Big5)	big5

LCID Property

The LCID property specifies the locale identifier (LCID) of the page that is sent to the browser. The LCID is a standard international abbreviation that uniquely identifies the locale; for instance the hex value 0409 (decimal 1033) represents the United States, with the default currency symbol '$', and the date format 'mm/dd/yy'.

This LCID can also be used in statements such as FormatCurrency, where there is an optional LCID argument.

```
Session.LCID = Long
Long = Session.LCID
```

For example, to set the Locale ID to the United States:

```
' VBScript
Session.LCID = &H0409
```

```
// JScript
Session.LCID = 0x0409;
```

The LCID for a page can also be set in the opening ASP processing directive, <%@ ... %>, and this overrides the setting in the LCID property of the session:

```
<%@ LANGUAGE="VBScript" LCID="1033" %>
```

A list of locales (and their associated LCID numbers) is given in the table below:

Country/Region	Language	LCID (Hex)
Albania	Albanian	041c
Algeria	Arabic	1401
Argentina	Spanish	2c0a
Australia	English	0c09
Austria	German	0c07
Bahrain	Arabic	3c01
Belarus	Belarusian	0423
Belgium	French	0813
Belize	English	2809
Bolivia	Spanish	400a
Brazil	Portuguese	0416
Brunei Darussalam	Malay	083e
Bulgaria	Bulgarian	0402
Canada	English	1009
Canada	French	0c0c
Caribbean	English	2409
Chile	Spanish	340a
Colombia	Spanish	240a
Costa Rica	Spanish	140a
Croatia	Croatian	041a
Czech Republic	Czech	0405
Denmark	Danish	0406
Dominican Republic	Spanish	1c0a

Country/Region	Language	LCID (Hex)
Ecuador	Spanish	300a
Egypt	Arabic	0c01
El Salvador	Spanish	440a
Estonia	Estonian	0425
Faeroe Islands	Faeroese	0438
Finland	Finnish	040b
France	French	040c
Germany	German	0407
Greece	Greek	0408
Guatemala	Spanish	100a
Honduras	Spanish	480a
Hong Kong	Chinese	0c04
Hungary	Hungarian	040e
Iceland	Icelandic	040f
India	Hindi	0439
Indonesia	Indonesian	0421
Iran	Farsi	0429
Iraq	Arabic	0801
Ireland	English	1809
Israel	Hebrew	040d
Italy	Italian	0410
Jamaica	English	2009
Japan	Japanese	0411
Jordan	Arabic	2c01
Kenya	Swahili	0441
Korea	Korean (Ext. Wansung)	0412
Korea	Korean (Johab)	0812
Kuwait	Arabic	3401
Latvia	Latvian	0426
Lebanon	Arabic	3401
Libya	Arabic	3001
Liechtenstein	German	1407
Lithuania	Classic Lithuanian	0827
Lithuania	Lithuanian	0427
Luxembourg	French	140c
Luxembourg	German	1007
Macau	Chinese	1404
Macedonia	Macedonian	042f

Country/Region	Language	LCID (Hex)
Malaysia	Malay	043e
Mexico	Spanish	080a
Monaco	French	180c
Morocco	Arabic	1801
Netherlands	Dutch	0413
New Zealand	English	1409
Nicaragua	Spanish	4c0a
Norway (Bokmal)	Norwegian	0414
Norway (Nynorsk)	Norwegian	0814
Oman	Arabic	2001
Pakistan	Urdu	0420
Panama	Spanish	180a
Paraguay	Spanish	280a
Peru	Spanish	280a
Philippines	English	3409
Poland	Polish	0415
Portugal	Portuguese	0816
PRC	Chinese	0804
Puerto Rico	Spanish	500a
Qatar	Arabic	4001
Romania	Romanian	0418
Russia	Russian	0419
Saudi Arabia	Arabic	0401
Serbia (Cyrillic)	Serbian	0c1a
Serbia (Latin)	Serbian	081a
Singapore	Chinese	1004
Slovakia	Slovak	041b
Slovenia	Slovene	0424
South Africa	English	1c09
South Africa	Afrikaans	0436
Spain	Basque	042d
Spain	Catalan	0403
Spain (Mod. Sort)	Spanish	0c0a
Spain (Trad. Sort)	Spanish	040a
Sweden	Swedish	041d
Switzerland	French	100c
Switzerland	German	0807

Country/Region	Language	LCID (Hex)
Switzerland	Italian	0810
Syria	Arabic	2801
Taiwan	Chinese	0404
Thailand	Thai	041e
Trinidad	English	2c09
Tunisia	Arabic	1c01
Turkey	Turkish	041f
U.A.E.	Arabic	3801
Ukraine	Ukrainian	0422
United Kingdom	English	0809
United States	English	0409
Uruguay	Spanish	380a
Venezuela	Spanish	200a
Vietnam	Vietnamese	042a
Yemen	Arabic	2401
Zimbabwe	English	3009

SessionID Property

The read-only `SessionID` property returns the session identifier for the current session. This is generated by the server when the session is started. It is unique only for the duration of the parent `Application` object, and so may be re-used when a new application is started.

```
String = Session.SessionID
```

Because session IDs are only guaranteed to be unique for the duration of the application, there is a security risk if you attempt to store these IDs permanently (for example, in a database), and this could result in one user being able to view another's session information.

Timeout Property

The `Timeout` property specifies the timeout period in minutes for the `Session` object. If the user does not refresh or request a page within the timeout period, the session ends. This can be changed on individual pages as required.

```
Session.Timeout = Long
Long = Session.Timeout
```

The default for ASP 3.0 is 10 minutes (20 minutes for ASP 2.0); however, shorter timeouts may be preferred on a high-usage site to reduce memory consumption caused by user sessions on the server. However, there is also a risk in setting the property too low: if you rely on session variables to process user data and the user has not been able to complete the processing of an identification form, the loss of session variables will cause all sorts of problems.

Value Property

The `Value` property (normally omitted) sets or returns the value of a variable stored in the `Session` object.

```
Session.Value = Variant
Variant = Session.Value(Variable_name)
```

For example:

```
Session.Value("FirstName") = "John"
FirstName = Session.Value("FirstName")
```

Session Object Events

The `Session` object exposes two events that are used in the `global.asa` file. These events occur when the session starts and ends.

A session **starts** when any user first requests an ASP page within the default application or a virtual application, if they do not already have an active session.

A session **ends** when that user has not loaded an ASP page within the timeout period specified for the session. The timeout can be set in script code using the `Session.Timeout` property, set individually for each application in its Properties dialog, or the default changed in the IIS metabase via the `IIS:ADSI` namespace provider. A session also ends after a page containing a call to the `Session.Abandon` method finishes executing.

OnStart Event

The `OnStart` event occurs when an ASP user session starts, before the page that the user requests is executed. It is used to initialize variables, create objects, or run other code.

For example, this code creates an instance of the Ad Rotator object, a variant array, and two other variables with session-level scope. It also retrieves a value from the client's request, and increments the number of session starts stored in an application-level variable:

```
Sub Session_OnStart()

    'Create an instance of the AdRotator component with session-level scope
    Set Session("ASPAdRotator") = Server.CreateObject("MSWC.AdRotator")

    Dim varArray(3)                         'Create a Variant array and fill it
    varArray(0) = "This is a"
    varArray(1) = "Variant array"
    varArray(2) = "stored in the"
    varArray(3) = "Session object"
    Session("Variant_Array") = varArray     'Store it in the Session
    Session("Start_Time") = CStr(Now)       'Store the date/time as a string
```

```
'We can access the contents of Request and Response in a Session_OnStart
'event handler for the page that initiated the session. This is the *only*
'place that the ASP page context is available like this.
'as an example, we can get the IP address of the user:
Session("Your_IP_Address") = Request.ServerVariables("REMOTE_ADDR")

Application.Lock                                'Prevent concurrent updates
intVisits = Application("Visit_Count") + 1     'Increment counter variable
Application("Visit_Count") = intVisits          'Store back in Application
Application.Unlock                             'Release lock on Application

End Sub
```

Or using JScript:

```
function Session_OnStart() {

   // Create an instance of the AdRotator component with session-level scope
   Session("ASPAdRotator") = Server.CreateObject("MSWC.AdRotator");

   Session("Start_Time") = String(Date())        // Store the date/time as a
string

   /* We can access the contents of the Request and Response in a
Session_OnStart
      event handler for the page that initiated the session. This is the
*only*
      place that the ASP page context is available like this.
      as an example, we can get the IP address of the user:
      Session("Your_IP_Address") = Request.ServerVariables("REMOTE_ADDR") */

   Application.Lock();                           //Prevent concurrent updates
   intVisits = Application("Visit_Count") + 1;   //Increment counter variable
   Application("Visit_Count") = intVisits;       //Store back in Application
   Application.UnLock();                         //Release lock on
Application
}
```

As stated above, JScript Array objects cannot be stored in the Session, although VBArray objects can.

> Note that this is only an example of the code that you use to create object instances. In general, you should refrain from creating object instances at session-level scope where possible. However, if you do require session-scoped objects, they should really be agile objects – both-threaded components which aggregate the Free Threaded Marshaler, or neutral-threaded components. Apartment-threaded components can be used, but should be avoided in high-volume sites. Single-threaded objects should *never* be instantiated with session-level scope. See Chapter 41 for more details.

OnEnd Event

The OnEnd event is raised when an ASP user session ends. This occurs when the predetermined session timeout period has elapsed since that user's last page request from the application, or when the Abandon method is called. All variables existing in the session are destroyed when it ends; however, it is good practice explicitly to destroy any objects you have used. It is also possible to end ASP user sessions explicitly in code using the Abandon method, and this event is raised when that happens.

For example:

```
' VBScript
Sub Session_OnEnd()
    'release the object instance
    Set Session("ASPAdRotator") = Nothing
End Sub
```

```
// JScript
function Session_OnEnd() {
    // release the object instance
    delete Session("ASPAdRotator");
}
```

Session Object Collections

The Session object has two collections: the Contents and StaticObjects collections.

The Contents Collection

The Contents collection is a collection of all variables and their values that are stored in this instance of the Session object, and which are *not* defined using an <OBJECT> element. This includes variant arrays and variant-type object instance references.

```
Session.Contents(Variable_name) = Variant
Variant = Session.Contents(Variable_name)
```

The Contents collection exposes the following methods and properties:

Methods	Properties
Remove	Count
RemoveAll	Item
	Key

Although the Contents collection can be used to set and retrieve session-scoped variables, normally it is only used to obtain lists of the session variables that are available. The Session object is typically accessed directly to set or retrieve the contents of each variable:

```
Session(variable_name) = Variant
Variant = Session(variable_name)
```

For example:

```
' VBScript
Session("BGColor") = "Blue"
strColor = Session("BGColor")
```

```
// JScript
Session('BGColor') = 'Blue';
strColor = Session('BGColor');
```

We can iterate through the Contents collection using the VBScript For Each...Next construct:

```
For Each objItem in Session.Contents
    If IsObject(Session.Contents(objItem)) Then
        Response.Write "Object reference: '" & objItem & "'<BR>"
    ElseIf IsArray(Session.Contents(objItem)) Then
        Response.Write "Array: '" & objItem & "' contents are:<BR>"
        varArray = Session.Contents(objItem)
        'Note: the following only works with a one-dimensional array
        For intLoop = 0 To UBound(varArray)
            Response.Write "  Index(" & intLoop & ") = " _
                             & varArray(intLoop) & "<BR>"
        Next
    Else
        Response.Write "Variable: '" & objItem & "' = " & _
                        Session.Contents(objItem) & "<BR>"
    End If
Next
```

Or in JScript, using an Enumerator object:

```
var objEnum = new Enumerator(Session.Contents)
for (;!objEnum.atEnd();objEnum.moveNext()) {
    var objItem = objEnum.item();
    Response.Write('Session("' + objItem + '") = ' + Session.Contents(objItem)
                    + '<BR>');
}
```

Contents Collection Methods

Remove Method

The Remove method removes a named variable from the Contents collection.

```
Session.Contents.Remove(variable_name)
```

Parameter	Data Type	Description
variable_name	Variant	The name of the variable to be removed from the Session.Contents collection.

RemoveAll Method

The `RemoveAll` method removes all variables from the `Contents` collection.

```
Session.Contents.RemoveAll()
```

Contents Collection Properties

The `Contents` collection has three properties, which we can use to access the information in the collection.

Count

The `Count` property returns the number of items in the collection:

```
Integer = Session.Contents.Count
```

Item

The `Item` property returns the value of a specific member of the collection.

```
Variant = Session.Contents.Item(variable_name)
```

This is equivalent to:

```
Variant = Session.Contents(variable_name)
```

We can specify the item to be accessed using its index in the collection, or using its name (key).

For example:

```
' VBScript
Session.Contents.Item("FirstName") = "John"
FirstName = Session.Contents.Item(1)
Response.Write "First Name = " &  FirstName
```

```
// JScript
Session.Contents.Item("FirstName") = "Fred";
FirstName = Session.Contents.Item(1);
Response.Write ("First Name = " +  FirstName);
```

Key

The `Key` property allows us to access the key of a specific member of the collection using its (one-based) ordinal position in the collection.

```
Variant = Session.Contents.Key(Index)
```

For example:

```
' VBScript
str_key = Session.Contents.Key(1)
str_item = Session.Contents.Item(str_key)
Response.Write "str_item = " & str_item
```

Session Object

```
// JScript
var str_key = Session.Contents.Key(1);
var str_item = Session.Contents.Item(str_key);
Response.Write ('str_item = ' + str_item);
```

StaticObjects Collection

The StaticObjects collection is a collection of all of the variables that are stored in an application-scoped object that is created by using an <OBJECT> element in the global.asa file. For example, the StaticObjects collection would contain the ASPContentLink object created as follows:

```
<OBJECT ID="ASPContentLink" RUNAT="Server" SCOPE="Session"
        PROGID="MSWC.NextLink">
</OBJECT>
```

The StaticObjects collection has the following methods and properties:

StaticObjects Methods	StaticObjects Properties
Remove	Count
RemoveAll	Item
	Key

Each member of the StaticObjects collection is read-only. Normally the StaticObjects collection is used only to obtain lists of variables that are available, whereas the Session object is accessed directly to retrieve the contents of each variable:

```
Variant = Session.StaticObjects(object_name)
```

We can also refer to this collection implicitly; for example:

```
objADCont = Session("ASPContentLink")
```

We can iterate through the StaticObjects collection using VBScript's For Each...Next construct using for example:

```
For Each objItem in Session.StaticObjects
   If IsObject(Session.StaticObjects(objItem)) Then
      Response.Write "OBJECT element with ID=" & objItem & "<BR>"
   End if
Next
```

Or in JScript, using an Enumerator object:

```
var objEnum = new Enumerator(Session.StaticObjects);
for (; !objEnum.atEnd(); objEnum.moveNext()) {
   var objItem = objEnum.item();
   Response.Write("OBJECT element ID = " + objItem + "<BR>");
}
```

StaticObjects Collection Methods

Remove Method

The `Remove` method removes a named variable from the `StaticObjects` collection.

```
Session.StaticObjects.Remove(Variable_name)
```

Parameter	Data Type	Description
Variable_name	Variant	The name of the variable to be removed from the Session.StaticObjects collection.

Note that objects cannot be removed from the `Session.StaticObjects` collection at run-time.

RemoveAll Method

The `RemoveAll` method removes all variables from the `StaticObjects` collection.

```
Session.StaticObjects.RemoveAll()
```

Note that variables cannot be removed from the `Session.StaticObjects` collection at run-time.

StaticObjects Collection Properties

The `StaticObjects` collection has three properties, which we can use to access information about the objects in the collection.

Count

The `Count` property returns the number of items in the collection.

```
Integer = Session.StaticObjects.Count
```

Item

The `Item` property sets or returns a specific member of the `StaticObjects` collection.

```
Session.StaticObjects.Item(object_name) = Variant
Variant = Session.StaticObjects.Item(object_name)
```

This is the default property for the `StaticObjects` collection, so it can also be omitted:

```
Session.StaticObjects(object_name) = Variant
Variant = Session.StaticObjects(object_name)
```

We can specify the item to be accessed using its index in the collection, or using its name (key).

Key

The Key property allows us to access the key of a specific member of the StaticObjects collection using its (one-based) ordinal position in the collection.

```
Variant = Session.StaticObjects.Key(variant)
```

Problems with Sessions

Sessions provide a great way to store values that are specific to each user. However, there are some issues to consider:

❏ Remember that some browsers and web servers are case sensitive as far as URLs, paths and filenames are concerned (for example, Netscape Navigator and Unix/Linux-based servers). If you place hyperlinks in a page to a URL without ensuring that the case is exactly the same, they are *not* treated as being the same in these browsers. Likewise, if the path or filename case is not identical, it is treated as a different directory or file by the browser. This is not important as far as locating the resource on the server is concerned, because IIS is not case-sensitive so will accept any mix of upper case and lower case, and return a file with the same letters in a different combination of case. However, if a cookie has a path specified, and it is different to the path specified in a hyperlink in terms of case, the browser may not return it to the server with the request for a page from that directory. This means a user session that depends on that cookie will not be located, and the Session object will not be in scope (i.e. any values in it will not be available). Hence, it's a good idea to stick to all lower case, or an obvious mix of letter case, in all your directory and page names.

❏ In previous versions of IIS and ASP, there were also some minor bug-associated problems with nested applications. Sometimes, when the user left a nested ASP virtual application and returned to the default ASP application level, any global variables with the same name as local variables that they had defined within the nested application failed to reappear. Also, when the session was intentionally terminated, using the Session.Abandon method, any code in the global.asa file failed to execute. These have been fixed in ASP 3.0.

❏ Remember that sessions depend on cookies. Visitors that have cookies disabled, or whose browser doesn't support them, won't get a session started and so will not have access to a Session object.

❏ Sessions can time out on users and cause all the data for the session to be lost. We can fix this by specifying a higher Session.Timeout value, but this can have a performace cost.

Disabling Sessions

The activity of sending and decoding the session cookies, and matching them to the respective users, takes up processing cycles and memory on the server. If you don't need state to be maintained, you can disable sessions to save these resources.

To disable all sessions for the entire web site, you edit the properties for the Default Web site application. To disable sessions for a specific application you edit the properties for that virtual application. Open the Properties dialog for the appropriate application or virtual application in the Internet Services Manager console, and in the Home Directory page click the Configuration button. In the Configuration dialog that appears, open the App Options tab. Here, you can enable or disable sessions for this entire application, and also change the default session timeout value:

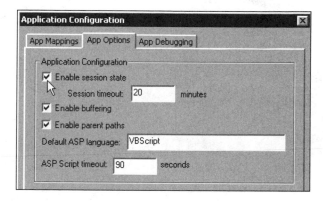

To disable sessions for specific pages, while allowing them to be created and used in other pages of the same application, add an entry to the ASP processing directive for that particular page. It is appended to the default language statement (or can be used alone if you aren't specifying a default language):

```
<%@ LANGUAGE="VBScript" ENABLESESSIONSTATE="False" %>
```

Summary

The Session object equates to the concept in ASP of a user session. ASP applications allow us to allocate special properties to a set of pages that define how IIS and ASP will manage these pages, and any other components that they use. As with the Application object, the main reason for using ASP sessions is often to maintain state automatically when moving between pages in the application.

The Scripting Objects

The Scripting Objects

As well as the intrinsic objects discussed in the previous section, we can instantiate and use other objects to extend the capability of our Active Server Pages. There is a whole range of objects from scripting objects to installable components. Installable objects can include those provided with the standard IIS/ASP installation, those bought from third parties, and those downloaded from the Internet or built by ourselves.

In this section we consider the scripting objects provided by the VBScript and JScript that we would generally use in ASP. These scripting objects are implemented in the Microsoft Scripting Runtime Library (`scrrun.dll`), and are therefore normally called the **Scripting Runtime Library** objects or scripting objects). This DLL is installed with the default **Active Scripting** engines, VBScript and JScript, as well as with a number of other applications such as Office 2000.

Microsoft provides three main objects as part of the Scripting Runtime Library.

- ❑ The **Dictionary object** is a useful object that we can use to store values, which can then be accessed and referenced by name (or key) rather than by numerical index as in a normal script array.

- ❑ The **FileSystemObject object** enables access to the server's file system. We can use the `FileSystemObject` object to access the local and networked drives, folders and files available to the server. The `FileSystemObject` object provides us with access to the following objects and collections:

  - ❑ The **Drive object** and **Drives collection**

  - ❑ The **Folder object** and **Folders collection**

  - ❑ The **File object** and **Files collection**

- ❑ The **TextStream object** provides access to files stored on disk and is used in conjunction with the `FileSystemObject` object. It allows us to read from and write to text files. It can only be instantiated via the `FileSystemObject` object, so we might also think of this as a child of that object.

Accessing our File System

The `FileSystemObject` object enables us to access the file system of the web server itself, as well as the pages available as part of our ASP application. This allows us to:

- ❑ Get and manipulate information on all of the drives available to the server.

- ❑ Get and manipulate information on the folders and subfolders in a drive.

- ❑ Get and manipulate information on the files stored in a folder.

With this information, there is a broad range of things that we can do with the file system. Aside from setting security information, just about anything that you can do with the file system using Windows Explorer or File Manager can also be done using the `FileSystemObject`.

By combining the file and folder manipulation capabilites of the FileSystemObject with the web server configuration functionality of ADSI (covered in Chapter 37), you can build your own web-based server management tool. The advantage of this is that it allows us to perform basic management functions such as copying files, moving folders, and creating virtual web directories remotely.

The FileSystemObject object exposes a series of other objects and collections that are used to interact with the file system: the Drives, Folders and Files collections, which are the collections of the Drive, Folder or File objects respectively.

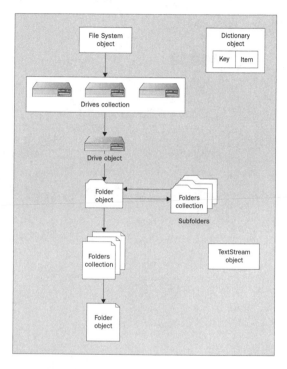

The FileSystemObject object and the TextStream object are inexorably linked, as we must use them both to access the contents of the files on the server's drives. A TextStream object can be created to reference any file on the system, and through it we can read from and write to that file. Files can be in ASCII or in Unicode format.

This combination of navigation and read/write capabilities allows us to exert complete control over the file system of the server. We can also use these objects (with limitations) in script code running on a client machine.

The following diagram illustrates the relationships between each object, and the methods and properties which we can use to access these objects.

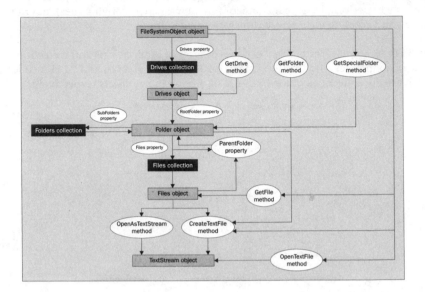

The Dictionary Object

The Dictionary object is one of the Scripting Runtime Objects that are available in the Microsoft Scripting Run-time Library, scrrun.dll. This library can be accessed through the scripting engine when programming in VBScript or JScript.

A Dictionary object stores values that can be accessed and referenced by a name, known as a **key**, rather than by an index as in an array. It can, for example, store the name/value pairs that we retrieve from the ASP Request object. A Dictionary object consists of a set of **key/item pairs**. It is thus like a two-dimensional array in which each element consists of a key and the related item of data.

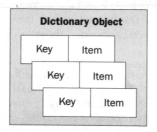

The methods and properties of the Dictionary object are used to access the data. The data cannot be accessed directly as with an array. Keys and items both have Variant as their data types, so a dictionary can be used to store any type of data.

The Dictionary object exposes the following methods and properties:

Methods	Properties
Add	CompareMode
Exists	Count
Items	Item
Keys	Key
Remove	
RemoveAll	

Creating a Dictionary Object

Before we use a Dictionary object, we must first create an instance of it. This can be done either by using the Server.CreateObject object or in an <OBJECT> element.

For example, using Server.CreateObject in VBScript:

```
Dim objDictionary
Set objDictionary = Server.CreateObject("Scripting.Dictionary")
```

Or in JScript:

```
var objDictionary = Server.CreateObject('Scripting.Dictionary');
```

An example of using the <OBJECT> element to create a Dictionary object is given below:

```
<!-- Server-side with an OBJECT element -->
<OBJECT RUNAT="SERVER" SCOPE="PAGE" ID="objDictionary"
        PROGID="Scripting.Dictionary">
</OBJECT>
```

These objects are normally created with **page scope**, which means they exist only as long as the page is executing in ASP and are automatically destroyed after the current page has completed and the results sent back to the client browser. Where application- and session-level scope objects are needed these can be created in global.asa.

> **Performance will downgrade if you store a** Dictionary **object with session scope, and storing it with application scope may even crash your web server. This is due to a bug in the** Dictionary **object (which was originally intended for client-side use). Microsoft's** Lookuptable **component enables you to pass this kind of information between pages. This is available from:**
>
> http://msdn.microsoft.com/workshop/server/downloads/l
> kuptbl.asp
>
> **Further information about this error and how to avoid it can be found at:**
>
> http://msdn.microsoft.com/msdn-
> online/MSDNchronicles2.asp

The Dictionary Object Methods

The Dictionary object has the Add, Exists, Items, Keys, Remove, RemoveAll methods:

Add Method

The Add method adds a key/item pair. An error occurs if the key is already being used.

```
Dictionary.Add(Key, Item)
```

Parameter	Data Type	Description
Key	Variant	The key that will be added.
Item	Variant	The item that will be associated with the key.

For example in VBScript:

```
objDictionary.Add "Blue", "Bleu"
Dim strKey
Dim strItem
strKey = "Green"
strItem = "Vert"
objDictionary.Add strKey, strItem
```

Or in JScript:

```
objDictionary.Add('Blue', 'Bleu');
var strKey = 'Green';
var strItem = 'Vert';
objDictionary.Add(strKey, strItem);
```

Exists Method

The Exists method returns a boolean that is true if the key exists.

```
Boolean = Dictionary.Exists(Key)
```

Parameter	Data Type	Description
Key	Variant	The key whose existence is in question.

For example in VBScript:

```
blnRed = objDictionary.Exists("Red")
```

Or in JScript:

```
var blnRed = objDictionary.Exists('Red');
```

Items Method

The Items method returns a variant array containing all the items in the Dictionary object.

```
VariantArray = Dictionary.Items()
```

The following code example uses the Items and Keys method along with the Count property, to retrieve all the keys and values from a Dictionary object called objDictionary. In VBScript and JScript, arrays always start at index zero, so we must iterate through the array from 0 to Count - 1.

In VBScript for example:

```
arrKeys = objDictionary.Keys                'get all the keys into an array
arrItems = objDictionary.Items              'get all the items into an array

For intLoop = 0 To objDictionary.Count - 1  'iterate through the array
   strThisKey = arrKeys(intLoop)              'this is the key value
   strThisItem = arrItems(intLoop)            'this is the item (data) value
   Response.Write strThisKey & " = " & strThisItem & "<BR>"
Next
```

Or in JScript:

```
// get VB-style arrays using the Keys() and Items() methods
var arrKeys = new VBArray(objDictionary.Keys()).toArray();
var arrItems = new VBArray(objDictionary.Items()).toArray();
for (intLoop = 0; intLoop < objDictionary.Count; intLoop++) {
   // Iterate through the arrays
   strThisKey = arrKeys[intLoop];         // this is the key value
   strThisItem = arrItems[intLoop];       // this is the item (data) value
   Response.Write(strThisKey + ' = ' + strThisItem + '<BR>')
}
```

Alternatively to list the items in the array, we could use the VBScript For Each...Next construct and the Items method:

```
arrItems = objDictionary.Items              'get all the items into an array
For Each objItem in arrItems
   Response.Write objItem & "<BR>"
Next
```

Keys Method

The Keys method returns a variant array that contains all the keys in the Dictionary object. It takes no parameters.

```
VariantArray = Dictionary.Keys()
```

An example of using the Keys method can be found under the Items method above.

Remove Method

The Remove method removes a key/item pair from the dictionary. An error occurs if the specified key does not exist.

```
Dictionary.Remove(Key)
```

Parameter	Data Type	Description
Key	Variant	The key for the key/item pair that will be removed from the dictionary.

For example in VBScript:

```
objDictionary.Remove("Red")
```

Or in JScript:

```
objDictionary.Remove("Red");
```

RemoveAll Method

The `RemoveAll` method removes all key/item pairs from the `Dictionary` object. It takes no parameters.

```
Dictionary.RemoveAll()
```

Dictionary Object Properties

CompareMode Property

The `CompareMode` property sets or returns an integer that sets or returns the string comparison mode for the keys. The string comparison mode determines how keys are matched when doing searches, or when looking up a key. You can either treat the keys as being case-sensitive or as being non-case sensitive.

```
Dictionary.CompareMode = Integer
Integer = Dictionary.CompareMode
```

It has the following possible values:

Value	Constant	Description
0	BinaryCompare	Binary (case-sensitive) comparisons.
1	TextCompare	Case-insensitive comparisons.

If you want to use the named constants above, then you must include the scripting runtime type library in your page or `global.asa` file:

```
<!-- METADATA TYPE="TypeLib" FILE="C:\WinNT\System32\scrrun.dll" -->
```

An error occurs if you try to change its value when the `Dictionary` object already contains data.

The following script illustrates the difference between the two modes of comparison:

```vbscript
' VBScript
Dim objDictionary
Set objDictionary = Server.CreateObject("Scripting.Dictionary")
objDictionary.CompareMode = 0    'binary (case-sensitive) comparison

objDictionary.Item("Red") = "Rouge"
objDictionary.Item("red") = "rouge"

Response.write objDictionary("RED") & "<HR>"
Response.write objDictionary("Red") & "<HR>"
Response.write objDictionary("red") & "<HR>"
```

```jscript
// JScript
var objDictionary = Server.CreateObject("Scripting.Dictionary");
objDictionary.CompareMode = 0;       //binary (case-sensitive) comparison

objDictionary.Item("Red") = "Rouge";
objDictionary.Item("red") = "rouge";
Response.write(objDictionary("RED") + '<HR>');
Response.write(objDictionary("Red") + '<HR>');
Response.write(objDictionary("red") + '<HR>');
```

With CompareMode set to 0, the JScript code gives (in VBScript the top line is blank):

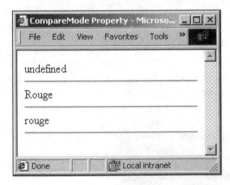

However, if we change the value of CompareMode to 1, the output of this page will be:

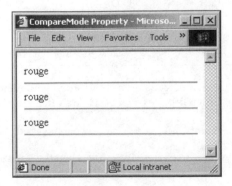

Count Property

The Count property returns an integer that tells us the number of key/item pairs in the Dictionary object. The Count property is read-only.

```
Integer = Dictionary.Count
```

Item Property

The Item property sets or returns a variant that specifies the item associated to a key.

```
Dictionary.Item(Key) = Variant
Variant = Dictionary.Item(Key)
```

If this property is set using a key that does not already exist, then a new key/item pair will be created. It can be used either to read or change the value of an existing item to created, or to create a new item.

For example in VBScript:

```
objDictionary.Item("Red") = "Rouge"
```

Or in JScript:

```
objDictionary.Item('Red') = 'Rouge';
```

Key Property

The write-only Key property is used to change the value of a key:

```
Dictionary.Key(OldKey) = Variant
```

Where *OldKey* is the existing key value and *Variant* is the name of the new key.

For example in VBScript:

```
objDictionary.Add "Blue", "Bleu"
objDictionary.Key("Blue") = "NewBlue"
```

Or in JScript:

```
objDictionary.Add('Blue', 'Bleu');
objDictionary.Key('Blue') = 'NewBlue';
```

Using the Dictionary Object

The following example uses the Dictionary object to store the values of a series of radio buttons which are provided to give feedback on a web site:

```
<HTML>
<HEAD>
   <TITLE>Demo of the Dictionary object</TITLE>
</HEAD>
<BODY>
<H1>How did you find our web site?</H1>
```

Dictionary Object

195

```
<FORM ACTION="dict_js.asp" METHOD="POST">
<TABLE CELLSPACING=10>
<TR><TD>How do you rate our web site overall?</TD>
<TD><INPUT TYPE="RADIO" NAME='Web Site Overall'
            VALUE="Very Good">Very Good</INPUT>
<TD><INPUT TYPE="RADIO" NAME='Web Site Overall'
            VALUE="Good">Good</INPUT></TD>
<TD><INPUT TYPE="RADIO" NAME='Web Site Overall'
            VALUE="OK">OK</INPUT></TD>
<TD><INPUT TYPE="RADIO" NAME='Web Site Overall'
            VALUE="Poor">Poor</INPUT></TD></TR>
<TR></TR>

<TR><TD>How are our web site contents?</TD>
<TD><INPUT TYPE="RADIO" NAME='Web Site Content'
            VALUE="Very Good">Very Good</INPUT></TD>
<TD><INPUT TYPE="RADIO" NAME='Web Site Content'
            VALUE="Good">Good</INPUT></TD>
<TD><INPUT TYPE="RADIO" NAME='Web Site Content'
            VALUE="OK">OK</INPUT></TD>
<TD><INPUT TYPE="RADIO" NAME='Web Site Content'
            VALUE="Poor">Poor</INPUT><BR></TD></TR>
<TR></TR>

<TR><TD>How is our look and feel?</TD>
<TD><INPUT TYPE="RADIO" NAME='Web Site Look and Feel'
            VALUE="Very Good">Very Good</INPUT></TD>
<TD><INPUT TYPE="RADIO" NAME='Web Site Look and Feel'
            VALUE="Good">Good</INPUT></TD>
<TD><INPUT TYPE="RADIO" NAME='Web Site Look and Feel'
            VALUE="OK">OK</INPUT></TD>
<TD><INPUT TYPE="RADIO" NAME='Web Site Look and Feel'
            VALUE="Poor">Poor</INPUT></TD></TR>
</TABLE>

<INPUT TYPE="SUBMIT" VALUE="Submit">
</FORM><HR>

<%
If Request.Form.Count > 1 Then
   Set objMyDict = Server.CreateObject("Scripting.Dictionary")
   For Each objItem In Request.Form
      objMyDict.Add objItem, Request.Form(objItem)
   Next
   Response.Write "<P>You submitted the following " & _
                  "key/item pairs:</P>"
   arrKeys = objMyDict.Keys()
   arrItems = objMyDict.Items()
   For intLoop = 0 To objMyDict.Count -1
      strThisKey = arrKeys(intLoop)
      strThisItem = arrItems(intLoop)
      Response.Write "<P>    " & strThisKey & _
                  " = " & strThisItem & "</P>"
   Next
   Response.Write "<P><B>Thank you for completing " & _
                  "our feedback form.</B></P>"
   objMyDict.RemoveAll
End If

%>
</BODY>
</HTML>
```

The equivalent in JScript is:

```
<HTML>
<HEAD>
  <TITLE>Demo of the Dictionary object</TITLE>
</HEAD>
<BODY>
<H1>How did you find our web site?</H1>

<FORM ACTION="dict_js.asp" METHOD="POST">

<TABLE CELLSPACING=10>
<TR><TD>How do you rate our web site overall?</TD>
<TD><INPUT TYPE="RADIO" NAME='Web Site Overall'
        VALUE="Very Good">Very Good</INPUT>
<TD><INPUT TYPE="RADIO" NAME='Web Site Overall'
        VALUE="Good">Good</INPUT></TD>
<TD><INPUT TYPE="RADIO" NAME='Web Site Overall'
        VALUE="OK">OK</INPUT></TD>
<TD><INPUT TYPE="RADIO" NAME='Web Site Overall'
        VALUE="Poor">Poor</INPUT></TD></TR>
<TR></TR>

<TR><TD>How are our web site contents?</TD>
<TD><INPUT TYPE="RADIO" NAME='Web Site Content'
        VALUE="Very Good">Very Good</INPUT></TD>
<TD><INPUT TYPE="RADIO" NAME='Web Site Content'
        VALUE="Good">Good</INPUT></TD>
<TD><INPUT TYPE="RADIO" NAME='Web Site Content'
        VALUE="OK">OK</INPUT></TD>
<TD><INPUT TYPE="RADIO" NAME='Web Site Content'
        VALUE="Poor">Poor</INPUT><BR></TD></TR>
<TR></TR>

<TR><TD>How is our look and feel?</TD>
<TD><INPUT TYPE="RADIO" NAME='Web Site Look and Feel'
        VALUE="Very Good">Very Good</INPUT></TD>
<TD><INPUT TYPE="RADIO" NAME='Web Site Look and Feel'
        VALUE="Good">Good</INPUT></TD>
<TD><INPUT TYPE="RADIO" NAME='Web Site Look and Feel'
        VALUE="OK">OK</INPUT></TD>
<TD><INPUT TYPE="RADIO" NAME='Web Site Look and Feel'
        VALUE="Poor">Poor</INPUT></TD></TR>
</TABLE>

<INPUT TYPE="SUBMIT" VALUE="Submit">
</FORM><HR>
<%
if (Request.Form.Count>1) {
   objMyDict = Server.CreateObject('Scripting.Dictionary');
   var enmRadio = new Enumerator(Request.Form);
   for (; !enmRadio.atEnd(); enmRadio.moveNext()) {
      var objItem = enmRadio.item();
      objMyDict.Add(objItem, Request.Form(objItem));
   }
   Response.Write('<P>You submitted the following ' +
               'key/item pairs:</P>');
   var arrKeys = new VBArray(objMyDict.Keys()).toArray();
   var arrItems = new VBArray(objMyDict.Items()).toArray();
   for (intLoop = 0; intLoop < objMyDict.Count; intLoop++) {
      strThisKey = arrKeys[intLoop];
      strThisItem = arrItems[intLoop];
      Response.Write('<P>    ' + strThisKey +
               ' = ' + strThisItem + '</P>');
   }
```

Dictionary Object

197

```
        Response.Write('<P><B>Thank you for completing ' +
                       'our feedback form.</B></P>')
        objMyDict.RemoveAll();
}

%>
</BODY>
</HTML>
```

The page contains a form consisting of three sets of identically named radio buttons and a submit button. The radio buttons allow the user to rate different aspects of the web site. When the form is submitted, we store all the name/value pairs from the Request.Form collection in a Dictionary object. Finally, we iterate through the Dictionary to display the user's ratings.

The resulting web page looks like this:

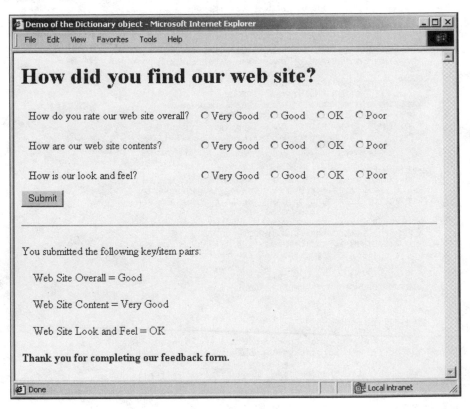

Summary

In this chapter, we've looked at the Dictionary object that is always available when we use ASP with one of the default scripting languages, VBScript or JScript. It is implemented by the scripting run-time library, in the file scrrun.dll.

The Dictionary object provides a useful way to store values that are indexed and accessed by name, rather than by a numerical index as in an array. It's ideal for storing things like the name/value pairs in the intrinsic ASP Request collections.

In this chapter we have considered:

❑   Creating a Dictionary object using Server.CreateObject and using the <OBJECT> element

❑   The methods and properties of the Dictionary object

❑   An example of using the Dictionary object to create pairs of data values from a web site questionnaire.

10

The Drive Object and the Drives Collection

The Drive Object

A Drive object can represent either a drive on the local machine or a mapped network drive. As a subsiduary object of the FileSystemObject object, it is a Scripting Runtime Object. It is therefore available in the Microsoft Scripting Run-time Library, scrrun.dll.

Accessing a Drive Object

A Drive object can be accessed through the Drives collection or through the GetDrive method of a FileSystemObject object. For example, using the Drives collection:

```
' VBScript
Set objFSO = Server.CreateObject("Scripting.FileSystemObject")
Set colDrives = objFSO.Drives
Set objDrive = colDrives.Item("C")
```

```
// JScript
objFSO = Server.CreateObject('Scripting.FileSystemObject');
colDrives = objFSO.Drives;
objDrive = colDrives.item("C");
```

An example of using the GetDrive method of a FileSystemObject object is:

```
' VBScript
Set objFSO = Server.CreateObject("Scripting.FileSystemObject")
Set objDrive = objFSO.GetDrive("C")
```

```
// JScript
objFSO = Server.CreateObject('Scripting.FileSystemObject');
objDrive = objFSO.GetDrive('C');
```

Drive Object Properties

The Drive object exposes the following 12 properties, which provide information about the drive:

Properties	
AvailableSpace	Path
DriveLetter	RootFolder
DriveType	SerialNumber
FileSystem	ShareName
FreeSpace	TotalSize
IsReady	VolumeName

AvailableSpace Property

The AvailableSpace property is a read-only property that returns the amount of space available to this user on the drive (in bytes). This value takes into account quotas and other restrictions.

```
Long = Drive.AvailableSpace
```

DriveLetter Property

The read-only DriveLetter property returns the drive letter of the drive, such as "C".

```
String = Drive.DriveLetter
```

DriveType Property

The read-only DriveType property returns an integer indicating the type of the drive.

```
Integer = Drive.DriveType
```

It can take any of the following values:

Value	Constant	Description
0	Unknown	The drive type cannot be determined.
1	Removable	A removable disk drive, such as a floppy disk drive.
2	Fixed	A fixed drive, such as a hard drive.
3	Remote	A network drive.
4	CDROM	A CD ROM drive.
5	RamDisk	A RAM disk drive.

These constants can be accessed in an ASP script by including the Scripting Runtime DLL in a METADATA directive. For example:

```
<!-- METADATA TYPE="TypeLib"
             FILE="C:\WINNT\system32\scrrun.dll" -->
<%
Set objFSO = Server.CreateObject("Scripting.FileSystemObject")
Set objDrive = objFSO.GetDrive("C")
Select case objDrive.DriveType
   Case Removable
      strDriveType = "Removable"
   Case Fixed
      strDriveType = "Fixed"
   Case Remote
      strDriveType = "Network"
   Case CDROM
      strDriveType = "CD-ROM"
   Case RamDisk
      strDriveType = "RAM Disk"
   Case Else
      strDriveType = "Unknown"
End Select
%>
```

Or in JScript:

```
<!-- METADATA TYPE="TypeLib"
             FILE="C:\WINNT\system32\scrrun.dll" -->
<%
objFSO = Server.CreateObject("Scripting.FileSystemObject");
objDrive = objFSO.GetDrive("C");
switch (objDrive.DriveType) {
   case Removable:
      strDriveType = "Removable";
      break;
   case Fixed:
      strDriveType = "Fixed";
      break;
   case Remote:
      strDriveType = "Network";
      break;
   case CDROM:
      strDriveType = "CD-ROM";
      break;
   case RamDisk:
      strDriveType = "RAM Disk";
      break;
   default:
      strDriveType = "Unknown";
}
%>
```

FileSystem Property

The FileSystem property returns the type of file system for the drive. Possible values include "FAT", "NTFS" and "CDFS". It is a read-only property.

```
String = Drive.FileSystem
```

FreeSpace Property

The FreeSpace property returns a value that indicates the free space available on the drive to the current user. It is a read-only property.

```
Variant = Drive.FreeSpace
```

IsReady Property

The IsReady property indicates whether the drive is available for use. For example, it will return false if there is no disk in a removable drive. It is a read-only property.

```
Boolean = Drive.IsReady
```

This property will always return false for network drives or for empty disk drives or CD-ROM drives.

Path Property

The Path property returns the path for the drive as a string consisting of the drive letter followed by a colon (e.g. "C:"). It is a read-only property.

```
String = Drive.Path
```

RootFolder Property

The read-only RootFolder property returns a Folder object that represents the root folder of the drive.

```
Folder = Drive.RootFolder
```

Every drive can have only one root folder (e.g. "C:\"). This contains all the files and subfolders on the drive.

For example:

```
' VBScript
Set objRootFolder = objDrive.RootFolder
```

```
// JScript
var objRootFolder = objDrive.RootFolder;
```

SerialNumber Property

The SerialNumber property returns a decimal serial number that uniquely identifies a disk volume. It is a read-only property.

```
Long = Drive.SerialNumber
```

ShareName Property

The ShareName property returns the network share name (in UNC format) of a remote drive. It is read-only.

```
String = Drive.ShareName
```

TotalSize Property

The TotalSize property returns the total size of the drive (including both free and used space) in bytes. It is read-only.

```
Variant = Drive.TotalSize
```

VolumeName Property

The VolumeName property indicates the volume name of the drive if it is a local drive. It is a read/write property, so you can use this to assign a new name to the drive volume.

```
Drive.VolumeName = String
String = Drive.VolumeName
```

The Drives Collection

The Drives collection represents the drives that are available either from the local machine or as mapped network drives. This collection can be obtained through the Drives property of the FileSystemObject object.

```
colDrives = FileSystemObject.Drives
```

The Drives collection exposes the following two properties:

Properties
Count
Item

Count Property

The Count property returns the number of Drive objects in the collection.

```
Long = Drives.Count
```

Item Property

The Item property returns a Drive object. It takes the Drive object's drive letter as input, rather than a number.

```
Drive = Drives.Item(Drive_letter)
```

Note that the *Drive_letter* must be a string, so you may get an error in VBScript if you use a variable rather a string literal without explictly converting it. This is because all variables are variants in VBScript. So, while we can write:

```
Set objDrive = colDrives.Item("C")
```

We can't use:

```
strDrive = "C"
Set objDrive = colDrives.Item(strDrive)
```

Instead, we need to write:

```
Set objDrive = colDrives.Item(CStr(strDrive))
```

In JScript, we can simply write:

```
var strDrive = "C";
var objDrive = colDrives.item(strDrive);
```

Using the Drives Collection

We can use the `Drives` collection of the `FileSystemObject` object to show the details of the various drives available on our system.

We start by instantiating our `FileSystemObject` and getting a reference to its `Drives` collection. We then iterate through the collection, adding the `DriveLetter` for each `Drive` object to a `<SELECT>` element. The page submits to itself, so we then check the `Request.Form` collection to see if one of these options has been selected. If so, we print out the type of the selected drive and, if the drive is ready, all of the remaining properties.

In VBScript, the code looks like this:

```
<HTML>
<HEAD>
   <TITLE>The Drives Collection</TITLE>
</HEAD>
<BODY>
   <H2>The Drive Object and Drives Collection</H2>
<HR>

<%
dim objFSO, colDrives, objDrive, strLetter, strDriveType
Set objFSO = Server.CreateObject("Scripting.FileSystemObject")
Set colDrives = objFSO.Drives
Response.Write "Number of available drives = " & colDrives.Count & "<HR>"
%>

Please select a drive letter:
<FORM METHOD="POST" ACTION="Drives.asp">
<SELECT NAME="driveLetter">

<%
for each objDrive in colDrives
   Response.Write "<OPTION>" & objDrive.DriveLetter & "</OPTION>"
next
%>

</SELECT><BR><BR>
<INPUT TYPE="SUBMIT" NAME="submit" VALUE="View Properties">
</FORM>
<HR>
<B>Properties of selected drive:</B><BR><BR>

<%
strLetter = Request.Form("driveLetter")
```

```
If strLetter <> "" Then
   Set objDrive = colDrives.Item(CStr(strLetter))
   Response.Write "Drive letter = " & objDrive.DriveLetter & "<BR>"
   Select case objDrive.DriveType
      Case 1
         strDriveType = "Removable"
      Case 2
         strDriveType = "Fixed"
      Case 3
         strDriveType = "Network"
      Case 4
         strDriveType = "CD-ROM"
      Case 5
         strDriveType = "RAM Disk"
      Case Else
         strDriveType = "Unknown"
   End Select
   Response.Write "Drive type = " & strDriveType & "<BR>"
   If objDrive.IsReady = false then
      Response.Write "Drive " & strLetter & " is not ready."
   Else
      Response.Write "File system = " & objDrive.FileSystem & "<BR>"
      Response.Write "Available space = " & objDrive.AvailableSpace & "<BR>"
      Response.Write "Free space = " & objDrive.FreeSpace & "<BR>"
      Response.Write "Total size = " & objDrive.TotalSize & "<BR>"
      Response.Write "Path = " & objDrive.Path & "<BR>"
      Response.Write "Root folder = " & objDrive.RootFolder & "<BR>"
      Response.Write "Serial number = " & objDrive.SerialNumber & "<BR>"
      Response.Write "Share name = " & objDrive.ShareName & "<BR>"
      Response.Write "Volume name = " & objDrive.VolumeName & "<BR>"
   End If
End If
%>
```

The same thing in JScript looks like this:

```
<%@ LANGUAGE="JScript" %>
<HTML>
<HEAD>
   <TITLE>The Drives Collection</TITLE>
</HEAD>
<BODY>
   <H2>The Drive Object and Drives Collection</H2>
<HR>

<%
objFSO = Server.CreateObject('Scripting.FileSystemObject');
colDrives = objFSO.Drives;
Response.Write('Number of available drives = ' + colDrives.Count + '<HR>');
%>

Please select a drive letter:
<FORM METHOD="POST" ACTION="Drives.asp">
<SELECT NAME="driveLetter">

<%
enmDrives = new Enumerator(colDrives);
for (; !enmDrives.atEnd(); enmDrives.moveNext()) {
   objDrive = enmDrives.item();
   Response.Write('<OPTION>' + objDrive.DriveLetter + '</OPTION>');
```

```
}
%>

</SELECT><BR><BR>
<INPUT TYPE="SUBMIT" NAME="submit" VALUE="View Properties">
</FORM>
<HR>
<B>Properties of selected drive:</B><BR><BR>

<%
strLetter = Request.Form('driveLetter');
if (String(strLetter) != "undefined") {
   objDrive = colDrives.Item(strLetter);
   Response.Write('Drive letter = ' + objDrive.DriveLetter + '<BR>');
   switch (objDrive.DriveType) {
      case 1:
         strDriveType = 'Removable';
         break;
      case 2:
         strDriveType = 'Fixed';
         break;
      case 3:
         strDriveType = 'Network';
         break;
      case 4:
         strDriveType = 'CD-ROM';
         break;
      case 5:
         strDriveType = 'RAM Disk';
         break;
      default:
         strDriveType = 'Unknown';
   }
   Response.Write('Drive type = ' + strDriveType + '<BR>');
   if (!objDrive.IsReady) {
      Response.Write('Drive ' + strLetter + ' is not ready.');
   } else {
      Response.Write('File system = ' + objDrive.FileSystem + '<BR>');
      Response.Write('Available space = ' + objDrive.AvailableSpace +
                     '<BR>');
      Response.Write('Free space = ' + objDrive.FreeSpace + '<BR>');
      Response.Write('Total size = ' + objDrive.TotalSize + '<BR>');
      Response.Write('Path = ' + objDrive.Path + '<BR>');
      Response.Write('Root folder = ' + objDrive.RootFolder + '<BR>');
      Response.Write('Serial number = ' + objDrive.SerialNumber + '<BR>');
      Response.Write('Share name = ' + objDrive.ShareName + '<BR>');
      Response.Write('Volume name = ' + objDrive.VolumeName + '<BR>');
   }
}
%>
```

One point to note is that, for network drives and when you don't have a disk or CD-ROM in your machine, you can only access the DriveLetter and DriveType properties.

The result of the code example looks like this:

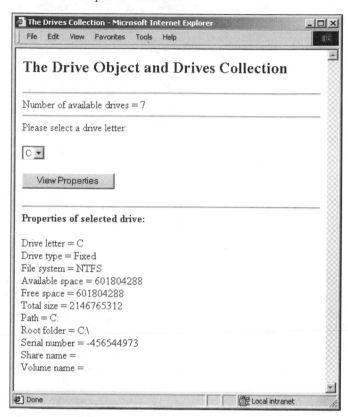

Summary

In this chapter, we've looked at the Drive object and the Drives collection. These are always available when we use ASP with one of the default scripting languages, VBScript or JScript, as they are implemented by the scripting run-time library, in the file scrrun.dll.

A Drive object can represent either a drive on the local machine or a mapped network drive. The Drives collection is accessible through the FileSystemObject and contains a Drive object for each drive that is available to the web server machine.

In this chapter we have looked at:

- ❑ Accessing the Drive object using the GetDrive method of a FileSystemObject object and through the Drives collection.

- ❑ The properties of the Drive object.

- ❑ The properties of the Drives collection.

- ❑ An example of using a Drive object and the Drives collection to give the details of the drives on your system.

The File Object and the Files Collection

The File Object

The File object represents a file in the server's file system; it gives us access to the properties of the file, and has methods that manipulate the file. As a descendant object of the FileSystemObject object, it is a Scripting Runtime object and is thus available in the Microsoft Scripting Runtime Library, scrrun.dll.

Accessing a File Object

A File object can be accessed through the Files collection of a Folder object, or through the GetFile method of a FileSystemObject object.

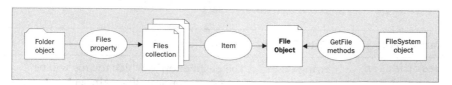

For example using the Files collection:

```
' VBScript
Set colFiles = objFolder1.Files
Set objFile = colFiles.Item("ASP_ProgRef.txt")
```

or in JScript:

```
colFiles = objFolder1.Files;
objFile = colFiles.Item('ASP_ProgRef.txt');
```

An example of using the GetFile method of a FileSystemObject object, with VBScript is:

```
Set objFSO = Server.CreateObject("Scripting.FileSystemObject")
Set objFile = objFSO.GetFile("C:\MyFile.txt")
```

or in JScript:

```
objFSO = Server.CreateObject('Scripting.FileSystemObject');
objFile = objFSO.GetFile('C:\MyFile.txt');
```

File Object Members

The File object exposes the following methods and properties:

Methods	Properties	
Copy	Attributes	ParentFolder
Delete	DateCreated	Path
Move	DateLastAccessed	ShortName
OpenAsTextStream	DateLastModified	ShortPath
	Drive	Size
	Name	Type

The File Object Methods

The File object exposes the following methods:

Copy Method

The Copy method copies the file to a specified folder.

```
FileObject.Copy(destination, [overwrite])
```

Parameters	Data Type	Description
destination	String	The destination to which the file will be copied. If it ends with a path separator (\), it is assumed to be a folder into which the copied file will be placed. Otherwise, it is assumed to be a full path name and a new file will be created if necessary.
overwrite	Boolean	Optional. Determines whether the destination file will be overwritten if it already exists. An error occurs if this parameter is set to false and the destination already exists. The default is true.

For example in VBScript:

```
objFile.Copy("C:\MyFile2.txt")
```

Or in JScript:

```
objFile.Copy('C:\\MyFile3.txt');
```

Delete Method

The Delete method deletes the file.

```
FileObject.Delete([force])
```

Parameter	Data Type	Description
force	Boolean	Optional. Specifies whether to force the file to be deleted even if it is read-only. The default is false.

> This will generate a **Permission denied** error if the user does not have the necessary permissions on the file. If anonymous access is enabled, the page will be running as the IUSR_MACHINENAME user, and the problem can be overcome by granting administrator privileges to this user and restarting the web server. However, this should never be done on a live web site.

Move Method

The Move method moves the file to a specified folder.

```
FileObject.Move(destination, [overwrite])
```

Parameters	Data Type	Description
destination	String	The destination to which the file will be copied. If it ends with a path separator (\), it is assumed to be a folder into which the copied file will be placed. Otherwise, it is assumed to be a full path name and a new file will be created if necessary.
overwrite	Boolean	Optional. Determines whether the destination will be overwritten if it already exists. An error occurs if this parameter is set to false and the destination already exists. The default is true.

File Object & Files Collection

For example in VBScript:

```
objFile.Move("C:\MyFile.txt")
```

Or in JScript:

```
objFile.Move('C:\\MyFile5.txt');
```

> This will generate a **Permission denied** error if the user does not
> have the necessary permissions on the file. If anonymous access is
> enabled, the page will be running as the IUSR_MACHINENAME user,
> and the problem can be overcome by granting administrator
> privileges to this user and restarting the web server. However, this
> should never be done on a live web site.

OpenAsTextStream Method

The OpenAsTextStream method opens the file and returns a new TextStream
object that can be used to read from, write to, or append to the file.

```
TextStream = FileObject.OpenAsTextStream([iomode], [format])
```

Parameter	Data Type	Description
iomode	Integer	Optional. The type of access required.
format	Integer	Optional. The format of the data to be read from or written to the file.

The possible values for iomode are:

Value	Constant	Description
1	ForReading	The TextStream object can be used for reading from a text stream (the default).
2	ForWriting	The TextStream object can be used for writing to a text stream.
8	ForAppending	The TextStream object can be used for appending a string of text to a text stream.

The possible values for format are:

Value	Constant	Description
0	TristateFalse	ASCII (default).
-1	TristateTrue	Unicode.
-2	TristateUseDefault	The system default format.

For example:

```
' VBScript
Const ForReading = 1, ForWriting = 2, ForAppending = 8
Const TristateDefault = -2, TristateTrue = -1, TristateFalse = 0
Set objTextStream = objFile.OpenAsTextStream(ForAppending, false)
objTextStream.Write "This is MORE new text"
```

```
// JScript
var ForReading = 1, ForWriting = 2, ForAppending = 8;
var TristateDefault = -2, TristateTrue = -1, TristateFalse = 0;
objTextStream = objFile.OpenAsTextStream(ForAppending, false);
objTextStream.Write('This is MORE new text');
```

> **For further details, see Chapter 14, The TextSteam Object.**

The File Object Properties

The properties of the File object can be used to obtain information about the file, and to change its name.

Attributes Property

The Attributes property sets or returns the attributes of the file.

```
FileObject.Attributes = Integer
Integer = FileObject.Attributes
```

Its value can be a combination of any of the following:

Value	Attribute	Description	Read/Write Attribute
0	Normal	Normal	N/A
1	ReadOnly	Read-only	Read/Write
2	Hidden	Hidden	Read/Write
4	System	System	Read/Write
8	Volume	Directory Volume name	Read-only
16	Directory	Folder or Directory	Read-only
32	Archive	Changed since last backup	Read/Write
1024	Alias	Link or Shortcut	Read-only
2048	Compressed	Compressed file	Read-only

The Attributes value for a file (or folder) can be ascertained by adding the values for the attributes which apply to that file/folder. For example, a hidden read-only file would have the value 3.

In order to determine whether a given file has a specific attribute, we must perform a bitwise AND operation on the total Attributes value and the value for the attribute we want to check for. For example, to check whether a folder is hidden, we need to AND the folder's Attributes property and 2. If the result of this operation is true (that is, if it returns a number greater than zero), we know that the folder is hidden. Things are slightly more complex if we want to check that our file has two particular attributes. First, we must add the values for the two attributes, and perform a binary AND operation on this value and the file's Attributes property, and compare that to the sum of our two attributes. So if we want to check for a hidden, read-only file, we must use:

```
If (objFile.Attributes And 3) = 3 Then
   ' File is read-only and hidden
End If
```

This operation is much easier to understand if we consider the binary representations of the values. The binary equivalent of 3 is 11, which is comprised of 10 (hidden) plus 01 (read-only). Suppose our file has an Attributes property equal to 7 (hidden, read-only and system). In this case our AND operation looks like this:

```
  111     (our file's Attributes property)
& 011     (read-only and hidden)
  011
```

The result is 3, so our file is indeed both read-only *and* hidden. But what if the file were read-only and not hidden. In that case, our AND operation is:

```
  101
& 011
  001
```

The result 1 informs us that the file is read-only, but does not have any of the other properties we checked for. This is why we need to compare the result of the AND with the sum of the values to check for: this operation returns true (a non-zero result), even though not all of the attributes are present. However, if we only want to check whether *one* of the specified attributes is present, we can still just check that the result is true.

So, to check whether a given file (or folder) is read-only and/or hidden we could perform the following test:

```
intAttrib = objFile.Attributes
' To test whether a file is a read-only hidden file
If (intAttrib And 3) Then
    Response.Write "This file has read-only and hidden atttributes."
Else
    Response.Write "This file is not read-only " & _
                   "and/or not a hidden file."
End If
```

```
// JScript
intAttrib = objFile.Attributes
if (intAttrib & 3) {
    Response.Write("This file has read-only and hidden atttributes.");
```

```
} else {
  Response.Write("This file is not read-only " +
            "and/or not a hidden file.");
}
```

> This will generate a **Permission denied** error if the user does not
> have the necessary permissions on the file. If anonymous access is
> enabled, the page will be running as the IUSR_*MACHINENAME* user,
> and the problem can be overcome by granting administrator
> privileges to this user and restarting the web server. However, this
> should never be done on a live web site.

DateCreated Property

The DateCreated property returns the date and time that the file was created.

```
Date = FileObject.DateCreated
```

DateLastAccessed Property

The DateLastAccessed property returns the date and time that the file was last accessed.

```
Date = FileObject.DateLastAccessed
```

DateLastModified Property

The DateLastModified property returns the most recent date and time when the file was modified.

```
Date - FileObject.DateLastModified
```

Drive Property

The Drive property returns a Drive object that represents the drive on which the file resides.

```
Drive = FileObject.Drive
```

Name Property

The Name property sets or returns the name of the file.

```
FileObject.Name = String
String = FileObject.Name
```

For example:

```
' VBScript
strFileName = objFile.Name
Response.Write "strFileName = " & strFileName & "<BR>"
objFile.Name = "NewName.txt"
Response.Write "strFileName.Name = " & objFile.Name & "<BR>"
```

File Object & Files Collection

```
// JScript
strFileName = objFile.Name;
Response.Write('strFileName = ' + strFileName + '<BR>');
objFile.Name = "NewName2.txt";
Response.Write('NewName2.txt = ' + objFile.Name + '<BR>');
```

> Setting the name of a file will generate a **Permission denied** error if the user does not have the necessary permissions on the file. If anonymous access is enabled, the page will be running as the *IUSR_MACHINENAME* user, and the problem can be overcome by granting administrator privileges to this user and restarting the web server. However, this should never be done on a live web site.

ParentFolder Property

The ParentFolder property returns the Folder object representing the directory in which the file resides.

```
Folder = FileObject.ParentFolder
```

Path Property

The Path property returns the absolute path of the file, using long file names where appropriate.

```
String = FileObject.Path
```

ShortName Property

The ShortName property returns the DOS-style 8.3 version of the file name.

```
String = FileObject.ShortName
```

ShortPath Property

The ShortPath property returns the DOS-style 8.3 version of the absolute path of this file.

```
String = FileObject.ShortPath
```

Size Property

The Size property returns the size of the file, in bytes.

```
Variant = FileObject.Size
```

Type Property

The Type property returns a string that is a description of the file type. This is stored in the Registry, and is the value that appears in the **Type** column of Windows Explorer.

```
String = FileObject.Type
```

The Files Collection

The `Files` collection contains `File` objects representing all the files in the folder. The `Files` collection can be accessed through the `Files` property of its parent `Folder` object, the collection containing a `File` object corresponding to each file in the directory.

The `Files` collection exposes the following properties:

Properties
Count
Item

Count Property

The `Count` property returns the number of files in the folder.

```
Long = Files.Count
```

Item Property

The `Item` property returns a `File` object. Notice that we can't use a numeric index to reference an item in a `Files` collection – we have to reference it by its name.

```
File = Files.Item(Index)
```

For example:

```
' VBScript
Set objFile = objFolder1.Files.Item("ASP_ProgRef.doc")
```

```
// JScript
objFile = objFolder1.Files.Item('ASP_ProgRef.doc');
```

File Object Example

We can use the `File` object to display the details of a file on your system. To keep this example reasonably concise, this code requires the full path of the file to be specified. See Chapter 13 on the `Folder` object and `Folders` collection for an example of how we can browse through the folders on your system.

The VBScript version of the code is:

```
<HTML>
<HEAD>
    <TITLE>Details of a File</TITLE>
</HEAD>
<BODY>
    <H2>Details of a File - Using the File Object</H2>
```

```
Please enter your file name (including its full path):
<FORM METHOD="POST" ACTION="Files.asp">
<INPUT NAME="FilePath"></INPUT><BR><BR>
<INPUT TYPE="SUBMIT" NAME="submit" VALUE="View Details">
</FORM>
<HR>

<%
Dim strFilePath

If Request.Form("FilePath")<> "" Then
    strFilePath = Request.Form("FilePath")

    Set objFSO = Server.CreateObject("Scripting.FileSystemObject")
    Set objFile = objFSO.GetFile(strFilePath)

    Response.Write "<B>Properties of your file:</B><BR>"
    Response.Write "Name: " & objFile.Name & "<BR>"
    Response.Write "ShortName: " & objFile.ShortName & "<BR>"
    Response.Write "Size: " & objFile.Size & " bytes <BR>"
    Response.Write "Type: " & objFile.Type & "<BR>"
    Response.Write "Path: " & objFile.Path & "<BR>"
    Response.Write "ShortPath: " & objFile.ShortPath & "<BR>"
    Response.Write "Created: " & objFile.DateCreated & "<BR>"
    Response.Write "LastModified: " & objFile.DateLastModified & "<P>"
End If
%>
```

The equivalent in JScript looks like this:

```
<HTML>
<HEAD>
    <TITLE>Details of a File</TITLE>
</HEAD>
<BODY>
    <H2>Details of a File - Using the File Object</H2>

Please enter your file name (including its full path):
<FORM METHOD="POST" ACTION="Files.asp">
<INPUT NAME="FilePath"></INPUT><BR><BR>
<INPUT TYPE="SUBMIT" NAME="submit" VALUE="View Details">
</FORM>
<HR>

<%
var strFilePath = Request.Form('FilePath');

if (String(strFilePath) != 'undefined') {
    objFSO = Server.CreateObject('Scripting.FileSystemObject');
    objFile = objFSO.GetFile(strFilePath);

    Response.Write('<B>Properties of your file:</B><BR>');
    Response.Write('Name: ' + objFile.Name + '<BR>');
    Response.Write('ShortName: ' + objFile.ShortName + '<BR>');
    Response.Write('Size: ' + objFile.Size + ' bytes <BR>');
    Response.Write('Type: ' + objFile.Type + '<BR>');
    Response.Write('Path: ' + objFile.Path + '<BR>');
    Response.Write('ShortPath: ' + objFile.ShortPath + '<BR>');
    Response.Write('Created: ' + objFile.DateCreated + '<BR>');
    Response.Write('LastModified: ' + objFile.DateLastModified + '<P>');
}
%>
```

The result of both these code fragments is :

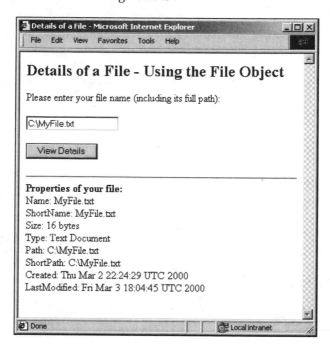

Summary

In this chapter, we looked at the File object and the Files collection. These are available through the FileSystemObject, and can be found in the Scripting Runtime library (scrrun.dll).

The File object provides us with access to the properties of the file, and has methods that manipulate the file. The Files collection contains File objects representing all the files in a folder.

In this chapter, we looked at:

❑ Accessing the File object using the GetFile method of a FileSystemObject object and through the Files collection.

❑ The methods and properties of the File object.

❑ The properties of the Files collection.

❑ An example of using a File object to display the details of a file.

The FileSystemObject Object

The FileSystemObject object is one of the Scripting Runtime Objects that are available in the Microsoft Scripting Runtime Library, scrrun.dll. It provides access to the server's file system and can be used to manipulate the machine's local and networked drives, files, and folders. The FileSystemObject allows us to access the drives available to the server's file system through the Drives collection, through which we can get access to the folders and files on each drive. The FileSystemObject object also has two methods for working with text streams.

> See the introduction to this section for more details of the
> relationships between the FileSystemObject object and the other
> objects and collections within the Scripting Runtime Library.

The FileSystemObject object exposes the following methods and properties:

Methods			Properties
BuildPath	FileExists	GetFileName	Drives
CopyFile	FolderExists	GetFolder	
CopyFolder	GetAbsolutePath Name	GetParentFolderN ame	
CreateFolder	GetBaseName	GetSpecialFolder	
CreateTextFile	GetDrive	GetTempName	
DeleteFile	GetDriveName	MoveFile	
DeleteFolder	GetExtensionName	MoveFolder	
DriveExists	GetFile	OpenTextFile	

Creating a FileSystemObject Object

A `FileSystemObject` object can be created using either the
`Server.CreateObject` method or using the `<OBJECT>` element. A
`FileSystemObject` object must be created in order to use any of the methods and
properties that are associated with the `Drive` object and `Drives` collection, the
`Folder` object and `Folders` collection and the `File` object and `Files` collection.

We can create an instance of the `FileSystemObject` object for example using the
`Server.CreateObject` method:

```
' VBScript
Dim objMyFSO
Set objMyFSO = Server.CreateObject("Scripting.FileSystemObject")
```

```
// JScript
var objMyFSO = Server.CreateObject('Scripting.FileSystemObject');
```

Alternatively, using the `<OBJECT>` element:

```
<!-- Server-side with an OBJECT element -->
<OBJECT RUNAT="SERVER" SCOPE="PAGE" ID="objFSO"
        PROGID="Scripting.FileSystemObject">
</OBJECT>
```

We can add a reference to the `FileSystemObject` type library in an ASP page, so
that we can use the intrinsic constants that it defines directly, rather than their numeric
equivalents. The type library for the complete scripting runtime library can be added
to any ASP page (or to the `global.asa`) with the following code:

```
<!-- METADATA TYPE="typelib" FILE="C:\WinNT\System32\scrrun.dll" -->
```

We must change the `FILE` attribute value if Windows is installed in a folder other than
the default, or if drive other than `"C:"` is in use.

The FileSystemObject Methods

The `FileSystemObject` object provides a range of methods for manipulating the
subsidiary objects such as the `Drive`, `Folder`, and `File` objects. It also implements
the two methods for working with `TextStream` objects: `CreateTextFile` and
`OpenTextFile`.

Several of the methods of the `FileSystemObject` can be used to get references to
other objects, so that we can navigate through the file system of the server and any
networked drives:

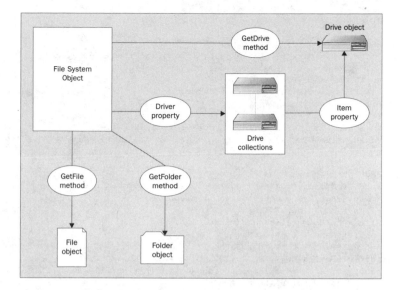

The complexity is due to the extremely high level of flexibility we have in how we access different parts of the file system. For example, we can navigate from the root FileSystemObject down to a file on any drive through the various subsidiary objects. Starting from the Drives collection, we go to a Drive object, then to the root Folder object of that drive, then to a subfolder Folder object, then to the Files collection in that folder, and finally to a File object within that collection.

Alternatively, if we know which drive, file or folder we want, we can access them using the GetDrive, GetFolder, GetSpecialFolder or GetFile methods.

BuildPath Method

The BuildPath method adds a file or folder to an existing path string inserting a separator character (\) if necessary.

```
String = FileSystemObject.BuildPath(path, name)
```

Parameter	Data Type	Description
path	String	An existing path.
name	String	The name of the file or folder to be added to the path.

The resulting string is a concatenation of path and name, with a backslash (\) inserted between them. Note that the BuildPath method doesn't create directories and folders in your hardware – it just produces "well-formed" path names.

For example:

```
' VBScript
Set objMyFSO = Server.CreateObject("Scripting.FileSystemObject")
Set objFolder = objMyFSO.GetFolder("C:\mydocuments")
Set colFiles = objFolder.Files
Set objFile = colFiles.Item("aardvarks.txt")
strFileName = objFile.Name
strFilePath = objFolder.Path
strFullPath = objMyFSO.BuildPath(strFilePath, strFileName)
Response.Write "The well-formatted path for " & strFileName & " is " & _
                strFullPath
```

```
// JScript
objMyFSO = Server.CreateObject('Scripting.FileSystemObject');
objFolder = objMyFSO.GetFolder('C:\\mydocuments');
colFiles = objFolder.Files;
objFile = colFiles.Item('aardvarks.txt');
var strFileName = objFile.Name;
var strFilePath = objFolder.Path;
var strFullPath = objMyFSO.BuildPath(strFilePath, strFileName);
Response.Write('The well-formatted path for ' + strFileName + ' is ' +
                strFullPath);
```

CopyFile Method

The CopyFile method copies one or more files to a folder.

```
FileSystemObject.CopyFile(source, destination, [overwrite])
```

Parameters	Data Type	Description
source	String	The path name of the file or files that will be copied. This parameter may contain wildcards.
destination	String	The destination to which the file will be copied.
overwrite	Boolean	Optional. Determines whether the destination will be overwritten if it already exists. The default is true.

If source contains wildcards or if destination ends with a path separator character (\), then destination is assumed to be a folder into which the copied file or files will be placed. Otherwise, destination is assumed to be a full path name.

An error occurs if the overwrite parameter is set to false and the destination already exists. To avoid such errors, the CopyFile method should be used in combination with the FileExists method where a file may have been moved:

```
' VBScript
If Not objMyFSO.FileExists("d:\mybusiness\profits.doc") Then
   objMyFSO.CopyFile "d:\mybusiness\profits.doc", _
                     "d:\mydocuments\businessprofits.doc"
Else
   Response.Write "The file d:\mybusiness\profits.doc " & _
                  "already exists."
End If
```

```
// JScript
if (!objMyFSO.FileExists('d:\\mybusiness\\profits.doc')) {
   objMyFSO.CopyFile('d:\\mybusiness\\profits.doc',
                     'd:\\mydocuments\\businessprofits.doc');
} else {
   Response.Write('The file d:\\mybusiness\\profits.doc ' +
                  'already exists.');
}
```

CopyFolder Method

The CopyFolder method copies one or more folders.

```
FileSystemObject.CopyFolder(source, destination, [overwrite])
```

Parameters	Data Type	Description
source	String	The path name of the file or files that will be copied. This parameter may contain wildcards.
destination	String	The destination to which the file will be copied.
overwrite	Boolean	Optional. Determines whether the destination will be overwritten if it already exists. The default is true.

An error occurs if the *overwrite* parameter is set to false and the destination already exists. To avoid such errors, the CopyFolder method should be used in combination with the FolderExists method where a folder may have been moved:

```
' VBScript
If Not objMyFSO.FolderExists("d:\mybusiness") Then
   objMyFSO.CopyFolder "d:\mydocuments", "d:\mybusiness"
Else
   Response.Write "The folder d:\mybusiness already exists."
End If
```

Or in JScript:

```
if (!objMyFSO.FolderExists('d:\\mybusiness')) {
   objMyFSO.CopyFolder('d:\\mydocuments', 'd:\\mybusiness')
} else {
   Response.Write('The folder d:\\mybusiness already exists.');
}
```

CreateFolder Method

The CreateFolder method creates a new folder.

```
FileSystemObject.CreateFolder(foldername)
```

Parameter	Data Type	Description
foldername	String	The path and name of the new folder.

FileSystemObject Object

If a folder with this path and name already exists, an error results. Therefore the `CreateFolder` method is often used in conjunction with the `FolderExists` method.

CreateTextFile Method

The `CreateTextFile` method creates a new text file on disk and returns a `TextStream` object that refers to it.

```
TextStream = FileSystemObject.CreateTextFile(filename, [overwrite],
[unicode])
```

Parameter	Data Type	Description
filename	String	The name of the file that will be created.
overwrite	Boolean	Optional. Determines whether any existing file with the same path and name will be overwritten. The default is false.
unicode	Boolean	Optional. Determines whether the contents of the file will be stored in Unicode format. The default is false.

For example in VBScript:

```
Set objTextStream = objFSO.CreateTextFile("C:\MyFile2.txt", true, false)
objTextStream.Write "This is new text"
' some line of code here ...
objTextStream.Close
```

Or in JScript:

```
objTextStream = objFSO.CreateTextFile('C:\\MyFile2.txt', true, false);
objTextStream.Write('This is new text');
// some line of code here ...
objTextStream.Close();
```

> For further details on the `TextSteam` object, see Chapter 14.

DeleteFile Method

The `DeleteFile` method deletes one or more files.

```
FileSystemObject.DeleteFile(filespec, force)
```

Parameter	Data Type	Description
filespec	String	The file or files that will be deleted. This parameter may contain wildcards.
force	Boolean	Optional. Determines whether the file or files are deleted if they are read-only. The default is false.

DeleteFolder Method

The `DeleteFolder` method deletes one or more folders.

```
FileSystemObject.DeleteFolder(folderspec, [force])
```

Parameter	Data Type	Description
folderspec	String	The folder or folders that will be deleted. This parameter may contain wildcards.
force	Boolean	Optional. Determines whether the folder or folders will be deleted if they or any of their contents are read-only. The default is `false`.

DriveExists Method

The `DriveExists` method returns `true` if a drive with the specified name exists, and `false` otherwise.

```
Boolean = FileSystemObject.DriveExists(drivespec)
```

Parameter	Data Type	Description
drivespec	String	The name of the drive whose existence is in question. This parameter can be a drive letter as a string or a full absolute path for a folder or file.

We can get a list of available drive letters using the `DriveExists` method:

```vbscript
' VBScript
Set objFSO = Server.CreateObject("Scripting.FileSystemObject")
For intCode = 65 To 90    'ANSI codes for 'A' to 'Z'
   strLetter = Chr(intCode)
   If objFSO.DriveExists(strLetter) Then
      Response.Write "Found drive " & strLetter & ":<BR>"
   End If
Next
```

```jscript
// JScript
var objFSO = Server.CreateObject('Scripting.FileSystemObject');
for (var intCode = 65; intCode <= 90; intCode++) {
   strLetter = String.fromCharCode(intCode);
   if (objFSO.DriveExists(strLetter))
      Response.Write('Found drive ' + strLetter + ':<BR>');
}
```

The result of both these code fragments is:

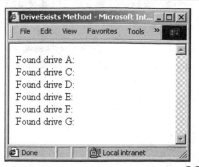

FileExists Method

The FileExists method returns true if a file with the specified name exists, and false otherwise.

```
Boolean = FileSystemObject.FileExists(filespec)
```

Parameter	Data Type	Description
filespec	String	The name of the file whose existence is in question. This parameter can be an absolute or relative path for the file, or just a file name in the current folder.

The FileExists method is commonly used with the other methods of the FileSystemObject object that are responsible for moving items around as well as creating and deleting them. To keep the code clean, it's a good idea to keep tabs on whether the item you're dealing with actually exists – it can make a big difference to the outcome of the command! For example, attempting to delete a non-existent file using DeleteFile will generate an error.

The solution to avoiding these errors is to use these methods in conjunction with the FileExists method. For example, here's a simple way to avoid an error when using DeleteFile:

```
' VBScript
If objFSO.FileExists("d:\mybusiness\myreport.txt") Then
    objFSO.DeleteFile("d:\mybusiness\myreport.txt")
    Response.Write "File deleted"
Else
    Response.Write "Error. File does not exist"
End If
```

```
// JScript:
if (objFSO.FileExists('d:\\mybusiness\\myreport.txt')) {
    objFSO.DeleteFile('d:\\mybusiness\\myreport.txt');
    Response.Write('File deleted');
} else {
    Response.Write('Error. File does not exist');
}
```

FolderExists Method

The FolderExists method returns true if a folder with the specified name exists and false otherwise.

```
Boolean = FileSystemObject.FolderExists(folderspec)
```

Parameter	Data Type	Description
folderspec	String	The name of the folder whose existence is in question. This parameter can be an absolute or relative path for the folder, or just a folder name in the current folder.

As described above, many of the other methods of the `FileSystemObject` object are responsible for moving items around, creating and deleting them. To avoid problems it's a good idea to check that the item you're dealing with currently exists.

Here's how to avoid a possible error when using `CreateFolder` caused when the folder already exists:

```
' VBScript
If Not objFSO.FolderExists("d:\mybusiness\") Then
    objFSO.CreateFolder("d:\mybusiness\")
    Response.Write("Folder created")
Else
    Response.Write("Error - Folder already exists")
End If
```

```
// JScript
if (!objFSO.FolderExists('d:\\mybusiness\\')) {
    objFSO.CreateFolder('d:\\mybusiness\\');
    Response.Write('Folder created');
} else {
    Response.Write('Error - Folder already exists');
}
```

GetAbsolutePathName Method

The `GetAbsolutePathName` method returns a full path name for a file or folder as a string taking into account the current folder's path.

```
String = FileSystemObject.GetAbsolutePathName(pathspec)
```

Parameter	Data Type	Description
pathspec	String	A path that identifies a file or folder relative to the current folder.

For example, if the current folder is `"c:\docs\sales\"` and *pathspec* is `"jan"`, then `"c:\docs\sales\jan"` is returned.

GetBaseName Method

The `GetBaseName` method returns the name of a file omitting the path and any extension. For example, for a file `C:\My Documents\sales.xml`, the base name will be `"sales"`.

```
String = FileSystemObject.GetBaseName(filespec)
```

Parameter	Data Type	Description
filespec	String	File path and name from which the base name of the file is determined.

GetDrive Method

The GetDrive method returns a Drive object. This method is important since it enables us to create instances of the Drive object.

```
Drive = FileSystemObject.GetDrive(drivespec)
```

Parameter	Data Type	Description
drivespec	String	The name of the drive. This parameter can include the colon, path separator or be a network share, e.g. "c", "c:", "c:\", or "\\machine\sharename".

An example of using the GetDrive method of a FileSystemObject object is:

```
' VBScript
Set objFSO = Server.CreateObject("Scripting.FileSystemObject")
Set objDrive = objFSO.GetDrive("C")
```

```
// JScript
objFSO = Server.CreateObject('Scripting.FileSystemObject');
objDrive = objFSO.GetDrive('C');
```

GetDriveName Method

The GetDriveName method returns a string value representing the name of a drive.

```
String = FileSystemObject.GetDriveName(drivespec)
```

Parameter	Data Type	Description
drivespec	String	An absolute path to a file or folder, or just the drive letter such as "c:" or just "c".

GetExtensionName Method

The GetExtensionName method returns just the file extension of a file with the path and file name removed.

```
String = FileSystemObject.GetExtensionName(filespec)
```

Parameter	Data Type	Description
filespec	String	File path and name from which the file extension is determined.

GetFile Method

The GetFile method returns a File object that represents a file. This method is particularly important, as it enables us to instantiate a File object without having to first refer to the Files collection, possibly one or more subfolders' Folders collections, a Folder object, and a Drive object from the Drives collection.

```
File = FileSystemObject.GetFile(filespec)
```

Parameter	Data Type	Description
filespec	String	A relative or absolute path to the required file.

An example of using the GetFile method of a FileSystemObject object is:

```
' VBScript
Set objFSO = Server.CreateObject("Scripting.FileSystemObject")
Set objFile = objFSO.GetFile("C:\MyFile.txt")
```

```
// JScript
objFSO = Server.CreateObject('Scripting.FileSystemObject');
objFile = objFSO.GetFile('C:\\MyFile.txt');
```

GetFileName Method

The GetFileName method returns the name part of the path and filename specified in pathspec, or the last folder name if there is no file name. It does not check for the existence of the file or folder.

```
String = FileSystemObject.GetFileName(pathspec)
```

Parameter	Data Type	Description
pathspec	String	The path of the file whose name we seek.

GetFolder Method

The GetFolder method returns a Folder object corresponding to the folder specified in folderspec. This can be a relative or absolute path to the required folder or just a folder name in the current folder.

```
Folder = FileSystemObject.GetFolder(folderspec)
```

Parameter	Data Type	Description
folderspec	String	The name of the folder that is sought.

This method returns a Folder object. It is an important way to access a Folder object without having to go through the Drives collection and a Drive object first.

Using the `GetFolder` method of a `FileSystemObject` object, we can create an instance of the `Folder` object immediately after creating the `FileSystemObject` object:

```
' VBscript
Set objFSO = Server.CreateObject("Scripting.FileSystemObject")
Set objFolder = objFSO.GetFolder("C:\test")
```

```
// JScript
objFSO = Server.CreateObject('Scripting.FileSystemObject');
objFolder = objFSO.GetFolder('C:\\test');
```

GetParentFolderName Method

The `GetParentFolderName` method returns the name of the parent folder of the file or folder specified in *pathspec*.

String = *FileSystemObject*.GetParentFolderName(*pathspec*)

Parameter	Data Type	Description
pathspec	String	A path of the parent folder.

GetSpecialFolder Method

The `GetSpecialFolder` method returns a `Folder` object corresponding to one of the special folders on the machine, such as the Windows directory, the System directory or the Temporary directory.

Folder = *FileSystemObject*.GetSpecialFolder(*folderspec*)

Parameter	Data Type	Description
folderspec	Special Folder Constant	The value or pre-defined name of the special folder we seek.

Where the parameter *folderspec* has one of the following values:

Value	Constant	Description
0	WindowsFolder	The **%Windows%** directory, by default `WinNT` (or `Windows` on a non-NT/2000 machine).
1	SystemFolder	The **%System%** directory, by default `WinNT\System32` (or `Windows\System` on a non-NT/2000 machine).
2	TemporaryFolder	The **%Temp%** directory, by default `WinNT\Temp` (or `Windows\Temp` on a non-NT/2000 machine).

To get a reference to a special folder, we supply the appropriate pre-defined constant as a parameter of the `GetSpecialFolder` method:

```vbscript
' VBScript
Const WindowsFolder = 0, SystemsFolder = 1, TemporaryFolder =2

Set objFSO = Server.CreateObject("Scripting.FileSystemObject")
Set objFolder = objFSO.GetSpecialFolder(WindowsFolder)
Response.Write "GetSpecialFolder(WindowsFolder) returned:<BR>"
Response.Write "Path: " & objFolder.Path & "<P>"

Set objFolder = objFSO.GetSpecialFolder(SystemsFolder)
Response.Write "GetSpecialFolder(SystemsFolder) returned:<BR>"
Response.Write "Path: " & objFolder.Path & "<P>"

Set objFolder = objFSO.GetSpecialFolder(TemporaryFolder)
Response.Write "GetSpecialFolder(TemporaryFolder) returned:<BR>"
Response.Write "Path: " & objFolder.Path & "<P>"
```

```jscript
// JScript
var WindowsFolder = 0, SystemsFolder = 1, TemporaryFolder = 2;

objFSO = Server.CreateObject('Scripting.FileSystemObject');
objFolder = objFSO.GetSpecialFolder(WindowsFolder);
Response.Write('GetSpecialFolder(WindowsFolder) returned:<BR>');
Response.Write('Path: ' + objFolder.Path + '<P>');

objFolder = objFSO.GetSpecialFolder(SystemsFolder);
Response.Write('GetSpecialFolder(SystemsFolder) returned:<BR>');
Response.Write('Path: ' + objFolder.Path + '<P>');

objFolder = objFSO.GetSpecialFolder(TemporaryFolder);
Response.Write('GetSpecialFolder(TemporaryFolder) returned:<BR>');
Response.Write('Path: ' + objFolder.Path + '<P>');
```

The result is shown:

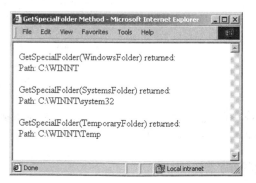

GetTempName Method

The `GetTempName` method returns a randomly generated file name that can be used for performing operations that require a temporary file or folder.

```
String = FileSystemObject.GetTempName()
```

MoveFile Method

The MoveFile method moves one or more files to a different directory.

```
FileSystemObject.MoveFile(source, destination)
```

Parameter	Data Type	Description
source	String	The path name for the file or files that will be moved. This parameter can contain wildcards (to move multiple files).
destination	String	The path name for the folder to which the file or files will be moved.

If *source* contains wildcards or if *destination* ends with a path separator character (\), then the destination will be a folder; otherwise, it will be a full path name for the new file.

An error will occur if a destination file already exists. It is good practice to use this in conjunction with the FileExists method.

MoveFolder Method

The MoveFolder method moves one or more folders to a different parent folder.

```
FileSystemObject.MoveFolder(source, destination)
```

Parameter	Data Type	Description
source	String	The path name for the file or files that will be moved. This parameter can contain wildcards (to move multiple folders).
destination	String	The path name for the folder to which the file or files will be moved.

An error will occur if a destination folder already exists. It is good practice to use this in conjunction with the FolderExists method.

OpenTextFile Method

The OpenTextFile method opens a text file. If the required file does not exist, it can be created.

```
objTextStream = FileSystemObject.OpenTextFile(filename, [iomode],
                                              [create], [format])
```

Parameter	Data Type	Description
filename	String	An absolute or relative path name for the file that will be opened or created.
iomode	IOMode	Optional. Specifies the required input/output mode. The default is ForReading.
create	Boolean	Optional. Specifies whether a file with the required path name will be created if one does not already exist. The default is false.
format	Tristate	Optional. Specifies the format of the data that will be read from or written to the file. The default is Tristatefalse.

The *iomode* parameter may have the following values:

Value	Constant	Description
1	ForReading	The TextStream object can be used for reading from a text stream (default).
2	ForWriting	The TextStream object can be used for writing to a text stream.
8	ForAppending	The TextStream object can be used for appending a string of text to a text stream.

The possible values for *format* are:

Value	Constant	Description
0	TristateFalse	ASCII (default).
-1	TristateTrue	Unicode.
-2	TristateUseDefault	The system default format.

For example:

```vbscript
' VBScript
Const ForReading = 1, ForWriting = 2, ForAppending = 8
Const TristateDefault = -2, TristateTrue = -1, TristateFalse = 0
Set objTextStream = objFSO.OpenTextFile _
            ("C:\mydocuments\writing.txt", ForAppending, false)
objTextStream.Write "This is some new text"
```

```jscript
// JScript
var ForReading = 1, ForWriting = 2, ForAppending = 8;
var TristateDefault = -2, TristateTrue = -1, TristateFalse = 0;
objTextStream = objFSO.OpenTextFile('C:\\mydocuments\\writing.txt',
                                ForAppending, false);
objTextStream.Write('This is some new text');
```

FileSystemObject Object

FileSystemObject Properties

Drives

The Drives property returns an instance of the Drives collection. This collection contains a Drive object for each drive available to the file system.

```
Drives = FileSystemObject.Drives
```

> See Chapter 10 for more information on the Drives collection and the Drive object.

To retrieve a reference to the Drives collection:

```
' VBScript
Set objFSO = Server.CreateObject("Scripting.FileSystemObject")
Set colDrives = objFSO.Drives
```

```
// JScript
objFSO = Server.CreateObject('Scripting.FileSystemObject');
colDrives = objFSO.Drives;
```

Summary

In this chapter, we've looked at the FileSystemObject object which allows us to access the file system of the server from our ASP pages. This is located in the Scripting Runtime library, scrrun.dll. The FileSystemObject object provides access to drives, folders (directories) and files. It has properties and methods that we can use to retrieve information about these, or to move, copy, or delete them. It also has two methods for working with text streams.

In this chapter we have looked at:

❑ Creating a FileSystemObject object using the Server.CreateObject method or using the <OBJECT> element.

❑ The methods and properties exposed by the FileSystemObject object.

13

The Folder Object and the Folders Collection

The Folder Object

The `Folder` object represents a folder, or directory, in a file system. As a subsiduary object of the `FileSystemObject` object, it is a Scripting Runtime Object and is thus available in the Microsoft Scripting Runtime Library, `scrrun.dll`.

A `Folder` object can be accessed in a number of different ways. These are explained in the next section. They include four different cases – using the `RootFolder` property of a `Drive` object, the `SubFolders` collection of a `Folder` object, the `GetFolder` method of a `FileSystemObject` object, and the `ParentFolder` property of a `Folder` object.

Accessing a Folder Object

An instance of the `Folder` object can be accessed using:

- ❑ The `RootFolder` property of a `Drive` object, if the folder is the drive's root folder.

- ❑ The `ParentFolder` property of a `File` or `Folder` object that resides within the folder.

- ❑ The `SubFolders` collection of a `Folder` object that represents the folder's parent folder.

- ❑ The `GetFolder` method of a `FileSystemObject` object.

> **Special Folders, such as the Windows directory, the System directory and the Temporary directory, can also be accessed through the `FileSystemObject.GetSpecialFolder` method discussed in the previous chapter.**

The following diagram shows how we can create various instances of the Folder object.

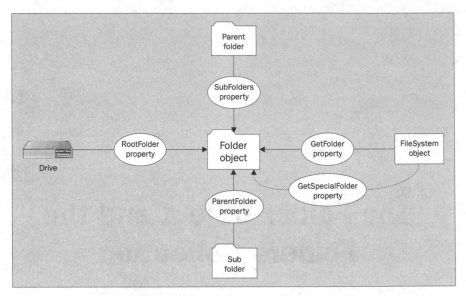

A Folder object that is the root folder of a drive can be accessed using the RootFolder property of a Drive object:

```
' VBscript
Set objFSO = Server.CreateObject("Scripting.FileSystemObject")
Set objDrive = objFSO.GetDrive("C")
Set objFolder1 = objDrive.RootFolder
```

```
// JScript
objFSO = Server.CreateObject('Scripting.FileSystemObject');
objDrive = objFSO.GetDrive('C');
objFolder1 = objDrive.RootFolder;
```

The Folder object that is returned by the RootFolder property of a Drive object can access all of the contents of the drive. We can use the ParentFolder and SubFolders properties of the Folder object to navigate through the folders in a drive.

A Folder object can also be accessed using the ParentFolder property of a File or Folder object that resides within the folder:

```
' VBScript
Set objParentFolder = objFolder.ParentFolder
```

```
// JScript
objParentFolder = objFolder.ParentFolder;
```

Thirdly, a Folder object can be accessed through the SubFolders collection of a Folder object that represents the folder's parent folder:

```
' VBScript
Set colFolders = objFolder1.SubFolders
Set objFolder2 = colFolders.Item("test")
```

```
// JScript
colFolders = objFolder1.SubFolders;
objFolder2 = colFolders.Item('test');
```

And finally, a `Folder` object can be accessed using the `GetFolder` method of the `FileSystemObject` object:

```
' VBScript
Set objFSO = Server.CreateObject("Scripting.FileSystemObject")
Set objFolder3 = objFSO.GetFolder("C:\test")
```

```
// JScript
objFSO = Server.CreateObject('Scripting.FileSystemObject');
objFolder3 = objFSO.GetFolder('C:\\test');
```

Folder Object Members

The `Folder` object exposes the following methods and properties:

Methods	Properties	
Copy	Attributes	ParentFolder
CreateTextFile	DateCreated	Path
Delete	DateLastAccessed	ShortName
Move	DateLastModified	ShortPath
	Drive	Size
	Files	SubFolders
	IsRootFolder	Type
	Name	

Many of the methods and properties of the `Folder` object are similar to the methods and properties of the `File` object. When you think about this, it makes a lot of sense – there are many aspects of files and folders which can obviously be handled in the same way (e.g. parent directory, path, date of creation properties; creation, deletion methods, etc.). Of course, folders and files are not exactly the same, so there are also differences between the interfaces of the `Folder` and `File` objects.

The Folder Object Methods

The `Folder` object has methods that can be used to copy, delete and move the folder that it represents. They are similar to the `CopyFolder`, `DeleteFolder` and `MoveFolder` methods of the `FileSystemObject` object, but they do not, of course, require a `source` parameter.

Three of the `Folder` object methods are shared by the `File` object, as shown overleaf:

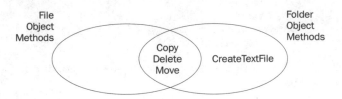

The remaining method, CreateTextFile, is similar to the FileSystemObject object's method of the same name.

Copy Method

The Copy method copies the folder and all its contents to another folder.

```
FolderObject.Copy(destination, [overwrite])
```

Parameters	Data Type	Description
destination	String	The path for the destination folder. If this parameter ends with a path separator character (\) then it represents a folder into which the copied folder will be placed; otherwise, a new folder will be created.
overwrite	Boolean	Optional. Determines whether the destination will be overwritten if it already exists. The default is true.

An error will occur if the destination folder already exists and the *overwrite* parameter is set to false. It is advisable to check first whether the destination folder exists using the FolderExists method of the FileSystemObject object, and hence avoid an error.

For example, placing a copy of the mybusiness directory into the temp directory, we could create a subfolder if C:\Temp already exists:

```
' VBScript
Set objFSO = Server.CreateObject("Scripting.FileSystemObject")
Set objFolder = objFSO.GetFolder("C:\mybusiness")
If Not objFSO.FolderExists("C:\temp") Then
    objFolder.Copy("C:\temp")
Else
    Response.Write "temp folder already exists - " & _
                   "folder copied to subfolder of this"
    objFolder.Copy("C:\temp\mybusiness_copy")
End If
```

```
// JScript
objFSO = Server.CreateObject('Scripting.FileSystemObject');
objFolder = objFSO.GetFolder('C:\\mybusiness');
if (!objFSO.FolderExists('C:\\temp') ) {
    objFolder.Copy('C:\\temp');
} else {
```

```
      Response.Write('temp folder already exists - ' +
                     'folder copied to subfolder of this');
      objFolder.Copy('C:\\temp\\mybusiness_copy');
}
objFolder.Copy('C:\\temp');
```

CreateTextFile Method

The `CreateTextFile` method creates and opens a text file in the folder and returns a new `TextStream` object associated with the new file.

```
TextStream = FolderObject.CreateTextFile(filename, [overwrite], [unicode])
```

Parameter	Data Type	Description
filename	String	The name of the file that will be created.
overwrite	Boolean	Optional. Determines whether an existing file with the required name will be overwritten. The default value is false.
unicode	Boolean	Optional. Determines whether the file will be stored as Unicode text. The default value is false.

For example, to create a `FileSystemObject` object, check whether the new text file name already exists, create this new file if not, and write to it:

```
' VBScript
If objFSO.FileExists(objFolder.Path & '\' & "myreport.txt") Then
   Response.Write "A file myreport.txt already exists"
Else
   Set objTextStream = objFolder.CreateTextFile("myreport.txt", _
                                                true, false)
   objTextStream.Write "This is new text created using " & _
                       "Folder object CreateTextFile"
   ' Some lines of code here ....
   objTextStream.Close
End If
```

Or in JScript:

```
if (objFSO.FileExists(objFolder.Path + '\\' + 'myreport.txt')) {
   Response.Write('A file myreport.txt already exists');
} else {
   objTextStream = objFolder.CreateTextFile('myreport.txt', true,
                                            false);
   objTextStream.Write('This is new text created using ' +
                       'Folder object CreateTextFile');
   // Some lines of code here ....
   objTextStream.Close();
}
```

Folder Object & Folders Collection

Delete Method

The Delete method deletes an empty folder.

```
FolderObject.Delete([force])
```

Parameter	Data Type	Description
force	Boolean	Optional. Determines whether the folder will be deleted if it is read-only. The default value is false.

Move Method

The Move method moves the folder and all its contents from its current location to another folder specified by the destination parameter. Properties such as Name, ParentDirectory and Drive are updated to reflect the new location of the folder.

```
FolderObject.Move(destination)
```

Parameter	Data Type	Description
destination	String	The destination for the folder. If this parameter ends with a path separator character (\) then it represents a folder into which the moved folder will be placed; otherwise a new folder will be created. An error will occur if the destination folder already exists.

The Move method is used like the Copy method above. Again your code will be cleaner if you check for existing folders (using the FileSystemObject.FolderExists method) before using the Move method.

The Folder Object Properties

The properties of the Folder object properties are similar to those of the File object, as shown below:

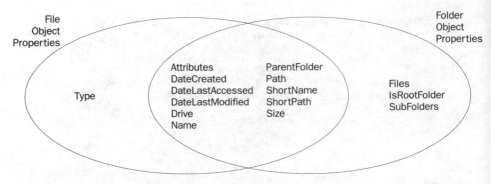

Some `Folder` object properties return objects or collections as shown in the figure below:

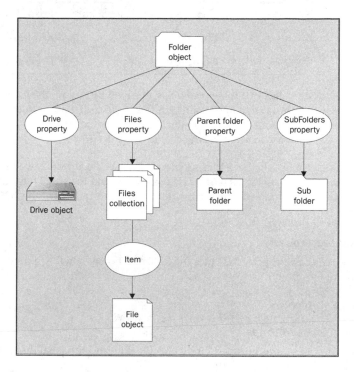

Attributes Property

The `Attributes` property sets or returns the attributes value for the folder.

```
FolderObject.Attributes = Integer
Integer = FolderObject.Attributes
```

This value can be a combination of any of the following values.

Value	Attribute	Description	Read/Write Attribute
0	Normal	Normal	N/A
1	ReadOnly	Read-only	Read/Write
2	Hidden	Hidden	Read/Write
4	System	System	Read/Write
8	Volume	Directory volume name	Read-only
16	Directory	Folder or directory	Read-only

Folder Object & Folders Collection

Value	Attribute	Description	Read/Write Attribute
32	Archive	Changed since last backup	Read/Write
1024	Alias	Link or shortcut	Read-only
2048	Compressed	Compressed	Read-only

The `Attributes` value for a folder can be ascertained by adding the values for the attributes which apply to that folder. Since the value 16 designates a folder, all folders will have an `Attributes` property greater than or equal to 16. For example, a read-only, hidden folder will have an `Attributes` value of $1 + 2 + 16 = 19$.

In order to determine whether a given folder has a specific attribute, we must perform a binary AND operation on the total `Attributes` value and the value for the attribute we want to check for. For more detail see the `Attributes` property of the `File` object in Chapter 11.

DateCreated Property

The `DateCreated` property indicates the date and time when the folder was created. It is a read-only property.

```
Date = FolderObject.DateCreated
```

DateLastAccessed Property

The `DateLastAccessed` property indicates the date and time that the folder was last accessed. It is a read-only property.

```
Date = FolderObject.DateLastAccessed
```

DateLastModified Property

The `DateLastModified` property indicates the date and time that the folder was last modified. It is a read-only property.

```
Date = FolderObject.DateLastModified
```

Drive Property

The `Drive` property returns a `Drive` object corresponding to the drive that contains the folder. It is a read-only property.

```
Drive = FolderObject.Drive
```

Files Property

The `Files` property of the `Folder` object returns a `Files` collection which contains a set of `File` objects.

```
FilesCollection = Folder.Files
```

See Chapter 11 for more information on the `File` object and the `Files` collection.

IsRootFolder Property

The IsRootFolder property returns a Boolean value that indicates whether the folder is the root folder for its drive. This is a read-only property.

```
Boolean = FolderObject.IsRootFolder
```

Name Property

The Name property is a string value that sets or returns the name of the folder.

```
FolderObject.Name = String
String = FolderObject.Name
```

For example:

```
' VBScript
strName = objFolder.Name
Response.Write "strName = " & strName & "<BR>"
objFolder.Name = "Mytest"
Response.Write "objFolder.Name = " & objFolder.Name & "<BR>"
```

```
// JScript
strName = objFolder.Name;
Response.Write('strName = ' + strName + '<BR>');
objFolder.Name = 'Mytest';
Response.Write('strFolderName.Name = ' + objFolder.Name + '<BR>');
```

ParentFolder Property

The ParentFolder property returns the Folder object for the parent folder of the current Folder object.

```
Folder = FolderObject.ParentFolder
```

Path Property

The Path property returns the absolute path of the folder using long file names where appropriate.

```
String = FolderObject.Path
```

For example in VBScript:

```
Set objFSO = Server.CreateObject("Scripting.FileSystemObject")
Set objFolder = objFSO.GetFolder("C:\mybusiness")
Response.Write "The path of " & objFolder.Name & " is " & _
               objFolder.Path
```

Or in JScript:

```
objFSO = Server.CreateObject('Scripting.FileSystemObject');
objFolder = objFSO.GetFolder('C:\\mybusiness');
Response.Write('The path of ' + objFolder.Name + ' is ' +
               objFolder.Path);
```

ShortName Property

The ShortName property returns the DOS-style 8.3 version of the folder name. The Folder object's ShortName property returns a truncated string when the name of the folder exceeds 8 characters.

```
String = FolderObject.ShortName
```

For example the following code:

```
' VBScript
Set objFSO = Server.CreateObject("Scripting.FileSystemObject")
Set objFolder = objFSO.GetFolder("C:\mybusiness\mydocuments")
strShortName = objFolder.ShortName
Response.Write "The short name of " & objFolder.Name & " is " & strShortName
```

```
// JScript
objFSO = Server.CreateObject('Scripting.FileSystemObject');
objFolder = objFSO.GetFolder('C:\\mybusiness\\mydocuments');
var strShortName = objFolder.ShortName;
Response.Write('The short name of ' + objFolder.Name + ' is ' +
strShortName);
```

Gives the output: The short name of mydocuments is MYDOCU~1.

ShortPath Property

The ShortPath property returns the DOS-style 8.3 version of the absolute path of this folder.

```
String = FolderObject.ShortPath
```

For example, the following code:

```
' VBScript
Set objFSO = Server.CreateObject("Scripting.FileSystemObject")
Set objFolder = objFSO.GetFolder("C:\mybusiness\mydocuments")
strShortName = objFolder.ShortPath
Response.Write "The short path of " & objFolder.Name & _
               " is " & strShortName
```

```
objFSO = Server.CreateObject('Scripting.FileSystemObject');
objFolder = objFSO.GetFolder('C:\\mybusiness\\mydocuments');
var strShortPath = objFolder.ShortPath;
Response.Write('The short path of ' + objFolder.Name +
               ' is ' + strShortPath);
```

Gives the output: The short path of mydocuments is C:\MYBUSI~1\MYDOCU~1.

Size Property

The Size property returns the size in bytes of all files and subfolders contained in the folder.

```
Variant = FolderObject.Size
```

SubFolders Property

The SubFolders property returns a Folders collection containing a Folder object for each subfolder in the directory.

```
Folders = Folder.SubFolder
```

Type Property

The Type property returns a string that is a description of the folder type (such as "File Folder", "System Folder" or "Recycle Bin"), if available.

```
String = FolderObject.Type
```

The Folders Collection

A Folders collection contains a set of Folder objects. We can use a Folders collection to represent any set of folders we like. For example, when we use an instance of the Folder object to represent a folder, its SubFolders property is a Folders collection that consists of all the subfolders of the folder.

The Folders collection exposes the following methods and properties:

Methods	Properties
Add	Item
	Count

Folders Collection Methods

Add Method

The Add method creates a new folder in the Folders collection. An error will be raised if the folder already exists.

```
Folder = FolderCollection.Add(Name)
```

Parameter	Data Type	Description
Name	String	The name of the folder to be created.

For example:

```
' VBScript
Set objFSO = Server.CreateObject("Scripting.FileSystemObject")
Set objFolder = objFSO.GetFolder("C:\mybusiness")
Set objSubFoldCol = objFolder.SubFolders
Response.Write "Number of subfolders in " & objFolder.Name & _
               " is " & objSubFoldCol.Count
objSubFoldCol.Add("addtest")
Response.Write "<BR>Number of subfolders is now " & _
               objSubFoldCol.Count
```

```
// JScript
objFSO = Server.CreateObject('Scripting.FileSystemObject');
objFolder = objFSO.GetFolder('C:\\mybusiness');
objSubFoldCol = objFolder.SubFolders;
Response.Write('Number of subfolders in ' + objFolder.Name + ' is ' +
               objSubFoldCol.Count);
objSubFoldCol.Add('addtest');
Response.Write('<BR>Number of subfolders is now ' +
               objSubFoldCol.Count);
```

Folders Collection Properties

Count Property

The Count property returns the number of folders in the Folders collection. As with other collections the Count property can be used to iterate through the objects in the collection.

```
Long = FolderCollection.Count
```

Item Property

The Item property returns a named Folder object in the Folders collection. Notice that the *Index* cannot be specified by a number, but should be specified by the Folder name.

```
Folder = FolderCollection.Item(Index)
```

Using the Folder Object and Folders Collection

The following example shows a simple file system browser using the Folder object and the Folders collection. The page contains three forms containing selection boxes for each drive in the file system, for each folder in selected folder (or in the drive's root folder if none has been selected), and for each file in the selected folder. Previously selected options are stored in HTML HIDDEN <INPUT> elements, so that we can keep track of where the user has navigated to in the file system. When a specific file has been selected, we display its contents in an HTML <TEXTAREA>.

The VBScript for this page is:

```
<HTML>
<HEAD>
   <TITLE>The Folders Collection</TITLE>
</HEAD>

<BODY>
<H2>A Simple File System Browser</H2>

<FORM METHOD="POST" ACTION="folders.asp">
Select drive: <SELECT NAME="driveLetter">

<%
strDrive = Request.Form("driveLetter")
```

```
Set objFSO=Server.CreateObject("Scripting.FileSystemObject")
For Each objDrive in objFSO.Drives
   Response.Write "<OPTION"
   If objDrive.DriveLetter=strDrive Then
      Response.Write " SELECTED"
   End If
   Response.Write ">" & objDrive.DriveLetter & "</OPTION>"
Next
%>
</SELECT><INPUT TYPE="SUBMIT" NAME="submit" VALUE="OK">
</FORM>
<HR>


<%
If strDrive <> "" Then
   Set objDrive = objFSO.GetDrive(CStr(strDrive))
   If Not objDrive.IsReady Then
      Response.Write "Drive is not available.<HR>"
   Else
      strFolder = Request.Form("folderPath")
      If strFolder = "" Then
         Set objFolder = objDrive.RootFolder
      Else
         strFolderName = Request.Form("folderName")
         If strFolderName <> "" Then
            If strFolderName = "[Up one level]" Then
               strFolder = strFolder & "\.."
            Else
               strFolder = strFolder & "\" & strFolderName
            End If
         End If
         Set objFolder = objFSO.GetFolder(CStr(strFolder))
      End If
      Response.Write "Folder path = " & objFolder.Path & "<BR>"
%>

      <FORM METHOD="POST" ACTION="folders.asp">
      <INPUT TYPE="HIDDEN" NAME="driveLetter"
            VALUE="<%= objDrive.DriveLetter %>">
      <INPUT TYPE="HIDDEN" NAME="folderPath"
            VALUE="<%= objFolder.Path %>">
      Select folder:
      <SELECT NAME="folderName">
<%
         If Not objFolder.IsRootFolder Then
            Response.Write "<OPTION SELECTED>[Up one level]" & _
                           "</OPTION>"
         End If
         For Each objSubFolder in objFolder.SubFolders
            Response.Write "<OPTION>" & objSubFolder.Name & _
                           "</OPTION>"
         Next
%>
      </SELECT><INPUT TYPE="SUBMIT" NAME="submit" VALUE="OK">
      </FORM>
      <HR>
      <FORM METHOD="POST" ACTION="folders.asp">
      <INPUT TYPE="HIDDEN" NAME="driveLetter"
            VALUE="<%= objDrive.DriveLetter %>">
      <INPUT TYPE="HIDDEN" NAME="folderPath"
            VALUE="<%= objFolder.Path %>">
```

```
<%
     If objFolder.Files.Count > 0 Then
        Response.Write "Select file: <SELECT NAME=""fileName"">"
        For Each objFile in objFolder.Files
            Response.Write "<OPTION>" & objFile.Name & _
                           "</OPTION>" & vbCrLf
        Next
        Response.Write "</SELECT><INPUT TYPE=""SUBMIT"" " & _
                       "NAME=""submit"" VALUE=""OK"">"
     Else
        Response.Write "No files to view."
     End If
     Response.Write "</FORM><HR>"
     strFileName = Request.Form("fileName")
     If strFileName <> "" Then
        Set objFile=objFSO.GetFile(objFolder.Path & "\" & _
                                    strFileName)
        Response.Write "Filename = " & objFile.Name
        on error resume next
        strText = objFile.OpenAsTextStream.ReadAll
        If err.number <> 0 Then
            Response.Write "<BR><BR>Sorry, that file " & _
                           "cannot be opened."
        Else
            Response.Write "<FORM><TEXTAREA NAME=""objTextArea""" & _
                           " COLS=50 ROWS=10>"
            Response.Write  strText
            Response.Write  "</TEXTAREA></FORM>"
        End If
     End If
   End If
End If
%>

</FORM>
</BODY>
</HTML>
```

The equivalent in JScript looks like this:

```
<%@ LANGUAGE = "JScript" %>
<HTML>
<HEAD>
   <TITLE>The Folders Collection</TITLE>
</HEAD>

<BODY>
<H2>A Simple File System Browser</H2>

<FORM METHOD="POST" ACTION="folders.asp">
Select drive: <SELECT NAME="driveLetter">

<%
strDrive = Request.Form('driveLetter');
objFSO=Server.CreateObject('Scripting.FileSystemObject');

enmDrives = new Enumerator(objFSO.Drives);
for (; !enmDrives.atEnd(); enmDrives.moveNext()) {
   objDrive = enmDrives.item();
   Response.Write('<OPTION');
   if (objDrive.DriveLetter == strDrive) {
     Response.Write(' SELECTED');
```

```
    }
    Response.Write('>' + objDrive.DriveLetter + '</OPTION>');
}
%>

</SELECT><INPUT TYPE="SUBMIT" NAME="submit" VALUE="OK">
</FORM>
<HR>

<%
strDrive=String(strDrive);
if (strDrive != 'undefined') {
    objDrive = objFSO.GetDrive(strDrive);
    if (!objDrive.IsReady) {
      Response.Write('Drive is not available.<HR>');
    } else {
        strFolder = String(Request.Form('folderPath'));
        if (strFolder == 'undefined') {
            objFolder = objDrive.RootFolder;
        } else {
            strFolderName = String(Request.Form('folderName'));
            if (strFolderName != 'undefined')  {
                if (strFolderName == '[Up one level]') {
                    strFolder = strFolder + '\\..';
                } else {
                    strFolder = strFolder + '\\' + strFolderName;
                }
            }
            objFolder = objFSO.GetFolder(strFolder);
        }
        Response.Write('Folder path = ' + objFolder.Path + '<BR>');
%>

        <FORM METHOD="POST" ACTION="folders.asp">
        <INPUT TYPE="HIDDEN" NAME="driveLetter"
            VALUE="<%= objDrive.DriveLetter %>">
        <INPUT TYPE="HIDDEN" NAME="folderPath"
            VALUE="<%= objFolder.Path %>">
        Select folder:
        <SELECT NAME="folderName">
<%

            if (!objFolder.IsRootFolder) {
                Response.Write('<OPTION SELECTED>[Up one level]' +
                            '</OPTION>');
            }
            var enmFolders = new Enumerator(objFolder.SubFolders);
            for (; !enmFolders.atEnd(); enmFolders.moveNext()) {
                objSubFolder = enmFolders.item();
                Response.Write('<OPTION>' + objSubFolder.Name +
                            '</OPTION>');
            }
%>
        </SELECT><INPUT TYPE="SUBMIT" NAME="submit" VALUE="OK">
        </FORM>
        <HR>
        <FORM METHOD="POST" ACTION="folders.asp">
        <INPUT TYPE="HIDDEN" NAME="driveLetter"
            VALUE="<%= objDrive.DriveLetter %>">
        <INPUT TYPE="HIDDEN" NAME="folderPath"
            VALUE="<%= objFolder.Path %>">
<%
```

```
        if (objFolder.Files.Count > 0) {
            Response.Write('Select file: <SELECT NAME=\"fileName\">');
            var enmFiles = new Enumerator(objFolder.Files);
            for (; !enmFiles.atEnd(); enmFiles.moveNext()) {
                objFile = enmFiles.item();
                Response.Write('<OPTION>' + objFile.Name + '</OPTION>\n');
            }
            Response.Write('</SELECT><INPUT TYPE=\"SUBMIT\" NAME=\"submit\"
VALUE=\"OK\">');
        } else {
            Response.Write('No files to view.');
        }
        Response.Write('</FORM><HR>');
        strFileName = String(Request.Form('fileName'));
        if (strFileName != 'undefined') {
            objFile=objFSO.GetFile(objFolder.Path + '\\' + strFileName);
            Response.Write('Filename = ' + objFile.Name);
            try {
                strText = objFile.OpenAsTextStream().ReadAll();
                Response.Write('<FORM><TEXTAREA NAME=\"objTextArea\" ' +
                               'COLS=50 ROWS=10>');
                Response.Write(strText);
                Response.Write('</TEXTAREA></FORM>');
            }
            catch(e) {
                Response.Write('<BR><BR>Sorry, that file cannot be opened.');
            }
        }
    }
}
%>

</FORM>
</BODY>
</HTML>
```

The output of this is:

Summary

In this chapter, we've looked at the Folder object and the Folders collection implemented by the Scripting Runtime library, in the file scrrun.dll. These are accessible through the FileSystemObject discussed in Chapter 12.

The Folder object has methods that can be used to copy, delete, and move the folder that it represents. They are similar to the CopyFolder, DeleteFolder, and MoveFolder methods of the FileSystemObject object, but they do not, of course, require a source parameter. The Folders collection contains all the Folder objects for a parent folder.

In this chapter we have looked at:

❑　Accessing the Folder object using the RootFolder property of a Drive object, the SubFolders property of a Folder object, the GetFolder method of a FileSystemObject object and the ParentFolder property of a Folder object.

❑　The methods and properties of the Folder object.

❑　The properties of the Folders collection.

❑　An example of using a Folder object and Folders collection in a simple file system browser.

Folder Object & Folders Collection

The TextStream Object

The TextStream object provides access to the contents of text files stored on disk, and is used with the FileSystemObject object. The TextStream object can read from or write to text files – so you can use the TextStream object to get sequential access to files of type .txt, .html, .asp, and so on.

It can only be created through the FileSystemObject object, so it is effectively a child of that object.

The FileSystemObject, Folder, and File objects all provide methods for creating, reading from or writing to text files via a TextStream object. We use the FileSystemObject object or one of its subsidiary objects to create a TextStream object for access to the contents of a disk file.

Accessing a TextStream Object

We can create an instance of the TextStream object using one of three different methods:

❑   The CreateTextFile method of the Folder object or the FileSystemObject object

❑   The OpenTextFile method of the FileSystemObject object

❑   The OpenAsTextStream method of the File object

Once we've used one of these methods to create a new text file, or to open an existing one, we have a TextStream object reference to it, and we can manipulate the file using the methods and properties of the TextStream object.

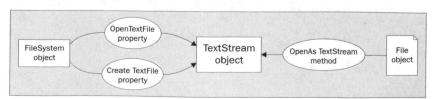

Creating a New Text File

The CreateTextFile method creates a new text file (or overwrites an existing one) on disk with the specified filename. It returns a TextStream object that refers to it and that we can use to read from or write to the file. The CreateTextFile method of the Folder object or the FileSystemObject object has the following syntax:

```
TextStream = FileSystemObject.CreateTextFile(filename, [overwrite],
                                                       [unicode])
```

If the optional overwrite parameter is set to true, any existing file with the same path and filename will be overwritten. The default for overwrite is false. If the optional unicode parameter is set to true, the content of the file will be stored as unicode text. Again, the default is false.

This example uses VBScript to create an ASCII (i.e. non-Unicode) file named MyFile.txt, replacing any existing file with the same name:

```
Set objFSO = Server.CreateObject("Scripting.FileSystemObject")
Set objTStream = objFSO.CreateTextFile("C:\TextFiles\MyFile.txt", True, _
                                        False)
objTStream.Write "This is new text"
' some line of code here ...
objTStream.Close
```

To do the same in JScript we can use:

```
var objFSO = Server.CreateObject('Scripting.FileSystemObject');
var objTStream = objFSO.CreateTextFile('C:\\TextFiles\\MyFile.txt', true,
                                        false);
objTStream.Write('This is new text');
// some line of code here ...
objTStream.Close();
```

Once the file has been created, we can use the objTStream reference (which is a reference to the TextStream object) to work with the file.

Opening an Existing Text File

The OpenTextFile method opens an existing text file. It returns a TextStream object that we can use to read from or append data to the file. Again, we first create a FileSystemObject object, then use it to create a TextStream object. The OpenTextFile method of the FileSystemObject object has the following syntax:

```
objTextStream = FileSystemObject.OpenTextFile(filename, [iomode], [create],
                                                        [format])
```

The *filename* parameter can contain an absolute or relative path. The *iomode* parameter specifies the type of access required. The permissible values are ForReading (1 – the default), ForWriting (2), and ForAppending (8). If the *create* parameter is set to true when writing or appending to a file that does not exist, a new file will be created. The default for *create* is false. The *format* parameter specifies the format of the data to be read from or written to the file. Permissible values are TristateFalse (0 – the default) to open the file in ASCII format, TristateTrue (-1) to open it as Unicode, and TristateUseDefault (-2) to open it using the system default format. These constants are not available by default, so if you want to use them rather than the literal values, you will need to define them manually.

This VBScript example opens a file named MyFile.txt ready to read the contents:

```
Const ForReading = 1, ForWriting = 2, ForAppending = 8
Const TristateDefault = -2, TristateTrue = -1, TristateFalse = 0
Set objFSO = Server.CreateObject("Scripting.FileSystemObject")
Set objTStream = objFSO.OpenTextFile("C:\myfile.txt", ForReading)
```

The same in JScript is:

```
var ForReading = 1, ForWriting = 2, ForAppending = 8;
var TristateDefault = -2, TristateTrue = -1, TristateFalse = 0;
var objFSO = Server.CreateObject('Scripting.FileSystemObject');
var objTStream = objFSO.OpenTextFile('C:\\myfile.txt');
```

To open the file for writing, creating a new file if the one specified doesn't already exist, we could use in VBScript:

```
Set objTStream = objFSO.OpenTextFile("C:\myfile.txt", ForWriting, True)
objTStream.Write "This is some new text"
```

Or in JScript:

```
var objTStream = objFSO.OpenTextFile('C:\\myfile.txt', ForWriting, true);
objTStream.Write('This is some new text');
```

If we want to open an existing Unicode file ready to append data to it, but *not* create a new file if the one specified doesn't already exist, we could use, in VBScript:

```
Set objTStream = objFSO.OpenTextFile("C:\myfile.txt", ForAppending, False, _
                                     TristateTrue)
objTStream.Write "This is some new text"
```

Or in JScript:

```
var objTStream = objFSO.OpenTextFile('C:\\myfile.txt', ForAppending, false,
                                     true);
objTStream.Write('This is some new text');
```

Note that in Windows 2000, Notepad now gives us several options for the format in which we save a text file, so we can use this old favorite to create a file in Unicode format.

TextStream Object

Opening a TextStream From a File Object

The OpenAsTextStream method of the File object opens the file that this object refers to and returns a TextStream object that can be used to read from, write to, or append to the file. The OpenAsTextStream method of the File object has the following syntax:

```
TextStream = FileObject.OpenAsTextStream([iomode], [format])
```

The *iomode* parameter specifies the type of access required. The permissible values are ForReading (1 – the default), ForWriting (2), and ForAppending (8). The *format* parameter specifies the format of the data to be read from or written to the file. Permissible values are TristateFalse (0 – the default) to open the file in ASCII format, TristateTrue (-1) to open it as Unicode, and TristateUseDefault (-2) to open it using the system default format.

So, given a File object (not a FileSystemObject in this case) named objFile, we can open it for appending as an ASCII (i.e. not Unicode) TextStream object method like this in VBScript:

```
Const ForReading = 1, ForWriting = 2, ForAppending = 8
Const TristateDefault = -2, TristateTrue = -1, TristateFalse = 0
Set objTextStream = objFile.OpenAsTextStream(ForAppending, false)
objTextStream.Write "This is new text to be appended to the file"
```

The equivalent code in JScript looks like:

```
var ForReading = 1, ForWriting = 2, ForAppending = 8;
var TristateDefault = -2, TristateTrue = -1, TristateFalse = 0;
objTextStream = objFile.OpenAsTextStream(ForAppending, false);
objTextStream.Write('This is new text to be appended to the file');
```

Writing to a Text File

Once we've created a TextStream object that refers to a file, using the CreateTextFile, OpenTextFile or OpenAsTextStream method with the ForWriting or ForAppending parameter, we can write to it and close it using VBScript like this:

```
objTStream.WriteLine "At last I can create files with VBScript!"
objTStream.WriteLine
objTStream.WriteLine "Here are three blank lines:"
objTStream.WriteBlankLines 3
objTStream.Write "... and this is "
objTStream.WriteLine "the last line."
objTStream.Close
```

Or using JScript:

```
objTStream.WriteLine('At last I can create files with JScript!');
objTStream.WriteLine();
objTStream.WriteLine('Here are three blank lines:');
objTStream.WriteBlankLines(3);
objTStream.Write('... and this is ');
objTStream.WriteLine('the last line.');
objTStream.Close();
```

The resulting file looks
like this:

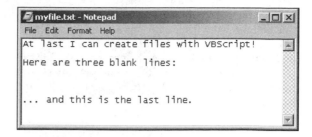

Reading from a Text File

Once we've created a TextStream object that refers to a file, using the
CreateTextFile, OpenTextFile, or OpenAsTextStream method with the
ForReading parameter, we can read from it and close it using VBScript like this:

```
' Read one line at a time until the end of the file is reached
Do While Not objTStream.AtEndOfStream
    'Get the line number
    intLineNum = objTStream.Line
    'Format it as a 4-character string with leading zeros
    strLineNum = Right("000" & CStr(intLineNum), 4)
    'Get the text of the line from the file
    strLineText = objTStream.ReadLine
    Response.Write strLineNum & ": " & strLineText & "<BR>"
Loop
objTStream.Close
```

Or using JScript:

```
// Read one line at a time until the end of the file is reached
while (!objTStream.AtEndOfStream) {
    // Get the line number
    intLineNum = objTStream.Line;
    // Format and convert to a string
    strLineNum = '000' + intLineNum;
    strLineNum = strLineNum.substr(strLineNum.length - 4, 4);
    // Get the text of the line from the file
    strLineText = objTStream.ReadLine();
    Response.Write(strLineNum + ': ' + strLineText + '<BR>');
}
objTStream.Close();
```

TextStream Object Members

The TextStream object exposes the following methods and properties:

Methods		Properties
Close	SkipLine	AtEndOfLine
Read	Write	AtEndOfStream
ReadAll	WriteLine	Column
ReadLine	WriteBlankLines	Line
Skip		

TextStream Object

A key concept to understand, before looking at the properties and methods, is that of a **file pointer**. With each TextStream instance, there is an internal pointer that indicates the current position in the file. When the stream is first opened, the file pointer points to the position immediately before the first character in the file. As we manipulate the TextStream using its methods and properties, the position indicated by the file pointer changes, and subsequent method calls will read from or write to the file starting at the new position.

TextStream Object Methods

The TextStream object has nine methods which we can use to read from or write to the stream, to move the position of the file pointer, or to close the file.

Close Method

The Close method closes a text file. After closing a file, the TextStream object is destoryed and we can no longer use the properties and methods of the TextStream object associated with it.

```
TextStreamObject.Close()
```

Read Method

The Read method reads a specifed number of characters from the file and returns them as a string.

```
String = TextStreamObject.Read(numchars)
```

Parameter	Data Type	Description
numchars	Integer	The number of characters to be read.

Note that we need to have opened the file in read mode in order to use any of the read methods – if we open the file for writing and attempt to use a read method, a Bad File Mode error will be raised.

ReadAll Method

The ReadAll method reads the entire file and returns the result as a string.

```
String = TextStreamObject.ReadAll()
```

ReadLine Method

The ReadLine method reads a line (up to the next carriage return or line feed) from the file and returns it (excluding the newline character) as a string.

```
String = TextStreamObject.ReadLine()
```

Skip Method

The Skip method skips a specified number of characters from the file. The number of characters to be skipped can be a positive or negative number.

```
TextStreamObject.Skip(numchars)
```

Parameter	Data Type	Description
numchars	Long	The number of characters to be skipped.

The Skip method moves the file pointer forwards or backwards the specified number of characters in the stream. If the numchars parameter is positive, the file pointer will move forward; if it is negative, it will move backwards. This method can only be used if a file has been opened for reading.

SkipLine Method

The SkipLine method skips the next line from the file; that is, it moves the file pointer from its current position to the beginning of the next line.

```
TextStreamObject.SkipLine()
```

This method can only be used when reading a file. In order to write a blank line to a file, we must use the WriteBlankLines method.

Write Method

The Write method writes a string to the file.

```
TextStreamObject.Write(String)
```

Parameter	Data Type	Description
String	String	The text to be added to the file.

Where the text is written in the file is based on the input/output mode that you selected when opening the file. If you selected ForAppending, the text will be added to the end of the file. If you chose ForWriting, the first write to the file will be at the beginning of the file and any subsequent writes will be appended to it.

WriteLine Method

The WriteLine method writes an optional string followed by a newline character to the file.

```
TextStreamObject.WriteLine([String])
```

Parameter	Data Type	Description
String	String	Optional. The string to be written to the file before the newline character.

WriteBlankLines Method

The WriteBlankLines method writes the specified number of newline characters to the file.

```
TextStreamObject.WriteBlankLines(n)
```

TextStream Object

Parameter	Data Type	Description
n	Long	The number of newline characters to be written to the file.

TextStream Object Properties

The TextStream properties provide information about the current position of the file pointer within the file. They are all read-only.

AtEndOfLine Property

The read-only AtEndOfLine property returns True if the file pointer is positioned immediately before the end of a line marker. It is only available if the file is opened with iomode of ForReading. Using it otherwise will cause an error.

```
Boolean = TextStreamObject.AtEndOfLine
```

AtEndOfStream Property

The read-only AtEndOfStream property returns True if the file pointer is positioned at the end of the file. It is only available if the file is opened with iomode of ForReading. Using it otherwise will cause an error.

```
Boolean = TextStreamObject.AtEndOfStream
```

Column Property

The read-only Column property returns the column number of the current position in the file. Column 1 represents the first character in each line.

```
Long = TextStreamObject.Column
```

Line Property

The read-only Line property returns a long integer which gives the current line number in the file, starting from 1.

```
Long = TextStreamObject.Line
```

Using the TextStream Object

In this example, we will use the TextStream object to enhance the way that ASP files can be viewed when trying to teach people about your code. One of the best ways to learn how to program on the web is to look at people's source code. You can learn many HTML tricks by looking at the source code of your favorite pages.

How can you use this same approach to learn the insides of ASP? With ASP, the source is interpreted on the server, and all the client sees is the completed HTML. In this example, we will create an ASP script that displays the source of any of the ASP files on your server. The file name will be passed in as a URL parameter. We will also show how to link it to an existing ASP page.

When you view the example from chapter 10, you will now see a new entry at the bottom of the page.

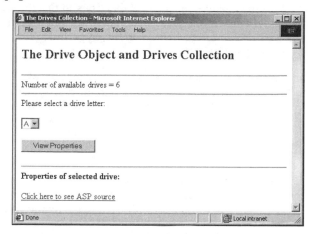

When you click on this hyperlink, you will see:

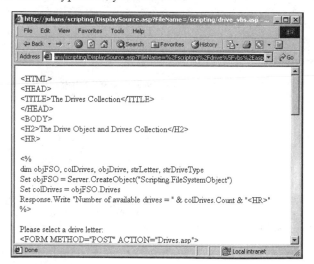

How It Works

We've used `Drives.asp` (from Chapter 10) as the starting point for this example – we could have used any ASP page. In order to make the ASP code of the page available to the user, we've added the following single line of code:

```
<A HREF="DisplaySource.asp?FileName="<%= Server.URLEncode
(Request.ServerVariables("PATH_INFO")) %>">Click here to see ASP source</A>
```

This hyperlink will request the page `DisplaySource.asp`. This line will look for `DisplaySource.asp` in the same directory as the current ASP file (generally, you need to reference `DisplaySource.asp` via a relative filepath). One parameter, called `FileName`, will be passed in the `QueryString`. This will contain the virtual path to the file, as contained in the `PATH_INFO` server variable.

267

Since this information is going to be passed on the URL string, we will need to ensure that it is properly formatted. We *could* go through and replace each space with "%20" – but an easier way is to employ some method that does all this for us. Luckily, the URLEncode method of the Server object will make sure that the string is properly formatted to be a URL. When the user clicks on this hyperlink, the DisplaySource.asp page is displayed.

Let's walk through the code sections of DisplaySource.asp. We'll be using some methods of the TextStream object that require parameters. Rather than just passing the numerical value, we'll create constants that represent the possible values:

```
<%
    Const ForReading = 1, ForWriting = 2, ForAppending = 3
    Const TristateUseDefault = -2, TristateTrue = -1, TristateFalse = 0
```

You will see later how this makes the code more readable. Also, in order to create a TextStream object, we need to start with a valid File object for the file we are interested in. To get this, we substitute the value passed in on the URL line:

```
    Dim strPathInfo, strPhysicalPath
    strPathInfo = Request.QueryString("FileName")
    strPhysicalPath = Server.MapPath(strPathInfo)
    Dim objFSO, objFile
    Set objFSO = CreateObject("Scripting.FileSystemObject")
    set objFile = objFSO.GetFile(strPhysicalPath)
%>
```

Once we have the valid File object, the next step is to open that file as a text file. To do this, we use the OpenAsTextStream method of the File object:

```
<%
    Dim objFileTextStream
    set objFileTextStream = objFile.OpenAsTextStream(ForReading, _
                                                     TristateUseDefault)
```

This method will return a reference to a TextStream object that contains the contents of the file. Since we are not interested in modifying the file, we will open it ForReading only. You should usually open the file in the default format mode, unless you are absolutely sure that the contents are not of the default type.

Once the file is open, we can begin reading the information from the file. There are plenty of different methods that allow us to do this in different ways. For example, we could read the file all at once, using ReadAll – it's the easiest to implement, but it doesn't work too well for large files. Instead, we'll read it line-by-line, using the ReadLine method.

We need some indication as to when we've run out of file to read. The TextStream object provides the AtEndOfStream property, which returns true when the file pointer is at the end of the file:

```
    Dim strLine, strFileLine
    Do While objFileTextStream.AtEndOfStream <> True
        strFileLine = objFileTextStream.ReadLine
```

If we simply use `Response.Write strFileLine` now, we'll probably get some messy results – first we need to handle any special characters in the string. This is particularly relevant in this case, because we're trying to display HTML and ASP code – the HTML tags are a particular problem. When a client displays an HTML page, it looks for HTML tags (bounded by < >) and uses them as formatting instructions. We need to format these symbols so that they'll be interpreted as text characters instead. The `Server` object's `HTMLEncode` method does just that. We'll also use the `Replace` method to replace tab characters with ` ` (explicit space characters), to retain the tab formatting in the original file:

```
        strLine = Server.HTMLEncode(strFileLine)
        strLine = Replace (strLine, Chr(9), "    ")
```

Now that the whole line is properly formatted, we can output it to the client using the `Response.Write` method. Since the client will ignore any carriage returns in the text file, we need to add our own line break to the displayed source code:

```
        Response.Write strLine
        Response.Write "<BR>" + vbCrLf
    Loop
    objFileTextStream.Close
%>
```

The JScript equivalent for the entire code is:

```
<%
    var ForReading = 1, ForWriting = 2, ForAppending = 3;
    var TristateUseDefault = -2, TristateTrue = -1, TristateFalse = 0;
    var strPathInfo, strPhysicalPath;
    strPathInfo = Request.QueryString("FileName");
    strPhysicalPath = Server.MapPath(strPathInfo);
    var objFSO, objFile;
    objFSO = Server.CreateObject("Scripting.FileSystemObject");
    objFile = objFSO.GetFile(strPhysicalPath);
%>
<%
    var objFileTextStream = objFile.OpenAsTextStream(ForReading,
                                        TristateUseDefault);
    var strLine, strFileLine;
    while (!objFileTextStream.atEndOfStream) {
        strFileLine = objFileTextStream.ReadLine();
        strLine = Server.HTMLEncode(strFileLine);
        objRE = /\t/g;
        strLine.replace(objRE, "    ");
        Response.Write(strLine);
        Response.Write("<BR>\n");
    }
    objFileTextStream.Close();
%>
```

The only point to note here is that we use the `String.replace` method to replace tab characters, which takes as its first parameter a Regular Expression object which represents the pattern to be replaced. We want to replace all tabs, so our regular expression is simply `/\t/g` – the forward slashes mark the start and end of the pattern, the expression `\t` matches a tab character, and the flag `g` indicates that the replace is to be global – all tab characters found are to be replaced.

TextStream Object

DisplaySource.asp can be referenced from any ASP page on your web server, so you can see that it makes it very easy to add documentation to your pages for other developers to see how you actually created the page. And since the documentation is generated from the actual page itself, you never have to worry about the documentation becoming out of sync with the real code.

Summary

In this chapter, we've looked at the TextStream object that is always available when we use ASP with VBScript or JScript through the scripting run-time library, scrrun.dll. The TextStream object is inexorably linked to the FileSystemObject object, since we use them both to access the contents of disk drives that are available on our server or networked (mapped) to it.

A TextStream object can be created to reference any file on the system, and through it we can read from and write to that file. It is treated as a text file for reading and writing, and we can even handle Unicode-format files. This combination of navigation and read/write capabilities allows us to exert complete control over the file system of the server. We can also use these objects (with limitations) in script code running on a client machine.

In this chapter we have considered:

❑   The different ways of accessing a TextStream object.

❑   Using the methods of the TextStream object to read from and write to text files.

❑   Using the properties of the TextStream object to navigate within the file.

❑   An example which used the TextStream object to display the source code for an ASP page.

Active Server Components

The Ad Rotator Component

The Ad Rotator component can be used to display different advertisements on our pages, each time the page is referenced from a browser. This component automatically rotates images (typically advertisements – hence the name) according to a specified schedule, stored in the **rotator schedule file**. The ads are rotated on the server when another client requests the page, or when the client refreshes the page. We can also make the image a hyperlink and specify redirection to another URL when the ad is clicked, using the **redirection file**.

The Ad Rotator component is found in adrot.dll and can be instantiated using the Server.CreateObject method with a ProgID of "MSWC.AdRotator":

```
' VBScript
Set MyAD = Server.CreateObject("MSWC.AdRotator")
```

```
// JScript
MyAD = Server.CreateObject("MSWC.AdRotator");
```

Alternatively, we can use an HTML <OBJECT> tag with a RUNAT="SERVER" attribute:

```
<OBJECT ID="MyAd" RUNAT="SERVER" PROGID="MSWC.AdRotator"></OBJECT>
```

However, before using the Ad Rotator component, we first need to create a schedule file, and make sure that we have set all the properties of the Ad Rotator that we require.

The Rotator Schedule File

The Ad Rotator component obtains all the information it needs from the rotator schedule file. This is a specially formatted text file that consists of two sections, separated by a line containing a single asterisk. The first section (optional) contains values that will apply to all advertisements; the second section has values specific to each advertisement.

The format of the file is:

```
REDIRECT URL
WIDTH width
HEIGHT height
BORDER border
*
adURL
adHomePageURL
altText
impressions
```

In the first section we set the default values for the attributes that apply to all advertisement images in the schedule. If we skip this section, our rotator schedule file should still start with a single asterisk in the first line. The second section contains details of the individual advertisements. The attributes which can be included in the file are:

Name	Type	Description
REDIRECT	URL	Specifies the virtual path and name of the DLL, CGI application or ASP file that will implement redirection to the URL specified with AdHomePageURL below when the advertisement is clicked. This can be either the full URL (for example, http://localhost/ads-demo/redirect.asp), or the path relative to the virtual directory (for example, /ads-demo/redirect.asp).
WIDTH	Number	Specifies the width of the advertisement. Default value is 440 pixels.
HEIGHT	Number	Specifies the height of the advertisement. Default value is 60.
BORDER	Number	Specifies the width of the border around the advertisement. Default value is 1 pixel.
adURL	URL	The location of the advertisement image file. This should be a virtual path and file name. This can be a graphics file in JPEG, GIF or PNG format.
adHomePageURL	URL	The URL to which the client will be redirected, usually the advertiser's home page. If there is no URL supplied, place the hyphen (-) symbol here.

Name	Type	Description
`altText`	String	Alternative text for browsers that do not support graphics.
`impressions`	Number	A number between 0 and 4,294,967,295 that indicates the relative weight of the advertisement. The higher the `impressions` value for the advertisement, the more frequently it will appear on the page.

Below is an example of a simple rotator schedule file with two ads:

```
REDIRECT /ads-demo/redirect.asp
WIDTH 440
HEIGHT 60
BORDER 1
*
http://www.wrox.com/images/wroxlogo.gif
http://www.wrox.com/
Best programmer's books
20
http://www.asptoday.com/images/asptoday.gif
http://www.asptoday.com
Up-to-the minute articles on ASP
20
```

In this example rotator schedule file, we have two advertisements that have the same value for the impressions parameter, meaning that each advertisement is equally likely to appear.

The Redirection File

As we've just seen, we can specify a file in the `Redirect` property of the rotator schedule file, which will handle redirection to the URL specified with the `adHomePageURL` property.

This file could consist simply of a single line of code to redirect the user to the appropriate site:

```
Response.Redirect(Request.QueryString("url"))
```

However, we can also add code to the redirection file that will perform other useful functions, before we redirect the client. For instance, we might want to record statistics, such as the number of users who have jumped from our page to the home page of one or other advertiser. We have the URL value passed as part of the query string to tell us which ad the user has chosen, and we can either store this information in a file, using the `TextStream` object discussed in Chapter 14, or write the statistics to a database

Ad Rotator Component

using ADO. This would allow us to gauge the success of an ad, or prove to the advertisers that our site is attracting potential customers for them, and bill the advertisers accordingly.

Ad Rotator Component Members

The AdRotator component exposes one method and three properties:

Methods	Properties
GetAdvertisement	Border
	Clickable
	TargetFrame

Ad Rotator Component Methods

The single method exposed by the Ad Rotator component allows us to retrieve an image from the schedule file.

GetAdvertisement Method

This method gets details of the next advertisement from the rotator schedule file and returns the appropriate HTML code for displaying the image in the browser. It retrieves the next scheduled advertisement each time the script is invoked – when a user either opens the ASP file or refreshes it. The GetAdvertisement method has the following syntax:

```
String = AdRotator.GetAdvertisement(Path)
```

Parameter	Data Type	Description
Path	String	The location of the rotator schedule file relative to the virtual directory

The GetAdvertisement method returns an HTML-formatted string that can be used to display the advertisement in the current page. We can call the method as follows:

```
' VBScript
Set MyAd = Server.CreateObject("MSWC.AdRotator")
Response.Write MyAd.GetAdvertisement("new-ads/schedule.txt")
```

```
' JScript
MyAd = Server.CreateObject("MSWC.AdRotator");
Response.Write(MyAd.GetAdvertisement("new-ads/schedule.txt"));
```

In this example, we assume that the schedule file called schedule.txt is stored in the /new-ads/ folder within the current folder where our application runs. The output of this call will be a section of HTML text for the new advertisement to be displayed, which should look something like this:

```
<A HREF="redirect.asp?url=http://www.wrox.com/&image=http://www.wrox.com/ads/
                                                            site-ad.gif">
   <IMG SRC="http://www.wrox.com/images/wroxlogo.gif" ALT="The best
                                                    programmer's books"
        WIDTH=440 HEIGHT=60 BORDER=1>
</A>
```

Ad Rotator Properties

The Ad Rotator component has three properties which can be used to set characteristics of all the images displayed.

Border Property

The `Border` property returns or sets the size of the border around the advertisement:

```
Integer = AdRotator.Border
AdRotator.Border = Integer
```

The default value can be set in the header of the rotator schedule file and changed with this property. A value of 0 indicates that there should be no border around the advertisement. The larger the value, the greater the thickness of the border. For example:

```
' VBScript
Set MyAd = Server.CreateObject("MSWC.AdRotator")
MyAd.Border = 3        ' This sets the size of the border 3 pixels wide
```

```
// JScript
MyAd = Server.CreateObject("MSWC.AdRotator");
MyAd.Border = 3        // This sets the size of the border 3 pixels wide
```

Clickable Property

The `Clickable` property enables us to specify whether the advertisements are displayed as hyperlinks.

```
Long = AdRotator.Clickable
AdRotator.Clickable = Long
```

The default value is `true` (the URL is defined by the `adHomePageURL` attribute in the rotator schedule file), but if you don't need this functionality, you can assign the value `false` to this property. For example:

```
' VBScript
Set MyAd = Server.CreateObject("MSWC.AdRotator")
MyAd.Clickable = False     ' Show ads as static graphics
```

```
// JScript
MyAd = Server.CreateObject("MSWC.AdRotator");
MyAd.Clickable = False;       // Show ads as static graphics
```

Ad Rotator Component

TargetFrame Property

The `TargetFrame` property allows us to set the name of the frame into which the hyperlink (the one that is defined by the `adHomePageURL` attribute in the rotator schedule file) from the banner will be loaded.

```
String = AdRotator.TargetFrame
AdRotator.TargetFrame = String
```

This property works the same way as the `TARGET` attribute of the HTML `<ANCHOR>` element. The value of this parameter can be the name of any frame within the page, or one of the following predefined HTML frame identifiers such as `"_top"`, `"_new"`, `"_child"`, `"_self"`, `"_parent"`, or `"_blank"`. The default value of the `TargetFrame` property is `"NO FRAME"`.

Using the Ad Rotator Component

The following code demonstrates how to set up a page with rotating advertisements. We will use two images, for Wrox and ASPToday, defined in the following rotator schedule file:

```
REDIRECT redirect.asp
WIDTH 200
HEIGHT 200
BORDER 0
*
http://www.wrox.com/ads-demo/wroxlogo.gif
http://www.wrox.com
Best programmer's books
20
http://www.asptoday.com/ads-demo/asptoday.gif
http://www.asptoday.com
Up-to-the minute articles on ASP
20
```

We just define two advertisements, for the Wrox and ASPToday sites, with equal `impressions` values of 20, so they will appear equally frequently. We also define a redirection page, where we will count the number of users who clicked on each image.

The ASP script which sends the advertisement to the browser really couldn't be much simpler: we just instantiate the object and then call its `GetAdvertisement` method. In VBScript, the code is:

```
<%
Set MyAD=Server.CreateObject("MSWC.AdRotator")
Response.write MyAD.GetAdvertisement("schedule.txt")
%>
<H3>Rest of the page goes here...</H3>
```

Or in JScript:

```
<%
MyAD=Server.CreateObject("MSWC.AdRotator");
Response.write(MyAD.GetAdvertisement("schedule.txt"));
%>
<H3>Rest of the page goes here...</H3>
```

When we view this script in the browser, we see a page similar to the following:

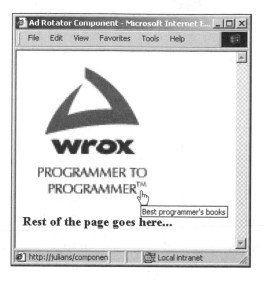

Finally, we must define our redirection page. In this case, we will simply check the value of the url parameter in the query string and increment an application variable according to which image was clicked. We will then display a table containing the values of these variables:

```
<% ' in VBScript
Response.expires=-1000
strURL=Request.QueryString("url")
Select Case strURL
   Case "http://www.wrox.com/"
      Application("Wrox") = Application("Wrox") + 1
   Case "http://www.asptoday.com"
      Application("ASPToday") = Application("ASPToday") + 1
End Select

%>
<TABLE CELLPADDING=10>
   <TR>
      <TD>Wrox Press</TD>
      <TD><%= Application("Wrox") %></TD>
   </TR>
   <TR>
      <TD>ASPToday</TD>
      <TD><%= Application("ASPToday") %></TD>
   </TR>
</TABLE>
```

Or in JScript:

```
<% // in JScript
Response.expires=-1000;
strURL=Request.QueryString("url");
switch (strURL) {
   case "http://www.wrox.com/":
      Application("Wrox") = Application("Wrox") + 1;
      break;
   case "http://www.asptoday.com":
      Application("ASPToday") = Application("ASPToday") + 1;
}

%>
<TABLE CELLPADDING=10>
   <TR>
      <TD>Wrox Press</TD>
      <TD><%= Application("Wrox") %></TD>
   </TR>
   <TR>
      <TD>ASPToday</TD>
      <TD><%= Application("ASPToday") %></TD>
   </TR>
</TABLE>
```

Summary

The Ad Rotator component allows us to rotate advertisements or other images, so that a random graphic is sent to the browser each time the page is requested. In this chapter we looked at:

❑ The rotator schedule file, where we specify which images will appear, the relative frequency of each image, and attributes such as the size and border width of the image.

❑ The redirection file, which allows us to redirect users to another page when they click on the image.

❑ The methods and properties of the Ad Rotator component.

❑ Using the Ad Rotator component in an ASP page.

❑ Using the redirection file to compile statistics on which images users click.

Ad Rotator Component

16

The Browser Capabilities Component

The **Browser Capabilities** component can be used to obtain information about the client's web browser. We can use it to check, for example, that a client's browser supports a particular feature, before we generate client-side logic (HTML or scripting) which requires that feature.

This component consists of a single DLL, browscap.dll, and a text file named browscap.ini, which should reside in the same directory as the DLL. The component takes the browser name and version information from the HTTP_USER_AGENT environment variable which is sent by the browser, and compares the contents of this variable with the entries in the browscap.ini file. If a match is found, the Browser Capabilities component makes available the appropriate properties for that browser. If no match is found, the values for the default browser are returned, unless there is no default browser defined in the browscap.ini file, when all the properties will be set to the value "UNKNOWN".

To instantiate the component we can use either the Server.CreateObject method or an HTML <OBJECT> tag. In both cases, we need to supply a ProgID of "MSWC.BrowserType":

```
' VBScript
Set objBrowserType = Server.CreateObject("MSWC.BrowserType")
```

```
// JScript
objBrowserType = Server.CreateObject('MSWC.BrowserType');
```

```
<!-- HTML OBJECT tag -->
<OBJECT RUNAT="SERVER" ID="objBrowserType"
PROGID="MSWC.BrowserType"></OBJECT>
```

The browscap.ini File

Let's look at the format of the `browscap.ini` file. As we have already said, this is a text file, so we are able to browse through it, and even edit its contents and update it when new versions of browsers appear. Here is a simple `browscap.ini` file, with cut-down entries for two browsers, IE 2.0 and Mozilla 1.22, and a default browser:

```
;Browsers - last updated xx/yy/zz;;;

[IE 2.0]
browser=IE
version=2.0

[Mozilla/1.22 (compatible; MSIE 2.0; Mac_PowerPC)]
parent=IE 2.0
platform=MacPPC


;Default Browser

[Default Browser Capability Settings]
browser=Default
Version=0.0
```

Our example `browscap.ini` file begins with a comment – one or more lines that start with a semicolon (`;`). Comments are ignored by the Browser Capabilities component and can be placed anywhere in the file.

The beginning of an entry for a particular browser is marked by the `[HTTPUserAgentHeader]` line – such as `[IE 2.0]` in the example above. This is the value that the Browser Capabilities component compares with the `HTTP_USER_AGENT` entry of the `Request.ServerVariables` collection (discussed in Chapter 5), and it should be unique for each browser. The asterisk (`*`) character can be used as a wildcard to replace one or more characters if needed.

Next come browser features. Each line should start with an alphabetic character and should be no longer than 255 characters. There is no limit on the number of lines for a browser. All of the attributes for the particular browser are available through the Browser Capabilities component. Some of the most significant are listed in the following table:

Property	Description
`ActiveXControls`	Specifies whether the browser supports ActiveX control.
`backgroundsounds`	Specifies whether the browser supports background sounds.
`beta`	Specifies whether the browser is beta software.
`browser`	Specifies the name of the browser.

Property	Description
cdf	Specifies whether the browser supports the Channel Definition Format (CDF) for webcasting.
cookies	Specifies whether the browser supports cookies.
frames	Specifies whether the browser supports frames.
javaapplets	Specifies whether the browser supports Java applets.
javascript	Specifies whether the browser supports JavaScript or JScript.
platform	Specifies the platform that the browser runs on.
tables	Specifies whether the browser supports tables.
vbscript	Specifies whether the browser supports VBScript.
version	Specifies the version number of the browser.

The [parent=browserDefinition] line indicates that the browser "inherits" all the characteristics of its "parent" browser. In our example file above the entry for Mozilla 1.22 specifies that it will have all the same properties as IE 2.0, in addition to any other properties subsequently listed.

The [Default Browser Capability Settings] section defines the properties of the "default browser" – the one that will be used if the Browser Capabilities component can't find any match for the HTTP header in other sections.

Browser Capabilities Component Methods

Since the component stores its values in the browscap.ini text file, it only needs to expose a single method, which is used to extract these values:

Method
Value

Value Method

The Value method is used to retrieve a specific value from the browscap.ini file for the current user agent.

```
Variant = BrowserType.Value(attribute)
```

Parameter	Data Type	Description
attribute	String	The name of the browser attribute for which the value will be returned.

The `Value` method returns the value of the specified attribute which is associated with the current user agent. For example, to check whether the browser supports VBScript:

```
Set objBrowserType = Server.CreateObject("MSWC.BrowserType")
Response.Write objBrowserType.Value("vbscript")
```

Or using JScript:

```
var objBrowserType = Server.CreateObject('MSWC.BrowserType');
Response.Write(objBrowserType.Value('vbscript'));
```

Because `Value` is the default method, we don't need to state explicitly that this is the method being called:

```
objBrowserType('vbscript')
```

Alternatively, we can use the *object.property* syntax, as though these attributes were real properties of the `BrowserType` object:

```
objBrowserType.vbscript
```

Using the Browser Capabilities Component

As you may have already gathered, the Browser Capabilities component can be very useful in situations when we use Active Server Pages to generate HTML contents dynamically for the client browser. Knowing what the client browser can do and what features it supports allows us to avoid sending Java applets to the Mozilla 1.0 browsers, ActiveX components to the Sun platforms, or using VBScript code with Netscape Navigator. Even better, we can simply redirect our clients to the appropriate versions of our pages.

When we've instantiated the component, we can check the features of the client browser through the newly created instance, using any of the three syntaxes outlined above. For example, we can check if the client supports JavaScript (or JScript):

```
Set objBrowscap = Server.CreateObject("MSWC.BrowserType")
If objBrowscap.javascript Then
   Response.Write "JavaScript supported. " & _
               "You will be redirected to a different version of the
site."
   Response.Redirect "/new/dhtml.asp"
Else
   Response.Write "JavaScript is not supported. " & _
               "You will be redirected to the plain HTML version of the
site."
   Response.Redirect "/old/plain.asp"
End If
```

Or in JScript:

```
var objBrowscap = Server.CreateObject("MSWC.BrowserType");
if (objBrowscap.javascript) {
   Response.Write("JavaScript supported. " +
               "You will be redirected to a different version of the
site.")
   Response.Redirect("new/dhtml.asp");
} else {
   Response.Write("JavaScript is not supported. " +
               "You will be redirected to the plain HTML version of the
site.");
   Response.Redirect("old/plain.asp");
}
```

The clientCaps Behavior

A new feature introduced into IE5 is the ability to attach components known as
behaviors to the elements of an HTML document. These components can include code
that reacts to events in the document, and they can expose methods, properties and
events of their own. Although these components can be created with languages such as
Visual Basic and Visual C++, or with XML and script code, Microsoft provides a
number of ready-made components installed with IE5+. One of these, the
clientCaps behavior interacts with the Browser Capabilities component to extend
the range of information about the client accessible to our ASP scripts. Whereas the
Browser Capabilities component on its own can only tell us about the built-in features
of the browser, the clientCaps behavior can tell us about the browser's current
settings.

*For more information on IE5 behaviors, see XML in IE5 Programmer's
Reference, ISBN 1-861001-57-6, from Wrox Press.*

The clientCaps behavior exposes thirteen properties, which provide information on
the current settings for the client browser. If these properties are written to a cookie
using client-side script, they can subsequently be accessed through the Browser
Capabilities component.

Property	Description
availHeight	Returns the available height of the screen in pixels, excluding toolbars, etc.
availWidth	Returns the available width of the screen in pixels, excluding toolbars, etc.
bufferDepth	Returns the number of bits per pixel for the screen buffer on the client.
colorDepth	Returns the number of bits per pixel that can be displayed on the client screen.

Browser Capabilities Component

Property	Description
connectionType	Returns the type of network connection that the client is using.
cookieEnabled	Returns true if the client browser is set to accept cookies.
cpuClass	Returns the type of processor in use, for example 'x86'.
height	Returns the overall height of the screen in pixels, including toolbars, etc.
javaEnabled	Returns true if the client browser has Java code execution enabled.
platform	Returns the type of operating system in use, for example 'Win32'
systemLanguage	Returns the language code set in the client's operating system
userLanguage	Returns the language code set in the client's browser.
width	Returns the overall width of the screen in pixels, including toolbars, etc.

To make use of the clientCaps behavior in this way, we simply need to create an HTML page in which the behavior is attached to one of the elements, and which creates the cookie. We attach the behavior to a custom XML element, which we have named <MYCAPS>. We do this by adding a STYLE attribute with a value of "behavior:url(#default#clientCaps)" to the element's opening tag. We also add an onLoad event handler to the <BODY> tag, which calls a JavaScript function named createCookie(). This simply builds up a string of key/item pairs using the clientCaps component's property names and their current value:

```
<HTML>
   <HEAD>
      <SCRIPT LANGUAGE="JavaScript">
         function createCookie() {
            strCookie = "Browscap="
            strCookie += "availHeight=" + clientCaps.availHeight;
            strCookie += "&availWidth=" + clientCaps.availWidth;
            strCookie += "&bufferDepth=" + clientCaps.bufferDepth;
            strCookie += "&colorDepth=" + clientCaps.colorDepth;
            strCookie += "&connectionType=" + clientCaps.connectionType;
            strCookie += "&cookieEnabled=" + clientCaps.cookieEnabled;
            strCookie += "&cpuClass=" + clientCaps.cpuClass;
            strCookie += "&height=" + clientCaps.height;
            strCookie += "&javaEnabled=" + clientCaps.javaEnabled;
            strCookie += "&platform=" + clientCaps.platform;
            strCookie += "&systemLanguage=" + clientCaps.systemLanguage;
            strCookie += "&userLanguage=" + clientCaps.userLanguage;
            strCookie += "&width=" + clientCaps.width;
```

```
            document.cookie=strCookie;
        }
    </SCRIPT>
</HEAD>
<BODY ONLOAD="createCookie()">
    <MYCAPS ID="clientCaps" STYLE="behavior:url(#default#clientCaps)" />
</BODY>
</HTML>
```

This creates a cookie with contents similar to the following:

```
Browscap=availHeight=740&availWidth=1024&bufferDepth=0&colorDepth=16&connecti
onType=lan&cookieEnabled=true&cpuClass=x86&height=768&javaEnabled=true&platfo
rm=Win32&systemLanguage=en-us&userLanguage=en-us&width=1024
```

In order to make these values accessible to our ASP script, we need first to ensure that this HTML page is sent to the browser before any ASP page that uses these settings. We can achieve this by including a METADATA directive in our ASP pages:

```
<!-- METADATA TYPE="Cookie" NAME="Browscap" SRC="clientCaps.htm" -->
```

The contents of the cookie can now be accessed through the Browser Capabilities component in the normal way:

```
blnJava=objBrowserType.Value("javaEnabled")
```

Or:

```
blnJava=objBrowserType.javaEnabled
```

Of course, you can add any other values to the cookie, besides the
clientCaps properties. You could add the values of any DHTML
properties, for example. Remember, though, that this technique will only work
for IE5+ browsers, even when cross-browser properties such as
screen.availHeight are used.

Summary

The Browser Capabilities component allows us to modify the content we send to the client from ASP script according to the type of browser in use. The component examines the HTTP_USER_AGENT variable and compares it to a list of browsers and their supported features in a text file named browscap.ini. It then makes available to the script code a number of attributes which indicate whether a given feature is supported by the current browser. So, in this chapter we looked at:

❑   The browscap.ini file where the list of browsers and their supported features is maintained.

❑   Instantiating the component.

❑   The Value method of the Browser Capabilities component and accessing the attributes for the current browser.

❑   Using the component.

❑   How the Browser Capabilities component can be extended for IE5+ browsers using the clientCaps behavior.

Browser Capabilities Component

17

The Content Linking Component

The **Content Linking** component allows us to order the pages on our site into a specific sequence. It manages a list of URLs that can be used to create tables of contents, navigation links and other structures, which can be represented as a set of related web pages. This list of URLs is stored in a special text file on the server, called the **content linking list file** (or just **list file**). If we later need to alter this sequence, we simply have to update the text file, for example by rearranging the order of the files in the content linking list file.

The Content Linking List File

The **content linking list file** contains a list of page URLs, in the order in which they are to be displayed. For each URL in the list, there must be one line of text in the list file. This line consists of two or three parts, separated from each other by a *tab* character (spaces won't work), and ends with a carriage return:

```
PageURL  Description      [Comment]
```

Where:

❑ *PageURL* contains the virtual or relative URL of the file we want to include in the list. This can include not only HTML and ASP files, but also other file types supported by the client browser, such as image files or (IE5+ only) XML files. Absolute URLs, which start with "http:", "//", or "\\", are not supported.

❑ *Description* contains text used to display a descriptive link to the page.

❑ *Comment* is optional, and may contain explanatory text which is ignored by the component and which cannot be viewed by the user.

A typical list file might look something like this:

```
0100.asp     Sales for January
0200.asp     Sales for February     incomplete
0300.asp     Sales for March
Home.asp     This month so far     Last updated xx/yy/zz
```

If we need a menu which contains absolute URLs, we can build a redirection page using ASP and specify this in the content linking list file, specifying the real page we want to link to as a query string added to the URL. For example, we could have a page named `redirect.asp` containing simply this code:

```
<%
'redirect the request to the site specified in the query string
Response.Clear
Response.Redirect Request.QueryString("url")
%>
```

We can then use this in our content linking list file with the appropriate query strings appended:

```
redirect.asp?url=http://www.wrox.com/        The SA fileUp Component Web Pages
redirect.asp?url=http://www.stonebroom.com/swindex.htm      The Stonebroom
RegEx Web Pages
```

Instantiating the Content Linking Component

Once we've created our content linking file, we can add the component to our pages. The Content Linking component is found in `nextlink.dll` and can be instantiated using the `CreateObject` method of the `Server` object, passing in a Prog ID of `"MSWC.NextLink"`. For example, in VBScript:

```
Set objNextLink = Server.CreateObject("MSWC.NextLink")
```

And in JScript:

```
var objNextLink=Server.CreateObject(' MSWC.NextLink');
```

Alternatively, we can use an HTML `<OBJECT>` tag with a `RUNAT="SERVER"` attribute:

```
<OBJECT RUNAT="SERVER" ID="objNextLink" PROGID="MSWC.NextLink"></OBJECT>
```

Content Linking Component Members

The Content Linking component has one property and eight methods:

Methods	Properties
GetListCount	About
GetListIndex	
GetNextURL	
GetNextDescription	
GetPreviousURL	

Methods	Properties
GetPreviousDescription	
GetNthURL	
GetNthDescription	

Content Linking Component Methods

The methods are mainly used to retrieve various entries from the content linking list file, either relative to the current page entry or as an absolute entry using an index number. The index number of the first item is 1.

GetListCount Method

This method allows us to determine the number of items in a content linking list file.

```
Integer = NextLink.GetListCount(links_file)
```

Parameter	Data Type	Description
links_file	String	The path and filename of the content linking list file to be used.

The GetListCount method returns an integer indicating the number of files in the specified content linking list file.

The following example iterates through all the entries in the content linking file and creates a list of the pages as hyperlinks:

```
<%
Set objNextLink = Server.CreateObject("MSWC.Nextlink")
intCount = objNextLink.GetListCount("contlink.txt")
For intLoop = 1 To intCount
%>
    <A HREF="<% = objNextLink.GetNthURL("contlink.txt", intLoop) %>">
        <% = objNextLink.GetNthDescription("contlink.txt", intLoop) %>
    </A>
<%
Next
%>
```

The JScript equivalent of this code would be:

```
<%
var objNextLink = Server.CreateObject('MSWC.Nextlink');
intCount = objNextLink.GetListCount('contlink.txt');
for (i=1; i<=intCount; i++) {
%>
    <A HREF="<%= objNextLink.GetNthURL('contlink.txt', i) %>">
        <%= objNextLink.GetNthDescription('contlink.txt', i) %>
    </A> <BR>
<%
}
%>
```

Content Linking Component

This code first creates a **Content Linking** object. We then call the `GetListCount` method to find out how many entries there are in the list file, and iterate through the file. For each entry, we create an `<A>` element with the `HREF` attribute set to the URL for that entry (the return value of the `GetNthURL` method), and the text within the link to the associated description (retrieved using the `GetNthDescription` method).

Notice that in this case our content list file is in the same folder as the ASP page that uses it. If it weren't, we could provide either a relative physical path, or a full virtual path, to it:

```
intCount = objNextLink.GetListCount("links\contlink.txt") 'physical path
intCount = objNextLink.GetListCount("/demo/contlink.txt") 'virtual path
```

GetListIndex Method

This method allows us to determine the position of the current page in the sequence specified in the content linking list file.

```
Integer = NextLink.GetListIndex(links_file)
```

Parameter	Data Type	Description
links_file	String	The path and filename of the content linking list file to be used.

The `GetListIndex` method returns an integer indicating the index of the current page in the specified content linking list file. If the page isn't in the content linking file, `GetListIndex` returns zero.

For example, to display the number of the current page from a total page count (e.g. **Page 1 of 7**), we could use the code:

```
<% 'in VBScript:
Set objNextLink = Server.CreateObject("MSWC.NextLink")
strListFile = "contlnk.txt"
intThisPage = objNextLink.GetListIndex(strListFile)
intPageCount = objNextLink.GetListCount(strListFile)
Response.write "<H3>Page " & intThisPage & " of " & intPageCount & "</H3>"
%>
```

Or in JScript:

```
<% // in JScript:
var objNextLink = Server.CreateObject("MSWC.NextLink");
strListFile = "contlnk.txt";
intThisPage = objNextLink.GetListIndex(strListFile);
intPageCount = objNextLink.GetListCount(strListFile);
Response.write("<H3>Page " + intThisPage + " of " + intPageCount + "</H3>");
%>
```

GetNextURL Method

This method allows us to determine the URL of the page listed immediately after the current page in the content linking list file.

```
String = NextLink.GetNextURL(links_file)
```

Parameter	Data Type	Description
links_file	String	The path and filename of the content linking list file to be used.

The GetNextURL method returns a string containing the URL of the next page in the specified content linking list file. If the current page is the last page in the file, the URL for the first page in the content linking list file will be returned. If the current page is not included in the list file at all, GetNextURL will return the URL for the last page.

We can use this method, for example, to redirect the client to the next page after a specific event (such as a button click):

```
<INPUT TYPE=BUTTON VALUE="Next &gt;"
       ONCLICK="location.href='<%= objNextLink.GetNextURL("contlink.txt")
%>';">
```

We will see a more detailed example of using this method in the section on 'Using the Content Linking Component' later in this chapter.

GetNextDescription Method

This method is used to retrieve the description of the page listed immediately after the current page in the content linking list file.

```
String = NextLink.GetNextDescription(links_file)
```

Parameter	Data Type	Description
links_file	String	The path and filename of the content linking list file to be used.

The GetNextDescription method returns the descriptive string associated with the next page in the specified content linking list file. If the current page is the last page in the file, the description for the first page in the content linking list file will be returned. If the current page is not included in the list file at all, GetNextDescription will return the description for the last page.

For example, we could use the GetNextDescription method to display a more informative hyperlink rather than the simple Next button we used in the previous example:

```
<A HREF="<%= objNextLink.GetNextURL("contlink.txt") %>>
   <%= objNextLink.GetNextDescription("contlink.txt") %>
</A>
```

Content Linking Component

GetPreviousURL Method

This method allows us to determine the URL of the page listed immediately before the current page in the content linking list file.

```
String = NextLink.GetPreviousURL(links_file)
```

Parameter	Data Type	Description
links_file	String	The path and filename of the content linking list file to be used.

The GetPreviousURL method returns a string containing the URL of the previous page in the specified content linking list file. If the current page is the first page in the file, the URL for the last page in the content linking list file will be returned. If the current page is not included in the list file at all, GetPreviousURL will return the URL for the first page.

GetPreviousDescription Method

This method is used to retrieve the description of the page listed immediately before the current page in the content linking list file.

```
String = NextLink.GetPreviousDescription(links_file)
```

Parameter	Data Type	Description
links_file	String	The path and filename of the content linking list file to be used.

The GetPreviousDescription method returns the descriptive string associated with the previous page in the specified content linking list file. If the current page is the first page in the file, the description for the last page in the content linking list file will be returned. If the current page is not included in the list file at all, GetPreviousDescription will return the description for the first page.

GetNthURL Method

This method allows us to determine the URL of a page at a specific position in the content linking list file.

```
String = NextLink.GetNthURL(links_file, n)
```

Parameter	Data Type	Description
links_file	String	The path and filename of the content linking list file to be used.
n	Integer	The (one-based) index of the page in the content linking list file.

The GetNthURL method returns a string containing the URL of the page with the specified index in the content linking list file. This index is one-based, so the first page has an index of one.

This method can be used to create a contents list, by iterating through the pages in the list file and creating an <A> element for each item with its HREF attribute set to the return value of this method. The code below (in the section on 'Creating a Contents Page') demonstrates this technique.

GetNthDescription Method

This method allows us to retrieve the description of a page at a specific position in the content linking list file.

```
NextLink.GetNthDescription(links_file, n)
```

Parameter	Data Type	Description
links_file	String	The path and filename of the content linking list file to be used.
n	Integer	The (one-based) index of the page in the content linking list file.

The GetNthDescription method returns a string containing the description associated with the page with the specified index in the content linking list file. Again, the index is one-based.

Content Linking Component Properties

The only property exposed by the Content Linking Component is the About property.

About Property

The read-only About property returns information about the version of the component in use.

```
String = NextLink.About
```

For example:

```
' VBScript
Set objNextLink = Server.CreateObject("MSWC.NextLink")
Response.Write objNextLink.About
```

```
// JScript
var objNextLink = Server.CreateObject("MSWC.NextLink");
Response.Write(objNextLink.About);
```

This returns:

"MSWC Content Linking Object Library (Release), built Oct 21 1999 at 14:14:29"

Content Linking Component

Using the Content Linking Component

As we've already seen, the Content Linking Component can be used to create a contents page for a set of pages on a site. The code to do this is simply that listed under the `GetListCount` method above. For example, if we have a page for each section in this book, we might have a list file as follows:

```
Section1.asp      The ASP Intrinsic Objects
Section2.asp      The Scripting Objects
Section3.asp      Active Server Components
Section4.asp      ActiveX Data Objects
Section5.asp      Extending ASP
Section6.asp      Performance and Security
Section7.asp      Miscellaneous Reference
```

We can now create a table of contents for these pages using the Content Linking component:

```asp
<%@ LANGUAGE="VBScript" %>
<H1>ASP 3.0 Programmer's Reference</H1><HR>
<%
Set objNextLink = Server.CreateObject("MSWC.NextLink")
strListFile = "contlink.txt"
intListCount = objNextLink.GetListCount(strListFile)
%>
<TABLE CELLSPACING=10>
   <TH><TR>
      <TD><B>Section</B></TD>
      <TD><B>Title</B></TD>
   </TR></TH>
   <TBODY>
<%
    For intCount = 1 To intListCount
%>
       <TR>
          <TD><%= intCount %></TD>
          <TD>
             <A HREF="<%= objNextLink.GetNthURL(strListFile, intCount) %>">
                <%= objNextLink.GetNthDescription(strListFile, intCount) %>
             </A>
          </TD>
       </TR>
<%
    Next
%>
   </TBODY>
</TABLE>
```

In JScript, this code would be:

```asp
<%@ LANGUAGE="JScript" %>
<H1>ASP 3.0 Programmer's Reference</H1><HR>
<%
var objNextLink = Server.CreateObject("MSWC.NextLink");
var strListFile = "contlink.txt";
var intListCount = objNextLink.GetListCount(strListFile);
%>
```

```
<TABLE CELLSPACING=10>
   <TH><TR>
      <TD><B>Section</B></TD>
      <TD><B>Title</B></TD>
   </TR></TH>
   <TBODY>
<%
      for (i=1; i<=intListCount; i++) {
%>
      <TR>
         <TD><%= i %></TD>
         <TD>
            <A HREF="<%= objNextLink.GetNthURL(strListFile, i) %>">
               <%= objNextLink.GetNthDescription(strListFile, i) %>
            </A>
         </TD>
      </TR>
<%
      }
%>
   </TBODY>
</TABLE>
```

Using the list file given above, the output of this code is:

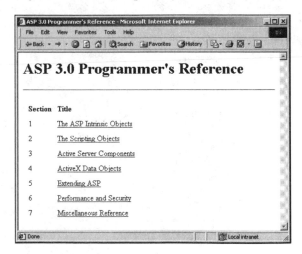

Adding Navigation Buttons to a Page

As well as allowing us to create tables of contents in this way, the Content Linking component can be used to provide navigation buttons, so that the user can move through the sequence of pages in the list file in order. For example, we can use the GetNextURL and GetPreviousURL methods to create Back and Next buttons. We can also allow the user to jump straight to the start or end of the sequence by calling the GetNthURL method with a value of 1 or with the return value of the GetListCount method respectively.

*It's an obvious point, but remember that we can't use the
'redirect.asp' technique if we're browsing through pages in this way,
because the actual page being viewed won't be in the list file.*

The following code adds Start, Back, Next and End buttons to a page. We can either
add this code to each of the pages in the list file, or insert it with an SSI #include
directive:

```
<%@ LANGUAGE="VBScript" %>
<%
   Set objNextLink = Server.CreateObject("MSWC.NextLink")
   strListFile = "contlink.txt"
   intListIndex = objNextLink.GetListIndex(strListFile)
   intListCount = objNextLink.GetListCount(strListFile)
%>
<H1>Page <%= intListIndex %> of <%= intListCount %></H1><HR>
<FORM>
<%
   If intListIndex > 1 Then
%>
      <INPUT TYPE=BUTTON VALUE="|<< Start"
             ONCLICK="location='<% = objNextLink.GetNthURL(strListFile, 1)
%>';">

      <INPUT TYPE=BUTTON VALUE="< Back"
             ONCLICK="location='<% = objNextLink.GetPreviousURL(strListFile)
%>';">
<%
   End If
   If intListIndex < intListCount Then
%>
      <INPUT TYPE=BUTTON VALUE="Next >"
             ONCLICK="location='<%= objNextLink.GetNextURL(strListFile)
%>';">

      <INPUT TYPE=BUTTON VALUE="End >>|"
             ONCLICK="location='<% = objNextLink.GetNthURL(strListFile,
                                  intListCount) %>';">
<%
   End If
%>
</FORM>
```

The JScript equivalent for this code is:

```
<%@ LANGUAGE="JScript" %>
<%
   var objNextLink = Server.CreateObject("MSWC.NextLink");
   var strListFile = "contlink.txt";
   var intListIndex = objNextLink.GetListIndex(strListFile);
   var intListCount = objNextLink.GetListCount(strListFile);
%>
<H1>Page <%= intListIndex %> of <%= intListCount %></H1><HR>
<FORM>
<%
   if (intListIndex > 1) {
%>
```

```
        <INPUT TYPE=BUTTON VALUE="|<< Start"
              ONCLICK="location='<% = objNextLink.GetNthURL(strListFile, 1)
%>';">

        <INPUT TYPE=BUTTON VALUE="< Back"
              ONCLICK="location='<% = objNextLink.GetPreviousURL(strListFile)
%>';">
<%
    }
    if (intListIndex < intListCount) {
%>
        <INPUT TYPE=BUTTON VALUE="Next >"
              ONCLICK="location='<%= objNextLink.GetNextURL(strListFile)
%>';">

        <INPUT TYPE=BUTTON VALUE="End >>|"
              ONCLICK="location='<% = objNextLink.GetNthURL(strListFile,
                                    intListCount) %>';">
<%
    }
%>
</FORM>
```

After we've instantiated our Content Linking object, we create variables to store the name of the list file, the current page index, and the total number of pages in the list file. We use the latter two variables to print out the current position in the sequence (for example, Page 2 of 7).

We then add the navigation buttons to the page. We don't need to display the Start or Back buttons if we're on the first page, so we include the HTML code for these buttons in an `if` statement which checks whether the list index is greater than one. Similarly, we don't want Next or End buttons on the last page, so the code for these is placed in an `if` statement which checks that the list index is less than the total number of pages.

The buttons themselves are created using standard HTML `<INPUT>` elements of type `"BUTTON"`. The navigation is performed by setting the `ONCLICK` attribute to alter the `location` of the window. For the Back and Next buttons, we call the `GetPreviousURL` and `GetNextURL` methods respectively to determine the URL for the new `location`. For the Start and End buttons, we call `GetNthURL` with a value of either 1, or our `intListCount` variable, in which we stored the number of pages in the list file.

The result of this is a page such as the following:

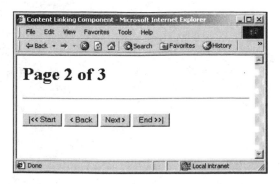

Content Linking Component

Summary

The Content Linking component provides an easy way of ordering pages into a sequence, keeping track of the position of the current page in that sequence, and navigating through the pages. In this chapter we looked at:

❑   The content linking list file used to store the sequence of pages.

❑   The methods of the Content Linking component.

❑   Creating a contents page with the Content Linking component.

❑   Providing a way for the user to navigate through the pages in sequence.

18

The Content Rotator Component

The **Content Rotator component** works in a very similar way to the Ad Rotator component we looked at in Chapter 15, except that it allows us to rotate any HTML and text content, rather than just predetermined images. As with the Ad Rotator component, the component uses a text file (called the **content schedule file**) to store the content to be rotated and the weighting which specifies the frequency with which each section of content appears. The Content Rotator component provides methods for displaying one or all of these content sections.

The Content Schedule File

The content schedule file has a very simple structure:

```
%% priority // First entry
<!-- First HTML and text content section goes here -->

%% priority // Second entry
<!-- Second HTML and text content section -->

... etc. ...
```

Each content section is preceded by a line consisting of two percentage signs (%%) and the `priority`, which specifies the relative weighting for the content section (how often the section will appear in returned pages). This line can also contain a comment, which is prefixed, JavaScript-style, by two forward slashes.

For example:

```
%% 2
<IMG SRC="http://www.wrox.com/images/wroxlogo.gif>

%% 1
<H3><A HREF="http://www.wrox.com">Visit the Wrox web site!</A></H3>

%% 2
<IMG SRC="http://www.asptoday.com/images/asptoday.gif>
```

```
%% 1
<H3><A HREF="http://www.asptoday.com">Up-to-the-minute articles on
ASP!</A></H3>
```

The schedule file above has four different sections of HTML content. These are given priorities of 2, 1, 2, and 1, so the first section will appear on roughly one third of pages (2 out of 6), the second on one sixth, etc. Each time content is requested, the actual section is chosen at random, so in any given sequence of returned pages, a particular section will not necessarily occur in exactly the proportions specified.

Instantiating the Content Rotator Component

The Content Rotator component can be found in the file ContRot.dll. As with the other installable components, we can instantiate the Content Rotator using either the Server.CreateObject method or an <OBJECT> tag. The ProgID for the component is "MSWC.ContentRotator".

For example, using Server.CreateObject:

```
' VBScript
Set objContRot = Server.CreateObject("MSWC.ContentRotator")
```

```
// JScript
objContRot = Server.CreateObject("MSWC.ContentRotator");
```

Or with an <OBJECT> tag:

```
<OBJECT ID="objContRot" RUNAT="Server" PROGID="MSWC.ContentRotator"></OBJECT>
```

Content Rotator Component Methods

The Content Rotator component has two methods. These are used to retrieve content from a specific content schedule file:

Methods
ChooseContent
GetAllContent

ChooseContent Method

The ChooseContent method retrieves the next content section from the schedule file without displaying it.

```
String = ContentRotator.ChooseContent(ScheduleFile)
```

Parameter	Data Type	Description
ScheduleFile	String	The schedule file from which the content is to be retrieved

This method extracts the next HTML content section from the named schedule file and returns it as a string, which we can then send to the browser using `Response.Write`. If the schedule file resides in a different directory to the current page, we can specify either a full virtual path or a physical path relative to the web site's root directory.

For example in VBScript:

```
Set objContRot = Server.CreateObject("MSWC.ContentRotator")

strPath = "/ASPComponents/content.txt"          ' Full virtual path (excluding
                                                ' server name)
' Or:
strPath = "\ProgRef\Components\content.txt"      ' Physical path relative to
                                                ' root directory

strContent = objContRot.ChooseContent(strPath)
Response.Write strContent
```

Or in JScript:

```
objContRot = Server.CreateObject("MSWC.ContentRotator");

strPath = "/ASPComponents/content.txt";              // Full virtual path
// Or:
strPath = "\\ProgRef\\Components\\content.txt";       // Relative physical path

strContent = objContRot.ChooseContent(strPath);
Response.Write(strContent);
```

GetAllContent Method

The Content Rotator's `GetAllContent` method displays all of the content sections from the schedule file.

```
ContentRotator.GetAllContent(ScheduleFile)
```

Parameter	Data Type	Description
ScheduleFile	String	The schedule file from which the content is to be retrieved.

This method sends all of the content in the named schedule file to the browser. The content sections are sent in the order in which they are listed in the file, and are separated by <HR> elements. As with the `ChooseContent` method, the path to the schedule file may be a full virtual path or a physical path relative to the web site's root directory.

Content Rotator Component

For example:

```
' VBScript
Set objContRot = Server.CreateObject("MSWC.ContentRotator")

strPath = "/ASPComponents/content.txt"        ' Full virtual path (excluding
                                              ' server name)
' Or:
strPath = "\ProgRef\Components\content.txt"   ' Physical path relative to
                                              ' root directory

objContRot.GetAllContent strPath
```

```
// JScript
objContRot = Server.CreateObject("MSWC.ContentRotator");

strPath = "/ASPComponents/content.txt";            // Full virtual path
// Or:
strPath = "\\ProgRef\\Components\\content.txt";     // Relative physical path

objContRot.GetAllContent(strPath);
```

Using the Content Rotator Component

Before using the Content Rotator, we will of course need first to write our content schedule file. We will include three short adverts for Wrox, ASPToday and Stonebroom software, each containing an image and a slogan which is also a hyperlink:

```
%% 1
<IMG SRC="wroxlogo.gif">
<H3><A HREF="http://www.wrox.com">The best programming books!</A></H3>

%% 1
<IMG SRC="asptoday.gif">
<H3><A HREF="http://www.asptoday.com">Up-to-the-minute articles on
ASP!</A></H3>

%% 1
<IMG SRC="sslogo.gif">
<H3><A HREF="http://www.stonebroom.com">Specialist and bespoke
software</A></H3>
```

We assign the same priority (%% 1) to each advertisement, so each will occur roughly the same number of times. In the following code, we will assume that this file is saved as content.txt in the same directory as the ASP page which accesses it.

Next, we must write our ASP page. To demonstrate both of the component's methods, we will display first one of the content selections (retrieved using the ChooseContent method), and then the entire content (displayed with the GetAllContent method):

```
<% ' VBScript
Dim objContRot, strPath
Set objContRot = Server.CreateObject("MSWC.ContentRotator")
strPath = "content.txt"
```

```
Response.Write "Selected content:<HR>"
Response.write objContRot.ChooseContent(strPath)

Response.Write "<HR>Entire content:"
objContRot.GetAllContent strPath
%>
```

The same page written in JScript would be:

```
<% // JScript
var objContRot, strPath;
objContRot = Server.CreateObject("MSWC.ContentRotator");
strPath = "content.txt";

Response.Write("Selected content:<HR>");
Response.write(objContRot.ChooseContent(strPath));

Response.Write("<HR>Entire content:");
objContRot.GetAllContent(strPath);
%>
```

The result is something like this:

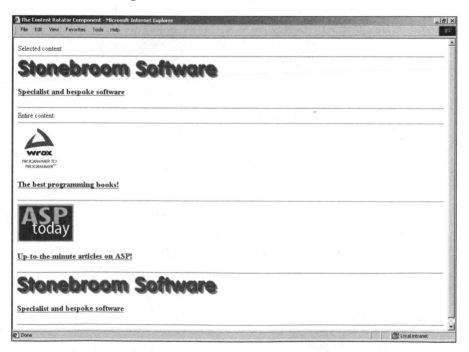

The first image and slogan are chosen with the ChooseContent method and therefore will vary; each time the page is requested, one of three sections will be chosen at random. The remainder of the page, however, will remain identical every time the page is viewed.

Summary

The Content Rotator component allows us to display different sections of text and HTML code chosen at random each time a page is viewed. This component works in a very similar way to the Ad Rotator component, but allows us greater freedom, in that we can use it to rotate any text and HTML content, not just images. In this chapter we looked at:

❑ The content schedule file where we define the content sections set their priority levels.

❑ How to retrieve and display one of these content sections with the `ChooseContent` method.

❑ How to send all of the content sections to a page with the `GetAllContent` method.

The Counters Component

The **Counters** component can be used to keep count of any value on an ASP page, from anywhere within our ASP application. Like many of the ASP components, the data is stored in a single text file on the server, so we only need one instance of the Counters component for our entire application, and we can use this to create as many counters as we want.

Each counter is distinguished by a string name and contains an integer value. We can set, update or retrieve this value through the methods of the Counters component. The names and values of all these counters are stored in a text file called Counters.txt, which resides in the /WinNT/System32/inetsvr/data directory. The component itself can be found in a file named counters.dll.

Because we should only have one instance of the Counters component, it is a good idea to instantiate this in the global.asa file with application scope. To do this, we can either use an <OBJECT> tag:

```
<OBJECT ID="objCounters" RUNAT="SERVER" SCOPE="Application"
PROGID="MSWC.Counters">
</OBJECT>
```

Or we can instantiate the object in the Application_OnStart event handler. For example, in VBScript:

```
Sub Application_OnStart
    Set Application("objCounters") = Server.CreateObject("MSWC.Counters")
End Sub
```

Or in JScript:

```
function Application_OnStart() {
    Application("objCounters") = Server.CreateObject("MSWC.Counters");
}
```

Counters Component Methods

The Counters component has four methods which we can use to create and remove counters and to manipulate their values:

Methods
Get
Increment
Remove
Set

Get Method

The Get method allows us to retrieve a value from a named counter.

```
Long = Counters.Get(CounterName)
```

Parameter	Data Type	Description
CounterName	String	The name of the counter for which the value is to be retrieved

If the counter does not already exist, it is created with a value of zero.

For example, in VBScript:

```
Response.Write objCounters.Get("Wrox")          ' Get value of "Wrox" counter
```

Or in JScript:

```
Response.Write(objCounters.Get("ASPToday"));    // Get value of "ASPToday"
                                                // counter
```

Increment Method

This method increases the value of the specfied counter by one.

```
Long = Counters.Increment(CounterName)
```

Parameter	Data Type	Description
CounterName	String	The name of the counter for which the value is to be incremented

The `Increment` method increments the value stored in the named counter and returns the new value. If the counter does not already exist, it is created and its value set to one.

For example, in VBScript:

```
lngNewValue = objCounters.Increment("Wrox")
```

Or in JScript:

```
lngNewValue = objCounters.Increment("Wrox");
```

Remove Method

The `Remove` method destroys the named counter.

```
Counters.Remove(CounterName)
```

Parameter	Data Type	Description
CounterName	String	The name of the counter to be destroyed

On calling this method, the specified counter will be removed from the Counters object and the corresponding entry will be removed immediately from the `Counters.txt` file.

For example, in VBScript:

```
objCounters.Remove "Wrox"
```

Or in JScript:

```
objCounters.Remove("Wrox");
```

Set Method

The `Set` method allows us to set the value of a particular counter.

```
Long = Counters.Set(CounterName, Value)
```

Parameter	Data Type	Description
CounterName	String	The name of the counter for which the value is to be set.
Value	Long	The new value for the counter.

This method sets the named counter to the supplied value and returns this new value. If the counter does not already exist, it will be created and set to the specified value. This is the usual method of creating counters.

Counters Component

For example, to create a counter named "Wrox" and set its value to 1:

```
' in VBScript
objCounters.Set "Wrox", 1
```

```
// in JScript
objCounters.Set("Wrox", 1);
```

If the counter does not already exist, this will cause the following line to be added to the Counters.txt file:

```
Wrox:1
```

Otherwise, an existing line in the file will be updated to reflect the new value.

Using the Counters Component

To illustrate the use of the Counters component, we will modify the redirect.asp page used by the Ad Rotator component in Chapter 15. In this page, we stored statistics for the number of click-throughs for each image in a rotator schedule file. The original page stored these statistics in application variables, but a more efficient approach is to use counters.

To do this, first we must modify our global.asa file to instantiate the Counters component. We will also create "Wrox" and "ASPToday" counters in the Application_OnStart event handler and set their values to zero:

```
<OBJECT ID="objCounters" RUNAT="SERVER" SCOPE="Application"
PROGID="MSWC.Counters">
</OBJECT>
<SCRIPT RUNAT="SERVER" LANGUAGE="VBScript">
Sub Application_OnStart
    objCounters.Set "Wrox, 0
    objCounters.Set "ASPToday", 0
End Sub
</SCRIPT>
```

Or in JScript:

```
<OBJECT ID="objCounters" RUNAT="SERVER" SCOPE="Application"
PROGID="MSWC.Counters">
</OBJECT>
<SCRIPT RUNAT="SERVER" LANGUAGE="JScript">
function Application_OnStart() {
    objCounters.Set("Wrox, 0);
    objCounters.Set("ASPToday", 0);
}
</SCRIPT>
```

Now we simply have to update the `redirect.asp` page to replace references to the application variables with references to the counters. We will call the `Increment` method to increase the value for the appropriate counter each time one of the links is followed and `redirect.asp` is called. On this page, we also display a table of the current statistics. We use the `Get` method to retrieve the value for each counter:

```
<%
Response.expires=-1000
strURL=Request.QueryString("url")
Select Case strURL
   Case "http://www.wrox.com/"
      objCounters.Increment "wrox"
   Case "http://www.asptoday.com"
      objCounters.Increment "ASPToday"
End Select
%>
<TABLE CELLPADDING=10>
   <TR>
      <TD>Wrox Press</TD>
      <TD><%= objCounters.Get("Wrox") %></TD>
   </TR>
   <TR>
      <TD>ASPToday</TD>
      <TD><%= objCounters.Get("ASPToday") %></TD>
   </TR>
</TABLE>
```

Summary

The Counters component is useful for keeping track of any set of numbers which is referenced by pages in our ASP application. Because the data is stored in a text file, we can actually persist this information beyond application scope. In this chapter we saw:

❑   How to instantiate the Counters component.

❑   How to use the component's methods to create and destroy counters and update their values.

❑   How to use the Counters component in an ASP page.

Counters Component

The Logging Utility Component

The **Logging Utility** component, a new addition in ASP 3.0, allows us to access the information stored in IIS's log files and to append log entries to the files.

To instantiate the component, we use the Prog ID of "MSWC.IISLog", and we can, as usual, use either the Server.CreateObject method or an <OBJECT> tag:

```
' VBScript
Set objLog = Server.CreateObject("MSWC.IISLog")

// JScript
objLog = Server.CreateObject("MSWC.IISLog");

<!-- OBJECT tag -->
<OBJECT RUNAT="SERVER" ID="objLog" PROGID="MSWC.IISLog"></OBJECT>
```

The Logging Utility Component Members

The Logging Utility component has six methods and twenty properties:

Methods	Properties	
AtEndOfLog	BytesReceived	ServerIP
CloseLogFiles	BytesSent	ServerName
OpenLogFile	ClientIP	ServerPort
ReadFilter	Cookie	ServiceName
ReadLogRecord	CustomFields	TimeTaken
WriteLogRecord	DateTime	URIQuery
	Method	URIStem
	ProtocolStatus	UserAgent
	ProtocolVersion	UserName
	Referer	Win32Status

Logging Utility Componant Methods

AtEndOfLog Method

The AtEndOfLog method is similar to a normal end-of-file method, and indicates whether the end of the log file has been reached.

```
Boolean = IISLog.AtEndOfLog()
```

This method returns true if the end of the log has been reached when iterating through the file, or false if there are still records to be read. This method is usually used with the ReadLogRecord method:

```
' VBScript
Do Until objLog.AtEndOfLog
   objLog.ReadLogRecord
Loop
```

```
// JScript
while (!objLog.AtEndOfLog()) {
   objLog.ReadLogRecord();
}
```

CloseLogFiles Method

The CloseLogFiles method is used to close open log files.

```
IISLog.CloseLogFiles([IOMode])
```

Parameter	Data Type	Description
IOMode	Integer	Optional. This can be one of the IOMode values (see below) and indicates the type of log files which will be closed.

Where IOMode is one of the following values:

Constant	Value	Description
ForReading	1	Close only log files opened for reading.
ForWriting	2	Close only log file opened for writing.
AllOpenFiles	32	Close all open log files.

OpenLogFile Method

The OpenLogFile method allows us to open a log file for reading or writing.

```
IISLog.OpenLogFile(Filename, IOMode, ServiceName, ServiceInstance,
               OutputFormat)
```

Parameter	Data Type	Description
Filename	String	The filename of the log to open. This should be the full qualified path name.
IOMode	IOMode	This value can be ForWriting (2) or ForReading (1; the default).
ServiceName	String	The name of the service to open the log file for, e.g. "W3SVC".
ServiceInstance	Long	Service instance number e.g. 1 (for the default site).
OutputFormat	String	This parameter indicates the format to use when writing to the file.

ReadFilter Method

The ReadFilter method will limit those records returned from reading the file to within a time and date range. Both parameters are optional, and if omitted the *start* is the first record in the file(s) and the *end* is the last record.

```
IISLog.ReadFilter ([start], [end])
```

Parameter	Data Type	Description
start	Date	Optional. The start date and time from which records should be retrieved.
end	Date	Optional. The end date and time upto which records should be retrieved.

ReadLogRecord Method

The ReadLogRecord method reads the next log record from the current log file(s) that is opened by the OpenLogFile method.

```
IISLog.ReadLogRecord()
```

WriteLogRecord Method

The WriteLogRecord method writes log records from a file that has been opened for reading to a file that has been opened for writing. The parameter is an object variable referencing the Logging Utility component instance that holds the source records.

```
IISLog.WriteLogRecord(logging_object)
```

Parameter	Data Type	Description
logging_object	IISLog	The log to write to the file.

Logging Utility Component

323

Logging Utility Componant Properties

The Logging Utility component also provides twenty properties that correspond to the fields in an IIS log record. These are all read-only.

BytesReceived Property

The read-only `BytesReceived` property returns the number of bytes received from the browser as the request.

```
Long = IISLog.BytesReceived
```

BytesSent Property

The read-only `BytesSent` property returns the number of bytes sent back to the browser as the response.

```
Long = IISLog.BytesSent
```

ClientIP Property

The read-only `ClientIP` property returns the IP address of the client or their host (i.e. proxy server).

```
String = IISLog.ClientIP
```

Cookie Property

The read-only `Cookie` property returns the contents of any cookie sent in the request.

```
String = IISLog.Cookie
```

CustomFields Property

The read-only `CustomFields` property returns an array of any custom headers that were added to the request.

```
Variant = IISLog.CustomFields
```

DateTime Property

The read-only `DateTime` property returns the date and time of the request as GMT.

```
Date = IISLog.DateTime
```

Method Property

The read-only `Method` property returns the operation type, such as `"GET"` or `"POST"`.

```
String = IISLog.Method
```

ProtocolStatus Property

The read-only `ProtocolStatus` property returns the status code to the client, for example 200 (for 'OK').

```
Long = IISLog.ProtocolStatus
```

ProtocolVersion Property

The read-only `ProtocolVersion` property returns the protocol version string, such as "HTTP/1.1".

> *String* = *IISLog*.ProtocolVersion

Referer Property

The read-only `Referer` property returns the URL of a page that contained the link that initiated this request, if available.

> *String* = *IISLog*.Referer

ServerIP Property

The read-only `ServerIP` property returns the IIS machine's IP address.

> *String* = *IISLog*.ServerIP

ServerName Property

The read-only `ServerName` property returns the machine name of the IIS server.

> *String* = *IISLog*.ServerName

ServerPort Property

The read-only `ServerPort` property returns the port number that the request was received on, such as 80.

> *Long* = *IISLog*.ServerPort

ServiceName Property

The read-only `ServiceName` property returns the service name, such as "MSFTPSVC" or "W3SVC".

> *String* = *IISLog*.ServiceName

TimeTaken Property

The read-only `TimeTaken` property returns the total processing time to retrieve and create the returned page.

> *Long* = *IISLog*.TimeTaken

URIQuery Property

The read-only `URIQuery` property returns any parameters in the query string appended to the URL in the request.

> *String* = *IISLog*.URIQuery

URIStem Property

The read-only URIStem property returns the target URL that was requested.

```
String = IISLog.URIStem
```

UserAgent Property

The read-only UserAgent property returns the user agent string sent by the client.

```
String = IISLog.UserAgent
```

UserName Property

The read-only UserName property returns the logon name of the user if they are not accessing the server anonymously.

```
String = IISLog.UserName
```

Win32Status Property

The read-only Win32Status property returns the Win32 status code returned after processing the request.

```
Long = IISLog.Win32Status
```

Using the Logging Utility Component

The most common use of the Logging Utility component is likely to be for custom querying of the log files. The ability to write new files that are made up of selected records from an existing file means that we can summarize certain types of entry or selectively pick out records for further investigation.

To use the ForReading, ForWriting, and AllOpenFiles constants that are exposed by the component, remember to include a METADATA directive in the <HEAD> section of the page:

```
<!-- METADATA TYPE="typelib"
            FILE="C:\WINNT\system32\inetsrv\logscrpt.dll" -->
```

To iterate through the records, we just need to open the file and call the ReadLogRecord method repeatedly until the AtEndOfLog method returns true. In this example, we're also filtering the records so that we get only those for the last 24 hours (i.e. from yesterday until today):

```
'create the component instance
Set objLogUtil = Server.CreateObject("MSWC.IISLog")

'open the log file for reading, for the W3SVC instance number 1
objLogUtil.OpenLogFile "extend#.log", ForReading, "W3SVC", 1

'set a filter for the last day's records only
objLogUtil.ReadFilter DateAdd("d", -1, Now), Now
'loop through the records
```

```
Do While Not objLogUtil.AtEndOfLog
    objLogUtil.ReadLogRecord      'read the next record
    Response.Write "Request received for page " & objLogUtil.URIStem & " on " _
              & objLogUtil.DateTime & " from IP address " _
              & objLogUtil.ClientIP & ".<BR>"
Loop
objLogUtil.CloseLogFiles(ForReading)    'close the file(s)
```

> It should be noted that this method does not work as specified. To
> make this work you will need to dynamically generate the full
> qualified path and name for the log file including the drive letter
> when using the OpenLogFile method.

Logging Utility Example

This example demonstrates the Logging Utility component in use. Before we can run it
from the main 'ASP Installable Components' menu, we need to make sure that we
disable anonymous access in Internet Services Manager for the directory containing
the sample files or for the loggingutility.asp file, or we won't be able to access
the log files. We then open the Directory Security page of the Properties dialog for the
appropriate directory or the loggingutility.asp file. Then we click the Edit button
in the 'Anonymous access and authentication control' section of this dialog page to
open the Authentication Methods dialog, and turn off the 'Anonymous access' option.

We also edit the
page to change
the filename of
the log file to suit
our machine. We
turned on W3C
Extended
Logging in the
Web Site page of
the Properties
dialog for the
Default Web Site:

In this dialog,
click the
Properties
button to open
the Extended
Logging
Properties
dialog.

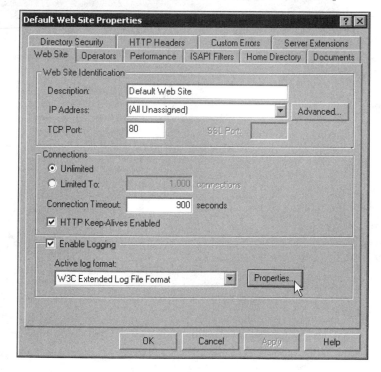

There we can check the file name that will be used for the files. We chose the fixed-size log file option, so the file names will be `extend1.log`, `extend2.log`, etc:

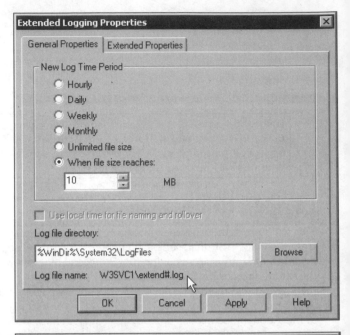

We then also open the **Extended Properties** page and make sure that all the values we want to log are selected:

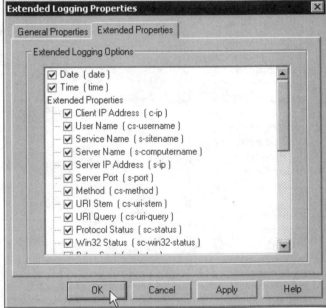

Now, we can run the sample page and see the results. We've chosen to display the values in a normal HTML table using the following code:

```
<!-- METADATA TYPE="typelib" FILE="C:\WINNT\system32\inetsrv\logscrpt.dll" -->
...
<%
```

```
Set objLogUtil = Server.CreateObject("MSWC.IISLog")
objLogUtil.OpenLogFile "c:\logs\w3scv1\extend1.log", ForReading, "W3SVC", 1,
0
objLogUtil.ReadFilter DateAdd("d", -1, Now), Now

%>
<TABLE CELLPADDING="10">
<TR>
<TH>Date/Time</TH>
<TH>Client IP</TH>
<TH>Bytes Sent</TH>
<TH>Target URL</TH>
</TR>
<%
Do While Not objLogUtil.AtEndOfLog
    objLogUtil.ReadLogRecord   'read the next record
%>
<TR>
<TD><% = objLogUtil.DateTime %></TD>
<TD><% = objLogUtil.ClientIP %></TD>
<TD><% = objLogUtil.BytesSent %></TD>
<TD><% = objLogUtil.URIStem %></TD>
</TR>
<%
Loop
objLogUtil.CloseLogFiles(ForReading)
%>
...
```

In the code above you'll see that I have redirected the logging to a folder called 'logs' from the default (normally under the System32 folder of your system folder). The **w3scv1** folder is created automatically by the extended logging properties manager.

And here's the result:

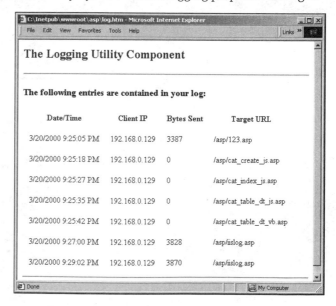

Summary

In this chapter we saw how the Logging Utility component enables us to access the information stored in IIS's log files and to append log entries to the files.

MyInfo Component

The **MyInfo** component (`myinfo.dll`) allows us to store pieces of personal information in the form of dynamic properties. This information is persisted in a text file in pseudo-XML format named `myinfo.xml`, located in the `WinNT\System32\inetsrv\Data` directory.

Using the MyInfo Component

Because the data for the MyInfo component is stored in a single text file, we should only create one instance of the component, and make this instance available to all the pages on our website. Note that having a single file means that the same data will be available to all clients: we can't use this component to store information specific to a given session.

As usual, the component can be instantiated using an <OBJECT> element in `global.asa`:

```
<OBJECT RUNAT="SERVER" SCOPE="Application" PROGID="MSWC.MyInfo"
ID="objMyInfo"></OBJECT>
```

Alternatively, we can use `Server.CreateObject`:

```
' VBScript
Set objMyInfo = Server.CreateObject("MSWC.MyInfo")
```

```
// JScript
var objMyInfo = Server.CreateObject("MSWC.MyInfo");
```

The MyInfo component has no properties or methods by default, but we can add dynamic properties, simply by setting them to a specific value. For example, we could set a default greeting which we display to all users and which appears on several pages. We will store this value in a dynamic property named `greeting`, which we can set just as if it were a normal property:

```
<% ' in VBScript
objMyInfo.greeting = "Happy Christmas!"
%>
```

```
<% // in JScript
objMyInfo.greeting = "Happy Christmas!";
%>
```

We can also retrieve the value as for any normal property:

```
<% ' in VBScript
Response.Write "<H1>" & objMyInfo.greeting & "</H1>"
%>
```

```
<% // in JScript
Response.Write("<H1>" + objMyInfo.greeting + "</H1>");
%>
```

The value can also be retrieved according to its position in the text file. For example, objMyInfo(0) will return the value of the first property.

When the user leaves the page where the value was set, or when the page is refreshed, the value will be stored in an element in the myinfo.xml file:

```
<XML>
<greeting>Happy Christmas!</>
</XML>
```

This is a convenient way of storing information which is used in a number of places but which is likely to change in the future, since it means we don't have to change the value on every page where it occurs.

MyInfo Example

In order to demonstrate the dynamic properties of the MyInfo component, the following sample page allows the user to add new properties, or to view the value of a property which has already been added. The page contains a form which submits to itself, giving the user the option either of viewing the value of an existing property (chosen from a <SELECT> drop-down list), or of adding a new property with a new value:

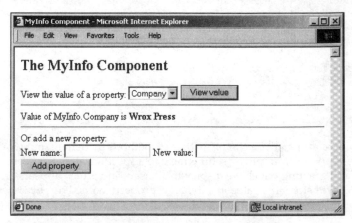

The form contains two submit buttons, so we check which of these was pressed to see what action to take. If the **Add property** button was pressed, we check whether the property is already in our list, and if not, we add the name of the property to a string stored with session scope, surrounded by <OPTION> ... </OPTION> tags. This string is written to the page in the <SELECT> element, so this forms a way of allowing the user to choose one of the properties that has already been added. We also add the property to the MyInfo component and set its value. If the **View value** button was pressed, we simply display the value for the selected property.

The VBScript version of this code is:

```
<HTML>
<TITLE>MyInfo Component</TITLE>
<H2>The MyInfo Component</H2>
<%
Set objMyInfo = Server.CreateObject("MSWC.MyInfo")
If IsEmpty(Session("strPropNames")) Then
    Session("strPropNames") = ""
End If

If Request.Form("submit") = "Add property" Then
    strName = Request.Form("txtName")
    strValue = Request.Form("txtValue")
    strOption = "<OPTION>" & strName & "</OPTION>"
    ' Only add the new property to the list if it's not already there
    If Instr(Session("strPropNames"), strOption) = 0 Then
        Session("strPropNames") = Session("strPropNames") & _
                                  strOption & vbCrLf
    End If
    objMyInfo(strName) = strValue
End If
%>
<FORM ACTION="myinfo_vbs.asp" METHOD="POST">
View the value of a property:
<SELECT NAME="propName">
    <%= Session("strPropNames") %>
</SELECT>
<INPUT TYPE="SUBMIT" NAME="submit" VALUE="View value">
<BR>

<%
If Request.Form("submit") = "View value" Then
    strProp = Request.Form("propName")
    Response.Write "<HR>Value of MyInfo." & strProp & _
                   " is <B>" & objMyInfo(strProp) & "</B>"
End If
%>
<HR>
Or add a new property:<BR>
New name:
<INPUT TYPE="TEXT" NAME="txtName">
New value:
<INPUT TYPE="TEXT" NAME="txtValue">
<INPUT TYPE="SUBMIT" NAME="submit" VALUE="Add property">
</HTML>
```

And the JScript equivalent:

```
<HTML>
<TITLE>MyInfo Component</TITLE>
<H2>The MyInfo Component</H2>
<%
// Instantiate component, and if it doesn't already exist
// initialize the session variable which holds the property names
var objMyInfo = Server.CreateObject("MSWC.MyInfo");
if (String(Session("strPropNames")) == "undefined") {
   Session("strPropNames") = "";
}
if (Request.Form("submit") == "Add property") {
   strName = Request.Form("txtName");
   strValue = Request.Form("txtValue");
   strOption = "<OPTION>" + strName + "</OPTION>"
   // Only add the new property to the list if it's not already there
   if (Session("strPropNames").indexOf(strOption) == -1) {
      Session("strPropNames") += strOption + "\n";
   }
   // Set the property of the MyInfo component
   objMyInfo(strName) = strValue;
}
%>
<FORM ACTION="myinfo2_js.asp" METHOD="POST">
View the value of a property:
<SELECT NAME="propName">
   <%= Session("strPropNames") %>
</SELECT>
<INPUT TYPE="SUBMIT" NAME="submit" VALUE="View value">
<%
if (Request.Form("submit") == "View value") {
   strProp = Request.Form("propName");
   // Retrieve the value for the requested property
   Response.Write("<HR>Value of MyInfo." + strProp +
                  " is <B>" + objMyInfo(strProp) + "</B>");
}
%>
<BR>
<HR>
Or add a new property:<BR>
New name:
<INPUT TYPE="TEXT" NAME="txtName">
New value:
<INPUT TYPE="TEXT" NAME="txtValue">
<INPUT TYPE="SUBMIT" NAME="submit" VALUE="Add property">
</HTML>
```

Summary

The MyInfo component allows us to store information in dynamic properties, which we can retrieve at any time, from anywhere in our application. Because this information is stored in a text file, we don't lose it when the application is restarted. However, this means that the properties will return the same values for all users, so the MyInfo component is probably best suited to storing values which are always the same, on all pages in an application, but which are liable to change. So in this chapter, we looked at:

- ❑ Instantiating the MyInfo component.

- ❑ Setting and retrieving the values of the dynamic properties.

- ❑ An example page which allows the user to set or retrieve values in the MyInfo component.

MyInfo Component

22

Page Counter Component

The **Page Counter** component allows us to store the number of times a particular page has been requested. This data is saved in a text file called the **hit count data file** (HitCnt.cnt, located in the WinNT\System32\inetsvr\Data directory), and the value can be retrieved for any page where the component has been instantiated.

To instantiate the component, we can use either the Server.CreateObject method or an HTML <OBJECT> element. The ProgID is "MSWC.PageCounter":

```
' Server.CreateObject in VBScript
Set objPageCount = Server.CreateObject("MSWC.PageCounter")

// Server.CreateObject in JScript
objPageCount = Server.CreateObject("MSWC.PageCounter");

<!-- HTML OBJECT tag -->
<OBJECT RUNAT="SERVER" ID="objPageCount" PROGID="MSWC.PageCounter"></OBJECT>
```

Page Counter Component Methods

The Page Counter component can be found in PageCnt.dll. The Page Counter component provides three methods which allow us to retrieve the hit count for a given page, to increment the hit count for the current page, or to reset a page's hit count to zero:

Methods
Hits
PageHit
Reset

Hits Method

The Hits method allows us to retrieve the current hit count for any page where the Page Counter is instantiated (and which consequently has an entry in the hit count data file).

```
Long = PageCounter.Hits([PagePath])
```

Parameter	Data Type	Description
PagePath	String	Optional. The URL (excluding domain name) of the page for which the hit count will be returned. If omitted, the hit count for the current page will be returned.

This method returns the value currently stored in the hit count data file for the specified page. If that page does not have an entry in the data file (for example, if the page doesn't exist or if the Page Counter isn't instantiated on it), this method will return zero.

For example:

```
' VBScript
Dim objPageCount
Set objPageCount = Server.CreateObject("MSWC.PageCounter")
Response.Write "Current page hit count: " & objPageCount.Hits & "<BR>"
Response.Write "Some other page: " &
objPageCount.Hits("/ASPComponents/somepage.asp")
```

```
// JScript
var objPageCount = Server.CreateObject("MSWC.PageCounter");
Response.Write("Current page hit count: " + objPageCount.Hits() + "<BR>");
Response.Write("Some other page: " +
objPageCount.Hits("/ASPComponents/somepage.asp"));
```

PageHit Method

The PageHit method increases the hit count for the current page by one in the hit count data file.

```
Long = PageCounter.PageHit
```

The method returns the new hit count for the page.

For example:

```
' VBScript
Dim objPageCount
Set objPageCount = Server.CreateObject("MSWC.PageCounter")
Response.Write "New hit count: " & objPageCount.PageHit
// JScript
var objPageCount = Server.CreateObject("MSWC.PageCounter");
Response.Write("New hit count: " + objPageCount.PageHit());
```

Reset Method

The Reset method sets the hit count for a given page to zero.

```
PageCounter.Reset([PagePath])
```

Parameter	Data Type	Description
PagePath	String	Optional. The URL (excluding domain name) of the page for which the hit count will be reset. If omitted, the hit count for the current page will be reset.

For example:

```
' VBScript
Dim objPageCount
Set objPageCount = Server.CreateObject("MSWC.PageCounter")
objPageCount.Reset                                          ' Reset the
current page
objPageCount.Reset "\ASPComponents\somepage.asp"            ' Reset another
page
```

```
// JScript
var objPageCount = Server.CreateObject("MSWC.PageCounter");
objPageCount.Reset();                                       // Reset the
current page
objPageCount.Reset("\ASPComponents\somepage.asp");          // Reset another
page
```

Using the Page Counter Component

To demonstrate the Page Counter component, we'll write two nearly equivalent pages in VBScript and JScript. Each page will display the current page count for both of these pages, and provide options for resetting the count for each page. We will also add a button which allows the count for the current page to be incremented. This is how the JScript version appears when displayed in the browser:

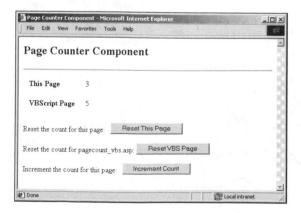

The code for the VBScript version of this page is as follows:

```
<H2>Page Counter Component</H2><HR>
<%
Dim objPageCount, strSubmit
Set objPageCount = Server.CreateObject("MSWC.PageCounter")
strSubmit = Request.Form("submit")
If strSubmit = "Reset This Page" Then
    objPageCount.Reset
ElseIf strSubmit = "Reset JS Page" Then
    objPageCount.Reset "/components/pagecount_js.asp"
Else
    objPageCount.PageHit
End If
%>
<TABLE BORDER=0 CELLPADDING=10>
    <TR>
        <TD><B>This Page</B></TD>
        <TD><%= objPageCount.Hits() %></TD>
    </TR>
    <TR>
        <TD><B>JScript Page</B></TD>
        <TD><%= objPageCount.Hits("/components/pagecount_js.asp") %></TD>
    </TR>
</TABLE>

<FORM METHOD="POST" ACTION="pagecount_vbs.asp">
Reset the count for this page:  
<INPUT TYPE="SUBMIT" NAME="submit" VALUE="Reset This Page"><BR><BR>
Reset the count for pagecount_js.asp:
<INPUT TYPE="SUBMIT" NAME="submit" VALUE="Reset JS Page"><BR><BR>
Increment the count for this page:  
<INPUT TYPE="SUBMIT" NAME="submit" VALUE="Increment Count">
</FORM>
```

And the JScript version:

```
<H2>Page Counter Component</H2><HR>
<%
var objPageCount = Server.CreateObject("MSWC.PageCounter");
var strSubmit = Request.Form("submit");
if (strSubmit=="Reset This Page") {
    objPageCount.Reset();
} else {
    if (strSubmit=="Reset VBS Page") {
        objPageCount.Reset("/components/pagecount_vbs.asp");
    } else {
        objPageCount.PageHit();
    }
}
%>
<TABLE BORDER=0 CELLPADDING=10>
    <TR>
        <TD><B>This Page</B></TD>
        <TD><%= objPageCount.Hits() %></TD>
    </TR>
    <TR>
        <TD><B>VBScript Page</B></TD>
        <TD><%= objPageCount.Hits("/components/pagecount_vbs.asp") %></TD>
```

```
    </TR>
</TABLE>

<FORM METHOD="POST" ACTION="pagecount_js.asp">
Reset the count for this page:  
<INPUT TYPE="SUBMIT" NAME="submit" VALUE="Reset This Page"><BR><BR>
Reset the count for pagecount_vbs.asp:
<INPUT TYPE="SUBMIT" NAME="submit" VALUE="Reset VBS Page"><BR><BR>
Increment the count for this page:  
<INPUT TYPE="SUBMIT" NAME="submit" VALUE="Increment Count">
</FORM>
```

When the page loads, we first instantiate the Page Counter component, and then we check the Request.Form collection to see what action to take. The page has a form with three submit buttons, and with an ACTION attribute set to the page itself. Each of the three submit buttons has the name "submit" but a different value, so the value of Request.Form("submit") tells us which of the buttons was pressed.

If the Reset This Page button was clicked, we call the Reset method with no parameter, so the page count of the current page is reset to zero. If the user selected to reset the count for the other version of the page, we call the same method, but add the URL of that page as a parameter. Otherwise, we increase the page count for the current page.

We then display a table containing the current page counts for both pages, which we retrieve using the Hits method. Again, for the current page we call the method with no parameter, but supply the URL in order to retrieve the count for the other version of the page.

Summary

The Page Counter provides a very easy way of keeping track of the number of visits a particular page has received. We simply need to instantiate the component and call its Hits methods once on a page, and the component will keep a hit count of that page, increasing the count each time the page is executed. So in this chapter, we saw:

❑   How to instantiate the Page Counter component.

❑   How to use the component's methods to retrieve, increment or reset the count for a page.

❑   How to retrieve or reset the hit count for another page on which the component is instantiated.

Page Counter Component

23

The Permission Checker Component

The **Permission Checker** component allows a script to check whether the user account has the necessary permissions to access a specific file or resource. It can also be used to hide links to resources for which the current user does not have permissions.

The Permission Checker component can be found in the file `PermChk.dll` and can be instantiated using the `Server.CreateObject` method or an `<OBJECT>` tag. The Prog ID is `"MSWC.PermissionChecker"`:

```
' VBScript
Set objPermChk = Server.CreateObject("MSWC.PermissionChecker")
```

```
// JScript
objPermChk = Server.CreateObject("MSWC.PermissionChecker");
```

```
<!-- OBJECT tag -->
<OBJECT RUNAT="SERVER" ID="objPermChk"
PROGID="MSWC.PermissionChecker"></OBJECT>
```

Permission Checker Methods

The Permission Checker component has a single method, `HasAccess`.

HasAccess Method

The `HasAccess` method indicates whether the user account under which the ASP script is running has the right to access to a given file.

```
Boolean = PermissionChecker.HasAccess(FilePath)
```

Parameter	Data Type	Description
FilePath	String	The path to the file or resource for which we want to check the user's permissions. This can be either a virtual or physical path.

This returns true if the account has access to the specified resource, or false if the account does not have access to the resource, or if it does not exist.

How the Permission Checker Component Works

Generally, unless we specify otherwise, our users will be accessing the pages anonymously, and therefore IIS will access resources on their behalf using its own Windows account. By default this is IUSR_machinename, for example IUSR_WROXBOX. So, the Permission Checker component will check if the IUSR_machinename account has access to the specified page or resource.

However, by turning off the Allow Anonymous Access option in Internet Services Manager for a web site or a specific directory, we force IIS to prompt the user for a username and password of a valid user account. This account is then used to access the resources for which anonymous access is denied. Access control is specified in the Internet Services Manager, in the Directory Security page of the Properties dialog for a site or directory. Click the Edit button in the 'Anonymous access and authentication control' section of this dialog page to open the Authentication Methods dialog, and turn off the 'Anonymous access' option:

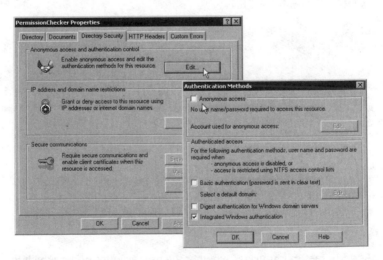

When the Permission Checker component is instantiated in a page that is accessed by a user under their own account (rather than IUSR_machinename), it checks to see if their account has permission to access the specified resource. So, if we disable anonymous access so that all users have to supply their account details, we can use Windows Explorer to set up specific permissions on each file or resource – in the Security page of the Properties dialog for that resource:

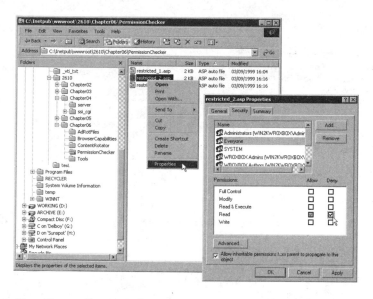

Using the Permission Checker Component

We can use the Permission Checker component to check whether the current user has permission to access any other page (anywhere on our site) with the `HasAccess` method. In the following example we use a form to check which file a user wishes to access, and then print a message telling the user whether they have the permissions to do this or not.

Our VBScript code looks like this:

```asp
<%@ LANGUAGE="VBScript" %>
<TITLE>Permissions Checker Component</TITLE>
<H2>The Permissions Checker Component</H2>
Please enter the path of a file on the system:
<FORM ACTION="permchk_vbs.asp" METHOD="POST">
    <INPUT TYPE="TEXT" NAME="txtPath">  
    <INPUT TYPE="SUBMIT" VALUE="Check Permissions">
</FORM><HR>

<%
strPath = Request.Form("txtPath")
If strPath <> "" Then
    Set objPermChk = Server.CreateObject("MSWC.PermissionChecker")
    If objPermChk.HasAccess(strPath) Then
        Response.Write "The current user has access to the file <B>" & _
                    strPath & "</B>"
    Else
        Response.Write "The current user does not have access " & _
                    "to the file <B>" & strPath & "</B>"
    End If
End If
%>
```

Or in JScript:

```
<%@ LANGUAGE="JScript" %>
<TITLE>Permissions Checker Component</TITLE>
<H2>The Permissions Checker Component</H2>
Please enter the path of a file on the system:
<FORM ACTION="permchk_js.asp" METHOD="POST">
   <INPUT TYPE="TEXT" NAME="txtPath">  
   <INPUT TYPE="SUBMIT" VALUE="Check Permissions">
</FORM><HR>

<%
strPath = Request.Form("txtPath");
if (strPath != null) {
   objPermChk = Server.CreateObject("MSWC.PermissionChecker");
   if (objPermChk.HasAccess(strPath)) {
      Response.Write("The current user has access to the file <B>" +
                     strPath + "</B>");
   } else {
      Response.Write("The current user does not have access " +
                     "to the file <B>" + strPath + "</B>");
   }
}
%>
```

The screen output looks like this:

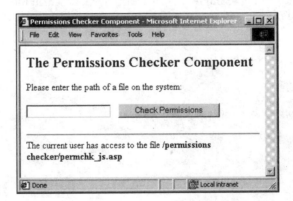

Summary

In this chapter we looked at the Permission Checker component and demonstrated how to use it in an ASP page to enable a user to access a file or deny them access to it.

24

The Tools Component

The **Tools** component provides a number of miscellaneous useful methods. These allow us to check whether a particular file exists, to generate an ASP page dynamically based on a template, and to generate a random integer. There are also two methods available only for the Apple Macintosh that check whether a plug-in is installed on the server and check whether the current user is the owner of the web site.

The Tools component resides in a file named `Tools.dll`, and to instantiate it we use the normal `Server.CreateObject` method or the HTML `<OBJECT>` tag, passing in a Prog ID of `"MSWC.Tools"`:

```
' VBScript
Set objTools = Server.CreateObject("MSWC.Tools")
```

```
// JScript
objTools = Server.CreateObject("MSWC.Tools");
```

```
<!-- OBJECT tag -->
<OBJECT RUNAT="SERVER" ID="objTools" PROGID="MSWC.Tools"></OBJECT>
```

Tools Component Methods

The Tools component has five methods, two of which are available only on the Apple:

Methods
FileExists
Owner (Apple only)
PluginExists (Apple only)
ProcessForm
Random

FileExists Method

The `FileExists` method allows us to determine whether or not a specific file exists.

```
Boolean = Tools.FileExists(RelativeURL)
```

Parameter	Data Type	Description
RelativeURL	String	The full virtual path (excluding domain name) of the file to check for.

This method returns `true` if the file does exist, or `false` if it does not.

The following example allows the user to input a URL and uses the `FileExists` method to check whether that file exists:

```
<FORM ACTION="fileExists_vbs.asp" METHOD="POST">
Please type a file URL:
<INPUT TYPE="TEXT" NAME="file"><BR>
<INPUT TYPE="SUBMIT" NAME="submit">
</FORM>
<HR>
<%
Dim objTools, strFile
Set objTools = Server.CreateObject("MSWC.Tools")
strFile = Request.Form("file")
If strFile <> "" Then
   If objTools.FileExists(strFile) Then
      Response.Write "The file <B>" & strFile & "</B> exists."
   Else
      Response.Write "The file <B>" & strFile & _
                     "</B> does not exist."
   End If
End If
Set objTools = Nothing
%>
```

The JScript equivalent of this code is:

```
<FORM ACTION="fileExists_js.asp" METHOD="POST">
Please type a file URL:
<INPUT TYPE="TEXT" NAME="file"><BR>
<INPUT TYPE="SUBMIT" NAME="submit">
</FORM>
<HR>
<%
var objTools = Server.CreateObject("MSWC.Tools");
var strFile = Request.Form("file");
if (strFile != "") {
   if (objTools.FileExists(strFile)) {
      Response.Write("The file <B>" + strFile + "</B> exists.");
   } else {
      Response.Write("The file <B>" + strFile +
                     "</B> does not exist.");
   }
}
delete objTools;
%>
```

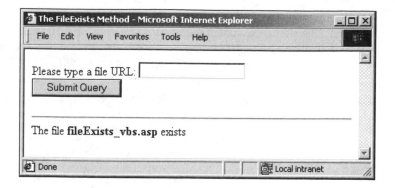

Owner Method

The Owner method indicates whether the current user is the web site's owner.

```
Boolean = Tools.Owner()
```

On the Apple Macintosh, this method will return true if the current user account is the owner of the web site, or otherwise false, but on Windows 2000 this will always return false.

PluginExists Method

The PluginExists method can be used on the Apple to determine whether a particular plug-in is installed on the server.

```
Boolean = Tools.PluginExists(PluginName)
```

Parameter	Data Type	Description
PluginName	String	The name of the plug-in.

This method returns true if the named plug-in exists on the server, or false otherwise. Again, this will always return false on Windows 2000.

ProcessForm Method

The ProcessForm method allows us to generate an ASP page dynamically, usually based on the values submitted by a user through an HTML form. The generated page is based on a template which can contain both normal ASP code (executed when the page is loaded) and script in special <%% ... %%> tags which is executed when the page is generated.

```
Tools.ProcessForm(OutputFile, TemplateFile, [InsertionPoint])
```

Parameter	Data Type	Description
OutputFile	String	The full URL (excluding domain name) of the output file into which the generated content will be written.
TemplateFile	String	The full URL (excluding domain name) of the template file upon which the generated output file will be based.
InsertionPoint	String	Optional. A string which determines where in the output file the generated content will be placed. If preceded by an asterisk (*), the content will be inserted before the first occurrence of the string; otherwise, it will be placed after it. If this parameter is omitted, the entire contents of the output file will be replaced. Note that in early versions of the Tools component, this parameter is ignored, and the entire contents are always replaced.

The Output File

Note that, although in current versions of the component, the contents of the output file are always entirely replaced, this file must exist before we call the method. In addition, IIS must have write permissions on the file and on the directory in which it resides. Otherwise, IIS will not be able to open the file and the ProcessForm method will generate an 'MSWC.Tools error 80004005 Couldn't open output file' error. The easiest way to get round this is to open up the Properties pages for the file and directory and, for each one, grant Full Control to the Everyone group:

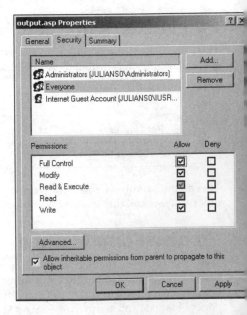

Because the file's contents will be entirely replaced, it doesn't really matter what this file contains – a blank text file will do nicely. However, because the generated file can contain ASP script, you will probably want to save it with an .asp extension.

Creating the Template

After creating the output file and setting its permissions, we need to create the template file. This file contains the content that will be written to the output file. As we have mentioned, it can contain normal ASP script code, and this will be executed whenever the output page is loaded, just like a normal ASP page. However, it can also contain code in special <%% ... %%> tags which will be executed when the content is generated. We can use these tags to enter information entered by the user in an HTML form. This will be written into the output page, and remain constant whenever the page is loaded (until the ProcessForm method is called again, and the page's content replaced once more).

To illustrate this, we will use an HTML form where users can input their favorite color, and generate a page with this as the background color. So, our first page is a simple HTML page with a form and a <SELECT> element:

```
<HTML>
<FORM METHOD="POST" ACTION="ProcessForm.asp">
Please choose your favorite color:
<SELECT NAME="color">
   <OPTION SELECTED>blue</OPTION>
   <OPTION>green</OPTION>
   <OPTION>red</OPTION>
   <OPTION>yellow</OPTION>
   <OPTION>white</OPTION>
</SELECT>
<INPUT TYPE=SUBMIT NAME="submit">
</FORM>

</HTML>
```

The ACTION of the form is set to the ASP page where we will actually call the ProcessForm method. We will see this page shortly, but first – our template:

```
<HEAD>
<TITLE>Tools.ProcessForm Method</TITLE>
</HEAD>

<BODY BGCOLOR=<%%= Request.Form("color") %%>>

<H1>This page is generated by the Tools component</H1>

Generated <%%= Now %%><BR>

Page served <%= Now %>

</BODY>
```

This template simply writes in the value of the color select box taken from the form, and sets it as the background color in the <BODY> tag. Because this is enclosed in <%% ... %%> tags, the value will be written into the page as a literal. We also include the date and time that the page was generated (again in <%% ... %%> tags, so this will remain the same however often the generated page is executed), and the time when the page was served. This is in a normal ASP script section in <% ... %> tags, which will be inserted directly into the output file, and executed when the page is loaded.

The output from this template will be a page such as the following:

```
<HEAD>
<TITLE>Tools.ProcessForm Method</TITLE>
</HEAD>

<BODY BGCOLOR=yellow>

<H1>This page is generated by the Tools component</H1>

Generated 3/5/2000 6:42:59 PM<BR>

Page served <%= now %>

</BODY>
```

Generating the New Page

Our final task is to write the page ProcessForm.asp, where the method is actually called. This contains just three lines:

```
<%
Set objTools = Server.CreateObject("MSWC.Tools")
objTools.ProcessForm "/components/output.asp", _
                     "/components/template.asp"
Server.Transfer "output.asp"
%>
```

Or in JScript:

```
<%
objTools = Server.CreateObject("MSWC.Tools");
objTools.ProcessForm("/components/output.asp",
                     "/components/template.asp");
Server.Transfer("output.asp");
%>
```

We simply instantiate the Tools component, call the ProcessForm method and then use the new Server.Transfer method to transfer to our newly generated page. When we run this, we will see something like the following:

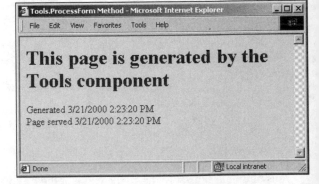

Since we transfer to the page straight after generating it, the two times displayed are identical. However, if we were later to load output.asp (without regenerating it), the Page served date would be updated, but the Generated date would remain constant.

Random Method

The Random method allows us to incorporate a random element into our web pages by generating a random integer.

```
Integer = Tools.Random()
```

This returns an integer between −32768 and 32767. We can use the Abs function to ensure a positive result. For example:

```
Set objTools = Server.CreateObject("MSWC.Tools")
intRand = Abs(objTools.Random)
```

Or in JScript, we would use the Math.abs method:

```
objTools = Server.CreateObject("MSWC.Tools");
intRand = Math.abs(objTools.Random());
```

To get a positive floating-point number between 0 and 1, we can simply divide this by 32767:

```
' VBScript
intRand = Abs(objTools.Random) / 32767
```

```
// JScript
intRand = Math.abs(objTools.Random()) / 32767;
```

Or, to get a positive value between zero and a given positive integer, we can use the modulus operator. For example, to get a random integer between zero and nine:

```
' VBScript
intRand = Abs(objTools.Random) mod 10
```

```
// JScript
intRand = Math.abs(objTools.Random()) % 10;
```

The following example uses the Random method to display one of three quotations chosen at random:

```
<%
Set objTools = Server.CreateObject("MSWC.Tools")
intRand = Abs(objTools.Random) mod 3
Select Case intRand
    Case 0
        strQuot = "<P>I agree with no man's opinions. I have some of my
own.</P>" & _
                  "<P>Ivan Turgenev</P>"
    Case 1
        strQuot = "<P>A classic is something that everybody wants to have read,
but nobody wants to read.</P>" & _
                  "<P>Mark Twain</P>"
    Case 2
        strQuot = "<P>'What is the use of a book,' thought Alice, 'without
pictures or conversations?'</P>" & _
                  "<P>Lewis Carroll</P>"
End Select
Response.Write strQuot
%>
```

Or in JScript:

```
<%
var objTools = Server.CreateObject("MSWC.Tools");
intRand = Math.abs(objTools.Random()) % 3
switch (intRand) {
    case 0:
        strQuot = "<P>I agree with no man's opinions. I have some of my
own.</P>" +
                  "<P>Ivan Turgenev</P>"
        break;
    case 1:
        strQuot = "<P>A classic is something that everybody wants to have read,
but nobody wants to read.</P>" +
                  "<P>Mark Twain</P>"
        break;
    case 2:
        strQuot = "<P>'What is the use of a book,' thought Alice, 'without
pictures or conversations?'</P>" +
                  "<P>Lewis Carroll</P>"
}
Response.Write(strQuot);
%>
```

Summary

The Tools component provides three useful but unrelated methods for the PC, as well as two more which can only be used on the Macintosh. In this chapter we looked at:

❑ Instantiating the Tools component.

❑ Checking whether a given file exists with the FileExists method.

❑ Using the ProcessForm method to generate an ASP page dynamically using a predefined template and the information submitted in a form.

❑ Using the Random method to select one of a number of options at random.

Tools Component

25

Third-Party Components

In this chapter we briefly outline some of the popular commercial and free third-party server components that you can use with ASP. Two of the common tasks you have to accomplish when developing web sites are managing compatibility and uploading files to the server. We look at a couple of components that can help out. We also look at a component that can be used instead of the Microsoft sample Registry Access component, which appears to have been withdrawn from their web site.

The BrowserHawk Component

While many people are happy with the **Browser Capabilities** component that is supplied with IIS and ASP, it suffers from the problem that the browser definition file `browscap.ini` requires regular maintenance or replacement to keep up with new browser releases.

CyScape, the company that provides updated versions of `browscap.ini`, also offers its own component that carries out browser detection, both on the server and on the client. What's more, it provides a handy graphical interface that can be used to view and modify its own browser definition file:

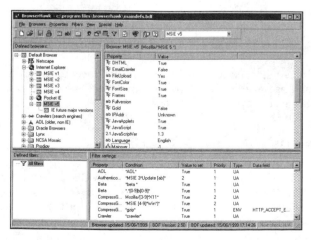

You can see that there are many more properties available for each browser type, such as Dynamic HTML, style sheets, the JavaScript version, file upload capabilities, Secure Sockets Layer support, operating system details, and language. And, like the Microsoft Browser Capabilities component, you can add your own as well. There is also a useful Wizard-style feature that helps you to add new browsers to the definition file:

Some of the nice tricks that **BrowserHawk** has up its sleeve are the ability to recognize new browsers (using a special pattern-matching algorithm), and a far wider range of browsers supported by default – including Opera, WebTV, etc. New properties are also easy to add using the filtering feature.

However, probably the biggest advantage with BrowserHawk is the ability to automatically check periodically for new versions of the browser definition file from the CyScape website, and merge the additions into your current definition file. This means that you don't have to keep copying the definition files to all your Web servers.

Using the BrowserHawk component is easy, as it is compatible with the Microsoft Browser Capabilities component. The only requirement is to change the ProgID in your Server.Create method or <OBJECT> element that creates the component instance from "MSWC.BrowserType" to "cyScape.browserObj":

```
'VBScript
Set objBCap = Server.CreateObject("cyScape.browserObj")
```

```
//JScript
Set objBCap = Server.CreateObject("cyScape.browserObj")
```

However, you should check out the BrowserHawk documentation regarding a few issues that can arise. You can download a copy of BrowserHawk yourself from the CyScape web site at http://www.cyscape.com/.

The SA-FileUp Component

One regular requirement on many web sites is the ability to accept files that are posted from the client to the server. In IIS4.0, Microsoft provided a component known as the **Posting Acceptor** which did just that. This component is no longer included with a standard installation of IIS5.0 and ASP 3.0, though it is included if you install Site

Server Express. You can also download it from the Microsoft web site at
`http://www.microsoft.com/windows/software/webpost/post_accept.htm`.

However, many people find the Posting Acceptor both limited in features and difficult
to program. One of the popular alternatives is the **SA-FileUp** component from **Software
Artisans**. Unlike Posting Acceptor (which is an ISAPI filter), SA-FileUp is a true
ActiveX DLL server component, and integrates easily into ASP pages. This means that
the same techniques for setting security on pages and limiting user access can be used
as in any other ASP pages or components. It can also be run within the MTS/COM+
out-of-process environment like any other ActiveX DLL.

A full tutorial for using SA-FileUp is provided at
`http://www.activeserverpages.com/upload/`, so we will only show you the
results here. You can download a copy of **SA-FileUp** yourself from the **Software
Artisans** web site at `http://www.softartisans.com/`.

Using the SA-FileUp Component

The sample pages provided with SA-FileUp create a simple page containing a
`FileUpload` element and a button, using the HTML `INPUT` elements:

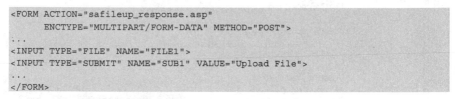

```
<FORM ACTION="safileup_response.asp"
      ENCTYPE="MULTIPART/FORM-DATA" METHOD="POST">
...
<INPUT TYPE="FILE" NAME="FILE1">
<INPUT TYPE="SUBMIT" NAME="SUB1" VALUE="Upload File">
...
</FORM>
```

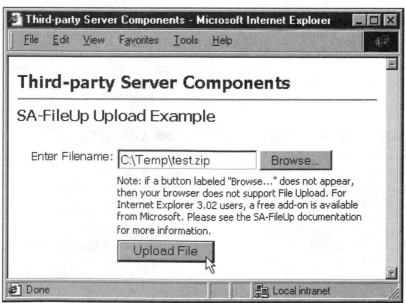

When the user submits the form, the contents are posted to the server and an ASP page there creates an instance of the component and starts the upload process. Afterwards the component returns a series of values that describe the file that was uploaded:

SA-FileUp fetches the file and stores it temporarily on the server, where it can be saved as a normal disk file or placed in a database as binary data. You can also control the upload process with ASP, limiting the size of the upload or even discarding it. You can also change the name and location of the uploaded file dynamically.

The RegEx Registry Access Component

One of the sample components that Microsoft provided with IIS 4.0 was capable of accessing the system Registry on the server, which is useful for checking things like which version of a particular item of software is installed, or various parameters being used by IIS or the operating system.

This component has disappeared from IIS 5.0, but there are other commercial versions available if you need this functionality. One of them is **RegEx**, which provides access to any part of the local machine's Registry, providing that the current user has sufficient permissions. Remember that in an ASP page that is accessed anonymously, the current user is the IUSR_machinename account.

The RegEx Component Members

The RegEx component provides four methods to read and write Registry values, and one method to access the internal component version information. Full information and documentation is provided with the component and an evaluation version can be downloaded from http://www.stonebroom.com/. The example pages that come with it are included in the samples we provide for this book, though you will need to download the component yourself:

Method	Description
GetRegValue (*RegistryHive*, *SubKeyString*)	This returns the 'Default' value of a given sub-key from the Registry or an empty string if the value cannot be accessed.
SetRegValue (*RegistryHive*, *SubKeyString*, *NewValue*)	This creates or updates the 'Default' value within the specified sub-key, setting the data-type to REG_SZ (String). Returns True if the update is successful or False otherwise.
GetRegValueEx (*RegistryHive*, *SubKeyString*, *ValueName*, *ValueType*)	This returns a named value from the specified sub-key, updating the variable specified in the last parameter of the method with the data-type of the returned value. Returns an empty string, and REG_ERROR as the data-type, if the value cannot be accessed.
SetRegValueEx (*RegistryHive*, *SubKeyString*, *ValueName*, *NewValue*, *ValueType*)	This creates or updates a named value within the specified sub-key, setting the data-type to that specified in the last parameter of the method. Returns True if the update is successful or False otherwise.
GetInternal VersionNumber()	This returns the internal version number of the component. If it is an evaluation version, the return value will contain this information as well.

Using the RegEx Component

The RegEx component is supplied with an example application written in Visual Basic, which allows you to experiment with the methods that it exposes. This application uses the RegEx component to allow you to read and write values to any part of the system Registry, in any of the supported data types or as the default String-type values. A warning is displayed before any updates are made to prevent accidental changes.

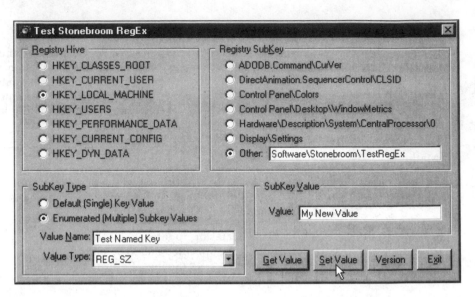

There is also a simple ASP example that displays some values from the Web server's Registry, and allows you to read and set a 'test' sub-key as well. Again, this page can be modified and used without limitation in your own applications. Here is the result when run on IIS4 on NT4:

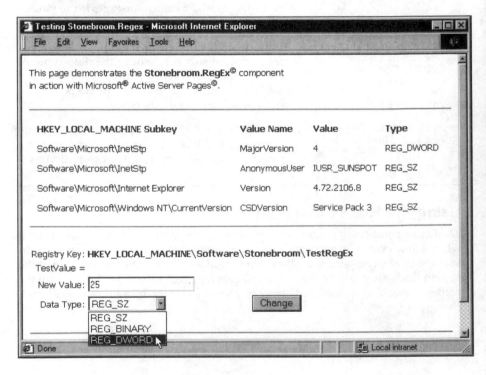

> Remember that changing values in the Registry can prevent your system from running properly. You should always back up the Registry files before editing the contents.

Data Access and Conversion Components

ActiveDOM – enables XML and XHTML files to be loaded, created and manipulated from just about any product or programming language that supports Microsoft COM. Implements the W3C DOM 1.0 Level 1 interfaces and is designed to be fully compatible with MSXML.
See: http://www.vivid-creations.com/dom/index.htm

ActiveSAX – enables XML files of any size to be parsed from just about any product or programming language that supports Microsoft COM.
See: http://www.vivid-creations.com/sax/index.htm

ASP2XML – creates XML documents from any OLE DB or ODBC enabled data source, and can update the original data as well.
See: http://www.stonebroom.com/swindex.htm

Data Validation – validates a wide variety of data through a series of functions and methods.
See: http://www.a-href.com/products/ahrefdvc.html

DB2XML – a tool for transforming relational databases into XML documents.
See: http://www.informatik.fh-wiesbaden.de/~turau/DB2XML/index.html

RSConvert – a control for converting DAO or ADO recordsets to MDB or DBF files. It allows direct output of MDB or DBF files from ASP pages.
See: http://www.pstruh.cz/help/RSConv/library.htm

SaveForm – automatically persists form data in an ASP Session, and to a database or text file between sessions. Can also send it as an e-mail message via CDONTS.
See: http://www.stonebroom.com/swindex.htm

XML-DBMS – Java Packages for Transferring Data between XML Documents and Relational Databases.
See: http://www.informatik.tu-darmstadt.de/DVS1/staff/bourret/xmldbms/readme.html

XMLServlet – A Java Servlet that uses XML instructions to combine XML or HTML templates with one another and with live database values.
See: http://www.beyond.com/PKSN102998/prod.htm

Third-Party Components

E-Mail ASP Components

AspMail – allows you to send SMTP mail directly from an ASP page, and provides almost all the e-mail message features you might want.
See: http://www.serverobjects.com/products.htm

AspQMail – works just like AspMail except that messages are queued for delivery. A companion NT service is notified when messages are added to the queue and attempts delivery while your ASP script is free to continue.
See: http://www.serverobjects.com/products.htm

JMail – free, very capable e-mail component.
See: http://www.dimac.net/

OCX Mail/ASP – can be used to read SMTP mail that contains attachments.
See: http://www.flicks.com/ASPMail

Web Essentials Listcaster – a mailing list server and SMTP/POP3 server with ASP-based setup and administration.
See: http://www.download.com/pc/software/0,332,0-57624-s,1000.html

File Management Components

AspUpload – enables an ASP application to accept, save and manipulate files uploaded from a browser through one or more <INPUT TYPE=FILE> elements.
See: http://www.aspupload.com/

File I/O – lets you perform disk directory scans, read and write INI files, create and delete files and directories, read the <TITLE> from Web documents, etc.
See: http://www.tarsus.com/asp/io2/

LastMod – gets a file's last modified date/time from within an ASP page.
See: http://www.serverobjects.com/products.htm

ScriptUtilities – lets you work with safearray binary data. It enables binary file upload to ASP and multiple files/folders download from ASP with on-the-fly compression or generation of binary data.
See: http://www.pstruh.cz/help/ScptUtl/library.htm

ServerZip – performs on-demand compression of user-selected files into ZIP files on the server ready for downloading.
See: http://www.stonebroom.com/swindex.htm

Networking Components

AspDNS – does forward and reverse DNS lookups returning either the IP address or the host name.
See: http://www.serverobjects.com/products.htm

AspHTTP – allows you to GET/POST/HEAD documents via the HTTP protocol. Exposes HTTP response headers, supports transferring requests to a file (including binary transfers), password authentication support, and more.
See: http://www.serverobjects.com/products.htm

AspInet – allows you to remotely GET and PUT files via FTP from Active Server Pages.
See: http://www.serverobjects.com/products.htm

ASPLogin – provides basic security for any webpage or collection of pages without using Windows own security system and risking compromising system passwords over the Net.
See: http://www.oceantek.com/asplogin/

AspPing – allows you to check the connection with any URL through the echo protocol from within ASP.
See: http://www.serverobjects.com/products.htm

FTP/X – provides easy, high-level access to the complete FTP client protocol (RFC 959). Can make the results available as an ADO Recordset, and has built-in features to support debugging and non-standard servers using the Quote method.
See: http://www.mabry.com/ftpx/index.htm

RAS/X – a RAS Dialer. Remote Access Services allows a computer to connect to an Internet server as though it was on a LAN.
See: http://www.mabry.com/rasx/index.htm

ShotIp – enables ASP scripts to connect to other machines over the 'Net using TCP/IP.
See: http://download.proxy.ru/mike/shotip/

SOCKET/X – a WinSock ActiveX Control that provides full access to Windows 'Sockets', making it easy to write TCP/IP or UDP client and server software.
See: http://www.mabry.com/socketx/index.htm

TCPIP - provides simple IP address and host name resolution.
See: http://www.pstruh.cz/help/tcpip/library.htm

TraceRoute – allows the route followed by a TCP/IP packet to be examined.
See: http://www.pstruh.cz/help/tcpip/library.htm

URL Replacer – an ISAPI filter that replaces specific parts of the URL sent from a browser, allowing ASP to specify different static resources for the same request.
See: http://www.pstruh.cz/help/urlrepl/library.htm

Third-Party Components

UserManager – contains simple objects for creating, deleting, managing and enumerating user accounts and groups. Allows removal and addition of users to groups.
See: `http://www.pstruh.cz/help/usrmgr/library.htm`

WHOIS/X – follows the WhoIs/NICNAME protocol and allows queries of InterNIC or other RFC 954 servers to obtain information about a user, domain or host.
See: `http://www.mabry.com/whoisx/index.htm`

Content Creation Components

AspBible – allows you to dynamically generate texts from the Bible.
See: `http://www.serverobjects.com/products.htm`

ASPointer – extracts content from XML documents, HTML and ASP pages using a syntax that is based on XPointer, and can optionally insert new content into the document.
See: `http://www.stonebroom.com/swindex.htm`

Content Link Generator – generates content links across subdirectories.
See: `http://www.serverobjects.com/products.htm`

ListView – creates 4 different list views. Comes with an interactive designer and HTML source generator. The output is pure HTML.
See: `http://www.visualasp.com/Components.asp?ProductID=3`

ShotGraph – creates pictures on the fly and allows ASP script to work with them. It lets you create interactive inline images for your webpages.
See: `http://download.proxy.ru/mike/shotgraph/`

Strings – contains everything you need to manipulate strings in ASP code. Can also filter out HTML tags and other content (like profanities), and format strings in different ways.
See: `http://www.tarsus.com/asp/ts/`

Text2HTML – converts URL and e-mail addresses that are plain text to HTML anchors. It also properly formats Access memo fields for output to an HTML page.
See: `http://members.home.net/pjsteele/asp/`

TreeView – creates dynamically expandable and collapsible tree nodes in 8 different styles. Comes with an interactive designer and HTML source generator. The output is pure HTML.
See: `http://www.visualasp.com/Components.asp?ProductID=2`

Miscellaneous Components

10 components in one pack – Calendar, Contact Form, FAQ, Help System, Home Page, Links, Message Board, Scrapbook, User Administration, and Whats New components
See: `http://www.compo.net/products/default.asp`

AspExec – allows you to execute DOS and Windows apps from within ASP.
See: http://www.serverobjects.com/products.htm

AspProc – allows you to get a variant array of process IDs and process names, and to terminate a particular process by process ID. Does not work on WinNT 3.5x and Win95 systems.
See: http://www.serverobjects.com/products.htm

AspCrypt – duplicates the one-way algorithm used by Crypt on Unix.
See: http://www.serverobjects.com/products.htm

EnhancedLog – an IIS ISAPI add-in that allows redirection and customized error messages for each file/directory, extended logging, RAW data logging, POST data logging, and unique cookies.
See: http://www.pstruh.cz/el/enhlog.asp

GUIDMaker – creates globally unique identifiers (GUIDs) from within ASP.
See: http://www.serverobjects.com/products.htm

RegEx – provides full access to the system Registry, including extended keys.
See: http://www.stonebroom.com/swindex.htm

WaitFor – allows you to pause your ASP pages for a specified time, wait until a file exists, or wait until the component can get exclusive read/write permissions to a file.
See: http://www.serverobjects.com/products.htm

Sites that List ASP Components

Many ASP-oriented web sites provide lists of ASP components that are available, and often provide downloads as well. Some of the better-known sites are:

15 Seconds Free Resources Center at http://www.15seconds.com/

Active Server Pages Resources Site at http://www.activeserverpages.com/

ASP 101 Resources Site at http://www.asp101.com/

ASP Hole IIS and ASP Guide at http://www.asphole.com/

ASP Toolbox at http://www.tcp-ip.com/

ASP Watch at http://www.tcp-ip.com/

ASPXtras at http://www.aspwatch.com/

ComponentSource at http://www.componentsource.com/

Microsoft ASP Component Catalog at
http://msdn.microsoft.com/workshop/server/components/catalog.asp

ServerObjects at `http://www.serverobjects.com/`

The ASP Resource Index at `http://www.aspin.com/`

Ultimate ASP at `http://www.ultimateasp.com/`

Wynkoop BackOffice Pages at `http://www.swynk.com/`

Summary

In this chapter we consider some useful third party components that are available including: BrowserHawk component, SA-FileUp component and RegEx Registry Access component. We also list components for data access and conversions, e-mail ASP, file management, networking, content creation and other components.

*Our thanks to the following readers who helped to compile these lists: **Aaron Bertrand, Adam Wilson, Mikhail Tchikalov, Antonin Foller, Bruce Knapton, Richard Anderson, Andrew White, Jay McVinney, and Neil Holmes.***

Third-Party Components

ActiveX Data Objects

In this section we consider Microsoft's **ActiveX Data Objects** (ADO) technology, which enables our ASP to access data from data sources. ADO provides an easy-to-use object-based interface to the underlying OLE DB technology that gives the actual access to the underlying data.

Data Access Techniques

By data we simply mean any piece (or pieces) of information, regardless of the contents. A data store is, quite simply, the place where the data is kept. Although databases like Microsoft Access or SQL Server are an obvious type of data source, data can also be found in many other locations, for example, in:

- ❑ Spreadsheets
- ❑ Mail systems
- ❑ File systems
- ❑ Documents such as those used by Microsoft Word
- ❑ Web pages, such as the contents of an HTML page, or the XML data that can exist in a "Data Island" within an HTML page.

These diverse data sources each have their own way of formatting and storing information. The challenge is to access this information without having to use different methods for each specific type of data source.

Universal Data Access (UDA) is a Microsoft's strategy that aims to provide high performance access to data regardless of its data source. The ADO technology, combined with the underlying OLE DB goes some way towards implementing this in practice. For example, we can build a web application that uses ADO for its data access and this could then (using OLE DB) access data from a number of different data sources, *without* us needing to know the details of how to communicate with each through their individual data formats.

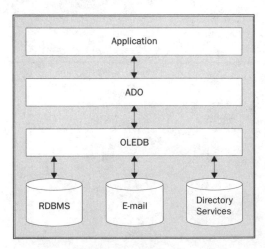

Before considering ADO in detail, let's just look at various data access techniques that are available and see how they fit into the UDA concept.

ODBC (Open DataBase Connectivity) was a first step towards the goal of universal data access. It was designed (by Microsoft and other database systems vendors) to provide a **cross-platform,** independent method to access data from relational databases using API calls. However, it did not have an object model associated with it, and hence was perceived as difficult to use.

DAO (Data Access Objects) was introduced with Microsoft Access and provided a strictly hierarchical set of objects for manipulating data in Jet, other ISAM and SQL databases. Since the objects were available through Visual Basic, DAO rapidly became a popular way to access data from VB programs. In principle, since DAO overlays ODBC, applications that made use of DAO could interact with multiple data sources. In practice, however, DAO was optimized for the Microsoft Jet ODBC engine, and offered a much poorer performance when accessing other databases. On account of this DAO is rapidly becoming deprecated and Microsoft are now only producing bug fixes, not new versions, despite DAO being quite a bit faster than ADO for accessing Access databases.

OLE DB was developed by Microsoft as the successor to ODBC. It provided for the increased focus on data access over the Internet, enabled access to data stored in non-relational data sources such as mail systems, and also delivered a COM-based interface for data access. OLE DB defines a set of COM interfaces for data access regardless of the data store (however, whereas ODBC was cross-platform, OLE DB is only available for platforms that support COM). OLE DB components consist of **data providers** that contain and expose data, **data consumers** that use data, and **service providers** that process and transport data (such as query processors and cursor engines). Since there is an OLE DB data provider for ODBC, it enables continued support for existing ODBC database drivers. The following diagram shows how an application (OLE DB Consumer) interacts with the data source through OLE DB.

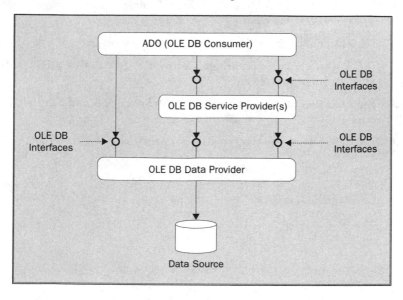

RDS (Remote Data Services) are used to transport data from a server to a client computer, where it is cached. The client machine can then be disconnected from the server and hence RDS facilitates **data remoting** within the same programming model as ADO. The RDS client-side components can run under an ActiveX-enabled browser and use HTTP to communicate with the web server, or they can be part of a server component communicating with the database. When a client enters a request, the client-side RDS component sends a query to the server, which is then processed and sent to the database server. The information is then sent back via the server to the client.

> More information on RDS and data remoting can be found in 'Professional ADO 2.5 RDS Programming with ASP 3.0' by Wrox Press.

ADO provides an object-based interface to OLE DB. This is needed since the complex COM interfaces can only be used from low-level languages like C++, and not from higher-level languages such as Visual Basic and the scripting languages used by, for example, ASP. It is becoming a very widely-used technology. ADO is implemented with a small footprint, minimal network traffic in key scenarios, and optimized interaction between the front end and data source. It uses the familiar COM automation interface, and is therefore available from scripting languages within ASP. Finally, since ADO was an evolutionary step from previous technologies, developers can quickly take advantage of its benefits.

The ADO Object Model

In common with other Microsoft technologies such as ASP, ADO has its own object model. The main objects in the ADO object model are:

- ❑ The ADO **Command object** enables us to interact with the stored procedure capabilities of the database.

- ❑ The ADO **Connection object** is used to create a connection to a data source.

- ❑ The ADO **Record object** represents a row in a recordset, or a file or directory in a file system or web resource.

- ❑ The ADO **Recordset object** gives us the ability to view and manipulate the data in a data store.

- ❑ The ADO **Stream object** represents a stream of text or binary data.

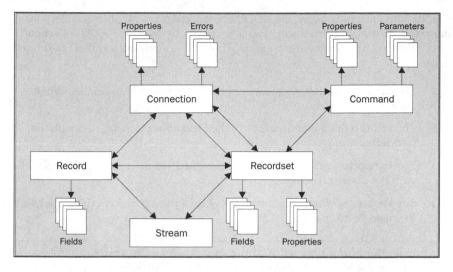

The ADO object model defines the objects that make it up and their hierarchy. However, unlike DAO for example, the hierarchical model for ADO is relatively flat, i.e. the requirement for having every object within it being instantiated has been relaxed. For example, the three main objects within the ADO object model (Connection, Command and Recordset) can each exist independently within our code. This means that, for example, in order to create a Command object, we do not first have to create a Connection object – ADO will do this automatically when a connection is required.

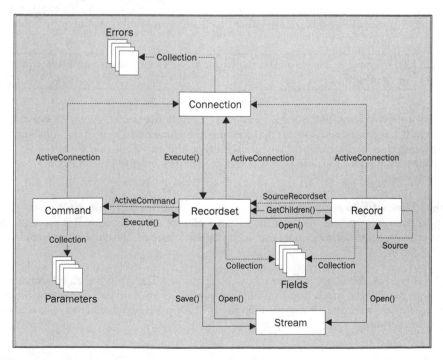

In addition to the main objects, the ADO object model has a number of collections comprising zero or more instances of its associated objects. These ADO collections must be derived from their parent objects. The ADO collections and their associated objects are:

❑ The **Errors collection** of instances of the **Error object** is associated with the `Connection` object.

❑ The **Fields collection** of instances of the **Field object** is associated with the `Recordset` and `Record` objects.

❑ The **Parameters collection** of instances of the **Parameter object** is associated with the `Command` object.

❑ The **Properties collection** of instances of the **Property object** can be used with all the main ADO objects.

> **The methods and properties of the** `Errors`, `Fields` **and** `Parameters` **collections and their associated** `Error`, `Field` **and** `Parameter` **objects are described in the chapters for their parent objects. In addition the** `Properties` **collection that contains instances of the** `Property` **object is described in Chapter 26, The Command Object.**

ADO Constants

When using components such as ADO libraries from ASP, we often need to pass the values of particular constants to the methods used in our code. These constants, for example `adLockReadOnly`, can either be passed as a numeric value or by name.

> **The names, values and descriptions of ADO constants can be found in Appendix D.**

There are two ways that our ASP script can identify the named constant. We can either include a file in our ASP script that contains the name and value of the constant we are interested in, or alternatively we can use a **type library** – a file that contains information about the objects, types, and constants supported by an ActiveX component.

Including a file in our ASP script will generally include **all** the constants for a particular library, such as the `adovbs.inc` file for ADO. Since ASP is processed as a script language, the more data that each page has to read, the slower it is to deliver to the client.

Improved performance is achieved by using a type library, a file with information about the objects, types, and constants supported by an ActiveX component. Since type libraries are already in binary format, the ASP script engine doesn't have to recompile them every time.

A type library is declared using the <METADATA> tag in the global.asa file for our
application. For example, to declare the ADO type library, we use the following
statement:

```
<!--METADATA TYPE="typelib" FILE = "c:\program files\common
files\system\ado\msado15.dll" -->
```

or, using its class ID:

```
<!--METADATA TYPE="typelib" uuid="00000205-0000-0010-8000-00AA006D2EA4" -->
```

We can then refer to the ADO constants declared in the type libraries from any script
in the same application as the global.asa file, without having to include the
adovbs.inc file, thus improving performance.

> If you plan to use a hosting service for your web site, the
> msado15.dll file may be in a different location, so using the UUID
> will be more reliable.

The Command Object

The Command object is one of the main objects in the ADO object model. It is designed to run commands, particularly those involving parameters, against a data store. Where the commands require parameters, they are typically stored procedures or stored queries. These are basically the same: Jet 4 database supports stored queries, whereas SQL Server and other SQL-based database servers support stored procedures. A Command operation either returns no information, or returns a Recordset object, for example where rows of information are returned.

Using the Command object provides much greater functionality and flexibility than executing commands through the Connection object and gives increased performance by avoiding continual referral to default values. The Command object allows us to specify the exact details (such as datatype and length) of the parameters, as well as use output parameters and return values, which accept values back from the command.

It's not actually a requirement that data providers support the Command object in the ADO model, however where it is supported it proves not only useful, but essential in some areas. For example, when using stored procedures that have output parameters, we have to use a Command object. The Command object's Parameters collection allows the passing of parameters into and out of stored procedures, as well as allowing a recordset to be passed back to the application.

Command Object Members

The Command object exposes the following methods and properties:

Methods	Properties	
Cancel	ActiveConnection	Parameters
CreateParameter	CommandText	Prepared
Execute	CommandTimeout	Properties
	CommandType	State
	Name	

The interface of the Command object allows us to define the operation that the object will execute, the parameters that will be used within the operation, which Connection to associate the command with, and to initiate the operation. The Parameters collection, which contains all of the parameters associated with the command, is accessed through the Parameters property of the Command object.

Command Object Methods

Cancel Method

The Cancel method cancels execution of a pending Execute or Open call.

```
Command.Cancel
```

The Cancel method is particularly important when we allow users to submit their own queries. We use it in the implementation of a Cancel button on screen that the user can press if the execution time is too long. Note that a run-time error will result if we try to cancel an Execute call that was used without the adExecuteAsync option.

CreateParameter Method

The CreateParameter method creates a new Parameter object.

```
Parameter = Command.CreateParameter([Name], [DataType], [Direction],
                                    [Size], [Value])
```

Parameter	Type	Description	Default
Name	String	Optional. Name of parameter.	
DataType	DataTypeEnum (Long)	Optional. Data type of parameter.	adEmpty
Direction	Parameter DirectionEnum (Long)	Optional. Direction of parameter.	adParamInpout
Size	Long	Optional. Maximum length of parameter value in bytes. This can be omitted for fixed length fields.	0
Value	Variant	Optional. Value of parameter.	

The values of the ParamDirectionEnum constants are: adParamUnknown, adParamInput, adParamOutput, adparamInputOutput, and adParamReturnValue. The list of DataTypeEnum constants is quite long. The lists of the constants and their descriptions can be found in Appendix D.

The CreateParameter method is used to create parameters that are passed to stored procedures and stored queries. It can either be used with all of its arguments specified, or without any arguments where these are defined later in the code. We must then manually add our parameter (or parameters) to the Parameters collection using the Parameters.Append method.

The following two VBScript code examples are equivalent:

```
Set objCmd = Server.CreateObject("ADODB.Command")
dbConnection.Open strConnect
objCmd.ActiveConnection = dbConnection
objCmd.CommandType = adCmdStoredProc
objCmd.CommandText = "byroyalty"
Set objParam = objCmd.CreateParameter
objParam.Name = "percentage"
objParam.Type = adInteger
objParam.Direction = adParamInput
objParam.Value = 40
objCmd.Parameters.Append objParam
```

or:

```
Set objCmd = Server.CreateObject("ADODB.Command")
dbConnection.Open strConnect
objCmd.ActiveConnection = dbConnection
objCmd.CommandType = adCmdStoredProc
objCmd.CommandText = "byroyalty"
Set objParam = objCmd.CreateParameter("percentage", adInteger, _
                                      adParamInput, 40)
objCmd.Parameters.Append objParam
```

In JScript these two code snippets look like:

```
objCmd = Server.CreateObject("ADODB.Command");
dbConnection.Open(strConnect);
objCmd.ActiveConnection = dbConnection
objCmd.CommandType = adCmdStoredProc
objCmd.CommandText = "byroyalty"
objParam = objCmd.CreateParameter();
objParam.Name = "percentage";
objParam.Type = adInteger;
objParam.Direction = adParamInput;
objParam.Value = 40;
objCmd.Parameters.Append(objParam);
```

and

```
objCmd = Server.CreateObject("ADODB.Command");
dbConnection.Open(strConnect);
objCmd.ActiveConnection = dbConnection
objCmd.CommandType = adCmdStoredProc
objCmd.CommandText = "byroyalty"
objParam = objCmd.CreateParameter("percentage", adInteger,
                                  adParamInput, 40);
objCmd.Parameters.Append(objParam);
```

Command Object

Alternatively, we can avoid creating the temporary variable that holds a reference to the `Parameter` object and simply apply both functions in one statement using for example in VBScript:

```
' VBScript
objCmd.Parameters.Append objCmd.CreateParameter("percentage", _
                  adInteger, adParamInput, 40)
```

or in JScript:

```
// JScript
objCmd.Parameters.Append(objCmd.CreateParameter("percentage",
                  adInteger, adParamInput, 40));
```

Note that it is important, when adding parameters to the `Parameters` collection, to add them in the same order that they are defined in the stored procedure.

Execute Method

The `Execute` method executes the query, SQL statement, or stored procedure specified in the `CommandText` property.

```
Recordset = Command.Execute([RecordsAffected], [Parameters], [Options])
```

Parameter	Type	Description	Default
RecordsAffected	Long	Optional. This is where the provider returns the number of records affected by the operation.	
Parameters	Variant	Optional. The array of parameter values passed with a SQL statement. (Output parameters will not return correct values if passed here.)	
Options	Long	Optional. This indicates how the provider shoud interpret the `CommandText` property.	-1

The `Execute` method can return its results as a `Recordset` object, or nothing if the work being done doesn't return any information. If a `Recordset` is returned, then it will have a forward-only, read-only cursor. The only way to get other cursor or locking types is to explicitly use a `Recordset` object to gather the data.

The `Execute` method is either used with zero or more optional parameters. For example in its simplest form we can use it with no parameters. For example in VBScript:

```
Set dbConnection = Server.CreateObject("ADODB.Connection")
Set cmdExample = Server.CreateObject("ADODB.Command")
dbConnection.Open strConnect

cmdExample.ActiveConnection = dbConnection
cmdExample.CommandText = strSQL
cmdExample.CommandType = adCmdText
Set rsExample = cmdExample.Execute
```

Or in JScript:

```
dbConnection = Server.CreateObject("ADODB.Connection");
cmdExample = Server.CreateObject("ADODB.Command");
dbConnection.Open(strConnect);

cmdExample.ActiveConnection = dbConnection;
cmdExample.CommandText = strSQL;
cmdExample.CommandType = adCmdText;
rsExample = cmdExample.Execute();
```

The RecordsAffected parameter contains the number of records that were affected by the execution of the command. This only returns a value for stored procedures and action queries, therefore will not be set in a SELECT statement.

The Parameters parameter of the Execute method can contain parameters to be passed to a stored procedure. These values must be stored as an array of variables or scalar values. They will override any values in the Parameters collection. If any of the parameters in the stored procedure are output parameters, then their values will *not* be set properly using this approach. In order to handle parameters in a more robust manner, we must utilize the Parameters collection of the Command object.

The Options parameter can take one of the constants of the CommandText property. This indicates the type of statement to be executed, for example adCmdTable, indicates that the command text is to be interpreted as the name of a table. The Options parameter can also combine execution options using AND or OR. For example we could also add adAsyncExecute to make the command execute asynchronously and adAsyncFetch or adAsyncFetchNonBlocking to make the recordset be returned asynchronously.

Command Object Properties

ActiveConnection Property

The ActiveConnection property indicates the Connection object to which the Command object currently belongs.

```
Command.ActiveConnection = Variant
Variant = Command.ActiveConnection
Command.ActiveConnection = Connection
Connection = Command.ActiveConnection
```

Command Object

The `ActiveConnection` property can be used either with an existing `Connection` object or a connection string. The difference between the two can be seen, for example, in the following code snippets: the first two use an existing `Connection` object, whereas the second two implicitly create a new connection:

```
' VBScript
dbConnection.Open "Provider=SQLOLEDB; Data Source=Test_server; " & _
                  "Initial Catalog=pubs; User ID=sa; Password =;"
cmdExample.ActiveConnection = dbConnection
```

```
// JScript
dbConnection.Open("Provider=SQLOLEDB; " +
                  "Data Source=Test_server; Initial Catalog=pubs;" +
                  "User ID=sa; Password =;");
cmdExample.ActiveConnection = dbConnection;
```

```
' VBScript
cmdExample.ActiveConnection = "Provider=SQLOLEDB; " & _
                 "Data Source=Test_server; Initial Catalog=pubs;" & _
                 "User ID=sa; Password =;"
```

```
// JScript
cmdExample.ActiveConnection = "Provider=SQLOLEDB; " +
                 "Data Source=Test_server; Initial Catalog=pubs;" +
                 "User ID=sa; Password =;";
```

CommandText Property

The `CommandText` property sets or returns the executable text of a command to be issued against a data provider.

```
Command.CommandText = String
String = Command.CommandText
```

The `CommandText` property is a string usually containing either the text of a SQL query or the name of a stored procedure. We can also include a table name or the name of a view. The `CommandText` property functions the same way as the `CommandText` property in the `Recordset` object. See Appendix D for a list of the constants.

For example, to set the command text to a SQL string, we can do the following:

```
' VBScript
objComm.CommandText = "SELECT * FROM contacts WHERE state = 'CA'"
```

```
// JScript
objComm.CommandText = "SELECT * FROM contacts WHERE state = 'CA'";
```

The `CommandText` property can also be used to pass parameters to a stored procedure in SQL Server, by passing the procedure and its arguments as a text command. For example:

```
' VBScript
objCmd.CommandText = "byroyalty (40)"
objCmd.CommandType = adCmdStoredProc
Set rsAuth = objCmd.Execute
```

```
// JScript
objCmd.CommandText = "byroyalty (40)";
objCmd.CommandType = adCmdStoredProc;
rsAuth = objCmd.Execute();
```

Alternatively we can use the `Parameters` argument of the `Execute` method as follows:

```
' VBScript
objCmd.CommandText = "byroyalty"
objCmd.CommandType = adCmdStoredProc
Set rsAuth = objCmd.Execute(,Array(40))
```

```
// JScript
objCmd.CommandText = "byroyalty";
objCmd.CommandType = adCmdStoredProc;
rsAuth = objCmd.Execute(0, 40);
```

CommandTimeout Property

The `CommandTimeout` property sets or returns how long to wait, in seconds, while executing a command before terminating the command and generating an error. The default is 30 seconds.

```
Command.CommandTimeout = Long
Long = Command.CommandTimeout
```

Note: This property bears no relation to the `CommandTimeOut` property of the `Connection` object.

CommandType Property

The `CommandType` property sets or returns the type of `Command` object.

```
Command.CommandType = CommandTypeEnum
CommandTypeEnum = Command.CommandType
```

This is used to optimize the processing of the command to improve the performance of our code. For example if we know that our command will not return any data then we should use the `adExecuteNoRecords` in conjunction with `adCmdText` or `adCmdStoredProc`. See Appendix D for a list of the contents

Name Property

The `Name` property sets or returns the name of the `Command` object.

```
Command.Name = String
String = Command.Name
```

In most cases this won't be used, however it could be used to uniquely identify a `Command` object in a collection of commands.

Command Object

Parameters Property

The Parameters property can be used to access the Parameters collection which contains all of the Parameter objects for a Command object.

```
Parameters = Command.Parameters
```

Prepared Property

The Prepared property sets or returns a boolean value that indicates whether or not to save a compiled version of a command before execution.

```
Command.Prepared = Boolean
Boolean = Command.Prepared
```

Setting the Prepared property to true will cause the data source to save a compiled version of the query after it is run. This is useful if we want to repeat the command several times. Although setting the Prepared property to true, will cause the first execution of the command to be slower, all subsequent executions of the same CommandText will be faster.

> Also see Appendix E for ADO's dynamic properties and how to use them.

Properties Property

The Properties property contains all of the Property objects for a Command object.

```
Properties = Command.Properties
```

State Property

The State property describes whether the Command object is open, closed, executing an asynchronous query, or fetching something.

```
Long = Command.State
```

State can be one of the following constants: adStateClosed, adStateOpen, adStateExecuting, or adStateFetching.

The Parameters Collection and Parameter Object

The Command object is the only way that we can pass explicit parameters to a database operation. This is done by populating the Parameters collection, which is part of the Command object. This collection contains a set of Parameter objects, which represent the various input and output parameters of the stored procedure or query. By using stored procedures with parameters, we can remove nearly all of the native SQL database text from our ASP pages and encapsulate the database logic within the database itself. This allows for a separation of the data manipulation logic from the page display logic in ASP and makes it easy to change the ASP code when we want to refer to a new database.

Parameters Collection

The Parameters collection contains all the Parameter objects for a Command object. There is one element in the collection for each parameter in the stored procedure. Normally this collection is not populated by default by ADO, so we must fill it manually using the Append method (or use the Refresh command).

The Parameters collection exposes the following methods and properties:

Methods	Properties
Append	Count
Delete	Item
Refresh	

Parameters Collection Methods

Append Method

The Append method appends a Parameter object to the Parameters collection.

```
Parameters.Append(Object)
```

Parameter	Type	Description
Object	Parameter	The Parameter object to be appended to Parameters collection.

Once parameters have been created by the CreateParameter method of the Command object, they need to be added to the Parameters collection. This is either achieved using the Append method or using the Refresh method to query the data provider for their details. Although the Append method is more cumbersome to code than the Refresh method, its usage is much more efficient since it minimizes the total number of calls made to the provider.

The following code examples are equivalent:

```
' VBScript
Set objParam = objCmd.CreateParameter
objParam.Name = "percentage"
objParam.Type = adInteger
objParam.Direction = adParamInput
objParam.Value = 40
objCmd.Parameters.Append objParam
```

```
// JScript
objParam = objCmd.CreateParameter();
objParam.Name = "percentage";
objParam.Type = adInteger;
objParam.Direction = adParamInput;
objParam.Value = 40;
objCmd.Parameters.Append(objParam);
```

Command Object

389

We can combine the `CreateParameter` and `Append` methods into a single line of code.

```
' VBScript
objCmd.Parameters.Append objCmd.CreateParameter("percentage", _
                         adInteger, adParamInput, 40)
```

```
// JScript
objCmd.Parameters.Append(objCmd.CreateParameter("percentage",
                         adInteger, adParamInput, 40));
```

Note that before calling the `Append` method we must set the `Type` property of the `Parameter` object.

Delete Method

The `Delete` method deletes a `Parameter` object from the `Parameters` collection.

Parameters.Delete(Parameter)

Parameter	Type	Description
Value	Variant	The name or number of the parameter to be removed from the `Parameters` collection.

The `Parameter` object's index or name can be used to delete it from the `Parameters` collection. Note that we cannot use an object variable.

For example in VBScript:

```
cmdExample.Parameters.Delete("@lolimit")
cmdExample.Parameters.Delete(2)
```

Alternatively in JScript:

```
cmdExample.Parameters.Delete("@lolimit");
cmdExample.Parameters.Delete(2);
```

Refresh Method

The `Refresh` method updates the `Parameter` objects in the `Parameters` collection.

Parameters.Refresh

The `Refresh` method has the effect of querying the provider for the details of the parameters. They can then be accessed by name or index.

The `Refresh` method should only be used when we are willing to accept the performance hit of the provider re-querying the data source for the parameter details. This is particularly inefficient when the same set of parameters is used frequently.

If we do not create our own `Parameters` for a command and access the `Parameters` collection, then ADO will call `Refresh` automatically to fill the collection. A return value is always created as the first parameter, irrespective of whether the command returns a value.

The Refresh method will query into the data source and will populate the Parameters collection with all of the parameters of the stored procedure we are calling. This can be quite powerful when developing an ASP page to work with a specific stored procedure. The drawback with this method is that it requires a lot of data to be transferred between the data source and the ASP page. In a production web site, this would probably be seriously detrimental to the performance of the page. But this does not mean that the Refresh method should not be used at all. Simply write our page to create the Command object, Refresh the parameters, and then output to the browser the detail about each parameter in the collection. Take that output and rewrite our ASP page to call CreateParameter for each parameter, and take out the Refresh method.

Parameters Collection Properties

Count Property

As with other collections, the read-only Count property returns a long integer that gives the number of Parameter objects in the Parameters collection.

```
Long = Parameters.Count
```

Item Property

The read-only Item property allows indexing in the Parameters collection to reference a specific Parameter object.This is the default property of the Parameters collection.

```
Parameter = Parameters.Item(Index)
```

Parameter Object

The Parameter object comprises all the information for a single parameter to be used in a stored procedure or query. They are only used in conjunction with ADO's Command object. Parameter objects are created using the CreateParameter method of the Command object and added to the Parameters collection using the Append method of the collection. It is important to note that parameters should be added to the Parameters collection in the order that they are defined in the stored procedure.

The Parameter object exposes the following methods and properties:

Methods	Properties	
AppendChunk	Attributes	Properties
	Direction	Size
	Name	Type
	NumericScale	Value
	Precision	

Command Object

Parameter Object Methods

The `Parameter` object only exposes one method: `AppendChunk`.

AppendChunk Method

The `AppendChunk` method appends data to a large or binary `Parameter` object.

```
Parameter.AppendChunk(Data)
```

Parameter	Type	Description
Data	Variant	Data to be appended to the `Parameter`.

The first `AppendChunk` call after editing the parameter details writes the data to the parameter, overwriting any existing data. Subsequent `AppendChunk` calls add to this data. The `AppendChunk` method is commonly used to put images into tables.

The `AppendChunk` method of the `Parameter` object is functionally the same as the `AppendChunk` method of the `Field` object, discussed in the `Recordset` chapter. The only difference is that the base object is different.

Parameter Object Properties

The properties of the `Parameter` object allow us to modify or set a parameter's characteristics after it has been created.

Attributes Property

The `Attributes` property indicates one or more characteristics of a `Parameter` object.

```
Parameter.Attributes = ParameterAttributesEnum
ParameterAttributesEnum = Parameter.Attributes
```

Parameter	Type	Description	Default
ParameterAttributes Enum	Long	The characteristics of the `Parameter` object.	adParamSigned

This can be one or more of the following values: `adParamSigned` (the parameter accepts signed values), `adParamNullable` (the parameter accepts null values), and `adParamLong` (the parameter accepts long values such as binary data).

Direction Property

The `Direction` property indicates whether the `Parameter` object represents an input parameter, an output parameter, or both, or whether the parameter is a return value from a stored procedure.

```
Parameter.Direction = ParameterDirectionEnum
ParameterDirectionEnum = Parameter.Direction
```

An example of the use of the `Direction` property , in VBScript is:

```
Select Case parm.Direction
   Case 1
      strDir = "Input"
   Case 2
      strDir = "Output"
   Case 3
      strDir = "Input/Output"
   Case 4
      strDir = "Return"
End Select
Response.Write "The parameter is a " & strDir & "object. <BR>"
```

Or in JScript:

```
switch (parm.Direction) {
   case 1:
      strDir = "Input";
      break;
   case 2:
      strDir = "Output";
      break;
   case 3:
      strDir = "Input/Output";
      break;
   case 4:
      strDir = "Return"
}
Response.Write("The parameter is a" + strDir + "<object. <BR>>");
```

The `Direction` property is identical to the value that can be set during the `CreateParameter` method of the `Command` object. The values of the `ParamDirectionEnum` constants are: `adParamUnknown`, `adParamInput`, `adParamOutput`, `adparamInputOutput`, and `adParamReturnValue`. Further details can be found in Appendix D.

The return value is always the first parameter in the `Parameters` collection and it is named RETURN_VALUE. If we're creating parameters, we'll need to create the return value first. For example in VBScript:

```
objCmd.CreateParameter("RETURN_VALUE", adVarInteger, _
                       adParamReturnValue, 0, lngRetVal)
```

Or in JScript:

```
objCmd.CreateParameter('RETURN_VALUE', adVarInteger,
                       adParamReturnValue, 0, lngRetVal);
```

The return value should be declared as a long integer. Note that if we use `Refresh` to create our parameters, a return value is always created, irrespective of whether the command returns a value.

> **Microsoft Access does not have output parameters or return values.**

Command Object

393

Name Property

The Name property sets and returns the name of the Parameter object.

```
Parameter.Name = String
String = Parameter.Name
```

The Name property can also be set by the CreateParameter method of the Command object. This name does not have to be the same as the name of the parameter in the stored procedure or query; however, keeping the same name makes our code easier to read and maintain.

NumericScale Property

The NumericScale property indicates the number of digits there are to the right of the decimal point of numeric values of the Parameter object.

```
Parameter.NumericScale = Byte
Byte = Parameter.NumericScale
```

Both the NumericScale and the Precision properties are required in order to process SQL numeric data correctly. The NumericScale and Precision properties cannot be set via the CreateParameter method of the Command object. In order to set these values we need to create an explicit Parameter object and set its properties before appending it to the Parameters collection.

Precision Property

The Precision property indicates the degree of precision for numeric values in the Parameter object, i.e. the maximum number of digits that are used to represent a numeric value.

```
Parameter.Precision = Byte
Byte = Parameter.Precision
```

The Precision property, like the NumericScale property, is needed for the correct processing of numeric SQL data. For more information about using the Precision property see the notes on the NumericScale property above.

Size Property

The Size property sets and returns the *maximum* size, in bytes or characters, of a Parameter object.

```
Parameter.Size = Long
Long = Parameter.Size
```

The Size property is identical to the value that can be set during the CreateParameter method of the Command object. There are a few things to note when using the Size property:

- ❑ You must always set the Size for variable-length parameters, so that the provider knows how much space to allocate for the parameter. An error will result if no size is set.

❑   If you use the `Refresh` method to force the provider to fill in the parameter details the maximum size and memory is often allocated for variable-length parameters.

❑   You must be specific about the size of a parameter for binary data. For example if you have a parameter of type image and you `Refresh` the parameters, the size returned is 2147483647. If you create the parameters yourself, use this size, and then `AppendChunk` to add data to the parameter there are no problems – but creating the parameter with the actual size of the binary data doesn't work; this is because `Size` is the maximum size of the parameter, not its actual size.

Type Property

The `Type` property indicates the data type of the `Parameter` object.

```
Parameter.Type = DataTypeEnum
DataTypeEnum = Parameter.Type
```

The `Type` property is identical to the value that can be set during the `CreateParameter` method of the `Command` object. A full list of the `DataTypeEnum` values is shown in Appendix D.

There are a few things to note:

❑   If your parameters are the wrong type they can cause your code to fail.

❑   Date parameters in SQL Server don't map to the obvious `adDate` datatype, but rather to the `adDBTimeStamp` datatype; and the SQL Server `timestamp` datatype maps to `adVarBinary` for SQL Server 6.5 and `adBinary` for SQL Server 7.0.

❑   If you are creating your parameters using `Command.CreateParameters` and have problems matching the correct datatypes or sizes then a simple trick to try is to temporarily call the `Refresh` method and examine the `Parameters` collection using the code below. (Don't forget to remove your `Refresh` once you've sorted out your parameters if you want to avoid the performance hit.)

For example we can iterate through the objects in the `Parameters` collection checking the size and datatype of each parameter as follows:

```
' VBScript
For Each objParam in objCmd.Parameters
    Response.Write "<B>" & objParam.Name & "</B>"
    Response.Write " has size: " & objParam.Size & " "
    Response.Write " and datatype: " & objParam.Type & "<BR>"
Next
```

```
//JScript
enmParm=new Enumerator(cmdExample.Parameters);
while (!enmParm.atEnd()) {
    parm=enmParm.item();
    Response.Write('<B>' + parm.Name + '</B> ');
    Response. Write(' has size: ' + parm.Size + ' ');
    Response. Write(' and datatype: ' + parm.Type + ' <BR>');
    enmParm.moveNext();
}
```

Command Object

Value Property

The Value property indicates the value assigned to the Parameter object.

```
Parameter.Value = Variant
Variant = Parameter.Value
```

When a stored procedure sets a value of a parameter, it will only be read once by ADO from the data source. Depending on the provider, when a recordset is returned, we will need to close that recordset before ADO is able to read the output parameters from the provider. The Value property is the default property for the Parameter object.

Properties Collection and Property Object

The Properties collection contains zero or more Property objects, to indicate the extended properties of the applicable object. The relationship of the properties collection to the ADO object model is shown in the diagram below.

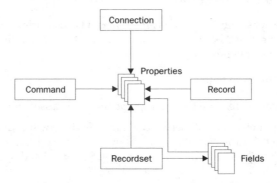

The reason we have a Properties collection in ADO is because it is designed to work with many different data sources, each of which could have different facilities. By making the Properties a collection, it is dynamic, and can therefore change according to the data provider. For example the OLE DB provider for Jet allows us to access the Jet specific security properties. By telling ADO which OLE DB Provider we are using, it can fill in the Properties collection with the default values for the provider.

> **For more information on the** Properties **collection see ADO 2.1**
> **Programmers Reference published by Wrox Press, ISBN 1-861002-68-8**

The following code demonstrates the Properties collection and Property object. In VBScript:

```
<TABLE
border=1><TR><TH>Name</TH><TH>Type</TH><TH>Value</TH><TH>Attributes</TH></TR>
<%
' Properties collection
Response.Write "<B>The Properties collection and Property object</B>
<BR><BR>"
```

```
Response.Write "Props Count = " & cmdExample.Properties.Count & "<BR>"
Response.Write "Props Item(0) = " & cmdExample.Properties.Item(0).Name &
"<BR><BR>"

For Each prop In cmdExample.Properties
   Response.Write "<TR>"
   Response.Write "<TD>" & prop.Name & "</TD>"
   Response.Write "<TD>" & prop.Type & "</TD>"
   Response.Write "<TD>" & prop.Value & "</TD>"
   Response.Write "<TD>" & prop.Attributes & "</TD>"
  Response.Write "</TR>"
Next
Response.Write "</TABLE>"
```

In JScript:

```
<TABLE
BORDER=1><TR><TH>Name</TH><TH>Type</TH><TH>Value</TH><TH>Attributes</TH></TR>
<%

// Properties collection
Response.Write('<B>The Properties collection and Property object</B>
<BR><BR>');

Response.Write('Props Count = ' + cmdExample.Properties.Count + '<BR>');
Response.Write('Props Item(0) = ' + cmdExample.Properties.Item(0).Name +
'<BR><BR>');

enmProp=new Enumerator(cmdExample.Properties);
while (!enmProp.atEnd()) {
   prop=enmProp.item();
   Response.Write('<TR>');
   Response.Write('<TD>' + prop.Name + '</TD>');
   Response.Write('<TD>' + prop.Type + '</TD>');
   Response.Write('<TD>' + prop.Value + '</TD>');
   Response.Write('<TD>' + prop.Attributes + '</TD>');
   Response.Write('</TR>');
   enmProp.moveNext();
}
Response.Write('</TABLE>');
delete enmProp;
```

The screen output looks like this:

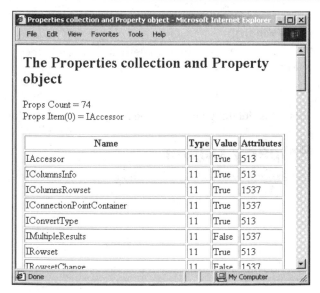

Properties Collection

The Properties collection exposes the following methods and properties.

Methods	Properties
Refresh	Count
	Item

Properties Collection Methods

Refresh Method

The Refresh method updates the Property objects in the Properties collection with the details from the provider.

```
Property = Properties.Refresh
```

This is useful for the Properties collection since the default provider is the OLE DB provider for ODBC. If we have the Provider property of the Connection object (see the next chapter) pointing to a different provider, then we can use the Refresh method to ensure that the properties relate to the relevant provider.

Properties Collection Properties

Count Property

As with other collections, the read-only Count property indicates the number of Property objects in the Properties collection. This can be used to loop through the objects in the collection.

```
Long  = Properties.Count
```

Item Property

The read-only Item property allows indexing into the Properties collection to refer to a specific Property object.

```
Property = Properties.Item(Variant)
```

This is the default property of the Properties collection.

Property Object

The Property object has no methods. It exposes the following properties:

Properties
Attributes
Name
Type
Value

Property Object Properties

Attributes Property

The Attributes property sets or returns one or more characteristics of a Property object.

```
Property.Attributes = PropertyAttributesEnum
PropertyAttributesEnum = Property.Attributes
```

The Attributes can be of one or more of the PropertyAttributesEnum values: adPropNotSupported, adPropRequired, adPropOptional, adPropRead, and adPropWrite. More details can be found in Appendix D.

Name Property

The Name property returns the name of the Property object. This is a read-only property.

```
String = Property.Name
```

Type Property

The Type property returns the data type of the Property object. This is a read-only property.

```
DataTypeEnum = Property.Type
```

For example, the UserID property of a connection has a value of BStr, which indicates a string. See Appendix D for the list of DataTypeEnum constants.

Value Property

The Value property sets or returns the value assigned to the Property object.

```
Property.Value = Variant
Variant = Property.Value
```

Retrieving Output Parameters

The ability to retrieve information from stored procedures in parameters can be extremely useful, however there are a few things to note:

Firstly, not all providers support output values, for example Microsoft Access does not!

Secondly, it is important to establish at what stage we should read the output parameters (whether as soon as the parameter becomes available or only after the recordset has been closed). The reason to watch out for the latter is that ADO will only allow us to read the parameter values once and if the parameter has been read before it may not be available after the recordset is closed.

Command Object

We can check which of the modes our provider supports by examining the OutputParameterAvailability custom property for the connection. This will return one of the three DBPROPVAL_OA constant values: DBPROPVAL_OA_ATEXECUTE, DBPROPVAL_OA_ATROWRELEASE, or DBPROPVAL_OA_NOTSUPPORTED. More details of this can be found in the next chapter and in Appendix D.

We could check these values with code like this: In VBScript:

```
objCmd.ActiveConnection = dbConnection
objCmd.CommandText = "usp_ProcedureWithOutputParam"
objCmd.CommandType = adCmdStoredProc
objCmd.Parameters.Append objCmd.CreateParameter("output_param", _
    adVarChar, adParamOutput,20)
Set rsExample = objCmd.Execute

intParamAvail = dbConnection.Properties("Output Parameter Availability")
' If Parameter not available until recordset is closed
' DBPROPVAL_OA_ATROWRELEASE = 4
If intParamAvail = 4 Then
    rsExample.Close
End If

strOutParam = objCmd.Parameters("output_param")
Response.Write strOutParam
```

Or in JScript:

```
objCmd.ActiveConnection = dbConnection;
objCmd.CommandText = "usp_ProcedureWithOutputParam";
objCmd.CommandType = adCmdStoredProc;
objCmd.Parameters.Append(objCmd.CreateParameter("output_param",
    adVarChar, adParamOutput,20));
rsExample = objCmd.Execute();

intParamAvail = dbConnection.Properties("Output Parameter Availability");
// If Parameter not available until recordset is closed
// DBPROPVAL_OA_ATROWRELEASE = 4
if (intParamAvail == 4) {
    rsExample.Close();
}

strOutParam = objCmd.Parameters("output_param");
Response.Write(strOutParam);
```

A solution to the problem of parameters not being available until the recordset is closed involves the naming of stored procedures using the Name property of the Command object. In VBScript this looks like:

```
objCmd.CommandText = "usp_ProcedureWithOutputParam"
objCmd.CommandType = adCmdStoredProc

Set objParam = _
    objCmd.CreateParameter("output_param", _
    adVarChar, adParamOutput,20)

objCmd.Parameters.Append objParam
objCmd.Name = "StoredProcedureName"
Set objCmd.ActiveConnection = dbConnection

dbConnection.StoredProcedureName
```

Or in JScript:

```
objCmd.CommandText = "usp_ProcedureWithOutputParam";
objCmd.CommandType = adCmdStoredProc;

objParam = objCmd.CreateParameter("output_param",
                          adVarChar, adParamOutput,20);
objCmd.Parameters.Append(objParam);
objCmd.Name = "StoredProcedureName";
objCmd.ActiveConnection = dbConnection;

dbConnection.StoredProcedureName();
```

Examples of Using the Command Object

In this example, we will use the Command object to execute a SQL query. This query will join together two tables in the pubs database and will output the information in a table to the browser.

```
<!-- METADATA TYPE="typelib"
     FILE="C:\Program Files\Common Files\System\ado\msado15.dll" -->

<%
Dim dbConnection, rsExample, strConnect, strSQL, cmdExample
strConnect = Application("DBConnection")
strSQL = "SELECT title, au_lname, price, ytd_sales, pub_id " & _
         "FROM authors INNER JOIN titleauthor " & _
         "ON authors.au_id = titleauthor.au_id INNER JOIN " & _
         "titles ON titleauthor.title_id = titles.title_id;"

Set dbConnection = Server.CreateObject("ADODB.Connection")
Set cmdExample = Server.CreateObject("ADODB.Command")
dbConnection.Open strConnect

cmdExample.ActiveConnection = dbConnection
cmdExample.CommandText = strSQL
cmdExample.CommandType = adCmdText
Set rsExample = cmdExample.Execute

Dim strTable
strTable = rsExample.GetString(adClipString, ,"</TD><TD>", _
                               "</TD></TR>" & vbCrlf & "<TR><TD>")
strTable = left(strTable,len(strTable) - 8)
Response.Write "<TABLE BORDER=1><TR><TD>" & strTable & "</TABLE>"

rsExample.Close
Set cmdExample = Nothing
dbConnection.Close
Set rsExample = Nothing
Set dbConnection = Nothing
%>
```

The JScript version of this is:

```
<%@ LANGUAGE=JScript %>
<!-- METADATA TYPE="typelib"
     FILE="C:\Program Files\Common Files\System\ado\msado15.dll" -->

<%
strConnect = Application("DBConnection");
strSQL = "SELECT title, au_lname, price, ytd_sales, pub_id " +
         "FROM authors INNER JOIN titleauthor " +
         "ON authors.au_id = titleauthor.au_id INNER JOIN " +
         "titles ON titleauthor.title_id = titles.title_id;";
```

Command Object

401

```
dbConnection = Server.CreateObject("ADODB.Connection");
cmdExample = Server.CreateObject("ADODB.Command");
dbConnection.Open(strConnect);

cmdExample.ActiveConnection = dbConnection;
cmdExample.CommandText = strSQL;
cmdExample.CommandType = adCmdText;
rsExample = cmdExample.Execute();

var strTable = rsExample.GetString(adClipString, -1, "</TD><TD>",
                                   "</TD></TR>\n<TR><TD>");
strTable = strTable.substring(0,strTable.length - 8);
Response.Write("<TABLE BORDER=1><TR><TD>" + strTable + "</TABLE>");

rsExample.Close();
delete cmdExample;
dbConnection.Close();
delete rsExample;
delete dbConnection;
%>
```

Our first step is to instantiate our variables. In this example we use a SQL statement that is held in a string, and create a Command object. We create a variable to hold a Recordset, but do not explicitly create a Recordset object. Once we have opened the database connection, we can begin to work with the Command object.

We first have to attach the Command object to the database connection via the ActiveConnection property. We could have passed in the strConnect variable, in which case an implicit Connection object would have been created for this Command object. Since we already have a valid Connection object created and opened, we just use a reference to it. The CommandText property holds the SQL query that we created earlier. Since this is a textual SQL statement, we set the CommandType property to adCmdText.

With all the information on the object properly set, we can call the Execute method. Since this is a SELECT query, the RecordsAffected parameter will not be set, so there is no reason to capture it. This method will return a Recordset object containing the results of the query. We will assign this to the variable rsExample that we declared at the top of the page. ADO has internally created a Recordset object, just like in the Execute method of the Connection object.

Using this Recordset object, we can output the results to the browser as a table using the GetString method of the Recordset object, that returns the Recordset as a string. Once the information is sent back, we can go about closing all of our ADO objects, and then releasing their references before the page ends.

Using the Command Object with Stored Procedures

In this example, we will use the Command object to let us work with a stored procedure. The example comes in two parts. This first part will be a helper page, which will output the information returned by the data provider when the Refresh method is called on the Parameters collection.

```
<!-- METADATA TYPE="typelib"
            FILE="C:\Program Files\Common Files\System\ado\msado15.dll" -->
<%
Dim dbConnection, rsExample, strConnect, cmdExample
strConnect = Application("DBConnection")

Set dbConnection = Server.CreateObject("ADODB.Connection")
Set cmdExample = Server.CreateObject("ADODB.Command")
dbConnection.Open strConnect

cmdExample.ActiveConnection = dbConnection
cmdExample.CommandText = "reptq3"
cmdExample.CommandType = adCmdStoredProc
```

Once we have connected to the database, we will start working with our Command object. It will be attached to the Connection object via the ActiveConnection property. The CommandText value will be set to the name of the stored procedure that we will be calling in the database. In this example, the name of the stored procedure is reptq3 (in the pubs database). We will set the CommandType parameter to indicate this is a stored procedure. You can see from this example that ADO would have no easy way of knowing if the value in CommandText was a table name or a stored procedure. By looking at the CommandType parameter, it is much more efficient for ADO.

```
cmdExample.Parameters.Refresh
%>
<TABLE
border=1><TR><TH>Name</TH><TH>Type</TH><TH>Size</TH><TH>Direction</TH></TR>
<%
For Each parm In cmdExample.Parameters
    Response.Write "<TR>"
    Response.Write "<TD>" & parm.Name & "</TD>"
    Response.Write "<TD>" & parm.Type & "</TD>"
    Response.Write "<TD>" & parm.Size & "</TD>"
    Select Case parm.Direction
        Case 1
            strDir = "Input"
        Case 2
            strDir = "Output"
        Case 3
            strDir = "Input/Output"
        Case 4
            strDir = "Return"
    End Select
    Response.Write "<TD>" & strDir & "</TD>"
    Response.Write "</TR>"
Next
Response.Write "</TABLE>"
```

This part of the example represents the helper code to get and display the set of parameters. The Refresh method will populate the collection from the database. Since this is a standard collection, we can use, for example, the VBScript For Each statement to iterate through each entry in the collection. With each entry, we will output the key properties. The Type property will be returned as a numeric value, but it is a simple matter of looking in the appendix to see which data type the number corresponds to. In the case of the Direction property (where the number of possibilities is much smaller than for the datatype), a short Select Case statement allows the name of the direction to be output instead of the numeric value.

Command Object

403

```
Set cmdExample = Nothing
dbConnection.Close
Set dbConnection = Nothing
%>
```

The JScript equivalent of the above code is:

```
<%@ LANGUAGE="JScript" %>
<!-- METADATA TYPE="typelib"
               FILE="C:\Program Files\Common Files\System\ado\msado15.dll" -->
<%
var dbConnection, rsExample, strConnect, cmdExample;
strConnect = Application("DBConnection");

dbConnection = Server.CreateObject("ADODB.Connection");
cmdExample = Server.CreateObject("ADODB.Command");
dbConnection.Open(strConnect);

cmdExample.ActiveConnection = dbConnection;
cmdExample.CommandText = "reptq3";
cmdExample.CommandType = adCmdStoredProc;
cmdExample.Parameters.Refresh();
%>
<TABLE
border=1><TR><TH>Name</TH><TH>Type</TH><TH>Size</TH><TH>Direction</TH></TR>
<%
enmParm=new Enumerator(cmdExample.Parameters);
while (!enmParm.atEnd()) {
   parm=enmParm.item();
   Response.Write("<TR>");
   Response.Write("<TD>" + parm.Name + "</TD>");
   Response.Write("<TD>" + parm.Type + "</TD>");
   Response.Write("<TD>" + parm.Size + "</TD>");
   switch (parm.Direction) {
     case 1:
        strDir = "Input";
        break;
     case 2:
        strDir = "Output";
        break;
     case 3:
        strDir = "Input/Output";
        break;
     case 4:
        strDir = "Return"
   }
   Response.Write("<TD>" + strDir + "</TD>");
   Response.Write("</TR>");
   enmParm.moveNext();
}
Response.Write('</TABLE>');
delete enmParm;
delete cmdExample;
dbConnection.Close();
delete dbConnection;
%>
```

Our output page displays the details of each parameter required by the stored procedure, so that we can now code our ASP script to add the correct parameters to the Command object:

With the data that is returned from this page, we can set out to write the ASP page that will actually use the stored procedure and display the data returned by it.

```
<!-- METADATA TYPE="typelib"
     FILE="C:\Program Files\Common Files\System\ado\msado15.dll" -->
<%
Dim dbConnection, rsExample, strConnect, cmdExample
strConnect = Application("DBConnectionString")

Set dbConnection = Server.CreateObject("ADODB.Connection")
Set cmdExample = Server.CreateObject("ADODB.Command")
dbConnection.Open strConnect

cmdExample.ActiveConnection = dbConnection
cmdExample.CommandText = "reptq3"
cmdExample.CommandType = adCmdStoredProc
```

The opening part of the example page is exactly the same as the helper page. We have connected to the data source and begun configuration of the Command object. The change comes in the next section, where, instead of calling Refresh, we will populate the Parameters collection manually. It seems like more code, but given the inefficiencies of the Refresh method, it is definitely more efficient. By doing the work ourselves at coding time and not forcing the data provider to do it EVERY time the page is accessed, we will end up with a more efficient running page.

```
cmdExample.Parameters.Append cmdExample.CreateParameter _
                      ("return",adInteger, adParamReturnValue)
cmdExample.Parameters.Append cmdExample.CreateParameter _
                      ("@lolimit", adCurrency, adParamInput)
cmdExample.Parameters.Append cmdExample.CreateParameter _
                      ("@hilimit", adCurrency, adParamInput)
cmdExample.Parameters.Append cmdExample.CreateParameter _
                      ("@type", adVarChar, adParamInput, 12)
```

Based on the information that was returned by our helper page, we will create four parameters. These are created in the same order in which they were displayed on the helper page. The return parameter is always the first parameter in the collection. We have used the same names as were returned by the Refresh method, but this is not a requirement. For each parameter, we define the data type and direction, but not the value.

```
cmdExample.Parameters("@lolimit").Value = 10
cmdExample.Parameters("@hilimit").Value = 20
cmdExample.Parameters("@type") = "psychology"
```

Command Object

We will then set the values of the three input parameters. This shows that we can have one common set of code to initialize the `Parameters` collection, and then set the value of each parameter separately. This is a key advantage of using stored procedures, in that the parameters are very easy to set and to change. Notice that since the `Value` property is the default property of the `Parameter` object, we can omit it as we did when setting the @type parameter.

```
Set rsExample = cmdExample.Execute

Dim strTable
strTable = rsExample.GetString(adClipString, , "</TD><TD>",
                                       "</TD></TR><TR><TD>")
Response.Write "<TABLE BORDER=1><TR><TD>" & strTable & "</TABLE>"
rsExample.Close
Response.Write "Return value = " & _
               cmdExample.Parameters("return").Value
```

After we execute the stored procedure, we can then output the resulting `Recordset` to the browser. Since our stored procedure also had a return value, we want to output that as well. As we mentioned earlier, we have to close the `Recordset` that was returned before we can access any of the returned parameters. This is the case for both return values and output parameters.

```
Set cmdExample = Nothing
dbConnection.Close
Set rsExample = Nothing
Set dbConnection = Nothing
%>
```

Finally, we will close the database connection and release all of our variables before ending the page.

Our output looks, for example, like this, though this obviously depends on the stored procedure we are using:

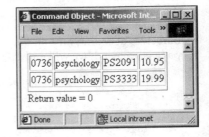

The JScript version of this code is:

```
<%@ LANGUAGE = JScript %>
<!-- METADATA TYPE="typelib"
     FILE="C:\Program Files\Common Files\System\ado\msado15.dll" -->
<%
strConnect = Application("DBConnection");

dbConnection = Server.CreateObject("ADODB.Connection");
cmdExample = Server.CreateObject("ADODB.Command");
dbConnection.Open(strConnect);

cmdExample.ActiveConnection = dbConnection;
cmdExample.CommandText = "reptq3";
cmdExample.CommandType = adCmdStoredProc;
```

```
cmdExample.Parameters.Append(cmdExample.CreateParameter
                            ("return", adInteger, adParamReturnValue));
cmdExample.Parameters.Append(cmdExample.CreateParameter
                            ("@lolimit", adCurrency, adParamInput));
cmdExample.Parameters.Append(cmdExample.CreateParameter
                            ("@hilimit", adCurrency, adParamInput));
cmdExample.Parameters.Append(cmdExample.CreateParameter
                            ("@type", adVarChar, adParamInput, 12));

cmdExample.Parameters("@lolimit").Value = 10;
cmdExample.Parameters("@hilimit").Value = 20;
cmdExample.Parameters("@type") = "psychology";

rsExample = cmdExample.Execute();

strTable = rsExample.GetString(adClipString, -1, "</TD><TD>",
                            "</TD></TR><TR><TD>");
Response.Write("<TABLE BORDER=1><TR><TD>" + strTable + "</TABLE>");
rsExample.Close();
Response.Write("Return value = " +
                cmdExample.Parameters("return").Value);

delete cmdExample;
dbConnection.Close();
delete rsExample;
delete dbConnection;
%>
```

Summary

In this chapter, we examined the ADO Command object, which is designed to run commands, particularly those involving parameters, against a data store. Although many commands can be executed using the Connection object, using the Command object provides much greater functionality and flexibility, and is more efficient. The Command object allows us to specify the exact details (such as datatype and length) of the parameters, as well as use output parameters and return values, which accept values back from the command.

In this chapter, we considered:

❑   The methods and procedures supported by the Command object.

❑   The methods and procedures exposed by the Parameters collection and Parameter object.

❑   The methods and procedures exposed by the Properties collection and Property object.

❑   Examples of using the Command object in ASP pages to execute a SQL query and work with a stored procedure.

Command Object

27

The Connection Object

The Connection object is the hub of ADO, providing the methods that we need to connect to data stores. It is through the Connection object that we can specify which OLE DB provider we wish to use, the security details needed to connect to the data store and other details specific to the datastore.

Although the Connection object is fundamental to ADO and provides the means by which we connect to the data, it is not necessary to create a Connection object explicitly before creating a Command, Recordset or Record object. For example, if we create a Recordset object directly, passing in the connection information, behind the scenes, ADO will automatically create an implicit Connection object for us.

We can create the connection through the Recordset object:

```
' VBScript
Dim strConn, rsData
strConn = Application("DBConnectionString")        'Create a string with the
                                                   'Connection details
Set rsData = Server.CreateObject("ADODB.Recordset") 'Create a Recordset
                                                   'object
rsData.Open "authors", strConn                     'Create an implicit
                                                   'Connection object
```

```
// JScript
var strConn = Application("DBConnectionString");
rsData = Server.CreateObject('ADODB.Recordset');   // Create a Recordset
                                                   // object
rsData.Open('authors', strConn);                   // Create an implicit
                                                   // Connection object
```

It makes sense, however, to use an explicit Connection object if we are going to be creating a number of Command or Recordset objects in our page that connect to the same database. This is because if we rely on ADO to create the connection automatically, then it will open a new connection each time we want to access the recordset, which has major performance implications. By explicitly creating our own Connection object, and providing it to the Command, Recordset, or Record objects that we are using, we need only one connection to the database.

Before we consider the methods and properties exposed by the Connection object, the events it supports, and the associated Errors collection and Error object, we will first take a look at the subject of connecting to data stores.

Connecting to Data Stores

ADO can connect to many different types of data store due to its underlying use of OLE DB as the data provider – the conduit between the data store and the ADO object model. There are different OLE DB providers for the various types of data stores that we can access. When we install the data access components that come with Windows 2000, we are supplied with the following OLE DB providers:

Provider	Description
MSDASQL	OLE DB Provider for ODBC, which allows access to existing ODBC data sources.
Microsoft.Jet.SQLOLEDB.4.0	OLE DB Provider for Jet, for connecting to Microsoft Access databases.
SQLOLEDB	OLE DB Provider for SQL Server.
MSDAORA	OLE DB Provider for Oracle.
MSIDXS	OLE DB Provider for Microsoft Index Server.
ADSDSOObject	OLE DB Provider for Active Directory Services, for connection to the Microsoft Active Directory.
MSDataShape	Data Shape Provider, for connecting to hierarchical recordsets.
MSPersist	Persist, for locally saved recordsets.
MSDAOSP	Simple provider, for creating our own provider for simple text data.
MSDAIPP	OLE DB Provider for Internet Publishing.
MSOLAP	OLE DB Provider for On-Line Analytical Processing – used with ADOMD.

There are several different ways that we can connect to a data source, using:

❑ A **connection string**: this is simply a string which contains the information required by the provider to make a connection to the data source. The advantages are that the details are kept within your ASP page (or pages if you have several pages that access the data). A solution to the problem of maintenance caused by having multiple occurrences of the connection string is to declare this in an ASP include file, or alternatively to store it in an application-scope variable declared in our global.asa file.

❑   A **data link file**: this is a file (with a `.udl` extension) that contains the connection details.

❑   We can connect to ODBC data sources using predefined connection information known as a **DSN** or Data Source Name.

One of the major differences between providers is in the **connection string** used to establish the connection. Each provider has different parameter requirements to connect to the data store. ADO itself only recognises four of these parameters, and passes any other supplied parameters on to the data provider.

We can connect to a relational data source either via the OLE DB Provider for ODBC (e.g. using a DSN), or using a **native provider** (using an OLE DB provider specifically written for the data source in question). Using a native provider, where one is available, is the preferred method since the performance is better. Using ODBC imposes another layer between the ADO and the data source, as is shown by the two sides of the following diagram:

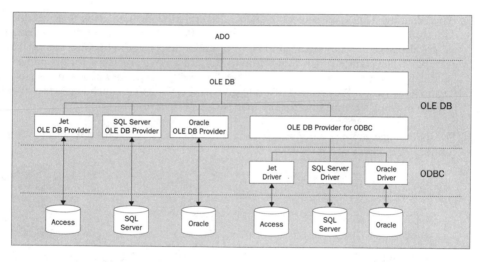

DSN Connections between ADO and Data Stores

To use a DSN to connect to a data source, we first need to create the DSN. This is done using the **ODBC Data Source Administrator** dialog, found under Data Sources (ODBC) in **Administrative Tools**. When we bring this dialog up, the existing DSNs available are displayed, and we are also given the option to add a new DSN. There are a number of types of DSN that we can create, but for use with ASP, we will need to create a System DSN, which is accessible to all users of the system.

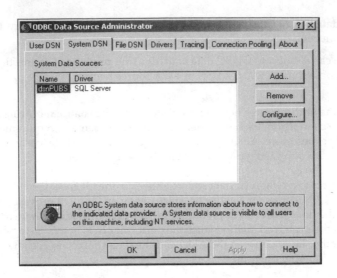

When creating a DSN, we select the ODBC driver that we will be using to access the data store (e.g. the ODBC driver for SQL Server). Based on the type of driver selected, we are also asked to provide additional information to configure the data source. For example, when configuring a connection to SQL Server, we are asked for the name of the database server and the name of the database within SQL Server, as well as a user ID and a password. We are also asked to give the DSN a name which is used to refer to it when opening a connection to the database.

The following example demonstrates how the name dsnPUBS is used when creating a connection to the pubs database via DSN:

```
' VBScript
Dim strDSN, db
'Create a string with the DSN name
strDSN = "dsnPUBS"
Set db = Server.CreateObject("ADODB.Connection")
'Open the DSN connection
db.Open strDSN , "sa", ""
```

```
// JScript
var strDSN = "dsnPUBS";
db = Server.CreateObject("ADODB.Connection");
db.Open(strDSN , "sa", "");
```

Note that when using a DSN to connect to a data store, we will always be using an ODBC connection to that data store. Even if there is a valid OLE DB provider for that data source, the use of a DSN means that we will connect through an ODBC connection. This generally yields slower performance than a DSN-less connection, as we are forcing the database calls through an additional software layer. In fact, using a DSN is also slightly slower than using an ODBC connection with a connection string, since ODBC has to look up the connection information on the hard drive.

Connecting through Native Providers

Using a native provider for a data source is the preferred method for connecting to a data store. We must specify all of the parameters needed to connect to the database that are within the connection string. This means that we will be providing the detailed information necessary to connect to the database directly when we open the connection. The two key pieces of information that we will supply in this string are the database provider name and the location of the data source. The actual contents of the parameters will differ depending on the provider that we are using.

Examples for accessing two different data sources are given at the end of this chapter.

Connection Object Members

The Connection object exposes the following methods, properties and events:

Methods	Properties		Events
BeginTrans	Attributes	Properties	BeginTransComplete
Cancel	CommandTimeout	Provider	CommitTransComplete
Close	ConnectionString	State	ConnectComplete
CommitTrans	ConnectionTimeout	Version	Disconnect
Execute	CursorLocation		ExecuteComplete
Open	DefaultDatabase		InfoMessage
OpenSchema	Errors		RollbackTransComplete
RollbackTrans	IsolationLevel		WillConnect
	Mode		WillExecute

Connection Object Methods

The methods of the Connection object can be grouped into two categories. The first set of methods allows us to work with the Connection object. The second set allows us to interact with the transactional capabilities of ADO and OLE DB. The key methods that we will be working with in ASP are the Open, Close and Execute methods.

Connection Object

BeginTrans Method

The BeginTrans method begins a new transaction or nested transaction.

```
Long = Connection.BeginTrans()
```

A transaction provides atomicity to a series of data changes to a recordset (or recordsets) within a connection, allowing changes to take place either all at once, or not at all. Once a transaction has been started, any changes to a recordset that uses the connection are cached until the transaction is either complete or aborted. At this stage, all of the changes are either written to the data store or discarded.

The return value of the BeginTrans method indicates the level of nested transactions. It will be 1 for a top-level transaction and is incremented by one for each nested transaction.

Not all providers support transactions. This can be checked by checking the "Transaction DDL" property in the Properties collection. For example in VBScript:

```
intSupported = objConnection.Properties("Transaction DDL")
' The "Transaction DDL" property returns 8 (DBPROPVAL_TC_ALL)
' if transactions are fully supported
If intSupported = 8 Then
    objConnection.BeginTrans
End If
```

Or in JScript:

```
intSupported = objConnection.Properties("Transaction DDL");
// The "Transaction DDL" property returns 8 (DBPROPVAL_TC_ALL);
// if transactions are fully supported
if (intSupported == 8) {
    objConnection.BeginTrans();
}
```

See also the CommitTrans and RollbackTrans methods.

Cancel Method

The Cancel method cancels the execution of a pending asynchronous Execute or Open operation.

```
Connection.Cancel()
```

The Cancel method is particularly useful for applications which allow a user to submit a query, so that you can provide a Cancel button which enables the user to stop the query if it is taking too long.

A run-time error results if the Cancel method is called when adRunAsync was not used as one of the Options on the Execute or Open operation.

Close Method

The Close method closes an open connection and any dependant objects.

```
Connection.Close()
```

Note that closing a connection does not remove it from memory. In order to do this we must delete the Connection object. To ensure no error message arises, we may want to check that the connection object is still open before we close it. This is done as follows (in VBScript):

```
If objConnection.State Then
    objConnection.Close
End If
Set objConnection = Nothing
```

Or in JScript:

```
if (objConnection.State) {
    objConnection.Close();
}
delete objConnection
```

When the Close method is used Command objects associated with the connection will persist. Recordset objects may or may not persist, depending whether you used the Save command of the Recordset object. If you call a Close method while there is a transaction in progress, a run-time error is generated.

CommitTrans Method

The CommitTrans method saves any changes and ends the current transaction.

```
Connection.CommitTrans()
```

All changes made since the previous BeginTrans method call will be written to the data source. This only affects the most recently-opened transaction and, as with RollbackTrans, you must resolve lower-level transactions before resolving higher ones.

If the Connection object's Attributes property is set to adXactCommitRetaining, then the provider automatically starts a new transaction.

See also the BeginTrans and RollbackTrans methods.

Connection Object

Execute Method

The Execute method executes the query, SQL statement, stored procedure, or provider-specific text.

```
Recordset = Connection.Execute(CommandText, [RecordsAffected], [Options])
```

Parameter	Type	Description	Default
CommandText	String	This contains the SQL statement, table name, relative URL, stored procedure call or provider-specific text to execute.	
RecordsAffected	Long	This is where the provider returns the number of records affected.	
Options	Long	Optional. This indicates how the provider should interpret the CommandText parameter.	-1 (adCmd Unspecified)

The optional Options parameter can be one or more of the CommandTypeEnum or ExecuteOptionsEnum constants. For more details, see Appendix D. One parameter we can include here is the adExecuteNoRecords parameter, which tells ADO not to create and return a recordset to the caller.

The Recordset object that is returned has a read-only, forward-only cursor associated with it.

The Execute method will execute a SQL query or stored procedure and return a Recordset object.

We can use the Execute method either with or without parameters. For example:

```
' VBScript
Dim strConn, objConnection
Set objConnection = Server.CreateObject("ADODB.Connection")
strConn = Application("DBConnectionString")
objConnection.Open strConn

Dim strSQL, iNumRecords, rsPublishers
strSQL = "SELECT pub_name, city, state, country FROM publishers;"
Set rsPublishers = objConnection.Execute(strSQL, , adCmdText)
'...The recordset now contains the results of the query
```

```
// JScript
objConnection = Server.CreateObject("ADODB.Connection");
strConn = Application("DBConnectionString");
objConnection.Open(strConn);

strSQL = "SELECT pub_name, city, state, country FROM publishers;";
rsPublishers = objConnection.Execute(strSQL, 1, adCmdText);
//...The recordset now contains the results of the query
```

Open Method

The Open method opens a connection to a data source, so that commands can be executed against it.

```
Connection.Open([ConnectionString], [UserID], [Password], [options])
```

Parameter	Type	Description	Default
ConnectionString	String	This is a string value containing connection information.	Empty String (" ")
UserID	String	Optional. User ID for security.	Empty String (" ")
Password	String	Optional. Password.	Empty String (" ")
Options	Long	Optional. Extra connection options.	-1 or adConnectUnspecified (Synchronous operation)

The ConnectionString parameter contains the DSN or DSN-less connection string. The UserID and Password parameters contain any necessary login information for the database. The Options parameter can contain one of the ConnectOptionsEnum constants in Appendix D. An asynchronous connection is defined using adConnectAsych, and adConnectUnspecified indicates that the connection mode is not specified.

We can use an Open method with a connection string that is either defined in the ASP page or, say, as an application variable in global.asa:

```
' VBScript
Dim strConn
strConn = Application("DBConnectionString")    'Create a string with the
                                               'Connection details
rsData.Open "authors", strConn                 'Create an implicit Connection
                                               'object
```

Connection Object

```
// JScript
var strConn = Application("DBConnectionString");    // Create a string with
                                                     // the Connection details
rsData.Open('authors', strConn);                     // Create an implicit
                                                     // Connection object
```

Alternatively, we can just include the details in the Open line:

```
' VBScript
Set objConn = Server.CreateObject("ADODB.Connection")
objConn.Open "Provider=SQLOLEDB; Data Source=julians;" & _
            "Initial Catalog=pubs; User ID=sa; Password="
```

```
// JScript
objConn = Server.CreateObject("ADODB.Connection");
objConn.Open("Provider=SQLOLEDB; Data Source=julians;" +
            "Initial Catalog=pubs; User ID=sa; Password=");
```

OpenSchema Method

The OpenSchema method obtains database schema information from the provider.

```
Recordset = Connection.OpenSchema(Schema, [Restrictions], [SchemaID])
```

Parameter	Type	Description
Schema	SchemaEnum	The type of schema to run.
Restrictions	Variant	An array of query constraints for each schema option.
SchemaID	Variant	The provider-specific schema GUID, if adSchemaProviderSpecific supported.

SchemaEnum is one of a large list of constants given in Appendix D.

This method is most useful for obtaining table and procedure names from a data store:

```
' VBScript
Set objRecSet = objconn.OpenSchema(adSchemaTables)
objRecSet.MoveFirst
Do While Not objRecSet.EOF
    Response.Write objRecSet("TABLE_NAME") & "    "
    Response.Write objRecSet("TABLE_TYPE") & "<BR>"
    objRecSet.MoveNext
Loop
```

```
// JScript
objRecSet = objConn.OpenSchema(adSchemaTables);
objRecSet.MoveFirst();
while (!objRecSet.EOF) {
    Response.Write(objRecSet("TABLE_NAME") + "    ");
    Response.Write(objRecSet("TABLE_TYPE") + "<BR>");
    objRecSet.MoveNext();
}
```

For multi-dimensional providers using adSchemaMembers, the restrictions can either be the columns in the members schema or one of the MDTREEOP constants (see Appendix H). An alternative to obtaining schema information is to use the ADOX library as described in Chapter 32.

RollbackTrans Method

The RollbackTrans method cancels any changes made during the current transaction and ends the transaction.

```
Connection.RollbackTrans
```

All changes made since the previous BeginTrans method call will be canceled. This only affects the most recently opened transaction and, as with CommitTrans, you must resolve lower-level transactions before resolving higher ones.

See also the BeginTrans and CommitTrans methods.

Connection Object Properties

The properties of the Connection object are used to define the characteristics of the connection to the database. Most of the values contained in the connection string are accessible via properties of the Connection object. The key properties of the Connection object that we will use with ASP are the CommandTimeout, CursorLocation, and the ConnectionTimeout properties.

Attributes Property

The Attributes property sets or returns one or more characteristics of a Connection object. The default is zero.

```
Connection.Attributes = Long
Long = Connection.Attributes
```

This indicates the transactional facilities of the Connection object. The returned value is one or more of the adXactAttributes constants: dXactCommitRetaining, dXactAbortRetaining, or a combination of both (using OR) to indicate that a new transaction is started automatically after an existing transaction is finished.

Not all providers support transactions. Also, beware of automatic transaction enlistment when using nested transactions.

CommandTimeout Property

The CommandTimeout property sets or returns how long, in seconds, to wait while executing a command before terminating the command and generating an error. The default is 30 seconds.

```
Connection.CommandTimeout = Long
Long = Connection.CommandTimeout
```

Connection Object

If the timeout period is reached before the command completes execution, then an error is generated and the command is canceled. Setting this to a value of zero forces the provider to wait indefinitely.

For example, the following ensures an error is generated if the command doesn't complete within 10 seconds:

```
objConn.CommandTimeout = 10
```

ConnectionString Property

The ConnectionString property sets or returns the information used to establish a connection to a data source.

```
Connection.ConnectionString = String
String = Connection.ConnectionString
```

ADO supports only the following four arguments for the connection string:

- ❑ Provider – This identifies the provider.

- ❑ FileName – This identifies the name of the provider-specific file containing the connection information (e.g. a UDL).

- ❑ Remote Provider – This is the name of a provider that should be used when opening a client-side connection (only appropriate for RDS).

- ❑ Remote Server – This is the path name for the server that should be used when opening a client-side connection (only appropriate for RDS).

Any additional arguments are ignored by ADO and passed directly to the provider.

You cannot pass both the Provider and FileName arguments. Specifying a FileName will cause ADO to load the provider – the provider details will be stored in this file.

The connection string may be changed by the provider after the connection has been established.

For example in VBScript:

```
Set objConn = Server.CreateObject("ADODB.Connection")
objConn.ConnectionString = "Provider=SQLOLEDB; Data Source=julians;" & _
            "Initial Catalog=pubs; User ID=sa; Password="
objConn.Open
```

Or in JScript:

```
objConn = Server.CreateObject("ADODB.Connection");
objConn.ConnectionString = "Provider=SQLOLEDB; Data Source=julians;" +
            "Initial Catalog=pubs; User ID=sa; Password=";
objConn.Open();
```

ConnectionTimeout Property

The `ConnectionTimeout` property sets or returns how long, in seconds, to wait while establishing a connection before terminating the attempt and generating an error. The default is 15 seconds.

```
Connection.ConnectionTimeout = Long
Long = Connection.ConnectionTimeout
```

A run-time error results if the timeout period is reached before the connection is established. Setting this property to zero forces the provider to wait indefinitely.

This property cannot be changed once a connection has been opened.

CursorLocation Property

The `CursorLocation` property determines whether a client-side or a server-side cursor will be used. Cursors are discussed in more detail in Chapter 29.

```
Connection.CursorLocation = CursorLocationEnum
CursorLocationEnum = Connection.CursorLocation
```

`CursorLocationEnum` is one of the following constants:

- ❏ `adUseClient`. The OLE DB Client Cursor Engine will be used.

- ❏ `adUseServer`. The data source's cursor service will be used.

- ❏ `adUseNone`. No cursor service will be used.

See Appendix D for more information. There is also a constant `adUseClientBatch`, which has the same value as `adUseClient`, and is supported for backwards compatibility only. The default is `adUseServer`, which indicates a cursor on the database server.

The `Recordset` object created against the `Connection` object will inherit the `CursorLocation` set by the `Connection` object. A disconnected recordset can only be achieved by setting the `CursorLocation` property to `adUseClient`. Changing this property has no effect on existing connections.

DefaultDatabase Property

The `DefaultDatabase` property sets or returns a default database for a `Connection` object.

```
Connection.DefaultDatabase = String
String = Connection.DefaultDatabase
```

You can access objects in other databases by fully qualifying the objects, if the data source or provider supports this.

Connection Object

For example in VBScript:

```
Set objConn = Server.CreateObject("ADODB.Connection")
objConn.Open "Provider=SQLOLEDB; Data Source=julians;" & _
             "User ID=sa; Password="
objConn.DefaultDatabase = "pubs"

Set rsData = Server.CreateObject("ADODB.Recordset")
rsData.open "authors", objConn ,adOpenStatic, adLockReadOnly, adCmdTable

Set rsData2 = Server.CreateObject("ADODB.Recordset")
rsData2.open "Northwind..Orders", objConn ,adOpenStatic, adLockReadOnly, _
             adCmdTable
```

Or in JScript:

```
objConn = Server.CreateObject("ADODB.Connection");
objConn.Open("Provider=SQLOLEDB; Data Source=julians;" +
             "User ID=sa; Password=");
objConn.DefaultDatabase = "pubs";

rsData = Server.CreateObject("ADODB.Recordset");
rsData.open("authors", objConn ,adOpenStatic, adLockReadOnly, adCmdTable);

rsData2 = Server.CreateObject("ADODB.Recordset");
rsData2.open("Northwind..Orders", objConn ,adOpenStatic, adLockReadOnly,
             adCmdTable);
```

Errors Property

The Errors property contains all of the Error objects created in response to a single failure involving the provider.

```
Errors = Connection.Errors
```

IsolationLevel Property

The IsolationLevel property sets or returns the level of transaction isolation for a Connection object.

```
Connection.IsolationLevel = IsolationLevelEnum
IsolationLevelEnum = Connection.IsolationLevel
```

IsolationLevelEnum is one of the following constants:

❑ adXactUnspecified. The provider cannot determine the isolation level of the transaction.

❑ adXactChaos. A higher-level transaction has control over the records, and pending changes from another user cannot be overwritten.

❑ adXactBrowse or adXactReadUncommited. Uncommitted changes in another transaction may be viewed.

❑ adXactCursorStability or adXactReadCommitted. Changes in other transactions can only be viewed once they have been committed.

❑ adXactRepeatableRead. Changes in other transactions may only be viewed if the recordset is requeried.

❑ adXactIsolated or adXactSerializable. Transactions are completely isolated from each other.

See Appendix D for more information. The default is adXactReadCommitted.

Mode Property

The Mode property indicates the available permissions for modifying data in a Connection.

```
Connection.Mode = ConnectModeEnum
ConnectModeEnum = Connection.Mode
```

ConnectModeEnum is one of the following constants:

❑ adModeUnknown. Permissions cannot be determined.

❑ adModeRead. Read-only permissions.

❑ adModeWrite. Write-only permissions.

❑ adModeReadWrite. Read-write permissions.

❑ adModeShareDenyRead. Other users are prevented from opening a connection with read permissions.

❑ adModeShareDenyWrite. Other users are prevented from opening a connection with write permissions.

❑ adModeShareExclusive. Other users are prevented from opening a connection.

❑ adModeShareDenyNone. Other users are prevented from opening a connection with any permissions.

See Appendix D for more information.

You can use this property to set or return the provider access permission for the current connection. The property can't be set on open connections.

Properties Property

The Properties property returns the Properties collection containing all of the Property objects for a Connection object.

```
Properties = Connection.Properties
```

Provider Property

The Provider property sets or returns the name of the OLE DB provider for a Connection object.

```
Connection.Provider = String
String = Connection.Provider
```

Connection Object

423

This can also be set in the `ConnectionString` property.

If no provider is specified, then the default is `MSDASQL`, the Microsoft OLE DB Provider for ODBC. See the list at the start of this chapter for the providers supplied with the Windows 2000 data access components. Note that specifying the provider in more than one place may have unexpected results.

State Property

The read-only `State` property describes whether the `Connection` object is open or closed.

```
Long = Connection.State
```

This is one of the `ObjectStateEnum` constants, `adStateOpen` or `adStateClosed`.

For example in VBScript:

```
If objConn.State = adStateOpen Then
    objConn.Close
End If
```

Or in JScript:

```
if (objConn.State == adStateOpen) {
    objConn.Close();
}
```

Version Property

The `Version` property is a read-only property that returns the ADO version number.

```
String = Connection.Version
```

The version number of the provider can be obtained from the `Connection` objects `Properties` collection.

Connection Object Events

We provide a list of these events for completeness. COM events cannot be used by ASP.

Name	Description
`BeginTransComplete`	This event fires after a `BeginTrans` operation finishes executing.
`CommitTransComplete`	This event fires after a `CommitTrans` operation finishes executing.
`ConnectComplete`	This event fires after a connection starts.

Name	Description
Disconnect	This event fires after a connection ends.
ExecuteComplete	This event fires after a command has finished executing.
InfoMessage	This event fires whenever a ConnectionEvent operation completes successfully and additional information is returned by the provider.
RollbackTransComplete	This event fires after a RollbackTrans operation finished executing.
WillConnect	This event fires before a connection starts.
WillExecute	This event fires before a pending command executes on the connection.

Error Object

Error Object

Each Error object contains a set of properties that describe the error. The provider generates these errors, as an ADO error will generate a run-time error within the ASP page.

The Error object exposes the following properties:

Properties	
Description	Number
HelpContextID	Source
HelpFile	SQLState
NativeError	

Error Object Properties

Description Property

The Description property returns a string associated with the error. It is a read-only property.

```
String = Error.Description
```

This is the default property of the Error object, so the .Description can be omitted from the code.

HelpContextID Property

The `HelpContextID` property returns the `ContextID` in the help file for the associated error. It is a read-only property.

```
Long = Error.HelpContextID
```

HelpFile Property

The `HelpFile` property returns a string with the name of the help file. It is a read-only property.

```
String = Error.HelpFile
```

NativeError Property

The `NativeError` property returns a long integer that indicates the provider-specific error code for the associated error. It is a read-only property.

```
Long = Error.NativeError
```

Number Property

The `Number` property returns the number that uniquely identifies an `Error` object. It is a read-only property.

```
Long = Error.Number
```

Source Property

The `Source` property returns a string that is the name of the object or application that originally generated the error. It is a read-only property.

```
String = Error.Source
```

SQLState Property

The `SQLState` property returns a string that indicates the SQL state for a given `Error` object. It is a five-character string that follows the ANSI SQL standard. The `SQLState` property is a read-only property.

```
String = Error.SQLState
```

Example of Using the Error Object

We can find out information about an error as follows. In VBScript this looks like:

```
<%
On Error Resume Next
Set objConn = Server.CreateObject("ADODB.Connection")
objConn.Open "Provider=SQLOLEDB; Data Source=myserver;" & _
             "Initial Catalog=pubs; User ID=Fred; Password="
```

```
Response.Write objConn.Errors(0).Description & "<BR>"
Response.Write objConn.Errors(0).NativeError & "<BR>"
Response.Write objConn.Errors(0).Number & "<BR>"
Response.Write objConn.Errors(0).Source & "<BR>"
Response.Write objConn.Errors(0).SQLState & "<BR>"
%>
```

In JScript this looks like:

```
<%@ LANGUAGE=JScript %>
<%
try {
objConn = Server.CreateObject("ADODB.Connection");
objConn.Open("Provider=SQLOLEDB; Data Source=myserver;" +
          "Initial Catalog=pubs; User ID=Fred; Password=");
}

catch(e) {
Response.Write(objConn.Errors(0).Description + "<BR>");
Response.Write(objConn.Errors(0).NativeError + "<BR>");
Response.Write(objConn.Errors(0).Number + "<BR>");
Response.Write(objConn.Errors(0).Source + "<BR>");
Response.Write(objConn.Errors(0).SQLState + "<BR>");
}
%>
```

The screen output looks like this: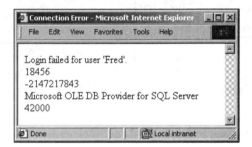

Errors Collection

The Errors collection is a set of the Error objects that are created in response to a single failure involving the connection to the data source. This collection is cleared before it is populated whenever an ADO operation generates an error. This collection can contain warnings and status messages as well as errors, so we should not rely on checking for entries in this collection to see if errors have occurred in an ADO operation. We need to check each Error object individually.

The Errors collection exposes the following methods and properties:

Methods	Properties
Clear	Count
Refresh	Item

Connection Object

We can iterate through the `Errors` collection as follows. For example in VBScript:

```
For Each objErr In objConn.Errors
    Response.Write objErr.Number & " " & objErr.Description
Next
```

Or in JScript:

```
enmErr = new Enumerator(objConn.Errors);
while (!enmErr.atEnd()) {
    objErr=enmErr.item();
    Response.Write(objErr.Number + ' ' + objErr.Description);
}
```

Errors Collection Methods

Clear Method

The `Clear` method removes all of the `Error` objects from the `Errors` collection.

```
Errors.Clear
```

Refresh Method

The `Refresh` method updates the `Error` objects with information from the provider.

```
Errors.Refresh
```

Errors Collection Properties

Count Property

The read-only `Count` property indicates the number of `Error` objects in the `Errors` collection.

```
Long = Errors.Count
```

Item Property

The read-only `Item` property allows indexing into the `Errors` collection to reference a specific `Error` object.

```
Error = ErrorsCol.Item(Variant)
```

Examples of Using the Connection Object

Now that we have looked at the various properties and methods of the Connection object and its associated objects, we will consider some examples that show how to use the Connection object from within an ASP page.

Connecting to Jet 4 (Microsoft Access)

To connect to a Microsoft Access or Jet 4 database using a connection string, we will use a string such as:

```
Provider=Microsoft.OLEDB.4.0; Data Source=filepath; User ID=userID;
Password=password;
```

Where the parameters are:

Parameter	Usage
Provider	For Access or Jet 4 databases, this parameter is Microsoft.OLEDB.4.0.
Data Source	This parameter indicates the physical path to the .MDB file that contains the database to connect to. We do not need to specify an Initial Catalog or Database parameter, since an .MDB file can only contain one Access database.
User ID	The user ID passed to the database when the connection is opened.
Password	The password associate with the User ID to validate access to the database.

In this example, we are connecting to the standard Northwind database, stored in the nwind.mdb file. Using VBScript, this looks like:

```
<%
Dim strConn
Dim objConnection
Set objConnection = Server.CreateObject("ADODB.Connection")
strConn = "Provider=Microsoft.Jet.OLEDB.4.0; " & _
          "Data Source= C:\Program Files\Microsoft Visual
Studio\VB98\NWIND.MDB"
objConnection.Open strConn

Dim rsData
Set rsData = Server.CreateObject("ADODB.Recordset") 'Create a Recordset
                                                     'object
rsData.Open "Customers", objConnection

rsData.MoveFirst
do While Not rsData.EOF
   Response.Write rsData(1) & "<BR>"
   rsData.MoveNext
Loop
%>
```

Or with JScript:

```
<%
objConnection = Server.CreateObject("ADODB.Connection");
strConn = "Provider=Microsoft.Jet.OLEDB.4.0; " +
          "Data Source=C:\\Program Files\\Microsoft " +
          "Visual Studio\\VB98\\NWIND.MDB"
objConnection.Open(strConn);

rsData = Server.CreateObject("ADODB.Recordset");
rsData.Open("Customers", objConnection);

rsData.MoveFirst();
while (!rsData.EOF) {
   Response.Write(rsData(1) + "<BR>");
   rsData.MoveNext();
}
%>
```

The primary difference in this example is in the connection string. We will be using an OLE DB provider to connect to the Access database. Note that the `Data Source` parameter is a physical path, not a virtual path. If we wanted to use a virtual path to the database, we would need to use the `Server.MapPath` to convert the virtual path to a physical path. By dynamically creating the physical path to the database file, it makes it much easier to move the ASP application from server to server. For example in VBScript:

```
strConn = "Provider=Microsoft.Jet.OLEDB.4.0; Data Source=" & _
          Server.MapPath("/data/nwind.mdb")
objConnection.Open strConn
```

Or in JScript:

```
strConn = "Provider=Microsoft.Jet.OLEDB.4.0; Data Source=" +
          Server.MapPath("/data/nwind.mdb");
objConnection.Open(strConn);
```

Connecting to SQL Server

To connect to a SQL Server or MSDE database using a native provider, we can use the following connection string. (MSDE, the Microsoft Data Engine, is a free, but limited, version of the SQL Server database engine.)

```
Provider=SQLOLEDB; Data Source=serverName; Initial Catalog=databaseName; User
ID=userID; Password=password;
```

Where the parameters are:

Parameter	Description
Provider	This parameter is used to indicate the name of the OLE DB provider. To access SQL Server, this will be SQLOLEDB.
Data Source	The server where the database resides. It can be a machine name, a valid DNS name, IP address, or (local) which indicates the current machine.

Parameter	Description
Initial Catalog	The name of the database within SQL Server to connect to. This can also be passed as the Database parameter.
User ID	The user ID passed to the database when the connection is opened.
Password	The password associate with the UID to validate access to the database.

In this example, we open a connection to a SQL Server database. We are interested in opening the pubs database on that server, a machine called MYSERVER. In VBScript this looks like:

```
<%
Dim strConn
Dim objConnection
Set objConnection = Server.CreateObject("ADODB.Connection")
strConn = "Provider=SQLOLEDB; Data Source=MYSERVER; " & _
          "Initial Catalog=pubs; User ID=sa; Password="
objConnection.Open strConn

Dim rsData
Set rsData = Server.CreateObject("ADODB.Recordset") 'Create a Recordset
object
rsData.Open "titles", objConnection

rsData.MoveFirst
do While Not rsData.EOF
   Response.Write rsData(1) & "<BR>"
   rsData.MoveNext
Loop
%>
```

And in JScript it looks like:

```
<%@ LANGUAGE = JScript %>
<%
objConnection = Server.CreateObject("ADODB.Connection");
strConn = "Provider=SQLOLEDB; Data Source=MYSERVER; " +
          "Initial Catalog=pubs; User ID=sa; Password=";
objConnection.Open(strConn);

rsData = Server.CreateObject("ADODB.Recordset");
rsData.Open("titles", objConnection);

rsData.MoveFirst();
while (!rsData.EOF) {
   Response.Write(rsData(1) + "<BR>")
   rsData.MoveNext();
}
%>
```

Connection Object

This connection string is again the only change to the example. We can begin to see the advantages of ADO, in that we are connecting to two completely different databases, yet all we have to do is change one string and everything else stays the same. Note that with SQL Server, we pass in a user ID and password, so all access using this connection will be accomplished using the rights of the sa database user, which in this example has no password.

Using a Global Connection String

One advantage of using OLE DB connections to data sources is that OLE DB has built-in connection pooling. This means that when connections are closed, instead of being destroyed they are returned to a 'pool' of available connections. If an identical connection is required later, an existing connection can be taken from this pool, without the need for the creation of a new connection. One requirement of connection pooling is that, in order for a connection to be reused, it can only be reused following a request for the exact same connection. The easiest way to ensure this in an ASP application is to store the connection string in only one place. An application-level variable is a convenient place to store this.

In our ASP application's global.asa file, we add this entry to the Application_OnStart method. Using VBScript this looks like:

```
Sub Application_OnStart
    ' ... Any existing code
    Application.Lock
    Application("DBConnectionString") = "Provider=SQLOLEDB; " & _
                "Data Source=MYSQLSERVER; Database=pubs; User ID=sa"
    Application.Unlock
End Sub
```

Alternatively using JScript we have:

```
function Application_OnStart() {
    Application.Lock();
    Application("DBConnectionString") = "Provider=SQLOLEDB; " +
                "Data Source=julians; Initial Catalog=pubs; " +
                "User ID=sa; Password=";
    Application.Unlock();
}
```

Then we can use this when we open a database connection. For example in VBScript:

```
<%
Dim strConn
Dim objConnection
Set objConnection = Server.CreateObject("ADODB.Connection")
strConn = Application("DBConnectionString")
objConnection.Open strConn
%>
```

Or in JScript:

```
<%
objConnection = Server.CreateObject('ADODB.Connection');
var strConn = Application('DBConnectionString');
objConnection.Open(strConn);
%>
```

Note that we don't need to lock the Application object when we retrieve the value, since we are only reading and not changing its value. If we store our connection string in this way then, if we ever need to change the connection information for the database, we only have to change it in one place.

Executing a SQL Query

One of the most common uses of the Connection object is to use its Execute method to perform database operations without having explicitly to create a Recordset or Command object. In this example, we will show how to issue a SQL SELECT query that returns a Recordset object containing the results of the query. We will also execute a DELETE query against the database, which will not return anything to the caller. In VBScript this looks like:

```
<%
Dim strConn
Dim objConnection
Set objConnection = Server.CreateObject("ADODB.Connection")
strConn = Application("DBConnectionString")
objConnection.Open strConn

Dim strSQL, iNumRecords, rsPublishers
strSQL = "SELECT pub_name, city, state, country FROM publishers;"
Set rsPublishers = objConnection.Execute(strSQL, , adCmdText)
' ...The recordset now contains the results of the Query

strSQL = "DELETE FROM publishers WHERE country = 'England';"
objConnection.Execute strSQL, , adExecuteNoRecords
%>
```

Alternatively, in JScript we have:

```
<%@ LANGUAGE=JScript %>
<%
objConnection = Server.CreateObject("ADODB.Connection");
var strConn = Application("DBConnectionString");
objConnection.Open(strConn);

var strSQL = "SELECT pub_name, city, state, country FROM publishers;";
rsPublishers = objConnection.Execute(strSQL,1, adCmdText);
// ...The recordset now contains the results of the Query

var strSQL = "DELETE FROM publishers WHERE country = 'England';";
objConnection.Execute(strSQL, 1, adExecuteNoRecords);
%>
```

As we saw in the previous example, we use the global connection string stored in an application-level variable. The first example performs a SQL SELECT statement against the database, and any information returned by that statement would be represented by the Recordset object referred to by rsPublishers. Since the operation being performed consists of a SQL text query, we have set the Options parameter to adCmdText. The component could figure out on its own that this was a text query, but by explicitly setting the Option parameter, we avoid any ambiguity.

The second part of the example shows a different type of query. The DELETE query will delete each row from the database table in which the WHERE clause is true. This type of query does not return any information, so the operation is not part of a SET statement. By default, ADO will create an empty recordset while performing its processing. This can cause an unnecessary drain on system resources. To indicate that we do not want a recordset to be created, we have set the Options parameter to adExecuteNoRecords. Note that we are not interested in the second parameter, so we have left a place for it by placing two commas next to each other. Since VBScript does not have named parameters, we need to indicate an optional parameter in this manner.

Summary

In this chapter, we have considered the ADO Connection object. As mentioned in our introduction, the Connection object is the hub of ADO, providing the methods that we need to connect to data stores. It is through the Connection object that we can specify which OLE DB provider we wish to use, the security details needed to connect to the data store, and other details specific to the datastore.

We have looked at:

❑   ODBC connections using a DSN.

❑   DSN-less connections including accessing SQL Server using OLE DB and Accessing Microsoft Access using OLE DB.

❑   The methods and properties of the Connection object.

❑   The methods and properties of the Errors collection and Error object.

❑   Some examples of using the Connection object.

28

The Record Object

The Record object (along with the Stream object) was introduced with ADO 2.5 for dealing with semi-structured data stores such as mail systems and file systems. These non-relational data stores generally have a hierarchical structure, like a directory tree, where each level of the tree can have a mixture of different types of object, for example both files *and* subfolders in the case of a file system. This makes such semi-structured material difficult to map onto a Recordset (which assumes the data is arranged neatly in rows and columns, where each row has exactly the same columns as the other rows), or even a series of nested Recordsets which assumes all objects within it are the same type.

The Record object enables us to access our data in spite of the complexity of a semi-structured data store. For a directory system, we have a collection of entries at each level, with some properties in common, but with each entry also having unique properties. With the introduction of the Record object, we map the collection to a Recordset, and each individual entry to a Record object, whose properties are described by the Fields collection.

Like the Recordset and Command objects, the Record object can either be used with an existing connection, or with a Connection object created implicitly by ADO when the Record is opened. Given that these non-relational types of data exist in data sources outside traditional databases, ADO is now supplied with a new data provider for Internet Publishing (this was first shipped with ADO 2.1, but the version shipped with ADO 2.5 has much increased functionality). This provider gives us a new way of referring to the data source: instead of specifying a DSN or OLE DB connection string, we can now use a URL to specify a data source.

Each Record contains a Fields collection that contains a set of Field objects. These Field objects can include representation of the data itself, for example the columns of a Recordset row, and also information supplied by the data provider.

Note that with the initial release of Windows 2000, the only use of the Record object is with the OLE DB Provider for Internet Publishing. When Microsoft Exchange 2000 ships, there will be an OLE DB Provider that will offer access to the Exchange Information Store in a similar method, using recordsets and records.

> Note that many people have experienced security problems using the
> Record object from ASP. We can work around this problem by
> adding the IUSR_*MachineName* user account to the Administrators
> group, but this should not be done on a live web server.

WebDAV

WebDAV (Web Distributed Authoring and Versioning) is a W3C standard that
extends HTTP 1.1 to include a set of new commands allowing the management of web
resources. With WebDAV built into your web server, you automatically get a new set
of functions for managing web resources. These functions support the retrieval of
properties, the updating of properties, the creation of new collections, and the copying
and moving of resources within a namespace.

The real problem of course, is how you use these new functions. First, you need IIS5,
which fully supports the standard. Second, you need a client to make these command
requests, and since not many people use HTTP commands directly, Microsoft has
created the OLE DB Provider for Internet Publishing. The whole idea behind this
provider is that it's built on top of WebDAV, and uses the native HTTP commands.
The great advantage of this is that you don't have to learn how to do all that nasty
HTTP stuff, because ADO does it all for you.

The Internet Publishing Provider is designed to manage resources on a web site. So we
are talking about files and directories, and a Record points at an individual file or
directory. The contents of a single directory (that is the files and directories directly
under it) can be managed in a Recordset. The easy way to think of this is that a
single item is a Record and a collection of items is a Recordset.

> More information about WebDAV can be found at
> http://www.webDAV.org and
> http://www.ics.uci.edu/pub/ietf/webdav/.

Record Object Members

The Record object exposes the following methods and properties:

Methods		Properties	
Cancel	GetChildren	ActiveConnection	Properties
Close	MoveRecord	Fields	RecordType
CopyRecord	Open	Mode	Source
DeleteRecord		ParentURL	State

The Record object also exposes the Fields collection that has a set of Field objects.
As with the Recordset object, the Fields collection enables us to examine some of
the properties of our Record object.

Record Object Methods

Cancel Method

The `Cancel` method cancels the execution of an asynchronous method (i.e. `CopyRecord`, `DeleteRecord`, `MoveRecord`, or `Open`).

```
Record.Cancel()
```

This is useful when we allow users to submit their own queries, as it enables us to give them a way to cancel the query if it is taking too long. A runtime error will result if we try to use the cancel method on a record that is not asynchronous.

Close Method

The `Close` method closes the open record and releases the associated data and any exclusive access rights.

```
Record.Close()
```

Closing a record does not delete it from memory, therefore we should do this explicitly. Also, to avoid any errors, you should check that the record is open before closing it:

```
' VBScript
If objRec.State = adStateOpen Then
   objRec.Close
End If
Set objRec = Nothing
```

```
// JScript
if (objRec.state == adStateOpen) {
   objRec.close();
}
delete objRec;
```

CopyRecord Method

The `CopyRecord` method copies the file or directory represented by the `Record` object, from one location to another.

```
String = Record.CopyRecord([Source], [Destination], [UserName],
                        [Password], [Options], [Async])
```

Where the parameters are as follows:

Parameter	Type	Description	Default
Source	String	The URL of the source file. If blank then the Record object becomes the source.	An empty string
Destination	String	The URL of the destination file.	An empty string

Table Continued on Following Page

Parameter	Type	Description	Default
UserName	String	Optional. The user name for connecting to the destination URL.	
Password	String	Optional. The password for connecting to the destination URL.	
Options	CopyRecords OptionsEnum	Optional. This specifies extra options for the CopyRecord method. It can take the constants adCopyOverWrite, adCopyNonRecursive, or adCopyAllowDataLoss. See Appendix D for more details.	adCopyUns pecified
Async	Boolean	If this is true then CopyRecord executes asynchronously.	false

The CopyRecord method returns a string, which depends on the provider, but is typically the destination URL. A run-time error will result if the source and destination are the same.

DeleteRecord Method

The DeleteRecord method deletes a file or directory and subdirectories.

```
Record.DeleteRecord([Source], [Async])
```

Where the parameters are:

Parameter	Type	Description	Default
Source	String	The URL of the source file. An empty string deletes the file or directory represented by the record itself.	An empty string
Async	Boolean	If this is true then DeleteRecord executes asynchronously.	false

GetChildren Method

The GetChildren method opens a Recordset whose rows contain information about the files and directories within a directory that is represented by the Record object.

```
Record.GetChildren
```

The provider itself determines the information that is contained in the fields of the recordset.

For example in VBScript:

```
Set objRec= Server.CreateObject("ADODB.Record")
objRec.Open "", "URL=http://localhost/"
Set rsChildren = objRec.GetChildren
```

Or in JScript:

```
objRec= Server.CreateObject("ADODB.Record");
objRec.Open("", "URL=http://localhost/");
rsChildren = objRec.GetChildren();
```

MoveRecord Method

The MoveRecord method moves the object represented by the Record object, or a file or directory and subdirectories, from one location to another.

```
String = Record.MoveRecord([Source], [Destination], [UserName], [Password],
                           [Options], [Async])
```

Where the parameters are as follows:

Parameter	Type	Description	Default
Source	String	The URL of the source file. If blank then the Record object becomes the source.	An empty string
Destination	String	The URL of the destination file.	An empty string
UserName	String	Optional. The user name for connecting to the destination URL.	
Password	String	Optional. The password for connecting to the destination URL.	
Options	Copy Records Options Enum	Optional. This specifies extra options for the CopyRecord method. It can take the constants adCopyOverWrite, adCopyNonRecursive, or adCopyAllowDataLoss. See Appendix D for more details.	adCopy Unspecified
Async	Boolean	If this is true then CopyRecord executes asynchronously.	false

Record Object

Open Method

The Open method opens an existing file or directory or creates a new one.

```
Record.Open([Source], [ActiveConnection], [Mode], [CreateOptions], [Options],
[UserName], [Password])
```

Where the parameters are:

Parameter	Type	Description	Default
Source	Variant	This is the URL of the file or directory represented by the Record object, or a row of an open Recordset object.	An empty string
Active Connection	Variant	This is the connection string, or Connection object.	An empty string
Mode	Connect ModeEnum	This can be one or more of the connection modes for the Record object. See Appendix D for the list of constants.	adMode Unknown
Create Options	RecordCreate OptionsEnum	This specifies whether to open an existing directory/file or create a new one when the Record object opens. See Appendix D for the list of constants.	adFailIfNot Exists
Options	RecordOpen OptionsEnum	This can specify one or more extra options used when the Record is opened. See Appendix D for the list of constants.	adOpenRecord Unspecified
UserName	String	The user name for secure connections.	
Password	String	The password for secure connections.	

The first step in working with a Record object is to open it. Normally only the first two parameters are used in the Open method. The simplest use of the Open method is to open either a single file or a directory. For example code to open a virtual directory on the server would look like the following in VBScript:

```
Set objRec = Server.CreateObject("ADODB.Record")
objRec.Open "", "URL=http://localhost/ADO"
```

Or in JScript:

```
objRec = Server.CreateObject('ADODB.Record');
objRec.Open('', 'URL=http://localhost/ADO');
```

This opens the Record object and points it at the ProgRef directory on a machine called myserver. In this example we are implicitly creating a connection (rather than using an exsiting connection). Note that we have specified URL= at the beginning of the connection details to switch from the default OLE DB provider, which doesn't recognise URLs, to the OLE DB Provider for Internet Publishing.

To open the subfolder SubDir1 under the ProgRef directory use the following command. In VBScript:

```
Set objRec= Server.CreateObject("ADODB.Record")
objRec.Open "ADO", "URL=http://localhost"
```

Or in JScript:

```
objRec = Server.CreateObject('ADODB.Record');
objRec.Open('ADO', 'URL=http://localhost');
```

This will open a Record object and point it at the SubDir1 directory in the ProgRef directory on myserver.

If we open a Record from an existing Recordset, then the Connection associated with the Recordset will be passed to the Record:

```
' VBScript
Set objRecSet = Server.CreateObject("ADODB.Recordset")
' ...
Set objRec = Server.CreateObject("ADODB.Record")
objRec.Open objRecSet
```

```
// JScript
objRecSet = Server.CreateObject("ADODB.Recordset");
// ...
objRec = Server.CreateObject("ADODB.Record");
objRec.Open(objRecSet);
```

Record Object Properties

The properties of the Record object allow us to configure how the object interacts with its data source as well as reading information retrieved from the data source.

ActiveConnection Property

The ActiveConnection property sets or returns the Connection object to which the Record object belongs.

```
Record.ActiveConnection = Variant
Variant = Record.ActiveConnection
```

The `ActiveConnection` property can be set to a pre-existing `Connection` object:

```
' VBScript
Set objConn = Server.CreateObject("ADODB.Connection")
objConn.Open "URL=http://localhost"

Set objRec = Server.CreateObject("ADODB.Record")
objRec.ActiveConnection = objConn
objRec.Open
```

```
// JScript
objConn = Server.CreateObject('ADODB.Connection');
objConn.Open('URL=http://localhost');

objRec = Server.CreateObject('ADODB.Record');
objRec.ActiveConnection = objConn;
objRec.Open();
```

Alternatively we can use a connection string or a URL, in which case an implicit `Connection` object is created by ADO. For example in VBScript:

```
Set objRec = Server.CreateObject("ADODB.Record")
objRec.ActiveConnection = "URL=http://localhost"
objRec.Open
```

Or in JScript:

```
objRec = Server.CreateObject("ADODB.Record");
objRec.ActiveConnection = "URL=http://localhost";
objRec.Open();
```

Fields Property

The read-only `Fields` property returns a collection containing all of the `Field` objects for the current `Record` object.

```
Fields = Record.Fields
```

For example:

```
' VBScript
For Each objField in objRec.Fields
   Response.Write "Field: " & objField & "<BR>"
Next
```

```
// JScript
for (i=0; i<objRec.Fields.Count; i++) {
   objField=objRec.Fields(i);
   Response.Write("Field " + objField + "<BR>");
}
```

Mode Property

The `Mode` property indicates the available permissions for modifying data in a `Connection`.

```
Record.Mode = ConnectModeEnum
ConnectModeEnum = Record.Mode
```

Details of the constants and values for the Mode property can be found under ConnectModeEnum in Appendix D. The default is adModeRead, which indicates read-only permissions.

The Mode property not only sets the read/write values for the Record, it is also used to define what access is permitted by other resources accessing the same data source.

ParentURL Property

The ParentURL property is a read-only property that returns a string indicating the absolute URL of the parent Record of the current Record.

```
String = Record.ParentURL
```

If the current Record is at the root of a directory, then the ParentURL property is Null. This value may also indicate that the Record does not logically have a parent, for example, it is a Record derived from a Recordset.

Properties Property

The read-only Properties property returns a collection containing all of the Property objects for the current Record object. This collection is identical to the Properties collection of the Command object (see Chapter 26).

```
Properties = Record.Properties
```

RecordType Property

The read-only RecordType property indicates whether the record is a simple record, a structured document, or a collection.

```
RecordTypeEnum = Record.RecordType
```

The RecordType property can be one of:

❑   adSimpleRecord, which indicates a record that doesn't contain any child nodes.

❑   adCollectionRecord, which indicates a record that contains child nodes.

❑   adStructDoc, which indicates the record represents a COM structured document.

See Appendix D for a list of the values.

Source Property

The Source property indicates the entity that the Record represents, i.e. a directory, a file, or a reference to an open Recordset.

```
Variant = Record.Source
```

Record Object

This returns the value passed as the Source parameter in the Open method. If the Record was opened from a Recordset, then this property will contain a reference to that Recordset object. If the ActiveConnection property is set to a URL value, then the Source property will be considered a relative reference from the URL in the ActiveConnection property.

State Property

The read-only State property indicates whether the Record is currently open or closed. If it is open, the State property gives the state of asynchronous actions.

```
ObjectStateEnum = Record.State
```

For example:

```
' VBScript
If objRec.State = adStateOpen Then
   objRec.Close
End If
Set objRec = Nothing
```

```
// JScript
if (objRec.State == adStateOpen) {
   objRec.Close();
}
delete objRec;
```

Fields Collection and Field Objects

Like the Recordset object, the Record object exposes a Fields collection that contains a set of Field objects. These enable us to examine some of the properties of our Record or Recordset object.

The methods and properties of the Fields collection and of the Field object for the Record are identical to those of the Recordset Fields collection and Field object.

However, as in the Properties collection, the *objects* that populate the Fields collection depend on the the provider and the entity that we are considering; that is, whether the Record object is a file, directory row of a recordset, or a Recordset object.

For the Record object, each Field object contains information describing the Record. In addition, the Fields collection of the Record object has two special fields which give the default Stream for the Record and the URL for the Record as a string. These use the two constants FieldEnum: adDefaultStream (-1) and adRecordURL (-2).

If we open the Record object against the OLE DB Provider for Internet Publishing, its Fields collection will be populated with two sets of fields:

❑ Fields provided by Microsoft OLE DB Provider for Internet Publishing

❑ The official DAV (Distributed Authoring and Versioning) fields

These sets of fields are broadly equivalent, each DAV field mapping onto one of the Internet Publishing Provider fields (with the single exception of DAV:getetag). The reason for having these two sets of fields is that the Microsoft OLE DB Provider for Internet Publishing is built on top of the WebDAV protocol. IIS5 is a WebDAV server, and it is therefore possible to use any WebDAV client to access IIS5; so it must also support the official set of WebDAV fields.

A list of the Field objects provided by Microsoft OLE DB Provider for Internet Publishing is shown below. Descriptions of the data types can be found in Appendix D under DataTypeEnum:

Field	Type	Description
RESOURCE_PARSENAME	adVarWChar	The URL of the resource.
RESOURCE_PARENTNAME	adVarWChar	The URL of the parent resource.
RESOURCE_ABSOLUTEPARSENAME	adVarWChar	The absolute URL, including path.
RESOURCE_ISHIDDEN	adBoolean	Indicates whether or not the resource is hidden.
RESOURCE_ISREADONLY	adBoolean	Indicates whether or not the resource is read-only.
RESOURCE_CONTENTTYPE	adVarWChar	The likely use of the resource.
RESOURCE_CONTENTCLASS	adVarWChar	The MIME type of the resource.
RESOURCE_CONTENTLANGUAGE	adVarWChar	The resource language.
RESOURCE_CREATIONTIME	adFileTime	The time the resource was created.
RESOURCE_LASTACCESSTIME	adFileTime	The time the resource was last accessed.
RESOURCE_LASTWRITETIME	adFileTime	The time the resource was updated.
RESOURCE_STREAMSIZE	adUnsigned BigInt	Size of the default Stream.
RESOURCE_ISCOLLECTION	adBoolean	Indicates whether or not the resource is a collection – i.e. has children.
RESOURCE_ISSTRUCTUREDDOCUMENT	adBoolean	Indicates whether or not the resource is a structured document – e.g. a Word document.
DEFAULT_DOCUMENT	adVarWChar	The URL of the default document for a folder.
RESOURCE_DISPLAYNAME	adVarWChar	Display name of the resource.
RESOURCE_ISROOT	adBoolean	Indicates whether or not the resource is the root of a collection.
RESOURCE_ISMARKEDFOROFFLINE	adBoolean	Indicates whether or not the resource is marked for offline usage.

Record Object

You should note that RESOURCE_CONTENTTYPE and RESOURCE_CONTENTCLASS might have their values reversed. At the time of writing they were as documented above, but this may have been corrected for the release.

The table below lists the names of the Field objects as defined as the official DAV (Distributed Authoring and Versioning) properties (which begin with DAV:) and shows how these map onto the fields provided by Microsoft OLE DB Provider for Internet Publishing.

Internet Publishing Field	DAV Field
RESOURCE_PARSENAME	DAV:lastpathsegment
RESOURCE_PARENTNAME	DAV:parentname
RESOURCE_ABSOLUTEPARSENAME	DAV:href
RESOURCE_ISHIDDEN	DAV:ishidden
RESOURCE_ISREADONLY	DAV:isreadonly
RESOURCE_CONTENTTYPE	DAV:getcontenttype
RESOURCE_CONTENTCLASS	DAV:getcontentclass
RESOURCE_CONTENTLANGUAGE	DAV:getcontentlanguage
RESOURCE_CREATIONTIME	DAV:creationtime
RESOURCE_LASTACCESSTIME	DAV:lastaccessed
RESOURCE_LASTWRITETIME	DAV:getlastmodified
RESOURCE_STREAMSIZE	DAV:getcontentlength
RESOURCE_ISCOLLECTION	DAV:iscollection
RESOURCE_ISSTRUCTUREDDOCUMENT	DAV:isstructureddocument
DEFAULT_DOCUMENT	DAV:defaultdocument
RESOURCE_DISPLAYNAME	DAV:displayname
RESOURCE_ISROOT	DAV:isroot
	DAV:getetag

Example of Using the Record Object

We will now take a look at how to use the Record object to view the contents of a URL. This URL can either be a directory or an individual file. In VBScript this looks like:

```
<%
Dim recNode, fldNode
Set recNode= Server.CreateObject("ADODB.Record")

recNode.Open "", "URL=http://localhost/ADO/record_example.asp"
```

```
Response.Write "<TABLE BORDER=1>"
For each fldNode in recNode.Fields
    Response.Write "<TR><TD>" & fldNode.Name & "</TD><TD>" & fldNode.Value &
                   "</TD></TR>"
Next
Response.Write "</TABLE>"

recNode.Close
Set recNode = Nothing
%>
```

Alternatively in JScript we have:

```
<%@ LANGUAGE="JScript" %>
<%
var recNode, fldNode;
recNode= Server.CreateObject("ADODB.Record");

recNode.Open("", "URL=http://localhost/ADO/record_example.asp");

Response.Write("<TABLE BORDER=1>");
for (i-0; i<recNode.Fields.Count; i++) {
    fldNode=recNode.Fields(i);
    Response.Write("<TR><TD>" + fldNode.Name + "</TD><TD>" + fldNode.Value +
                   "</TD></TR>");
}
Response.Write("</TABLE>");

recNode.Close();
delete recNode;
%>
```

We first create a `Record` object and then open it. Then we pass a URL as the `ActiveConnection` parameter to the `Open` method. By passing a blank string for the `Source` parameter, we open a `Record` that points to the directory itself. Next, we iterate through all of the `Field` objects in the `Fields` collection of the `Record` object. This lets us view all of the information that the URL provider has returned to ADO.

This gives a table similar to this:

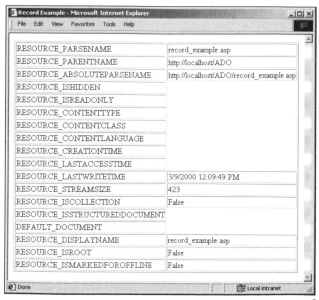

Summary

In this chapter we considered the Record object which is new to ADO 2.5. The Record object can represent and manipulate data that exists in a non-relational format. Each Record object either represents a file, a directory or a row in a Recordset.

We looked at:

❑   WebDAV, the W3C standard that extends HTTP 1.1 to include a set of new commands allowing the management of Web resources.

❑   The methods and properties of the Record object.

❑   The fields exposed by the Record object.

❑   An example of using the Record object to view the properties of a URL.

29

The Recordset Object

The Recordset object represents a set of records returned from a database query. It is used to examine and manipulate data within a database. Combined with the cursor service, it enables us to move through the records, find particular records that fit certain criteria, sort records in a particular order, and update records.

The Recordset object is probably the most commonly used ADO object. It has a rather more complex interface than the other objects in the ADO object model which exposes many more methods and properties. Once we have created and populated a recordset, we can then use other parts of the interface to work with the contents of the recordset.

A Recordset object allows us to access individual records (the rows of the database) and fields (the columns). The set of fields associated with a recordset (and with each individual record) is accessible through the Fields collection and Field object, which are described later in this chapter.

Like the Command and Record objects, a Recordset can either exist on its own or be attached to a Connection. The latter is the preferred option when we are creating several recordsets within a page, because it means that the connection to the data doesn't have to be opened each time we create a recordset. We can either update records within a recordset one record at a time, or we can batch a set of changes to various records, and then execute the database update in one step. Recordset objects can also be disconnected from a data store, so that changes can be made to the data in an off-line state, and then updated when the recordset is reconnected to the database. This allows for the movement of entire recordsets from the server to client for update and manipulation.

Before we consider the many methods and properties exposed by the Recordset object, let us briefly consider two important related subjects – cursors and locking.

Cursors

Cursors provide a means for us to order the rows held within the recordset. Cursors expose the entire recordset, but present the records as though they were sequentially ordered, and allow us to iterate through the records one at a time. Cursors can be located on the client (in which case they are provided by the OLE DB Cursor Service), or on the server (supplied by the OLE DB provider).

> A cursor manages the set of records and the current location within the recordset, the latter being handled by the current record pointer.

There are four different types of cursor available in ADO which determine how the current record pointer can move through our data:

❑ A **static** cursor (adOpenStatic) maintains a static copy of the records; i.e. the data is fixed at the time the recordset was created. Movement both forwards and backwards through the recodset is allowed.

❑ A **forward-only** cursor (adOpenForwardOnly) is the default cursor type and is identical to the static cursor, except that we can only move forwards through the recordset.

❑ A **dynamic** cursor (adOpenDynamic) doesn't have a fixed set of records, i.e. any data changes, additions or deletions by other users is visible in the recordset. Both forwards and backwards movement through the recordset is allowed.

❑ A **keyset** cursor (adOpenKetset) is like a dynamic cursor, except that the set of records is fixed. You can see changes made by other users, but new records are not visible. If users delete records, these are marked as inaccessible within the recordset.

Another cursor we should mention is a **firehose cursor**. Firehose cursors are read-only, forward-only cursors and can lead to a great improvement in performance. Not all cursor types are supported by all providers.

We can specify the properties of our cursor either in our Open statement or using the CursorLocation and CursorType properties before the Recordset is opened. For example in VBScript:

```
rsExample.Open "titles", strConn, adOpenDynamic, _
          adLockOptimistic, adCmdTable
```

Or in JScript:

```
rsExample.Open("titles", strConn, adOpenDynamic,
          adLockOptimistic, adCmdTable);
```

Locking

Locking is the method by which we ensure the integrity of our data, making sure that changes aren't made simultaneously. For example, if a sales column in a database contains the number 20 and one user updates that by 5 on making a sale, the figure will now be 25. If another user also makes a sale and updates the column by 3, the new value should be 28. However, if the two updates are nearly simultaneous, there is a risk that the second user will change the value to 23 before the first update has been completed, thus corrupting the data. The solution to this is to 'lock' the data while a record is being edited, so that no further editing can be done until the first user has finished.

There are four different lock types used by ADO:

❑ **Read only** (adLockReadOnly). This is the default locking type, where the recordset is read-only and records cannot be modified.

❑ **Pessimistic** (adLockPessimistic). This locks a record as soon as some editing takes place to guarantee the successful editing of a record.

❑ **Optimistic** (adLockOptimistic). The record is not locked until the changes to the record are committed to the datastore, by way of the Update method.

❑ **Batch optimistic** (adLockBatchOptimistic). This allows multiple records to be modified and the records are only locked when the UpdateBatch method is called.

We can set the type of locking either in our Open statement or by using the LockType property prior to opening a Recordset.

Recordset Object Members

The Recordset object exposes some 25 methods and 28 properties. It also has 10 events which are listed below for completeness. However, since these are not relevant to ASP, we don't cover them in further detail.

The Recordset object exposes the following methods:

Methods			
AddNew	Delete	MoveNext	Seek
Cancel	Find	MovePrevious	Supports
CancelBatch	GetRows	NextRecordset	Update
CancelUpdate	GetString	Open	UpdateBatch
Clone	Move	Requery	
Close	MoveFirst	Resync	
CompareBookmarks	MoveLast	Save	

Recordset Object

The Recordset object exposes the following properties:

Properties			
AbsolutePage	CursorLocation	Filter	Properties
AbsolutePosition	CursorType	Index	RecordCount
ActiveCommand	DataMember	LockType	Sort
ActiveConnection	DataSource	MarshalOptions	Source
BOF	EditMode	MaxRecords	State
Bookmark	EOF	PageCount	Status
CacheSize	Fields	PageSize	StayInSync

The Recordset object supports the following events:

Events	
EndOfRecordset	RecordsetChangeComplete
FetchComplete	WillChangeField
FetchProgress	WillChangeRecord
FieldChangeComplete	WillChangeRecordset
MoveComplete	WillMove

Recordset Object Methods

There are three broad categories of methods that are commonly used with the Recordset object. The first category deals with the population of a recordset with data; the next deals with the navigation through the recordset, and the third deals with the manipulation of data in the recordset.

❑ The **population methods** populate the recordset with data. These include the Open, Close, Clone, Requery and Save methods.

❑ The **manipulation methods** allow us to change the information in the data source that is represented by the recordset. We can also use the manipulation methods to extract bulk information from the recordset. The current lock type that was set when the recordset was opened will affect the methods that allow us to change data. The manipulation methods include the AddNew, Update and CancelUpdate methods.

❑ The **navigation methods** allow us to move the cursor within the recordset. The basic move methods allow us to move to the next record, previous record, first record, or last record. The navigation methods include the Move, MoveNext, MovePrevious, MoveLast, MoveFirst and Find methods.

AddNew Method

The AddNew method creates a new record in the recordset, and sets it as the current record.

```
Recordset.AddNew([FieldList], [Values])
```

Parameter	Type	Description	Default
FieldList	Variant	Optional. A single name or an array of field names.	A blank record is inserted.
Values	Variant	A single name or an array of the values corresponding to each field passed in the FieldList parameter.	

We can only use the AddNew method when the recordset supports addition of new records. This can be checked using the Supports method as follows:

```
' VBScript
If rsExample.Supports(adAddNew) Then
    Response.Write "Recordset supports additions<BR>"
End If
```

```
// JScript
if (rsExample.Supports(adAddNew)) {
    Response.Write('Recordset supports additions');
}
```

The AddNew method can be used in two ways. Firstly, we can use it without any arguments. It places the current pointer on a new record and we can then set the values for the new record and save the changes with Update or UpdateBatch. Alternatively, the changes are also saved by moving off the field using, for example one of the MoveFirst, MoveLast, MoveNext or MovePrevious methods. We can for example use the AddNew method as follows:

```
' VBScript
rsExample.AddNew
rsExample("title_id") = "BF1234"
rsExample("title") = "ASP Prog Ref 3.0"
rsExample.Update
```

```
// JScript
rsExample.AddNew();
rsExample("title_id") = "BF1234";
rsExample("title") = "ASP Prog Ref 3.0";
rsExample.Update();
```

Recordset Object

457

The second method of using the AddNew method uses the arguments to pass in an array of fields and values:

```
' VBScript
rsExample.AddNew Array("title_id", "title"), _
                 Array("BF1234", " ASP Prog Ref 3.0")
rsExample.Update
```

```
// JScript
rsExample.AddNew(Array("title_id", "title"),
                 Array("BF1234", " ASP Prog Ref 3.0"));
rsExample.Update ();
```

After calling the AddNew method, the EditMode property is set to adEditAdd. Also see the 'Changing Data Using a Recordset' example at the end of this chapter.

Cancel Method

The Cancel method cancels execution of a pending asynchronous Open operation.

```
Recordset.Cancel()
```

This is particularly useful when you allow users to submit their own queries, as you can provide them with a means of cancelling the query if it is taking too long.

CancelBatch Method

The CancelBatch method cancels a pending batch update when in batch update mode.

```
Recordset.CancelBatch([AffectRecords])
```

Parameter	Type	Description	Default
AffectRecords	AffectEnum	Optional. This determines which records will be affected by batch cancel.	adAffectAll

AffectEnum is one of the following constants: adAffectAll, adAffectAllChapters, adAffectCurrent or adAffectGroup. See Appendix D for more information. Care should be taken with adAffectGroup as this only deletes records that match the current filter.

You should always check the Errors collection after using the CancelBatch method. Also it is always sensible to set the current record position to a known record after this call, as the current record can be left in an unknown position after a CancelBatch method call.

CancelUpdate Method

The `CancelUpdate` method reverses any changes made to the current record being edited or a new record.

```
Recordset.CancelUpdate()
```

You can use this to cancel the addition of a new record, in which case the current record becomes the record you were on before adding the new record. A run-time error results if no changes have been made to the data in the current row before the `CancelUpdate` method call.

Clone Method

The `Clone` method creates a `Recordset` object that exactly duplicates the current one. Cloning a recordset allows us to quickly move between two points within the recordset – we simply have to move from one recordset to the other, without having to jump back and forth between records.

```
Recordset = Recordset.Clone([LockType])
```

Parameter	Type	Description	Default
LockType	LockTypeEnum	Optional. This specifies whether the cloned object has the same lock type (adLockUnspecified) or adLockReadOnly.	adLock Unspecified

In this case, LockTypeEnum is a subset of the full list of constants and should be either `adLockUnspecified` or `adLockReadOnly`. See Appendix D for more information.

The `Clone` method creates a duplicate object that represents the same data as the current recordset. Each recordset will point to the same underlying data, so if the cursor type supports it, changes made in one are reflected in the other. It is much faster to clone an existing recordset than to open a new one.

Cloning is only allowed on bookmarkable recordsets. You can check this using the `Supports` method. For example in VBScript:

```
Dim strConn, rsExample, rsExampleClone
strConn = Application("DBConnectionString")
Set rsExample = Server.CreateObject("ADODB.Recordset")
rsExample.CursorLocation = adUseClient
rsExample.Open "authors", strConn, adOpenStatic, _
            adLockOptimistic, adCmdTable

If rsExample.supports(adBookmark) Then
    Set rsExampleClone1 = rsExample.Clone
        rsExampleClone1.MoveFirst
```

Recordset Object

459

```
do While Not rsExampleClone1.EOF
      Response.Write rsExampleClone1(1) & "<BR>"
      rsExampleClone1.MoveNext
   Loop
Else
   Response.Write "Bookmarks, and hence cloning, not supported<BR>"
End If
```

Or in JScript:

```
var strConn = Application("DBConnectionString");
rsExample = Server.CreateObject('ADODB.Recordset');
rsExample.CursorLocation = adUseClient
rsExample.Open("authors", strConn, adOpenStatic,
               adLockOptimistic, adCmdTable);

if (rsExample.supports(adBookmark)) {
   rsExampleClone = rsExample.Clone();

   rsExampleClone.MoveFirst();
   while (!rsExampleClone.EOF) {
      Response.Write(rsExampleClone(1) + "<BR>");
      rsExampleClone.MoveNext();
   }
} else {
   Response.Write("Bookmarks, and hence cloning, not supported<BR>");
}
```

Close Method

The Close method closes an open Recordset object.

```
Recordset.Close()
```

Note that when changes are in place when the recordset is closed, this will lead to a run-time error in immediate update mode, or the changes will be lost if in batch update mode.

Closing a recordset does not delete the object from memory, this needs to be done explicitly. In order to avoid any errors, we can also check that the recordset is open first:

```
' VBScript
If rsExample.State = adStateOpen Then
   rsExample.Close
End If
Set rsExample = Nothing
```

```
// JScript
if (rsExample.State == adStateOpen) {
   rsExample.Close();
}
delete rsExample;
```

CompareBookmarks Method

The CompareBookmarks method compares two bookmarks and returns an indication of the relative positions, e.g the first bookmark is after the second, before the second etc.

```
CompareEnum = Recordset.CompareBookmarks(Bookmark1, Bookmark2)
```

Parameter	Type	Description
Bookmark1	Variant	The first bookmark
Bookmark2	Variant	The second bookmark

CompareEnum is one of the following constants: adCompareLessThan, adCompareEqual, adCompareGreaterThan, adCompareNotEqual or adCompare. See Appendix D for more information.

The return value is the position of the first bookmark relative to the second bookmark. Note that this compares the actual bookmarks, *not* the values in the records that the bookmarks point to.

Delete Method

The Delete method deletes the current record in the recordset.

```
Recordset.Delete([AffectRecords])
```

Parameter	Type	Description	Default
AffectRecords	AffectEnum	Optional. This determines which records will be affected by the deletion.	adAffectAll

AffectEnum is one of the following constants: adAffectAll, adAffectAllChapters, adAffectCurrent or adAffectGroup. See Appendix D for more information.

If we have a read-only lock type set for this recordset, then calling the Delete method causes a run-time error to be generated. Once we delete a recordset, we can no longer retrieve values from the fields in the record.

Recordset Object

Find Method

The Find method searches the recordset for a row that matches the specified criteria.

    Recordset.Find(Criteria, [SkipRows], [SearchDirection], [Start])

Parameter	Type	Description	Default
Criteria	String	This specifies the column name, comparison operator, and value to check against for the search.	
SkipRows	Long	Optional. This specifies the row offset from which to begin the search.	0 (i.e. start at the current row)
Search Direction	Search DirectionEnum	Optional. This specifies in which direction from the current position to search.	adSearchForward (searches towards the end of the recordset)
Start	Variant	Optional. This indicates a bookmark at which to begin the search.	

SearchDirectionEnum can be one of adSearchForwards or adSearchBackwards. See Appendix D for more information. The Start parameter can be a valid bookmark or one of the BookmarkEnum constants: adBookmarkCurrent, adBookmarkFirst or adBookmarkLast.

We can only specify a single search value in the Criteria argument. Using multiple search values with AND or OR causes an error. We can use the asterisk (*) as a wildcard operator at the end of the value in the criterion string.

If you do need to use multiple criteria values then you should create a new recordset, or use a Filter, which does accept multiple values.

Lets look at an example of using the Find method. We'll search in the titles table for a record with the title_id of 'PC1035':

```
' VBScript
Dim strConn, rsExample
'Create a string with the Connection details
strConn = Application("DBConnectionString")
'Create a Recordset object
Set rsExample = Server.CreateObject("ADODB.Recordset")
rsExample.Open "titles", strConn, adOpenDynamic, _
            adLockOptimistic, adCmdTable
rsExample.Find "title_id = 'PC1035'"
Response.Write rsExample("title_id") & " " & _
            rsExample("title") & "<BR>"
```

And in JScript:

```
// JScript
var strConn = Application("DBConnectionString");
// Create a Recordset object
rsExample = Server.CreateObject('ADODB.Recordset');
rsExample.Open("titles", strConn, adOpenDynamic,
            adLockOptimistic, adCmdTable);
rsExample.Find("title_id = 'PC1035'");
Response.Write(rsExample("title_id") + " " +
            rsExample("title") + "<BR>");
```

See also the 'Changing Data Using a Recordset' example at the end of this chapter.

GetRows Method

The GetRows method retrieves multiple records from the recordset into an array.

```
Variant = Recordset.GetRows([Rows], [Start], [Fields])
```

Parameter	Type	Description	Default
Rows	Long	This indicates the number of records from the recordset to retrieve.	-1 (All records)
Start	Variant	The bookmark from which to start the retrieval.	
Fields	Variant	An array of field names to be retrieved into the array.	

The Start parameter can be a valid bookmark or one of the BookmarkEnum constants: adBookmarkCurrent, adBookmarkFirst or adBookmarkLast. If no Start parameter is set, the retrieval begins at the current record of the recordset.

The GetRows method returns a two-dimensional array, with the first dimension indicating the field, and the second dimension indicating the row (record). If we do not specify the Rows parameter, all of the rows in the database are returned. After calling this method, the current record moves past the end of the recordset and the EOF property is set to true.

463

GetString Method

The GetString method returns the Recordset as a string.

```
String = Recordset.GetString([StringFormat], [NumRows],
                             [ColumnDelimiter], [RowDelimiter],
                             [NullExpr])
```

Parameter	Type	Description	Default
StringFormat	StringFormat Enum	This defines how the string should be formatted on return.	adClipString
NumRows	Long	The number of rows in the recordset.	-1 (All rows are converted)
Column Delimiter	String	This defines the string delimiter that is inserted between each column in a row.	A tab character
RowDelimiter	String	This defines the string delimiter that is inserted between each record in the string.	A carriage return character
NullExpr	String	This defines the string value that is inserted in place of a null value in the field of the recordset.	Empty String

The only valid value for StringFormatEnum is adClipString.

The GetString method is similar to the GetRows method, in that it retrieves multiple records from the recordset. We can also format the returned string. This method returns the information stored in the rows, but will not return any schema data. There is no automatic way to reconstruct a recordset from the string generated by this method.

The GetString method is very useful for example for creating HTML tables in ASP:

```
' VBScript
strTable = rsExample.GetString(adClipString, , "</TD><TD>", _
                               "</TD></TR><TR><TD>")
strTable = Left(strTable, Len(strTable)-8)
Response.Write "<TABLE BORDER=1><TR><TD>" & strTable & "</TABLE>"
```

```
// JScript
strTable = rsExample.GetString(adClipString,-1,"</TD><TD>",
                               "</TD></TR><TR><TD>");
strTable = strTable.substring(0,strTable.length - 8);
Response.Write("<TABLE BORDER=1><TR><TD>" + strTable +
               "</TD></TR></TABLE>");
```

See also the 'Changing Data Using a Recordset' example at the end of this chapter.

Move Method

The Move method moves the position of the current record within a recordset.

```
Recordset.Move(numRecords, [Start])
```

Parameter	Type	Description	Default
numRecords	Long	The number of records to move.	
Start	Variant	Optional. This indicates a Bookmark from which to start the move.	adBookmarkCurrent

The Start parameter can be a valid bookmark or one of the BookmarkEnum constants: adBookmarkCurrent, adBookmarkFirst or adBookmarkLast.

The numRecords parameter indicates the number of records to move. This can be a positive number, in which case the record pointer moves towards the end of the recordset. If it is negative, then the record pointer moves towards the beginning. The cursor must support backwards movement in order for this to work.

For example, to iterate backwards through a recordset moving three records at a time:

```
' VBScript
rsExample.MoveLast
Do While Not rsExample.BOF
   Response.Write rsExample(1) & "<BR>"
   rsExample.Move -3
Loop
```

```
// JScript
rsExample.MoveLast();
while (!rsExample.BOF) {
   Response.Write(rsExample(1) + "<BR>");
   rsExample.Move(-3);
}
```

See also the 'Navigating a Recordset' example at the end of this chapter.

MoveFirst Method

The `MoveFirst` method moves the current record to the first record in the recordset. If the recordset has a forward-only cursor, then calling this method may cause the `Requery` method to be called.

```
Recordset.MoveFirst()
```

You should be aware that some providers (e.g. SQL Server) implement the `MoveFirst` by resubmitting the query to the database server, having the effect of reopening the recordset, thus placing you back on the first record. This could have serious performance implications, but only occurs with server-side cursors.

If the current record has been changed, but you haven't yet called `Update`, then a `MoveFirst` will implicitly call `Update`. Use `CancelUpdate` before using this method call if you want to keep your changes.

See also the 'Navigating a Recordset' example at the end of this chapter.

MoveLast Method

The `MoveLast` method moves the cursor to the last record in the recordset. A run-time error is generated with a forward-only cursor (`adOpenForwardOnly`).

```
Recordset.MoveLast()
```

If the current record has been changed, but you haven't yet called `Update`, then a `MoveLast` will implicitly call `Update`. Use `CancelUpdate` before using this method call if you want to keep your changes.

See also the 'Navigating a Recordset' example at the end of this chapter.

MoveNext Method

The `MoveNext` method moves the cursor to the next record in the recordset. If you are currently at the last record, the `EOF` property is set to `true`.

```
Recordset.MoveNext()
```

If the current record has been changed, but you haven't yet called `Update`, then a `MoveNext` will implicitly call `Update`. Use `CancelUpdate` before using this method call if you want to keep your changes.

See also the 'Navigating a Recordset' example at the end of this chapter.

MovePrevious Method

The `MovePrevious` method moves the cursor to the preceding record in the recordset. If you are currently at the first record, the `BOF` property is set to `true`. A run-time error results with a forward-only cursor (`adOpenForwardOnly`).

```
Recordset.MovePrevious()
```

If the current record has been changed, but you haven't yet called `Update`, then a `MovePrevious` will implicitly call `Update`. Use `CancelUpdate` before using this method call if you want to keep your changes.

See also the 'Navigating a Recordset' example at the end of this chapter.

NextRecordset Method

The `NextRecordset` method clears the current `Recordset` object and returns the next `Recordset` for use by our code.

```
Recordset = Recordset.NextRecordset([RecordsAffected])
```

Parameter	Type	Description
RecordsAffected	Long	Optional. A long integer into which the provider returns the number of records that the operation affected.

`RecordsAffected` is only meaningful for a non-row-returning recordset.

The `NextRecordset` method is useful if you wish to build up a set of SQL statements and send them to the provider in one go. However not all the data may be reurned in one batch so you may have to make a round trip to the server for each recordset.

For example we can produce two lists using the two recordsets generated by the following SQL stored procedure:

```
CREATE PROCEDURE sp_pubs
AS
BEGIN
    SELECT * FROM authors
    SELECT * FROM titles
END
```

Our ASP code calls this stored procedure to open these two recordsets, and then iterates through each recordset in turn:

```
<%
Dim strConn, rsExample
strConn = Application("DBConnectionString")
Set dbConnection = Server.CreateObject("ADODB.Connection")
Set cmdExample = Server.CreateObject("ADODB.Command")
Set rsExample = Server.CreateObject("ADODB.Recordset")
dbConnection.Open strConn
```

Recordset Object

467

```
cmdExample.ActiveConnection = dbConnection
cmdExample.CommandType = adCmdStoredProc

rsExample.Open "sp_pubs", dbConnection, adOpenForwardOnly, _
               adLockReadOnly, adCmdStoredProc
Response.Write "<HR><B>List of Authors: </B><BR><BR>"
Do While Not rsExample.EOF
   Response.Write rsExample(1) & "<BR>"
   rsExample.MoveNext
Loop

Response.Write "<HR><B>List of Titles: </B><BR><BR>"
Set rsTitles = rsExample.NextRecordset
Do While Not rsTitles.EOF
   Response.Write rsTitles(1) & "<BR>"
   rsTitles.MoveNext
Loop
%>
```

Or in JScript:

```
<%
var strConn = Application("DBConnectionString");
dbConnection = Server.CreateObject("ADODB.Connection");
cmdExample = Server.CreateObject("ADODB.Command");
rsExample = Server.CreateObject("ADODB.Recordset");
dbConnection.Open(strConn);

cmdExample.ActiveConnection = dbConnection;
cmdExample.CommandType = adCmdStoredProc;

rsExample.Open("sp_pubs", dbConnection, adOpenForwardOnly,
               adLockReadOnly, adCmdStoredProc);
Response.Write("<HR><B>List of Authors: </B><BR><BR>");
while (!rsExample.EOF) {
   Response.Write(rsExample(1) + "<BR>");
   rsExample.MoveNext();
}

Response.Write("<HR><B>List of Titles: </B><BR><BR>");
rsTitles = rsExample.NextRecordset;
while (!rsTitles.EOF) {
   Response.Write(rsTitles(1) + "<BR>");
   rsTitles.MoveNext();
}
%>
```

> **Note that not all providers support the** NextRecordset **method.**

468

Open Method

The Open method opens a connection to a data source.

```
Recordset.Open([Source], [ActiveConnection], [CursorType], [LockType],
               [Options])
```

Parameter	Type	Description	Default
Source	Variant	The source of the data that populates the recordset.	If not set, the recordset itself is used as the source.
Active Connection	Variant	A reference to an existing, open Connection object, or to a valid data source connection string.	
CursorType	CursorType Enum	The cursor type to use when opening the recordset.	adOpen Unspecified (-1)
LockType	LockTypeEnum	The locking type to use when opening the recordset.	adLockReadOnly
Options	Long	One or more of CommandTypeEnum or ExecuteOptionEnum.	-1 (Unspecified)

CursorTypeEnum is one of the following constants: adOpenForwardOnly, adOpenKeyset, adOpenDynamic and adOpenStatic. LockTypeEnum is one of the following constants: adLockReadOnly, adLockPessimistic, adLockOptimistic and adLockBatchOptimistic. See Appendix D for more information.

Options should be set to one or more of the following constants: adCmdText, adCmdTable, adCmdStoredProcedure, adCmdUnknown, adCmdTableDirect, adCmdFile, adAsyncFetch or adAsyncFetchNonBlocking. If you don't set the Options parameter, then ADO has to figure out for itself what the Source parameter represents. This has a slight performance cost.

Recordset Object

We can open up a recordset with a pre-existing connection. In VBScript this looks like:

```
Dim strConn, rsExample
strConn = Application("DBConnectionString")
Set dbConnection = Server.CreateObject("ADODB.Connection")
Set rsExample = Server.CreateObject("ADODB.Recordset")
dbConnection.Open strConn
rsExample.Open "titles", dbConnection, adOpenDynamic, _
               adLockOptimistic
```

Or in JScript:

```
var strConn = Application("DBConnectionString");
dbConnection = Server.CreateObject('ADODB.Connection');
rsExample = Server.CreateObject('ADODB.Recordset');
dbConnection.Open(strConn);
rsExample.Open("titles", dbConnection, adOpenDynamic,
               adLockOptimistic);
```

We can also open a recordset without an existing `Connection` object. For example in VBScript:

```
Dim strConn, rsExample
strConn = Application("DBConnectionString")
Set rsExample = Server.CreateObject("ADODB.Recordset")
rsExample.Open "titles", strConn, adOpenDynamic, adLockOptimistic
```

Or in JScript:

```
var strConn = Application("DBConnectionString");
rsExample = Server.CreateObject('ADODB.Recordset');
rsExample.Open("titles", strConn, adOpenDynamic, adLockOptimistic);
```

The example at the end of this chapter on 'Opening a Recordset' demonstrates a number of ways of opening a recordset.

Requery Method

The `Requery` method repopulates the recordset by re-executing the original `Source` property.

```
Recordset.Requery([Options])
```

Parameter	Type	Description	Default
Options	Long	Optional. This defines the options to use when requerying the string.	adExecuteUnspecified (-1)

The `Options` parameter is a long value or one of the `ExecuteOptionEnum` constants `adAsyncExecute`, `adAsyncFetch`, `adAsyncFetchNonBlocking`, `adAsyncNoRecords` and `adExecuteUnspecified`.

This could be rerunning a stored procedure, reopening a table, or running a SQL query again. This is equivalent to calling `Close` and `Open` in succession. We cannot call this method if we are currently editing a record.

Resync Method

The `Resync` method refreshes the data in the current `Recordset` object from the underlying database.

```
Recordset.Resync([AffectRecords], [ResyncValues])
```

Parameter	Type	Description	Default
AffectRecords	AffectEnum	This defines how many records are affected.	adAffectAll
ResynchValues	ResynchEnum	This specifies whether the underlying values are overwritten.	adResynch AllValues

`AffectEnum` is one of the following: `adAffectAll`, `asAffectAllChapters`, `adAffectCurrent` and `adAffectGroup`.

`ResynchEnum` is either `adResynchAllValues` or `adResynchUnderlyingValues`. See Appendix D for more information.

Not all providers support the `Resync` method.

Save Method

The `Save` method saves the current recordset information into a `Stream` object or to a file.

```
Recordset.Save([Destination], [PersistFormat])
```

Parameter	Type	Description	Default
Destination	Variant	The filename that the recordset is saved to, or a Stream object that holds the information.	
PersistFormat	PersistFormat Enum	This indicates the format used to save the file in.	adPersistADTG

PersistFormatEnum is either adPersistADTG (Advanced Data TableGram format) or adPersistXML (Extensible Markup Language format). ADTG is Microsoft's proprietary format. XML is a standard, cross-platform format, so you should choose this option if you need the file to be accessible to applications which do not use ADO. However, note that recordsets saved as XML are significantly larger than the same recordsets saved in ADTG format.

Using Save means the following actions apply:

❑ Only records in the current Filter are saved.

❑ The first row becomes the current row once the save is complete.

❑ If the recordset is being fetched asynchronously then the Save will be blocked until all records are fetched.

The following example calls the Save method to persist a recordset as an XML file with a filename based on the session ID:

```
' VBScript
strFileName = Server.MapPath(CStr(Session.SessionID) & ".xml")
rsExample.Save strFileName, adPersistXML
```

```
// JScript
var strFileName = Server.MapPath(String(Session.SessionID) + ".xml");
rsExample.Save(strFileName, adPersistXML);
```

The Save method allows data to be saved locally and reopened with the Open method. This enables the same application to be used by connected and disconnected users alike. For example it works for people who use laptops to enter say an order, which does not get processed until they return say to the office, where the master copy of the data is entered. An example of 'Persisting a Recordset' is given at the end of this chapter.

Seek Method

The Seek method searches the recordset index to locate a the row with the specified value or values.

```
Recordset.Seek(keyValues, SeekOptions)
```

Parameter	Type	Description
KeyValues	Variant	An array containing the set of values to compare against.
SeekOptions	SeekEnum	The comparison type to be made.

SeekEnum is one of the following constants: adSeekFirstEQ, adSeekLastEQ, adSeekAfterEQ, adSeekAfter, adSeekBeforeEQ and adSeekBefore. See Appendix D for more information.

If the record being sought is not found then no error is returned and the current record is placed at EOF.

Not all providers support the Seek method. To check this you should use adSeek of with the Supports method.

Supports Method

The Supports method determines whether a specified Recordset object supports particular functionality.

```
Boolean = Recordset.Supports(CursorOptions)
```

Parameter	Type	Description
CursorOptions	CursorOptionEnum	One or more values to identify the functionality to be supported.

CursorOptionEnum is one or more of the following CursorOptionEnum constants: adAddNew, adApproxPosition, adBookmark, adDelete, adFind, adHoldRecords, adIndex, adMovePrevious, adNotify, adResync, adSeek, adUpdate or adUpdatebatch. See Appendix D for more information.

In this chapter we have demonstrated many examples of calling the Supports method with particular constants to check whether a particular method or property is supported by the data provider. An example looks like this in VBScript:

```
If rsExample.supports(adBookmark) Then
    Set rsExampleClone1 = rsExample.Clone
Else
    Response.Write "Bookmarks, and hence cloning, not supported<BR>"
End If
```

Or in JScript:

```
if (rsExample.supports(adBookmark)) {
    rsExampleClone = rsExample.Clone();
} else {
    Response.Write("Bookmarks, and hence cloning, not supported<BR>");
}
```

Note that even if a provider supports the particular feature, the underlying data may make it unavailable.

Recordset Object

Update Method

The Update method saves any changes made to the current row of the recordset.

```
Recordset.Update([Fields], [Values])
```

Parameter	Type	Description
Fields	Variant	An array containing the names of the fields to update
Values	Variant	An array of the values corresponding to the field names given above.

We can update in two ways as follows: firstly we can assign values to fields and then call the Update method. For example in VBScript:

```
rsExample.AddNew
rsExample("title_id") = "BF1774"
rsExample("title") = "ASP Prog Ref 3.0"
rsExample.Update
```

Or in JScript:

```
rsExample.AddNew();
rsExample("title_id") = "BF1774";
rsExample("title") = "ASP Prog Ref 3.0";
rsExample.Update();
```

Secondly we can pass either one or multiple fields and values. For example in VBScript:

```
rsExample.Update Array("title_id", "title"), _
                 Array("BF1234", "ASP Prog Ref 3.0")
```

Or in JScript:

```
rsExample.Update(Array("title_id", "title"),
                 Array("BF1234", "ASP Prog Ref 3.0"));
```

Using any of the Move methods automatically updates your data.

UpdateBatch Method

The UpdateBatch method writes all pending batch updates to disk.

```
Recordset.UpdateBatch([AffectRecords])
```

Parameter	Type	Description	Default
AffectRecords	AffectEnum	The number of affected records.	adAffectAll

`AffectEnum` is one of the following constants: `adAffectAll`, `asAffectAllChapters`, `adAffectCurrent` and `adAffectGroup`. See Appendix D for more information.

Using `UpdateBatch` allows changes to be cached until such time as you request the underlying datastore to be updated.

A failure to update will cause the `Errors` collection to be populated, and can use the `Filter` property to see which records failed.

Recordset Object Properties

The properties of the `Recordset` object fall into three categories:

❑ The **position properties** are related to the position of the current record within the recordset.

❑ The **configuration properties** are related to the current configuration of the recordset.

❑ The **viewability properties** control what portions of the recordset can be seen.

AbsolutePage Property

The `AbsolutePage` property sets or returns a value denoting the page in which the current record resides.

```
Recordset.AbsolutePage = PositionEnum
PositionEnum = Recordset.AbsolutePage
```

`PositionEnum` can be a valid page number, or one of the constants `adPosBOF`, `adPosEOF` or `adPosUnknown`. See Appendix D for more information.

When setting the value of the `AbsolutePage` property, the record pointer is set to the first record of the specified page. Hence setting the `AbsolutePage` property to 1 sets the record counter to the first record in the recordset. This is used in conjunction with the `PageSize` property.

Also see the "Paging through a Recordset" example at the end of this chapter.

AbsolutePosition Property

The `AbsolutePosition` property sets or returns the ordinal position of a `Recordset` object's current record.

```
Recordset.AbsolutePosition = PositionEnum
PositionEnum = Recordset.AbsolutePosition
```

`PositionEnum` can be a valid record number, or one of the following constants `adPosBOF`, `adPosEOF` and `adPosUnknown`. See Appendix D for more information.

Recordset Object

The `AbsolutePosition` property can't be used to identify a record uniquely since it changes as records are added or deleted from the recordset or `Sort` or `Index` is used to change the order of records in the recordset. A bookmark should be used to identify a record despite sorts etc.

ActiveCommand Property

The read-only `ActiveCommand` property returns a reference to the `Command` object that created the associated `Recordset` object.

```
Command = Recordset.ActiveCommand
```

When a recordset was created from a command the `ActiveCommand` property can be used to access the `Command` object's properties and parameters.

For example in VBScript:

```
Dim rsExample
Set rsExample = Server.CreateObject("ADODB.Recordset")
rsExample.Open "SELECT * FROM authors", strConn, adOpenForwardOnly, _
               adLockOptimistic, adCmdText
Response.Write rsExample.ActiveCommand.CommandText
```

Or in JScript:

```
var strConn = Application("DBConnectionString");
rsExample = Server.CreateObject('ADODB.Recordset');
rsExample.Open("SELECT * FROM authors", strConn, adOpenForwardOnly,
               adLockOptimistic, adCmdText);
Response.Write(rsExample.ActiveCommand.CommandText);
```

ActiveConnection Property

The `ActiveConnection` property sets or returns to which `Connection` object the specified `Recordset` object currently belongs.

```
Recordset.ActiveConnection = Variant
Variant = Recordset.ActiveConnection
```

We can use this property prior to opening the recordset to indicate the data source for the data. It can be used with a pre-existing `Connection` object as follows. For example in VBScript:

```
Dim strConn, rsExample
strConnect = Application("DBConnectionString")
Set dbConnection = Server.CreateObject("ADODB.Connection")
dbConnection.Open strConnect
Set rsExample = Server.CreateObject("ADODB.Recordset")
rsExample.ActiveConnection = dbConnection
rsExample.Open "authors"
```

Or in JScript:

```
var strConnect = Application("DBConnectionString");
dbConnection = Server.CreateObject("ADODB.Connection");
dbConnection.Open(strConnect);
rsExample = Server.CreateObject('ADODB.Recordset');
rsExample.ActiveConnection = dbConnection;
rsExample.Open("authors");
```

Alternatively we can set up the connection implicitly. For example in VBScript:

```
Dim rsExample
Set rsExample = Server.CreateObject("ADODB.Recordset")
rsExample.ActiveConnection = "Provider=SQLOLEDB; " & _
    "Data Source=myServer; Initial Catalog=pubs; " & _
    "User ID=sa; Password="
rsExample.Open "authors"
```

Or in JScript:

```
rsExample = Server.CreateObject('ADODB.Recordset');
rsExample.ActiveConnection = "Provider=SQLOLEDB; " +
    "Data Source=myServer; Initial Catalog=pubs; " +
    "User ID=sa; Password=";
rsExample.Open("authors");
```

The `ActiveConnection` property may also be modified by the provider to allow access to provider-specific connection information.

If the recordset is already open, then this is read-only and represents the `Connection` object that was used to create the recordset. Disconnected recordsets are created by setting the `ActiveConnection` property to `Nothing` after the recordset has been opened (if the `CursorLocation` is set to `adUseClient`).

BOF Property

The read-only BOF property indicates whether the current record is before the first record in a `Recordset` object.

```
Boolean = Recordset.BOF
```

The BOF (Beginning Of File) property and EOF (End Of File) property are the two most common position properties that we use in ASP. A number of examples of using BOF and EOF are given at the end of this chapter under "Navigating a Recordset".

We can use the BOF property for example to display a table backwards. For example in VBScript:

```
rsExample.MoveLast
Do While Not rsExample.BOF
    Response.Write rsExample("title_id") & "<BR>" & vbCRLF
    rsExample.MovePrevious
loop
```

Or in JScript:

```
rsExample.MoveLast();
while (!rsExample.BOF) {
    Response.Write(rsExample('title_id') + '<BR>' + '\n');
    rsExample.MovePrevious();
}
```

Bookmark Property

The Bookmark property returns a bookmark that uniquely identifies the current record in a Recordset object, or sets the current record to the record identified by a valid bookmark.

```
Variant = Recordset.Bookmark
```

Bookmarks are used to store the position in the recordset temporarily, allowing you to return to that position at a later date. For example in VBScript:

```
varBkmk = rsExample.Bookmark
' ... some processing that changes the current record...
rsExample.Bookmark = varBkmk
```

Or in JScript:

```
var varBkmk = rsExample.Bookmark;
// ... some processing that changes the current record...
rsExample.Bookmark = varBkmk;
```

Bookmarks can be used for example after a search to return to a bookmarked position. You chould check the adBookmark value (using the Support method of the Recordset object) to verify the cursors.

Bookmarks between recordsets. created using the Clone method are the same, whereas bookmarks from different recordsets are not interchangable, even if the recordsets were created from the same source or command.

CacheSize Property

The CacheSize property sets or returns the number of records from a Recordset object that are cached locally in memory. The default is 1.

```
Recordset.CacheSize = Long
Long = Recordset.CacheSize
```

The cache size affects how many records are fetched from the server in one go and held locally. This has an effect on performance and memory usage. Note that records in the cache do not reflect underlying changes made by other users until the Resync method is used or until recordset navigation causes the records to be reread.

A run-time error results if the CacheSize is set to 0. An undocumented and not officially supported feature is that negative CacheSize values cause the records to be fetched backwards from the current row.

CursorLocation Property

The CursorLocation property sets or returns the location of the cursor engine, i.e. whether the cursor resides on the client (if the OLE DB cursor service is used) or the server (if the provider's own cursor service is used).

```
Recordset.CursorLocation = CursorLocationEnum
CursorLocationEnum = Recordset.CursorLocation
```

CursorLocationEnum is one of the following constants: adUseNone, adUseClient or adUseServer. See Appendix D for more information.

Once the Recordset object has been opened, this becomes a read-only property.

For example in VBScript:

```
Dim strConn, rsExample, rsExampleClone
strConn = Application("DBConnectionString")
Set rsExample = Server.CreateObject("ADODB.Recordset")
rsExample.CursorLocation = adUseClient
rsExample.Open "authors", strConn, adOpenStatic,
          adLockOptimistic, adCmdTable
```

Or inJScript:

```
var strConn = Application("DBConnectionString");
rsExample = Server.CreateObject('ADODB.Recordset');
rsExample.CursorLocation = adUseClient
rsExample.Open("authors", strConn, adOpenStatic,
          adLockOptimistic, adCmdTable);
```

CursorType Property

The CursorType property indicates the type of cursor used in a Recordset object.

```
Recordset.CursorType = CursorTypeEnum
CursorTypeEnum = Recordset.CursorType
```

CursorTypeEnum is one of the following constants: adOpenForwardOnly, adOpenKeyset, adOpenDynamic and adOpenStatic. See Appendix D for more information.

This value can be read at any time, but it can only be changed when the recordset is closed. There are four types of cursors for ADO, as described in the 'Cursors' section at the start of this chapter.

Not all providers support all cursor types and the actual cursor type used may depend on the cursor location (found using the CursorLocation property). For keyset cursors, we can control the visibility of inserted or deleted records with the use of the dynamic properties "Remove Deleted Rows", "Own Inserts Visible" and "Others' Inserts Visible".

Recordset Object

For example:

```
' VBScript
Dim rsExample
' Create a Recordset object
Set rsExample = Server.CreateObject("ADODB.Recordset")
rsExample.CursorType = adOpenStatic
rsExample.Open "authors", strConn, , adLockOptimistic, adCmdTable
```

```
// JScript
var strConn = Application("DBConnectionString");
rsExample = Server.CreateObject('ADODB.Recordset');
rsExample.CursorType = adOpenStatic
rsExample.Open("authors", strConn, adLockOptimistic, adCmdTable);
```

DataMember Property

The write-only DataMember property sets or returns the name of the data member to retrieve from the object referenced by the DataSource property.

```
Recordset.DataMember = String
String = Recordset.DataMember
```

DataSource Property

The DataSource property specifies an object containing data to be represented as a Recordset object. It identifies the object to which the DataMember belongs.

```
Recordset.DataSource = Object
Object = Recordset.DataSource
```

EditMode Property

The read-only EditMode property returns the editing status of the current record.

```
EditmodeEnum = Recordset.Editmode
```

EditmodeEnum is one of the following constants: adEditNone, adEditInProgress, adEditAdd and adEditDelete. See Appendix D for more information.

You could use this in an interactive application that allows users to edit and move records around. Since moving records around intrinsically calls the Update method, you could use this in some code that offers users the ability to cancel an update.

EOF Property

The read-only EOF property indicates whether the current record is after the last record in a Recordset object.

```
Boolean = Recordset.EOF
```

The BOF (Beginning Of File) property and EOF (End Of File) property are the two most common position properties that we use in ASP. A number of examples of using BOF and EOF are given at the end of this chapter under "Navigating a Recordset".

We can use the EOF property when iterating through a recordset:

```
' VBScript
rsExample.MoveFirst
Do While Not rsExample.EOF
    Response.Write rsExample(1) & "<BR>"& vbCRLF
    rsExample.MoveNext
Loop
```

```
// JScript
rsExample.MoveFirst();
while (!rsExample.EOF) {
    Response.Write(rsExample(1) + "<BR>" + "\n");
    rsExample.MoveNext();
}
```

Fields Property

The Fields property contains all of the Field objects for the current Recordset object.

```
Fields = Recordset.Fields
```

Filter Property

The Filter property sets or returns a filter for data in the Recordset.

```
Variant = Recordset.Filter([Criteria])
```

The Filter property is used to screen out records selectively in the current recordset. Once the Filter property is set, the cursor is moved to the first record that matches the filter criterion.

The Filter property can be set to a valid filter string, which is made up of one or more clauses concatenated with AND or OR operators. The format of the string uses the same syntax as a standard SQL WHERE clause.

Alternatively the Filter property can be an array of bookmarks or one of the FilterGroupEnum constants: adFilterNone, adFilterPendingRecords, adFilterAffectedRecords, adFilterFetchedRecords, adFilterPredicate or adFilterConflictRecords. See Appendix D for more information.

We can clear any existing filter by setting the property to a blank string (" ") or by setting it to the adFilterNone constant.

Recordset Object

The following example filters the recordset so that only records where the pub_id field has the value "0877" are displayed:

```
rsExample.Filter = "pub_id=0877"
If rsExample.EOF Then
   Response.Write "No Matching Titles<BR>"
Else
   Do While Not rsExample.EOF
      Response.Write rsExample("pub_id") & " - " & _
                     rsExample("Title") & "<BR>" & vbCRLF
      rsExample.MoveNext
   Loop
End If
```

Or in JScript:

```
rsExample.Filter = "pub_id=0877";
if (rsExample.EOF) {
   Response.Write('No Matching Titles<BR>');
} else {
   while (!rsExample.EOF) {
      Response.Write(rsExample('pub_id') + ' - ' +
                     rsExample('Title') + '<BR>\n');
      rsExample.MoveNext();
   }
}
```

The screen looks like this:

Index Property

The Index property sets or returns the name of the index currently in use.

```
Recordset.Index = String
String = Recordset.Index
```

The Index property refers to a table index that can either have been created on the base table or an ADOX Index object. Changing an index may change the current row position and therefore update the current record.

Not all providers support the Index property. This can be checked using adIndex with the Supports method. The Index property is not related to the indexing used by the dynamic Optimize property.

LockType Property

The LockType property sets or returns the type of lock placed on records during editing.

```
LockTypeEnum = Recordset.LockType
Recordset.LockType = LockTypeEnum
```

LockTypeEnum is one of the following constants: adLockReadOnly, adLockPessimistic, adLockOptimistic or adLockBatchOptimistic. See Appendix D for more information.

The LockType property indicates the way in which records are locked when they are being edited. Which method you should choose depends on your application. Like the CursorType property, this property can be read at any time, but can only be set prior to opening the recordset. Only adLockBatchOptimistic and adLockReadOnly are supported by client-side cursors. If you attempt to use any other lock type you'll get adLockBatchOptimistic.

See also the section on "Locking" at the start of this chapter and the examples on "Navigating a Recordset" and "Changing Data Using a Recordset" at the end of this chapter.

MarshalOptions Property

The MarshalOptions property indicates which records are to be marshaled back to the server.

```
Recordset.MarshalOptions = MarshalOptionsEnum
MarshalOptionsEnum = Recordset.MarshalOptions
```

MarshalOptionsEnum is one of the following constants: adMarshalAll or adMarshalModifiedOnly. See Appendix D for more information.

Marshaling is the name given to transferring a recordset between two processes. This could be between the client and the server in a two-tier system or between the client and a middle-tier in an n-tier system.

This property is only applicable when using disconnected, client-side recordsets. By marshaling only the modified records (rather than all records) we can greatly improve performance. If only a few records are modified locally, less data needs to be sent back to the server process.

You can use this quite effectively when using n-tier client/server architecture, using a business object on the server to supply recordsets. These can be modified locally, and only the records which have changed are sent back to the business process for updating.

Recordset Object

MaxRecords Property

The MaxRecords property sets or returns the maximum number of records to return to a Recordset object from a query. The default is zero (no limit).

```
Recordset.MaxRecords = Long
Long = Recordset.MaxRecords
```

You can only set this property while the recordset is closed. It is quite useful for big applications that allow users to submit queries, since it enables you to limit their set of records if it is too big. The MaxRecords property is not supported by all providers.

PageCount Property

The read-only PageCount property indicates how many pages of data the Recordset object contains.

```
Long = Recordset.PageCount
```

The recordset consists of a number of pages, each of which contains a number of records specified by the PageSize property (apart from the last page, which may contain fewer). If the PageSize is not set then the PageCount value will be -1.

For example, to move to the first record of the last page:

```
' VBScript
rsExample.AbsolutePage = rsExample.RecordCount/rsExample.PageCount
```

```
// JScript
rsExample.AbsolutePage = rsExample.RecordCount/rsExample.PageCount;
```

Also see the 'Paging through a Recordset' example at the end of this chapter.

PageSize Property

The PageSize property sets or returns an integer which shows how many records constitute one page in the recordset.

```
Long = Recordset.PageSize
Recordset.PageSize = Long
```

For example, the following displays six records per page:

```
' VBScript
rsExample.Open "titles", strConn, adOpenStatic, adLockOptimistic
rsExample.PageSize = 6
Response.Write "Number of records in recordset = " & _
               rsExample.RecordCount & "<BR>"
Response.Write "Number of pages in recordset = " & _
               rsExample.PageCount & "<BR>"
```

```
// JScript
rsExample.Open("titles", strConn, adOpenStatic, adLockOptimistic);
rsExample.PageSize = 6;
```

```
Response.Write("Number of records in recordset = " +
               rsExample.RecordCount + "<BR>");
Response.Write("Number of pages in recordset = " +
               rsExample.PageCount + "<BR>");
```

The `PageSize` property is not supported by all providers. See also the 'Paging through a Recordset' example at the end of this chapter.

Properties Property

The `Properties` property returns a reference to a `Properties` collection which contains all of the `Property` objects for the current `Recordset` object.

```
Properties = Recordset.Properties
```

The `Properties` collection is discussed in Chapter 26.

RecordCount Property

The read-only `RecordCount` property indicates the current number of records in the `Recordset` object.

```
Long = Recordset.RecordCount
```

The `RecordCount` property returns the number of records in the current recordset (or -1 if the record count can't be determined accurately). This property only works with certain cursor types (except server-side forward-only cursors and server-side dynamic cursors), and can also cause a significant resource drain, since the entire recordset could have to be retrieved from the data source in order to compute this property. For forward-only cursors, this property returns -1 until we have traversed through the recordset to the end.

The `RecordCount` property will only be accurate for recordsets that support approximate positioning or bookmarks. If this is not the case we must fully populate the recordset before an accurate `RecordCount` value can be returned.

Sort Property

The `Sort` property specifies one or more field names the recordset is sorted on, and the direction of the sort.

```
Recordset.Sort = String
String = Recordset.Sort
```

The sort string is a comma-separated list of columns to dictate the sort order, each optionally followed by the sort direction ("ASC" or "DESC"). The default sort direction is "ASC". The primary sort field is listed first, followed by the secondary sort field, etc. For example, to sort first by the author's last name (in ascending order) and then by first name (in descending order):

485

```
' VBScript
Dim strConn, rsExample
strConn = Application("DBConnectionString")
Set rsExample = Server.CreateObject("ADODB.Recordset")
rsExample.CursorLocation = adUseClient
rsExample.Open "authors", strConn, adOpenstatic, adLockOptimistic
rsExample.Sort = "au_lname ASC, au_fname DESC"
rsExample.MoveFirst
do While Not rsExample.EOF
    Response.Write rsExample(1) & "<BR>"
    rsExample.MoveNext
Loop
```

```
// JScript
var strConn = Application("DBConnectionString");
rsExample = Server.CreateObject('ADODB.Recordset');
rsExample.CursorLocation = adUseClient;
rsExample.Open("authors", strConn, adOpenDynamic, adLockOptimistic);
rsExample.Sort = "au_lname ASC, au_fname DESC";
rsExample.MoveFirst();
while (!rsExample.EOF) {
    Response.Write(rsExample(1) + "<BR>");
    rsExample.MoveNext();
}
```

Sorting is performed by the OLE DB cursor service, so CursorLocation needs to be set to adUseClient.

Source Property

The Source property sets or returns the source for the data in a Recordset object.

```
Recordset.Source = Variant
Variant = Recordset.Source
```

This is useful for identifying the actual command text used to create the recordset.

State Property

The read-only State property indicates whether the recordset is open or closed, or whether it is executing an asynchronous operation.

```
ObjectStateEnum = Recordset.State
```

ObjectStateEnum is one of the following constants: adStateClosed, adStateOpen, adStateConnecting, adStateExecuting or adStateFetching. See Appendix D for more information.

When the recordset is opened asynchronously, you should use a logical AND operation to test these values:

```
' VBScript
If (objRecSet.State And adStateFetching) = adStateFetching Then
    Response.Write "Recordset still fetching Records ..."
End If
```

```
// JScript
if ((objRecSet.State & adStateFetching) == adStateFetching) {
   Response.Write('Recordset still fetching Records ...');
}
```

Status Property

The read-only Status property indicates the status of the current record with respect to match updates or other bulk operations.

```
Integer = Recordset.Status
```

RecordStatusEnum is one of a number of constants. See Appendix D for more information.

StayInSync Property

The StayInSync property indicates, for a hierarchical Recordset object, whether the parent row should change when the set of underlying child records changes.

```
Recordset.StayInSync = Boolean
Boolean = Recordset.StayInSync
```

The default is true. If set to false, a reference to a child recordset will remain pointing to the old recordset, even though the parent may have changed. Hierarchical recordsets are covered in more detail in Chapter 31 (Data Shaping).

Recordset Object Events

Name	Description
EndOfRecordset	This event fires when there is an attempt to move to a row past the end of the recordset.
FetchComplete	This event fires after all the records in an asynchronous operation have been retrieved into the recordset.
FetchProgress	This event fires periodically during a length asynchronous operation, to report how many rows have currently been retrieved.
FieldChangeComplete	This event fires after the value of one or more Field object has been changed.
MoveComplete	This event fires after the current position in the recordset changes.
RecordChangeComplete	This event fires after one or more records change.

Recordset Object

487

Name	Description
RecordsetChangeComplete	This event fires after the recordset has changed.
WillChangeField	This event fires before a pending operation changes the value of one or more Field object.
WillChangeRecord	This event fires before one or more rows in the recordset change.
WillChangeRecordset	This event fires before a pending operation changes the recordset.
WillMove	This event fires before a pending operation changes the current position in the recordset.

Fields Collection and Field Objects

Both the Recordset object and the Record object expose a Fields collection that contains a set of Field objects. These enable us to examine some of the properties of our Recordset or Record object.

The methods and properties of the Fields collection for both the Record and the Recordset object are the same. Also, the Field objects in the Record and Recordset Fields collections have the same methods and properties.

However, as in the Properties collection, the actual objects that populate the Fields collection depend on the the provider and the entity that we are considering, i.e. whether we are talking about a Record object that is a file, directory or row of a recordset, or a Recordset object.

For the Recordset object, there will be one Field object for each column in existing recordsets. When creating new recordsets you append Field objects to the Fields collection.

For the Record object, the Fields collection is populated with a subset of available fields by providers such as the OLEDB Provider for Internet Publishing. See the previous chapter on the Record object for more information.

The most important properties of a Field object are Value, OriginalValue and UnderlyingValue.

A Field object's Value sets or returns the *current* value for a Field within the cached rowset. This may not reflect the actual value in the data source because of changes made to the cached rowset or changes to the data source made by other users. The CancelUpdate and CancelBatch methods can reset it to its original value, effectively undoing the changes.

The `OriginalValue` property returns the value stored in the field before any changes were made on the cached rowset. The `UnderlyingValue` property returns the value of the field as stored in the data source. It can be manually refreshed be calling the `Recordset`'s `Resync` method.

Fields Collection

The `Fields` collection exposes the following methods and properties:

Methods	Properties
Append	Count
CancelUpdate	Item
Delete	
Refresh	
Resync	
Update	

The `Fields` collection is the default collection of the `Recordset` object. This means that the following two lines are equivalent:

```
fldVal = Recordset(fldName).Value
```

And:

```
fldVal = Recordset.Fields(fldName).Value
```

We can iterate through the `Fields` collection using the usual scripting language techniques:

```
' VBScript
For Each objField in rsExample.Fields
   Response.Write "The field name is " & objField.Name & "<BR>"
Next
```

```
// JScript
enmField=new Enumerator(rsExample.Fields);
while (!enmField.atEnd()) {
   fld=enmField.item();
   Response.Write("The field name is " + fld.Name + "<BR>");
   enmField.moveNext();
}
```

Recordset Object

Fields Collection Methods

Append Method

The Append method appends a Field object to the Fields collection.

```
Variant = Fields.Append(Name, DataType, [DefinedSize],
                        [FieldAttrib], [FieldValue])
```

Parameter	Type	Description	Default
Name	String	The name of the new Field object; this must not be the same as any existing fields in the collection	
DataType	DataTypeEnum	The data type of the new field	adEmpty
DefinedSize	Long	The size of the new field; this can be bytes or characters	That the data type is specified.
FieldAttrib	FieldAttribute Enum	Specifies the attributes for this object	adFldDefault which gets its attributes from the Type.
FieldValue	Variant	Optional; a field value can be specified here	Null value

A full list of the possible values for FieldAttributeEnum and DataTypeEnum can be found in Appendix D.

This method is used to append fields to a closed fabricated recordset. A run-time error results if the Append method is called while a Recordset is open, or has an active connection.

CancelUpdate Method

The CancelUpdate method will reverse any changes made to the Fields collection.

```
Fields.CancelUpdate()
```

This can be used to reset a field's value to its original value in the data source, effectively undoing any changes.

Delete Method

The Delete method deletes a Field object from the Fields collection.

```
Recordset.Fields.Delete(Field)
```

Parameter	Type	Description
Field	Variant	Either the field object's name or its index position.

A run-time error results if the Delete method is called while a Recordset is open or has an active connection. It is only really useful to cancel fields appended to fabricated recordsets.

Refresh Method

The Refresh method updates the Field objects in the Fields collection from the provider. Any changes will be reflected in the collection.

```
Fields.Refresh()
```

Resync Method

The Resync method refreshes the data from the underlying database.

```
Fields.Resync([ResyncValues])
```

Parameter	Type	Description	Default
ResyncValues	ResyncEnum	This specifies whether the underlying values are overwritten	adResynchAll Values

ResyncEnum is either adResynchAllValues or adResynchUnderlyingValues. See Appendix D for more information.

The UnderlyingValue property returns the value of the field as stored in the data source. It can be manually refreshed by calling the Recordset's Resync method.

Update Method

The Update method saves any changes made to the Fields collection.

```
Fields.Update()
```

Fields Collection Properties

Count Property

The read-only `Count` property indicates the number of `Field` objects in the `Fields` collection.

```
Long = Fields.Count
```

For example:

```
' VBScript
Response.Write rsExample.Fields.Count & "<BR>"
```

```
// JScript
Response.Write( rsExample.Fields.Count + "<BR>");
```

Item Property

The read-only `Item` property allows indexing into the `Fields` collection to reference a specific `Field` object.

```
Field = Fields.Item(Variant)
```

This is the default property of the `Fields` collection, so the following lines of code are equivalent:

```
' VBScript
Response.Write rsExample.Fields.Item(0).Name & "<BR>"
Response.Write rsExample.Fields(0).Name & "<BR>"
Response.Write rsExample.Fields("title_id").Name & "<BR>"
Response.Write rsExample.Fields.Item("title_id").Name & "<BR>"
```

```
// JScript
Response.Write(rsExample.Fields.Item(0).Name + "<BR>");
Response.Write(rsExample.Fields(0).Name + "<BR>");
Response.Write(rsExample.Fields("title_id").Name + "<BR>");
Response.Write(rsExample.Fields.Item("title_id").Name + "<BR>");
```

Field Object

The `Field` object has properties that allow us to examine the characteristics of the field along with the data contained within the field. The methods of the `Field` object allow us to manipulate any binary or character information that may be contained in the field.

The `Field` object exposes the following methods and properties:

Methods	Properties		
AppendChunk	ActualSize	NumericScale	Type
GetChunk	Attributes	OriginalValue	UnderlyingValue

Methods	Properties		
	DataFormat	Precision	Value
	DefinedSize	Properties	
	Name	Status	

The default property of the Field object is the Value property. This allows us to set or retrieve the value contained in that field within the current row of the recordset. We can access this property using two methods:

```
fldVal = Recordset.Fields.Item(fldName).Value
```

Or:

```
fldVal = Recordset(fldName)
```

As you can see, the second method is much easier to write and to read.

Field Object Methods

AppendChunk Method

The AppendChunk method appends data to a large or binary Field object.

```
Field.AppendChunk(Data)
```

Parameter	Type	Description
Data	Variant	The data to append to the field

The first call to AppendChunk (after you have started to edit a field) writes data to the field, overwriting any existing data in the buffer. Subsequent calls append further data to this existing data.

This method is most often used with Binary Large Objects (BLOBs) such as images or large text files stored in databases.

GetChunk Method

The GetChunk method returns all or a portion of the contents of a large or binary Field object.

```
Variant = Field.GetChunk(Length)
```

Parameter	Type	Description
Length	Long	The number of bytes (or characters) to read from the field

Recordset Object

The first call retrieves data starting at the start of the field. Subsequent calls start where the last call left off.

Like the AppendChunk method, the GetChunk method is most used with BLOBs such as images.

Field Object Properties

ActualSize Property

The read-only ActualSize property indicates the actual length of a field's value.

```
Long = Field.ActualSize
```

This property is used when you need to know how large a field actually is, rather than how large it can be (found using the DefinedSize). These two properties are equivalent for fixed length data types, but may differ for variable-length data.

Attributes Property

The Attributes property indicates one or more characteristics of a Field object.

```
Field.Attributes = Long
Long = Field.Attributes
```

The characteristics can be one or more of the FieldAttributeEnum constants. The full list is given in Appendix D.

We can use a logical AND operation to check whether any specific attribute is present in this bitmask value. For example, to check whether the field can contain null values:

```
' VBScript
If (fld.Attributes AND adFldMayBeNull) = adFldMayBeNull Then
    Response.Write "Field may be null"
End If
```

```
// JScript
if ((fld.Attributes && adFldMayBeNull) == adFldMayBeNull) {
    Response.Write("Field may be null");
}
```

The Attributes property is read/write when you are fabricating your own recordsets, but becomes read-only once they are opened.

DataFormat Property

The DataFormat property sets or returns the format that the data should be displayed in.

```
Field.DataFormat = DataFormat
DataFormat = Field.DataFormat
```

This is used in conjunction with Visual Basic and Visual J++.

DefinedSize Property

The DefinedSize property returns the defined size of the Field object.

```
Field.DefinedSize = Long
Long = Field.DefinedSize
```

For variable-width fields, the DefinedSize property gives the maximum width of the field rather than its actual size. This property is read/write when fabricating your own recordsets, but is read-only for opened recordsets.

Name Property

The read-only Name property returns the name of the Field object.

```
String = Field.Name
```

For example, to iterate through the Fields collection and display the name of each field:

```
' VBScript
For Each objField in rsExample.Fields
    Response.Write "The field name is " & objField.Name & "<BR>"
Next
```

```
// JScript
enmField=new Enumerator(rsExample.Fields);
while (!enmField.atEnd()) {
    fld=enmField.item();
    Response.Write("The field name is " + fld.Name + "<BR>");
    enmField.moveNext();
}
```

NumericScale Property

The NumericScale property indicates the number of digits there are to the right of the decimal point of numeric values of the Field object.

```
Field.NumericScale = Byte
Byte = Field.NumericScale
```

This property is read/write when fabricating your own recordsets, but is read-only for opened recordsets.

OriginalValue Property

The read-only OriginalValue property indicates the value of a Field object that existed in the record before any changes were made.

```
Variant = Field.OriginalValue
```

Recordset Object

The `OriginalValue` is the value stored in the field before any changes were saved to the provider. This value enables the provider to return to the original value if a `CancelBatch` or `CancelUpdate` method is called. For example in VBScript:

```
' Assume this field contains the value 29.95
Set fld = rsExample.Fields("price")
Response.Write fld & "<BR>" & vbCRLF
fld.Value = 50.00
Response.Write fld.OriginalValue & "<BR>"    'Prints 29.95
Response.Write fld.Value & "<BR>"            'Prints 50.00
rsExample.CancelUpdate
Response.Write fld & "<BR>"                   'Prints 29.95
```

Or in JScript:

```
// Assume this field contains the value 29.95
fld = rsExample.Fields("price");
Response.Write(fld + "<BR>");
fld.Value = 50.00;
Response.Write(fld.OriginalValue + "<BR>");   //Prints 29.95
Response.Write(fld.Value + "<BR>");           //Prints 50.00
rsExample.CancelUpdate();
Response.Write(fld + "<BR>");                  //Prints 29.95
```

Also see the related properties `Value` and `UnderlyingValue`.

Precision Property

The `Precision` property indicates the degree of precision for numeric values in the `Field` object, i.e. the maximum number of significant digits that are used to represent a number.

```
Field.Precision = Byte
Byte = Field.Precision
```

Like the `NumericScale` property, the `Precision` property is read/write when fabricating your own recordsets, but is read-only for opened recordsets.

Properties Property

The `Properties` property returns a reference to the `Properties` collection which contains all of the `Property` objects for a `Field` object.

```
Properties = Field.Properties
```

The `Properties` collection of a `Field` object is identical to that for the other ADO objects, and is discussed in the `Command` object chapter (Chapter 26).

Status Property

The `Status` property indicates whether a `Field` object has been added to or deleted from the `Fields` collection (these are cached until `Update` is called).

```
FieldStatusEnum = Field.Status
```

The possible values for `FieldStatusEnum` are listed in Appendix D.

Type Property

The Type property sets or returns the data type of the Field object.

```
Field.Type = DataTypeEnum
DataTypeEnum = Field.Type
```

A full list of *DataTypeEnum* constants can be found in Appendix D. Not all providers support all datatypes. When creating recordsets, you can use all types and the provider will convert any types it doesn't support to the appropriate supported type. This property is read/write when creating your own recordset, but read-only when using an open recordset.

UnderlyingValue Property

The read-only UnderlyingValue property indicates a Field object's current value in the database.

```
Variant = Field.UnderlyingValue
```

The underlying value differs from the original value, as the UnderlyingValue property holds the current value of the field as stored in the data source. For example, this will hold the value if another user has changed the value of a field. In order to be sure that the UnderlyingValue property contains the latest value, it must be refreshed by calling the Resync method – it will not automatically change when the value changes in the data source.

Also see the related properties Value and OriginalValue.

Value Property

The Value property sets or returns the current value assigned to the Field object.

```
Field.Value = Variant
Variant = Field.Value
```

Also see the related properties OriginalValue and UnderlyingValue.

Examples of Using the Recordset Object

We consider some examples that show how to work with a Recordset object and with the underlying information within the recordset. In each example, we assume that a valid connection string is stored within the application-level variable named DBConnectionString. We also assume that the ADO type library has been included in the global.asa file as well. The use of these techniques was seen earlier in the chapter.

Opening a Recordset

The first step in working with a recordset is to open one. Both the Command and the Connection objects expose Execute methods, which allow us to open a recordset without first creating a Recordset object. In this example, we look at different ways of explicitly creating and opening a recordset.

Recordset Object

In VBScript the code is:

```
<%
' First create and open the Connection
Dim dbConnection, rsExample, strConnect, strSQL
strConnect = Application("DBConnectionString")
Set dbConnection = Server.CreateObject("ADODB.Connection")
Set rsExample = Server.CreateObject("ADODB.Recordset")
dbConnection.Open strConnect

' Open a database table as a recordset
rsExample.Open "authors", dbConnection, , , adCmdTable
' ... use this data
rsExample.Close

' Open a recordset using a SQL Query
strSQL = "SELECT title, price, notes FROM titles;"
rsExample.Open strSQL, dbConnection, adOpenStatic, _
                adLockOptimistic, adCmdText
' ... use this data
rsExample.Close

' Open a recordset without a Connection object
rsExample.Open "titles", strConnect, adOpenDynamic, _
                adLockPessimistic, adCmdTable
' ... use this data
rsExample.Close

dbConnection.Close
Set rsExample = Nothing
Set dbConnection = Nothing
%>
```

Or in JScript:

```
<%@ LANGUAGE = JScript %>
<%
// Create and open the Connection
var strConnect = Application("DBConnectionString");
dbConnection = Server.CreateObject("ADODB.Connection");
rsExample = Server.CreateObject("ADODB.Recordset");
dbConnection.Open(strConnect);

// Open a database table as a recordset
rsExample.Open("authors", dbConnection, adCmdTable);
// ... use this data
rsExample.Close();

// Open a recordset using a SQL Query
var strSQL = "SELECT title, price, notes FROM titles;";
rsExample.Open(strSQL, dbConnection, adOpenStatic,
                adLockOptimistic, adCmdText);
// ... use this data
rsExample.Close();

// Open a recordset without a Connection object
rsExample.Open("titles", strConnect, adOpenDynamic,
                adLockPessimistic, adCmdTable);
// ... use this data
rsExample.Close();
```

```
dbConnection.Close();
delete rsExample;
delete dbConnection;
%>
```

This example shows three ways of opening a recordset. Prior to this, we have declared some variables to use in this example and have created two ADO objects. The Connection object is opened using the connection string stored in an application-level variable, which we saw with the ADO Connection object in Chapter 27.

The first example opens an entire table of the pubs database as a recordset. This creates a recordset that contains all of the fields and rows within the authors table in the pubs database. We have accepted the default lock and cursor types, which mean we get a forward-only, read-only cursor. This is also known as a **firehose cursor**. Since we are directly opening a table, we let ADO know this by passing in the adCmdTable parameter.

In the second example, we populate our recordset with the results of a SQL query. This query returns three fields, title, price, and notes, from the titles table. All rows in the table are returned. Since the recordset is a dynamic picture of the underlying data source, we can edit the data returned by this query, so we want to set a lock type other than read-only. By setting a static cursor type, we are able to move backwards and forwards through the records, and to update the data as well as read it.

The third example shows how to open a recordset without using an existing Connection object. Instead of passing the reference to the Connection object, dbConnection, to the Open method, we are passing in a connection string. ADO implicitly creates a Connection object, and use it to work with this recordset. It cannot be used for any other database manipulation in the page. Since we already have a Connection object already created and open, this would be a waste of resources in real life.

Finally, once we are done with all of our database manipulations, we close the connection to the database. With both the Connection and the Recordset objects closed, we can release these objects by setting their reference to Nothing. This is not exactly necessary, as VBScript will do this for us when the page ends, but it is good programming practice to release resources as soon as they are no longer needed. Especially on a web server, where resources are at a premium, all resource savings have direct performance benefits.

Navigating a Recordset

In the previous example, we saw how to open a recordset. Once we have that recordset open, the first thing we want to do is navigate through it. For navigation, we have the five Move... methods and the Find method. This example shows how to use these methods by navigating the books table of the pubs database.

```
<%
Dim dbConnection, rsExample, strConnect, strSQL
strConnect = Application("DBConnectionString")
Set dbConnection = Server.CreateObject("ADODB.Connection")
Set rsExample = Server.CreateObject("ADODB.Recordset")
dbConnection.Open strConnect
```

Recordset Object

499

```
' Open a database table as a recordset
rsExample.Open "titles", dbConnection, adOpenStatic, _
            adLockReadOnly, adCmdTable

' Navigate through the entire table
Do While Not rsExample.EOF
    Response.Write rsExample("Title") & "<BR>" & vbCRLF
    rsExample.MoveNext
Loop
Response.Write "<HR>" & vbCRLF
```

The first part of the example is exactly the same as the previous example. We open a connection to the database using our global connection string, then open a recordset that contains the contents of the `titles` table. The first thing we are going to do is navigate through the entire recordset. This is probably the most common type of ADO code that you will see. The EOF property remains `false` until we navigate past the end of the recordset. This allows us to set up a `Do While` loop, which executes as long as EOF is not `true`. Within each iteration of the loop, we output the contents of the `title` field, by retrieving it from the `Field` object that represents that column. To move to the next row in the table, we call the `MoveNext` method.

```
' Display the table backwards
rsExample.MoveLast
Do While Not rsExample.BOF
    Response.Write rsExample("title_id") & "<BR>" & vbCRLF
    rsExample.MovePrevious
Loop
Response.Write "<HR>" & vbCRLF
```

In this step, we use code that is similar to the above step, but this time we move through the recordset backwards. This means that we want to start at the end of the recordset, which we can reach by calling the `MoveLast` method. The `Do While` loop continues to iterate as long as the BOF property is not `true`. After outputting the contents of a field in the current record, we move to the previous record by calling `MovePrevious`.

```
' Display every other record
rsExample.MoveFirst
Do While Not rsExample.EOF
    Response.Write rsExample("title") & _
                "<BR>*** Skip One ***<BR>" & vbCRLF
    rsExample.Move 2
Loop
Response.Write "<HR>" & vbCRLF
```

Next, we go through the recordset from beginning to end, but this time we skip every other record in the recordset. We could issue two back-to-back calls to `MoveNext`, but this has the following drawbacks: firstly, it is inefficient to make two separate calls to the database object. Secondly, if the first call to `MoveNext` moves the cursor past the end of the table, and we don't check EOF between calls, then the second call to `MoveNext` generates a run-time error. Instead, we use the `Move` method, and pass a `numRecords` parameter of 2, which moves the cursor to every other row in the recordset.

```
' Show only certain titles
rsExample.Filter = "pub_id=0877"
If rsExample.EOF Then
    Response.Write "No Matching Titles<BR>"
Else
    Do While Not rsExample.EOF
        Response.Write rsExample("pub_id") & " - " & _
                                rsExample("Title") & "<BR>"
        rsExample.MoveNext
    Loop
End If
Response.Write "<HR>" & vbCRLF
```

The last part of the example shows how to navigate through just a portion of the recordset. We only want to display the titles that correspond to a particular publisher. We could close the recordset and reopen it with a SQL query as its source, but that would be an inefficient use of resources. We can just use the Filter property to set criteria that restricts our recordset to only showing the records that match it.

After setting the Filter property, but before navigating through the recordset, we want to check to see if the Filter property caused an empty recordset to be created. If the EOF property is true immediately after setting the Filter property, we output a message indicating that there were no titles that matched the criterion. If there are matching records, then we use our standard looping code to display the matching titles.

```
rsExample.Close
dbConnection.Close
Set rsExample = Nothing
Set dbConnection = Nothing
%>
```

Once we are done using the ADO objects in this example, we need to clean them up properly. The first step is to Close the Recordset and Connection objects. Once that has been done, we also want to release the memory used by these objects. This is done by setting their references to Nothing. This makes the system resources used by these two objects available to the system again.

The complete code in JScript is:

```
<%@ LANGUAGE = JScript %>
<%
var strConnect = Application("DBConnectionString");
dbConnection = Server.CreateObject("ADODB.Connection");
rsExample = Server.CreateObject("ADODB.Recordset");
dbConnection.Open(strConnect);

// Open a database table as a recordset
rsExample.Open("titles", dbConnection, adOpenStatic,
               adLockReadOnly, adCmdTable);

// Navigate through the entire table
while (!rsExample.EOF) {
    Response.Write(rsExample("Title") + "<BR>\n");
    rsExample.MoveNext();
}
Response.Write("<HR>\n");
```

Recordset Object

501

```
// Display the table backwards
rsExample.MoveLast();
while (!rsExample.BOF) {
   Response.Write(rsExample("title_id") + "<BR>\n");
   rsExample.MovePrevious();
}
Response.Write("<HR>\n");

// Display every other record
rsExample.MoveFirst();
while (!rsExample.EOF) {
   Response.Write(rsExample("title") + "<BR>*** Skip One ***<BR>\n");
   rsExample.Move(2);
}
Response.Write("<HR>\n");

// Show only certain titles
rsExample.MoveFirst();
rsExample.Filter = "pub_id=0877";
if (rsExample.EOF) {
   Response.Write("No Matching Titles<BR>\n");
} else {
   while (!rsExample.EOF) {
      Response.Write(rsExample("pub_id") + " - " +
                    rsExample("title") + "<BR>\n");
      rsExample.MoveNext();
   }
}
Response.Write("<HR>\n");

rsExample.Close();
dbConnection.Close();
delete rsExample
delete dbConnection
%>
```

Paging through a Recordset

If the database information to be displayed in our ASP page contains a large number of rows, we may want to display only a subset of the data, and allow the user to page up and page down through the data. In this example, we look at an ASP page that allows us to do this, along with using the GetString method to output the contents of the recordset.

```
<%
Dim dbConnection, rsExample, strConnect, strSQL
strConnect = Application("DBConnectionString")
Set dbConnection = Server.CreateObject("ADODB.Connection")
Set rsExample = Server.CreateObject("ADODB.Recordset")
dbConnection.Open strConnect

Dim curPage, pageSize, numPages
pageSize = 6 ' display 6 records per page
If Request.QueryString("page") <> "" Then
   curPage = CInt(Request.QueryString("page"))
Else
   curPage = 1
End If
```

With our database connection opened in the same way as the previous examples, we can first deal with the page number that we need to display. A local variable, pageSize, holds the size of the pages that we want to display. A query string parameter can be passed into this page to indicate which page to display. If there is no page parameter passed, then we position the recordset at the first page. If a parameter is passed in, we use that as the current page to display.

```
rsExample.Open "titles", dbConnection, adOpenStatic, adLockReadOnly
rsExample.PageSize = pageSize
numPages = rsExample.PageCount
If curPage > numPages Then curPage = numPages
rsExample.AbsolutePage = curPage
```

We open the recordset using a static read-only cursor. It contains all of the fields and records from the titles table. Once the recordset is opened, we can set the PageSize property to the value stored in our local variable. With the PageSize set, we can check the PageCount property to see the total number of pages in the recordset. If the intended current page is greater than the number of pages, then we set the current page, stored in the curPage local variable, to the last page in the recordset. Finally, we set the cursor position to the first record on the desired page by setting the AbsolutePage property to the value stored in the curPage variable.

```
Dim strTable
strTable = rsExample.GetString(adClipString, pageSize, "</TD><TD>", _
                               "</TD></TR><TR><TD>")
strTable = Left(strTable, Len(strTable)-8)
Response.Write "<TABLE BORDER=1><TR><TD>" & strTable & "</TABLE><HR>"
```

To output the records on the current page, we could again use a Do While loop, but in this example we use the GetString method. This method returns the contents of the recordset formatted with row and column delimiters. We are very selective in specifying these delimiters, and the result is a formatted table. Our table has each record on one row, and each column represents a field. So between each column, we want to terminate the current table cell and start a new one. Hence, our column delimiter parameter is </TD><TD>. Between each record, we want to end the current row and start a new one. When we end the row, we also need to end the current table cell, and likewise start a new table cell after starting a new row. This makes our row delimiter </TD></TR><TR><TD>.

With the string created, we can output it to the browser. We need to include our own prefix to create the table and to start the first row and table cell. Following the body of the table, we need to pass in a closing </TABLE> tag.

```
If curPage > 1 Then
   Response.Write "<A HREF=""paging.asp?page=" & (curPage-1)
   Response.Write """>Previous Page</A><BR>"
End If
If curPage < numPages Then
   Response.Write "<A HREF=""paging.asp?page=" & (curPage+1) & """>Next
Page</A>"
End If
```

Recordset Object

The last step is to provide the navigation buttons. We want to display the navigation buttons only if the navigation is appropriate. This means that the Next Page button should appear on every page except the last, and the Previous Page button on all but the first. The link that each button has reference the current ASP page, and pass in a parameter to indicate the page to jump to. This new page is computed by either adding or subtracting from the current page number, stored in the curPage variable.

```
rsExample.Close
dbConnection.Close
Set rsExample = Nothing
Set dbConnection = Nothing
%>
```

Finally, we use our standard clean-up routine of closing both the Recordset and Connection objects, and releasing them by setting their references to Nothing.

The complete JScript code is:

```
<%@ LANGUAGE = JScript %>
<%
var strConnect = Application("DBConnectionString");
dbConnection = Server.CreateObject("ADODB.Connection");
rsExample = Server.CreateObject("ADODB.Recordset");
dbConnection.Open(strConnect);

var pageSize = 6;      // display 6 records per page
if (String(Request.QueryString("page")) != "undefined") {
   var curPage = Request.QueryString("page");
} else {
   var curPage = 1;
}

rsExample.Open("titles", dbConnection, adOpenStatic, adLockReadOnly);
rsExample.PageSize = pageSize;
numPages = rsExample.PageCount;
if (curPage > numPages) { curPage = numPages; }
rsExample.AbsolutePage = curPage;

var strTable = rsExample.GetString(adClipString, pageSize,
                          "</TD><TD>","</TD></TR><TR><TD>");
strTable = strTable.substring(0,strTable.length - 8);
Response.Write("<TABLE BORDER=1><TR><TD>" + strTable +
            "</TABLE><HR>");

if (curPage > 1) {
   Response.Write("<A HREF=" + "paging.asp?page=" + (curPage-1));
   Response.Write("" + ">Previous Page</a><BR>");
}
if (curPage < numPages) {
   Response.Write("<A HREF=" + "paging.asp?page=" + (Number(curPage+1)) +
                  "" + ">Next Page</A>");
}

rsExample.Close();
dbConnection.Close();
delete rsExample;
delete dbConnection;
%>
```

Changing Data Using a Recordset

The preceding examples have shown how to retrieve information from a data source and display it in different ways using a recordset. Once we have retrieved this data, we can also edit it in addition to viewing it. In this example, we retrieve some data from the data source and edit an existing record. We also add some new information to the data source.

```
<%
Dim dbConnection, rsExample, strConnect, strSQL
strConnect = Application("DBConnectionString")
Set dbConnection = Server.CreateObject("ADODB.Connection")
Set rsExample = Server.CreateObject("ADODB.Recordset")
dbConnection.Open strConnect

rsExample.Open "SELECT title_id, title, price FROM titles", _
        dbConnection, adOpenDynamic, adLockOptimistic, adCmdText
```

After using our now familiar code to open the connection to the database, we populate the recordset with the results of a SQL query. This query returns three columns from the `titles` table. Since we plan to edit the information contained in the recordset, we set the lock type to optimistic locking. This means that the information in the data source is locked only when we go to update the record. We could also call this considerate locking, since it has the least effect on other users of the data source.

```
rsExample.Find "title_id = 'PC1035'"
If Not rsExample.EOF Then
   rsExample("title") = "This is the new title"
   rsExample("price") = 125.00
   rsExample.Update
End If
```

The first part of the example edits an existing record. To locate that record, we use the `Find` method of the recordset. This moves the cursor to the record that matches the criteria passed in as the first parameter. Since we are doing a find on the primary key of the database, we know that we can find at most one record, which is the one we are interested in. If the matching record is not found, then the `EOF` property is true.

Once the cursor is at the record we are interested in, we can begin to use the `Field` objects for each column we want to edit. We change these values by modifying the `Value` property of the `Field` object, which happens to be the default property of the object. After making changes to two of the fields in the record, we commit those changes to the data source by calling the `Update` method.

```
rsExample.AddNew
rsExample("title_id") = "BF1234"
rsExample("title") = "ASP Prog Ref 3.0"
rsExample("price") = 29.95
rsExample.Update
```

In addition to editing existing records, we can add new records to the recordset. Even though we are only looking at a view of the database table as a result of the SQL query, we can still add new records through this view. To start adding a new record, we first call the `AddNew` method.

Recordset Object

This creates a blank record, and sets the cursor to that record. We can then use the Field objects for each column we want to set in the record. We need to ensure that we meet all of the database requirements for the table we are editing. In this case, that means that our title_id value must be unique. Once we have set all of the values, the call to Update commits this new record to the database.

```
rsExample.MoveFirst
Dim strTable
strTable = rsExample.GetString(adClipString, , "</TD><TD>",
                                    "</TD></TR><TR><TD>")
strTable = Left(strTable, Len(strTable)-8)
Response.Write "<TABLE BORDER=1><TR><TD>" & strTable & "</TABLE><HR>"
```

The newly added record is now the current record in the recordset, so if we want to display the entire contents of the recordset, we need to move back to the top before displaying the data. The MoveFirst method moves the cursor to the first record in the recordset. The GetString method, which we saw in the previous example, then outputs all of the records in the recordset to the browser.

```
rsExample.Close
dbConnection.Close
Set rsExample = Nothing
Set dbConnection = Nothing
%>
```

As should hopefully become common practice, remember to always close our database objects and release them explicitly at the end of the page.

In JScript, the equivalent code is:

```
<%@ LANGUAGE = JScript %>
<%
var strConnect = Application("DBConnectionString");
dbConnection = Server.CreateObject("ADODB.Connection");
rsExample = Server.CreateObject("ADODB.Recordset");
dbConnection.Open(strConnect);

rsExample.Open("SELECT title_id, title, price FROM titles",
          dbConnection, adOpenDynamic, adLockOptimistic, adCmdText);

rsExample.Find("title_id = 'PC1035'");
if (!rsExample.EOF) {
   rsExample("title") = "This is the new title";
   rsExample("price") = 125.00;
   rsExample.Update();
}

rsExample.AddNew();
rsExample("title_id") = "BF1234";
rsExample("title") = "ASP Prog Ref 3.0";
rsExample("price") = 29.95;
rsExample.Update();

rsExample.MoveFirst();
var strTable = rsExample.GetString(adClipString, 1, "</TD><TD>",
                                    "</TD></TR><TR><TD>");
```

```
strTable = strTable.substring(0,strTable.length - 8);
Response.Write("<TABLE BORDER=1><TR><TD>" + strTable + "</TABLE><HR>");

rsExample.Close();
dbConnection.Close();
delete rsExample;
delete dbConnection;
%>
```

Persisting a Recordset

One of the newer features in ADO is the ability to persist a recordset to a file. This file can then be transferred to another system, where a `Recordset` object can be loaded with the data or it can be read by a system that expects information in a different file format, such as XML. In this example, we take the data from a recordset and save it out as a temporary XML file, then read in that file and output the response from the ASP page as an XML stream.

```
<%
Dim dbConnection, rsExample, strConnect, strSQL
strConnect = Application("DBConnectionString")
Set dbConnection = Server.CreateObject("ADODB.Connection")
Set rsExample = Server.CreateObject("ADODB.Recordset")
dbConnection.Open strConnect

rsExample.Open "authors", dbConnection
```

We will work with the `authors` table in the `pubs` database for this example. Since we are only extracting information from the recordset, we can accept the default cursor and lock types. If you don't recall, this gives us a firehose cursor.

```
Dim strFileName
strFileName = Server.MapPath(CStr(Session.SessionID) & ".xml")
rsExample.Save strFileName, adPersistXML
```

For our example, we want to output the XML created by persisting the recordset back to the browser. The `Save` method allows us to convert the recordset to XML, but then only to a file. In order to create a temporary file for each possible user of the ASP page, we need a unique file name. The `SessionID` property can help us create a unique file name. Once we have the proper file name, represented as a physical path, then we can call the `Save` method, and pass in the appropriate parameter to save the file as XML.

```
Dim fso, ts, strContent, objFile
Set fso = Server.CreateObject("Scripting.FileSystemObject")
Set ts = fso.OpenTextFile(strFileName, 1)
strContent = ts.ReadAll
ts.Close
Set objFile = fso.GetFile(strFileName)
objFile.Delete
```

With the XML information now written out to a temporary file on the server, we want to read that information back into the ASP script so that we can output it to the browser. We use the `Scripting.FileSystemObject` and `Scripting.TextStream` objects to do this.

Recordset Object

507

The `OpenTextFile` method opens the temporary file as a `TextStream` object, and the `ReadAll` method returns the entire contents of the file as a string. Once we have read the information from the stream, we close it, and use the `GetFile` and `Delete` methods of the `FileSystemObject` to delete the temporary file from the server.

```
Response.ContentType = "text/xml"
Response.Write strContent
```

Finally, we want the response to this ASP script to be an XML stream. To change this, we need to modify the `ContentType` property of the `Response` object to be "text/xml." This change needs to be made before any information is written out to the browser. Once we have done this, we can simply use the `Response.Write` method to output the contents of the temporary file directly to the browser.

```
Set fso = Nothing
rsExample.Close
dbConnection.Close
Set rsExample = Nothing
Set dbConnection = Nothing
%>
```

As we saw earlier, it is good programming practice explicitly to close and release all objects that we have used, even though it is technically not necessary. But since we have used some additional objects in the page, namely those related to the file handling, we properly close and release these as well.

In JScript this code looks like:

```
<%@ LANGUAGE = JScript %>
<%
var strConnect = Application("DBConnectionString");
dbConnection = Server.CreateObject("ADODB.Connection");
rsExample = Server.CreateObject("ADODB.Recordset");
dbConnection.Open(strConnect);
rsExample.Open("authors", dbConnection);

var strFileName = Server.MapPath(String(Session.SessionID) + ".xml");
rsExample.Save(strFileName, adPersistXML);

fso = Server.CreateObject("Scripting.FileSystemObject");
ts = fso.OpenTextFile(strFileName, 1);
var strContent = ts.ReadAll();
ts.Close();
objFile = fso.GetFile(strFileName);
objFile.Delete();

Response.ContentType = "text/xml";
Response.Write(strContent);

delete fso;
rsExample.Close();
dbConnection.Close();
delete rsExample
delete dbConnection
%>
```

And the resulting output looks like this (so long as it's viewed in IE5):

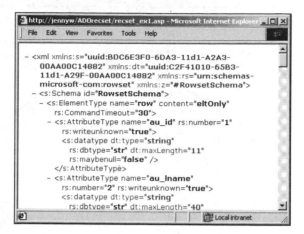

Summary

In this chapter, we looked at the Recordset object, which is probably the most commonly used ADO object. The Recordset object is used to examine and manipulate data within a database. It enables us to move through the records, find particular records that fit certain criteria, sort records in a particular order, and update records.

We have looked at:

- ❏ Cursors and locking types.
- ❏ The methods and properties of the Recordset object.
- ❏ The Fields collection and Field object.
- ❏ Examples of opening a recordset, navigating a recordset, paging through a recordset and changing data using a recordset.

Recordset Object

The Stream Object

In dealing with files and directories with the `Record` and `Recordset` objects, we have been looking at the pointers in the file system that represent these items. To deal with the *contents* of a file, we need to use the `Stream` object.

The `Stream` object contains a stream of binary or text data. It can be used to get access to the contents of a file, when the `Stream` is in effect just a holder for a block of memory, and can read and write data within it. We can open a `Stream` either directly from a URL, or from an existing `Record` object. We can also explicitly create our own `Stream` object, and use it to store our own data. Alternatively, we can persist an ADO recordset to a `Stream` object and send that to the browser (since in ASP 3.0, the `Response` and `Request` objects also support the `IStream` interface).

Stream Object Members

The `Stream` object exposes the following methods and properties:

Methods		Properties
Cancel	SaveToFile	Charset
Close	SetEOS	EOS
CopyTo	SkipLine	LineSeparator
Flush	Write	Mode
LoadFromFile	WriteText	Position
Open		Size
Read		State
ReadText		Type

Stream Object Methods

The methods of the Stream object allow us to open and close a stream, read from or write to the stream, write the data from the Stream back to the data source, and save and restore data from files.

Cancel Method

The Cancel method cancels execution of a pending asynchronous Open operation.

```
Stream.Cancel()
```

Close Method

The Close method closes an open Stream.

```
Stream.Close()
```

Note that this closes the Stream object, but does not remove it from memory. This needs to be explicitly done. Also, to avoid errors it is worth checking the stream is open before closing it. For example:

```
' VBScript
If stmExample.State = adStateOpen Then
    stmExample.Close
End If
Set stmExample = Nothing
```

```
// JScript
if (stmExample.State == adStateOpen) {
    stmExample.Close();
}
delete stmExample;
```

CopyTo Method

The CopyTo method copies characters or bytes from one Stream object to another. The number of characters copied can be specified in the optional CharNumber parameter, this defaults to −1 if it is not specified, in which case all the characters from current position to EOS will be copied.

```
Stream.CopyTo(DestStream, [CharNumber])
```

Parameter	Type	Description	Default
DestStream	Stream object	An open destination Stream object.	
CharNumber	Long	The number of characters to copy.	−1

For example:

```
' VBScript
Set stmCopy = Server.CreateObject("ADODB.Stream")
stmCopy.Open
stmOriginal.CopyTo stmCopy
stmCopy.SaveToFile "C:\test\streamcopy.xml"
Response.Write stmCopy.ReadText
```

```
// JScript
stmCopy = Server.CreateObject("ADODB.Stream");
stmCopy.Open();
stmOriginal.CopyTo(stmCopy);
stmCopy.Position = 0;
Response.Write(stmCopy.ReadText);
```

Flush Method

The Flush method flushes the contents of the stream to the underlying object.

```
Stream.Flush()
```

The Flush method will force ADO to send the information contained in the Stream object to the underlying data source. This ensures that all changes to the data are properly represented in the data source.

LoadFromFile Method

The LoadFromFile method loads a Stream from a file. The converse method is SaveToFile, which is used to load the contents of a file into a Stream object. Any information that is currently in the Stream will be overwritten when the file is read in. If the Stream is associated with a data source, then that association is unaffected.

```
Stream.LoadFromFile(FileName)
```

Parameter	Type	Description
FileName	String	The fully qualified name of the file to load from.

The FileName parameter must be either a physical location or a valid UNC name.

For example:

```
' VBScript
Response.ContentType = "text/xml"
Dim rsExample, strConnect, stmExample, strExample
Set stmExample = Server.CreateObject("ADODB.Stream")
stmExample.Open
stmExample.LoadFromFile("C:\test\streamtest.xml")
```

```
// JScript
Response.ContentType = "text/xml";
stmExample = Server.CreateObject("ADODB.Stream");
```

Stream Object

```
stmExample.Open
stmExample.LoadFromFile("C:\\test\\streamtest.xml");
var strExample = stmExample.ReadText(adReadAll);
```

Open Method

The Open method opens a Stream object from a URL or an existing Record, or creates a blank Stream. It connects to a data source to populate the contents of the Stream object.

Stream.Open([Source], [Mode], [OpenOptions], [UserName], [Password])

Parameter	Type	Description	Default
Source	Variant	Optional. The source for the data for the Stream, as an absolute or relative URL or a reference to an open Record. If no source is specified the object will be opened with no underlying source.	
Mode	ConnectMode Enum	Optional. This specifies the permissions for modifying data.	adMode Unkown
Options	StreamOpen OptionsEnum	Optional. This specifies options for the Open method.	adOpen Stream Unspecified
UserName	String	Optional. User name for source security.	
Password	String	Optional. Password for source security.	

❑ ConnectModeEnum is one of the constants adModeRead, adModeReadWrite, adModeRecursive, adModeShareDenyNone, adModeShareDenyRead, adModeShareDenyWrite, adModeShareExclusive, adModeUnknown or adModeWrite.

❑ StreamOpenOptionsEnum is one of the following: adOpenStreamUnspecified, adOpenStreamAsync or adOpenStreamFromRecord. Note: adOpenStreamFromURL does not appear in the type library; however it has a value of 8.

See Appendix D for more information on these constants.

The Open method can be used to create a blank Stream object. For example in VBScript:

```
Dim stmExample
Set stmExample = Server.CreateObject("ADODB.Stream")
stmExample.Open
```

Or in JScript:

```
stmExample = Server.CreateObject("ADODB.Stream");
stmExample.Open();
```

Alternatively we can open an existing URL or `Record`. For example in VBScript:

```
Dim stmExample, strExample
Set stmExample = Server.CreateObject("ADODB.Stream")
stmExample.Open "URL=http://localhost/streamtest.txt", adModeReadWrite, 8
' where StreamOpenOptionsEnum = 8 (adOpenStreamFromURL)

stmExample.Charset = "ascii"
Response.Write stmExample.ReadText
```

Or in JScript:

```
stmExample = Server.CreateObject("ADODB.Stream");
stmExample.Open("URL=http://localhost/streamtest.txt", adModeReadWrite, 8);
// where StreamOpenOptionsEnum = 8 (adOpenStreamFromURL)

stmExample.Charset = "ascii";
Response.Write(stmExample.ReadText);
```

Read Method

The `Read` method reads from the stream a specified number of bytes from the current position to the end of the stream. It returns this information as a variant.

```
Variant = Stream.Read(numBytes)
```

Parameter	Type	Description	Default
numBytes	Long	The number of bytes to read.	adReadAll

If no data is available to be read, then the value returned will contain a `Null`.

ReadText Method

The `ReadText` method reads a number of characters from a text stream.

```
String = Stream.ReadText([NumChars])
```

Parameter	Type	Description	Default
NumChars	Long	Optional. The number of characters to be read or a StreamReadEnum value.	adReadAll

The `StreamReadEnum` constants are `adReadAll` (-1) and `adReadLine` (-2). See Appendix D for further details.

Stream Object

Like its counterpart the Read method, the ReadText method reads the specified number of characters from the current position to the end of the stream. The return value is a Variant containing the data or NULL if no data was read. The SkipLine method can be used in conjunction with this method in text data:

```
' VBScript
stmExample.LoadFromFile("C:\test\streamtest.xml")
strExample = stmExample.ReadText(adReadAll)
```

```
// JScript
stmExample.LoadFromFile("C:\\test\\streamtest.xml");
var strExample = stmExample.ReadText(adReadAll);
```

SaveToFile Method

The SaveToFile method saves an open Stream object to a file. In addition to writing a Stream back to its original data store, we can use the SaveToFile method to save the contents to a disk file. This has no effect on the data that is stored in the original data source.

```
Stream.SaveToFile(FileName, [Options])
```

Parameter	Type	Description	Default
FileName	String	The fully qualified name of the file or a valid UNC.	
Options	SaveOptions Enum	Optional. This specifies file save options.	adSaveCreate NotExist

The SaveOptionsEnum constant is either one or both of: adSaveCreateNotExist and adSaveCreateOverwrite. See Appendix D for further details.

For example:

```
' VBScript
rsExample.Open "authors", strConnect
rsExample.Save stmExample, adPersistXML
rsExample.Close
Set rsExample = Nothing
stmExample.SaveToFile "C:\test\streamtest.xml"
```

```
// JScript
rsExample.Save(stmExample, adPersistXML);
rsExample.Close();
delete rsExample;
stmExample.SaveToFile("C:\\test\\streamtest.xml");
```

SetEOS Method

The SetEOS method sets the current position as the end of the Stream.

```
Stream.SetEOS()
```

SkipLine Method

The SkipLine method skips a line when reading from a text stream. The current position remains at EOS (end of stream) if you call this method when EOS has already been reached.

```
Stream.SkipLine()
```

Write Method

The Write method is used to write *binary* information into the stream. To add text information, use the WriteText method.

```
Stream.Write(Buffer)
```

Parameter	Type	Description
Buffer	Variant	The array of bytes to be written.

The data is added at the current position, and the size of the stream will increase as needed to accommodate the new data.

WriteText Method

The WriteText method writes text data to a Stream.

```
Stream.WriteText(data, [Options])
```

Parameter	Type	Description
data	String	The string of the text to be written to the object.
Options	StreamWriteEnum	Optional. This indicates if a line separator character should be appended to the end of the string.

The StreamWriteEnum is either adWriteChar or adWriteLine. See Appendix D for more details.

For example:

```
' VBScript
stmExample.Open
stmExample.WriteText ("this text is written to the stream.")
strExample = stmExample.ReadText(adReadAll)
Response.Write strExample
```

```
// JScript
stmExample.Open();
stmExample.WriteText("this text is written to the stream.");
strExample = stmExample.ReadText(adReadAll);
Response.Write(strExample);
```

Stream Object

517

Stream Object Properties

The properties of the Stream object allow us to specify the character set of the stream, control the current position within the stream, see if we are at the end of the stream, determine the size of the stream, and control the access mode of the stream.

Charset Property

The Charset property identifies the character set used by the Stream.

```
Stream.Charset = String
String = Stream.Charset
```

The Charset property is important when the data will need to be translated to a readable character set. A list of the character sets known by a system, can be found in the Windows Registry under HKEY_CLASSES_ROOT\MIME\Database\Charset.

For example, to set the character set to ASCII:

```
' VBScript
stmExample.Charset = "ascii"
Response.Write stmExample.ReadText
```

```
// JScript
stmExample.Charset = "ascii";
Response.Write(stmExample.ReadText);
```

EOS Property

The read-only EOS property returns true if the current pointer position is at the end of the stream.

```
Boolean = Stream.EOS
```

This is very useful, for example, in conditional statements:

```
' VBScript
stmExample.Position = 0
Do While Not stmExample.EOS
    Response.Write stmExample.ReadText(20) & "<BR>"
Loop
```

```
// JScript
stmExample.Position = 0;
while (!stmExample.EOS) {
    Response.Write(stmExample.ReadText(20) + "<BR>");
}
```

LineSeparator Property

The LineSeparator property sets or returns the character used to separate lines in a text stream.

```
Stream.LineSeparator = LineSeparatorEnum
LineSeparatorEnum = Stream.LineSeparator
```

The default is adCRLF (carriage return and line feed). As shown in Appendix D, other options are adCR (carriage return) and adLF (line feed).

Mode Property

The Mode property indicates the available permissions for modifying data in a Connection.

```
Stream.Mode = ConnectModeEnum
ConnectModeEnum = Stream.Mode
```

The possible values for ConnectModeEnum are: adModeUnknown, adModeRead, adModeWrite, adModeReadWrite, adModeShareDenyRead, adModeShareDenyWrite, adModeShareExclusive, adModeShareDenyNone and adModeRecursive.

For more information on these constants, see Appendix D.

Position Property

The Position property specifies the current position of the pointer in the Stream.

```
Stream.Position = Long
Long = Stream.Position
```

Size Property

The read-only Size property returns the length of the Stream in bytes.

```
Long = Stream.Size
```

State Property

The read-only State property indicates whether the Stream is open or closed, and if open the state of asynchronous actions.

```
ObjectStateEnum = Stream.State
```

ObjectStateEnum is one of the following: adStateClosed (the default), adStateConnecting, adStateExecuting, adStateFetching or adStateOpen. See Appendix D for more information.

This property should be checked before closing a stream, since attempting to close a closed stream will generate an error:

```
' VBScript
If stmExample.State = adStateOpen Then
    stmExample.Close
End If
Set stmExample = Nothing
```

```
// JScript
if (stmExample.State == adStateOpen) {
    stmExample.Close();
}
delete stmExample;
```

Stream Object

Type Property

The Type property indicates whether the Stream contains text or binary data.

```
Stream.Type = StreamTypeEnum
StreamTypeEnum = Stream.Type
```

StreamTypeEnum is either adTypeBinary or adTypeText.

Example of Using the Stream Object

The Stream object lets us work with textual or binary information inside an ASP page. We can either deal with that information in our script, send it to the browser via the Response object, or write it out to the server's disk using the SaveToFile method.

Persisting a Recordset with Streams

In this example, we will look at persisting a Recordset in XML format to a Stream object, which we can then read into a string and manipulate as desired. In VBScript this looks like:

```
<!-- METADATA TYPE="typelib"
    FILE="C:\Program Files\Common Files\System\ado\msado15.dll" -->
<%
Response.ContentType = "text/xml"
Dim rsExample, strConnect, stmExample, strExample
strConnect = Application("DBConnectionString")
Set rsExample = Server.CreateObject("ADODB.Recordset")
Set stmExample = Server.CreateObject("ADODB.Stream")

rsExample.Open "authors", strConnect
rsExample.Save stmExample, adPersistXML
rsExample.Close
Set rsExample = Nothing

strExample = stmExample.ReadText(adReadAll)

stmExample.Close
Set stmExample = Nothing

Response.Write strExample
%>
```

The JScript equivalent is:

```
<%@ LANGUAGE="JScript" %>
<!-- METADATA TYPE="typelib"
    FILE="C:\Program Files\Common Files\System\ado\msado15.dll" -->
<%
var rsExample, strConnect, stmExample, strExample;
strConnect = Application("DBConnectionString");
rsExample = Server.CreateObject("ADODB.Recordset");
stmExample = Server.CreateObject("ADODB.Stream");

rsExample.Open("authors", strConnect);
rsExample.Save(stmExample, adPersistXML);
rsExample.Close();
```

```
delete rsExample;

strExample = stmExample.ReadText(adReadAll);

stmExample.Close();
delete stmExample;

Response.ContentType="text/xml";
Response.Write(strExample);
%>
```

In this example, we combine `Recordset` persistence with streams. The `Recordset` object is opened to refer to the `Authors` table in the `pubs` database. We then use the `Save` method of the `Recordset` object that we saw last chapter to persist the recordset. We pass the reference to the `Stream` as the destination parameter, and then tell ADO that we want the data in XML format. Once it is persisted to the in-memory `Stream`, we can close the `Recordset` and release it. To bring the contents of the `Stream` into a local string variable, we use the `ReadText` method. With the information stored in a local variable, we can use the `Response.Write` method to output it for display on the browser.

The screen looks like this:

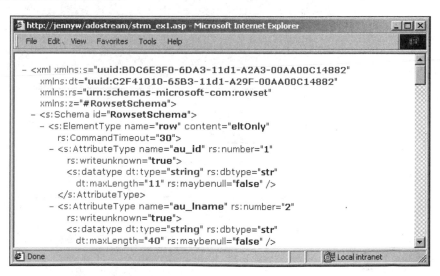

Summary

The `Stream` object provides the means to read, write, and manage the stream of binary information that comprises the non-relational storage mechanism.

In this chapter we have looked at:

❑   The methods and properties of the `Stream` object.

❑   An example of using the `Stream` object to persist a `Recordset`.

31

Data Shaping

Data shaping is a powerful and efficient way to create sophisticated data analysis and reporting applications using complex hierarchical data relationships. It allows us to represent a tree-like structure of related recordsets. This is achieved by having a field in a recordset which itself contains a recordset, i.e. **hierarchical recordsets**. Data shaping enables database relationships to be expressed, and multiple recordsets to be returned in a single call.

> A hierarchical recordset (the parent) is one that contains a field that is a pointer to another recordset (a child), which is related in some way to the parent recordset.

As an example let us consider a recordset of customer information (e.g. from the Northwind database supplied with Access and SQL Server). This could contain a field called `orders` which itself contains a recordset of all the orders placed by that particular customer:

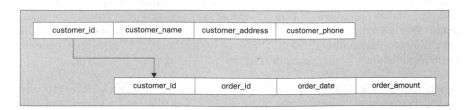

Using data shaping, we can generate this parent-child relationship between the customer data and the particular customer order data using the following SHAPE command:

```
SHAPE {SELECT * FROM customers}
   APPEND ({SELECT * FROM orders} AS rsOrders
      RELATE customer_id TO customer_id)
```

The syntax and commands used in this SHAPE command and the Shape language are covered later in this chapter. For now, simply note that we have a way of generating the information needed for, say, a report listing the customer's details and the orders for that customer, in some very succinct code. The fact that we can return all of this information with just one command enables us to build complex hierarchical recordsets with relative ease.

To demonstrate the benefits of data shaping, let us consider implementing the same example using a query that makes use of the SQL JOIN command to join the customer and order tables. This results in the following table:

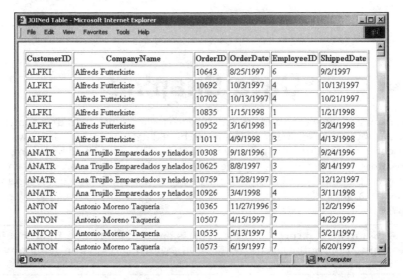

Immediately we notice a high degree of duplication, since the customer information is the same for all orders from a particular customer. The resulting recordset would be much larger than the two tables from which it derived.

What the SHAPE command produces is a recordset for all the customers, with an extra column containing another recordset for the orders from a particular customer. Child recordsets, such as the orders recordset here, are often called **chapters**, and the datatype of the column would be adChapter. The child column actually contains the details that relate the parent to the child. When you access the child (orders) column, the child recordset is filtered, so that only the correct rows are shown that relate to the particular customer you are considering.

When building the ADO connection string for a shaped recordset, we must specify two providers (unless we are manually creating recordsets that are not part of a relational database). The first provider is the service provider, which will be the **Data Shape Provider**. We must use the MSDataShape provider in order to execute a SHAPE command. The second provider is the data provider, which will supply the data for the recordsets. This is the same provider that we would use for a normal connection.

We use SHAPE commands by issuing them when opening a Recordset object, or alternatively we can set the CommandText property of the Command object to adCmdText and call the Execute method.

At first sight data shaping looks rather off-putting, since we have to use the following:

❑ The MSDataShape OLE DB service provider, which is provided as part of MDAC SDK.

❑ A special Shape language, which is not ANSI-SQL compliant, but is a set of extensions to the SQL language that allows us to construct the hierarchies.

However, it can be a very effective and efficient way of producing reports and data analysis applications.

The Data Shape Provider – MSDataShape

We consider in this section what actually happens when we use a SHAPE command for the parent-child relationship outlined in our example.

The SHAPE command is not used directly by the data provider, but instead passed to an intermediary service provider, MSDataShape. This acts as a translation layer between the SHAPE command and the (non-optimized) SQL queries that are sent to the OLE DB provider or ODBC driver and hence the database. The relationships between these objects are displayed in the following diagram.

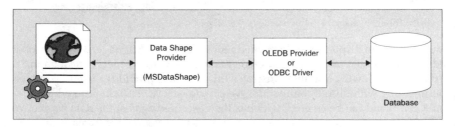

Using (for example) SQL Trace in SQL Server 6.5 or SQL Profiler in SQL Server 7.0, we can see that the SHAPE command has the effect for our customers/orders example of sending two statements to the database:

```
SELECT * FROM Customers
SELECT * FROM Orders
```

These are sent from the Data Shape Provider in one command and returned in one go as multiple recordsets. So the client machine is sent two 'small' recordsets, rather than one 'big' one resulting from a table join, and resource usage is kept to a minimum. The processing operation is then performed by the Data Shape Provider, and now actually takes place on the client machine.

With the above picture in mind it is clear why, when we write code to create a SHAPE and navigate through the records of our parent and child databases, we need to change the connection string. We should set the Provider in our connection string to "MSDataShape", rather than the OLE DB provider and database, since these are just the suppliers of the data.

However, we also need to specify the appropriate data provider for the data source from which we will take the data (e.g. SQLOLEDB for SQL Server or MSDAORA for Oracle). We do this by setting the Data Provider in the connection string. Hence our connection string contains something like the following:

```
Provider=MSDataShape; Data Provider=SQLOLEDB; ...
```

The remainder of the connection string is formed as normal.

Accessing Hierarchical Recordsets

Before we go on to look at the Shape language in detail, we need first to see how we can access our hierarchical recordsets once we have created them. In fact, this is very logical, and also very easy. Since the child recordset is the contents of a field in the parent recordset, we simply set our recordset to the Value property of the field which contains it:

```
' VBScript
Set rsChild = rsParent.Fields("Orders").Value
```

```
// JScript
rsChild = rsParent.Fields("Orders").Value;
```

If we are going to display all the returned records in an HTML page, we will probably need to create nested tables or <UL> elements to cope with the hierarchical nature of the data. The following example illustrates this, and also provides a useful page for experimenting with SHAPE commands. We provide a <TEXTAREA> into which a SHAPE command can be entered, which is then executed against the data source. We display the results using a recursive function which creates a table for each recordset, and which is originally called for our outermost recordset. Each field in the recordset is displayed as a column in the table. We check the Field object's Type property to see if it is a child recordset (adChapter, or 136). If so, we call the same recursive function (from within the function itself), passing in the Value of the Field object, to build a nested table for the child recordset. The VBScript code for this example is:

```
<% Response.Buffer = False %>
<TITLE>Data Shaping</TITLE>
<FORM ACTION="shape_vbs.asp" METHOD="POST">
    <TEXTAREA NAME="txtShape" ROWS=15 COLS=100></TEXTAREA><BR><BR>
    <INPUT TYPE=SUBMIT>
</FORM>

<%
If Request.Form("txtShape") <> "" Then
    strShape = Request.Form("txtShape")
```

```
    ' ********** Configure this connection string **********
    strConnect = "Provider=MSDataShape;Data Provider=SQLOLEDB;" & _
                 "Initial Catalog=Northwind;Data Source=ServerName;" & _
                 "User ID=sa;Password=;"
    Set cnShape = Server.CreateObject("ADODB.Connection")

    cnShape.Open strConnect

    Set rsParent = cnShape.Execute(strShape)
    Response.Write "<BR>Results of SHAPE command <B>" & strShape & "</B>:<HR>"
    RecurseChildren rsParent
End If

Sub RecurseChildren(rsChild)
%>
<TABLE BORDER=1><THEAD><TR>
<%
For Each objField In rsChild.Fields
    Response.Write "<TH>" & objField.Name & "</TH>"
Next
%>
</TR></THEAD>
<TBODY>
<%
    Do Until rsChild.EOF
        Response.Write "<TR>"
        Dim objField
        For Each objField In rsChild.Fields
            Response.Write "<TD>"
            If objField.Type = 136 Then
                Response.Write "<TABLE BORDER=1 WIDTH='100%'>"
                RecurseChildren objField.Value
                Response.Write "</TABLE>"
            Else
                Response.Write objField.Value
            End If
            Response.Write "</TD>"
        Next
        rsChild.MoveNext
        Response.Write "</TR>"
    Loop
End Sub
%>
</TBODY></TABLE>
```

And the JScript equivalent:

```
<% Response.Buffer = False; %>
<TITLE>Data Shaping</TITLE>
<FORM ACTION="shape_js.asp" METHOD="POST">
    <TEXTAREA NAME="txtShape" ROWS=15 COLS=100></TEXTAREA><BR><BR>
    <INPUT TYPE=SUBMIT>
</FORM>

<%
if (String(Request.Form("txtShape")) != "undefined") {
    strShape = Request.Form("txtShape");
```

Data Shaping

```
    // ********** Configure this connection string **********
    strConnect = "Provider=MSDataShape;Data Provider=SQLOLEDB;" +
                 "Initial Catalog=Northwind;Data Source=ServerName;" +
                 "User ID=sa;Password=;";
    cnShape = Server.CreateObject("ADODB.Connection");

    cnShape.Open(strConnect);

    rsParent = cnShape.Execute(strShape);
    Response.Write("<BR>Results of SHAPE command <B>" +
                 strShape + "</B>:<HR>");
    RecurseChildren(rsParent);
}

function RecurseChildren(rsChild) {
%>
<TABLE BORDER=1><THEAD><TR>
<%
var enmFieldNames = new Enumerator(rsChild.Fields);
for (; !enmFieldNames.atEnd(); enmFieldNames.moveNext()) {
    Response.Write("<TH>" + enmFieldNames.item().Name + "</TH>");
}
%>
</TR></THEAD>
<TBODY>
<%
    while (!rsChild.EOF) {
        Response.Write("<TR>");
        var objField;
        var enmFields = new Enumerator(rsChild.Fields);
        for (; !enmFields.atEnd(); enmFields.moveNext()) {
            objField = enmFields.item();
            Response.Write("<TD>");
            if (objField.Type == 136) {
                Response.Write("<TABLE BORDER=1 WIDTH='100%'>");
                RecurseChildren(objField.Value);
                Response.Write("</TABLE>");
            } else {
                Response.Write(objField.Value);
            }
            Response.Write("</TD>");
        }
        rsChild.MoveNext();
        Response.Write("</TR>");
    }
}
%>
</TBODY></TABLE>
```

The output of this page when a valid SHAPE command is entered is:

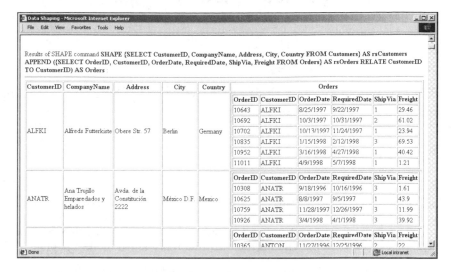

The Shape Language

The other new part of data shaping is the Shape language. This language has its own grammar and keywords, but it is based on SQL, so it should be easy to understand with a little work.

SHAPE statements fall into two basic types: APPEND commands, which are used to create child recordsets; and COMPUTE commands, which are used to create a new parent recordset. We will look at the syntax for these two types of command in detail in the following section. However, since the syntax of the Shape language is somewhat daunting, let's look first at a simple example to clarify the situation. A common Shape command just relates a parent and a child database with one column in common. The syntax is:

```
SHAPE parent_command AS parent_table_alias
    APPEND (child_command AS child_table_alias
        RELATE parent_column TO child_column) AS column_name
```

Using an example from the SQL Server pubs database, we can relate the Publishers and Titles tables with the SHAPE command:

```
SHAPE {SELECT * FROM Publishers} AS Publishers
    APPEND ({SELECT * FROM Titles} AS Titles
        RELATE Pub_ID TO Pub_ID) AS rsTitles
```

When this command is executed, we will get back a recordset that contains all of the fields in the Publishers table along with an additional field named rsTitles. This field will contain a recordset containing all of the records from the Titles table joined on the Pub_ID field.

Shape Language Reference

This contains a table of the recordset column types and a list of the commands and keywords of the Shape language.

Recordset Column Types

A shaped recordset can consist of the following types of columns (fields):

Column Type	Description
Data column	These are fields from a recordset that are either returned from a query command sent to a data provider or a table or previously shaped recordset.
Chapter column (child recordset)	This column type refers to another recordset called a chapter. The parent in a parent-child relationship is the recordset containing the chapter column and the child is the recordset represented by the chapter.
Aggregate column	The data in this column type is derived from executing an aggregate function on all the rows, or a column of all the rows of a child Recordset. The aggregate functions are: ANY, AVG, COUNT, MAX, MIN, STDEV and SUM.
Calculated column	The data in this column type is derived by calculating a Visual Basic for Applications expression on columns in the same row of the Recordset. The expression is the argument to the CALC function.
New column	This is an empty column which can be subsequently populated with data. It is defined with the NEW keyword.

Shape Commands and Keywords

The Shape language has the following commands, keywords and functions:

ANY	BY	MAX	RELATE	TABLE
APPEND	CALC	MIN	SHAPE	TO
AS	COMPUTE	NEW	STDEV	
AVG	COUNT	PARAMETER	SUM	

ANY

The ANY operator will produce a non-calculated field on the parent recordset that the COMPUTE command creates.

```
ANY(recordset_name.column_name)
```

COMPUTE command creates.

```
ANY(recordset_name.column_name)
```

It is an aggregate function of a recordset used in a Shape COMPUTE clause. We use this flag to specify a static field (which is the same for all rows). For example, if we want to add the customer's name then we would specify ANY(CustomerName) to the COMPUTE query.

APPEND

The APPEND (...) command appends chapter columns (from a child recordset) or one or more other columns to the parent recordset. This includes the *required* parentheses. The general SHAPE command with an APPEND clause is rather complicated and looks like this:

```
SHAPE [parent_command [[AS] parent_table_alias]]
    APPEND (column_list [[[AS] child_table_alias]
        [RELATE parent_column TO child_column], ...])
            [[AS] chapter_alias]
        [, ... More APPEND and RELATE lines
        in the case of multiple children]
```

> **Note that the square brackets [...] are *not* part of the Shape language, but are used here to show optional terms in syntax.**

This SHAPE command is composed of the following parts:

❑ SHAPE – The keyword denoting a data shaping operation.

❑ *parent_command* – A command related to the parent recordset. This may be omitted or one of:

   ❑ A query command for the data provider, delimited by curly braces ({ }), that returns the parent Recordset object, such as {SELECT * FROM Customers}. The command is issued to the underlying data provider, so its syntax depends on the dialect of SQL (or other language) used by the data provider.

   ❑ The name of a previously shaped recordset. See the 'Reshaping' section later in this chapter.

   ❑ Another SHAPE command, embedded in *required* parentheses, e.g. (APPEND ...) for a parent-child-grandchild hierarchy. See the section on 'Relational Recordsets' later in the chapter.

   ❑ The keyword TABLE, followed by the name of a table to be used for the parent recordset.

❑ [AS] *parent_table_alias* – Optional. The syntax used when a table alias is specified. The keyword AS is optional, but recommended for clarity. The table alias is an optional reference to the parent recordset, e.g. rsCustomers. This is useful, for example, when we may want to reshape our recordsets (see the 'Reshaping' section later in this chapter).

❑ APPEND (...) – A data shaping command that appends chapter columns (from a child recordset) or one or more other columns to the parent recordset. This includes the *required* parentheses.

❑ `column_list` – This is one or more of the following:

    ❑ A `child_column` (chapter column from a child recordset). The command for the data provider usually takes the form of a query command, delimited by curly braces, { }, that returns a child Recordset object. A SQL example is {SELECT * FROM Orders}. The command is issued to the underlying data provider; therefore its syntax depends on the language used by the data provider.

    ❑ The name of a previously shaped Recordset. See the 'Reshaping' section later in this chapter.

    ❑ Another SHAPE command, e.g. APPEND (...).

    ❑ The keyword TABLE, followed by the name of a table.

    ❑ An aggregate column which contains data derived by aggregating all rows or a column of all rows in the child recordset.

    ❑ A calculated column which contains data related to other columns in the same row.

    ❑ A new column created by the NEW clause.

❑ [AS] `child_table_alias` – Optional. The syntax used when a `child_table_alias` is specified. The keyword AS is optional, but recommended for clarity. The `child_table_alias` is an optional reference to the child recordset, e.g. rsOrders. This is useful, for example, when we may want to reshape our recordsets (see the 'Reshaping' section later in this chapter).

❑ `child_table_alias` – A reference to the child recordset returned by the command.

❑ RELATE ... TO ... – This defines how parent and child record sets are related to each other. This has a comma-delimited list of one or more fields in the parent recordset that are joined to the fields containing the same data in the child recordset.

❑ `parent_column` – A column in the parent recordset returned by the `parent_command`.

❑ `child_column` – A column in the child recordset returned by the `child_command` that contains the same data as the `parent_column`. The `parent_column` and `child_column` must be of the same datatype and length. You should follow the same rules as you would with a standard SQL JOIN command.

❑ `chapter_alias` – An alias that refers to the column appended to the parent recordset.

AS

The optional AS keyword denotes that the following name is an alias for the recordset returned from the *parent_command* or *child_command*.

```
SHAPE [parent_command [[AS] parent_table_alias]]
   APPEND (column_list [[[AS] child_table_alias]
      [RELATE parent_column TO child_column], ...])
      [[AS] chapter_alias]
```

For example, to create a parent recordset from the Publishers table with a child recordset consisting of the fields of the Titles table:

```
SHAPE {SELECT * FROM Publishers} AS Publishers
   APPEND ({SELECT * FROM Titles} AS Titles
      RELATE Pub_ID TO Pub_ID) AS rsTitles
```

AVG

The AVG command calculates the average of the values in the specified column. It is an aggregate function of a recordset used in a Shape COMPUTE clause.

```
AVG(recordset_name.column_name)
```

BY

The BY keyword is covered in the section on the COMPUTE command. If the COMPUTE command does not contain a BY clause, there will be only one parent row, whereas a BY clause will contain multiple parent rows for each unique value in the BY clause.

CALC

The CALC function allows us to calculate the values for a new column. These values are calculated using a VBA (Visual Basic for Applications) function acting on the specified *Column_name*.

```
CALC(function(Column_name))
```

Where *function* may be one of the following VBA functions:

Data Shaping

533

Abs	Cos	Error	IsDate	LTrim$	Rate	Sqr	Trim$
Asc	CSng	Error$	IsEmpty	Mid	RGB	Str	TypeName
Atn	CStr	Exp	IsError	Mid$	Right	Str$	UCase
CBool	Cvar	Fix	IsNull	Minute	RightB	StrComp	UCase$
CByte	CVDate	Format	IsNumeric	MIRR	Right$	StrConv	Val
CCur	CVErr	Format$	IsObject	Month	RightB$	String	VarType
CDate	Date	FV	LCase	Now	Rnd	String$	Weekday
CDbl	Date$	Hex	LCase$	NPer	RTrim	SYD	Year
Chr	DateAdd	Hex$	Left	NPV	RTrim$	Tan	
ChrB	DateDiff	Hour	LeftB	Oct	Second	Time	
ChrW	DatePart	IIF	Left$	Oct$	Sgn	Time$	
Chr$	DateSerial	InStr	LeftB$	Pmt	Sin	Timer	
ChrB$	DateValue	Int	Len	PPmt	SLN	TimeSerial	
CInt	Day	IPmt	Log	PV	Space	TimeValue	
CLng	DDB	IRR	LTrim	QBColor	Space$	Trim	

For example, if we want to create a field containing the rounded values of the order totals for individual customers in our recordset, we could use the Int function (with + 0.5 to round to the nearest integer, rather than to round down). The SHAPE command for this is:

```
SHAPE {SELECT * FROM Orders}
   APPEND (({SELECT [Order Details].OrderID,
              [Order Details].UnitPrice*[Order Details].Quantity AS
              ExtendedPrice FROM [Order Details]}
       RELATE OrderID TO OrderID) As rsOrderDetails,
   SUM(rsOrderDetails.ExtendedPrice) AS OrderTotal,
   CALC(Int(OrderTotal + 0.5)) AS RoundedTotal
```

COMPUTE [... BY ...]

The COMPUTE clause generates a parent recordset from calculated values. This is very useful for generating reports from a set of data. A COMPUTE clause differs from the APPEND clause, in that it involves only one source dataset. The new recordset that it generates is a new *parent* rather than a new child recordset.

The COMPUTE command can be used with or without the BY statement, which specifies how the rows in the child recordset are grouped. This is similar to a SQL GROUP BY statement and rows with a common column value are grouped together. Aggregate columns are formed using SUM, AVG, MIN, MAX, COUNT, STDEV, ANY and CALC.

```
SHAPE {child_command} [AS] child_table_alias
   COMPUTE child_table_alias [[AS] name], appended_column_list]
      [BY group_field_list]
```

Where the parts are:

❑ *child_command* – A command related to the child recordset. This is one of:

    ❑ A query command for the data provider, delimited by curly braces, "{ }", that returns the child Recordset object. A SQL example is {SELECT * FROM Orders}. The command is issued to the underlying data provider, so its syntax depends on the language used by the data provider.

    ❑ The name of a previously shaped recordset. See the 'Reshaping' section later in this chapter.

    ❑ Another SHAPE command, embedded in *required* parentheses, e.g. (APPEND ...) for a parent-child-grandchild hierarchy. See the section on 'Relational Recordsets' later in the chapter.

    ❑ The keyword TABLE, followed by the name of a table to be used for the child recordset.

❑ *child_table_alias* – A reference to the child recordset returned by the command.

- ❏ *appended_column_list* – A list where each element defines a column in the generated parent recordset. Each element may be one of:

  - ❏ A chapter column.

  - ❏ A new column.

  - ❏ A calculated column.

  - ❏ A value resulting from an aggregate function on the child recordset.

- ❏ *group_field_list* – A list of columns in the parent and child recordsets that specifies how rows should be grouped in the child. This specifies the group order of the child recordset. This is equivalent to the GROUP BY clause in normal SQL syntax.

A simple example of using COMPUTE in the Shape language is:

```
SHAPE {SELECT * FROM Customers} AS rsCustomers
    COMPUTE rsCustomers BY CustomerID
```

If the COMPUTE command does not contain a BY clause, there will be only one parent row. If a BY clause is included, the parent recordset will contain multiple rows for each unique value in the BY clause.

See the section on 'Grouped/Aggregated Recordsets' for more details on using the COMPUTE command.

COUNT

COUNT is an aggregate function of a recordset used in a Shape COMPUTE clause. This counts the number of rows in the recordset or column. For the COUNT function, the *column_name* is an optional parameter, since the number of rows in the column and the recordset are equal.

```
COUNT(recordset_name.[column_name])
```

MAX

The MAX command calculates the maximum value in the specified column. This is an aggregate function of a recordset used in a Shape COMPUTE clause.

```
MAX(recordset_name.column_name)
```

MIN

The MIN command calculates the minimum value in the specified column. This is an aggregate function of a recordset used in a Shape COMPUTE clause.

```
MIN(recordset_name.column_name)
```

NEW

A NEW command adds an empty column of the specified type to the recordset.

```
NEW (field_type [(width | scale [, precision])])
```

The *field_type* and optional *width* or *scale* (and *precision*) parameters depend on the data provider in use. For example, where the Data Provider is set to NONE, we would use VBScript code such as the following to create a shaped recordset programmatically:

```
Dim dbConnection, rsParent, rsChild
Set dbConnection = Server.CreateObject("ADODB.Connection")
dbConnection.Open "Provider=MSDataShape; Data Provider=NONE;"
strSHAPE = "SHAPE APPEND " & _
           "NEW adInteger AS ClientID, " & _
           "NEW adVarChar(50) AS ClientName, " & _
           "(( SHAPE APPEND " & _
              "NEW adVarChar(4) AS StockID, " & _
              "NEW adVarChar(20) AS StockName, " & _
              "NEW adInteger AS ClientID) " & _
           "RELATE ClientID TO ClientID) AS Portfolio"
Set rsParent = Server.CreateObject("ADODB.Recordset")
rsParent.CursorLocation = adUseClient
rsParent.Open strSHAPE, dbConnection, adOpenStatic, adLockOptimistic

With rsParent
   .AddNew
   .Fields("ClientID") = 1
   .Fields("ClientName") = "Chris Mawbey"
   .Update
   '... etc
End with

Set rsChild = rsParent.Fields("Portfolio").Value
With rsChild
   .AddNew
   .Fields("ClientID") = 1
   .Fields("StockID") = "AOL"
   .Fields("StockName") = "America OnLine"
   .Update
   '... etc
End with
```

Or in JScript:

```
dbConnection = Server.CreateObject("ADODB.Connection");
dbConnection.Open("Provider=MSDataShape; Data Provider=NONE;");
var strSHAPE = "SHAPE APPEND " +
               "NEW adInteger AS ClientID, " +
               "NEW adVarChar(50) AS ClientName, " +
               "(( SHAPE APPEND " +
                  "NEW adVarChar(4) AS StockID, " +
                  "NEW adVarChar(20) AS StockName, " +
                  "NEW adInteger AS ClientID) " +
               "RELATE ClientID TO ClientID) AS Portfolio";
rsParent = Server.CreateObject("ADODB.Recordset");
rsParent.CursorLocation = adUseClient;
rsParent.Open(strSHAPE, dbConnection, adOpenStatic, adLockOptimistic);

with (rsParent) {
   AddNew();
   Fields("ClientID") = 1;
   Fields("ClientName") = "Chris Mawbey";
```

Data Shaping

```
   Update();
   //... etc
}

rsChild = rsParent.Fields("Portfolio").Value;
with (rsChild) {
   AddNew();
   Fields("ClientID") = 1;
   Fields("StockID") = "AOL";
   Fields("StockName") = "America OnLine";
   Update();
   //... etc
}
```

PARAMETER

The PARAMETER keyword is used when a parameterized query is made. PARAMETER 0 dynamically populates the *child_column_name* = ? parameter each time we move in the parent recordset.

```
SHAPE [parent_command]
   APPEND ({native_SQL_query WHERE child_column_name = ?}
      RELATE parent_column TO PARAMETER 0)
```

Using parameters is more efficient than the non-parameterized syntax, because the data for the child recordset is fetched on an as-needed basis, whereas a standard SHAPE command will pull all of the necessary data and generate the child records on the client. However, we cannot disconnect a recordset shaped with parameters. We can only disconnect a recordset that uses the standard APPEND syntax. Keep that point in mind, since we may need to decide between speed, bandwidth and server resources.

For example:

```
SHAPE {SELECT * FROM Publishers}
   APPEND ({SELECT * FROM Titles WHERE Pub_ID=?} AS Titles
      RELATE Pub_ID TO PARAMETER 0) AS rsTitles
```

Parameterized recordsets are discussed in more detail below.

RELATE

The RELATE ... TO ... command defines how parent and child recordsets are related to each other. This has a comma-delimited list of one or more fields in the parent recordset that are joined to the fields containing the same data in the child recordset.

```
RELATE parent_column TO child_column
```

Where:

- ❑ *parent_column* – A column in the parent recordset returned by the *parent_command*.

- ❑ *child_column* – A column in the child recordset returned by the *child_command* that contains the same data as the *parent_column*. The *parent_column* and *child_column* must be of the same datatype and length. You should follow the same rules as you would with a standard SQL JOIN command.

For example:

```
SHAPE {SELECT * FROM Publishers} AS Publishers
    APPEND ({SELECT * FROM Titles} AS Titles
        RELATE Pub_ID TO Pub_ID) AS rsTitles
```

SHAPE

The SHAPE keyword denotes a command in the Shape language that is interpreted by the MSDataShape Provider. This contains an APPEND statement or a COMPUTE statement.

```
SHAPE ... APPEND (...) RELATE (... TO ...)
SHAPE ... COMPUTE ...
```

Nested SHAPE commands are used for parent-child-grandchild and higher relation-based hierarchies.

Any command not starting with SHAPE is passed through to the data provider. This is equivalent to issuing a SHAPE command of the form SHAPE{*provider_command*}. In this case, the command does not need to return a hierarchical recordset. This feature means that both normal provider and SHAPE commands can share the same connection and transaction.

STDEV

The STDEV command calculates the standard deviation of the values in the specified column. It is an aggregate function of a recordset used in a Shape COMPUTE clause.

```
STDEV(recordset_name.column_name)
```

SUM

The SUM command calculates the sum of the values in the specified column. It is an aggregate function of a recordset used in a Shape COMPUTE clause.

```
SUM(recordset_name.column_name)
```

For example:

```
SHAPE {SELECT * FROM Orders}
    APPEND ({SELECT [Order Details].OrderID,
            [Order Details].UnitPrice*[Order Details].Quantity AS
            ExtendedPrice FROM [Order Details]}
        RELATE OrderID TO OrderID) AS rsOrderDetails,
        SUM(rsOrderDetails.ExtendedPrice) AS OrderTotal
```

TABLE

The TABLE keyword is used to precede the name of a table which represents the parent or child recordset, included as part of a *child_command* or *parent_command* in an APPEND or COMPUTE clause.

```
TABLE recordset_name.column_name
```

Data Shaping

For example:

```
SHAPE TABLE Publishers
    APPEND (TABLE Titles
        RELATE Pub_ID to Pub_ID) AS rsTitles
```

TO

The keyword TO is used with the RELATE clause in a Shape APPEND statement. See the section on the RELATE command.

Types of Hierarchical Recordsets

Data shaping supports three types of hierarchies:

❑ **Relation-based hierarchies**: These use the most basic form of SHAPE command, where there is a recordset that contains a related child recordset. They can be parent-child (with a single child or multiple children) or parent-child-granchild relationships (with three or more "generations").

❑ **Parameterized hierarchies**: These are similar to relational recordsets, except that each child recordset is fetched only as needed when a parent moves the record pointer. Parameterized recordsets are also used when calling stored procedures that take parameters.

❑ **Grouped hierarchies**: The Shape language also allows us to create a new parent recordset with computed values, which we can use to group the child recordsets.

Relational Recordsets

In a relation-based hierarchy the client fetches two recordsets (a parent and a child recordset) which are related on a common field (column of data). This is more efficient and flexible than a standard SQL JOIN. Since we can have nested SHAPE commands, the relationships between the recordsets can be not only parent-child, but also parent-multiple child, parent grandchild, parent-multiple grandchild, and we can even have great grandchildren!

Parent-Child

A parent-child relationship is created by a simple Shape APPEND syntax between two tables. A parent child relationship is similar to using a table join in standard SQL, but without the redundant row-by-row data that a JOIN returns. Alternatively, if we wanted a list of customers and orders, we could return two recordsets and write code for every time we move in either recordset, rather than returning the data as one table as for a JOIN query. The single table solution is the most common, but most inefficient, because we are returning customer information on every row that has order information. If a customer has placed, say, 50 orders with us, we will duplicate the entire customer table 50 times. This makes for large recordsets and wasted network bandwidth. We can use the SHAPE command to produce the same results in a more efficient manner.

To relate customers and orders we would use the SHAPE syntax to generate the following command, in the Shape language:

```
SHAPE {select * FROM customers}
   APPEND ({select * FROM orders} AS rsOrders
      RELATE customerID TO customerID)
```

Executing this SHAPE command will give the structure shown below. The entire Orders table is a child of the Customers table.

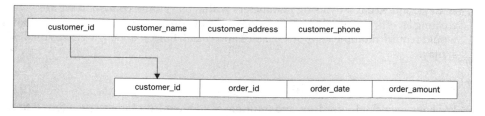

The key point to note here is that we are not duplicating customer data for each order row. Each parent record from the customers table has a field called rsOrders that contains a reference to the child recordset from the orders table and contains all of the fields from the orders table. As we move through the customer recordset we requery the child recordset to generate only the required information.

Multiple Children

A parent record can have more than one child recordset. For instance, we would like to see all orders over 30 days old in one recordset and all new orders less than 30 days old in another recordset. We can use the SHAPE command to generate these two recordsets under the parent customer table. If we modify our code to look like the following, we will produce two child recordsets.

```
SHAPE {SELECT * FROM Customers}
   APPEND ({SELECT * FROM Orders
              WHERE OrderDate < getdate() - 30 AND CustomerID = ?}
         RELATE CustomerID TO PARAMETER 0) AS rsOver30Days,
         ({SELECT * FROM Orders
              WHERE OrderDate >= getdate() - 30 AND CustomerID = ?}
         RELATE CustomerID TO PARAMETER 0) AS rsUnder30Days
```

Note that the getdate() function used here is specific to SQL Server's Transact-SQL. An alternative would be to pass the date in from your script code when building the SQL statement.

In the above command we are using a parameterized query, where PARAMETER 0 dynamically populates the CustomerID = ? parameter each time we move in the parent recordset. The structure of the recordset lists the Orders table twice as a child of the customer SHAPE since we have generated two distinct recordsets for the customers to be joined with. The figure below displays the Customers recordset with the two child recordsets for the orders over 30 days old as well as the recordset for the orders less than 30 days old.

Data Shaping

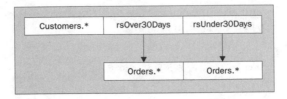

We can create as many child recordsets as necessary. We could follow this syntax to generate a shaped recordset of an invoice-aging summary for under 30 days, 30 days, 60 days, and 90 days. By using parameters within our SHAPE command we are creating an efficient means of data retrieval, and we are retrieving data in ways that would require multiple temporary tables and calculations if done with traditional SQL syntax.

Parent-Child-Grandchild

We have seen child recordsets and multiple child recordsets (otherwise referred to as nested SHAPEs) with ADO, but we can continue to add children to child recordsets. This is known as a parent-child-grandchild relationship. Taking our first example one step further, we can append the order details information to the recordset in order to see all of the line items of a given order for a specific customer. The syntax for this stays the same, with the exception of an additional APPEND and SHAPE command.

This is the source that has been updated to reflect the new grandchild OrderDetails table. In the Shape language this looks like:

```
SHAPE {SELECT * FROM Customers}
    APPEND ((SHAPE {SELECT * FROM Orders} AS rsOrders
        APPEND ({SELECT * FROM [Order Details]} AS rsOrderDetails
            RELATE OrderID TO OrderID) AS rsOrderDetails)
        RELATE CustomerID TO CustomerID)
```

This yields the following structure:

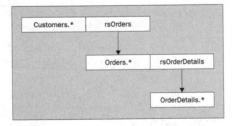

As we can see, we add a grandchild to a child by adding another APPEND clause to the current SHAPE command. We can go even further by appending to a grandchild through another APPEND clause. There is virtually no limit to the levels that we can create in an ADO shaped recordset.

Parameterized Recordsets

We looked at the simple SHAPE command in our first example, and we can take the same code and generate a parameterized hierarchy. In the following we change our Shape code from:

```
SHAPE {SELECT * FROM Customers}
    APPEND ({SELECT * FROM Orders} AS rsOrders
        RELATE CustomerID TO CustomerID)
```

to:

```
SHAPE {SELECT * FROM Publishers}
    APPEND ({SELECT * FROM Titles WHERE Pub_ID=?} AS Titles
        RELATE Pub_ID TO PARAMETER 0) AS rsTitles
```

This produces the same results but is more efficient because the data for orders is fetched on an as-needed basis, whereas a standard SHAPE command will pull all of the necessary data and generate the child records on the client. However, we cannot disconnect a recordset shaped with parameters. Remember, we can only disconnect a recordset that uses the standard Shape APPEND syntax.

We are able to use parameters on multiple levels of a SHAPE command, for example in the parent-child-grandchild relationship used earlier, which is much more efficient than the non-parameterized code. We lose the ability to disconnect from this recordset and we cannot marshal this recordset out of process, as that the recordset is built on an as-needed basis. If we send the recordset from a middle tier to a client, there is no way for the recordset to fetch the child records on subsequent calls.

Grouped/Aggregate Recordsets

The Shape language contains a COMPUTE command that we can use to generate a parent recordset on calculated values or to group data. This is very useful for generating reports from a set of data.

The COMPUTE command differs from the APPEND command in that it involves only one set of data: it generates a new *parent* rather than a new child recordset. This is similar to a GROUP BY SQL statement and rows with a common column value are grouped together and aggregate columns formed (e.g. using SUM, AVG etc.).

Although only one set of data, or source recordset, is used, two recordsets are returned by a COMPUTE command. These are the parent recordset, containing the group and aggregate data, and the child recordset with the details of the actual rows.

Before we COMPUTE a recordset, let's first consider using an aggregate function within a normal SHAPE command. We can produce a report of the total order price for each customer and order using the SUM aggregate as follows in the Shape language:

Data Shaping

```
SHAPE {SELECT * FROM Orders}
    APPEND ({SELECT [Order Details].OrderID,
            [Order Details].UnitPrice*[Order Details].Quantity
            AS ExtendedPrice FROM [Order Details]}
        RELATE OrderID TO OrderID) As rsOrderDetails,
        SUM(rsOrderDetails.ExtendedPrice) AS OrderTotal
```

This returns a recordset that has shaped the `OrderTotal` information within the parent recordset:

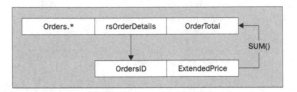

Using the SUM function rolls up data to the parent recordset. The COMPUTE statement, on the other hand, creates a new parent recordset. The following SHAPE statement uses the COMPUTE command to produce a recordset that groups Customers by CustomerID. In the Shape language this looks like:

```
SHAPE {SELECT * FROM Customers} AS rsCustomers
    COMPUTE rsCustomers BY CustomerID
```

The above code doesn't do much apart from illustrate the creation of a new parent recordset as shown below:

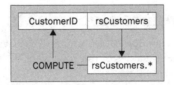

We can expand this SHAPE statement into something more meaningful by adding more detail information. If we take our query above, where we are calculating the line item total (ExtendedPrice) and roll the information up to a customer level to find the order totals, then we can produce a very detailed order report. We use the next SHAPE query to produce the desired output. In the Shape language this looks like:

```
SHAPE(SHAPE {SELECT Customers.CustomerID, Orders.OrderID
    FROM Customers INNER JOIN Orders
    ON Customers.CustomerID = Orders.CustomerID}
    APPEND ({SELECT [Order Details].OrderID,
        [Order Details].UnitPrice * [Order Details].Quantity
        AS ExtendedPrice FROM [Order Details]} AS rsOrderDetails
    RELATE OrderID TO OrderID),
    SUM(rsOrderDetails.ExtendedPrice) AS OrderTotal) AS rsOrders
    COMPUTE rsOrders,
    SUM(rsOrders.OrderTotal) AS CustomerTotal
        BY CustomerID
```

This looks pretty complex now, so let's break the query down into manageable parts. First, we have the query that we used previously to find the line item totals. If we take the `rsOrders` and `rsOrderDetails` out of the SHAPE query, then we are left with the changes that we made:

```
SHAPE
    <OLD SHAPE QUERY>
        COMPUTE rsOrders,
        SUM(rsOrders.OrderTotal) AS CustomerTotal
        BY CustomerID
```

All we have added is the COMPUTE and SUM sections of the new SHAPE command. What we are creating is a new parent recordset that adds all of the order totals and groups by customer. This produces an outline with the parent totals:

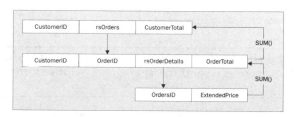

The `rsOrders` and `rsOrderDetails` recordsets are the recordsets returned by the original query, and the COMPUTE command has added the new parent recordset that contains the `CustomerTotal` and `CustomerID` fields.

COMPUTE clauses can be the most confusing aspect of data shaping, since the generation of a new parent recordset changes the entire hierarchy of the recordset structure. However, with just a little practice we will be able to generate complex COMPUTE queries with little trouble.

Reshaping

Recordsets that have been created with the Data Shape Provider can be reshaped. This allows us to take recordsets built from the same connection and shape them as we would with a single SHAPE statement. We can take an existing recordset that has already been created and shape the recordset to display new data. We can use the AS operator to assign a name to a shaped recordset.

> **The reshaped recordset must have the same** `Connection` **object as the original recordset.**

Data reshaping utilizes the names given to recordsets in SHAPE commands. For example, if we had the SHAPE command:

```
SHAPE {SELECT * FROM Customers} as rsCustomers
    APPEND ((SHAPE {SELECT * FROM Orders} AS rsOrders
        APPEND ({SELECT * FROM [Order Details]} AS rsOrderDetails
            RELATE OrderID TO OrderID) AS OrderDetails)
        RELATE CustomerID TO CustomerID)
```

What reshaping allows us to do is to take the rsCustomers, rsOrders or rsOrderDetails recordsets and use them in another SHAPE command. This enables us to break complex Shape statements into much smaller statements and reuse existing recordsets without the need to transmit the same data to the client for each request.

For instance as an illustration of the concept, we can take the SHAPE command:

```
SHAPE {select * FROM customers} AS rsCustomers
    APPEND ({select * FROM orders} AS rsOrders
        RELATE customer_id TO customer_id)
```

Then we would be able to reshape both rsCustomers and rsOrders. For instance, we can reshape rsOrders by running a COMPUTE statement. This would look like:

```
SHAPE {rsOrders}
    COMPUTE rsOrders BY CustomerID
```

> You cannot reshape a parameterized recordset or a recordset involved in a COMPUTE clause, or perform aggregate operations on any recordset resulting from reshaping.

Benefits and Limitations of Reshaping

The main benefit of reshaping is for persisted recordsets. We can generate a complex SHAPE command and use the ADO Recordset's Save method to persist the recordset. At a later time, we can generate reports or further analyze the data. This can be a very valuable tool if, for example, we have a traveling sales force who would like the ability to analyze sales data while traveling away from the main system.

The limitations when reshaping data are:

❏ The SHAPE command must refer to recordsets created by the same process on the same computer.

❏ The APPEND clause cannot be used to add new columns to an existing recordset.

❏ Reshaping of parameterized recordsets is not supported.

❏ We cannot reshape recordsets in an intervening COMPUTE clause or perform aggregate operations on any recordset other than the one being reshaped.

Example of Using Data Shaping

In this example, we will take a look at how to create a hierarchical recordset using the MSDataShape provider and the Shape query language.

```
Application("DBShapingConnection") = "Provider=MSDataShape; " & _
        "Data Provider=SQLOLEDB; Data Source=Server_name; " & _
        "Initial Catalog=pubs; User ID=sa; Password =;"
```

First, we add a line to our `global.asa` file to represent the new connection string that we need to use the `MSDataShape` provider. All of the other connection information is the same – we have just added the proper provider and changed our SQLOLEDB provider to be a Data Provider.

```
<!-- METADATA TYPE="TypeLib"
     FILE="C:\Program Files\Common Files\System\ado\msado15.dll" -->
<%
Dim dbConnection, rsPubs, strConnect, strSHAPE, rsTitles, rsEmp
strConnect = Application("DBShapingConnection")
strSHAPE = "SHAPE {SELECT Pub_ID, Pub_Name FROM Publishers} " & _
           "APPEND ({SELECT Pub_ID, title FROM Titles} " & _
           "RELATE Pub_ID to Pub_ID) AS rsTitles, " & _
           "({SELECT * FROM Employee} " & _
           "RELATE Pub_ID TO Pub_ID) AS rsEmployees"
```

We set up our example to relate together the publishers, titles and employees in the SQL Server `pubs` database. Our parent recordset will contain the records from the `Publishers` table. This will contain four fields – two from the `Publishers` table itself, one containing a recordset of the titles for the publisher, and one containing a recordset of the employees that work for the publisher.

```
Set dbConnection = Server.CreateObject("ADODB.Connection")
Set rsPubs = Server.CreateObject("ADODB.Recordset")
dbConnection.Open strConnect

rsPubs.Open strSHAPE, dbConnection
```

We connect to the database in the same way that we are used to. We will open a `Connection` object and then use that object to open the `Recordset`. Instead of passing a SQL `SELECT` statement to the `Open` method, we are passing the SHAPE statement. Since our provider is now `MSDataShape`, it understands how to interpret this text.

```
Response.Write "<UL>" & vbCrLf
Do While Not rsPubs.EOF
   Response.Write "<LI>" & rsPubs("Pub_Name") & vbCrLf
   Response.Write "<UL>Titles<UL>" & vbCrLf
   Set rsTitles = rsPubs("rsTitles").Value
   Do While Not rsTitles.EOF
      Response.Write "<LI>" & rsTitles("title") & vbCrLf
      rsTitles.MoveNext
   loop
   Response.Write "</UL></UL>" & vbCrLf
```

Since the publishers information is our parent in the hierarchy, we will loop through this recordset. Within each record in this recordset, we will want to display the child recordsets. To access this child recordset, we will take the value from the `rsTitles` field and assign it to a local variable. This now represents the child recordset, and we can navigate through it in the same way that we have become accustomed to.

```
Response.Write "<UL>Employees<UL>" & vbCrLf
Set rsEmp = rsPubs("rsEmployees").Value
Do While Not rsEmp.EOF
   Response.Write "<LI>" & rsEmp("fname") & " " & _
```

Data Shaping

```
                         rsEmp("lname") & vbCrLf
        rsEmp.MoveNext
    Loop
    Response.Write "</UL></UL>" & vbCrLf
    rsPubs.MoveNext
Loop
```

Once we have displayed all of the titles associated with this publisher, we can then display all of the employees. We will obtain a reference to this child recordset in the same way – this time retrieving it from the rsEmployees field in the parent recordset. Once we have output all of the employee information, we can move to the next publisher in the list.

```
Response.Write "</UL>"

rsPubs.Close
dbConnection.Close
Set rsTitles = Nothing
Set rsPubs = Nothing
Set rsEmp = Nothing
Set dbConnection = Nothing
%>
```

We can see from this example how easy it is to create and display hierarchical recordsets. Data shaping doesn't automatically improve performance, but when used correctly it can. For the SELECT statements in the SHAPE statement, the tables are fetched from the data source in their entirety, so using a WHERE clause will not optimize the retrieval of information that forms the child recordsets.

The JScript equivalent of this code is:

```
<%@ LANGUAGE="JScript" %>
<!-- METADATA TYPE="typelib"
    FILE="C:\Program Files\Common Files\System\ado\msado15.dll" -->
<%
var dbConnection, rsPubs, strConnect, strSHAPE, rsTitles, rsEmp;
strConnect = Application("DBShapingConnection");
strSHAPE = "SHAPE {SELECT Pub_ID, Pub_Name FROM Publishers} " +
           "APPEND ({SELECT Pub_ID, title FROM Titles} " +
           "RELATE Pub_ID to Pub_ID) AS rsTitles, " +
           "({SELECT * FROM Employee} " +
           "RELATE Pub_ID TO Pub_ID) AS rsEmployees";
dbConnection = Server.CreateObject("ADODB.Connection");
rsPubs = Server.CreateObject("ADODB.Recordset");
dbConnection.Open(strConnect);

rsPubs.Open(strSHAPE, dbConnection);
Response.Write("<UL>\n");
while (!rsPubs.EOF) {
    Response.Write("<LI>" + rsPubs("Pub_Name") + "\n");
    Response.Write("<UL>Titles\n<UL>\n");
    rsTitles = rsPubs("rsTitles").Value;
    while (!rsTitles.EOF) {
        Response.Write("<LI>" + rsTitles("title") + "\n");
        rsTitles.MoveNext();
    }
    Response.Write("</UL>\n</UL>\n");
    Response.Write("<UL>Employees\n<UL>\n");
        rsEmp = rsPubs("rsEmployees").Value;
```

```
    while (!rsEmp.EOF) {
        Response.Write("<LI>" + rsEmp("fname") + " " +
                        rsEmp("lname") + "\n");
        rsEmp.MoveNext();
    }
    Response.Write("</UL>\n</UL>\n");
    rsPubs.MoveNext();
}
Response.Write("</UL>");

rsPubs.Close();
dbConnection.Close();
delete rsTitles;
delete rsPubs;
delete rsEmp;
delete dbConnection;
%>
```

The output of this is:

Summary

In this chapter we considered data shaping, the concept of building hierarchical recordsets. A hierarchical recordset (the parent) is one that contains a field that is a pointer to another recordset (a child), which is related in some way to the parent recordset. Data shaping allows us to develop hierarchical recordsets through an extension of regular SQL syntax, called the Shape language. Data shaping uses a special service provider, the Data Shape Provider (MSDataShape).

In this chapter we looked at:

❑   The concept of data shaping.

❑   The MSDataShape service provider.

❑   The Shape language, which allows us to construct the hierarchies.

❑   The types of hierarchies supported by data shaping: relation-based, parameterized and grouping/aggregate hierarchies.

❑   The concept of reshaping which enables us to take existing shaped recordsets and modify the data that they represent.

❑   An example of generating a report using data shaping.

Data Shaping

549

32

ADOX

ADO Extensions for Data Definition Language and Security (ADOX) provides us with a rich set of tools for accessing the structure, security model, and procedures stored in a database. It allows the manipulation of the data store through a standardized object model, thus removing the necessity to learn the explicit syntax of the data provider, in keeping with Microsoft's UDA (Universal Data Object) strategy.

As its full name suggests, ADOX provides two new sets of tools: The ADOX object model contains objects which allow us to manage database security, and also to perform **Data Definition Language** (DDL) operations.

Data Definition Language refers to the set of SQL commands used to modify the schema of a database. DDL is used to build a framework in which programmers and end users can place their data rather than inserting data into the database, performing searches, or retrieving data. This first aspect of ADOX is designed to abstract the DDL features of individual data providers into a simple set of components. This enables us to access metadata, create tables and procedures, etc., without knowing the specific language that the data store uses.

The second aspect of ADOX covers security. The SQL language contains another sub-language, known as **Data Control Language** (DCL), which is used to manage the security of a database. DCL comprises a number of of SQL commands for assigning or denying permissions to particular users or groups of users and for assigning users to or removing them from groups. Again, ADOX abstracts these DCL operations so that we don't need to know the SQL syntax used by the data store.

ADOX is most closely linked with the Jet Engine in Microsoft Access, but it can also be used to manipulate SQL Server though the SQLOLEDB provider, or Oracle databases through the MSDAORA provider. It is, however, most fully supported for the Access engine. Other OLE DB Providers currently available may not support all properties and methods. If you wish to use ADOX, you should consult the provider's documentation for more details on supported properties for ADOX.

Given that the Jet Engine in Access is the only provider that gives full support for ADOX, you could ask the question: "Why should I bother with ADOX?". The answer is that although the technology is still very new, it is hoped both that support for ADOX will grow, and that its limitations will be resolved as new providers are released. This would then give us a more-or-less provider-neutral Application Programming Interface (API) for all our DDL and security needs (although there will always be some anomalies, such as data types that are available for some providers and not others). One of the reasons for the success of ADO it that its object model is supported by many data providers, and it is hoped that this success will in time translate to ADOX. If you want to migrate from DAO to ADOX, http://msdn.microsoft.com/library/officedev/off2000/achowDAOToADOX.htm provides the DAO-to-ADOX object map.

Before using any ADOX constants, we need to reference the type library in msadox.dll. This is usually installed in the Program Files\Common Files\System\Ado directory. We will also need to reference the ADO type library if we want to use any constants associated with the ADO Command objects, for example when creating new procedures and views. When developing in VBScript for the web, notice that the ADOX constants are not defined in adovbs.inc, and for example, the following reference could be added in our global.asa:

```
<!-- METADATA TYPE="TypeLib"  VERSION="2.5"
          NAME="Microsoft ADO Ext. 2.5 for DDL and Security"
          UUID="{00000600-0000-0010-8000-00AA006D2EA4}" -->
```

ADOX Object Model

The object model for ADOX provides support for creating, modifying, and deleting database objects, such as tables and stored queries. It also provides an object interface to the security aspects of the database, allowing us to control users and groups, along with assigning permissions to objects.

The ADOX object model observes more of a hierarchy than the ADO object model, but that's because of the nature of the objects it contains. This means that there is a parent object and several child objects:

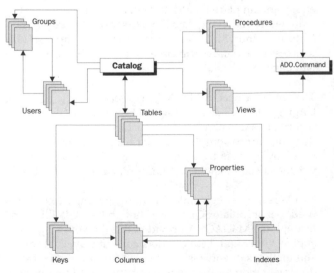

The objects in the ADOX object model are:

Object		
Catalog	Indexes	Tables
Column	Key	Table
Columns	Keys	User
Group	Procedure	Users
Groups	Procedures	View
Index	Properties	Views

ADOX Object Overview

Before we look at the ADOX objects and their methods and properties in detail, it is useful to briefly introduce each object. The ADOX object model consists of the following objects and collections:

❑ The **Catalog object** is really just a container for all of the other objects. It allows us to connect to a data source (using the ActiveConnection property) and drill-down to its components. It's also possible to obtain and set the owner of various objects without using the collections.

❑ The **Column object** represents an individual column of a Table, Index or Key object. This is similar to the ADO Field object, but rather than storing the details of a recordset, it holds the details of a stored column, such as its name, its data type, etc. For Key columns it contains details of the related columns, and for Index columns it contains details of the clustering and sorting.

❑ The **Columns collection** contains all of the columns for a particular Table, Key or Index object.

❑ The **Group object** identifies a particular security group, containing a list of users in the catalog. It allows the retrieval and setting of permission for a named group of users, and enables us to access the Users collection, which contains a list of all users belonging to this group.

❑ The **Groups collection** contains a list of Group objects that belong to a particular catalog, or a list of Group objects that a particular user belongs to.

❑ The **Index object** contains the details for a single index on a table. Its Column objects contain information like the index name, whether the index is unique, whether it allows nulls, etc.

❑ The **Indexes collection** contains all of the Index objects for a particular Table.

❑ The **Key object** contains the information about a table key. Its Column objects contain information like its name, whether it is a primary or foreign key, the related table, etc.

❑ The **Keys collection** contains a list of keys for a Table.

ADOX

❑ The **Procedure object** identifies a stored procedure in a catalog. The Procedure object identifies the details about the stored procedure (such as its name and when it was last modified), while the Command object identifies the internal details of the procedure (such as the SQL test, etc.). The Procedure object has very few properties, mainly because one of these properties represents an ADO Command object.

❑ The **Procedures collection** contains a Procedure object for each stored procedure in the Catalog.

❑ The **Property object** and **Properties collection** are identical to their ADO equivalents.

❑ The **Table object** identifies a single table in a catalog. Its Column objects contain information like the table name and the last modified date. It is also a container for the Columns, Indexes and Keys collections

❑ The **Tables collection** contains a Table object for each table in the catalog. An example of the Tables and Columns collections is shown in a moment (after we've introduced the Columns collection).

❑ The **User object** contains details of a single user of the data store. It contains the user name, the unique ID of the user, and methods to read and write permissions. The User object also contains a Groups collection, which is a list of groups to which the user belongs. You should be careful about writing recursive procedures that traverse the Users and Groups collections, because they point to each other.

❑ The **Users collection** contains a list of all users in a catalog.

❑ The **View object** identifies a single view in a catalog. A view represents a set of records or a virtual table. Like the Procedure object, the View contains a Command object, allowing access to the view command.

❑ The **Views collection** contains a list of View objects, one for each view in the catalog.

The Catalog Object

The Catalog object is the parent object for all ADOX objects. It can deal with information from catalogs or data stores.

The Catalog object contains a set of collections that represent all of the elements of the database. It is the Catalog object that is associated with a particular database through the use of its ActiveConnection property. This property refers to an ADO Connection object which provides the actual link to the database. The set of collections of the Catalog object are Tables, Groups, Users, Procedures, and Views. Within each of these collections are sets of objects that follow the standard naming convention. That is, the Tables collection is a group of Table objects. Each of these collections has an Append method, which is the way to add a new object to the database. Conversely, each collection also has a Delete method, used to remove an object from the database.

The Catalog object exposes the following properties and methods:

Methods	Properties
Create	ActiveConnection
GetObjectOwner	Groups
SetObjectOwner	Procedures
	Tables
	Users
	Views

Catalog Object Methods

The Catalog object exposes the methods Create, GetObjectOwner and SetObjectOwner.

Create Method

The Create method sets or returns a new Catalog – a new database in most cases.

```
Variant = Catalog.Create(ConnectString)
```

Parameter	Data Type	Description
ConnectString	String	The connection string used to connect to the data source.

The return value is either the connection string for the Catalog or an ADODB Connection object depending on how you call the method. For example in VBScript, using Set returns a Connection object, which can then use all the methods and properties of the ADO Connection object, whereas without it, the connection string is returned. Hence in VBScript:

```
Set objCat = Server.CreateObject("ADOX.Catalog")
strConn = objCat.Create("Provider= Microsoft.Jet.OLEDB.4.0; " & _
                        "Data Source=C;\temp\newdb.mdb")
Response.write objCat.ActiveConnection
```

Or in JScript:

```
objCat = Server.CreateObject("ADOX.Catalog");
strConn = objCat.Create("Provider= Microsoft.Jet.OLEDB.4.0; " +
                        "Data Source=C:\\temp\\newdb.mdb");
Response.Write(objCat.ActiveConnection);
```

Note that not all providers support the Create method. It is currently not supported in SQL Server or Oracle. If we try to use the Create method on a provider that does not support it (such as SQL Server), we will receive an error such as the following:

-2147467262 – No such interface supported

ADOX

We can't delete a database in ADOX. For an Access MDB, we would have to use a file system command (such as `kill`) and for SQL Server, we can use the SQL-DMO `Database` object. For other systems, please consult the vendor documentation.

To open an existing database use the `ActiveConnection` property of the `Catalog` object.

GetObjectOwner Method

The `GetObjectOwner` method returns the user or group name of the owner of the specified object.

```
String = Catalog.GetObjectOwner(ObjectName, ObjectType, [ObjectTypeId])
```

Parameter	Data Type	Description
ObjectName	String	The name of the object.
ObjectType	ObjectTypeEnum	The type of the object
ObjectTypeId	Variant	Optional. A GUID. If the ObjectType is provider-specific and not a standard OLE DB object type, ObjectType must be set to adPermObjProviderSpecific.

`ObjectTypeEnum` can be one of the following constants: `adPermObjColumn`, `adPermObjDatabase`, `adPermObjProcedure`, `adPermObjProviderSpecific`, `adPermObjTable`, and `adPermObjView`. See Appendix F for more details.

For example, to retrieve the name of the owner of a table called `tblNewTable`:

```
' VBScript
Set objTable = objCat.Tables("tblNewTable")
Response.Write objCat.GetObjectOwner(objTable.Name, adPermObjTable)
```

```
' JScript
objTable = objCat.Tables("tblNewTable");
Response.Write (objCat.GetObjectOwner(objTable.Name, adPermObjTable));
```

SetObjectOwner Method

The `SetObjectOwner` method sets the user or group as the owner of the specified object.

```
Catalog.SetObjectOwner(ObjectName, ObjectType, UserName, [ObjectTypeId])
```

Parameter	Data Type	Description
ObjectName	String	The name of the object.
ObjectType	ObjectTypeEnum	The type of the object.
UserName	String	The name of the user or group who will be the new owner of the object.

Parameter	Data Type	Description
ObjectTypeId	Variant	Optional. A GUID. If the object type is provider specific and not a standard OLE DB object type, ObjectType must be set to adPermObjProviderSpecific.

ObjectTypeEnum can be one of the following constants: adPermObjColumn, adPermObjDatabase, adPermObjProcedure, adPermObjProviderSpecific, adPermObjTable, and adPermObjView. See Appendix F for more details.

In the case of an Access database, the security database must be explicitly set in the connection string. For example:

```
' VBScript
strConnectionString = "Provider=Microsoft.Jet.OLEDB.4.0; " & _
    "Data Source=C:\pubs.mdb; Jet OLEDB:System database=" & _
    "C:\Program Files\Microsoft Office 2000\Office\system.mdw;"
```

```
// JScript
strConnectionString = "Provider=Microsoft.Jet.OLEDB.4.0; " +
    "Data Source=C:\\pubs.mdb; Jet OLEDB:System database=" +
    "C:\\Program Files\\Microsoft Office 2000\\Office\\system.mdw;";
```

You may also need to ensure that no other users are currently accessing the workgroup file.

For example, to make a user named "Fred" the owner of the Authors table, we would use:

```
' VBScript
objCat.SetObjectOwner "Authors", adPermObjTable, "Fred"
```

```
// JScript
objCat.SetPbjectOwner("Authors", adPermObjTable, "Fred");
```

Fred must already exist in the Users collection and, in the case of an Access database, the security database must be explicitly set in the connection string (as above). If we want to add a user to the Users collection, then we can use the Append method (we discuss the Users collection in more detail below):

```
' VBScript
objCat.Users.Append "Fred", "FredsNewPassword"
```

```
// JScript
objCat.Users.Append("Fred", "FredsNewPassword");
```

ADOX

557

Catalog Object Properties

The `Catalog` object exposes the `ActiveConnection` property and five properties for accessing the `Tables`, `Groups`, `Users`, `Procedures`, and `Views` collections.

ActiveConnection Property

The `ActiveConnection` property sets or returns the information detailing the connection to the data store.

```
Catalog.ActiveConnection = Variant
Variant = Catalog.ActiveConnection
```

This property can be set to or return either an ADODB `Connection` object, or a connection string.

For example to get a reference to the ADO `Connection` object for the `Catalog`:

```
' VBScript
Set objConn = objCat.ActiveConnection
```

```
// JScript
objConn = objCat.ActiveConnection;
```

Groups Property

The `Groups` property returns a collection of the user group accounts that are contained in this catalog.

```
Groups = Catalog.Groups
```

Procedures Property

The `Procedures` property returns a collection of the stored procedures that are contained in this catalog.

```
Procedures = Catalog.Procedures
```

Tables Property

The `Tables` property returns a collection of the tables that are contained in the `Catalog`. This is the default property for the `Catalog` object and can be referred to implicitly.

```
Tables = Catalog.Tables
```

Users Property

The `Users` property returns the collection of the user accounts that are contained in this catalog.

```
Users = Catalog.Users
```

Views Property

The `Views` property returns a collection of the views that are contained in this catalog.

```
Views = Catalog.Views
```

The Column Object

The Column object relates to an individual column, or field, in a Key, Table or Index. This object allows us to view or set the name, data type, size, and other properties of the column.

The Column object exposes no methods, but has the following properties:

Properties	
Attributes	Precision
DefinedSize	Properties
Name	RelatedColumn
NumericScale	SortOrder
ParentCatalog	Type

Column Object Properties

Attributes Property

The Attributes property sets or returns the individual characteristics of a Column.

```
Column.Attributes = ColumnAttributesEnum
ColumnAttributesEnum = Column.Attributes
```

ColumnAttributesEnum can be either one or both of the following values: adColFixed, to indicate that the column is of a fixed length and adColNullable, to indicate that the column may contain null values. See Appendix F for more details.

The default value has neither of these attributes set. We should use bitwise operations to set multiple values, or to retrieve individual attributes.

DefinedSize Property

The DefinedSize property sets or returns the maximum size of a column.

```
Column.DefinedSize = Long
Long = Column.DefinedSize
```

For variable-length columns this indicates the maximum amount of data that the column may contain. It defaults to 0, and a value is not explicitly required for fixed-length data types.

We can only set this value on Column objects before they are appended to the Columns collection.

Name Property

The Name property sets or returns the name of a column. This is the default property of the Column object.

```
Column.Name = String
String = Column.Name
```

ADOX

NumericScale Property

The NumericScale property sets or returns the scale for a numeric column. This is only applicable to columns of type adNumeric or adDecimal, and any value in this property will be ignored for all other column types. The default value is 0.

```
Column.NumericScale = Byte
Byte = Column.NumericScale
```

ParentCatalog Property

The ParentCatalog property sets or returns the Catalog to which this column belongs.

```
Catalog = Column.ParentCatalog
Column.ParentCatalog = Catalog
```

Precision Property

The Precision property sets or returns the maximum precision of data in the column. This is only applicable to columns that are numeric, and is ignored for other column types. The default value is 0.

```
Column.Precision = Long
Long = Column.Precision
```

Properties Property

The Properties property returns the Properties collection associated with the Column.

```
Properties = Column.Properties
```

The Properties collection contains provider specific properties, and behaves exactly the same as the Properties collection of ADO.

RelatedColumn Property

For key columns, the RelatedColumn property sets or returns the name of the column in the related table.

```
Column.RelatedColumn = String
String = Column.RelatedColumn
```

We can only set this value on Column objects before they are appended to the Columns collection. An error will be generated if we try to read this value for columns which are not part of keys.

SortOrder Property

For a Column in an Index the SortOrder property indicates the order in which the column is sorted.

```
Column.SortOrder = SortOrderEnum
SortOrderEnum = Column.SortOrder
```

`SortOrderEnum` can be either `adSortAscending` or `adSortDescending`. The default sort order is ascending.

Accessing this property on a column which is not part of an index will generate an error.

Type Property

The `Type` property sets or returns the data type for the values that will be held in the column.

```
Column.Type = DataTypeEnum
DataTypeEnum = Column.Type
```

Because of its size, the listing for `DataTypeEnum` is not shown here, but can be found in Appendix D. The default value is `adVarWChar`.

The Columns Collection

The `Columns` collection is a collection of `Column` objects for a table, an index or a key.

The `Columns` collection exposes the following methods and properties:

Methods	Properties
Append	Count
Delete	Item
Refresh	

Columns Collection Methods

As we drill further into the object model, we see that the `Columns` collection is a set of `Column` objects. As with the collections of the `Catalog` object, these collections support both the `Append` and `Delete` methods. The `Column` object represents the individual columns of the table.

Append Method

The `Append` method adds an new `Column` to the collection.

```
Columns.Append(Item, [Type], [DefinedSize])
```

Parameter	Data Type	Description
Item	Variant	A Column object to append or the name of a new column to create and append.
Type	DataTypeEnum	Optional. The data type of the object to append; the default is adVarWChar.
DefinedSize	Long	Optional. The maximum column size; the default size is 0.

ADOX

Because of its size, the listing for `DataTypeEnum` is not shown here, but can be found in Appendix D.

Delete Method

The `Delete` method deletes a `Column` object from the collection.

```
Columns.Delete(Item)
```

Parameter	Data Type	Description
`Item`	Variant	The ordinal index number or name of the object to be deleted.

Refresh Method

The `Refresh` method refreshes the collection from the provider. This ensures that any deleted objects will no longer be shown and new objects are available so that any changes made by other users sharing the catalog will be reflected in our collection.

```
Columns.Refresh()
```

Columns Collection Properties

Count Property

The `Count` property returns the number of items within the collection.

```
Long = Columns.Count
```

Item Property

The `Item` property returns the object referenced by name or index number.

```
Column = Columns.Item(Index)
```

The Group Object

The `Group` object identifies a security group account, i.e. it represents a particular group of users of the database. This object contains a collection of `User` objects, which refer to the individual users of the group. Through the `Append` and `Delete` methods of this collection, we can add or remove users from a group in the database. The `User` object represents a user account within the database. It has methods that allow us to change the password for the user, or read and modify the permissions of the user. Note that each user may belong to more than one group, so each `User` object also has a `Groups` collection.

It exposes the following methods and properties:

Methods	Properties
GetPermissions	Name
SetPermissions	Users

Group Object Methods

GetPermissions Method

The GetPermissions method returns the permissions the group has on that object or class of object.

```
RightsEnum = Group.GetPermissions(Name, ObjectType, [ObjectTypeId])
```

Parameter	Data Type	Description
Name	Variant	The name of the object to retieve the permissions for
ObjectType	ObjectTypeEnum	The type of object
ObjectTypeID	Variant	Optional. If the object is not a standard OLE DB object type, the GUID should be provided. The ObjectType must be set to adPermObjProviderSpecific.

ObjectTypeEnum can be one of the following ObjectTypeEnum constants: adPermObjColumn, adPermObjDatabase, adPermObjProcedure, adPermObjProviderSpecific, adPermObjTable and adPermObjView. See Appendix F for more details.

SetPermissions Method

The SetPermissions method sets the permissions the group has on an object or class of object.

```
Group.SetPermissions(Name, ObjectType, Action, Rights, [Inherit],
                     [ObjectTypeId])
```

Parameter	Data Type	Description
Name	Variant	The name of the object for which to set permissions.
ObjectType	ObjectTypeEnum	The object type.
Action	ActionEnum	The type of permission action to set.
Rights	RightsEnum	The individual permissions to set.

Table Continued on Following Page

ADOX

Parameter	Data Type	Description
Inherit	InheritTypeEnum	Optional. This indicates the type of permissions inheritance for containers and objects. The default is adInheritNone
ObjectTypeId	Variant	Optional. A GUID. If the object type is provider-specific and not a standard OLE DB object type, ObjectType must be set to adPermObjProviderSpecific.

ObjectTypeEnum can be one of the following ObjectTypeEnum constants: adPermObjColumn, adPermObjDatabase, adPermObjProcedure, adPermObjProviderSpecific, adPermObjTable and adPermObjView. See Appendix F for more details.

The ADOX documentation mentions adPermObjSchema, adPermObjDomain, adPermObjCollation, adPermObjSchemaRowset, adPermObjCharacterSet, adPermObjTranslation as allowable options for the object type. This is incorrect, as these constants are not supported.

Action can be one of the following ActionEnum constants: adAccessDeny, adAccessGrant, adAccessRevoke, adAccessSet.

Rights can be one or more of the RightsEnum constants, a list of which is shown in Appendix F, and indicates the permissions to be set on the object for the group.

Inherit can be one of the InheritTypeEnum constants, and allows us to specify whether containers inherit permissions from the object that we are setting permissions for, the options are: adInheritBoth, adInheritContainers, adInheritNone, adInheritNoPropogate or adInheritObjects.

To set more than one right, we should combine them with a bitwise OR operation:

```
' VBScript
lngRights = adRightInsert Or adRightUpdate
```

```
// JScript
lngRights = adRightInsert | adRightUpdate;
```

Group Object Properties

Name Property

The Name property sets or returns the name of the group account. This is the default property.

```
Group.Name = String
String = Group.Name
```

Users Property

The Users property will return the collection containing all of the User accounts that belong to this group.

```
Users = Group.Users
```

To list all of the users in a particular group, we can use the VBScript For..Each construct or a JScript Enumerator.

The Groups Collection

The Groups collection contains a Group object for each of the group accounts in the catalog (Catalog.Groups), or to which a specific user belongs (User.Groups). It exposes the following properties and methods:

Methods	Properties
Append	Count
Delete	Item
Refresh	

Groups Collection Methods

Append Method

The Append method adds a new Group object to the collection.

```
Group.Append(Item)
```

Parameter	Data Type	Description
Item	Variant	A Group object or the name of the group to be added

Delete Method

The Delete method deletes an item from the collection.

```
Groups.Delete(Item)
```

Parameter	Data Type	Description
Item	Variant	The ordinal index number or name of the object to be deleted.

Refresh Method

The Refresh method refreshes the collection from the provider. This ensures that any deleted objects will no longer be shown and new objects are available so that any changes made by other users sharing the catalog will be reflected in our collection.

```
Groups.Refresh()
```

ADOX

Groups Collection Properties

Count Property

The Count property returns the number of items within the collection.

```
Long = Groups.Count
```

Item Property

The Item property returns the object referenced by name or index number.

```
Group = Groups.Item(Index)
```

The Index Object

The Index object contains all of the details for an index on a table. It exposes the following properties.

Properties	
Clustered	PrimaryKey
Columns	Properties
IndexNulls	Unique
Name	

Index Object Properties

Clustered Property

The Clustered property indicates whether or not the index is a clustered index. By default, indexes are not clustered.

```
Index.Clustered = Boolean
Boolean = Index.Clustered
```

We can only set this property before appending an Index to the Indexes collection.

Columns Property

The Columns property returns a collection of the columns in the index.

```
Columns = Index.Columns
```

IndexNulls Property

The IndexNulls property indicates what happens to index entries that contain Null values.

```
Index.IndexNulls = AllowNullsEnum
AllowNullsNum = Index.IndexNulls
```

AllowNullsEnum can be one of the following constants: adIndexNullsAllow, adIndexNullsDisallow, adIndexNullsIgnore or adIndexNullsIgnoreAny. See Appendix F for more details.

We cannot change this property on Index objects that already exist in the Indexes collection.

Name Property

The Name property sets or returns the name of the index. This is the default property of the Index object.

```
Index.Name = String
String = Index.Name
```

PrimaryKey Property

The PrimaryKey property indicates whether or not the index forms the primary key of the table. The default value is False, and we can only set this value for Index objects that have not yet been added to the Indexes collection.

```
Index.PrimaryKey = Boolean
Boolean = Index.PrimaryKey
```

Properties Property

The Properties property returns an ADODB Properties collection containing a Property object for each of the provider-specific properties available for the Index object.

```
Properties = Index.Properties
```

Unique Property

The Unique property indicates whether or not the keys in the index must be unique. The default value is false, and we can only set this value for Index objects that have not yet been added to the Indexes collection.

```
Index.Unique = Boolean
Boolean = Index.Unique
```

The Indexes Collection

The Indexes collection contains all of the information for an index on the table. It exposes the following properties and methods:

Methods	Properties
Append	Count
Delete	Item
Refresh	

ADOX

Indexes Collection Methods

Append Method

The Append method adds a new index to the collection.

```
Indexes.Append(Item, [Columnns])
```

Parameter	Data Type	Description
Item	Variant	An Index object or the name of the index to be added to the collection.
Columns	Variant	Optional. An array listing the names of the columns contained in the index.

For example:

```
' VBScript
objIndex.Name = "NameIndex"
objIndex.Columns.Append "FirstName", adVarWChar, 10
objIndex.Columns.Append "LastName", adVarWChar, 10
objTable.Indexes.Append objIndex
```

```
// JScript
objIndex.Name = "NameIndex";
objIndex.Columns.Append("FirstName", adVarWChar, 10);
objIndex.Columns.Append("LastName", adVarWChar, 10);
objTable.Indexes.Append(objIndex);
```

Delete Method

The Delete method deletes an item from the collection.

```
Indexes.Delete(Item)
```

Parameter	Data Type	Description
Item	Variant	The ordinal index number or name of the object to be deleted.

Refresh Method

The Refresh method refreshes the collection from the provider. This ensures that any deleted objects will no longer be shown and new objects are available so that any changes made by other users sharing the catalog will be reflected in our collection.

```
Indexes.Refresh()
```

Indexes Collection Properties

Count Property

The Count property returns the number of items within the collection.

```
Long = Indexes.Count
```

Item Property

The Item property returns the object referenced by name or index number.

```
Index = Indexes.Item(Index)
```

The Key Object

The Key object represents the key column(s) in a table, whether unique, foreign or the primary one. It has no methods but exposes the following properties.

Properties	
Columns	RelatedTable
DeleteRule	Type
Name	UpdatedRule

Key Object Properties

Columns Property

The Columns property returns a Columns collection containing a Column object for each column in the key.

```
Columns = Key.Columns
```

DeleteRule Property

The DeleteRule property indicates what happens when a primary key is deleted.

```
Key.DeleteRule = RuleEnum
RuleEnum = Key.DeleteRule
```

RuleEnum can be one of the following constants: adRICascade, adRINone, adRISetDefault, or adRISetNull. See Appendix F for more details.

We can only set this value on keys before we add them to the Keys collection.

Name Property

The Name property indicates the name of the Key.

```
Key.Name = String
String = Key.Name
```

ADOX

RelatedTable Property

If the key is a foreign key, then the `RelatedTable` property represents the name of the related table.

```
Key.RelatedTable = String
String = Key.RelatedTable
```

Type Property

The `Type` property indicates whether the key is a primary, foreign or unique key.

```
Key.Type = KeyTypeEnum
KeyTypeEnum = Key.Type
```

`KeyTypeEnum` can be one of the following constants: `adKeyForeign`, `adKeyPrimary` and `adKeyUnique`. See Appendix F for more details.

UpdateRule Property

The `UpdateRule` property indicates what should happen when primary keys are updated.

```
Key.UpdateRule = RuleEnum
RuleEnum = Key.UpdateRule
```

`RuleEnum` can be one of the following constants: `adRICascade`, `adRINone`, `adRISetDefault` or `adRISetNull`. See Appendix F for more details.

We can only set this value on keys before we add them to the `Keys` collection.

The Keys Collection

The `Keys` collection manages keys in a collection. It exposes the following properties and methods:

Methods	Properties
Append	Count
Delete	Item
Refresh	

Keys Collection Methods

Append Method

The `Append` method add new keys to the collection.

```
Keys.Append(Item, [Type], [Column], [RelatedTable], [RelatedColumn])
```

Parameter	Data Type	Description
Item	Variant	A Key object or the name of the key to append.
Type	KeyTypeEnum	Optional. The type of the key. The default is adKeyPrimary.
Column	Variant	Optional. The column that the key applies to.
RelatedTable	String	Optional. For a foreign key, the Table that the key points to.
RelatedColumn	String	Optional. For a foreign key, the Column in the RelatedTable that the key points to.

The Type parameter is one of the KeyTypeEnum constants: adKeyForeign (to indicate the key is a foreign key), adKeyPrimary (to indicate the key is a primary key) or adKeyUnique (to idicate the key is unique). See Appendix F for more details.

Delete Method

The Delete method deletes an item from the collection.

```
Keys.Delete(Item)
```

Parameter	Data Type	Description
Item	Variant	The ordinal index number or name of the object to be deleted.

Refresh Method

The Refresh method refreshes the collection from the provider. This ensures that any deleted objects will no longer be shown and new objects are available. This ensures that any changes made by other users sharing the catalog will be reflected in our collection.

```
Collection.Refresh()
```

Keys Collection Properties

Count Property

The Count property returns the number of items within the collection.

```
Long = Keys.Count
```

Item Property

The Item property returns the Key object referenced by name or index number.

```
Object = Keys.Item(Item)
```

ADOX

The Procedure Object

The Procedure object contains the details of a stored procedure. It does not directly contain the SQL text associated with the stored procedure, but identifies the procedure in the catalog. To access the SQL that makes up the procedure, we use the Command property of the Procedure object, which returns an ADODB Command object. The CommandText property of this object will contain the SQL code for the stored procedure.

The Procedure object allows us to manipulate a stored procedure in the database. We can use this object in conjunction with a Command object to create a new stored query in the database. By doing this, we can use ADO to create stored procedures rather than having to rely on the database's CREATE PROCEDURE SQL statement, which can differ from provider to provider. In the same way, the View object, which represents the views in the database, can work with the Command object to create new database views.

It exposes the following properties:

Properties
Command
DateCreated
DateModified
Name

Procedure Object Properties

Command Property

The Command property sets or returns the ADO Command object that contains the procedure details.

```
Command = Procedure.Command
Procedure.Command = Command
```

The following providers do *not* support the Command property and will return an error if we try reference it:

- ❑ OLE DB Provider for SQL Server

- ❑ OLE DB Provider for ODBC

- ❑ OLE DB Provider for Oracle

This is the default property for the Procedure object.

DateCreated Property

The DateCreated property returns the date that the procedure was created. We will need to Refresh the collection to see this value for newly appended procedures.

```
Variant = Procedure.DateCreated
```

DateModified Property

The DateModified property indicates the date the procedure was last modified. We will need to Refresh the collection to see this value for newly appended procedures.

```
Variant = Procedure.DateModified
```

Name Property

The Name property returns the name of the procedure.

```
String = Procedure.Name
```

The Procedures Collection

The Procedures collection exposes the following properties and methods:

Methods	Properties
Append	Count
Delete	Item
Refresh	

Procedures Collection Methods

Append Method

The Append method adds a new procedure to the collection.

```
Procedures.Append(Name, Command)
```

Parameter	Data Type	Description
Name	String	The name of the new procedure.
Command	ADODB.Command	An ADODB Command object containing the procedure details.

Like the Command property, this method is not supported by all providers. For providers that do support this, we can easily create new stored procedures.

ADOX

Delete Method

The `Delete` method deletes a procedure from the collection.

```
Procedures.Delete(Item)
```

Parameter	Data Type	Description
`Item`	Variant	The ordinal index number of name of the object to be deleted.

Refresh Method

The `Refresh` method refreshes the collection from the provider. This ensures that any deleted objects will no longer be shown and new objects are available. This ensures that any changes made by other users sharing the catalog will be reflected in our collection.

```
Procedures.Refresh()
```

Procedures Collection Properties

Count Property

The `Count` property returns the number of items within the collection.

```
Long = Procedures.Count
```

Item Property

The `Item` property returns the object referenced by name or index number.

```
Procedure = Procedure.Item(Item)
```

The Table Object

The `Table` object represents an individual table within the database. Each `Table` object has `Columns`, `Indexes`, `Keys` and `Properties` collections.

It exposes the following properties:

Properties	
Columns	Name
DateCreated	ParentCatalog
DateModified	Properties
Indexes	Type
Keys	

The following example uses the properties and collections of the `Tables` collection and the `Table` object to add a new table named `tblNewTable` to an Access database. To this table, we add columns named `FirstName`, `LastName` and `Age`. We also add a validation rule which specifies that the `Age` must be greater than 17:

```
' VBScript
Dim strConn
Dim objCat

Set objCat = Server.CreateObject("ADOX.Catalog")
Set objTbl = Server.CreateObject("ADOX.Table")

objCat.ActiveConnection = "Provider= Microsoft.Jet.OLEDB.4.0; " & _
                          "Data Source=C:\temp\newdb.mdb"

objTbl.Name = "tblNewTable"
objTbl.Columns.Append "FirstName", adVarWChar, 25
objTbl.Columns.Append "LastName", adVarWChar, 25
objTbl.Columns.Append "Age", adInteger

Set objTbl.ParentCatalog = objCat
objTbl.Properties("Jet OLEDB:Table Validation Rule") = "[Age]>17"
objTbl.Properties("Jet OLEDB:Table Validation Text") = _
    "Age must be 18 or over"

objCat.Tables.Append objTbl
```

```
// JScript
var strConn;
var objCat;

objCat = Server.CreateObject("ADOX.Catalog");
objTbl = Server.CreateObject("ADOX.Table");

objCat.ActiveConnection = "Provider= Microsoft.Jet.OLEDB.4.0; " +
                          "Data Source=C:\\temp\\newdb.mdb";

objTbl.Name = "tblNewTable";
objTbl.Columns.Append("FirstName", adVarWChar, 25);
objTbl.Columns.Append("LastName", adVarWChar, 25);
objTbl.Columns.Append("Age", adInteger);

objTbl.ParentCatalog = objCat;
objTbl.Properties("Jet OLEDB:Table Validation Rule") = "[Age]>17";
objTbl.Properties("Jet OLEDB:Table Validation Text") =
    "Age must be 18 or over";

objCat.Tables.Append(objTbl);
```

ADOX

Table Object Properties

Columns Property

The `Columns` property returns the collection for this table. This is the default property that can be referred to implicitly.

```
Columns = Table.Columns
```

DateCreated Property

The read-only `DateCreated` property identifies the date on which the table was created.

```
Variant = Table.DateCreated
```

DateModified Property

The read-only `DateModified` property identifies the date on which the table was last modified.

```
Variant = Table.DateModified
```

Indexes Property

The `Indexes` property returns the `Indexes` collection associated with the table.

```
Indexes = Table.Indexes
```

Keys Property

The `Keys` property returns a `Keys` collection containing a `Key` object for each primary, foreign and unique key in the table.

```
Keys = Table.Keys
```

Name Property

The `Name` property can be used to set or return the name of the table.

```
Table.Name = String
String = Table.Name
```

For some providers (for example those for SQL Server and Oracle), the `Name` property is read-only.

ParentCatalog Property

The `ParentCatalog` property returns the `Catalog` object to which the `Table` belongs.

```
Catalog = Table.ParentCatalog
Table.ParentCatalog = Catalog
```

We can use the `ParentCatalog` property to set provider-specific properties before the table is added to the catalog.

Properties Property

The `Properties` property returns an ADODB `Properties` collection containing the provider-specific properties for the table.

```
Properties = Table.Properties
```

Type Property

The `Type` property identifies the type of table.

```
String = Table.Type
```

The possible values for this string include: "TABLE" (for a normal table), "SYSTEM TABLE" (for a provider system table) or "GLOBAL TEMPORARY" (for a temporary table).

The Tables Collection

The Tables collection contains a Table object for each table in the catalog, and allows us to manage the Table objects by iterating through the items in the collection, adding tables to the collection and deleting them.

The Tables collection exposes the following properties and methods:

Methods	Properties
Append	Count
Delete	Item
Refresh	

We can iterate through the collection using the normal scripting techniques:

```
' VBScript
Set objTables = Server.CreateObject("ADOX.Catalog")
objCat.ActiveConnection = "Provider= Microsoft.Jet.OLEDB.4.0; " & _
                          "Data Source=C:\\temp\\newdb.mdb"

Set objTables = objCat.Tables
For Each objTable in objTables
   Response.Write objTable.Name
Next
```

Or in JScript:

```
objCat = Server.CreateObject("ADOX.Catalog");
objCat.ActiveConnection = "Provider= Microsoft.Jet.OLEDB.4.0; " +
                          "Data Source=C:\\temp\\newdb.mdb";

objTables = objCat.Tables;
for (i = 0; i < objTables.Count; i++) {
   Response.Write(objTables(i).Name);
}
```

Tables Collection Methods

Append Method

The Append method adds a new Table to the collection.

```
Tables.Append(Item)
```

Parameter	Data Type	Description
Item	Variant	A Table object or the name of the table to add to the collection.

ADOX

Delete Method

The Delete method deletes a Table from the collection.

```
Tables.Delete(Item)
```

Parameter	Data Type	Description
Item	Variant	The ordinal index number or name of the object to be deleted.

Refresh Method

The Refresh method refreshes the collection from the provider. This ensures that any deleted objects will no longer be shown and new objects are available and that any changes made by other users sharing the catalog will be reflected in our collection.

```
Tables.Refresh()
```

Tables Collection Properties

Count Property

The Count property returns the number of items within the collection.

```
Long = Tables.Count
```

Item Property

The Item property returns the object referenced by name or index number.

```
Table = Tables.Item(Index)
```

The User Object

The User object contains the details of a single user account. Each user may belong to a number of groups, so each User object has a Groups collection; but since groups will normally contain a number of users, each Group object has a Users collection. Because of this circular relation, you need to be very careful when using recursion on these objects!

Methods	Properties
ChangePassword	Groups
GetPermissions	Name
SetPermissions	

User Object Methods

ChangePassword Method

The ChangePassword method allows us to change the user's password.

```
User.ChangePassword(OldPassword, NewPassord)
```

Parameter	Data Type	Description
OldPassword	String	The existing user password.
NewPassord	String	The new user password.

To clear a password, or to represent a blank password, we should use an empty string. For example, to clear the password for objUser:

```
' VBScript
objUser.ChangePassword "abc123", ""
```

```
// JScript
objUser.ChangePassword (abc123", "");
```

GetPermissions Method

The GetPermissions method retrieves the permissions the user has on an object.

```
RightsEnum = User.GetPermissions(Name, ObjectType, [ObjectTypeId])
```

Parameter	Data Type	Description
Name	Variant	The name of the object to retrieve the permissions for.
ObjectType	ObjectTypeEnum	The type of object.
ObjectTypeID	Variant	Optional. If the object is not a standard OLE DB object type, the GUID should be provided. The ObjectType must be set to adPermObjProviderSpecific.

Usage of the SetPermission method for a User object is exactly the same as the SetPermissions method for the Group object.

ObjectTypeEnum can be one of the following constants: adPermObjColumn, adPermObjDatabase, adPermObjProcedure, adPermObjProviderSpecific, adPermObjTable, and adPermObjView. See Appendix F for more details.

SetPermissions Method

The SetPermissions method sets the user permissions for an object, or for a class of object.

```
User.SetPermissions(Name, ObjectType, Action, Rights, [Inherit],
[ObjectTypeId])
```

ADOX

Parameter	Data Type	Description
Name	Variant	The name of the object for which to set permissions.
ObjectType	ObjectTypeEnum	The object type.
Action	ActionEnum	The type of permission action to set.
Rights	RightsEnum	The individual permissions to set.
Inherit	InheritTypeEnum	Optional. Indicates the type of permissions inheritance for containers and objects. Default is adInheritNone.
ObjectTypeId	Variant	Optional. A GUID. If the object type is provider specific and not a standard OLE DB object type, ObjectType must be set to adPermObjProviderSpecific.

Usage of the GetPermission method for a User object is exactly the same as the GetPermissions method for the Group object.

ObjectTypeEnum can be one of the following constants: adPermObjColumn, adPermObjDatabase, adPermObjProcedure, adPermObjProviderSpecific, adPermObjTable, and adPermObjView. See Appendix F for more details.

User Object Properties

Groups Property

The Groups property returns a collection of the group accounts to which the user belongs.

```
Groups = User.Groups
```

Name Property

The Name property identifies the name of the user. This is the default property of the User object and can be referred to implicitly.

```
User.Name = String
String = User.Name
```

The Users Collection

The Users collection exposes the following properties and methods.

Methods	Properties
Append	Count
Delete	Item
Refresh	

Users Collection Methods

Append Method

The Append method adds a new user to a group or to a catalog.

```
Users.Append(Item, [Password])
```

Parameter	Data Type	Description
Item	Variant	A user object or the name of the user to add.
Password	String	Optional. The user password.

Item can be either a valid User object or the name of a user:

```
objUser.Name = "Jan"
objCat.Users.Append objUser
```

or in JScript:

```
objUser.Name = "Jan";
objCat.Users.Append(objUser);
```

We must ensure that a User is added to the Catalog before adding the User to a Group. This is because the User must be a valid user account before it can be added to a Group.

Delete Method

The Delete method deletes a User from the collection.

```
Users.Delete(Item)
```

Parameter	Data Type	Description
Item	Variant	The ordinal index number of name of the object to be deleted.

ADOX

581

Refresh Method

The Refresh method refreshes the collection from the provider. This ensures that any deleted objects will no longer be shown and new objects are available. This ensures that any changes made by other users sharing the catalog will be reflected in our collection.

```
Users.Refresh()
```

Users Collection Properties

Count Property

The Count property returns the number of User objects within the collection.

```
Long = Users.Count
```

Item Property

The Item property returns the object referenced by name or index number.

```
User = Users.Item(Item)
```

The View Object

The View object contains details of views in the catalog. For Microsoft Access, this includes standard select queries. The View object exposes the following properties:

Properties
Command
DateCreated
DateModified
Name

View Object Properties

Command Property

The Command property sets or returns an ADODB Command object that contains the view details.

```
Command = View.Command
View.Command = Command
```

The following providers do *not* support the Command property and will return an error if we try to reference it:

❑ OLE DB Provider for SQL Server

❑ OLE DB Provider for ODBC

❑ OLE DB Provider for Oracle

This is the default property for the View object.

DateCreated Property

The `DateCreated` property returns the date the view was created.

```
Variant = View.DateCreated
```

DateModified Property

The `DateModified` property returns the date the view was last modified.

```
Variant = View.DateModified
```

Name Property

The `Name` property identifies the name of the view.

```
String = View.Name
```

The Views Collection

The `Views` collection exposes the following properties and methods.

Methods	Properties
Append	Count
Delete	Item
Refresh	

Views Collection Methods

Append Method

The `Append` method adds a new view to the catalog.

```
Views.Append(Name, Command)
```

Parameter	Data Type	Description
Name	String	The name of the new procedure.
Command	ADODB.Command	An ADO `Command` object containing the procedure details.

Like the `Command` property, this method is not supported by all providers. For providers that do support this, we can easily create new views.

Delete Method

The `Delete` method deletes a `User` from the collection.

```
Views.Delete(Item)
```

ADOX

Parameter	Data Type	Description
Item	Variant	The ordinal index number or name of the object to be deleted.

Refresh Method

The Refresh method refreshes the collection from the provider. This ensures that any deleted objects will no longer be shown and new objects are available. This ensures that any changes made by other users sharing the catalog will be reflected in our collection.

```
Views.Refresh()
```

Views Collection Properties

Count Property

The Count property returns the number of View objects within the collection.

```
Variant = Views.Count
```

Item Property

The Item property returns the object referenced by name or index number.

```
View = Views.Item(Index)
```

Summary

The ADO Extensions for Data Definition Language and Security (or ADOX) provides us with a rich set of tools for gaining access to the structure and security model of a database. It allows the manipulation of the data store through ADO objects and methods, thus removing the necessity to learn the explicit syntax of the data provider.

ADOX is a set of companion objects to the core ADO objects. The object model for ADOX provides support for creating, modifying, and deleting database objects, such as tables and stored queries. It also provides an object interface to the security aspects of the database, allowing us to control users and groups, and to assign them permissions to access objects in the database.

ADOX is most closely linked with the Jet database engine (used for Microsoft Access), but it can also be used to manipulate SQL Server though the SQLOLEDB provider, or Oracle databases through MSDAORA. However, it is most fully supported for the Access engine. Other OLE DB providers currently available may not support all properties and methods. If you wish to use ADOX, you should consult the provider's documentation for more details on supported properties for ADOX.

ADOX

33

ADO Multi-Dimensional

ADOMD, or ADO for Multi-Dimensional data to give it its full title, is a companion to the standard ADO library and was introduced with ADO 2.1. It comprises a set of objects specially developed to integrate with Online Analytical Processing (OLAP) servers. OLAP is a technique for allowing data to be analyzed according to multiple "dimensions".

A business survives by having the most up-to-date information, and being able to act on that data accordingly. If you can't analyze the data correctly, then your business might not be performing as well as it can. OLAP makes this analysis easier, by pre-processing frequently used data, representing the data in a multi-dimensional way, and defining a special query language to keep the data extraction easy.

Online Analytical Processing (OLAP)

So what is OLAP? You won't be surprised to learn that it focuses around the manipulation of data. Since the rise of the PC, and especially the relational database, we've been storing increasing amounts of data. Relational databases are great for storing data, and great for simple data extraction, but SQL isn't really designed for complex data analysis. It's great for standard set-based stuff, such as lists of items and simple summaries, but it's not so good at deep analysis using several different tables and levels of complexity.

This is where OLAP comes in, since its whole basis is the analysis of data from different viewpoints. For example, sales of products by time, location, consumer type, and so on. While this is possible with standard SQL, it's much easier with OLAP. OLAP provides three features which facilitate this analysis:

- ❑ It pre-processes frequently used data. This speeds up the analysis because less calculation is required.
- ❑ It represents the data in a multi-dimensional way. Most relational systems only consider rows and columns, but OLAP allows more than two dimensions.
- ❑ It defines a special query language to extend the capabilities of SQL.

These combine to allow the abstraction of the operational storage and provide an easier view for data analysis:

With OLAP systems, users don't access the actual operational data. Instead they request the data from the OLAP system, which stores the data in a format designed for analysis. This takes the form of one of the following:

❑ **Multidimensional OLAP (MOLAP)**, where a multidimensional structure is used to store a copy of, and aggregations of, the original data. Since a complete copy of the data is held by the OLAP service, this provides the fastest response to queries, and is ideal for situations where the OLAP service is frequently queried.

❑ **Relational OLAP (ROLAP)**, where only the aggregations are managed by the OLAP service. This type of storage provides slower response to queries than MOLAP, and is therefore more suited to data that isn't frequently queried.

❑ **Hybrid OLAP (HOLAP)** combines aspects of MOLAP and ROLAP, and is a compromise between the two storage types. The response time depends upon the query being issued. This type of storage is most suitable for summaries of large amounts of data, where queries require a rapid response.

Which of the three you use depends on what sort of queries you are going to be processing, the number of users, the amount of data, and how fast the queries need to be processed. In all three the OLAP service processes the query and returns the data appropriately, which removes some of the load from the source database. This is even more of an advantage if the OLAP service is running on a separate machine to the source database.

OLAP Servers

To use ADOMD, we're obviously going to need access to an OLAP server – Microsoft SQL Server comes with an OLAP server, so check out the documentation. The OLAP server for SQL 7.0 is extremely easy to set up and use, and can be obtained (along with SQL Server 7.0 itself) as a time-limited evaluation. The limit is 120 days, which should give us plenty of time to get to know it.

To use ADO with OLAP we will need to install the Client components when we install the OLAP Services, ensuring that the PivotTable Service is installed. This is the service that provides the interface from ADO into the OLAP Service. The SQL 7.0 installation CD contains a set of ADOMD examples, in a variety of languages.

OLAP Data

To understand how OLAP works, let's take a quick look at an example of some OLAP data. First, though, we need to introduce some new terminology. A **cube** is a subset of the data that is to be processed, and contains several elements. The first is a **fact table**, which contains the actual data to be analyzed. Next are **dimensions**, which identify how the data in the fact table is analyzed. The OLAP Services for SQL Server support a maximum of 63 dimensions, so don't think you are restricted to only the three dimensions that make up our physical world, although using more than three does tend to make the data rather difficult to visualize. Finally there are **levels**, which are **dimensions** broken down into sub-categories.

A sample comes provided with OLAP Services for SQL Server (called `FoodMart`), which we'll look at to get an understanding of how multi-dimensional data works. This sample contains the sales details for a supermarket chain. The following screenshot shows the relationship diagram upon which the `FoodMart` data is based:

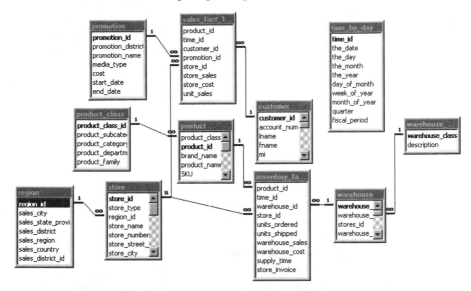

This is isn't too complex, but still complex enough to make in-depth analysis quite tricky. There are tables for the product, the stores, the regions, types of products, the warehouse, and so on. Trying to produce figures linking all of these together would be very complex. What OLAP does is to extract this information into a more manageable set of information. The following diagram concentrates on the warehouse side:

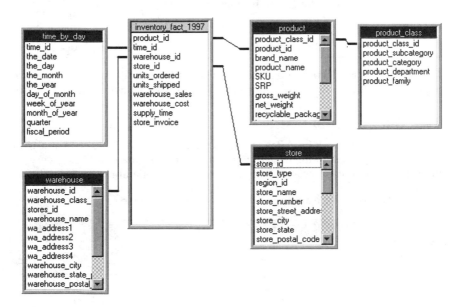

ADOMD

This diagram is a visual representation of the cube we defined earlier. The fact table corresponds to the `inventory_fact` table. This table contains key fields (`product_id`, `time_id`, `warehouse_id` and `store_id`), which relate to the dimensions tables. It also contains the actual data we want to analyze: the units ordered and shipped, etc.

The difference between `Dimensions` and `Levels` is a subtle one, and introduces the concept of a category of data and sub-categories. For example, in the data above the `Dimensions` would be:

Dimension	Description
Store	The stores and locations.
Time	The years, months and quarters.
Product	The product names, groups, and brands.
Store Size in SqFt	The size of the stores in square feet.
Store Type	The types of the stores (Supermarket, Grocery, etc.).
Warehouse	The warehouse names and locations.

The `Product` dimension has several different levels:

Level Number	Name	Example
1	Product Family	Food
2	Product Department	Produce
3	Product Category	Fruit
4	Product Subcategory	Fresh Fruit
5	Brand Name	High Top
6	Product Name	High Top Cantaloupe

This splitting of a category into levels gives the ability to drill down to a narrower focus. You'll see how this can be important when constructing queries a little later.

Two Dimensional Data

The greatest point about OLAP is that it allows us to view data from an analytical viewpoint, regardless of the underlying structure of the database. This is very important, since databases are often designed from an operational perspective.

One of the things we are aiming to do is produce figures like this:

Store Type	+ Product Family All Products	+ Drink	+ Food	+ Non-Consumable
All	102,278.41	9,218.35	73,367.55	19,692.51
Deluxe Supermarket	32,251.87	3,554.97	22,143.27	6,553.63
Gourmet Supermarket	5,132.90	590.42	3,635.13	907.35
Mid-Size Grocery	5,274.34	437.32	3,661.14	1,175.88
Small Grocery	3,132.05	281.24	2,342.09	508.73
Supermarket	56,487.25	4,354.41	41,585.92	10,546.92

If you're used to relational databases, then this is similar to a crosstab query, and this is precisely why OLAP analysis is so good. Microsoft Access has special commands to perform crosstabs, but in standard SQL it's not so easy. You can do it using an intermediate table or by using some advanced SQL, but it's not very efficient. The OLAP services pre-process the data to make this kind of analysis easy.

To understand OLAP, and the data shown in the above diagram, we have to introduce some more new terms – **axes** and **axis**. Looking at the diagram these should be obvious – there are two Axes, one for the **Rows** and one for the **Columns**. When you are analyzing data using OLAP you'll always be dealing with at least these two axes. What we've done with the above data is to map a dimension (which is a representation of the structure of the data) onto an axis (which is a representation of the way the data is analyzed in a single query).

Three Dimensional Data

The above diagram shows a simple set of data using two dimensions, where each Dimension was shown on an **Axis**. We have the product types along the **Columns** and the store types along the **Rows**. But OLAP has the facility to manage more Axes. In fact, the use of the term cube is pretty good, because this automatically brings to mind three dimensions. For example, imagine that we wanted to add countries to this analysis. Using the third dimension could give us something like this:

Store Type	All Products	+Drink	+Food	+Non-Consumable
All	102,278.41	9,218.35	73,367.55	19,692.51
Deluxe Supermarket	32,251.87	3,554.97	22,143.27	6,553.63
Gourmet Supermarket	5,132.90	590.42	3,635.13	907.35
Mid-Size Grocery	5,274.34	437.32	3,661.14	1,175.88
Small Grocery	3,132.05	281.24	2,342.09	508.73
Supermarket	56,487.25	4,354.41	41,585.92	10546.92

Now we have the addition of a third axis – called **Pages**. Each page contains the data for a country, with a page for the summary information for all pages. With the OLAP facilities at hand this is pretty easy to do. You could equate this to the pages in a spreadsheet.

n-Dimensional Data

As we've mentioned, SQL OLAP Services support a maximum of 63 Axes, so don't think you are restricted to only three. For example, if you wanted to extend the analysis shown in the above diagram by adding the Time Dimension onto a fourth Axis, you would end up with:

ADOMD

1998 table:

Store Type	All Products	+Drink	+Food	+Non-Consumable
All	102,278.41	9,218.35	73,367.55	19,692.51
Deluxe Supermarket	32,251.87	3,554.97	22,143.27	6,553.63
Gourmet Supermarket	5,132.90	590.42	3,635.13	907.35
Mid-Size Grocery	5,274.34	437.32	3,661.14	1,175.88
Small Grocery	3,132.05	281.24	2,342.09	508.73
Supermarket	56,487.25	4,354.41	41,585.92	10546.92

1997 table:

Store Type	All Products	+Drink	+Food	+Non-Consumable
All	102,278.41	9,218.35	73,367.55	19,692.51
Deluxe Supermarket	32,251.87	3,554.97	22,143.27	6,553.63
Gourmet Supermarket	5,132.90	590.42	3,635.13	907.35
Mid-Size Grocery	5,274.34	437.32	3,661.14	1,175.88
Small Grocery	3,132.05	281.24	2,342.09	508.73
Supermarket	56,487.25	4,354.41	41,585.92	10546.92

I've shown the fourth Axis as an extension in time. Conceptually however, it doesn't matter which way you extend the Axes.

Multiple Data per Axis

Something else that is also pretty easy in OLAP is the ability to show multiple sets of data on the same axis. If you wanted to show both the Store Type and the Country on the rows, you can end up with this:

Store Type	+ Store Country	+ Product Family All Products	+ Drink	+ Food	+ Non-Consumable
All	All Stores	196,770.89	18,010.60	141,147.92	37,612.37
	+ Canada				
	+ Mexico				
	+ USA	196,770.89	18,010.60	141,147.92	37,612.37
Deluxe Supermarket	All Stores	61,860.15	6,923.76	42,380.16	12,556.22
	+ Canada				
	+ Mexico				
	+ USA	61,860.15	6,923.76	42,380.16	12,556.22
Gourmet Supermarket	All Stores	10,156.50	1,241.74	7,075.10	1,839.66
	+ Canada				
	+ Mexico				
	+ USA	10,156.50	1,241.74	7,075.10	1,839.66
Mid-Size Grocery	All Stores	10,212.20	882.69	7,226.60	2,102.92
	+ Canada				
	+ Mexico				
	+ USA	10,212.20	882.69	7,226.60	2,102.92
Small Grocery	All Stores	5,931.58	510.98	4,451.55	969.05
	+ Canada				
	+ Mexico				
	+ USA	5,931.58	510.98	4,451.55	969.05
Supermarket	All Stores	108,610.46	8,451.44	80,014.51	20,144.52
	+ Canada				
	+ Mexico				
	+ USA	108,610.46	8,451.44	80,014.51	20,144.52

Here we have the Store Type as the main category, and the Country as the sub-category.

Multi-Dimension Extensions

The problem is, to get the data in this sort of form you can't use standard SQL because it is not designed to cope with multi-dimensional data. The answer to this lies in a special set of extesions to the SQL language, known as Multi-Dimension Extensions (MDX), which allow us to process OLAP queries.

The basic query syntax is pretty much the same as a standard SQL query:

```
SELECT <axis_specification> [,<axis_specification>]
   FROM <cube_specification>
   WHERE <slicer_specification>
```

The difference is the *axis_specification*, which allows us not only to select the source of the data, but which axis it is to be placed on. The MDX extensions allow the use of OLAP names (Members, Levels, and so on) in SQL queries. The *slicer_specification* is a filter to select only specific data; **slicing** is simply an OLAP term for filtering the data. For example, to select the product on the columns and the store type on the rows from the Warehouse cube, limiting the query to figures for 1998, we would use:

```
SELECT product.Children ON COLUMNS,
       [Store Type].Children ON ROWS
   FROM Warehouse
   WHERE ([1998])
```

We can also use a CROSSJOIN statement if we want multiple data sets on a single axis. Resultsets from a CROSSJOIN can be quite large.

For more information on multi-dimensional queries, consult the MDX documentation in the Data Access SDK, at http://msdn.microsoft.com/library/psdk/dasdk/olap55v8.htm.

ADOMD Object Model

This diagram depicts the entire ADOMD object model:

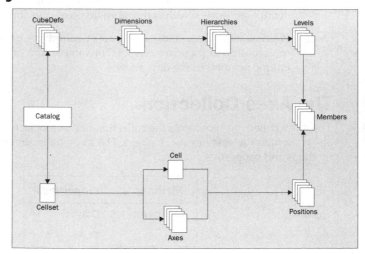

Let's explain the objects in more detail. The first set of objects (along the top in the above diagram) represent the structure of the data as held by the OLAP Services:

❑ **Catalog**, which is the container for all OLAP objects. This identifies the OLAP server, and the actual data server that supplies the original data.

❑ **CubeDef**, which is a container for a set of data. A CubeDef doesn't represent how the data is shown – it just represents what the structures are and what they contain.

❑ **Dimension**, which is a distinct set of items. You've already seen that Time, Store and Store Type are dimensions – these are the top-level items upon which queries can be based.

❑ **Hierarchy**, which identifies the different ways in which the members of a Dimension can be aggregated.

❑ **Level**, which identifies the sub-elements in an individual Hierarchy. So, for the Time dimension we have three Levels: Year, Quarter and Month.

❑ **Member**, which represents a unique item in a Level.

The second set of OLAP objects represent the data as it has been queried. So if you run a query against an OLAP server you get a set of data, which comprises:

❑ **Axis**, which represents one of the physical axes of the CellSet. For example, the diagram above would require an Axis for the Rows and another Axis for the Columns. A third Axis for the Pages would be included if requested.

❑ **Cell**, which is a single cell, or item of data.

❑ **CellSet**, which represents the whole set of data. The data is represented as an *n*-dimensional array, where there is a dimension for each Axis.

❑ **Measure**, which is a quantitative, numerical column, and is usually the name of the item that is shown in each cell. In our examples the measure has been the default measure, which is the Store Invoice – the amount invoiced by the store.

❑ **Position**, which is an individual row or column. A position represents a unique row, column or page in a cell set. The intersection of Positions gives the unique position in the data array.

The Axes Collection

The Axes collection represents the collection of Axis objects in the CellSet. This always contains a least one Axis object. The Axes collection exposes the following methods and properties:

Methods	Properties
Refresh	Count
	Item

Axes Collection Methods

Refresh Method

The Refresh method updates the collection from the provider so that any changes are reflected on the system.

```
Axes.Refresh()
```

Axes Collection Properties

Count Property

The Count property returns the number of objects in the collection.

```
Long = Axes.Count
```

Item Property

The Item property returns the object referenced by its name or ordinal index number.

```
Object = Axes.Item(Index)
```

The Index is the number or name of the object in the collection in the zero-based index.

This is the default property and so it can be called implicitly. For example, the following lines are identical:

```
Set Object = Axes.Item(1)
```

```
Set Object = Axes(1)
```

The Axis Object

The Axis object represents one of the physical axes of the CellSet. The Axis object has the following properties.

Properties
DimensionCount
Name
Positions
Properties

Axis Object Properties

DimensionCount Property

The DimensionCount property returns the number of Dimensions on this Axis.

```
Long = Axis.DimensionCount
```

Name Property

The Name property returns the name of the Axis.

```
String = Axis.Name
```

Positions Property

The Positions property returns a collection of Position objects.

```
Positions = Axis.Positions
```

Using the Positions collection allows us to iterate through the unique rows and columns in a query.

Properties Property

The Properties property returns an ADODB Properties collection.

```
Properties = Axis.Properties
```

The Catalog Object

The Catalog object is the container for all OLAP objects; it identifies the OLAP server that contains the structures to be used for OLAP queries.

The Catalog object has three properties and no methods.

Properties
ActiveConnection
CubeDefs
Name

Catalog Object Properties

ActiveConnection Property

The ActiveConnection property sets or returns the ADO Connection to the OLAP data provider.

```
Connection = Catalog.ActiveConnection
Catalog.ActiveConnection = Connection
String = Catalog.ActiveConnection
Catalog.ActiveConnection = String
```

This can be an existing ADODB Connection object or an ADO connection string.

CubeDefs Property

The CubeDefs property returns the CubeDefs collection for the Catalog.

```
CubeDefs = Catalog.CubeDefs
```

We can use the CubeDefs collection to access individual CubeDef objects:

```
Set objCubeDef = objCatalog.CubeDefs("AllSales")
```

Name Property

The Name property returns the name of the catalog.

```
String = Catalog.Name
```

The Cell Object

The Cell object represents a single cell, e.g. the quantity of cars sold. This is much like a cell in a spreadsheet and is uniquely identified by the Positions along the axes.

A cell represents a single item of data, at the intersection of a number of axes in a CellSet. The Cell object has the following properties and no methods:

Properties
FormattedValue
Ordinal
Positions
Properties
Value

Cell Object Properties

FormattedValue Property

The FormattedValue property sets or returns the formatted value of the cell.

```
Cell.FormattedValue = String
String = Cell.FormattedValue
```

The value from this property is the Value property formatted according to its type.

Ordinal Property

The Ordinal property returns the ordinal index number of the cell which uniquely identifies a cell within a CellSet.

```
Long = Cell.Ordinal
```

The cellset notionally identifies each cell as though the cellset were a multi-dimensional array, and each array element had a unique number. Cells are numbered starting from 0, and the Ordinal can be used in the Item property of the CellSet to quickly locate a cell.

Positions Property

The Positions property returns a collection of Position objects.

```
Positions = Cell.Positions
```

ADOMD

Each CellSet comprises a number of Axes, and each Axis contains a number of Position objects. Each Position object uniquely identifies a row or column in the Axis.

We can use the Positions collection to iterate through each Position:

```
For Each objPos In objCell.Positions
    Response.Write objPos.Name
Next
```

Properties Property

The Properties property returns the ADODB Properties collection associated with the Cell.

```
Properties = Cell.Properties
```

Value Property

The Value property sets or returns the value contained within the Cell.

```
Cell.Value = Variant
Variant = Cell.Value
```

The CellSet Object

A CellSet object contains the results of a multi-dimensional query against an OLAP server. It contains collections of Cell objects, a collection of Axis objects and details of the connection and query. The CellSet object has the following methods and properties:

Methods	Properties
Close	ActiveConnection
Open	Axes
	FilterAxis
	Item
	Properties
	Source
	State

CellSet Object Methods

Open Method

The Open method opens a new CellSet based upon a multi-dimensional query.

```
CellSet.Open([DataSource], [ActiveConnection])
```

Parameter	Type	Description
DataSource	Variant	The multi-dimensional query that will retrieve the data.
ActiveConnection	Variant	Either an ADODB Connection object or an ADO connection string.

The *DataSource* argument corresponds to the Source property of the CellSet. Multi-dimensional queries use their own variant of the SQL language. For example:

```
' VBScript
strQuery = "SELECT [Books].MEMBERS ON ROWS," & _
            " [Stores].MEMBERS ON COLUMNS" & _
        " FROM [PubsOLAP]"

objCellSet.Open strQuery, objConn
```

```
// JScript
strQuery = "SELECT [Books].MEMBERS ON ROWS," +
            " [Stores].MEMBERS ON COLUMNS" +
        " FROM [PubsOLAP]";

objCellSet.Open(strQuery, objConn);
```

For more information on multi-dimensional queries, consult the MDX documentation in the Data Access SDK, at http://msdn.microsoft.com/library/psdk/dasdk/olap55v8.htm.

The *ActiveConnection* argument corresponds to the ActiveConnection property.

Close Method

The Close method closes an open CellSet. Closing a CellSet will release any child collections associated with the CellSet.

```
CellSet.Close()
```

CellSet Object Properties

ActiveConnection Property

The ActiveConnection property sets or returns the connection to which the CellSet or Catalog belongs.

```
Connection = CellSet.ActiveConnection
CellSet.ActiveConnection = Connection
String = CellSet.ActiveConnection
CellSet.ActiveConnection = String
```

This can be a valid ADODB Connection object or an ADO connection string. Like ADO, if the string method is used then a new connection is made.

ADOMD

If the *ActiveConnection* argument of the Open method was used to specify the connection, then the ActiveConnection property inherits the value from the argument.

Axes Property

The Axes property returns the Axes collection for this CellSet.

```
Axes = CellSet.Axes
```

This collection will always contain at least one Axis object. We can iterate through the Axes collection to examine the data in the CellSet. For example, consider the following OLAP query:

```
SELECT Publishers.Members ON COLUMNS,
       Geography.Members ON ROWS,
       Dates.Members ON PAGES
    FROM AllSales
```

This creates three Axis objects in the collection, for Publishers, Geography, and Dates.

FilterAxis Property

If filtering has been used to restrict the data returned during the query, then the FilterAxis property will return an Axis object, usually containing one row with the filter information.

```
Axis = CellSet.FilterAxis
```

Item Property

The Item property allows indexing into the CellSet collection to reference a specific Cell object.

```
Cell = CellSet.Item(Index)
```

The index is the number of the Cell in the collection.

Properties Property

The Properties property returns the ADODB Properties collection for this CellSet.

```
Properties = CellSet.Properties
```

Source Property

The Source property returns or sets the multi-dimensional query used to return the data.

```
Variant = CellSet.Source
CellSet.Source = Variant
```

If the *DataSource* argument of the Open method was used to specify the query, then the Source property inherits its value from the argument.

State Property

The State property returns the current state of the CellSet.

```
Long = CellSet.State
```

The State can be one of the following ADO ObjectStateEnum constants: adStateOpen, to indicate the CellSet is open; or adStateClosed, to indicate the CellSet is closed.

The CubeDef Object

The CubeDef object is a container for a set of data, it contains all the related dimensions of multi-dimensional data. It contains the structures in which the data is set out and the data these structures contain. For example, a CarSales CubeDef might contain Sales, Date and VehicleModel structures (or dimensions).

The CubeDef object has four properties and no methods.

Properties
Description
Dimensions
Name
Properties

CubeDef Object Properties

Description Property

The Description property returns a description of the CubeDef.

```
String = CubeDef.Description
```

Dimensions Property

The Dimensions property returns the Dimensions collection for the CubeDef.

```
Dimensions = CubeDef.Dimensions
```

Name Property

The Name property identifies the name of the CubeDef.

```
String = CubeDef.Name
```

We can use the Name property to index into the Catalog object's CubeDefs collection:

```vbscript
' VBScript
Set objCubeDef = objCatalog.objCubeDefs("AllSales")
```

```jscript
// JScript
objCubeDef = objCatalog.objCubeDefs("AllSales");
```

ADOMD

Properties Property

The `Properties` property returns the ADODB `Properties` collection for each provider-specific property for the `CubeDef`.

```
Properties = CubeDef.Properties
```

The CubeDefs Collection

The `CubeDefs` collection contains all of the `CubeDef` objects for the catalog. This collection has the following methods and properties:

Methods	Properties
Refresh	Count
	Item

CubeDefs Collection Methods

Refresh Method

The `Refresh` method updates the collection from the provider so that any changes are reflected on the system.

```
CubeDefs.Refresh()
```

CubeDefs Collection Properties

Count Property

The `Count` property returns the number of objects in the collection.

```
Long = Cubedefs.Count
```

Item Property

The `Item` property returns the object referenced by its name or ordinal index number.

```
CubeDef = CubeDefs.Item(Index)
```

The `Index` is the number or name of the object in the collection in the zero-based index.

This is the default property and so it can be called implicitly. For example, the following lines are identical:

```
Set objCubeDef = objCat.CubeDefs.Item(1)
```

```
Set objCubeDef = objCat.CubeDefs(1)
```

The Dimension Object

The `Dimension` object represents a single dimension from a cube in a multi-dimensional query.

The `Dimension` object has the following properties:

Properties
Description
Hierarchies
Name
Properties
UniqueName

Dimension Object Properties

Description Property

The `Description` property returns a description for the `Dimension`.

```
String = Dimension.Description
```

Hierarchies Property

The `Hierarchies` property returns the `Hierarchies` collection associated with the `Dimension` object.

```
Hierarchies = Dimension.Hierarchies
```

Name Property

The `Name` property identifies the name of the `Dimension`.

```
String = Dimension.Name
```

We can use the `Name` property to index into the `Dimensions` collection of the `CubeDef` object:

```
' VBScript
Set objDimension = objCubeDef.Dimensions("Geography")
```

```
// JScript
objDimension = objCubeDef.Dimensions("Geography");
```

Properties Property

The `Properties` property returns the ADODB `Properties` collection containing each provider-specific property for the dimension.

```
Properties = Dimension.Properties
```

ADOMD

603

UniqueName Property

The `UniqueName` property returns the unique name for the `Dimension` object.

```
String = Dimension.UniqueName
```

Because of the complexity of dimensions, it's possible that we may find ourselves using two (or more) `Dimension` objects with the same `Name` property. In such cases, `UniqueName` can be used to provide an unambiguous name for each `Dimension` object.

The Dimensions Collection

This is the collection of `Dimension` objects for a `CubeDef` and exposes the following methods and properties:

Methods	Properties
Refresh	Count
	Item

Dimensions Collection Methods

Refresh Method

The `Refresh` method updates the collection from the provider so that any changes are reflected on the system.

```
Dimensions.Refresh()
```

Dimensions Collection Properties

Count Property

The `Count` property returns the number of objects in the collection.

```
Long = Dimension.Count
```

Item Property

The `Item` property returns the object referenced by its name or ordinal index number.

```
Dimension = Dimensions.Item(Index)
```

The `Index` is the number or name of the object in the collection.

The Hierarchies Collection

The `Hierarchies` object is the collection of `Hierarchy` objects for a dimension and exposes the following methods and properties:

Methods	Properties
Refresh	Count
	Item

Hierarchies Collection Methods

Refresh Method

The Refresh method updates the collection from the provider so that any changes are reflected on the system.

```
Hierarchies.Refresh()
```

Hierarchies Collection Properties

Count Property

The Count property returns the number of objects in the collection.

```
Long = Hierarchies.Count
```

Item Property

The Item property returns the object referenced by its name or ordinal index number.

```
Hierarchy = Hierarchies.Item(Index)
```

The Index is the number or name of the object in the collection.

The Hierarchy Object

The Hierarchy object identifies a single way in which data from a Dimension can be represented. This is often called an **aggregation** or a roll-up.

The Hierarchy object identifies the relationship of the items within a Dimension. So, for the Dates dimension, we might have three hierarchies: Year, Quarter, and Month. The hierarchies give us sub-headings. It has the following properties:

Properties
Description
Levels
Name
Properties
UniqueName

Hierarchy Object Properties

Description Property

The Description property returns a description of the Hierarchy object.

```
String = Hierarchy.Description
```

ADOMD

Levels Collection

The `Levels` property returns the `Levels` collection for the hierarchy.

```
Levels = Hierarchy.Levels
```

Name Property

The `Name` property identifies the `Hierarchy` object within the `Hierarchies` collection of a `Dimension`.

```
String = Hierarchy.Name
```

Properties Collection

The `Properties` property returns the ADODB `Properties` collection for each provider-specific property.

```
Properties = Hierarchy.Properties
```

UniqueName Property

The `UniqueName` property provides a unique name with which to identify the `Hierarchy` in the collection.

```
String = Hierarchy.UniqueName
```

The `UniqueName` property allows us to uniquely identify a `Hierarchy` object where several `Hierarchy` objects may have the same `Name`.

The Level Object

The `Level` object contains the elements in an individual `Hierarchy`. For the `Dates` dimension, we might have a `Hierarchy` called `Year` – each year in the `Dimension` is a `Level`.

The `Level` object has the following properties:

Properties
Caption
Depth
Description
Members
Name
Properties
UniqueName

Level Object Properties

Caption Property

The Caption property identifies the text to show when the Level is displayed.

```
String = Level.Caption
```

Depth Property

The Depth property identifies how deep in the hierarchy this Level is.

```
Integer = Level.Depth
```

The Level object's Depth property is the number of levels between the root of the hierarchy and the Level object. For example, if we have a Hierarchy object called Dates, the levels of this hierarchy (and their depths) might be as follows:

Level Name	Depth
(All)	0
Year	1
Quarter	2
Month	3
Day	4

Description Property

The Description property returns a textual description of the Level object.

```
String = Level.Description
```

Members Collection

The Members property returns the Members collection for the Level object.

```
Members = Level.Members
```

Name Property

The Name property identifies the name of the Level object.

```
String = Level.Name
```

Properties Collection

The Properties property returns the Properties collection for the Level object.

```
Properties = Level.Properties
```

UniqueName Property

The UniqueName property provides a unique name for the Level object. This property allows for Level objects with the same name.

```
String = Level.UniqueName
```

ADOMD

The Levels Collection

The Levels object is a collection of levels and exposes the following methods and properties.

Methods	Properties
Refresh	Count
	Item

Levels Collection Methods

Refresh Method

The Refresh method updates the collection from the provider so that any changes are reflected on the system.

```
Levels.Refresh()
```

Levels Collection Properties

Count Property

The Count property returns the number of objects in the collection.

```
Long = Levels.Count
```

Item Property

The Item property returns the object referenced by its name or ordinal index number.

```
Level = Levels.Item(Index)
```

The Index is the number or name of the object in the collection. This is the default property and so it can be called implicitly.

The Member Object

The Member object represents the data in a dimension. It has the following properties.

Properties	
Caption	Name
ChildCount	Parent
SChildren	ParentSameAsPrev
Description	Properties
DrilledDown	Type
LevelDepth	UniqueName
LevelName	

Member Object Properties

Caption Property

The Caption property returns the caption which is displayed with the data.

```
String = Member.Caption
```

ChildCount Property

The ChildCount property returns the number of child members of the Member object.

```
Long = Member.ChildCount
```

The child members can be retrieved via the Children property.

Children Property

The Children property returns the child members of which this Member is the parent.

```
Members = Member.Children
```

To make this clearer, consider the Dates hierarchy again. This has levels for the different types of date measurement (all dates, years, quarters, months, and days). OLAP allows us to look at data from a variety of different ways – to implement this, each Member (in the Members collection of each Level) has a collection of Member objects, which are the children of the current Member. We can see this more clearly in the table below:

Level Name	Member	Child Member
(All)	All Dates	1992
		1993
		1994
Year	1992	Quarter 2
	1993	Quarter 1
		Quarter 2
		Quarter 4
	1994	Quarter 3
Quarter	Quarter 2	June
	Quarter 1	February
		March
	Quarter 2	May
Month	June	15
	May	22
		24

Description Property

The Description property returns a description of the member.

```
String = Member.Description
```

DrilledDown Property

The DrilledDown property indicates whether the Member is contained in the deepest level of the hierarchy – that is, whether we have *drilled down* as far as possible. If so, this property returns true. Otherwise (that is, the Member possesses child members) this property returns False.

```
Boolean = Member.DrilledDown
```

LevelDepth Property

The LevelDepth property identifies how deep this Member is, within the Level's hierarchy.

```
Long = Member.LevelDepth
```

The LevelDepth property is the same as the Depth property for the Level, and it is included for a Member because we can access Member objects from their positions in a CellSet, and not just from the Levels collection.

LevelName Property

The LevelName property returns the name of the Level to which the Member belongs.

```
String = Member.LevelName
```

Name Property

The Name property returns the name of the Member.

```
String = Member.Name
```

Parent Property

The Parent property returns the parent object of this Member.

```
Member = Member.Parent
```

ParentSameAsPrev Property

The ParentSameAsPrev property identifies whether the parent of this member is the same as the parent of the preceding Member in the Members collection.

```
Boolean = Member.ParentSameAsPrev
```

We can use this property to identify siblings – Member objects that are on the same level.

Properties Property

The Properties property returns the ADODB Properties collection for this Member.

```
Properties = Member.Properties
```

Type Property

The Type property returns the type of the Member; the default is adMemberRegular.

```
Member.Type = MemberTypeEnum
```

MemberTypeEnum can be one of the following constants: adMemberRegular, adMemberMeasure, adMemberFormula, adMemberAll, or adMemberUnknown. See Appendix H for further information.

UniqueName Property

The UniqueName property returns the unique name for the Member.

```
String = Member.UniqueName
```

The Members Collection

This is the collection of Member objects for a Position, and exposes the following methods and properties:

Methods	Properties
Refresh	Count
	Item

Members Collection Methods

Refresh Method

The Refresh method updates the collection from the provider so that any changes are reflected on the system.

```
Members.Refresh()
```

Members Collection Properties

Count Property

The Count property returns the number of objects in the collection.

```
Long = Members.Count
```

Item Property

The Item property returns the object referenced by its name or ordinal index number.

```
Member = Members.Item(Index)
```

The Index is the number or name of the object in the collection. This is the default property and so it can be called implicitly.

ADOMD

The Position Object

The Position object represents an individual row or column in an axis. A Position object contains the members of those dimensions that identify a point along a specific axis. The Position object contains the following two properties

Properties
Members
Ordinal

Position Object Properties

Members Property

The Members property returns the Members collection for the Position object.

```
Members = Position.Members
```

Ordinal Property

The Ordinal property returns a position along an axis.

```
Long = Position.Ordinal
```

The Ordinal is a unique identifier for a position and corresponds to the Index of the position in the Positions collection.

The Positions Collection

The Positions object is a collection of Position objects. It exposes the following methods and properties.

Methods	Properties
Refresh	Count
	Item

Positions Collection Methods

Refresh Method

The Refresh method updates the collection from the provider so that any changes are reflected on the system.

```
Positions.Refresh()
```

Positions Collection Properties

Count Property

The Count property returns the number of objects in the collection.

```
Long = Positions.Count
```

Item Property

The Item property returns the object referenced by its name or ordinal index number.

```
Object = Positions.Item(Index)
```

The *Index* is the number or name of the object in the collection. This is the default property and so it can be called implicitly.

Summary

In this chapter, we have taken a whirlwind tour through the world of ADOMD. We looked quickly at the concept of Online Analytical Processing, or OLAP, and its various 'flavors' (MOLAP, ROLAP and HOLAP), and the way that OLAP allows us to analyze data according to multiple dimensions.

This multi-dimensional data cannot be accessed using normal SQL queries, but there is a special set of extensions (known as Multi-Dimension Extensions, or MDX), which allow us to formulate multi-dimensional queries.

Finally, we looked at the ADOMD object model itself, giving the methods and properties for each object. ADOMD is a complex topic, and isn't central to an ASP book, so unfortunately we've had to rush through this very quickly. However, we hope that this chapter has provided you with enough information to get started, and will be an important reference once you have mastered the basics.

ADOMD

Extending ASP

34

Transactions and Message Queuing

In this chapter we consider two separate services, **Microsoft Transaction Server** (MTS) and **Microsoft Message Queuing** (MSMQ), which simplify our work creating accurate and scalable web applications: Although with Windows 2000 both MTS and MSMQ are now included within COM + Services, they perform different functions and are considered separately here and referred to as MTS and MSMQ .

In the first half of this chapter we look at Microsoft Transaction Server (MTS). This benefits applications that perform operations that consist of multiple steps all of which must be completed successfully for the operation to be completed successfully.

The second half of the chapter looks at Microsoft Message Queuing (MSMQ). Using MSMQ makes an application more scalable and more resistant to say a server not being available. It provides the foundation for building an application using asynchronous methods.

Transactions

A transaction is an operation which has one or more steps that either successfully completes or fails to complete as a unit. A transaction either succeeds or fails as a whole, it is not possible for parts of it to complete and others to fail.

The transactions managed by Microsoft Transaction Server (MTS) have **ACID** properties of:

- ❏ **Atomicity** – The transaction is either completed in full, or fails in full.
- ❏ **Consistency** – If a transaction fails, no parts of it are committed, and the system is stable. If the transaction succeeds, all parts are commited, and the system is stable.

❏ **Isolation** – All transactions execute separately from each other, and are each treated as having exclusive access to the system.

❏ **Durability** – Any changes committed in a transaction are final.

Using a transaction processor like MTS, means that these properties are already taken care of for us. This saves us, as developers, from having to anticipate all the possible problems the could occur with our code, guess the error codes and create error-handling code to restore the system to its original state.

As a useful illustration of the concept of a transaction, let us consider a very simple operation that we might want to do with our bank, to transfer money from one of our accounts (say a savings account) to another (a checking account). Our money is first deducted from the savings account and then added to the checking account. If these two operations are handled separately then we could have the situation where the deduction succeeds, but the addition fails. In this case we may have "lost" our money and the system may be in an inaccurate/invalid state.

If instead, our money transfer is handled as a transaction, the behaviour is different. The steps are the same, but their effect is not immediate. First there is a call to deduct the money from our savings account. Then if this succeeds there us a call to add the same amount to the checking account. If that call succeeds then both of the changes are **committed** and the money is transferred. Until this commitment happens, the changes can be undone. For example in the event that the addition to the destination account fails, then the operation of deduction from the original account would be rolled back and the system returned to its state before the transaction was started.

Prior to Windows 2000, MTS was a standalone product (still available through the Windows NT 4 Option Pack), however it is now a part of the COM + services built into Windows 2000.

Distributed Transaction Coordinator

Our simple banking example assumed that all of the operations were performed on the same system. However in the real world, this isn't necessarily the case: Many applications are more complex and may be interacting with data from different data sources and data on servers which may be in various locations. In this situation we need to be able to support **distributed transactions**. The **Microsoft Distributed Transaction Coordinator**, MS DTC, handles complex scenarios like this. MS DTC was first shipped with SQL Server, however it is now another part of the COM + services built into Windows 2000.

Due to the extra complexity of different data sources and servers, the distributed transactions using MS DTC, are executed in a different way from the single data source (or machine) transactions of MTS. There is now a two stage process for committing changes (called **two-phase commit**). First, each of the data sources is in the **Prepare** phase. In this phase the transactions are executed, but the result is not written to the data. Once *all* data sources have succeeded in the **Prepare** phase then they will move on to the **Commit** phase. In this phase, *all* data source changes are committed. If there is an error in this phase then the entire transaction, and all changes in all data sources, are rolled back.

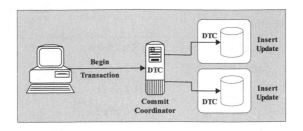

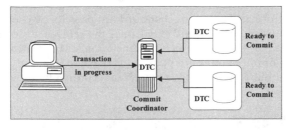

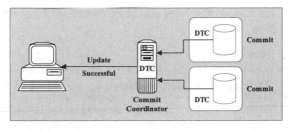

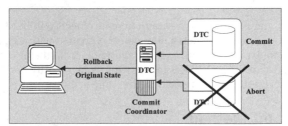

Transaction Object Model

There is only one object in the Transaction object model of interest to ASP programmers: The ObjectContext object.

ObjectContext Object

Lets look at how to programmatically create a transaction and control its results. The simplest method of controlling a transaction is to use the ObjectContext object. This exposes the following methods

Transactions & Message Queuing

Methods	
CreateInstance	IsInTransaction
DisableCommit	IsSecurityEnabled
EnableCommit	SetAbort
IsCallerInRole	SetComplete

It's worth noting that an object should not pass its `ObjectContext` to another object. This would invalidate the reference since the object context ties it to the real object and has no meaning for third parties. Also a real object should not pass a reference to itself, otherwise it could be called directly, rather than by its context wrapper.

CreateInstance Method

The `CreateInstance` method creates another transaction object within the activity of the calling application.

```
ObjectContext.CreateInstance(ProgID)
```

Parameter	Data Type	Description
ProgID	String	This is the programmatic ID of the new object's component

The `CreateInstance` method is the way to create objects within MTS, that work together within a transaction. When a new object is created with `CreateInstance` MTS copies the context information of the creating object to the new object's context object. This means that the new object inherits the same security and transactional environment as its creator and runs within the same activity.

DisableCommit Method

The `DisableCommit` method changes the transaction object's internal state, to indicate that it has not finished its current work and that its transactional updates are in a potentially inconsistant state.

```
ObjectContext.DisableCommit()
```

EnableCommit Method

The `EnableCommit` method changes the object's internal state to indicate that its work isn't necessarily finished, but its transactional updates are in a consistent state. This is the default state for a newly-created object.

```
ObjectContext.EnableCommit()
```

IsCallerInRole Method

The `IsCallerInRole` method indicates whether the object's direct caller is in a specified role (either directly or as part of a group).

```
Long = ObjectContext.IsCallerInRole(Role)
```

Parameter	Data Type	Description
Role	String	This is the name of the role in which we want to determine whether the caller is acting

The `IsInRole` method returns either `true` (meaning either that the caller is in the specified role, or that security is not enabled) or `false`.

IsInTransaction Method

The `IsInTransaction` method indicates whether the object is currently executing within a transaction. This method can be used to enforce the transaction requirements of a component.

```
ObjectContext.IsInTransaction()
```

IsSecurityEnabled Method

The `IsSecurityEnabled` method indicates whether security is enabled. MTS security is enabled unless the object is running in the client's process (when configured as a library package), or MTS is running under Windows 9X.

```
ObjectContext.IsSecurityEnabled()
```

SetAbort Method

The `SetAbort` method declares that the object has failed to complete its work and can be deactivated once the currently-executing method has returned.

```
ObjectContext.SetAbort()
```

It should be called to indicate that transactional updates are in an inconsistent state or that some sort of unrecoverable error occurred. This means that the transaction (in which the object was executing) must be aborted. If any object executing within a transaction returns to its client after calling `SetAbort`, the entire transaction is doomed to abort.

SetComplete Method

The `SetComplete` method declares that the object has completed its work and can be deactivated once the currently executing method has returned.

```
ObjectContext.SetComplete()
```

For objects that are executing within the scope of a transaction, it also indicates that the object's transactional updates can be committed. When an object that is the root of a transaction calls `SetComplete`, MTS attempts to commit the transaction on return from the current method.

Example of Using Transactions

The implementation of transactions varies depending on the system and application being used. This book covers ASP therefore we focus on two important transaction implementations IIS/COM+ integrated transactions and COM+ transactions. First we look at the different ways that we can make use of transactions from within an ASP page and then we create a sample application using COM+ transactions.

IIS/COM+ Transactions

Although MTS functionality was available with IIS 4.0, it is only with Windows 2000 that MTS becomes fundamental to the operating system. We can now create ASP code that is executed as a transaction, that shares a transaction with COM+ object or that responds to events in the COM+ object related to the transaction.

Transactional ASP Pages

An ASP page can be defined as a transaction. This means that if any of the operations within the ASP code fail, then all of the operations affecting MS DTC compliant data sources (Access, SQL Server,etc) are rolled back. Any operations that do not affect a data source, for example changes made to session- or application-scope variables, and changes affecting non-MS DTC compliant data sources, cannot be rolled back.

Consider for example the case where we want to update a table in a database from a static ASP page that uses transactions. Lets say an error occurs when trying to make the connection command. This causes the transaction to be aborted and any changes to be rolled back: However if the same page assigned a value to a session variable, this would not be reversed, unlike the account data which is in the same state it was in before the ASP page interacted with the data source.

In IIS4, a transaction directive covered all of the operations on a single ASP page. Although IIS5 makes it possible for a transaction to include operations on multiple ASP pages, normally all the steps are contained on one ASP page. Using the money transfer example, the ASP page would make the method call to deduct the money from the savings account and then also make the method call to add the money to the checking account.

In order to create a transactional page,we add a **Transaction Directive** to our ASP Page. The directive must be the first line of the ASP page and would look like this:

```
<%@ [Any_Other_Directives] TRANSACTION = Value [Any_Other_Directives] %>
```

where *Value* is one of the following:

Value	Description
Disabled	The component is not involved in transactions
Requires_New	This creates a new transaction regardless if one already exists
Required	This creates a new transaction if one does not already exist
Supported	This uses an existing transaction if available, but will not create a new one
Not_Supported	This will not use an existing transaction

For example the directive statement if we want to use JScript and create a new transaction, would look like this:

```
<%@ LANGUAGE=JScript TRANSACTION=Required %>
```

When the ASP page completes execution and no Commit or Abort methods have been called, the transaction is assumed to have succeeded and is committed.

Transactions Including ASP Pages and COM+ Objects

As well as ASP code executing as a transaction, we can also write ASP pages that share transactions with other component objects created within the ASP page. This is done using the ObjectContext object, which is the same ObjectContext object that is available to COM + components written for transactions.

Here we consider an example of an ASP page that uses a COM + object called Bank.AcctTransfer. This COM + object is similar to one described later in this chapter, with the only differences being how SetComplete and SetAbort are called. The Bank.AcctTransfer object provides two methods. The Withdrawal method withdraws a specified amount of money from a specified account. The Deposit method that deposits a specified amount of money into a specified account. If either of these methods fails to execute successfully, it returns 0 and the transaction isn't committed.

Our application would also require a second ASP (or HTML) page which contains a form for the user to complete giving details of the two accounts and the amount of money to be transferred. When this form is submitted then the data would be passed to our main ASP page as a query string. (The code for this page is given in the User interface section of our larger COM+ example. It is just an HTML form tha generates the query string that is used in our main ASP page.)

Here's what our main ASP page for interacting with the COM+ Bank.AcctTransfer object via the ObjectContext object, looks like, in VBScript:

```
<%@ LANGUAGE=VBScript TRANSACTION=Required %>
<%
Dim objTransfer, TransAmount, OrigAccountNum, DestAccountNum
```

```
'Get information passed in from the Account Transfer request form page
TransAmount = Request.QueryString("Amount")
OrigAccountNum = Request.QueryString("OrigAcctNum")
DestAccountNum = Request.QueryString("DestAcctNum")

' Create our COM+ object that is used for transfers
Set objTransfer = Server.CreateObject("Bank.AcctTransfer")

' First, try to deduct the money using the Withdrawal method
If objTransfer.Withdrawal(CInt(OrigAccountNum),
                          CInt(TransAmount)) <> 0 Then
   ObjectContext.SetAbort    ' Rollback transaction if Withdrawal fails,

' If the Withdrawal succeeds, deposit the money using Deposit method
   Response.Write "Withdrawal Aborted"
Elseif  objTransfer.Deposit(CInt(DestAccountNum),
                            CInt(TransAmount)) <> 0 Then
   ObjectContext.SetAbort        ' Rollback transaction if Deposit fails,
   Response.Write "Aborted"
Else
   ObjectContext.SetComplete     ' Commit transaction when both succeed
   Response.Write "Succeeded"
End If

Set objTransfer = Nothing
%>
```

Or in JScript this is:

```
<%@ LANGUAGE=JScript TRANSACTION=Required %>
<%
/*Get the information that was passed in from
the Account Transfer request form page*/
TransAmount = Request.QueryString("Amount");
OrigAccountNum = Request.QueryString("OrigAcctNum");
DestAccountNum = Request.QueryString("DestAcctNum");

// Create our COM+ object that is used for transfers
objTransfer = Server.CreateObject("Bank.AcctTransfer");

// First, try to deduct the money using the Withdrawal method
if (objTransfer.Withdrawal(OrigAccountNum,
                           TransAmount) != 0) {
   ObjectContext.SetAbort();        // Rollback transaction if Withdrawal
fails,

// If the Withdrawal method succeeds, deposit the money using the Deposit
method
   Response.Write("Withdrawal Aborted");
} else {

   if (objTransfer.Deposit(DestAccountNum,TransAmount) != 0) {
      ObjectContext.SetAbort();     // Rollback transaction if Deposit fails
      Response.Write("Aborted");
   } else {
      ObjectContext.SetComplete(); // Commit transaction when both succeed
           Response.Write("Succeeded");
   }

}
delete objTransfer
%>
```

The transaction directive at the top of this ASP page creates a new transaction when it executed. This means that this page and all the components used within the page are all operating within this same transaction (as long as the components have **Required** or **Supported** for their Transaction Support attribute).

Once the transaction is created, the page will continue to execute. The originating account number, destination account number, and transfer amount are all gathered from the query string generated using the form page. The Bank.AcctTransfer object is then created and its Withdrawal and Deposit methods called. The return values from those methods are checked, and if they is not correct, then the page will force the transaction to abort by calling the SetAbort method. If both of the methods return the expected value then the code will execute the SetComplete method and cause the changes to be committed.

Including the SetComplete and SetAbort methods in the ASP code (rather than in the COM+ component) gives us the option of performing other operations if the SetAbort method is called.

ASP Pages Responding to Transaction Events of COM+ Objects

We have seen that an ASP page can be a transaction and can affect a transaction. Our ASP page can also repond to events generated by transactions. There are two events associated with transactions, namely:

❑   OnTransactionCommit, which is fired when the SetComplete method is called

❑   OnTransactionAbort, which is fired when SetAbort is called

Here is an example of code that responds to either of these two events:

```
<%@ LANGUAGE=VBScript TRANSACTION=Required %>

<%
Dim objTransfer, TransAmount, OrigAccountNum, DestAccountNum

TransAmount = Request.QueryString("Amount")
OrigAccountNum = Request.QueryString("OrigAcctNum")
DestAccountNum = Request.QueryString("DestAcctNum")

Set objTransfer = Server.CreateObject("Bank.AcctTransfer")

objTransfer.Withdrawal CInt(OrigAccountNum),CInt(TransAmount)

objTransfer.Deposit CInt(DestAccountNum),CInt(TransAmount)

Set objTransfer = Nothing

'// This subroutine is called when the transaction is committed
Sub OnTransactionCommit()
   Response.Write "Transfer has succeeded"
End Sub
```

```
'// This subroutine is called when the transaction is aborted
Sub OnTransactionAbort()
   Response.Write "Transfer has failed"
End Sub
```

Or in JScript:

```
<%@ LANGUAGE=JScript TRANSACTION=Required %>

<%
TransAmount = Request.QueryString("Amount");
OrigAccountNum = Request.QueryString("OrigAcctNum");
DestAccountNum = Request.QueryString("DestAcctNum");

objTransfer = Server.CreateObject("Bank.AcctTransfer");

objTransfer.Withdrawal(OrigAccountNum,TransAmount);

objTransfer.Deposit(DestAccountNum,TransAmount);

delete objTransfer;

// This subroutine is called when the transaction is committed
function OnTransactionCommit() {
   Response.Write("Transfer has succeeded");
}

// This subroutine is called when the transaction is aborted
function OnTransactionAbort() {
   Response.Write("Transfer has failed");
}

%>
```

The execution of this page is similar to the example that used the ObjectContext method. The difference is that the previous example checked and responded to the return values of the Withdrawal and Deposit methods. In this case the COM object handles the call to the SetAbort or SetComplete methods and our ASP code has the event handlers to respond to either the committing or aborting of the transaction.

When the transaction is commited (i.e. SetComplete is called within the COM object), then the OnTransactionCommit method will be executed. If the transaction is aborted (i.e. SetAbort is called within the COM Object), then the OnTransactionAbort method is called instead. In this example either of the two methods just prints out a message to the browser detailing the transaction results. Obviously other actions may be appropriate for other applications.

COM+ Transactions

In our previous examples we demonstrated how we can use transactions from our ASP pages and showed how these transactions can also extend to a COM+ object that requires or supports them. In real world situations a more common scenario is to use a transactional COM+ component that is called from an ASP page. This is in keeping with the good design practice of separating the logical tiers of an application (described in Chapter 2). In most applications ASP code is used for the presentation of the website, formatting and displaying results rather than performing a large amount of the business services or data services operation. In this section we describe how to create an application that does just this, using ASP for the presentation and using a COM+ component for the business operations and interacting with a database.

For our example application, we again use the very simple example of transferring money between two bank accounts. This illustrates the key points of using transactions in COM+ components. The basic design of the application is that of a typical three tier application: database, middle tier COM+ component, and an ASP-generated user interface.

Example COM+ Component

Although the user interface and the database are important parts of the application, the majority of the transaction work is done within the middle tier component.

For this example, we will create the component using VB and developing on a server with access to the COM+ services. We start by creating an ActiveX DLL project which we call "Bank". We then need to add project references to "Microsoft ActiveX Data Objects" and to the "COM+ Services Type Library". The project references dialog should look like this:

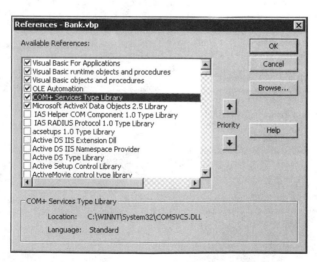

In this project we will only need one class file, that we'll call `AcctMgt.cls`. This class has two main functions: The `GetAccountList` function which retrieves a list of accounts for a user, and the `TransferMoney` method which transfers money between accounts.

Transactions & Message Queuing

We will also need to set the transactional model for our class to **Requires Transactions**.

The first task is handled with the `GetAccountList` function. This takes one parameter, `strAccountName`, and returns a recordset containing all the accounts belonging to that person. This function will also support transactions.

Before implementing any of the code to perform the query, it can be useful to first create the code to handle errors and commit or abort the transaction. In this case, the error handling is provided by the `GetAccountList_Error` handler.

```
On Error GoTo GetAccountList_Error
```

All the handler does is to call `SetAbort` to notify COM+ that the transaction should be aborted. Execution then changes to the `GetAccountList_Exit` function and cleanup is done.

If there are no errors in the code then the transaction is committed when this code is executed:

```
If Not objContext Is Nothing Then
    objContext.SetComplete
End If
```

The full text of the `GetAccountList` function, including the code to execute the query is:

```
Public Function GetAccountList(ByVal strAccountName As String) As
ADODB.Recordset
    Dim objContext As COMSVCSLib.ObjectContext
    Dim rsAccountList As ADODB.Recordset

    On Error GoTo GetAccountList_Error

    Set objContext = GetObjectContext()
    Set rsAccountList = New ADODB.Recordset

    With rsAccountList
        .ActiveConnection = "Provider=SQLOLEDB.1;User ID=sa;" & _
                            "Initial Catalog = AccountDB;Data
Source=BankServer"
        .CursorLocation = adUseClient
        .CursorType = adOpenStatic
        .LockType = adLockReadOnly
        .Source = "Select * from Accounts WHERE OwnerName = '" & strAccountName
& "'"
        .Open

        Set .ActiveConnection = Nothing      ' Release the connection
    End With

    Set GetAccountList = rsAccountList

    If Not objContext Is Nothing Then
        objContext.SetComplete
    End If
```

```
GetAccountList_Exit:
    Set objContext = Nothing
    Exit Function

GetAccountList_Error:
    ' Unexpected error occurred, abort
    If Not objContext Is Nothing Then
        objContext.SetAbort
    End If

    Resume GetAccountList_Exit

End Function
```

You may wonder why the GetAccountList function uses transactions since there is no information being updated. However, the use of a transaction here allows the program to notify the COM+ when their resources can be reclaimed.

The function that handles the actual money transfer between accounts also needs to be in the middle tier. This application calls the method TransferMoney which takes three parameters: intOrigAcct, intDestAcct, and intAmount. The error handling for this method is the same as for GetAccountList.

Once the database connection is created and opened, there are two key operations that this method performs. First, it attempts to withdraw money from the original account, OrigAcct:

```
.Execute "UPDATE Accounts SET AcctBalance = (Select AcctBalance " & _
        " FROM Accounts WHERE AcctID=" & intOrigAcct & ") - " & _
        intAmount & " WHERE AcctID = " & intOrigAcct
```

If there is no error thrown in that operation, then the code proceeds to attempt to deposit that money into the destination account, DestAcct:

```
.Execute "UPDATE Accounts SET AcctBalance = (Select AcctBalance" & _
        " FROM Accounts WHERE AcctID=" & intDestAcct & ") + " & _
        intAmount & " WHERE AcctID=" & intDestAcct
```

If both of these calls complete without any errors then the changes are committed when the following code is executed:

```
If Not objContext Is Nothing Then
    objContext.SetComplete
End If
```

Once that executes the transfer is complete.

The full source code for the TransferMoney method is:

```
Public Sub TransferMoney(ByVal intOrigAcct As Integer, ByVal intDestAcct As Integer, _
                        ByVal intAmount As Integer)

    Dim objContext As COMSVCSLib.ObjectContext
    Dim cnUpdateConn As ADODB.Connection
```

```
On Error GoTo TransferMoney_Error

Set objContext = GetObjectContext()
Set cnUpdateConn = New ADODB.Connection

With cnUpdateConn
   .ConnectionString = "Provider=SQLOLEDB.1;User ID=sa;" & _
                       "Initial Catalog=AccountDB;Data Source=BankServer"
   .Open

   ' Remove the money from the originating account
   .Execute "UPDATE Accounts SET AcctBalance = (Select AcctBalance " & _
            " FROM Accounts WHERE AcctID=" & intOrigAcct & ") - " & _
            intAmount & " WHERE AcctID = " & intOrigAcct

   ' And place it in the destination account
   .Execute "UPDATE Accounts SET AcctBalance = (Select AcctBalance" & _
            " FROM Accounts WHERE AcctID=" & intDestAcct & ") + " & _
            intAmount & " WHERE AcctID=" & intDestAcct
End With

If Not objContext Is Nothing Then
   objContext.SetComplete
End If

TransferMoney_Exit:
   Set objContext = Nothing
   Exit Sub

TransferMoney_Error:
   ' Unexpected error occurred, abort
   If Not objContext Is Nothing Then
      objContext.SetAbort
   End If

   Resume TransferMoney_Exit

End Sub
```

Installing the Component

Once the component has been built and compiled, there are a couple more steps that must be completed before it will support transactions. First it must be configured/installed as a COM+ application. This is done using the **Component Services Manager**. When you launch **Component Services Manager**, the resulting window will look something like:

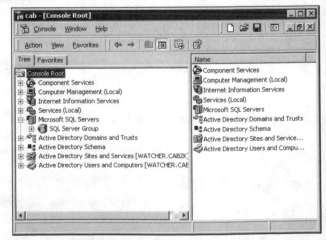

To create a new COM+ application, we will expand the Component Services node and expand down to the Component Services\Computers\My Computer\Com+ Applications node.

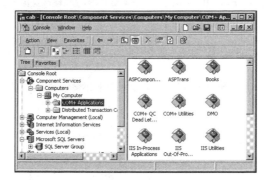

Now, to create a new application we right-click on the COM+ Applications node, select New, and then select Application. This launches the COM Application Install wizard. At the first screen, just click the Next button. On the second step you will be prompted to either Install pre-built application(s) or to Create an empty application. We are creating an empty one, so click on the button with the empty box.

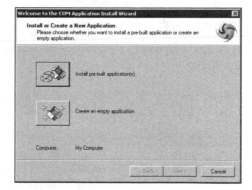

Next, we are prompted for a name and details of the application.

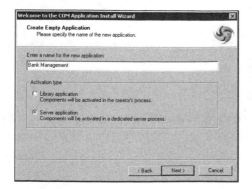

You can see that we have specifed BankManagement as the application name. This name can be anything we like, and need to not be the same name as the component. In the Activation type frame there are two choice for how components will be instantiated. For creating a component in the same process as it's creator, select Library application. For most objects used in ASP pages, it is preferable (and more reliable) to create the objects in their own process. Clicking the Next button will allow us to specify the account under which the application will run. The application will have only the permissions assigned to that account.

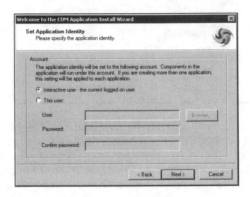

In cases where it is desired to restrict the object's access to certain resources, the component should be set to run with a specific user account. The permissions and priviliges on that account would then be set to limit its access. For this application, accepting the default of Interactive User is acceptable. Click the Next button and then click Finish and our new application will be created.

Now that we have an application, we need to add our component. First expand the COM+ Applications node and click on the Components folder.

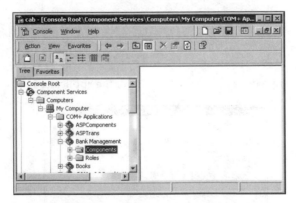

Now right-click on the Component folder and select New, then Component. Click Next at the wizard introduction dialog and you will then be prompted for what type of component to install.

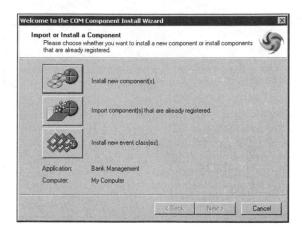

When copying the DLL from a development machine to the web server, you will usually select Install new component(s). If you have already registered the DLL on the machine, then you will select Import component(s) that are already registered. The Install new event class(es) is for adding new events to the system. For our example, we will select the first option. When you click on the button you will then see a browse dialog. Use this dialog to browse to the DLL we created. When you locate and add the object created above, you will see the following:

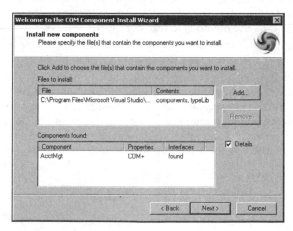

Click Next and then click Finish and you are done. The component is now treated as a COM+ application and has full transaction support and we should see something like this:

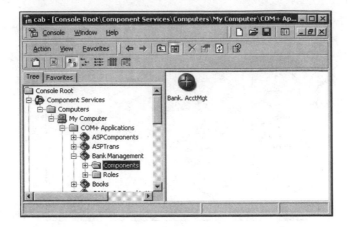

Next, we look at how to incorporate our object into an ASP application.

User Interface

Our banking example is only concerned with one process, that of transferring money between two accounts belonging to the same person. We therefore need two ASP pages: The first ASP page (`Transfer.asp`) contains a form which allows the user to enter which account to transfer their money from, which account to transfer to, and how much money to transfer. The second ASP page (`DoTransfer.asp`) creates the COM+ object and calls the methods to transfer the money.

Transfer.asp

The first action that the page executes is to get the list of accounts available to the user. In our simplified example we have hard coded the user name to be "John Smith", but in a real application the user name would be passed in the query string or specified in a session variable. Once that name is obtained, we instantiate the `Bank.AcctMgt` object. Using that object, we can make a call to the `GetAccountList` method and get back a recordset containing the account information for the current user.

```
' Create the Bank.AcctMgt object
Set objAcctMgt = Server.CreateObject("Bank.AcctMgt")

' Then get a list of the user's accounts
Set rsAcctList = objAcctMgt.GetAccountList(OwnerName)
```

Or in JScript:

```
// Create the Bank.AcctMgt object
objAcctMgt = Server.CreateObject("Bank.AcctMgt");

// Then get a list of the user's accounts
rsAcctList = objAcctMgt.GetAccountList(OwnerName);
```

The next step generates the contents of the account listbox. This code loops through the `rsAcctList` recordset and generates the correct HTML for the listbox. When creating the listbox, the account name is shown to the user, but the account ID is the value that is passed from the form. The user doesn't have to see the account ID, they refer to the account by it's name.

```
      <TD><SELECT id=OrigAcct name=OrigAcct style="HEIGHT: 22px; WIDTH: 154px">
<%
   While Not rsAcctList.EOF
%>
      <OPTION value=<%= rsAcctList.Fields("AcctID") %>> <%=
rsAcctList.Fields("AcctType") %>
      </OPTION>
<%      rsAcctList.MoveNext
   Wend
%>

   </SELECT></TD>
```

Or in JScript:

```
      <TD><SELECT id=OrigAcct name=OrigAcct style="HEIGHT: 22px; WIDTH: 154px">
<%
   while (!rsAcctList.EOF) {
%>
      <OPTION value=<%= rsAcctList.Fields("AcctID") %>> <%=
rsAcctList.Fields("AcctType") %>
      </OPTION>
<%       rsAcctList.MoveNext();
   }
%>

   </SELECT></TD>
```

Another interesting piece of code handles user feedback.

```
' Let the customer know whether their transfer worked or not.
If Request.QueryString("Commit") = "False" Then
   Response.Write "Sorry, your transfer failed to complete.<BR>"
Elseif Request.QueryString("Commit") = "True" Then
   Response.Write "Your transfer has succeeded.<BR>"
End If
```

Or in JScript:

```
// Let the customer know whether their transfer worked or not.
if (Request.QueryString("Commit") == "False") {
   Response.Write("Sorry, your transfer failed to complete.<BR>");
} else {
   Response.Write("Your transfer has succeeded.<BR>");
}
```

Once the user enters their transfer request, that information is sent to another page (`Transfer.asp`).

When `Transfer.asp` completes its processing it redirects the browser back to this page. This redirection appends a query string that specifies whether the transaction was successfully completed or not. When we look at the `Transfer.asp` page it will be clearer as to how this works. Each application may want to handle the outcomes differently. In this case, we are just illustrating providing some user feedback.

Transactions & Message Queuing

635

Here is the full source of the `Transfer.asp` page:

```
</HEAD>
<BODY>

<%
Dim OwnerName
Dim objAcctMgt
Dim rsAcctList

OwnerName = "John Smith"  ' Normally obtained via a query string

' Create the Bank.AcctMgt object
Set objAcctMgt = Server.CreateObject("Bank.AcctMgt")

' Then get a list of the user's accounts
Set rsAcctList = objAcctMgt.GetAccountList(OwnerName)
%>
<P><FONT SIZE=6><EM>Welcome, <% =OwnerName %>,</EM></FONT></P>

<%
' Let the customer know whether their transfer worked or not.
If Request.QueryString("Commit") = "False" Then
    Response.Write "Sorry, your transfer failed to complete.<BR>"
Elseif Request.QueryString("Commit") = "True" Then
    Response.Write "Your transfer has succeeded.<BR>"
End If
%>

<P>Please specify your transfer details:</P>
<P>
<FORM NAME=AcctTransfer Action="DoTransfer.asp" METHOD=GET>
<TABLE border="0" cellPadding="1" cellSpacing="1" width="300">

  <TR>
    <TD>Amount</TD>
    <TD><INPUT Type=Text id=intAmount name=intAmount></TD></TR>
  <TR>
    <TD>Originating Account</TD>
    <TD><SELECT id=OrigAcct name=OrigAcct
style="HEIGHT: 22px; WIDTH: 154px">
<%
   While Not rsAcctList.EOF
%>
     <OPTION value=<%= rsAcctList.Fields("AcctID") %>> <%=

rsAcctList.Fields("AcctType") %>
     </OPTION>
<%      rsAcctList.MoveNext
   Wend
%>

   </SELECT></TD>
   </TR>
   <TR>
    <TD>Destination Account</TD>
    <TD><SELECT id=DestAcct name=DestAcct style="HEIGHT: 22px; WIDTH: 154px">
<%
   rsAcctList.MoveFirst
   While Not rsAcctList.EOF
%>
```

```
       <OPTION value= <%= rsAcctList.Fields("AcctID") %> >
<%= rsAcctList.Fields("AcctType") %>
       </OPTION>
<%
      rsAcctList.MoveNext
   Wend
%>

</SELECT></TD></TR></TABLE></P>
<INPUT type="Submit" value="Execute Transfer"
id=btnExecute name=btnExcute>
</FORM>

</BODY>
</HTML>
```

Or in JScript:

```
<%@ LANGUAGE=JScript TRANSACTION=Required %>
<% Response.buffer = false %>
<HTML>
<HEAD>
<TITLE>Account Transfer Page</TITLE>
</HEAD>
<BODY>

<%
OwnerName = "John Smith";  // Normally obtained via a query string

// Create the Bank.AcctMgt object
objAcctMgt = Server.CreateObject("Bank.AcctMgt");

// Then get a list of the user's accounts
rsAcctList = objAcctMgt.GetAccountList(OwnerName);
%>
<P><FONT SIZE=6><EM>Welcome, <% =OwnerName %>,</EM></FONT></P>

<%
// Let the customer know whether their transfer worked or not.
if (Request.QueryString("Commit") == "False") {
   Response.Write("Sorry, your transfer failed to complete.<BR>");
} else {
   Response.Write("Your transfer has succeeded.<BR>");
}
%>

<P>Please specify your transfer details:</P>
<P>
<FORM NAME=AcctTransfer Action="DoTransfer.asp" METHOD=GET>
<TABLE border="0" cellPadding="1" cellSpacing="1" width="300">

  <TR>
    <TD>Amount</TD>
    <TD><INPUT Type=Text id=intAmount name=intAmount></TD></TR>
  <TR>
    <TD>Originating Account</TD>
    <TD><SELECT id=OrigAcct name=OrigAcct style="HEIGHT: 22px; WIDTH: 154px">
<%
   while (!rsAcctList.EOF) {
%>
```

```
      <OPTION value=<%= rsAcctList.Fields("AcctID") %>> <%=
rsAcctList.Fields("AcctType") %>
      </OPTION>
<%      rsAcctList.MoveNext();
  }
%>

  </SELECT></TD>
  </TR>
  <TR>
   <TD>Destination Account</TD>
   <TD><SELECT id=DestAcct name=DestAcct style="HEIGHT: 22px; WIDTH: 154px">
<%
  rsAcctList.MoveFirst();
  while (!rsAcctList.EOF) {
%>
      <OPTION value= <%= rsAcctList.Fields("AcctID") %> >
<%= rsAcctList.Fields("AcctType") %>
      </OPTION>
<%
      rsAcctList.MoveNext();
  }
%>

</SELECT></TD></TR></TABLE></P>
<INPUT type="Submit" value="Execute Transfer"
id=btnExecute name=btnExcute>
</FORM>

</BODY>
</HTML>
```

When viewed in the browser it `Transfer.asp` looks like this:

DoTransfer.asp

Once the user has entered the amount to transfer, they specify the Originating and Destination accounts and then click the **Execute Transfer** button. When that happens, the form information is passed on to the `DoTransfer.asp` page. The source for `DoTransfer.asp` is:

```asp
<%@ LANGUAGE=VBScript TRANSACTION=Required %>

<%
Dim objAcctMgt
Dim intOrigAcct
Dim intDestAcct
Dim intAmount

' Get the information from the query string
intOrigAcct = Request.QueryString("OrigAcct")
intDestAcct = Request.QueryString("DestAcct")
intAmount = Request.QueryString("intAmount")

' Create the object
Set objAcctMgt = server.CreateObject("Bank.AcctMgt")

' Call the method to transfer the money
objAcctMgt.TransferMoney intOrigAcct,intDestAcct,intAmount

' Release the object
Set objAcctMgt = nothing

Sub OnTransactionCommit()
   Response.Redirect "Transfer.asp?Commit=True"
End Sub

Sub OnTransactionAbort()
 Response.Redirect "Transfer.asp?Commit=False"
End Sub

%>
```

Or in JScript:

```asp
<%@ LANGUAGE=JScript TRANSACTION=Required %>

<%
// Get the information from the query string
intOrigAcct = Request.QueryString("OrigAcct");
intDestAcct = Request.QueryString("DestAcct");
intAmount = Request.QueryString("intAmount");

// Create the object
objAcctMgt = server.CreateObject("Bank.AcctMgt");

// Call the method to transfer the money
objAcctMgt.TransferMoney(intOrigAcct,intDestAcct,intAmount);

// Release the object
delete objAcctMgt;

function OnTransactionCommit() {
   Response.Redirect("Transfer.asp?Commit=True");
}

function OnTransactionAbort() {
 Response.Redirect("Transfer.asp?Commit=False");
}

%>
```

Database

For our application transferring money between two accounts, we have a very simplified database. For our Bank application this should either be a SQL Server 6.5 or 7.0 database. There is only one table, and its design is as follows:

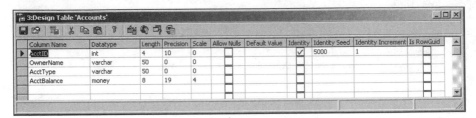

This table will contain all of the data for the fictional bank that we are building. The contents of the table are:

Table Field	Contents
AcctID	The Account number of the account
OwnerName	The name of the account holder
AcctType	The description of the account type (Checking, Saving)
AcctBalance	The current balance of the account.

Message Queuing

The COM+ Services built into Windows 2000 include many components. We have just looked at the transaction services. In this section we will change our focus to another of the COM+ services, Message Queuing which we refer to as MSMQ.

The use of Message Queuing makes applications more scalable since it provides the ability to make asynchronous communications. Those communications are sent as messages to a queue and are hence more reliable. If a message queue is not available when a client tries to send it a message, that message can be delivered at a later time, when the server is available again. The messsage is not lost if the server is not immediately available. In a similar vein, MSMQ guarantees that a message will be delivered to the server once and once only.

> When covering Message Queuing, it is assumed that the reader has a Message Queue server fully configured. If Message Queueing has not been installed and configured on the machine, the examples give in this section will not function.
>
> MSMQ provides a COM component that developers can use to add messaging support to their applications. This is provided in the MQOA.dll that is included as a core part of Windows 2000.

Messages

The key part of a message queuing system is the message which contains the information that is being communicated from one machine/process to another. It is useful to think of these messages as "e-mail for applications", being very closely analgous to e-mails, but *between applications* rather than between people.

A message has three main parts: **Label, Body**, and **DestinationQueue**. Using the e-mail analogy, the label of a message is similar to the e-mail subject line. This can be used to distinguish and/or group multiple messages residing in a queue. The body of a message is like the body of an e-mail message. The core information being communicated is passed in the body. For MSMQ, a message body can contain just about anything: variants, strings, persistable objects, arrays, persistable classes, are all valid body information. The DestinationQueue is similar to the "To recipient" of an e-mail, and specifies into which queue the message is to be delivered.

Message Queue

Again using the "e-mail for applications" analogy, the message queue is similar to the mail server that stores the e-mail messages. A message queue is a queue that contains any number of messages. These are removed from the queue when the message is read, expires, or the queue is cleared.

Using MSMQ, a machine can host any number of queues: Each queue resides only on one system, but any system can store multiple queues. The queue manager handles the management and routing of messages into the queues. Any messages sent to that machine are delivered to the destination queue if it resides on the system, or forwarded on as soon as the system is available if the destination is a remote queue.

A message queue has three key pieces of information to identify itself: **Label, ID**, and **TypeID** . The queue's **Label** is a string that identified the queue. The **ID** of a queue is a GUID (Globally Unique IDentifier - pronounced goo-id) which uniquely identifies that queue.

The **TypeID** is an identifier that specifies the type of queue. For MSMQ , there are four different types of message queues:

❑ **Public** queues are those that applications can access and use. The majority of queues that reside on a server will be public queues. A public queue on a MSMQ machine is known to all other machines in the enterprise, and can be utilized by any of those machines.

❑ A **Private** queue is a queue that resides on a server and is accessible to applications. The difference between a private and a public queue is that the private queue is not known to the whole enterprise, and it can only be accessed by applications running on the local machine. An application on a remote machine would not be able to send a message to a private queue.

❑ A **System** queue is only available to MSMQ. An example of a system queue is the dead-letter queue that MSMQ uses to store messages that cannot be delivered: Applications cannot directly add messages to the dead-letter queue.

❑ The **Outgoing** queue is used when a message is destined for a remote machine but has not yet been delivered. This may be due to the message having only just been sent, or alternatively due to the destination server not yet being available. This will happen very frequently in disconnected system. An example of a disconnected system is the package delivery business. Drivers have client machines that customers use to sign for deliveries. Those signatures are 'sent' to the corporate server, but are stored on the machine until the machine established communications. When communication is restored, the client machines send the information. An outgoing queue is like a system queue, as it is only used by MSMQ and is not available to applications.

Benefits and Limitations of MSMQ in ASP Applications

Looking from a reliability standpoint, it is common for servers and machines to go down. When this happens to a database server that handles order processing for a web application, the whole application comes to a stop. If the application were designed to communicate with the database server using MSMQ, then the application would still be able to execute. This would result in a backlog of orders waiting to be processed, but the application would still be up and running.

For scalability, MSMQ can be useful when an application is handling a number of concurrent requests for an operation. If the operation takes a significant amount of time, then it is possible for the application to timeout while waiting for it to complete. If instead, the application uses a message to communicate the information the operations requires, then the application does not need to wait for processing to complete. The total processing time will not be reduced, but the processing can be handled without errors or inordinate delays for the user.

The most common reason for *not* using MSMQ is when the application depends on the return value from the operations. If we were to make request to a database and have it return records, MSMQ would not be at all appropriate for that task. Another example is when synchronous processing is required, since MSMQ is, by definition, asynchronous communications. MSMQ could not be used when it is important to have three operations (A, B, & C) all happen in a specific order. As MSMQ is asynchronus, it is not possible to force (or know) the order in which the operations will be performed.

MSMQ Object Model

Now that we have a better understanding of messages and message queuing, we will move on to investigate the COM components that provide MSMQ support. MSMQ provides a COM component that developers can use to add messaging support to their applications. This is provided in the MQOA.dll that is included as a core part of Windows 2000. Although the DLL is on the system, unless MSMQ is properly configured you will not be able to run these examples.

```
┌─────────────────────────────────┐
│      MSMQApplication            │
└─────────────────────────────────┘
┌─────────────────────────────────┐
│      MSMQQuery                  │
└─────────────────────────────────┘
    ┌─────────────────────────────────┐
    │      MSMQQueueInfos             │
    └─────────────────────────────────┘
        ┌─────────────────────────────────┐
        │      MSMQQueueInfo              │
        └─────────────────────────────────┘
            ┌─────────────────────────────────┐
            │      MSMQQueue                 │
            └─────────────────────────────────┘
                ┌─────────────────────────────────┐
                │      MSMQMessage               │
                └─────────────────────────────────┘
```

```
┌─────────────────────────────────┐
│   MSMQTransactionDispenser      │
└─────────────────────────────────┘
    ┌─────────────────────────────────┐
    │      MSMQTransaction           │
    └─────────────────────────────────┘
┌──────────────────────────────────────┐
│ MSMQCoordinatedTransactionDispenser   │
└──────────────────────────────────────┘
    ┌─────────────────────────────────┐
    │      MSMQTransaction           │
    └─────────────────────────────────┘

┌─────────────────────────────────┐
│      MSMQEvent                 │
└─────────────────────────────────┘
```

The objects in the MSMQ object model are:

Object	
MSMQApplication	MSMQQueue
MSMQCoordinatedTransactionDispenser	MSMQQueueInfo
MSMQMessage	MSMQQueueInfos
MSMQTransaction	MSMQQuery
MSMQTransactionDispenser	

Although there are a number of objects that the component exposes, ASP developers really need only focus on MSMQQueueInfo, MSMQQueue, and MSMQMessage objects.

MSMQApplication Object

The main use of the MSMQApplication object is for getting machine names and certificate information. The MSMQApplication object has the following methods and properties:

Methods	Properties
MachineIdOfMachineName	IsDSEnabled
MachineNameOfMachineId	MSMQVersionBuild
RegisterCertificate	MSMQVersionMajor
	MSMQVersionMinor

MSMQApplication Object Methods

MachineIdOfMachineName Method

The MachineIdOfMachineName method translates the machine name and returns it's ID.

```
String = MQApplication.MachineIdOfMachineName (MachineName)
```

Parameter	Data Type	Description
MachineName	String	This is the machine name

MachineNameOfMachineID Method

The MachineNameOfMachineID method translates the machine's ID and returns it's name.

```
String = MSMQApplication.MachineNameOfMachineID (MachineID)
```

Parameter	Data Type	Description
MachineID	String	This is the machine ID

RegisterCertificate Method

The read-only RegisterCertificate method is used to register an additional certificate with directory services. The certificate can be either external or internal.

```
MSMQApplication.RegisterCertificate(Flags, [ExternalCertificate])
```

Parameter	Data Type	Description
Flags	String	Where flags determine when the certificate is registered. There are two possible values for flags: MQCERT_REGISTER_ALWAYS – Always register the certificate MQCERT_REGISTER_IF_NOT_EXIST – Only register the certificate if it is not already registered
External Certific ate	Variant	The externalCertificate parameter is optional. When provided, it is specified as a byte array that represents the external certificate.

MSMQApplication Object Properties

IsDSEnabled Property

The read-only IsDSEnabled property is true if the MQ machine is using Directory Services.

```
Boolean = MSMQApplication.IsDSEnabled
```

MSMQVersionBuild Property

The read-only `MSMQVersionBuild` property returns the version/build number of the local MSMQ machine.

```
Short = MSMQApplication.MSMQVersionBuild
```

MSMQVersionMajor Property

The read-only `MSMQVersionMajor` property returns the major version number of the local MSMQ machine.

```
Short = MSMQApplication.MSMQVersionMajor
```

MSMQVersionMinor Property

The read-only `MSMQVersionMinor` property returns the minor version number of the local MSMQ machine.

```
Short = MSMQApplication.MSMQVersionMinor
```

MSMQCoordinatedTransactionDispenser Object

The `MSMQCoordinatedTransactionDispenser` is used for MSDTC transactions, as we covered earlier in the chapter. The transaction can involve more than one resource manager. As an example involving multiple resources managers would be a transaction that updates a database and also sends a message to a queue.

Methods
BeginTransaction

BeginTransaction Method

The `BeginTransaction` method returns a newly created `MSMQTransaction` object.

```
MSMQTransaction = MSMQCoordinatedTransactionDispenser.BeginTransaction
```

MSMQMessage Object

This `MSMQMessage` object represents a message in the queue. A message is the key to the message queuing system.

The `MSMQMessage` object only has two methods: `Send` and `AttachCurrentSecurityContext`.

Methods	Properties	
AttachCurrent SecurityContext	Ack	IsFirstInTransaction
Send	AdminQueueInfo	IsLastInTransaction

Table Continued on Following Page

Methods	Properties	
	AppSpecific	Journal
	ArrivedTime	Label
	Authentication ProviderName	MaxTimeToReachQueue
	Authentication ProviderType	MaxTimeToReceive
	AuthLevel	MsgClass
	Body	Priority
	BodyLength	PrivLevel
	Class	Received AuthenticationLevel
	Connector TypeGUID	ResponseQueueInfo
	CorrelationID	SenderCertificate
	Delivery	SenderID
	Destination QueueInfo	SenderIDType
	Destination SymmetricKey	SenderVersion
	Encrypt Algorithm	SentTime
	Extension	Signature
	HashAlgorigthm	SourceMachineGUID
	ID	Trace
	Is Authenticated	TransactionID
		Transaction StatusQueueInfo

MSMQMessage Object Methods

AttachCurrentSecurityContext Method

The `AttachCurrentSecurityContext` method is used to send a large number of message with the same certificate.

```
MSMQMessage.AttachCurrentSecurityContext
```

The method attaches the certificate in `SenderCertificate`. MSMQ will provide an internal certificate is the `SenderCertificate` property is not set.

Send Method

The Send method has the following syntax:

```
MSMQMessage.Send(DestinationQueue, [Transaction])
```

Parameter	Data Type	Description
DestinationQueue	DestinationQueue	This references the destination queue object.
Transaction	String	Optional. This specifies whether the send method is involved in a transaction.

The DestinationQueue parameter takes an MSMQQueue object, which is the queue to which the message is intended to be delivered. The possible values for Transaction can be found in Appendix J.

MSMQMessage Object Properties

There are 42 properties that are available for an MSMQMessage object.

Ack Property

The read/write Ack property specifies the type of acknowledgement returned by MSMQ.

```
Long = MSMQMessage.Ack
MSMQMessage.Ack = Long
```

The MQMSG_ACKNOWLEDGMENT values can be found in Appendix J.

AdminQueueInfo Property

The AdminQueueInfo property sets or returns the queue object used for message acknowledgments.

```
MSMQQueueInfo = MSMQMessage.AdminQueueInfo
MSMQMessage.AdminQueueInfo = MSMQQueueInfo
```

AppSpecific Property

The AppSpecific property sets or returns the application specific information for message filtering.

```
Long = MSMQMessage.AppSpecific
MSMQMessage.AppSpecific = Long
```

ArrivedTime Property

The read-only ArrivedTime property returns the date and time the message arrived in queue.

```
Date = MSMQMessage.ArrivedTime
```

Transactions & Message Queuing

AuthenticationProviderName Property

The `AuthenticationProviderName` property sets or returns the name of provider that authenticated the message.

```
String = MSMQMessage.AuthenticationProviderName
MSMQMessage.AuthenticationProviderName = String
```

AuthenticationProviderType Property

The `AuthenticationProviderType` property sets or returns the type of provider that authenticated the message.

```
Long = MSMQMessage.AuthenticationProviderType
MSMQMessage.AuthenticationProviderType = Long
```

AuthLevel Property

The `AuthLevel` property determines if the message need be authenticated when received.

```
Long = MSMQMessage.AuthLevel
MSMQMessage.AuthLevel = Long
```

Body Property

The `Body` property specifies the body of the message.

```
Variant = MSMQMessage.Body
MSMQMessage.Body = Variant
```

BodyLength Property

The `BodyLength` property returns the size of the message in bytes.

```
Long = MSMQMessage.BodyLength
```

Class Property

The `Class` property returns the class/type of the message.

```
Long = MSMQMessage.Class
```

ConnectorTypeGUID Property

The `ConnectorTypeGUID` property returns the properties set by the sending application.

```
String = MSMQMessage.ConnectorTypeGUID
MSMQMessage.ConnectorTypeGUID = String
```

CorrelationID Property

The `CorrelationID` property returns the correlation identifier.

```
Variant = MSMQMessage.CorrelationID
MSMQMessage.CorrelationID = Variant
```

Delivery Property

The `Delivery` property sets or returns the method of delivery for the message.

```
Long = MSMQMessage.Delivery
MSMQMessage.Delivery = Long
```

DestinationQueueInfo Property

The `DestinationQueueInfo` property determines the queue where the message was sent.

```
MSMQQueueInfo = MSMQMessage.DestinationQueueInfo
```

DestinationSymmetricKey Property

The `DestinationSymmetricKey` property sets or returns the symmetric key used when encrypting the message.

```
Variant = MSMQMessage.DestinationSymmetricKey
MSMQMessage.DestinationSymmetricKey = Variant
```

EncryptAlgorithm Property

The `EncryptAlgorithm` property sets or returns the algorithm used to encrypt message.

```
Long = MSMQMessage.EncryptAlgorithm
MSMQMessage.EncryptAlgorithm = Long
```

Extension Property

The `Extension` property sets or returns the additional application defined information, it typically contains additional information to enable the application to deal with the message.

```
Variant = MSMQMessage.Extension
MSMQMessage.Extension = Variant
```

HashAlgorithm Property

The `HashAlgorithm` property sets or returns the hash algorithm used when authenticating the message.

```
Long = MSMQMessage.HashAlgorithm
MSMQMessage.HashAlgorithm = Long
```

ID Property

The read-only `ID` property returns the identifier for the message.

```
Variant = MSMQMessage.ID
```

IsAuthenticated Property

The read-only `IsAuthenticated` property determines if message was authenticated by MSMQ.

```
Short = MSMQMessage.IsAuthenticated
```

IsFirstInTransaction Property

The read-only `IsFirstInTransaction` property determines if the message was the first message in a transaction.

```
Short = MSMQMessage.IsFirstInTransaction
```

IsLastInTransaction Property

The read-only `IsLastInTransaction` property determines if the message was the last message in a transaction.

```
Short = MSMQMessage.IsLastInTransaction
```

Journal Property

The `Journal` property determines if a copy of the message is stored in the journal.

```
Long = MSMQMessage.Journal
MSMQMessage.Journal = Long
```

Label Property

The `Label` property sets or returns the label/title of the message; the purpose and setting of this is defined by the application.

```
String = MSMQMessage.Label
MSMQMessage.Label = String
```

MaxTimeToReachQueue Property

The `MaxTimeToReachQueue` property sets or returns the maximum amount of time for the message to be delivered.

```
Long = MSMQMessage.MaxTimeToReachQueue
MSMQMessage.MaxTimeToReachQueue = Long
```

MaxTimeToReceive Property

The `MaxTimeToReceive` property sets or returns the maximum amount of time the receiver has to retrieve the message.

```
Long = MSMQMessage.MaxTimeToReceive
MSMQMessage.MaxTimeToReceive = Long
```

MsgClass Property

The `MsgClass` property sets or returns the class/type of message.

```
Long = MSMQMessage.MsgClass
MSMQMessage.MsgClass = Long
```

This value is normally set by MSMQ and gives information about what type of message it is and if it is an acknowlegment the type of acknowledgement. It can be used to identify why the message what type of message this is. The possible values are `positive ack`, `negative ack`, `message` or a `report`.

Priority Property

The `Priority` property sets or returns the message priority. This value is an integer between 0 and 7 with the default being 3.

```
Long = MSMQMessage.Priority
MSMQMessage.Priority = Long
```

PrivLevel Property

The `PrivLevel` property determines if the message is private/encrypted.

```
Long = MSMQMessage.PrivLevel
MSMQMessage.PrivLevel = Long
```

ReceivedAuthenticationLevel Property

The `ReceivedAuthenticationLevel` property returns the authentication level of the sending application, this is different for MSMQ 1.0 and 2.0.

```
Short = MSMQMessage.ReceivedAuthenticationLevel
```

ResponseQueueInfo Property

The `ResponseQueueInfo` property sets or returns the queue to send message response to.

```
MSMQQueueInfo = MSMQMessage.ResponseQueueInfo
MSMQMessage.ResponseQueueInfo = MSMQQueueInfo
```

SenderCertificate Property

The `SenderCertificate` property sets or returns the senders certificate as an array of bytes.

```
Variant = MSMQMessage.SenderCertificate
MSMQMessage.SenderCertificate = Variant
```

SenderID Property

The `SenderID` property returns the ID of the message sender.

```
Variant = MSMQMessage.SenderID
MSMQMessage.SenderID = Variant
```

SenderIDType Property

The `SenderIDType` property sets or returns the specified type of sender identified by `SenderID`.

```
Long = MSMQMessage.SenderIDType
MSMQMessage.SenderIDType = Long
```

SenderVersion Property

The read-only `SenderVersion` property returns the version of MSMQ that sender used. This property, naturally enough, is only available with MSMQ 2.0 and can be either 0x0010 for MSMQ 1.0 or 0x0020 for MSMQ 2.0.

```
Long = MSMQMessage.SenderVersion
```

SentTime Property

The read-only `SentTime` property returns the date and time message was sent.

```
Variant = MSMQMessage.SentTime
```

Signature Property

The `Signature` property sets or returns the digital signature used to authenticate the message.

```
Variant = MSMQMessage.Signature
MSMQMessage.Signature = Variant
```

SourceMachineGUID Property

The `SourceMachineGUID` property returns the GUID of the computer from which the message was sent.

```
String = MSMQMessage.SourceMachineGUID
```

Trace Property

The `Trace` property determines whether to trace the message or not.

```
Long = MSMQMessage.Trace
MSMQMessage.Trace = Long
```

The default for this is `MSMQSG_TRACE_NONE`. If the message should be traced a report is issued every hop.

TransactionID Property

The read-only `TransactionID` property returns the transaction identifier of the message.

```
Variant = MSMQMessage.TransactionID
```

TransactionStatusQueueInfo Property

The read-only `TransactionStatusQueueInfo` property determines the transaction status Queue when retrieving transactions sent to a foreign queue.

```
MSMQQueueInfo = MSMQMessage.TransactionStatusQueueInfo
```

MSMQQuery Object

The MSMQQuery object gives a developer an easy method of quering for pulibic message queues. There is only one method on the object - `LookupQueue`.

Methods
LookupQueue

MSMQQuery Object Methods

LookupQueue Method

The method will return a MSMQQueueInfos object.

```
Query.LookupQueue( [GUID], [ServiceTypeGUID],
   [Label], [CreateTime], [ModifyTime],
      [RelServiceType], [RelLabel], [RelCreateTime], [RelModifyTime])
```

Parameter	Data Type	Description
QueueGUID	Variant	Optional. The GUID of the queue
ServiceTypeGUID	Variant	Optional. The service Type of the queue
Label	Variant	Optional. The queue's Label
CreateTime	Variant	Optional. The time the queue was created
ModifyTime	Variant	Optional. The time queue was last modified
RelServiceType	Variant	Optional. The relational parameter for ServiceTypeGUID
RelLabel	Variant	Optional. The relational parameter for Label
RelCreateTime	Variant	Optional. The relational parameter for CreateTime
RelModifyTime	Variant	Optional. The relational parameter for ModifyTime

The Relational parameters are used to add boolean operators to the criteria. The possible operators are:

Operator	Description
REL_EQ	Equals
REL_NEQ	Not Equals
REL_LT	Less Than
REL_GT	Greater Than
REL_LE	Less Than or Equal To
REL_GE	Greater Than or Equal To

MSMQQuery Object Properties

The MSMQQuery object exposes no properties.

MSMQQueue Object

The MSMQQueue object represents a single queue. This object has been retrieved by using the MSMQQueueInfo object and the Open method.

The MSMQQueue object has the following methods and properties:

Methods	Properties
Close	Access
EnableNotification	Handle
Peek	IsOpen
PeekCurrent	QueueInfo
PeekNext	ShareMode
Receive	
ReceiveCurrent	
Reset	

MSMQQueue Object Methods

Close Method

The Close method will close the currently open queue. It does not take any parameters.

```
MSMQQueue.Close()
```

EnableNotification Method

The EnableNotification method on the MSMQQueue object provides a means of asynchronous message handling using events. Once the EnableNotification method has been called, it is then possible for applications to have event handlers respond to events in the queue (MessageArrived, for example). Unfortunately, ASP applications are only able to process messages synchronously, so this method is not useful to the ASP developer.

```
MSMQQueue.EnableNotification(Event, [Cursor], [RecieveTimeout])
```

Parameter	Data Type	Description
Event	MSMQEvent	This references an MSMQEvent object
Cursor	Variant	Optional. This specifies the action of the cursor.
RecieveTimeout	Variant	Optional. This specifies how long MSMQ waits for a message in milliseconds.

Peek Method

The Peek group of methods allows the developer to retrieve a copy of a message from the queue. The Peek method will return the first message in the queue without removing it from the queue. If there is no message in the queue MSMQ will wait for one.

```
MMSMQMessage = MSMQQueue.Peek([WantDestinationQueue], [WantBody],
    [ReceiveTimeout])
```

Parameter	Data Type	Description
WantDestination Queue	Variant	Optional. This specifies whether the message's DestinationQueueInfo property should be updated. The default is false.
WantBody	Variant	Optional. This indicates whether MSMQ should retrieve the body of the message. The default is true.
ReceiveTimeout	Variant	Optional. This gives the time in milliseconds MSMQ will wait for a message to arrive if the queue is empty. The default is for MSMQ to halt execution until a message arrives.

This allows us to traverse through the messages in a queue if they are looking for a specific message. For time optimization if possible do not include the body and allow update of the queue.

PeekCurrent Method

The PeekCurrent method allows the developer to retrieve a copy of a message from the queue at the current queue position. It will not move the cursor to the next message.

```
MMSMQMessage = MSMQQueue.PeekCurrent([WantDestinationQueue], [WantBody],
    [ReceiveTimeout])
```

Parameter	Data Type	Description
WantDestination Queue	Variant	Optional. This specifies whether the message's DestinationQueueInfo property should be updated. The default is false.
WantBody	Variant	Optional. This indicates whether MSMQ should retrieve the body of the message. The default is true.
ReceiveTimeout	Variant	Optional. This gives the time in milliseconds MSMQ will wait for a message to arrive if the queue is empty. The default is for MSMQ to halt execution until a message arrives.

PeekNext Method

The Peeknext method allows the developer to retrieve a copy of a message after the current one in the queue without removing it from the queue. MSMQ will move the cursor from the current message and look at the next message.

```
MSMQMessage = MSMQQueue.PeekNext([WantDestinationQueue], [WantBody],
    [ReceiveTimeout])
```

Parameter	Data Type	Description
WantDestination Queue	Variant	Optional. This specifies whether the message's DestinationQueueInfo property should be updated. The default is false.
WantBody	Variant	Optional. This indicates whether MSMQ should retrieve the body of the message. The default is true.
ReceiveTimeout	Variant	Optional. This gives the time in milliseconds MSMQ will wait for a message to arrive if the queue is empty. The default is for MSMQ to halt execution until a message arrives.

Receive Method

The Receive method will receive the first message in the queue.

```
MSMQMessage = MSMQQueue.Receive([Transaction], [WantDestinationQueue],
    [WantBody], [RecieveTimeout])
```

Parameter	Data Type	Description
Transaction	MSMQ Transaction	Optional. This specifies whether the call is part of the current transaction, part of an external transaction or not part of a transaction.
WantDestination Queue	Variant	Optional. If true the destination queue is updates when the message is read from the queue.
WantBody	Variant	Optional. If false we do not need to read the body of the message.
RecieveTimeout	Variant	Optional. This determines the time in milliseconds that MSMQ waits for a message.

The MSMQTransaction constants can be found in Appendix J.:
The Receive and ReceiveCurrent methods allow us to retrieve a message from the queue. These methods will return an MSMQMessage object with the message information, and then remove the message from the queue. Once a message is received by one application it no longer exists in the queue.

ReceiveCurrent Method

The Receive and ReceiveCurrent methods allow us to retrieve a message from the queue.

```
MSMQMessage = MSMQQueue.ReceiveCurrent([Transaction], [WantDestinationQueue],
[WantBody], [RecieveTimeout], [WantConnectionType])
```

Parameter	Data Type	Description
Transaction	MSMQ Transaction	Optional. This specifies whether the call is part of the current transaction, part of an external transaction or not part of a transaction.
WantDestination Queue	Variant	Optional. If true the destination queue is updates when the message is read from the queue.
WantBody	Variant	Optional. If false we do not need to read the body of the message.
RecieveTimeout	Variant	Optional. This determines the time in milliseconds that MSMQ waits for a message.

Transactions & Message Queuing

The *MSMQTransaction* constant is one or more of the values listed in appendix J.

The ReceiveCurrent method will receive the message that is at the current cursor location (in the case of traversing messages in a queue). It returns an MSMQMessage object with the message information, and then remove the message from the queue. Once a message is received by one application it no longer exists in the queue.

Reset Method

The Reset method will reset the cursor to the start of the queue. It does not take any parameters.

```
MSMQQueue.Reset()
```

MSMQQueue Object Properties

Access Property

The read-only Access property determines the access rights for the queue. A list of returned values can be found in Appendix J.

```
Long = MSMQQueue.Access
```

Handle Property

The read-only Handle property returns the handle to the queue.

```
Long = MSMQQueue.Handle
```

IsOpen Property

The read-only IsOpen property returns 0 or 1 depending whether the queue is open or closed: 1 TRUE, 0 FALSE.

```
Short = MSMQQueue.IsOpen
```

QueueInfo Property

The QueueInfo property returns the MSMQQueueInfo object that was used to access the queue. This retrieves the stored settings used to open the queue.

```
MSMQQueueInfo = MSMQQueue.QueueInfo
```

ShareMode Property

The ShareMode property returns the share mode of the queue. This returns the last share mode of the queue even if it currently closed and can be restricted to this process or available to be shared by everyone.

```
Long = MSMQQueue.IsOpen
```

MSMQQueueInfo Object

The MSMQQueueInfo object allows the developer to have queue management capabilities in their applications. This enables the application to create, open, modify,

ShareMode Property

The `ShareMode` property returns the share mode of the queue. This returns the last
share mode of the queue even if it currently closed and can be restricted to this process
or available to be shared by everyone.

```
Long = MSMQQueue.IsOpen
```

MSMQQueueInfo Object

The `MSMQQueueInfo` object allows the developer to have queue management
capabilities in their applications. This enables the application to create, open, modify,
or delete a queue. For most messaging applications, this object will be the starting
point for any message related operations.

Methods	Properties
Create	Authenticate
Delete	BasePriority
Open	CreateTime
Refresh	FormatName
Update	IsTransactional
	IsWorldReadable
	Journal
	JournalQuota
	Label
	ModifyTime
	PathName
	PathNameDNS
	PrivLevel
	QueueQUID
	Quota
	ServiceTypeGUID

MSMQQueueInfo Object Methods

Create Method

The `Create` method is used to create a new queue. The syntax of the method is:

```
MSMQQueueInfo.Create([Transactional], [WorldReadable])
```

Parameter	Data Type	Description
Transactional	Variant	Optional. True to make the queue require messages to be sent as part of a transaction. Default is False.
WorldReadable	Variant	Optional. True to make messages in the queue readable by anyone. Default is False.

Delete Method

The Delete method allows the developer to delete existing queues. The method will delete the queue that is currently referenced by the MSMQQueueInfo object.

```
MSMQQueueInfo.Delete()
```

Open Method

The Open method will open a queue so that an applications can interact with the messages within. The method will return an MSMQQueue object that represents the queue. The syntax of the method is:

```
MSMQQueue = MSMQQueueInfo.Open(AccessType, ShareMode)
```

Parameter	Data Type	Description
Access	Long	This specifies the access that is being requested
ShareMode	Long	This determines which users can access the queue

The AccessType parameter specifies the access that is being requested. The ShareMode parameter determines which users can access the queue. The possible values for these constants are listed in Appendix J.

Refresh Methods

The Refresh method will simple refresh the property values for the currently referenced queue.

```
MSMQQueueInfo.Refresh()
```

Update Method

The Update method is used to commit changes that have been made to any of the property values.

```
MSMQQueueInfo.Update()
```

MSMQQueueInfo Object Properties

Authenticate Property

The `Authenticate` property determines whether the queue requires authenticated messages. It can be one of the following self-explanatory two values: `MQ_AUTHENTICATE_NONE` or `MQ_AUTHENTICATE`.

```
Long = MSMQQueueInfo.Authenticate
MSMQQueueInfo.Authenticate = Long
```

BasePriority Property

The `BasePriority` property sets or returns the default priority assigned to messages.

```
Long = MSMQQueueInfo.BasePriority
MSMQQueueInfo.BasePriority = Long
```

This defaults to 0 but can be any integer value between –32768 and 32767.

CreateTime Property

The read-only `CreateTime` property returns the date and time the queue was created.

```
Variant = MSMQQueueInfo.CreateTime
```

FormatName Property

The `FormatName` property is used to identify the queue, if this is not provided MSMQ will derive one from the path name.

```
String = MSMQQueueInfo.FormatName
MSMQQueueInfo.FormatName = String
```

IsTransactional Property

The read-only `IsTransactional` property specifies if the queue supports transactions, possible values are 1 (yes) and (0) no.

```
Short = MSMQQueueInfo.IsTransactional
```

IsWorldReadable Property

The read-only `IsWorldReadable` property specifies if everyone is able to read the messages in the queue, (1) everyone can read this, (0) the default – only the queue owner can read the message.

```
Short = MSMQQueueInfo.IsWorldReadable
```

Journal Property

The `Journal` property specifies whether retrieved messages are stored in the Journal queue. The default for this is `MQ_JOURNAL_NONE`, no journal entry is made. If you need a the message to be entered in the journal queue set this value to `MQ_JOURNAL`.

```
Long = MSMQQueueInfo.Journal
MSMQQueueInfo.Journal = Long
```

JournalQuota Property

The JournalQuota property is an optional property specifying the maximum size of the journal in kB, the default for this is INFINITE.

```
Long = MSMQQueueInfo.JournalQuota
MSMQQueueInfo.JournalQuota = Long
```

Label Property

The Label property returns a description of the queue, this value is defined by the application that uses it.

```
String = MSMQQueueInfo.Label
MSMQQueueInfo.Label = String
```

ModifyTime Property

The ModifyTime property returns the time of the last change to the queue's properties

```
Variant = MSMQQueueInfo.ModifyTime
```

PathName Property

The PathName property returns the MSMQ path to the queue. Although most of the properties are self-explanatory, there is more information to know about the PathName property. This property specified the full path to the Queue. For most queues it will be *MachineName\QueueName*. In the case where the path is to the local machine, it is possible to use a period (".") instead of the local machine's name. This is used in the below code examples.

```
String = MSMQQueueInfo.PathName
MSMQQueueInfo.PathName = String
```

PathNameDNS Property

The PathNameDNS property returns a string value containing the DNS path to the queue

```
String = MSMQQueueInfo.PathNameDNS
```

PrivLevel Property

The PrivLevel property specifies the privacy level of the queue.

```
Long = MSMQQueueInfo.PrivLevel
MSMQQueueInfo.PrivLevel = Long
```

Possible values are:

Value	Description
MQ_PRIV_LEVEL_NONE	This means it will accept only messages that are not encrypted.
MQ_PRIV_LEVEL_BODY	This means it will accept only encrypted messages.
MQ_PRIV_LEVEL_OPTIONAL	This is the default, object will accept any messages.

QueueGUID Property

The QueueGUID property returns the GUID of the queue represented by the MSMQQueueInfo object. This is set by MSMQ when the queue is first created.

```
String = MSMQQueueInfo.QueueGUID
```

Quota Property

The Quota property returns the maximum size of the queue.

```
Long = MSMQQueueInfo.Quota
MSMQQueueInfo.Quota = Long
```

This value defaults to INFINITE, it can be set as a long integer in kB. It is worth noting that the term INFINITE is relative and will be governed by the available memory.

ServiceTypeGUID Property

The ServiceTypeGUID property specifies the queue's service type.

```
String = MSMQQueueInfo.ServiceTypeGUID
MSMQQueueInfo.ServiceTypeGUID = String
```

MSMQQueueInfos Object

The MSMQQueueInfos object is provided to allow for moving through the collection of public queues returned by the LookupQueue method of the MSMQQuery object. The object has only two methods: Next and Reset.

Methods
Next
Reset

MSMQQueueInfos Object Methods

Next Method

The Next method will return the next MSMQQueueInfo object in the collection.

```
MSMQQueueInfo = MSMQQueueInfos.Next
```

Reset Method

The Reset method will reset the cursor back to the start of the collection.

```
MSMQQueueInfos.Reset()
```

MSMQQueueInfos Object Properties

The MSMQQueueInfos object does not expose any properties.

MSMQTransaction Object

The MSMQTransaction object is used to represent and identify a MSMQ transaction. The object is capable of representing both internal and MSDTC created transactions. As with the ObjectContext object in the MTS section, this object can be used for committing or aborting the transaction. The methods provided by the object are: Abort, Commit, and InitNew.

Methods	Properties
Abort	Transaction
Commit	
InitNew	

MSMQTransaction Object Methods

Abort Method

The Abort method has the following syntax:

```
MSMQTransaction.Abort([Retaining], [Async])
```

Parameter	Data Type	Description
Retaining	Variant	Optional. The Retaining parameter value must be false.
Async	Variant	Optional. The Async parameter determines if the abort is to be performed asynchronusly.

For most applications, we will not specify either of these optional parameters.

Commit Method

The Commit method is used to commit the curent transaction. The syntax of the method is:

```
MSMQTransaction.Commit([Retaining], [Sync], [Reserved])
```

Parameter	Data Type	Description
Retaining	Variant	Optional. This parameter is reserved for MSDTC internal use
Sync	Variant	Optional. This specifies whether the transaction is to be synchronus or asynchronus.
Reserved	Variant	Optional. This parameter reserved for MSDTC internal use

The Sync parameter is either XACTTC_ASYNC, where the call returns as soon as commit is initiated, or XACTTC_SYNCPHASEONE, where the call returns after phase one (of 2) is committed.

InitNew Method

The InitNew method is used to create a new transaction object that is based on an existing transaction.

```
MSMQTransaction.InitNew(ExistingTransaction)
```

Where objExistingTransaction is an existing transaction object that supports the ITransaction interface. An example of this would be an SQL transaction. If the SQL transaction object already existed, then InitNew would provide a MSMQTransaction object that would be able to perform MSMQ actions on the existing SQL transaction.

MSMQTransaction Object Properties

Transaction Property

The Transaction property returns a transaction object that represents the underlying transaction.

```
MSMQTransaction.Transaction
```

MSMQTransactionDispenser

The MSMQTransactionDispenser object is used to obtain a new MSMQTransaction object. That object can then be used for sending and receiving messages as part of a transaction.

MSMQTransactionDispenser is used only for MSMQ internal transactions. A MSMQ internal transaction is one which only sends and receives messages, and has no other operations within it. As they only involve MSMQ and its resource manager, the internal transactions are less costly.

Methods
BeginTransaction

BeginTransaction Method

The `BeginTransaction` method returns a newly created `MSMQTransaction` object.

```
MSMQTransaction = MSMQTransactionDispenser.BeginTransaction
```

MSMQ Example

Let's look at using MSMQ in practice. We will modify the example that we used for
Transaction Services: an application for transferring money between two different
bank accounts owned by the same person. We will update the application so that it
sends transfer requests to a queue. Then, we create a new application that will run on
the server and handle requests as they are posted to the queue.

Updating Bank.AcctMgt

Earlier in this chapter we described how to create the COM+ component
`Bank.AcctTransfer`. The first step for adding MSMQ support to the middle tier
object, and hence upgrading it to `Bank.AcctMgt`, is to add a reference to the **Microsoft
MessageQueue 2.0 Object library**. The references dialog should now look like this:

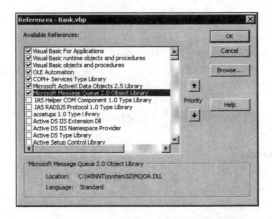

The main change that's needed to the DLL will be to the `TransferMoney` method,
where we remove the code that performed the transfer and replace it with code to send
a message. We also add a context object to both the `Transfer` and `GetAccounts`
methods. The DLLs will, of course, need to be recompiled too. The updated source
looks like this:

```
Option Explicit

Public Sub TransferMoney(ByVal intOrigAcct As Integer, ByVal intDestAcct As
Integer, _
                         ByVal intAmount As Integer)

    Dim objQueueInfo As New MSMQ.MSMQQueueInfo
    Dim objTransferQueue As New MSMQ.MSMQQueue
    Dim objMessage As New MSMQ.MSMQMessage
    Dim objContext As COMSVCSLib.ObjectContext
```

```
On Error GoTo Error_handler

Set objContext = GetObjectContext
    ' First, open the Transfer queue
    With objQueueInfo
        .PathName = ".\Transfers"
        Set objTransferQueue = objQueueInfo.Open(MQ_SEND_ACCESS, MQ_DENY_NONE)
    End With

    ' Then create and send the message
    With objMessage
        .Body = intOrigAcct & ";" & intDestAcct & ";" & intAmount
        .Label = "AcctTransfer"
        .Send objTransferQueue, MQ_TRANSACTIONAL
    End With

    If Not objContext Is Nothing Then
        objContext.SetComplete
    End If

Exit_handler:
    Set objContext = Nothing
    Exit Sub

Error_handler:

    If Not objContext Is Nothing Then
        objContext.SetAbort
    End If
    Resume Exit_handler
End Sub
```

```
Public Function GetAccountList(ByVal strAccountName As String) As
ADODB.Recordset
    Dim objContext As COMSVCSLib.ObjectContext
    Dim rsAccountList As ADODB.Recordset

    On Error GoTo GetAccountList_Error

    Set objContext = GetObjectContext()
    Set rsAccountList = New ADODB.Recordset

    With rsAccountList
        .ActiveConnection = "Provider=SQLOLEDB.1;User ID=sa;" & _
                            "Initial Catalog = Bank;Data Source=Watcher"
        .CursorLocation = adUseClient
        .CursorType = adOpenStatic
        .LockType = adLockReadOnly
        .Source = "Select * from Accounts WHERE OwnerName = '" & strAccountName
& "'"
        .Open

        Set .ActiveConnection = Nothing       ' Release the connection
    End With

    Set GetAccountList = rsAccountList

    If Not objContext Is Nothing Then
        objContext.SetComplete
    End If
```

```
GetAccountList_Exit:
   Set objContext = Nothing
   Exit Function

GetAccountList_Error:
   ' Unexpected error occurred, abort
   If Not objContext Is Nothing Then
      objContext.SetAbort
   End If

   Resume GetAccountList_Exit

End Function
```

The message that is built will specify the originating account, destination account, and amount to be transferred. For our purpose, however, we will pass the data in a simple semi-colon delimited list. (For more complicated information, creating an XML document would be a better means of passing the information). Other than that change, there are no modifications to the existing `Transfer.asp` application. There is, however, a need for a new component that will respond to the messages being posted to the `Transfers` queue. That will be handled by the `TransferProcessor` application, which we will now build.

TransferProcessor Application

With the `Transfer` application having been updated to place transfer requests into a queue, we now need to implement a processor that will act on those requests. We will also need to create our queue using **Computer Management**, and expanding the nodes: **Services and Applications** and **Message Queuing**. We then right-click on the **Public Queues**, mouse over **New** and click on **Public Queue**. We can then enter **AcctTransfer** as the name of our queue and make this transactional. When a new message is placed on our queue, the processor will gather the information from the messages and perform the transfer within our application.

The first step in creating this processor is to create a new VB Project. This will be a new **Standard EXE** project. Then, add a reference to the **Microsoft Message Queue 2.0 Object library** and the **Microsoft ActiveX Data Objects 2.5 library** (just as we did with the `Bank` project).

By default, a standard EXE project will include a form in the project. We open this form up and add a listbox to it. This listbox is used to show which transfer requests have been processed. The name of the form should be set to **frmStatus** and the listbox should be named **lbxTransfers**. The form should look like this (with its **Caption** changed to **Transfers Processed**):

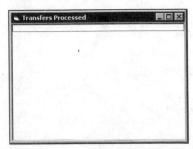

In addition to displaying the transfers that have been processed, this form will also contain the code for handling the `MessageArrived` events. The full source code behind the form looks like:

```
Option Explicit

Dim WithEvents m_objMSMQEvent As MSMQEvent
Dim m_objQueue As MSMQQueue

Private Sub Form_Load()
    Dim objQueueInfo As MSMQQueueInfo

    ' Retrieve the TransfersQueue object
    Set objQueueInfo = New MSMQQueueInfo
    With objQueueInfo
        .PathName = ".\Transfers"
        Set m_objQueue = .Open(MQ_RECEIVE_ACCESS, MQ_DENY_NONE)
    End With

    ' Register the message arrived event
    Set m_objMSMQEvent = New MSMQEvent
    m_objQueue.EnableNotification m_objMSMQEvent

    Set objQueueInfo = Nothing

End Sub
```

```
Private Sub m_objMSMQEvent_Arrived(ByVal Queue As Object, ByVal Cursor As
Long)
    Dim objMessage As New MSMQMessage
    Dim strTransferDetails As String
    Dim intOrigAcct As Integer
    Dim intDestAcct As Integer
    Dim intAmount As Integer

    Set objMessage = Queue.ReceiveCurrent
    strTransferDetails = objMessage.Body

    intOrigAcct = CInt(GetNextToken(strTransferDetails))
    intDestAcct = CInt(GetNextToken(strTransferDetails))
    intAmount = CInt(GetNextToken(strTransferDetails))

    TransferMoney intOrigAcct, intDestAcct, intAmount
    m_objQueue.EnableNotification m_objMSMQEvent

End Sub
```

```
Public Function GetNextToken(ByRef strData As String)

Dim intPosition As Integer
Dim strReturnValue As String

    intPosition = InStr(1, strData, ";", vbTextCompare)
    If intPosition <> 0 Then
        strReturnValue = Left(strData, intPosition - 1)
        strData = Mid(strData, intPosition + 1)
    Else
        strReturnValue = strData
```

```
        strData = ""
   End If

   GetNextToken = strReturnValue

End Function
```

```
Public Sub TransferMoney(ByVal intOrigAcct As Integer, ByVal intDestAcct As
Integer, _
                     ByVal intAmount As Integer)

   Dim rsUpdateConn As ADODB.Connection
   Dim strStatus As String

   Set rsUpdateConn = New ADODB.Connection

   With rsUpdateConn
      .ConnectionString = "Provider=SQLOLEDB.1;User ID=sa;Initial
Catalog=Bank;" & _
                        "Data Source=Watcher"
      .Open

      ' Remove the money from the originating account
      .Execute "UPDATE Accounts SET AcctBalance = (Select AcctBalance " & _
               "FROM Accounts WHERE AcctID=" & intOrigAcct & _
               ") - " & intAmount & " WHERE AcctID = " _
               & intOrigAcct

      ' And place it in the destintion account
      .Execute "UPDATE Accounts SET AcctBalance = (Select AcctBalance " & _
               "FROM Accounts WHERE AcctID=" & intDestAcct & _
               ") + " & intAmount & " WHERE AcctID=" & intDestAcct

   End With

   strStatus = intAmount & " from " & intOrigAcct & " to " & intDestAcct
   frmStatus.lbxTransfers.AddItem strStatus
End Sub
```

The two interesting subss to look at are: Form_Load and m_objMSMQEvent_Arrived. In the Form_Load event is where the TranfersQueue object is retrieved, using this code:

```
' Retrieve the TransfersQueue object
Set objQueueInfo = New MSMQQueueInfo
With objQueueInfo
   .PathName = ".\Transfers"
   Set m_objQueue = .Open(MQ_RECEIVE_ACCESS, MQ_DENY_NONE)
End With
```

Then, the code will use that MSMQQQueue object to set up an event handler. That event handler can then respond to the Arrived event of the queue.

```
' Register the message arrived event
Set m_objMSMQEvent = New MSMQEvent
m_objQueue.EnableNotification m_objMSMQEvent
```

When a message arrives our event handler code will retrieve that message. It will then parse the body of the message to determine the originating and destination account numbers, as well as the amount to transfer, and pass that data along to the `TransferMoney` sub. This is the same as the `TransferMoney` method of our original Bank application, but with the transactional code removed, since a standard EXE cannot support MTS transactions.

Summary

We have seen in this chapter how the MSMQ and MTS services provided by COM+ do a great deal to help ASP developers develop reliable and scalable applications. The objects and functionality provided by these important COM+ tools enable developers to focus on their application and its logic.

Transactions are valuable when there are several operations that must be completed as a whole. We also considered the purpose of Distributed Transaction Coordinators, the use of the ObjectContext interface and the Transaction Services object model.

We saw several examples of different ways of using transactions in both ASP and COM components.

We considered the MSMQ object model which makes enables us developers to incorporate message queuing into our applications. Used with care, the gains and scalability that can come out of using MSMQ can provide considerable benefits.

35

The XML DOM

XML, or **Extensible Markup Language**, is rapidly becoming an important tool for persisting and transmitting structured and semi-structured information. Microsoft has provided a library for the manipulation of XML documents. This library is Microsoft's implementation of the World Wide Web Consortium's (W3C) Document Object Model (DOM) specification for XML. It may be found in `msxml.dll`, which is installed automatically when Internet Explorer 5.0 or higher is installed, and is a standard component of Windows 2000.

What is the XML DOM?

The XML DOM is the mechanism defined by the W3C for structural access and modification of XML documents. It allows XML documents to be viewed as a tree of objects, rather than serialized text. This has several advantages over manipulating the text directly:

❑   Using the XML DOM guarantees that any document you create will be well-formed; since the document is created as a tree of nodes, rather than serialized text, problems like forgetting to write the end tag for an element to a stream just cannot occur.

❑   Using the XML DOM allows documents being read to be parsed for well-formedness and validity (if a DTD or schema is supplied for the document).

❑   Using the XML DOM allows documents to be created ad-hoc, with the serialization to a stream only happening after the document has been constructed as a tree.

❑   Using the XML DOM allows the use of XSL patterns (and, in version 2.6, XPath expressions) to search XML documents and retrieve nodes quickly.

Let's take a look at a quick example to understand how the tree view of XML documents works.

For example, if we have the XML document below:

```
<Catalog>
   <Book author="Kevin Williams">
      <Chapter>Chapter 1</Chapter>
      <Chapter>Chapter 2</Chapter>
      <!-- This book needs more chapters! -->
   </Book>
</Catalog>
```

This document is parsed by the DOM into a tree of nodes: a document node (which is always the topmost node in any document), containing a <Catalog> element. This contains a single <Book> element, which itself contains two <Chapter> elements and a comment. The <Chapter> elements and the comment contain text nodes representing their string values. The DOM generates a tree in memory that looks something like this:

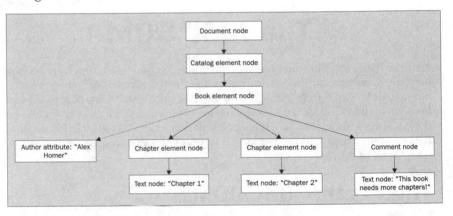

Note the dotted line going to the Author attribute – this is because attributes are treated as special node types in the DOM. There are methods and properties specifically dedicated to the manipulation of attribute values.

Which Version Should You Use?

The version of msxml.dll that ships with Internet Explorer 5 is version 2.0. This version provides support for XSL-style transformations, as well as all of the DOM functionality. Version 2.6 is available as a download from Microsoft (as of press time), and adds full support for newer XSLT-style transformations. The new objects in version 2.6 are clearly marked in the reference section; if you don't need to take advantage of this functionality, you don't need to obtain the newer version of the DLL. Also, if you choose to use version 2.6, be sure to read the documentation carefully – to ensure backwards compatibility, Microsoft has elected to embed the 2.6 functionality (for the purposes of this release, at least) in a separate DLL, msxml2.dll. You can choose to replace the existing msxml.dll with the newer msxml2.dll at install time if you like, or run both side-by-side. The package also includes a version of msxml.dll that fixes some performance problems with multiple connections from IIS, so it's worth a look as well.

Version 2.6 of the Microsoft XML libraries, together with an SDK containing documentation on the new objects, may be downloaded from:

```
http://msdn.microsoft.com/downloads/webtechnology/xml/msxml.asp
```

Using XML from ASP

Before we go on to look at the objects provided by the DOM in detail, we'll first have a quick look at some of the tasks that are commonly performed when manipulating XML documents from ASP, and give some introductory examples:

❑   Accessing stand-alone documents from ASP

❑   Creating an XML document from scratch

❑   Sending an XML document to the client

❑   Storing an XML document to a file

Accessing Stand-alone Documents from ASP

Stand-alone documents are accessed from ASP using the objects encapsulated in msxml.dll. The XMLDOMDocument object represents an entire XML document, and is used to load and parse XML files, either from in-memory strings or streams. This object should always be the first one created when working with the XML DOM objects; the other objects will then be accessible via factory methods or properties of the XMLDOMDocument object. To access a stand-alone document from a URL, you need to create an instance of the XMLDOMDocument object:

```
Dim xmldocument
Set xmldocument = Server.CreateObject("Microsoft.XMLDOM")
```

For the purposes of this example, we'll set the document to load synchronously (if you want to load asynchronously, you'll need to set an event handler on the onreadystatechange event):

```
xmldocument.async = false
```

Then, the document can be loaded and parsed by calling the load method of the newly-created object:

```
xmldocument.load("http://myServer/xml/books.xml")
```

> We must specify either a full URL or a full physical path in the Load method.

This will load the document from the remote resource and parse it. This document is retrieved using HTTP, so all the same restrictions for other operations that take place over HTTP pertain here: do all intervening firewalls allow HTTP traffic? Is the document protected? If a proxy server is being used, is the system configured to allow proxied access to the document over HTTP?

XML DOM

Since we set the document to load synchronously, once control is returned to us we know that the document has been loaded and parsed. We can now check to see if the document parsed correctly:

```
If xmldocument.parseError.errorCode <> 0 Then
    ' the parse failed - take some corrective action
Else
    ' the parse succeeded - continue normally
End If
```

The JScript equivalent for this code is:

```
var xmldocument = Server.CreateObject('Microsoft.XMLDOM');
xmldocument.async = false;
xmldocument.load('books.xml');

if (xmldocument.parseError.errorCode != 0) {
    // the parse failed - take some corrective action
} else {
    // the parse succeeded - continue normally
}
```

A complete list of the errors that may be generated by the MSXML parsing engine may be found in Appendix M.

Alternatively, if you want to load the document asynchronously, you can set the async property to true, and then set an event handler for the onreadystatechange event:

```
xmldocument.async = true
xmldocument.onreadystatechange = "HandleDocStateChange"
```

Or, in JScript:

```
xmldocument.async = 1;
xmldocument.onreadystatechange = "HandleDocStateChange";
```

After calling the load method, script execution will continue while the document is loaded and parsed in the background. The handler you have specified (in this case, HandleDocStateChange) will then be called as the XMLDOMDocument object's state changes, from "uninitialized" to "loading" to "loaded" to "interactive" (some data is available, but the parsing has not yet been completed) to "complete". You may write code in the event handler to take action once the parse of the document has completed.

Creating an XML Document from Scratch

To create an XML document in memory without loading a document, we must first create an empty instance of the XMLDOMDocument object:

```
Dim xmldocument
Set xmldocument = Server.CreateObject("Microsoft.XMLDOM")
```

Or, in JScript:

```
var xmldocument;
xmldocument = Server.CreateObject("Microsoft.XMLDOM");
```

Next, we create our various nodes and attach them to the node tree as we create them. For example, to create the root `<Book>` element for our document, we could do the following:

```
Dim xmlelement
Set xmlelement = xmldocument.createElement("Book")
xmldocument.appendChild(xmlelement)
```

Or, in JScript:

```
var xmlelement;
xmlelement = xmldocument.createElement("Book");
xmldocument.appendChild(xmlelement);
```

The entire document may be built in memory in this way.

If we have information in a serialized format that would lend itself to generation of XML text directly, we can also construct the document this way. Simply construct the XML text in a string:

```
Dim xmltext
xmltext = "<Book>"
xmltext = xmltext & "<Author>"
xmltext = xmltext & "Kevin Williams"
xmltext = xmltext & "</Author>"
xmltext = xmltext & "</Book>"
```

Or, in JScript:

```
var xmltext;
xmltext = "<Book>";
xmltext += "<Author>";
xmltext += "Kevin Williams";
xmltext += "</Author>";
xmltext += "</Book>";
```

If we then want to manipulate the document using the XML DOM, we can create an XMLDOMDocument and use the loadXML method on that document:

```
Dim xmldocument
Set xmldocument = Server.CreateObject("Microsoft.XMLDOM")
xmldocument.loadXML(xmltext)
```

Or, in JScript:

```
var xmldocument;
xmldocument = Server.CreateObject("Microsoft.XMLDOM");
xmldocument.loadXML(xmltext);
```

The parser will parse the document and populate the parseError object accordingly, making this method a good way to verify that you have created a well-formed document in your string variable:

```
If xmldocument.parseError.errorCode <> 0 Then
    ' the parse failed - we must not have created it correctly
Else
    ' the parse succeeded - continue normally
End If
```

Or, in JScript:

```
if (xmldocument.parseError.errorCode != 0) {
    // the parse failed - we must not have created it correctly
} else {
    // the parse succeeded - continue normally
}
```

Sending an XML Document to the Client

Once you have modified an existing XML document or created a new one in memory, you will probably want to do something with it. The simplest possibility is just to send the document to the client without formatting. To do this, we just need to set the `Response.ContentType` to `"text/xml"` and then write the contents of the document to the `Response` object:

```
Response.ContentType = "text/xml"
Response.Write xmldocument.xml
```

Any associated stylesheet will be applied in the browser. Otherwise, the browser's default stylesheet will be used:

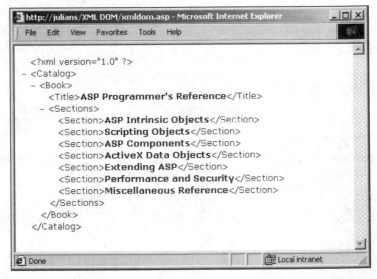

However, this will only produce meaningful results if we can guarantee that the browser supports XML (at the moment, this effectively means IE5+). A more useful technique over the Internet is to use an XSLT stylesheet to transform the XML into HTML before sending it to the client by calling the `XMLDOMDocument`'s `transformNode` method:

```
' VBScript
Dim objXML, objXSL

' Create XMLDOMDocument objects for the XML file and the stylesheet
objXML=Server.CreateObject("Microsoft.XMLDOM")
objXSL=Server.CreateObject("Microsoft.XMLDOM")
```

```
' Set synchronous loading
objXML.async=false
objXSL.async=false

' Load the XML files into our objects
objXML.load "http://myserver/books.xml"
objXSL.load "http://myserver/books.xsl"

' Transform the XML document and send it to the browser
strXML = objXML.transformNode(objXSL.documentElement)
Response.Write strXML
```

```
// JScript

// Create XMLDOMDocument objects for the XML file and the stylesheet
var objXML=Server.CreateObject("Microsoft.XMLDOM");
var objXSL=Server.CreateObject("Microsoft.XMLDOM");

// Set synchronous loading
objXML.async=false;
objXSL.async=false;

// Load the XML files into our objects
objXML.load("http://myserver/books.xml");
objXSL.load("http://myserver/books.xsl");

// Transform the XML document and send it to the browser
var strXML=objXML.transformNode(objXSL.documentElement);
Response.Write(strXML);
```

XSLT stylesheets are discussed in depth in the next chapter.

Storing an XML Document to a File

An alternative is to **persist** the document to a file. This is simple – the Microsoft implementation of the XML DOM includes a save method of the XMLDOMDocument object for just this purpose:

```
xmldocument.save("c:\xml\newbooks.xml")
```

Or, in JScript:

```
xmldocument.save("c:\\xml\\newbooks.xml");
```

Note that this only allows persistence to a local file, not across the Internet. Also, this method cannot be used inside a secured environment such as a web browser, as these environments are prevented from accessing the local file system directly because of the potential for abuse by hackers. We should therefore only use this method on the server.

The XML Document Object Model (DOM)

Manipulation of XML documents is performed via the Document Object Model libraries provided as part of Internet Explorer 5.0 and above. Some of the objects exposed by the Microsoft XML DOM libraries are base objects that other objects inherit from. The inheritance tree for the Microsoft XML DOM is shown in the following picture:

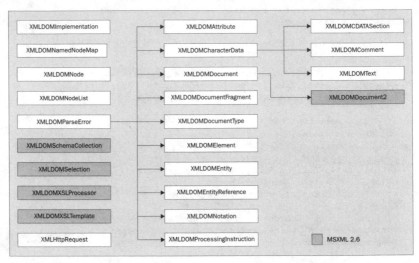

Only three of these objects may be instantiated directly: the XMLDOMDocument, which is the root node of the entire document; XMLHttpRequest, which is a helper object created to facilitate the transmission of XML documents across the Web; and the XSLTemplate object, which is used to cache compiled XSL templates. The other objects must be either referenced through properties of, or created by factory methods of, the XMLDOMDocument object.

XMLDOMAttribute

The XMLDOMAttribute object represents an attribute in an XML document. It has a name property representing the name of the attribute, and a value property representing the value stored in the attribute. For example, in the following document fragment:

```
<Book Author="Kevin Williams" />
```

There would be one XMLDOMAttribute object in the node tree, with a name of Author and a value of "Kevin Williams". This value is actually contained in a child text node, but can be accessed directly through the XMLDOMAttribute object.

The XMLDOMAttribute objects representing the attributes associated with a particular element may be accessed by examining the getattribute, getattributenode, setattribute, setattributenode, removeattribute, and removeattributenode methods of the XMLDOMElement object, as well as its attributes property.

For example, to retrieve a reference to an XMLDOMAttribute using the getAttributeNode method of the element node to which the attribute belongs:

```
' VBScript
Dim xmlAuthorAttribute
' get the Author attribute for the Book element referenced by the
' xmlBookElement variable
Set xmlAuthorAttribute = xmlBookElement.getAttributeNode("Author")
```

```
// JScript
/* get the Author attribute for the Book element referenced by the
   xmlBookElement variable */
var xmlAuthorAttribute = xmlBookElement.getAttributeNode("Author");
```

Alternatively, we can access an attribute through the XMLDOMNamedNodeMap for the element:

```
' VBScript
Dim xmlNamedNodeMap, xmlAuthorAttribute
' get the Author attribute for the Book element referenced by the
' xmlBookElement variable
Set xmlNamedNodeMap = xmlBookElement.attributes
Set xmlAuthorAttribute = xmlNamedNodeMap.getNamedItem("Author")
```

```
// JScript
/* get the Author attribute for the Book element referenced by the
   xmlBookElement variable */
var xmlNamedNodeMap = xmlBookElement.attributes;
var xmlAuthorAttribute = xmlNamedNodeMap.getNamedItem("Author");
```

We can also create an attribute using its parent element's setAttribute method:

```
' VBScript
' create an Author attribute for the Book element referenced by the
' xmlBookElement variable
xmlBookElement.setAttribute "Author", "Kevin Williams"
```

```
// JScript
/* create an Author attribute for the Book element referenced by the
   xmlBookElement variable */
xmlBookElement.setAttribute("Author","Kevin Williams");
```

The XMLDOMAttribute object is derived from the XMLDOMNode object. In addition to the name and value properties described below, see the methods, and properties defined for the XMLDOMNode object for additional functionality available through the XMLDOMAttribute object.

Methods	Properties	
appendChild*	attributes*	nodeTypedValue*
cloneNode*	baseName*	nodeTypeString*
hasChildNodes*	childNodes*	nodeValue*
insertBefore*	dataType*	ownerDocument*
removeChild*	definition*	parentNode*

XML DOM

Methods	Properties	
replaceChild*	firstChild*	parsed*
selectNodes*	lastChild*	prefix*
selectSingleNode*	name	previousSibling*
transformNode*	namespaceURI*	specified*
transformNodeToObject*	nextSibling*	text*
	nodeName*	value
	nodeType*	xml*

* See section on XMLDOMNode methods and properties.

Additional Methods

There are no additional methods defined for the XMLDOMAttribute object.

Additional Properties

The XMLDOMAttribute object has two properties which are not inherited from XMLDOMNode: name and value.

name

The read-only name property returns a string containing the name of the attribute.

```
String = XMLDOMAttribute.name
```

For example, the following code checks the name of the first attribute of an element, and if it is equal to "Author", stores the value in the variable strAuthor.

```
' VBScript
' get the name of the first attribute for the xmlBookElement element
Dim xmlAttribute, strAuthor
xmlAttribute = xmlBookElement.attributes(0)
If xmlAttribute.name = "Author" Then
    strAuthor = xmlAttribute.value
End If
```

```
// JScript
// get the name of the first attribute for the xmlBookElement element
var xmlAttribute, strAuthor;
xmlAttribute = xmlBookElement.attributes(0);
if (xmlAttribute.name == "Author") {
    strAuthor = xmlAttribute.value;
}
```

value

The value property gives the value of the attribute.

```
Variant = XMLDOMAttribute.value
```

If the attribute has more than one child node, this will be the value after parsing all entity references and concatenating the text. For example, suppose we have an entity &wrox; defined as:

```
<!ENTITY wrox "Wrox Press Limited">
```

If this is used within the Copyright attribute of an element such as:

```
<Book Copyright="Copyright 2000 &wrox;"> ... </Book>
```

Then the value property of this attribute will return:

```
"Copyright 2000 Wrox Press Limited"
```

XMLDOMCDATASection

The XMLDOMCDATASection object represents an escaped block of text in the XML document; this text is ignored by the XML parser, and may therefore contain characters which are otherwise illegal in XML, without needing each character to be escaped individually. They are therefore used to enclose sections of text which include many illegal characters.

The objects may be found in the child node lists in the node tree corresponding to their positions in the original document. For example, in the following document:

```
<SampleXML>
    <![CDATA[<Book Author="Kevin Williams"></Book>]]>
</SampleXML>
```

The SampleXML XMLDOMElement node would have one XMLDOMCDATASection node in its child node list, with the value <Book Author="Kevin Williams"></Book>.

XMLDOMCDATASection nodes may be accessed by finding them in the XMLDOMNodeList returned by the childNodes property of any node type that is allowed to contain escaped text blocks. For example, to get a reference to the CDATA section above, we would use:

```
xmlSampleXMLElement.childNodes.item(0)
```

The XMLDOMCDATASection object is derived from the XMLDOMCharacterData object, that itself is derived from the XMLDOMNode object. In addition to the splitText method of the XMLDOMCDATASection object, see the methods and properties defined for the XMLDOMCharacterData and XMLDOMNode objects for additional functionality available through the XMLDOMCDATASection object.

Methods	Properties	
appendChild*	attributes*	ownerDocument*
appendData†	baseName*	parentNode*
cloneNode*	childNodes*	parsed*

Table Continued on Following Page

Methods	Properties	
deleteData†	data†	prefix*
hasChildNodes*	dataType*	previousSibling*
insertBefore*	definition*	specified*
insertData†	firstChild*	text*
removeChild*	lastChild*	xml*
replaceChild*	length†	
replaceData†	namespaceURI*	
selectNodes*	nextSibling*	
selectSingleNode*	nodeName*	
splitText	nodeType*	
substringData†	nodeTypedValue*	
transformNode*	nodeTypeString*	
transformNodeToObject*	nodeValue*	

* See section on XMLDOMNode methods and properties.
† See section on XMLDOMCharacterData methods and properties.

We can embed an entire XML document in a CDATA section and then create a new node tree from that:

```
' VBScript
' Create a new node tree from the XML embedded in the xmlCatalogXML
' XMLDOMCDataSection object
Dim xmlCatalogDocument
Set xmlCatalogDocument = Server.CreateObject("Microsoft.XMLDOM")
xmlCatalogDocument.loadXML xmlCatalogXML.data
If xmlCatalogDocument.parseError.errorCode <> 0 Then
    ' the document did not parse - act accordingly
Else
    ' the document parsed - act accordingly
End If
```

```
// JScript
// Create a new node tree from the XML embedded in the xmlCatalogXML
// XMLDOMCDataSection object
var xmlCatalogDocument;
xmlCatalogDocument = Server.CreateObject("Microsoft.XMLDOM");
xmlCatalogDocument.loadXML (xmlCatalogXML.data);
if (xmlCatalogDocument.parseError.errorCode != 0) {
    // the document did not parse - act accordingly
} else {
    // the document parsed - act accordingly
}
```

Additional Methods

splitText

The `splitText` method splits the specified node into two nodes, breaking the data content apart at the *offset* location. It then creates an adjacent sibling node of the same type and inserts it at the appropriate location in the node tree.

```
xmlNewCDATASection = XMLDOMCDATASection.splitText(offset)
```

Parameter	Data Type	Description
offset	Long	Position at which node is split into two siblings

For example, if we take the XML element given above:

```
<SampleXML>
   <![CDATA[<Book Author="Kevin Williams"></Book>]]>
</SampleXML>
```

We can split this into two separate CDATA sections using the `splitText` method:

```
' VBScript
' xmlCatalogXML points to the CDATA section
Dim xmlNewCatalogCDATA
xmlNewCatalogCDATA = xmlCatalogXML.splitText(30)
```

```
// JScript
var xmlNewCatalogCDATA = xmlCatalogXML.splitText(30);
```

The `<SampleXML>` element now contains two CDATA sections:

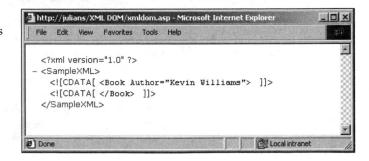

```
<?xml version="1.0" ?>
- <SampleXML>
    <![CDATA[ <Book Author="Kevin Williams"> ]]>
    <![CDATA[ </Book> ]]>
  </SampleXML>
```

Additional Properties

There are no additional properties associated with the XMLDOMCDATASection object.

XMLDOMCharacterData

The XMLDOMCharacterData object is not used directly by the Microsoft XML libraries. Instead, it is used as a common ancestor to other objects representing character data, namely XMLDOMCDataSection, XMLDOMComment, and XMLDOMText. Whenever a method or property of an object in the DOM returns one of these three types of objects, that object will support the methods and properties listed below.

The XMLDOMCharacterData object is derived from the XMLDOMNode object. In addition to the methods and properties described below, see the properties, methods, and events defined for the XMLDOMNode object for additional functionality available through the XMLDOMCharacterData object .

Methods	Properties	
appendChild*	attributes*	nodeValue*
appendData	baseName*	ownerDocument*
cloneNode*	childNodes*	parentNode*
deleteData	data	parsed*
hasChildNodes*	dataType*	prefix*
insertBefore*	definition*	previousSibling*
insertData	firstChild*	specified*
removeChild*	lastChild*	text*
replaceChild*	length	xml*
replaceData	namespaceURI*	
selectNodes*	nextSibling*	
selectSingleNode*	nodeName*	
substringData	nodeType*	
transformNode*	nodeTypedValue*	
transformNodeToObject*	nodeTypeString*	

* See section on XMLDOMNode methods and properties.

Additional Methods

There are five methods which are not inherited from the XMLDOMNode object: appendData, deleteData, insertData, replaceData, and substringData.

appendData

The appendData method appends the string in the *data* parameter to the end of the data currently contained in this node.

```
XMLDOMCharacterData.appendData(data)
```

Parameter	Data Type	Description
data	String	The data to be appended.

For example:

```
' VBScript
' modify the XMLDOMText node in xmlAuthorText to contain the author's whole
' name
If xmlAuthorText.data = "Williams" Then
   xmlAuthorText.appendData(", Kevin")
End If
```

```
// JScript
/* modify the XMLDOMText node in xmlAuthorText to contain the author's whole
   name */
if (xmlAuthorText.data == "Williams") {
   xmlAuthorText.appendData(", Kevin");
}
```

deleteData

The deleteData method deletes the substring of the data currently contained in this node beginning at the *offset* position (with zero indicating the first character in the string) and extending for *count* characters. If this extends beyond the end of the data currently in the node, the method deletes the data to the end of the string.

```
XMLDOMCharacterData.deleteData(offset, count)
```

Parameter	Data Type	Description
offset	Long	The position of the data to be deleted, i.e. characters from the start of the string
count	Long	The number of characters of data to be deleted

For example:

```
' VBScript
' modify the XMLDOMText node in xmlAuthorText to remove the author's first
' name
If xmlAuthorText.data = "Kevin Williams" Then
   xmlAuthorText.deleteData 0, 6
End If
```

```
// JScript
/* modify the XMLDOMText node in xmlAuthorText to remove the author's first
   name */
if (xmlAuthorText.data == "Kevin Williams") {
   xmlAuthorText.deleteData(0, 6);
}
```

insertData

The insertData method inserts the text specified in the data parameter into the data currently contained in this node at the offset position (with zero indicating the first character in the string).

```
XMLDOMCharacterData.insertData(offset, data)
```

Parameter	Data Type	Description
offset	Long	The position where the data is to be added, i.e. characters from the start of the string.
data	String	The data to be added.

```
' VBScript
' insert the author's first name into the xmlAuthorText XMLDOMText node
If xmlAuthorText.data = "Williams" Then
    xmlAuthorText.insertData 0, "Kevin "
End If
```

```
// JScript
// insert the author's first name into the xmlAuthorText XMLDOMText node
if (xmlAuthorText.data == "Williams") {
    xmlAuthorText.insertData(0, "Kevin ");
}
```

replaceData

The replaceData method deletes the substring of the data currently contained in this node beginning at the *offset* position (with zero indicating the first character in the string) and extending for *count* characters. It then inserts the text specified in the *data* parameter into the data currently contained in this node at the *offset* position.

```
XMLDOMCharacterData.replaceData(offset, count, data)
```

Parameter	Data Type	Description
offset	Long	The position of the data to be replaced, i.e. characters from the start of the string.
count	Long	The number of characters of data to be replaced.
data	String	The data to be added.

For example:

```
' VBScript
' correct the author's name in the XMLDOMText node xmlAuthorText
If xmlAuthorText.data = "George Williams" Then
    xmlAuthorText.replaceData 0, 6, "Kevin"
End If
```

```
// JScript
// correct the author's name in the XMLDOMText node xmlAuthorText
if (xmlAuthorText.data == "George Williams") {
    xmlAuthorText.insertData(0, 6, "Kevin");
}
```

substringData

The substringData method returns the portion of the data currently contained in this node beginning at the *offset* position (with zero indicating the first character in the string) and extending for *count* characters.

```
String = XMLDOMCharacterData.substringData(offset, count)
```

Parameter	Data Type	Description
offset	Long	The position of the data to be returned, i.e. characters from the start of the string.
count	Long	The number of characters of data to be returned.

For example:

```
' VBScript
' check to see if this book was written by a person named Kevin
Dim blnWrittenByKevin
blnWrittenByKevin = False
If xmlAuthorText.substringData(0, 5) = "Kevin" Then
    blnWrittenByKevin = True
End If
```

```
// JScript
// check to see if this book was written by a person named Kevin
var blnWrittenByKevin;
blnWrittenByKevinWilliams = false;
if (xmlAuthorText.substringData(0, 5) == "Kevin") {
    blnWrittenByKevin = true;
}
```

Additional Properties

As well as the properties inherited from XMLDOMNode, the XMLDOMCharacterData object exposes two properties of its own: data and length.

data

The data property sets or returns a string representing the data contained in this node.

```
XMLDOMCharacterData.data = String
String = XMLDOMCharacterData.data
```

```
' VBScript
' set the xmlAuthorText node's value to Unknown
xmlAuthorText.data = "Unknown"
```

```
// JScript
// set the xmlAuthorText node's value to Unknown
xmlAuthorText.data = "Unknown";
```

length

The read-only length property returns the number of characters in the data contained in this node.

```
Long = XMLDOMCharacterData.length
```

```
' VBScript
' get the length of the xmlAuthorText node's text and store it in a variable
Dim intAuthorLength
intAuthorLength = xmlAuthorText.length
```

```
// JScript
// get the length of the xmlAuthorText node's text and store it in a variable
var intAuthorLength = xmlAuthorText.length;
```

XML DOM

XMLDOMComment

The XMLDOMComment object represents a comment in the original XML document. The objects may be found in the child node lists in the node tree corresponding to their position in the original document. For example, in the following document:

```
<!-- This is the first comment -->
<Book Author="Kevin Williams">
   <!-- This is the second comment -->
</Book>
```

Two XMLDOMComment nodes would appear in the node tree: one with the text "This is the first comment", as the first child of the XMLDOMDocument object, and the second with the text "This is the second comment", as the first child of the XMLDOMElement object corresponding to the <Book> element.

XMLDOMComment nodes may be accessed by finding them in the XMLDOMNodeList returned by the childNodes property of any node type that is allowed to contain comments. For example, the first comment in the XML document above could be referenced using:

```
xmlDocument.childNodes.item(0)
```

The XMLDOMComment object is derived from the XMLDOMCharacterData object, that itself is derived from the XMLDOMNode object. There are no methods or properties unique to the XMLDOMComment object, so please see the methods and properties defined for the XMLDOMCharacterData and XMLDOMNode objects for the functionality available through the XMLDOMComment object.

Methods	Properties	
appendChild*	attributes*	nodeValue*
appendData†	baseName*	ownerDocument*
cloneNode*	childNodes*	parentNode*
deleteData†	data†	parsed*
hasChildNodes*	dataType*	prefix*
insertBefore*	definition*	previousSibling*
insertData†	firstChild*	specified*
removeChild*	lastChild*	text*
replaceChild*	length†	xml*
replaceData†	namespaceURI*	
selectNodes*	nextSibling*	
selectSingleNode*	nodeName*	
substringData†	nodeType*	
transformNode*	nodeTypedValue*	
transformNodeToObject*	nodeTypeString*	

* See section on XMLDOMNode methods and properties.
† See section on XMLDOMCharacterData methods and properties.

The following code retrieves all comment nodes for a <Book> element and
concatenates them together into one string:

```
' VBScript
Dim i, strAllComments
strAllComments = ""
For i = 0 To xmlBookElement.childNodes.length - 1
    ' Check if this child node is a comment (COMMENT_NODE = 8)
   If xmlBookElement.childNodes(i).nodeType = NODE_COMMENT Then
       strAllComments = strAllComments & " " &
xmlBookElement.childNodes(i).data
   End If
Next
```

```
// JScript
var i, strAllComments;
strAllComments = "";
for (i = 0; i < xmlBookElement.childNodes.length; i++) {
   // Check if this child node is a comment (COMMENT_NODE == 8)
   if (xmlBookElement.childNodes(i).nodeType == 8) {
       strAllComments += " " + xmlBookElement.childNodes(i).data;
   }
}
```

XMLDOMDocument

The XMLDOMDocument object represents an entire XML document. This is therefore
the topmost node of the XML DOM tree. It will always be the first object your script
references – typically by either creating a new instance and building the node tree from
scratch, or using the load or loadXML methods to initialize the node tree.

A new XMLDOMDocument object may be obtained by using the appropriate object
creation function to create an instance of XMLDOMDocument:

```
' VBScript
Dim xmlDocument
Set xmlDocument = Server.CreateObject("Microsoft.XMLDOM")
```

```
// JScript
var = Server.CreateObject("Microsoft.XMLDOM");
```

The XMLDOMDocument object is derived from the XMLDOMNode object. In addition to
the 15 methods, 10 properties, and three events of the XMLDOMDocument object
detailed below, see the properties, methods, and events defined for the XMLDOMNode
object for additional functionality available through the XMLDOMDocument object.

Methods	Properties	Events
abort	async	ondataavailable
appendChild*	attributes*	onreadystatechang
cloneNode*	baseName*	ontransformnode
createAttribute	childNodes*	
createCDATASection	dataType*	
createComment	definition*	
createDocumentFragment	doctype	
createElement	documentElement	
createEntityReference	firstChild*	
createNode	implementation	
createProcessing Instruction	lastChild*	
createTextNode	namespaceURI*	
getElementsByTagName	nextSibling*	
hasChildNodes*	nodeName*	
insertBefore*	nodeType*	
load	nodeTypedValue*	
loadXML	nodeTypeString*	
nodeFromID	nodeValue*	
removeChild*	ownerDocument*	
replaceChild*	parentNode*	
save	parsed*	
selectNodes*	parseError	
selectSingleNode*	preserveWhite Space	
transformNode*	previousSibling*	
transformNodeToObject*	readyState	
	resolveExternals	
	specified*	
	text*	
	url	
	validateOnParse	
	xml*	

* See section on XMLDOMNode methods and properties.

Additional Methods

abort

The abort method aborts the current load and parse operation if there is one in progress. Any portion of the XML node tree that has been built is discarded.

```
XMLDOMDocument.abort()
```

createAttribute

The createAttribute method creates a new XMLDOMAttribute object with the given name.

```
XMLDOMAttribute = XMLDOMDocument.createAttribute(name)
```

Parameter	Data Type	Description
name	String	The name of the attribute to be created.

This returns the new XMLDOMAttribute object. Note that the attribute will still need to be added to the child attribute list of the element to which it corresponds. If you need to create a namespace-qualified attribute, use the createNode method instead. The value of the attribute may be set by calling the setAttribute method on the new object.

For example, the following code creates an Author attribute in the xmlCatalogDocument document on the xmlBookElement element:

```vbscript
' VBScript
Dim xmlAuthorAttribute
Set xmlAuthorAttribute = xmlCatalogDocument.createAttribute("Author")
xmlAuthorAttribute.value = "Kevin Williams"
xmlBookElement.setAttributeNode(xmlAuthorAttribute)
```

```jscript
// JScript
var xmlAuthorAttribute = xmlCatalogDocument.createAttribute("Author");
xmlAuthorAttribute.value = "Kevin Williams";
xmlBookElement.setAttributeNode(xmlAuthorAttribute);
```

createCDATASection

The createCDATASection method creates a new XMLDOMCDATASection object with the given data.

```
XMLDOMCDATASection = XMLDOMDocument.createCDATASection(data)
```

Parameter	Data Type	Description
data	String	The data to be inserted into the new XMLDOMCDATASection object.

The new XMLDOMCDATASection object is returned. Note that the XMLDOMCDATASection object will still need to be added to the node tree in the appropriate location.

```
' VBScript
' Create a CDATASection child node in the xmlRawCodeElement element
Dim xmlRawCodeCDATA
Set xmlRawCodeCDATA = xmlCatalogDocument.createCDATASection("<Book></Book>")
xmlRawCodeElement.appendChild xmlRawCodeCDATA
```

```
// JScript
// Create a CDATASection child node in the xmlRawCodeElement element
var xmlRawCodeCDATA;
xmlRawCodeCDATA = xmlCatalogDocument.createCDATASection("<Book></Book>");
xmlRawCodeElement.appendChild(xmlRawCodeCDATA);
```

createComment

The createComment method creates a new XMLDOMComment object with the given text.

```
XMLDOMComment = XMLDOMDocument.createComment(data)
```

Parameter	Data Type	Description
data	String	The data to be inserted into the newly-created XMLDOMComment object.

This method returns the new XMLDOMComment object. Note that the XMLDOMComment object will still need to be added to the node tree in the appropriate location.

createDocumentFragment

The createDocumentFragment method creates a new, empty XMLDOMDocumentFragment object.

```
XMLDOMDocumentFragment = XMLDOMDocument.createDocumentFragment(name)
```

Parameter	Data Type	Description
name	String	The name of the XMLDOMDocumentFragment object to be created.

This method returns the new XMLDOMDocumentFragment object. Note that the XMLDOMDocumentFragment object will still need to be added to the node tree in the appropriate location once it has been populated.

createElement

The createElement method creates a new XMLDOMElement object with the given tag name.

```
XMLDOMElement = XMLDOMDocument.createElement(tag_name)
```

Parameter	Data Type	Description
tag_name	String	The name of the element to be created.

This method returns the new XMLDOMElement object. Note that the XMLDOMElement object will still need to be added to the node tree in the appropriate location. If you need to create a namespace-qualified element, use the createNode method instead.

createEntityReference

The createEntityReference method creates a new XMLDOMEntityReference object with the given name.

```
XMLDOMEntityReference = XMLDOMDocument.createEntityReference(name)
```

Parameter	Data Type	Description
name	String	The name of XMLDOMEntityReference object to be created.

This method returns the new XMLDOMEntityReference object. Note that the XMLDOMEntityReference object will still need to be added to the node tree in the appropriate location.

createNode

The createNode method creates a new XMLDOMNode object with the given type, name, and namespace URI. The possible types are enumerated in the XMLDOMNodeType enumeration. If the specified name contains a namespace prefix, that namespace prefix will be associated with the provided URI; otherwise, it will be treated as the default namespace.

```
XMLDOMNode = XMLDOMDocument.createNode(type, name, namespaceURI)
```

Parameter	Data Type	Description
type	Long	The type of XMLDOMNode object to be created. For possible values, see the nodeType property of the XMLDOMNode object.
name	String	The name of the node to be created.
namespace URI	String	The definition for the node's namespace.

This method returns the new XMLDOMNode object. For nodes that do not have names, the name parameter should be passed as an empty string. Note that the XMLDOMNode object will still need to be added to the node tree in the appropriate location.

For example:

```
' VBScript
' Create an xlink:simple element in the xmlBookElement element
Dim xmlXLinkSimpleElement
Set xmlXLinkSimpleElement = xmlCatalogDocument.createNode (NODE_ELEMENT, _
                                           "xlink:simple", _
                                           "http://www.w3.org/1999/xlink")
xmlBookElement.appendChild(xmlXLinkSimpleElement)
```

```
// JScript
// Create an xlink:simple element in the xmlBookElement element
var xmlXLinkSimpleElement;
xmlXLinkSimpleElement = xmlCatalogDocument.createNode (NODE_ELEMENT,
                                           "xlink:simple",
                                           "http://www.w3.org/1999/xlink");
xmlBookElement.appendChild(xmlXLinkSimpleElement);
```

This adds an `<xlink:simple>` element as the final child node of the `<Book>` element:

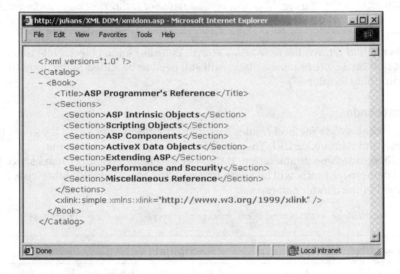

createProcessingInstruction

The `createProcessingInstruction` method creates a new `XMLDOMProcessingInstruction` object with the given target and data.

```
XMLDOMProcessingInstruction =
                XMLDOMDocument.createProcessingInstruction(target, data)
```

Parameter	Data Type	Description
target	String	The name of the application which will process the instruction
data	String	The data to be passed to the external application

This method returns the new XMLDOMProcessingInstruction object. Note that the XMLDOMProcessingInstruction object will still need to be added to the node tree in the appropriate location.

createTextNode

The createTextNode method creates a new XMLDOMText object with the given text data.

```
XMLDOMTextNode = XMLDOMDocument.createTextNode(data)
```

Parameter	Data Type	Description
data	String	The data the new XMLDOMText object will contain.

This method returns the new XMLDOMText object. Note that the XMLDOMText object will still need to be added to the node tree in the appropriate location.

getElementsByTagName

The getElementsByTagName method returns an XMLDOMNodeList object containing all the elements in the document with the specified *tagname*, in the order in which they appear in the original document. If no elements in the document have the specified *tag_name*, an empty XMLDOMNodeList is returned.

```
XMLDOMNodeList = XMLDOMDocument.getElementsByTagName(tag_name)
```

Parameter	Data Type	Description
tag_name	String	The name of the elements to search for.

```vbscript
' VBScript
' Select all the Book elements in the document
Dim xmlBookNodeList
Set xmlBookNodeList = xmlCatalogDocument.getElementsByTagName("Book")
```

```jscript
// JScript
// Select all the Book elements in the document
var xmlBookNodeList = xmlCatalogDocument.getElementsByTagName("Book");
```

load

The load method loads the XML document at the specified URL and parses it.

```
Boolean = XMLDOMDocument.load(filename)
```

Parameter	Data Type	Description
filename	Variant	The full URL or physical path of the XML file to be loaded into the document.

This method returns `true` if the document was loaded successfully, or `false` otherwise. If the URL cannot be resolved or does not contain an XML document, this method returns an error. Calling this method clears the current node tree for the document. If parsing errors are encountered when parsing the document, they are indicated in the `parseError` property of the `XMLDOMDocument` object.

```
' VBScript
Dim xmlCatalogDocument
Set xmlCatalogDocument = Server.CreateObject(Microsoft.XMLDOM)
xmlCatalogDocument.load "http://myserver/books.xml"
```

```
// JScript
var xmlCatalogDocument = Server.CreateObject("Microsoft.XMLDOM");
xmlCatalogDocument.load("http://myserver/books.xml");
```

loadXML

The `loadXML` method loads the XML document contained in the *xmlString* parameter and parses it.

```
Boolean = XMLDOMDocument.loadXML(xmlString)
```

Parameter	Data Type	Description
xmlString	String	The XML document to be loaded.

The method returns `true` if the XML string was loaded successfully, or `false` otherwise. Calling this method clears the current node tree for the document.

nodeFromID

The `nodeFromID` method returns the `XMLDOMNode` object for the element in the document with an `ID` attribute that matches the *idString* parameter. If no node matches the provided `ID`, this method returns `NULL`.

```
XMLDOMNode = XMLDOMDocument.nodeFromID(idString)
```

Parameter	Data Type	Description
idString	String	The value of the `ID` attribute to be sought in the document.

For this method to work, the node being sought must have an attribute defined as type `ID` in the DTD. For example, if we have a `<Book>` element with a unique identifying attribute called `BookID`, this attribute might be defined in the DTD as:

```
<!ATTLIST Book BookID ID #REQUIRED>
```

We can then use this attribute to provide a unique identifier for each `<Book>` element:

```
<Book BookID="ASP3ProgRef">
```

And we can easily retrieve this node (without needing to know its position in the XML document) using the `nodeFromID` method:

```
' VBScript
Dim xmlBookElement
Set xmlBookElement = xmlCatalogDocument.nodeFromID("ASP3ProgRef")
```

```
// JScript
var xmlBookElement = xmlCatalogDocument.nodeFromID("ASP3ProgRef");
```

save

The `save` method saves the XML for the current document to the target specified in the *objTarget* parameter.

```
XMLDOMDocument.save(objTarget)
```

Parameter	Data Type	Description
objTarget	Variant	If objTarget is a string, it represents a local filename to which the XML is to be written. If the file already exists, it is replaced. In a multi-user scenario, this could result in the file being overwritten and data lost, unless precautions are taken to ensure that the file is given a unique name each time it is saved.
		If objTarget is the Response object, the XML is sent back as the response to the calling client.
		If objTarget is an XMLDOMDocument object, the entire object is cloned and recreated in the new XMLDOMDocument object's node tree. Note that this actually persists the original document as text and then reparses it to create the new object's node tree, making this a good way to verify the persistability of your document.
		If objTarget is any other COM object that provides an IStream, IPersistStream, or IPersistStreamInit interface, the XML will be passed to that interface and the object will act on the XML accordingly.

We can use the `save` method to send an XML document to the browser by specifying the `Response` object as the target:

```
' VBScript
Dim xmlCatalogDocument
Set xmlCatalogDocument = Server.CreateObject("Microsoft.XMLDOM")
xmlCatalogDocument.async = false
xmlCatalogDocument.load "http://servername/xml/books.xml"
xmlCatalogDocument.save Response
```

XML DOM

```
// JScript
var xmlCatalogDocument = Server.CreateObject("Microsoft.XMLDOM");
xmlCatalogDocument.async = false;
xmlCatalogDocument.load("http://servername/xml/books.xml");
xmlCatalogDocument.save(Response);
```

Additional Properties

async

The async property is a boolean flag that indicates whether asynchronous operation is permitted.

```
XMLDOMDocument.async = Boolean
Boolean = XMLDOMDocument.async
```

When set to true (the default), control will return immediately to your script after calling the load or loadXML methods. If you want to use the XMLDOMDocument object asynchronously, you should set an event handler for the onreadystatechange event (see the onreadystatechange property below) before loading your document.

doctype

The doctype property is a read-only property that returns the XMLDOMDocumentType object that contains information about the Document Type Definition associated with the document. If there is no DTD for the document, or the document is not XML, this property returns NULL.

```
XMLDOMDocumentType = XMLDOMDocument.doctype
```

documentElement

The documentElement property sets or returns the XMLDOMElement node representing the outermost element of the document. Every XML document may have only one element immediately below the document root (although it may have other nodes, such as comments or processing instructions).

```
XMLDOMDocument.documentElement = XMLDOMElement
XMLDOMElement = XMLDOMDocument.documentElement
```

For example:

```
' VBScript
Dim xmlNewDocument
Set xmlNewDocument = Server.CreateObject("Microsoft.XMLDOM")
Set xmlNewDocument.documentElement = xmlNewDocument.createElement("Catalog")
```

```
// JScript
var xmlNewDocument = Server.CreateObject("Microsoft.XMLDOM");
xmlNewDocument.documentElement = xmlNewDocument.createElement("Catalog");
```

Implementation

The read-only `implementation` property returns the `XMLDOMImplementation` object that contains information about the version of the XML parser used to create or parse this document.

```
XMLDOMImplementation = XMLDOMDocument.implementation
```

parseError

The read-only `parseError` property returns an `XMLDOMParseError` object describing the status of the last parse performed by this instance of the XML DOM. You should always check the `parseError` property of a document after calling the `load` or `loadXML` methods to ensure that the document has been parsed correctly. A list of errors raised by the MSXML parse can be found in Appendix M.

```
XMLDOMParseError = XMLDOMDocument.parseError
```

For example:

```vbscript
' VBScript
' Check to see if the document parsed successfully
If xmldocument.parseError.errorCode <> 0 Then
    ' the parse failed - take some corrective action
Else
    ' the parse succeeded - continue normally
End If
```

```jscript
// JScript
// Check to see if the document parsed successfully
if (xmlDocument.parseError.errorCode != 0) {
    // the parse failed - take some corrective action
} else {
    // the parse succeeded - continue normally
}
```

preserveWhiteSpace

The `preserveWhiteSpace` property is a Boolean flag indicating whether whitespace should be preserved in the values of the `text` and `xml` properties for nodes in this document. If this flag is set to `true`, whitespace will always be preserved as if there were an `xml:space="preserve"` attribute on every element in the document. If the flag is set to `false`, whitespace will only be preserved for nodes where the `xml:space="preserve"` attribute is present. The default is `false`.

```
XMLDOMDocument.preserveWhiteSpace = Boolean
Boolean = XMLDOMDocument.preserveWhiteSpace
```

This property is unlikely to have any effect when sending an XML document to the browser.

readyState

The read-only `readyState` property returns a long integer that describes the status of the `load` or `loadXML` method.

```
Long = XMLDOMDocument.readyState
```

The possible values are:

- 0 ("unitialized"), i.e. the object has been created but the load method has not yet been executed.

- 1 ("loading"), i.e. the document is loading, but has not yet entered the parsing step.

- 2 ("loaded"), i.e. the document has been loaded and is being parsed.

- 3 ("interactive"), i.e. the document has been partially parsed, and a read-only version of the object model is available.

- 4 ("complete"), i.e. the document has been completely parsed, successfully or unsuccessfully.

For example:

```
' VBScript
Function checkCatalogDocumentState()
   ' This function handles the onreadystatechange event for the Catalog
   ' document load
   If xmlCatalogDocument.readyState = 4 Then ' Complete
      If xmldoc.parseError.errorCode = 0 Then
         blnCatalogParsedSuccessfully = True
      Else
         blnCatalogParsedSuccessfully = False
      End If
   End If
Set checkCatalogDocumentState = xmlCatalogDocument
End Function
```

```
// JScript
function checkCatalogDocumentState() {
   // This function handles the onreadystatechange event for the Catalog
   // document load
   if (xmlCatalogDocument.readyState == 4) { // Complete
      if (xmldoc.parseError.errorCode == 0) {
         blnCatalogParsedSuccessfully = 1;
      } else {
         blnCatalogParsedSuccessfully = 0;
      }
   }
}
```

resolveExternals

The resolveExternals property is a boolean flag indicating whether external definitions (resolvable namespaces, DTD external subsets, and external entity references) should be resolved at parse time. The default value is true.

```
XMLDOMDocument.resolveExternals = Boolean
Boolean = XMLDOMDocument.resolveExternals
```

url

The read-only url property returns a string containing the URL of the document that was last successfully loaded using the load method. If no document has been loaded with this method, this property returns NULL.

```
String = XMLDOMDocument.url
```

validateOnParse

The `validateOnParse` property is a Boolean flag indicating whether the parser should validate the document against a DTD or schema if one is present. If this flag is false, the parser will ignore a provided DTD or schema and only parse for well-formedness. The default value is `true`.

```
XMLDOMDocument.validateOnParse = Boolean
Boolean = XMLDOMDocument.validateOnParse
```

Events

The event handlers for the XML DOM are defined in VBScript and JScript by setting the value of a write-only property with the same name as the event to the name of the callback procedure used to respond to the event. Note that in VBScript a Type mismatch error will be raised if this event handler isn't a function which returns an object.

ondataavailable

The `ondataavailable` event is fired whenever a new chunk of data has been successfully loaded from a remote source. It could be used to indicate the status of a large document load to the user.

```
' VBScript
' set up an event handler for the ondataavailable event
xmlCatalogDocument.ondataavailable = checkCatalogDataAvailable

Function checkCatalogDataAvailable()
    ' handle the ondataavailable event for the Catalog document
    Set checkCatalogDataAvailable = xmlCatalogDocument
End Function
```

```
// JScript
// set up an event handler for the ondataavailable event
xmlCatalogDocument.ondataavailable = checkCatalogDataAvailable;

function checkCatalogDataAvailable() {
    // handle the ondataavailable event for the Catalog document
}
```

onreadystatechange

The `onreadystatechange` event is fired whenever the value of the `readyState` property for the object changes. When used in conjunction with the `async` property, this allows your script to continue executing while waiting for an XML document to be loaded.

```
' VBScript
' set up an event handler for the onreadystatechange event
xmlCatalogDocument.onreadystatechange = checkCatalogReadyStateChange

Function checkCatalogReadyStateChange()
    ' handle the onreadystatechange event for the Catalog document
    Set checkCatalogReadyStateChange = xmlCatalogDocument
End Function
```

```
// JScript
// set up an event handler for the onreadystatechange event
xmlCatalogDocument.onreadystatechange = checkCatalogReadyStateChange;

function checkCatalogReadyStateChange() {
    // handle the onreadystatechange event for the Catalog document
}
```

ontransformnode

The ontransformnode event is fired each time a node in a source document is about to be transformed using a node in a stylesheet. This event could be used to report the status of a long transformation to the user.

```
' VBScript
' set up an event handler for the ontransformnode event
xmlCatalogDocument.ontransformnode = checkCatalogTransformNode

Function checkCatalogTransformNode()
    ' handle the ontransformnode event for the Catalog document
    Set checkCatalogTransformNode = xmlCatalogDocument
End Function
```

```
// JScript
// set up an event handler for the ontransformnode event
xmlCatalogDocument.ontransformnode = checkCatalogTransformNode;

function checkCatalogTransformNode() {
    // handle the ontransformnode event for the Catalog document
}
```

XMLDOMDocument2

The XMLDOMDocument2 object extends the XMLDOMDocument object with additional functionality. It does not replace the original XMLDOMDocument object for reasons of backward compatibility. It supports schema caching and additional validation features, as well as providing support for XPath.

> This object is only available in version 2.6 of MSXML.

A new XMLDOMDocument2 object may be obtained by using the appropriate object creation function to create an instance of XMLDOMDocument2:

```
' VBScript
Dim xmlDocument2
Set xmlDocument2 = Server.CreateObject(MSXML2.DOMDocument)
```

```
// JScript
var xmlDocument2;
xmlDocument2 = Server.CreateObject("MSXML2.DOMDocument");
```

The XMLDOMDocument2 is by default apartment-threaded, but it is also available in a free-threaded version. This version exposes exactly the same methods and properties, and can be instantiated using the Prog ID "MSXML2.FreethreadedDOMDocument". As a general rule, it is probably a good idea to avoid using free-threaded objects in ASP.

The XMLDOMDocument2 object extends the functionality of the XMLDOMDocument object. In addition to the 4 methods and 2 properties of the XMLDOMDocument object detailed below, see the properties, methods, and events defined for the XMLDOMDocument object for additional functionality available through the XMLDOMDocument2 object.

Methods	Properties	Events
abort†	async†	ondataavailable†
appendChild*	attributes*	onreadystatechange†
cloneNode*	baseName*	ontransformnode†
createAttribute†	childNodes*	
createCDATASection†	dataType*	
createComment†	definition*	
createDocumentFragment†	doctype†	
createElement†	documentElement†	
createEntityReference†	firstChild*	
createNode†	implementation†	
createProcessing Instruction†	lastChild* namespaces	
createTextNode†	namespaceURI*	
getElementsByTagName†	nextSibling*	
getProperty	nodeName*	
hasChildNodes*	nodeType*	
insertBefore*	nodeTypedValue*	
load†	nodeTypeString*	
loadXML†	nodeValue*	
nodeFromID†	ownerDocument*	
removeChild*	parentNode*	
replaceChild*	parsed*	
save†	parseError†	
selectNodes‡	preserveWhiteSpace†	
selectSingleNode*	previousSibling*	
setProperty	readyState†	

Table Continued on Following Page

Methods	Properties	Events
transformNode*	resolveExternals†	
	schemas	
transformNodeToObject*	specified*	
validate	text*	
	url†	
	validateOnParse†	
	xml*	

* See section on XMLDOMNode methods and properties.

† See section on XMLDOMDocument methods properties and events.

‡ The XMLDOMDocument2 object redefines this method.

Additional Methods

getProperty

The getProperty method is used to obtain the value of a named property for the document. In version 2.6, the only supported property is "SelectionLanguage" which may have the value "XPath" or "XSLPattern". The value of this property governs the way queries passed to selectNode and selectSingleNode are interpreted for nodes in this document.

```
String = XMLDOMDocument2.getProperty(name)
```

Parameter	Data Type	Description
name	String	The name of the property to be returned by this call.

selectNodes

The selectNodes method is used to retrieve a set of nodes from the document. For the XMLDOMDocument2 object, an XMLDOMSelection object is returned. The parameter still represents the XSLT or XSL pattern query (based on the value of the SelectionLanguage property – see setProperty and getProperty) that will be used to create the result.

```
XMLDOMSelection = XMLDOMDocument2.selectNodes(strExpr)
```

Parameter	Data Type	Description
strExpr	String	The XSL pattern or XPath expression string used to execute the query.

For example, to find all the <Chapter> elements in the document:

```
' VBScript
Dim xmlSelectionChapterElements
xmlSelectionChapterElements = xmlCatalogDocument2.selectNodes("//Chapter")
```

```
// JScript
// find all the Chapter elements in the node
var xmlSelectionChapterElements;
xmlSelectionChapterElements = xmlCatalogDocument2.selectNodes("//Chapter");
```

setProperty

The `setProperty` method is used to set the value of a named property for the
document. In version 2.6, the only supported property is `"SelectionLanguage"`; it
may have the value `XPath` or `XSLPattern`. The value of this property governs the
way queries passed to `selectNode` and `selectSingleNode` are interpreted for
nodes in this document.

```
XMLDOMDocument2.setProperty(name, value)
```

Parameter	Data Type	Description
name	String	The name of the property that is to be set.
value	String	The value to which the property is to be set.

For example, to set the selection language to XPath:

```
' VBScript
xmlCatalogDocument2.setProperty("SelectionLanguage", "XPath")
```

```
// JScript
xmlCatalogDocument2.setProperty("SelectionLanguage", "XPath");
```

validate

The `validate` method performs runtime validation of a document using the currently
loaded DTD, schema, or schema collection. It returns error information indicating
what error, if any, was encountered while validating the document.

```
Integer = XMLDOMDocument2.validate
```

Additional Properties

namespaces

The `namespaces` property returns an `XMLDOMSchemaCollection` object that
contains a list of the namespaces used in the document. This property is read-only.

```
XMLDOMSchemaCollection = XMLDOMDocument2.namespaces
```

schemas

The `schemas` property sets or returns an `XMLDOMSchemaCollection` object that
contains a list of the precached schemas to be used in the validation of a document
loaded with the `load` or `loadXML` methods.

```
XMLDOMSchemaCollection = XMLDOMDocument2.schemas
XMLDOMDocument2.schemas = XMLDOMSchemaCollection
```

XML DOM

707

XMLDOMDocumentFragment

The XMLDOMDocumentFragment object does not correspond directly to any part of an XML document *per se*. Instead, it represents a well-formed fragment of a node tree, and may be used to construct a portion of an XML document before attaching it to the main document. When the XMLDOMDocumentFragment node is attached to the main document's node tree, all of the child nodes of the fragment are attached in its place.

A new XMLDOMDocumentFragment object for a document may be obtained by calling the createDocumentFragment method on the XMLDOMDocument object for that document.

The XMLDOMDocumentFragment object is derived from the XMLDOMNode object. The XMLDOMDocumentFragment object exposes no additional methods or properties, so see the XMLDOMNode section for the functionality available through this object.

Methods	Properties	
appendChild*	attributes*	nodeTypedValue*
cloneNode*	baseName*	nodeTypeString*
hasChildNodes*	childNodes*	nodeValue*
insertBefore*	dataType*	ownerDocument*
removeChild*	definition*	parentNode*
replaceChild*	firstChild*	parsed*
selectNodes*	lastChild*	prefix*
selectSingleNode*	namespaceURI*	previousSibling*
transformNode*	nextSibling*	specified*
transformNodeToObject*	nodeName*	text*
	nodeType*	xml*

* See section on XMLDOMNode methods and properties.

XMLDOMDocumentType

The XMLDOMDocumentType object contains information about the document type definition (DTD) associated with a particular document. If there is no DTD associated with a document, no XMLDOMDocumentType object will be available.

The XMLDOMDocumentType object for a particular document may be obtained through the doctype property of the XMLDOMDocument object for that document. For example, if we have an XML document with an internal DTD such as:

```
<?xml version="1.0"?>
<!DOCTYPE Catalog [
   <!ELEMENT Catalog (Book+)>
   <!ELEMENT Book (Publisher, Sections)>
   <!ELEMENT Publisher (#PCDATA)>
   <!ELEMENT Sections (Section+)>
```

```
    <!ELEMENT Section (#PCDATA)>
    <!ENTITY wrox "Wrox Press Limited">
]>
<Catalog>
    <Book>
        <Publisher>&wrox;</Publisher>
        <Sections>
            <Section>ASP Intrinsic Objects</Section>
            <Section>Scripting Objects</Section>
            <Section>ASP Components</Section>
            <Section>ActiveX Data Objects</Section>
            <Section>Extending ASP</Section>
            <Section>Miscellaneous Reference</Section>
        </Sections>
    </Book>
</Catalog>
```

We can get a reference to the XMLDOMDocumentType using the code:

```
' VBScript
Dim xmlCatalogDocument, xmlDoctype
Set xmlCatalogDocument = Server.CreateObject("Microsoft.XMLDOM")
xmlCatalogDocument.async = false
xmlCatalogDocument.load("http://servername/xml/books.xml")
Set xmlCatalogDoctype = xmlCatalogDocument.doctype
```

```
// JScript
var xmlCatalogDocument = Server.CreateObject("Microsoft.XMLDOM");
xmlCatalogDocument.async = false;
xmlCatalogDocument.load("http://servername/xml/books.xml");
var xmlCatalogDoctype = xmlCatalogDocument.doctype;
```

The XMLDOMDocumentType object is derived from the XMLDOMNode object. In addition to the three properties detailed below, see the methods and properties defined for the XMLDOMNode object for additional functionality available through the XMLDOMDocumentType object.

Methods	Properties	
appendChild*	attributes*	nodeTypedValue*
cloneNode*	baseName*	nodeTypeString*
hasChildNodes*	childNodes*	nodeValue*
insertBefore*	dataType*	notations
removeChild*	definition*	ownerDocument*
replaceChild*	entities	parentNode*
selectNodes*	firstChild*	parsed*
selectSingleNode*	lastChild*	prefix*
transformNode*	name	previousSibling*
transformNodeToObject*	namespaceURI*	specified*
	nextSibling*	text*
	nodeName*	xml*
	nodeType*	

* See section on XMLDOMNode methods and properties.

Additional Methods

There are no additional methods associated with the XMLDOMDocumentType object.

Additional Properties

entities

The read-only entities property returns an XMLDOMNamedNodeMap object containing a list of all the entities, both internal and external, that are declared in the document's DTD.

```
XMLNamedNodeMap = XMLDOMDocumentType.entities
```

For example:

```
' VBScript
Dim xmlCatalogEntities, xmlCatalogDoctype
Set xmlCatalogDoctype = xmlCatalogDocument.doctype
Set xmlCatalogEntities = xmlCatalogDoctype.entities
```

```
// JScript
var xmlCatalogDoctype = xmlCatalogDocument.doctype;
var xmlCatalogEntities = xmlCatalogDoctype.entities;
```

For the XML document above, the returned XMLDOMNamedNodeMap will contain just one item: the entity &wrox;.

name

The read-only name property returns the name of the document type. This will be the same as the tag of the root element of the document tree (in the example given above, this will be "Catalog").

```
String = XMLDOMDocumentType.name
```

notations

The read-only notations property returns an XMLNamedNodeMap object containing a list of all the notations declared in the document's DTD.

```
XMLNamedNodeMap = XMLDOMDocumentType.notations
```

XMLDOMElement

The XMLDOMElement object represents an element in the XML document. For example, in this document:

```
<Book>
    <Chapter>Chapter 1</Chapter>
</Book>
```

There would be two XMLDOMElement elements: one for the <Book> element and one for the <Chapter> element.

A new XMLDOMElement object may be created for a document by calling the createElement method on the XMLDOMDocument object for that document. Existing XMLDOMElement objects may be obtained by calling the getElementsByTagName method on any document or element:

```
' VBScript
' Get first Chapter element in document
Dim xmlChapterElement
Set xmlChapterElement = xmlDocument.getElementsByTagName("Chapter").item(0)
```

```
// JScript
// Get first Chapter element in document
var xmlChapterElement = xmlDocument.getElementsByTagName("Chapter").item(0);
```

Alternatively, we can look in the `childNodes` list directly:

```
' VBScript
Dim xmlChapterElement
Set xmlChapterElement = xmlBookElement.childNodes.item(0)
```

```
// JScript
var xmlChapterElement = xmlBookElement.childNodes.item(0);
```

The XMLDOMElement object is derived from the XMLDOMNode object. In addition to the methods and properties described below, please see the properties, methods, and events defined for the XMLDOMNode object for additional functionality available through the XMLDOMElement object.

Methods		Properties	
appendChild*	selectNodes*	attributes*	nodeType String*
cloneNode*	selectSingleNode*	baseName*	nodeValue*
getAttribute	setAttribute	childNodes*	ownerDocument *
getAttributeNode	setAttributeNode	dataType*	parentNode*
getElementsBy TagName	transformNode*	definition*	parsed*
hasChildNodes*	transformNodeTo Object*	firstChild*	prefix*
insertBefore*		lastChild*	previous Sibling*
normalize		namespace URI*	specified*
removeAttribute		nextSibling*	tagName
removeAttribute Node		nodeName*	text*
removeChild*		nodeType*	xml*
replaceChild*		nodeTyped Value*	

* See section on XMLDOMNode methods and properties.

Additional Methods

getAttribute

The `getAttibute` method returns a string containing the value of the attribute with the specified name for this element. If the attribute is not present but has a default value in the document's DTD, that value is returned; otherwise, this method returns the empty string.

```
Variant = XMLDOMElement.getAttribute(name)
```

Parameter	Data Type	Description
name	String	Name of the string attribute whose value is sought.

For example, if we have a `<Book>` element with an author attribute:

```
<Book Author="Kevin Williams">
```

We can retrieve the value from this attribute using the following code:

```
' VBScript
Dim strAuthor
strAuthor = xmlBookElement.getAttribute("Author")
```

```
// JScript
var strAuthor = xmlBookElement.getAttribute("Author");
```

getAttributeNode

The `getAttributeNode` method returns an `XMLDOMAttribute` object representing the attribute with the specified name for this element. If the attribute does not exist for this element, this method returns `NULL`.

```
XMLDOMAttribute = XMLDOMElement.getAttributeNode(name)
```

Parameter	Data Type	Description
name	String	Name of the attribute node to retrieve.

We could modify the previous example to retrieve a reference to the attribute node rather than to the value of the attribute:

```
' VBScript
Dim xmlAuthorAttribute
Set xmlAuthorAttribute = xmlBookElement.getAttributeNode("Author")
```

```
// JScript
var xmlAuthorAttribute = xmlBookElement.getAttributeNode("Author");
```

getElementsByTagName

The `getElementsByTagName` method returns an `XMLDOMNodeList` object containing a list of all the elements in this element's descendant tree with the specified *tag_name*, in the order they appear in the original document. If no elements in this element's descendant tree have the specified *tag_name*, an empty `XMLDOMNodeList` is returned.

```
XMLDOMNodeList = XMLDOMElement.getElementsByTagName(tag_name)
```

Parameter	Data Type	Description
tag_name	String	The name of the elements which will be retrieved.

For example, to retrieve all the `<Chapter>` descendants of a `<Book>` element into a node list:

```
' VBScript
Dim xmlChapterNodeList
Set xmlChapterNodeList = xmlBookElement.getElementsByTagName("Chapter")
```

```
// JScript
var xmlChapterNodeList = xmlBookElement.getElementsByTagName("Chapter");
```

normalize

The `normalize` method normalizes the descendant nodes of this element into a form where no two text nodes are adjacent. If adjacent text node siblings exist in the descendant nodes, they are combined into one node and the extra node is removed from the node tree.

```
XMLDOMElement.normalize
```

removeAttribute

The `removeAttribute` method removes the attribute with the specified name from this element's attribute list. If the attribute has a default value in the document's DTD, the attribute is instead replaced with one containing the default value for it defined in the DTD.

```
XMLDOMElement.removeAttribute(name)
```

Parameter	Data Type	Description
name	String	Name of attribute to be removed or changed.

removeAttributeNode

The `removeAttributeNode` method removes the specified attribute from this element's attribute list. If the attribute has a default value in the document's DTD, the attribute is instead replaced with one containing the default value for it defined in the DTD. This method returns the removed `XMLDOMAttribute` object.

```
XMLDOMNode = XMLDOMElement.removeAttributeNode(attr_node)
```

Parameter	Data Type	Description
attr_node	XMLDOMAttribute object	The attribute node removed from the element.

setAttribute

The `setAttribute` method sets the value of the attribute with the provided name to the specified value. If the attribute does not already exist for this element, it is created.

```
XMLDOMElement.setAttribute(name, value)
```

Parameter	Data Type	Description
name	String	Name of attribute whose value is to be set.
value	Variant	Value of attribute.

For example, to set the value of an existing `Author` attribute to `"Kevin Williams"`, or to create a new attribute with that value, we would write:

```
' VBScript
xmlBookElement.setAttribute("Author", "Kevin Williams")
```

```
// JScript
xmlBookElement.setAttribute("Author", "Kevin Williams");
```

setAttributeNode

The `setAttributeNode` method adds the attribute provided to the element. If an attribute with the same name already exists for this element, it is replaced with the new attribute. This method differs from `setAttribute` in that it returns the `XMLDOMAttribute` object.

```
XMLDOMAttribute = XMLDOMElement.setAttributeNode(attr_node)
```

Parameter	Data Type	Description
attr_node	XMLDOMAttribute object	Attribute node to be added to element.

Additional Properties

tagName

The read-only `tagName` property returns a string containing the element's name.

```
String = XMLDOMElement.tagName
```

XMLDOMEntity

The `XMLDOMEntity` object represents a parsed or unparsed entity in the XML document. The Microsoft XML DOM expands all external entities (except for binary ones) before returning the node tree. For example, in the following fragment of a DTD:

```
<!ENTITY ProgRef "Programmer's Reference">
```

The xmlBook entity would be represented by a XMLDOMEntity object. Note that this object only represents the entity definition; it does not represent the references to this entity within the XML document; these can be accessed through the XMLDOMEntityReference object.

We can reference this entity using the entities property of the XMLDOMDocumentType object:

```
' VBScript
Dim xmlDoctype, xmlEntity
Set xmlDoctype = xmlDocument.doctype
' Get reference to first entity in DTD
Set xmlEntity = xmlDoctype.entities(0)
```

```
// JScript
var xmlDoctype = xmlDocument.doctype;
// Get reference to first entity in DTD
var xmlEntity = xmlDoctype.entities(0);
```

The XMLDOMEntity object is derived from the XMLDOMNode object. In addition to the notationName, publicId, and systemId properties, please see the properties, methods, and events defined for the XMLDOMNode object for additional functionality available through the XMLDOMEntity object.

Methods	Properties	
appendChild*	attributes*	nodeValue*
cloneNode*	baseName*	notationName
hasChildNodes*	childNodes*	ownerDocument*
insertBefore*	dataType*	parentNode*
removeChild*	definition*	parsed*
replaceChild*	firstChild*	prefix*
selectNodes*	lastChild*	previousSibling*
selectSingleNode*	namespaceURI*	publicId
transformNode*	nextSibling*	specified*
transformNodeToObject*	nodeName*	systemId
	nodeType*	text*
	nodeTypedValue*	xml*
	nodeTypeString*	

* See section on XMLDOMNode methods and properties.

Additional Methods

There are no additional methods associated with the XMLDOMEntity object.

Additional Properties

notationName

The read-only `notationName` property returns a string containing the notation name for this entity. This is the name following the `NDATA` declaration, if there is one. For parsed entities, this property returns an empty string.

```
String = XMLDOMEntity.notationName
```

publicId

The read-only `publicId` property returns a string containing the public identifier for this entity. This is the string following the `PUBLIC` declaration, if one exists. If the public identifier is not specified, this property returns an empty string.

```
String = XMLDOMEntity.publicId
```

systemId

The read-only `systemId` property returns a string containing the system identifier for this entity. This is the string following the `SYSTEM` declaration, if one exists. If the system identifier is not specified, this property returns an empty string.

```
String = XMLDOMEntity.systemId
```

XMLDOMEntityReference

The `XMLDOMEntityReference` object represents an entity reference within an XML document.

For example, suppose we have an element such as the following containing an entity reference:

```
<Title>ASP &ProgRef;</Title>
```

The `<Title>` element has two child nodes: the first is a text node containing the string `"ASP "`, and the second is an entity reference with the name `"ProgRef"`. Since this is the second child node, we can get a reference to it using `xmlTitleElement.childNodes(1)`.

If the entity information about the entity being referenced is available, the `XMLDOMEntityReference` object's child tree will reflect the internal structure of that entity. For example, if the `ProgRef` entity is defined as:

```
<!ENTITY ProgRef "Programmer's Reference">
```

The entity reference will have a single child node: a text node containing the expanded text, `"Programmer's Reference"`.

The `XMLDOMEntityReference` object is derived from the `XMLDOMNode` object. It exposes no new methods, properties or events, so see the `XMLDOMNode` object for the functionality available through the `XMLDOMEntityReference` object.

Methods	Properties	
appendChild*	attributes*	nodeTypedValue*
cloneNode*	baseName*	nodeTypeString*
hasChildNodes*	childNodes*	nodeValue*
insertBefore*	dataType*	ownerDocument*
removeChild*	definition*	parentNode*
replaceChild*	firstChild*	parsed*
selectNodes*	lastChild*	prefix*
selectSingleNode*	namespaceURI*	previousSibling*
transformNode*	nextSibling*	specified*
transformNodeToObject*	nodeName*	text*
	nodeType*	xml*

* See section on XMLDOMNode methods and properties.

XMLDOMImplementation

The XMLDOMImplementation object allows the developer to query msxml.dll to determine what features it supports. This may be used to discover whether newer features are available from the version of the parser being used.

The XMLDOMImplementation object for a particular document may be accessed via the implementation property of the XMLDOMDocument object for that document.

Methods
hasFeature

Methods

hasFeature

The hasFeature method returns a boolean indicating whether the specified feature is supported by the current version of msxml.dll. For msxml.dll, valid features are "XML", "DOM", and "MS-DOM". At the time of writing, only version 1.0 of the DOM is supported by msxml.dll.

```
Boolean = XMLDOMImplementation.hasFeature(feature, version)
```

Parameter	Data Type	Description
feature	String	Specified feature
version	String	Version of that feature to check

XML DOM

717

The following example use the `hasFeature` method to check whether the current parser supports MSXML version 2.6 methods:

```
' VBScript
Dim xmlCatalogImplementation
Set xmlCatalogImplementation = xmlCatalogDocument.implementation
If xmlCatalogImplementation.hasFeature("MS-DOM", "2.6") Then
    Response.Write "2.6 objects, methods, and properties are supported."
Else
    Response.Write "2.6 objects, methods, and properties are not supported."
End If
```

```
// JScript
var xmlCatalogImplementation = xmlCatalogDocument.implementation;
if (xmlCatalogImplementation.hasFeature("MS-DOM", "2.6")) {
    Response.Write("2.6 objects, methods, and properties are supported.");
} else {
    Response.Write("2.6 objects, methods, and properties are not supported.");
}
```

Properties

There are no properties associated with the XMLDOMImplementation object.

XMLDOMNamedNodeMap

The XMLDOMNamedNodeMap collection contains an unordered set of nodes. They may be referenced by their name as well as by an ordinal position, although the ordinal position does not imply anything else about the node (it's simply a convenience for iterating through the set). An XMLDOMNamedNodeMap is used to represent the collection of attributes for an element node, and may be accessed through the attributes property of an element node.

Methods		Properties
getNamedItem	removeNamedItem	length
getQualifiedItem	removeQualifiedItem	
item	reset	
nextNode	setNamedItem	

Methods

getNamedItem

The getNamedItem method returns the XMLDOMNode object for the node in the collection with the specified name. If the node with the specified name is not in the collection of nodes, this method returns NULL.

```
XMLDOMNode = XMLDOMNamedNodeMap.getNamedItem(name)
```

Parameter	Data Type	Description
name	String	Name of node object.

For example:

```
' VBScript
' get the attribute list for the Book element
Dim xmlBookAttributes, xmlAuthorAttribute
xmlBookAttributes = xmlBookElement.attributes
' find the Author attribute in the attribute list
xmlAuthorAttribute = xmlBookAttributes.getNamedItem("Author")
```

```
// JScript
// get the attribute list for the Book element
var xmlBookAttributes, xmlAuthorAttribute;
xmlBookAttributes = xmlBookElement.attributes;
// find the Author attribute in the attribute list
xmlAuthorAttribute = xmlBookAttributes.getNamedItem("Author");
```

getQualifiedItem

The getQualifiedItem method returns the XMLDOMNode object for the attribute in the collection with the specified attribute name and namespace prefix. Note that, even though the second parameter is called *namespace_uri*, it actually corresponds to the namespace prefix. If an attribute matching the specified base name and namespace prefix is not in the collection of nodes, this method returns NULL.

```
XMLDOMNode = XMLDOMNamedNodeMap.getQualifiedItem(base_name, namespace_uri)
```

Parameter	Data Type	Description
base_name	String	The name of the item excluding the namespace prefix.
namespace_uri	String	The namespace prefix of the item.

item

The item method returns the XMLDOMNode at the position indicated by the index parameter. The XMLDOMNamedNodeMap collection is zero-based, so the index parameter must be between 0 and length - 1. If the index is out of range, this method returns NULL.

```
XMLDOMNode = XMLDOMNamedNodeMap.item(index)
```

Parameter	Data Type	Description
index	Long	Position of XMLDOMNode object.

For example, to get the first attribute for a <Book> element:

```
' VBScript
' get the attribute list for the Book element
Dim xmlBookAttributes, xmlFirstAttribute
Set xmlBookAttributes = xmlBookElement.attributes
' get the first attribute for the Book element
Set xmlFirstAttribute = xmlBookAttributes.item(0)
```

```
// JScript
// get the attribute list for the Book element
var xmlBookAttributes, xmlFirstAttribute;
xmlBookAttributes = xmlBookElement.attributes;
// get the first attribute for the Book element
xmlFirstAttribute = xmlBookAttributes.item(0);
```

nextNode

The nextNode method returns the next node in the list from the current iterator position. When the XMLDOMNamedNodeMap object is created, the iterator starts before the first node in the list, so all of the nodes may be iterated through by repeatedly calling nextNode until it returns a NULL, indicating that there are no more nodes in the list beyond the iterator position. Note again that the iterator is a convenience only and does not imply any sort of order to the nodes in the named node map.

```
XMLDOMNode = XMLDOMNamedNodeMap.nextNode()
```

removeNamedItem

The removeNamedItem method removes the node with the specified name from the collection. It returns an XMLDOMNode object representing the removed node. If the node with the given name does not exist in the collection, this method returns NULL.

```
XMLDOMNode = XMLDOMNamedNodeMap.removeNamedItem(name)
```

Parameter	Data Type	Description
name	String	Name of item to be removed.

removeQualifiedItem

The removeQualifiedItem method removes the XMLDOMNode object with the specified attribute name and namespace prefix from the collection. Note that, even though the second parameter is called namespace_uri, it actually corresponds to the namespace prefix. The removed XMLDOMNode object is returned. If an attribute matching the specified base name and namespace prefix is not in the collection of nodes, this method returns NULL.

```
XMLDOMNode = XMLDOMNamedNodeMap.removeQualifiedItem(base_name, namespace_uri)
```

Parameter	Data Type	Description
base_name	String	Name of XMLDOMNode object.
namespace_uri	String	Namespace of XMLDOMNode object

reset

The reset method resets the position of the iterator on the collection to before the first node in the list.

```
XMLDOMNamedNodeMap.reset()
```

setNamedItem

The setNamedItem method adds the specified XMLDOMNode object to the collection. If the collection already contains an attribute node with the same name as the new node, it is replaced. If the node being added is not an attribute, setNamedItem returns an error.

```
XMLDOMNode = XMLDOMNamedNodeMap.setNamedItem(new_item)
```

Parameter	Data Type	Description
new_item	XMLDOMNode	Name of XMLDOMNode to be set

For example, to add an Author attribute with the value "Kevin Williams" to a <Book> element:

```
' VBScript
' get the attribute list for the Book element
Dim xmlBookAttributes, xmlAuthorAttribute
Set xmlAuthorAttribute = xmlCatalogDocument.createAttribute("Author")
xmlAuthorAttribute.value = "Kevin Williams"
Set xmlBookAttributes = xmlBookElement.attributes
' set the Author attribute
Set xmlAuthorAttribute = xmlBookAttributes.setNamedItem(xmlAuthorAttribute)
```

```
// JScript
// get the attribute list for the Book element
var xmlBookAttributes, xmlAuthorAttribute;
xmlAuthorAttribute = xmlCatalogDocument.createAttribute("Author");
xmlAuthorAttribute.value = "Kevin Williams";
xmlBookAttributes = xmlBookElement.attributes;
// set the Author attribute
xmlAuthorAttribute = xmlBookAttributes.setNamedItem(xmlAuthorAttribute);
```

Properties

length

The read-only length property returns the number of XMLDOMNode objects in the collection.

```
Long = XMLDOMNamedNodeMap.length
```

XMLDOMNode

The XMLDOMNode object is the base object for all of the different node types expressed in the DOM node tree. It includes many generic methods that may be used to manipulate the various nodes without regard to the type of node represented by the object. Also, the XMLDOMNode object must be used to create objects with namespaces, as the specific node implementation objects do not provide this functionality.

Methods	Properties	
appendChild	attributes	nodeTypedValue
cloneNode	baseName	nodeTypeString
hasChildNodes	childNodes	nodeValue
insertBefore	dataType	ownerDocument
removeChild	definition	parentNode
replaceChild	firstChild	parsed
selectNodes	lastChild	prefix
selectSingleNode	namespaceURI	previousSibling
transformNode	nextSibling	specified
transformNodeToObject	nodeName	text
	nodeType	xml

Methods

appendChild

The appendChild method appends the newChild node to the end of the child list for this node. It returns a reference to the newChild node.

```
XMLDOMNode = XMLDOMNode.appendChild(new_child)
```

Parameter	Data Type	Description
new_child	XMLDOMNode object	New child node to be appended to child list.

The appendChild method must be called to add an element to the node tree after it has been created with the XMLDOMDocument's createElement method:

```
' VBScript
' create a new Chapter element
Dim xmlChapterElement
xmlChapterElement = xmlCatalogDocument.createElement("Chapter")
' append it to the Book element
xmlBookElement.appendChild(xmlChapterElement)
```

```
// VBScript
// create a new Chapter element
var xmlChapterElement;
xmlChapterElement = xmlCatalogDocument.createElement("Chapter");
// append it to the Book element
xmlBookElement.appendChild(xmlChapterElement);
```

cloneNode

The `cloneNode` method makes an exact copy of the current node and returns it. If the `deep` flag is set to `true`, it also recursively copies all of the child nodes in this node's subtree; otherwise, the new node will only have the attributes of the original, and its child node list will be blank.

```
XMLDOMNode = XMLDOMNode.cloneNode(deep)
```

Parameter	Data Type	Description
`deep`	Boolean	Flag which indicates whether child nodes are to be copied

For example, to clone a node, including all its descendant nodes:

```
' VBScript
' clone the Book node and all of its subtree
Dim xmlBookElement2
Set xmlBookElement2 = xmlBookElement.cloneNode(True)
```

```
// JScript
// clone the Book node and all of its subtree
var xmlBookElement2;
xmlBookElement2 = xmlBookElement.cloneNode(1);
```

Note that this creates a new, independent node, not a new reference to the existing node (so changing the text in one of these elements will not change the text in the other).

hasChildNodes

The `hasChildNodes` method returns a Boolean value indicating whether this node has children. It will always return `false` for node types that cannot have children.

```
Boolean = XMLDOMNode.hasChildNodes()
```

We should call this method before iterating through an element's children (for example, when parsing a document recursively):

```
' VBScript
' Check to see if the Book element has any children
If xmlBookElement.hasChildNodes Then
    ' there are children - process them
Else
    ' there are no children - continue
End If
```

```
// JScript
// Check to see if the Book element has any children
if (xmlBookElement.hasChildNodes()) {
    // there are children - process them
} else {
    // there are no children - continue
}
```

InsertBefore

The `insertBefore` method inserts the child specified by the *new_child* parameter into the child list of this node, to the left of the node specified by the *ref_child* parameter. If the *ref_child* parameter is NULL, the *new_child* node is added at the end of the parameter list.

```
XMLDOMNode = XMLDOMNode.insertBefore(new_child, ref_child)
```

Parameter	Data Type	Description
new_child	XMLDOMNode object	Child node to be inserted.
ref_child	Variant	The node before which the new child is to be inserted.

It returns the *new_child* node. Note that if a document fragment node is added using this method, instead of the document fragment node being inserted, all of the root-level elements of the fragment will be inserted at the same location. If the insertion being attempted contravenes any of the rules of the DOM (for example, that attributes may not be the children of other attributes), this method will return an error code.

```vbscript
' VBScript
' create a new Chapter element
Dim xmlChapterElement, xmlFirstChildNode
Set xmlChapterElement = xmlCatalogDocument.createElement("Chapter")
Set xmlFirstChildNode = xmlBookElement.firstChild
' insert it before the first child node of the Book element
xmlBookElement.insertBefore(xmlChapterElement, xmlFirstChildNode)
```

```jscript
// JScript
// create a new Chapter element
var xmlChapterElement = xmlCatalogDocument.createElement("Chapter");
var xmlFirstChildNode = xmlBookElement.firstChild;
// insert it before the first child node of the Book element
xmlBookElement.insertBefore(xmlChapterElement, xmlFirstChildNode);
```

removeChild

The `removeChild` method removes the specified child node from the child list of the current node and returns a reference to that child node. Note that even though the child node has been "disconnected" from the rest of the document, it will still exist, along with any nodes that make up its subtree; reattaching the node somewhere else in the tree will also reattach all of the subnodes. If the specified child node cannot be removed from the tree, this method will return an error code.

```
XMLDOMNode = XMLDOMNode.removeChild(old_child)
```

Parameter	Data Type	Description
old_child	XMLDOMNode object	Child to be removed from child list

For example, to remove the first child of an element:

```
' get the first subnode of the Book element
Dim xmlFirstElement
xmlFirstElement = xmlBookElement.firstChild
' remove it
xmlBookElement.removeChild(xmlFirstElement)
```

```
// JScript
// get the first element in the Book element
var xmlFirstElement;
xmlFirstElement = xmlBookElement.firstChild;
// remove it
xmlBookElement.removeChild(xmlFirstElement);
```

replaceChild

The `replaceChild` method allow us to replace the child node of the current node specified by the *old_child* parameter with the node specified by the *new_child* parameter. If a document fragment is added using this method, instead of the document fragment node being used to replace the old child node, the document fragment node's children will be inserted at the same location. If the replacement cannot be made, or the replacement would contravene any of the rules of the DOM, this method will return an error.

```
XMLDOMNode = XMLDOMNode.replaceChild(new_child, old_child)
```

Parameter	Data Type	Description
new_child	XMLDOMNode object	The new node which will replace the old
old_child	XMLDOMNode object	Old child node to be replaced

For example:

```
' VBScript
' create a new Chapter element
Dim xmlChapterElement
xmlChapterElement = xmlCatalogDocument.createElement("Chapter")
' replace the first child node of the Book element with the new chapter
' element
xmlBookElement.replaceChild(xmlBookElement.childNodes(0), xmlChapterElement)
```

```
// JScript
// create a new Chapter element
var xmlChapterElement;
xmlChapterElement = xmlCatalogDocument.createElement("Chapter");
// replace the first child node of the Book element with the new chapter
// element
xmlBookElement.replaceChild(xmlBookElement.childNodes(0), xmlChapterElement);
```

selectNodes

The `selectNodes` method applies the XSL pattern query specified by the *pattern_string* parameter using this node as the context node, and returns an XMLDOMNodeList containing the list of nodes selected by the query. If no nodes match the pattern query, an empty XMLDOMNodeList is returned.

```
XMLDOMNode = XMLDOMNode.selectNodes(pattern_string)
```

XML DOM

725

Parameter	Data Type	Description
pattern_string	String	Query to be executed on the subtree

For example, to select all `<Book>` elements with an `Author` attribute set to `"Kevin Williams"`:

```
' VBScript
Dim xmlBookElements
Set xmlBookElements = xmlCatalogDocument.selectNodes
                      ("//Book[@Author='Kevin Williams']")
```

```
// JScript
var xmlBookElements = xmlCatalogDocument.selectNodes
                      ("//Book[@Author='Kevin Williams']");
```

selectSingleNode

The `selectSingleNode` method applies the XSL pattern query specified by the `patternString` parameter using this node as the context node, and returns an XMLDOMNode that corresponds to the first node that matches the query. If no nodes match the query, this method returns NULL.

```
XMLDOMNode = XMLDOMNode.selectSingleNode(pattern_string)
```

Parameter	Data Type	Description
pattern_string	String	Query to be executed on the subtree

For example, to find the first `<Chapter>` element at any level in the document:

```
' VBScript
Dim xmlChapterElement
xmlChapterElement = xmlCatalogDocument.selectSingleNode("//Chapter")
```

```
// JScript
var = xmlCatalogDocument.selectSingleNode("//Chapter");
```

transformNode

The `transformNode` method applies the XSL stylesheet or fragment specified in the `stylesheet` parameter to the current node and returns a string containing the output of that transformation. The stylesheet may be specified either as an XMLDOMDocument object that references an entire stylesheet, or an XMLDOMNode object that references a fragment of a stylesheet.

```
XMLDOMNode = XMLDOMNode.transformNode(stylesheet)
```

Parameter	Data Type	Description
stylesheet	XMLDOMNode or XMLDOMDocument object	The stylesheet to be applied to the subtree

The following code transforms an XML document, storing the result as a string, and then sends this XML string to the browser. Transforming an XML document on the server in this way avoids problems caused by browsers which don't support XML and/or XSL.

```vbscript
' VBScript
Dim xmlDocument, xslDocument
Set xmlDocument=Server.CreateObject("Microsoft.XMLDOM")
Set xslDocument=Server.CreateObject("Microsoft.XMLDOM")

xmlDocument.async=false
xslDocument.async=false

xslDocument.load "http://myserver/books.xml"
xslDocument.load "http://myserver/books.xsl"

strXML = xmlDocument.transformNode(xslDocument.documentElement)
Response.Write strXML
```

```jscript
// JScript
var xmlDocument=Server.CreateObject("Microsoft.XMLDOM");
var xslDocument=Server.CreateObject("Microsoft.XMLDOM");

xmlDocument.async=false;
xslDocument.async=false;

xslDocument.load("http://myserver/books.xml");
xslDocument.load("http://myserver/books.xsl");

strXML = xmlDocument.transformNode(xslDocument.documentElement);
Response.Write(strXML);
```

transformNodeToObject

The transformNodeToObject method applies the XSL stylesheet or fragment specified in the *stylesheet* parameter to the current node. If the *output_object* parameter is an XMLDOMDocument object, the document is constructed with the results of the transformation; if the *output_object* parameter is a stream, the results of the transformation are written to that stream.

```
Variant = XMLDOMNode.transformNodeToObject(stylesheet, output_object)
```

Parameter	Data Type	Description
stylesheet	XMLDOMNode stylesheet	Stylesheet to be applied to subtree.
output_object	Variant	If the *output_object* parameter is an XMLDOMDocument object, the document is constructed with the results of the transformation. If the *output_object* parameter is a stream, the results of the transformation are written to that stream.

This code does the same as the previous example, but this time the transformed XML is stored in an XMLDOMDocument object rather than a string, so if we want, we could perform additional operations on the XML before sending it to the client:

```
' VBScript
Dim xmlDocument, xslDocument, xmlNewDocument
Set xmlDocument = Server.CreateObject("Microsoft.XMLDOM")
Set xslDocument = Server.CreateObject("Microsoft.XMLDOM")

xmlDocument.async=false
xslDocument.async=false

xslDocument.load "http://myserver/books.xml"
xslDocument.load "http://myserver/books.xsl"

Set xmlNewDocument = Server.CreateObject("Microsoft.XMLDOM")
xmlDocument.transformNodeToObject xslDocument.documentElement, xmlNewDocument
Response.Write xmlNewDocument.xml
```

```
// JScript
var xmlDocument, xslDocument, xmlNewDocument;
xmlDocument = Server.CreateObject("Microsoft.XMLDOM");
xslDocument = Server.CreateObject("Microsoft.XMLDOM");

xmlDocument.async = false;
xslDocument.async = false;

xslDocument.load("http://myserver/books.xml");
xslDocument.load("http://myserver/books.xsl");

xmlNewDocument = Server.CreateObject("Microsoft.XMLDOM");
xmlDocument.transformNodeToObject(xslDocument.documentElement,
                                  xmlNewDocument);
Response.Write(xmlNewDocument.xml);
```

Properties

attributes

The read-only attributes property returns an XMLNamedNodeMap containing an unordered list of the attributes for this node. Note that this will only be meaningful for nodes whose nodeType is NODE_ELEMENT, NODE_ENTITY, or NODE_NOTATION; all other nodeTypes will return NULL. For entity and notation nodes, the attributes must be either PUBLIC, SYSTEM, or NDATA.

```
XMLDOMNamedNodeMap = XMLDOMNode.attributes
```

baseName

The read-only baseName property returns the string containing the base name of the node. For non-namespace-qualified nodes, this will always be the name of the node; for namespace-qualified nodes, this will be the portion of the name following the colon – i.e., if the node's name is abc:def, baseName will return def.

```
String = XMLDOMNode.baseName
```

childNodes

The read-only `childNodes` property returns an `XMLDOMNodeList` containing an ordered list of the children of this node. If the node does not have children, or is not permitted to have children because of its type (for example, a `NODE_COMMENT` node), an `XMLDOMNodeList` is still returned with a length of zero.

```
XMLDOMNodeList = XMLDOMNode.childNodes
```

We can use this property to parse an XML document recursively. The following example defines a function `fnRecurse()` which takes a node object and an integer as parameters. The integer defines the number of spaces which will be printed out before the node's name and value, according to its depth in the node tree. After storing the requisite number of non-breaking spaces in a string, the function adds the name and value of the node. We then iterate through its `childNodes` and call the *same* function on each of these, before returning the resulting string. The rest of the script simply loads an XML document, calls our `fnRecurse` function on it, and finally writes this string into the contents of a `<SPAN>` element.

```
<HTML>
<%
Dim xmlDocument
Set xmlDocument=Server.CreateObject("Microsoft.XMLDOM")
xmlDocument.async=false
xmlDocument.load "http://myserver/xml/books.xml"
strXML = fnRecurse(xmlDocument, 0)

Function fnRecurse(objNode, intSpaces)
    Dim strXML
    strXML = ""
    For intCount=1 To intSpaces
        strXML = strXML & " "
    Next
    strXML = strXML & objNode.nodeName & ": " & _
            objNode.nodeValue & "<BR>"
    Dim intChildren
    intChildren = objNode.childNodes.length
    Dim intChildCount
    For intChildCount = 0 To intChildren - 1
        Dim objChild
        Set objChild=objNode.childNodes(intChildCount)
        strXML = strXML & fnRecurse(objChild, intSpaces+2)
    Next
    fnRecurse = strXML
End Function
%>
<SPAN STYLE="font-family: courier"><%= strXML %></SPAN>
</HTML>
```

Or in JScript:

```
<HTML>
<%
var xmlDocument=Server.CreateObject("Microsoft.XMLDOM");
xmlDocument.async=false;
xmlDocument.load("http://myserver/xml/books.xml");
strXML = fnRecurse(xmlDocument, 0);
```

```
function fnRecurse(objNode, intSpaces) {
   var strXML="";
   for (var i=0; i<intSpaces; i++) {
      strXML+=" ";
   }
   strXML+=objNode.nodeName+": "+objNode.nodeValue+"<BR>";
   var intChildren=objNode.childNodes.length;
   for (var j=0; j<intChildren; j++) {
      var objChild=objNode.childNodes[j];
      strXML+=fnRecurse(objChild, intSpaces+2);
   }
   return strXML;
}
%>
<SPAN STYLE="font-family: courier"><%= strXML %></SPAN>
</HTML>
```

The result is a display of the document's node tree, with the name and value of each node:

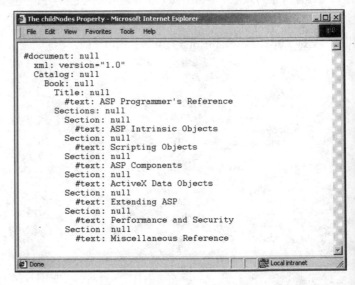

dataType

The dataType property sets or returns the string description of the data type for this node. For attribute and element nodes, this will be the string representation of the data type specifier included in the schema, or NULL if no data type was defined for the element or attribute. For entity references, this value will only be non-NULL if the entity referenced has exactly one top-level element; otherwise, it will return NULL. Attempts to assign the data type for an entity reference will be ignored. This property will always return NULL if the XML document is not associated with a schema.

```
XMLDOMNode.dataType = String
Variant = XMLDOMNode.dataType
```

definition

The read-only definition property returns an XMLDOMNode that is the definition of this node in the DTD or schema.

```
XMLDOMNode = XMLDOMNode.definition
```

If the node is an entity reference, the value returned will be the node in the DOCTYPE node's entity collection that corresponds to the referenced entity. If the node is an unparsed entity, the value returned will be the node in the DOCTYPE node's notation collection that corresponds to the entity. If the node is an attribute, and an XML-Data schema is being used, the node corresponding to the AttributeType declaration in the schema will be returned. If the node is an element and an XML-Data schema is being used, the node corresponding to the ElementType declaration in the schema will be returned. All other node types return NULL for this property.

firstChild

The read-only firstChild property returns the XMLDOMNode that is the first child node of this node. If this node has no children, or the node type is not allowed to have children, this property returns NULL.

```
XMLDOMNode = XMLDOMNode.firstChild
```

lastChild

The read-only lastChild property returns the XMLDOMNode that is the last child node of this node. If this node has no children, or the node type is not allowed to have children, this property returns NULL.

```
XMLDOMNode = XMLDOMNode.lastChild
```

namespaceURI

The read-only namespaceURI property returns the string corresponding to the URI of the namespace containing this node. If there is no namespace declared for the node, this property returns an empty string.

```
String = XMLDOMNode.namespaceURI
```

nextSibling

The read-only nextSibling property returns an XMLDOMNode that is the next sibling node of this node (that is, the next child node in the ordered child list of this node's parent). If the node does not have siblings following it, or the node is not allowed to have siblings (document nodes, document fragment nodes, and attribute nodes), this property returns NULL.

```
XMLDOMNode = XMLDOMNode.nextSibling
```

nodeName

The read-only nodeName property returns a string containing the fully-qualified name of the node. This string will include the namespace prefix for the node name if it is present. For nodes that do not have names, a constant string will always be returned; for example, a text node will always have a nodeName of #text.

```
String = XMLDOMNode.nodeName
```

The standard values for nodeName are:

Node Type	Node Name
Text node	"#text"
CDATA section	"#cdata-section"
Comment	"#comment"
Document	"#document"
Document fragment	"#document-fragment"

nodeType

The read-only nodeType property returns a value in the DOMNodeType enumeration indicating the type of node. See the description of the DOMNodeType enumeration later in the text for more details on the possible values for the nodeType property.

```
DOMNodeType = XMLDOMNode.nodeType
```

The possible values for nodeType are:

Name	Value	Definition
NODE_INVALID	0	The node is not a valid XML node.
NODE_ELEMENT	1	This node represents an element.
NODE_ATTRIBUTE	2	This node represents an attribute of an element.
NODE_TEXT	3	This node represents the text content of a tag.
NODE_CDATA_SECTION	4	This node represents a CDATA section (an escaped, unparsed block of text).
NODE_ENTITY_REFERENCE	5	This node represents a reference to an entity.
NODE_ENTITY	6	This node represents an expanded entity.
NODE_PROCESSING_INSTRUCTION	7	This node represents a processing instruction.
NODE_COMMENT	8	This node represents a comment.
NODE_DOCUMENT	9	This node represents a document. Note that it must have exactly one element child node, representing the root element in the document.
NODE_DOCUMENT_TYPE	10	This node represents the document type declaration.
NODE_DOCUMENT_FRAGMENT	11	This node represents a document fragment.
NODE_NOTATION	12	This node represents a notation.

If you want to use the constants rather than the numerical values, you will need to add a reference to the type library to your page, using a METADATA directive:

```
<!-- METADATA TYPE="TypeLib"
            FILE="C:\WinNT\System32\msxml2.dll" -->
```

If using the earlier version of MSXML, you will need to make the reference to msxml.dll rather than msxml2.dll.

nodeTypedValue

The nodeTypedValue property sets or returns the typed value for the node. For instance, if an attribute is declared to be of type float in a document's schema, this value will be a variant containing a floating-point integer value. Note that this works for text values in elements as well; if the containing element is typed, reading this property on the text node will return a value in the type of the containing element.

```
XMLDOMNode.nodeTypedValue = Variant
Variant = XMLDOMNode.nodeTypedValue
```

nodeTypeString

The read-only nodeTypeString property returns a string value for the node type.

```
String = XMLDOMNode.nodeTypeString
```

Possible values are: "attribute", "cdatasection", "comment", "document", "documentfragment", "documenttype", "element", "entity", "entityreference", "notation", "processinginstruction", and "text".

nodeValue

The nodeValue property sets or returns the string value for a node. If you want to work with the typed value of the node instead, use nodeTypedValue.

```
XMLDOMNode.nodeValue = Variant
Variant = XMLDOMNode.nodeValue
```

Note that the nodeValue of an element node will always return NULL; the value of any text content of the element is contained in a child text node.

ownerDocument

The read-only ownerDocument property returns the XMLDOMDocument object that corresponds to the document that contains this node. If the node has been removed from its document, this property will return the document that last contained this node.

```
XMLDOMDocument = XMLDOMNode.ownerDocument
```

parentNode

The read-only parentNode property returns the XMLDOMNode object for the parent node of this node. If the node does not have a parent (attribute nodes, document nodes, and document fragment nodes), this property returns NULL.

```
XMLDOMNode = XMLDOMNode.parentNode
```

XML DOM

733

parsed

The read-only `parsed` property returns a Boolean indicating whether the node has been completely parsed yet or not. This property is useful for asynchronous operation, to determine whether the parser has finished parsing a node.

```
Boolean = XMLDOMNode.parsed
```

prefix

The read-only `prefix` property returns a string containing the namespace prefix for the node; that is, if the node's name is `abc:def`, this property returns `abc`. If no namespace is declared for the node, or if the node's name may not contain a namespace, this property returns an empty string.

```
String = XMLDOMNode.prefix
```

previousSibling

The read-only `previousSibling` property returns an `XMLDOMNode` that is the previous sibling node of this node (that is, the previous child node in the ordered child list of this node's parent). If the node does not have siblings preceding it, or the node is not allowed to have siblings (document nodes, document fragment nodes, and attribute nodes), this property returns `NULL`.

```
XMLDOMNode = XMLDOMNode.previousSibling
```

specified

The read-only `specified` property returns a Boolean indicating whether the value for this node was specified, or was assigned by a default definition in a DTD or schema. This value will only be `false` for attribute nodes that take their values from defaults in the DTD or schema; for all other node types, the value returned will always be `true`.

```
Boolean = XMLDOMNode.specified
```

text

The `text` property sets or returns the text for a node.

```
XMLDOMNode.text = String
String = XMLDOMNode.text
```

This actually corresponds to the concatenated text of all the children of this node as well as this node, in document order, with whitespace normalized according to the current whitespace settings. For example, for a document like this:

```
<Book>ASP Programmer's Reference
    <Section>Intrinsic Objects</Section>
    <Section>Scripting Objects</Section>
    <Section>ASP Components</Section>
</Book>
```

The `text` property would return the string `"ASP Programmer's Reference Intrinsic Objects Scripting Objects ASP Components"`.

xml

The read-only xml property returns a string that contains the XML representation of this node and all its descendants. This property should be used when a document has been manipulated in script using the DOM and the modified version now needs to be sent to the client or persisted to a file.

```
String = XMLDOMNode.xml
```

XMLDOMNodeList

The XMLDOMNodeList object is a collection containing an ordered list of XMLDOMNode objects. It is returned when requesting the children of a node, or when executing an XSL pattern query against an XML document. For example:

```
' VBScript
Dim xmlNodeList
Set xmlNodeList = xmlBookElement.childNodes
```

```
// JScript
var xmlNodeList = xmlBookElement.childNodes;
```

Normal ASP collection coding techniques (such as a VBScript For...Next loop or a JScript Enumerator) may be used to access the individual members of this collection:

```
' VBScript
For Each xmlNode In xmlBookElement.childNodes
    Response.Write xmlNode.nodeName & ": " & xmlNode.text & "<BR>"
Next
```

```
// JScript
var enmNodeList = new Enumerator(xmlBookElement.childNodes);
for (; !enmNodeList.atEnd(); enmNodeList.moveNext()) {
    var xmlNode = enmNodeList.item();
    Response.Write(xmlNode.nodeName + ": " + xmlNode.text + "<BR>");
}
```

Methods	Properties
item	length
nextNode	
reset	

Methods

Item

The item method returns the XMLDOMNode at the position indicated by the *index* parameter. The XMLDOMNodeList collection is zero-based, so the *index* parameter must be between 0 and length - 1. If the index is out of range, this method returns NULL.

```
XMLDOMNode = XMLDOMNodeList.item(index)
```

Parameter	Data Type	Description
index	Long	The position of the node in the nodelist.

nextNode

The nextNode method returns the next node in the list from the current iterator position. When the XMLDOMNodeList object is created, the iterator starts before the first node in the list, so all of the nodes may be iterated through by repeatedly calling nextNode until it returns a NULL, indicating that there are no more nodes in the list beyond the iterator position. The iterator position can be reset to the start using the reset method.

```
XMLDOMNode = XMLDOMNodeList.nextNode()
```

reset

The reset method resets the position of the iterator on the collection to before the first node in the list.

```
XMLDOMNodeList.reset()
```

Properties

length

The read-only length property returns the number of XMLDOMNode objects in the collection.

```
Long = XMLDOMNodeList.length
```

XMLDOMNotation

The XMLDOMNotation object represents a notation declaration in the document's DTD or schema. Notations are used to associate certain special attributes with external applications which are used to process data which cannot be handled by the XML parser (such as images). For example, for the following notation declaration:

```
<!NOTATION jpeg PUBLIC "www.jpeg.org">
```

There would be one XMLDOMNotation object in the XMLDOMDocumentType associated with the document.

The XMLDOMNotation objects for a document may be accessed by accessing the notations property of the XMLDOMDocumentType object associated with the document.

The XMLDOMNotation object is derived from the XMLDOMNode object. In addition to the publicId and systemId properties of this object, see the methods and properties, methods defined for the XMLDOMNode object for additional functionality available through the XMLDOMNotation object.

Methods	Properties	
appendChild*	attributes*	nodeTypeString*
cloneNode*	baseName*	nodeValue*
hasChildNodes*	childNodes*	ownerDocument*
insertBefore*	dataType*	parentNode*
removeChild*	definition*	parsed*
replaceChild*	firstChild*	prefix*
selectNodes*	lastChild*	previousSibling*
selectSingleNode*	namespaceURI*	publicId
transformNode*	nextSibling*	specified*
transformNodeToObject*	nodeName*	systemId
	nodeType*	text*
	nodeTypedValue*	xml*

* See section on XMLDOMNode methods and properties.

Additional Methods

There are no additional methods associated with the XMLDOMNotation object.

Additional Properties

publicId

The read-only publicId property returns a string containing the public identifier for this entity (e.g., for the example above, this would return "www.jpeg.org"). If the public identifier is not specified, this property returns an empty string.

```
Variant = XMLDOMNotation.publicId
```

systemId

The read-only systemId property returns a string containing the system identifier for this entity. If the system identifier is not specified, this property returns an empty string.

```
Variant = XMLDOMNotation.systemId
```

XMLDOMParseError

The XMLDOMParseError object contains information about parsing errors encountered by the XMLDOMDocument object while attempting to parse an XML document. We can get a reference to this object using the parseError property of the XMLDOMDocument object:

```
' VBScript
Set xmlParseError = xmlCatalogDocument.parseError
```

XML DOM

737

```
// JScript
var xmlParseError = xmlCatalogDocument.parseError;
```

The XMLDOMParseError object may be tested after loading an XML document to see if errors were encountered while attempting to parse the document. A list of the possible parse errors can be found in Appendix M.

Properties
errorCode
filepos
line
linepos
reason
srcText
url

The following sample displays all the properties of the XMLDOMParseError object:

```
' VBScript
Dim xmlParseError
Set xmlParseError = xmlCatalogDocument.parseError
If xmlParseError.errorCode <> 0 Then
    strError = "<H2>Error " & xmlParseError.errorCode & "</H2>"
    strError = strError & xmlParseError.reason & "<BR>"
    strError = strError & xmlParseError.url
    strError = strError & ", line " & xmlParseError.line
    strError = strError & ", position " & xmlParseError.filepos & ":<BR>"
    strError = strError & Server.HTMLEncode(xmlParseError.srcText) & "<BR>"
    Response.Write strError
End If
```

```
// JScript
var xmlParseError = xmlCatalogDocument.parseError;
if (xmlParseError.errorCode != 0) {
    strError = "<H2>Error " + xmlParseError.errorCode + "</H2>";
    strError += xmlParseError.reason + "<BR>";
    strError += xmlParseError.url;
    strError += ", line " + xmlParseError.line;
    strError += ", position " + xmlParseError.filepos + ":<BR>";
    strError += Server.HTMLEncode(xmlParseError.srcText) + "<BR>";
    Response.write(strError);
}
```

This produces a simple generic error page:

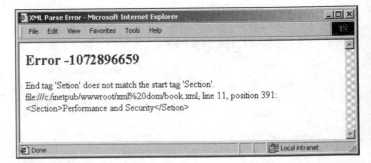

Methods

There are no methods associated with the XMLDOMParseError object.

Properties

errorCode

The read-only errorCode property returns the error code of the last parse error encountered, in decimal.

```
Long = XMLDOMParseError.errorCode
```

filepos

The read-only filepos property returns the absolute file position (offset in characters expressed as a long integer) where the reported error occurred.

```
Long = XMLDOMParseError.filepos
```

line

The read-only line property returns the line number (expressed as a long integer) where the reported error occurred.

```
Long = XMLDOMParseError.line
```

linepos

The read-only linepos property returns the offset in the current line (expressed as a long integer) where the reported error occurred.

```
Long = XMLDOMParseError.linepos
```

reason

The read-only reason property returns a string containing a description of the error.

```
String = XMLDOMParseError.reason
```

srcText

The read-only srcText property returns a string containing the entire line on which the error occurred.

```
String = XMLDOMParseError.srcText
```

url

The read-only url property returns a string containing the URL of the file being parsed when the error was encountered. If the document is being built in memory, this property will return NULL.

```
String = XMLDOMParseError.url
```

XMLDOMProcessingInstruction

The XMLDOMProcessingInstruction object corresponds to a processing instruction declared in the document. Processing instructions are data passed directly to the application which will process the XML document. For example, in the following document fragment:

```
<Book>
    <?Indexer IGNORE_BOOK ?>
</Book>
```

The <Book> element would have one XMLDOMProcessingInstruction object in its list of child nodes. We could therefore get a reference to this XMLDOMProcessingInstruction object using:

```
' VBScript
Dim xmlPI
Set xmlPI = xmlBookElement.childNodes(0)
```

```
// JScript
var xmlPI = xmlBookElement.childNodes(0);
```

The XMLDOMProcessingInstruction object is derived from the XMLDOMNode object. In addition to the data and target properties described below, please see the properties, methods, and events defined for the XMLDOMNode object for additional functionality available through the XMLDOMProcessingInstruction object.

Methods	Properties	
appendChild*	attributes*	nodeTypeString*
cloneNode*	baseName*	nodeValue*
hasChildNodes*	childNodes*	nodeTypedValue*
insertBefore*	data	ownerDocument*
removeChild*	dataType*	parentNode*
replaceChild*	definition*	parsed*
selectNodes*	firstChild*	prefix*
selectSingleNode*	lastChild*	previousSibling*
transformNode*	namespaceURI*	specified*
transformNodeToObject*	nextSibling*	target
	nodeName*	text*
	nodeType*	xml*

* See section on XMLDOMNode methods and properties.

Additional Methods

There are no additional methods associated with the XMLDOMProcessingInstruction object.

Additional Properties

data

The read-only data property sets or returns the string representing the content of the processing instruction with the exception of the target.

```
XMLDOMProcessingInstruction.data = String
String = XMLDOMProcessingInstruction.data
```

target

The read-only target property returns the string containing the target of the processing instruction.

```
String = XMLDOMProcessingInstruction.target
```

In the example above, the target would be "Indexer".

XMLDOMSchemaCollection

The XMLDOMSchemaCollection object provides a way to store namespace and schema information as a collection. This object allows us to manage the schemas and namespaces associated with an XML document and to access the nodes in a schema.

> This object is only available in version 2.6 of MSXML.

An XMLDOMSchemaCollection object may be obtained by reading the namespaces and schemas properties of XMLDOMDocument2. For example, if we have an XML document like this:

```
<?xml version="1.0"?>
<Catalog xmlns="x-schema:schema.xml">
   <Book>
      <Sections>
         <Section>ASP Intrinsic Objects</Section>
         <Section>Scripting Objects</Section>
         <Section>ASP Components</Section>
         <Section>ActiveX Data Objects</Section>
         <Section>Extending ASP</Section>
         <Section>Miscellaneous Reference</Section>
      </Sections>
   </Book>
</Catalog>
```

The schema for this might be as follows:

```
<Schema name="bookschema" xmlns="urn:schemas-microsoft-com:xml-data"
        xmlns:dt="urn:schemas-microsoft-com:datatypes">
   <ElementType name="Section" content="textOnly"
                model="closed" dt:type="string" />
   <ElementType name="Sections" content="eltOnly"
                model="closed">
```

XML DOM

```
    <element type="Section" minOccurs="1" maxOccurs="*" />
  </ElementType>
  <ElementType name="Book" content="eltOnly"
               model="closed">
    <element type="Sections" minOccurs="1" maxOccurs="1" />
  </ElementType>
  <ElementType name="Catalog" content="eltOnly"
               model="closed">
    <element type="Book" minOccurs="1" maxOccurs="*" />
  </ElementType>
</Schema>
```

To access the XMLDOMSchemaCollection for this document, we would use:

```
' VBScript
Dim xmlSchemas
Set xmlSchemas = xmlCatalogDocument.namespaces
```

```
// JScript
var xmlSchemas = xmlCatalogDocument.namespaces;
```

Methods	Properties
add	length
addCollection	
get	
namespaceURI	
remove	

Methods

add

The add method is used to add a new schema to the collection. The first parameter is the definition of the namespace to be associated with the schema. The second parameter is the schema to be loaded. If the parameter is a string, it is treated as the URL of a schema. If the parameter is an XMLDOMDocument object, that object is loaded as if it were a schema and added to the collection. If the parameter is NULL, any schema for the namespace specified is removed from the collection.

```
XMLDOMSchemaCollection.add(namespaceURI, schema)
```

Parameter	Data Type	Description
namespace URI	String	The namespace definition to be associated with the schema
schema	Object	The schema to be loaded into the collection, or NULL if the schema corresponding to the specified namespace is to be removed

For example:

```
' VBScript
' Add the schema in the xmlCatalogSchema document to the
' XMLCatalogSchemaCollection
xmlCatalogSchemaCollection.add("http://www.wrox.com/Catalog",
xmlCatalogSchema)
```

```
// JScript
// Add the schema in the xmlCatalogSchema document to the
// XMLCatalogSchemaCollection
xmlCatalogSchemaCollection.add("http://www.wrox.com/Catalog",
xmlCatalogSchema);
```

addCollection

The addCollection method is used to add all of the schemas from another existing XMLDOMSchemaCollection to the current XMLDOMSchemaCollection. If there are namespace collisions, the schemas in the existing XMLDOMSchemaCollection are replaced by the ones in the new XMLDOMSchemaCollection with the same namespace.

```
XMLDOMSchemaCollection.addCollection(objXMLDOMSchemaCollection)
```

Parameter	Data Type	Description
objXMLDOMSchema Collection	XMLDOMSchema Collection	Collection of schemas to be added to the current collection.

get

The get method is used to obtain the XMLDOMNode for the <Schema> element for the cached schema in the collection with the specified namespaceURI.

```
XMLDOMNode = XMLDOMSchemaCollection.get(namespaceURI)
```

Parameter	Data Type	Description
namespaceURI	String	The namespace for which the schema is to be returned.

For example, to access the <Schema> element of the schema given above, we would use:

```
' VBScript
Dim xmlSchemaNode
Set xmlSchemaNode = xmlSchemas.get("x-schema:schema.xml")
```

```
// JScript
var xmlSchemaNode = xmlSchemas.get("x-schema:schema.xml");
```

We can then access the other nodes in the schema through this. For example, we could access the first <ElementType> element as xmlSchemaNode.firstChild.

namespaceURI

The `namespaceURI` method is used to retrieve the namespace at the specified index in the collection. Information about any associated schema can then be discovered by using the `get` method on the returned `namespaceURI`.

```
String = XMLDOMSchemaCollection.namespaceURI(index)
```

Parameter	Data Type	Description
index	Long	Index of the namespace in the collection to be returned.

In the example XML document and associated schema given above, `xmlSchemas.namespaceURI(0)` would return `"x-schema:schema.xml"`.

remove

The `remove` method is used to remove the specified namespace from the collection.

```
XMLDOMSchemaCollection.remove(namespaceURI)
```

Parameter	Data Type	Description
namespaceURI	String	The namespace to be removed from the collection.

Properties

length

The `length` property returns the number of namespaces currently in the collection. This property is read-only.

```
Integer = XMLDOMSchemaCollection.length
```

XMLDOMSelection

The `XMLDOMSelection` object represents the list of nodes that match a particular XSL pattern or XPath expression. XPath expressions are discussed in-depth in the next chapter.

> This object is only available in version 2.6 of MSXML.

An `XMLDOMSchemaCollection` object is obtained by calling the `selectNodes` method of `XMLDOMDocument2`. For example, given the following XML document:

```xml
<?xml version="1.0"?>
<Catalog>
   <Book>
      <Sections>
         <Section Author="Alex Homer">ASP Intrinsic Objects</Section>
         <Section Author="Alex Homer">Scripting Objects</Section>
         <Section Author="Alex Homer">ASP Components</Section>
         <Section Author="Brian Francis">ActiveX Data Objects</Section>
         <Section Author="Various">Extending ASP</Section>
         <Section Author="Wrox">Miscellaneous Reference</Section>
      </Sections>
   </Book>
</Catalog>
```

We could retrieve an XMLDOMSelection containing all of the <Section> elements where the Author attribute is set to "Alex Homer" using:

```vbscript
' VBScript
Dim xmlCatalogDocument, xmlSelection
Set xmlCatalogDocument = Server.CreateObject("MSXML2.DOMDocument")
xmlCatalogDocument.async = false
xmlCatalogDocument.load("http://servername/xml/books.xml")
Set xmlSelection = xmlCatalogDocument.selectNodes("//Section[@Author='Alex
                                                   Homer']")
```

```jscript
// JScript
var xmlCatalogDocument = Server.CreateObject("MSXML2.DOMDocument");
xmlCatalogDocument.async = false;
xmlCatalogDocument.load("http://servername/xml/books.xml");
var xmlSelection = xmlCatalogDocument.selectNodes("//Section[@Author='Alex
                                                  Homer']");
```

Methods	Properties
clone	context
matches	expr
getProperty	length
item	
nextNode	
peekNode	
removeAll	
removeNext	
reset	

Methods

clone

The clone method creates an exact copy of the current XMLDOMSelection object with the same position and context.

```
XMLDOMSelection = XMLDOMSelection.clone()
```

matches

The matches method checks to see if the XMLDOMNode object passed in is part of the result set in the XMLDOMSelection object.

```
XMLDOMNode = XMLDOMSelection.matches(objXMLDOMNode)
```

Parameter	Data Type	Description
objXMLDOMNode	XMLDOMNode	The node to be checked against the XMLDOMSelection.

> **During testing, this method always returned** Nothing.

getProperty

The getProperty method is used to look up a property of the XMLDOMSelection object. For version 2.6 of MSXML, the only valid value for this property is "SelectionLanguage"; it will be either "XSLPattern" or "XPath", based on the selection method used to create the XMLDOMSelection object.

```
Variant = XMLDOMSelection.getProperty(name)
```

Parameter	Data Type	Description
name	String	The name of the property to look up the value of. Currently, this can only be "SelectionLanguage".

item

The item method is used to access individual nodes in the XMLDOMSelection collection.

```
XMLDOMNode = XMLDOMSelection.item(index)
```

Parameter	Data Type	Description
index	Long	The ordinal position of the node in the selection which will be retrieved.

nextNode

The nextNode method is used to retrieve the next node in the XMLDOMSelection collection. Calling this method increments the iterator for the collection, so that calling it repeatedly will retrieve all elements in the collection.

```
XMLDOMNode = XMLDOMSelection.nextNode()
```

peekNode

The peekNode method is used to retrieve the next node in the XMLDOMSelection collection. Calling this method does not increment the iterator for the collection, so that calling it repeatedly will continue to retrieve the node just beyond the current iterator position.

```
XMLDOMNode = XMLDOMSelection.peekNode()
```

removeAll

The removeAll method is used to remove all of the nodes in the XMLDOMSelection object from the document.

```
XMLDOMSelection.removeAll()
```

removeNext

The removeNext method is used to remove the next node in the XMLDOMSelection collection from the document.

```
XMLDOMSelection.removeNext()
```

reset

The reset method is used to reset the position of the iterator on the XMLDOMSelection object to the beginning of the list.

```
XMLDOMSelection.reset()
```

Properties

context

The context property sets or returns the node for which the results in the XMLDOMSelection object apply. Setting this property reinitializes the object for the specified node.

```
XMLDOMNode = XMLDOMSelection.context
XMLDOMSelection.context = XMLDOMNode
```

expr

The expr property sets or returns the XSL pattern or XPath expression for which the results in the XMLDOMSelection object apply. In the example above, expr would return "//Section[@Author='Alex Homer']". Setting this property reinitializes the object using the specified query string.

```
String = XMLDOMSelection.expr
XMLDOMSelection.expr = String
```

length

The length property returns the number of nodes in the XMLDOMSelection object. This property is read-only.

```
Long = XMLDOMSelection.length
```

XML DOM

747

XMLDOMText

The XMLDOMText object represents a text node which is used to contain the parsed character data contained in an XML element or attribute: element and attribute nodes do not themselves contain any text; their content is always contained in a child text node.

We can access a text node using the normal XMLDOMNode object properties, so if we have an XML element:

```
<Title>ASP Programmer's Reference</Title>
```

We can get a reference to the text node using:

```
' VBScript
Dim xmlTextNode
Set xmlTextNode = xmlTitleElement.firstChild
```

```
// JScript
var xmlTextNode = xmlTitleElement.firstChild;
```

We can also access the text node's content as a string using the element's text property.

This object is derived from the XMLDOMCharacterData object, that itself is derived from the XMLDOMNode object. In addition to the splitText method of the XMLDOMText object, see the methods and properties defined for the XMLDOMCharacterData and XMLDOMNode objects for additional functionality available through the XMLDOMText object.

Methods	Properties	
appendChild*	attributes*	ownerDocument*
appendData†	baseName*	parentNode*
cloneNode*	childNodes*	parsed*
deleteData†	data†	prefix*
hasChildNodes*	dataType*	previousSibling*
insertBefore*	definition*	specified*
insertData†	firstChild*	text*
removeChild*	lastChild*	xml*
replaceChild*	length†	
replaceData†	namespaceURI*	
selectNodes*	nextSibling*	
selectSingleNode*	nodeName*	
splitText	nodeType*	
substringData†	nodeTypedValue*	
transformNode*	nodeTypeString*	
transformNodeToObject*	nodeValue*	

* See section on XMLDOMNode methods and properties.
† See section on XMLDOMCharacterData methods and properties.

Additional Methods

splitText

The `splitText` method splits the specified node into two nodes, breaking the data content apart at the *offset* location. It then creates an adjacent sibling node of the same type and inserts it at the appropriate location at the node tree. The nodes can be rejoined using the element's `normalize` method.

```
XMLDOMText = XMLDOMText.splitText(offset)
```

Parameter	Data Type	Description
offset	Long	Position in text node where it is to be split.

Additional Properties

There are no additional properties associated with the XMLDOMText object.

XMLHttpRequest

The `XMLHttpRequest` object is used to transmit XML documents over HTTP. It is used primarily on the client side to access information that is available through the `Request` and `Response` objects on the server, so we won't look at it in too much detail here. A typical application of this object might be to transmit an XML document from a client to a server application of some kind, which processes the XML document and returns another XML document to the client. It can be instantiated using the Prog ID "`Microsoft.XMLHTTP`".

Methods	Properties	Events
abort	readyState	onreadystatechange
getAllResponseHeaders	responseBody	
getResponseHeader	responseStream	
open	responseText	
send	responseXML	
setRequestHeader	status	
	statusText	

Methods

abort

The `abort` method cancels the current request. This returns the object to an uninitialized state, and the `open` method must be called again before continuing.

```
XMLHttpRequest.abort()
```

getAllResponseHeaders

The getAllResponseHeaders method returns the header information sent in response to a call to the send method. The information is returned as a sequence of name-value pairs, separated by carriage-return linefeed pairs.

```
String = XMLHttpRequest.getAllResponseHeaders()
```

getResponseHeader

The getResponseHeader method returns the value of the header with the specified name from the headers sent in response to a call to the send method.

```
String = XMLHttpRequest.getResponseHeader(header)
```

Parameter	Data Type	Description
header	String	The name of the header to be retrieved.

For example, to get the "last-modified" header:

```
' VBScript
Dim strCatalogLastModified
strCatalogLastModified =
                    xmlCatalogHttpRequest.getResponseHeader("last-modified")
```

```
// JScript
var sCatalogLastModified =
                    xmlCatalogHttpRequest.getResponseHeader("last-modified");
```

open

The open method initializes a request, and sets information regarding that request. The method parameter is the HTTP method to be used for the request: GET, POST, and so on. The url parameter is the URL of the request. The async flag is used to set synchronous or asynchronous operation for the request (the default is asynchronous). The user and password parameters are used to specify security information for the requested object. Note that the actual request does not take place until the send method is called.

```
XMLHttpRequest.open(method, url, [async], [user], [password])
```

Parameter	Data Type	Description
method	String	The HTTP method, e.g. GET, POST etc.
url	String	URL of the request.
async	Variant	Optional. Determines whether synchronous or asynchronous operation will be used.
user	Variant	Optional security information.
password	Variant	Optional security information.

For example:

```
' VBScript
' Open the catalog XML document
xmlCatalogHttpRequest.open "GET", "catalog.xml"
```

```
// JScript
// Open the catalog XML document
xmlCatalogHttpRequest.open("GET", "catalog.xml");
```

send

The send method issues the request to the URL selected in the call to the open method. From VBScript, you can pass it a string containing the request information, an array of unsigned bytes, or an XMLDOMDocument object. For strings and arrays of unsigned bytes, use setRequestHeader to assign the content type and character set.

```
XMLHttpRequest.send(var_header)
```

Parameter	Data Type	Description
var_header	Variant	String of request information, array of unsigned bytes, or an XMLDOMDocument object.

setRequestHeader

The setRequestHeader method sets a value for a header on a request, and should be called if necessary after calling the open method but before calling the send method. The two parameters are the name of the header and its value, respectively. If another header has already been set with the same name, it is replaced.

```
XMLHttpRequest.setRequestHeader(bstr_header, bstr_value)
```

Parameter	Data Type	Description
bstr_header	String	The HTTP request header to be set.
bstr_value	String	The value to be set on the request header.

Properties

readyState

The read-only readyState property returns a long integer that describes the status of the request.

```
Long = XMLHttpRequest.readyState
```

The possible values are:

- ❏ 0 ("uninitialized"), i.e. the object has been created but the load method has not yet been executed.

- ❏ 1 ("loading"), i.e. the reply is loading, but has not yet entered the parsing step.

- ❏ 2 ("loaded"), i.e. the reply has been loaded and is being parsed.

- ❏ 3 ("interactive"), i.e. the reply has been partially parsed and a read-only version of the object model is available.

- ❏ 4 ("complete"), i.e. the reply has been completely parsed, successfully or unsuccessfully.

responseBody

The read-only responseBody property returns an array of unsigned bytes containing the raw response from the server. Note that this may contain encoded data depending on what the server transmitted.

```
Variant = XMLHttpRequest.responseBody
```

responseStream

The read-only responseStream property returns a stream object representing the raw response from the server. Note that this may contain encoded data depending on what the server transmitted.

responseText

The read-only responseText property returns a string representing the response from the server. The object attempts to decode the response as a Unicode string, so this field may contain meaningless information if the response is a BLOB or some other non-text response.

```
String = XMLHttpRequest.responseText
```

responseXML

The read-only responseXML property returns an XMLDOMDocument representing the returned document as parsed by the Microsoft parser. This property will only be populated if the MIME type of the response is correctly set to "text/xml". Note that the returned document is not validated against its DTD or schema (if one is present) by the parser before being returned.

```
XMLDOMDocument = XMLHttpRequest.responseXML
```

status

The read-only status property returns a long integer containing the HTTP status code received in response to a request.

```
Long = XMLHttpRequest.status
```

statusText

The read-only `statusText` property returns a string containing the HTTP response line status received in response to a request.

```
String = XMLHttpRequest.statusText
```

Events

onreadystatechange

The `onreadystatechange` event is fired whenever the value of the `readyState` property for the object changes. When used in conjunction with the `async` property, this allows your script to continue executing while waiting for an XML HTTP request to return. Event handlers are defined in VBScript and JScript by setting the value of a write-only property with the same name as the event to the name of the callback procedure used to respond to the event. See below for an example of this.

```
XMLHttpRequest.onreadystatechange = String
```

```
' VBScript
' set up an event handler for the onreadystatechange event
xmlCatalogHttpRequest.onreadystatechange = checkCatalogReadyStateChange
...
Sub checkCatalogReadyStateChange()
    ' handle the onreadystatechange event for the Catalog document
    ...
End Sub
```

```
// JScript
// set up an event handler for the onreadystatechange event
xmlCatalogHttpRequest.onreadystatechange = checkCatalogReadyStateChange;
...
function checkCatalogReadyStateChange() {
    // handle the onreadystatechange event for the Catalog document
    ...
}
```

XSLProcessor

The `XSLProcessor` object is used to perform transformations using compiled stylesheets.

This object is only available in version 2.6 of MSXML.

An `XSLProcessor` object may be obtained by calling the `createProcessor` method of the `XSLTemplate` object:

```
' VBScript
Dim xslTemplate, xslProcessor
Set xslTemplate = Server.CreateObject("MSXML2.XSLTemplate")
Set xslProcessor = xslTemplate.createProcessor
```

```
// JScript
var xslTemplate = Server.CreateObject("MSXML2.XSLTemplate");
var xslProcessor = xslTemplate.createProcessor();
```

The following code shows an example of using these two objects. We must first load our XML document and stylesheet as normal, except that we must use the free-threaded version of the `XMLDOMDocument2` object, or an error will be generated (due to the use of mixed threading models). We then instantiate our `XSLTemplate` object and set its `stylesheet` property to our XSL document and create the `XSLProcessor` object. Now we just need to set its `input` property (the XML node object which will be transformed, in this case our `xmlCatalogDocument`) and `output` property (the object to which the transformed XML will be sent; here, we send it directly to the browser). Finally we call the `XSLProcessor` object's `transform` method to perform the actual transformation.

The VBScript version of this code is:

```
Set xmlCatalogDocument = _
                        Server.CreateObject("MSXML2.FreeThreadedDOMDocument")
xmlCatalogDocument.async = false
xmlCatalogDocument.load("http://servername/xml/books.xml")

Set xslCatalogDocument = _
                        Server.CreateObject("MSXML2.FreeThreadedDOMDocument")
xslCatalogDocument.async = false
xslCatalogDocument.load("http://servername/xml/books.xsl")

Set xmlXSLTemplate = Server.CreateObject("MSXML2.XSLTemplate")
Set xmlXSLTemplate.stylesheet = xslCatalogDocument
Set xmlXSLProcessor = xmlXSLTemplate.createProcessor

xmlXSLProcessor.input = xmlCatalogDocument
xmlXSLProcessor.output = Response
xmlXSLProcessor.transform
```

And the JScript:

```
var xmlCatalogDocument =
                        Server.CreateObject("MSXML2.FreeThreadedDOMDocument");
xmlCatalogDocument.async = false;
xmlCatalogDocument.load("http://servername/xml/books.xml");

var xslCatalogDocument =
                        Server.CreateObject("MSXML2.FreeThreadedDOMDocument");
xslCatalogDocument.async = false;
xslCatalogDocument.load("http://servername/xml/books.xsl");

var xmlXSLTemplate = Server.CreateObject("MSXML2.XSLTemplate");
xmlXSLTemplate.stylesheet = xslCatalogDocument;
var xmlXSLProcessor = xmlXSLTemplate.createProcessor();

xmlXSLProcessor.input = xmlCatalogDocument;
xmlXSLProcessor.output = Response;
xmlXSLProcessor.transform();
```

Methods	Properties
addObject	input
addParameter	output
reset	readyState
setStartMode	startMode
transform	startModeURI
	stylesheet
	ownerTemplate

Methods

addObject

The `addObject` method is used to pass objects to a stylesheet. Numbers are converted to doubles, other values are converted to strings, and objects return an error.

```
XSLProcessor.addObject(obj, [namespaceURI])
```

Parameter	Data Type	Description
obj	Object	The object to be passed to the stylesheet.
namespaceURI	String	Optional. The namespace URI of the object to be passed to the stylesheet.

For example:

```
' VBScript
' Pass catalog information as parameters to the xmlCatalogProcessor object
xmlCatalogProcessor.addObject("catalog", "http://www.wrox.com/Catalog")
```

```
// JScript
// Pass catalog information as parameters to the xmlCatalogProcessor object
xmlCatalogProcessor.addObject("catalog", "http://www.wrox.com/Catalog");
```

addParameter

The `addParameter` method is used to pass values to a stylesheet that may be referenced by using the `<xsl:param>` element.

```
XSLProcessor.addParameter(baseName, parameter, [namespaceURI])
```

Parameter	Data Type	Description
baseName	String	The base name of the parameter to be passed to the stylesheet.
parameter	String	The value of the parameter to be passed to the stylesheet.
namespace URI	String	Optional. The namespace URI of the parameter.

reset

The `reset` method is used to abort any processing currently being performed by the `XSLProcessor` object and discard any results.

```
XSLProcessor.reset()
```

setStartMode

The `setStartMode` method is used to set the processing mode to be used by the `XSLProcessor` object. This will only apply those templates in the stylesheet that match the mode provided.

```
XSLProcessor.setStartMode(mode, [namespaceURI])
```

XML DOM

755

Parameter	Data Type	Description
mode	String	The mode in which the template is to be processed.
namespace URI	String	Optional. The namespace of the mode in which the template is to be processed.

For example:

```
' VBScript
' Set the catalog processor to operate in Public mode
xmlCatalogProcessor.setStartMode "public"
```

```
// JScript
// Set the catalog processor to operate in Public mode
xmlCatalogProcessor.setStartMode("public");
```

transform

The transform method starts or resumes a transformation operation using the XSLProcessor object. It returns false if the transformation did not complete successfully, or true if it did.

```
Boolean = XSLProcessor.transform()
```

Properties

input

The input property specifies the node at the top of the node tree to be transformed. Setting this property resets the state of the XSLProcessor object.

```
XMLDOMNode = XSLProcessor.input
XSLProcessor.input = XMLDOMNode
```

output

The output property specifies a target for the XSLProcessor object to write its output to. This may be any object that supports the IStream or IPersistStream interface (such as the ADO Stream object or the Response object); it may also be an XMLDOMDocument object. If this property is read from, it returns a string that is the incrementally-buffered output of the transformation process; successive reads to this property will return successive portions of the transformation result.

```
XSLProcessor.output = Variant
Variant = XSLProcessor.output
```

ownerTemplate

The ownerTemplate property returns the XSLTemplate object for the template that was used to create this XSLProcessor object.

```
XCMLDOMXSLTemplate = XSLProcessor.ownerTemplate
```

readyState

The read-only `readyState` property returns a long integer that describes the status of the current transformation.

```
Long = XSLProcessor.readyState
```

The possible values are:

- ❏ 0 (`"READYSTATE_UNINITIALIZED"`) i.e. the object has been created but the required properties has not yet been set.
- ❏ 1 (`"READYSTATE_LOADED"`) i.e. all properties have been set but the `transform` method has not yet been called.
- ❏ 2 (`"READYSTATE_INTERACTIVE"`) i.e. the transformation has begun but not completed.
- ❏ 3 (`"READYSTATE_COMPLETE"`) i.e. the transformation has completed and all the resultant output is available.

startMode

The `startMode` property returns the basename part of the starting mode for the processor. The default start mode is an empty string (i.e., no mode). This property is read-only – to set the start mode, invoke the `setStartMode` method.

```
String = XSLProcessor.startMode
```

startModeURI

The `startModeURI` property returns the URI of the namespace part of the starting mode for the processor. The default start mode is an empty string (i.e., no mode). This property is read-only – to set the start mode, invoke the `setStartMode` method.

```
String = XSLProcessor.startModeURI
```

stylesheet

The `stylesheet` property sets or returns the XMLDOMNode object representing the stylesheet that is to be used by the processor.

```
XMLDOMNode = XSLProcessor.stylesheet
XSLProcessor.stylesheet = XMLDOMNode
```

XSLTemplate

The `XSLTemplate` object is used to cache compiled XSL templates.

> **This object is only available in version 2.6 of MSXML.**

An `XSLTemplate` object may be instantiated using the `Server.CreateObject` function with a Prog ID of `"MSXML2.XSLTemplate"`:

```
' VBScript
Dim xslTemplate
Set xslTemplate = Server.CreateObject("MSXML2.XSLTemplate")
```

XML DOM

```
// JScript
var xslTemplate = Server.CreateObject("MSXML2.XSLTemplate");
```

Methods	Properties
createProcessor	stylesheet

Methods

createProcessor

The createProcessor method is used to create a new XSLProcessor object that may be used to transform documents using the cached stylesheet.

```
XSLProcessor = XSLTemplate.createProcessor()
```

Properties

stylesheet

The stylesheet property sets or returns the XMLDOMNode object representing the stylesheet to be used when creating processors from this template. Setting this property will replace the currently cached stylesheet.

```
XMLDOMNode = XSLProcessor.stylesheet
XSLProcessor.stylesheet = XMLDOMNode
```

Summary

In this rather long chapter, we've had a look at the objects of Microsoft's implementation of the XML DOM and their methods and properties. These objects allow us to manipulate an XML document before it is sent to the client, and also to transform it through an XSL stylesheet. Because of the amount of material we've had to cover, we've had to be very concise. We don't expect this chapter to help you learn XML from scratch, but once you've mastered the basics, we think you'll find that this reference will be more and more useful.

"Professional XML" by Wrox Press deals with the concept of XML with particular focus on real-world applications.

36

XSLT and XPath

XML is great for transferring data between applications, but, even though it's human-readable to some degree, we can't really expect users to be very impressed by raw XML data. The solution is to use a **stylesheet** to format the XML before it is displayed in the client browser. There are two formats for writing XML stylesheets: **Cascading Style Sheets** (CSS) and **Extensible Stylesheet Language** (XSL). CSS has been around for a while and is also used to format normal HTML. CSS has two main advantages: because we've been using it for some time with plain HTML pages, it should be familiar to web developers by now; and CSS styling of XML documents will be supported by Navigator 6.0.

However, there are also disadvantages. The functionality of CSS is limited to formatting, and CSS stylesheets can only be applied on the client. The disadvantage of this is that older browsers don't support XML, with or without CSS formatting, so if we send XML documents directly to the client, they will only be viewable in the most modern browsers. XSL doesn't have this problem, because we can apply an XSL stylesheet on the server using the XML DOM objects we saw in the previous chapter, and send just HTML code to the browser, so even older browsers should have no trouble displaying the page. This is possible because XSL is far more powerful than CSS, and can be used to transform an XML document into another XML document, creating, modifying and deleting nodes. And because of the relationship between XML and HTML, this new document can be HTML (so long as it is still valid XML).

XSL is managed by the World Wide Web Consortium (W3C). The version of XSL implemented in the XML parser that comes with Internet Explorer 5 and Windows 2000 is based on the December 1998 W3C Working Draft of XSL. This draft contains transformations, patterns and formatting objects. Microsoft's XML parser implemented transformations and patterns, but not formatting objects.

Since the December 1998 draft, the W3C has separated out transformations into XSLT and patterns into XPath. XSLT defines the rules used to describe transformations to be applied to an XML document. XPath is the selection syntax used within XSLT to describe which nodes are to be transformed. Both XSLT and XPath are W3C Recommendations as of November 1999. Microsoft has implemented a subset of XSLT and XPath in the Microsoft XML Parser Technology Preview Release (available at `http://msdn.microsoft.com/downloads/webtechnology/xml/msxml.asp`). Microsoft intends to implement the full specification for XSLT and XPath in the next version of their XML parser. You can convert XSL stylesheets based on the December 1998 Working Draft to use XSLT and XPath using a conversion program available from Microsoft, which we will look at briefly towards the end of this chapter.

This chapter outlines XSLT and XPath as implemented in the XML Parser Preview released February 3, 2000. Microsoft has made the bug list for this parser publicly available at `http://msdn.microsoft.com/workshop/xml/general/msxml_buglist.asp`.

Writing an XSLT Stylesheet

Although this book is intended as a reference work, in this section we'll try to provide a very quick tutorial to help you get started writing XSLT stylesheets. An important point to remember about XSLT is that it is itself an XML application. That means that an XSLT document must conform to the rules of XML and that an XML Document Type Definition (DTD) exists that specifies which elements can be used within an XSLT document. XSLT uses a number of predefined elements with the `xsl:` namespace prefix to transform the XML.

All XSL and XSLT stylesheets have an outer element `<xsl:stylesheet>`. This element must define the `xsl:` namespace, and in XSLT, must also specify the version number (`"1.0"`):

```
<xsl:stylesheet version="1.0"
                xmlns:xsl="http://www.w3.org/1999/XSL/Transform">
...
</xsl:stylesheet>
```

In the version of XSL implemented in IE5, we don't need to declare the version and the namespace is slightly different:

```
<xsl:stylesheet xmlns:xsl="http://www.w3.org/TR/WD-xsl">
...
</xsl:stylesheet>
```

Within the stylesheet, we define templates which match specific sets of nodes (or **node-sets**) using the `<xsl:template>` element. We specify the nodes in the template using XPath pattern matching syntax (which we will look at in detail in the first half of the reference section of this chapter). The outermost template usually matches the root node of the document (`"/"`). Within this template, we can specify other templates which will be applied as the current template is processed. We can also specify text and XML (or HTML, since the transformed XML will probably be written to a browser) elements, which will be output directly. We can also include XML comments:

```
<xsl:template match="/">
   <!-- match all Book elements below the current node -->
   <xsl:apply-templates select="//Book" />
</xsl:template>

<xsl:template match="Book">
   <!-- print out value of current node (.) and a horizontal rule -->
   <xsl:value-of select="." /><HR />
</xsl:template >
```

*Note that because every XSL file must adhere to the rules for well-formed XML, 'empty' HTML elements (such as <BR>) cannot be used in this way in an XSL stylesheet. Instead, we either have to add the closing slash (<BR />), or add an end element (
</BR>).*

If we apply this template to the following XML document:

```
<Catalog>
   <Book>ASP 3.0 Programmer's Reference</Book>
   <Book>Beginning ASP 3.0</Book>
   <Book>Professional ASP 3.0</Book>
</Catalog>
```

This will generate the following HTML code:

```
ASP 3.0 Programmer's Reference<HR />
Beginning ASP 3.0<HR />
Professional ASP 3.0<HR />
```

This is a very simple example, so before we move on, let's look at a slightly more complex stylesheet.

A Sample XSLT Stylesheet

The XML document we will be transforming contains the details of a couple of Wrox internet programming books. We include details of the title, a list of the authors, the book code and a reference to an image of the cover:

```
<?xml version="1.0"?>
<Catalog>
   <Book>
      <Title>XML in IE5 Programmer's Reference</Title>
      <Code>1576</Code>
      <Authors>
         <Author>Alex Homer</Author>
      </Authors>
      <Cover>XmlIE5.png</Cover>
   </Book>
   <Book>
      <Title>Professional ASP 3.0</Title>
      <Code>2610</Code>
      <Authors>
      <Author>Alex Homer</Author>
      <Author>Dave Sussman</Author>
      <Author>Brian Francis</Author>
</Authors>
      <Cover>ProASP3.png</Cover>
   </Book>
   <Book>
      <Title>Instant Netscape Dynamic HTML</Title>
```

```
      <Code>1193</Code>
      <Authors>
          <Author>Alex Homer</Author>
          <Author>Chris Ullman</Author>
      </Authors>
      <Cover>NCDHTML.png</Cover>
   </Book>
</Catalog>
```

Now we can write our stylesheet. First we need the opening `<xsl:stylesheet>` tag and the outermost template. Within this template, we'll include a title and heading for our output HTML page, and a reference for a template to match each `<Book>` element in the XML document:

```
<?xml version="1.0"?>
<xsl:stylesheet version="1.0"
                xmlns:xsl="http://www.w3.org/1999/XSL/Transform">

<xsl:template match="/">
    <TITLE>Wrox Catalog</TITLE>
    <H1 ALIGN="CENTER">Some Wrox Internet Books</H1>
    <xsl:apply-templates select="//Book" />
</xsl:template>
```

Next, we define the 'Book' template. We'll display each book in an HTML table with two cells. The left-hand cell will include another table with three rows, containing the book's title, list of authors, and code. The right-hand cell will include the book's cover image. We simply include the HTML elements for building this table within the template. For the title and code, we just print out the value of the relevant element, with a bit of text and HTML formatting. We need to do a bit more processing on the author list and image cover, though, so we apply sub-templates for each of these:

```
<xsl:template match="Book">
    <TABLE WIDTH="80%" CELLPADDING="10">
      <TR><TD WIDTH="80%">
          <TABLE>
            <TR><TD>
                <H2><xsl:value-of select="Title" /></H2>
            </TD></TR>
            <TR><TD>
                <xsl:apply-templates select="Authors" />
            </TD></TR>
            <TR><TD>
                Code: <xsl:value-of select="Code" />
            </TD></TR>
          </TABLE>
      </TD><TD>
          <xsl:apply-templates select="Cover" />
      </TD></TR>
    </TABLE>
    <HR />
</xsl:template>
```

We want to print out the authors in the form "By X, Y and Z". We need to decide for each author what should follow the author's name. This will be the word "and" (if the author is the penultimate in the list), nothing (if it's the last), or a comma (in other cases). We use an <xsl:for-each> element to iterate through each <Author> child element of the <Authors> element. We then use the <xsl:choose> ... <xsl:when> ... <xsl:otherwise> elements to test where in the list the name comes. These work very similarly to a VBScript If...ElseIf...Else construct: the outer <xsl:choose> element is used to signal that we're entering a conditional loop, and contains a number of <xsl:when> elements which we use to test specific conditions. Content within these elements will be output only if the condition is evaluates to true. The <xsl:choose> element can also contain one <xsl:otherwise> element which will be applied only if all the <xsl:when> conditions evaluated to false.

Now for the tricky bit: we use the XPath function position() to check the position of the current element in the list. We can find the total number of <Author> elements in <Authors> using the count() function, which takes an XPath expression signifying a set of nodes as a parameter, and returns the number of nodes in that node-set. We want to specify all the <Author> elements which are children of the <Authors> element, i.e. all siblings of the current node. The XPath expression parent::* specifies the current node's parent (* signifies 'all nodes', so this means 'all nodes which are the parent of the current node'; we will look at the double-colon syntax in more detail later), and parent::*/Author denotes all <Author> elements which are children of the current node's parent. So, finally, we can work out whether the author is the last in the list using the expression position() = count(parent::*/Author), and whether it's the last but one using count(parent::*/Author)-1. This is quite complex, but it does illustrate the power of XSL: we couldn't do anything like this with CSS!

```
<xsl:template match="Authors">
   By
   <xsl:for-each select="Author">
      <xsl:choose>
         <xsl:when test="position() = count(parent::*/Author)">
            <B><xsl:value-of select="." /></B>
         </xsl:when>
         <xsl:when test="position() = count(parent::*/Author)-1">
            <B><xsl:value-of select="." /></B> and
         </xsl:when>
         <xsl:otherwise>
            <B><xsl:value-of select="." /></B>,
         </xsl:otherwise>
      </xsl:choose>
   </xsl:for-each><BR /><BR />
</xsl:template>
```

Now we just need to display the cover image. We'll do this by transforming the <Cover> element into an HTML <IMG> element. We can create this element just by adding the opening and closing tags within the template, but we also need to create a SRC attribute pointing to the image file. Here again XSL shows its power: the <xsl:attribute> element, placed inside our <IMG>...</IMG> tags will add an attribute to the <IMG> element. We specify the attribute's name using the <xsl:attribute> element's name attribute, and the value of the attribute is contained within the <xsl:attribute> element (we get this from the contents of the <Cover> element). We also add an ALT attribute for good measure. Finally, we close the <xsl:stylesheet> element:

```
<xsl:template match="Cover">
   <IMG>
      <xsl:attribute name="SRC">
         <xsl:value-of select="." />
      </xsl:attribute>
      <xsl:attribute name="ALT">Book Cover</xsl:attribute>
   </IMG>
</xsl:template>

</xsl:stylesheet>
```

Well, that was hard work, but the result is much more useful than a plain XML file:

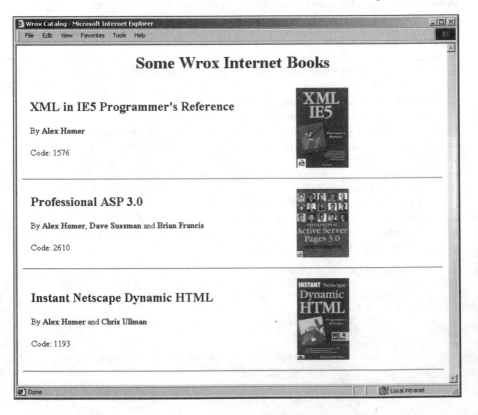

Applying XSLT to an XML Document

An XSL stylesheet can be applied to an XML document in a number of ways. One way is to embed a processing instruction within the XML document, which will cause the stylesheet to be applied when the document is viewed in the browser. Alternatively, we can transform the document on the server using the XMLDOMDocument's transformNode or transformNodeToObject method. A third possibility is to load a stylesheet into an XSLProcessor object and apply it to a number of XML documents.

Using a Processing Instruction

Processing instructions are used with an XML document to signal to the XML processor that some additional work has to be performed. The processing instruction contains a target that identifies the application to which the instruction is directed.

To apply an XSL style sheet to an XML document the xml-stylesheet processing instruction is used. This processing instruction must appear in the prolog of the XML document (the part of an XML document before the outermost element).

The xml-stylesheet processing instruction may contain the following attributes:

Attribute	Required	Description
href	Yes	The URL for the XSL stylesheet.
type	Yes	The content type of the content available in the target address. For an XSL stylesheet this value is "text/xsl".
title	No	A description of the XSL stylesheet.
media	No	The intended rendering medium that the style information applies to.
charset	No	Specifies the character encoding of the resource designated by the link in the href attribute.
alternate	No	Specifies whether the stylesheet is an alternate or not. Has the value of "yes" or "no".

The following example shows how to associate an XSL stylesheet with an XML document:

```
<?xml version="1.0"?>
<?xml-stylesheet type="text/xsl" href="myStyles.xsl"?>
<Catalog>
   ...
</Catalog>
```

Embedding a stylesheet within a document is usually done so that the document is rendered by the client as HTML. In this case, the client XML Parser is used. Since the XML Parser Preview is not yet embedded in Microsoft Internet Explorer (but will be in IE 5.5), the XSLT syntax used in this chapter may not work. As mentioned previously, Internet Explorer 5.0 conforms to the December 1998 XSL draft.

Microsoft provides a tool (named xmlinst.exe) for replacing an existing XML parser with the XML Parser Preview (MSXML version 2.6). This would allow you to try the new functionality with existing applications. The tool and instructions for using it are included in the Software Development Kit (SDK) for the XML Parser Preview (available for download from the same URL).

XSLT & XPath

In some cases, the stylesheet may be applied on the web server. The Microsoft XSL ISAPI Extension discussed later in this chapter is a way to enable this functionality for Microsoft Internet Information Server (IIS).

Transforming XML on the Server

A stylesheet can be applied to any XML document without it having a processing instruction with it.

The simplest way is to load both the XML and XSL documents first and then to call the transformNode method, as in the following example:

```
' VBScript
Dim objDocument
Dim objTransform
Dim strXML

Set objDocument = Server.CreateObject("MSXML2.DOMDocument")
Set objTransform = Server.CreateObject("MSXML2.DOMDocument")

objDocument.Load "c:\xmlcode\src.xml"
objTransform.Load "c:\xmlcode\transform.xsl"

strXML = objDocument.transformNode(objTransform)
```

```
// JScript
var objDocument = Server.CreateObject("MSXML2.DOMDocument");
var objTransform = Server.CreateObject("MSXML2.DOMDocument");

objDocument.load("c:\xmlcode\src.xml");
objTransform.load("c:\xmlcode\transform.xsl");

var strXML = objDocument.transformNode(objTransform);
```

The variable strXML will contain the transformed document. We can send this straight to the browser:

```
Response.Write strXML
```

However, when debugging a stylesheet, it is often useful to see the transformed XML, so we can see exactly what's going wrong. We can do this by calling the Server.HTMLEncode method:

```
Response.Write Server.HTMLEncode(strXML)
```

This will display the raw XML which results from the transformation:

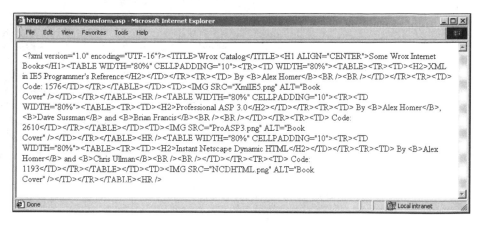

Error handling has been omitted from the code above for the sake of simplicity. However, it is always wise to ensure that your XML document has loaded and parsed correctly, using the XMLDOMParseError object (covered in the previous chapter). For example:

```
' VBScript
objDocument.Load "c:\xmlcode\src.xml"
If objDocument.parseError.errorCode <> 0 Then
    Response.Write "XML Source error: " & objDocument.parseError.reason
    Response.Write "line: " & objTransform.parseError.Line
    Response.End
End If
```

```
// JScript
objDocument.load("c:\\xmlcode\\src.xml");
if (objDocument.parseError.errorCode != 0) {
    Response.Write("XML Source error: " + objDocument.parseError.reason);
    Response.Write("line: " + objTransform.parseError.line);
    Response.End();
}
```

Sending Parameters to a Stylesheet

If you need parameters within your XSL document or want to reuse a stylesheet, it is best to use the XSLProcessor object. This object can be used to cache a parsed stylesheet, resulting in a performance increase for stylesheets that are re-used.

To use this object, we must first instantiate an XSLTemplate object and set its stylesheet property to a loaded XSL stylesheet. We can then create an XSLProcessor object by calling the XSLTemplate's createProcessor method. We set the XSLProcessor's input as usual to the XML document we wish to transform, and optionally also the output (e.g. if we want to send the output straight to the Response object). Now we can call the addParameter method, which we use to send our parameter to the stylesheet. This method can take three arguments: the name of the parameter in the stylesheet, the value to be passed in (you may need to convert this from a variant to the appropriate data type), and (optionally) the namespace URI for the parameter. Finally, we call the processor's transform method to cause the actual transform to take place.

XSLT & XPath

Let's modify our stylesheet to allow us to sort by either the book's title or its code number. The following code demonstrates how to pass in the parameter from ASP (for the sake of clarity, we'll just hard-code in the value "Title" here):

```
' VBScript
Dim objDocument, objTransform, objTemplate, objProcessor, strXML

Set objDocument = Server.CreateObject("MSXML2.FreeThreadedDOMDocument")
Set objTransform = Server.CreateObject("MSXML2.FreeThreadedDOMDocument")
Set objTemplate = Server.CreateObject("MSXML2.XSLTemplate")

objDocument.Load "c:\xmlcode\src.xml"
objTransform.Load "c:\xmlcode\transform.xsl"

Set objTemplate.stylesheet = objTransform
Set objProcessor = objTemplate.createProcessor
objProcessor.input = objDocument.documentElement
objProcessor.addParameter "sortBy", "Title"
objProcessor.transform
strXML = objProcessor.output
```

```
// JScript
var objDocument, objTransform, objTemplate, objProcessor, strXML;

objDocument = Server.CreateObject("MSXML2.FreeThreadedDOMDocument");
objTransform = Server.CreateObject("MSXML2.FreeThreadedDOMDocument");
objTemplate = Server.CreateObject("MSXML2.XSLTemplate");

objDocument.load("c:\\xmlcode\\src.xml");
objTransform.load("c:\\xmlcode\\transform.xsl");

objTemplate.stylesheet = objTransform;
objProcessor = objTemplate.createProcessor();
objProcessor.input = objDocument.documentElement;
objProcessor.addParameter("sortBy", "Title");
objProcessor.transform();
strXML = objProcessor.output;
```

Again, the variable strXML will contain the transformed document.

In order to access this parameter within our stylesheet, we need to create an <xsl:param> element with a name attribute set to the name of our parameter. The parameter can then be referenced within the stylesheet by this name prefixed with a dollar sign, e.g. $sortBy. We will place this element at the top level of the stylesheet, before our opening <xsl:template> element, so that it is globally available.

Now we just need to sort the books according to the value passed in. A template can be sorted by adding a an <xsl:sort> element as a child of the corresponding <xsl:apply-templates> element. The <xsl:sort> element takes a select attribute which specifies the pattern by which the template is to be sorted. You might think we could just write select="$sortBy". However, the parameter has a string value, and can't be used directly as an XPath expression. The way round this is to use the XPath expression "*[name()=$sortBy]". We'll look at XPath syntax in detail in the next section, but this means "all nodes which have a name with the same value as the $sortBy parameter". The first elements of our stylesheet thus become:

```
<xsl:stylesheet version="1.0"
                xmlns:xsl="http://www.w3.org/1999/XSL/Transform">
<xsl:param name="sortBy" />
<xsl:template match="/">
   <TITLE>Wrox Catalog</TITLE>
   <H1 ALIGN="CENTER">Some Wrox Internet Books</H1>
   <xsl:apply-templates select="//Book">
      <xsl:sort select="*[name()=$sortBy]" order="ascending" />
   </xsl:apply-templates>
</xsl:template>

... Rest of stylesheet
```

XPath Selection Language

As we have seen, the power of XSLT relies on our ability to choose specific nodes in the XML document and apply transformations selectively to those nodes. We use the XPath selection language to specify the nodes within the XML document which we wish to transform. Therefore, before we look in detail at the predefined XSL elements, we'll first look at the syntax of the XPath language.

Like the XML DOM, XPath uses a data model which represents the XML document as a tree containing nodes. XPath distinguishes seven types of node:

❑   Root nodes

❑   Element nodes

❑   Attribute nodes

❑   Text nodes

❑   Namespace nodes

❑   Processing instruction nodes

❑   Comment nodes

Every document has a root node and all other nodes are descendents of the root node. An element node exists for each XML element within the document. If an element has attributes, its element node will have an associated set of attribute nodes. Any character data, such as content within an element, is represented as a text node. Finally any namespaces, processing instructions and comments are also represented as distinct nodes within the tree.

XPath Syntax

The name XPath derives from its ability to represent a path of nodes from the node currently being processed (the **context node**) through the tree representing an XML document. This path can be selected using a combination of axes, node tests, predicates and expressions.

An **axis** specifies the hierarchical path from the context node to the nodes we wish to select. For example, `parent` or `child` to specify the parent or child nodes of the context node.

We further refine the selected node-set by using a **node test** to specify the types of node we want to select. This can be a built-in keyword or the name of a node. Axes and node-sets are specified using the syntax `axis::node-set`; For example, to specify `<Book>` elements which are children of the context node, we would use `child::Book`. An XPath expression can consist of a number of these axis/node-set pairs, separated by a forward slash character (/). So, to select the `Title` attribute of a child `<Book>` element, we would use `child::Book/attribute::Title`.

We can also test for specific properties of the nodes to be selected, such as only selecting elements with a given attribute. To do this, we use a **predicate**, which is enclosed in square brackets after the node test. This can simply be another axis/node-set path, as in the expression `child::Book[attribute::Title]`, which would select only `<Book>` child elements which have a `Title` attribute. However, we can also include mathematical and logical operators to build fully-formed conditions, such as `[attribute::Title='Professional ASP 3.0']`, which would check for elements with a `Title` attribute with a value of `"Professional ASP 3.0"`. Finally, there are also a number of **XPath functions** which we can use within these predicates.

We'll now look in turn at each of these parts of an XPath expression.

Axes

The primary method of navigating an XML document tree is by using axes. An axis specifies the relationship between the context node and the nodes to be selected in the tree. The following table shows the axes that are available:

Axis	Description	Example
ancestor	Selects the ancestors of the context node. This will always include the root node unless the context node is the root node.	`ancestor::para` selects all `<para>` ancestors of the context node.
ancestor-or-self	Selects the context node and its ancestors.	`ancestor-or-self::section` selects the `<section>` ancestors of the context node and, if the context node is a `<section>` element, the context node as well.
attribute	Selects the attributes of the context node. If the context node is not an element, nothing will be selected.	`attribute::author` selects the `<author>` attribute of the context node.
child	Selects the immediate children of the context node.	`child::title` selects all the `<title>` child nodes of the context node.

Axis	Description	Example
descendant	Selects the descendants of the context node. The descendant axis will never contain attribute or namespace nodes.	descendant::div selects all the <div> elements that are descendents of the context node.
descendant -or-self	Selects the context node and its descendants.	descendant-or-self::para selects the <para> element descendants of the context node and, if the context node is a <para> element, the context node as well.
parent	Selects the parent of the context node, if there is one.	parent::node() selects the parent node of the context node.
self	Selects the context node itself.	self::div selects the context node if it is a <div> element and otherwise selects nothing.

Abbreviated Syntax

Because these expressions can rapidly become very long, XPath also provides a number of abbreviations for the more common axes and axis/node test pairs:

Abbreviation	Description	Example
//	Abbreviation for /descendant-or-self::node()/	//para will select all <para> element descendants and the context node if it is a <para> element.
@	Abbreviation for attribute::	para[attribute::level= "advanced"] can be shortened to para[@level="advanced"].
. (period)	Abbreviation for self::node()	self::node()/descendant-or-self::node()/child::abstract can be shortened to .//abstract.
.. (double period)	Abbreviation for parent::node()	parent::node()/child::abstract can be shortened to ../abstract.

Also note that the child:: specifier can be omitted. For instance, child::h1/child:para can be abbreviated to h1/para.

Node Tests

As well as specifying a node's name as the node test, we can test for specific node types within an XPath expression using built-in keywords. Every axis has a **principal node type**. The principal node type is an element if the axis can contain elements, otherwise it is of the type of the nodes the axis can contain. For example, for the `attribute` axis, the principle node type is attibute. The following can be used to select nodes of various types.

Test	Description
`node()`	Returns `true` for any node of any type.
`text()`	Returns `true` for any text node.
`comment()`	Returns `true` for any comment node.
`processing-instruction()`	Returns `true` for any processing instruction node.
`*`	Returns `true` for any node of the principal node type. For example, `attribute::*` will return select all the attributes of the context node.

XPath Predicates and Expressions

Once an axis is specified, it can be filtered using an XPath predicate to create a new node-set. For each node in the node-set specified by the axis, the expression is evaluated with that node as the context node. If the expression evaluates to `true`, the node is included in the new node-set.

The expression will be converted to a Boolean to determine if a node should be included in the new node-set. If the expression result is a number, it will be converted to `true` if the number is equal to the context position. If the result is not a number, the result will be converted by the same rules as used by the `boolean` function (see below).

The following operators can be used in an expression for performing comparisons. They are listed in order of precedence with the highest precedence first:

❑ `<=, <, >=, >`

❑ `=, !=`

❑ `and`

❑ `or`

Before being evaluated, the `and` and `or` operators evaluate their operands and convert them to Booleans. Comparison of node-sets is performed by first converting the node-sets to their string-values and comparing the strings.

> Since an XSL document is an instance of an XML document, it must
> adhere to the XML rules. Therefore, when an XPath expression occurs
> in an XSL document, any < and <= operators must be quoted
> according to XML 1.0 rules by using < and <=. For example,
> the following expression tests if the level attribute is less than 5:
> <xsl:if test="@level < 5">...</xsl:if>.

The following operators can be used with numbers within an expression:

- +
- –
- *
- div
- mod

The div operator performs a division of the first operand by the second operand. The mod operator returns the remainder of a division of the first operand by the second operand. For example, item[position() mod 2 = 1] would select all item nodes that are odd-numbered children of their parent node.

XPath Functions

XPath has a set of functions that can be used within expressions. They are divided here into five categories: Boolean functions, node-set functions, number functions, string functions, and XSLT functions.

Boolean Functions

The XPath Boolean functions are used to convert XPath objects to Booleans.

boolean

Converts its argument to a Boolean based on the following rules:

- If a number is not zero and not "Not a Number" (NaN), it is true.
- If a node-set is not empty, it is true.
- If a string's length is greater than zero (i.e. it isn't an empty string), it is true.
- An object of a type other than those listed above is converted to a Boolean in a way that is dependent on that type.

```
Boolean boolean(object)
```

XSLT & XPath

Parameter	Data Type	Required	Description
object	Object	Yes	The object being tested.

For example, boolean(0) returns false, and boolean("I like coding") returns true.

false

Returns false.

```
Boolean False()
```

not

Returns true if the parameter is false, and true otherwise.

```
Boolean not(value)
```

Parameter	Data Type	Required	Description
value	Boolean	Yes	The object being tested.

For example, not(0) returns true and not("I like coding") returns false.

true

Returns true.

```
Boolean true()
```

Node-set Functions

The XPath node-set functions return information about nodes which we can use within an XPath expression.

count

Returns the number of nodes in the node-set passed as a parameter.

```
Number count(node-set)
```

Parameter	Data Type	Required	Description
node-set	Node-set	Yes	The node set for which the number of nodes is to be determined.

For example, count(descendant::order) returns the number of <order> descendants for the context node.

id

Selects elements by their unique ID.

```
Node-set id(object)
```

Parameter	Data Type	Required	Description
object	Object	Yes	An object that determines which nodes will be returned. If the parameter is a single ID then a single node is returned. Multiple nodes can be selected by passing a white space delimited list of ID's. If the parameter is a node-set then the string-value of each of the nodes in the node-set will be used as the selection criteria.

For example, `<xsl:template match="id('item1')">` would select the node with the unique ID `"item1"`. For an example of assigning a unique ID to an XML element, see the `nodeFromID` method of the `XMLDOMDocument` object in the previous chapter.

last

Returns the position number of the last node in the context node set. This is the total number of nodes in the node-set.

```
Number last()
```

This example returns the last `<product>` element in a list of products:
`products/product[position() = last()]`.

local-name

Returns the local part (i.e. the base name, excluding any namespace prefix) from the expanded name of the node in the specified `node-set` that comes first in the XML document. If the `node-set` argument is empty, an empty string is returned.

```
String local-name([node-set])
```

Parameter	Data Type	Required	Description
node-set	Node-set	No	If no parameter is provided, it defaults to a node-set with the context node as its only member.

For example, for a node with the expanded name `"Wrox:Title"`, `local-name()` will return `"Title"`.

name

Returns the expanded name of the node in the parameter node-set that is first in document order. If the argument node-set is empty, an empty string is returned. The expanded name of a node consists of the local part and any namespace prefix.

```
String name([node-set])
```

Parameter	Data Type	Required	Description
node-set	Node-set	No	If no parameter is provided, it defaults to a node-set with the context node as its only member.

namespace-uri

Returns the namespace URI of the node in the parameter node-set that is first in document order. This is the definition associated with any namespace prefix in the node's expanded name. The namespace-uri will be either null or a string. If the argument node-set is empty, or the first node has no expanded name, an empty string is returned.

```
String namespace-uri([node-set])
```

Parameter	Data Type	Required	Description
node-set	Node-set	No	If no parameter is provided, it defaults to a node-set with the context node as its only member.

For example, if we have a node defined as:

```
<Wrox:Book Title="ASP 3.0 Programmer's Reference"
           xmlns:Wrox="http://www.wrox.com" />
```

Then the namespace-uri for this element will be "http://www.wrox.com".

position

The position function returns a number equal to the context position from the expression evaluation context.

```
Number position()
```

The following example returns the second product in a list of products:
products/products[position() = 2].

Number Functions

The XPath number functions are used within an XPath expression to convert XPath objects to numbers .

number

Returns its parameter as a number according to the following rules:

❏ A string is converted to the IEEE 754 number that is nearest (according to the IEEE 754 round-to-nearest rule – see Institute of Electrical and Electronics Engineers, IEEE Standard for Binary Floating-Point Arithmetic, ANSI/IEEE Std 754-1985 for details) to the mathematical value represented by the string. Any other string is converted to NaN ("Not a number").

❏ A Boolean true is converted to 1 and a Boolean false is converted to 0.

❏ A node-set is first converted to a string as if by a call to the string function and then converted in the same way as a string argument.

```
Number number([object])
```

Parameter	Data Type	Required	Description
object	Object	No	The object to be converted to a number. If the parameter is omitted, it defaults to a node-set with the context node as its only member.

String Functions

The XPath string functions allow us to convert XPath objects to strings and to manipulate string objects.

concat

Returns a string that is the concatenation of its parameters. Any number of strings to be concatenated can be provided as parameters.

```
String concat(string1, [string2], ..., [stringn])
```

Parameter	Data Type	Required	Description
string[n]	String	n/a	The string(s) to be concatenated.

For example, concat("one ", "two ", "three") would return the stirng "one two three".

contains

Returns `true` if the first parameter contains the string in the second parameter. Otherwise this function returns `false`.

```
Boolean contains(string1, string2)
```

Parameter	Data Type	Required	Description
string1	String	Yes	The string to be searched.
string2	String	Yes	The string to search for.

For example, `contains("Rock and roll", "roll")` would return `true`.

normalize-space

Returns the parameter with whitespace normalized by stripping leading and trailing whitespace and replacing sequences of whitespace characters by a single space.

```
String normalize-space([string])
```

Parameter	Data Type	Required	Description
string	String	No	The string to be normalized. If no argument is passed, then the context node is converted to a string and normalized.

starts-with

Returns `true` if the first argument string starts with the second argument string, and otherwise returns `false`.

```
Boolean starts-with(string1, string2)
```

Parameter	Data Type	Required	Description
string1	String	Yes	The string to be tested.
string2	String	Yes	The string to test with.

For example, `starts-with ("In the beginning", "In")` would return `true`.

string

Converts an object to a string.

```
String string([object])
```

Parameter	Data Type	Required	Description
object	String	No	The object to convert to a string. If no parameter is provided, it defaults to a node-set with the context node as its only member.

Objects are converted to strings according to the following rules:

❑ A node-set is converted to a string by returning the string-value of the node in the node-set that is first in document order. If the node-set is empty, an empty string is returned.

❑ A number is converted to a string as follows:

  ❑ NaN is converted to the string "NaN".

  ❑ Positive zero is converted to the string "0".

  ❑ Negative zero is converted to the string "0".

  ❑ Positive infinity is converted to the string "Infinity".

  ❑ Negative infinity is converted to the string "-Infinity".

  ❑ If the number is an integer, the number is represented in base 10 as a number with no decimal point and no leading zeros, preceded by a minus sign (-) if the number is negative.

  ❑ Otherwise, the number is represented in decimal form as a number including a decimal point with at least one digit before the decimal point and at least one digit after the decimal point, preceded by a minus sign (-) if the number is negative. There will be no leading zeros before the decimal point, apart from the required digit immediately before the decimal point. Beyond the one required digit after the decimal point, there must be as many, but only as many, more digits as are needed to uniquely distinguish the number from all other IEEE 754 numeric values.

❑ The Boolean false value is converted to the string "false". The Boolean true value is converted to the string "true".

❑ The rules for objects which do not belong to one of the four basic types are dependent on the type of object.

string-length

Returns the number of characters in a string.

```
Number string-length([srcString])
```

Parameter	Data Type	Required	Description
srcString	String	No	The string to find the length of. If no argument is passed, then the context node is converted to a string and the length of that string is returned.

substring

Returns the substring of the first parameter starting at the position specified by the second parameter and length specified by the third parameter.

```
String substring(srcString, startPos, [length])
```

Parameter	Data Type	Required	Description
srcString	String	Yes	The string from which a substring will be obtained.
startPos	Number	Yes	The index position to start at. The first character is at position 1.
length	Number	No	The number of characters to return in the substring. If this argument is not provided, the substring from startPos to the end will be returned.

For example, substring("I like coding", 8) returns "coding", and substring("I like coding", 3, 4) returns "like".

substring-after

Returns the substring of the first parameter from the character position that follows the first occurrence of the second parameter to the end of the string. An empty string is returned if the second parameters is not contained in the first parameter.

```
String substring-after(srcString, searchString)
```

Parameter	Data Type	Required	Description
srcString	String	Yes	The string to search.
searchString	String	Yes	The string to search with.

For example, substring-after("1999/04/01", "/") returns "04/01", and substring-after("1999/04/01", "19") returns "99/04/01":

substring-before

Returns a substring of the first parameter starting at the first character and ending at the character preceding the first occurrence of the second parameter. An empty string is returned if the second parameter is not contained in the first parameter.

```
String substring-before(srcString, searchString)
```

Parameter	Data Type	Required	Description
srcString	String	Yes	The string to search.
searchString	String	Yes	The string to search with.

For example, substring-before("1999/04/01", "/") returns "1999".

translate

Returns the first argument with occurences of characters in the second argument replaced by the character at the corresponding position in the third argument.

```
String translate(string1, string2, string3)
```

Parameter	Data Type	Required	Description
string1	String	Yes	The source string to be translated.
string2	String	Yes	The characters to search for.
string3	String	Yes	The characters to perform replacement with.

For example, translate("abcd", "ac", "YZ") would return the string "YbZd", and translate("Version A.B", "AB", "20") would return the string "Version 2.0".

XSLT Functions

There are also a few functions for special use within XSLT.

current

Returns a node-set consisting solely of the current node.

```
Node-set current()
```

In most cases, this will be identical to " . ", which signifies the context node. However, there is a subtle difference. The context node changes as the XPath expression is processed – it walks down the path, if you like – whereas the current node remains the same throughout the expression. For example, we could modify our XML catalog from the start of the chapter to include a "Book of the Month" which is indicated by its code number:

```
<Catalog>
    <BookOfTheMonth>2610</BookOfTheMonth>
    <Book>
        <Title>XML in IE5 Programmer's Reference</Title>
        <Code>1576</Code>
    </Book>
    <Book>
        <Title>Professional ASP 3.0</Title>
        <Code>2610</Code>
    </Book>
    <Book>
        <Title>Instant Netscape Dynamic HTML</Title>
        <Code>1193</Code>
    </Book>
</Catalog>
```

If we want an XSL stylesheet which will output only the title of this book of the month, we could use something like this:

```
<xsl:template match="/">
    <xsl:apply-templates select="//Catalog" />
</xsl:template>

<xsl:template match="Catalog">
    <xsl:value-of select="Book[Code=current()/BookOfTheMonth]/Title" />
</xsl:template>
```

The XPath expression we use to select this title checks the contents of the <Code> child element for each <Book> against the <BookOfTheMonth> element which is a child of the <Catalog> element: the template being applied matches <Catalog>, so current() in this expression refers to that element.

If we were to change this expression to:

```
Book[Code=./BookOfTheMonth]/Title
```

This wouldn't find any matches, because " . " occurs in a predicate of the Book node test. The context node has moved down the path, and now " . " refers to the <Book> element.

element-available

Checks to see whether the specified `element` is available and may be used as an instruction in the stylesheet.

```
Boolean element-available(element)
```

Parameter	Data Type	Required	Description
element	String	Yes	The name of the element (including namespace prefix) to check for.

For example: `element-available('xsl:template')` (returns `true`).

format-number

Returns a string containing the supplied *number* in the specified *format*.

```
String format-number(number, format)
```

Parameter	Data Type	Required	Description
number	Number	Yes	The number to format.
format	String	Yes	The format for the number (see below).

The `format` parameter may contain the following characters:

- ❑ . (period). Used to mark the position of the decimal point. Digits after the decimal point are not included unless marked by a zero or pound placeholder. Rounding occurs if digits are not included.

- ❑ , (comma). Used as a thousands separator. If placed after the decimal point, it will be ignored.

- ❑ # (pound). Used as a placeholder for significant digits. Insignificant digits in these positions will be ignored.

- ❑ 0 (zero). Used to indicate that zeroes in these positions must be displayed, even if not significant.

For example: `format-number(123,'#.0')` returns `"123.0"`; `format-number(1002.38,'#,###.0')` returns `"1,002.4"`; and `format-number(1222333,'#,###.#')` returns `"1,222,33."`.

function-available

Checks to see whether the specified `function` is available in the stylesheet.

```
Boolean function-available(element)
```

Parameter	Data Type	Required	Description
function	String	Yes	The name of the function to check for. A namespace must be included if this isn't an XPath or XSL function.

For example: `function-available('boolean')` (returns `true`).

generate-id

Returns a unique identifier for the node in the supplied `node-set` which comes first in the XML document.

```
String generate-id([node-set])
```

Parameter	Data Type	Required	Description
node-set	Node-set	No	The node-set for the first node of which the ID will be generated. If omitted, the default is the context node.

system-property

Indicates the value of the specified `property`, which returns information about the XSLT implementation in use.

```
Variant system-property(property)
```

Parameter	Data Type	Required	Description
property	String	Yes	The name of the system property for which the value will be returned.

The system properties that can be checked are:

❑ `'msxsl:version'`. The version number of MSXML in use. This currently returns `2.6`.

❑ `'xsl:vendor'`. The name of the vendor of the XSLT implementation. For MSXML, this returns `"Microsoft"`.

❑ `'xsl:vendor-url'`. The URL of the vendor of the XSLT implementation. For MSXML, this returns `"http://www.microsoft.com"`.

❑ `'xsl:version'`. The version of XSLT implemented by the processor. This currently returns `1`.

XSLT

As we have seen, XSLT is a language for transforming XML into other XML documents. XSLT is designed for use within XSL, but can be used independently of XSL (as is the case with Microsoft's implementation).

An XSLT stylesheet is expressed as a well-formed XML document. The stylesheet may contains both elements that belong to the XSLT namespace, and elements which are defined in another namespace. XSLT is therefore essentially a definition of a set of elements that may be used within a document to describe a transformation.

XSLT Elements

To keep the syntax definition concise, the following symbols are used to define how often an element (or set of elements) may occur as children of another element:

- ❑ * an element or elements may occur zero or more times
- ❑ + an element or elements may occur one or more times
- ❑ ? an element must occur exactly once

The pipe (|) character is used to indicate that any one of a number of elements may occur in this position.

For example, the following is the syntax definition for `<xsl:apply-templates>`:

```
<xsl:apply-templates
    select = node-set-expression mode = modeName>
    <!-- Content: (xsl:sort | xsl:with-param)* -->
</xsl:apply-templates>
```

We will discuss shortly what this means in more detail, but it shows that the `<xsl:apply-templates>` element has two attributes, `select` and `mode`, and that the content within a `<xsl:apply-templates>` element can be any number of `<xsl:sort>` and/or `<xsl:with-param>` elements.

As mentioned, a stylesheet may contain both elements from the XSLT namespace and elements from another namespace. To indicate where non-XSLT elements are permitted the term *output_elements* is used.

xsl:apply-templates

Informs the processor to find the template to apply to the nodes selected. The processor looks for an `<xsl:template>` element whose `match` parameter specifies the same node as that being processed.

```
<xsl:apply-templates
    select = node-set-expression mode = modeName>
    <!-- Content: (xsl:sort | xsl:with-param)* -->
</xsl:apply-templates>
```

Attribute	Required	Description
select	No	An expression that specifies which child nodes to process. If a `select` attribute is not specified, all the children of the current node will be processed since the default value is `node()`.
mode	No	Indicates the mode specified for the execution of the templates. This mode must be a valid qualified name (consisting of a namespace prefix and a local name). A mode allows an element to be processed multiple times. If a template has a mode, it will only be used with an `<xsl:apply-templates>` element that has a `mode` attribute of the same value.

The following example processes all the `<list-item>` children of a `<list>` element:

```
<xsl:template match="list">
   <OL>
      <xsl:apply-templates select="list-item" />
   </OL>
</xsl:template>
```

xsl:attribute

Used to create an attribute and add it to the output stream.

```
<xsl:attribute
   name = attributeName
   namespace = uri-reference>
   <!-- Content: (#PCDATA | xsl:choose | xsl:copy | xsl:eval |
                  xsl:for-each | xsl:if | xsl:value-of)* -->
</xsl:attribute>
```

Attribute	Required	Description
name	Yes	Name of the attribute to create.
namespace	No	An XPath expression that evaluates to a Boolean. If the result is true, the content template is created and inserted into the output stream.

The content of the `<xsl:attribute>` element will be transformed into the value of the attribute which is created. For example, if we have the XML element:

```
<Cover>XmlIE5.png</Cover>
```

Then we can use the following XSL template:

```
<template match="Cover">
   <IMG>
      <xsl:attribute name="SRC">
         <xsl:value-of select="." />
      </xsl:attribute>
   </IMG>
</template>
```

This will transform the element into an HTML `<IMG>` element which will be displayed in the browser. The output would be:

```
<IMG SRC="XmlIE5.png"></IMG>
```

xsl:choose

This element is used to select one among a number of possible alternatives. It is used with a sequence of `<xsl:when>` elements followed by an optional `<xsl:otherwise>` element.

```
<xsl:choose>
    <!-- Content: (xsl:when+, xsl:otherwise?) -->
</xsl:choose>
```

In the following example, the amount attributes of each `<balance>` element will be displayed in a `<SPAN>` and colored red if negative, blue if positive, and black otherwise.

```
<xsl:template match="balanceSheet">

<xsl:for-each select="balance">
   <xsl:choose>
      <xsl:when test="@amount[. &lt; 0]">
         <SPAN>
            <xsl:attribute name="style">color:red</xsl:attribute>
            <xsl:value-of select="@amount" />
         </SPAN>
      </xsl:when>
      <xsl:when test="@amount[. > 0]">
         <SPAN>
            <xsl:attribute name="style">color:blue</xsl:attribute>
            <xsl:value-of select="@amount" />
         </SPAN>
      </xsl:when>
      <xsl:otherwise>
         <SPAN>
            <xsl:attribute name="style">color:black</xsl:attribute>
            <xsl:value-of select="@amount" />
         </SPAN>
      </xsl:otherwise>
   </xsl:choose>
</xsl:for-each>

</xsl:template>
```

Applied to an XML document like this:

```
<balanceSheet>
   <balance amount="1000" />
   <balance amount="0" />
   <balance amount="-500" />
</balanceSheet>
```

We get the following output:

```
<SPAN style="color:blue">1000</SPAN>
<SPAN style="color:black">0</SPAN>
<SPAN style="color:red">-500</SPAN>
```

xsl:comment

This element is used to generate a comment in the output stream.

```
<xsl:comment>
    <!-- Content: (#PCDATA | xsl:apply-templates | xsl:choose |
                   xsl:copy | xsl:eval | xsl:for-each | xsl:if |
                   xsl:value-of)* -->
</xsl:comment>
```

For example, the following XSL:

```
<xsl:comment>Start of table block.</xsl:comment>
```

Would create the comment:

```
<!-- Start of table block.-->
```

xsl:copy

This element is used to make a copy of the current node set. Attributes and children are not copied automatically. Use `<xsl:apply-templates>` within `<xsl:copy>` to process child nodes.

```
<xsl:copy>
    <!-- Content: (#PCDATA | xsl:apply-templates | xsl:attribute | xsl:choose
    | xsl:comment | xsl:copy | xsl:element | xsl:for-each | xsl:if |
    xsl:processing-instruction | xsl:value-of | output_elements)* -->
</xsl:copy>
```

The following example performs an identity transform on the entire document: each node in the source will be copied to the output to provide a logically equivalent tree. It is not a character-by-character copy, so, for instance, entities will be expanded and white space not marked as significant may be removed.

```
<xsl:template match="@*|node()">
   <xsl:copy>
      <xsl:apply-templates select="@*|node()" />
   </xsl:copy>
</xsl:template>
```

xsl:copy-of

Used to copy a node-set or a result tree fragment to the result tree according the evaluation of the select expression. The select expression may evaluate either to a node-set, in which case the entire node set will be copied, or to a result tree fragment, in which case that entire fragment will be copied to the result tree.

```
<xsl:copy-of
    select=node-set-expression />
```

Attribute	Required	Description
select	Yes	Expression that determines what will be copied.

In the following example, each `<product>` element with a `sku` attribute equal to `"X2000"` would be output to the result tree (including its entire contents):

```
<xsl:template match="/">
   <xsl:copy-of select="products/product[@sku='X2000']" />
</xsl:template>
```

xsl:element

Used to insert an element into the output stream.

```
<xsl:element
   name = elementName
   namespace = uri-reference
   <!-- Content: (#PCDATA | xsl:apply-templates | xsl:attribute  | xsl:choose
   | xsl:comment | xsl:copy | xsl:element | xsl:for-each | xsl:if
   | xsl:processing-instruction | xsl:value-of | output_elements)* -->
</xsl:element>
```

Attribute	Required	Description
name	Yes	The name of the element or an expression that evaluates to an element name.
namespace	No	The namespace of the element or an expression that evaluates to a namespace.

xsl:for-each

Used to apply a template repeatedly to a set of nodes. The `<xsl:for-each>` element determines which nodes will be iterated through. The XSLT elements within the loop are applied to each of the selected nodes.

```
<xsl:for-each
   select = node-set-expression>
   <!-- Content: (#PCDATA | xsl:apply-templates | xsl:attribute | xsl:choose
   | xsl:comment | xsl:copy | xsl:element | xsl:for-each | xsl:if |
   xsl:processing-instruction | xsl:sort | xsl:value-of | output_elements)* -->
</xsl:for-each>
```

Attribute	Required	Description
select	Yes	XPath query evaluated from the current context to determine the set of nodes to iterate over.

The following example formats a set of items into an alphabetically ordered list:

```
<xsl:template match="items">
   <xsl:for-each select="item">
      <xsl:sort select="." />
      <LI>
         <xsl:value-of select="." />
      </LI>
   </xsl:for-each>
</xsl:template>
```

xsl:if

Used to create template fragments based on a simple conditional expression. The other element used for conditional processing is <xsl:choose>, which allows us to perform multiple conditional tests.

```
<xsl:if
    test = boolean-expression>
    <!-- Content: (#PCDATA | xsl:apply-templates | xsl:attribute | xsl:choose
    | xsl:comment | xsl:copy | xsl:element | xsl:for-each | xsl:if
    | xsl:processing-instruction | xsl:value-of | output_elements)* -->
</xsl:if>
```

Attribute	Required	Description
test	Yes	An XPath expression that evaluates to a Boolean. If the result is true, the content template is created and inserted into the output stream.

The following example shows how to alternate the background colour of the rows in a table:

```
<xsl:template match="/">
    <TABLE WIDTH="500">
        <xsl:apply-templates select="//item" />
    </TABLE>
</xsl:template>

<xsl:template match="item">
    <TR>
        <xsl:if test="position() mod 2 = 0">
            <xsl:attribute name="bgcolor">lightgrey</xsl:attribute>
        </xsl:if>
        <xsl:value-of select="." />
    </TR>
</xsl:template>
```

If we apply this template to an XML document such as:

```
<items>
    <item>ASP 3.0 Programmer's Reference</item>
    <item>XML in IE5 Programmer's Reference</item>
    <item>Professional ASP 3.0</item>
    <item>Beginning ASP 3.0</item>
</items>
```

Then the outcome will be an XML table with alternate white and gray rows:

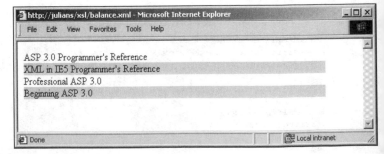

xsl:include

Used to include another XSLT stylesheet within an XSLT stylesheet. A stylesheet directly or indirectly including itself is considered an error. The resource located by the `href` attribute is parsed and inserted into the stylesheet, replacing the `<xsl:include>` element.

```
<xsl:include
    href = uri-reference />
```

Attribute	Required	Description
href	Yes	A URI specifying the resource representing the XSLT stylesheet to include.

xsl:otherwise

This element is used as the default case when performing conditional processing with `<xsl:choose>` and `<xsl:when>`.

```
<xsl:otherwise>
    <!-- Content: (#PCDATA | xsl:apply-templates | xsl:attribute | xsl:choose
    | xsl:comment | xsl:copy | xsl:element | xsl:for-each | xsl:if |
    xsl:processing-instruction | xsl:value-of | output_elements)* -->
</xsl:otherwise>
```

For an example, see `<xsl:choose>`.

xsl:output

Used to indicate how the result tree should be output. The `xsl:output` element is only allowed as a top-level element. Multiple `<xsl:output>` elements may be used. All `<xsl:output>` elements are merged into a single 'virtual' `<xsl:output>`. For conflicting attributes, the value used is that with the highest import precedence. If there is still a conflict, the attribute value used is that which is last specified in the stylesheet.

```
<xsl:output
    method = "xml"
    version = "1.0"
    encoding = string
    omit-xml-declaration = "yes" | "no"
    standalone = "yes" | "no"
    indent = "yes" | "no" />
```

Attribute	Required	Description
method	No	At the time of writing, `"xml"` is the only supported value. Future values will include `"html"` and `"text"`.
version	No	At the time of writing, `"1.0"` is the only supported value.

Attribute	Required	Description
encoding	No	The encoding of the output text. The value should either be a charset registered with the Internet Assigned Numbers Authority (IANA) or start with x- indicating it is experimental.
omit-xml-declaration	No	Specifies whether or not to omit an XML declaration before the output.
standalone	No	Specifies whether the XSLT processor should output a standalone document declaration.
indent	No	Specifies whether or not to indent the output tree.

xsl:param

Used to declare a parameter for use within an XSLT stylesheet.

```
<xsl:param
   name = parameterName
   select = expression>
   <!-- Content: template -->
</xsl:param>
```

Attribute	Required	Description
name	Yes	The name of the parameter to be used within parameter references. To reference the value of the parameter, use the $parameterName syntax.
select	No	The XPath expression that will be evaluated to give the default value of the parameter.

The values for parameters can be sent to the stylesheet via the XSL processor before the transformation takes place:

```
objProcessor.addParameter("myParam", "testval", "");
objXslProcessor.transform();
```

The following XSL code declares myParam and outputs its value to the transformed document:

```
<xsl:param name="myParam" />
<xsl:template match="/">
   <xsl:value-of select="$myParam" />
</xsl:template>
```

For a fuller example, see the section on 'Sending Parameters to a Stylesheet' towards the start of the chapter.

xsl:processing-instruction

Generates a processing instruction in the stylesheet.

```
<xsl:processing-instruction
   name = piName>
   <!-- Content: (#PCDATA | xsl:apply-templates | xsl:choose |
                  xsl:copy | xsl:for-each | xsl:if | xsl:value-of |
                  output_elements -->
</xsl:processing-instruction>
```

Attribute	Required	Description
name	Yes	The name of the processing instruction. The value of the attribute is interpreted as an attribute value template. The name used should be a processing instruction recognized by the XML Parser being used.

For example, the following element:

```
<xsl:processing-instruction name="xml-stylesheet">
   href="book.css" type="text/css"
</xsl:processing-instruction>
```

Would create the following processing instruction in the output:

```
<?xml-stylesheet href="book.css" type="text/css"?>
```

As in this example, we could use the <xsl:processing-instruction> element to link a stylesheet dynamically to an XML document. We could use this technique to format an XML document on the client after transforming it on the server, for browsers that support CSS formatting of XML, but not XSL.

xsl:sort

This element specifies the order that templates will be applied. Sorting is specified by adding <xsl:sort> elements as children of an <xsl:apply-templates> or <xsl:for-each> element. The first <xsl:sort> child specifies the primary sort key, the second <xsl:sort> child specifies the secondary sort key, and so on.

```
<xsl:sort
   select = string-expression
   order = "ascending" | "descending" />
```

Attribute	Required	Description
select	yes	An expression indicating the node on which the sort should be based.
order	No	Specifies whether the sort should be ascending or descending. The default is "ascending".

The following template will order a list of stores in ascending order, first by province and then by city:

```
<xsl:template match="stores">
   <xsl:apply-templates select="store">
      <xsl:sort select="province" />
      <xsl:sort select="city" />
   </xsl:apply-templates>
</xsl:template>
```

This template will then display the sorted list:

```
<xsl:template match="store">
   <xsl:value-of select="name" />,
   <xsl:value-of select="city" />,    <xsl:value-of select="province" /><BR />
</xsl:template>
```

xsl:stylesheet

The `<xsl:stylesheet>` element indicates that the XML document it contains is an XSL stylesheet. This element must be the outermost element of every XSL stylesheet. It can contain any number of `<xsl:template>` elements. An element occurring as a child of an `<xsl:stylesheet>` element is called a top-level element. It follows that this element cannot have a parent element.

```
<xsl:stylesheet
   version = number>
   <!-- Content: (xsl:template*) -->
</xsl:stylesheet>
```

Attribute	Required	Description
version	Yes	The version of XSLT that the stylesheet conforms to. Currently this value must be "1.0".

The `<xsl:stylesheet>` element requires the `xsl:` namespace to be declared, or it will generate an error. For the current version of XSLT, the XSL namespace is as shown below:

```
<xsl:stylesheet version="1.0"
                xmlns:xsl="http://www.w3.org/1999/XSL/Transform">
```

xsl:template

Used to specify a template rule. The template rule defines the type of nodes that will be output.

```
<xsl:template
   match = pattern
   priority = number
   mode = modeName>
   <!-- Content: (#PCDATA | xsl:apply-templates | xsl:attribute | xsl:choose
   | xsl:comment | xsl:copy | xsl:element | xsl:for-each | xsl:if
   | xsl:processing-instruction | xsl:value-of | output_elements)* -->
</xsl:template>
```

Attribute	Required	Description
match	Yes	The pattern that identifies the source node or nodes to which the template rule applies.
priority	No	The priority number for the template; this number is used to resolve conflicts when two templates match the same element.
mode	No	The mode for the template. A mode allows an element to be processed a number of times. If a template has a mode it will only be used with an xsl:apply-templates element that has a mode attribute of the same value.

In the following example, the template will match all <heading> elements and place a <B> element around them.

```
<xsl:template match="heading">
  <B>
     <xsl:apply-templates/>
  </B>
</xsl:template>
```

xsl:value-of

Used to insert the value of the selected node in the output stream.

```
<xsl:value-of
   select = string-expression
   disable-output-escaping = "yes" | "no" />
```

Attribute	Required	Description
select	Yes	An expression specifying the nodes to select. This expression is evaluated and the resulting object is converted to a string, as if by a call to the string() function.
disable-output-escaping	No	Specifies whether the text node output by the <xsl:value-of> element should have any escaping. The default value is "no".

In the following example, any elements that match <book> will have the value of their title and author attributes displayed:

```
<xsl:template match="book">
  <P>
     <xsl:value-of select="@title" />
     <BR />
     <xsl:value-of select="@author" />
  </P>
</xsl:template>
```

xsl:variable

Sets a variable for use within an XSLT stylesheet.

```
<xsl:variable
    name = variableName
    select = expression>
    <!-- Content: none -->
</xsl:variable>
```

Attribute	Required	Description
name	Yes	The name of the variable to be used within variable references.
select	No	The value of the variable. This can be an XPath expression that evaluates to the new value. To reference the value of the variable, use the $variableName syntax.

In the following example, when a `<footer>` element is encountered a link to /default.htm will be output:

```
<xsl:variable name="homePage">/default.htm</xsl:variable>

<xsl:template match="footer">
    <A>
        <xsl:attribute name="HREF">
            <xsl:value-of select="$homePage" />
        </xsl:attribute>
        Home Page
    </A>
</xsl:template>
```

xsl:when

Used in conjuction with `<xsl:choose>` and `<xsl:otherwise>` to specify one among a number of possible alternatives.

```
<xsl:when
    test = boolean-expression>
    <!-- Content: (#PCDATA | xsl:apply-templates | xsl:attribute | xsl:choose
| xsl:comment | xsl:copy | xsl:element | xsl:for-each | xsl:if
| xsl:processing-instruction | xsl:value-of | output_elements)* -->
</xsl:when>
```

Attribute	Required	Description
test	Yes	XPath expression evaluating to a Boolean. If this expression returns true, and the test pattern succeeds, the contents of xsl:when are placed in the output. If one of these tests fails, the next xsl:when is tested for evaluation or the xsl:otherwise element is evaluated.

See `<xsl:choose>` for an example of this element.

xsl:with-param

Used to pass parameters to templates. The parameter within the template is declared with `<xsl:param>`.

```
<xsl:with-param
   name = parameterName
   select = expression>
   <!-- Content: none -->
</xsl:with-param>
```

Attribute	Required	Description
name	Yes	The name of the parameter to be used within parameter references. To reference the value of the parameter, use the $parameterName syntax.
select	No	An XPath expression that evaluates to the value of the parameter.

msxsl:script

Defines functions for script extensions. Note that this tag is a Microsoft extension to XSLT and therefore has a different namespace to the standard W3C XSLT elements: `xmlns:msxsl="urn:schemas-microsoft-com:xslt"`.

```
<msxsl:script
   language = language-name
   implements-prefix = namespace-prefix>
   <!-- Content: #PCDATA -->
</ msxsl:script>
```

Attribute	Required	Description
language	No	Active Scripting language used for the functions defined within this element. If left unspecified, the current scripting language is used, as specified by a language attribute on an ancestor.
implements -prefix	No	The user-defined namespace associated with the `<msxsl:script>` block. One or more blocks can be associated with a single namespace.

The following example shows how script can be used within an XSLT document, including the use of a COM component:

```
<xsl:stylesheet version="1.0"
                xmlns:xsl="http://www.w3.org/1999/XSL/Transform"
                xmlns:msxsl="urn:schemas-microsoft-com:xslt"
                xmlns:myNS="urn:my-script-blocks">
   <msxsl:script language="VBScript" implements-prefix="myNS">
      Function CalcTax(amount)
         Set objTax = CreateObject("taxComponent")
         CalcTax = objTax.CalcTax(amount)
      End Function
   </msxsl:script>
<xsl:template match="/products/product">
   <TD>
```

```
<xsl:value-of select="@description"/>
    </TD>
    <TD>
        <xsl:value-of select="myNS:CalcTax(number(@price))"/>
    </TD>
  </xsl:template>
</xsl:stylesheet>
```

XSL to XSLT Converter 1.0

The Microsoft XML Technology Preview Parser maintains backward compatibility with Internet Explorer 5, meaning that it will process XSL stylesheets that conform to the December 1998 W3C Working Draft. However, these stylesheets are not compliant with the final W3C XSLT and XML Recommendations. It is recommended that you convert your stylesheets so that they adhere to the XSLT and XPath Recommendations.

To help you perform this task, Microsoft has provided a tool to perform this conversion for you. It will perform the following changes:

❑ Changes XSL and related namespaces

❑ Adds required attributes and previously defaulted attribute values

❑ Converts nested templates to modes

❑ Converts <xsl:eval> and <xsl:script> blocks to an XSLT-conformant extension mechanism

❑ Adds JScript implementations of XTLRuntime functions where necessary

❑ Converts XSL Pattern syntax to XPath

Microsoft makes the following statement about the converted stylesheet:

"The resulting style sheet will conform to the subset of the XSLT and XPath recommendations implemented in the Microsoft XML Technology Preview Parser but might also contain <msxsl:script> elements that will not be processed by XSLT processors from other vendors. Vendor-specific implementations of extension functions will need to be added for full interoperability."

Another point about the conversion tool is that most of it is embedded in an XSL stylesheet. Since both a December 1998 XSL stylesheet and an XSLT stylesheet are XML documents, the most efficient way to transform one to the other is through the use of a stylesheet.

XSL ISAPI Extension 1.1

A big advantage of using XML and XSL is the ability to separate data from styling information. This makes it easy to render the same information in many different ways. However, browser support for XSL is not yet widespread or consistent. In addition, there may be some cases where you don't want the entire XML document sent to the client for security reasons. The solution to these problems is to apply the stylesheet to the XML document on the web server and send the result to the client. This is the purpose of the Microsoft XSL ISAPI extension available from
http://msdn.microsoft.com/downloads/webtechnology/xml/xslisapi.asp

The XSL ISAPI Extension provides the following features:

- Automatic application of XSL stylesheets to XML documents on the web server
- Selection of stylesheets based on browser type
- Caching of stylesheets to improve performance
- Ability to specify output encodings
- Customizable error messages

Together, these features create a way to build a web site that automatically adapts rendering information based on the client.

The XSL ISAPI Extension is written in C++ and the source code is available.

The XSL ISAPI Extension is easy to install. A pre-compiled version is included with the download, so you don't have to have a C++ compiler. Once intalled and compiled any XML document requested on the web site will go through the XSL ISAPI extension. The first operation performed is to look for a stylesheet processing instruction within the document such as the following:

```
<?xml-stylesheet type="text/xsl" href="myStyle.xsl"?>
```

If the processing instruction is not found or the type is not `text/xsl`, the XML document is passed to the client without any processing.

Configuration

You may want to change the default handling of XML documents. For instance, XML is passed directly to clients reporting `MSIE 5` (Microsoft Internet Explorer 5). You may want to change this behavior if portions of the XML document should not be available on the client.

Configuration is performed through a file named `config.xml` placed in the same directory as `xslisapi.dll`. Configuration files are optional and are automatically reloaded into the XSL ISAPI extension if they are modified.

A sample configuration file looks like the following:

```
<config>
    <client name="MSIE 5.0; Windows NT 5.0" href=" href" />
    <cache cleanup="3600" />
    <output encoding="utf-16" />
</config>
```

The following section describes the elements that can be used within this configuration file.

XSLT & XPath

<client>

Used to associate a user agent string with a resource name representing the stylesheet to use.

Attribute	Description
name	A user agent string indicating the browser type.
href	The name of an attribute added to the stylesheet processing instruction, whose value indicates which stylesheet to use.

For example, the following code in the config file:

```
<client name="MSIE 5.0; Windows NT 5.0" href="ie5-href"/>
```

And the following code in the stylesheet processing instruction:

```
<?xml-stylesheet type="text/xsl"
                 href="otherBrowsers.xsl"
                 ie5-href="ie5.xsl"?>
```

Would have IE5 browsers use the ie5.xsl stylesheet and all other browsers use otherBrowsers.xsl.

<cache>

Used to determine how long an XSL document will be held in memory before being deleted. The default value is one hour.

Attribute	Description
cleanup	Number of minutes a document is held in the cache.

For example, the following code would cause an XSL document to be cached for 3 hours before removing it from memory:

```
<cache cleanup="180"/>
```

<output>

Used to determine the output encoding from the server XSL processing.

Attribute	Description
encoding	Type of encoding. Supported values are "ucs-2", "utf-16", "utf-8", and "windows-nnnn", where nnnn is an installed Windows codepage.

For example, the following code sets the encoding type to "ucs-2".

```
<output encoding="ucs-2"/>
```

Error Handling

The XSL ISAPI extension has the flexibility of allowing you to provide your own error messages. Possible errors include not finding a specified XSL stylesheet or being giving an invalid XML document.

Errors generated by the XSL ISAPI extension are output as an XML file. You then have the opportunity to process the error XML document by applying a XSL stylesheet. The XSL document to handle errors must be called `errors.xsl` and be placed in the same directory as the XSL ISAPI extension.

The following is a sample file provided with the XSL ISAPI extension to illustrate an instance of XML document representing an error:

```
<?xml version="1.0"?>
<!-- This is a sample file for testing your errors.xsl stylesheet -->
<?xml-stylesheet href="errors.xsl" type="text/xsl"?>
<error>
    <status-code>404</status-code>
    <url>foobar.xml</url>
    <info>Some more information goes here...</info>
</error>
```

The stylesheet would then be applied to this document to create the rendering that the end user would see on the client.

Resources

The following URLs provide further information on XSLT stylesheets. They cover both the W3C specification, as well as Microsoft's implementation of it, and the additional tools available from Microsoft.

- XSLT W3C Recommendation: `http://www.w3c.org/tr/XSLT`
- XPath W3C Recommendation: `http://www.w3c.org/tr/XPath`
- XSL W3C Working Draft: `http://www.w3c.org/xsl`
- Associating Stylesheets with XML documents: `http://www.w3.org/TR/xml-stylesheet/`
- Microsoft XML Parser Preview: `http://msdn.microsoft.com/downloads/webtechnology/xml/msxml.asp`
- XSL to XSLT Converter 1.0: `http://msdn.microsoft.com/downloads/webtechnology/xml/xsltconv.asp`
- Microsoft ISAPI Extension 1.1: `http://msdn.microsoft.com/downloads/webtechnology/xml/xslisapi.asp`
- Active Bug List for XML Parser Preview: `http://msdn.microsoft.com/workshop/xml/general/msxml_buglist.asp`

XSLT & XPath

Summary

XSLT is a very powerful technology for transforming an XML document into a completely new XML or HTML document, so we've had to cover a lot of ground in this chapter. We looked at:

❑ Writing an XSLT stylesheet.

❑ Transforming an XML document on the client and on the server.

❑ Passing parameters to an XSLT stylesheet from ASP.

❑ The XPath selection language used within XSLT to specify a node-set.

❑ The XSLT elements used to transform an XML document.

❑ A quick glimpse at two handy utilities provided by Microsoft for use with XSLT stylesheets.

In the next chapter, we will go on to look at working with Directory Services and using the ADSI interfaces from ASP.

37

ADSI

In this chapter we consider the Active Directory Services Interfaces (ADSI), which is an API developed by Microsoft to enable us to read data from any directory that supports the ADSI COM components.

In Section IV of this book we considered how ADO (ActiveX Data Objects) enables us to access information from data sources through our ASP pages. ADO is designed as a very general-purpose set of components that allow us to connect to a wide variety of data sources, notably including relational databases such as SQL server. However, the very general-purpose nature of ADO can mean that it is less than optimal for some specialized data sources. One such category is directories. Although ADO provides limited access to some directories, if you want your ASP pages to be able to read and modify data in directories, you will need to use ADSI.

Directory Concepts and Active Directory

Directories have many of the characteristics of databases, but since they are used primarily to look up data, they are optimized for read access. Thay are also normally structured in a hierarchical, tree-like manner, in much the same way as the folders and files in a file system.

There are a large number of directories which are accessible using ADSI, including:

❑ **Active Directory** – This is the directory of domain resources in Windows 2000. It is at the heart of Windows 2000 and includes network resources such as computers, printers, security information etc.

❑ The **IIS Metabase** – This is the set of IIS settings.

❑ The **WinNT namespace** (formerly known as the CIM repository) – This is not strictly a directory; but is, roughly speaking, a set of information about the domains on your local network, together with some information concerning items such as services, print queues and user accounts on the machines within those domains. ADSI presents this information in a way that makes it appear to be a single directory on domains controlled by NT4 and Windows 2000 domain controllers.

❑ The **Novell Netware directories** – These do a similar job to Active Directory for Novell networks.

❑ Any other directory that is compliant with the **LDAP** (Lightweight Directory Access Protocol) standard. LDAP is an industry-wide standard governing access to directories. Directories that meet this standard include Active Directory, the Exchange Directory, the Site Server Membership Directory, Netscape Directory Server, and the OpenLDAP Directory Server.

This chapter concentrates for the most part on ADSI rather than on any specific directory. Most of our examples use the Microsoft's Active Directory, however the programming techniques we demonstrate should, in the main, be applicable to other directories.

> For a more detailed introduction to ADSI see Professional ADSI Programming, also published by Wrox Press.

The easiest way to find out about the information available in Active Directory is to use the `adsvw.exe` tool that is available from Microsoft as part of the ADSI SDK. This can be downloaded from `http://www.microsoft.com/adsi`. Although `adsvw.exe` is also known as the Active Directory Browser, it can also be used to examine any other directory that is accessible using ADSI.

The following screenshot shows `adsvw.exe` being used to look at an installation of Active Directory. (Note that when we first run `adsvw.exe` we are presented with a dialog asking effectively if we want to look at an object or do a search (query). We select **Object Viewer** to obtain the screenshot as shown here).

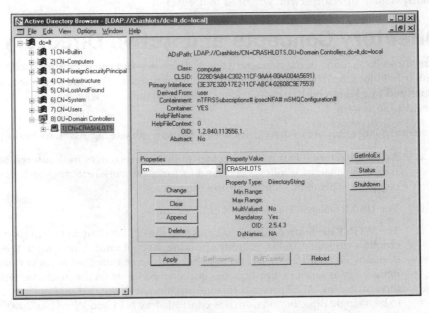

> Note that although you will always be able to run `adsvw.exe`, you will only be able to use it to look at Active Directory if you have Active Directory installed! You will have Active Directory if your domain controller is running Windows 2000. Otherwise, you should use the ADSI WinNT namespace to look at the structure of your domain.

Our domain in question is a small domain, `LT.local`, which has one domain controller, a machine called `CRASHLOTS`. Usually the name of the domain in Windows 2000 would correspond to your registered internet domain name, however this particular domain is not connected to the Internet, and hence has a name ending in `.local`, rather than, say, `.com`. The name `LT` is simply the name chosen for the domain.

> `LT.local` is a way of writing the domain name which corresponds to the usual format for internet domain names. Active Directory, however, prefers using a format for names that is based on the style favoured by the LDAP protocol. Accordingly the domain name `LT.local` becomes `DC=LT, DC=local`. where `DC` stands for domain component. Note that the name is not case-sensitive: It could equally well be written `dc=lt,dc=local`.

The screenshot shows the tree-like structure of Active Directory in the left hand pane. The topmost node is named `dc=lt`, and corresponds to the name. The `dc=lt` node contains seven child nodes which contain information about different types of objects in the domain. Here we've opened up the **Domain Controllers** node, and selected the object inside this node that corresponds to the domain controller machine, `CRASHLOTS`. The right hand pane of the `adsvw.exe` user interface shows information about the selected object and features various controls allowing the user to modify the attributes of the object.

The name of the object as far as ADSI is concerned is known as the **ADsPath** and is displayed near the top of the right-hand pane. The ADsPath plays a similar role to the full file system path in the Windows file system: by concatenating various components, it provides a unique name which may be used to identify the object to the ADSI runtime. The ADsPath plays a crucial role in ADSI since it is the name that must be supplied when instantiating an ADSI COM component corresponding to the required directory object.

For the case of Active Directory, the ADsPath consists of three parts:

❑ The prefix, `LDAP://`, indicates the ADSI **Namespace** that our directory resides in. In the case of Active Directory, the prefix is `LDAP://` because Active Directory is LDAP-compliant.

❑ The part of the ADsPath following the prefix depends on the particular `Namespace` object. For the case of the LDAP ADsPath shown, the next component is the name of the server against which requests are made – the domain controller, `CRASHLOTS`, followed by another forward slash. This part of the ADsPath for Active Directory is optional.

ADSI

❑   The final part of the ADsPath identifies the object we are interested in. It is formed by working up the directory tree from the object in question, at each stage concatenating the name of the next object in the tree. Note that this means the name of the object at the top of the directory tree comes last.

For the domain controller in our screenshot, the ADsPath is:

```
LDAP://Crashlots/CN=CRASHLOTS,OU=Domain Controllers,dc=lt,dc=local
```

(Compare this with the directory hierarchy shown in the left hand pane of the adsvw.exe screenshot. OU stands for Organizational Unit.)

Other directories have different formats for constructing ADsPaths. For example, ADsPaths in WinNT have the prefix WinNT:// followed by the names of the objects going *down* the tree (rather than up it), and they are separated by forward slashes, resulting in names like WinNT://CRASHLOTS/Administrator for the administrator user account. The IIS Metabase has a similar format, except that the initial WinNT:// is replaced by IIS://. For example, in the IIS provider, the web sites hosted are consecutively numbered 1, 2, 3 etc., and all appear under the container W3SVC, so on my network the ADsPath of the object representing my default (first) web site is IIS://Crashlots/W3SVC/1.

In all cases, the prefix is case-sensitive, but the rest of the ADsPath is not.

Data Stored in Active Directory

The data that is stored by default in Active Directory can best be understood by considering the top-level nodes in the earlier adsvw.exe screenshot. These are as follows:

Node Name	Description
BuiltIn	The domain groups
Computers	The registered computer accounts for machines that are not domain controllers
ForeignSecurity Principals	The security principals from external sources
Infrastructure	The various system settings
LostAndFound	Objects that are orphaned get placed here. (This might happen, for example, if an new object is created on one server's copy of AD at the same time as its parent is being deleted on another server)
System	The other system settings
Users	The domain user accounts
DomainControllers	The computer accounts for the domain controllers.

It should be noted, however, that this is the default information stored in Active Directory, and which is used by the Windows 2000 operating system. Active Directory is extensible, and provided you have suitable access rights, you can add any other information you wish, which you consider might be usefully stored there.

Browsing and Searching

When dealing with directories, it is important to understand the difference between browsing and searching. **Browsing** is what we were doing in our earlier adsvw.exe screenshot. It means systematically moving around the directory to see what objects are placed at certain locations. **Searching** is what we do when we want to find objects with certain characteristic properties but we don't know whereabouts in the directory hierarchy such objects might be located. For example, we might want to find all users who are not administrators, or all computers with names beginning with P. When we want this kind of information we will make a search request against the directory. Search requests are not supported by all ADSI directories; for example, while Active Directory and all LDAP-compliant directories support searching, WinNT and IIS do not.

The ADSI interfaces are designed to support browsing. Searching is actually done using the same ADO objects that we have been using throughout this book, and we'll cover that topic separately in the next section.

Searching Directories

The ADSI interfaces are designed to efficiently support browsing through our directories. There's no need for separate interfaces to support searching, since this can be done using ADO, via an OLE DB ADSI provider that Microsoft provide.

The OLE DB ADSI provider is an OLE DB provider which is able to make search requests against directories using ADSI. We need to use this provider to carry out searches from ASP pages. This means using an ADO Command object, as described in Chapter 26.

> Note that the current OLE DB ADSI provider can only be used for search requests. It cannot be used to modify the directory.

The following code shows a typical search request. This retrieves all user accounts in my Active Directory installation.

```
<%@ LANGUAGE="VBScript" %>
<HTML>
<HEAD>
<TITLE> ASP ProgRef Samples </TITLE>
</HEAD>
<BODY>
<H1> Searching with ADSI and ADO </H1>

<%
On Error Resume Next
```

ADSI

```
Dim objConnection, objCommand

Set objConnection = Server.CreateObject("ADODB.Connection")
Set objCommand = Server.CreateObject("ADODB.Command")

objConnection.Provider = "ADsDSOObject"
objConnection.Open "Active Directory Provider"
Set objCommand.ActiveConnection = objConnection
Response.Write "<P><P><P>"

Dim strCommand
strCommand = "<LDAP://CRASHLOTS/DC=LT,DC=local>;" & _
             "(objectCategory=Person);sAMAccountName,ADsPath;subtree"
objCommand.CommandText = strCommand

Response.Write "<P>This page displays the results from the " & _
               "following search request:" & _
               objCommand.CommandText & "<P>"

Dim objRecordset
Set objRecordset = objCommand.Execute(strCommand)

While Not objRecordset.EOF
   For Each objField In objRecordset.Fields
      Response.Write objField.Value & "<BR>"
   Next
   objRecordset.MoveNext
   Response.Write "<BR>"
Wend
%>

</BODY>
</HTML>
```

The JScript equivalent of this code is:

```
<%@ LANGUAGE="JScript" %>
<HTML>
<HEAD>
<TITLE> ASP ProgRef Samples </TITLE>
</HEAD>
<BODY>
<H1> Searching with ADSI and ADO </H1>

<%
objConnection = Server.CreateObject("ADODB.Connection");
objCommand = Server.CreateObject("ADODB.Command");

objConnection.Provider = "ADsDSOObject";
objConnection.Open("Active Directory Provider");
objCommand.ActiveConnection = objConnection;
Response.Write("<P><P><P>");

strCommand = "<LDAP://CRASHLOTS/DC=LT,DC=local>;" +
             "(objectCategory=Person);sAMAccountName," +
             "ADsPath;subtree";
objCommand.CommandText = strCommand;
```

```
Response.Write("<P>This page displays the results from the " +
               "following search request:" +
               objCommand.CommandText + "<P>");

objRecordset = objCommand.Execute(strCommand);

while (!objRecordset.EOF) {
   var enumFields = new Enumerator(objRecordset.Fields);
   for (;!enumFields.atEnd();enumFields.moveNext()) {
      var objFieldsItem = enumFields.item();
      Response.Write(objFieldsItem.Value + "<BR>")
   }
   objRecordset.MoveNext();
Response.Write("<BR>");
}
%>

</BODY>
</HTML>
```

This code shouldn't require much explanation since it simply runs through the standard ADO procedure for setting up `Connection` and `Command` objects and using them to execute a command. The results of the command get returned as a recordset, which is displayed in the standard way. The only points to note are that the required connection and provider strings, `ADsDSOObject` and Active Directory Provider, and the strange syntax of the command string.

We'll look at the command string next, but first check out the output produced by the script, which looks like this.

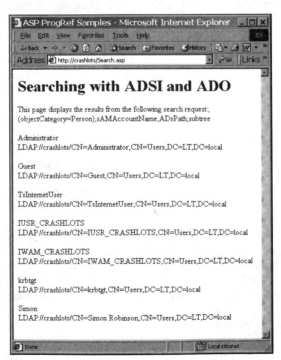

ADSI

Note from this output that each object returned constitutes one record, and the fields correspond to the attributes returned.

The Command String

Let's have a closer look at the command string we've passed to the OLE DB ADSI provider. This looks like:

```
<LDAP://CRASHLOTS/DC=LT,DC=local>;(objectCategory=Person);sAMAccountName,
ADsPath;subtree
```

This string tells the provider what we are searching for and also gives it some idea of where the objects we want might be found. It contains four pieces of information, separated by semicolons. We consider each of these bits of information below, namely the search base, the search filter, the properties and the scope of the search.

The **Search Base** is the first part of the string:

```
<LDAP://CRASHLOTS/DC=LT,DC=local>
```

This consists of the ADsPath of the point in the directory at which the search should start, enclosed in angled brackets. The lower down the directory we place the search base, the more efficient our search is. If we have no idea where in the directory the objects we're looking for are, we should use the root of the directory as our search base, as in this example.

The **Search Filter** tells the directory what we're looking for. In our case we have specified a search filter of:

```
(objectCategory=Person)
```

This indicates that we wish to find all users. The search filter follows a precise syntax, which is laid down by the LDAP standards. The rules for this syntax are complex and beyond the scope of this book, but full details may be found in **Request for Comments (RFC) 2254**, found at `http://www.ietf.org/rfc/`.

Essentially the search filter contains a series of conditions of the form (attribute=value) that specify the values of certain attributes. In our case, the filter `(objectCategory=Person)` works because all user accounts in Active Directory have an attribute called `objectCategory` which by default has the value `Person` only for user accounts.

Each condition must be surrounded by round brackets, and the conditions may be joined by the logical operators AND (&), OR (|) and NOT (!). Note that these operators precede the conditions they join rather that comig between them as you might intuitively expect. Wildcards may be used in the property values. For example, to find all users whose names begin with A, we would use the search filter:

```
(&(objectCategory=Person)(sAMAccountName=A*))
```

The **Properties** consist of a comma-separated list of the properties of the objects returned, that we are interested in. If you want all properties returned you should set this part of the command string to *. In our case, we have requested the username and the ADsPath. Have a look at the screenshot to see that this is exactly what was retrieved.

The **Scope** is the final part of the command string. It indicates how much of the directory you want to search in for the objects and is one of three strings: base, onelevel or subtree.

If the scope is set to base then only the object specified as the Search Base will be examined. If this satisfies the search filter then its details will be returned, otherwise no results are returned. This might seem pointless, however the option exists because LDAP distinguishes returning the properties of an object from searching: setting the search filter to base and executing a search is the standard way of retrieving the properties of an object with the LDAP protocol.

If the scope is set to onelevel then only the immediate children of the base object (not including the base object itself) will be examined. This provides an alternative to the IADsContainer interface for enumerating the children of a container.

If the scope is set to subtree then every object below the search base in the directory hierarchy (including the search base too) will be examined. This is the normal option for searching for objects in a directory.

Before leaving the subject of command strings, we note that the OLE DB ADSI provider does support an alternative, SQL-based, format for the command string, in which the different portions of the string (the filter, properties, etc.) are linked together in an SQL-like manner rather than separated by semi-colons. This format is slightly more readable, at the expense of leading to longer command strings. The equivalent of the above command in SQL command syntax is:

```
SELECT sAMAccountName,ADsPath FROM 'LDAP://CRASHLOTS/DC=LT,DC=local' WHERE
objectCategory='Person'
```

Full details of this alternative syntax are available in MSDN, under the Platform SDK/Networking and Directory Services/ADSI section.

The ADSI Object Model

The ADSI object model is based on providers, in a similar way to the object model in ADO. An ADSI provider is the set of COM objects that allow a client to talk to a particular directory using ADSI, as shown in the diagram.

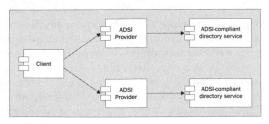

ADSI

Because of this similarity, we will explain the ADSI object model by comparing it to ADO. It should be noted, however, that there are significant differences between ADSI and ADO specifically in how the objects within a provider are implemented, and in the method of binding to an object. These differences will be explained.

Comparison of ADSI and ADO

ADO and its underlying technology, OLE DB, are based on the concept of a provider, which is a set of components that allow interaction with a particular data source, such as a database. However, when writing ADO clients we do not generally directly instantiate any components within a provider. Rather, we instantiate a Connection or Command object – a generic object which is able to connect to whichever provider we require. We pass a command string to this object, which identifies the provider we will be using, and then rely on the Command or Connection object to talk to the appropriate provider on our behalf. For example, we might typically write:

```
Dim objConnection
Set objConnection = Server.CreateObject("ADODB.Connection")
objConnection.Provider = "SQLOLEDB"
```

This code instantiates a Connection object. This object can, in principle, connect to any provider, but we indicate that we want to use a SQLOLEDB provider (to get to a SQL Server database) by setting its Provider property.

A consequence of this is that we only need to know a small number of ADO objects (the Command, Connection, Recordset, Record and Stream objects) to communicate with any data source supported by OLE DB.

ADSI is also COM-based, and to use it, we also instantiate components and call the methods of those components. However, in ADSI, there is no real equivalent of the ADO Command or Connection objects. Instead, the object model is based on the concept that each time we access a different item in a directory, we instantiate a separate COM object which acts as a proxy for that directory object, and communicates with the directory object on our behalf. As far as the client is concerned, it is talking directly to the directory, the proxy is invisible to it.

A consequence of this is that, whereas in ADO there is only one type of Command object, which can direct commands to any data source, in ADSI we must directly instantiate a COM object corresponding to the directory object we are interested in. If we then wish to access a different directory object, we must instantiate a different COM object to do so.

Of course, since ADSI can in principle be used to access *any* directory, as long as a suitable provider has been written, and since many directories can contain a huge number of different types of directory objects, the result is that there is a huge number of different types of ADSI COM components that we might need to instantiate. In addition, it is not possible to list the types of object as we did for ADO, since that information is not documented for the Microsoft providers. In any case, anyone writing a new ADSI provider would define new types of ADSI objects.

In fact, in ADSI you are not expected to know the type of object that you want to instantiate. In order to instantiate an ADSI object, you need to supply the name of the directory object you are interested in, in other words the ADsPath (Active Directories Path) of the object in question. This will automatically cause an object that acts as a proxy for the appropriate directory object to be instantiated, without you needing to know what type of object this actually is. We also do not use the Server.CreateObject method to instantiate any objects, but rather we use the function GetObject. The difference between CreateObject and GetObject is that CreateObject takes the name of the *type* of object, the ProgID, while GetObject takes as a parameter the name of the object, which for ADSI means the ADsPath.

For example, to instantiate the object in ASP, corresponding to the domain controller CRASHLOTS in the Active Directory install using the LDAP provider, we could use:

```
' VBScript
Dim objDC
Set objDC = GetObject("LDAP://CRASHLOTS/CN=CRASHLOTS,
                       OU=Domain Controllers,DC=LT,DC=local")
```

```
// JScript
var objDC = GetObject("LDAP://CRASHLOTS/CN=CRASHLOTS,
                       OU=Domain Controllers,DC=LT,DC=local");
```

Alternatively using the WinNT namespace to access the domain controller, looks like:

```
' VBScript
Dim objDC
Set objDC = GetObject("WinNT://CRASHLOTS")
```

```
// JScript
var objDC = GetObject("WinNT://CRASHLOTS");
```

Don't be fooled by the huge string passed to GetObject() for the LDAP provider – that's just because the ADsPath of this particular object happens to be quite long. The underlying method used to instantiate the object is very simple, just call GetObject() with the appropriate ADsPath.

To reiterate, in ADO it is sufficient to use Server.CreateObject because the type of object provides sufficient information for you to instantiate the object. For example, there is only one type of Connection object and you can use it to bind to any ADO provider. However, in ADSI there is no equivalent to the Connection object. We need to give the ASP interpreter sufficient information to locate the directory object we are interested in and so we use GetObject to bind directly to an object that is part of the required provider and which represents the item in the directory we want to examine.

Introducing Interfaces

As we've indicated there are many different types of objects in ADSI. This causes a problem, as we do not know which methods, properties and collections each ADSI object implements. This problem does not exist for ADO or the intrinsic ASP objects, the small number of objects means we can list the methods etc. implemented by each object – clearly we cannot do this with ADSI.

ADSI

817

This is where interfaces come in. An interface is a group of properties, methods and events that an object exposes. If certain methods or properties or collections serve a similar purpose, they will be grouped together into the same interface. The class or component then provides an implementation of those methods, properties and events. Take, for example, the Response object: we know that it implements several methods and properties, including the Write method. The Write method is defined in an interface called IResponse, and the Response object implements the IResponse interface. A COM component may implement any number of interfaces to support the various functions it performs or to allow different services such as transaction support and messaging.

Any client of that object can then find out the methods and properties of that object by requesting the interface (or interfaces) for that object. The client does not need to know how the interface is implemented to use the object. One reason why this approach comes in is for applications that may run on several different platforms. The core application would be identical while platform-specific information could be encapsulated within components.

> **The difference between interfaces and objects is also discussed in Chapter 38, CDO for Windows 2000.**

In fact, for scripting languages it's somewhat more complex than we've just explained. Due to restrictions in their design, scripting languages are unable to talk to most interfaces directly. To solve this problem, all components that can be used by scripting languages expose a second interface called IDispatch. This interface contains methods that indirectly call methods on the interfaces an object implements, but as far as we are concerned, this is an implementation detail of ASP that we don't need to be concerned about.

This use of interfaces is completely transparent to scripting languages – there is normally no need for an ASP programmer to be aware even of their existence, because the scripting interpreter deals with these details on your behalf. The reason for mentioning interfaces here is this: although there are many different types of ADSI objects, they generally all expose the same interfaces. This makes it easy for us to know which methods, properties and collections are likely to be available on an ADSI object, we simply need to know the standard ADSI interfaces.

For example, all ADSI objects that you would bind to using GetObject, without exception, expose an interface called IADs that allows us to get and set the attributes of the directory object. If the ADSI object corresponds to a directory object that can contain other objects (or in other words, it is a container, not a leaf, in the directory hierarchy), the ADSI object will also implement an interface called IADsContainer, which exposes methods to navigate down the tree. There are a number of other interfaces that are implemented by certain types of object, but those are the main interfaces, and accordingly are the ones that we will explore in this chapter.

ADSI Schema Management

ADSI is designed to interface with a wide variety of namespaces (i.e. a variety of the different directories). Though many of the objects in these namespaces are similar, there are characteristics of these namespaces that may vary widely. A provider may include an object that is not among the predefined objects of ADSI. The **Active Directory Interfaces Schema Management** provides the extensibilty of directory service. These objects enable the client to browse the definitions of defined objects and extend the definition of objects.

The ADSI Schema Management object model consists of:

❑ The **Schema container** object, which contains the schema objects.

❑ The **Class** object (also called the schema object or the class schema object), which provides information about objects of a particular type in the directory.

❑ The **Property** object, which is one of the pieces of information that is attached to an object.

❑ The **Syntax** object, which identifies the data type to the computer.

Graphically the hierarchy looks like this:

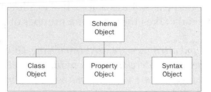

As we can see, the schema container is a tree that contains class, property and syntax definitions. New classes and properties can be added to extend the schema if necessary, making our ADSI development efforts more future-proof.

The ADSI Interface Reference

ADSI exposes a large number of interfaces. In this section we look in detail at just a few of them, which between them provide most of the generic directory operations you will want to carry out.

The interfaces we cover here are:

❑ The **IADs interface** – This is interface is exposed by all **directory objects**. It allows access to all the data describing the object and enables us to retrieve information needed to manipulate objects, such as the name and class of the object. The IADs interface also provides access to the properties and methods that manage the object's data in the **property cache**, which is a local copy of the attributes in the underlying directory object.

❑ The **IADsContainer interface** – Along with IADs interface, the IADsContainer interface is used by most directory objects. It is implemented by **container objects** i.e. objects that can contain other objects. It exposes methods and properties for managing object creation, moving, copying, binding child objects to a given object, or creating or deleting child objects.

ADSI

819

- ❏ The **IADsOpenDSObject interface** – This is exposed only by **namespace objects**, the objects at the top of each directory hierarchy with ADsPaths such as `IIS:`, `LDAP:`, and `WinNT:`. The IADsOpenDSObject interface enables us to supply authentication credentials to that namespace, which can then be automatically used when binding to objects in that directory.

- ❏ The **IADsClass interface** – This is implemented by **class schema objects**, the objects that describe a class of object, and which you can locate by using the `Schema` property of the `IADs` interface.

- ❏ The **IADsProperty interface** – This is implemented by **property objects**, the objects that describe individual properties. The `IADsProperty` interface exposes properties which determine information such as whether the property is multi-valued and what syntax is used to store the values.

- ❏ The **IADsSyntax interface** – This is implemented by **Syntax objects**, which describe particular syntaxes.

The IADs Interface

IADs is an interface that is exposed by all directory objects. Its purpose is to enable retrieval of certain standard information that is essential in order to manipulate objects, such as the name and class of the object. It also allows access to all the data that describes the object. This data takes the form of a number of **properties** or **attributes**.

The terms properties and attributes are used interchangeably – and we will follow that practice by using either term interchangeably in this chapter. It should however be noted that directory object properties are not the same as the automation properties that we are used to accessing on COM components. Directory object properties are the pieces of information that make up an item in a directory. Automation properties are similar but are the properties exposed specifically by COM components.

Methods	Properties
Get	AdsPath
GetEx	Class
GetInfo	GUID
GetInfoEx	Name
Put	Parent
PutEx	Schema
SetInfo	

The Property Cache

The property cache is a concept that needs to be explained before we actually list the properties and methods of the IADs interface. We said earlier that the COM component we instantiate acts as a proxy for the actual directory object, in most regards this means that as far as the ADSI client is concerned this component is indistinguishable from the directory object. However, there is one exception to this rule: the COM component carries a local copy of the attributes in the underlying directory object known as the property cache. Doing things this way enhances performance since the component is an in-process component, so communication with it is very fast. The underlying directory object may reside on another machine on the network or the Internet, so there is a clear need to minimize the number of network calls to it. Maintaining a local property cache means that network calls are only needed occasionally to copy the cache to the underlying directory object and vice versa when the client wishes, and specific IADs methods are available to do this.

IADs Methods

Get Method

The Get method returns the value of a named property. If the property concerned has more than one value, then the Get method returns an array containing the values.

```
Variant = Object.Get(PropertyName)
```

Parameter	Data Type	Description
PropertyName	String	The name of the property

This code snippet demonstrates retrieval of the Description property from the object representing the Administrator user account in my domain, using the WinNT provider:

```
' VBScript example
Set objObject = GetObject("WinNT://CRASHLOTS/Administrator")
Response.Write "Description using Get:<BR>" & _
               objObject.Get("Description")
```

```
//JScript example
var objObject = ActiveXObject("WinNT://CRASHLOTS/Administrator");
Response.Write("Description using Get:<BR>" +
               objObject.Get("Description") + "<P>");
```

The Description property of user objects simply contains a descriptive piece of text.

GetEx Method

The GetEx method is similar to the Get method, and takes the same parameter. However, GetEx will *always* return an array containing the value(s), even if this means returning an array that only contains one value. Whether you use Get or GetEx to obtain values of properties is to some extent a matter of personal preference. In general, though, you will find GetEx more useful if you do not know in advance whether the value is multivalued, since in that case you won't know whether Get will return the value(s) in an array or not.

ADSI

```
Variant = Object.GetEx(PropertyName)
```

Parameter	Data Type	Description
PropertyName	String	The name of the property

The following snippet from an ASP page expands the previous example of use of the Get method: this uses both Get and GetEx to retrieve the single-valued attribute, Description, from the Adminstrator user account using the WinNT provider, allowing us to compare how the two methods are used. This attribute is a textual description of what the account is there for.

```
<%@ LANGUAGE="VBScript" %>
<HTML>
<HEAD>
<TITLE> ASP Prog Ref Sample Code</TITLE>
</HEAD>
<BODY>
<H1> Get and GetEx Demo </H1>

<%
Set objObject = GetObject("WinNT://CRASHLOTS/Administrator")
Response.Write "<P>"

' display automation properties if we have bound to an object
If (Err.number = 0) Then
    Response.Write "Description using Get:<BR>" &
                    objObject.Get("Description")

& "<P>"
    For Each Value in objObject.GetEx("Description")
        Response.Write "Description using GetEx:<BR>" & Value & "<BR>"
    Next
End If
%>
</BODY>
</HTML>
```

In JScript, the equivalent code would read:

```
<%@ LANGUAGE="JScript" %>
<HTML>
<HEAD>
<TITLE> ASP Prog Ref Sample Code </TITLE>
</HEAD>
<BODY>
<H1> Get and GetEx Demo </H1>

<%
var objObject = ActiveXObject("WinNT://CRASHLOTS/Administrator");
Response.Write("<P>");

// Display automation properties if we have bound to an object
try {
    Response.Write("Description using Get:<BR>" +
                    objObject.Get("Description") + "<P>");
```

```
        var arrValues=new VBArray(objObject.GetEx("Description"));
        for (i=0; i<=arrValues.ubound(); i++) {
            Response.Write("Description using GetEx:<BR>" +
                           arrValues.getItem(i) + "<BR>");
        }
    }
    catch(e) {
        Response.Write(e.description);
    }
    %>
    </BODY>
    </HTML>
```

Notice the Get and GetEx methods retrieve data from the cache rather than from the underlying directory object. You might think that this would mean you'd have to call GetInfo first to ensure the cache does contain valid data, but in fact GetInfo is always called implicitly on your behalf the first time you make attempt to access data from the cache. You only need to call GetInfo explicitly if for some reason you think the data in the underlying directory object may have changed, and so the cache needs to be refreshed.

GetInfo Method

The GetInfo method refreshes the property cache from the underlying directory. You do not normally need to call this method since it is implicitly called for you the first time you use Get or GetEx to obtain a value from the cache. However you can use GetInfo to force the cache to be updated if you suspect that the information in the underlying directory may have changed since the cache was last updated. GetInfo does not take any parameters.

```
Object.GetInfo()
```

GetInfoEx Method

The GetInfoEx method is similar to GetInfo method, but it currently takes one parameter, a list of names of properties whos values are to be retrieved. (A second parameter currently isn't used.)

```
Object.GetInfoEx(Properties)
```

Parameter	Data Type	Description
Properties	String	An array of names of the properties to load into the directory.

The GetInfoEx method has two uses: it can save on network traffic by retrieving only certain properties from the underlying directory. Its other use is that there are some properties in some directories which are not by default retrieved into the cache when GetInfo is called. These are typically operational properties whose main purpose is for internal auditing and administration of the directory, and which are not considered useful to the casual user (for example, most LDAP directories have a property with each entry that stores the time that that entry was last modified, which falls into this category). If you want to examine these properties, you will need to use GetInfoEx to retrieve them.

ADSI

Put Method

The Put method sets the value of a property in the property cache. It takes two parameters, the name of the property, and the new value.

```
Object.Put(PropertyName, Value)
```

Parameter	Data Type	Description
PropertyName	String	The name of the property
Value	Variant	The value of the property.

The following example shows how to set the Description of the administrator's account using the Put method. Put only updates the value in the cache, so we call SetInfo afterwards to actually write the change to the directory object. The value is not changed until SetInfo is called. Note, however, that if changing multiple attributes, you only need to call SetInfo once, after making all the changes.

```
' VBScript example
Set objObject = GetObject("WinNT://CRASHLOTS/Administrator")
objObject.Put "Description", "This is the put & setinfo code"
```

```
//JScript example
var objObject = ActiveXObject("WinNT://CRASHLOTS/Administrator");
objObject.Put("Description", "This is the put & setinfo code");
```

Note the call to SetInfo following the call to Put. This is necessary to write the change to the underlying directory.

PutEx Method

The PutEx method is similar to Put but a bit more sophisticated in that it accepts a third parameter, an integer that indicates exactly how the new value is to be placed in the property and which is appropriate to multivalued properties.

```
Object.PutEx(Mode, PropertyName, Value)
```

Parameter	Data Type	Description
Mode	Long	An ADS_PROPERTY_OPERATION_ENUM which specifies an Append, Delete, Replace or Remove
PropertyName	String	The name of the property
Value	Variant	The value of the property.

SetInfo Method

The SetInfo method writes the current copy of the cache to the underlying directory. Note that you *must* call this method after making changes to the cache using Put or PutEx and before calling GetInfo again if you want your changes to be copied back to the directory. Failure to do so will result in any changes being lost. SetInfo does not take any parameters.

```
Object.SetInfo()
```

IADs Properties

ADsPath Property

The `ADsPath` property returns the ADsPath of an object. Normally the same as the string we use to bind to the object using `GetObject`.

```
String = Object.ADsPath
```

For example, let's look at the following code:

```
' VBScript example
Set objObject = GetObject("WinNT://LT/CRASHLOTS/Administrator")
Response.Write objObject.ADsPath & "<P>"
```

```
//JScript example
var objObject = ActiveXObject("WinNT://LT/CRASHLOTS/Administrator");
Response.Write(objObject.ADsPath + "<P>")
```

This will cause the text WinNT://LT/CRASHLOTS to be sent to the HTML page.

Although the `ADsPath` property may not seem particularly useful if you've just supplied the ADsPath to bind to the object, bear in mind that there are other methods of binding to ADSI objects which we discuss later in the chapter and which don't require an ADsPath. Also note that some ADSI providers allow alternative forms for some ADsPaths. (For example, the WinNT provider optionally allows the domain name to be omitted). In these cases, the value returned by the `ADsPath` property might not be the same as the string used to bind to the object.

Class Property

The `Class` property returns the class of the object, the string that identitifies the type of object, for example, user, domain, group, or computer.

```
String = Object.Class
```

Since CRASHLOTS is the name of a computer running on my network, this sample will return the text Computer.

```
' VBScript example
Set objObject = GetObject("WinNT://LT/CRASHLOTS")
Response.Write objObject.Class & "<P>"
```

```
//JScript example
var objObject = ActiveXObject("WinNT://LT/CRASHLOTS");
Response.Write(objObject.Class + "<P>");
```

GUID Property

The `GUID` property returns the GUID, the Global Unique Identifier, of the `Directory` object. This is a 128-bit number which uniquely identifies an object (or for some providers the class of an object).

```
String = Object.GUID
```

ADSI

Name Property

The Name property returns the name of the object, that is to say the part of the
ADsPath that identifies that object once you've already identified the container the
object is in.

```
String = Object.Name
```

The following code will return the text Administrator.

```
' VBScript example
Set objObject = GetObject("WinNT://LT/CRASHLOTS/Administrator")
Response.Write objObject.Name & "<P>"
```

```
//JScript example
var objObject = ActiveXObject("WinNT://LT/CRASHLOTS/Administrator");
Response.Write(objObject.Name + "<P>");
```

Parent Property

The Parent property returns the ADsPath of the parent that contains the current
object.

```
String = Object.Parent
```

It's useful for navigating up the directory tree. For example, this code binds to the
Administrator account, then retrieves the ADsPath of its parent,
WinNT://LT/CRASHLOTS.

```
' VBScript example
Set objObject = GetObject("WinNT://LT/CRASHLOTS/Administrator")
Response.Write objObject.Parent & "<P>"
```

```
//JScript example
var objObject = ActiveXObject("WinNT://LT/CRASHLOTS/Administrator");
Response.Write(objObject.Parent + "<P>");
```

Schema Property

The Schema property is similar to the Class property, but instead of returning just
the name of the class, it returns the full ADsPath to a so-called class-schema object
which describes objects of the given class. The class-schema object can be used, for
example, to identify the mandatory and optional properties of objects of a given class.

```
String = Object.Schema
```

For example:

```
' VBScript example
Set objObject = GetObject("WinNT://LT/CRASHLOTS")
Response.Write objObject.Schema & "<P>"
Set objSchema = GetObject(objObject.Schema)
```

```
//JScript example
var objObject = ActiveXObject("WinNT://LT/CRASHLOTS");
Response.Write(objObject.Schema + "<P>");
objSchema = GetObject(objObject.Schema);
```

This code writes the ADsPath of the class schema object for computers (which for the WinNT provider happens to be `WinNT://LT/Schema/Computer`) and then binds to this object.

The IADsClass Interface

The `IADsClass` interface is implemented by class schema objects, that is to say, the objects that describe a class of object, and which you can locate by using the `Schema` property of the `IADs` interface.

`IADsClass` is derived from `IADs`, so it implements all the `IADs` properties and methods.

In addition it implements the following methods and properties:

Methods	Properties
Qualifiers	Abstract
	AuxDerivedFrom
	Auxiliary
	Container
	Containment
	CLSID
	DerivedFrom
	HelpFileContext
	HelpFileName
	MandatoryProperties
	NamingProperties
	OID
	OptionalProperties
	PossibleSuperiors
	PrimaryInterface

Note that `IADsClass` properties are all read/write. While this is strictly true in principle, in practice few providers will allow you to write to any of these properties and then only if you have very high access rights. This is because these properties are describing the schema implemented by the provider – so writing to them implies that the schema is being modified. That is a pretty major operation, which not all providers support. For example, WinNT never allows you to write to any `IADsClass` properties, while Active Directory only allows you to if you are logged in under an account that is a member of the Schema Administrators group. The same applies to the `IADsProperty` and `IADsSyntax` properties. So in practice, you should usually treat all these properties as read-only.

IADsClass Methods

Qualifiers Method

The Qualifiers method is a provider-specific property and is not always implemented. This method takes no parameters and returns a reference to a collection object, which can be used, for example, in a For Each loop in VBScript to enumerate other requirements that objects of this class must satisfy.

```
Object = Object.Qualifiers()
```

IADsClass Properties

Abstract Property

The Abstract property sets or returns a boolean that indicates whether this class of object is Abstract. An Abstract class cannot be instantiated, but simply acts as a base class for derivation of further classes.

```
Boolean = Object.Abstract
Object.Abstract = Boolean
```

AuxDerivedFrom Property

The AuxDerivedFrom property sets or returns the names of any auxiliary classes that this class is derived from. A class may be derived from any number of auxiliary classes as well as at most one structural or Abstract class.

```
Variant = Object.AuxDerivedFrom
Object.AuxDerivedFrom = Variant
```

Auxiliary Property

The Auxiliary property sets or returns a boolean that indicates whether this class is auxiliary. An auxiliary class cannot be instantiated, but is instead simply a way of grouping together some additional properties that may be useful in some objects.

```
Boolean = Object.Auxiliary
Object.Auxiliary = Boolean
```

CLSID Property

The CLSID property sets or returns the CLSID of the COM object that implements ADSI objects representing this class. You don't really need this information since you should *never* instantiate the objects using CreateObject, so this property is often not implemented.

```
Object.CLSID = String
String = Object.CLSID
```

Container Property

The Container property sets or returns a boolean that indicates whether instances of this classes are containers that implement the IADsContainer interface.

```
Object.Container = Boolean
Boolean = Object.Container
```

Containment Property

The Containment property sets or returns the names of any classes that can be contained by instances of this class. Such classes will presumably name this class as one of the possible containing classes in the PossibleSuperiors property.

```
Variant = Object.Containment
Object.Containment = Variant
```

DerivedFrom Property

The DerivedFrom property sets or returns the class (if any) that this class is derived from. There should be only at most one such class, although this property is stored as an array of strings.

```
Variant = Object.DerivedFrom
Object.DerivedFrom = Variant
```

HelpFileContext Property

The HelpFileContext property sets or returns a string containining context information about where the information in the help file relating to this class can be found. Like HelpFileName this property is not always implemented.

```
String = Object.HelpFileContext
Object.HelpFileContext = String
```

HelpFileName

The HelpFileName property is provider-specific and often not implemented. It contains the name of a file that contains information about this class.

```
String = Object.HelpFileName
Object.HelpFileName = String
```

MandatoryProperties Property

The MandatoryProperties property sets or returns an array of strings that lists the names of all mandatory properties of this class of object, that is to say those properties which must be present and must have at least one value for every instance of this class of object.

```
Variant = Object.MandatoryProperties
Object.MandatoryProperties = Variant
```

For example, the following code snippet displays the names of the mandatory properties of the DHCP service on the machine CRASHLOTS, using the WinNT provider:

ADSI

```
' VBScript example
Dim objObject
NewADsPath = "WinNT://LT/CRASHLOTS/Dhcp"
Set objObject = GetObject(NewADsPath)

Dim objSchema
Set objSchema = GetObject(objObject.Schema)
Response.Write "<STRONG>MANDATORY PROPERTIES</STRONG><BR>"
For Each strProp In objSchema.MandatoryProperties
   Response.Write strProp & ":<BR>"
   For Each Value In objObject.GetEx(strProp)
      Response.Write "      " & Value & "<BR>"
   Next
Next
```

```
//JScript example
var NewADsPath = "WinNT://LT/CRASHLOTS/Dhcp";
var objObject = GetObject(NewADsPath);
var objSchema = GetObject(objObject.Schema);

Response.Write("<STRONG>MANDATORY PROPERTIES</STRONG><BR>");

var arrMandProps=new VBArray(objSchema.MandatoryProperties);

for (i=0; i<=arrMandProps.ubound(); i++) {
   var strProp = arrMandProps.getItem(i);
   Response.Write(strProp + ":<BR>");
   var arrValues = new VBArray(objObject.GetEx(strProp));
   for (j=0; j<=arrValues.ubound(); j++) {
      Response.Write("      " +
                     arrValues.getItem(j) + "<BR>");
   }
}
```

NamingProperties Property

The NamingProperties property sets or returns an array of strings that lists the prefixes by which instances of this class may be referred to. This is only really used in the LDAP provider, and indicates the prefixes such as CN or OU.

```
Variant = Object.NamingProperties
Object.NamingProperties = Variant
```

OID Property

The OID property sets or returns a string that indicates the object identifier (OID) that uniquely identifies the class of object. An OID is a set of numbers separated by dots, for example most Active Directory classes defined by Microsoft begin 1.2.840.123556. etc. Each number indicates the next level down a hierarchy that leads to the organization that created the object, and in this case the 1.2.840.123556 uniquely identifies Microsoft. Once an organization has been given an initial set of numbers, it can then add further numbers as it wishes in order to uniquely identify the classes it creates.

```
String = Object.OID
Object.OID = String
```

OptionalProperties Property

The OptionalProperties property sets or returns an array of strings that lists the names of those properties that may optionally be present for every instance of this class of object.

```
Variant = Object.OptionalProperties
Object.OptionalProperties = Variant
```

The following example repeats the sample that displays mandatory properties of the DHCP service, but instead displays the optional properties:

```
' VBScript example
Dim objObject
NewADsPath = "WinNT://LT/CRASHLOTS/Dhcp"
Set objObject = GetObject(NewADsPath)

Dim objSchema
Set objSchema = GetObject(objObject.Schema)
Response.Write "<STRONG>OPTIONAL PROPERTIES</STRONG><BR>"
For Each strProp In objSchema.OptionalProperties
    Response.Write strProp & ":<BR>"
    For Each Value In objObject.GetEx(strProp)
        Response.Write "      " & Value & "<BR>"
    Next
Next
```

```
//JScript example
var NewADsPath = "WinNT://LT/CRASHLOTS/Dhcp";
var objObject = GetObject(NewADsPath);
var objSchema = GetObject(objObject.Schema);

Response.Write("<STRONG>OPTIONAL PROPERTIES</STRONG><BR>");

var arrOptProps=new VBArray(objSchema.OptionalProperties);

for (i=0; i<=arrOptProps.ubound(); i++) {
    var strProp = arrOptProps.getItem(i);
    Response.Write(strProp + ":<BR>");
    var arrValues = new VBArray(objObject.GetEx(strProp));
    for (j=0; j<=arrValues.ubound(); j++) {
        Response.Write("      " +
                        arrValues.getItem(j) + "<BR>");
    }
}
```

PossibleSuperiors Property

The PossibleSuperiors property sets or returns the names of any classes of object that are permitted to contain instances of this class. For example, in the WinNT provider, domains can contain computers and users, while computers can also contain users. On the other hand, it wouldn't make sense for a computer to contain a domain.

```
Variant = Object.PossibleSuperiors
Object.PossibleSuperiors = Variant
```

ADSI

PrimaryInterface Property

The read-only `PrimaryInterface` property returns the IID of the main ADSI interface that objects of this class implement, for example `IADs` or `IADsUser`. This information is only really relevant for clients written in C++, since VB and scripting languages cannot use the IIDs.

```
String = Object.PrimaryInterface
```

IADsClass Example: Retrieving Values of all the Properties of an Item

So far we've listed all the methods and properties of the interfaces we've covered, and given sample code snippets for the more important ones. There is one task however that you will often have to do, which involves several of the interface methods and properties of both `IADs` and `IADsClass`. That is the task of listing the values of all the properties of a given directory item. Since you'll often need to do something like this, we've given this as a separate example.

We'll present a sample that lists *all* the attributes of a particular object when you don't necessarily know the names of any of them. The way to do this involves looking up the class schema object, specifically the `MandatoryProperties` and `OptionalProperties` properties.

The steps we need to take in the sample are:

1. To locate and bind to the class schema object corresponding to the object we are interested in.

2. To look up the names of the attributes using the `IADsClass::MandatoryProperties` and `OptionalProperties` properties of the class schema object.

3. Now we have the names, use `IADs::Get` to return the actual values in the normal way.

Recall that although we are referring to the interface names here, that's just a convenience in order to make it easier to recall which methods and properties are implemented by which objects. You never actually use the interfaces explicitly when coding ASP pages.

We can now show the code to retrieve the values of all attributes. This time in order to demonstrate the variety of tasks you can do using ADSI, we'll examine the DHCP service running on my local computer.

Since this is a more complex page, we've presented the code in full here:

```
<%@ LANGUAGE="VBScript" %>
<HTML>
<HEAD>
<TITLE> ASP ProgRef Sample Code </TITLE>
</HEAD>
<BODY>
<H1> Display Properties of DHCP Service </H1>
```

```
<%
' attempt to bind to ADSI object & display message if succeeded

On Error Resume Next
Dim objObject
NewADsPath = "WinNT://JULIANS/DHCP"
Set objObject = GetObject(NewADsPath)
If Not (Err.number = 0) Then
   Response.Write "Failed to bind to object <STRONG>" & _
                  NewADsPath & "</STRONG>"
Else
   Response.Write "Currently viewing object at <STRONG>" & _
                  objObject.ADsPath & "</STRONG><BR>"
End If
Response.Write "<P>"

' display automation properties if we have bound to an object
If (Err.number = 0) Then

   Dim oSchema
   Set oSchema = GetObject(objObject.Schema)
   ' should do some more error checking here but have left
   ' it for clarity

   Response.Write "Bound to Schema object at <STRONG>" & _
                  oSchema.ADsPath & "</STRONG><P>"

   Response.Write "<STRONG>MANDATORY PROPERTIES</STRONG><BR>"
   For Each strProp In oSchema.MandatoryProperties
      Response.Write strProp & ":<BR>"
      For Each Value In objObject.GetEx(strProp)
         Response.Write "      " & Value & "<BR>"
      Next
   Next

   Response.Write "<STRONG>OPTIONAL PROPERTIES</STRONG><BR>"
   For Each strProp In oSchema.OptionalProperties
      Response.Write strProp & ":<BR>"
      For Each Value In objObject.GetEx(strProp)
         Response.Write "      " & Value & "<BR>"
      Next
   Next

End If
%>

</BODY>
</HTML>
```

The JScript version of the code runs

```
<%@ Language="JScript" %>
<HTML>
<HEAD>
<TITLE> ASP ProgRef Sample Code </TITLE>
</HEAD>
<BODY>
<H1> Display Properties of DHCP Service </H1>

<%
// attempt to bind to ADSI object and display message if succeeded
```

```
try {
   var NewADsPath = "WinNT://JULIANS/Dhcp";
   var objObject = GetObject(NewADsPath);
   Response.Write("Currently viewing object at <STRONG>" +
                  objObject.ADsPath + "</STRONG><BR>");
   Response.Write("<P>");

   var oSchema = GetObject(objObject.Schema);

   Response.Write("Bound to Schema object at <STRONG>" +
                  oSchema.ADsPath + "</STRONG><P>");

   Response.Write("<STRONG>MANDATORY PROPERTIES</STRONG><BR>");

   var arrMandProps=new VBArray(oSchema.MandatoryProperties);

   for (i=0; i<=arrMandProps.ubound(); i++) {
      var strProp = arrMandProps.getItem(i);
      Response.Write(strProp + ":<BR>");
      var arrValues = new VBArray(objObject.GetEx(strProp));
      for (j=0; j<=arrValues.ubound(); j++) {
         Response.Write("      " +
                        arrValues.getItem(j) + "<BR>");
      }
   }

   Response.Write("<STRONG>OPTIONAL PROPERTIES</STRONG><BR>");

   var arrOptProps=new VBArray(oSchema.OptionalProperties);

   for (i=0; i<=arrOptProps.ubound(); i++) {
      var strProp = arrOptProps.getItem(i);
      Response.Write(strProp + ":<BR>");
      var arrValues = new VBArray(objObject.GetEx(strProp));
      for (j=0; j<=arrValues.ubound(); j++) {
         Response.Write("      " +
                        arrValues.getItem(j) + "<BR>");
      }
   }
}
catch(e) {
   Response.Write("Failed to bind to object <STRONG>" +
                  NewADsPath + "</STRONG>");
}
%>

</BODY>
</HTML>
```

This code produces the following output:

The IADsContainer Interface

The IADsContainer interface is implemented by those objects which are able to contain other objects. Recall that such objects are known as containers.

IADsContainer acts as a collection. It exposes a couple of properties, and a couple of methods that enable us to browse through and bind to the various children of the given object. In addition it exposes a number of methods to carry out operations such as moving, copying, creating or deleting children.

Methods	Properties
CopyHere	Count
Create	Filter
Delete	Hints
GetObject	
MoveHere	

If you treat an object that exposes IADsContainer as a collection (by putting the object in a For Each loop in VBScript) then you will get back references to all the objects that are children of the container.

IADsContainer Methods

CopyHere Method

The `CopyHere` method copies an object in exactly the same way as `MoveHere` method moves an object, except that is creates a copy of the object in the current container.

```
Object = Object.CopyHere(Source, [Name])
```

Parameter	Data Type	Description
Source	String	The ADsPath for the object to be copied
Name	String	Optional. We can specify a name for this object.

Create Method

You can either check the schema for the provider you are using to check what the mandatory properties of the class of object in question, or check the ADSI documentation in MSDN, which lists the properties needed for some common objects.

This all means that creating an object in ADSI is a three-stage process:

- ❏ Call `IADsContainer::Create` to create a blank object. Usually the ADSI provider will fill in default values for as many properties as it can.

- ❏ Use `IADs::Put` or `IADs::PutEx` to fill in the values for any other attributes that need to be set

- ❏ Use `IADs::SetInfo` to actually commit the changes to the directory. Until this step is completed the new object does not exist in the directory.

The `Create` method is needed to create a blank object, which is the first step towards creating a new object in ADSI. Usually the ADSI provider will fill in default values for as many properties as it can.The syntax for it is:

```
Object = Object.Create(ClassName, ObjectName)
```

Parameter	Data Type	Description
ClassName	String	The name of the (schema) class object to be created
ObjectName	String	The name of the object as it is known to the underlying directory

Delete Method

The `Delete` method deletes an object, and it works instantly on the underlying directory. Deleting an object is simpler than creating one since there are no properties to be filled in.

```
Object.Delete(ClassName, ObjectName)
```

Parameter	Data Type	Description
ClassName	String	The schema class name of the object
ObjectName	String	The name of the object as it is known to the underlying directory

There is no need to call SetInfo afterwards but unless you do the object will not actually be removed from the underlying directory. (In practise, we may want our ASP page to ask the user for confirmation that they really want to do this first. Deleting a user account is a rather one-way kind of operation!)

GetObject Method

The GetObject method is used to bind to an object with a given name. This method differs from the usual GetObject function in VBScript in that it requires the name of the object rather than its ADsPath, so it can be useful if you don't know the full ADsPath. Note, however, that the IADsContainer method also requires the class of the object as the first parameter, and must be called against the container of the object you want to bind to.

```
Object = Object.GetObject(ClassName, ObjectName)
```

Parameter	Data Type	Description
ClassName	String	The schema class name of the object
ObjectName	String	The name of the object as it is known to the underlying directory

For example the following code shows how to bind to the Administrator user account in Active Directory using GetObject.

```
<%
Dim objObject
Set objObject = GetObject("LDAP://CRASHLOTS/CN=Users,DC=LT,DC=local")
Response.Write "Bound to object <STRONG>" & _
               objObject.ADsPath & "</STRONG><P>"

Dim objChild
Set objChild = objObject.GetObject("User", "cn=Administrator")

Response.Write "Now bound to child:<BR>"
Response.Write "Name: " & objChild.name & "<BR>"
Response.Write "ADsPath: " & objChild.ADsPath

Set objChild = Nothing
Set objObject = Nothing
%>
```

The equivalent JScript version of this code is

```
<%@ LANGUAGE="JScript" %>
<%
var objObject = ActiveXObject("LDAP://CRASHLOTS/CN=Users," +
                             "DC=LT,DC=local");
Response.Write("Bound to object <STRONG>" +
               objObject.ADsPath + "</STRONG><P>");

var objChild = objObject.GetObject("User", "CN=Administrator");

Response.Write("Now bound to child:<BR>");
Response.Write("Name: " + objChild.name + "<BR>");
Response.Write("ADsPath: " + objChild.ADsPath);

delete objChild;
delete objObject;
%>
```

MoveHere Method

The MoveHere method enables us to rename or move an object.

```
Object = Object.MoveHere(Source, NewName)
```

Parameter	Data Type	Description
Source	String	The ADsPath for the object to be moved to.
Name	String	We can specify a new name for this object, if this is set to NULL it will not be renamed.

It is not necessary to supply the full new ADsPath since the object will automatically be moved to become a child of the container you are calling MoveHere against, if the object in question is not already a child of that container. Note again that moving objects around is the sort of operation that is likely to require higher privileges than simply examining objects.

For example, the following code renames the domain administrator account to 'Hidden'. Note that the MoveHere method actually returns a reference to the moved object which can be used if desired to perform further operations on the object.

IADsContainer Properties

Count Property

The Count property indicates the number of children the container has which satisfy the Filter, in other words, how many children will be returned if an attempt is made to enumerate over them. Note that this property is not always implemented, for example it doesn't currently appear to be implemented by the WinNT provider.

```
Long = Object.Count
```

Filter Property

The `Filter` property is the most commonly-used property.

```
Object.Filter = Variant
Variant = Object.Filter
```

The `Filter` property can be illustrated by using the previous code sample which enumerated all the users and groups in my domain. `Filter` contains an array of the names of all the classes of object you are interested in. By default it is empty, which indicates that all objects of whatever class should be returned.

Hints Property

The `Hints` property works like the `Filter` property in that it contains an array of values that is used to restrict the information returned when enumerating the children of a container.

```
Object.Hints = Variant
Variant = Object.Hints
```

However, where `Filter` contains the names of classes to be returned, `Hints` contains the names of properties, and is used to optimize network access by indicating that only those properties need to be loaded into the property cache for each object. Its implementation is to some extent provider–dependent.

The IADsNamespaces Interface

The `IADsNamespaces` interface is implemented in a `Namespaces` object and used for managing `Namespace` objects, that correspond to the root node of each directory tree. The `Namespaces` object allows us to count the number of `Namespace` objects.

Methods
DefaultContainer

The `IADsOpenDSObject` interfaces exposes no methods, and just one property, `DefaultContainer`.

IADsNamespaces Methods

The `IADsOpenDSObject` interfaces exposes no methods.

IADsNamespaces Property

DefaultContainer Property

The `DefaultContainer` property sets or returns the path to a container object.

```
String = Object.DefaultContainer
Object.DefaultContainer = String
```

ADSI

839

The IADsOpenDSObject Interface

The IADsOpenDSObject interface is exposed only by namespace objects, the objects at the top of each directory hierarchy, and which have ADsPaths like IIS:, LDAP:, and WinNT:. Its purpose is to allow supplying of authentication credentials to that namespace, which can then be automatically used when binding to objects in that directory.

Methods
OpenDSObject

The IADsOpenDSObject interfaces exposes no properties, and just one method, OpenDSObject, which binds to an object.

IADsOpenDSObject Methods

OpenDSObject Method

The OpenDSObject method binds to an object, supplying appropriate authentication credentials.

```
Object = Object.OpenDSObject(Name, UserName, Password, AuthFlags)
```

Parameter	Data Type	Description
Name	String	The ADsPath for the object to be moved to.
UserName	String	The user name for namespace server security
Password	String	The password for namespace server security
AuthFlags	Long	An integer that indicates preferences about the means of authentication. (See below for more details).

The precise meaning of the integer passed as the AuthFlags parameter is to some extent provider-dependent. However, some of the values that may commonly be passed are:

1	This requests secure authentication, using NTLM for NT4 machines, and Kerberos for machines that are running Windows 2000. This is the setting you will normally use.
2	This specifies that data should be encrypted over the network.
4	If you are running NT4 domain controllers, this indicates that backup domain controllers may be used, possibly speeding network access, but restricting yourself to operations that involve reading (not writing) domain information.

Any of these flags may be combined using the bitwise OR operation.

You would typically use OpenDSObject as follows to bind to the object WinNT://LT/Crashlots. For example:

```
Dim objNamespace, objObject
Set objNamespace = GetObject("WinNT:")
Set objObject = objNamespace.OpenDSObject("WinNT://LT/Crashlots", _
                                 "MyUserName","MyPassword", 1)
```

IADsOpenDSObject Properties

The IADsOpenDSObject Interface does not expose any properties.

The IADsProperty Interface

The IADsProperty interface is implemented by property objects, that is to say, objects that describe individual properties, providing such information as whether the property is multivalued and what syntax is used to store the values.

IADsProperty is derived from IADs so it implements all the IADs properties and methods.

In addition it also exposes the following methods and properties:

Methods	Properties
Qualifiers	MaxRange
	MinRange
	MultiValued
	OID
	Syntax

IADsProperty Methods

Qualifiers Method

This is similar to the Qualifiers method fo the IADsClass interface. It is provider-specific and so not always implemented, and returns a reference to a collection object, which may be used to obtain further information about the property.

```
Object = Object.Qualifiers()
```

IADsProperty Properties

MaxRange Property

The MaxRange property sets or returns an integer indicating a maximum value for this property. If the values are strings, this will typically be interpreted as the maximum length of the strings. If the values are integers, this is more likely to be interpreted as the maximum value for the integer.

```
String = Object.MaxRange
Object.MaxRange = String
```

MinRange Property

The MinRange property sets or returns an integer as for MaxRange but containing the minimum possible value.

```
String = Object.MinRange
Object.MinRange = String
```

MultiValued Property

The MultiValued property sets or returns a boolean value that indicates whether this property is multivalued.

```
String = Object.MultiValued
Object.MultiValued = String
```

OID Property

The OID property sets or returns a string containing an object identifier that uniquely identifies this property. Object identifiers were explained with the IADsClass::OID property.

```
String = Object.OID
Object.OID = String
```

Syntax Property

The Syntax property sets or returns the name of the syntax (eg. Boolean, String) which is used to store the values of this property.

```
String = Object.Syntax
Object.Syntax = String
```

Syntaxes in ADSI are recognised as objects in their own right. You'll need to look up the syntax object (that is to say, the ADSI object whose name is given by the syntax) to identify the meaning of this syntax, the actual automation Variant data type corresponding to this syntax, if you need the information.

The following code snippet displays the syntax of the Description property in the WinNT provider. The syntax of this property is String.

```
' VBScript example
Dim objProp
Set objProp = GetObject("WinNT://JULIANS/Schema/Description")
Response.Write objProp.Syntax & "<BR>"
```

```
//JScript example
objProp = GetObject("WinNT://JULIANS/Schema/Description");
Response.Write(objProp.Syntax + "<BR>");
```

The IADsSyntax Interface

The IADsSyntax interface is implemented by Syntax objects, which describe
particular syntaxes. It is derived from IADs, and so implements all the IADs
interface's methods and properties, besides one extra property of its own,
OleAutoDataType.

Properties
OleAutoDataType

OleAutoDataType Property

The OleAutoDataType property sets or returns a number that indicates the
automation Variant datatype that this syntax corresponds to. This information isn't
really relevant to scripting clients, since scripting languages handle Variants and any
associated data types automatically. When coding ASP pages you never need to worry
about whether data is stored as a string or as an integer for example as those sorts of
details are always handled for you, with every variable treated as a Variant. The
OleAutoDataType property may, however, be relevant to clients written in C++,
which need to code up different automation data types explicitly.

```
Long = Object.OleAutoDataType
Object.OleAutoDataType = Long
```

Summary

In this chapter we've covered a brief summary of ADSI. We've shown why ADSI
rather than ADO is better suited to browsing and manipulating the tree-like
hierarchical structures that form most directories. We've also, however, shown that for
the case of searching directories, ADO still has a role to play in conjunction with the
OLE DB ADSI provider.

ADSI consists of a large number of COM components and therefore exposes a large
number of interfaces. We looked in detail at a few of these, which between them
provide most of the generic directory operations you will want to carry out. The
interfaces covered were IADs and IADsContainer, which are used by most directory
objects, IADsOpenDSObject used for authenticating, and IADsClass,
IADsProperty and IADsSyntax, which are used in defining the syntax of the
directory, what types of object can be stored and what properties these types (classes)
of object can contain.

With the arrival of Active Directory and the increasing trend for organizations to store
information in central directories that are accessible over intranets via ASP pages,
ADSI is likely to play an increasingly important role in the pages that we write.

ADSI

38

CDO for Windows 2000

In this and the next chapter we'll look at **Collaboration Data Objects**. CDO enables us to enhance our ASP applications with messaging and collaboration features. This is a large topic, so we'll focus on the technologies that are more directly accessible to the ASP developer. Basic messaging features certainly are the most common requirement for collaborative applications, and we'll see soon that IIS 5.0 offers a very straightforward way to achieve that.

In this chapter we first introduce collaboration data objects and the various different technologies that are covered by this general term. The main focus for this chapter is CDO for Windows 2000, with a section at the end on CDO for Exchange 2000. CDO for Windows NT Server (CDONTS) is considered in the next chapter.

There are many ways that our applications can be enhanced with mailing capabilities, such as online order confirmations, administrative alerts, e-mail advertisements etc. We can deliver compelling messaging solutions using ASP and the IIS mailing services; however, complex collaboration issues (such as appointment and calendar managing or online discussion) may require third-party services (such as Microsoft Exchange).

Collaboration Data Objects

Collaboration Data Objects (CDO) is the name under which Microsoft harmonizes its nomenclature for messaging and collaboration COM libraries for high-level development tools and languages. These technologies were previously known as OLE Messaging, Active Messaging etc. Despite this naming consolidation, CDO encompasses *quite unrelated* technologies – and hence object models – which address specific programming issues.

❑ **CDO for Windows 2000** – This is an integral part of the Windows 2000 operating system, and enables us to develop both client-side, and server-side, applications dealing with SMTP, NNTP and MIME standards. CDO for Windows 2000 is the preferred way to access mailing services from IIS 5.0 and ASP 3.0, even though CDONTS is supported under Windows 2000.

❑ **CDO for Windows NT Server** (CDONTS) - This is a server-side library that allows us to send messages quickly and efficiently with little coding effort. It relies on an SMTP (Simple Mail Transfer Protocol) server to deliver the messages.

❑ **CDO for Exchange Server** – This is the automation interface, for Windows NT, used to access Exchange and MAPI-compliant services (there are really two different libraries). The most prevalent example of CDO programming is Outlook Web Access.

❑ **CDO for Exchange 2000** (previously known as CDO 3.0) – With the release of Exchange 2000 (still in beta at the time of writing), CDO for Exchange 2000 will supercede CDO for Exchange Server. It also incorporates CDO Workflow objects for Microsoft Exchange, and CDO for Exchange Management. Also, since the Exchange 2000 library is a *superset* of the Windows 2000 library, on a machine with Exchange 2000, we can simply use the single CDO for Exchange 2000 library to obtain all the functionality found in the CDO for Windows 2000 library plus the whole range of messaging and collaboration enhancements provided by Exchange 2000.

Comparison of CDO, CDONTS and CDO2000

Some useful guidelines for the choice of the CDO technology that best fits your requirements are given below.

CDO for Windows 2000 should be used when we need the following:

❑ A faster path to messaging services, especially unauthenticated outgoing messaging

❑ A simple server configuration

❑ Native support for SMTP, NNTP and MIME

❑ Strong features for managing MHTML messaging

❑ Very high message throughput for mass e-mailing scenarios

❑ Good programmatic configuration capabilities

❑ Strong features to manage/load/save message templates

❑ Direct SMTP sending over the network without requiring a companion SMTP service

CDONTS should be used when we need the following:

❑ ASP 2.0 backward compatibility

❑ Fast path to messaging services, especially unauthenticated outgoing messaging

❑ Native SMTP support

❑ Basic MHTML features

❑ Simple built-in inbox screening

❑ Good performance under heavy messaging load

CDO for Exchange and **CDO for Exchange 2000** should be used when we need the following:

❑ Exchange and MAPI-compliant messaging features

❑ Personal Information Management features, like calendar, etc.

❑ Rich collaborative web applications that use the Exchange's infostores to share information

❑ Strong authentication and security

❑ Distributed architecture encompassing multiple Exchange servers

❑ Automatic rendering of collaboration objects into HTML

Other Emerging Collaborative Technologies

In this section we briefly introduce two other emerging collaboration technologies: Distributed Authoring and Versioning (DAV) and Microsoft Office Server Extensions (OWS).

Distributed Authoring and Versioning

Distributed Authoring and Versioning (also known as DAV or WebDAV), is an industry standard that defines a set of HTTP extensions to manage and control the access to resources on a web server. If this definition seems vague, we could add that IIS 5.0 web folders are implemented through DAV (whereas IIS 4.0 used the proprietary FrontPage protocol). DAV is implemented at the HTTP protocol level defining a set of commands that extend the semantic of the HTTP request. These are listed below (in order to make things easier we talk about files and directories on the web server, rather than generic resources and collections):

Command	Description
COPY	This copies a file/directory from one location to another.
MOVE	This moves a file/directory from one location to another.
MKCOL	This creates a directory.
PROPFIND	This gets the properties of a file/directory.
PROPPATCH	This sets the properties of a file/directory.
LOCK	This places a lock on a file for managing concurrent changes.
UNLOCK	This removes a lock on a file.
SEARCH	This searches a specific file/directory.

Microsoft has encapsulated a DAV client in its OLE DB Provider for Internet Publishing (see Chapter 29), so we can access the resources on a DAV server using ADO. With the `Recordset`, `Record` and `Stream` objects we can add, modify and delete the contents of a web server. Although it makes more sense to use DAV directly from the web client, we can exploit it from ASP too. However, we should bear in mind that using ADO in ASP code to access DAV-managed resources means issuing a new HTTP request from inside the processing of an HTTP request, even if we access the same IIS server processing the ASP script.

Microsoft Office Server Extensions, OWS

Another interesting technology is represented by the **Microsoft Office Server Extensions** (OWS) that ships with Office 2000 (but isn't installed by default). This provides an NT service for notification tasks, a database that holds collaborative data, and some COM components for extra functionality. With OWS we can easily create an ASP application that provides online discussion and collaboration on the documents available on a web server. The following picture shows the standard discussion application that ships with OWS. It is implemented using ASP and the OWS COM components.

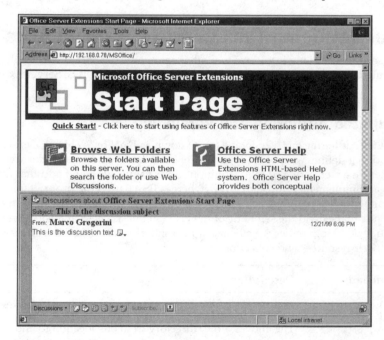

Although OWS is tightly integrated with IE5, it can also be accessed, for example, from Netscape Navigator. OWS also offers components to manage web folders from ASP (that is displaying web folders content, searching documents, etc.). These are server-side and are not based on DAV.

CDO for Windows 2000

CDO for Windows 2000 is used for sending and managing messages according to Internet standards, namely SMTP (Simple Mail Transfer Protocol), MIME (Multipurpose Internet Mail Extensions) and NNTP (Internetwork News Transfer Protocol). It is a COM component that ships as an integral part of the Microsoft Windows 2000. The library is implemented by cdosys.dll.

Throughout this chapter we use the short name "CDO2000" to refer to CDO for Windows 2000, however this should not be confused with CDO for Exchange Server 2000, which is discussed at the end of this chapter.

CDO2000 enables us to create client-side, as well as server-side applications, which offer rich features with a great deal of flexibility. The core concept is that CDO2000 can work either by queuing messages on the file system and relying on the IIS SMTP server to deliver them, or alternatively, by sending messages directly over the network to a specific SMTP server (without the helper IIS SMTP server).

Here are some other benefits of CDO2000:

❑   Its object model is tightly coupled with the underlying technologies, especially with the MIME specifications.

❑   It just offers SMTP and NNTP capabilities, that is, no other collaboration features (calendaring, etc.).

Here are some limitations of CDO2000:

❑   It offers no built-in user authentication and security features.

❑   It lacks the logon feature, useful for managing inboxes, provided by CDONTS.

Server Configuration

> **For information on the IIS SMTP configuration see the next chapter about CDONTS.**

CDO2000 can directly send outgoing messages using SMTP protocol over the network and doesn't require the mandatory presence of the companion SMTP service (necessary for CDONTS). Obviously however, if we use CDO2000 to manage Inboxes and incoming messages, the SMTP service is essential. CDO2000 also offers configuration capabilities and we can fine-tune the library, by adapting our script code according to our requirements.

Integration with ADO

CDO2000 is integrated with ADO 2.5, meaning that CDO2000's objects expose some of their functionality via the standard ADO interfaces. We therefore need to include the ActiveX Data Objects 2.5 Library (ADO DB) library in all applications. The `Metadata` directives required to import all the constants used by CDO2000 are:

```
<!--METADATA TYPE="typelib" NAME="CDO for Windows 2000 Type Library"
           UUID="CD000000-8B95-11D1-82DB-00C04FB1625D" -->
<!--METADATA TYPE="typelib"  NAME="ADODB Type Library"
           UUID="00000205-0000-0010-8000-00AA006D2EA4" -->
```

> Note that the Prog ID for the CDO2000 library is just `"CDO"`. For
> example, the Prog ID for `Message` is `"CDO.Message"`.

All the configurable CDO2000 interfaces (namely `IMessage`, `IBodyPart`, and `IConfiguration`) expose via the `Fields` property an `ADODB.Fields` collection containing a set of fields we can use to set the properties of the objects. These fields overlap with the standard properties of the interfaces, but allow a more robust run-time extension of the features exposed by an object.

CDO for Windows 2000 Object Model

Before we look at the object model, let us first briefly consider the differences between a COM object's **CoClass**, and its **interface**. CDO2000 is the first Microsoft COM library that is addressed to high-level languages such as VBScript and JScript, and the first time that ASP developers need to make a clear distinction between a COM object and the interfaces exposed by the object.

An **interface** defines the methods, properties and events that an object exposes. It does not provide any implementation of those methods, properties and events. Instead, it allows us to use an object without being concerned with how the object implements them. As ASP developers, we normally think of a one-to-one relationship between interfaces and objects. However, COM allows multiple interfaces on a single object. Each interface exposes a set of methods and properties associated with a particular set of functionality of the object. Development of the component may mean alternative methods, which perform the task more efficiently, or reflect different functionality. We can just think of different interfaces on the same object as different *views* of an *object's identity*.

The **CoClass**, or Component Object Class, is the COM implementation of the interface. For each method, property and event that the interface defines, the class provides an implementation of it. For each interface that the class implements, the class must implement the methods, properties and events defined in that interface. Sometimes interfaces may define methods that are identical in name and have the same parameters (both number and data type), in which case the method would only be implemented once. The same is true for events and properties.

The distinction between objects and interfaces is blurred by **automation technology** (IDispatch), which allows one component to use objects defined in another component. The reasons behind this are complex, and concern COM marshaling, which is beyond the scope of this book. However, the net result is that a typical automation object exposes just one dispatch interface. Furthermore, since VBScript and JScript are 'typeless' languages, it is hard to bind variables to the multiple interfaces exposed by an object identity, since the variables have no type.

The CDO2000 object model offers three CoClasses (i.e. directly creatable objects): Message, Configuration, and DropDirectory. There is also another COM object (BodyPart) and two collections (BodyParts and Messages) that cannot be created directly, but are created from the first three objects.

The CDO2000 Message object exposes not one, but three different interfaces: IMessage (the default), IBodyPart, and IDataSource. When we create a Message object using Server.CreateObject and assign it to a variable in JScript or VBScript, this variable holds a reference to the default interface (IMessage) of the object. We can navigate through the different interfaces provided by the object using its GetInterface method. Alternatively, we can use the particular property of the object to return the required interface. For example, the IMessage.BodyPart property returns the IBodyPart interface on the object. This mimics the COM standard interface navigation capability (IUnknown::QueryInterface in raw COM, or the type system in VB and Java) in the Automation/Scripting environment.

Finally, it's worth noting that the substitute techniques for interface navigation only work if the COM objects are context-neutral, i.e. if they aggregate the COM Free Threaded Marshaler (FTM), as CDO2000 does. The FTM allows a component to override the ordinary COM marshaling behavior to return a direct pointer to the server object (i.e. no proxy and stub) to the component's client. In other words, the FTM is essential to overrule the default COM marshaling workings and allow an automation object to expose more than one interface.

CDO for Windows 2000 Objects

The object model for CDO for Windows 2000 looks like this:

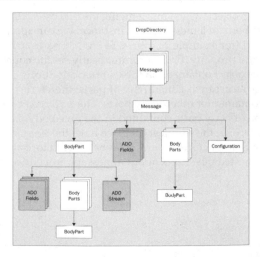

These objects and collections in the CDO for Windows 2000 object model are used as follows:

❑ The **BodyPart object** enables us to manage a body part of a message, for example, we can specify the nature of the data in the body part, or programmatically set the content.

❑ The **BodyParts collection** contains all of the body parts for a particular Message.

❑ The **Configuration object** is the stand-alone object used to configure the way a message is processed from CDO2000, for example whether the message should be queued or sent directly over the network. All configurable options are exposed via a set of name/value pairs, the ADODB.Fields collection.

❑ The **DropDirectory object** is used to access the file system directories containing messages, such as the default SMTP service drop directory. It contains a single method, the GetMessages method which exposes the Messages collection.

❑ The **Message object** is the most important object in the CDO2000 object model. As mentioned it implements three interfaces: IMessage, IBodyPart, and IDataSource. The IMessage interface enables us to work with the message at the higher level, for instance to set the recipient and send the message. Complex messages that contain more than plain text must be subdivided into parts. The Message object then acts as the root of a body parts hierarchy, and implements the IBodyPart interface (via the BodyPart property, or the GetInterface method). The IDataSource interface of the Message object allows us to manage the process of saving/loading the message to/from other objects.

❑ The **Messages collection** contains all the Message objects in a particular DropDirectory.

The BodyPart Object

Using the BodyPart object, which implements the IBodyPart interface, we can wholly manage the body of a message. For instance, we can specify the nature of the data in the body part (for example "text/plain", "image/gif", etc.) using the ContentMediaType property, or programmatically set the content of the part using the ADODB.Stream object obtained via the GetDecodedContentStream method. The MIME message structure is a hierarchy of parts, therefore a given BodyPart object can be the container for other body parts. The BodyParts property allows us to access the collection of body parts contained in the give body part using the IBodyParts interface. In the simplest case, we have the Message object as the root part that contains a flat structure of parts (maybe one or more attachments), but the hierarchy could be nested (just think about a message embedded in another message).

For example inVBScript:

```
Sub DisplayAttachment(bp)
   Dim stream, strBP

   Set stream = bp.GetStream()
   strBP = Server.HTMLEncode (stream.ReadText())

   Response.Write "<HR>"
   Response.Write "Body part: " & bp.FileName & "<BR>"
   Response.Write "Content Class: " & bp.ContentClass & "<BR>"
   Response.Write "Content Media Type: " & bp.ContentMediaType & _
                  "<BR>"
   Response.Write "Content Transfer Encoding: " & _
                  bp.ContentTransferEncoding & "<BR>"
   Response.Write "Content:" & "<P>"
   Response.Write strBP
   Response.Write "<HR>"

   Set stream = Nothing
End Sub
```

Or in JScript:

```
function DisplayAttachment(bp) {
   stream = bp.GetStream();
   strBP = Server.HTMLEncode (stream.ReadText());

   Response.Write("<HR>");
   Response.Write("Body part: " + bp.FileName + "<BR>");
   Response.Write("Content Class: " + bp.ContentClass + "<BR>");
   Response.Write("Content Media Type: " + bp.ContentMediaType +
                  "<BR>");
   Response.Write("Content Transfer Encoding: " +
                  bp.ContentTransferEncoding + "<BR>");
   Response.Write("Content:" + "<P>");
   Response.Write(strBP);
   Response.Write("<HR>");

   delete stream;
}
```

The BodyPart object exposes the following properties and methods:

Methods	Properties
AddBodyPart	BodyParts
GetDecodedContentStream	CharSet
GetEncodedContentStream	ContentClass
GetFieldParameter	ContentClassName
GetInterface	ContentMediaType

Table Continued on Following Page

Methods	Properties
GetStream	ContentTransferEncoding
SaveToFile	DataSource
	FieldName
	Fields
	Parent

BodyPart Object Methods

The BodyPart object exposes the following methods: AddBodyPart, GetDecodedContentStream, GetEncodedContentStream, GetFieldParameter, GetInterface, GetStream, and SaveToFile.

AddBodyPart Method

The AddBodyPart method adds a BodyPart object to the BodyParts collection.

```
BodyPart = BodyPart.AddBodyPart([Index])
```

Parameter	Data Type	Description
Index	Long	Optional. This sets the insertion point of the object from 1 to count. The default value of -1 appends the object to the end of the collection.

GetDecodedContentStream Method

The GetDecodedContentStream method returns an ADO Stream object that contains the contents of the body part in decoded format.

```
ADODB.Stream = BodyPart.GetDecodedContentStream()
```

For example in VBScript:

```
Set objStream = objBodyPart.GetDecodedContentStream
objStream.WriteText "This content has been produced on the " & _
                    "fly by ASP script."
objStream.Flush
```

Or in JScript:

```
objStream = objBodyPart.GetDecodedContentStream();
objStream.WriteText("This content has been produced on the " +
                    "fly by ASP script.");
objStream.Flush();
```

GetEncodedContentStream Method

The GetEncodedContentStream method returns an ADO Stream object that contains the body part content in encoded format.

```
ADODB.Stream = BodyPart.GetEncodedContentStream()
```

854

GetFieldParameter Method

The GetFieldParameter method returns the value of the specified parameter for the specified MIME header file. A typical example would be to retrieve the character set in a Content-Type header.

```
String = BodyPart.GetFieldParameter(FieldName, Parameter)
```

Parameter	Data Type	Description
FieldName	String	The fully qualified field name.
Parameter	String	The name of the parameter.

GetInterface Method

The GetInterface method returns the specified interface of the object.

```
Object = BodyPart.GetInterface(Interface)
```

Parameter	Data Type	Description
Interface	String	The name of the required interface.

GetStream Method

The GetStream method returns a reference to an ADO Stream object which contains the headers and content of the BodyPart.

```
ADODB.Stream = BodyPart.GetStream()
```

SaveToFile Method

The SaveToFile method saves the decoded content of the BodyPart to disk.

```
BodyPart.SaveToFile(FileName)
```

Parameter	Data Type	Description
FileName	String	The full, local drive, path and filename URL.

BodyPart Object Properties

BodyParts Property

The BodyParts property returns the BodyParts collection for the object.

```
BodyParts = BodyPart.BodyParts
```

CharSet Property

The CharSet property sets or returns the character set for the body part.

```
String = BodyPart.CharSet
BodyPart.CharSet = String
```

ContentClass Property

The ContentClass property sets or returns the content class value of the body part.

```
String = BodyPart.ContentClass
BodyPart.ContentClass = String
```

ContentClassName Property

The ContentClassName property is deprecated and not used.

```
String = BodyPart.ContentClassName
BodyPart.ContentClassName = String
```

ContentMediaType Property

The ContentMediaType property sets or returns the MIME type and subtype of body part content.

```
String = BodyPart.ContentMediaType
BodyPart.ContentMediaType = String
```

ContentTransferEncoding Property

The ContentTransferEncoding property defines the encoding mechanism used when sending the object. If none is defined it will default to simple 7-bit ASCII.

```
String = BodyPart.ContentTransferEncoding
BodyPart.ContentTransferEncoding = String
```

The encoding options are as follows:

Constant	Value	Description
cdo7bit	"7bit"	Simple 7-bit ASCII
cdo8bit	"8bit"	8-bit encoding with line termination characters
cdoBase64	"base64"	3 octets encoded into 4 sextets with offset
cdoBinary	"binary"	Arbitrary binary stream
cdoMacBinHex40	"mac-binhex40"	Macintosh binary-to-hex encoding
cdoQuotedPrintable	"quoted-printable"	Mostly 7-bit, with 8-bit characters encoded as "=HH"
cdoUuencode	"uuencode"	UNIX UUEncode encoding

For example:

```
' VBScript
' now we change the encoding rule applied to the Word document
objBodyPart.ContentTransferEncoding = cdoUuencode
```

```
// JScript
// now we change the encoding rule applied to the Word document
objBodyPart.ContentTransferEncoding = cdoUuencode;
```

DataSource Property

The DataSource property returns the IDataSource interface of the object. This property can only be used on a Message object. It is not implemented on the BodyPart object provided with CDO2000 and will raise an exception if used.

```
DataSource = BodyPart.DataSource
```

Fields Property

The Fields property returns the Fields collection for the object.

```
Fields = BodyPart.Fields
```

FileName Property

The FileName property returns the content disposition. There is no specifically defined presentation behavior for the FileName property. The default value is an empty string. If CDO does not recognize the disposition of the body part it is treated as an attachment.

```
String = BodyPart.FileName
```

Parent Property

The Parent property returns a reference to the parent BodyPart object.

```
BodyPart = BodyPart.Parent
```

The BodyParts Collection

The BodyParts collection exposes the following methods and properties:

Methods	Properties
Add	Count
Delete	Item
DeleteAll	

BodyParts Collection Methods

The `BodyParts` collection exposes the `Add`, `Delete`, and `DeleteAll` methods:

Add Method

The `Add` method adds a new `BodyPart` object to the collection.

```
BodyPart = BodyParts.Add(Index)
```

Parameter	Data Type	Description
`Index`	Long	The index position in which to add the new `BodyPart` from 1 to `Count`. The default a value of -1 appends the `BodyPart` to the collection.

Delete Method

The `Delete` method removes the specified `BodyPart` object from the collection.

```
BodyParts.Delete(Item)
```

Parameter	Data Type	Description
`Item`	Variant	This parameter is either the index number or a reference to the `BodyPart` that is to be removed.

DeleteAll Method

The `DeleteAll` method removes all the `BodyPart` objects from the collection.

```
BodyParts.DeleteAll()
```

BodyParts Collection Properties

Count Property

The `Count` property returns the number of `BodyPart` objects in the collection.

```
Long = BodyParts.Count
```

Item Property

The `Item` property returns the `BodyPart` specified by index number.

```
BodyPart = Bodyparts.Item(Index)
```

The Configuration Object

The `Configuration` object is a stand-alone object that exposes the `IConfiguration` interface. We use this object to configure the way a message is processed from CDO2000, for instance if the message should be queued or sent directly over the network. The `IConfiguration` interface is pretty simple as all configurable options are exposed via a set of name/value pairs, the `ADODB.Fields` collection in the `Fields` property.

The Configuration object exposes the following methods and properties:

Methods	Properties
Load	Fields
GetInterface	

Creating a Configuration Object

We can create an Configuration object as follows:

For example in VBScript:

```
Set objCfg = Server.CreateObject("CDO.Configuration")
```

Or in JScript

```
objCfg = Server.CreateObject("CDO.Configuration");
```

Configuration Object Methods

The Configuration object exposes the Load and GetInterface methods:

Load Method

The Load method loads the specific configuration.

```
Configuration.Load(LoadFrom, [URL])
```

Parameter	Data Type	Description
LoadFrom	CdoConfigSource	This specifies which configuration to load.
URL	String	Optional. This is currently ignored & reserved for future use.

CdoConfigSource is one of the following: cdoSourceDefaults (which loads all the relevant default values), cdoSourceIIS (loads any default value from IIS), or cdoSourceOutlookExpress (loads default values from Microsoft Outlook Express).

GetInterface Method

The GetInterface method returns the specified interface on the object.

```
Object = Configuration.GetInterface(Interface)
```

Parameter	Data Type	Description
Interface	String	The name of the interface to return.

Configuration Object Properties

Fields Property

The Fields property returns the Fields object which currently contains the configuration settings.

```
Fields = AddressEntry.Address
```

For example in VBScript:

```
Set objCfgFlds = objCfg.Fields
With objCfgFlds
  .Item(cdoSendUsingMethod) = cdoSendUsingPort
  .Item(cdoSMTPServer) = "test-server"
  .Item(cdoSMTPAuthenticate) = cdoAnonymous
  .Item(cdoSMTPConnectionTimeout) = 20
  .Update
End With
```

Or in JScript:

```
objCfgFlds = objCfg.Fields;
with (objCfgFlds) {
  Item(cdoSendUsingMethod) = cdoSendUsingPort;
  Item(cdoSMTPServer) = "test-server";
  Item(cdoSMTPAuthenticate) = cdoAnonymous;
  Item(cdoSMTPConnectionTimeout) = 20;
  Update();
}
```

The DropDirectory Object

The DropDirectory object implements the IDropDirectory interface, and is used to access the file system directories containing messages, such as the default SMTP service drop directory.

The DropDirectory object exposes one method and no properties:

Method
GetMessages

Creating a DropDirectory Object

We can create a DropDirectory object as follows:

For example in VBScript:

```
Set objDropDir = Server.CreateObject("CDO.DropDirectory")
Set objMsgsColl = objDropDir.GetMessages
```

or in JScript:

```
var objDropDir = Server.CreateObject("CDO.DropDirectory");
var objMsgsColl = objDropDir.GetMessages();
```

DropDirectory Object Methods

GetMessages Method

The GetMessages method returns a collection containing the messages in the directory specified.

```
Messages = DropDirectory.GetMessages([DirName])
```

Parameter	Data Type	Description
DirName	String	Optional. The path to a directory that contains the messages. If an empty string is used it will default to the currently defined SMTP drop directory.

The GetMessages method returns an IMessages interface to iterate over the Message objects contained in the collection. The IMessages interface is a standard collection interface, but offers a couple of additional features to manage the collection of messages, such as the FileName method, which returns the name of the file that holds in the a specific message file system.

DropDirectory Object Properties

The DropDirectory object does not expose any properties.

The Message Object

The Message object is the most important object and, as mentioned previously, it implements three interfaces: IMessage, IBodyPart, and IDataSource. The IMessage interface enables us to work with the message at the higher level, for instance to set the recipient and Send the message.

A message can be a quite complex entity. The CDO2000 architecture is modeled on the MIME specification, and by default the message body content is constructed using MIME encoding rules. This behavior is controlled using the MimeFormatted property; which if set to false means that the message is processed using UUENCODE format.

A complex message that contains more than plain text must be subdivided into parts following the encoding rule. In this case, the Message object acts as the root of the MIME bodyparts hierarchy, and therefore it implements the IBodyPart interface. We access this interface via the BodyPart property, or using the GetInterface method. Bear in mind that the new reference we get still references the same object, not a new one. It merely allows us access to alternate functionality of the object.

The `Message` object exposes the following methods and properties:

Methods	Properties
ActiveConnection	ActiveConnection
AddAttachment	Attachments
AddBodyPart*	AutoGenerateTextBody
AddRelatedBodyPart	BCC
CreateHTMLBody	BodyPart
Forward	BodyParts*
GetDecodedContentStream*	CC
GetEncodedContentStream*	CharSet*
GetFieldParameter*	Configuration
GetInterface*	ContentClass*
GetStream*	ContentClassName*
Open	ContentMediaType*
OpenObject	ContentTransferEncoding*
Post	DataSource*
PostReply	DSNOptions
Reply	EnvelopeFields
ReplyAll	FieldName*
Save	Fields*
SaveTo	FollowUpTo
SaveToContainer	From
SaveToFile*	HTMLBody
SaveToObject	HTMLBodyPart
Send	IsDirty
	Keywords
	MDNRequested
	MimeFormatted
	Newsgroups
	Organization
	Parent*
	ReceivedTime

Methods	Properties
	ReplyTo
	Sender
	SentOn
	Source
	SourceClass
	SourceURL
	Subject
	TextBody
	TextBodyPart

* Please see CDO Windows 2000 BodyPart object reference.

Creating a Message Object

We can create a Message object using the following VBScript code:

```
Dim objMsg
Set objMsg = Server.CreateObject("CDO.Message")
```

Or in JScript:

```
var objMsg = Server.CreateObject("CDO.Message");
```

Message Object Methods

The Message object exposes the following methods:

ActiveConnection Method

The ActiveConnection method is currently not implemented. This method is defined in the IDataSource interface.

AddAttachment Method

The AddAttachment method adds an attachment to the message.

```
BodyPart = Message.AddAttachment(URL, [UserName], [Password])
```

Parameter	Data Type	Description
URL	String	The full path and filename of the attachment.

Table Continued on Following Page

Parameter	Data Type	Description
UserName	String	Optional. A user name to use for authentication purposes.
Password	String	Optional. A password to use for authentication.

For example in VBScript:

```
With objMsg
    ' To, From, Subject, TextBody etc lines
    .AddAttachment "http://test-server/postinfo.html"
    .AddAttachment "C:\Attachments\Word attachment.doc"
    .AddAttachment "C:\Attachments\Simple text attachment.txt"
    .AddAttachment "C:\Attachments\HTML attachment.htm"
    .Send
End With
```

Or in JScript:

```
with (objMsg) {
    // To, From, Subject, TextBody etc lines
    AddAttachment("http://test-server/postinfo.html");
    AddAttachment("file://C:\\Attachments\\Word attachment.doc");
    AddAttachment("C:\\Attachments\\Simple text attachment.txt");
    AddAttachment("C:\\Attachments\\HTML attachment.htm");
    Send();
}
```

AddRelatedBodyPart Method

The AddRelatedBodyPart method adds the content referred to by URL to the BodyParts collection of the message as a BodyPart object.

```
BodyPart = Message.AddRelatedBodyPart(URL, Reference, ReferenceType,
                                [UserName], [Password])
```

Parameter	Data Type	Description
URL	String	The fully path and filename of the resource.
Reference	String	The ContentID or ContentLocation to reference to the new body part with.
ReferenceType	CdoReferenceType	The method of referencing the new body part.
UserName	String	Optional. This parameter can be used for authentication.
Password	String	Optional. The password for authentication

CreateMHTMLBody Method

The `CreateMHTMLBody` method converts the contents of a web page into a MIME encapsulation of MHTML formatted message body.

```
Message.CreateMHTMLBody(URL, [Flags], [UserName], [Password])
```

Parameter	Data Type	Description
URL	String	The full path and filename of the web page.
Flags	CdoMHTLFlags	Optional. The A bit mask controlling the inclusion of items as related body parts.
UserName	String	Optional. The user name for authentication purposes.
Password	String	Optional. The password for authentication.

The values for `CdoMHTLFlags` can be found in Appendix K.

For example in VBScript:

```
objMsg.CreateMHTMLBody "file://C:\Attachments\Compliments.htm"
```

Or in JScript:

```
objMsg.CreateMHTMLBody("file://C:\\Attachments\\Compliments.htm");
```

Forward Method

The `Forward` method creates and returns a new message which can be used to forward this message. The original message is formatted to text.

```
Message = Message.Forward()
```

GetStream Method

The `GetStream` method returns the `Stream` object which contains the message.

```
ADODB.Stream = Message.GetStream()
```

Open Method

The `Open` method is currently not implemented. This is from the `IDataSource` interface.

Post Method

The `Post` method submits this message to a specified newgroup.

```
Message.Post()
```

PostReply Method

The PostReply method creates and returns a new message that can be used to reply to this message, the Newsgroup property is copied over but any attachments are removed. The original message headers are formatted into text.

```
Message = Message.PostReply()
```

Reply Method

The Reply method creates and returns a new message that can be used to reply to the sender of the message, all attachments and recipients are removed. If the ReplyTo is set, it is used to set the To property otherwise the From property of this message is used.

```
Message = Message.Reply()
```

ReplyAll Method

The ReplyAll method creates and returns a new Message object which can be used to reply to the sender and all recipients. If the ReplyTo property is set it is used to set the To property as well as the CC and BCC properties, otherwise the From property is used.

```
Message = Message.ReplyAll()
```

Save Method

The Save method saves local changes to the currently bound data source. This method is exposed by the IDataSource interface.

```
Message.Save()
```

SaveTo Method

The SaveTo method is currently not implemented. This method is exposed by the IDataSource interface.

SaveToContainer Method

The SaveToContainer method is currently not implemented. This method is exposed by the IDataSource interface.

SaveToObject Method

The SaveToObject method binds to and saves data into the specified object. This method is exposed by the IDataSource interface.

```
Message.SaveToObject(Source, Interface)
```

Parameter	Data Type	Description
Source	Variant	The interface on the object in which to save the data.
Interface	String	A string indicating the type of interface passed in the first argument.

Send Method

The Send method sends the message.

```
Message.Send()
```

Message Object Properties

ActiveConnection Property

The ActiveConnection property is currently not implemented.

Attachments Property

The Attachments property is the collection of message attachments.

```
BodyParts = Message.Attachments
```

AutoGenerateTextBody Property

The AutoGenerateTextBody property indicates whether the TextBody property of the message should be generated from the contents of the HTMLBody property for an alternative or multipart message.

```
Boolean = Message.AutoGenerateTextBody
Message.AutoGenerateTextBody = Boolean
```

BCC Property

The BCC property specifies the blind carbon copy recipients for this message.

```
String  = Message.BCC
Message.BCC = String
```

BodyPart Property

The BodyPart property specifies the IBodyPart interface on this object.

```
BodyPart = Message.BodyPart
```

CC Property

The CC property specifies the secondary recipients of this message.

```
String = Message.CC
Message.CC = String
```

Configuration Property

The Configuration property returns the reference to the Configuration object that is associated with the Message object.

```
Configuration = Message.Configuration
Message.Configuration = Configuration
```

DataSource Property

The DataSource property returns the data source for this object:

```
DataSource = Message.DataSource
```

DSNOptions Property

The DSNOptions property sets or returns the type of DSN (Delivery Status Notification) option set for the message.

```
CdoDSNOptions = Message.DNSOptions
Message.DNSOptions = CdoDSNOptions
```

The values of CdoDSNOptions are found in Appendix K.

EnvelopeFields Property

The EnvelopeFields property specifies the fields for the SMTP or NNTP transport envelope for this message. The EnvelopeFields property returns the ADO Fields collection for this property:

```
ADODB.Fields = Message.EnvelopeFields
```

Fields Property

The Fields property returns the ADO Fields collection for this property:

```
ADODB.Fields = Message.Fields
```

FollowUpTo Property

The FollowUpTo property lists the newsgroups to which any responses to this group should be posted.

```
String = Message.FollowUpTo
Message.FollowUpTo = String
```

From Property

The From property lists the e-mail addresses of the principal author(s) of this message.

```
String = Message.From
Message.From = String
```

HTMLBody Property

The HTMLBody property contains the HTML representation of this message.

```
String = Message.HTMLBody
Message.HTMLBody =  String
```

HTMLBodyPart Property

The HTMLBodyPart property returns the BodyPart that contains the HTML representation of the message.

```
BodyPart = Message.HTMLBodyPart
```

IsDirty Property

The IsDirty property sets or returns a boolean value indicating whether the local data has changed since the last time it was saved to the currently bound data object. This is from the IDataSource interface.

```
Boolean = Message.IsDirty
Message.IsDirty = Boolean
```

Keywords Property

The Keywords property is a list of the keywords for the message.

```
String = Message.Keywords
Message.Keywords = String
```

MDNRequested Property

The MDNRequested property is a boolean value indicating whether a Message Disposition Notification is requested for the message.

```
Boolean = Message.MDNRequested
Message.MDNRequested = Boolean
```

MimeFormatted Property

The MimeFormatted property indicates whether this message is to be formatted according to the MIME formatting scheme.

```
Boolean = Message.MimeFormatted
Message.MimeFormatted = Boolean
```

Newsgroups Property

The Newsgroups property is a list of the newsgroup recipients of this message.

```
String = Message.Newsgroups
Message.Newsgroups = String
```

Organization Property

The Organization property indicates the sender's organization if set, e.g. Any Company, IT dept. The default value for this property is an empty string.

```
String = Message.Organization
Message.Organization = String
```

ReceivedTime Property

The ReceivedTime property specifies the date and time the message was delivered to the server.

```
Date = Message.ReceivedTime
```

ReplyTo Property

The ReplyTo property specifies the address or addresses to which replies should be sent.

```
String = Message.ReplyTo
Message.ReplyTo = String
```

Sender Property

The Sender property specifies the address of the sender.

```
String = Message.Sender
Message.Sender = String
```

SentOn Property

The SentOn property specifies the date and time that the message was sent on.

```
Date = Message.SentOn
```

Source Property

The Source property returns the currently bound data object. This is from the IDataSource interface.

```
Object = Message.Source
```

SourceURL Property

The SourceURL property is currently not implemented. This is from the IDataSource interface.

Subject Property

The Subject property specifies the subject of the message.

```
String = Message.Subject
Message.Subject = String
```

TextBody Property

The TextBody property returns the plain text representation of the message.

```
String = Message.TextBody
Message.TextBody = String
```

TextBodyPart Property

The TextBodyPart property returns the BodyPart object which contains the plain text representation.

```
BodyPart = Message.TextBodyPart
```

To Property

The To property sets or returns the main recipient of the message:

```
String = Message.TextBodyPart
Message.TextBodyPart = String
```

The Messages Collection

The Messages collection exposes the following methods and properties:

Methods	Properties
Delete	Count
DeleteAll	Item
	FileName

Messages Collection Methods

The Messages object exposes the Delete and DeleteAll methods:

Delete Method

The Delete method deletes the message from the collection and the file system folder.

```
Messages.Delete(Index)
```

Parameter	Data Type	Description
Index	Long	The ordinal index of the message object to delete.

DeleteAll Method

The DeleteAll method deletes all the Message objects from the collection and the associated files on the file system.

```
Messages.DeleteAll()
```

Messages Collection Properties

Count Property

The Count property returns the number of Message objects in the collection.

```
Long = Messages.Count
```

Item Property

The Item property returns a single Message object from the Messages collection according to that specified by Index.

```
Message = Messages.Item(Index)
```

Where Index is the ordinal number or a reference to a particular message.

CDO for Windows 2000 Examples

CDO2000 objects can be safely used as page-, session- or application-scoped objects without incurring performance penalties since they aggregate the COM Free Threaded Marshaler (FTM).

The METADATA directives required to import all the constants defined in the type libraries are:

```
<!--METADATA TYPE="typelib" NAME="CDO for Windows 2000 Type Library"
             UUID="CD000000-8B95-11D1-82DB-00C04FB1625D" -->
<!--METADATA TYPE="typelib"  NAME="ADODB Type Library"
             UUID="00000205-0000-0010-8000-00AA006D2EA4" -->
```

Creating and Configuring a Simple Message

This example shows the code needed to send a simple "text/plain" mail message. We create a Message object and use the default interface IMessage. Notice that strings that represent the addresses are in the form "displayable name" <email address>, where the displayable name is enclosed in double quotes inside the whole string. In VBScript this looks like:

```
Set objMsg = Server.CreateObject("CDO.Message")
With objMsg
    .To       = """User 33"" <user.33@test-server>"
    .From     = """User 1"" <user.1@dev02>"
    .Subject  = "This is the subject"
    .TextBody = "This is the body."
    .Send
End With
```

In JScript this looks like:

```
<%@ LANGUAGE = JScript %>
<!--METADATA TYPE="typelib" NAME="CDO for Windows 2000 Type Library"
             UUID="CD000000-8B95-11D1-82DB-00C04FB1625D" -->
<!--METADATA TYPE="typelib"  NAME="ADODB Type Library"
             UUID="00000205-0000-0010-8000-00AA006D2EA4" -->
    NAME="ADODB Type Library" -->
<TITLE> CDO2k_?.asp</TITLE>
<%
objMsg = Server.CreateObject("CDO.Message");
with (objMsg) {
    To       = "\"User 33 \" <user.33@test-server>";
    From     = "\"User 1 \" <user.1@dev02>";
    Subject  = "This is the subject";
    TextBody = "This is the body.";
    Send();
}
%>
```

When we run this code in an ASP page, CDO2000 uses the default configuration of the local SMTP Service and queues the message as a file in the default pickup directory. CDO2000 offers configuration capabilities through the Configuration object that implements the IConfiguration interface. The configuration settings are exposed as an ADODB.Fields collection (the IConfiguration.Fields property), and we access each individual option as a field in the collection.

The constants used to identify each field are defined in the CDO2000 type library (see Appendix K). We can use the symbolic constant or the string itself. In the following snippet of code we create and configure a CDO.Configuration object in order to send the message directly over the network (cdoSendUsingMethod field) to the TCP port 25 of the test-server machine (cdoSMTPServer), using an anonymous SMTP transaction (cdoSMTPAuthenticate) with a 20 seconds SMTP connection timeout (cdoSMTPConnectionTimeout).

```
<%
Set objCfg = Server.CreateObject("CDO.Configuration")
Set objCfgFlds = objCfg.Fields
With objCfgFlds
  .Item(cdoSendUsingMethod) = cdoSendUsingPort
  .Item(cdoSMTPServer) = "test-server"
  .Item(cdoSMTPAuthenticate) = cdoAnonymous
  .Item(cdoSMTPConnectionTimeout) = 20
  .Update
End With

Set objMsg = Server.CreateObject("CDO.Message")

With objMsg
  Set .Configuration = objCfg
  .To      = """User 33"" <user.33@test-server>"
  .From    = """User 1"" <user.1@dev02>"
  .Subject = "This is the subject"
  .TextBody = "This is the body."
  .Send
End With
%>
```

The equivalent using JScript is:

```
<%@ LANGUAGE = JScript %>
<!--METADATA TYPE="typelib" NAME="CDO for Windows 2000 Type Library"
          UUID="CD000000-8B95-11D1-82DB-00C04FB1625D" -->
<!--METADATA TYPE="typelib"  NAME="ADODB Type Library"
          UUID="00000205-0000-0010-8000-00AA006D2EA4" -->
<TITLE> CDO2k_?.asp</TITLE>
<%
objCfg = Server.CreateObject("CDO.Configuration");
objCfgFlds = objCfg.Fields;
with (objCfgFlds) {
  Item(cdoSendUsingMethod) = cdoSendUsingPort;
  Item(cdoSMTPServer) = "test-server";
  Item(cdoSMTPAuthenticate) = cdoAnonymous;
  Item(cdoSMTPConnectionTimeout) = 20;
  Update();
}

objMsg = Server.CreateObject("CDO.Message");

with (objMsg) {
  Configuration = objCfg;
  To      = "\"User 33\" <user.33@test-server>";
  From    = "\"User 1\" <user.1@dev02>";
  Subject = "This is the subject";
  TextBody = "This is the body of the JScript message.";
  Send();
}
%>
```

The other constants, such as cdoSendUsingPort, are just standard type library enums (see Appendix K). In order to apply this configuration to the message object, we assign the Configuration object to the .Configuration property. With CDO2000 we can configure the SMTP pickup directory too. For instance, the following configuration instructs CDO2000 to place a file message in the C:\Another Pickup directory:

```
' VBScript version
objCfgFlds.Item(cdoSMTPServerPickupDirectory) = "c:\Another Pickup"
```

```
// JScript version
objCfgFlds.Item(cdoSMTPServerPickupDirectory) = "c:\\Another Pickup";
```

We should be aware that this code doesn't affect the IIS SMTP service configuration, so if the SMTP server is configured to use the standard pickup directory, messages placed in another directory will not be processed. This offers us a great deal of flexibility. For example, we can easily send messages through multiple SMTP services. Finally we look at how we can access message headers not available as object properties and add custom headers to the mail message:

```
With objMsg
    ' The following two statements are equivalent;
    ' they both set the standard approved header of the message
    .Fields.Item("urn:schemas:mailheader:approved") = _
                                        "moderator@company.com"
    '.Fields.Item(CdoMailHeader.cdoApproved) = _
    '                                    "moderator@company.com"

    ' This statement creates a custom header in the message
    .Fields.Item("urn:schemas:mailheader:Custom-header") = _
                                        "This is the value"

    .Fields.Update
    .Send
End With
```

In JScript this looks like:

```
with (objMsg) {
    // The following two statements are equivalent;
    // they both set the standard approved header of the message
    Fields.Item("urn:schemas:mailheader:approved") =
                                        "moderator@company.com";
    //Fields.Item(CdoMailHeader.cdoApproved) =
                                        "moderator@company.com";

    // This statement creates a custom header in the message
    Fields.Item("urn:schemas:mailheader:Custom-header") =
                                        "This is the value";

    Fields.Update();
    Send();
}
```

The `urn:schemas:mailheader:` namespace defines the fields for internet standard message headers. We can access a standard message header using the full name string (e.g. `urn:schemas:mailheader:approved`) or the symbolic constant defined in the type library, `CdoMailHeader.cdoApproved`). To add a custom header we create a new field appending the custom header name to the root namespace, e.g. `urn:schemas:mailheader:Custom-header`, and set the value of the field. This means that the message generated by CDO2000 carries our header in the form `"Custom-header: This is the value"`.

Advanced Configuration

When a `Configuration` object is created, it loads the default configuration options, i.e. the local SMTP settings on a typical server machine. On a client machine the default configuration is provided by the Outlook Express settings (remember we can use CDO2000 as client-side library). The `IConfiguration.Load` method allows us to specify what configuration we want to load. The following VBScript example allows us to experiment with the various configuration options available. It loads and shows in a table the default configuration and then the configuration as changed by the code.

```vbscript
<%@ LANGUAGE = VBScript %>
<!--METADATA TYPE="typelib" NAME="CDO for Windows 2000 Type Library"
            UUID="CD000000-8B95-11D1-82DB-00C04FB1625D" -->
<!--METADATA TYPE="typelib" NAME="ADODB Type Library"
            UUID="00000205-0000-0010-8000-00AA006D2EA4" -->
<%
Option Explicit

Sub DisplayCfgTable( cfgObj )
Dim strTableHeader, strTableFooter
   strTableHeader = "<P><TABLE WIDTH=""100%"" BORDER=""1""" & _
                    "BGCOLOR=""Silver"" CELLSPACING=""1"" " & _
                    "CELLPADDING=""1""><TR BGCOLOR=""Yellow"">" & _
                    "<TD><B>Field</B></TD><TD><B>Value</B></TD></TR>"
   strTableFooter = "</TABLE><P>"

   Response.Write strTableHeader

   Dim field
   For Each field In cfgObj.Fields
      Response.Write "<TR><TD>" & field.Name & "</TD>"
      Response.Write "<TD>" & CStr(field.Value) & "</TD></TR>"
   Next

   Response.Write strTableFooter
End Sub

Dim objCfg, objMsg, objCfgFlds, strFrom, strTo, strSubject, strBody
%>

<HTML>
<HEAD>
<TITLE>CDO2000 sample 1 - Sending a simple message</TITLE>
</HEAD>
<BODY>

<%
strFrom = """User 1"" <user.1@dev02>"
```

```
strTo = """User 33"" <user.33@test-server>"
strSubject = "This is the subject"
strBody = "This is the body."

Set objMsg = Server.CreateObject("CDO.Message")
Set objCfg = Server.CreateObject("CDO.Configuration")
objCfg.Load cdoIIS
%>

These are the default IIS/SMTP configuration settings:
<% DisplayCfgTable(objCfg) %>

Now we are changing the configuration ...<BR>
<%
Set objCfgFlds = objCfg.Fields
With objCfgFlds
  .Item(cdoSendUsingMethod) = cdoSendUsingPort
  .Item(cdoSMTPServer) = "test-server"
  .Item(cdoSMTPConnectionTimeout) = 20
  .Item(cdoSMTPAuthenticate) = cdoAnonymous
  ' the following line is meaningful with cdoSendUsingMethod
  ' equal tocdoSendUsingPickup
  .Item(cdoSMTPServerPickupDirectory) = "c:\Another Pickup"
  .Update
End With
%>
These are the new configuration settings:
<% DisplayCfgTable(objCfg) %>
Now we are sending the message ... <BR>
<%
With objMsg
   Set .Configuration = objCfg
   .To       = strTo
   .From      = strFrom
   .Subject   = strSubject
   .TextBody = strBody
   .Send
End With

Set objCfgFlds = Nothing
Set objCfg = Nothing
Set objMsg = Nothing
%>
We have sent a message to <%= strTo %>.<BR>
</BODY>
</HTML>
```

In JScript this is:

```
<%@ LANGUAGE = JScript %>
<!--METADATA TYPE="typelib" NAME="CDO for Windows 2000 Type Library"
          UUID="CD000000-8B95-11D1-82DB-00C04FB1625D" -->
<!--METADATA TYPE="typelib"  NAME="ADODB Type Library"
          UUID="00000205-0000-0010-8000-00AA006D2EA4" -->
<%
function DisplayCfgTable(cfgObj) {
   strTableHeader = "<P><TABLE WIDTH=\"100%\" BORDER=\"1\"" +
                    "BGCOLOR=\"Silver\" CELLSPACING=\"1\" " +
                    "CELLPADDING=\"1\"><TR bgcolor=\"Yellow\">" +
                    "<TD><B>Field</B></TD><TD><B>Value</B></TD></TR>"
   strTableFooter = "</TABLE><P>";
```

```
      Response.Write(strTableHeader);

   var objEnum = new Enumerator(cfgObj.Fields);
   for (;!objEnum.atEnd();objEnum.moveNext()) {
      var objItem = objEnum.item();
      Response.Write("<TR><TD>" + objItem.Name + "</TD>");
      Response.Write("<TD>" + objItem.Value + "</TD></TR>");
   }

   Response.Write(strTableFooter);
}
%>


<HTML>
<HEAD>
<TITLE>CDO2000 sample 1 - Sending a simple message</TITLE>
</HEAD>
<BODY>


<%
strFrom = "\"User 1\" <user.1@dev02>";
strTo = "\"User 33\" <user.33@test-server>";
strSubject = "This is the subject";
strBody = "This is the body.";

objMsg = Server.CreateObject("CDO.Message");
objCfg = Server.CreateObject("CDO.Configuration");
objCfg.Load(cdoIIS);
%>

These are the default IIS/SMTP configuration settings:
<%
DisplayCfgTable(objCfg);
 %>

Now we are changing the configuration ...<BR>
<%
objCfgFlds = objCfg.Fields;
with (objCfgFlds) {
  Item(cdoSendUsingMethod) = cdoSendUsingPort;
  Item(cdoSMTPServer) = "test-server";
  Item(cdoSMTPConnectionTimeout) = 20;
  Item(cdoSMTPAuthenticate) = cdoAnonymous;
  // the following line is meaningful with cdoSendUsingMethod
  // equal to cdoSendUsingPickup
  Item(cdoSMTPServerPickupDirectory) = "c:\Another Pickup"
  Update();
}
%>
These are the new configuration settings:
<% DisplayCfgTable(objCfg) %>
Now we are sending the message ... <BR>
<%
with (objMsg) {
   Configuration = objCfg;
   To      = strTo;
   From    = strFrom;
   Subject = strSubject;
   TextBody = strBody;
   Send
}
```

```
delete objCfgFlds;
delete objCfg;
delete objMsg;
%>
We have sent a message to <%= strTo %>.<BR>
</BODY>
</HTML>
```

At the end of the script we send the message according to the configuration applied. This script can be the starting point to explore the various options CDO2000 offers. Here is a sample screenshot:

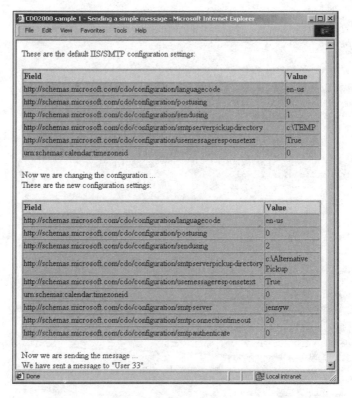

The available configuration options allow us a great deal of flexibility in configuring how a message is processed. For example, we can configure the language and time zone information, authentication fields to access protected network resources, and even the network access through a proxy server.

As a final point, we note that explicitly managing the Configuration object can improve performance. In fact, not relying on loading default configuration for each message sent (as we may guess this is an expensive operation) increases the overall system throughput. The CDO2000 objects aggregate the COM Free Threaded Marshaler. So we can safely create a global Configuration object, store it with session or application-scope and reuse it for each message sent without compromising performance.

Adding Attachments

The simplest way of adding attachments to our message uses the
IMessage.AddAttachment method. For example, the following code adds four
attachments to our message:

```
<%@ LANGUAGE = VBScript %>
<!--METADATA TYPE="typelib" NAME="CDO for Windows 2000 Type Library"
             UUID="CD000000-8B95-11D1-82DB-00C04FB1625D" -->
<!--METADATA TYPE="typelib" NAME="ADODB Type Library"
             UUID="00000205-0000-0010-8000-00AA006D2EA4" -->
<TITLE>Adding Attachments</TITLE>

<%
Set objMsg = Server.CreateObject("CDO.Message")

With objMsg
   .To       = """User 33"" <user.33@test-server>"
   .From     = """User 1"" <user.1@dev02>"
   .Subject  = "This is the subject"
   .TextBody = "This is the body."
   .AddAttachment "http://test-server/postinfo.html"
   .AddAttachment "file://C:\Attachments\Word attachment.doc"
   .AddAttachment "C:\Attachments\Simple text attachment.txt"
   .AddAttachment "C:\Attachments\HTML attachment.htm"
   .Send
End With

Set objMsg = Nothing
%>
```

The equivalent in JScript look like:

```
<%@ LANGUAGE = JScript %>
<!--METADATA TYPE="typelib" NAME="CDO for Windows 2000 Type Library"
             UUID="CD000000-8B95-11D1-82DB-00C04FB1625D" -->
<!--METADATA TYPE="typelib" NAME="ADODB Type Library"
             UUID="00000205-0000-0010-8000-00AA006D2EA4" -->
<TITLE>Adding Attachments</TITLE>

<%
objMsg = Server.CreateObject("CDO.Message");

with (objMsg) {
   To       = "\"User 33\" <user.33@test-server>";
   From     = "\"User 1\" <user.1@dev02>";
   Subject  = "This is the subject";
   TextBody = "This is the body.";
   AddAttachment("http://test-server/postinfo.html");
   AddAttachment("file://C:\\Attachments\\Word attachment.doc");
   AddAttachment("C:\\Attachments\\Simple text attachment.txt");
   AddAttachment("C:\\Attachments\\HTML attachment.htm");
   Send();
}

delete objMsg;
%>
```

The following are added as attachments: the default page of a web server, a Word document referenced through the URL notation that uses the `file` protocol, a text file, and an HTML document referenced through the full path on the server. We can therefore create a pretty complex MIME message with `Content-Type` equal to `multipart/mixed`. This is the message as displayed by Outlook Express 5.0:

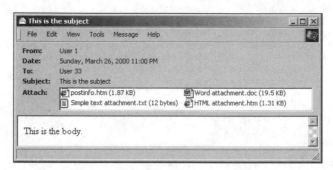

The `AddAttachment` method returns an object that exposes the `IBodyPart` interface and represents the attachment as part of the body message. Using that reference we can manage and modify the attachment. For example let's examine this VBScript code:

```
<%@ LANGUAGE = VBScript %>
<!--METADATA TYPE="typelib" NAME="CDO for Windows 2000 Type Library"
             UUID="CD000000-8B95-11D1-82DB-00C04FB1625D" -->
<!--METADATA TYPE="typelib" NAME="ADODB Type Library"
             UUID="00000205-0000-0010-8000-00AA006D2EA4" -->

<%
Option Explicit

Sub DisplayAttachment(bp)
   Dim stream, strBP

   Set stream = bp.GetStream()
   strBP = Server.HTMLEncode (stream.ReadText())

   Response.Write "<HR>"
   Response.Write "Body part: " & bp.FileName & "<BR>"
   Response.Write "Content Class: " & bp.ContentClass & "<BR>"
   Response.Write "Content Media Type: " & bp.ContentMediaType & _
                  "<BR>"
   Response.Write "Content Transfer Encoding: " & _
                  bp.ContentTransferEncoding & "<BR>"
   Response.Write "Content:" & "<P>"
   Response.Write strBP
   Response.Write "<HR>"

   Set stream = Nothing
End Sub

Dim objMsg, objBodyPart, strFrom, strTo, strSubject, strBody
%>

<HTML>
<HEAD>
<TITLE>CDO2000 Sample #2 - Adding attachments</TITLE>
```

```
</HEAD>
<BODY>
<H3>Creating a message with attachments. Let's take a look at the
MIME representation of attachments:</H3>

<%
strFrom="""User 1"" <user.1@dev02>"
strTo="""User 33"" <user.33@test-server>"
strSubject = "This is the subject"
strBody= "This is the body."

Set objMsg = Server.CreateObject("CDO.Message")

With objMsg
    .To       = strTo
    .From     = strFrom
    .Subject  = strSubject
    .TextBody = strBody

    Set objBodyPart = .AddAttachment ("http://test-server/postinfo.html")
    DisplayAttachment(objBodyPart)
    Set objBodyPart = Nothing

    Set objBodyPart = .AddAttachment ("file://C:\Attachments\Word
attachment.doc")
    DisplayAttachment(objBodyPart)
    ' now we change the encoding rule applied to the Word document
    objBodyPart.ContentTransferEncoding = cdoUuencode
    DisplayAttachment(objBodyPart)
    Set objBodyPart = Nothing

    Set objBodyPart = .AddAttachment ("C:\Attachments\Simple text
attachment.txt")
    DisplayAttachment(objBodyPart)
    Set objBodyPart = Nothing

    Set objBodyPart = .AddAttachment ("C:\Attachments\HTML " & _
                                      "attachment.htm")
    DisplayAttachment(objBodyPart)
    Set objBodyPart = Nothing

    .Send
End With
%>
<H3>Here is the list of attachments obtained via the
BodyParts collection of the message object:</H3>

<%
Dim  objMsgBP
Dim  objAttBP
Set objMsgBP = objMsg.BodyPart
For Each objAttBP In objMsgBP.BodyParts
    Response.write objAttBP.filename
    Response.Write "<BR>"
Next
Set objMsgBP = Nothing
Set objMsg = Nothing

Response.Write "<HR>"
%>
```

```
<H3>We have sent a message to <% = strTo %>.</H3>
<BR>
</BODY>
</HTML>
```

Or in JScript:

```
<%@ LANGUAGE = JScript %>
<!--METADATA TYPE="typelib" NAME="CDO for Windows 2000 Type Library"
             UUID="CD000000-8B95-11D1-82DB-00C04FB1625D" -->
<!--METADATA TYPE="typelib" NAME="ADODB Type Library"
             UUID="00000205-0000-0010-8000-00AA006D2EA4" -->

<%
function DisplayAttachment(bp) {
    stream = bp.GetStream();
    strBP = Server.HTMLEncode (stream.ReadText());

    Response.Write("<HR>");
    Response.Write("Body part: " + bp.FileName + "<BR>");
    Response.Write("Content Class: " + bp.ContentClass + "<BR>");
    Response.Write("Content Media Type: " + bp.ContentMediaType +
                "<BR>");
    Response.Write("Content Transfer Encoding: " +
                bp.ContentTransferEncoding + "<BR>");
    Response.Write("Content:" + "<P>");
    Response.Write(strBP);
    Response.Write("<HR>");

    delete stream;
}
%>

<HTML>
<HEAD>
<TITLE>CDO2000 Sample #2 - Adding attachments</TITLE>
</HEAD>
<BODY>
<H3>Creating a message with attachments. Let's take a look at the
MIME representation of attachments:</H3>

<%
strFrom="\"User 1\" <user.1@dev02>";
strTo="\"User 33\" <user.33@test-server>";
strSubject = "This is the subject";
strBody= "This is the body.";

objMsg = Server.CreateObject("CDO.Message");

with (objMsg) {
    To       = strTo;
    From     = strFrom;
    Subject  = strSubject;
    TextBody = strBody;

    objBodyPart = AddAttachment ("http://test-server/postinfo.html");
    DisplayAttachment(objBodyPart);
    delete objBodyPart;

    objBodyPart = AddAttachment("file://C:\\Attachments\\" +
```

```
                                    "Word attachment.doc");
   DisplayAttachment(objBodyPart);
   // now we change the encoding rule applied to the Word document
   objBodyPart.ContentTransferEncoding = cdoUuencode;
   DisplayAttachment(objBodyPart);
   delete objBodyPart;

   objBodyPart = AddAttachment ("C:\\Attachments\\" +
                                "Simple text attachment.txt")
   DisplayAttachment(objBodyPart);
   delete objBodyPart;

   objBodyPart = AddAttachment("C:\\Attachments\\HTML " +
                                "attachment.htm")
   DisplayAttachment(objBodyPart);
   delete objBodyPart;

   Send();
}
%>
<H3>Here is the list of attachments obtained via the
BodyParts collection of the message object:</H3>

<%
objMsgBP = objMsg.BodyPart();
var objEnum = new Enumerator(objMsgBP.BodyParts);
for (;!objEnum.atEnd(); objEnum.moveNext()) {
   var objItem = objEnum.item();
   Response.Write(objItem.filename + "<BR>");
}

delete objMsgBP;
delete objMsg;

Response.Write("<HR>");
%>

<H3>We have sent a message to <% = strTo %>.</H3>
<BR>
</BODY>
</HTML>
```

We get the body part object related to each attachment, and then call the DisplayAttachment function to display the attachment in the HTML page. This gets the ADODB.Stream object reference containing the headers and content of this body part and writes this data in the page along with the other IBodyPart properties: FileName, ContentMediaType, ContentClass, and ContentTransferEncoding. If we run the code, we see that the default encoding rule that applies to the Word document is *base64* (cdoBase64), therefore, if we change the encoding to *uuencode* (cdoUuencode) the attachment is sent using this encoding rule. Obviously, we can also access all the attachments of a message using the IMessage.Attachments collection. Alternatively we can get the IBodyPart interface of the message object (using the BodyPart property) and access the attachments via the BodyParts collection.

Advanced Techniques for Managing Attachments

With CDO2000 we can produce message's attachments on the fly in the ASP script, meaning that we can create the attachments' content programmatically (rather than loading it from file). Let's suppose, for instance, we have a collection of standard attachments we want to add to our advertising messages, which are being stored in a SQL Server database. The following snippet of VBScript code is the foundation to programmatically produce the attachments' content :

```
<%@ LANGUAGE = VBScript %>
<!--METADATA TYPE="typelib" NAME="CDO for Windows 2000 Type Library"
            UUID="CD000000-8B95-11D1-82DB-00C04FB1625D" -->
<!--METADATA TYPE="typelib" NAME="ADODB Type Library"
            UUID="00000205-0000-0010-8000-00AA006D2EA4" -->
<%
Option Explicit

Dim objMsg, objBodyPart, objBPfields, objStream, strFrom
Dim strTo, strSubject, strBody
%>

<HTML>
<HEAD>
<TITLE>CDO2000 Sample #3 - Advanced techniques for
managing attachments</TITLE>
</HEAD>
<BODY>

<%
strFrom="""User 1"" <user.1@dev02>"
strTo="""User 33"" <user.33@test-server>"
strSubject = "This is the subject"
strBody= "This is the body."

Set objMsg = Server.CreateObject("CDO.Message")

With objMsg
    .To       = strTo
    .From      = strFrom
    .Subject   = strSubject
    .TextBody  = strBody
    Set objBodyPart = .Attachments.Add
End With

Set objBPfields = objBodyPart.Fields

With objBPfields
    .Item("urn:schemas:mailheader:content-type") = "text/plain;" & _
                        " name=Simple text attachment.txt"
    .Item("urn:schemas:mailheader:content-transfer-encoding") = _
"quoted-printable"
    .Update
End With

Set objBPfields = Nothing
```

```
Set objStream = objBodyPart.GetDecodedContentStream
objStream.WriteText "This content has been produced on the " & _
                    "fly by ASP script."
objStream.Flush
Set objStream = Nothing

objMsg.Send
Set objMsg = Nothing
%>

We have sent a message to <% = strTo %> with an attachment
produced on the fly by ASP script.<BR>
</BODY>
</HTML>
```

The equivalent in JScript looks like:

```
<%@ LANGUAGE = JScript %>
<!--METADATA TYPE="typelib" NAME="CDO for Windows 2000 Type Library"
            UUID="CD000000-8B95-11D1-82DB-00C04FB1625D" -->
<!--METADATA TYPE="typelib" NAME="ADODB Type Library"
            UUID="00000205-0000-0010-8000-00AA006D2EA4" -->
<HTML>
<HEAD>
<TITLE>CDO2000 Sample #3 - Advanced techniques for
managing attachments</TITLE>
</HEAD>
<BODY>

<%
strFrom="\"User 1\" <user.1@dev02>";
strTo="\"User 33\" <user.33@test-server>";
strSubject = "This is the subject";
strBody= "This is the body.";

objMsg = Server.CreateObject("CDO.Message");

with (objMsg) {
    To      = strTo;
    From    = strFrom;
    Subject = strSubject;
    TextBody = strBody;
    objBodyPart = Attachments.Add();
}

objBPfields = objBodyPart.Fields;

with (objBPfields) {
    Item("urn:schemas:mailheader:content-type") = "text/plain;" +
                " name=Simple text attachment.txt"
    Item("urn:schemas:mailheader:content-transfer-encoding") =
                "quoted-printable"
    Update();
}

delete objBPfields;

objStream = objBodyPart.GetDecodedContentStream();
objStream.WriteText("This content has been produced on the " +
```

```
                        "fly by ASP script.");
objStream.Flush();
delete objStream;

objMsg.Send();
delete objMsg;
%>

We have sent a message to <% = strTo %> with an attachment
produced on the fly by ASP script.<BR>
</BODY>
</HTML>
```

We create an empty attachment (an object exposing the `IBodyPart` interface), using the `Add` method of the `Attachments` collection of the message object. We then configure this, accessing the required fields in the `ADODB.Fields` collection exposed via the `Fields` property, as we saw with the `IConfiguration` interface. Alternatively, we could have configured the attachment using the `ContentMediaType` and `ContentTransferEncoding` properties directly instead of accessing the `Fields` collection. To load content in the attachment we get an `ADODB.Stream` object using the `GetDecodedContentStream` method. Then we write a simple text in the stream and flush it. In this sample we used a plain text attachment, but we could also work with binary attachments.

Creating MHTML Messages

CDO2000 offers a straightforward way of producing a MHTML messages using the `CreateMHTMLBody` method. With just one line of code we can create a very complex and glitzy mail message.

```
' VBScript
objMsg.CreateMHTMLBody "file://C:\Attachments\Compliments.htm"
```

```
// JScript
objMsg.CreateMHTMLBody("file://C:\\Attachments\\Compliments.htm");
```

This method accepts a URL to scan for links (e.g. images), and creates the appropriate MHTML body parts of the message. We can control the amount of information that is placed in the message via the second optional parameter, which allows us to control the inclusion of items from the web page as related body parts. The third and fourth optional parameters of the method can be used for authentication (i.e. User name and password).

The `CreateMHTMLBody` method automatically creates a message with `Content-Type` equal to `multipart/alternative`. This means that we get the MHTML content and a `text/plain` body part containing the plain text extracted from the HTML, referenced via the `TextBody` property. We can also overwrite the plain text automatically created with another content. This way any mail user agent that is not able to handle MHTML can display the text body part of the message.

It's worth noting that we can use the file protocol in a URL, for example, `file://c:\HTMLtemplates\ad1.htm`. This makes it very simple to create a set of standard messages as HTML files, place them on a private section of the disk and produce an attractive mail message with just a few lines of code. We can also create a MHTML message from scratch working with the body parts hierarchy of the message, but the easiest way to cope with complex MHTML messages is to load a template with `CreateMHTMLBody` and modify the message in the script to customize the content. That's precisely what the following code does:

```
<%@ LANGUAGE = VBScript %>
<!--METADATA TYPE="typelib" NAME="CDO for Windows 2000 Type Library"
            UUID="CD000000-8B95-11D1-82DB-00C04FB1625D" -->
<!--METADATA TYPE="typelib" NAME="ADODB Type Library"
            UUID="00000205-0000-0010-8000-00AA006D2EA4" -->


<%
Option Explicit

Sub ReplaceInBodyPart(bp)
    Const strTokentoFind = "SIGNATURE"
    Const strTokenToReplace = "Marco Gregorini"
    Dim objStream, strContent

    Set objStream = bp.GetDecodedContentStream
    strContent = objStream.ReadText
    strContent = Replace (strContent, strTokentoFind, strTokenToReplace)

    objStream.Position = 0
    objStream.SetEOS
    objStream.WriteText strContent
    objStream.Flush
    Set objStream =Nothing
End Sub

Sub ModifyHtmlAndTextBodyParts(msg)
    Dim objBP

    Set objBP = msg.HTMLBodyPart
    ReplaceInBodyPart objBP
    Set objBP = Nothing

    Set objBP = msg.TextBodyPart
    ReplaceInBodyPart objBP
    Set objBP = Nothing
End Sub

Dim objMsg, strFrom, strTo, strSubject, strBody
%>

<HTML>
<HEAD>
<TITLE>CDO2000 Sample #4 - Creating MHTML messages</TITLE>
</HEAD>
<BODY>

<%
strFrom="""User 1"" <user.1@dev02>"
strTo="""User 33"" <user.33@test-server>"
strSubject = "With compliments"
```

```
Set objMsg = Server.CreateObject("CDO.Message")

With objMsg
   .To       = strTo
   .From     = strFrom
   .Subject  = strSubject
   .CreateMHTMLBody "file://C:\Attachments\Compliments.htm"
End With

ModifyHtmlAndTextBodyParts objMsg
objMsg.Send

Set objMsg = Nothing
%>

We have sent a MHTML message to <% = strTo %>.<BR>
</BODY>
</HTML>
```

The equivalent in JScript looks like:

```
<%@ LANGUAGE = JScript %>
<!--METADATA TYPE="typelib" NAME="CDO for Windows 2000 Type Library"
            UUID="CD000000-8B95-11D1-82DB-00C04FB1625D" -->
<!--METADATA TYPE="typelib" NAME="ADODB Type Library"
            UUID="00000205-0000-0010-8000-00AA006D2EA4" -->

<%
function ReplaceInBodyPart(bp) {
   re = /SIGNATURE/g;
   var strTokenToReplace = "Marco Gregorini";
   objStream = bp.GetDecodedContentStream();
   var strContent = objStream.ReadText();
   strContent = strContent.replace(re, strTokenToReplace);

   objStream.Position = 0;
   objStream.SetEOS();
   objStream.WriteText(strContent);
   objStream.Flush();
   delete objStream;
}

function ModifyHtmlAndTextBodyParts(msg) {
   objBP = msg.HTMLBodyPart;
   ReplaceInBodyPart(objBP);
   delete objBP;

   objBP = msg.TextBodyPart;
   ReplaceInBodyPart(objBP);
   delete objBP;
}
%>

<HTML>
<HEAD>
<TITLE>CDO2000 Sample #4 - Creating MHTML messages</TITLE>
</HEAD>
<BODY>
```

```
<%
strFrom="\"User 1\" <user.1@dev02>";
strTo="\"User 33\" <user.33@test-server>";
strSubject = "With compliments";

objMsg = Server.CreateObject("CDO.Message");

with (objMsg) {
    To        = strTo;
    From      = strFrom;
    Subject   = strSubject;
    CreateMHTMLBody("file://C:\\Attachments\\Compliments.htm");
}

ModifyHtmlAndTextBodyParts(objMsg);
objMsg.Send();

delete objMsg;
%>

We have sent a MHTML message to <% = strTo %>.<BR>
</BODY>
</HTML>
```

Having created the MHTML message we modify it according to our requirement in the `ModifyHtmlAndTextBodyParts` sub. The `IMessage.HTMLBodyPart` property is the quickest way to access the `IBodyPart` object reference to the object that contains the HTML representation of the message. This way we avoid enumerating the body parts hierarchy of the message seeking the object with `Content-Type` set to `"text/html"`. Once we have a reference to the HTML body part, we call the `ReplaceInBodyPart` method, passing this reference as parameter. Inside this function we get the `ADODB.Stream` object that contains the body part content in decoded format, exactly as in the previous sample.

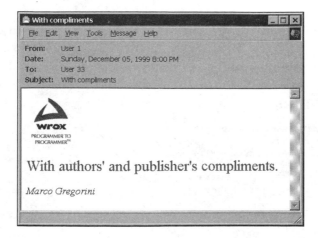

This stream enables us to read the content of the part, i.e. the HTML that represents the message, and replace a predefined token with the customized string, in this case the signature. Finally we write the changed content back to the stream and flush it (note that we must take care to completely overwrite the original content). Our script repeats this process for the body part containing the plain text version of the message, referenced via the `IMessage.TextBodyPart` property (in this case this part is produced automatically by CDO2000 extracting the test from the HTML). The coding effort required for this is quite trivial, but the net result of this technique can be fairly impressive.

Working with Drop Directories

The SMTP Service of Windows 2000 does not provide direct mailbox support. Instead, all the incoming mail messages are delivered to the same physical disk directory, the `DropDirectory` configured via the default local domain, and placed in files with the `.eml` extension. We can work with incoming messages using the CDO2000 `DropDirectory` object, which implements the simple `IDropDirectory` interface. There is just one method defined by this interface, `GetMessages`, which takes as an optional parameter the path to a directory that contains the messages (if we don't specify a path, the SMTP default setting is used) and returns the collection of messages (`IMessages`) contained in this directory. There is no functionality-equivalent to `CDONTS Session.LogonSMTP`, that allows us to automatically filter the messages addressed to a specific mailbox, so the collection of messages returned by `GetMessages` contains all the messages in the directory.

`GetMessages` allows us to use whatever directory we want, so it's reasonably easy to create and manage multiple directories that act as individual mailboxes. For instance, the following ASP page opens the default `Drop` directory and moves all messages to `c:\mailboxes`.

```
<%@ LANGUAGE = VBScript %>
<!--METADATA TYPE="typelib" NAME="CDO for Windows 2000 Type Library"
             UUID="CD000000-8B95-11D1-82DB-00C04FB1625D" -->
<!--METADATA TYPE="typelib" NAME="ADODB Type Library"
             UUID="00000205-0000-0010-8000-00AA006D2EA4" -->

<%
Option Explicit

Function MsgFileName (msgsColl, msg)
   Dim strFileName
   strFileName = msgsColl.FileName(msg)
   strFileName = Right(strFileName, Len(strFileName) - _
                       InStrRev(strFileName,"\") )
   MsgFileName = strFileName
End Function

Sub DisplayMsgsTable( msgsColl )

   Dim strTableHeader, strTableFooter
   strTableHeader = "<P><TABLE WIDTH=""100%"" BORDER=""1""" & _
                    "BGCOLOR=""Silver"" CELLSPACING=""1"" " & _
                    "CELLPADDING=""1""><TR BGCOLOR=""Yellow"">" & _
                    "<TD><B>From</B></TD><TD><B>Subject</B></TD></TR>"
   strTableFooter = "</TABLE><P>"
```

```
        Response.Write strTableHeader

    Dim   objMsg
    For Each objMsg In msgsColl
        Response.Write "<TR><TD>" & objMsg.From & "</TD>"
        Response.Write "<TD>" & objMsg.Subject & "</TD>"
        Response.Write "<TD>" & MsgFileName(msgsColl, objMsg)
        Response.Write  "</TD></TR>"
    Next

    Response.Write strTableFooter
End Sub

Const  strNewDropPath = "c:\mailboxes"

Dim objDropDir, objMsgsColl, objMsg, objStream, lngCounter
%>

<HTML>
<HEAD>
<TITLE>CDO2000 sample 5 - Working with Drop Directories</TITLE>
</HEAD>
<BODY>
We are moving the following message files from the default
SMTP drop directory to the " <%= strNewDropPath%>" directory.
<P>
<%
Set objDropDir = Server.CreateObject("CDO.DropDirectory")
Set objMsgsColl = objDropDir.GetMessages

DisplayMsgsTable(objMsgsColl)
lngCounter = 0

For Each objMsg In objMsgsColl
Set objStream = objMsg.GetStream
    objStream.SaveToFile strNewDropPath & "\" & _
                        MsgFileName(objMsgsColl, objMsg)
    objStream.Close
    Set objStream = Nothing
    lngCounter = lngCounter + 1
Next

objMsgsColl.DeleteAll
Set objMsgsColl = Nothing
%>
<P>We have moved <%= CStr(lngCounter) %> messages
to the new location.<BR>
Now we are opening the " <%= strNewDropPath%>" drop directory
that contains the following messages.

<P>
<%
Set objMsgsColl = objDropDir.GetMessages(strNewDropPath)
DisplayMsgsTable(objMsgsColl)

Set objMsgsColl = Nothing
Set objDropDir = Nothing
%>
</BODY>
</HTML>
```

We create the `DropDirectory` object and get the collection of messages contained in the default SMTP drop directory, we then display in a table the sender, subject and file name for each message in to the collection. Using the `ADODB.Stream` interface we save each message in the new location and then delete messages in the default drop directory using the `DeleteAll` method of the `IMessages` collection. Finally, we get the messages collection in the `c:\mailboxes` directory and display a table of messages. It's not very hard to programmatically filter the `Messages` collection using the `IMessage.To` property (but an automatic screening feature such as that provided by CDONTS would be appreciated).

The same code in JScript looks like:

```
<%@ LANGUAGE = JScript %>
<!--METADATA TYPE="typelib" NAME="CDO for Windows 2000 Type Library"
            UUID="CD000000-8B95-11D1-82DB-00C04FB1625D" -->
<!--METADATA TYPE="typelib" NAME="ADODB Type Library"
            UUID="00000205-0000-0010-8000-00AA006D2EA4" -->

<%
function MsgFileName (msgsColl, msg) {
   strFileName = msgsColl.FileName(msg);
   strFileName = strFileName.substring(strFileName.lastIndexOf ("\\")+1,
strFileName.length);
   return strFileName;
   }

function DisplayMsgsTable (msgsColl) {
   strTableHeader = "<P><TABLE WIDTH=\"100%\" BORDER=\"1\"" +
                    "BGCOLOR=\"Silver\" CELLSPACING=\"1\" " +
                    "CELLPADDING=\"1\"><TR BGCOLOR=\"Yellow\">" +
                    "<TD><B>From</B></TD><TD><B>Subject</B></TD></TR>";
   strTableFooter = "</TABLE><P>";
   Response.Write(strTableHeader);
   var objEnum = new Enumerator(msgsColl);
   for (;!objEnum.atEnd();objEnum.moveNext()) {
      var objItem = objEnum.item();
      Response.Write("<TR><TD>" + objItem.From + "</TD>");
      Response.Write("<TD>" + objItem.Subject + "</TD>");
      Response.Write("<TD>" + MsgFileName(msgsColl, objItem));
      Response.Write( "</TD></TR>");
      }
   Response.Write(strTableFooter);
}

strNewDropPath = "c:\\mailboxes";
%>

<HTML>
<HEAD>
<TITLE>CDO2000 sample 5 - Working with Drop Directories</TITLE>
</HEAD>
<BODY>
We are moving the following message files from the default
SMTP drop directory to the " <%= strNewDropPath%>" directory.
<P>
<%
objDropDir = Server.CreateObject("CDO.DropDirectory");
objMsgsColl = objDropDir.GetMessages();
```

```
DisplayMsgsTable(objMsgsColl);
lngCounter = 0;

var objEnum = new Enumerator(objMsgsColl);
for (;!objEnum.atEnd();objEnum.moveNext()) {
    var objItem = objEnum.item();
    objStream = objItem.GetStream();
    objStream.SaveToFile(strNewDropPath + "\\" + MsgFileName(objMsgsColl,
                         objItem));
    objStream.Close();
    delete objStream;
    lngCounter++;
}

objMsgsColl.DeleteAll();
delete(objMsgsColl);
%>
<P>We have moved <%= lngCounter %> messages
to the new location.<BR>
Now we are opening the " <%= strNewDropPath%>" drop directory
that contains the following messages.

<P>
<%
objMsgsColl = objDropDir.GetMessages(strNewDropPath);
DisplayMsgsTable(objMsgsColl);

delete objMsgsColl;
delete objDropDir;
%>
</BODY>
</HTML>
```

Loading/Saving Messages from/to ADO Stream Objects

With the ADODB.Stream and CDO.IDataSource interfaces we can easily create a library of *pre-cooked* messages that we can load from file on demand. The following code shows us a couple of procedures we can use to accomplish this task. The CreateAndSaveMessageTemplate function creates a message and configures some of its properties (From, Subject and TextBody). It also creates a Configuration object to configure the message to be sent directly over the network. We then save the message to a file. This streaming process implies the use of the IDataSource interface of the Message object, or in other words, we exploit the Message object via an interface that is not the default IMessage interface. We can see there are three main steps to saving the message to a file:

❑ Create and open an ADODB.Stream object

❑ Save the data contained in the message object (e.g. the subject and the body's text) to the Stream object using the IDataSource.SaveToObject method

❑ Save the Stream object to a file on the disk using the ADODB.Stream.SaveToFile method.

In VBScript this looks like:

```
<%@ LANGUAGE = VBScript %>
<!--METADATA TYPE="typelib" NAME="CDO for Windows 2000 Type Library"
            UUID="CD000000-8B95-11D1-82DB-00C04FB1625D" -->
<!--METADATA TYPE="typelib" NAME="ADODB Type Library"
            UUID="00000205-0000-0010-8000-00AA006D2EA4" -->
<%
Option Explicit

Sub CreateAndSaveMessageTemplate( path )
   Const  strFrom="""User 1"" <user.1@dev02>"
   Const  strSubject = "This is the subject"
   Const  strBody= "This is the body."

   Dim objCfg, objMsg, objCfgFlds, objStream, itfDatasource

   Set objMsg = Server.CreateObject("CDO.Message")
   Set objCfg = Server.CreateObject("CDO.Configuration")

   objCfg.Load cdoIIS
   Set objCfgFlds = objCfg.Fields

   With objCfgFlds
       .Item(cdoSendUsingMethod) = cdoSendUsingPort
       .Item(cdoSMTPServer) = "test-server"
       .Item(cdoSMTPConnectionTimeout) = 20
       .Item(cdoSMTPAuthenticate) = cdoAnonymous
       .Update
   End With

   With objMsg
      Set .Configuration = objCfg
      .Sender   = strFrom
      .From     = strFrom
      .Subject  = strSubject
      .TextBody = strBody
   End With

   Set objStream = Server.CreateObject("ADODB.Stream")
   objStream.Open
   objStream.Type = adTypeText
   objStream.Charset = "US-ASCII"

   Set itfDatasource = objMsg.DataSource
   itfDatasource.SaveToObject objStream, CdoInterfaces.cdoAdoStream

   objStream.SaveToFile path, adSaveCreateOverWrite

   Set objStream = Nothing
   Set itfDatasource = Nothing
   Set objCfgFlds = Nothing
   Set objCfg = Nothing
   Set objMsg = Nothing
End Sub

Function GetMessageTemplateFromFile (path)
   Dim objStream, objMsg, itfDatasource
```

```
      Set objStream = Server.CreateObject("ADODB.Stream")
      objStream.Open
      objStream.LoadFromFile path
      Set objMsg = Server.CreateObject("CDO.Message")
      Set itfDatasource = objMsg.DataSource
      itfDatasource.OpenObject objStream, CdoInterfaces.cdoAdoStream
      Set GetMessageTemplateFromFile = objMsg
      Set objStream = Nothing
End Function

Const  strTemplatePath = "C:\CDO2000MsgTemplate.eml"

Dim strTo, objMsg
%>

<HTML>
<HEAD>
<TITLE>CDO2000 Sample #6 - Loading/saving messages from/to
ADO Stream objects</TITLE>
</HEAD>
<BODY>

We are creating and saving to a file. This message template
hasn't got a recipient ...<BR><BR>

<%
CreateAndSaveMessageTemplate(strTemplatePath)
%>
Now we are loading our template from file, setting the
recipient and sending it ...<BR><BR>

<%
strTo="""User 33"" <user.33@test-server>"
Set objMsg = GetMessageTemplateFromFile(strTemplatePath)
With objMsg
    .To = strTo
    .Send
End With
Set objMsg = Nothing
%>

We have sent a message to <% = strTo %>.
</BODY>
</HTML>
```

The equivalent in JScript looks like:

```
<%@ LANGUAGE = JScript %>
<!--METADATA TYPE="typelib" NAME="CDO for Windows 2000 Type Library"
            UUID="CD000000-8B95-11D1-82DB-00C04FB1625D" -->
<!--METADATA TYPE="typelib" NAME="ADODB Type Library"
            UUID="00000205-0000-0010-8000-00AA006D2EA4" -->
<%
function CreateAndSaveMessageTemplate(path) {
    strFrom="\"User 1\" <user1@test-server>";
    strSubject = "This is the subject";
    strBody= "This is the body.";

    objMsg = Server.CreateObject("CDO.Message");
    objCfg = Server.CreateObject("CDO.Configuration");
```

```
   objCfg.Load(cdoIIS);
   objCfgFlds = objCfg.Fields;

   with (objCfgFlds) {
      Item(cdoSendUsingMethod) = cdoSendUsingPort;
      Item(cdoSMTPServer) = "test-server";
      Item(cdoSMTPConnectionTimeout) = 20;
      Item(cdoSMTPAuthenticate) = cdoAnonymous;
      Update();
   }

   with (objMsg) {
      Configuration = objCfg;
      Sender   = strFrom;
      From     = strFrom;
      Subject  = strSubject;
      TextBody = strBody;
   }

   objStream = Server.CreateObject("ADODB.Stream");
   objStream.Open();
   objStream.Type = adTypeText;
   objStream.Charset = "US-ASCII";

   itfDatasource = objMsg.DataSource;
   itfDatasource.SaveToObject(objStream,
                                 CdoInterfaces.cdoAdoStream);

   objStream.SaveToFile(path, adSaveCreateOverWrite);

   delete objStream;
   delete itfDatasource;
   delete objCfgFlds;
   delete objCfg;
   delete objMsg;
}

function GetMessageTemplateFromFile(path) {
   objStream = Server.CreateObject("ADODB.Stream");
   objStream.Open();
   objStream.LoadFromFile(path);
   objMsg = Server.CreateObject("CDO.Message");
   itfDatasource = objMsg.DataSource;
   itfDatasource.OpenObject(objStream, CdoInterfaces.cdoAdoStream);
   return objMsg;
   delete(objStream);
}

strTemplatePath = "C:\\CDO2000MsgTemplate.eml"
%>

<HTML>
<HEAD>
<TITLE>CDO2000 Sample #6 - Loading/saving messages from/to
ADO Stream objects</TITLE>
</HEAD>
<BODY>

We are creating and saving to a file. This message template
hasn't got a recipient ...<BR><BR>
```

```
<%
CreateAndSaveMessageTemplate(strTemplatePath);
%>
Now we are loading our template from file, setting the
recipient and sending it ...<BR><BR>

<%
strTo="\"User 33\" <user.33@dev2.com>"
objMsg = GetMessageTemplateFromFile(strTemplatePath);


with (objMsg) {
   To = strTo;
   Send();
}
delete objMsg;
%>

We have sent a message to <% = strTo %>.
</BODY>
</HTML>
```

The inverse function, GetMessageTemplateFromFile, creates an empty Message object and performs the following steps to initialize it from the file we created earlier:

❑ Create and open an ADODB.Stream object

❑ Call the ADODB.Stream.LoadFromFile method in order to load the contents of the file into the stream object

❑ Finally it loads the data held by the stream object in the message object using the IDataSource.OpenObject method

We therefore have a message with some properties already set, and obviously we can pursue this technique with more complex messages (e.g. MHTML). Note that the configuration data (i.e. the sending options set via the Configuration object) for the message are not saved as part of the streaming process. We can verify that since we configured the message to be sent directly over the network in the CreateAndSaveMessageTemplate function, but when the message is actually sent, it goes through the pickup directory of the SMTP service.

Exploiting the SMTP Transport Event Sink

The Windows 2000 SMTP and NNTP services provide an architecture for the implementation of custom transport event sinks. This architecture is based upon the standard COM event infrastructure. An event sink is just a COM object that implements one or more **source interfaces** defined in the CDO for Windows 2000 type library. A source interface is an interface that is not implemented by the CDO2000 objects. We must implement it in an event sink object and register this event sink to be called by the SMTP/NNTP service. This is exactly the same situation we see with events of ActiveX controls: the control defines a source interface that we must implement in our program to allow the control to fire the events.

The CDO2000 type library defines four source interfaces, each one of which models specific event semantics. The SMTP/NNTP service calls the methods of such interfaces to allow the event sink object to synchronously intercept mail or news messages after the SMTP/NNTP service receives them, but before they are transported to a final storage destination, such as the drop directory. In other words, the event sink can preprocess the message before it comes to the recipients, performing tasks such as virus checking, blocking junk mail, etc.

Three source interfaces are related to the NNTP service, each one of which has just one method:

Source Interface Method	Description
INNTPOnPostEarly.OnPostEarly	This is called when message headers arrive at the NNTP service but before the message content has arrived.
INNTPOnPost.OnPost	This is called when a message has arrived at the NNTP service.
INNTPOnPostFinal.OnPostFinal	This is called after a message has been posted at the NNTP service.

The other source interface is related to the SMTP service:

Source Interface Method	Description
ISMTPOnArrival.OnArrival	This is called when a new message arrives at the SMTP service.

All the interfaces' methods have precisely the same parameters:

❑   IMessage interface on a CDO.Message object holding the message that arrived,

❑   A CdoEventStatusEnum value that indicates the status of the event (we can tell the SMTP/NNTP service to proceed notifying the next event sink, or skip any remaining sinks for the event).

We're now going to see a practical example of a SMTP event sink. Our aim is to automatically raise the importance of mail messages that come from a specific domain, in our case vips.com.

First of all we must implement the event sink. Notice that CDO2000 offers a framework that allows us to implement the event sink in scripting languages. This code should be saved to a file on disk (say c:\Sample SMTP event sink.vbs):

```
Sub ISMTPOnArrival_OnArrival(ByVal Msg, Status)
    Msg.Fields.Item("urn:schemas:httpmail:importance") = 2 ' cdoHigh
    Msg.Fields.Update
    Msg.DataSource.Save
    Status = 1 ' cdoSkipRemainingSinks
End Sub
```

Notice the name of the function: we are implementing the `OnArrival` method of the `ISMTPOnArrival` interface. The code is pretty simple: we set the `Importance` header of the mail message to the value 2 (`cdoHigh`). It's worth noting that we must call `Update` on the `Message.Fields` collection and `IDataSource.Save` on the `Message` object to commit the change. Obviously, we can write an event sink with Visual Basic, C++, or any COM-enabled tool too. A compiled language offers better performance, but VBScript give us a straightforward way to implement an event sink.

The next step is to register this event sink to be called by the SMTP service. Unfortunately, there is no straightforward GUI way to register an event sink and the registration process must be performed programmatically using a COM object (ProgID `Event.Manager`) implemented by `seo.dll`. Luckily there is a VBScript file that performs this task on our behalf: `SMTPReg.vbs`, in the **Platform SDK** (there is also a companion file, `NNTPReg.vbs`, to register NNTP event sinks).

Obviously, we cannot register our script file as `Sample SMTP event sink.vbs`: since the SMTP service expects to call a standard COM object. CDO for Windows 2000 implements a set of generic event sinks that can load a scripting engine and execute script code. The `ProgID` of the CDO generic event sink that implements the `ISMTPOnArrival` interface is `CDO.SS_SMTPOnArrivalSink`. We therefore perform a two-phase registration. First we tell the SMTP service to call the generic event sink, and then we tell the generic event sink to run our script file.

For the first phase we run the `SMTPReg.vbs` script with the following set of parameters (Here we use the `cscript.exe` interpreter, but we could equally well use the `wscript.exe` one):

```
cscript smtpreg.vbs /add 1 OnArrival "Sample SMTP event sink"
CDO.SS_SMTPOnArrivalSink
                "MAIL FROM=*@vips.com"
```

The first parameter (`/add`) tells the script to add a new event sink. We must then supply the following parameters in this order:

- ❑ The SMTP instance to work against (`1`)
- ❑ The SMTP event (can be only `OnArrival`)
- ❑ The display name of the event (`"Sample SMTP event sink"`)
- ❑ The ProgID of the event sink object (`CDO.SS_SMTPOnArrivalSink`)
- ❑ The rule to use for the event (`"MAIL FROM=*@vips.com"`)

The last parameter tells the SMTP service that the event sink must be called only for mail messages coming from the `vips.com` domain. The following command performs the second phase of the registration:

```
cscript smtpreg.vbs /setprop 1 OnArrival "Sample SMTP event sink" Sink
ScriptName
                "c:\Sample SMTP event sink.VBS"
```

The first parameter (/setprop) tells the script to set a property for an existing event sink. Then we must supply the other parameters in this order:

❑ The SMTP instance to work against (1)

❑ The SMTP event (can be only OnArrival)

❑ The display name of the event ("Sample SMTP event sink")

❑ The name of the PropertyBag the property belongs to (Sink)

❑ The name of the property to edit (ScriptName)

❑ The value to assign to the property (the path of the script file)

Now our event sink is set up so that it will be called for every message coming from the vips.com domain. We can view all the registered event sinks using this command:

```
cscript smtpreg.vbs /enum
```

If we need to remove the event sink, we should run these two commands:

```
cscript smtpreg.vbs /delprop 1 OnArrival "Sample SMTP event sink" Sink
ScriptName
cscript smtpreg.vbs /remove 1 OnArrival "Sample SMTP event sink"
```

Having set up our event sink, it's time to see it working. The quickest way to do that is using CDO2000 in a VBScript file to send a message to the target SMTP service:

```
Option Explicit

Dim objCfg, objMsg, objCfgFlds, strFrom, strTo, strSubject, strBody

strFrom="a.vip@vips.com"
strTo="""User 33"" <user.33@dev002.mcgreg.com>"
strSubject = "This is the subject"
strBody= "This is the body."

Set objMsg = CreateObject("CDO.Message")
Set objCfg = CreateObject("CDO.Configuration")
Set objCfgFlds = objCfg.Fields

With objCfgFlds
   .Item("http://schemas.microsoft.com/cdo/configuration/sendusing") _
       = 2 ' cdoSendUsingPort
   .Item("http://schemas.microsoft.com/cdo/configuration/smtpserver") _
       = "dev002.mcgreg.com"
   .Item("http://schemas.microsoft.com/cdo/configuration/" & _
       "smtpauthenticate") = 0 ' cdoAnonymous
   .Update
End With
Set objCfgFlds = Nothing

With objMsg
   Set .Configuration = objCfg
   .To       = strTo
```

```
    .From      = strFrom
    .Subject   = strSubject
    .TextBody = strBody
    .Fields.Item("urn:schemas:httpmail:importance") = 0 ' cdoLow
    .Fields.Update
    .Send
End With

Set objCfg = Nothing
Set objMsg = Nothing
```

Notice that we explicitly set the importance of the message to 0 (cdoLow). The content of the message's file found in the drop directory of the target SMTP server looks like this:

```
x-sender: a.vip@vips.com
x-receiver: user.33@dev002.mcgreg.com
Received: from dev002([192.168.0.3]) by dev002.mcgreg.com with Microsoft
SMTPSVC(5.0.2172.1); Sun, 5 Mar 2000 19:17:04 +0100
From: <a.vip@vips.com>
To: "User 33" <user.33@dev002.mcgreg.com>
Subject: This is the subject
Date: Sun, 5 Mar 2000 19:17:04 +0100
Message-ID: <000001bf86cf$022e1530$0300a8c0@mcgreg.com>
MIME-Version: 1.0
Content-Type: text/plain;
    charset="iso-8859-1"
Content-Transfer-Encoding: 7bit
X-Mailer: Microsoft CDO for Windows 2000
Thread-Index: Ab+GzwInODdpYXxdROuYEzNlBF+N/w==
Content-Class: urn:content-classes:message
Importance: high
X-MimeOLE: Produced By Microsoft MimeOLE V5.00.2919.6700
Return-Path: <a.vip@vips.com>
X-OriginalArrivalTime: 05 Mar 2000 18:17:04.0499(UTC)
FILETIME=[0252B430:01BF86CF]

This is the body.
```

Notice that now the importance of the message is high.

CDO2000 Performance: Testing and Issues

In this section we test the performance of CDO2000 (CDO for Windows 2000), comparing its two working modes, namely queued and direct operations. We also compare CDO2000 with CDONTS on IIS 5.0 using the same hardware/software configuration. The IIS application runs as isolated process.

Test #1 – Direct Sending

Our first test measures the performance of sending the messages directly from ASP over the network using SMTP protocol. We need to set the name of the machine hosting the SMTP server that CDO2000 will send the messages to. This is done using the following VBScript code:

CDO for Windows 2000

```
<%
strFrom = """"User 1"" <user.1@domain1.com>"
strTo = """"User 33"" <user.33@domain2.com>"
strSubject = "This is the subject"
strBody = "This is the body."

Set objMsg = Server.CreateObject("CDO.Message")
Set objCfg = Server.CreateObject("CDO.Configuration")
Set objCfgFlds = objCfg.Fields

With objCfgFlds
   .Item(cdoSendUsingMethod) = cdoSendUsingPort
   .Item(cdoSMTPServer) = "mailserver.domain2.com"
   .Item(cdoSMTPConnectionTimeout) = 20
   .Item(cdoSMTPAuthenticate) = cdoAnonymous
   .Update
End With

With objMsg
   Set .Configuration = objCfg
   .From      = strFrom
   .Subject   = strSubject
   .TextBody  = strBody

   For lngCycles=1 To 50
      .To = strTo
      .Send
   Next
End With
%>
```

Notice that with CDO2000 we can send the same `Message` object more than once. This means that we can create just one object and send multiple messages, even changing some properties (maybe the recipient) for each sending operation. The following picture shows the performance data for three consecutive executions of the test. The upper line is the ASP Request Execution Time: We can see that the test script takes about 18500 milliseconds to complete (note that the scale in the graph 1 :1000). The percentage Internetwork utilization rises to roughly 0.5% (the scale is multiplied by ten) and the network engagement is spread over about 18 to 20 seconds (there are four seconds between two consecutive vertical grid lines).

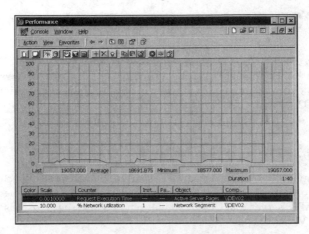

The CPU time consumption for the IIS application host process (DLLHost.exe) is about 250-300 milliseconds, whereas Inetinfo.exe, as we may expect, consumes virtually no CPU cycles (indeed the SMTP server executes no task).

Test #2 – Queued Sending

The code for this test is almost identical to the one shown above. We just change the configuration, queuing the messages to the Pickup directory of the IIS SMTP server, which in turn will send them over the network.

```
With objCfgFlds
    .Item(cdoSendUsingMethod) = cdoSendUsingPickup
    .Update
End With
```

The ASP Request Execution Time is now about 400 milliseconds (the scale is one-tenth) and the percentage Internetwork utilization reaches a peak of 1%.

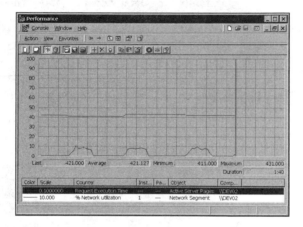

The CPU time consumption for the IIS application host process (DLLHost.exe) is virtually identical to Test #1 (about 300 milliseconds), whereas Inetinfo.exe uses about 400-500 milliseconds of CPU time to perform SMTP-related operations.

Comparison with CDONTS

We may reasonably expect CDO2000 has a higher message throughput than CDONTS. To quantify this performance difference we compare the results of Test #2 using CDO2000 and CDONTS. The major difference between the two tests lies in the one-to-one relationship between message and object enforced by CDONTS, whereas CDO2000 allows us to send multiple messages using a single object.

	CDONTS	CDO2000
ASP Request Execution Time	5,000 ms	400 ms
IIS application process CPU time	900 ms	300 ms
IIS main process CPU time	500 ms	400-500 ms

The Internetwork utilization pattern is almost identical in the two cases, however we can easily see that CDO2000 places a significantly lighter load on the system. Not only is the script notably more responsive, but also the overall CPU cycles consumption in this specific instance is almost half for CDO2000 with respect to CDONTS.

CDO2000 with Exchange's Internet Mail Service

As we saw above, CDO2000 offers rich programmatic configuration features, making it quite easy to send messages through the IMS provided with Exchange 5.5. Using the Configuration object we can instruct CDO2000 to send the message using the pickup directory of IMS:

```
objCfg.Fields.Item(cdoSMTPServerPickupDirectory) =
"c:\exchsrvr\imcdata\pickup"
```

However, we should bear in mind that the default configuration is always based on IIS SMTP, even if IMS has disabled it. So we must explicitly configure each message, otherwise it'll be placed in the IIS SMTP directory. As we said above the best way to achieve that is to create an ASP Application-wide configuration object and assign it to each message.

CDO for Exchange

CDO for Exchange is a complex topic that would require an entire book to explore all the features available in its object model from an ASP programmer's perspective. This brief section is only enough to give you a glimpse at this powerful tool. CDO for Windows 2000 and CDONTS offer a much faster path for SMTP-based messaging tasks. However, CDO for Exchange is Microsoft's response to the need to build fully-fledged collaborative applications, which deal with calendaring, appointments, public folders to share information, etc.

In this section we refer to CDO for Exchange by the shorter name of simply "CDO".

Firstly we note that CDO is complex because it's tightly bonded to MAPI (Messaging Application Programming Interface) and Exchange 5.X. To exploit CDO in our ASP application using Exchange as back-end messaging server, we need to install and configure Exchange. However even with Exchange already running on our network, we may still need to make some configurational changes, such as authentication.

> CDO for Exchange2000 supercedes CDO for Exchange. It has a totally different object model and its library is a superset of the CDO for Windows 2000 library. At time of press CDO for Exchange2000 had not yet been released.

Two separate libraries compose CDO for Exchange, of which the current, and probably last, version is 1.2.1. The main library exposes the messaging objects (e.g. Session and Message) and is implemented by cdo.dll. The ProgID for this library is MAPI, for instance MAPI.Session. This is both a client-side and a server-side library, and we can use it the same way, for instance, in ASP or in a client VB application. In fact, cdo.dll can access an Exchange server over the network, and the library is installed with Exchange or Outlook.

The second library in CDO is the rendering library that is implemented by `cdohtml.dll`. The ProgID for this library is AMHTML, for instance `AMHTML.Application` (the acronym comes from Active Messaging HTML). The role of the objects exposed by this server-side only library is to render in HTML the MAPI messaging objects, in other words to produce an HTML output that depicts the content of a displayable section of a collaborative application, let's say the Inbox or the Calendar. The rendering library has been exploited by Microsoft to realize **Outlook Web Access**, the web application that mimics the Outlook features from any web browser. We should be aware that a fully-fledged collaborative web application is complicated; for instance, Outlook Web Access consists of nearly 90 script files, corresponding to about 650 KB of code.

As a final point, we note that **Microsoft Exchange 2000** (available in the Beta at the time of writing) introduces a new version of CDO, oddly named "Microsoft CDO for Microsoft Exchange Library". This is an extension of the CDO for Windows 2000 and is implemented by `codex.dll`. Indeed, SMTP is the base protocol that Exchange 2000 uses to transport messages. So the library exposes the same objects and interfaces we previously discussed in connection with CDO for Windows 2000 (`IMessage`, `IBodyPart`, etc.) adding to those the objects and interface required to deal with appointments, contacts, etc. In fact, this library takes the place of `cdosys.dll`.

Exchange 2000 also comes with `cdo.dll` version 1.2.1, so we can hope for a certain degree of backwards compatibility. As a final point, we note that Exchange for Windows 2000 is tightly coupled with the Windows 2000's Active Directory and therefore cannot run on an NTLM-based domain.

Authentication

As mentioned above CDO requires authentication to work. The thread that is trying to access an Exchange mailbox must run in the security context of the NT account that is the owner of that mailbox. In the ASP world this means that we must enforce authentication on the pages that use CDO objects. We should be aware therefore of the old problems that torment the design of an authenticated IIS application that accesses the network. In brief, if we use IE 3+ and NT Challenge/Response authentication, we can only access the Exchange server located on the same machine as the IIS server. The thread that processes the ASP page cannot use an Exchange instance on another machine because the access token that represents the user's security context doesn't cache the authentication information required to make another hop on the network. With Basic Authentication there is no such a limitation (the thread impersonates the user's security context using the password sent as clear text and therefore the token caches the authentication information) and we can go over the network reaching the required Exchange server. We should bear in mind that Exchange can manage multiple servers belonging to the same *site* and therefore the architecture of an ASP/CDO distributed application can be quite complex and compelling. This description is based on the NTLM network security, and it applies to an IIS 5.0 server belonging to an NTLM-based domain. The situation changes with Windows 2000 domains and the Kerberos authentication protocol and the impersonation behaviour of distributed application relies on **delegation** and **cloaking** to allow the client's credentials making any number of network hops.

CDO for Exchange Example: Administrative Messaging

Here we give a simple example of CDO, based on the anonymous messaging concept presented in the CDO documentation. In fact, nothing is anonymous from Exchange's point of view; it's just anonymous in the ASP context. Let's imagine we need to post an administrative alert in an Exchange mailbox when a critical situation is detected during the processing of any ASP page belonging to our application. It doesn't matter if we use anonymous or authenticated access to our ASP application or a mixture of both. The key point is that it would be very tricky to manage authentication and security issues to allow a message to be sent potentially from every page. The simplest solution is to create a specialized page that sends the message, and let the other pages redirect to this page, passing the message information in a query string. Something like this:

```
<%
Dim strRedirect
strRedirect = "notifier.asp?Recipient=User one&Subject=" & _
              "This is the subject&" & "Body=This is the body."
Response.Redirect(strRedirect)
%>
```

The page that sends the message begins by reading the parameters (recipient, subject and message body) from the query string. As we can see from the following VBScript code the current CDO objects (not the CDO for Exchange 2000 objects) resemble the CDONTS ones. Indeed, the CDO object model is almost an extension of the CDONTS one, although there are some differences in the semantics of the methods.

We create the session and logon (let's pass over this point for a now and we will revisit it in a moment), get the Outbox Folder, add a new Message to the Messages collection of the Outbox and add a new Recipient to the Recipients collection of the new message. Then we set the recipient name, the message's subject and text and, finally, send the message.

```
<!--METADATA TYPE="typelib" NAME="Microsoft CDO 1.21 Library"
            UUID="3FA7DEA7-6438-101B-ACC1-00AA00423326"  -->

<%
Option Explicit

Dim objSession, objOutbox, objMessage, objRecipients, objRecipient
Dim strProfileInfo, strServer, strMailbox, strTo, strSubject, strBody
%>

<HTML>
<HEAD>
<TITLE>CDO for Exchange Sample #1 - Sending a simple message</TITLE>
</HEAD>
<BODY>

<%
strTo = Request.QueryString("Recipient")
strSubject = Request.QueryString("Subject")
strBody= Request.QueryString("Body")
```

```
Set ObjSession = Server.CreateObject("MAPI.Session")

strServer = "dev"
strMailbox = "AnonExchAspNotifier"
strProfileInfo = strServer + vbLF + strMailbox

ObjSession.Logon "", "", False, True, 0, True, strProfileInfo

Set objOutbox = objSession.Outbox
Set objMessage = objOutbox.Messages.Add
Set objRecipients = objMessage.Recipients
Set objRecipient = objRecipients.Add

objRecipient.Name =  strTo
objRecipient.Resolve
objMessage.Subject = strSubject
objMessage.Text =  strBody
objMessage.Send

Set objRecipient = Nothing
Set objRecipients = Nothing
Set objMessage = Nothing
Set objOutbox = Nothing
Set ObjSession = Nothing
%>

We have sent an administrative alert to <% = strTo %>.<BR>
</BODY>
</HTML>
```

The only parameter supplied to the Session.Logon method worth noting is the last one. This string is the concatenation of the name of the server that hosts Exchange and the name of the mailbox that we want to access in order to send outgoing messages. Also we must Resolve the recipient's address information (typically the Exchange mailbox name) into a full messaging address before sending the message. However we haven't yet talked about the security issue: Let's suppose in the code above we access the AnonExchAspNotifier mailbox and the NT account, i.e. the owner of that mailbox is COPRAS\AnonExchAspNotifier. We must therefore set the authentication method of the ASP page to anonymous and supply the username and password as shown below (to access this dialog box open the ASP page's **Properties** dialog in the Microsoft Management Console, then select the **File Security** tab, press the **Edit** button in the **Anonymous access and authentication control** group box, and finally press the **Edit** button in the **Anonymous access** group box).

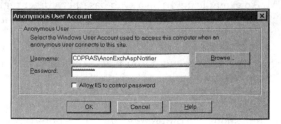

The following figure shows the message's recipient reading the message with Outlook Web Access. Obviously this is a very basic example, whose primary drawback is the impossibility of redirecting to the message-sender page if some page content is already written to the client (we shouldn't turn off response buffering). This solution requires an additional browser-server round trip too. However, we cannot use the new ASP 3.0's `Server.Transfer` or `Execute` methods because they continue the processing of the target page as an addendum of the caller page, so our CDO code wouldn't be processed in the required security context.

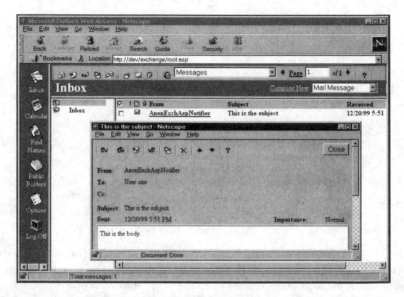

CDO for Exchange 2000

> Note that at the time this book went to press Exchange 2000 had not been released. All the related information is therefore subject to change by Microsoft without any notice.

The **CDO for Exchange 2000** library (sometimes known as CDO 3.0) ships as COM components that can be used in applications written in any programming languages that support COM. An example might be a web-based customer registration application using an Exchange 2000 public contacts folder, written using ASP and the new CDO for Exchange 2000 library.

CDO for Exchange 2000 is a *server-only* component. You cannot create client applications with it (except those using a web interface), even if you are running the workstation version of Windows 2000.

The following diagram shows the different ways applications can access Exchange 2000 – through CDO, directly through ADO 2.5 or via MAPI. Notice, however, that client applications operating with Outlook are not supported by CDO for Exchange 2000:

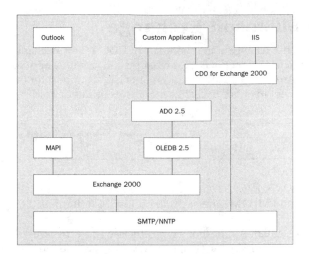

How does CDO for Exchange 2000 compare with CDO for Windows 2000? After all, both use the name CDO for their type libraries. The Exchange 2000 library is a **superset** of the Windows 2000 library. In fact, when Exchange 2000 is installed, the CDO for Windows 2000 component is automatically deregistered. In other words, on a machine with Exchange 2000, you simply use the single CDO for Exchange 2000 library to obtain all the functionality found in the CDO for Windows 2000 library, plus the whole range of messaging and collaboration enhancements provided by Exchange 2000.

Exchange 2000 actually includes three separate COM components, as shown in the following table:

Component	Description
CDO for Microsoft Exchange (cdoex.dll)	CDO component to create collaborative applications based upon Windows 2000 and Exchange 2000.
CDO Workflow Objects for Microsoft Exchange (cdowf.dll)	CDOWF component to build workflow functionality on top of Exchange 2000.
CDO for Exchange Management (emo.dll)	CDOEXM component to manage an Exchange server. Can be used to create, move and delete mailboxes or manage users, contacts, and groups etc.

In addition to these new components, Exchange 2000 also installs the cdo.dll and cdohtml.dll to provide backward compatibility for CDO 1.21 and HTML Rendering Library 1.21 applications.

CDO for Microsoft Exchange

CDO for Microsoft Exchange is the successor of CDO 1.2 for Exchange 5.x, implemented as a COM component for creating collaborative applications on top of Exchange 2000. Among its major enhancements is full support for calendar sevices and contact management in either Exchange mailboxes or Public Folders.

> The bad news is that it does not support tasks and journal entries as separate objects, only as Message objects.

As with CDO for Windows 2000, the CDO for Microsoft Exchange library fully supports MIME and MHTML messages to build HMTL formatted e-mail messages.

ADO skills are essential. Applications typically use ADO to manipulate folders as rowsets and use structured query language (SQL) queries to retrieve particular items.

> Because CDO in Exchange 2000 is tightly coupled with ADO 2.5 including the ActiveX Data Objects 2.5 Library (ADODB) library is required in all applications. ADO 2.5 ships with Windows 2000.

CDO Workflow Objects for Microsoft Exchange

The **CDO Workflow Objects for Microsoft Exchange** component is the successor to the Exchange Routing Objects introduced in Exchange Server 5.5 Service Pack 1 as a feature running on top of the Exchange Server Event Service.

Workflow objects can be used in two different kinds of applications that deal with item routing and decision-making:

❑ Applications connecting directly to the Exchange 2000 data store use what is called **database-style workflow**. In this case, a connection to the Exchange 2000 data store is required for the whole time while the workflow process is running, e.g. while a document is edited.

❑ Offline users interact with a workflow application by sending messages to a workflow-enabled folder on the Exchange 2000 Server. For such messaging-style workflows, CDO Workflow Objects provide mechanisms for identifying a message as part of an ongoing workflow process instance, initiating a new process instance based on an incoming message, and ensuring that the sender of the message has the proper authority to participate in the workflow:

CDO for Exchange Management

The **CDO for Exchange Management** component provides another set of new features to support applications that manage mailboxes, e.g. create, move, or delete mailboxes and manage users, external recipients and groups. While those features are also available via OLE DB 2.5 and ADSI, CDO for Exchange Management provides a high-level method to perform those tasks without going into raw OLE DB 2.5 and Active Directory management.

Outlook Web Access in Exchange 2000

Exchange 2000 does not provide an updated version of the cdohtml.dll rendering library. You no longer need to build ASP pages in order to display messages, appointments, or contacts in web pages in Exchange 2000. Instead, the rendering is handled natively by the new version of Outlook Web Access (OWA) in Exchange 2000. Items can be opened simply by specifying a URL, which includes the folder path and the name of the item.

Other new features in OWA include:

❑ Rendering via either DHTML for late-model browsers and HTML 3.2 for earlier browsers

❑ Default web forms for public folders

❑ A web store forms registry

❑ Support for cascading style sheets to define the formatting of folder views

Exchange Server Events in Exchange 2000

Server-based events in Exchange 2000 are vastly expanded from those available in Exchange Server 5.5. In addition, you can use Visual Basic to create event agents, not just VBScript or languages like C++. Events fire upon changes to not only individual items, but folders as well.

If you've ever been frustrated by the lack of a true Delete event in Exchange 5.5, you will want to examine the new OnSyncDelete event. Both it and the new OnSyncSave event are synchronous events: They give your program exclusive control over an item *before* it is saved or deleted and are cancellable events. These and other events are listed in the following table:

Event	Description
OnDelete	This event fires when a folder or item is deleted. Replaces the OnMessageDeleted event in Exchange Server 5.5. (*Asynchronous*)
OnMDBShutdown	This event fires when the Exchange store stops. (*New*)
OnMDBStartUp	This event fires when the Exchange store starts. (*New*)
OnSave	This event fires when a folder or item is saved. Replaces the OnMessageCreated and OnChange events in Exchange Server 5.5. (*Asynchronous*)
OnSyncDelete	This event fires when a folder or item is deleted. (*New, synchronous*)
OnSyncSave	This event fires when a folder or item is saved. (*New, synchronous*)
OnTimer	This event fires at an interval defined when the event-based application is installed.

> Exchange Server 5.5 supported only asynchronous item events so there was no guarantee that when the event fired, the item would still be available. With the introduction of synchronous events in Exchange 2000, you get greater control over what happens when items or folders are created, modified, or removed

Don't forget that, because CDO for Exchange 2000 replaces CDO for Windows 2000, you also have access to the SMTP and NNTP protocol events discussed earlier.

Summary

Collaboration Data Objects (CDO) enables us to enhance our ASP applications with messaging and collaboration features.

In this chapter we have considered:

❑ Collaborative data objects in general, when to use which technology and someof the emerging collaborative technologies.

❑ The CDO for Windows 2000 Object model and why it is important to distinguish between an interface and a CoClass object, since an object can expose more than one interface.

❑ The methods and properties of the CDO for Windows 2000 objects

❑ Examples of using CDO for Windows 2000 for creating and configuring a simple message, advanced configuration, adding and managing attachments, creating MHTML messages, working with drop directories, loading and saving messages from ADO `Stream` objects, exploiting SMTP transport event sinks.

❑ Performance and testing issues with CDO for Windows 2000

❑ CDO for Exchange and CDO for Exchange 2000

CDO for Windows 2000

39

CDO for NT Server

Having looked at CDO for Windows 2000 in the previous chapter, in this chapter we'll look at the other main messaging and collaboration library used from within ASP 3.0. **CDO for NT Server**, or CDONTS, is a lightweight server-side library which is intended to be used with IIS and its SMTP (Simple Mail Transfer Protocol) service, although it can also be used with Microsoft Exchange Server. CDONTS is less powerful that CDO for Windows 2000, but if you just want to send and receive e-mail messages, the simplicity of CDONTS is a big advantage. In fact, as we will see shortly, with CDONTS we can send an e-mail in just three lines of code.

What is CDONTS?

The CDONTS library is implemented by `cdonts.dll` (the current, and probably last, version is 1.2) and it is installed with IIS version 4.0/5.0, Microsoft Exchange Server version 5.5 (when the Internet Mail Service (IMS) Wizard is run) and Microsoft Commercial Internet System (MCIS). CDONTS has been designed as a lightweight server-side component offering the ASP developer a quick approach to enhancing their applications with mailing services. CDONTS has a number of limitations we should bear in mind:

❑ It's based on Simple Mail Transfer Protocol (SMTP) and therefore has no support for Post Office Protocol (POP) or Internet Message Access Protocol (IMAP).

❑ It's a server-side only library (it needs the IIS SMTP server to deliver messages).

❑ It only offers mailing capabilities; that is, no other collaboration features (calendaring, etc.).

❑ We cannot access remote servers, so CDONTS can only deliver mail through the SMTP server located on the same machine (we'll see more on this later).

❑ It can exploit either the SMTP Service provided by IIS or Exchange's Internet Mail Service, but not both.

❑ The SMTP-related configuration cannot be modified using the library itself and therefore CDONTS totally relies on the configuration of the host machine. In other words, we must properly configure the SMTP server of IIS or Exchange.

❑ It offers no built-in user authentication and security features.

We are basing our exposition about CDONTS on Windows 2000 Advanced Server, but everything we say in this chapter also applies to Windows NT Server 4.0 with Service Pack 5. In fact, the CDONTS library shipped with Windows 2000 is exactly the same version that comes with NT 4.0.

The Internal Workings of CDONTS

We stated above that CDONTS is SMTP-based. So it would be obvious to assume that the NewMail.Send method performs an SMTP transaction to deliver the message. However this is totally wrong: all the CDONTS operations are file system-based. From the point of view of CDONTS, the in-going and out-going messages are just files placed in a specific set of directories. For example, when we use NewMail.Send to send a message, it creates a file with contents similar to the following and puts it in the directory that holds the out-going messages:

```
X-Sender: sender@domain1.com
X-Receiver: recipient@domain2.com
From: <sender@domain1.com>
To: <recipient@domain2.com>
Subject: This is the subject
Date: Sun, 21 Nov 1999 15:30:03 +0100
X-MimeOLE: Produced By Microsoft MimeOLE V5.00.2314.1300

This is the very short mail message.
```

It's up to the SMTP server to retrieve that file, initiate a TCP connection on port 25 with the recipient's SMTP host and send the mail message. This architecture has some important consequences that we'll examine in the following sections. First and foremost, let's note that NewMail.Send hasn't got a return value to check the operation's outcome, as it just places a file in a directory; the message is accepted even if the SMTP server is not running and if the recipient can't be reached or doesn't exist. If the mail cannot be delivered, the SMTP server can eventually notify the sender with a non-delivery report.

The SMTP Service Directories

To use CDONTS, we must first ensure that the SMTP service on which it relies is properly configured. In the next section, we'll inspect the SMTP server that comes with IIS 5.0, but version 4.0 is almost identical (there are just some name changes and a few additions). We briefly examine the issues concerning the use of CDONTS with the Exchange's Internet Mail Service in a separate section. When we select to install the SMTP Service with IIS, a Default SMTP Virtual Server is created and automatically configured. We can inspect and modify this configuration using the Internet Services Manager Microsoft Management Console (MMC) or a web-based application (usually found at http://localhost/Mail/Smtp/Admin/). A Mailroot directory (with some subfolders) is also created under the standard Inetpub root:

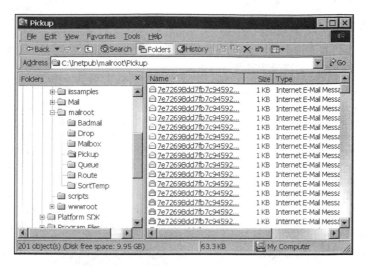

The `Pickup` directory you can see in the figure above is the folder where CDONTS puts out-going message files. When the SMTP service is running, every file placed in this directory is picked up, and the message is processed and sent. If the message cannot be delivered, it is placed in the `Queue` directory and the SMTP service attempts to re-send the message more times at regular intervals (more on this later). With IIS 4.0 this directory also contains text files that can be used to determine the reason for the non-delivery of a particular message, whereas IIS 5.0 writes events in the System Log if a message delivery fails. If a message hasn't been delivered after a specified number of attempts, it is placed in the `Badmail` folder. The `Drop` directory contains all incoming messages. The IIS SMTP service doesn't have anything like individual mailboxes – all messages for all recipients are stored in this folder. In the 'CDO for NT Server Examples' section below, we'll show how to deal with incoming mails.

How CDONTS Works

How does CDONTS know what directories it must use? It exploits the IIS Admin Service COM object that allows access to the IIS Metabase. This configuration database contains all the settings pertaining to IIS services (WWW, FTP, SMTP, etc.). CDONTS reads the values of the `PickupDirectory` and `DropDirectory` entries from the Metabase, and thus it knows where to put/find message files. It's worth noting that only the `BadMailDirectory` and `DropDirectory` can be configured through the MMC. To change the other directories, we need to access the Metabase using the Active Directory Service Interfaces (ADSI). Although this is not necessary in the ordinary operations, we'll see later an interesting application of this technique. A consequence of this *modus operandi* is that the account under which the ASP application runs must have access to the Metabase. This problem doesn't arise under IIS 5.0 and with IIS 4.0 in-process applications, but if you use CDONTS in an IIS 4.0 out-of-process application, you'll get a **Permission denied** error due to the fact that the `IWAM_MachineName` account does not have access to the Metabase. We therefore need to run CDONTS code as an in-process application. Otherwise, we must grant the default out-of-process application's account access to the Metabase (using the **Operators** tab of the SMTP Site **Properties** dialog; see below), or change the identity of the out-of-process application package under MTS. Both of these introduce a potential security risk.

CDONTS

917

Server Configuration

Because CDONTS relies so heavily on IIS's SMTP Service, it's worth taking a couple of minutes to look at the configuration of the service before we look at the CDONTS object model. Actually, configuring the SMTP Service is pretty simple: if we just want to perform some initial tests with CDONTS, we probably don't need to make any changes to the default configuration. Note, however, that the SMTP service doesn't have any automatic dial-up feature. If we're working on a LAN with a dial-up connection to the Internet, we should manually establish the connection to allow mail messages to be delivered outside the local environment. If the dial-up connection is established on the IIS machine, the SMTP service can go outside straight away. Alternatively, it might be necessary to configure some TCP routing options on the LAN – a typical configuration for SOHO (Small Office/Home Office) businesses, where there isn't a public registered domain and access to the Internet is through an ISP. Obviously, in such a situation our SMTP service is completely useless with incoming mail from the outside, but it works fine for out-going mail. With a permanent direct link to the Internet and a registered domain, our SMTP service could behave like a full-fledged server, unless security constraints forbid outside access to the IIS machine. The IIS SMTP Service has simple routing features that allow us to overcome this problem (we'll look at these shortly).

We can use Internet Services Manager MMC to inspect the SMTP configuration: select the **Default SMTP Virtual Server** and then **Properties** from the **Action** menu. We will just briefly mention the two tabs that are common to many IIS services and normally require no modification. The **General** tab allows us to configure IP address, TCP ports, connection constraints and logging. The **Security** tab grants operator permissions for the SMTP site. The **LDAP Routing** tab is a notable addition over IIS 4.0, but we cannot consider this here. The SMTP service can use Lightweight Directory Access Protocol (LDAP) to communicate with a directory service to retrieve information about mail clients and their mailboxes. The remaining three tabs allow us to adjust the SMTP server according to our requirements.

Messages

The **Messages** tab lets us set limits for the size of a single message, the size of the entire SMTP session, and the number of outbound messages per connection. If our server is heavily loaded, we need to understand these settings clearly, so that we can achieve the best configuration (see the online help for the Microsoft SMTP Service). In particular, the **Limit number of messages per connection to** setting is important, as it allows us to split the sending of a large number of messages over separate connections, thus improving performance.

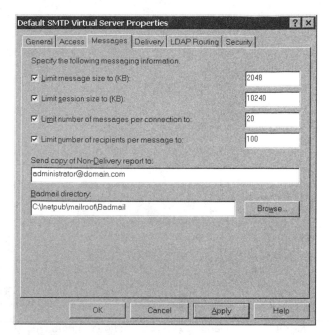

In the Send copy of Non-delivery report to text box, we can specify the e-mail address to which the non-delivery report (NDR) will be sent when a message is undeliverable (an undeliverable message is always returned to the sender with an NDR). This option can be very important with automatically generated mail, allowing us to track delivery problems.

Delivery

Here we can set the maximum number of times that SMTP will attempt to send a message (if it can't be delivered on the first attempt), and the intervals between these attempts. We set these parameters according to our system configuration: obviously, permanent and dial-up connections have different requirements. For instance, if we have a dial-up connection we might need to repeatedly try sending the message with short intervals.

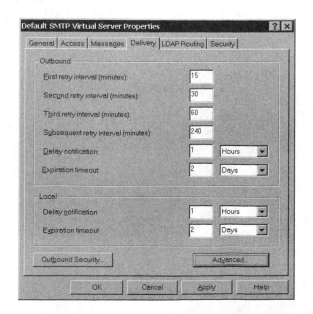

The Advanced button provides us with further delivery configuration options:

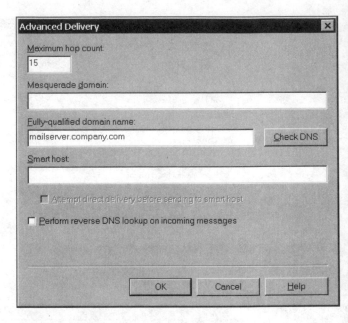

The Fully Qualified Domain Name text box by default contains the TCP address for the machine, but in some circumstances we might want to override the machine-wide configuration, specifying a host name here in the standard form: `host_name.subdomain.second-level_domain.top-level_domain`, e.g. `mailserver.dept.company.com`. If we only deal with out-going mail, we can safely ignore this setting. The Smart host is a very important field: it contains the name or IP address of an SMTP server to which our server will send all the messages. In other words, if we set this field, our SMTP service will send the out-going message to the smart host (instead of contacting the SMTP server of the recipient's domain), which will relay the message on our behalf. This configuration could be essential if the IIS machine is not allowed to access the Internet directly for security reasons – in this case the Smart host should be the organization-wide public SMTP host. If we use a dial-up connection, we could set the smart host to the SMTP server of our Internet Service Provider (ISP). Although this is not strictly required, it could improve the performance of the system because access to the ISP SMTP server should be faster than communication with the recipient's SMTP server. Obviously, the ISP's SMTP server must allow the message to be relayed (some don't, to prevent spam mails). We'll see shortly that we can have multiple smart hosts. The Outbound Security button allows us to specify whether the default out-going SMTP transaction will allow anonymous authentication. Alternatively, we can specify that our server should attempt to authenticate itself to the remote SMTP server using Basic Authentication or the Windows Security Package through Windows Security Support Provider Interface (NT Challenge/Response in the previous version of IIS). Typically, we should disable authentication unless our smart host requires it. It's worth noting that the typical ISP SMTP server allows anonymous connection.

Access

In this tab we can configure security for incoming SMTP transactions. We can allow anonymous access or require authentication (Basic Authentication or Windows Security Package). Furthermore, we can set up secure communication using Transport Layer Security (TLS) and deny or grant access to specific IP addresses. The Relay Restrictions is a feature that allows us to grant or deny permission to relay mail through the SMTP site.

Configuring Domains

We have almost finished discussing the IIS SMTP Service, but we should say something about domains. We can create (by selecting New | Domain from the Action menu) and configure both local and remote domains. A **local domain** is a domain that is serviced by the local SMTP server – the SMTP server will accept any incoming mail message addressed to such a domain and deliver it as a file to the Drop directory. There is by default one local domain and we can create multiple aliased local domains. The names of local domains are very important. For instance, if we created an aliased local domain with the name mycompany.com, the SMTP service would accept and deliver to the Drop directory all messages directed to someuser@mycompany.com. The name of the default local domain is automatically configured by IIS according to the machine's TCP address, but we can change it by creating a new aliased domain and setting this as the default. It's worth noting there is only one Drop directory for all local domains.

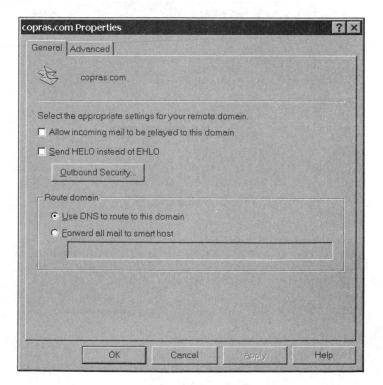

Remote domains are related to out-going mail messages. If we created a remote domain named yourcompany.com, we could override the default configuration for all outgoing messages sent to this domain. If we selected Forward all mail to smart host in the Route domain option, and in the text box we put the name or IP address of an SMTP server, our server would send all messages directed to yourcompany.com to this smart host. We could also configure the outbound security for this specific route. All these settings override the ones on the Delivery tab. This allows us to achieve a great deal of flexibility in mail delivery. Furthermore, we can instruct the SMTP service to initiate out-going SMTP sessions by issuing an EHLO command instead of the standard HELO command. This enables us to use the ESMTP (Extended SMTP) features provided by the remote SMTP server (such as message encryption).

Now that we've got our SMTP site configured, we can look at the CDONTS object model in detail.

The CDONTS Object Model

The simplicity of CDONTS is reflected in its object model, which exposes two creatable objects: CDONTS.NewMail and CDONTS.Session. All other objects can only be accessed (directly or indirectly) through the Session object. NewMail is a stand-alone object that is wholly unrelated to the hierarchy, and it offers the simplest way to deal with out-going mail. The hierarchy can be seen in the figure below:

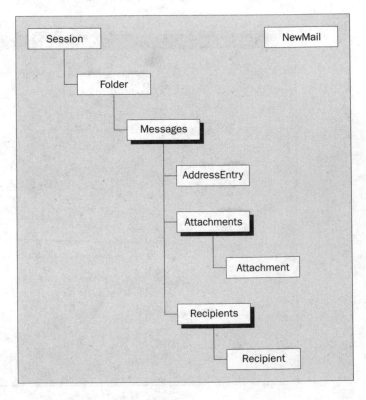

Sending Messages with CDONTS

This hierarchy is very simple, and intuitive. We can see how we work down this hierarchy when we send a mail. We can accomplish this in seven steps:

1. Create the Session object.

2. Log on using a display name and e-mail address.

3. Get the Outbox Folder object.

4. Create a new empty Message in the Outbox's Messages collection.

5. Set the Text and Subject properties of the Message object.

6. Add a new Recipient to the Recipients collection of the Message object.

7. Finally, Send the message.

And here's the code that accomplishes these steps, in exactly the same order:

```
' VBScript
Set objSession = Server.CreateObject("CDONTS.Session")
objSession.LogonSMTP "Sender Name", "sender@domain1.com"
Set objOutbox = objSession.Outbox

Set objNewMsg = objOutbox.Messages.Add
objNewMsg.Subject = "This is the subject"
objNewMsg.Text = "This is the very short mail message."
objNewMsg.Recipients.Add "Recipient Name", _
                    "recipient@domain2.com", CdoTo
objNewMsg.Send

objSession.Logoff
```

```
// JScript
objSession = Server.CreateObject("CDONTS.Session");
objSession.LogonSMTP("Sender Name", "sender@domain1.com");
objOutbox = objSession.Outbox;

objNewMsg = objOutbox.Messages.Add();
objNewMsg.Subject = "This is the subject";
objNewMsg.Text = "This is the very short mail message.";
objNewMsg.Recipients.Add("Recipient Name",
                    "recipient@domain2.com", CdoTo);
objNewMsg.Send();

objSession.Logoff();
```

Sending Mail with Three Lines of Code

Although the code above is pretty effortless, with CDONTS there's an even easier way of sending a mail from an ASP page. Using the NewMail object, we can do this with just these three lines of code:

```
Set objMailer = Server.CreateObject("CDONTS.NewMail")
objMailer.Send "sender@domain1.com", "recipient@domain2.com", _
            "This is the subject", _
            "This is the very short mail message."
Set objMailer = Nothing
```

Or in JScript:

```
var objMailer = Server.CreateObject("CDONTS.NewMail");
objMailer.Send("sender@domain1.com", "recipient@domain2.com",
               "This is the subject",
               "This is the very short mail message.");
delete objMailer;
```

The parameters for the NewMail.Send method are pretty self-explanatory, and they all are optional. In fact, we could achieve the same result setting some NewMail properties (From, To, Subject and Body) and calling the Send method without parameters. There also are other properties that allow us a finer-grained control on the out-going mail (we will look at the complete CDONTS object model in the following sections). The NewMail object has one peculiarity: we can use it only once, i.e. just for a single Send operation. Any attempt to set a property or call a method after the call to Send raises an error. If we need to deliver multiple messages, we should create multiple object instances. This design choice is also evident in the write-only nature of all its properties (except Version, which is read-only and can also be referenced after the call to Send). This is a characteristic that NewMail has in common with the Message object.

CDONTS Objects Reference

This section outlines the use of every object in the CDONTS object model, and gives the syntax of its methods and properties. In the following section, we will look at some code samples which demonstrate the use of these objects.

Four properties are common to almost all CDONTS objects, so we will cover these here, rather than repeating the information for each object.

Common Properties

Every CDONTS object (with the exception of NewMail) has the following four properties: Application, Class, Parent and Session. All of these properties are read-only.

Application Property

Returns the name of the current application.

```
Variant = Object.Application
```

For CDONTS, this always returns "Collaboration Data Objects for NTS version X" (Where X is the current CDONTS version).

Class

Returns the Class type of the current object.

```
Long = Object.Class
```

The possible return values for this are:

Constant	Value	Object Type
CdoSession	0	Session object
CdoFolder	2	Folder object
CdoMsg	3	Message object
CdoRecipient	4	Recipient object
CdoAttachment	5	Attachment object
CdoAddressEntry	8	AddressEntry object
CdoMessages	16	Messages collection
CdoRecipients	17	Recipients collection
CdoAttachments	18	Attachments collection

Parent

Returns a reference to the parent object of the current object.

```
Message = Object.Parent
```

Session

Returns a reference to the CDONTS Session object for the current session.

```
Session = Object.Session
```

The AddressEntry Object

The AddressEntry object contains all of the addressing information for the sender of the message, and can be retrieved using the Sender property of a Message object:

```
' VBScript
Dim objAddressEntry
Set objAddressEntry = objMessage.Sender
```

```
// JScript
var objAddressEntry = objMessage.Sender;
```

As the AddressEntry object contains all the addressing information for the sender of a message, a common use of the object is for automating replies. To have our application automatically reply to a message, the code would look like this:

```
' VBScript
dim objAddrEntry, objMessage, objNewMsg, objNewMail

' Add Code here to get the desired objMessage object
```

```
set objAddrEntry = objMessage.Sender
set objNewMail = Server.CreateObject("CDONTS.NewMail")

objNewMail.From = "Administrator@domain1.com"
objNewMail.To = objAddrEntry.Address
objNewMail.Body = objAddrEntry.Name & _
                  ", This is your automatic message reply"
objNewMail.Send
```

```
// JScript
var objAddrEntry, objMessage, objNewMsg, objNewMail;

// Add Code here to get the desired objMessage object

objNewMail.From = "Administrator@domain1.com";
objAddrEntry = objMessage.Sender;
objNewMail = Server.CreateObject("CDONTS.NewMail");

objNewMail.To = objAddrEntry.Address;
objNewMail.Body = objAddrEntry.Name +
                  ", This is your automatic message reply";
objNewMail.Send();
```

AddressEntry Properties

The `AddressEntry` object has no methods, but exposes the following seven properties, which provide information about the sender of the message:

Property	
Address	Parent*
Application*	Session*
Class*	Type
Name	

* See the section on 'Common Properties' earlier in the chapter.

Address

Returns the senders's e-mail address.

```
String = AddressEntry.Address
```

Name

Returns the sender's alias or friendly display name.

```
String = AddressEntry.Name
```

Type

Returns a string indicating the type of address associated with the `AddressEntry` object. For CDONTS, this is always "SMTP".

```
String = AddressEntry.Type
```

The Attachment Object

The Attachment object represents a message's attachment – a file or message attached to and sent with the message. Every Message object has an Attachments collection which contains one Attachment object for each attached file or message.

We can reference an Attachment object through the Attachment collection's Item method:

```
' VBScript
Set objAttachment = objMsg.Attachments.Item(1)
```

```
// JScript
objAttachment = objMsg.Attachments.Item(1);
```

Or we can create a new Attachment object using the Add method of the Attachments collection:

```
' VBScript
objMsg.Attachments.Add "A Word attachment.doc", CdoFileData, _
                       "C:\Attachments\Word attachment.doc"
```

```
// JScript
objMsg.Attachments.Add("A Word attachment.doc", CdoFileData,
                       "C:\\Attachments\\Word attachment.doc");
```

We can create an attachment for a NewMail object using that object's AttachFile and AttachURL methods. For a full example of working with attachments, see the 'CDO for NT Server Examples' section later on in the chapter.

The Attachment object exposes the following methods and properties:

Methods	Properties	
Delete	Application*	Name
ReadFromFile	Class*	Parent*
WriteToFile	ContentBase	Session*
	ContentID	Source
	ContentLocation	Type

* See the section on 'Common Properties' earlier in the chapter.

Attachment Object Methods

The Attachment object has three methods: Delete, ReadFromFile and WriteToFile.

Delete Method

The Delete method removes the attachment from the message's Attachments collection.

```
Attachment.Delete()
```

ReadFromFile Method

The `ReadFromFile` method replaces the contents of an attachment with those of the specified file. This method depends on the `Type` property of the `Attachment`, and isn't supported for messages of type `CdoEmbeddedMessage`.

```
Attachment.ReadFromFile(Filename)
```

Parameter	Data Type	Description
Filename	String	The name of the file from which to load the attachment's contents.

WriteToFile Method

The `WriteToFile` method saves the attachment to a file in the file system. This method depends on the `Type` property of the `Attachment`, and isn't supported for messages of type `CdoEmbeddedMessage`.

```
Attachment.ReadToFile(Filename)
```

Parameter	Data Type	Description
Filename	String	The name of the file to which the contents of the attachment are to be saved.

Attachment Object Properties

The six properties specific to the `Attachment` object return information about the attached file.

ContentBase Property

The `ContentBase` property returns the `content-base` header of the attachment. This indicates the base URL to use for a MIME HTML attachment if `ContentLocation` is a relative URL. See the example of 'Working with MIME HTML (MHTML)' later in the chapter for more information.

```
String = Attachment.ContentBase
```

ContentID Property

The `ContentID` property returns the `content-id` header of a MIME HTML attachment. This indicates a universally unique ID for this attachment. See the example of 'Working with MIME HTML (MHTML)' later in the chapter for more information.

```
String = Attachment.ContentID
```

ContentLocation Property

The `ContentLocation` property returns the `content-location` header of a MIME HTML attachment. This specifies the URL where the attachment is located. If this is a relative URL, the base URL will be returned by the `ContentBase` property. See the example of 'Working with MIME HTML (MHTML)' later in the chapter for more information.

```
String = Attachment.ContentLocation
```

Name Property

The Name property sets or returns the display name of the attachment. This is read-only for attachments on incoming messages.

```
Attachment.Name = String
String = Attachment.Name
```

Source Property

The Source property sets or returns the Message object to be embedded as an attachment for attachments of type CdoEmbeddedMessage. For attachments of type CdoFileData, the Source property is not used and will return an empty string (the source must be set using the Add method of the Attachments collection). This is read-only for attachments on incoming messages.

```
Attachment.Source = Variant
Variant = Attachment.Source
```

Note that the Type property must be set before Source is set.

Type Property

The Type property sets or returns the type of the attachment (whether the attachment is an embedded message or a file). This is read-only for attachments on incoming messages.

```
Attachment.Type = String
String = Attachment.Type
```

The possible values are:

Constant	Value	Description
CdoFileData	1	The attachment is a file (the default).
CdoEmbeddedMessage	4	The attachment is an embedded message.

The Attachments Collection

The Attachments collection contains all of the Attachment objects for a message and provides methods and properties for managing a message's attachments. We can retrieve a reference to the Attachments collection through the Attachments property of the Message object:

```
' VBScript
Set colAttachments = objMsg.Attachements
```

```
// JScript
colAttachments = objMsg.Attachments;
```

Note that the NewMail object does not have an Attachments collection, although we can create an attachment for a NewMail object using the AttachFile and AttachURL methods. For a full example of working with attachments, see the 'CDO for NT Server Examples' section later on in the chapter.

CDONTS

The `Attachments` collection exposes the following methods and properties:

Methods	Properties	
Add	Application*	Item
Delete	Class*	Parent*
	Count	Session*

* See the section on 'Common Properties' earlier in the chapter.

Attachments Collection Methods

The `Attachments` collection exposes methods which allow us to add attachments to and remove them from a message.

Add Method

The `Add` method creates and returns a new `Attachment` object in the `Attachments` collection.

```
Attachment = Attachments.Add([Name], [Type], [Source],
                        [ContentLocation], [ContentBase])
```

Parameter	Data Type	Description
Name	String	The display name for the new attachment. The default value is an empty string.
Type	Long	The type of the attachment. This may be either `CdoFileData` (1; the default) or `CdoEmbeddedMessage` (4).
Source	Variant	The full path and filename of the file (if `Type` is `CdoFileData`) or the message to be embedded (if `Type` is `CdoEmbeddedMessage`). The default value is an empty string.
ContentLocation	String	The URL for a body part of a MIME HTML attachment.
ContentBase	String	The base URL for a body part of a MIME HTML attachment.

For example, to add a Word document as an attachment to a message:

```
' VBScript
Set objAttach = objNewMsg.Attachments.Add("attachment.doc", _
            CdoFileData, "C:\ASPProgRef\CDONTS\attachment.doc")
```

```
// JScript
objAttach = objNewMsg.Attachments.Add("attachment.doc",
            CdoFileData, "C:\\ASPProgRef\\CDONTS\\attachment.doc");
```

Delete Method

The `Delete` method deletes all the attachments in the `Attachments` collection.

```
Attachments.Delete()
```

To remove only one attachment, you should use the `Attachment` object's `Delete` method.

Attachments Collection Properties

As well as the common properties, the `Attachments` collection exposes two properties, `Count` and `Item`.

Count Property

The `Count` property returns the number of `Attachment` objects in the collection.

```
Long = Attachments.Count
```

Item Property

The `Item` property returns a reference to the `Attachment` object with the specified (one-based) ordinal position in the collection.

```
Attachment = Attachments.Item(Index)
```

The `Index` is therefore a long between one and the number of items in the collection (which can be retrieved using the `Count` property).

The Folder Object

The `Folder` object represents a folder in the message store. For CDONTS, this will either be the Inbox (where incoming messages are stored) or the Outbox (where outgoing messages reside until they are sent) for the user currently logged on. Note that messages in the Inbox may not be modified (although they can be deleted). We include a full example of retrieving messages from the Inbox folder in the 'CDO for NT Server Examples' section later in the chapter.

We can get a reference to a `Folder` object using the `Session` object's `GetDefaultFolder`, `Inbox`, or `Outbox` methods. For example, to create a `Folder` object representing the Outbox using `GetDefaultFolder`:

```
' VBScript
Set objOutbox = objSession.GetDefaultFolder(CdoDefaultFolderOutbox)
```

```
// JScript
objOutbox = objSession.GetDefaultFolder(CdoDefaultFolderOutbox);
```

Or using the `Session`'s `Outbox` property:

```
' VBScript
Set objOutbox = objSession.Outbox
```

```
// JScript
objOutbox = objSession.Outbox;
```

CDONTS

The Folder object has no methods, but exposes the following properties:

Properties	
Application*	Name
Class*	Parent*
Messages	Session*

* See the section on 'Common Properties' earlier in the chapter.

Folder Object Properties

The Folder object exposes two properties beside the four common to all CDONTS objects.

Messages Property

The Messages property returns a Messages collection which contains a Message object for each message stored within the folder.

```
Messages = Folder.Messages
```

Name Property

The Name property returns the name of the Folder object.

```
String = Folder.Name
```

The Message Object

The Message object represents a mail message in either the Inbox or Outbox folder. Note that incoming messages cannot be modified in any way, although they can be deleted.

We can access a Message object through the Messages collection of the folder in which it resides. For example, to retrieve the first message in the Inbox:

```
' VBScript
Set objInbox = objSession.Inbox
Set objMessage = objInbox.Messages.Item(1)
```

```
// JScript
objInbox = objSession.Inbox;
objMessage = objInbox.Messages.Item(1);
```

We can create a new Message object using the Messages collection's Add method:

```
' VBScript
Set objOutbox = objSession.Outbox
Set objMessage = objOutbox.Messages.Add("This is the subject", _
                "This is the body.", CdoNormal)
```

```
// JScript
objOutbox = objSession.Outbox;
objMessage = objOutbox.Messages.Add("This is the subject",
                             "This is the body.", CdoNormal)
```

The Message object exposes the following methods and properties:

Methods	Properties		
Delete	Application*	HTMLText	Session*
Send	Attachments	Importance	Size
	Class*	MessageFormat	Subject
	ContentBase	Parent*	Text
	ContentID	Recipients	TimeReceived
	ContentLocation	Sender	TimeSent

* See the section on 'Common Properties' earlier in the chapter.

Message Object Methods

The methods of the Message object allow us to delete a message from the collection or to send the message.

Delete Method

The Delete method deletes the Message object.

```
Message.Delete()
```

Send Method

The Send method sends the message to the recipients through the messaging system.

```
Message.Send()
```

For an example of sending a mail with the Message object, see the section on 'Sending Messages with CDONTS' earlier in the chapter.

Message Object Properties

Attachments property

The Attachments property returns the Attachments collection for the message.

```
Attachments = Message.Attachments
```

ContentBase Property

The ContentBase property returns the content-base header of the message. This indicates the base URL to use for a MIME HTML message if ContentLocation is a relative URL. See the example of 'Working with MIME HTML (MHTML)' later in the chapter for more information.

```
Message.ContentBase = String
String = Message.ContentBase
```

This property is read-only for incoming messages.

ContentID Property

The ContentID property returns the content-id header of a MIME HTML message. This indicates a universally unique ID for this message. See the example of 'Working with MIME HTML (MHTML)' later in the chapter for more information.

```
String = Message.ContentID
```

ContentLocation Property

The ContentLocation property returns the content-location header of a MIME HTML message. This specifies the URL where the message body is located. If this is a relative URL, the base URL will be returned by the ContentBase property. See the example of 'Working with MIME HTML (MHTML)' later in the chapter for more information.

```
Attachment.ContentLocation = String
String = Attachment.ContentLocation
```

This property is read-only for incoming messages.

HTMLText Property

The HTMLText property sets or returns the body of a message in HTML format. Read-only for incoming messages.

```
Message.HTMLText = Variant
Variant = Message.HTMLText
```

In scripting languages, this property will always contain a string, although in C/C++ and Java it can contain an IStream object. CDONTS automatically synchronizes the HTMLText and Text properties, so setting this will cause the Text property to be set too.

Importance Property

The Importance property returns or sets the importance of the message. Read-only for incoming messages.

```
Message.Importance = Long
Long = Message.Importance
```

This can be one of the following values:

Constant	Value	Description
CdoLow	0	The message is of low importance.
CdoNormal	1	The message is of normal importance (the default).
CdoHigh	2	The message is of high importance.

MessageFormat Property

The MessageFormat property determines whether the message text will be in MIME or plain text format. This property is write-only and not used with incoming messages.

```
Message.MessageFormat = Long
```

The possible settings are:

Constant	Value	Description
CdoMime	0	The message is in MIME format.
CdoText	1	The message is in plain text format.

Recipients Property

The Recipients property returns the Recipients collection for the message.

```
Recipients = Message.Recipients
```

Sender Property

The Sender property returns an AddressEntry object representing the sender of the message.

```
AddressEntry = Message.Sender
```

Size Property

The Size property returns the approximate size of the message in bytes.

```
Long = Message.Size
```

Subject Property

The Subject property sets or returns a string containing the subject of the message. This property is read-only for incoming messages.

```
Message.Subject = String
String = Message.Subject
```

This is the default property of the Message object, so can be referred to implicitly.

Text Property

The Text property sets or returns the body of the message. Read-only for incoming messages.

```
Message.Text = Variant
Variant = Message.Text
```

In scripting languages, this property will always contain a string, although in C/C++ and Java it can contain an IStream object. CDONTS automatically synchronizes the HTMLText and Text properties, so setting this will cause the HTMLText property to be set too.

TimeRecieved Property

The TimeReceived property returns the date and time when the message was received.

```
Date = Message.TimeRecieved
```

TimeSent Property

The TimeSent property returns the date and time when the message was sent.

```
Date = Message.TimeSent
```

The Messages Collection

The Messages collection contains all the Message objects in the Inbox or Outbox folder. Note that messages in the Inbox folder cannot be modified in any way (except that they may be deleted). Also, the Messages collection of the Outbox is always empty, although we can use its Add method to create a new message for sending.

We can get a reference to the Messages collection of a folder through its Messages property:

```
' VBScript
Set objOutbox = objSession.Outbox
Set colMessages = objOutbox.Messages
```

```
// JScript
objOutbox = objSession.Outbox;
colMessages = objOutbox.Messages;
```

The Messages collection exposes the following methods and properties:

Methods	Properties
Add	Application*
Delete	Class*
GetFirst	Count
GetLast	Item
GetNext	Parent*
GetPrevious	Session*

* See the section on 'Common Properties' earlier in the chapter.

Messages Collection Methods

The Messages collection exposes six methods which allow us to navigate through the collection and to add and delete messages.

Add Method

The Add method adds a message to the Messages collection and returns the new Message object.

```
Message = Messages.Add([Subject], [Text], [Importance])
```

Parameter	Data Type	Description
Subject	Variant	The subject of the new message; the default is an empty string.
Text	Variant	The body of the message; this corresponds to the Text property. The default is an empty string.
Importance	Variant	The priority of the message. This may be CdoLow, CdoNormal, or CdoHigh; the default is CdoNormal.

Delete Method

The Delete method deletes all the messages in the Messages collection.

```
Messages.Delete()
```

To remove a single message from the folder, you should use the Delete method of the Message object.

GetFirst Property

The GetFirst method returns the first Message object in the Messages collection. It returns Nothing if the collection is empty (i.e. if there are no messages in the folder to which the collection belongs).

```
Message = Messages.GetFirst()
```

GetLast Method

The GetLast method returns the last Message object in the Messages collection. It returns Nothing if the collection is empty (i.e. if there are no messages in the folder to which the collection belongs).

```
Message = Messages.GetLast()
```

GetNext Method

The GetNext method returns the next Message object in the Messages collection. It returns Nothing if the last message has already been reached, or if the collection is empty (i.e. if there are no messages in the folder to which the collection belongs).

```
Message = Messages.GetNext()
```

GetPrevious Method

The GetPrevious method returns the previous Message object in the Messages collection. It returns Nothing if the current message is the first in the collection, or if the collection is empty (i.e. if there are no messages in the folder to which the collection belongs).

```
Message = Messages.GetPrevious()
```

Messages Collection Properties

As well as the four standard properties, the Messages collection exposes Count and Item properties.

Count Property

The Count property returns the number of Message objects in the collection.

```
Long = Messages.Count
```

This will always return 0 for the Messages collection of the Outbox.

Item Property

The Item property retrieves a Message object from the Messages collection.

```
Message = Messages.Item(Index)
```

The Index is the one-based ordinal position of the message in the collection. This is the default property for the Messages collection, so may be omitted.

The NewMail Object

The NewMail object provides a very quick way of creating and sending a mail message, without needing to log on to a session and work down the CDONTS object hierarchy, as we would with a Message object. In fact, the NewMail object simply 'floats' in the object model, without direct connections to any other CDONTS object. For example, the NewMail object doesn't have a Recipients or Attachments collections, but provides methods and properties for adding attachments and recipients. However, we cannot subsequently access these once they have been added.

We can create a NewMail object using the Server.CreateObject method:

```
' VBScript
Set objMailer = Server.CreateObject("CDONTS.NewMail")
```

```
// JScript
objMailer = Server.CreateObject("CDONTS.NewMail");
```

The NewMail object exposes the following methods and properties:

Methods	Properties	
AttachFile	Bcc	Importance
AttachURL	Body	MailFormat
Send	BodyFormat	Subject
SetLocaleIDs	Cc	To
	ContentBase	Value
	ContentLocation	Version
	From	

NewMail Object Methods

The NewMail object exposes the AttachFile, AttachURL, Send, and SendLocaleIDs methods:

AttachFile Method

The AttachFile method adds a file attachment to the mail.

```
NewMail.AttachFile(Source, [FileName], [EncodingMethod])
```

Parameter	Data Type	Description
Source	String	The full path and filename for the file. (If coding from C/C++ or Java, this can also be a pointer to an IStream object.)
FileName	String	The name for the attachment, which will show on the message; the default is the filename in the Source parameter.
EncodingMethod	Long	The encoding to use for the mail. Possible values are CdoEncodingUUencode (UUEncode format; the default) and CdoEncodingBase64 (Base 64 encoding).

AttachURL Method

The AttachURL method attaches a file to the message and associates the attachment with a URL.

```
NewMail.AttachURL(Source, [ContentLocation], [ContentBase], [EncodingMethod])
```

Parameter	Data Type	Description
Source	String	The full physical path and filename of the attachment. (If coding from C/C++ or Java, this can also be a pointer to an IStream object.)

Table Continued on Following Page

CDONTS

939

Parameter	Data Type	Description
ContentLocation	String	The relative or absolute URL to reference this attachment.
ContentBase	String	The base for a relative URL used to reference this attachment.
EncodingMethod	Long	The encoding to use for the mail. Possible values are CdoEncodingUUencode (UUEncode format; the default) and CdoEncodingBase64 (Base 64 encoding).

For example:

```
' VBScript
objMessage.AttachURL "C:\Templates\wrox_logo100.gif", _
                     "the_wrox_logo.gif"
```

```
// JScript
objMessage.AttachURL("C:\\Templates\\wrox_logo100.gif",
                     "the_wrox_logo.gif");
```

Send Method

The Send method sends the mail message. All the parameters are optional, and can instead be set through the NewMail object's properties before the mail is sent.

```
NewMail.Send([From], [To], [Subject], [Body], [Importance])
```

Parameter	Data Type	Description
From	String	The e-mail address of the sender.
To	String	A semi-colon delimited string containing the e-mail addresses of all the recipients.
Subject	String	The content of the mail's subject field.
Body	String	The body of the mail message.
Importance	Long	The priority of the message. This may be CdoLow, CdoNormal, or CdoHigh; the default is CdoNormal.

For example:

```
' VBScript
Set objMailer = Server.CreateObject("CDONTS.NewMail")
objMailer.Send "sender@domain1.com", _
               "recipient1@domain2.com; recipient2@domain3.com", _
               "This is the subject", _
               "This is the very short mail message."
Set objMailer = Nothing
```

```
// JScript
var objMailer = Server.CreateObject("CDONTS.NewMail");
objMailer.Send("sender@domain1.com",
               "recipient1@domain2.com; recipient2@domain3.com",
               "This is the subject",
               "This is the very short mail message.");
delete objMailer;
```

SetLocaleIDs Method

The SetLocaleIDs method sets the locale for the new message. This setting determines the character set for the mail, the date and currency format, etc. This does not affect the locale settings for any other Message or NewMail objects.

```
NewMail.SetLocaleIDs(CodePageID)
```

Parameter	Data Type	Description
CodePageID	Long	The ID for the code page to be used by this message.

NewMail Object Properties

The NewMail object does not have the four properties common to all the other CDONTS objects. However, it does expose 13 properties which we can use to set the body and subject of the message, its recipients, etc. These properties are all write-only, with the exception of the read-only Version property.

Bcc Property

The Bcc property sets the BCC recipients for the message. Each recipient should be represented by a full e-mail address. Multiple recipients should be separated in the string by semi-colons.

```
NewMail.Bcc = String
```

Body Property

The Body property sets the body text of the object.

```
NewMail.Body = Variant
```

In scripting languages, this property can only be set to a string, although in C/C++ and Java, it can also be set to an IStream object.

BodyFormat Property

The BodyFormat property specifies whether the body should be formatted as plain text or as HTML.

```
NewMail.BodyFormat = Long
```

The possible values for this property are:

Constant	Value	Description
CdoBodyFormatHTML	0	The body is in HTML format.
CdoBodyFormatText	1	The body will only contain plain text (the default).

Cc Property

The Cc property sets the secondary (CC) recipients of the message. Each recipient should be represented by a full e-mail address. Multiple recipients should be separated in the string by semi-colons.

```
NewMail.Cc = String
```

ContentBase Property

The ContentBase property sets the content-base header for the message. This indicates the base URL to use for any relative URLs pertaining to the body of a MIME HTML message. See the example of 'Working with MIME HTML (MHTML)' later in the chapter for more information.

```
NewMail.ContentBase = String
```

ContentLocation Property

The ContentLocation property sets the content-location header for a MIME HTML message. This specifies the URL for the body of the message. If this is a relative URL, the base URL will be set by the ContentBase property. See the example of 'Working with MIME HTML (MHTML)' later in the chapter for more information.

```
NewMail.ContentLocation = String
```

From Property

The From property sets the e-mail address for the sender of the mail. Note that multiple senders are not permitted, so this string cannot contain a semi-colon.

```
NewMail.From = String
```

Importance Property

The Importance property specifies whether the mail should be marked as low, normal or high priority.

```
NewMail.Importance = Long
```

The possible values for this property are:

Constant	Value	Description
CdoLow	0	The message is of low importance.
CdoNormal	1	The message is of normal importance (the default).
CdoHigh	2	The message is of high importance.

MailFormat Property

The `MailFormat` property determines whether the mail's body will be in MIME or plain text format.

```
NewMail.MessageFormat = Long
```

The possible settings are:

Constant	Value	Description
CdoMailFormatMime	0	The message is in MIME format.
CdoMailFormatText	1	The message is in plain text format (the default).

Subject Property

The `Subject` property sets the subject text for the mail.

```
NewMail.Subject = String
```

To Property

The `To` property sets the list of primary recipients for the message. Each recipient should be represented by a full e-mail address. Multiple recipients should be separated in the string by semi-colons.

```
NewMail.To = String
```

Value Property

The `Value` property allows us to specify custom headers alongside standard header such as `To`, `Subject`, etc.

```
NewMail.Value(Header_name) = String
```

Where `Header_name` is a string containing the name of the header to be set, and `String` is the value for that header.

This is the default property for the `NewMail` object, so can be referred to implicitly.

For example:

```
' VBScript
strReplyTo = "please@replyhere.com"
objMsg.Value("Reply-To") = strReplyTo
objMsg.Value("Custom-header") = "This is the value"
```

```
// JScript
strReplyTo = "please@replyhere";
objMsg.Value("Reply-To") = strReplyTo;
objMsg.Value("Custom-header") = "This is the value";
```

See also the 'Using Custom Message Headers' example later in the chapter.

Version Property

The read-only `Version` property returns the version number of the CDONTS library in use.

```
String = NewMail.Version
```

Currently, this returns `"1.2"`.

The Recipient Object

The `Recipient` object represents a recipient to whom a message will be sent. Each `Message` object has a `Recipients` collection, which contains one `Recipient` object for each user who will receive the message.

We can get a reference to an existing `Recipient` object through the `Recipients` collection of a `Message` object. For example, to get the first recipient for a message:

```
' VBScript
Set objRecip = objMessage.Recipients.Item(1)
```

```
// JScript
objRecip = objMessage.Recipients.Item(1);
```

To add a new recipient to a message, we use the `Add` method of the `Recipients` collection:

```
' VBScript
Set objRecip = objMessage.Recipients.Add("John Smith", _
                        "jsmith@mycompany.com", CdoTo)
```

```
// JScript
objRecip = objMessage.Recipients.Add("John Smith",
                        "jsmith@mycompany.com", CdoTo);
```

The `Recipient` object exposes the following methods and properties:

Methods	Properties	
Delete	Address	Parent*
	Application*	Session*
	Class*	Type
	Name	

* See the section on 'Common Properties' earlier in the chapter.

Recipient Object Methods

The `Recipient` object has only one method, `Delete`.

Delete Method

The `Delete` method removes the `Recipient` object from the message's `Recipients` collection.

```
Recipient.Delete()
```

Recipient Object Properties

Address Property

The Address property sets or returns the full e-mail address for the recipient. This is read-only for incoming messages.

```
Recipient.Address = String
String = Recipient.Address
```

Name Property

The Name property sets or returns the display name of the Recipient object. This is read-only for incoming messages.

```
Recipient.Name = String
String = Recipient.Name
```

This is the default property for the Recipient object.

Type Property

The Type property specifies whether the recipient is a To, CC, or BCC recipient. This is read-only for incoming messages.

```
Long = Recipient.Type
Recipient.Type = Long
```

This may be one of the following values:

Constant	Value	Description
CdoTo	1	The recipient is a primary (To) recipient (the default).
CdoCc	2	The recipient is a CC recipient.
CdoBcc	3	The recipient is a BCC recipient.

The Recipients Collection

The Recipients collection contains all the Recipient objects for a message and exposes methods and properties for managing the recipients. We can get a reference to the Recipients collection through the Recipients property of a Message object:

```
' VBScript
Set colRecipients = objMessage.Recipients
```

```
// JScript
colRecipients = objMessage.Recipients;
```

The Recipients collection exposes the following methods and properties:

Methods	Properties
Add	Application*
Delete	Class*
	Count
	Item
	Parent*
	Session*

* See the section on 'Common Properties' earlier in the chapter.

Recipients Collection Methods

The Recipients collection has two methods, which allow us to add recipients to and remove them from the message.

Add Method

The Add method adds a recipient to the message and returns the new Recipient object.

```
Recipient = Recipients.Add([Name], [Address], [Type])
```

Parameter	Data Type	Description
Name	Variant	The display name for the recipient; the default is an empty string.
Address	Variant	The full e-mail address to which the message will be sent; the default is an empty string.
Type	Variant	The type of recipient. This can be CdoTo (the default), CdoCc, or CdoBcc.

Delete Method

The Delete method removes all the Recipient objects from the Recipients collection.

```
Recipients.Delete()
```

If you want to delete a single recipient, you should use the Delete method of the Recipient object.

Recipients Collection Properties

Count Property

The Count property returns the number of Recipient objects in the collection.

```
Long = Recipients.Count
```

Item Property

The Item property returns a single Recipient object from the Recipients collection.

```
Recipient = Recipients.Item(Index)
```

The *Index* is the one-based ordinal position of the recipient in the collection. This is the default property for the Recipients collection, so may be omitted.

The Session Object

The Session object represents a CDONTS session. Before we access any of the CDONTS objects (with the exception of NewMail), we must first create and log on to a CDONTS session. No significant CDONTS activity can be performed before we have logged on to the session (we can, however, call the Session's SetLocaleIDs method). Once we have done this, we can access the Inbox and the Outbox folders through the Session object, and hence the messages in them.

To create a Session object and log on to a session, we use this code:

```
' VBScript
Set objSession = Server.CreateObject("CDONTS.Session")
objSession.LogonSMTP "John Smith", "jsmith@mycompany.com"
```

```
// JScript
objSession = Server.CreateObject("CDONTS.Session");
objSession.LogonSMTP("John Smith", "jsmith@mycompany.com");
```

For a fuller example, see the example of 'Using the Session' below.

The Session object exposes the following methods and properties:

Methods	Properties	
GetDefaultFolder	Application*	Outbox
Logoff	Class*	Parent*
LogonSMTP	Inbox	Session*
SetLocaleIDs	MessageFormat	Version
	Name	

Session Object Methods

The Session object exposes methods for logging on to and out of a CDONTS session, for accessing the default folders and for setting locale information.

GetDefaultFolder Method

The GetDefaultFolder method returns a reference to the specified Folder object (the Inbox or the Outbox).

```
Folder = Session.GetDefaultFolder(Type)
```

CDONTS

Parameter	Data Type	Description
Type	Variant	The default folder to retrieve; this can be either CdoDefaultFolderInbox (1) or CdoDefaultFolderOutbox (2).

For example, to get a reference to the Inbox:

```
' VBScript
Set objInbox = objSession.GetDefaultFolder(CdoDefaultFolderInbox)
```

```
// JScript
objInbox = objSession.GetDefaultFolder(CdoDefaultFolderInbox);
```

Logoff Method

The Logoff method logs off from the messaging system.

```
Session.Logoff()
```

After calling this method, the CDONTS objects will no longer be available, and attempts to access them will result in an error.

LogonSMTP Method

The LogonSMTP method logs on to the messaging system. Note that this method does not cause any authentication to take place, and any user name can be supplied. If CDONTS is being used with IIS, one Inbox will be shared for all users; however, only those e-mails addressed to the logged on user will be accessible. If Exchange is the mail server, the Inbox will be the logged on user's Inbox.

```
Session.LogonSMTP(DisplayName, Address)
```

Parameter	Data Type	Description
DisplayName	String	The display name for the user logging on.
Address	String	The full e-mail address for the user logging on.

SetLocaleIDs Method

The SetLocaleIDs method sets the locale for the current session. This setting determines the character set for the mail, the date and currency format, etc. This method can only be called before the call to LogonSMTP. If not called, the locale settings will be those from the user's Registry.

```
Session.SetLocaleIDs(CodePageID)
```

Parameter	Data Type	Description
CodePageID	Long	The ID for the code page to be used by this user.

Session Object Properties

The Session object also provides properties for retrieving references to the Inbox and Outbox, for setting the default message format and retrieving the user's display name, and for checking the current version of CDONTS in use.

Inbox Property

The Inbox property returns a Folder object representing the current user's Inbox folder.

```
Folder = Session.Inbox
```

MessageFormat Property

The MessageFormat property determines the default encoding for messages for the session.

```
Session.MessageFormat = Long
Long = Session.MessageFormat
```

The possible values are:

Constant	Value	Description
CdoMime	0	Messages will be in MIME format.
CdoText	1	Messages will be in plain text (the default).

Name Property

The Name property returns the display name of the currently logged on user (as specified in the LogonSMTP method call).

```
String = Session.Name
```

This is the default property for the Session object.

Outbox Property

The Outbox property returns a Folder object representing the current user's Outbox folder.

```
Folder = Session.Outbox
```

Version Property

The Version property returns the version number of the CDONTS library in use.

```
String = Session.Version
```

This is currently "1.2".

CDO for NT Server Examples

Before we look at the code samples, we must first raise some general issues. Firstly, the CDONTS objects are marked as ThreadingModel = both in the Registry, so they behave as page-scoped ASP objects. They don't aggregate the Free Threaded Marshaler (FTM), so they are not agile, and we must not store them with Session or Application scope, unless we clearly understand that this would severely hamper ASP's thread management. Secondly, if we want to refer to the CDONTS constants, we could create a virtual application and put the following METADATA directives in its global.asa file:

```
<!-- METADATA TYPE="typelib" NAME="Microsoft CDO for NTS 1.2 Library"
          UUID="0E064ADD-9D99-11D0-ABE5-00AA0064D470" -->
```

This directive imports all the constants defined in the type library, making them available to all the pages of the application. Alternatively, this directive could be placed in every individual ASP page where the CDONTS constants are required. Finally, note that the code given below omits error handling for the sake of clarity.

Using the Session

The Session object is the root of the CDONTS object hierarchy, and we need to create a Session object before we can work with any CDONTS objects (apart from NewMail). Using a Session object is fairly straightforward: first of all, we log on using the LogonSMTP method, then access a folder using either the Inbox or Outbox properties or the GetDefaultFolder method, and finally Logoff from the session:

```
' VBScript
Set objSession = Server.CreateObject("CDONTS.Session")
objSession.LogonSMTP "Sender Name", "sender@domain1.com"

Set objOutbox = objSession.Outbox
Set objInbox = objSession.GetDefaultFolder(CdoDefaultFolderInbox)

' working with message(s) in the folder(s)

objSession.Logoff
```

```
// JScript
objSession = Server.CreateObject("CDONTS.Session");
objSession.LogonSMTP("Sender Name", "sender@domain1.com");

objOutbox = objSession.Outbox;
objInbox = objSession.GetDefaultFolder(CdoDefaultFolderInbox);

// working with message(s) in the folder(s)

objSession.Logoff();
```

It's worth noting that the LogonSMTP method doesn't perform any authentication or validation of the two string parameters supplied, the display name and the e-mail address. It just sets this property for subsequent use, e.g. sending a message or accessing incoming messages.

Working with Attachments

We saw above (in the section on 'Sending Messages with CDONTS') the steps required to send a message, using either the `NewMail` object or the `Message` object and the CDONTS hierarchy. Either way, adding attachments is a matter of course. In the following ASP page, we first send an e-mail with two attachments (a Word document and an HTML file) using the `NewMail` object; then we send a message with a Word attachment using the `Message` object. The VBScript code for the page is:

```
<%
Option Explicit

Dim objMsg, objSession, objOutbox, objInbox
Dim strFrom, strTo, strSubject, strBody
%>

<HTML>
<HEAD>
<TITLE>CDONTS Sample #1 - Working with attachments</TITLE>
</HEAD>
<BODY >
<%
strFrom="""User 1"" <user.1@dev02>"
strTo="""User 33"" <user.33@test-server>"
strSubject = "This is the subject"
strBody = "This is the body"

' Using NewMail object
Set objMsg = Server.CreateObject("CDONTS.NewMail")

With objMsg
    .To = strTo
    .From = strFrom
    .Subject = strSubject
    .MailFormat = CdoMailFormatMime
    .AttachFile "C:/Attachments/Word attachment.doc", _
                "A Word attachment.doc"
    .AttachFile "C:/Attachments/HTML attachment.htm", _
                "An HTML attachment.htm"
    .Send
End With

Set objMsg = nothing

' Using Session-rooted hierachy
Set objSession = Server.CreateObject("CDONTS.Session")
objSession.LogonSMTP "Sender Name", "sender@domain1.com"
Set objOutbox = objSession.Outbox
'Set objInbox = objSession.GetDefaultFolder(CdoDefaultFolderInbox)

Set objMsg = objOutbox.Messages.Add
objMsg.Subject = "This is the subject"
objMsg.Text = "This is the very short mail message."
objMsg.Recipients.Add "Recipient Name", "recipient@domain2.com", CdoTo
objMsg.Attachments.Add "A Word attachment.doc" , CdoFileData, _
                    "C:/Attachments/Word attachment.doc"
objMsg.Send

Set objMsg = nothing
Set objOutbox = nothing
objSession.Logoff
Set objSession = nothing
%>
```

951

```
We have sent messages with attachments to <%= strTo %>.
<BR>
</BODY>
</HTML>
```

And the JScript equivalent for this is:

```
<%
var objMsg, objSession, objOutbox, objInbox;
var strFrom, strTo, strSubject, strBody;
%>

<HTML>
<HEAD>
<TITLE>CDONTS Sample #1 - Working with attachments</TITLE>
</HEAD>
<BODY >
<%
strFrom="\"User 1\" <user.1@dev02>";
strTo="\"User 33\" <user.33@test-server>";
strSubject = "This is the subject";
strBody = "This is the body";

// Using NewMail object
objMsg = Server.CreateObject("CDONTS.NewMail");

with (objMsg) {
   To = strTo;
   From = strFrom;
   Subject = strSubject;
   MailFormat = CdoMailFormatMime;
   AttachFile("C:/Attachments/Word attachment.doc",
           "A Word attachment.doc");
   AttachFile("C:/Attachments/HTML attachment.htm",
           "An HTML attachment.htm");
   Send();
}

delete objMsg;

// Using Session-rooted hierachy
objSession = Server.CreateObject("CDONTS.Session");
objSession.LogonSMTP("Sender Name", "sender@domain1.com");
objOutbox = objSession.Outbox;
// objInbox = objSession.GetDefaultFolder(CdoDefaultFolderInbox);

objMsg = objOutbox.Messages.Add();
objMsg.Subject = "This is the subject";
objMsg.Text = "This is the very short mail message.";
objMsg.Recipients.Add("Recipient Name", "recipient@domain2.com", CdoTo);
objMsg.Attachments.Add("A Word attachment.doc" , CdoFileData,
                     "C:/Attachments/Word attachment.doc");
objMsg.Send();

delete objMsg;
delete objOutbox;
objSession.Logoff();
delete objSession;
%>

We have sent messages with attachments to <%= strTo %>.
<BR>
</BODY>
</HTML>
```

There are obviously differences in the tasks we can do with attachments using these two approaches. With the `NewMail` object, we can only add attachments (using the `AttachFile` method), but we cannot modify or manage them. However, the `Message` object exposes its `Attachments` collection, allowing us to access and modify each individual `Attachment` object. The sample code above shows the quickest way to add an attachment object to the collection, passing the essential information to create the attachment to the `Attachments.Add` method. All these parameters are optional and the method returns an `Attachment` object; so we could create an empty attachment and then load the content using the `Attachment's` `ReadFromFile` method.

Working with MIME HTML (MHTML)

CDONTS offers rudimentary support for MIME HTML (MHTML), allowing us to create a message that contains in its body an HTML page with graphics and other HTML content. We used the term "rudimentary" because CDONTS doesn't give us complete control of the complex MHTML message's structure, and its features are quite weak compared to CDO2000's powerful integration with MIME standards. So, if we need MHTML support and use Windows 2000, we should positively exploit CDO2000. However, it's quite straightforward to create a basic MHTML message with CDONTS.

There are two slightly different ways to create a simple MHTML message using the `NewMail` object. This is the first approach:

```
<%
Option Explicit
Dim objMsg, strFrom, strTo, strSubject, strBody
%>
<HTML>
<HEAD>
<TITLE>CDONTS Sample #2 - Working with MHTML</TITLE>
</HEAD>
<BODY>
<%
strFrom="""User 1"" <user.1@dev02>"
strTo="""User 33"" <user.33@test-server>"
strSubject = "With compliments"

strBody = "<HTML><HEAD><TITLE>With compliments</TITLE></HEAD>" & _
          "<BODY><P><IMG src=""the_wrox_logo.gif""></P>" & _
          "<P><FONT color=red size=5> With authors' and " & _
          "publisher's compliments.</FONT></P>" & _
          "<P><FONT color=black><EM>" & _
          "The ""ASP 3.0 Programmer's Reference"" Team" & _
          "</EM></FONT></P></BODY></HTML>"

Set objMsg = Server.CreateObject("CDONTS.NewMail")

With objMsg
   .To = strTo
   .From = strFrom
   .Subject = strSubject
   .MailFormat = CdoMailFormatMime
   .BodyFormat = CdoBodyFormatHTML
   .Body = strBody
   .AttachURL "C:\Templates\wrox_logo100.gif", "the_wrox_logo.gif"
   .Send
End With
```

```
Set objMsg = nothing
%>
We have sent a MHTML message to <%= strTo %>.
<BR>
</BODY>
</HTML>
```

Or in JScript:

```
<%
var objMsg, strFrom, strTo, strSubject, strBody;
%>
<HTML>
<HEAD>
<TITLE>CDONTS Sample #2 - Working with MHTML</TITLE>
</HEAD>
<BODY>
<%
strFrom="\"User 1\" <user.1@dev02>";
strTo="\"User 33\" <user.33@test-server>";
strSubject = "With compliments";

strBody = "<HTML><HEAD><TITLE>With compliments</TITLE></HEAD>" +
          "<BODY><P><IMG SRC=\"the_wrox_logo.gif\"></P>" +
          "<P><FONT color=red size=5> With authors' and " +
          "publisher's compliments.</FONT></P>" +
          "<P><FONT color=black><EM>" +
          "The \"ASP 3.0 Programmer's Reference\" Team" +
          "</EM></FONT></P></BODY></HTML>";

objMsg = Server.CreateObject("CDONTS.NewMail");

with (objMsg) {
    To = strTo;
    From = strFrom;
    Subject = strSubject;
    MailFormat = CdoMailFormatMime;
    BodyFormat = CdoBodyFormatHTML;
    Body = strBody;
    AttachURL("C:\\Templates\\wrox_logo100.gif", "the_wrox_logo.gif");
    Send();
}

delete objMsg;
%>
We have sent a MHTML message to <%= strTo %>.
<BR>
</BODY>
</HTML>
```

This approach uses a string containing the HTML that represents the skeleton of the message. This HTML contains references to other elements forming a compound document, in this case the GIF image the_wrox_logo.gif. We appropriately set the format types of the message and body (CdoMailFormatMime and CdoBodyFormatHTML), then assign the HTML string to the Body property and finally use the AttachURL method to add the required image to the MHTML message. The first parameter is the physical path to the file, and the second is the string value of the Content-Location header of the generated MIME part, which must be identical to the SRC attribute of the image in the HTML. The Content-Location and Content-Base headers are defined to resolve URL references to other body parts. Let's take a look at a snippet of the MIME code produced by the script (we can find it in the file CDONTS puts in the pickup directory):

```
...
------=_NextPart_001_0069_01BF4005.1B28B510
Content-Type: text/html;
 charset="iso-8859-1"
Content-Transfer-Encoding: quoted-printable

<HTML><HEAD><TITLE>With compliments</TITLE></HEAD><BODY><P><IMG =
src=3D"the_wrox_logo.gif"></P><P><FONT color=3Dred size=3D5> With authors' =
and publisher's compliments.</FONT></P><P><FONT color=3Dblack><EM>The =
"ASP 3.0 Programmer's Reference" Team</EM></FONT></P></BODY></HTML>
------=_NextPart_001_0069_01BF4005.1B28B510--

------=_NextPart_000_0068_01BF4005.1B242130
Content-Type: image/gif
Content-Transfer-Encoding: base64
Content-Disposition: attachment
Content-Location: the_wrox_logo.gif
```

```
R0lGODlhZABkAPcAABgYECEhGCkhITEpKTExMTk5MUJCOUpCQlJKSlJSUlpaUmNaWmtjY2tra3Nz
c3t7c4R7e4yEhIyMjJSUlJyclKWcnKWlpa05Ma1COa2trbVKQrVSSrW1tb1aUr1aWr1jWr1rY729
vcZra8Zza8Z7c8a9vcbGxs6Ee86EhM6MhM6UjM7OztaUlNaclNacnNalnNbW1t6lpd6trd61rd7e
...
```

The first part is the HTML for the message, and the second one (which begins with _NextPart_000_0068_01BF4005.1B242130) is the GIF image. The mail user agent (e.g. Outlook Express) uses the Content-Location value of the second part to resolve the URL reference from the HTML, displaying a well-formatted HTML page:

The Content-Base header adds another level of indirection, allowing the mail user agent to resolve URL references. For instance, we could send the above message without embedding the GIF image, letting the mail user agent access the image over the Internet. To do that, we would have to add a Content-Base header to the HTML MIME part specifying a URL base to form a complete URL to the requested resource:

```
...
------=_NextPart_001_0069_01BF4005.1B28B510
Content-Type: text/html;
    charset="iso-8859-1"
Content-Transfer-Encoding: quoted-printable
Content-Base:http://www.wrox.com/images/

<HTML><HEAD><TITLE>With compliments</TITLE></HEAD><BODY><P><IMG =
src=3D"the_wrox_logo.gif"></P><P><FONT color=3Dred size=3D5> With authors' =
and publisher's compliments.</FONT></P><P><FONT color=3Dblack><EM>The =
...
```

In this case, the mail user agent will try to download the image from the Internet using the URL http://www.wrox.com/images/the_wrox_logo.gif. We can use the same approach even on an intranet, using a UNC (Universal Naming Convention) path. For instance, if the Content-Base header were \\MyServer\MyImages, the mail user agent would try to download and display the image from \\MyServer\MyImages\the_wrox_logo.gif. We can set the Content-Location and Content-Base headers using the ContentLocation and ContentBase property of the NewMail and Attachment objects, and with the appropriate parameters of the NewMail's AttachURL method.

The second CDONTS approach to MHTML messaging allows us to avoid managing the HTML as a string. We simply call the AttachURL method twice, once for the HTML file and once for the image file:

```
...
With objMsg
    .To = strTo
    .From = strFrom
    .Subject = strSubject
    .MailFormat = CdoMailFormatMime
    .BodyFormat = CdoBodyFormatHTML
    .AttachURL "C:\Templates\compliments.htm", "compliments.htm"
    .AttachURL "C:\Templates\wrox_logo100.gif", "the_wrox_logo.gif"
    .Send
End With
```

The exact MIME structure of the message created in the two cases is not identical, but Outlook Express displays the content in the same way. The first case also produces an alternative version of the HTML content in simple text (multipart/alternative). Also, the second method delivers both parts as attachments (i.e. with the MIME Content-Disposition header equal to "attachment"), making the order of the method calls critical. We must call AttachURL for the HTML file before calling it for the image file(s).

Using Custom Message Headers

With the NewMail's Value property (this is the default property, so .Value can be omitted as in the following example), we can easily set up additional headers and their values for the message. Let's suppose we need to use a standard message header that isn't available as an object property (e.g. Reply-To, Keywords, etc.), or we must add to the message a custom header that is recognized by a specific recipient. So, we can enhance our message using this syntax:

```
<%
Option Explicit

Dim objMsg, strFrom, strTo, strReplyTo, strSubject, strBody
%>

<HTML>
<HEAD>
<TITLE>CDONTS Sample #3 - Using custom message headers</TITLE>
</HEAD>
<BODY >

<%
strFrom="""User 1"" <user.1@dev02>"
strTo="""User 33"" <user.33@test-server>"
strReplyTo = "please@replyhere"
strSubject = "This is the subject"
strBody = "This is the body"

Set objMsg = Server.CreateObject("CDONTS.NewMail")

With objMsg
    .To = strTo
    .From = strFrom
    .Subject = strSubject
    .Body = strBody
    .Value("Reply-To") = strReplyTo
    .Value("Custom-header") = "This is the value"
    .Send
End With

Set objMsg = nothing
%>

We have sent a message with custom headers to <%= strTo %>.
<BR>
</BODY>
</HTML>
```

Or in JScript:

```
<%
var objMsg, strFrom, strTo, strReplyTo, strSubject, strBody;
%>

<HTML>
<HEAD>
<TITLE>CDONTS Sample #3 - Using custom message headers</TITLE>
</HEAD>
<BODY >

<%
strFrom="\"User 1\" <user.1@dev02>";
strTo="\"User 33\" <user.33@test-server>";
strReplyTo = "please@replyhere";
strSubject = "This is the subject";
strBody = "This is the body";

objMsg = Server.CreateObject("CDONTS.NewMail");

with (objMsg) {
    To = strTo;
    From = strFrom;
    Subject = strSubject;
    Body = strBody;
```

```
    Value("Reply-To") = strReplyTo;
    Value("Custom-header") = "This is the value";
    Send();
}

delete objMsg;
%>

We have sent a message with custom headers to <%= strTo %>.
<BR>
</BODY>
</HTML>
```

Here's the entire generated message; the `Reply-To` and `Custom-header` lines are highlighted in bold:

```
X-Receiver: user.33@test-server
X-Sender: user.1@dev02
Reply-To: <please@replyhere>
From: "User 1" <user.1@dev02>
To: "User 33" <user.33@test-server>
Subject: This is the subject
Date: Sat, 4 Mar 2000 17:06:41 +0100
Custom-header: This is the value
X-MimeOLE: Produced By Microsoft MimeOLE V5.00.2919.6700

This is the body
```

Obviously, from the CDONTS point of view, there is no difference at all between `Reply-To` and `Custom-header`; they are both processed as name-value pairs (although the first is a little special since CDONTS interprets it as an e-mail address and surrounds it in angle brackets).

Examining the Inbox Folder

We saw above (in the 'Using the Session' example) how to get the `Inbox` and `Outbox` folders from the `Session` object. A `Folder` object has just two properties: the `Name` (a string containing `"Inbox"` or `"Outbox"`) and the `Messages` collection. We used the `Messages.Add` method in conjunction with the Outbox folder to create a new outgoing `Message` object, and this is the only task we can perform with this collection. In other words, the `Messages` collection of the Outbox folder is always empty, and its `Count` property is always `0` (even if we use the `Messages.Add` method). On the other hand, the `Messages` collection of the Inbox folder doesn't allows us to call the `Add` method, but lets us iterate through the `Message` objects in the collection. So the question is: what messages are included in the Inbox collection?

Remember that when we logon using the `Session` object, we pass in an e-mail address as a parameter? Well, the `Messages` collection of the Inbox contains all the messages in the SMTP service's `Drop` directory that have an `X-receiver` header with this e-mail address (see the following sample for more information on this header). For instance, if we logged on to the mail system using the address `news.mng@dev02`, the collection would hold all the messages with the required header value; for example:

```
x-receiver: news.mng@dev02
From: postmaster@dev02
To: news.mng@dev02
Date: Wed, 8 Dec 1999 14:02:53 -0800
MIME-Version: 1.0
Content-Type: multipart/report; report-type=delivery-status;
   boundary="9B095B5ADSN=_01BF41C7AA12BDA000000002dev02"
Message-ID: <FRaqbC8wS00000002@dev02>
Subject: Delivery Status Notification (Failure)

... (message content omitted)
```

In the following ASP page, we define a subroutine named `DisplayMsgsTable` that accepts a generic `Folder` object as a parameter and displays certain message fields in a table. We can call this subroutine with both the Inbox and the Outbox folder, but the table will only be displayed for the former.

```
<%
Option Explicit

Sub DisplayMsgsTable(folder)

   Const strTableHeader = "<P><TABLE WIDTH=100% bgcolor=Silver " & _
                          "BORDER=1 CELLSPACING=1 CELLPADDING=1>" & _
                          "<TR BGCOLOR=Yellow><STRONG>" & _
                          "<TD>From</TD><TD>To</TD>" & _
                          "<TD>Subject</TD><TD>Message text</TD>" & _
                          "<TD>Attachment</TD><TD>Received</TD>" & _
                          "</STRONG></TR>"
   Const strTableFooter = "</TABLE><P>"

   Response.Write "<HR><H2>" & folder.Name & "</H2><BR>"

   If Not (folder.Messages.Count > 0) Then
      Response.Write "Sorry, the folder contains no messages<HR>"
      Exit Sub
   End If


   Response.Write strTableHeader

   Dim objMsg
   For Each objMsg In folder.Messages
      Response.Write "<TR><TD>" & objMsg.Sender.Name & " &lt;" & _
                     objMsg.Sender.Address & "&gt;</TD>"

      Dim strRecs
      If objMsg.Recipients.Count > 0 Then
         strRecs = objMsg.Recipients(1).Name & " &lt;" & _
                   objMsg.Recipients(1).Address & "&gt;"
         Dim idx
         For idx=2 To objMsg.Recipients.count
            strRecs = strRecs & "; " & _
                      objMsg.Recipients(idx).Name & " &lt;" & _
                      objMsg.Recipients(idx).Address & "&gt;"
         Next
      Else
         strRecs = "No recipient"
      End if

      Response.Write "<TD>" & strRecs & "</TD>"
      Response.Write "<TD>" & objMsg.Subject & "</TD>"
      Response.Write "<TD>" & objMsg.Text & "</TD>"
      Response.Write "<TD>" & CStr(objMsg.Attachments.Count>0) & _
                     "</TD>"
      Response.Write "<TD>" & FormatDateTime(objMsg.TimeReceived, _
                     vbShortDate) & "</TD></TR>"
```

```
      Next

      Response.Write strTableFooter
      Response.Write "<HR>"

End sub

Dim objSession, objOutbox, objInbox
%>
<HTML>
<HEAD>
<TITLE>CDONTS Sample #4 - Examining inbox and outbox folders</TITLE>
</HEAD>
<BODY >

<%
Set objSession = Server.CreateObject("CDONTS.Session")
objSession.LogonSMTP "Newsletter manager", "news.mng@dev02"
'Set objOutbox = objSession.Outbox
Set objOutbox = objSession.GetDefaultFolder(CdoDefaultFolderOutbox)
Set objInbox = objSession.GetDefaultFolder(CdoDefaultFolderInbox)

Response.Write "<H1> Welcome " & objSession.Name & "</H1><P>"

Response.Write "<H3> This is the content of your mail folders:</H3><P>"

' #####################
' We can use the following code to verify that we cannot add
' messages to the Inbox folder
'Dim objNewMsg
'Set objNewMsg = objInbox.Messages.Add
'Set objNewMsg = nothing
'#####################

DisplayMsgsTable objInbox

' #####################
' We can use the following code to verify that outbox's Messages
' collection is always empty
'Dim objNewMsg
'Set objNewMsg = objOutbox.Messages.Add
'objNewMsg.Subject = "This is the subject"
'objNewMsg.Text = "This is the very short mail message."
'objNewMsg.Recipients.Add "Recipient Name", _
'                         "recipient@domain2.com", CdoTo
'objNewMsg.Attachments.Add "A Word attachment.doc" , CdoFileData, _
'                          "C:/Wrox/Books/1999/ASP30PR/ch10/" & _
'                          "CDO2000/Attachments/Word attachment.doc"
' ### objOutbox.Messages.count is always 0
'Response.write objOutbox.Messages.count
'objNewMsg.Send
'Set objNewMsg = nothing
'#####################

DisplayMsgsTable objOutbox

Set objOutbox = nothing
Set objInbox = nothing
objSession.Logoff
Set objSession = nothing
%>

<BR>
</BODY>
</HTML>
```

Or in JScript:

```
<%
function DisplayMsgsTable(folder) {

   var strTableHeader = "<P><TABLE WIDTH=100% bgcolor=Silver " +
                        "BORDER=1 CELLSPACING=1 CELLPADDING=1>" +
                        "<TR BGCOLOR=Yellow><STRONG>" +
                        "<TD>From</TD><TD>To</TD>" +
                        "<TD>Subject</TD><TD>Message text</TD>" +
                        "<TD>Attachment</TD><TD>Received</TD>" +
                        "</STRONG></TR>";
   var strTableFooter = "</TABLE><P>";

   Response.Write("<HR><H2>" + folder.Name + "</H2><BR>");

   if (!folder.Messages.Count > 0) {
      Response.Write("Sorry, the folder contains no messages<HR>");
      return;
   }

   Response.Write(strTableHeader);

   var objEnum = new Enumerator(folder.Messages);
   for (; !objEnum.atEnd(); objEnum.moveNext()) {
      var objMsg = objEnum.item();
      Response.Write("<TR><TD>" + objMsg.Sender.Name + " &lt;" +
                     objMsg.Sender.Address + "&gt;</TD>");

      var strRecs
      if (objMsg.Recipients.Count > 0) {
         strRecs = objMsg.Recipients(1).Name + " &lt;" +
                   objMsg.Recipients(1).Address + "&gt;"
         var idx
         for (idx=2; idx<=objMsg.Recipients.Count; idx++) {
            strRecs += "; " + objMsg.Recipients(idx).Name +
                       " &lt;" + objMsg.Recipients(idx).Address +
                       "&gt;"
         }
      } else {
         strRecs = "No recipient" ;
      }

      Response.Write("<TD>" + strRecs + "</TD>");
      Response.Write("<TD>" + objMsg.Subject + "</TD>");
      Response.Write("<TD>" + objMsg.Text + "</TD>");
      Response.Write("<TD>" + String(objMsg.Attachments.Count>0) +
                     "</TD>");
      Response.Write("<TD>" + Date(objMsg.TimeReceived) +
                     "</TD></TR>");
   }

   Response.Write(strTableFooter);
   Response.Write("<HR>");

}

var objSession, objOutbox, objInbox;
%>
<HTML>
<HEAD>
<TITLE>CDONTS Sample #4 - Examining inbox and outbox folders</TITLE>
</HEAD>
<BODY >
```

CDONTS

```
<%
objSession = Server.CreateObject("CDONTS.Session");
objSession.LogonSMTP("Newsletter manager", "news.mng@dev02");
// objOutbox = objSession.Outbox;
objOutbox = objSession.GetDefaultFolder(CdoDefaultFolderOutbox);
objInbox = objSession.GetDefaultFolder(CdoDefaultFolderInbox);

Response.Write("<H1> Welcome " + objSession.Name + "</H1><P>");

Response.Write("<H3> This is the content of your mail folders:" +
               "</H3><P>");

/* #####################
We can use the following code to verify that we cannot add
messages to the Inbox folder
var objNewMsg
objNewMsg = objInbox.Messages.Add();
delete objNewMsg
##################### */

DisplayMsgsTable(objInbox);

/* #####################
We can use the following code to verify that outbox's Messages
collection is always empty
var objNewMsg
objNewMsg = objOutbox.Messages.Add();
objNewMsg.Subject = "This is the subject";
objNewMsg.Text = "This is the very short mail message.";
objNewMsg.Recipients.Add("Recipient Name",
                         "recipient@domain2.com", CdoTo);
objNewMsg.Attachments.Add("A Word attachment.doc" , CdoFileData,
                     "C:/Wrox/Books/1999/ASP30PR/ch10/" +
                     "CDO2000/Attachments/Word attachment.doc");
 ### objOutbox.Messages.count is always 0
Response.Write(objOutbox.Messages.count);
objNewMsg.Send();
delete objNewMsg
##################### */

DisplayMsgsTable(objOutbox);

delete objOutbox
delete objInbox
objSession.Logoff();
delete objSession
%>

<BR>
</BODY>
</HTML>
```

The code is pretty simple: we iterate through all the Message objects in the folder's Messages collection. For each message, we display the sender (using the AddressEntry object), the list of recipients (iterating through the message's Recipients collection), the message's subject and text, whether the message has any attachments, and, finally, the date the message was received. This is the resulting screenshot for a page that creates the Inbox Folder object and calls the above sub with it:

Note that the display name for the user currently logged on with
`Session.LogonSMTP` (in this case `"Newsletter manager"`) is available via the
`Session.Name` property.

Mass Mailings

Imagine the following common scenario: sending the same message to a multitude of
recipients from an ASP page, for example a newsletter managed via a web interface.
Obviously, we don't want to disclose our mailing list, and privacy considerations
require that a recipient must not know who the others are. So we cannot put multiple
addresses in the main (`To`) or secondary carbon-copy (`Cc`) lists of message's recipients.
On the other hand, sending a separate message to each recipient (i.e., creating a
separate `NewMail` object for each recipient) could easily be a performance nightmare.
The solution is to use the blind carbon-copy (`Bcc`) list of recipients. In order to see how
this all fits together, let's take a look at the `NewMail.Bcc` string in the following
simple code:

```
<%
Option Explicit

Dim objMsg, strFrom, strTo, strCc, strBcc, strSubject, strBody
%>
```

```
<HTML>
<HEAD>
<TITLE>CDONTS Sample #5 - Mass E-mailing</TITLE>
</HEAD>
<BODY >

<%
strFrom = """"Newsletter manager"" <news.mng@dev02>"
strTo = """"Our newsletter subscribers"" <newsletter@dev02>"
strCc = """"Newsletter manager"" <news.mng@dev02>"
strSubject = "This is the newsletter subject"
strBody = "This is the newsletter body"

strBcc =      """"User 33"" <user.33@domain1.com>;" & _
          """"User 98"" <user.98@domain1.com>;" & _
          """"User 16"" <user.16@domain2.com>;" & _
          """"User 25"" <user.25@domain3.com>;"

Set objMsg = Server.CreateObject("CDONTS.NewMail")

With objMsg
   .To = strTo
   .From = strFrom
   .Cc = strCc
   .Bcc = strBcc
   .Subject = strSubject
   .Body = strBody
   .Send
End With

Set objMsg = nothing
%>
We have mass-e-mailed our newsletter to <%= strBcc %>.
<BR>
</BODY>
</HTML>
```

Or in JScript:

```
<%
var objMsg, strFrom, strTo, strCc, strBcc, strSubject, strBody;
%>

<HTML>
<HEAD>
<TITLE>CDONTS Sample #5 - Mass E-mailing</TITLE>
</HEAD>
<BODY >

<%
strFrom = "\"Newsletter manager\" <news.mng@dev02>";
strTo = "\"Our newsletter subscribers\" <newsletter@dev02>";
strCc = "\"Newsletter manager\" <news.mng@dev02>";
strSubject = "This is the newsletter subject";
strBody = "This is the newsletter body";

strBcc =      "\"User 33\" <user.33@domain1.com>;" +
          "\"User 98\" <user.98@domain1.com>;" +
          "\"User 16\" <user.16@domain2.com>;" +
          "\"User 25\" <user.25@domain3.com>;";
```

```
objMsg = Server.CreateObject("CDONTS.NewMail");

with (objMsg) {
    To = strTo;
    From = strFrom;
    Cc = strCc;
    Bcc = strBcc;
    Subject = strSubject;
    Body = strBody;
    Send();
}
delete objMsg
%>
We have mass-e-mailed our newsletter to <%= strBcc %>.
<BR>
</BODY>
</HTML>
```

The entire file for the message placed by CDONTS in the pickup directory of the SMTP server is:

```
X-Receiver: newsletter@dev02
X-Sender: news.mng@dev02
X-Receiver: news.mng@dev02
X-Receiver: user.33@domain1.com
X-Receiver: user.98@domain1.com
X-Receiver: user.16@domain2.com
X-Receiver: user.25@domain3.com
From: "Newsletter manager" <news.mng@dev02>
To: "Our newsletter subscribers" <newsletter@dev02>
Cc: "Newsletter manager" <news.mng@dev02>
Subject: This is the newsletter subject
Date: Wed, 8 Dec 1999 13:36:41 -0800
X-MimeOLE: Produced By Microsoft MimeOLE V5.00.2919.5600

This is the newsletter body
```

As we can see, there is an X-Receiver header for each recipient in the To, Cc and Bcc lists, but although To and Cc recipients are also included in the respective headers, there is no Bcc header. The SMTP server servicing domain1.com will receive the following SMTP message:

```
x-sender: news.mng@dev02
x-receiver: user.33@domain1.com
x-receiver: user.98@domain1.com
Received: from dev02 ([192.168.0.3]) by mail.domain1.com with Microsoft
SMTPSVC(5.5.1877.977.9);
    Wed, 8 Dec 1999 13:58:57 +0100
Received: from mail pickup service by dev02 with Microsoft SMTPSVC;
    Wed, 8 Dec 1999 14:00:41 -0800
From: "Newsletter manager" <news.mng@dev02>
To: "Our newsletter subscribers" <newsletter@dev02>
Cc: "Newsletter manager" <news.mng@dev02>
Subject: This is the newsletter subject
Date: Wed, 8 Dec 1999 14:00:41 -0800
X-MimeOLE: Produced By Microsoft MimeOLE V5.00.2919.5600
Message-ID: <DEV02FRaqbC8wSA1Xvp00000003@dev02>
X-OriginalArrivalTime: 08 Dec 1999 22:00:41.0584 (UTC)
FILETIME=[AB2D6700:01BF41C7]
Return-Path: news.mng@dev02

This is the newsletter body
```

CDONTS

Notice that there is no evidence at all of recipients (i.e. X-Receiver headers) other than ones belonging to this specific domain. The message processing performed by the domain's mail system (e.g. the delivery to individual POP3 mailboxes) could further remove unrelated X-Receiver headers from the final version of the message. So, with a single CDONTS operation, we can perform a mass mailing, greatly improving performance compared with using multiple message objects. We can build the Bcc string in a number of ways, for example extracting e-mail address from a database. We experimented using this technique with 32,800 recipients and it worked well on the test system described in the 'Performance: Testing and Issues' section. As a final tip, note that we can optimize the performance of a mass e-mail operation using a file system-based approach: remember from the SMTP service's point of view, an outgoing message is just a file placed in the pickup directory. So we could undoubtedly devise some way of creating and managing a file containing a message template with our huge list of X-Receiver headers. The Send operation would then become a question of modifying the template with the current content and putting the file in the SMTP pickup directory.

Performance: Testing and Issues

The duration of an SMTP transaction can be very unpredictable, as it depends on the network latency. Obviously, this is a bad thing for ASP applications, chiefly for pages that perform mail-intensive tasks. With CDONTS, we can completely forget that problem. We saw above that sending an e-mail message just means queuing a file to the local disk, so control quickly returns to the ASP script. However, we should bear in mind that the computational load for sending the message is still on the SMTP server process, Inetinfo.exe, on the local machine. (At the end of this section, we'll see a trick we can use to *deceive* CDONTS in order to allow mail delivery through a remote SMTP server). It's very important to measure the performance of mail operations, to understand the related issues, and to make the appropriate design choice. So we're going to try to give some performance data.

Let's begin by defining our test environment. We're using a simple ASP page that sends the same messages repeatedly in a loop 50 times; the code for the page is basically as follows:

```
<%@ LANGUAGE="VBScript" %>

<%
Option Explicit

Dim objMailer
Dim strFrom
Dim strTo
Dim strSubject
Dim strBody
Dim lngImportance
Dim lngCycles
%>

<HTML>
<HEAD>
<TITLE>CDONTS test 1</TITLE>
</HEAD>
<BODY>
```

```
<%
strFrom = "user.1@domain1"
strTo = "user.33@domain2"
strSubject = "This is the subject"
strBody = "This is the body."
lngImportance = CdoNormal

For lngCycles=1 To 50
    Set objMailer = Server.CreateObject("CDONTS.NewMail")
    objMailer.Send strFrom,strTo,strSubject,strBody,lngImportance
    Set objMailer = Nothing
next
%>

We have sent <%= (lngCycles-1) %> messages.
<BR>
</BODY>
</HTML>
```

The test configuration is composed of two machines on a 10 Mbps LAN. The system running ASP is a Pentium III 500 MHz machine with 256 MB of RAM, running Windows 2000 Advanced Server. The other machine is a Pentium 90 with 64 MB of RAM running NT Server SP4; this machine hosts the SMTP site servicing the recipients' domain (this configuration allows us to simulate to some extent a busy SMTP server or a slow network link). We're going to test CDONTS code on Windows NT 4.0 Server too, with a dual Pentium II 400 MHz with 512 MB of RAM and a RAID subsystem (making performance comparison between Windows 2000 and NT 4.0 we should take into account the different hardware configurations). During the test, the systems, and the LAN too, aren't loaded with other significant computational tasks. We execute the ASP test script in an out-of-process IIS application; this way we can easily pinpoint the computational load due to the ASP script (which happens in the dllhost.exe process; mtx.exe for NT 4.0) and that due to the actual sending of the e-mail messages (which happens in the inetinfo.exe process).

We will be using two counters to track the performance of our mail server (see Chapter 41 for more information on performance counters):

❑ `Active Server Pages\Request Execution Time` (i.e. the number of milliseconds that it took to execute the request).

❑ `Internetwork segment\% Internetwork utilization` (i.e. the percentage of network bandwidth in use on the network segment).

We will track these counters using the NT/Windows 2000 **Performance Monitor**. We will also use **PView** (a Platform SDK tool supplied with Visual Studio) to monitor the amount of CPU time that the processes use. It's worth noting that the performance data we measured for the following tests shouldn't be taken as absolute values. However, they do allow us to make a quick comparison of the effectiveness of the different approaches.

CDONTS

Test #1 – Using the NewMail Object

The script code for this test is exactly the same as shown above. The following picture shows the performance data for three consecutive executions of the test. The upper line in the following screenshot represents the ASP Request Execution Time counter. We can see that the test script takes about 5,000 milliseconds to complete (the scale in the graph is one-hundredth of a millisecond). The percentage of network utilization (represented by the lower line) has a peak of roughly 0.9 % (the scale is multiplied by ten), and the network engagement is spread over about ten seconds (there are four seconds between two consecutive vertical grid lines).

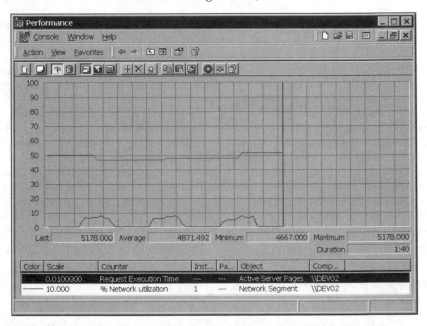

The amount of CPU time the DLLHost.exe process uses for each request is approximately 1,300 to 1,400 milliseconds. The Inetinfo.exe process consumes around 900 to 1,000 milliseconds for each request, approximately 400 of which are due to SMTP operations. As we expected, the net result is that CDONTS quickly returns control to the ASP script, while the SMTP service continues to process the messages after the script has completed. It is worth remembering that the SMTP service might not even be running when the ASP script executes, with the e-mail delivery scheduled while the web server is idle.

The performance data for the NT 4.0 test are:

- ❏ ASP Request Execution Time: 3,750 to 4,000 milliseconds.

- ❏ % Internetwork utilization: peak of 0.85% with the network engagement spread over about nine seconds.

- ❏ mtx.exe CPU time: 1,700 to 1,800 milliseconds.

- ❏ Inetinfo.exe CPU time: 900 to 1,000 milliseconds, approximately 400 of which are due to SMTP operations.

Finally, note that in such a situation (multiple messages addressed to the same domain), the SMTP service can be very effective sending more messages on the same SMTP session. If we recalled that the SMTP Limit number of messages per connection to setting has a default value of 20, we could deduce that the SMTP service opens three sessions with the remote server to deliver the 50 messages posted by the script. And that's exactly what happens in our test.

Test #2 – Using the Session Object

Although the NewMail object is easy to use, its stand-alone nature means that each time we create an object, it performs some sort of library initialisation. As we might expect, this means performance deterioration. The following code uses the CDONTS.Session object in order to log on to the library just once:

```
<%
strFrom = "user.1@domain1"
strTo = "user.33@domain2"
strSubject = "This is the subject"
strBody = "This is the body."

Set objSession = Server.CreateObject("CDONTS.Session")
objSession.LogonSMTP "User One", strFrom
Set objOutbox = objSession.Outbox

For lngCycles=1 to 50
    Set objNewMsg = objOutbox.Messages.Add (strSubject, strBody)
    objNewMsg.Recipients.Add strTo, strTo, CdoTo
    objNewMsg.Send
    Set objNewMsg = Nothing
Next

Set objOutbox = Nothing
objSession.Logoff
Set objSession = Nothing
%>
```

The relevant code is very simple. After initializing the session, we get the Outbox folder. We then create and send a new out-going message 50 times in a loop. It's worth noting that we can't send the same message object more than once. In other words, after the Send method is called we cannot, for example, modify the recipient and send the message again: we must create another Message object. The performance chart for ASP Request Execution Time and network utilization pattern are almost identical to Test #1, but the amount of CPU time the DLLHost.exe process uses for each request is now approximately 900 milliseconds. The Inetinfo.exe process consumes around 500 milliseconds for each request, 400 of which are due to SMTP operations (in fact, the CPU time consumed to dispatch the HTTP traffic and initialize CDONTS can be quantified as less then 100 milliseconds). So the difference in Inetinfo.exe CPU consumption between Test #1 and #2 lies entirely in the multiple initialization of the CDONTS library.

The performance data for the NT 4.0 test are:

❏ ASP Request Execution Time: about 2,000 milliseconds (that is in NT 4.0 the use of the Session object affects the responsiveness of the script too).

❏ % Internetwork utilization: peak of 0.85% with the network engagement spread over about nine seconds.

CDONTS

- ❏   `mtx.exe` CPU time: 1,200 to 1,300 milliseconds.
- ❏   `Inetinfo.exe` CPU time: 500 milliseconds, approximately 400 of which are due to SMTP operations.

Test #3 - Putting the Messages on a Remote Server

As we stated above, it's possible to change the `PickupDirectory` property of the local SMTP site using ADSI. The following VBScript code, run as shell script by a system administrator, achieves that result:

```
Dim objSMTPSvc
Set objSMTPSvc = GetObject("IIS://localhost/SmtpSvc/1")
objSMTPSvc.PickupDirectory = "c:\some\path"
objSMTPSvc.setInfo
```

If we set the property's value to the UNC path of the pickup directory of a remote SMTP site, CDONTS would put the message files in a directory where the SMTP server on the remote machine would process them. Obviously, we must stop the local SMTP server, relying solely on the remote one. It's worth noting that this technique requires IIS application to be configured to allow access to network files (this is beyond the scope of this chapter, but it can be achieved in several ways; see, for instance, the following MS Knowledge Base article: "HOWTO: Accessing Network Files from IIS Applications" ID: Q207671). The following figure shows the performance counters for the same script used in Test #2, with the pickup directory on a remote machine (the NT 4.0 dual Pentium II described above) connected through a 10 Mbps LAN:

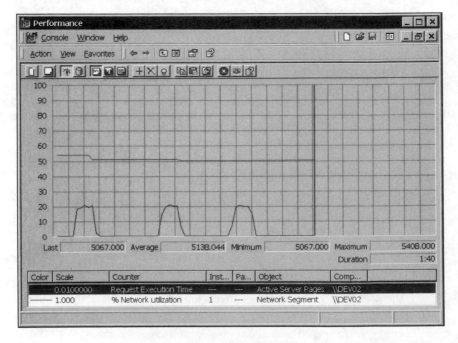

We can see that the ASP `Request Execution Time` is just a few milliseconds higher than Test #2, but the network utilization is quite high compared to previous tests (the peak is more than 20%; note that the value is not scaled). The amount of CPU time used by the `DLLHost.exe` process for each request is substantially the same as Test #2, i.e. about 1,000 milliseconds. Obviously, this approach saves the consumption of CPU cycles due to SMTP operations, which is moved onto the remote machine. It's hard to say if this unconventional use of CDONTS can be effective in a production environment; we lighten the load on the web server, but we increase the LAN traffic. Anyway, if we faced a situation with a heavily loaded web/SMTP server, we could try experimenting with this technique to relocate the SMTP load onto a separate machine.

The performance data for the NT 4.0 test are:

- ☐ ASP `Request Execution Time`: about 6 to 6,5 seconds.

- ☐ `% Internetwork utilization`: peak of 15%.

- ☐ `mtx.exe` CPU time: 1,300 milliseconds.

Using CDONTS with Exchange's Internet Mail Service

When we install the Internet Mail Service (IMS) provided with Exchange, it disables the IIS SMTP service. Obviously, IMS offers more features than IIS. For instance, we can inspect the delivery queues without examining the file system, or we can schedule Remote Access Service (RAS) connections to access the Internet at recurring intervals in order to deliver the messages. Although configuring IMS can be more difficult than the IIS SMTP server, we don't have to worry about this, and there is a good chance that we can start to exploit IMS in our ASP application with the default configuration provided by the IMS installation wizard (at least with out-going messages). From the CDONTS point of view, the key point is that the IMS SMTP server simply replaces the IIS SMTP server, and all the workings remain the same.

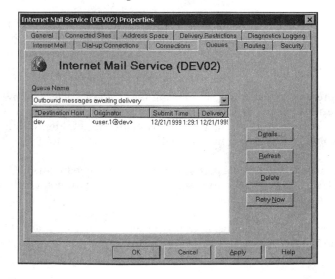

CDONTS

971

IMS has its own directory structure (usually rooted at `<Exchange_installation_path>\imcdata\`) that CDONTS uses to send and retrieve messages exactly as we saw above. One question arises: how does CDONTS know that it must use the IMS directories instead of the IIS ones? The answer lies in this registry key:

```
HKLM\SOFTWARE\Microsoft\Exchange\Active Messaging
```

If CDONTS finds this key with the named value `Use Exchange` set to `"0X01"`, it will use the IMS directory, which it will discover from the registry value:

```
HKLM\SYSTEM\CurrentControlSet\Services\MSExchangeIMC\
    Parameters\RootDir
```

Otherwise, CDONTS uses the IIS SMTP directories. This knowledge can be useful in troubleshooting CDONTS/IMS issues. Indeed, I found out that after IMS was installed on a Windows 2000 system, the IIS SMTP service was correctly disabled but the CDONTS code executed in ASP pages continued to use its directories instead of IMS ones. Moreover, the same ASP code executed as a shell script worked as expected. The problem lay in the security permissions of the above keys. If the security context of the thread that processes the ASP page is denied access to those keys, CDONTS will presume it must use the IIS SMTP service. The solution was to grant the `IUSR_MachineName` account (in the case of anonymous access) or the authenticated users' accounts (in the case of authenticated access) at least read permission to those keys.

Summary

In this chapter, we looked at the CDO for NT Server library, which provides a very quick and easy way of sending and receiving e-mail messages. CDONTS uses the SMTP service of the web server machine, so we started by looking at the configuration settings for this service.

We then looked at the object model provided by CDONTS. CDONTS provides two ways of sending email: using the `Message` object and the full object hierarchy, which requires logging on to a session; and using the stand-alone `NewMail` object, which is independent of the CDONTS hierarchy.

We then presented some examples of using the CDONTS objects, showing how to initialize a session, how to add attachments to a mail, examples of working with MIME HTML and custom headers, and how to access the Inbox folder. We also looked at issues involved with sending mass e-mails.

We also looked at some of the performance issues involved with CDONTS, carrying out three tests to check the performance of scripts using different coding techniques and server configurations.

Finally, we looked briefly at using CDONTS with Exchange's Internet Mail Service rather than the IIS SMTP service.

Indexing Services

As our world becomes more and more information-focused, the efficient storage and retrieval of our information is becoming increasingly important. The Microsoft **Indexing Service** provides one solution to the problem of retrieving our information from many data sources. The Indexing Service allows us to index diverse and distributed files and documents, and provides users with the ability to search the contents of these files and associated data.

The Indexing Service enables us to provide a quick and accurate way for users to search for information (usually via a web page search form), by providing us with ready-built tools and services to catalog the information and manage these catalogs. Using the Indexing Service to set up catalogs and handle the gathering of information becomes an administrative task. Three main activities are performed by the Indexing Sevice: managing, querying, and filtering. The most interesting of these to developers is the querying of data, i.e. the retrieval of information from the Indexing Service.

In this chapter, we will briefly look at creating catalogs, and then consider querying these catalogs and displaying the results of the query in greater detail. The Indexing Service allows us to provide users with an application that enables them to locate information quickly and precisely. This application usually takes the form of a web search page in which users enter details about the information they wish to access, combined with code to perform a query and display the results.

The Indexing Service provides a `Query` object that can be used to create search pages that have very specific search criteria. For example, we could create a web page that enables a user to enter the name of a product produced by a particular company, and search a central document repository of the company's products specifications (permissions allowing). The user would then get a list of the documents in the repository related to that product.

The search capabilites that are provided by the Indexing Service complement, rather than replace, web site navigation systems. Web search pages provide an essential additional means of accessing information of critical importance to large internet or intranet sites, particularly where the growth in the site has been 'organic', rather than closely managed, or where the number of pages is very large and split between a number of related sections of a web site.

The Microsoft Indexing Service, introduced with Windows 2000, evolved from Microsoft **Index Server**, available from the Windows NT 4.0 Option Pack. The expanded capabilities include:

❑   Cataloging and indexing of information from a web server and/or a file system.

❑   The ability to create and manage the indexes and to query these indexes. Three new objects were introduced with Indexing Service 3.0 to help administer the service. (These are outside the scope of this book – we will concentrate here on building and executing queries, which an ASP developer is more likely to face.)

❑   Integration into Windows 2000.

There are two languages that can be used for querying the Indexing Services – the **Indexing Service Query Language** (ISQL), and a special dialect of the **Structured Query Language** (SQL), the standard language for database queries. The former uses the ixsso.dll type library, whereas SQL uses ADO with the msidxs data provider. SQL is much more flexible than ISQL in the type of queries that can be done, and also faster. Queries using SQL are based on extensions to the SQL querying language designed for use with the Indexing Service.

The Indexing Service provides object models both for querying a recordset and administering the catalogs. The objects for querying the recordset, Query and Utility, are provided in ixsso.dll. The other objects, AdminIndexServer, CatAdm, and ScopeAdm, are provided by ciodm.dll. The administrative tasks they perform can also be accomplished using the Windows 2000 Computer Management tool.

Indexing Services Catalogs

An Indexing Service catalog stores information about documents either on a web site or on the file system. It is somewhat analogous to a database.

The information stored in the catalog can include details such as the type of the file, its size, contents etc. The files whose information is collated into the catalog are specified when the catalog is created. These could include, for example, all the files on a document repository machine, or the files on a web server. Once the catalog has been created and then indexed, we can then leverage the catalog and the Indexing Service to search for specific information quickly.

Creating a Catalog

The Indexing Service includes some default catalogs; however, these are typically broader than a specific application needs, and hence it is desirable to create a new catalog that only contains specific directories.

A new catalog can be created using the **Computer Management** tool provided in the **Administrative Tools** group of Windows 2000. Expand **Services and Applications** and click on **Indexing Service**. To create a new catalog, we right click-on the **Indexing Service** node, "mouse over" **New** and then click on **Catalog**. This brings up the **Add Catalog** dialog box:

The name of our new catalog is entered as well as a location where it will be stored. This location does not determine which directories are to be included in the catalog. For illustration, we enter "My Docs" as the name of the catalog and "C:\" for its location and then click **OK**. This causes a dialog box to appear, noting that our created catalog is offline until the service is restarted. When this dialog box is dismissed, the **Computer Management** tool looks something like this (with the **My Docs** catalog now shown in the right-hand panel when **Services and Applications** and **Indexing Services** are open):

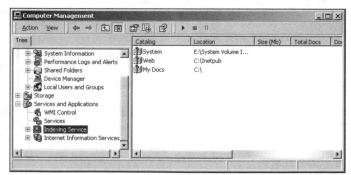

Once the catalog has been created, we then need to specify which directories will be indexed and included in the catalog. To do this, right-click on the catalog name, "mouse over" **New** and then click on **Directory**. This brings up the **Add Directory** dialog box:

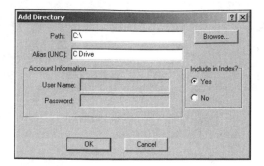

In the screenshot above, we have entered values for the **Path** and **Alias** fields, where the **Path** field specifies the path to the directory and the **Alias** field is optional for local directories. Clicking **OK** adds the C:\ directory to our catalog.

These steps can be repeated to add further directories to the catalog. It should be noted that we can add directories from remote machines to our catalog; for example, we could add "\\DocServer\Specifications" by entering this as the **Path** and entering values in the **User Name** and **Password** fields. These values specify the username and password that the service will use when accessing the remote path. Note that if the information entered is invalid, no error message appears, but the directory will simply fail to be indexed.

Finally, we need to restart the service and scan/index the new catalog and its directories.

Querying The Indexing Service

As we know, sharing information in a central resource is only useful if there is a quick and precise method of accessing the specific information that is required. The Indexing Service provides objects and mechanisms that can be used for retrieving information based on specific criteria. We will look at these objects and their methods and properties at the end of this chapter. Just as we can query a normal database by using specific criteria and statements, it is also possible to query a catalog using specific criteria.

The primary object used when creating and executing queries on the Indexing Service catalogs, is the Query object. We are able to submit a query and get results by setting the properties and calling methods on the Query object.

Let us first do a static query. The following ASP example shows how we can use the Query object to find all HTML files containing the name "Jeanie" and list them out. The VBScript code is:

```
<%
Dim objQuery, rsResults
' create a new query object
Set objQuery = Server.CreateObject("IXSSO.Query")

' Set the properties that determine the query
' and the information to return
' i.e. query the file system rather than a web server
objQuery.Catalog = "System"
objQuery.MaxRecords = 100          ' return a maximum of 100 records

' Specify HTML files containing the string "jeanie" in their names
objQuery.Query = "(#filename *.htm* )and jeanie"
' return the full path of files matching criteria
objQuery.Columns = "path"

' search for results & store as the rsResults recordset
Set rsResults = objQuery.CreateRecordset("sequential")
```

```
If rsResults.EOF Then
    Response.Write "No Results Found"
Else
    While not rsResults.EOF
        ' list results to browser
        Response.Write rsResults.fields(0).value & "<BR>"
        rsResults.MoveNext
    Wend
End If
%>
```

The JScript equivalent of this code is:

```
<%@ LANGUAGE = JScript %>
<%
objQuery = Server.CreateObject('IXSSO.Query');

/* Set the properties that determine the query
   and the information to return */
// use the "System" catalog
objQuery.Catalog = 'System';
// return a maximum of 100 records
objQuery.MaxRecords = 100;

// specify HTML files containing the string "jeanie" in their names
objQuery.Query = '(#filename *.htm* )and jeanie';
// return the full path of files matching criteria
objQuery.Columns = 'path';

// search for results & store as rsResults
rsResults = objQuery.CreateRecordset('sequential');

if (rsResults.EOF) {
    Response.Write('No Results Found');
} else {
    while (!rsResults.EOF) {
        // list results to browser
        Response.Write(rsResults.fields(0).value+'<BR>');
        rsResults.MoveNext();
    }
}
%>
```

This code gives a simple static example of using the Query object. Much more powerful use can be made of the Query object by formating the queries using either:

- ❑ The Indexing Service Query Language (ISQL).
- ❑ The Structured Query Language (SQL).

Indexing Service Query Language

The Indexing Service Query Language, ISQL, is the language provided by the Indexing Service for creating queries and hence searching using a variety of criteria.

There are in fact two varieties of ISQL, called **dialect 1** and **dialect 2** (introduced with Indexing Service 3.0). In most cases, dialect 2 is used. Normally the dialect 1 format is compatible with the dialect 2 format; however, a `Dialect` property of the `Query` object is provided for when this is not the case.

> **Detailed coverage of the language can be found at:**
> `http://msdn.microsoft.com/library/psdk/indexsrv/ixref`
> `qls_8eep.htm` **(dialect 1)**
> `http://msdn.microsoft.com/library/psdk/indexsrv/ixref`
> `qls_8eeq.htm` **(dialect 2).**

As we saw in the last example, a number of criteria can be used for a search. These include the file contents, its name, size, date, location and many other properties. Criteria can be combined using Boolean operators (e.g. AND and OR), proximity operators (e.g. NEAR) and regular expressions, leading to very powerful searches.

A **content query** is used for cases where specific contents are sought. There are two types of content query: **Phrase** and **FreeText**. Phrase queries search for the entire phrase and hence take into account the ordering of the words in the search string, whereas FreeText queries simply search on, say, two words, regardless of the order they appear in the document. For example, to search for the exact phrase `"Internet Explorer"`, we would use the code:

```
' VBScript
objQuery.Query = "{phrase}Internet Explorer{/phrase}"
```

```
// JScript
objQuery.Query = '{phrase}Internet Explorer{/phrase}';
```

Whereas, if we did not use the `{phrase}` tags, the query would have been in FreeText mode and would have returned any document with `"Internet"` and `"Explorer"` in it.

The `Contains` operator provides an alternative way to narrow the scope of a search to a specific property. For example, to look for files containing the phrase `"Internet Explorer"` we could use the query:

```
{prop name=Contents} Contains {phrase}Internet Explorer{/phrase}
```

Boolean operators can be used to combine multiple criteria and make a query that is more specific (and hence more useful in real life) . The Boolean operators are: AND, OR and NOT. For example if we want to search for files containing the text `"Internet Explorer"` but not `"Netscape"`, our query could look like this:

```
({phrase}Internet Explorer{/phrase}) AND Not (Netscape)
```

Another very powerful tool is the **proximity operator** NEAR. This can be used for querying for values within a distance of a certain number of units (words, paragraphs etc.) from one another within a text file. The keyword `dist` determines the number of units that can exist between the two words or phrases.

For example to search for documents that have the word "Netscape" within a certain range, say 10 words, of the phrase "Internet", the query would look like this:

```
{phrase}Internet Explorer{/phrase}
{near dist = 10, unit = word} Netscape
```

The units that can be used for the proximity operator are:

Value	Description
Chap	Chapter
Par	Paragraph
Sent	Sentence
Word	Word (default)

The distance dist = 0 is not allowed when the unit is "Word". For other units, a distance of 0 means that the words are contained in the same sentence, paragraph, or chapter as appropriate. The default unit is a word and the default distance is 50 units.

ISQL Example

In this example we look at a sample ASP web application which searches the catalog based on user input. This consists of two pages:

❑ An HTML page, search.htm, for the user to enter their query criterion.

❑ An ASP page, executequery.asp, where all the work is done to execute the query and display the results.

Search.htm

The following HTML code creates a page on which the user can enter their query criteion. It allows the user to enter the text for a search and specify whether they want to use phrase or free text queries.

```
<HTML>
<HEAD>
<TITLE>Search Page</TITLE>
</HEAD>

<BODY>
<FORM METHOD=GET ACTION="ExecuteQuery.asp">
<P><FONT size=7><STRONG>Search Page</STRONG></FONT></P>
<P>Please enter the text you would like to locate:</P>
<P><INPUT ID=txtSearchText NAME=txtSearchText
     STYLE="HEIGHT: 22px; WIDTH: 298px"></P>
<P>Select Search Type:
     <SELECT ID=cboSearchType NAME=cboSearchType
     STYLE="HEIGHT: 22px; WIDTH: 192px">
```

```
                <OPTION selected>FreeText</OPTION>
                <OPTION>Phrase</OPTION>
        </SELECT></P>
<P><INPUT ID=btnSearch NAME=btnSearch
        TYPE=SUBMIT VALUE="Search Now"></P>
</FORM>

</BODY>
</HTML>
```

This page looks like:

On this page the user will enter the text that they use to locate their information. Here we have entered `"apples oranges"` and selected to do a FreeText search. When this form is submitted, it will send the values to our `executequery.asp` page described below.

ExecuteQuery.asp

The `ExecuteQuery.asp` page is where the real work is done to execute the query and display the results. Using VBScript, the code of `ExecuteQuery.asp` is:

```
<HTML>
<BODY>
<%
Dim objQuery
Dim rsResults
Dim strSearchText
Dim strSearchType

strSearchText =Request.QueryString("txtSearchText")
strSearchType = Request.QueryString("cboSearchType")

Set objQuery = Server.CreateObject("IXSSO.Query")
Set rsResults = server.CreateObject("ADODB.Recordset")

objQuery.Catalog = "System"

If strSearchType = "Phrase" Then
    strSearchText = "{phrase}" & strSearchText & "{/phrase}"
End If
```

```
objQuery.Query = strSearchText
objQuery.Columns = "FileName, path"
Set rsResults = objQuery.CreateRecordset("sequential")

If rsResults.EOF Then
   Response.Write "<STRONG><FONT SIZE=+6 COLOR=BLUE>" & _
                  "No Results Found</FONT></STRONG>"
Else
%>
   <TABLE BORDER=0 WIDTH=100%>
      <TR>
         <TD><STRONG>File name</STRONG></TD>
         <TD><STRONG>File Location</STRONG></TD>
      </TR>
<%
      While Not rsResults.EOF
%>
         <TR>
            <TD><% =rsResults.Fields(0).Value %></TD>
            <TD><A HREF="<%= rsResults.fields(1).value %>">
               <%= rsResults.Fields(1).Value %></A></TD>
         </TR>
<%
         rsResults.MoveNext
      Wend
%>
   </TABLE>
<%
End If
Set objQuery = Nothing
Set rsResults = Nothing
%>
</BODY>
</HTML>
```

The code of `ExecuteQuery.asp` in JScript is looks like:

```
<HTML>
<BODY>
<%
var strSearchText = Request.QueryString("txtSearchText");
var strSearchType = Request.QueryString("cboSearchType");

var objQuery = Server.CreateObject("IXSSO.Query");
var rsResults = Server.CreateObject("ADODB.Recordset");

objQuery.Catalog = "System";

if (strSearchType == "Phrase") {
   strSearchText = "{phrase}" + strSearchText + "{/phrase}";
}

objQuery.Query = strSearchText;
objQuery.Columns = "FileName, path";
var rsResults = objQuery.CreateRecordset("sequential");

if (rsResults.EOF) {
   Response.Write("<STRONG><FONT SIZE=+6 COLOR=BLUE>" +
                  "No Results Found<FONT></STRONG>");
} else {
%>
```

```
<TABLE BORDER=0 WIDTH=100%>
    <TR>
        <TD><STRONG>File name</STRONG></TD>
        <TD><STRONG>File Location</STRONG></TD>
    </TR>
<%
    while (!rsResults.EOF) {
%>
        <TR>
            <TD><%= rsResults.Fields(0).Value %></TD>
            <TD><A HREF="<%= rsResults.Fields(1).Value %>">
                <%= rsResults.Fields(1).Value %></A>
        </TR>
<%
        rsResults.MoveNext();
    }
%>
    </TABLE>
<%
}
%>
</BODY>
</HTML>
```

If the user had clicked the Search button after entering "apples oranges" in the
Search.htm page, they would have seen something similar to this:

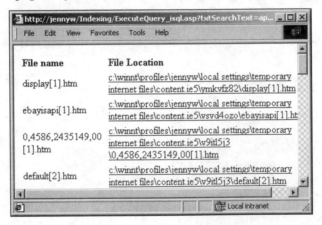

The results that you see when running this page may of course vary from these results,
depending on what directories your system is indexing. Having now seen the results
of this page, let's take a look at what the code was doing to display the results.

The first thing to happen on the page is to get the information that was sent from the
first page. Those values are then assigned to local variables.

Then, the next step is to create the query object and set its properties correctly.

Most of the code here is pretty straightforward, except for a couple of lines that deal
with handling Phrase or FreeText searches. Since the default search is FreeText,
nothing needs to be done unless the user selected "Phrase" on the Search.htm
page. To do a Phrase query instead of a FreeText query, we need to add the phrase tags
around the text.

By setting the `Columns` property, the developer can specify to retrieve the file name and path of the documents that are returned by the query:

```
objQuery.Columns = "FileName, path"
```

Then, the code executes the query and assigns the result set to the `rsResults` recordset. In VBScript this looks like:

```
' VBScript
Set rsResults = objQuery.CreateRecordset("sequential")
```

```
// JScript
var rsResults = objQuery.CreateRecordset("sequential");
```

The remaining code just loops through the returned recordset and lists out the names and locations of the files that matched the query. In doing so, the code uses the `path` property to generate a link to the file.

Structured Query Language

Let us now consider using Structured Query Language (SQL) against the Indexing Service. This is much more flexible than ISQL in the type of queries that can be performed, and also faster. Queries using SQL are based on extensions to the SQL language which are designed for use with the Indexing Service. We will revisit the example discussed earlier in this chapter where we search for all HTML documents with the name `"Jeanie"` in them.

If this is written using a SQL query, the VBScript version would be:

```
<HTML>
<BODY>
<%
Set rsResults = Server.CreateObject("ADODB.Recordset")

rsResults.Open "SELECT Path FROM System..SCOPE() " & _
               "WHERE (FileName LIKE '%.htm%') AND " & _
               "(CONTAINS(Contents, 'Netscape'))", "Provider=MSIDXS;"

If rsResults.EOF Then
   Response.Write "Empty Results"
End If

While Not rsResults.EOF
   Response.Write rsResults.Fields(0).Value & "<BR>"
   rsResults.MoveNext
Wend

%>
</BODY>
</HTML>
```

And the JScript version:

```
<HTML>
<BODY>
<%
rsResults = Server.CreateObject("ADODB.Recordset");

rsResults.Open("SELECT Path FROM System..SCOPE() WHERE " +
               "(FileName LIKE '%.htm%') AND " +
               "(CONTAINS(Contents, 'Netscape'))",
               "Provider=MSIDXS;");

if (rsResults.EOF) {
   Response.Write("Empty Results");
}

while (!rsResults.EOF) {
   Response.Write(rsResults.Fields(0).Value + "<BR>");
   rsResults.MoveNext();
}
%>
</BODY>
</HTML>
```

The most noticable difference between this code and the ISQL equivalent is that this doesn't use the Query object. As seen in the second argument of the Recordset Open statement, the code uses an OLE DB provider called MSIDX that enables us to access the Indexing Service through ADO.

Query Syntax of the SQL Query Language

The syntax of a typical SQL query language statement is as follows:

```
SELECT Column_list | *
    FROM_Clause
    [ WHERE_Clause ]
    [ ORDER_BY_Clause ]
```

We will look in turn at each of the individual parts of this query – the SELECT statement, FROM_Clause, WHERE_Clause, and ORDER_BY_Clause. The SELECT statement can also be preceded by a SET statement (which maps the document-specific properties to the column names or selects a ranking method for content searches), and a CREATEVIEW statement.

SELECT Statement

The SELECT statement defines the query that is specified as the source of the results recordset. This is the key to using ADO for querying the Indexing Service, and accessing the greater speed and capabilities provided by ADO.

The syntax for the SELECT statement is shown above. The Column_list is the list of columns retrieved in our search. This is the same list as for the Query object's Columns property. For example if we want to return the filename and size of all documents that match our criteria, we would use: SELECT FileName, Size .... We can use the wildcard "*", in place of column_list, to retrieve all columns, or those specified in a predefined view used in the FROM statement.

The simplest form of query is:

```
SELECT *
    FROM SCOPE()
```

For example:

```
rsResults.Open("SELECT Path FROM System..SCOPE()", _
                "Provider=MSIDXS;")
```

FROM Clause

The *FROM_Clause* in the SQL SELECT statement specifies the scope of the query. This
determines which physical or virtual paths are to be searched, and the depth to which
they are searched. The default is a deep search of the paths, including all the
subdirectories. The FROM clause is used in one of following ways:

```
FROM { [[Server].][[Catalog]..]SCOPE ([Arguments]) }
FROM { [[Server].][[Catalog]..]PredefinedView }
FROM { [[Catalog]..]View] }
```

Parameter	Description
Server	The name of the server which is queried.
Catalog	The name of the catalog which is used in the query.
PredefinedView	The name of either a predefined Indexing Service or Site Server view (see table below for details).
View	The name of a view created with the CreateView statement.

With a pre-defined view, we do not need to specify the column names in our SELECT
statement. Here is a list of the columns displayed for the results corresponding to the
predefined views created by the Indexing Service:

Predefined View Name	Columns to be Displayed
FILEINFO	Path, FileName, Write, Attrib, Size
FILEINFO_ABSTRACT	Path, FileName, Write, Attrib, Size, Characterization
EXTENDED_FILEINFO	Path, FileName, Size, Write, Attrib, DocTitle, DocAuthor, DocSubject, DocKeywords, Characterization
WEBINFO	Vpath, Path, FileName, Size, Write, Attrib, Characterization, DocTitle
EXTENDED_WEBINFO	Vpath, Path, Filename, Size, Write, Attrib, Characterization, Doctitle, Docauthor, Docsubject, Dockeywords

In the case where only basic file information is needed, we could either write a SQL statement like this:

```
SELECT Path, FileName, Write, Attrib, Size
    FROM SCOPE()
```

Or we could make use of the FILEINFO predefined view and write the statements like this:

```
SELECT *
    FROM Catalog_name..FILEINFO
```

For example:

```
' VBScript
Set rsResults = Server.CreateObject("ADODB.Recordset")
rsResults.Open "SELECT Path FROM System..FILEINFO", _
            "Provider=MSIDXS;"
While Not rsResults.EOF
    Response.Write rsResults.Fields(0).Value & "<BR>"
    rsResults.MoveNext
Wend
```

```
// JScript
rsResults = Server.CreateObject("ADODB.Recordset");
rsResults.Open("SELECT Path FROM System..FILEINFO",
            "Provider=MSIDXS;");
while (!rsResults.EOF) {
    Response.Write(rsResults.Fields(0).Value + "<BR>");
    rsResults.MoveNext();
}
```

It's clear from this example that any queries that always query for the same list of properties can be greatly assisted by the use of views. In addition to the predefined views, developers can create their own views by using the CreateView method, which we will cover later in the chapter.

WHERE Clause

The WHERE clause of the SELECT statement specifies the criteria that are used when querying the Indexing Service. Any documents in the scope of the query that match all of the criteria specified in the WHERE clause will be returned in the resultset. Those documents not matching all of the criteria in the WHERE clause will not be returned. The syntax of the clause is:

```
WHERE Condition [AND | OR | NOT Condition ...]
```

This allows us to specify multiple conditions and use the logical AND, OR, and NOT operators to build more specific queries. For the query to return all documents where the file had a size greater than 5000 bytes and contains the word 'apples', but not the word 'oranges', the WHERE clause would look like this:

```
...
WHERE (size > 5000) AND (Contains(Content, 'Apples'))
    AND (NOT CONTAINS(Content,'Oranges'))
...
```

In the WHERE clause it is possible to use logical operators, comparison operators, FreeText searches, wildcard characters, and regular expressions.

ORDER BY Clause

The ORDER BY clause of the SELECT statement determines the order of the items in the resultset that is returned. The syntax is:

```
ORDER BY ColumnName [ASC | DESC] [, ColumnName [ASC | DESC]]
```

In this clause, it is possible to specify multiple *ColumnNames* to use in sorting the resultset. The results will first be sorted based on the first *ColumnName* specified. Then, they are sorted on each subsequent *ColumnName* specified. The default sorting order is ascending (ASC). One catch to this is that once the sort order has been specified for a column in the list, each subsequent column will also have that sort order until a column specifies another sort order. To illustrate this, we will look at the results of this code:

```
ORDER BY FileName DESC, Size, Author ASC
```

This code would cause the results to be sorted in descending order for FileName and Size columns, but in ascending order for the Author column.

CREATE VIEW Statement

Although the predefined views are useful, there are many examples where we need a little more or a little less (or even something completely different) than the predefined views. In those cases, we can create our own view by using the CREATE VIEW statement. Any view that is created will only persist as long as the session/connection exists with the Indexing Service. The syntax of the statement is:

```
CREATE VIEW #ViewName AS
    SELECT ColumnsList
        FROM SCOPE()
```

The SELECT statement has the same syntax as we just covered in the previous section. The key point of this section is that when a select statement, or a group of columns, is commonly specified in the query statement it is normally better to create a view. Using the earlier sample application that only wanted the FileName and Path properties, we would create a view like this:

```
CREATE VIEW #NamePath AS
    SELECT FileName, Path
        FROM scope()
```

The next section shows an example of using ADO and the SQL language to query the Indexing Service.

SQL Example – Using ADO for the Query

For this example, we create a similar ASP application to that in our Query object example. The main benefit arising from using ADO to query the Indexing Service is that this search is more specific and powerful.

Search.htm

First, we will look at the Search.htm page. This page just contains an HTML form in which the user enters the criterion for a search:

```
<HTML>
<HEAD>
<TITLE>Search Page</TITLE>
</HEAD>
<BODY>
<P><FONT SIZE=7><STRONG>Search Page </STRONG></FONT></P>

<FORM ACTION=ExecuteSearch.asp METHOD=GET NAME=frmQuery>
<TABLE WIDTH="75%" ALIGN=CENTER>
   <TR>
      <TD>Author Name: </TD>
      <TD><INPUT ID=txtAuthor NAME=txtAuthor></TD>
   </TR>
   <TR>
      <TD>Title: </TD>
      <TD><INPUT ID=txtTitle NAME=txtTitle></TD>
   </TR>
   <TR>
      <TD>Keywords:</TD>
      <TD><INPUT ID=txtKeywords NAME=txtKeywords></TD>
   </TR>
   <TR>
      <TD>Contains:</TD>
      <TD><INPUT ID=txtContains NAME=txtContains></TD>
   </TR>
   <TR>
      <TD><P></TD>
      <TD><INPUT TYPE=submit VALUE="Search Now"
                ID=submit1 NAME=submit1></TD>
   </TR>
</TABLE>
</FORM>

</BODY>
</HTML>
```

When viewed in the browser, the page appears like:

As you can see, this page allows a user to search on any or all of four criteria: Author Name, the Title of the document, Keywords in the document, or the Contents of the document. Keep in mind that the `Author`, `Title`, and `Keywords` fields only apply to those ActiveX documents that store those properties. Most text and HTML files will not have those attributes.

From the page, the user will enter all of the criteria they have for the search. In this case, all of the criteria will be used to build a large `WHERE` statement. For a document to be found by the query, it will have to match each of the criteria that the user specifies in this page. When the user clicks the Search Now button, the page will submit the values for all of the criteria to the `ExecuteSearch.asp` page.

ExecuteSearch.asp

As in the first example, all of the real work for building and executing a query is done in the `ExecuteSearch.asp` page. If, in the previous page, the user had queried on files containing `"internet service"`, then they would see results similar to this:

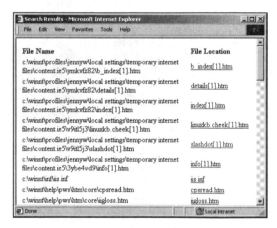

The full source of the `ExecuteSearch.asp` page is:

```
<% Option Explicit %>
<HTML>
<HEAD>
<TITLE>Search Results</TITLE>
</HEAD>
<BODY>

<%

Dim rsResults, strQuery, strWhereClause, strAuthor
Dim strTitle, strKeywords, strPrefix, strContains

strAuthor = Request.QueryString("txtAuthor")
strTitle = Request.QueryString("txtTitle")
strKeywords = Request.QueryString("txtKeywords")
strContains = Request.QueryString("txtContains")
```

```
strPrefix = " "
strWhereClause = ""

'// Build the Where clause based on the values being passed in.
If strAuthor <> "" Then
   strWhereClause = "CONTAINS(DocAuthor, '" & Chr(34) & _
                   strAuthor & Chr(34) & "')"
   strPrefix = " AND "
End If

If strTitle <> "" Then
   strWhereClause = strWhereClause & strPrefix & _
                   "CONTAINS(DocTitle, '" & Chr(34) & strTitle & _
                   Chr(34) & "')"
   strPrefix = " AND "
End If

If strKeywords <> "" Then
   strWhereClause = strWhereClause & strPrefix & _
                   "CONTAINS(DocKeywords, '" & Chr(34) & _
                   strKeywords & Chr(34) & "')"
End If

If strContains <> "" Then
   strWhereClause = strWhereClause & strPrefix & _
                   "CONTAINS(Contents, '" & Chr(34) & _
                   strContains & Chr(34) & "')"
End If

'// Then, build the full Query to be used
strQuery = "SELECT * FROM System..FILEINFO"

If strWhereClause <> "" Then
   strQuery =strQuery & " WHERE " & strWhereClause
End If

'// Execute the query and assign the results to the recordset
Set rsResults = Server.CreateObject("ADODB.Recordset")
rsResults.Open strQuery,"Provider=MSIDXS;"

'// Then, handle the results
If rsResults.EOF Then
%>
   <STRONG><FONT SIZE=+6 COLOR=BLUE>No Results Found<FONT></STRONG>
<%
Else
%>
   <TABLE BORDER=0 WIDTH=100%>
     <TR>
        <TD><STRONG>File Name</STRONG></TD>
        <TD><STRONG>File Location</STRONG></TD>
     </TR>
<%
     While Not rsResults.eof
%>
        <TR>
           <TD><%= rsResults.Fields(0).Value %></TD>
           <TD><A HREF="<%= rsResults.fields(1).value %>">
              <%= rsResults.fields(1).value %></A></TD>
        </TR>
<%
```

```
            rsResults.MoveNext
        WEnd
%>
    </TABLE>
<%
End If
%>

</BODY>
</HTML>
```

As you can see, there is a little bit more code involved in this example than in the Query object. Do not be concerned that using ADO to query the Indexing Service will cause you to need to write more code. The reason that this page has more code is mostly due to this page being more powerful than the other example. As we go through the code, you will see that most of the code is to handle building the WHERE clause and is not dealing with the executing of the query or handling the results.

As in the previous example, the first step of the code is to dim all the variables and to then retrieve the values from the ASP QueryString into local variables. As that code is not all that new or interesting, we will move on to the code that builds the query.

The next task to occur in the code is the handling of creating the SQL query WHERE clause. This is done using four If statements:

```
'// Build the Where clause based on the values being passed in.
If strAuthor <> "" Then
    strWhereClause = "CONTAINS(DocAuthor, '" & Chr(34) & _
                    strAuthor & Chr(34) & "')"
    strPrefix = " AND "
End If

If strTitle <> "" Then
    strWhereClause = strWhereClause & strPrefix & _
                    "CONTAINS(DocTitle, '" & _
                    Chr(34) & strTitle & Chr(34) & "')"
    strPrefix = " AND "
End If

If strKeywords <> "" Then
    strWhereClause = strWhereClause & strPrefix & _
                    "CONTAINS(DocKeywords, '" & Chr(34) & _
                    strKeywords & Chr(34) & "')"
End If

If strContains <> "" Then
    strWhereClause = strWhereClause & strPrefix & _
                    "CONTAINS(Contents, '" & Chr(34) & _
                    strContains & Chr(34) & "')"
End If
```

For each case in which the specific criterion does not have an empty value, the correct CONTAINS condition is added to the WHERE clause being built. The variable strPrefix is used so that the AND operator is correctly added to the WHERE clause when it is needed. As soon as one CONTAINS condition has been added to the WHERE clause, each subsequent CONTAINS condition will be prefixed by the necessary AND operator. The combination of this strPrefix and the building of the strWhere clause allows the code to correctly construct the WHERE clause that will be used in the query.

Once the WHERE clause has been created, the next step is to create the full text of the SQL query. This code handles the constructing of the full SQL query text:

```
'// Then, build the full Query to be used
strQuery = "SELECT * FROM System..FILEINFO"

If strWhereClause <> "" Then
    strQuery =strQuery & " WHERE " & strWhereClause
End If
```

Since it is possible for a user to not specify any criterion (thus returning all documents from the catalog), the code handles the possibility of the strWhereClause variable being empty.

And, for the final step, the ADO Recordset object is created and the query is executed.

```
'// Execute the query and assign the results to the recordset
Set rsResults = Server.CreateObject("ADODB.Recordset")
rsResults.Open strQuery, "Provider=MSIDXS;"
```

The Open method of the Recordset has a number of parameters, (see Chapter 29, which covers the Recordset object). For our purposes we are only concerned with two of them: Source and ActiveConnection. In this case, the source for the recordset is the query that the code built. The ActiveConnection is specified to be the Indexing Service, which we can access through the MSIDXS OLE DB provider with which ADO is able to communicate.

The remainder of the code handles the listing out of the results from the query, and is not significantly different to the code for the simple query application. As such, we will not go into any further detail on the remaining code.

The same program in JScript looks like:

```
<HTML>
<HEAD>
<TITLE>Search Results</TITLE>
</HEAD>
<BODY>

<%

strAuthor = Request.QueryString("txtAuthor");
strTitle = Request.QueryString("txtTitle");
strKeywords = Request.QueryString("txtKeywords");
strContains = Request.QueryString("txtContains");

strPrefix = " ";
strWhereClause = "";

// Build the Where clause based on the values being passed in.
if (!strAuthor == "undefined") {
    strWhereClause = "CONTAINS(DocAuthor, '" + Chr(34) +
                     strAuthor + Chr(34) + "')";
    strPrefix = " AND "
}
```

```
if (!strTitle == "undefined") {
   strWhereClause = strWhereClause + strPrefix +
                    "CONTAINS(DocTitle, '" +
                    Chr(34) + strTitle + Chr(34) + "')";
   strPrefix = " AND "
}

if (!strKeywords == "undefined") {
   strWhereClause = strWhereClause + strPrefix +
                    "CONTAINS(DocKeywords, '" + Chr(34) +
                    strKeywords + Chr(34) + "')";
}

if (!strContains == "undefined") {
   strWhereClause = strWhereClause + strPrefix +
                    "CONTAINS(Contents, '" + Chr(34) +
                    strContains + Chr(34) + "')";
}

// Then, build the full Query to be used
strQuery = "SELECT * FROM System..FILEINFO";

if (strWhereClause == "undefined") {
   strQuery =strQuery + " WHERE " + strWhereClause;
}

// Execute the query and assign the results to the recordset
Set rsResults = Server.CreateObject("ADODB.Recordset");
rsResults.Open strQuery, "Provider=MSIDXS;";

// Then, handle the results
if (rsResults.EOF) {
%>
   <STRONG><FONT SIZE=+6 COLOR=BLUE>No Results Found<FONT></STRONG>
<%
} else {
%>
   <TABLE BORDER=0 WIDTH=100%>
      <TR>
         <TD><STRONG>File Name</STRONG></TD>
         <TD><STRONG>File Location</STRONG></TD>
      </TR>
<%
      while (!rsResults.EOF) {
%>
         <TR>
            <TD><%= rsResults.Fields(0).Value %></TD>
            <TD><A HREF="<%= rsResults.fields(1).value %>">
                <%= rsResults.fields(1).value %></A></TD>
         </TR>
<%
         rsResults.MoveNext
      }
%>
   </TABLE>
<%
}
%>

</BODY>
</HTML>
```

Indexing Service Object Model

Earlier in this chapter, we demonstrated how we could interact with the Indexing Service using the **Computer Management** tool. In this section, we consider how our programs can interact with the Indexing Service using a set of components provided by Microsoft for VBScript, JScript, Visual Basic, Visual C/C++, and other programming languages that support COM automation.

The Indexing Service object model has the following objects: AdminIndexServer, CatAdmin, ScopeAdmin, Query and Utility. The Query and Utility objects are provided in the ixsso.dll, while the others are in ciodm.dll – a split which mirrors a division in functionality. The ciodm.dll objects are intended for administering the Indexing Service, whereas the ixsso.dll objects are used when working with queries.

Object
AdminIndexServer
CatAdm
Query
ScopeAdm
Utility

> We do not consider the three Indexing Service administration automation objects, AdminIndexServer, CatAdm, and ScopeAdm, since they are used to administer rather than query the Indexing Service. Information on them can be found at http://msdn.microsoft.com/library/psdk/indexsrv/ixref obj_3skz.htm.

Query Object

Querying of the catalog is the most common operation within Indexing Service. The Query object handles much of the work required to create and execute a query against the Indexing Service. By setting the properties of the Query object, it is possible to be very detailed and specific about the information to locate. This Query object is provided in the ixsso.dll, which is installed along with the Indexing Service.

Methods	Properties		
Create Recordset	Allow Enumeration	GroupBy	QueryIncomplete
Define Column	Catalog	GroupBy	QueryTimedOut
Query ToURL	CiFlags	LocaleID	Resource UseFactor

Methods	Properties		
Reset	CiScope	MaxRecords	SortBy
SetQuery FromURL	CodePage	OptimizeFor	StartHit
	Columns	OutOfDate	
	Dialect	Query	

Query Object Methods

CreateRecordset Method

The CreateRecordset method creates a recordset.

```
Recordset = Query.CreateRecordset(CursorType)
```

Parameter	Data Type	Description
CursorType	String	This specifies the type of recordset to return.

The CursorType parameter is either sequential or non-sequential. Sequential recordsets retrieve results as they are requested. Non-sequential recordsets have all of their results cached on the machine.

Once a Query object has been created and had all its properties set to the desired values, we can then get the results of the query. For the Query object, the results are retuned as an ADO Recordset object. In order to get access to this recordset, the Query object provides the CreateRecordset method.

For example:

```
' VBScript
Dim objQuery, rsResults
Set objQuery = Server.CreateObject("IXSSO.Query")
objQuery.Catalog = "System"
objQuery.Query = "(#filename *.htm* )and jeanie"
objQuery.Columns = "path"
Set rsResults = objQuery.CreateRecordset("sequential")
```

```
// JScript
objQuery = Server.CreateObject('IXSSO.Query');
objQuery.Catalog = 'System';
objQuery.Query = '(#filename *.htm* )and jeanie';
objQuery.Columns = 'path';
rsResults = objQuery.CreateRecordset('sequential');
```

Note that up until this method is called, the query has not actually executed. Calling the `CreateRecordset` method will execute the query and then return the results of that query. It is also possible that an error will be generated by the call to the `CreateRecodset` method. In this case, the usual cause is one of the Query object's properties having an invalid value and not due to an error in querying the Indexing Service. It is possible that the error is due to the Indexing Service, in which case you will get an error returned to the ASP page indicating the details.

DefineColumn Method

The `DefineColumn` method is very similar to the aliasing that is possible in SQL queries. By using `DefineColumn` it is possible to assign a friendly name to a column name.

```
Query.DefineColumn(strDefinition)
```

Where *strDefinition* is a string composed as follows:

```
FName [ (Type) ] = PropsetID [ PropID | PropName ]
```

Name	Description
FName	The friendly name for the property.
Type	The type of the column.
PropsetID	This is the GUID representing property set ID of the column.
PropID	The numeric ID of the property.
PropName	The property name (instead of `PropID`).

QueryToURL Method

The `QueryToURL` method is used to gather the Query object's `Catalog`, `SortBy`, `GroupBy`, `Query`, `MaxRecords`, and `AllowEnumeration` properties in order to create the query string portion of a URL.

```
String = Query.QueryToURL()
```

The returned string is the query string with characters which are illegal in URLs replaced by the corresponding character escape sequences (e.g. spaces converted to %20).

Reset Method

The `Reset` method clears all property settings for a Query object and resets the object's state. This can be useful when creating a new query that reuses the existing Query object.

```
Query.Reset()
```

SetQueryFromURL Method

The `SetQueryFromURL` method sets the properties on the query object of a Web client request and is the opposite of the `QueryToURL` method. It retrieves the `Catalog`, `SortBy`, `GroupBy`, `Query`, `MaxRecords`, and `AllowEnumeration` values from a URL and assigns the correct `Query` object properties to the object.

```
Query.SetQueryFromURL(QueryString)
```

Parameter	Data Type	Description
QueryString	String	This is the Query portion of the URL.

Query Object Properties

AllowEnumeration Property

The `AllowEnumeration` property returns `true` if enumeration is allowed.

```
Query.AllowEnumeration = Variant
Variant = Query.AllowEnumeration
```

Catalog Property

The `Catalog` property sets or returns the name of the `Catalog` associated with the query.

```
String = Query.Catalog
Query.Catalog = String
```

This value can contain multiple `Catalog` names, such as:

```
objQuery.Catalog = "System;Web"
```

We can specify a remote machine for the location of the catalog as follows:

```
query://Hostname/CatalogName
```

For example:

```
objQuery.Catalog = "query://DocumentServer/CatalogName"
```

When no hostname is provided, the local machine name is used. If the catalog name is not provided, then the default catalog on the machine is used.

CiFlags Property

The `CiFlags` property should not be used. It is deprecated in favor of the `Utility` object's `AddScopeToQuery` method.

```
String = Query.CiFlags
Query.CiFlags = String
```

Indexing Services

CiScope Property

The `CiScope` property should not be used. It is deprecated in favor of the `Utility` object's `AddScopeToQuery` method.

```
String = Query.CiScope
Query.CiScope = String
```

CodePage Property

The `CodePage` property returns the code page for the character set used.

```
Long = Query.CodePage
Query.CodePage = Long
```

Columns Property

The `Columns` property specifies the columns that will be returned in the result set. This property lets us determine what information about the file will be returned.

```
String = Query.Columns
Query.Columns = String
```

Here is a list of some common values for the `Columns` property:

Value	Information Returned
Directory	The directory in which the file was located
FileName	The filename of the file
Path	The fully qualified path to the document
Size	The size of the file
Attrib	The attribute flags for the file
Write	The date/time that the file was last written
Create	The date/time that the file was created
Access	The date/time that the file was last accessed
Change	The date/time that the file was last changed (only for the NTFS file system)
Contents	The textual contents of the file
ShortName	The 8.3-format (DOS-style) name of the file

For more information of the list of possible column property names, see `http://msdn.microsoft.com/library/psdk/indexsrv/ixuwebov_1qcn.htm` In the case where we only want to return the filename and path of the documents in the query resultset, the `Columns` property could be set to the following:

```
objQuery.Columns = "FileName, Path"
```

In addition to the standard file type properties, ActiveX documents expose other properties that can be specified in the columns:

Value	Information Returned
DocTitle	The title for the document
DocSubject	Subject information for the document
DocAuthor	Author information for the document
DocKeyWorks	The set of keywords for the document
DocComments	The set of comments for the document

Dialect Property

The Dialect property specifies whether the query is dialect 1 or dialect 2.

```
String = Query.Dialect
Query.Dialect = String
```

GroupBy Property

The GroupBy property returns the criteria for grouping of results.

```
String = Query.GroupBy
Query.GroupBy = String
```

LocaleID Property

The LocaleID property returns the LocaleID that is used when executing the query.

```
Long = Query.LocaleID
Query.LocaleID = Long
```

MaxRecords Property

The MaxRecords property sets or returns the maximum number of records for the query to return to the client browser.

```
Long = Query.MaxRecords
Query.MaxRecords = Long
```

OptimizeFor Property

The OptimizeFor property determines if queries are optimized for performance, or scalability.

```
String = Query.OptimizeFor
Query.OptimizeFor = String
```

OutOfDate Property

The OutOfDate property can be used to determine if content is out of date.

```
Boolean = Query.OutOfdate
```

Query Property

The Query property returns the query string (restriction) of the query.

```
String = Query.Query
Query.Query = String
```

This is the most important property of the Query object. It specifies the criteria for the search. If the value of the Query property is not set, or if it is assigned to an empty string, then an error will occur when the query is executed.

The Query property can only be set to a valid ISQL query. The Query object cannot interpret Structured Query Language (SQL) syntax, and will give an error if you attempt to use it in the value of the Query property. In the earlier section on ISQL we saw an example of valid syntax and usage of the Query property.

QueryIncomplete Property

The QueryIncomplete property returns true if the query string cannot be resolved.

```
Boolean = Query.QueryIncomplete
```

QueryTimedOut Property

The QueryTimedOut property returns true if the query timed out while executing.

```
Boolean = Query.QueryTimedOut
```

ResourceUseFactor Property

The ResourceUseFactor property is used internally by the Query object and is included here only for completeness.

```
Long = Query.ResourceUseFactor
Query.ResourceUseFactor = Long
```

SortBy Property

The SortBy property returns the specification for sorting the results.

```
String = Query.SortBy
Query.SortBy = String
```

StartHit Property

The StartHit property is used internally by the Query object.

```
Query.StartHit = Variant
Variant = Query.StartHit
```

Utility Object

The Utility object provides some utility functions that can be used in conjunction with the Query object. It is provided in ixsso.dll (along with the Query object).

The object exposes seven methods that can be very helpful when programming with the Query object.

Methods	
AddScopeToQuery	LocaleIDToISO
GetArrayElement	TruncateToWhitespace
HTMLEncode	URLEncode
ISOToLocaleID	

Utility Object Methods

AddScopeToQuery Method

The AddScopeToQuery method is used to add an additional search path to the query object. The syntax of the method is:

```
Utility.AddScopeToQuery(Query, Path, Depth)
```

Parameter	Data Type	Description
Query	String	The Query object that will be modified.
Path	String	The path to be added to the scope.
Depth	String	"Shallow" to include only the specified directory. "Deep" includes all subdirectories.

GetArrayElement Method

The GetArrayElement method enables us to access an element in an array.

```
Variant = Utility.GetArrayElement(Array, ID)
```

Parameter	Data Type	Description
Array	Array	The array to be used.
ID	Long	The item to return from the array.

HTMLEncode Method

The HTMLEncode method will apply HTML encoding the the specified string.

```
String = Utility.HTMLEncode(String, CodePage)
```

Parameter	Data Type	Description
String	String	The string to encode.
CodePage	Long	The code page to use in encoding.

ISOToLocaleID Method

The `ISOToLocaleID` method can be used to convert an ISO language code to a Windows Locale ID. The method has only one parameter, which is the value to be converted.

```
Long = Utility.ISOToLocaleID(Locale)
```

Parameter	Data Type	Description
Locale	String	The value to be converted.

LocaleIDToISO Method

The `LocaleIDToISO` method can be used to convert a Windows LocaleID to an ISO language code.

```
String = Utility.LocaleIDToISO(LCID)
```

Parameter	Data Type	Description
LCID	Long	The value to be converted.

TruncateToWhitespace Method

The `TruncateToWhitespace` method is used to truncate a string at the first occurrence of a whitespace character. The syntax is:

```
String = Utility.TruncateToWhitespace(String, MaxLength)
```

Parameter	Data Type	Description
String	String	The string to truncate.
MaxLength	Long	Maximum length of the string.

URLEncode Method

Similar to the URLEncode method of ASP, the `URLEncode` method will apply URL Encoding to the specified string.

```
String = Utility.URLEncode(String, CodePage)
```

Parameter	Data Type	Description
String	String	The string to encode.
CodePage	Long	The code page to use in encoding.

Summary

The Indexing Service can simplify the process of locating information either in a file system or on a web server. The developer is provided with a number of different methods to choose from when creating search applications. For most ASP developers, the Query object provides the easiest method for searching for information.

Administrative tasks, such as creating a new catalog be done using the Windows 2000 Computer Management tool (or via three objects provided by ciodm.dll not considered in this book).

There are two languages that can be used for queries, the **Indexing Services Query Language** (ISQL) and the **Structured Query Language** (SQL). The former uses a ixsso.Query object, where as SQL uses ADO with the provider specified as msidxs. SQL is much more flexible than ISQL in the type of queries that can be done, and also faster. Queries using SQL are based on extensions to the SQL querying language designed for use with the Indexing Service.

Finally, we looked at the object model that the Indexing Service provides for querying a recordset. These objects, Query and Utility, are provided in ixsso.dll.

Performance and Security

41

Optimizing ASP Performance

Achieving good performance in an ASP application is not a question of blindly applying a set of formulas, but requires understanding of, and experience with, the factors that can affect performance, and making tradeoffs between them to achieve optimal improvement.

Before we can achieve this Holy Grail of optimal performance, we first need to be able to evaluate our application's current performance. It is therefore important to understand how to measure performance, and then monitor how changes work for or against the desired result.

In this chapter, we will discuss:

- ❑ What performance is and how to measure it.
- ❑ Monitoring performance counters.
- ❑ How hardware affects performance.
- ❑ The impact of the database.
- ❑ Designing and using COM objects.
- ❑ How the `Session` and `Application` objects affect performance.
- ❑ Effectively caching data.
- ❑ How to select a process model.
- ❑ Scripting that's fast.
- ❑ Script profiling, HTTP compression and debugging.
- ❑ The performance-related metabase settings.

Performance is often a matter of perception. To the end user, the faster a response to the request for a page, the better the performance. To the Webmaster, the volume of requests a server can handle is indicative of its performance. To those watching the hardware, lower CPU utilization may indicate that performance is good. After all, there's no call for a faster machine. Since overall performance is really the combination of all these perspectives, it's important to understand how each is measured and how they are affected. That said, we want to maximize the performance from the user's perspective. Users don't care about hardware utilization and concurrency; they just want the page back quickly.

So, before we look at some suggestions for improving performance, we'll first look at some of the measurements we can take to monitor the performance of our site, and some of the software tools we can use to take those measurements.

Software Tools

The first step in improving the performance of a web application is to gain an understanding of its current behavior. One of the most important tools for achieving this is provided with the operating system: the Performance Monitor. This tool, which was a stand-alone application in NT4 and is now part of the Microsoft Management Console of System Tools, provides enormous amounts of detailed information about the operation of the system. To start it, click Start | Settings, and then select Control Panel. In the Control Panel open Administrative Tools and look for the Performance program. The Performance Monitor provides a number of counters which we can use to monitor our application's performance, such as the time taken for a script to execute. Explanations are provided there for each of the individual counters, but we will look at the counters which are most important for ASP shortly.

There are a number of tools available for purchase as well as download that are important for performance analysis. These tools are typically referred to as stress tools as they endeavor to apply real-world load on the server so that the performance can be measured while it is under stress. Their capabilities span a wide range and each has its own strengths and weaknesses.

Stress tools place a large load on the server to simulate the actions of many users working with the application at once. This provides data about the scalability of the site. However, the user is interested in how many other users are able to access the site only to the extent that it affects how fast they get a response. These two measurements are related. A thread can only handle one request at a time, and the sooner it has satisfied that request, the sooner it can move on to another. Performance work is a combination of establishing the hardware and architecture to support the number of concurrent users, and practicing coding procedures and tuning to satisfy single requests quickly. One tool that helps analyze performance and scalability is currently provided for free from Microsoft. It is available at http://webtool.rte.microsoft.com and is known as the Web Application Stress Tool or WAST.

The WAST web site has its own knowledge base and provides updated answers to frequently asked questions. The download provides a tutorial as well as a comprehensive set of help documents. There is even a mailing list where experts provide help. The tool coordinates the efforts of as many client machines as you have enlisted to put load on a designated server. It has rich reporting capabilities and a set of APIs that allow you to script its behavior. This allows you to vary the load programmatically to achieve the desired results. The tools can use multiple client machines using multiple threads to simulate the behavior of tens or hundreds of users. It ties in to the performance counters of the server being tested, so that you can effectively measure the behavior of the server and correlate it to the combined efforts of the clients.

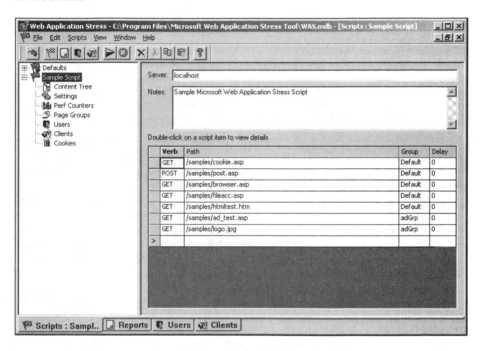

The WAST tool provides four views, as you can see from the tabs at the bottom of the screenshot above: Scripts, Reports, Users and Clients. The Scripts view is used to edit the settings associated with a particular set of tests. There are four methods for creating a test script. The Manual method requires entering by hand the test (e.g. POST or GET), and the path of the page to test. An easy way to capture all requests necessary for images and frames is the Record feature. A script is created as the WAST tool acts as a proxy for the browser. It records all of the requests into the script to use under stress. WAST can replay actual activity and multiply it with numerous clients by using the logs from the web server. And it can also create scripts simply by crawling a content directory at which it is pointed. By highlighting the Settings for the script, the number of threads each client will use can be modified as well as the duration of the test. The Warm Up time is useful for populating the cache after an application has just been started.

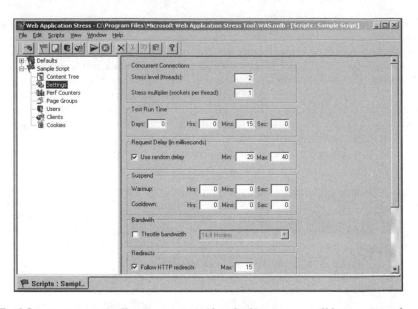

The **Perf Counters** setting allows us to specify which counters will be monitored on the server during the test. We will look at the performance counters to monitor in the next section. The minimum, maximum, and percentile values are then displayed in the report for the test. Script items belong to specific page groups, and unless specifically changed, all scripts are added to the default page group. When a separate page group is established, the amount of load placed on the group can be specified. This is especially useful when it is known that some specific parts of the application are accessed more or less frequently than others. Specific users and associated passwords can be established to test security performance and branching in the code, based on user rights. The **Scripts** page also allows custom cookies to be specified per user.

The **Reports** view displays the results of running a script. Executing the scripts allows us to capture performance numbers from the System Monitor, and the **Reports** view provides detailed information ranging from the number of times a script was executed to the average number of milliseconds it took to run. It also gives details about socket level activity that help to identify any network-level problems.

The **Clients** view is used to coordinate the efforts of all machines participating as clients for the stress test. The clients can also be controlled via a web interface. This allows tests to be started and stopped remotely, so that machines that can't be used during regular hours can easily be used as clients during off hours and controlled from home.

Ideally, a lab consisting of multiple clients and a server should be put aside for the stress-testing procedure. By isolating these machines from other duties, we alleviate the need to question changes in behavior because we know they are the result of our code changes and parameter tuning, and not because the machines have had to split their efforts. It does not take a large number of machines acting as clients to provide a substantial volume of requests for the server to process, but if it is difficult to dedicate machines for this purpose, WAST makes it easy to use these machines in the off hours when they are not typically being used.

The Web Application Stress Tool should be installed on all client machines that will participate in stressing the server. All of these 'clients' have the same executable running as a service on the machine. Any one of these clients can also act as the controller, where test scripts are established, reports are generated and tests are started and stopped. The machine acting as the controller is also responsible for gathering performance metrics from the machine being tested. Additionally, it participates in the effort by executing the tests against the server along with the other clients. It is possible to run the Web Application Stress Tool on the server being tested, but this is not recommended. The server should be carrying out the single job of servicing requests. The resources used by a controller may vary from test to test and could skew the results if running on the server.

Performance Metrics

Now that we've had a look at the most important tool we can use to measure performance, we can consider some of the things we need to measure. We can use these metrics to identify weak points in our application, and use them as a basis for improvements.

Megahertz Cost

Since we cannot measure and digest all of the possible ways that performance is perceived, we must begin to identify ways to quantify the performance. The Megahertz cost of a script is a good way to get an idea of the cost of executing a script, regardless of what hardware will be executing it. The Megahertz cost of a request is denoted as MHz per request per second. The Megahertz cost is the `(number of CPUs)` * `(MHz of the CPU)` * `(CPU utilization)`. This number is then divided by requests per second to give us the Megahertz cost of a request. For example, using a 400 Megahertz dual-processor machine we might achieve 120 requests per second. If the performance monitor shows us that at this request rate we are using 65% of the CPU's capacity, we have:

```
((2 CPUs) * (400 MHz) * (.65 CPU utilization)) / 120 requests per second
(800 * .65) / 120
520 / 120 = 4.33
```

This tells us that the average Megahertz cost for the pages being tested is 4.33. This number is a useful approximation, because it is fairly portable from system to system. You may be testing a web application on hardware that is not quite the same as the final destination machines. By using the Megahertz cost metric, it is easier to approximate the behavior of the application when in production, and plan accordingly so that you have the hardware necessary for the expected load.

Response Time

Probably the most important performance metric as far as the user is concerned is the response time. This is an indicator of the amount of time that elapses between the request for the page being issued by the browser and the page content being returned. This value is reported individually for each page element, including individual body text and each image. Even when considering this one metric, the matter of perception must again be considered. Is the response time the number of seconds or milliseconds until the first byte of the content arrives back at the browser, or is it the time until the last byte arrives? The approach adopted by WAST is to calculate and track both the mean time to first byte (TTFB) and mean time to last byte (TTLB).

This response time is a combination measurement. It includes the latency time; the time it takes for the request and response to travel across the network. This can be quite short in an intranet scenario or comparatively long when working on the Internet. It also includes queue time – the amount of time the request waits in the ASP queue for a thread to become available for processing. And, of course, it includes processing time which is the time actually taken to execute the script instructions.

The Web Application Stress Tool provides overall statistics of response time. It is also possible to quickly instrument specific pages to measure the processing time. At the top of the page, mark the current time. Then mark the time at the end and take the difference to find out how long a specific script was actually being processed by the script engine. Following is an example in JScript. The last line written to the browser is the processing time in milliseconds.

```
<%@ LANGUAGE="JScript" %>
<%
//top of page
var start = new Date();
//the rest of the page
...
//bottom of page
var end = new Date();
Response.Write(end - start);
%>
```

The execution time in seconds can be calculated using the following in VBScript:

```
<%@ LANGUAGE="VBScript" %>
<%
' top of page
dim startTime
startTime = now
' the rest of the page
...
' bottom of page
dim endTime
endTime = now
Response.Write endTime - startTime
%>
```

The ideal is for this time to remain fairly constant under increasing load. Even if a request must wait in the queue for longer periods of time before being processed, it is hoped that once it is being processed the results stay the same. If there is a marked increase in the contention for shared resources when under load, this time may rise. This can be the result of database resources being limited or competition for critical sections in an application-scoped COM object. For example, simple file operations may seem acceptable when testing as a single user. But locking a file for use can become a source of problems when the machine is servicing many requests simultaneously. The ideal is a linear scaling of the response time, but the best achievable result may be slightly less than linear. When the processing time changes dramatically under load, look for the source of the problem. Some possible trouble spots to look out for are scripts accessing a file or updating the same value in a database during a long-running transaction. Application-scoped COM objects may be holding critical sections longer than necessary, and may need to be modified or a replacement found.

Throughput

Throughput is the rate at which the server can deliver pages to all users. It is typically measured in requests per second. This number can be found using the Performance Monitor and can be gathered automatically in the Web Application Stress Tool. Try monitoring the Active Server Pages value for Requests/Sec to ascertain ASP throughput. To see throughput for all types of activity, monitor the Web Service counter value of Total Method Requests/Sec. One thing to remember here is that this measurement can be misleading. If you are stress-testing a page that does not exist, the 404 error message can be returned at an amazingly high rate. Check to see that you are measuring successful requests for pages that are representative of the application. Again, we must remind ourselves of the principle of perceived performance. Pages that are frequently accessed by the user count for more than those that are rarely used. For example, the home page is probably accessed much more than an order page or search page. It is less important in terms of perceived performance for a specialized page to be fast. The user judges an application based on first impressions and what they see in the majority of cases, not the page which takes the longest to return.

Obviously, page size affects throughput. Many lab tests have revealed that the network connection is the weakest link. A well-tuned application with a mix of static and dynamic content on a modern server can easily saturate a fractional T1 connection. If the server is able to handle the traffic but the packets aren't able to make it through the network because the network is saturated, the user perceives poor performance.

The web server provides detailed statistical information in a number of **performance counters** that can be viewed using the Performance Monitor. These will be discussed in the following section. There are two counters to view to monitor throughput:

❏   Web Service (_Total)\Get Requests/sec. This indicates throughput for .htm files and images.

❏   Active Server Pages\Requests/Sec. This corresponds to ASP throughput.

Performance Counters

To tune the server for performance, it is necessary to understand how it behaves. There are dozens of performance counters tracking vast amounts of information about the system operation. In this section, we will discuss the most important performance counters with respect to understanding and tuning the system. In IIS 4, run **perfmon** in order to launch the Management Console plugin and monitor values. In IIS 5, this results in a warning that the Performance MMC snapin should be used to monitor performance counters. This can be launched by running perfmon.msc or by clicking Start | Programs | Administrative Tools | Performance.

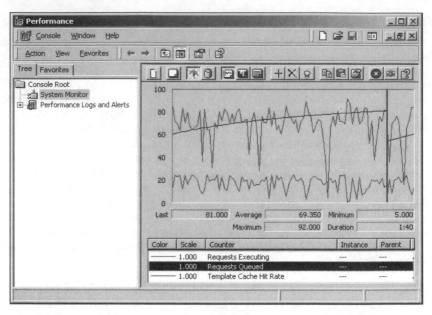

It is easy to add the most important counters and save those settings for future reference, as well as to log their values over time to see the effects of system tuning. Select the + button to launch the **Add Counters** dialog. The Web Application Stress Tool also invokes the **Add Counter** dialog to automate the gathering of performance data from the server during testing.

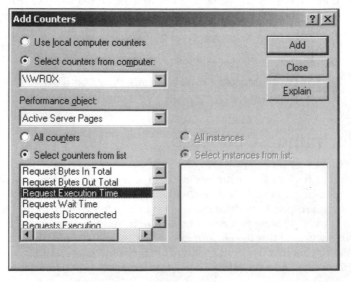

As soon as a counter is added, the performance monitor starts to display the values for it. By default, it will update the data every second. For monitoring trends over a period of time, it may be appropriate to select the properties tab and change this value so that updates occur less frequently.

ASP Sessions

```
Active Server Pages \ Session Duration
Active Server Pages \ Sessions Timed Out
Active Server Pages \ Sessions Current
Active Server Pages \ Sessions Total
```

The Session Duration corresponds to the duration, in milliseconds, of the most recent session. Remember that Sessions can be terminated in script and free their associated resources before waiting to time out. The Sessions Total figure is calculated since the service was started. If the application can explicitly end sessions, it is good for performance to do so. These counters allow us to see how effective our efforts are to curtail session inactivity and limit session overhead.

Memory

```
Active Server Pages \ Memory Allocated
Process(inetinfo) \ Private Bytes
Process(dllhost) \ Private Bytes
```

If the application protection level is set to Low (IIS Process), ASP runs in the inetinfo.exe process, which is the same process space as the core web server. In this case, it is possible to track the memory usage easily using the Process(inetinfo) \ Private Bytes counter. Otherwise, use the Active Server Pages \ Memory Allocated counter to watch memory use over time. If memory continues to increase steadily over time, it will become necessary to start isolating the usage of COM objects and ISAPI filters and extensions in order to identify what is responsible for the memory leak. Historically, memory leaks are a common problem, and they can be difficult to identify. Microsoft provides a tool (called the IIS Exception Monitor) that has proved very useful in identifying misbehaving code. It goes a long way in automating this process and minimizing the impact if it becomes necessary to run it on a production machine. However, this is never a recommended method for debugging. See a detailed explanation on how to use the IIS Exception monitor at http://msdn.microsoft.com/workshop/server/iis/ixcptmon.asp, as well as the Tech Net article that further discusses the technique, at http://www.microsoft.com/TechNet/iis/tools/ixcptmon.asp.

Script Templates

```
Active Server Pages \ Script Engines Cached
Active Server Pages \ Templates Cached
Active Server Pages \ Template Cache Hit Rate
Active Server Pages \ Template Notifications
```

These counters help us to understand how the cache is being used when we're setting the size of the ASP cache. If the cache hit rate is low, increasing the FileCacheSize (see the section on 'The Metabase' towards the end of the chapter) can reduce the extent that the server must go to the disk. It is also wise to check the Template Notifications counter to see if an unexpectedly high number of scripts are changing on the disk and forcing the cache to become invalidated. Many applications rely on other processes to generate and update scripts automatically, and tuning the activity of these processes to minimize template cache flushes is good for performance.

Requests Queued

```
Active Server Pages \ Requests Queued
```

This number can range from 0 to the value of the property for `RequestQueueMax` in the Metabase. It indicates how many requests have been received from clients that are waiting for processing. As they sit waiting, the response time increases. We should try to minimize this figure, as it is an indication of the number of requests that are doing nothing but waiting.

Requests Executing

```
Active Server Pages \ Requests Executing
```

This number can range from 0 to the number of processors times the value of `AspProcessorThreadMax` in the Metabase. Suppose the server has four processors and the default value of 25 for `AspProcessorThreadMax` is used. At most, there can be 4 * 25 = 100 threads executing requests at any given moment. While requests are executing, content is being created for the user. By decreasing the execution time of the ASP scripts, they get through this stage faster and keep response time to a minimum.

Execution Time

```
Active Server Pages \ Request Execution Time
```

The value for this counter is reported from a periodic sampling and corresponds to the most recent request at that time. If this number starts on an upward trend, it may be an indication of additional strain on a shared resource. Access to application-scoped COM objects may be getting slowed down due to increased load and contention for critical sections. Another potential cause is that a database may be being used in a way that prevents efficient access from others.

Wait Time

```
Active Server Pages \ Request Wait Time
```

This counter is also a periodic sampling. It gives a general idea of how long requests are waiting before they are processed. An increase in the wait time usually happens at the same time as the number of requests queued goes up. Obviously, the aim is to identify why, and bring the number back down.

Request Results

```
Active Server Pages \ Requests Total
Active Server Pages \ Requests Succeeded
Active Server Pages \ Requests Failed Total
```

These counters give a quick summary of activity since the service was started. The number of successful requests should be close to the total. Failed requests sum the values for errors, rejections, timeouts and authorization failures. It is probably impractical to expect no failures, but they indicate potential problems in the application that merit investigation.

```
Active Server Pages \ Requests Disconnected
```

There should be a certain amount of tolerance for general network problems. However, if this number changes dramatically, it may indicate a hardware failure. The figure also includes attempts by users to reload or refresh the page when content is not returned fast enough for them.

```
Active Server Pages \ Requests Rejected
```

The 'Server Too Busy' error is not an indicator of stellar performance. If this counter goes above zero, it is an indication that the request queue has filled to capacity, and there is a performance problem.

```
Active Server Pages \ Requests Timed Out
```

If a request waits in the queue longer than AspQueueConnectionTestTime or exceeds the value for Script Timeout, users have had to wait only to receive an error message. Consider increasing the number of threads using AspProcessorThreadMax (see the Metabase section), and carefully analyze why scripts are not passing through the execution phase more quickly.

```
Active Server Pages \ Requests Not Found
```

This is usually an indication of invalid, outdated, or misspelled links. It is also the result of probing algorithms in use today to identify characteristics of servers on the Web. A small number of 404 Not Found errors should be considered normal. An increase after launching new content should be interpreted as a warning about possible content problems.

```
Active Server Pages \ Requests Not Authorized
```

Unless the web application has no secure content, there will be requests that are not authorized. Whenever a user mistypes their password when accessing a secured resource, it is counted as an unauthorized request. If this number rises suddenly, it may indicate an organized attempt to breach the security of that content. Analyze the log file to ascertain what scripts are being targeted and to gain info about the attempt.

Performance Factors

Now that we've seen how to measure our application's performance, we can start to look at ways in which we can improve it. Because a typical ASP application relies on many different technologies, there are many factors which can have an effect on its performance and scalability. In the remainder of this chapter, we'll look at the most important of these factors, starting with the hardware we're using to run the application, and provide suggestions for ways in which we can best enhance these.

The System

The system used to host a web application consists of far more than just IIS and ASP. The software runs on hardware, and historically there have been (and probably will continue to be) enormous advances in the capabilities of the hardware. The server architecture of a multi-tiered web application also impacts the performance. Simple changes in the system can yield big gains in performance: upgrading the CPU can be a simple way to improve the overall system; adding memory can yield remarkable results. Improving a system can be as easy as moving a database to hardware dedicated solely to that purpose.

Hardware

When looking for gains in web application performance, it often pays off to throw money at the problem. Where that money is spent is an important choice. You don't want to pay for a faster CPU if the problem is a lack of memory. You don't want to buy faster disks if the code is effectively cached in memory. Don't be fooled into believing that bigger and better hardware is a solution to every problem, but if an application is well-tuned, better hardware may yield enormous returns. New hardware can buy time when a problem has been discovered and there will be a delay until the problem can be fixed.

If the level of CPU utilization is high enough that you are afraid of the next spike in traffic, consider upgrading to a faster CPU. The competition between the major chip manufacturers keeps them busy producing ever-faster processors so that it should soon be possible to buy a 1 Gigahertz CPU. If your web site is running on a server with two-year old 200 Megahertz CPUs, it may be worthwhile to upgrade. The CPU utilization can be viewed in the Performance Monitor under the counter `Processor (_Total)\% Processor Time`.

Another question you encounter when considering hardware is the number of CPUs. Until recently, adding additional CPUs had a significantly decreasing margin of additional benefit. However, Windows 2000 can achieve nearly linear scaling with the addition of processors. Previously, it wasn't practical to beyond two processors. Now, it makes sense to consider two-, four- and even eight-way machines. If the site is on the verge of outgrowing a single box, adding additional processors becomes quite compelling, especially as it may delay deploying multiple machines along with configuring and managing load sharing and load balancing software across the web farm.

Often, the cheapest and easiest way to improve performance when considering hardware is to add more memory. Slow trips to the hard disk can be avoided if memory is adequate to store many script engines and script templates in memory. I would recommend 256 Megabytes of RAM as the minimum. Again, there are diminishing returns when taking this to extremes. It is now conceivable, although expensive, to have multiple Gigabytes of RAM in a server. This money could probably be better spent elsewhere.

The effect of not having enough memory is that the operating system is forced to swap information out of memory to the hard disk. The next time the data is needed, it must swap something else out to make room for reading it back in. In the most extreme case, as IIS demands scripts and other content from the operating system continuously, the situation can worsen to a condition called thrashing. In this case, the data required to run is not in memory, so the OS removes data from memory to make room, but the data removed is immediately required to continue. The OS must again remove more data to bring this data in, and so on. The operating system is almost completely stymied by the relatively slow speed of the hard drive. You can view the rate at which the operating system is required to go to the disk by viewing the counter `Memory \ Pages/Sec`.

When a single machine just isn't enough, the next step is to spread the load across multiple machines. The two main possibilities for load balancing are: software to provide a cooperative environment between servers, and hardware that sits in front of the farm and spreads the incoming requests across the farm. Hardware to accelerate the use of SSL is available for applications that make heavy use of secured content. As more Application Service Providers work with confidential user information, these solutions will become increasingly prevalent. In selecting a load balancing solution, beware of setting up a single point of failure. It may be prudent to buy more than one device if all traffic must pass through it before being processed.

> Remember that ASP session state resides on a single box, and it becomes impractical to use in a web farm. Load balancing software or hardware may be required to ensure that a session is always directed to the same machine. It may be cheaper and easier to store session-specific data in a single database that is accessed by all servers in the farm.

Database Performance

Online applications are often projections of a database onto the web. The data is at the heart of most web applications and drives applications into the multi-tiered domain. Because databases require large amounts of memory and CPU in order to yield high performance, it becomes necessary to separate the database from the web server. Dedicating hardware to host just the database can yield vast improvements over forcing a machine to serve multiple purposes.

Do not use a database designed for single-client use as the web server database. For example, Microsoft Access is not designed for use with multiple concurrent requests from a web server and will be the root of problems if used in this fashion. Threads executing requests may be forced to wait for another thread that is already working in the Jet driver. These threads don't accomplish anything during this time, and the user is forced to wait.

A lot of database access from ASP is handled using ADO. By default, in order to accommodate databases that support only apartment-threaded access via ODBC, the ADO components are shipped in an apartment-threaded configuration. Fortunately, Microsoft provides the ability to change the threading model that is used with ADO to provide better performance when used with high performance databases capable of free-threaded access. A batch file located on the server hard drive in the `Program Files\Common Files\System\ado` directory called `makefre15.bat` changes the way ADO will be utilized. Yes, there is a corresponding file called `makeapt15.bat` provided to switch it back if you are so inclined. Although the version numbers for ADO have changed with new releases, the numbers on the file names have been frozen to reduce versioning difficulties.

When iterating through a recordset in ADO, first obtaining a reference to the fields or columns to be used and using this, instead of indexing into the row, yields better performance. For example:

```
Set rstCustomers = cnnOrders.Execute(strSQL)
Set fldCustomerID = rstCutomers("CustomerID")
Set fldCustomerName = rstCusomters("CustomerName")
Do Until rsCustomers.EOF
   Response.Write fldCustomerID & " - " & fldCustomerName & "<BR>"
   rstCustomers.MoveNext
Loop
```

Notice that it is not necessary to specify which field is being accessed in each iteration. The reference to the field has already been obtained and is used for the current row. This is faster than seeking the reference again and again, as in the following example:

```
Set rstCustomers = cnnOrders.Execute(strSQL)
Do Until rsCustomers.EOF
   Response.Write rstCustomer("CustomerID") & " - " & _
               rstCustomers("CustomerName") & "<BR>"
   rstCustomers.MoveNext
Loop
```

Process Model

The process model of IIS provides several options that yield different combinations of robustness and performance. The `inetinfo` process is the heart of the web server. By default, with IIS5, all ASP applications run in a separate process called `dllhost.exe`. The setting is referred to as Application Protection and can be changed on a per application basis on the properties page for the application in the Internet Services Manager. An application can be changed to run inside `inetinfo` by changing it to Low application protection, or it can run in its own `dllhost` without sharing the process with any other applications by setting the protection level to High:

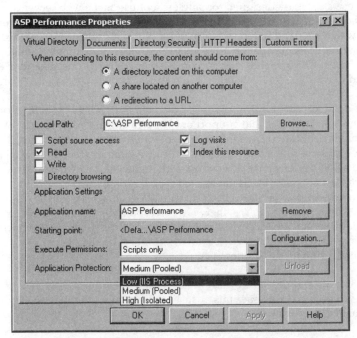

The best performance, theoretically, is when the application is running as part of the IIS process. This eliminates the need to communicate between processes, which is a relatively expensive operation. Running in a dedicated dllhost process yields better isolation from other applications, but there is a cost associated with numerous processes, so the protection comes at a price. Obviously, this is much better than a service regularly crashing and thus causing the whole system to crash.

It is also possible to isolate the application further from a possible crash in a COM object by using COM+ to run the COM objects in their own processes. Again, this comes at a performance price. As you can see in the diagram below, the fastest performance comes when everything is running in the same process, but a crash in any component or application results in the web server temporarily going down. Every step of isolation provides better reliability, but the cross-process communication is expensive in terms of performance:

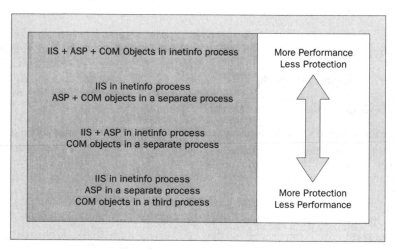

The impact of a failed application has been minimized with a new feature of Windows 2000. If a service fails, the Service Control Manager now allows the administrator to specify actions to take on the first, second, and any subsequent failures. The default setting is to **Take No Action**. The service can also be re-started, or a file specified for execution. It even offers the extreme option of rebooting the server.

This decision of what action to take because of a failure could have a big impact on the perceived performance. If unreliable objects are causing the service to fail and the machine to re-boot, it is not available to process requests. It is recommended to work with a new object running in a separate process until its reliability is known. At that point, it can be placed in **Low** isolation with more confidence that the recovery options will not need to be utilized. If they fail, Dllhost processes are automatically re-started at the next request that requires the resource.

Threading Models

Code that is written as script can be re-written as COM objects in a compiled language and provide better performance. The rule of thumb I have seen is that 1,000 lines of code usually warrant the effort of creating a COM object. When writing the object, the choice of what threading model to use is critical and affects the development time that must be invested. This choice has further impacts on how the object can be used from ASP. Some threading models are recommended for use only when the object is created and destroyed during the execution of the page. Others are intended for more robust performance and are suitable for storage in session or application scope. Others should not be used at all.

The choices for threading models include single-threaded, free-threaded, apartment-threaded, both-threaded, and both-threaded agile, as well as the new neutral threading model. The type of threading model can make a huge performance difference for objects used in ASP.

For those unfamiliar with threading, it pays to have a simple way to think about threading models. A thread can be thought of as a sequence of instructions that your computer is executing. Normally your computer will appear to be doing several things at once; for example, accepting input into a Word document and at the same time checking to see if you click on another window to do something else. Each of these lines of execution is known as a **thread**.

Each of these threads resides in an **apartment**. An apartment is essentially a context that prohibits all but one thread from invoking methods on an object. If another thread needs access to the object, COM steps in and marshals the call to the appropriate thread. Apartments can contain either a single thread (single-threaded apartment, or STA), or a multiple threads (multi-threaded apartment, or MTA). Single-threaded objects support only STAs, and can only service one client at a time. Apartment-threaded objects also support only STAs, but multiple instances of these components can be created within the process, so they can service more than one client at a time. Current versions of Visual Basic only allow us to created single- and apartment-threaded components.

Do not use single-threaded objects in ASP. A COM main thread is established for the process. Single-threaded COM objects must have their calls marshaled to the COM main thread. If this thread is already busy processing a call when an executing page attempts to invoke a method on the object, the request must wait for the thread to become available. When the COM main thread finishes processing its current request, it processes the next waiting request. When the server is under load, the requests can stack up waiting for access to that specific thread. These sorts of queuing get progressively worse as more scripts need access to the single-threaded object.

Free-threaded COM objects are also generally not advisable, even though they utilize multi-threaded apartments (MTAs). In this model, the component always runs in the MTA. Single- and free-threaded objects run under the system identity and therefore bypass some of the usual security enforcements of user ACLs. Free-threaded COM objects also require special attention to acquire the context necessary for access to the ASP intrinsic objects. They must be registered in Transaction Explorer (in NT 4) or in the COM Services Explorer (in Windows 2000). Other threading models are more appropriate for use in ASP, and avoid the extra registration step and extra code required to acquire the context.

Apartment-threaded objects can be used in ASP but should only be used at page-scope. In other words, they should be created using Server.CreateObject on the page and should not be stored in the Session or Application for future use. If stored in session state, the same thread that created the object must handle all subsequent requests in that session. This is akin to picking a counter at the grocery store, and insisting on using it each time you return to the store even if it has an enormous line and other counters have no one waiting.

It is possible to store an apartment-threaded object at application scope using the <OBJECT> syntax; however, this will result in all requests waiting for a single thread. If we consider this in the grocery store metaphor, it means that all customers would insist on using the same counter. Storing apartment-threaded objects in application scope has such serious implications that using Server.CreateObject to do it returns an error. For example, the following code fails:

```
Application("the_object") = Server.CreateObject("object.apartment");
```

The object syntax circumvents this check:

```
<OBJECT SCOPE="Application" RUNAT="SERVER" ID="the_object"
        PROGID="object.apartment">
```

So if performance is horrible with low CPU utilization and low paging, check the global.asa for objects that are not suitable for use outside of page scope. A further argument against using apartment-threaded objects at application scope is that they, like free-threaded objects, run under the system context.

In both-threading, COM effectively chooses the apartment threading or free threading model at runtime when the object is instantiated, depending on whether the component instance is being created in an STA or MTA. Both-threaded objects behave like apartment-threaded objects unless they aggregate the free-threaded marshaler (FTM). Components that perform this aggregation are termed **agile components**. By taking this extra step to become an agile component, the object eliminates the need for COM to run interference and marshal calls to a specific thread designated for the object. When using ATL to create both-threaded objects, aggregating the free-threaded marshaler is as easy as selecting a checkbox. Under most circumstances, there is no further code required on the part of the developer. When creating your own components, it is easy to take this extra step. When used in ASP, this allows calls to be made to the objects without extra thread switches and marshaling. IIS5 enforces storing only agile objects in Session and Application unless you change AspTrackThreadingModel to true in the Metabase. This is not recommended as changing it forces ASP to monitor the type of threading model and take extra measures to allow the use of non-agile components in this way.

This overhead can and should be reduced by using only agile components in Session and Application scope. The ability to change this setting is presumably provided only to help those making the transition from legacy code. Agile objects require extra effort to develop. Allowing multiple threads to execute code concurrently in the object introduces the need for critical sections to protect access to volatile data. Most code can be accessed simultaneously, but some pointers must be protected during initialization, and access to variables must be guarded to ensure that their values are changed synchronously. They can be called by any thread at any time and must guard the data where necessary.

Neutral components exploit a new threading model that can be used with IIS 5. They don't bind to an apartment and don't require calls from other apartments to be marshaled. There is no slow-down to acquire the context of the neutral apartment when called from a different thread. Since they can be called from any apartment, they are considered agile too. Thus, they can be used at `Session` and `Application` scope. The downside to neutral objects is that they are not compatible for use with IIS 4. Development of agile components usually takes more time and is more complex, but being able to store them with `Application` scope can eliminate the overhead required to create them for each page in which they are needed.

Session State

The HTTP protocol that is the foundation upon which web communication is built is stateless. Each request for a page looks like every other request for the page with respect to time or the sequence of the request. Web applications are not stateless and web developers need to be able to track information about a user to provide functionality. To provide this ability, ASP uses a temporary cookie called `ASPSessionID`. This cookie is not returned when you iterate through the `Cookies` collection. It is assumed that the web developer does not want it. The `ASPSessionID` cookie is not written to the client disk, so when the user closes the browser, the cookie disappears. The cookie is transmitted back and forth between the client and server just like a persistent cookie, but the browser only keeps it in memory.

Sessions are serialized. In other words, a script in a session cannot run at the same time as any other script in the same session when sessions are enabled. This fact is often overlooked or misunderstood and is best explained with an example. Suppose that four requests arrive simultaneously, or very close to it, all from the same client. This is the case when the page layout is a frameset with four individual frames. If one of those frames has disabled sessions it can run independently of the other three. The scripts that are participating in the session cannot run concurrently, so whichever request gets hold of the internal locking mechanism first will run first. The other two requests must wait for the first to finish execution before the next one can begin. Even if a thread becomes available while other requests are waiting, the waiting scripts must wait for the one in front to finish. This can be seen from the start and end times of the scripts running in the frames seen in this screenshot:

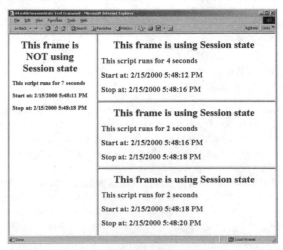

Notice that the frame on the left executed at the same time as the top frame on the right. The other two frames on the right had to get in line and wait for their turn to run as part of that session.

Sessions are useful and play an important part in many web applications. If they are not part of the application they should be turned off in the Internet Services Manager for the entire application or in the Metabase (see later discussion).

If they cannot be turned off for the entire application, they should only be left enabled for pages that need access to the session variables and objects. Adding one line to the top of each page that does not need access to the `Session` object can produce a boost in performance in an application with session state enabled:

```
<%@ EnableSessionState=false %>
```

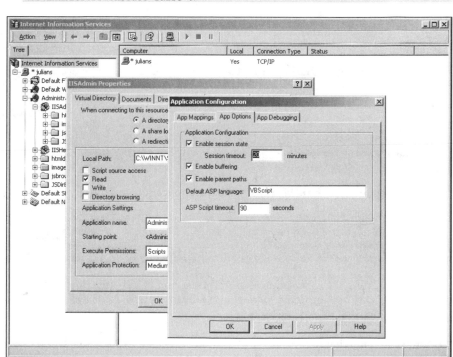

To disable session state for an entire application, start the Internet Information Services manager (Start | Programs | Administrative Tools | Internet Services Manger (or Start | Run (inetmgr)). Expand the listing of applications under the computer name and right-click on the application with which you are working and select Properties. On the Home Directory tab, click on the Configuration button and choose the App Options tab. There you will find the checkbox used to enable and disable support for sessions. If session state is disabled, any reference in script to the `Session` object will result in the Object expected error. The application will not incur the overhead of full-sessions, and consequently the object is not available.

Application State

The `Application` object also provides core functionality to many web applications. Using it appropriately can actually improve performance. However, using it incorrectly can impact performance severely.

The `Session` object does not have explicit `Lock` and `UnLock` methods as sessions are serialized (see the section on 'Session State'). The `Application` object is available to concurrently running scripts, so when modifying data it is sometimes necessary to call `Application.Lock`, modify the `Application` variable, followed by a call to `Application.UnLock`. Hold the lock only for as long as necessary. To improve performance, do not acquire the lock unnecessarily. It is a poor but common practice to acquire the lock to make a simple assignment into it. The point is to use locks only when necessary and hold them for as little time as possible.

```
Application.Lock();          //unnecessary
Application("weather_today") = "rainy";
Application.UnLock();
```

Taking locks like this is unnecessary. If a group of variables must be updated and must also always be in sync with each other, then it is necessary to acquire the lock. For example, suppose the following script is executed:

```
Application.Lock();
Application("weather_today") = "sunny";
Application("temperature_today") = "hot";
Application.UnLock();
```

Followed at some later date by a change to the application variables:

```
Application.Lock();
Application("weather_today") = "snowing";
Application("temperature_today") = "cold";
Application.UnLock();
```

Without acquiring the lock, some other script running at the same time may read `weather_today` as `"snowing"` along with `temperature_today` as `"hot"`. These types of group updates require locking.

Another situation that requires the lock is modifying an existing value based on its current value. Suppose that an application variable currently has the value 100. One script adds 30 to it and another script deducts 10. The final result should be that the value would increase by 20. Without appropriate locks something else might happen.

Script A:

```
Application("cash") = Application("cash") + 30;
```

Script B:

```
Application("cash") = Application("cash") - 10;
```

Suppose that Script A reads in the current value of 100. Before it is able to write back the new value of 130, Script B also reads in the current value of 100. Script A then writes back its new value of 130 followed by Script B writing back a new value of 90. Without correct locks, application variables can, and will, yield unpredictable results.

Caching Output and Input

Static content can be delivered by the web server much, much faster than dynamic content. When the amounts of data being transmitted are equal, the static file will always be returned more quickly. There are methods available to cache static images on the browser, and cache parts of dynamic content on the server. Dynamic content is vital for turning web pages into a web application, and it can't be sacrificed for speed. There are several methods for caching dynamic content so that the performance is maximized: output caching, input caching, and client-side caching.

Output Caching

Output caching refers to taking a piece of HTML content that has been dynamically generated, and storing it in a way that means it can be retrieved more quickly. This is ideal for data which doesn't change often. For example, suppose a drop-down list of products is populated from a database. The ASP page that displays this list should not have to go to the database each time it is executed unless the data has changed. If the products change from minute to minute, it is probably not an ideal candidate for output caching. Data that remains relatively stable is ideal for use in output caching.

The idea is to set an application variable with the HTML that is to be sent to the client. When the application starts, the variable will not be set, and therefore the trip to the database is necessary. Otherwise, it is just written to the client. Here's an example in JScript:

```
function display_products() {
    if (Application("select_products") != null) {
        Response.Write(Application("select_products"));
    } else {
        //get the data from the database
        //and store it in the Application variable
    }
}
```

The VBScript equivalent of this code is:

```
Sub display_products()
    If Application("select_products" <> "" Then
        Response.Write Application("select_products")
    Else
        'get the data from the database
        'and store it in the Application variable
    End If
End Sub
```

The only complication comes in automating a method for resetting the variable when the data changes. Automated processes can be put in place to run a script that resets the variable. Forcing periodic application re-starts produces a negative impact on performance, so the recommended method is to have an administrative script that is automatically executed when the data is updated or is executed each night so that values from the database are current for the duration of the following day. The update method depends on the needs of the application.

```
<SCRIPT LANGUAGE=JScript RUNAT="SERVER">
   Application.Contents.Remove("select_products");
</SCRIPT>
```

The next step in effectively using output caching is to be able to dynamically modify the output without incurring the overhead of returning to the database.

Input Caching

Another method for infrequently changing data is to periodically generate an include file. This only affects the scripts that require access to that data and that don't require populating the Application object. This is particularly effective when the data is needed by a smaller set of scripts in the application. Suppose the following data is stored in the Application variable "select_products":

```
<SELECT>
   <OPTION>shirts</OPTION>
   <OPTION>pants</OPTION>
   <OPTION>short pants</OPTION>
   <OPTION>sweaters</OPTION>
</SELECT>
```

Based on some user input, the developer may want to pre-select one of these options. The script can modify the contents of the HTML before sending it to the client without returning to the database. The data hasn't changed, but what needs to be done with it has:

```
// JScript
var cached_content = new String(Application("select_products");
var preference = Request("preference");
var regExp = new RegExp("<OPTION>" + preference, "ig");
cached_content = cached_content.replace(regExp, "<OPTION SELECTED>" +
                                       preference);
Response.Write(cached_content);
```

```
' VBScript
cached_content = Application("select_products")
preference = Request("preference")
Replace(cached_content, "<OPTION>" & preference, _
                   "<OPTION SELECTED>" & preference)
Response.Write cached_content
```

Client-Side Caching

Another performance enhancing method of caching is to cache content at the client. Images are a prime candidate for client-side caching. They are often big, are rarely dynamic and seldom change. IIS5 provides a simple method for asking the client to assume an image is good for a specified period of time. If the client complies, it will request the image just once and then use it in all other pages of the application where it is referenced until the specified time has past.

For example, the current Wrox logo image is more than 2K in size but it is not changed often. If the logo is requested for every page viewed on the site, it may account for a significant percentage of the request being delivered to the server. Although these requests can be handled with only a '304 Not Modified' instead of transmitting the entire image, it still places an unnecessary burden on the server. An easy way to reduce these extra round trips is to move images to a separate directory and enable expiration for the directory. If scripts reference copies that are not in this directory, the expiration information will not be sent to the browser and unnecessary requests for the image will persist. To enable expiration, open up the Internet Information Services snapin for MMC, find the directory, right-click for properties and enable content expiration:

The LookupTable Object

Another technique that we should mention in this discussion of caching involves the LookupTable object. This object provides the ability to retrieve sets of data from a database and store and then retrieve them from memory from then on. Eliminating trips to the database can greatly increase performance. Obviously, not all data is appropriate for storage this way, but some sets of data change very infrequently and merit the extra effort of periodically refreshing the contents of the LookupTable. Some examples of ideal data sets include product lists, product descriptions and products prices. Remember that this method does require memory, so it should be used on sets of data that are the appropriate size for the hardware. If vast amounts of memory are being stored this way, contention for memory to use for caching script templates and script engines may result in data being paged from memory to disk and back again. Page faults are expensive in terms of performance and this is one of the counters that should be monitored. Make sure you understand the effects of caching on memory paging by using the performance monitor to get graphs of the behavior before and after trying these techniques. Excessive paging should be avoided, so a marked increase in paging as a result of caching is an indication to rollback. However, used within reason, the LookupTable can provide in-memory access to data at much faster rates than a database.

This object can be downloaded at
`http://msdn.microsoft.com/workshop/server/downloads/lkuptbl.asp`,
and an article describing its use can be found at
`http://msdn.microsoft.com/workshop/management/planning/MSDNchron`
`icles2.asp`. The `LookupTable` object performs far better than the
`Scripting.DictionaryObject`, which was originally developed for use on the
client.

Server.Transfer

In ASP 3.0, the `Server` object has a new method which provides the opportunity to
increase performance. Once a script has determined that the client should start to
execute a different script, based on some set of criteria, the user will be re-directed to
that URL. Previously, this required a round-trip and an additional request to get the
user to the URL. Another method used is to carefully place functionality that might be
needed in this way in separate include files and use them only when necessary. Both of
these methods are inefficient. There is a cost associated with include files, and even if
the content from an included file is not used, it must still be parsed and will increase
the memory requirements for caching. A redirect is a perceptible slow-down to the
user, and puts the next request at the end of the queue for processing. The
`Server.Transfer` method eliminates the need to use either of these methods. The
transfer is accomplished without the need for extra includes and is transparent to the
user. Control is simply passed to the designated script. The developer can leave what
output has already been buffered so that it is sent when appropriate or can clear the
response buffer if desired. This provides all of the flexibility at a very small fraction of
the cost.

For example:

```
// JScript
if (user_should_be_redirected) {
    Response.Clear();
    Server.Transfer("some_other_script.asp");
}
```

```
' VBScript
If user_should_be_directed = True Then
    Response.Clear
    Server.Transfer "some_other_script.asp"
End If
```

CreateObject

The standard method for creating objects in ASP is to call `Server.CreateObject`.
Among other things, this provides the object with a special context. This
`ObjectContext` allows it to access and utilize the ASP intrinsic objects (`Response`,
`Request`, `Server`, `Application`, `Session`, and `ASPError`). This `ObjectContext`
is required in order to participate in a transaction. Without the context, it is not
possible to send output directly to the client, read or write cookies, access or modify
session and application variables. If it is known that the object being created does not
need the context, we can call `CreateObject` directly in VBScript (instead of using
`Server.CreateObject`), or to use `x = new ActiveXObject("...")` in JScript.

When using IIS 4, eliminating the overhead associated with the
`Server.CreateObject` call provided a substantial increase in performance. That is
no longer the case with IIS 5. From a performance perspective, there is essentially no
difference. Significant improvements introduced with COM+ have provided this
benefit.

For IIS 5, this is a moot discussion, but for IIS 4 it may be worth looking into the
possibility of using just `CreateObject`. Before deciding to use `CreateObject` over
`Server.CreateObject`, it is necessary to have detailed knowledge about the
implementation of the object, so that there are no doubts that it will not make use of
the `ObjectContext`. I don't believe it's safe to make this assumption about any object
unless it was authored in-house.

Scripting

The scripting habits of the ASP application's developer are at the heart of its
performance. All the tuning efforts in the world can't fix a poorly written application.
Fortunately, the platform is fairly forgiving, but it pays when looking to improve
performance to analyze the scripts themselves and make changes in the name of
performance where appropriate.

IsClientConnected

The `Response` object has a seldom used and often misunderstood method that
provides the opportunity to reduce server load. Reducing the work that must be done
for one script provides more resources to handle other incoming requests.
`Response.IsClientConnected`, when used appropriately, can eliminate
unnecessary work. Before executing expensive database queries or executing long-
running calls into COM objects, check to see that the client is still connected and
waiting for a response. If not, simply call `Response.End` and the overhead of doing
work for a client that isn't waiting is eliminated. The executing thread is able to process
another request that much sooner.

Which Script Language?

Use just one language per page. In version 4 of the script engines, there were
differences between JScript and VBScript that may have warranted switching between
the languages on a single page. Now, in version 5, JScript has introduced support for
`try...catch`, allowing error handling similar to VBScript's `On Error Resume
Next` statement. Additionally, there is a regular expression object available that can be
called from VBScript, a functionality previously reserved for those using the JScript
engine. There are also script engines available for other languages, including Perl and
Python. For better performance, use just one scripting language per page. When a page
makes calls with more than one language, it increases the burden on the IIS cache to
allow the page access to both. Even though this extra overhead may seem small when
looking at the Megahertz cost for a single page, it decreases performance dramatically
under load.

Know your language. Performing actions in code by brute force that are supported natively in the language is much slower. Script is interpreted and the opportunities for optimization on the part of the script engine during execution are very limited. If client-side scripting is required, it may prove beneficial to standardize on JScript to afford the greatest reach. From a performance perspective, the languages are nearly identical. Functionally, there are no longer compelling arguments for one language over the other. It pays to standardize on one language for the application and spend the time learning all the features of the chosen language. For example, parsing done in the script by going through large strings character by character may be an unnecessarily slow way to accomplish what can be done by the split method of JScript's String object. The object methods are coded in a compiled language and have been carefully tuned for performance. These native methods will always be faster than something written in the script to accomplish the same task. Script code is executed by the compiled code, so going straight to the compiled code yields a benefit.

Type Libraries

Use type libraries instead of include files. ADO provides adovbs.inc, which is commonly used to populate the namespace for a script with all of the constants. This file contains more than 500 lines. Type libraries provide performance advantage over included constants (except in the situation where only a few constants will be defined). They are not referenced until the local namespace has been searched and are therefore accessed only when needed. Furthermore, accessing a type library does not read in all of the other constants that are not needed into the namespace. The script engine does not have to search a large namespace to look up every constant because the use of a type library over an include file has kept the namespace small. Here is the code to be included in the global.asa to provide access to the ADO constants without using the include file (as mentioned previously the file numbers have been frozen, so the ADO 2.5 library is still called msado15.dll):

```
<!-- METADATA TYPE="typelib"
     FILE="C:\Program Files\Common Files\System\ado\msado15.dll" -->
```

It is also possible to use the UUID of the type library instead:

```
<!-- METADATA NAME="Microsoft ActiveX Data Objects 2.5 Library"
     TYPE="TypeLib" UUID="{00000205-0000-0010-8000-00AA006D2EA4}" -->
```

OnStart and OnEnd

The global.asa file is used for declaring objects that will be used in the page, providing access to type libraries and is, of course, where the OnStart and OnEnd methods for the Application and Session are placed. Do not include these methods as empty implementations. ASP does not check to see that something valuable is actually happening in these methods. Instead, it incurs the overhead of performing a function call that accomplishes nothing.

For legacy reasons, many developers still provide OnStartPage and OnEndPage methods for COM objects for use with ASP. They were required for use with IIS 3 and are still supported in IIS 4 and 5, but are no longer needed. Providing empty implementations of them incurs extra unnecessary cost. These methods should only be implemented when necessary.

For objects that will be stored in the `Session` or `Application` objects, use the `<OBJECT>` tag and declare them in the `global.asa`. ASP will create the object when it is needed, instead of when the session is first launched. This may prevent the need for a lengthy `Session_OnStart` method. The `OnStart` method is called for the user's first request, and first impressions mean a lot. Delaying object creation until it is necessary may provide a much better perceived performance for the user.

Arrays

Arrays are a convenient way to store and retrieve information. Associative arrays stored with application or session scope provide a means for handling data quickly without having to constantly access a database. When used to handle relatively small amounts of data, they can provide a performance boost. When the array is large, it can have a negative impact. The reason behind the potential problem is the fact that the array is copied when it is accessed. For example, suppose that 1,000 items are retrieved from a database and stored in an array that is put into the `Application` object. Perhaps it is a list of current products and associated descriptions. In theory, accessing the array instead of going back to the database should be a good thing, but in fact, it may not be. Each time the array is accessed, the entire contents of the array are copied into the local namespace. This can be a large amount of data to be moving around in memory. The functionality of the array without the associated problem of copying the elements can be achieved by using the `LookupTable` object from Microsoft (see the section on caching data above). XML data islands provide another method for accomplishing this.

Script Transitions

The number of transitions between script blocks and HTML code should be minimized. All HTML in an ASP page is eventually sent using a `Response.Write`, so there is no avoiding use of the intrinsic objects to send output (a common misconception). Interspersing the use of `<%=...%>` throughout HTML code keeps the page readable and provides for easier maintenance. The problem lies in the number of transitions from HTML to script and back again. For most scripts, this is not an issue, but those that contain hundreds or even thousands of transitions gain an advantage by re-writing to eliminate some of them. Parsing is an expensive task anyway, and complicating the process only serves to slow things down.

Variable Declarations

Each time a variable is referenced, the script engine must search the namespace in order to make use of it. It first searches the local namespace for a function, and then resorts to the global namespace. If the name is still not found, type libraries will then be accessed to complete the search. The global namespace is large when compared to the size of the namespace held by a function. When writing functions, look carefully at the variables being used and eliminate globals where possible. It may seem very convenient to have a global counter used in all the loops. Intuition leads to the belief that declaring the variable just once and using it throughout should be more efficient. In most cases, this is not true.

If writing in VBScript, make use of `Option Explicit`. This forces a variable to be declared with the `Dim` statement before it can be used. If a variable is not declared, it produces a compiler error. Using `Option Explicit` provides a substantial performance increase in VBScript code.

Script Profiling

The poor behavior of just one script affects the server. As long as one script is running, it is occupying the thread resource for which another script might be waiting. The so-called "Poor Man's Profiler" is a method used to help identify the specific line or lines within a script that are expensive to execute. The idea is to benchmark the script isolated from the other parts of the application, and then execute increasingly smaller parts of the script until the problem is identified.

The first step in profiling scripts is to get a clear picture of the script. To eliminate the potential confusion of included files, rename the ASP file with an `.stm` extension. Do not do this on a production machine or you risk downloading your code to the outside. Request this file with the `.stm` extension from the server and you get the script in a state where includes have been performed, but the ASP processing has not. Take this code and place it in a file for testing. It may be much larger than was expected if the developer has made heavy use of include files. Review the script to find out if sections of code have been duplicated by nested includes bringing in the same source more than once. This is a common mistake that places an unnecessary burden on the server.

Now that the include files have been expanded, proceed to the profiling steps. Run a stress tool against just that script to get a starting benchmark. Let's suppose that the result is ten pages per second. Move to the middle of the script and insert a `Response.End` call. Run the stress tool against the script again to find out the behavior of just the first half. If the throughput is still ten pages per second, it is safe to conclude that the top half of the script contains the problem. If the throughput has jumped significantly, the assumption is that the problem rests in the second half of the script. For either of these two cases, move the `Response.End` up or down as appropriate, and run the test again. The aim is to identify quickly the section of the script causing the bottleneck and then focus on identifying the exact line that is causing the blocking. Much of the time, the culprit is found as an expensive database request or call into a COM object that is experiencing contention over its resources under heavy use. The solution depends on the situation. An expensive database call may call for work on the database, or implementation of a way to cache the data. A call into a shared COM object may lead towards using a page-scoped object to reduce contention in accessing the resource. The difficult situation arises when the problem appears to be evenly distributed throughout the script. This may indicate that large amounts of script should be encapsulated in a COM object rather than run in script.

HTTP Compression

IIS5 provides the ability to transmit data to clients in a compressed format. By reducing the amount of data that must be transmitted, throughput can be increased. The value of this technique is greatly dependent on the nature of the traffic and the processing requirements of the application. Compressing and decompressing data is more costly in terms of CPU usage than just transmitting it. If the CPU is being well utilized to perform ASP script processing, the application may not be an appropriate candidate for HTTP compression. It doesn't have to be an all-or-nothing decision. The settings allow selecting individually to compress static content and application (dynamic) content. To access the dialog box where HTTP compression can be enabled, open the Internet Information Services MMC snap-in and select the Properties option for the appropriate server. Select the WWW Service option from the Master Properties drop-down box and then click the Edit button. The service tab has checkboxes for enabling HTTP compression. When experimenting with compression, be sure to monitor the CPU utilization in the Performance area of the System Monitor. If CPU usage climbs too high to handle spikes in traffic comfortably, the application and hardware may not be appropriate for compression.

Debugging

When an application that has been performing satisfactorily suddenly can't keep up with the load, the first thing to do is check that debugging has not been enabled. If the AdminScripts are on the server (typically found as a subdirectory of the InetPub directory) use adsutil.vbs to quickly find out the debug settings for all applications:

```
C:\Inetpub\AdminScripts>cscript adsutil.vbs enum_all | findstr Debug
AppAllowDebugging : (BOOLEAN) False
AppAllowClientDebug : (BOOLEAN) False
```

The setting will be repeated for any nested application that has explicitly defined it rather than inheriting the value from the web service root. If debugging has been enabled, the application is running with just one thread. All requests are waiting for all processing to be handled by that single debug-enabled thread. Debugging on a production machine is not recommended. Even if a problem is quickly identified and remedied, the setting is often forgotten and days are spent trying to find out what has gone wrong.

The Metabase

The Metabase is where IIS stores configuration settings. Many of the values can be modified and viewed using the Internet Information Services Management Console plugin. In Windows 2000, right-click on the My Computer icon and select Manage, expand Services and Applications and then choose Internet Information Services. By right-clicking on a site or virtual directory, the properties page can be accessed. The values displayed are stored in the metabase. For those values that cannot be accessed from MMC, we must use the ADSI interfaces. Fortunately this has been made very easy with the Windows Scripting Host. Several scripts are provided in the AdminScripts directory in the Inetpub directory.

The general-purpose script called `adsutil.vbs` (which we have just met) is useful for quickly viewing and updating Metabase values. It is run with the built-in `cscript` interpreter for the Windows Script Host. The first argument corresonds to the command that should be executed and can be one of the following values: `get`, `set`, `enum`, `delete`, `create`, `copy`, `appcreateinproc`, `appcreateoutproc`, `appcreatepoolproc`, `appdelete`, `appunload`, or `appgetstatus`.

The second argument corresponds to the path in the Metabase, which is a tree-like structure. The root of the web service is denoted by `/w3svc`. The first instance is identified as the number `1` and the default application is called `root`. The Metabase works on an inheritance basis. If a value is not defined at a specific node, it is inherited from above. If the value is not found above, a default value is used. This reduces the size of the data that must be stored. The third argument is used to set a particular value. In the following example, we just list all the values defined at the web service node and then use `findstr` on the output to get the entries that include ASP.

The result is this:

```
C:\Inetpub\AdminScripts>cscript adsutil.vbs enum /w3svc/ | findstr /i asp
DefaultDoc : (STRING) "Default.htm,Default.asp"
AspBufferingOn : (BOOLEAN) True
AspLogErrorRequests : (BOOLEAN) True
AspScriptErrorSentToBrowser : (BOOLEAN) True
AspScriptErrorMessage : (STRING) "An error occurred on the server when
  processing the URL. Please contact the system administrator."
AspAllowOutOfProcComponents : (BOOLEAN) True
AspScriptFileCacheSize : (INTEGER) 250
AspScriptEngineCacheMax : (INTEGER) 125
AspScriptTimeout : (INTEGER) 90
AspSessionTimeout : (INTEGER) 20
AspEnableParentPaths : (BOOLEAN) True
AspAllowSessionState : (BOOLEAN) True
AspScriptLanguage : (STRING) "VBScript"
AspExceptionCatchEnable : (BOOLEAN) True
AspCodepage : (INTEGER) 0
AspQueueTimeout : (INTEGER) -1
AspEnableAspHtmlFallback : (BOOLEAN) False
AspEnableChunkedEncoding : (BOOLEAN) True
AspEnableTypelibCache : (BOOLEAN) True
AspErrorsToNTLog : (BOOLEAN) False
AspProcessorThreadMax : (INTEGER) 25
AspTrackThreadingModel : (BOOLEAN) False
AspRequestQueueMax : (INTEGER) 3000
AspEnableApplicationRestart : (BOOLEAN) True
AspQueueConnectionTestTime : (INTEGER) 3
AspSessionMax : (INTEGER) -1
AspThreadGateEnabled : (BOOLEAN) False
AspThreadGateTimeSlice : (INTEGER) 1000
AspThreadGateSleepDelay : (INTEGER) 100
AspThreadGateSleepMax : (INTEGER) 50
AspThreadGateLoadLow : (INTEGER) 50
AspThreadGateLoadHigh : (INTEGER) 80
 ".asp,C:\WINNT\System32\inetsrv\asp.dll,1,GET,HEAD,POST,TRACE"
 ".cer,C:\WINNT\System32\inetsrv\asp.dll,1,GET,HEAD,POST,TRACE"
 ".cdx,C:\WINNT\System32\inetsrv\asp.dll,1,GET,HEAD,POST,TRACE"
 ".asa,C:\WINNT\System32\inetsrv\asp.dll,1,GET,HEAD,POST,TRACE"
```

AspBufferingOn

The default for IIS 5 is to enable buffering. For maximum performance, it should be left on. The effect of this is to allow headers to be written at any time during script processing. To write out content before a long running step, use `Respones.Flush`.

AspRequestQueueMax

When a request for an ASP page arrives at the server, it is placed in the request queue until a thread becomes available to process it. If requests are arriving faster than threads are becoming available the queue begins to fill. If the queue fills to the `AspRequestQueueMax` number, IIS doesn't place additional requests in the queue until the number drops below this setting. Instead, the client is sent a **500 Server Too Busy** error message. The default setting in IIS 4 was `500`. This has been increased in IIS 5 to `3000`. If CPU usage is low and the processing time for each script is too long, then it may be appropriate to increase this setting even further to accommodate high volumes. To view its value, use the following script with the Windows Scripting Host. Place the code in a file with a `.js` extension (or `.vbs` if using VBScript) and it is mapped to the WSH when executed.

The following JScript script retrieves the value of this setting:

```
var obj = GetObject("IIS://LocalHost/W3SVC/1/Root");
var RequestQueueMax = obj.AspRequestQueueMax;
WScript.Echo(RequestQueueMax);
```

To change it requires appropriate Administration privileges on the server:

```
var obj = GetObject("IIS://LocalHost/W3SVC/1/Root");
obj.AspRequestQueueMax = 3500;
obj.SetInfo();
```

New functionality in IIS 5 allows the error message sent for **Server Too Busy** to be customized. This at least allows us to ensure that the error page can maintain the look and feel of the rest of the application, and the message can be made somewhat less abrupt.

AspAllowSessionState

As discussed previously, sessions are not free from overhead cost. Disabling them for the site places less burden on the server. When using frames, it may increase the user's perceived performance significantly. Unfortunately, it is not possible to disable session state globally and enable it just in those pages where it is needed. If sessions are needed at all, it must be turned on for the application. All of the other pages that don't require session must then include the directive `<% @EnableSessionState=False %>` at the top of the page in order to turn sessions off for that script. To turn them off in the Metabase for the default application:

```
var obj = GetObject("IIS://LocalHost/W3SVC/1");
obj.AspAllowSessionState = false;
obj.SetInfo();
```

AspSessionTimeout

The default length of time a session has to be inactive before it is expired by IIS is 20 minutes. It may be prudent, if the number of users is high but the length of stay is short, to reduce this timeout.

AspSessionMax

The value of −1 in the Metabase means that IIS will not limit the number of concurrent sessions. If an application is using sessions and volume is heavy, it may be necessary to set a limit. In this situation, the number of active sessions can also be curtailed by reducing the AspSessionTimeout.

AspScriptFileCacheSize

The default value of 250 corresponds to the number of script files the server will try to cache in memory. Setting this to 0 causes no scripts to be cached and a value of −1 results in the server trying to cache everything. On a non-production machine, it is a worthwhile exercise to turn caching off and see the dramatic difference in response times. If the total number of scripts on the site is not unwieldy and memory is adequate, performance can be gained by increasing the AspScriptFileCacheSize.

AspScriptEngineCacheMax

The number of script engines kept in memory defaults to 125. This too should be adjusted up if the memory use is not high and the number of unique scripts on the server is. The performance gain is in ensuring that the most frequently accessed scripts have a cached script engine ready for use.

AspQueueTimeout

This property provides functionality not previously available in IIS 4, but it is turned off by default. If a request waits in the queue for longer than this setting allows, it will not be processed. Instead, a Server Too Busy message will be sent to the client. A value of −1 (the default) indicates no timeout value. Although it is not typically desirable to fail client requests, for some applications it is more appropriate to reduce the current load on the server by turning away those that have waited too long. Use this setting in conjunction with AspQueueConnectionTestTime to achieve better performance.

AspQueueConnectionTestTime

When a worker thread is ready to remove a request from the queue for processing, ASP will check that the client is still connected before processing the request if it has been in the queue longer than the AspQueueConnectionTestTime. This prevents ASP from doing unnecessary work.

AspProcessorThreadMax

ASP allocates a number of threads per processor at start up time. These threads are the workers that process requests. If the scripts of an application make long-running calls to external components, increasing the value of this property may have an increase in performance. Do not adjust the number of threads up from the default value in IIS5 of 25 without carefully monitoring the resulting behavior. Too many threads can result in a rapid decrease in overall responsiveness. With the number of threads, it is possible to have too much of a good thing.

Summary

When it comes to ASP web applications, performance is a lot of things: performance is the time it takes to satisfy a request; performance is the volume of requests that can be processed; performance is linear scaling under load. There is no simple way to define what is good performance. Get absolute numbers for how an application behaves and then set absolute goals for how it should behave. Improving throughput from ten requests per second to twenty is an enormous percentage increase, but may not be realistic for deployment. The number of things to consider when doing performance work may seem unwieldy, but the biggest gains are sometimes the easiest to achieve. Focus on one aspect of performance at a time until the behavior and impact is understood, then move on to something else. We have discussed how to measure performance and how to stress test an application. We have talked about how the choices about hardware affect the capabilities of the application. We have discussed how to monitor ASP and what key items relating to performance are available for tuning in the Metabase. We have discussed how scripting guidelines can be used to prevent bottlenecks and improve performance. If the impact of a decision is understood, it is far easier to decide.

42

Securing ASP Applications

With all the news lately about increased hacking activity on the Internet, we cannot afford to be lax about the overall general security of our ASP web sites, applications and the systems they run upon. We will discuss more than just programming in this chapter but fear not, there will also be ASP code discussions.

It is imperative in this day and age that programmers are concerned with security aspects of systems. Programmers and network/server administrators work closely together more than ever, due to the popularity of Active Server Pages. In fact, it is not uncommon that programmers do most of the system administration or vice versa. I personally hold a dual job role as a network administrator and an internet programmer. Having this ability to be on both sides of the programmer/administrator relationship, my skills both as a network administrator and as an internet programmer have flourished. Even if you are not the person held directly responsible for the administration and security of your web applications, I do recommend that you read this chapter. You should also read other security-related information to achieve a general understanding of the arena you work in. The aim of this chapter is to help you achieve that undersatanding.

This chapter will discuss many things related to the security of our ASP web sites and applications in a broad way including:

❑   Securing Microsoft Windows NT/Windows 2000

❑   Securing Microsoft Internet Information Server

❑   Securing Microsoft SQL Server 7.0

❑   Encryption Technology

❑   Effective ASP Code Surrounding Authentication

Securing Windows NT/ Windows 2000

A stock Microsoft Windows NT/2000 installation is by no means secure when you bring that server out into the public domain of the Internet. In fact, depending upon the knowledge level of internal employees, it may not be a very secure system for an internal Local Area Network either. There are many things that can be done to make this a more secure environment for a web server.

There are more aspects to securing a Windows NT server than can be mentioned in this chapter. In this section, we will investigate briefly some of the more important security issues with Windows NT servers. Let's take a look at what will be covered in this section:

❑   Hard disk formats

❑   Security Checklists

❑   Network Security

Hard Disk Formats

Windows 2000 supports three possible disk formats – FAT, FAT32 and NTFS. Each of these different disk formats has a level of compatibility, support, and security within Microsoft Windows 2000 servers. Within Windows NT 4.0, you only have two choices – FAT and NTFS. It is imperative that you investigate the differences and relationships between these different disk formats. Windows 2000 has the latest versions of the NTFS file system, NTFS 5. Whether you have chosen Windows NT 4.0 or Windows 2000 as your network Operating System, you will probably want to choose NTFS as your disk format of choice because of the following security features:

❑   **Access Control Lists (ACLs)** for objects, dictionaries and files. ACLs contain zero or more access control entries, each of which details a user's access rights to the object or file in question.

❑   **Disk Quotas**. Administrators can monitor and limit the amount of disk space any given user can consume. This is only available by default to Windows 2000 servers, but can be made available for Windows NT 4.0 with third party software.

❑   **Encrypted Files**. Windows 2000 NTFS disk format has the ability to encrypt sensitive files and information when it is saved to disk. This is not supported within Windows NT 4.0.

NTFS (New Technology File System) is a much more secure environment for sensitive data to be stored because of its ability to control access, and because of the extra attributes available on file and folder objects. This is the best choice when running ASP web sites or applications with security in mind. Again, getting to know these disk formats and understanding how they work are imperative for both administrators and programmers.

Disk and File Capacity

One of the more important issues concerning disk formats is the capacity of file size limits and partition sizes. This can definitely become an issue when dealing with databases because of unexpected growth. The disk partition and file size limits for each of the three disk formats are as follows:

❑ FAT can work with partitions no greater than 2Gb in size.

❑ FAT32 can work with partitions up to 2Tb in size. However, a file size limit does exist. Files can be no larger than 4Gb in size.

❑ NTFS can work with partitions up to 2Tb in size and file sizes are limited only by the size of the partition.

With the low cost of disk space and the high capacity of disk partition space and file size limits with NTFS, you can see another reason for using this disk format. When coupled with the security availability, it is easy to see why NTFS is a much better choice for your Windows NT/Windows 2000 server.

Security Checklist

For this section, it will be assumed that you have chosen Windows NT 4 or Windows 2000 as your network operating system for your ASP web site or application. This section provides a checklist to follow as a guideline when (re-)building your servers to provide a secure internet or intranet environment. There are a number of things to look for when securing your server, but first, a few words of caution:

> Some of the following advice involves making changes to the system Registry. Before making any changes, the Registry should be backed up. There is no damaging content in what is going to be done in this section, but for safety's sake you should back the registry up first. You can backup the registry simply by selecting Registry/Export Registry within `regedit32`.

Setting the Server's Role in the Domain

When installing Windows 2000, we are confronted with the question of what role we would like the server to play within the network – a Primary Domain Controller, Back-up Domain Controller or a Stand-Alone Server. It is safest to chose a stand-alone server to prevent the possibility of exposing any sensitive information contained in a domain, such as usernames or passwords.

Choosing a Disk Format

Earlier in this section, we looked at disk formats and said that you would probably want to use the NTFS file system. Therefore during the installation process, choose NTFS to format and create the partitions accordingly. If you have already installed Windows 2000, but did not choose NTFS during the installation process, you can safely convert to this format using the supplied `convert.exe` utility. However, please note that when you choose NTFS as your file system type as part of your installation, it will set default security values on your shares and directories. When the filesystem is converted, it will not apply any of this security information, so you will need to do this manually. To convert the file system:

❑ Open a command prompt window.

❑ Type convert c: /FS:NTFS (where c: is the drive to be converted) and follow the onscreen prompts.

> Note that you cannot reverse this procedure once it has taken place. It is important that you understand the implication of doing this: Any files stored on NTFS partitions on your drive will not be accessible to other operating systems.

Partitioning your Web Space

Dividing the hard drive in your web server into several partitions is a good idea. By putting all web files on an extended or logical partition, you will prevent any attackers gaining control of your primary boot partition, even if control of the web site is compromised. This is also dependent upon how your ACLs were set on the primary boot partition. In other words, if you were to give an account access on the primary partition and also on the logical or extended partition and this account were compromised, the boot partition and your web partition would be at the mercy of the attacker. For safety's sake, never give the accounts that are used on your web partition any access to the primary boot partition.

Latest Service Packs and Hot-fixes

Check to make sure that you have the latest service packs and hot-fixes installed on your server according to your security policy. Review all Microsoft Security Bulletins concerning all the software installed on your server. You should also add yourself to any security mailing lists for your operating systems and any software that you use. You can find these online at http://www.microsoft.com/security.

NTFS 8.3 Name Generation

NTFS provides some backward compatibility with 16-bit applications by automatically generating DOS-style 8.3 format filenames (e.g Progra~1\word.exe) when required. This facility should be turned off within a secure internet environment, to ensure that no 16-bit applications can be installed on the machine. To turn off NTFS 8.3 file name generation click Start | Run, and type regedit to open the registry editor. Then add the following registry entry:

Registry Hive	HKEY_LOCAL_MACHINE\SYSTEM
Registry Key	CurrentControlSet\Control\FileSystem
Name	NtfsDisable8dot3NameCreation
New Value	1

Note that this also results in an increase in performance.

Hiding the Last Logged On User

If more than one person logs onto the console of your server, it is quite handy to hide the last username for a few simple security reasons. If someone were to see the console, they would be presented with a valid user account name (with super user or Administrator privileges if the last logged on user belongs to the Administrators group), and they would then be half way to gaining access. We can edit the following entry in the Registry to hide the last username:

Registry Hive	HKEY_LOCAL_MACHINE\SOFTWARE
Registry Key	\Microsoft\Windows NT\Current Version\Winlogon
Name	DontDisplayLastUsername
New Value	1

Displaying a Legal Notice

Displaying a legal notice at logon time can be useful in scaring some people off, and it's also a requirement for a system to gain a C2 security certificate (US-only). This is issued by the NSA's National Computer Security Center and recognizes that the server has adhered to the baseline measurement for a secure operating system. To display a legal notice at logon time, we can edit the following keys in the Registry:

Registry Hive	HKEY_LOCAL_MACHINE\SOFTWARE
Registry Key	\Microsoft\Windows NT\Current Version\Winlogon
Name	Legal Notice Caption
New Value	The title of the message box that you want to appear (e.g. Important Notice!!).

Registry Hive	HKEY_LOCAL_MACHINE\SOFTWARE
Registry Key	\Microsoft\Windows NT\Current Version\Winlogon
Name	LegalNoticeText
New Value	The text of the message you want to appear. (E.g. "It is unlawful to access this computer without proper permission").

Check the Status of the Logon Screen Shutdown Button

As you may have noticed, it is initially possible to shutdown a Windows NT/ Windows 2000 server from the logon screen without actually having to log on to the server. Make sure that you have disabled this possibility by setting the following registry key:

Registry Hive	HKEY_LOCAL_MACHINE\SOFTWARE
Registry Key	\Microsoft\Windows NT\Current Version\Winlogon
Name	ShutdownWithoutLogon
New Value	0

Disable Anonymous Network Access

By default, Windows NT/ Windows 2000 also allows non-authenticated users to enumerate the users on a system. To disable this functionality, we need to edit the following key in the registry:

Registry Hive	HKEY_LOCAL_MACHINE\SYSTEM
Registry Key	\CurrentControlSet\Control\LSA
Name	RestrictAnonymous
New Value	1

Check Permissions in the Registry for Remote Access

Windows NT/ Window 2000 supports access to the Registry from remote locations. Some configuration is necessary to make this more secure. To change this setting, use the regedt32 utility rather than the regedit utility (this utility allows us to change security settings for registry entries). To set the proper permissions on the following keys, click Start | Run and type regedt32. Then locate the following entry in the Registry:

Registry Hive	HKEY_LOCAL_MACHINE\SYSTEM
Registry Key	\CurrentControlSet\Control\SecurePipeServers
Name	\winreg

Now click Security on the toolbar and select Permissions. You will notice that members of the Administrators group have full control, and Backup Operators have read access. You can remove the read access of the Backup Operators Group if your backup software is on the local machine. You can also remove it if your remote backup software does not backup the Registry, or if the account that the backup software runs under is not a member of the Backup Operators Group. It is a very bad idea not to back up the Registry, so any software that you are using that does not do this should be in question.

Other ACL-Critical Registry Keys

There are a few other critical Registry keys that you will want to set permissions on, because they can allow an attacker to install Trojan Horse or virus programs on your server. You will also want to audit access to these keys so that you will be notified if such an attempt were to occur.

Hive Key	HKEY_LOCAL_MACHINE\SOFTWARE\Microsoft\Windows NT\CurrentVersion\Run
Hive Key	HKEY_LOCAL_MACHINE\SOFTWARE\Microsoft\Windows NT\CurrentVersion\RunOnce
Hive Key	HKEY_LOCAL_MACHINE\SOFTWARE\Microsoft\Windows NT\CurrentVersion\RunOnceEx
Hive Key	HKEY_LOCAL_MACHINE\SOFTWARE\Microsoft\Windows NT\CurrentVersion\AeDebug
Hive Key	HKEY_LOCAL_MACHINE\SOFTWARE\Microsoft\Windows NT\CurrentVersion\WinLogon

You will notice that the current ACL settings for these keys are:

❑ Administrators (Full Control)

❑ System (Full Control)

❑ Creator Owner (Full Owner)

❑ Everyone (Read)

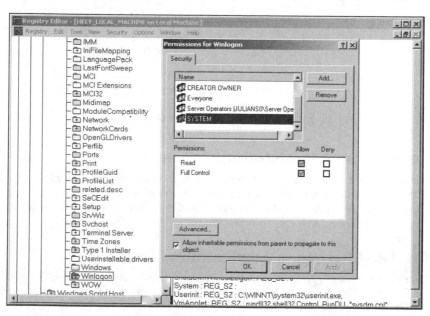

To secure this, click on Security in the toolbar and then select Permissions and set the following ACLs:

❑ Administrator Account username (Full Control)

❑ System (Full Control)

❑ Remove Create Owner

❑ Remove Everyone (Read)

As mentioned, you will also want to monitor attempts to modify these keys. To do this, click on Security in the toolbar then select Audit. Create a new audit process for the Everyone group for as many of these keys as possible for Success and Failures (click on Advanced and select the Auditing tab in the dialog box). This will create event log entries for all of the items which you have selected. This could possibly be a performance issue and take up some disk space for the event log entries. However, this performance issue should not be too serious, because these registry keys don't get modified often. If someone is repeatedly trying to modify these keys, it should definitely be logged and reviewed.

Disabling Autosharing for Net Shares

Windows NT/Windows 2000 allows for shared network drives to be created and will also auto-share all drives and create an ADMIN$ share on the %SYSTEMROOT% directory where NT/Windows 2000 was installed. This, of course, is a wonderful feature in a standard network situation, but not suitable for many reasons in an internet environment. To disable this functionality, we have to create the following key in the Registry:

Registry Hive	HKEY_LOCAL_MACHINE\SYSTEM
Registry Key	\CurrentControlSet\Services\LanmanServer\Parameters
Name	AutoShareServer
New Value	0

Note that this will not take effect until the server is rebooted.

Rename the Administrator Account

When hackers try to crack your system, they will commonly try to use the Administrator logon because it has the most power on the system. To circumvent this, you can rename the Administrator account and then create a fake Administrator account and give it zero access on the system.

Disabling Access to Administrator Tools

There are a few tools which only administrators should have access to. The easiest way to enforce this is by creating a new folder – for example, c:\admintools, copying these tools into this folder and then deleting the files from their original location. Then set the proper security settings so that only the administrator has access to these files. To set the permissions for this folder, all you have to do is open Windows Explorer and right-click on the folder, select the Properties tab, click the Security or the Permissions button and set the proper access rights to this folder:

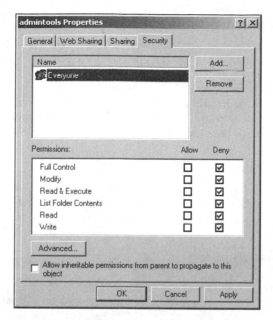

Here is a list of tools that you ought to consider moving and securing in this fashion.
You can of course add or exclude files as you see fit:

xcopy .exe	wscript. exe	cscript .exe	net.exe	ftp.exe	telnet .exe
arp .exe	edlin .exe	ping.exe	route .exe	at.exe	finger .exe
posix .exe	rsh.exe	atsvc .exe	qbasic .exe	runonce .exe	syskey .exe
cacls .exe	ipconfig .exe	rcp.exe	setfixup .exe	nbtstat .exe	rdisk .exe
debug .exe	regedt32 .exe	regedit .exe	edit.exe	netstat .exe	tracert .exe
Nslookup .exe	rexec .exe	cmd.exe	format .com	windisk .exe	Fdisk .com

Note that you will no longer be able to click on Start I Run and type cmd, for example.
You will need to type the path c:\admintools\cmd or modify the System
Environment Variable PATH to have c:\admintools invoked for your shell.

Strengthen Your Passwords

Ensuring that all passwords are at least 9 characters long will decrease the risk of
someone being able to find them out, as will encrypting the passwords for the domain
with a filter and ensuring that they contain a mix of numbers uppercase and lowercase
letters. You can specify each of these options (and a couple of others) by altering the
values stored in the Password Policy Folder under the Account Policies in Microsoft
Management Console with the Group Policy snap-in installed.

Account Lockout Securing

It is also possible to cause the system to lock out user accounts automatically if it becomes apparent that people are trying to guess the passwords for those accounts over and over again. To enable this feature, go into the Account Lockout Policy folder in the Local Security Settings MMC snap-in, and change the value for Account Lockout Count to the number of invalid password guesses you think your users may need to type their passwords correctly. You can also specify if you want to lock the account out for a certain amount of time and then re-enable it after the time limit has expired.

Limiting Access from the Network

Windows NT /2000 by default allows everyone access to the server from the network. This is definitely a big security risk. You can change this setting by going into the Local Policies folder (in the Local Security Settings snap-in), then selecting the User Rights Assignment folder:

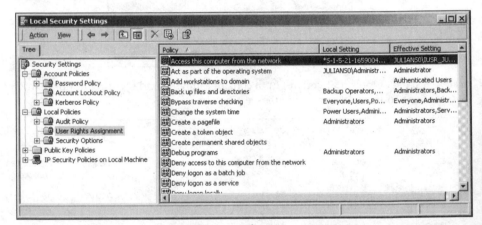

Double-click the Access this computer from the network icon and uncheck the Local Policy box for Everyone. Click the Add button and select Authenticated Users then click Add and then hit the OK button. You will be prompted to update your effective policy; choose Yes:

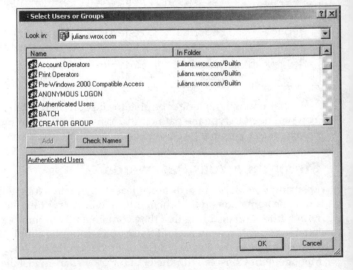

Auditing Logons to the Server

To write logon activity to the security event log, go into the Audit Policy folder (under Local Policies) and change the Audit account logon events and Audit logon events settings. You should check that both successful and unsuccessful attempts to log on to the server are being logged. This will give a good idea of the activity that is going on concerning user accounts.

Log Interval Overwrites

Depending upon how much activity and traffic your site receives, you will have to decide on how big a security log you should keep, and when to start overwriting parts of it. Set the file size high – around 5 Mb should do – for busy servers. You will need enough space to capture the current events and keep a decent backlog of events for your site. Again, your choice of overwrite policy depends on your needs, and you must judge that from experience. A good starting point is to Overwrite events as needed. However, if denial of service attacks are exercised against your server, this setting may hide that activity from you. You can also choose to not overwrite events, and have the server stop responding to network requests when it has filled up. This is the most secure setting (and is required for the C2 compliance that we mentioned earlier), but it does have its drawbacks.

You can edit this by opening the Event Viewer snap-in and by right-clicking the Security log and choosing Properties:

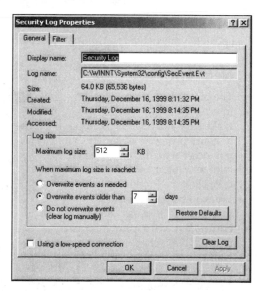

Network Security

Once we've dealt with usernames and passwords, we need to turn our attention towards the network settings to make sure they are correct and secure. These can be changed in the Local Area Connection Properties dialog. There several different ways to get to this screen within Windows 2000, but the simplest is to right-click on the My Network Places icon on the desktop and select Properties. From this dialog box, right-click Local Area Connection and select Properties again. For Windows NT, you can right-click the Network Neighborhood and select Properties to get this dialog box:

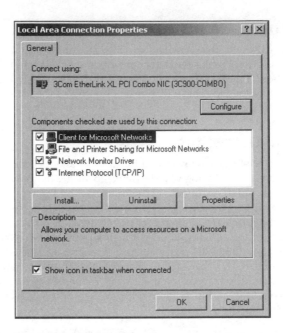

Many of these features will have an impact on your networking, so you might want to speak to your network administrator before carrying out any of the following.

Network Protocols

The only relevant protocol for internet servers is TCP/IP, so make sure you have no other network protocols installed that you don't actually need. Select Internet Protocol (TCP/IP) and then click the Properties button. You will be presented with your machine's IP address and DNS entries, but we're more interested in the WINS (Windows Internet Name Service) properties, which you will find by hitting the Advanced button:

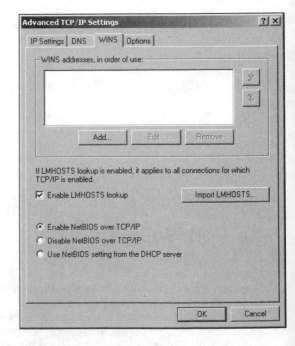

Disabling WINS

In a secure internet environment you would not want to run WINS on the server or use it on a remote server. There have been security issues in the past with servers running WINS and you should not feel any impact as the Internet is based purely on TCP/IP anyway. Oddly enough, the naming convention for the acronym WINS would lead you to believe otherwise. Remove any WINS servers that have been defined and then uninstall WINS itself. However, if your server is behind a firewall and functions within a normal Windows network, you can leave WINS running if it is needed. There is a known denial of service attack when running WINS. This code can be reviewed at:

```
http://rootshell.com/archive-
j457nxiqi3gq59dv/199805/coke.c.html.
```

Disabling NETBIOS

NetBIOS is the network protocol traditionally used for Windows network communications, but which TCP/IP easily supercedes if installed. Again, if your server is on an internal network, or behind a firewall and functions within a Windows network, you can leave this running because this protocol does have its place in networking. In an internet environment, this changes the scenario since the only valid protocol is TCP/IP. It also enables a few tools that could cause breaches in security. You can disable NetBIOS by selecting the Disable NetBIOS over TCP/IP option in the WINS tab.

Disabling LMHOSTS Lookup

The LMHOSTS file is used to map IP addresses to the computer names of Windows machines. So far, there have been no reports of security breaches as a result of enabling LMHOSTS lookup, but it's not really necessary, unless you can't traverse your network using IP addresses instead of computer names. You can disable LMHOSTS lookup by deselecting the relevant radio button in the WINS tab again.

TCP/IP Filtering

A large number of network ports are left open by default by the server, unless specified otherwise. Fortunately, as we know which particular ports HTTP, FTP, etc. use, we can shut down all but those we need on the server, even if it's already behind a firewall or proxy server. Still in the Advanced TCP/IP Settings dialog box, select the Options tab and then Properties for TCP/IP Filtering.

- ❑ Check the Enable TCP/IP Filtering (all Adapters) checkbox, if it isn't already checked.

- ❑ Under TCP ports, you should only add ports you know are being used, for example, port 21 for FTP, port 80 for HTTP, port 443 for SSL, and port 25 for SMTP. There may of course be others which you should add accordingly.

- ❑ You should allow no UDP ports unless needed (for example: Real Audio UDP 7070).

Check Security Resources Regularly

Below are some of the many widely available resources on the Internet pertaining to Windows NT security. These sites should referenced on a periodic basis for any updates with security issues and implementation changes.

- ❏ Main security site for Microsoft:
  `http://www.microsoft.com/security/default.asp`

- ❏ Subscribe to the Microsoft Security Notification Service
  `http://www.microsoft.com/technet/security/notify.asp`

- ❏ Microsoft Checklist for Internet Information Server Secure Server Implementation:
  `http://www.microsoft.com/technet/security/iischk.asp`

> **In the documentation above, Microsoft recommends that you remove the OS2 and POSIX subsystems from Windows NT. This is a very good idea, but if you follow Microsoft's instructions on this site it will render your system unusable! Instead, use the Windows NT Resource Kit C2 configuration utility to remove these subsystems safely.**

- ❏ Windows 2000 Security Walkthrough Site:
  `http://www.microsoft.com/windows2000/library/planning/default.asp`

- ❏ As part of a project for the National Security Agency (NSA), Trusted Systems has produced guidelines to be followed for security on Windows NT: `http://www.trustedsystems.com/NSAGuide.htm`; you may also want to check out `www.ntsecurity.net`.

Securing IIS

This section of the chapter will deal with the secure configuration of Internet Information Server and also investigate the authentication methods that can be used via the web. It is important to have a secure web server along with a secure operating system. Following these checklists for security issues is a recipe for success. You might also be surprised at some of the information in this section, because developers themselves have control over most of the security settings and files that are installed on the web server.

Install as Few Components as Possible

When you install Windows 2000, it will by default install certain selected items for Internet Information Server 5.0. From a security point of view, however, it may well not be in your best interests to use of all these default program installations. For instance, consider the following components:

- ❏ Front Page Server Extensions

- ❏ SMTP Server

- ❏ Remote Data Services

Front Page Server Extensions

Front Page Server extensions should not be used unless set up properly on the machine and configured by a security professional. If a user has write access to the FTP server for a web site on your machine, they can do something like this:

```
ftp host.com
mkdir _vti_bin
CDUP _vti_bin
Put trojanfile.exe
Exit
```

Then, if they type `http://somewhere.com/_vti_bin/trojanfile.exe` in their browser, the Trojan file will now be running on the server.

SMTP Server

If you do not plan to receive mail, or maybe even to send *or* receive mail, or if you will not be using CDO or CDONTS to send mail with your applications, you should not install the SMTP server. A user could email-bomb your web server to decrease its performance.

Remote Data Services

You should not install Remote Data Services on IIS for a few simple reasons. There are known denial of service attacks causing your server to be rendered in an unusable state. More information on this attack can be found at:

`http://support.microsoft.com/support/kb/articles/Q184/3/75.asp`

Users can also create forms on their local machine web server and try to connect to your database through OLE DB.

Don't worry, if you have already installed these components and wish to remove them. To uninstall any of these components all you have to do is open Add/Remove programs in the Control Panel, select Add/Remove Windows Components and then deselect the components you wish to get rid of.

Create a Logical Securable Directory Structure

A good web site structure also makes it simpler to manage security for the various applications within it. You should be able to define directories such that they contain only one type of file – executables, ASP Pages, server-side includes etc. – allowing you to define tight security permissions on a directory rather that a file basis in Windows Explorer, and making it easier to maintain. Below is an example structure:

Directory Name	Contains	File Extensions	Permission Settings
Webroot\exec	Executables files	`.exe`, `.dll`, `.pl`	Anonymous Web user (Read and Execute)
			Administrator (Full Control)
			System (Full Control)
Webroot\incs	Include files	`.inc`, `.shtml`, `.shtm`	Anonymous Web user (Read and Execute or just Execute)
			Administrator (Full Control)
			System (Full Control)
Webroot\asp	ASP Pages	`.asp`	Anonymous Web user (Read and Execute or just Execute)
			Administrator (Full Control)
			System (Full Control)
Webroot\html	HTML\Client-side script	`.htm`, `.html`	Anonymous Web user (Read Only)
			Administrator (Full Control)
			System (Full Control)
Webroot\imgs	Image Files	`.gif`, `.jpeg`, `.psd`	Anonymous Web user (Read Only)
			Administrator (Full Control)
			System (Full Control)

Authentication Methods

There are two major concepts that we need to understand in order to secure our system: authentication, ensuring that users are who they say they are, and authorization, validating that users have access rights the resource which has been requested. Both of these functions are usually fulfilled by getting users to input a username and password. In this section, we'll look at the ways in which we can validate this authentication.

Anonymous Authentication

When anonymous access has been enabled, IIS does not care about the user's identity and simply assigns a pre-specified user account and permissions to anyone accessing the files on the web server. By default, this anonymous user account is named IUSR_MACHINENAME where MACHINENAME is the name of the server that is specified during the installation of Windows NT/2000. This account is assigned to the Guests local account group, given a password that can be changed, and given the right to 'Log on Locally', which allows it to access the IISA 5.0 WWW Services.

For security reasons, you might consider changing the name of the
IUSR_MACHINENAME account, as we recommended earlier with the administrator
account.

Provided that Anonymous
Authentication has been
enabled, users accessing WWW
Services are allowed access to
those resources with the
permissions allocated to the
IUSR_MACHINENAME account.
We can change the
Anonymous authentication
setting through the
Authentication Methods dialog
box, which we can bring up by
selecting **Anonymous access
and authentication** control on
the **Directory Security** tab of the
web site's **Properties** dialog:

*IIS 5.0 also creates another user account called IWAM_MACHINENAME during
the installation process. When we create web applications that run out of
process from IIS, it will create an MTS package that is set to run under this
account. For security reasons, you might also consider changing the name of
the IWAM_MACHINENAME account.*

Pressing the top **Edit** button in this dialog box allows us to modify these permissions,
and the anonymous account itself.

Basic Authentication

If a user requests a resource to which the anonymous user account does not have
access, the request will be rejected and a **401 Access Denied** message will be returned
to the client. If either of the other two authentication methods are enabled, most
browsers will then prompt the user for a username and password and then submit
both of them and again request access to the server for verification.

The difference between Basic and Integrated Windows Authentication lies in the way
the username and passwords are transmitted. Under Basic Authentication, they are
transmitted as Base64-encoded strings, which are easily deciphered. The user ID can
either be declared simply (e.g. DomainName\dan), or, new to IIS 5.0, in the form
dan@domainname.com.

*The transmissions of usernames and passwords inclear cstring form can be
changed by using SSL encryption, which we will be discussion later in this
chapter.*

Integrated Windows Authentication

With IWA (Integrated Windows Authentication, formerly known as NTLM or Windows NT Challenge/Response Authentication in Windows NT 4.0), the user's password is never sent across the network, and so can never be revealed to an attacker. Instead, when challenged for user information by the server (IIS), the client responds with an encrypted security blob, which a server has previously issued. Blob here means a chunk of encrypted data. The way in which this blob is encrypted and exactly how it is verified is dependent upon which protocol Windows is using.

If both the client and the IIS server have a trusted connection to a Kerberos Key Distribution Center (KDC) and are both Active Directory compatible, IIS will use the Kerberos Network Authentication Protocol to verify the security blob. Kerberos is the new security model upon which Windows 2000 authentication is based. You can find more information about it at:

```
http://www.microsoft.com/security/tech/kerberos/
```

If the server, or, more likely, the client is not Kerberos-compatible, the server will fall back to the Windows NT Challenge/Response protocol. You can find more information about this at:

```
http://www.microsoft.com/NTServer/security/.
```

The details of these protocols aside, two points must be made clear with respect to IWA:

❑ The only time IWA is used is when anonymous access is either denied or when an anonymous user has come across a page which forces the user to authenticate before a connection is established to the content.

❑ IWA is compatible only with Internet Explorer 2+ browsers.

Securing SQL Server 7.0

As ASP applications are very often data-centric and use sensitive data, database security is an important issue. This topic is of course dependent on the database server in use, but as SQL Server is the most popular database for ASP applications, we will look at the issue of securing SQL Server.

Installation

During the installation of SQL Server 7.0 there are a few things to think about. You will be asked what accounts to run for the MSSQLServer and SQLAgent services. The default is the sa account. You will probably want to change this to make this more secure in case of an sa account break-in. You will also want to change this if you are going to be using the SQLMail service with Microsoft Outlook so you can take advantage of the Mail profiles. Also, during the installation process the system administrator's account password is set to NULL. You will need to change this first before any configuration is done on the server: to do this, open the SQL Server Enterprise Manager, expand the server group for your server, click on the Security folder to expand it and finally click on the Logins icon:

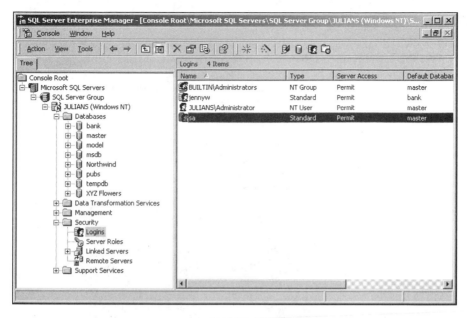

Double-click the sa account icon in the right-hand pane. When presented with the **SQL Server Login Properties** dialog box, enter the password you want the sa account to have. Make sure it is a strong password because this account has full access to all of your SQL databases for that server:

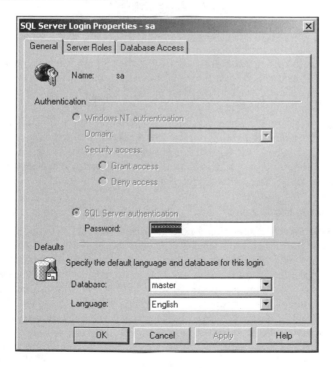

Adding Users to SQL Server

When we add users to a SQL Server database, we need to take certain measures to make this a secure environment. We will create a user account within SQL Server called odbc as an example account, and we will configure the access rights of this user to a database called application. First, right-click on Logins in Enterprise Manager, and select New Login. You will be presented with the SQL Server Login dialog box below:

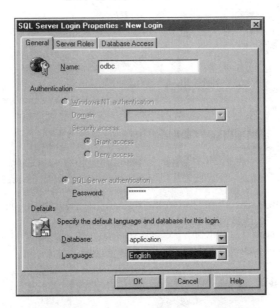

We can choose to authenticate our new user through Integrated Windows Authentication, or through SQL Server authentication. In this case, we want a SQL Server account, so I've gone for the latter option. As you can see, I have entered the account name odbc, given a password, selected the default database for this user, and also the default language. There are a few stock **Server Roles** that you can add users to. These can be seen simply by clicking the Server Roles tab. Unless you want this user to have special database access gearing towards administrative tasks, you would not want to add this user to any of those roles. This should never be done for configuring an account for an ASP web site or web application.

Granting Database Access

With the SQL Server Logins dialog box still open, you will need to grant access to a database, or to multiple databases. For this exercise, we will only grant access to the application database. To do this, simply click the Database Access tab and choose the database that this account will need to access. Once you check the database you want to grant access rights for, you will see that that user will automatically be added to the public role for that database. Any other roles that have been set up in that database will also be displayed. For now, we will just leave our new user in the public role. Finish creating the account by clicking the OK button.

Using Roles to Tighten Security

SQL Server 7.0 allows you to create server roles for each database user or set of users. SQL Server roles exist within a database and cannot extend more than a single database. There are major security advantages of using database roles. Some of the most important of these are:

- ❑ For any user, more than one database role can be active at a time.

- ❑ SQL Server roles can contain Windows NT groups and users, and SQL Server users and other roles providing all users, groups and roles exist in the current database.

- ❑ A user can belong to more than one role in the same database.

- ❑ A scalable model is provided for setting up the right level of security within a database.

Perhaps the most important advantage here is that the right level of security can be set within a database. This will provide us with a secure environment for our ASP database links when the role is tied to a user. Let's examine what security levels we can set for a role.

For tables including the system tables we have the ability to set access to the following:

- ❑ Select
- ❑ Insert
- ❑ Update
- ❑ Delete
- ❑ DRI (declarative referential integrity)

For views, we can set access to the following:

- ❑ Select
- ❑ Insert
- ❑ Update
- ❑ Delete

For stored procedures, we can set access to the following:

- ❑ Execute

Let's get more in depth with this and create a role for the odbc account that we created above. Expand the **Databases** folder and then expand the database that we granted the odbc account access to.

Locate the Roles icon and right-click and select New Database Role. You will then be presented with the Database Role Properties dialog box as shown here.

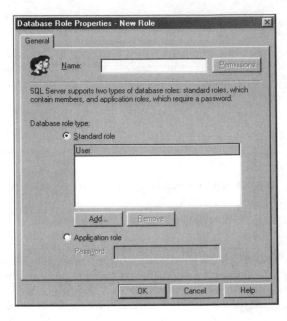

There are two things that we need to do here:

❑ Specify a role name

❑ Add the odbc user to the role

Let's name the role odbclink, and add the odbc account that we created above into this role. We must do this first, before we set any permissions for this role. When you have filled in the name of the role and added the odbc user, click OK. In the right pane you will see that the role has been created. Double-click the odbclink role icon and then click the permissions tab in the upper right-hand corner. The Database Role Properties dialog box will then be displayed. Currently I have created two tables in this database – Logins and Users.

Consider the following scenario:

❑ The Users table is used to store usernames and accounts.

❑ The Logins table is used to track when a user has logged in and stores their IP adddress and Session ID and whether or not the Session is enabled. In an ASP web application, this would allow us to track the user's status.

❑ I will grant SELECT access to the Users table and SELECT, INSERT, and UPDATE access to the Logins table. When configuring permissions for database roles, make sure you give the least degree of access possible. Once you have finished setting access permissions within the role, you can create the ODBC link (or use a native provider in your code) and use the odbc account's username and password that we created, and all of these security settings will be in effect. I would advise setting the role for the login as this simplifies maintenance; otherwise, we would have to set the access rights for each user.

Another possibility to consider is not granting any permissions to the web account, but instead abstracting access via stored procedures and granting `exec` permissions on those procedures. Direct access is disabled altogether and all operations are done with the use of the stored procedures thus any hacker is limited in what damage they can do to using your mechanisms.

Encryption

In this section, we will try to give a brief general overview of encryption with our web sites or web applications. We will discuss Secure Sockets Layer (SSL) and Digital Certificates on the server, otherwise known as Digital IDs. Several books can be written on this subject because of its complex nature, but rather than getting sidetracked into all the needless information surrounding encryption, we will discuss the following:

❑   What is encryption?

❑   How does it work?

❑   What are the benefits of encryption to our users and to us?

What is Encryption?

Encryption, put most simply, is the scrambling of data so that it is no longer human-readable.

When a user comes to a site under normal situations and enters data and submits it, that data transfers across the Internet in an easily accessible form. By using one of the numerous network software packages that knows how to decipher this information you can see the data that has been submitted. An example of one of these software packages would be `netmon.exe` within Windows NT/2000.

We can change the way in which this works by using encryption. You can see this sometimes when you have an `https://` prefix in your browsers address bar instead of the normal `http://` protocol in their browser address bar. This means that the connection with the server is a secure connection.

You should remember that encryption has a small performance cost on the server, but the benefits far outweigh this (minor) cost.

How Does it Work?

When using SSL with Server Digital IDs, data is encrypted using a system commonly known as **Public Key Encryption** or **asymmetric encryption**. This has two main parts that play a role in how the data is encrypted when data is transferred across the Internet. This system uses two keys:

❑   Private Key

❑   Public Key

The public key is used to encrypt the data, but cannot be used to decrypt the data. Only someone who has the private key can decrypt the data. This means that the public key can be given to anyone – in fact they are often published onsite – but only private key holders will be able to read the data.

This process is shown below:

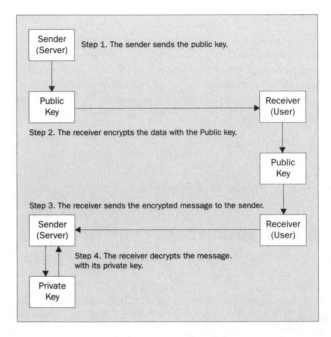

In addition, the owner of the private key can sign content with a "digital signature" which can be verified and which cannot be faked. Taken together, these provide a way of verfiying that you are who you say you are, by signing content and ensuring that the client and the data it sends hasn't been tampered with.

What are the Benefits of Encryption?

Using encryption benefits our users, as well as ourselves, in many ways: E-commerce, for example, is one scenario where I think everyone will realize the benefits of encryption. When a user wants to purchase something on an e-commerce site, they would normally enter their credit card information, so that they can be charged by the supplier. Using SSL during this process benefits users by reassuring them that their credit card information will be safe while the data is in transit. It also benefits us for a number of reasons, including the fact that the consumer is probably aware of the security issues surrounding the Internet and credit card data transfer. Using SSL makes us look good as a company, showing that we are taking the precautions necessary to make the data secure and we don't have to worry about someone intercepting and tampering with this data and charging that person's credit card. If this were to happen and we weren't using SSL, the user would probably know how their credit card information got intercepted. It is of course possible to intercept the data and send a dummy package with false card information, but is unlikely.

As you can imagine, any customer bitten while paying over the Internet is not likely to use your services, or any internet services, ever again.

See Appendix C for more information about certificate services on the server.

Effective ASP Code for Authentication

This section is geared towards the ASP developer and concerns effective code use when thinking about how to authenticate users securely. The previous section discussed encryption with SSL on the web server. These methods can be quite secure without using SSL, but there is no match for the level of security that can be attained with the addition of SSL.

Using global.asa

Many web sites and web applications do not make use of the global.asa file within Active Server Pages. It is largely unclear why this functionality is not taken advantage of. However, there are some general misunderstandings about the effective use of the global.asa file.

What Does the global.asa File Do?

The global.asa file allows us to use global variables and also gives access to use the OnStart and OnEnd events for the Application and Session object. It can never be read, and so can help us to manage state and also provide us with a secure place to initialize database connection strings and other values for later retrieval. You can also create event handlers for your site or application. Let's examine these event handlers in the global.asa file:

❑   Session_OnStart: runs the first time a user runs any page in your application.

❑   Session_OnEnd: runs when a user's session times out or quits your application.

❑   Application_OnStart: runs once when any user runs the first page of your application for the first time.

❑   Application_OnEnd: runs once when the web server shuts down or all sessions have finished.

As you can see, the word 'application' is used in the descriptions for all of the event handlers. The word application refers to the virtual applications within Internet Information Server. These applications are also configured when you specify an alias for a directory within a web site. The global.asa file must be contained in the root directory of the web application, or it will be ignored. Consider this directory structure with two virtual applications contained in the web site. One application is the root directory of the web site and the other is a virtual application on the folder named login. Of course, the virtual applications needs to be set up and configured.

❑ **C:\Inetpub\wwwroot** – Contains the global.asa file containing event handlers for your main web site in the root directory

❑ **C:\Inetpub\wwwroot\login** – Contains the global.asa file containing event handlers for your login virtual application.

How Does global.asa Provide Me with Security?

The global.asa file provides you with security in one main respect: Users cannot request this file from the web server from within a browser. You can take advantage of this by storing your database connection strings, which contain user names and passwords, in the global.asa file and referencing that application variable later on within the application. If a user were to make a request to the web server for the global.asa file from anywhere within a web site, even if a virtual application is not configured and/or directory browsing is allowed, they would receive the following error message:

HTTP/1.1 Requests for GLOBAL.ASA Not Allowed

Remember that NT ACLs for users who have FTP access to the web server need to be configured properly so they cannot download the global.asa file. Be sure not to allow anonymous access to an FTP site that starts in any virtual applications or root directories of web sites, or more simply don't allow FTP access to any directory that contains server-side code that can't be viewed by looking at the source from a web browser.

Storing database connection strings in the global.asa file is a safeguard against having to put usernames, passwords and data source names or other connection details within every ASP file within the web site or web application. This serves as a deterrent to people trying to see the actual code that gets processed by the server. In the past, there was a neat trick to view the source of an ASP file in this way. Microsoft used this as a debugging feature which was a secret until word got out about it, and it became a huge security hole within Internet Information Server/Personal Web Server. If you were to type in the following in a browser:

http://yourwebserver.com/file.asp::$DATA

You would see the source code of the ASP file for the file requested. There is also another occurrence of this with servers that have the showcode.asp file installed on the system, which was also specifically built to help debug ASP code, and which is installed by default. The showcode.asp file should be removed from the system entirely, but as you can see the global.asa file provides a workaround to any of the security loop holes as they are unveiled.

Code Examples

In this section, we'll look at good ASP coding techniques from the security perspective in practice by providing a few small code samples which illustrate some of the points we've been discussing.

Application_OnStart

Let's take a look at what we can do with the `Application_OnStart` event handler to store our database connection string. This example will use the SQL Server database. One point to bear in mind is that the variable is not set individually for each user, but for the whole application: we cannot have a variable with the value 6 for one user and 7 for another. We could place code similar to the following inside our `global.asa` file:

```
<SCRIPT LANGUAGE=VBScript RUNAT=Server>
Sub Application_OnStart
    'Database Connection String
    Application("strConn") = "Data Source=yourserver;" & _
        "Provider=SQLOLEDB;Initial Catalog=database;" & _
        "User ID=user;Password=passsword;"
End Sub
</SCRIPT>
```

Or in JScript:

```
<SCRIPT LANGUAGE=JScript RUNAT=Server>
function Application_OnStart() {
    Application("strConn") = "Data Source=yourserver;" +
        "Provider=SQLOLEDB;Initial Catalog=database;" +
        "User ID=user;Password=passsword;";
}
</SCRIPT>
```

Now, anywhere within this web application we can reference the `Application` `("strConn")` variable within an ASP page. For example:

```
' VBScript
Set Conn = Server.CreateObject("ADODB.Connection")
Conn.Open Application("strConn")
Set rs = Server.CreateObject("ADODB.RecordSet")
strSql = "SELECT * FROM Table_name"     ' Where Table_name is one of
                                        ' the tables in your Database
rs.Open strSql,Conn
```

```
// JScript
Conn = Server.CreateObject("ADODB.Connection");
Conn.Open(Application("strConn"));
rs = Server.CreateObject("ADODB.RecordSet");
strSql = "SELECT * FROM Table_name"     // Where Table_name is one of
                                        // the tables in your Database
rs.Open(strSql,Conn);
```

By utilizing this functionality you don't have to put the usernames, passwords, and connection strings in every ASP file. Suppose we changed any of the connection details, such as the database name or the username or password for the database connection. If we didn't use an application variable, we might need to go into every .asp file and change the username and password.

Application_OnEnd

When the application has ended, we can clear out any application variables that we have defined within the Application_OnStart event handler. For example, let's take the connection string we defined in the global.asa file above and clear it out:

```
Sub Application_OnEnd
    Set Application ("strConn") = Nothing
End Sub
```

Or in JScript:

```
function Application_OnEnd() {
    delete Application("strConn");
}
```

Session_OnStart

Let's take a look at what we can do with the Session_OnStart event handler. One thing to keep in mind is that a session variable set *is* set individually for each user, so, for example, we *can* have a variable with the value 6 for one user and 7 for another. For example, suppose we have a table called logins where we will write a cookie to the client to track how many times a user has come to our site, and we write this information to the database. We will also store the user's IP address in the database and store all of the information about the user's browser. This is just an example to show the use of the Session_OnStart. This could have possible performance issues in a production environment. We could do the following in VBScript:

```
Sub Session_OnStart
    If not(Request.Cookies("Name")("Visited") <> "") Then
        Response.Cookies("Name").Expires = "January 1, 2005"
        Response.Cookies("Name")("Visited") = "1"
        a = 1
    Else
        a = Request.Cookies("Name")("Visited")
        a = a + 1
        Response.Cookies("Name").Expires = "January 1, 2005"
        Response.Cookies("Name")("Visited") = a
    End If

    Set BrowserType = Server.CreateObject("MSWC.BrowserType")

    Set Conn = Server.CreateObject("ADODB.Connection")
    Conn.Open Application("strConn")

    Set rs = Server.CreateObject("ADODB.RecordSet")
    strSql = "SELECT * FROM [Logins]"
    rs.Open strSql, conn

    rs.Addnew
    rs.Fields("IP") = Request.ServerVariables("REMOTE_ADDR")
    rs.Fields("Referring_Site").value = _
        Request.ServerVariables("HTTP_REFERER")
    rs.Fields("Visited").value = Request.Cookies("Name")("Visited")
    rs.Fields("ActiveX").value = CStr(BrowserType.ActiveX)
    rs.Fields("Backgroundsounds").value = _
        CStr(BrowserType.Backgroundsounds)
    rs.Fields("Beta").value = CStr(BrowserType.Beta)
    rs.Fields("Cookies").value = CStr(BrowserType.Cookies)
    rs.Fields("Frames").value = CStr(BrowserType.Frames)
```

```
      rs.Fields("Javaapplets").value = CStr(BrowserType.Javaapplets)
      rs.Fields("Javascript").value = CStr(BrowserType.Javascript)
      rs.Fields("Majorver") = BrowserType.Majorver
      rs.Fields("Minorver") = BrowserType.Minorver
      rs.Fields("Parent") = BrowserType.Parent
      rs.Fields("Platform")= Request.ServerVariables("HTTP_USER_AGENT")
      rs.Fields("Tables").value = CStr(BrowserType.Tables)
      rs.Fields("Vbscript").value = CStr(BrowserType.Vbscript)
      rs.Fields("Version") = BrowserType.Version
      rs.Update
      rs.close
      conn.close
End Sub
```

Or in JScript:

```
function Session_OnStart() {
    if (Request.Cookies("Name")("Visited") != null) {
        Response.Cookies("Name").Expires = "January 1, 2005";
        Response.Cookies("Name")("Visited") = "1";
        a = 1;
    } else {
        a = Request.Cookies("Name")("Visited");
        a += 1;
        Response.Cookies("Name").Expires = "January 1, 2005";
        Response.Cookies("Name")("Visited") = a;
    }

    BrowserType = Server.CreateObject("MSWC.BrowserType");

    Conn = Server.CreateObject("ADODB.Connection");
    Conn.Open(Application("strConn"));

    rs = Server.CreateObject("ADODB.RecordSet");
    strSql = "SELECT * FROM [Logins]";
    rs.Open(strSql, Conn);

    rs.Addnew();
    rs.Fields("IP").value = Request.ServerVariables("REMOTE_ADDR");
    rs.Fields("Referring_Site").value =
        Request.ServerVariables("HTTP_REFERER");
    rs.Fields("Visited").value = Request.Cookies("Name")("Visited");
    rs.Fields("ActiveX").value = String(BrowserType.ActiveX);
    rs.Fields("Backgroundsounds").value =
        String(BrowserType.Backgroundsounds);
    rs.Fields("Beta").value = String(BrowserType.Beta);
    rs.Fields("Cookies").value = String(BrowserType.Cookies);
    rs.Fields("Frames").value = String(BrowserType.Frames);
    rs.Fields("Javaapplets").value = String(BrowserType.Javaapplets);
    rs.Fields("Javascript").value = String(BrowserType.Javascript);
    rs.Fields("Majorver") = BrowserType.Majorver;
    rs.Fields("Minorver") = BrowserType.Minorver;
    rs.Fields("Parent") = BrowserType.Parent;
    rs.Fields("Platform")= Request.ServerVariables("HTTP_USER_AGENT");
    rs.Fields("Tables").value = String(BrowserType.Tables);
    rs.Fields("Vbscript").value = String(BrowserType.Vbscript);
    rs.Fields("Version") = BrowserType.Version;
    rs.Update();
    rs.close();
    Conn.close();
}
```

Session_OnEnd

Finally, let's take a look at what we can do with the `Session_OnEnd` event handler. We can, for example, keep a log of sessions being ended. This doesn't really serve much purpose, because all sessions will eventually end. The default session timeout value is 20 minutes. But just to show how we use this event, we will create a log into a table of a session ending and when it ended:

```
Sub Session_OnEnd

    Set Conn = Server.CreateObject("ADODB.Connection")
    Conn.Open Application("strConn")

    Set rs = Server.CreateObject("ADODB.RecordSet")
    strSql = "SELECT * FROM [Logins]"
    rs.Open strSql, Conn
    rs.AddNew
    rs.Fields("State") = "Session Ended"
    rs.Fields("Date") = Now()
    rs.Update
    rs.Close
    Conn.Close
End Sub
```

Or in JScript:

```
function Session_OnEnd() {

    Conn = Server.CreateObject("ADODB.Connection");
    Conn.Open(Application("strConn"));

    rs = Server.CreateObject("ADODB.RecordSet");
    strSql = "SELECT * FROM [Logins]";
    rs.Open(strSql, Conn);
    rs.AddNew();
    rs.Fields("State") = "Session Ended";
    rs.Fields("Date") = Date();
    rs.Update();
    rs.Close();
    Conn.Close();
}
```

Using the Session Object

There are a few things we can do with sessions regarding authentication. For instance, we can keep track of the username and password of a user. Remember that the user's browser needs to be configured to accept cookies in order for these to work. The cookie will not actually be written to the client's `Temporary Internet Files` folder, but stays resident in memory for the length of the Session Timeout Value set either on the server or through code using the `Session.Timeout` method. For an example we will use SQL logins for each user when they login, and then set their username and password values equal to two session variables after they login, and use those sessions for all our database connection strings. Our first page will be `Index.htm`, a basic login screen that will post to `logincheck.asp`, which will attempt to connect to the database server with the user's credentials as the `User ID` and `Password` fields in our connection string. Then, if the login is successful, we will set two sessions to hold these values.

Index.htm

```html
<HTML>
<BODY>
<FORM NAME="login" METHOD="POST" ACTION="logincheck.asp">
<CENTER>
<BR>
    <TABLE BORDER="0">
        <TR>
            <TD>
                User Name:
            </TD>
            <TD>
                <input type="text" name="USR" value="">
            </TD>
        </TR>
        <TR>
            <TD>
                Password:
            </TD>
            <TD>
                <INPUT TYPE="PASSWORD" NAME="PWD" VALUE="">
            </TD>
        </TR>
    </TABLE>
    <INPUT TYPE="SUBMIT" VALUE="Login">
</CENTER>
</BODY>
</HTML>
```

logincheck.asp

```asp
<%
On Error Resume Next
If Request.Form("USR") <> "" AND Request.Form("PWD") <> "" Then
    Set Conn = Server.CreateObject("ADODB.Connection")
    strConn = "Provider=SQLOLEDB; Data Source=server" & _
              "Initial Catalog=database;User ID=user;" & _
              "Passsword=password;"
    Conn.Open strConn

    If err.number = 0  Then
        Session("USR") = Request.Form("USR")
        Session("PWD") = Request.Form("PWD")
        Conn.close
        Response.Redirect "main.asp"
    Else
        ' Couldn't open connection, or other error occurred
        If Conn.State = 1 Then    ' 1 = adStateOpen
            Conn.Close
        End If
        Response.Write "Sorry, we cannot verify your details."
    End If
Else
    Response.Redirect "index.htm"
End IF
%>
```

Or the equivalent in JScript:

```
<%
if (String(Request.Form("USR")) != "undefined" &
    String(Request.Form("PWD")) != "undefined") {
    try {
        Conn = Server.CreateObject("ADODB.Connection")
        strConn = "Provider=SQLOLEDB; Data Source=server" +
                  "Initial Catalog=database;User ID=user;" +
                  "Passsword=password;";
        Conn.Open(strConn);
        Session("USR") = Request.Form("USR");
        Session("PWD") = Request.Form("PWD");
        Conn.close();
        Response.Redirect("main.asp");
    }
    catch(e) {
        // Couldn't open connection, or other error occurred
        if (Conn.State == 1) {    // 1 = adStateOpen
            Conn.Close();
        }
        Response.Write("Sorry, we cannot verify your details.");
    }
} else {
    Response.Redirect("index.htm");
}
%>
```

Then, in all of the rest of our files, we can use the `Session("USR")` and `Session("PWD")` variables as our connection string criteria. In this example, the `logincheck.asp` will redirect to `main.asp`:

```
<% ' VBScript
Set Conn = Server.CreateObject("ADODB.Connection")
strConn = "Provider=SQLOLEDB; Data Source=server; " & _
          "Initial Catalog=database;User ID=" & Session("USR") & _
          ";Password=" & Session("PWD")
Conn.Open(strConn)
%>
```

```
<% // JScript
Conn = Server.CreateObject("ADODB.Connection");
strConn = "Provider=SQLOLEDB; Data Source=server; " +
          "Initial Catalog=database;User ID=" + Session("USR") +
          ";Password=" + Session("PWD");
Conn.Open(strConn);
%>
```

Using Cookies

We can use cookies to set values to be stored on the client machine that we can retrieve on a later visit or during the user's stay on the web site. This works only if the user accepts the cookie and does not delete it after leaving our site. We can specify how long the cookie is valid for on the client's machine with an expiration date. When the expiration date has passed, the cookie will disappear off of the user's machine. Cookies can be useful for tracking things such as how many times a user has been to our site. Also, we can use them to pre-populate forms on our web sites leaving less data entry for users the next time they encounter a form that requires them to enter data. We will use the same example as above, but instead use cookies. This example should use SSL because the username and password information are transferred over the Internet.

Index.htm

```
<HTML>
<BODY>
<FORM NAME="login" METHOD="POST" ACTION="logincheck.asp">
<CENTER>
<BR>
    <TABLE BORDER="0">
        <TR>
            <TD>
                User Name:
            </TD>
            <TD>
                <INPUT TYPE="TEXT" NAME="USR" VALUE="">
            </TD>
        </TR>
        <TR>
            <TD>
                Password:
            </TD>
            <TD>
                <INPUT TYPE="PASSWORD" NAME="PWD" VALUE="">
            </TD>
        </TR>
    </TABLE>
    <INPUT TYPE="SUBMIT" VALUE="Login">
</CENTER>
</BODY>
</HTML>
```

logincheck.asp

```
<%
' VBScript
On Error Resume Next
If Request.Form("USR") <> "" AND Request.Form("PWD") <> "" Then
    Set Conn = Server.CreateObject("ADODB.Connection")
    strConn = "Provider=SQLOLEDB;Data Source=server;" & _
              "Initial Catalog=database;User ID=" & _
              Request.Form("USR") & ";Password=" & Request.Form("PWD")
    Conn.Open strConn

    If err.number = 0  Then
        ' Couldn't open connection, or other error occurred
        Response.Cookies("APP")("USR") = Request.Form("USR")
        Response.Cookies("APP")("PWD") = Request.Form("PWD")
        Conn.close
        Response.Redirect "main.asp"
    Else

        If Conn.State = 1 Then
            Conn.Close
        End If
        Response.Write "Sorry, we cannot verify your details." & _
                       "</BODY></HTML>"
    End If
Else
    Response.Redirect "index.htm"
End IF
%>
```

Or in JScript:

```
<%
if (String(Request.Form("USR")) != "undefined" &
if  String(Request.Form("PWD")) != "undefined") {

    try {
        Conn = Server.CreateObject("ADODB.Connection")
        strConn = "Provider=SQLOLEDB; Data Source=server" +
                  "Initial Catalog=database;User ID=user;" +
                  "Passsword=password;";
        Conn.Open(strConn);
        Response.Cookies("APP")("USR") = Request.Form("USR");
        Response.Cookies("APP")("PWD") = Request.Form("PWD");
        Conn.close();
        Response.Redirect("main.asp");
    }
    catch(e) {
        // Couldn't open connection, or other error occurred
        if (Conn.State == 1) {
            Conn.Close();
        }
        Response.Write("Sorry, we cannot verify your details.");
    }
} else {
    Response.Redirect("index.htm");
}
%>
```

Now we can use `Request.Cookies("APP")("USR")` and
`Request.Cookies("APP")("PWD")` in the rest of our pages as our connection
string criteria. In this example the `logincheck.asp` redirects to `main.asp`.

And in `main.asp`, or any other file that requires a database connection, we can
connect to the database as follows:

```
<%
' VBScript
Set Conn = Server.CreateObject("ADODB.Connection")
strConn = "Provider=SQLOLEDB;Data Source=server;" & _
          "Initial Catalog=database;User ID=" & _
          Request.Cookies("APP")("USR") & ";Password=" & _
          Request.Cookies("APP")("PWD")
Conn.Open(strConn)
%>
```

```
<%
// JScript
Conn = Server.CreateObject("ADODB.Connection");
strConn = "Provider=SQLOLEDB;Data Source=server;" +
          "Initial Catalog=database;User ID=" +
          Request.Cookies("APP")("USR") + ";Password=" +
          Request.Cookies("APP")("PWD");
Conn.Open(strConn);
%>
```

Summary

Within Active Server Pages there are far more opportunities for security mishaps to occur than in static HTML pages. The basics of server setup/security, Internet Information Server setup/security, SQL 7.0 setup/security, Encryption, and Effective ASP Authentication Code have all been covered in this chapter.

The beauty of ASP is the functionality it allows with interfacing our web sites and web applications with a database. Although this technology is a great boon for internet applications, it also raises huge potential security problems. The simple reason is that this technology involves a great deal of functionality with many applications working together as a whole. Special attention needs to be given to each component, to ensure that we have a fully functional secure web site or application. These checklists were designed for just that and the scope of this chapter was designed to cover the most basic configurations that are the most popular with Active Server Page developers. Following these checklists will help deter attacks on your systems and prevent security breaches, which are most often due to misconfiguration.

Miscellaneous Reference

P2P.WROX.COM and Customer Support

We've tried to make this book as accurate and enjoyable as possible, but what really matters is what the book actually does for you.

All the source code for all the examples in this book is available for download at the Wrox Press Web site at www.wrox.com or at webdev.wrox.co.uk. You'll find more information about COM at a related Web site, www.comdeveloper.com.

We've made every effort to make sure that there are no errors in the text or the code. However, to err is human and as such we recognize the need to keep you informed of any mistakes as they're spotted and corrected. Errata sheets are available for all our books at www.wrox.com. If you find an error that hasn't already been reported, please let us know.

Our Web site acts as a focus for other information and support, including the code from all our books, sample chapters, previews of forthcoming titles, and articles and opinion on related topics.

This book also benefits from a totally comprehensive and unique customer support system. Wrox is committed to supporting you not just while you read the book, but once you start developing applications as well.

Please let us know your views, either by returning the reply card in the back of the book, or by contacting us via e-mail at feedback@wrox.com.

P2P.WROX.COM

Join the ASP 3.0 Programmer's Reference mailing lists for author and peer support. Our unique system provides **programmer to programmer™ support** on mailing lists, forums and newsgroups all in addition to our one-to-one email system. Be confident that your query is not just being examined by a support professional, but by the many Wrox authors and other industry experts present on our mailing lists.

We've extended our commitment to support beyond just while you read the book. We'll be there on this crucial second step of your learning as you develop applications. You have the choice of how to receive this information: you can either enroll onto one of several mailing lists, or you can just browse the online forums and newsgroups for an answer. Go to p2p.wrox.com. You'll find six different lists, each tailored to a specific subject area:

- **How To?**
  This is your first port of call if you encounter a problem with the book. If you think there's an error in the book, something you think the book should have talked about, something you'd just like to know more about, or a completely baffling problem with no solution, then this is your forum. If you're developing an application at work then chances are there's someone out there who's already done the same as you, and has a solution to your problem here.

- **Code Clinic**
  You've read the book, and you're sat at home, or work, developing your own application, but it doesn't work in the way you think it should: post your code here for advice and support from our authors and from people in the same position as yourself.

- **Beginning ASP**
  If you're a novice or newbie, then don't worry as friendly advice is at hand. Rather than offer jargonistic explanations, you'll find a sympathetic approach on this list. You'll also be joined by a lot of people in the same boat as you. This list is more heavily moderated to make sure that questions that can stop you dead in your tracks at an early stage of learning are answered quickly.

- **ASP Databases**
  Heavily moderated list containing only queries dealing with ASP and Databases. Discussion of ADO, ODBC, OLE-DB, integration of ASP with Access, SQL Server, Oracle, Informix or various legacy databases can all be discussed here. Off topic queries will be directed to either Beginning ASP or How To?

- **ASP CDO**
  Heavily moderated list containing only queries dealing with ASP and e-mail integration. Discussion of CDO, CDONTS, SMTP and Exchange are all fair game. Also difficulties with logging on to e-mail accounts will be supported here. Off topic queries will be directed to either Beginning ASP or How To?

- **ASP ECommerce**
  Heavily moderated list containing only queries dealing with E-Commerce and ASP. This book deals with queries about E-Commerce concerning personalization, security, creation of shopping baskets and specific queries relating to Wrox's Beginning E-Commerce book. Off topic queries will be directed to either the Beginning ASP or How To? lists.

How To Enroll For Support

Just follow this four-step system:

1. Go to p2p.wrox.com.

2. Click on the **ASP** button.

3. Click on the type of mailing list you wish to join.

4. Fill in your e-mail address and password (of at least 4 digits) and e-mail it to us.

Why This System Offers the Best Support

You can choose to join the mailing lists or you can receive them as a weekly digest. If you don't have the time or facility to receive the mailing list, then you can search our online archives. You'll find the ability to search on specific subject areas or keywords. As these lists are moderated, you can be confident of finding good, accurate information quickly. Mails can be edited or moved by the moderator into the correct place, making this a most efficient resource. Junk and spam mail are deleted, and your own e-mail address is protected by the unique Lyris system from web-bots that can automatically hoover up newsgroup mailing list addresses. Any queries about joining, leaving lists or any query about the list should be sent to: moderatorasp3progref@wrox.com.

Wrox also continues to provide our one-to-one email system using support.wrox.com. If you have a query about the book you can send an e-mail to this address. Please include the book ISBN and relevent page number.

ASP Resources

Wrox Press provides three sites that contain useful information for ASP and web developers in general:

- ❑ **The Wrox Web Developer Site** (http://webdev.wrox.co.uk/)
  The main site for sample code for all the web-developer books we publish. Run the samples on-line or download code to run on your own server. Also contains chapters and extracts from our books, industry news, and a series of useful reference tools and other resources.

- ❑ **The Wrox P2P.Wrox.com** (http://p2p.wrox.co.uk/)
  This is our support site. See Appendix A for more information.

- ❑ **ASPToday** (http://www.asptoday.com/)
  Read focused and useful articles on ASP and other web programming techniques from a range of experts and industry gurus. A new article is available every day of the week, and you can search the archives for previous ones.

Finding ASP-friendly ISPs

ASP runs on Microsoft Windows servers, while the majority of ISPs still use Unix-based systems or an equivalent. While there are ASP clones that run on Unix or Linux, many people want to use the full spectrum of ASP functions (such as COM components and Windows services) on their sites. This tends to rule out many traditional ISPs.

Two or three years ago, it was very difficult to find an ISP that used Windows NT servers, and would allow you to install your own components or make use of Windows services in your Web applications. Thankfully, the situation is changing fast, and there are now hundreds of ISPs that do support ASP in full on Windows NT servers (predominantly Windows NT 4 at the time of writing, but no doubt this will change fairly quickly as Windows 2000 proves itself) – just check that they allow you to install your *own* components before you sign up.

A search on **InfoSeek** (http://www.infoseek.com/) for ASP-enabled Windows NT based ISPs (using the criteria '+asp +Web +hosting') returned 390 matches. Many of these offer ASP on Windows NT Server, plus support for applications such as SQL Server and others. Some of the sites found (at the time of writing) were:

Active Server (http://www.active-server.com/)
DataReturn (http://www.datareturn.com/)
IMC Online (http://www.imconline.net/)
Intermedia (http://www.intermedia.net/)
SiteCrafters Internet Services (http://www.sitecrafters.com/)
Softcom (http://www.softcomca.com)
Technocom plc (http://www.technocom.net/)
Virtualscape (http://www.virtualscape.com/)

There are also sites that allow you to search for ISPs based of a whole range of criteria, such as **Action Jackson** (http://www.actionjackson.com/hosts) and **Top Hosts** (http://www.tophosts.com).

Other ASP Web Sites

There are also many other sites that provide ASP, or general web-oriented information, for developers. This is just a selection of some of those we know of:

15 Seconds Free Resources Center (http://www.15seconds.com/)
Free resource for developers working with Microsoft Internet Solutions. 15 Seconds proclaims to be the biggest IIS and ASP development resource in the world, with over 2300 pages.

ActionJackson Web Developer Central (http://www.actionjackson.com)
A comprehensive resource of news, articles, books and links, including discussion forums, components, IIS hosts, jobs and much more.

Active Server Pages Resources Site (http://www.activeserverpages.com/)
This site specializes in Active Server Pages programming issues. Maintained by Charles Carroll, it contains online programming tutorials, references, and links to a wide range of resources and articles.

ASP 101 Resources Site (http://www.asp101.com/)
The purpose of this site is to provide both expert and novice developers with useful and timely information on the emerging technology of Active Server Pages.

ASP Forums (http://www.aspforums.com/)
This site provides a range of forums and discussion groups for ASP related topics, plus lists of related companies and their software designed for use with ASP.

ASP Hole IIS and ASP Guide (http://www.asphole.com/)
Intended to help the Active Server Pages professional locate ASP-related and IIS-related resources quickly and efficiently. A huge range of various resources is available.

ASP Toolbox (http://www.tcp-ip.com/)
Here you'll find a range of tutorials and other ASP-related information to help in
developing your dynamic web sites.

The ASP Resource Index (http://www.aspin.com/)
Find all the Active Server Pages (ASP) Resources you need in one place. Contains a
comprehensive list of ASP components, applications, code snippets, references, and
books.

ASPWatch (http://www.aspwatch.com/)
Provides real world Active Server Pages solutions and resources. This includes articles,
discussions and book lists.

Haneng (http://www.haneng.com/)
Provides content that is free to be used commercially and non-commercially.
Dedicated to ASP technology and created and maintained by Alexander Haneng on a
hobby basis.

JavaScript Source (http://javascript.internet.com/)
An excellent JavaScript resource with tons of cut & paste JavaScript examples for your
web pages. All for free!

Microsoft's NT Server and BackOffice Site
(http://www.microsoft.com/backoffice/)
This site is the main page for the Microsoft BackOffice products, including NT Server,
SQL Server, Exchange, and other components.

PowerASP Active Server Pages (http://powerasp.com/)
This site offers code snippets, hints & tips, a discussion board, a chat room and
newsletters – all related to ASP and general Web development topics.

Ultimate ASP (http://www.ultimateasp.com/)
An ever-expanding wealth of information for building dynamic web pages, including
help for beginners.

Website Abstraction (http://www.wsabstract.com/)
This site is a webmaster's learning center featuring tutorials on all aspects of JavaScript
and web site construction. It has been featured in many prestigious sources such as the
LA Times and Vancouver Province newspapers.

World Wide Web Consortium (http://www.w3.org/)
The home of the Web. W3C is the main body that sets and agrees the standards for
HTML and web-related technologies.

Wynkoop BackOffice Pages (http://www.swynk.com/)
Maintained by Steve Wynkoop, this site covers all Microsoft BackOffice technologies.
Ideal for those who want to combine ASP and corporate databases.

ASP Resources

Certificates and Certificate Services

Digital certificates can be used for user authentication and secure communication over the Web. The following text outlines the theory of the encryption techniques used in digital certificates, and discusses how they can be used in Windows 2000 and IIS. It also shows you how the new Microsoft **Certificate Services** can be used to create self-issued certificates. These are extremely useful if all you require is a simple and secure communication link for your site, or when you are just experimenting with these new technologies.

A Simple Guide To Encryption

There are two basic techniques for encrypting information: **symmetric encryption** (usually called *secret key* encryption) and **asymmetric encryption** (usually called *public key* encryption). We've chosen the names symmetric and asymmetric encryption because they are less confusing than 'secret key' and 'public key' encryption – ultimately both methods use a 'secret' key.

Symmetric Encryption

Symmetric encryption is the oldest and best-known technique, based on the one you used at school to encode your love letters or 'secret gang' messages. A secret key, which can be a number, a word, or just a string of random letters, is applied to the text of a message so as to change the content in a particular way. It might be as simple as shifting each letter along by a number of places in the alphabet. As long as both sender and recipient know the secret key, they can encrypt and decrypt all messages that use this key.

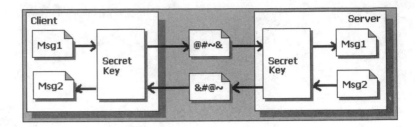

Asymmetric Encryption

The problem with secret keys is: how do you exchange them over the Internet or a large network while preventing them from falling into the wrong hands? Anyone who knows the secret key can decrypt the messages. The answer is asymmetric encryption, where there are two related keys – a key pair. The **public key** is made freely available to anyone who might want to send you a message. The second **private key** is kept secret, so that *only* you know it.

The way it works is that any message (text, binary files, documents, etc.) encrypted using the **public** key can only be decrypted by applying the same algorithm to it, but using the matching **private** key. Vice versa, any message encrypted using the **private** key can only be decrypted using the matching **public** key.

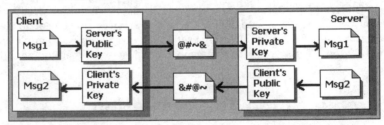

This means that you don't have to worry about passing public keys over the Internet – after all they're supposed to be public. The one problem with asymmetric encryption, however, is that it's quite slow compared to symmetric encryption, because it requires far more processing power to both encrypt and decrypt the content of the message.

About Digital Certificates

In order to use asymmetric encryption, there has to be a way for users to discover each other's public keys. The usual technique is the use of **digital certificates**. A certificate is simply a package of information that identifies a user or a server, containing things like the organization name, the organization that issued the certificate, the user's e-mail address, country, and of course their public key.

When a server and client require a secure encrypted communication, they send a query over the network to the other party, who sends back a copy of their certificate. The other party's public key can then be extracted from the certificate and used to encode the message. However, certificates can do more than this. Here we come back to authentication, because a certificate can also be used to uniquely identify the holder.

Certificate Authorities

Recognized and trusted organizations, called **Certificate Authorities** (CAs), issue certificates to individuals and corporations. These certificates contain not only details about the holder and their public key, but also the public key of the CA. As reputable CAs apply rigorous checks to see that applicants actually are who they claim to be (using tax and business registers, etc.) you are deemed to be able to trust the information in certificates they issue to be accurate. They also make available (through their Web site) their own **public** key certificate – this is their **root certificate**.

Many browsers come with the popular CA root certificates already installed. To see them in IE5, for example, open the Tools | Internet Options dialog, select the Content page, and click the Certificates button:

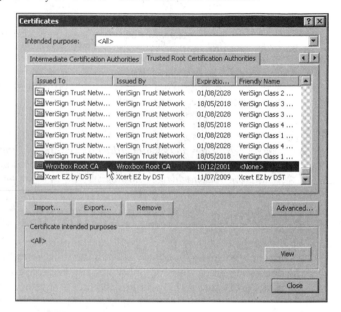

Before issuing a user with their own personal certificate, the CA digitally 'signs' it using their (the CA's) **private** key. This means that if you can decrypt this signature using the CA's **public** key, you know that it's a 'real' valid certificate from that CA.

Verifying Certificates

So one party can provide the other with their certificate, and at the same time send them an extract of it that is encrypted with that party's **private** key. This extract is usually called the **message digest**. The recipient can then check that the sender is who they claim to be by decrypting the message digest using the **public** key in the certificate, and seeing if the results agree with the certificate contents. If they do, the sender must know the private key that matches this certificate, and so they must be the legitimate holder of the certificate. All this usually happens behind the scenes automatically, but if you want to work with certificates you need to know at least the main principles.

> *Of course this all falls apart if the real holder of the certificate has allowed someone else to discover their private key, and it indicates how important it is to keep your own private keys safe. For a detailed explanation of the principles of digital certificates, check out the Tutorials available at*
> http://www.verisign.com/repository/index.html.

Using Digital Certificates

So, one way of easily adding security to web sites or web applications is to use certificates in our communication with clients. They provide two secure features:

❑ We can use digital certificates to authenticate visitors and to allow them to authenticate our server – so that both sides are convinced that they actually are connected to who they think they are.

❑ We can also use digital certificates to encrypt the communication, by using the other party's public keys that they contain. However, as we mentioned earlier, asymmetric (public key) encryption is slow. Instead, we use a combination of encryption methods to make it all work much more quickly.

The process of setting up a digital certificate on your server is quite complex, and is not covered in detail here. For more information check out the Help files for IIS and Certificate Services (http://loalhost/iishelp/).

> *Server certificates and client certificates are fundamentally the same. IIS can use the certificates that are stored in the browser that is installed on the server. This is one reason why you must have IE installed on your server.*

Windows 2000 Certificate Services

You've seen here how we can provide authentication and encryption by using digital certificates. Normally, to obtain a certificate, you would visit a CA's Web site and fill in the details required. However, now you can issue your own digital certificates using the new **Certificate Services** application that is supplied with Windows 2000 Server.

You can use Certificate Services to create a certificate hierarchy based on a CA's root certificate. However, you can also use it to create your own root certificate, and use Certificate Services to automatically generate and distribute client certificates to your visitors. This is the option we've chosen to demonstrate Certificate Services in action. The problem is that, because your certificates are rooted outside a widely-renown CA, visitors will get a warning in their browser that the certificate is not from a known issuer.

Whether this really is a problem depends on what you are using the certificates for. They will still provide secure communication across the network using encryption, and so are useful for Intranet and Extranet applications, even if you decide against using them on the Web as a whole.

> *If you are planning to set up your own CA using Certificate Services, remember that it's the CA itself that people have to trust and respect, not just the certificates. If the CA is unknown or cannot be trusted, the certificates it issues are worthless for the purpose of reliably identifying users.*

Installing Root Certificates

When you install Certificate Services, it prompts for the details of your company and automatically generates your enterprise's root certificate. You can then create client and server certificates by applying for them via a special Web page that is supplied with Certificate Services. You can also use the Certificate Services Web pages to install your root certificate on other machines (which you'll need to do if users are to be able to verify your client and server certificates), and to monitor requests for client certificates from users.

The main menu page is available through a mapped virtual root that the setup program creates, named /CertSrv, so you can open it using http://*servername*/certsrv/:

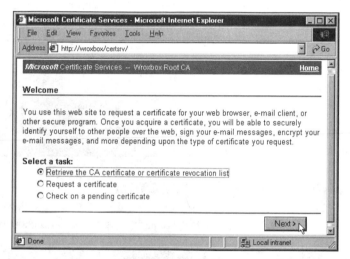

The first step is to retrieve the CA's root certificate, as shown above. The next page shows the certificates that are available from our Certificate Services machine:

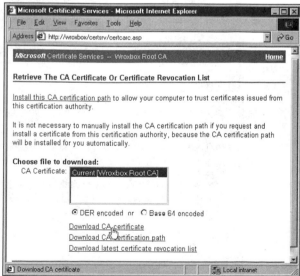

Selecting Download CA
Certificate opens the normal
'file download' dialog, and
here you should click 'Open'
rather than 'Save to disk'. The
downloaded certificate is
then displayed and you can
install it by clicking the Install
Certificate button:

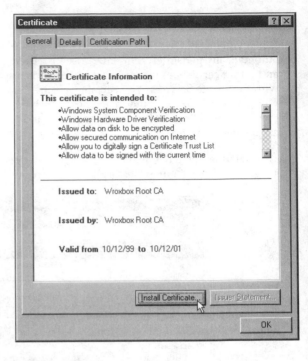

Delivering Client Certificates

The next step is for the user to apply for a client certificate. This is also done from the
/CertSrv menu page. This time, select 'Request a certificate' and click Next:

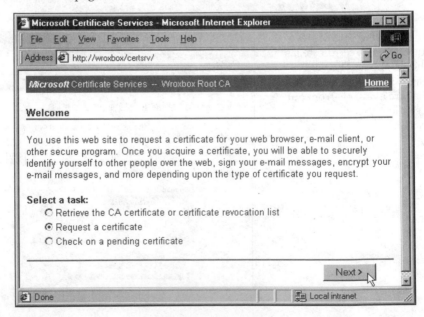

The next page allows you to select the type of certificate you require. For SSL use, this is a Web Browser Certificate:

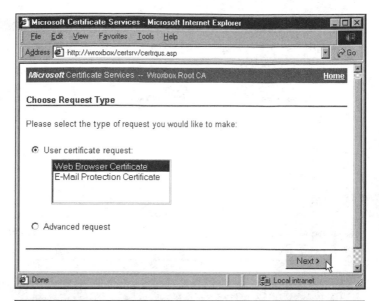

Clicking Next opens the page where you provide the information for the certificate. The More Options button can be used to tailor the request type for different CA's, but the default options are sufficient for Microsoft Certificate Services:

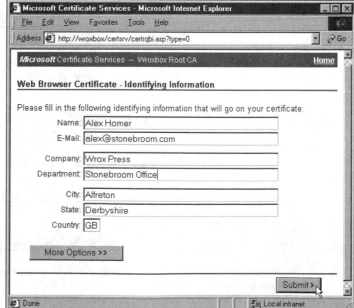

When the Submit button is clicked, the browser builds the certificate request and sends it to the server's Certificate Services application for processing. The browser provides instructions on how to return to collect the certificate once the CA has **issued** it (that is, has processed the request and granted a certificate):

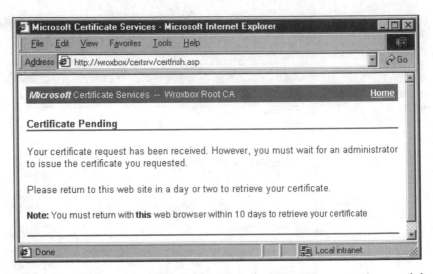

You can leave the browser open, as we'll issue the certificate now ourselves, and then install it in the browser.

Granting and Issuing Certificates

The client certificate request is received and stored on the server, and can be viewed and managed through the Certificate Services manager. Select Programs | Administrative Tools | Certification Authority from your server's Start menu to open the Certification Authority snap-in to the MMC:

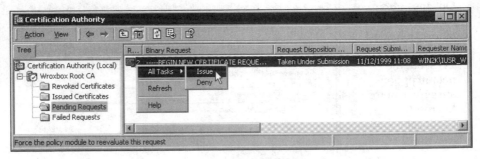

Here, the certificate request can be viewed (in the Pending Requests list). To grant and issue the certificate, simply right-click and select All Tasks | Issue, as shown above. The certificate is issued, and it appears in the Issued Certificates list. The certificate request is then deleted.

Now the user can collect the certificate using their browser. Click the Home link to go back the default /CertSrv page, and select 'Check on a pending certificate':

You should get a page that allows you to install the new client certificate into your browser:

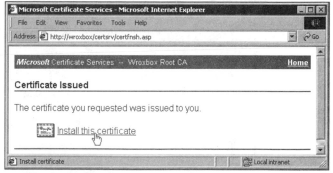

After doing so, the certificate can be viewed in the browser using the **Certificates** dialog (available from the **Content** page of the **Internet Options** dialog):

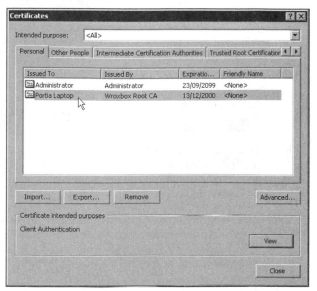

Obtaining and Installing Server Certificates in IIS

Server certificates are similar to client certificates, but are installed on the server so that IIS can use them to prove the server's identity to the browser; the public key they contain is then used by the browser to create the symmetric encryption key that will be used throughout this session. We'll use Microsoft Certificate Services to obtain a server certificate.

To apply for and install a server certificate for a Web site, or for a single virtual application within a site, we use the Internet Services Manager snap-in to the MMC. Open the Properties dialog for the Web site or virtual application and, in the Directory Security page, click the Server Certificate button:

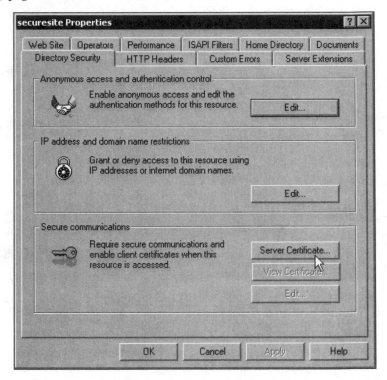

This starts a Wizard that guides you through the process of creating a new certificate, and then installs it into IIS for you. Note that you must request the certificate from a Certification Authority that is **not** on the same machine as this IIS Web server. If they are on the same machine, only offline certificates can be requested.

The Server Certificate Wizard collects the details for your server certificate, including the name and location of the organization and the server, then creates and installs the certificate automatically. Afterwards, you can view the contents of the certificate by clicking the View Certificate button in the Properties dialog of the site or virtual application.

After the certificate has been created and installed, open the Properties dialog again, and in the 'Secure communications' section of the Directory Security page click the Edit button to open the Secure Communications dialog:

'Turn on' SSL and the server certificate by selecting the 'Require secure channel (SSL)' checkbox. Then select the Client certificates option that you need. The last option, 'Require client certificates', will force the browser to send its client certificate so that you can verify who the user is. If you only need to provide secure communications for, say, accepting credit card numbers or personal details, you can select the 'Ignore client certificates' or 'Accept client certificates' option instead.

Certificate Issuing Policies

For the certificates you issue yourself via Certificate Services to be of any value, you'll want to confirm the details about users who request certificates before you issue them. By default, as you've just seen, Certificate Services simply waits for you to accept the request and issue each certificate using the Certification Authority application (unless you are querying the Enterprise root CA service). This is useful while you set up and test the system, or where you just need to implement secure (SSL) communication without authenticating visitors (through client certificates) and without mapping them to a Windows 2000 account.

However, you can configure Certificate Server to do more detailed checking of requests; detailed control of certificate issuing can be achieved by creating **custom policy modules** as COM components in VB or C++, and installing them into Certificate Services. For more information see the Writing Custom Policy Modules section in the Security | Certificate Services | Using Certificate Services section of the Windows 2000 Platform SDK.

D

ADO Constants

Standard Constants

The following constants are predefined by ADO. You can either include the .inc file, or set a reference to the type library with a METADATA tag:

```
<!-- METADATA TYPE="typelib" FILE="C:\Program Files\Common Files
                                      \System\ADO\msado15.dll" -->
```

AffectEnum

Name	Value	Description
adAffectAll	3	Operation affects all records in the recordset.
adAffectAllChapters	4	Operation affects all child (chapter) records.
adAffectCurrent	1	Operation affects only the current record.
adAffectGroup	2	Operation affects records that satisfy the current Filter property.

BookmarkEnum

Name	Value	Description
adBookmarkCurrent	0	Default. Start at the current record.
adBookmarkFirst	1	Start at the first record.
adBookmarkLast	2	Start at the last record.

CEResyncEnum

Name	Value	Description
adResyncAll	15	Resynchronizes the data for each pending row.
adResyncAutoIncrement	1	Resynchronizes the auto-increment values for all successfully inserted rows. This is the default.
adResyncConflicts	2	Resynchronizes all rows for which an update or delete operation failed due to concurrency conflicts.
adResyncInserts	8	Resynchronizes all successfully inserted rows, including the values of their identity columns.
adResyncNone	0	No resynchronization is performed.
adResyncUpdates	4	Resynchronizes all successfully updated rows.

CommandTypeEnum

Name	Value	Description
adCmdFile	256	Indicates that the provider should evaluate CommandText as a previously persisted file.
adCmdStoredProc	4	Indicates that the provider should evaluate CommandText as a stored procedure.

Name	Value	Description
adCmdTable	2	Indicates that the provider should generate a SQL query to return all rows from the table named in CommandText.
adCmdTableDirect	512	Indicates that the provider should return all rows from the table named in CommandText.
adCmdText	1	Indicates that the provider should evaluate CommandText as textual definition of a command, such as a SQL statement.
adCmdUnknown	8	Indicates that the type of command in CommandText is unknown.
adCmdUnspecified	-1	The command type is unspecified.

ADO Constants

CompareEnum

Name	Value	Description
adCompareEqual	1	The bookmarks are equal.
adCompareGreaterThan	2	The first bookmark is after the second.
adCompareLessThan	0	The first bookmark is before the second.
adCompareNotComparable	4	The bookmarks cannot be compared.
adCompareNotEqual	3	The bookmarks are not equal and not ordered.

ConnectModeEnum

Name	Value	Description
adModeRead	1	Indicates read-only permissions.
adModeReadWrite	3	Indicates read/write permissions.
adModeRecursive	32	Used in conjunction with the ShareDeny values to propagate sharing restrictions.
adModeShareDenyNone	16	Prevents others from opening connection with any permissions.

Name	Value	Description
adModeShareDenyRead	4	Prevents others from opening connection with read permissions.
adModeShareDenyWrite	8	Prevents others from opening connection with write permissions.
adModeShareExclusive	12	Prevents others from opening connection.
adModeUnknown	0	Default. Indicates that the permissions have not yet been set or cannot be determined.
adModeWrite	2	Indicates write-only permissions.

ConnectOptionEnum

Name	Value	Description
adAsyncConnect	16	Open the connection asynchronously.
adConnectUnspecified	-1	The connection mode is unspecified.

ConnectPromptEnum

Name	Value	Description
adPromptAlways	1	Always prompt for connection information.
adPromptComplete	2	Only prompt if not enough information was supplied.
AdPromptComplete Required	3	Only prompt if not enough information was supplied, but disable any options not directly applicable to the connection.
adPromptNever	4	Default. Never prompt for connection information.

CopyRecordOptionsEnum

Name	Value	Description
adCopyAllowEmulation	4	If the CopyRecord method fails, simulate it using a file download and upload mechanism.

Name	Value	Description
adCopyNonRecursive	2	Copy the current directory, but not sub-directories.
adCopyOverWrite	1	Overwrite the existing file or directory.
adCopyUnspecified	-1	No copy behavior specified.

CursorLocationEnum

Name	Value	Description
adUseClient	3	Use client-side cursors supplied by the local cursor library.
adUseClientBatch	3	Use client-side cursors supplied by the local cursor library.
adUseNone	1	No cursor services are used.
adUseServer	2	Default. Uses data provider driver supplied cursors.

CursorOptionEnum

Name	Value	Description
adAddNew	16778240	You can use the AddNew method to add new records.
adApproxPosition	16384	You can read and set the AbsolutePosition and AbsolutePage properties.
adBookmark	8192	You can use the Bookmark property to access specific records.
adDelete	16779264	You can use the Delete method to delete records.
adFind	524288	You can use the Find method to find records.
adHoldRecords	256	You can retrieve more records or change the next retrieve position without committing all pending changes.
adIndex	8388608	You can use the Index property to set the current index.

ADO Constants

Name	Value	Description
adMovePrevious	512	You can use the MoveFirst, MovePrevious, Move and GetRows methods.
adNotify	262144	The recordset supports Notifications.
adResync	131072	You can update the cursor with the data visible in the underlying database with the Resync method.
adSeek	4194304	You can use the Seek method to find records by an index.
adUpdate	16809984	You can use the Update method to modify existing records.
adUpdateBatch	65536	You can use the UpdateBatch or CancelBatch methods to transfer changes to the provider in groups.

CursorTypeEnum

Name	Value	Description
adOpenDynamic	2	Opens a dynamic type cursor.
adOpenForwardOnly	0	Default. Opens a forward-only type cursor.
adOpenKeyset	1	Opens a keyset type cursor.
adOpenStatic	3	Opens a static type cursor.
adOpenUnspecified	-1	Indicates an unspecified value for cursor type.

DataTypeEnum

Name	Value	Description
adBigInt	20	An 8-byte signed integer.
adBinary	128	A binary value.
adBoolean	11	A Boolean value.
adBSTR	8	A null-terminated character string.
adChapter	136	A chapter type, indicating a child recordset.

Name	Value	Description
adChar	129	A String value.
adCurrency	6	A currency value. An 8-byte signed integer scaled by 10,000, with 4 digits to the right of the decimal point.
adDate	7	A Date value. A Double where the whole part is the number of days since December 30 1899, and the fractional part is a fraction of the day.
adDBDate	133	A date value (yyyymmdd).
adDBFileTime	137	A database file time.
adDBTime	134	A time value (hhmmss).
adDBTimeStamp	135	A date-time stamp (yyyymmddhhmmss plus a fraction in billionths).
adDecimal	14	An exact numeric value with fixed precision and scale.
adDouble	5	A double-precision floating point value.
adEmpty	0	No value was specified.
adError	10	A 32-bit error code.
adFileTime	64	A DOS/Win32 file time. The number of 100 nanosecond intervals since Jan 1 1601.
adGUID	72	A globally unique identifier.
adIDispatch	9	A pointer to an IDispatch interface on an OLE object.
adInteger	3	A 4-byte signed integer.
adIUnknown	13	A pointer to an IUnknown interface on an OLE object.
adLongVarBinary	205	A long binary value.
adLongVarChar	201	A long String value.
adLongVarWChar	203	A long null-terminated string value.
adNumeric	131	An exact numeric value with a fixed precision and scale.

ADO Constants

Name	Value	Description
adPropVariant	138	A variant that is not equivalent to an Automation variant.
adSingle	4	A single-precision floating point value.
adSmallInt	2	A 2-byte signed integer.
adTinyInt	16	A 1-byte signed integer.
adUnsignedBigInt	21	An 8-byte unsigned integer.
adUnsignedInt	19	An 4-byte unsigned integer.
adUnsignedSmallInt	18	An 2-byte unsigned integer.
adUnsignedTinyInt	17	A 1-byte unsigned integer.
adUserDefined	132	A user-defined variable.
adVarBinary	204	A binary value.
adVarChar	200	A String value.
adVariant	12	An Automation Variant.
adVarNumeric	139	A variable width exact numeric, with a signed scale value.
adVarWChar	202	A null-terminated Unicode character string.
adWChar	130	A null-terminated Unicode character string.

EditModeEnum

Name	Value	Description
adEditAdd	2	Indicates that the AddNew method has been invoked and the current record in the buffer is a new record that hasn't been saved to the database.
adEditDelete	4	Indicates that the Delete method has been invoked.
adEditInProgress	1	Indicates that data in the current record has been modified but not saved.
adEditNone	0	Indicates that no editing is in progress.

ErrorValueEnum

Name	Value	Description
adErrProviderFailed	3000	The provider failed to perform the operation.
adErrInvalidArgument	3001	The application is using arguments that are the wrong type, are out of the acceptable range, or are in conflict with one another.
adErrOpeningFile	3002	An error occurred whilst opening the requested file.
adErrReadFile	3003	An error occurred whilst trying to read from the file.
adErrWriteFile	3004	An error occurred whilst trying to write to the file.
adErrNoCurrentRecord	3021	Either BOF or EOF is True, or the current record has been deleted. The operation requested by the application requires a current record.
adErrIllegalOperation	3219	The operation requested by the application is not allowed in this context.
adErrCantChangeProvider	3220	The provider cannot be changed during the operation.
adErrInTransaction	3246	The application cannot explicitly close a Connection object while in the middle of a transaction.
adErrFeatureNotAvailable	3251	The provider does not support the operation requested by the application.
adErrItemNotFound	3265	ADO could not find the object in the collection.

ADO Constants

Name	Value	Description
adErrObjectInCollection	3367	Can't append. Object already in collection.
adErrObjectNotSet	3420	The object referenced by the application no longer points to a valid object.
adErrDataConversion	3421	The application is using a value of the wrong type for the current application.
adErrObjectClosed	3704	The operation requested by the application is not allowed if the object is closed.
adErrObjectOpen	3705	The operation requested by the application is not allowed if the object is open.
adErrProxviderNotFound	3706	ADO could not find the specified provider.
adErrBoundToCommand	3707	The application cannot change the ActiveConnection property of a Recordset object with a Command object as its source.
adErrInvalidParamInfo	3708	The application has improperly defined a Parameter object.
adErrInvalidConnection	3709	The application requested an operation on an object with a reference to a closed or invalid Connection object.
adErrNotReentrant	3710	The operation is not reentrant - you cannot perform the operation whilst processing an event.

Name	Value	Description
adErrStillExecuting	3711	The operation cannot be performed during an asynchronous operation.
adErrOperationCancelled	3712	The operation was cancelled by the user.
adErrStillConnecting	3713	The operation cannot be performed during an asynchronous connection.
adErrInvalidTransaction	3714	The transaction is invalid.
adErrNotExecuting	3715	The operation is not executing.
adErrUnsafeOperation	3716	The operation is unsafe under these circumstances. The safety settings of the computer prohibit access to data from another domain.
adwrnSecurityDialog	3717	This page is accessing data on another domain. Do you want to allow this?
adwrnSecurityDialogHeader	3718	This page is accessing data on another domain. Do you want to allow this?
adErrIntegrityViolation	3719	The action failed due to a violation of data integrity.
adErrPermissionDenied	3720	The action failed because you do not have sufficient permission to complete the operation.
adErrDataOverflow	3721	The data was too large for the supplied data type.
adErrSchemaViolation	3722	The data conflicts with the data type or the field constraints.

ADO Constants

Name	Value	Description
adErrSignMismatch	3723	Data type conversion failed because the value was signed and the field data type is unsigned.
adErrCantConvertvalue	3724	The value cannot be converted for reasons other than a sign mismatch or a data overflow. Data truncation is an example of this.
adErrCantCreate	3725	The field data type is unknown, therefore the value cannot be set or retrieved; or the provider had insufficient resources to perform the operation.
adErrColumnNotOnThisRow	3726	The requested field is not contained on this row.
adErrURLDoesNotExist	3727	The URL does not exist.
adErrTreePermissionDenied	3728	You do not have sufficient permissions to access the tree or subtree.
adErrInvalidURL	3729	The supplied URL contains invalid characters.
adErrResourceLocked	3730	The resource identified by the URL is locked by another process.
adErrResourceExists	3731	The resource identified by the URL already exists. Specify adCopyOverwrite to replace the resource.
adErrCannotComplete	3732	The action could not be completed.
adErrVolumeNotFound	3733	The provider cannot find the storage device associated with the URL.

Name	Value	Description
adErrOutOfSpace	3734	The operation failed because the server could not obtain enough space to complete the operation.
adErrResourceOutOfScope	3735	The resource URL is outside the scope of the current Record.
adErrUnavailable	3736	The operation failed to complete and the status is unavailable.
AdErrURLNamedRowDoesNot Exist	3737	The URL in the named Record does not exists.
adErrDelResOutOfScope	3738	The resource URL cannot be deleted because it is out of the allowed scope of the current Record.
adErrPropInvalidColumn	3739	The property cannot be applied to the specified field.
adErrPropInvalidOption	3740	The property attribute is invalid.
adErrPropInvalidValue	3741	The property value is invalid.
adErrPropConflicting	3742	The property value conflicts with another property.
adErrPropNotAllSettable	3743	The property is read-only, or it cannot be set.
adErrPropNotSet	3744	The optional property value was not set.
adErrPropNotSettable	3745	The property is read-only and the value was not set.
adErrPropNotSupported	3746	The property is not supported by the provider.

ADO Constants

Name	Value	Description
adErrCatalogNotSet	3747	The action could not be completed because the ParentCatalog is not set.
adErrCantChangeConnection	3748	The connection cannot be changed.
adErrFieldsUpdateFailed	3749	The Update method of the Fields collection failed.
adErrDenyNotSupported	3750	The provider does not support sharing restrictions.
adErrDenyTypeNotSupported	3751	The provider does not support the requested type of sharing restriction.

EventReasonEnum

Name	Value	Description
adRsnAddNew	1	A new record is to be added.
adRsnClose	9	The object is being closed.
adRsnDelete	2	The record is being deleted.
adRsnFirstChange	11	The record has been changed for the first time.
adRsnMove	10	A Move has been invoked and the current record pointer is being moved.
adRsnMoveFirst	12	A MoveFirst has been invoked and the current record pointer is being moved.
adRsnMoveLast	15	A MoveLast has been invoked and the current record pointer is being moved.
adRsnMoveNext	13	A MoveNext has been invoked and the current record pointer is being moved.
adRsnMovePrevious	14	A MovePrevious has been invoked and the current record pointer is being moved.

Name	Value	Description
adRsnRequery	7	The recordset was requeried.
adRsnResynch	8	The recordset was resynchronized.
adRsnUndoAddNew	5	The addition of a new record has been cancelled.
adRsnUndoDelete	6	The deletion of a record has been cancelled.
adRsnUndoUpdate	4	The update of a record has been cancelled.
adRsnUpdate	3	The record is being updated.

EventStatusEnum

Name	Value	Description
adStatusCancel	4	Request cancellation of the operation that is about to occur.
adStatusCantDeny	3	A Will event cannot request cancellation of the operation about to occur.
adStatusErrorsOccurred	2	The operation completed unsuccessfully, or a Will event cancelled the operation.
adStatusOK	1	The operation completed successfully.
adStatusUnwantedEvent	5	Events for this operation are no longer required.

ExecuteOptionEnum

Name	Value	Description
adAsyncExecute	16	The operation is executed asynchronously.
adAsyncFetch	32	The records are fetched asynchronously.
adAsyncFetchNonBlocking	64	The records are fetched asynchronously without blocking subsequent operations.

ADO Constants

Name	Value	Description
adExecuteNoRecords	128	Indicates CommandText is a command or stored procedure that does not return rows. Always combined with adCmdText or adCmdStoreProc.

FieldAttributeEnum

Name	Value	Description
adFldCacheDeferred	4096	Indicates that the provider caches field values and that subsequent reads are done from the cache.
adFldFixed	16	Indicates that the field contains fixed-length data.
adFldIsChapter	8192	The field is a chapter field, and contains a rowset.
adFldIsCollection	262144	The field is a collection.
adFldIsDefaultStream	131072	The fields is the default Stream.
adFldIsNullable	32	Indicates that the field accepts Null values.
adFldIsRowURL	65536	The fields is a URL.
adFldKeyColumn	32768	The field is part of a key column.
adFldLong	128	Indicates that the field is a long binary field, and that the AppendChunk and GetChunk methods can be used.
adFldMayBeNull	64	Indicates that you can read Null values from the field.
adFldMayDefer	2	Indicates that the field is deferred, that is, the field values are not retrieved from the data source with the whole record, but only when you access them.
adFldNegativeScale	16384	The field has a negative scale.

Name	Value	Description
adFldRowID	256	Indicates that the field is some kind of record ID.
adFldRowVersion	512	Indicates that the field is a time or date stamp used to track updates.
adFldUnknownUpdatable	8	Indicates that the provider cannot determine if you can write to the field.
adFldUnspecified	-1	Attributes of the field are unspecified.
adFldUpdatable	4	Indicates that you can write to the field.

ADO Constants

FieldEnum

Name	Value	Description
adDefaultStream	-1	When used as the index into the Fields collection of a Record, returns the default Stream for the Record.
adRecordURL	-2	When used as the index into the Fields collection of a Record, returns the absolute URL for the Record.

FieldStatusEnum

Name	Value	Description
adFieldAlreadyExists	26	The field already exists.
adFieldBadStatus	12	An invalid status value has been sent from the OLE DB provider. This could be related to a an OLE DB 1.0 or 1.1 provider.
adFieldCannotComplete	20	The action cannot be completed by the server of the URL specified in the Source.
adFieldCannotDeleteSource	23	The field cannot delete the source of the field, after a move operation.

Name	Value	Description
adFieldCantConvertValue	2	The field cannot convert the value without data loss.
adFieldCantCreate	7	The field cannot be created because the provider exceeded its limitation.
adFieldDataOverflow	6	The data is too long to fit in the field.
adFieldDefault	13	The default value of the field was used.
adFieldDoesNotExist	16	The field does not exist.
adFieldIgnore	15	The field was skipped when setting values, and no value was set by the provider.
AdFieldIntegrity Violation	10	The field update failed because it is a calculated or derived field.
adFieldInvalidURL	17	The field contains invalid URL characters.
adFieldIsNull	3	The provider returned a null value.
adFieldOK	0	The field was successfully added or deleted.
adFieldOutOfSpace	22	The field ran out of space for storage.
adFieldPendingChange	262144	The field has been deleted from and then added to the Fields collection, but the provider has not yet been updated.
adFieldPendingDelete	131072	The field has been deleted from the Fields collection, but the provider has not yet been updated.
adFieldPendingInsert	65536	The field has been inserted into the Fields collection, but the provider has not yet been updated.
adFieldPendingUnknown	524288	The provider cannot determine the operation that caused the Status to be set.

Name	Value	Description
AdFieldPending UnknownDelete	1048576	The provider cannot determine the operation that caused the Status to be set, and the field will be deleted from the Fields collection.
adFieldPermissionDenied	9	Permission to modify the field failed because it is read-only.
adFieldReadOnly	24	The field in the data source is read-only.
adFieldResourceExists	19	The resource URL specified by the field already exists.
adFieldResourceLocked	18	The resource URL specified by the field is locked by another process.
AdFieldResource OutOfScope	25	The resource specified by the field is outside the scope of the current Record.
adFieldSchemaViolation	11	The field update failed due to a schema violation.
adFieldSignMismatch	5	The value returned by the provider was signed but the ADO field data type was unsigned.
adFieldTruncated	4	The field value was truncated.
adFieldUnavailable	8	The provider could not determine the value of the field.
adFieldVolumeNotFound	21	The volume specified by the URL was not found.

ADO Constants

FilterGroupEnum

Name	Value	Description
adFilterAffectedRecords	2	Allows you to view only records affected by the last Delete, Resync, UpdateBatch, or CancelBatch method.

Name	Value	Description
AdFilterConflicting Records	5	Allows you to view the records that failed the last batch update attempt.
adFilterFetchedRecords	3	Allows you to view records in the current cache.
adFilterNone	0	Removes the current filter and restores all records to view.
adFilterPendingRecords	1	Allows you to view only the records that have changed but have not been sent to the server. Only applicable for batch update mode.
adFilterPredicate	4	Allows you to view records that failed the last batch update attempt.

GetRowsOptionEnum

Name	Value	Description
adGetRowsRest	-1	Retrieves the remainder of the rows in the recordset.

IsolationLevelEnum

Name	Value	Description
adXactBrowse	256	Indicates that from one transaction you can view uncommitted changes in other transactions.
adXactChaos	16	Default. Indicates that you cannot overwrite pending changes from more highly isolated transactions.
adXactCursorStability	4096	Default. Indicates that from one transaction you can view changes in other transactions only after they have been committed.
adXactIsolated	1048576	Indicates that transactions are conducted in isolation from other transactions.

Name	Value	Description
adXactReadCommitted	4096	Same as adXactCursorStability.
adXactReadUncommitted	256	Same as adXactBrowse.
adXactRepeatableRead	65536	Indicates that from one transaction you cannot see changes made in other transactions, but that requerying can bring new recordsets.
adXactSerializable	1048576	Same as adXactIsolated.
adXactUnspecified	-1	Indicates that the provider is using a different IsolationLevel than specified, but that the level cannot be identified.

LineSeparatorEnum

Name	Value	Description
adCR	13	The carriage return character.
adCRLF	-1	The carriage return and line feed characters.
adLF	10	The line feed character.

LockTypeEnum

Name	Value	Description
adLockBatchOptimistic	4	Optimistic batch updates.
adLockOptimistic	3	Optimistic locking, record by record. The provider locks records when Update is called.
adLockPessimistic	2	Pessimistic locking, record by record. The provider locks the record immediately upon editing.
adLockReadOnly	1	Default. Read only, data cannot be modified.
adLockUnspecified	-1	The clone is created with the same lock type as the original.

MarshalOptionsEnum

Name	Value	Description
adMarshalAll	0	Default. Indicates that all rows are returned to the server.
adMarshalModifiedOnly	1	Indicates that only modified rows are returned to the server.

MoveRecordOptionsEnum

Name	Value	Description
adMoveAllowEmulation	4	If the attempt to move the record fails, allow the move to be performed using a download, upload and delete set of operations.
adMoveDontUpdateLinks	2	Do not update hyperlinks of the source record.
adMoveOverWrite	1	Overwrite the target if it already exists.
adMoveUnspecified	-1	No specific move options are set. The default applies.

ObjectStateEnum

Name	Value	Description
adStateClosed	0	Default. Indicates that the object is closed.
adStateConnecting	2	Indicates that the object is connecting.
adStateExecuting	4	Indicates that the object is executing a command.
adStateFetching	8	Indicates that the rows of the recordset are being fetched.
adStateOpen	1	Indicates that the object is open.

ParameterAttributesEnum

Name	Value	Description
adParamLong	128	Indicates that the parameter accepts long binary data.
adParamNullable	64	Indicates that the parameter accepts Null values.
adParamSigned	16	Default. Indicates that the parameter accepts signed values.

ParameterDirectionEnum

Name	Value	Description
adParamInput	1	Default. Indicates an input parameter.
adParamInputOutput	3	Indicates both an input and output parameter.
adParamOutput	2	Indicates an output parameter.
adParamReturnValue	4	Indicates a return value.
adParamUnknown	0	Indicates parameter direction is unknown.

PersistFormatEnum

Name	Value	Description
adPersistADTG	0	Default. Persist data in Advanced Data TableGram format.
adPersistXML	1	Persist data in XML format.

PositionEnum

Name	Value	Description
adPosBOF	-2	The current record pointer is at BOF.
adPosEOF	-3	The current record pointer is at EOF.

ADO Constants

Name	Value	Description
adPosUnknown	-1	The Recordset is empty, the current position is unknown, or the provider does not support the AbsolutePage property.

PropertyAttributesEnum

Name	Value	Description
adPropNotSupported	0	Indicates that the property is not supported by the provider.
adPropOptional	2	Indicates that the user does not need to specify a value for this property before the data source is initialized.
adPropRead	512	Indicates that the user can read the property.
adPropRequired	1	Indicates that the user must specify a value for this property before the data source is initialized.
adPropWrite	1024	Indicates that the user can set the property.

RecordCreateOptionsEnum

Name	Value	Description
adCreateCollection	8192	Create a new collection record (directory) at the specified URL.
adCreateNonCollection	0	Create a new record at the specified URL.
adCreateOverwrite	67108864	Overwrite any existing record at the specified URL.
adCreateStructDoc	-2147483648	Create a new structured document record at the specified URL.
adFailIfNotExists	-1	Fail if the URL does not exist.
adOpenIfExists	33554432	Open the record at the specified URL if it exists.

RecordOpenOptionsEnum

Name	Value	Description
adDelayFetchFields	32768	Delay fetching fields until they are requested.
adDelayFetchStream	16384	Delay fetching the Stream until it is requested.
adOpenAsync	4096	Open the Record asynchronously.
adOpenSource	8388608	Open the source document at the URL, rather than the executed contents.
adOpenURLBind	1024	Indicates the connection string contains a URL.

RecordStatusEnum

Name	Value	Description
adRecCanceled	256	The record was not saved because the operation was cancelled.
adRecCantRelease	1024	The new record was not saved because of existing record locks.
adRecConcurrency Violation	2048	The record was not saved because optimistic concurrency was in use.
adRecDBDeleted	262144	The record has already been deleted from the data source.
adRecDeleted	4	The record was deleted.
adRecIntegrityViolation	4096	The record was not saved because the user violated integrity constraints.
adRecInvalid	16	The record was not saved because its bookmark is invalid.
adRecMaxChangesExceeded	8192	The record was not saved because there were too many pending changes.
adRecModified	2	The record was modified.

ADO Constants

1125

Name	Value	Description
adRecMultipleChanges	64	The record was not saved because it would have affected multiple records.
adRecNew	1	The record is new.
adRecObjectOpen	16384	The record was not saved because of a conflict with an open storage object.
adRecOK	0	The record was successfully updated.
adRecOutOfMemory	32768	The record was not saved because the computer has run out of memory.
adRecPendingChanges	128	The record was not saved because it refers to a pending insert.
adRecPermissionDenied	65536	The record was not saved because the user has insufficient permissions.
adRecSchemaViolation	131072	The record was not saved because it violates the structure of the underlying database.
adRecUnmodified	8	The record was not modified.

RecordTypeEnum

Name	Value	Description
adCollectionRecord	1	The record is a collection type (directory).
adSimpleRecord	0	The record is a simple file.
adStructDoc	2	The record is a structured document.

ResyncEnum

Name	Value	Description
adResyncAllValues	2	Default. Data is overwritten and pending updates are cancelled.
AdResyncUnderlyingValues	1	Data is not overwritten and pending updates are not cancelled.

SaveOptionsEnum

Name	Value	Description
adSaveCreateNotExist	1	Create a new file if the file does not already exist.
adSaveCreateOverWrite	2	Overwrite any existing file.

SchemaEnum

Name	Value	Description
adSchemaAsserts	0	Request assert information.
adSchemaCatalogs	1	Request catalog information.
adSchemaCharacterSets	2	Request character set information.
adSchemaCheckConstraints	5	Request check constraint information.
adSchemaCollations	3	Request collation information.
adSchemaColumnPrivileges	13	Request column privilege information.
adSchemaColumns	4	Request column information.
adSchemaColumnsDomainUsage	11	Request column domain usage information.
AdSchemaConstraintColumn Usage	6	Request column constraint usage information.
AdSchemaConstraintTable Usage	7	Request table constraint usage information.
adSchemaCubes	32	For multi-dimensional data, view the Cubes schema.
adSchemaDBInfoKeywords	30	Request the keywords from the provider.
adSchemaDBInfoLiterals	31	Request the literals from the provider.
adSchemaDimensions	33	For multi-dimensional data, view the Dimensions schema.

ADO Constants

Name	Value	Description
adSchemaForeignKeys	27	Request foreign key information.
adSchemaHierarchies	34	For multi-dimensional data, view the Hierarchies schema.
adSchemaIndexes	12	Request index information.
adSchemaKeyColumnUsage	8	Request key column usage information.
adSchemaLevels	35	For multi-dimensional data, view the Levels schema.
adSchemaMeasures	36	For multi-dimensional data, view the Measures schema.
adSchemaMembers	38	For multi-dimensional data, view the Members schema.
adSchemaPrimaryKeys	28	Request primary key information.
adSchemaProcedureColumns	29	Request stored procedure column information.
adSchemaProcedureParameters	26	Request stored procedure parameter information.
adSchemaProcedures	16	Request stored procedure information.
adSchemaProperties	37	For multi-dimensional data, view the Properties schema.
adSchemaProviderSpecific	-1	Request provider specific information.
adSchemaProviderTypes	22	Request provider type information.
AdSchemaReferential Constraints	9	Request referential constraint information.
AdSchemaReferential Constraints	9	Request referential constraint information.
adSchemaSchemata	17	Request schema information.

Name	Value	Description
adSchemaSQLLanguages	18	Request SQL language support information.
adSchemaStatistics	19	Request statistics information.
adSchemaTableConstraints	10	Request table constraint information.
adSchemaTablePrivileges	14	Request table privilege information.
adSchemaTables	20	Request information about the tables.
adSchemaTranslations	21	Request character set translation information.
adSchemaTrustees	39	Request trustee information.
adSchemaUsagePrivileges	15	Request user privilege information.
adSchemaViewColumnUsage	24	Request column usage in views information.
adSchemaViews	23	Request view information.
adSchemaViewTableUsage	25	Request table usage in views information.

ADO Constants

Due to a misspelling in the type library adSchemaReferentialConstraints is included twice – once for the original spelling and once for the corrected spelling.

SearchDirectionEnum

Name	Value	Description
adSearchBackward	-1	Search backward from the current record.
adSearchForward	1	Search forward from the current record.

SeekEnum

Name	Value	Description
adSeekAfter	8	Seek the key just after the match.

Name	Value	Description
adSeekAfterEQ	4	Seek the key equal to or just after the match.
adSeekBefore	32	See the key just before the match.
adSeekBeforeEQ	16	Seek the key equal to or just before the match.
adSeekFirstEQ	1	Seek the first key equal to the match.
adSeekLastEQ	2	Seek the last key equal to the match.

StreamOpenOptionsEnum

Name	Value	Description
adOpenStreamAsync	1	Opens the Stream asynchronously.
adOpenStreamFromRecord	4	Opens the Stream using an existing Record as the source.
adOpenStreamFromURL	8	Opens the Stream using a URL as the source.

StreamReadEnum

Name	Value	Description
adReadAll	-1	Reads all bytes from the Stream, from the current position to the end of the stream.
adReadLine	-2	Reads the next line from the Stream. Uses the LineSeparator property to identify the end of the line.

StreamTypeEnum

Name	Value	Description
adTypeBinary	1	The Stream contains binary data.
adTypeText	2	The Stream contains text data.

StreamWriteEnum

Name	Value	Description
adWriteChar	0	Writes the specified string to the Stream.
adWriteLine	1	Writes the specified string and a line separator to the Stream.
stWriteChar	0	Writes the specified string to the Stream.
stWriteLine	1	Writes the specified string and a line separator to the Stream.

StringFormatEnum

Name	Value	Description
adClipString	2	Rows are delimited by user defined values.

XactAttributeEnum

Name	Value	Description
adXactAbortRetaining	262144	The provider will automatically start a new transaction after a RollbackTrans method call.
adXactAsyncPhaseOne	524288	Perform an asynchronous commit.
adXactCommitRetaining	131072	The provider will automatically start a new transaction after a CommitTrans method call.
adXactSyncPhaseOne	1048576	Performs an synchronous commit.

ADO Dynamic Properties

The `Properties` collection deals with dynamic properties that are specific to the provider. All ADO objects have a fixed set of properties (such as `Name`), but since ADO is designed for use with different providers, a way was needed to allow providers to specify their own properties. The `Properties` collection contains these properties, and this appendix deals with which properties are supported by which providers, and what these properties actually do.

Some of the properties refer to `Rowsets`. This is just the OLE DB term for `Recordsets`.

Property Usage

As you can see from the tables in this appendix, there are very many properties – however, using them is actually quite simple. You simply index into the `Properties` collection, by using the property name itself. For example, to find out the name the provider gives to procedures you could do this:

```
Print objConn.Properties("Procedure Term")
```

For SQL Server, this returns `stored procedure` and for Access this returns `STORED QUERY`.

You can iterate through the entire set of properties very simply:

```
For Each objProp In objConn.Properties
   Print objProp.Name
   Print objProp.Value
Next
```

This will print out the property name and value.

For those properties that return custom types, you need to identify whether these return a bitmask or a simple value – the property description identifies this, as it says 'one of' or 'one or more of'. In its simplest forms, these properties will just return a single value. For example, to find out whether your provider supports output parameters on stored procedures you can query the Output Parameter Availability property. This is defined as returning values of type DBPROPVAL_OA, which are as follows:

Constant	Value
DBPROPVAL_OA_ATEXECUTE	2
DBPROPVAL_OA_ATROWRELEASE	4
DBPROPVAL_OA_NOTSUPPORTED	1

Examining this property when connected to SQL Server gives you a value of 4, indicating that output parameters are available when the recordset is closed. Access, on the other hand, returns a value of 1, indicating that output parameters are not supported.

For those properties that return a bitmask, you'll need to use Boolean logic to identify which values are set. For example, to query the provider and examine what features of SQL are supported, you can use the SQL Support property. For Access this returns 512, which corresponds to DBPROPVAL_SQL_SUBMINIMUM, indicating that not even the ANSI SQL92 entry-level SQL facilities are provided. On the other hand, SQL Server returns 283, but there isn't a single value for this, so it must be a combination of values. In fact, it corresponds to the sum of the following:

Constant	Value
DBPROPVAL_SQL_ESCAPECLAUSES	256
DBPROPVAL_SQL_ANSI92_ENTRY	16
DBPROPVAL_SQL_ANDI89_IEF	8
DBPROPVAL_SQL_CORE	2
DBPROPVAL_SQL_MINIMUM	1

In order to see whether a specific value is set, use the Boolean AND operator. For example:

```
lngSQLSupport = oConn.Properties("SQL Support")
If (lngSQLSupport AND DBPROPVAL_SQL_CORE) = DBPROPVAL_SQL_CORE Then
   'core facilities are supported
End If
```

A full description of the constants is given in Appendix D.

Property Support

The following table shows a list of all OLE DB properties, and indicates which of them are supported by three widely used drivers: the Microsoft OLE DB driver for Jet, the Microsoft OLE DB driver for ODBC, and the Microsoft OLE DB driver for SQL Server. Since this list contains dynamic properties, not every property may show up under all circumstances. Other providers may also implement properties not listed in this table.

A tick (✓) indicates that the property is supported, and a blank space indicates it is not supported. Note that support for recordset properties may depend upon the locking type, cursor type and cursor location.

> Note. This list doesn't include the Iproperty (such as IRowset, etc) properties. Although these are part of the collection, they are not particularly useful for the ADO programmer.

For the *Object Type* column, the following applies:

- ❏ RS = Recordset
- ❏ R = Record
- ❏ C = Connection
- ❏ F = Field

Property Name	Object Type (RS/R/F/C)	ODBC	Jet	SQL Server	Internet Publishing (IIS5)	MSDataShape	Persist	Remote	Indexing Service	Directory Services	Exchange
Access Order	RS	✓	✓	✓		✓	✓	✓	✓	✓	
Accessible Procedures	C	✓									
Accessible Tables	C	✓									
Active Sessions	C	✓	✓	✓					✓	✓	✓
Active Statements	C	✓									
ADSI Flag										✓	
Alter Column Support	C		✓								

Table Continued on Following Page

ADO Dynamic Properties

Property Name	Object Type (RS/R/F/C)	ODBC	Jet	SQL Server	Internet Publishing (IIS5)	MSDataShape	Persist	Remote	Indexing Service	Directory Services	Exchange
Always use content index	RS								✓		
Append-Only Rowset	RS	✓	✓	✓		✓	✓	✓	✓	✓	
Application Name	C			✓							
Asynchable Abort	C	✓	✓	✓							✓
Asynchable Commit	C	✓	✓	✓							✓
Asynchronous Processing	C					✓					
Asynchronous Rowset Processing	RS	✓	✓	✓		✓	✓	✓	✓	✓	✓
Auto Recalc	RS	✓	✓	✓		✓	✓	✓	✓	✓	
Auto Translate	C			✓							
Autocommit Isolation Levels	C	✓	✓	✓		✓	✓	✓	✓	✓	✓
Background Fetch Size	RS	✓	✓	✓	✓	✓	✓	✓	✓		
Background thread Priority	RS	✓	✓	✓	✓	✓	✓	✓	✓		
BASECATALOGNAME	F	✓	✓	✓	✓	✓	✓	✓	✓		
BASECOLUMNNAME	F	✓	✓	✓	✓	✓	✓	✓	✓		
BASESCHEMANAME	F	✓	✓	✓	✓	✓	✓	✓	✓		
BASETABLENAME	F	✓	✓	✓	✓	✓	✓	✓	✓		
Batch Size	RS	✓	✓	✓	✓	✓	✓	✓	✓		
Bind Flags	C				✓	✓					
BLOB accessibility on Forward Only cursor	RS	✓									
Blocking Storage Objects	RS	✓	✓	✓		✓	✓	✓	✓		
Bookmark Information	RS	✓		✓							
Bookmark Type	RS	✓	✓	✓		✓	✓	✓	✓	✓	✓
Bookmarkable	RS	✓	✓	✓	✓	✓	✓	✓	✓	✓	✓

ADO Dynamic Properties

Property Name	Object Type (RS/R/F/C)	ODBC	Jet	SQL Server	Internet Publishing (IIS5)	MSDataShape	Persist	Remote	Indexing Service	Directory Services	Exchange
Bookmarks Ordered	RS	✓	✓	✓		✓	✓	✓	✓	✓	✓
Cache Aggressively	C				✓						
Cache Authentication	C		✓			✓	✓				
Cache Child Rows	RS	✓	✓	✓		✓	✓	✓	✓	✓	
Cache Deferred Columns	RS	✓	✓	✓		✓	✓	✓	✓	✓	✓
CALCULATIONINFO	F	✓	✓	✓		✓	✓	✓	✓	✓	
Catalog Location	C	✓	✓	✓					✓	✓	
Catalog Term	C	✓	✓	✓					✓	✓	
Catalog Usage	C	✓		✓					✓	✓	
Change Inserted Rows	RS	✓	✓	✓		✓	✓	✓			✓
Chapter	C						✓				
CLSID	F	✓									
COLLATINGSEQUENCE	F	✓	✓								
Column Definition	C	✓	✓	✓					✓		
Column Privileges	RS	✓	✓	✓		✓	✓	✓	✓	✓	✓
Column Set Notification	RS	✓	✓	✓		✓	✓	✓	✓	✓	
Column Writable	RS	✓	✓	✓		✓	✓	✓	✓	✓	
Command Properties	C							✓			
Command Time Out	RS	✓	✓	✓	✓	✓	✓	✓	✓	✓	
COMPUTEMODE	F	✓									
Connect Timeout	C	✓		✓	✓	✓	✓	✓		✓	
Connection Status	C	✓		✓							
Current Catalog	C	✓	✓	✓					✓		

Table Continued on Following Page

Property Name	Object Type (RS/R/F/C)	ODBC	Jet	SQL Server	Internet Publishing (IIS5)	MSDataShape	Persist	Remote	Indexing Service	Directory Services	Exchange
Current DFMode	C							✓			
Current Language	C			✓							
Cursor Engine Version	RS	✓	✓	✓		✓	✓	✓	✓	✓	
Data Provider	C					✓					
Data Source	C	✓	✓	✓	✓	✓		✓	✓	✓	✓
Data Source Name	C	✓	✓	✓						✓	✓
Data Source Object Threading Model	C	✓	✓	✓		✓		✓	✓	✓	✓
Datasource Type	C				✓						✓
DATETIMEPRECISION	F	✓		✓							
DBMS Name	C	✓	✓	✓					✓		✓
DBMS Version	C	✓	✓	✓					✓		✓
DEFAULTVALUE	F	✓									
Defer Column	RS	✓	✓	✓		✓	✓	✓	✓	✓	✓
Defer scope and security testing	RS								✓		
Delay Storage Object Updates	RS	✓	✓	✓		✓	✓	✓	✓	✓	
DFMode	C							✓			
DOMAINCATALOG	F	✓									
DOMAINNAME	F	✓									
DOMAINSCHEMA	F	✓									
Driver Name	C	✓									
Driver ODBC Version	C	✓									
Driver Version	C	✓									
Enable Fastload	C			✓							

ADO Dynamic Properties

Property Name	Object Type (RS/R/F/C)	ODBC	Jet	SQL Server	Internet Publishing (IIS5)	MSDataShape	Persist	Remote	Indexing Service	Directory Services	Exchange
Encrypt Password	C		✓			✓		✓		✓	
Extended Properties	C	✓	✓	✓		✓		✓		✓	
Fastload Options	RS			✓							
Fetch Backwards	RS	✓	✓	✓	✓	✓	✓	✓	✓	✓	✓
File Usage	C	✓									
Filter Operations	RS	✓	✓	✓		✓	✓	✓	✓	✓	
Find Operations	RS	✓	✓	✓		✓	✓	✓	✓	✓	
Force no command preparation when executing a parameterized command	RS	✓									
Force no command reexecution when failure to satisfy all required properties	RS	✓									
Force no parameter rebinding when executing a command	RS	✓									
Force SQL Server Firehose Mode cursor	RS	✓									
Generate a Rowset that can be marshalled	RS	✓									
General Timeout	C	✓		✓							
Generate URL	C				✓						
GROUP BY Support	C	✓	✓	✓						✓	
Handler	C							✓			
HASDEFAULT	F	✓									
Heterogeneous Table Support	C	✓	✓	✓						✓	
Hidden Columns	RS	✓	✓	✓		✓	✓	✓	✓	✓	

Table Continued on Following Page

Property Name	Object Type (RS/R/F/C)	ODBC	Jet	SQL Server	Internet Publishing (IIS5)	MSDataShape	Persist	Remote	Indexing Service	Directory Services	Exchange
Hold Rows	RS	✓	✓	✓	✓	✓	✓	✓	✓	✓	✓
Identifier Case Sensitivity	C	✓	✓	✓							
Ignore Cached Data	C				✓						
Immobile Rows	RS	✓	✓	✓		✓	✓	✓	✓	✓	✓
Impersonation Level	C					✓		✓			
Include SQL_FLOAT, SQL_DOUBLE, and SQL_REAL in QBU where clauses	RS	✓									
Initial Catalog	C	✓		✓		✓		✓			
Initial Fetch Size	RS	✓	✓	✓		✓	✓	✓	✓	✓	
Initial File Name	C			✓							
Integrated Security	C			✓		✓		✓		✓	
Integrity Enhancement Facility	C	✓									
Internet Timeout	C							✓			
ISAUTOINCREMENT	F	✓	✓	✓		✓	✓	✓	✓		
ISCASESENSITIVE	F	✓	✓	✓							
Isolation Levels	C	✓	✓	✓					✓		✓
Isolation Retention	C	✓	✓	✓					✓		✓
ISSEARCHABLE	F	✓		✓							
ISUNIQUE	F	✓									
Jet OLEDB:Bulk Transactions	RS		✓								
Jet OLEDB:Compact Reclaime Space Amount	C		✓								

ADO Dynamic Properties

Property Name	Object Type (RS/R/F/C)	ODBC	Jet	SQL Server	Internet Publishing (IIS5)	MSDataShape	Persist	Remote	Indexing Service	Directory Services	Exchange
Jet OLEDB:Compact Without Replica Repair	C	✓									
Jet OLEDB:Connection Control	C		✓								
Jet OLEDB:Create System Database	C		✓								
Jet OLEDB:Database Locking Mode	C		✓								
Jet OLEDB:Database Password	C	✓									
Jet OLEDB:Don't Copy Locale on Compact	C		✓								
Jet OLEDB:Enable Fat Cursors	RS		✓								
Jet OLEDB:Encrypt Database	C		✓								
Jet OLEDB:Engine Type	C		✓								
Jet OLEDB:Exclusive Async Delay	C		✓								
Jet OLEDB:Fat Cursor Cache Size	RS		✓								
Jet OLEDB:Flush Transaction Timeout	C		✓								
Jet OLEDB:Global Bulk Transactions	C		✓								
Jet OLEDB:Global Partial Bulk Ops	C		✓								
Jet OLEDB:Grbit Value	RS		✓								

Table Continued on Following Page

Property Name	Object Type (RS/R/F/C)	ODBC	Jet	SQL Server	Internet Publishing (IIS5)	MSDataShape	Persist	Remote	Indexing Service	Directory Services	Exchange
Jet OLEDB:Implicit Commit Sync	C		✓								
Jet OLEDB:Inconsistent	RS		✓								
Jet OLEDB:Lock Delay	C		✓								
Jet OLEDB:Lock Retry	C		✓								
Jet OLEDB:Locking Granularity	RS		✓								
Jet OLEDB:Max Buffer Size	C		✓								
Jet OLEDB:Max Locks Per File	C		✓								
Jet OLEDB:New Database Password	C		✓								
Jet OLEDB:ODBC Command Time Out	C		✓								
Jet OLEDB:ODBC Parsing	C		✓								
Jet OLEDB:ODBC Pass-Through Statement	RS		✓								
Jet OLEDB:Page Locks to Table Lock	C		✓								
Jet OLEDB:Page Timeout	C		✓								
Jet OLEDB:Partial Bulk Ops	RS		✓								
Jet OLEDB:Pass Through Query Bulk-Op	RS		✓								
Jet OLEDB:Pass Through Query Connect String	RS		✓								
Jet OLEDB:Recycle Long-Valued Pages	C		✓								
Jet OLEDB:Registry Path	C		✓								

Property Name	Object Type (RS/R/F/C)	ODBC	Jet	SQL Server	Internet Publishing (IIS5)	MSDataShape	Persist	Remote	Indexing Service	Directory Services	Exchange
Jet OLEDB:Reset ISAM Stats	C		✓								
Jet OLEDB:Sandbox Mode	C		✓								
Jet OLEDB:SFP	C		✓								
Jet OLEDB:Shared Async Delay	C		✓								
Jet OLEDB:Stored Query	RS		✓								
Jet OLEDB:System database	C		✓								
Jet OLEDB:Transaction Commit Mode	C		✓								
Jet OLEDB:Use Grbit	RS		✓								
Jet OLEDB:User Commit Sync	C		✓								
Jet OLEDB:Validate Rules On Set	RS		✓								
Keep Identity	RS			✓							
Keep Nulls	RS			✓							
KEYCOLUMN	F	✓	✓	✓		✓	✓	✓	✓	✓	
Like Escape Clause	C	✓									
Literal Bookmarks	RS	✓	✓	✓		✓	✓	✓	✓	✓	✓
Literal Row Identity	RS	✓	✓	✓		✓	✓	✓	✓	✓	✓
Locale Identifier	C	✓	✓	✓	✓	✓			✓	✓	✓
Location	C	✓				✓		✓	✓	✓	
Lock Mode	RS		✓	✓							
Lock Owner	C				✓						
Maintain Change Status	RS	✓	✓	✓	✓	✓	✓	✓	✓	✓	

Table Continued on Following Page

ADO Dynamic Properties

Property Name	Object Type (RS/R/F/C)	ODBC	Jet	SQL Server	Internet Publishing (IIS5)	MSDataShape	Persist	Remote	Indexing Service	Directory Services	Exchange
Maintain Property Values	C						✓				
Mark For Offline	C				✓						
Mask Password	C		✓			✓		✓			
Max Columns in Group By	C	✓									
Max Columns in Index	C	✓									
Max Columns in Order By	C	✓									
Max Columns in Select	C	✓									
Max Columns in Table	C	✓									
Maximum BLOB Length	RS			✓							
Maximum Index Size	C	✓	✓	✓							
Maximum Open Chapters	C			✓					✓		
Maximum Open Rows	RS	✓	✓	✓		✓	✓	✓	✓	✓	✓
Maximum Pending Rows	RS	✓	✓	✓		✓	✓	✓	✓		
Maximum Row Size	C	✓	✓	✓					✓	✓	✓
Maximum Row Size Includes BLOB	C	✓	✓	✓							
Maximum Rows	RS	✓	✓	✓		✓	✓	✓	✓	✓	✓
Maximum Tables in SELECT	C	✓	✓	✓					✓		
Memory Usage	RS	✓	✓	✓		✓	✓	✓	✓	✓	
Mode	C	✓	✓		✓	✓		✓		✓	✓
Multi-Table Update	C	✓	✓	✓							
Multiple Connections	C			✓							
Multiple Parameter Sets	C	✓	✓	✓					✓	✓	
Multiple Results	C	✓	✓	✓		✓		✓	✓		✓

Property Name	Object Type (RS/R/F/C)	ODBC	Jet	SQL Server	Internet Publishing (IIS5)	MSDataShape	Persist	Remote	Indexing Service	Directory Services	Exchange
Multiple Storage Objects	C	✓	✓	✓					✓		✓
Network Address	C			✓							
Network Library	C			✓							
Notification Granularity	RS	✓	✓	✓		✓	✓	✓	✓	✓	
Notification Phases	RS	✓	✓	✓		✓	✓	✓	✓	✓	
NULL Collation Order	C	✓	✓	✓					✓		
NULL Concatenation Behavior	C	✓	✓	✓							
Numeric Functions	C	✓									
Objects Transacted	RS	✓	✓	✓		✓	✓	✓	✓	✓	
OCTETLENGTH	F	✓		✓							
ODBC Concurrency Type	RS	✓									
ODBC Cursor Type	RS	✓									
OLE DB Services	C	✓						✓			
OLE DB Version	C	✓	✓	✓	✓			✓	✓	✓	✓
OLE Object Support	C	✓	✓	✓					✓	✓	✓
OLE Objects	C				✓						
Open Rowset Support	C	✓	✓	✓							
OPTIMIZE	F	✓	✓	✓		✓	✓	✓	✓	✓	
ORDER BY Columns in Select List	C	✓	✓	✓					✓		
Others' Changes Visible	RS	✓	✓	✓		✓	✓	✓	✓	✓	✓
Others' Inserts Visible	RS	✓	✓	✓		✓	✓	✓	✓	✓	✓
Outer Join Capabilities	C	✓									

ADO Dynamic Properties

Table Continued on Following Page

Property Name	Object Type (RS/R/F/C)	ODBC	Jet	SQL Server	Internet Publishing (IIS5)	MSDataShape	Persist	Remote	Indexing Service	Directory Services	Exchange
Outer Joins	C	✓									
Output Parameter Availability	C	✓	✓	✓				✓	✓		
Own Changes Visible	RS	✓	✓	✓		✓	✓	✓	✓	✓	✓
Own Inserts Visible	RS	✓	✓	✓		✓	✓	✓	✓	✓	✓
Packet Size	C			✓							
Pass By Ref Accessors	C	✓	✓	✓					✓	✓	✓
Password	C	✓	✓	✓	✓	✓		✓		✓	✓
Persist Encrypted	C					✓					
Persist Format	C						✓				
Persist Schema	C						✓				
Persist Security Info	C	✓		✓		✓		✓			
Persistent ID Type	C	✓	✓	✓					✓	✓	✓
Position on the last row after insert	RS	✓									
Prepare Abort Behavior	C	✓	✓	✓							✓
Prepare Commit Behavior	C	✓	✓	✓							✓
Preserve on Abort	RS	✓	✓	✓		✓	✓	✓	✓	✓	✓
Preserve on Commit	RS	✓	✓	✓		✓	✓	✓	✓	✓	✓
Procedure Term	C	✓	✓	✓							
Prompt	C	✓	✓	✓	✓	✓		✓	✓	✓	
Protection Level	C					✓		✓			
Protocol Provider	C				✓						
Provider Friendly Name	C	✓	✓	✓					✓	✓	✓
Provider Name	C	✓	✓	✓	✓				✓	✓	✓

ADO Dynamic Properties

Property Name	Object Type (RS/R/F/C)	ODBC	Jet	SQL Server	Internet Publishing (IIS5)	MSDataShape	Persist	Remote	Indexing Service	Directory Services	Exchange
Provider Version	C	✓	✓	✓	✓			✓	✓	✓	✓
Query Based Updates/Deletes/Inserts	RS	✓									
Query Restriction	RS								✓		
Quick Restart	RS	✓	✓	✓		✓	✓	✓	✓	✓	✓
Quoted Catalog Names	C			✓							
Quoted Identifier Sensitivity	C	✓		✓							
Read-Only Data Source	C	✓	✓	✓					✓	✓	✓
Reentrant Events	RS	✓	✓	✓		✓	✓	✓	✓	✓	✓
RELATIONCONDITIONS	F	✓	✓	✓		✓	✓	✓	✓	✓	
Remote Provider	C							✓			
Remote Server	C							✓			
Remove Deleted Rows	RS	✓	✓	✓		✓	✓	✓	✓	✓	✓
Report Multiple Changes	RS	✓	✓	✓		✓	✓	✓	✓	✓	✓
Reshape Name	RS	✓	✓	✓	✓	✓	✓	✓			
Reset Datasource	C	✓		✓					✓		
Resync Command	RS	✓	✓	✓		✓	✓	✓	✓	✓	
Return Pending Inserts	RS	✓	✓	✓		✓	✓	✓	✓	✓	
Return PROPVARIANTs in variant binding	RS								✓		
Row Delete Notification	RS	✓	✓	✓		✓	✓	✓	✓	✓	
Row First Change Notification	RS	✓	✓	✓		✓	✓	✓	✓	✓	
Row Insert Notification	RS	✓	✓	✓		✓	✓	✓	✓	✓	
Row Privileges	RS	✓	✓	✓		✓	✓	✓	✓	✓	✓

Table Continued on Following Page

Property Name	Object Type (RS/R/F/C)	ODBC	Jet	SQL Server	Internet Publishing (IIS5)	MSDataShape	Persist	Remote	Indexing Service	Directory Services	Exchange
Row Resynchronization Notification	RS	✓	✓	✓		✓	✓	✓	✓	✓	
Row Threading Model	RS	✓	✓	✓		✓	✓	✓	✓	✓	✓
Row Undo Change Notification	RS	✓	✓	✓		✓	✓	✓	✓	✓	
Row Undo Delete Notification	RS	✓	✓	✓		✓	✓	✓	✓	✓	
Row Undo Insert Notification	RS	✓	✓	✓		✓	✓	✓	✓	✓	
Row Update Notification	RS	✓	✓	✓		✓	✓	✓	✓	✓	
Rowset Conversions on Command	C	✓	✓	✓					✓	✓	
Rowset Fetch Position Change Notification	RS	✓	✓	✓		✓	✓	✓	✓	✓	
Rowset Query Status	RS								✓		
Rowset Release Notification	RS	✓	✓	✓		✓	✓	✓	✓	✓	
Schema Term	C	✓	✓	✓							
Schema Usage	C	✓	✓	✓							
Scroll Backwards	RS	✓	✓	✓		✓	✓	✓	✓	✓	✓
Server Cursor	RS	✓	✓	✓		✓	✓	✓	✓	✓	✓
Server Data on Insert	RS		✓	✓							
Server Name	C	✓		✓							
Skip Deleted Bookmarks	RS	✓	✓	✓		✓	✓	✓	✓	✓	✓
Special Characters	C	✓									
SQL Content Query Locale String	RS								✓		
SQL Grammar Support	C	✓									
SQL Support	C	✓	✓	✓					✓	✓	✓

ADO Dynamic Properties

Property Name	Object Type (RS/R/F/C)	ODBC	Jet	SQL Server	Internet Publishing (IIS5)	MSDataShape	Persist	Remote	Indexing Service	Directory Services	Exchange
Stored Procedures	C	✓									
String Functions	C	✓									
Strong Row Identity	RS	✓	✓	✓		✓	✓	✓	✓	✓	✓
Structured Storage	C	✓	✓	✓					✓		✓
Subquery Support	C	✓	✓	✓					✓		
System Functions	C	✓									
Table Term	C	✓	✓	✓							✓
Time/Date Functions	C	✓									
Transact Updates	C							✓			
Transaction DDL	C	✓	✓	✓					✓		✓
Treat As Offline	C				✓						
Unicode Comparison Style	C			✓							
Unicode Locale Id	C			✓							
Unique Catalog	RS	✓	✓	✓		✓	✓	✓	✓	✓	
Unique Reshape Names	C					✓					
Unique Rows	RS	✓	✓	✓		✓	✓	✓	✓	✓	
Unique Schema	RS	✓	✓	✓		✓	✓	✓	✓	✓	
Unique Table	RS	✓	✓	✓		✓	✓	✓	✓	✓	
Updatability	RS	✓	✓	✓	✓	✓	✓	✓	✓	✓	✓
Update Criteria	RS	✓	✓	✓		✓	✓	✓	✓	✓	
Update Resync	RS	✓	✓	✓		✓	✓	✓	✓	✓	
URL Generation	C										✓
Use Bookmarks	RS	✓	✓	✓	✓	✓	✓	✓	✓	✓	✓

Table Continued on Following Page

Property Name	Object Type (RS/R/F/C)	ODBC	Jet	SQL Server	Internet Publishing (IIS5)	MSDataShape	Persist	Remote	Indexing Service	Directory Services	Exchange
Use Procedure for Prepare	C			✓							
User ID	C	✓	✓	✓	✓	✓		✓		✓	✓
User Name	C	✓	✓	✓						✓	
Window Handle	C	✓	✓	✓	✓	✓		✓	✓	✓	
Workstation ID	C			✓							

For the RC3 beta of Windows 2000 this was reported as 'Integrated Security '. This has an addition space and point mark at the end of the property name. The final release may have cured this.

Object Properties

This section details the properties by object type, including the enumerated values that they support. These values are not included in the standard adovbs.inc include file but can be found in adoconvb.inc and adoconjs.inc for ASP, in VBScript and JScript format from the supporting web site.

Some properties in this list are undocumented, and I've had to make an educated guess as to their purpose. I've marked these properties with a * symbol in their description field.

The Connection Object's Properties

Property Name	Description	DataType
Access Permissions	Identifies the permissions used to access the data source. Read/Write.	ConnectModeEnum
Accessible Procedures	Identifies accessible procedures. Read-only.	Boolean
Accessible Tables	Identifies accessible tables. Read-only.	Boolean

Property Name	Description	DataType
Active Sessions	The maximum number of sessions that can exist at the same time. A value of 0 indicates no limit. Read-only.	Long
Active Statements	The maximum number of statements that can exist at the same time. Read-only.	Long
Alter Column Support	Identifies which portions of the column can be altered.	DBCOLUMNDESCFLAG
Application Name	Identifies the client application name. Read/Write.	String
Asynchable Abort	Whether transactions can be aborted asynchronously. Read-only.	Boolean
Asynchable Commit	Whether transactions can be committed asynchronously. Read-only.	Boolean
Asynchronous Processing	Specifies the asynchronous processing performed on the rowset. Read/Write.	DBPROPVAL_ASYNCH
Auto Translate	Indicates whether OEM/ANSI character conversion is used. Read/Write.	Boolean
Autocommit Isolation Level	Identifies the transaction isolation level while in auto-commit mode. Read/Write.	DBPROPVAL_OS
Bind Flags	Identifies the binding behavior for resources. Allows binding to the results of a resource rather than the resource itself.	DBBINDURLFLAG
Cache Aggressively	Identifies whether or not the provider will download and cache all properties of the resource, and its stream.	Boolean
Cache Authentication	Whether or not the data source object can cache sensitive authentication information, such as passwords, in an internal cache. Read/Write.	Boolean

Table Continued on Following Page

ADO Dynamic Properties

Property Name	Description	DataType
Catalog Location	The position of the catalog name in a table name in a text command. Returns 1 (DBPROPVAL_CL_START) if the catalog is at the start of the name (such as Access with \Temp\Database.mdb), and 2 (DBPROPVAL_CL_END) if the catalog is at the end of name (such as Oracle with ADMIN.EMP@EMPDATA). Read/Write.	DBPROPVAL_CL
Catalog Term	The name the data source uses for a catalog, e.g. 'catalog' or 'database'. Read/Write.	String
Catalog Usage	Specifies how catalog names can be used in text commands. A combination of zero or more of DBPROPVAL_CU constants. Read/Write.	DBPROPVAL_CU
Column Definition	Defines the valid clauses for the definition of a column. Read/Write.	DBPROPVAL_CD
Command Properties	The dynamic properties of the Command.*	String
Connect Timeout	The amount of time, in seconds, to wait for the initialization to complete. Read/Write.	Long
Connection Status	The status of the current connection. Read-only.	DBPROPVAL_CS
Current Catalog	The name of the current catalog. Read/Write.	String
Current DFMode	Identifies the actual version of the Data Factory on the server. Can be: "21" (the default) for version 2.1 "20" for version 2.0 "15" for version 1.5	String
Current Language	Identifies the language used for system messages selection and formatting. The language must be installed on the SQL Server or initialization of the data source fails. Read/Write.	Boolean

Property Name	Description	DataType
Data Provider	For a shaped (hierarchical) recordset, this identifies the provider who supplies the data.	String
Data Source	The name of the data source to connect to. Read/Write.	String
Data Source Name	The name of the data source. Read-only.	String
Data Source Object Threading Model	Specifies the threading models supported by the data source object. Read-only.	DBPROPVAL_RT
Datasource Type	The type of data source.	DBPROPVAL_DST
DBMS Name	The name of the product accessed by the provider. Read-only.	String
DBMS Version	The version of the product accessed by the provider. Read-only.	String
DFMode	Identifies the Data Factory mode. Can be: "21" (the default) for version 2.1 "20" for version 2.0 "15" for version 1.5	String
Driver Name	Identifies the ODBC Driver name. Read-only.	String
Driver ODBC Version	Identifies the ODBC Driver version. Read-only.	String
Driver Version	Identifies the Driver ODBC version. Read-only.	String
Enable Fastload	Indicates whether bulk-copy operations can be used between the SQL Server and the consumer.	Boolean
Encrypt Password	Whether the consumer required that the password be sent to the data source in an encrypted form. Read/Write.	Boolean
Extended Properties	Contains provider specific, extended connection information. Read/Write.	String

Table Continued on Following Page

ADO Dynamic Properties

1153

Property Name	Description	DataType
File Usage	Identifies the usage count of the ODBC driver. Read-only.	Long
Generate URL	Identifies the level of support of the Internet Server for generating URL suffixes.	DBPROPVAL_GU
General Timeout	The number of seconds before a request times out. This applies to requests other than the connection opening or a command execution.	Long
GROUP BY Support	The relationship between the columns in a GROUP BY clause and the non-aggregated columns in the select list. Read-only.	DBPROPVAL_BG
Handler	The name of the server-side customization program, and any parameters the program uses.	String
Heterogeneous Table Support	Specifies whether the provider can join tables from different catalogs or providers. Read-only.	DBPROPVAL_HT
Identifier Case Sensitivity	How identifiers treats case. Read-only.	DBPROPVAL_IC
Ignore Cached Data	Identifies whether the provider should ignore any cached data for this resource.	Boolean
Impersonation Level	Identifies the level of client impersonation the server can take whilst performing actions on behalf of the client.	DB_IMP_LEVEL
Initial Catalog	The name of the initial, or default, catalog to use when connecting to the data source. If the provider supports changing the catalog for an initialized data source, a different catalog name can be specified in the Current Catalog property. Read/Write.	String
Initial File Name	The primary file name of an attachable database. *	String
Integrated Security	Contains the name of the authentication service used by the server to identify the user. Read/Write.	String

Property Name	Description	DataType
Integrity Enhancement Facility	Indicates whether the data source supports the optional Integrity Enhancement Facility. Read-only.	Boolean
Internet Timeout	The maximum number of milliseconds to wait before generating an error.	Long
Isolation Levels	Identifies the supported transaction isolation levels. Read-only.	DBPROPVAL_TI
Isolation Retention	Identifies the supported transaction isolation retention levels. Read-only.	DBPROPVAL_TR
Jet OLEDB:Compact Reclaimed Space Amount	The approximate amount of space that would be reclaimed by a compaction. This is not guaranteed to be exact.	Long
Jet OLEDB:Compact Without Replica Repair	Indicates whether or not to find and repair damaged replicas.	Boolean
Jet OLEDB:Compact Without Relationships	Indicates whether or not to copy relationships to the new database.	Boolean
Jet OLEDB:Connecti on Control	Identifies the state of the connection, indicating whether other users are allowed to connect to the database or not.	DBPROPVAL_JCC
Jet OLEDB:Create System Database	Indicates whether or not a system database is generated when creating a new data source.	Boolean
Jet OLEDB:Database Locking Mode	Identifies the mode to use when locking the database. The first person to open a database identifies the mode.	DBPROPVAL_DL
Jet OLEDB:Database Password	The database password. Read/Write.	String
Jet OLEDB:Don't Copy Locale on Compact	Indicates that the database sort order should be used when compacting, rather that the locale.	Boolean
Jet OLEDB:Encrypt Database	Indicates whether or not to encrypt the new database.	Boolean

Table Continued on Following Page

ADO Dynamic Properties

Property Name	Description	DataType
Jet OLEDB:Engine Type	Identifies the version of the database to open, or the version of the database to create.	JET_ENGINETYPE
Jet OLEDB:Exclusive Async Delay	The maximum time (in milliseconds) that Jet will delay asynchronous writes to disk, when the database is open in exclusive mode.	Long
Jet OLEDB:Flush Transaction Timeout	Amount of time of inactivity before the asynchronous write cache is written to the disk.	Long
Jet OLEDB:Global Bulk Transactions	Identifies whether bulk operations are transacted.	DBPROPVAL_BT
Jet OLEDB:Global Partial Bulk Ops	Identifies whether Bulk operations are allowed with partial values. Read/Write.	DBPROPVAL_BP
Jet OLEDB:Implicit Commit Sync	Indicates whether or not implicit transactions are written synchronously.	Boolean
Jet OLEDB:Lock Delay	The number of times to repeat attempts to access a locked page.	Long
Jet OLEDB:Lock Retry	The number of attempts made to access a locked page.	Long
Jet OLEDB:Max Buffer Size	The largest amount of memory (in Kb) that can be used before it starts flushing changes to disk.	Long
Jet OLEDB:Max Locks Per File	The maximum number of locks that can be placed on a database. This defaults to 9500.	Long
Jet OLEDB:New Database Password	Sets the database password.	String
Jet OLEDB:ODBC Command Time Out	The number of seconds before remote ODBC queries timeout.	Long
Jet OLEDB:ODBC Parsing	Indicates whether or not Jet should attempt parsing of ODBC SQL syntax, or only use native Jet syntax.	Boolean

Property Name	Description	DataType
Jet OLEDB:Page Locks to Table Lock	The number of page locks to apply to a table before escalating the lock to a table lock. 0 means the lock will never be promoted.	Long
Jet OLEDB:Page Timeout	The amount of time (in milliseconds) that are waited before Jet checks to see if the cache is out of date with the database.	Long
Jet OLEDB:Recycle Long-Valued Pages	Indicates whether or not Jet aggressively tries to reclaim BLOB pages when they are freed.	Boolean
Jet OLEDB:Registry Path	The registry key that contains values for the Jet database engine. Read/Write.	String
Jet OLEDB:Reset ISAM Stats	Determines whether or not the ISAM statistics should be reset after the information has been returned.	Boolean
Jet OLEDB:Sandbox Mode	Indicates whether the database is in Sandbox mode. *	Boolean
Jet OLEDB:Shared Async Delay	The maximum time (in milliseconds) to delay asynchronous writes when in multi-user mode.	Long
Jet OLEDB:System database	The path and file name for the workgroup file. Read/Write.	String
Jet OLEDB:Transaction Commit Mode	A value of 1 indicates that the database commits updates immediately, rather than caching them.	Long
Jet OLEDB:User Commit Sync	Indicates whether or not explicit user transactions are written synchronously.	Boolean
Like Escape Clause	Identifies the LIKE escape clause. Read-only.	String
Locale Identifier	The locale ID of preference for the consumer. Read/Write.	Long

Table Continued on Following Page

ADO Dynamic Properties

Property Name	Description	DataType
Location	The location of the data source to connect to. Typically this will be the server name. Read/Write.	String
Lock Owner	The string to show when you lock a resource and other users attempt to access that resource. Ignored for the WEC protocol, used with FrontPage Server Extensions. Read/Write.	String
Log text and image writes	Identifies whether writes to text and images fields are logged in the transaction log. Read/Write.	Boolean
Maintain Property Values	Indicates whether or not the property values are persisted along with the data when saving a recordset. Defaults to True. *	Boolean
Mark For Offline	Indicates that the URL can be marked for offline use. *	Integer
Mask Password	The consumer requires that the password be sent to the data source in masked form. Read/Write.	Boolean
Max Columns in Group By	Identifies the maximum number of columns in a GROUP BY clause. Read-only.	Long
Max Columns in Index	Identifies the maximum number of columns in an index. Read-only.	Long
Max Columns in Order By	Identifies the maximum number of columns in an ORDER BY clause. Read-only.	Long
Max Columns in Select	Identifies the maximum number of columns in a SELECT statement. Read-only.	Long
Max Columns in Table	Identifies the maximum number of columns in a table. Read-only.	Long
Maximum Index Size	The maximum number of bytes allowed in the combined columns of an index. This is 0 if there is no specified limit or the limit is unknown. Read-only.	Long
Maximum Open Chapters	The maximum number of chapters that can be open at any one time. If a chapter must be released before a new chapter can be opened, the value is 1. If the provider does not support chapters, the value is 0. Read-only.	Long

Property Name	Description	DataType
Maximum OR Conditions	The maximum number of disjunct conditions that can be supported in a view filter. Multiple conditions of a view filter are joined in a logical OR. Providers that do not support joining multiple conditions return a value of 1, and providers that do not support view filters return a value of 0. Read-only.	Long
Maximum Row Size	The maximum length of a single row in a table. This is 0 if there is no specified limit or the limit is unknown. Read-only.	Long
Maximum Row Size Includes BLOB	Identifies whether Maximum Row Size includes the length for BLOB data. Read-only.	Boolean
Maximum Sort Columns	The maximum number of columns that can be supported in a View Sort. This is 0 if there is no specified limit or the limit is unknown. Read-only.	Long
Maximum Tables in SELECT	The maximum number of tables allowed in the FROM clause of a SELECT statement. This is 0 if there is no specified limit or the limit is unknown. Read-only.	Long
Mode	Specifies the access permissions. Read/Write.	DB_MODE
Multi-Table Update	Identifies whether the provider can update rowsets derived from multiple tables. Read-only.	Boolean
Multiple Connections	Identifies whether the provider silently creates additional connections to support concurrent Command, Connection or Recordset objects. This only applies to providers that have to spawn multiple connections, and not to providers that support multiple connections natively. Read/Write.	Boolean
Multiple Parameter Sets	Identifies whether the provider supports multiple parameter sets. Read-only.	Boolean

Table Continued on Following Page

ADO Dynamic Properties

Property Name	Description	DataType
Multiple Results	Identifies whether the provider supports multiple results objects and what restrictions it places on those objects. Read-only.	DBPROPVAL_MR
Multiple Storage Objects	Identifies whether the provider supports multiple, open storage objects at the same time. Read-only.	Boolean
Network Address	Identifies the network address of the SQL Server. Read/Write.	String
Network Library	Identifies the name of the Net-Library (DLL) used to communicate with SQL Server. Read/Write.	String
NULL Collation Order	Identifies where NULLs are sorted in a list. Read-only.	DBPROPVAL_NC
NULL Concatenation Behavior	How the data source handles concatenation of NULL-valued character data type columns with non-NULL valued character data type columns. Read-only.	DBPROPVAL_CB
Numeric Functions	Identifies the numeric functions supported by the ODBC driver and data source. Read-only.	SQL_FN_NUM
OLE DB Services	Specifies the OLE DB services to enable. Read/Write.	DBPROPVAL_OS
OLE DB Version	Specifies the version of OLE DB supported by the provider. Read-only.	String
OLE Object Support	Specifies the way in which the provider supports access to BLOBs and OLE objects stored in columns. Read-only.	DBPROPVAL_OO
OLE Objects	Indicates the level of binding support for OLE Objects.	DBPROPVAL_OO
Open Rowset Support	Indicates the level of support for opening rowsets.	DBPROPVAL_ORS
ORDER BY Columns in Select List	Identifies whether columns in an ORDER BY clause must be in the SELECT list. Read-only.	Boolean

Property Name	Description	DataType
Outer Join Capabilities	Identifies the outer join capabilities of the ODBC data source. Read-only.	SQL_OJ
Outer Joins	Identifies whether outer joins are supported or not. Read-only.	Boolean
Outer Join Capabilities	Identifies the outer join capabilities of the ODBC data source. Read-only.	SQL_OJ
Output Parameter Availability	Identifies the time at which output parameter values become available. Read-only.	DBPROPVAL_OA
Packet Size	Specifies the network packet size in bytes. It must be between 512 and 32767. The default is 4096. Read/Write.	Long
Pass By Ref Accessors	Whether the provider supports the DBACCESSOR_PASSBYREF flag. Read-only.	Boolean
Password	The password to be used to connect to the data source. Read/Write.	String
Persist Encrypted	Whether or not the consumer requires that the data source object persist sensitive authentication information, such as a password, in encrypted form. Read/Write.	Boolean
Persist Format	Indicates the format for persisting data.	PersistFormat Enum
Persist Schema	Indicates whether or not the schema is persisted along with the data.	Boolean
Persist Security Info	Whether or not the data source object is allowed to persist sensitive authentication information, such as a password, along with other authentication information. Read/Write.	Boolean
Persistent ID Type	Specifies the type of DBID that the provider uses when persisting DBIDs for tables, indexes and columns. Read-only.	DBPROPVAL_PT
Prepare Abort Behavior	Identifies how aborting a transaction affects prepared commands. Read-only.	DBPROPVAL_CB

Table Continued on Following Page

ADO Dynamic Properties

Property Name	Description	DataType
Prepare Commit Behavior	Identifies how committing a transaction affects prepared commands. Read-only.	DBPROPVAL_CB
Procedure Term	Specifies the data source providers name for a procedure, e.g. 'database procedure' or 'stored procedure'. Read-only.	String
Prompt	Specifies whether to prompt the user during initialization. Read/Write.	DBPROMPT
Protection Level	The level of protection of data sent between client and server. This property applies only to network connections other than RPC. Read/Write.	DB_PROT_LEVEL
Protocol Provider	The protocol to use when using the IPP to connect to a resource. This should be WEC to use the FrontPage Web Extender Client protocol, and DAV to use the Web Distributed Authoring and Versioning (WebDAV) protocol.	String
Provider Friendly Name	The friendly name of the provider. Read-only.	String
Provider Name	The filename of the provider. Read-only.	String
Provider Version	The version of the provider. Read-only.	String
Quoted Catalog Names	Indicates whether or not quoted identifiers are allowed for catalog names.	Boolean
Quoted Identifier Sensitivity	Identifies how quoted identifiers treat case. Read-only.	DBPROPVAL_IC
Read-Only Data Source	Whether or not the data source is read-only. Read-only.	Boolean
Remote Provider	The data provider used to supply the data from a remote connection.	String
Remote Server	The name of the server supplying data from a remote connection.	String

Property Name	Description	DataType
Reset Datasource	Specifies the data source state to reset. Write only.	DBPROPVAL_RD
Rowset Conversions on Command	Identifies whether callers can enquire on a command and about conversions supported by the command. Read-only.	Boolean
Schema Term	The name the data source uses for a schema, e.g. 'schema' or 'owner'. Read-only.	String
Schema Usage	Identifies how schema names can be used in commands. Read-only.	DBPROPVAL_SU
Server Name	The name of the server. Read-only.	String
Sort on Index	Specifies whether the provider supports setting a sort order only for columns contained in an index. Read-only.	Boolean
Special Characters	Identifies the data store's special characters. Read-only.	String
SQL Grammar Support	Identifies the SQL grammar level supported by the ODBC driver. 0 represents no conformance, 1 indicates Level 1 conformance, and 2 represents Level 2 conformance. Read-only.	Long
SQL Support	Identifies the level of support for SQL. Read-only.	DBPROPVAL_SQL
SQLOLE execute a SET TEXTLENGTH	Identifies whether SQLOLE executes a SET TEXTLENGTH before accessing BLOB fields *. Read-only.	Boolean
Stored Procedures	Indicates whether stored procedures are available. Read-only.	Boolean
String Functions	Identifies the string functions supported by the ODBC driver and data source. Read-only.	SQL_FN_STR
Structured Storage	Identifies what interfaces the rowset supports on storage objects. Read-only.	DBPROPVAL_SS

ADO Dynamic Properties

Table Continued on Following Page

Property Name	Description	DataType
Subquery Support	Identifies the predicates in text commands that support subqueries. Read-only.	DBPROPVAL_SQ
System Functions	Identifies the system functions supported by the ODBC Driver and data source. Read-only.	SQL_FN_SYS
Table Term	The name the data source uses for a table, e.g. 'table' or 'file'. Read-only.	String
Time/Date Functions	Identifies the time/date functions supported by the ODBC Driver and data source. Read-only.	SQL_SDF_CURRENT
Transact Updates	Indicates whether or not updates on the remote server are transacted. *	Boolean
Transaction DDL	Indicates whether Data Definition Language (DDL) statements are supported in transactions. Read-only.	DBPROPVAL_TC
Treat As Offline	Indicates whether or not the resource should be treated as an offline resource.	Boolean
Unicode Comparison Style	Determines the sorting options used for Unicode data.	Long
Unicode Locale Id	The locale ID to use for Unicode sorting.	Long
Unique Reshape Names	Indicates whether or not the value of the Name property of a recordset would conflict with an existing name, resulting in a unique name being generated.	Boolean
URL Generation	Indicates whether the provider requires data store generated URLs.	DBPROPVAL_GU
Use Procedure for Prepare	Indicates whether SQL Server is to use temporary stored procedures for prepared statements. Read/Write.	SSPROPVAL_USEPROCFORPREP

Property Name	Description	DataType
User Authentication mode	Indicates whether Windows NT Authentication is used to access SQL Server. Read/Write.	Boolean
User ID	The User ID to be used when connecting to the data source. Read/Write.	String
User Name	The User Name used in a particular database. Read-only.	String
Window Handle	The window handle to be used if the data source object needs to prompt for additional information. Read/Write.	Long
Workstation ID	Identifies the workstation. Read/Write.	String

ADO Dynamic Properties

The Recordset Object's Properties

Property Name	Description	DataType
Access Order	Indicates the order in which columns must be accessed on the rowset. Read/Write.	DBPROPVAL_AO
Always use content index	Indicates whether or not to use the content index to resolve queries, even if the index is out of date.	Boolean
Append-Only Rowset	A rowset opened with this property will initially contain no rows. Read/Write.	Boolean
Asynchronous Rowset Processing	Identifies the asynchronous processing performed on the rowset. Read/Write.	DBPROPVAL_ ASYNCH
Auto Recalc	Specifies when the MSDataShape provider updates aggregated and calculated columns. Read/Write.	ADCPROP_ AUTORECALC_ENUM
Background Fetch Size	The number of rows to fetch in each batch, during asynchronous reads.	Long
Background thread Priority	The priority of the background thread for asynchronous actions. Read/Write.	ADCPROP_ ASYCTHREADPRIORITY_ ENUM

Table Continued on Following Page

Property Name	Description	DataType
Batch Size	The number of rows in a batch. Read/Write.	Integer
BLOB accessibility on Forward-Only cursor	Indicates whether or not BLOB columns can be accessed irrespective of their position in the column list. If True then the BLOB column can be accessed even if it is not the last column. If False then the BLOB column can only be accessed if it the last BLOB column, and any non-BLOB columns after this column will not be accessible. Read/Write.	Boolean
Blocking Storage Objects	Indicates whether storage objects might prevent use of other methods on the rowset. Read/Write.	Boolean
Bookmark Information	Identifies additional information about bookmarks over the rowset. Read-only.	DBPROPVAL_BI
Bookmark Type	Identifies the bookmark type supported by the rowset. Read/Write.	DBPROPVAL_BMK
Bookmarkable	Indicates whether bookmarks are supported. Read-only.	Boolean
Bookmarks Ordered	Indicates whether boomarks can be compared to determine the relative position of their rows in the rowset. Read/Write.	Boolean
Bulk Operations	Identifies optimizations that a provider may take for updates to the rowset. Read-only.	DBPROPVAL_BO
Cache Child Rows	Indicates whether child rows in a chaptered recordset are cached, or whether they are re-fetched when the rows are accessed. Read/Write.	Boolean
Cache Deferred Columns	Indicates whether the provider caches the value of a deferred column when the consumer first gets a value from that column. Read/Write.	Boolean
Change Inserted Rows	Indicates whether the consumer can delete or update newly inserted rows. An inserted row is assumed to be one that has been transmitted to the data source, as opposed to a pending insert row. Read/Write.	Boolean

Property Name	Description	DataType
Column Privileges	Indicates whether access rights are restricted on a column-by-column basis. Read-only.	Boolean
Column Set Notification	Indicates whether changing a column set is cancellable. Read-only.	DBPROPVAL_NP
Column Writable	Indicates whether a particular column is writable. Read/Write.	Boolean
Command Time Out	The number of seconds to wait before a command times out. A value of 0 indicates an infinite timeout. Read/Write.	Long
Concurrency control method	Identifies the method used for concurrency control when using server based cursors. Read/Write.	SSPROPVAL_CONCUR
Cursor Engine Version	Identifies the version of the cursor engine. Read-only.	String
Defer Column	Indicates whether the data in a column is not fetched until specifically requested. Read/Write.	Boolean
Defer scope and security testing	Indicates whether or not the search will defer scope and security testing.	Boolean
Delay Storage Object Updates	Indicates whether, when in delayed update mode, storage objects are also used in delayed update mode. Read/Write.	Boolean
Fastload Options	Indicates the options to use when in Fastload mode.	String
Fetch Backward	Indicates whether a rowset can fetch backwards. Read/Write.	Boolean
Filter Operations	Identifies which comparison operations are supported when using Filter on a particular column. Read-only.	DBPROPVAL_CO
Find Operations	Identifies which comparison operations are supported when using Find on a particular column. Read-only.	DBPROPVAL_CO
FOR BROWSE versioning columns	Indicates the rowset contains the primary key or a timestamp column. Only applicable with rowsets created with the SQL FOR BROWSE statement. Read/Write.	Boolean

ADO Dynamic Properties

Table Continued on Following Page

Property Name	Description	DataType
Force no command preparation when executing a parameterized command	Identifies whether or not a temporary statement is created for parameterized commands. *. Read/Write.	Boolean
Force no command reexecution when failure to satisfy all required properties	Identifies whether or not the command is reexecuted if the command properties are invalid. *. Read/Write.	Boolean
Force no parameter rebinding when executing a command	Identifies whether or not the command parameters are rebound every time the command is executed *. Read/Write.	Boolean
Force SQL Server Firehose Mode cursor	Identifies whether or not a forward-only, read-only cursor is always created *. Read/Write.	Boolean
Generate a Rowset that can be marshalled	Identifies whether or not the rowset that is to be created can be marshalled across process boundaries *. Read/Write.	Boolean
Hidden Columns	Indicates the number of hidden columns in the rowset added by the provider to uniquely identify rows.	Long
Hold Rows	Indicates whether the rowset allows the consumer to retrieve more rows or change the next fetch position whilst holding previously fetched rows with pending changes. Read/Write.	Boolean
Immobile Rows	Indicates whether the rowset will reorder insert or updated rows. Read/Write.	Boolean
Include SQL_FLOAT, SQL_DOUBLE, and SQL_REAL in QBU where clauses	When using a query-based update, setting this to True will include REAL, FLOAT and DOUBLE numeric types in the WHERE clause, otherwise they will be omitted. Read/Write.	Boolean
Initial Fetch Size	Identifies the initial size of the cache into which records are fetched. Read/Write.	Long

Property Name	Description	DataType
Jet OLEDB:Bulk Transaction	Determines whether bulk operations are transacted.	DBPROPVAL_BT
Jet OLEDB:Enable Fat Cursors	Indicates whether or not Jet caches multiple rows for remote row sources.	Boolean
Jet OLEDB:Fat Cursor Cache Size	The number of rows that should be cached if the dynamic property Jet OLEDB:Enable Fat Cursors is set to True.	Long
Jet OLEDB:Inconsistent	Indicates whether or not inconsistent updates arc allowed on queries.	Boolean
Jet OLEDB:Locking Granularity	Identifies the lock mode used to open a table. This only applies if Jet OLEDB:Database Locking Mode is set to DBPROPVAL_DL_ALCATRAZ.	DBPROPVAL_LG
Jet OLEDB:ODBC Pass-Through Statement	Identifies the statement used for a SQL Pass through statement. Read/Write.	String
Jet OLEDB:Partial Bulk Ops	Indicates whether on not bulk operations will complete if some of the values fail.	
Jet OLEDB:Pass Through Query Bulk-Op	Indicates whether or not the pass-through query is a bulk operation.	Boolean
Jet OLEDB:Pass Through Query Connect String	Identifies the Connect string for an ODBC pass through query. Read/Write.	String
Jet OLEDB:Stored Query	Indicates whether or not the command should be interpreted as a stored query.	Boolean
Jet OLEDB:Validate Rules On Set	Indicates whether Jet validation rules are applied when the value in a column is set (True) or when the changes are commited (False).	Boolean
Keep Identity	Indicates whether or not IDENTITY columns should keep the values if supplied by the client during an INSERT.	Boolean

Table Continued on Following Page

ADO Dynamic Properties

Property Name	Description	DataType
Keep Nulls	Indicates whether or not NULL values supplied by the client should be kept if DEFAULT values exist on the columns.	Boolean
Literal Bookmarks	Indicates whether bookmarks can be compared literally, i.e. as a series of bytes. Read/Write.	Boolean
Literal Row Identity	Indicates whether the consumer can perform a binary comparison of two row handles to determine whether they point to the same row. Read-only.	Boolean
Lock Mode	Identifies the level of locking performed by the rowset. Read/Write.	DBPROPVAL_LM
Maintain Change Status	Indicates whether or not to maintain the status of a row if a conflict happens during row updates. *	Boolean
Maximum BLOB Length	Identifies the maximum length of a BLOB field. Read-only.	Long
Maximum Open Rows	Specifies the maximum number of rows that can be active at the same time. Read/Write.	Long
Maximum Pending Rows	Specifies the maximum number of rows that can have pending changes at the same time. Read/Write.	Long
Maximum Rows	Specifies the maximum number of rows that can be returned in the rowset. This is 0 if there is no limit. Read/Write.	Long
Memory Usage	Estimates the amount of memory that can be used by the rowset. If set to 0 the amount is unlimited. If between 1 and 99 it specifies a percentage of the available virtual memory. If 100 or greater it specifies the number of kilobytes. Read/Write.	Long
Notification Granularity	Identifies when the consumer is notified for methods that operate on multiple rows. Read/Write.	DBPROPVAL_NT
Notification Phases	Identifies the notification phases supported by the provider. Read-only.	DBPROPVAL_NP

Property Name	Description	DataType
Objects Transacted	Indicates whether any object created on the specified column is transacted. Read/Write.	Boolean
ODBC Concurrency Type	Identifies the ODBC concurrency type. Read-only.	Integer
ODBC Cursor Type	Identifies the ODBC cursor type. Read-only.	Integer
Others' Changes Visible	Indicates whether the rowset can see updates and deletes made by someone other that the consumer of the rowset. Read/Write.	Boolean
Others' Inserts Visible	Indicates whether the rowset can see rows inserted by someone other than the consumer of the rowset. Read/Write.	Boolean
Own Changes Visible	Indicates whether the rowset can see its own updates and deletes. Read/Write.	Boolean
Own Inserts Visible	Indicates whether the rowset can see its own inserts. Read/Write.	Boolean
Position on the last row after insert	Identifies whether or not the cursor is placed on the last row after an insert. * Read-only.	Boolean
Preserve on Abort	Indicates whether, after aborting a transaction, the rowset remains active. Read/Write.	Boolean
Preserve on Commit	Indicates whether after committing a transaction the rowset remains active. Read/Write.	Boolean
Query Based Updates/Deletes/Inserts	Identifies whether or not queries are used for updates, deletes, and inserts. * Read/Write.	Boolean
Quick Restart	Indicates whether RestartPosition is relatively quick to execute. Read/Write.	Boolean
Query Restriction	Indicates the restriction to use for a query.	String
Reentrant Events	Indicates whether the provider supports reentrancy during callbacks. Read-only.	Boolean
Remove Deleted Rows	Indicates whether the provider removes rows it detects as having been deleted from the rowset. Read/Write.	Boolean

Table Continued on Following Page

ADO Dynamic Properties

Property Name	Description	DataType
Report Multiple Changes	Indicates whether an update or delete can affect multiple rows and the provider can detect that multiple rows have been updated or deleted. Read-only.	Boolean
Reshape Name	Indicates the name of the recordset that can be used in reshaping commands.	String
Resync Command	The command string that the Resync method will use to refresh data in the Unique Table.	String
Return PROPVARIANTs in variant binding	Indicates whether or not to return PROPVARIANTS when binding to variant columns.	Boolean
Return Pending Inserts	Indicates whether methods that fetch rows can return pending insert rows. Read-only.	Boolean
Row Delete Notification	Indicates whether deleting a row is cancellable. Read-only.	DBPROPVAL_NP
Row First Change Notification	Indicates whether changing the first row is cancellable. Read-only.	DBPROPVAL_NP
Row Insert Notification	Indicates whether inserting a new row is cancellable. Read-only.	DBPROPVAL_NP
Row Privileges	Indicates whether access rights are restricted on a row-by-row basis. Read-only.	Boolean
Row Resynchronization Notification	Indicates whether resynchronizing a row is cancellable. Read-only.	DBPROPVAL_NP
Row Threading Model	Identifies the threading models supported by the rowset. Read/Write.	DBPROPVAL_RT
Row Undo Change Notification	Indicates whether undoing a change is cancellable. Read-only.	DBPROPVAL_NP
Row Undo Delete Notification	Indicates whether undoing a delete is cancellable. Read-only.	DBPROPVAL_NP
Row Undo Insert Notification	Indicates whether undoing an insert is cancellable. Read-only.	DBPROPVAL_NP
Row Update Notification	Indicates whether updating a row is cancellable. Read-only.	DBPROPVAL_NP

Property Name	Description	DataType
Rowset Fetch Position Change Notification	Indicates whether changing the fetch position is cancellable. Read-only.	DBPROPVAL_NP
Rowset Release Notification	Indicates whether releasing a rowset is cancellable. Read-only.	DBPROPVAL_NP
Scroll Backward	Indicates whether the rowset can scroll backward. Read/Write.	Boolean
Server Cursor	Indicates whether the cursor underlying the rowset (if any) must be materialized on the server. Read/Write.	Boolean
Server Data on Insert	Indicates whether, at the time an insert is transmitted to the server, the provider retrieves data from the server to update the local row cache. Read/Write.	Boolean
Skip Deleted Bookmarks	Indicates whether the rowset allows positioning to continue if a bookmark row was deleted. Read/Write.	Boolean
SQL Content Query Locale String	The locale string to use for queries.	String
Strong Row Identity	Indicates whether the handles of newly inserted rows can be compared. Read-only.	Boolean
Unique Catalog	Specifies the catalog, or database name containing the table named in the Unique Table property.	String
Unique Rows	Indicates whether each row is uniquely identified by its column values. Read/Write.	Boolean
Unique Schema	Specifies the schema, or owner of the table named in the Unique Table property.	String
Unique Table	Specifies the name of the base table upon which edits are allowed. This is required when updateable recordsets are created from one-to-many JOIN statements.	String

Table Continued on Following Page

ADO Dynamic Properties

Property Name	Description	DataType
Updatability	Identifies the supported methods for updating a rowset. Read/Write.	DBPROPVAL_UP
Update Criteria	Specifies which fields can be used to detect conflicts during optimistic updates. Read/Write.	ADCPROP_ UPDATECRITERIA_ ENUM
Update Operation	For chaptered recordsets, identifies the operation to be performed with a requery. Read/Write.	String
Update Resync	Specifies whether an implicit Resync method is called directly after an UpdateBatch method.	CEResyncEnum
Use Bookmarks	Indicates whether the rowset supports bookmarks. Read/Write.	Boolean

The Field Object's Properties

The field property names are different from the other properties, because they are less readable and appear more like the schema column names.

Property Name	Description	DataType
BASECATALOGNAME	The name of the catalog. Read-only.	String
BASECOLUMNNAME	The name of the column. Read-only.	String
BASESCHEMANAME	The name of the schema. Read-only.	String
BASETABLENAME	The table name. Read-only.	String
CALCULATIONINFO	This is only available for client cursors.	Binary
CLSID	The class id of the field.	GUID
COLLATINGSEQUENCE	The locale ID of the sort sequence.	Long
COMPUTEMODE	Indicates the mode of recalculation for computed fields.	DBCOMPUTEMODE

Property Name	Description	DataType
DATETIMEPRECISION	The number of digits in the fractional seconds portion of a datetime column. Read-only.	Long
DEFAULTVALUE	The default value of the field.	Variant
DOMAINCATALOG	The name of the catalog containing this column's domain.	String
DOMAINNAME	The name of the domain of which this column is a member.	String
DOMAINSCHEMA	The name of the schema containing this column's domain.	String
HASDEFAULT	Indicates whether or not the field has a default value.	Boolean
ISAUTOINCREMENT	Identifies whether the column is an auto-increment column, such as an Access Autonumber or a SQL Server IDENTITY column. Read-only.	Boolean
ISCASESENSITIVE	Identifies whether the contents of the column are case sensitive. Useful when searching. Read-only.	Boolean
ISSEARCHABLE	Identifies the searchability of the column. Read-only.	DB_SEARCHABLE
ISUNIQUE	Indicates whether or not the field uniquely identifies the row.	Boolean
KEYCOLUMN	Identifies whether or not the column is a key column, used to uniquely identify the row. Read-only.	Boolean
OCTETLENGTH	The maximum column length in bytes, for character or binary data columns. Read-only.	Long
OPTIMIZE	Identifies whether the column is indexed locally. This is only available of client cursors. Read/Write.	Boolean
RELATIONCONDITIONS	Identifies the relationship between fields. This is only available on client cursors. *	Binary

ADOX Constants

ActionEnum

Constant Name	Value	Description
adAccessDeny	3	Deny the specific permissions to the Group or User.
adAccessGrant	1	Grant the specific permissions to the Group or User. Other permissions may remain in effect.
adAccessRevoke	4	Revoke any specific access rights to the Group or User.
adAccessSet	2	Set the exact permissions for the Group or User. Other permissions will not remain in effect.

Note: The documentation indicates that adAccessAuditSuccess *and* adAccessAuditFailure *are allowable values for the* Action. *This is incorrect – these constants are not supported.*

AllowNullsEnum

Constant Name	Value	Description
adIndexNullsAllow	0	Key columns with null values have index values.
adIndexNullsDisallow	1	Do not allow index entries if the key columns are Null.
adIndexNullsIgnore	2	Null values in key columns are ignored and an index entry is not created.
adIndexNullsIgnoreAny	4	Null values in any part of the key (for multiple columns) are ignored, and an index entry is not created.

ColumnAttributesEnum

Constant Name	Value	Description
adColFixed	1	The column is of a fixed length.
adColNullable	2	The column may contain null values.

DataTypeEnum

The ADOX data type constants are the same as the ADO data type constants. See the listing for DataTypeEnum in Appendix D.

InheritTypeEnum

Constant Name	Value	Description
adInheritBoth	3	Permissions for the object are inherited by both objects and other containers.
adInheritContainers	2	Permissions for the object are inherited by other containers.
adInheritNone	0	No permissions are inherited.
adInheritNo Propogate	4	The adInheritObjects and adInheritContainers permissions are not propagated to child objects.
adInheritObjects	1	Permissions are only inherited by objects that are not containers.

Note: The documentation states that adInheritOnly is an allowable option for the InheritType. This is incorrect – this constant is not supported.

KeyTypeEnum

Constant Name	Value	Description
adKeyForeign	2	The key is a foreign key.
adKeyPrimary	1	The key is a primary key.
adKeyUnique	3	The key is unique.

ObjectTypeEnum

Constant Name	Value	Description
adPermObjColumn	2	The object is a column.
adPermObjDatabase	3	The object is a database.
adPermObjProcedure	4	The object is a procedure.
adPermObjProviderSpecific	-1	The object is of a provider-specific type.
adPermObjTable	1	The object is a table.
adPermObjView	5	The object is a view.

Note: The documentation mentions adPermObjSchema, adPermObjDomain, adPermObjCollation, adPermObjSchemaRowset, adPermObjCharacterSet, adPermObjTranslation *as allowable options for the object type. This is incorrect – these constants are not supported.*

RightsEnum

Constant Name	Value	Description
adRightCreate	16384	The User or Group has permission to create the object.
adRightDelete	65536	The User or Group has permission to delete the object.
adRightDrop	256	The User or Group has permission to drop the object.
adRightExclusive	512	The User or Group has permission to obtain exclusive access to the object.

Table Continued on Following Page

ADOX Constants

Constant Name	Value	Description
adRightExecute	536870912	The User or Group has permission to execute the object.
adRightFull	268435456	The User or Group has full permissions on the object.
adRightInsert	32768	The User or Group has permission to insert the object.
adRightMaximumAllowed	33554432	The User or Group has the maximum number of permissions allowed by the provider.
adRightNone	0	The User or Group has no permissions on the object.
adRightRead	-2147483648	The User or Group has permission to read the object.
adRightReadDesign	1024	The User or Group has permission to read the design of the object.
adRightReadPermissions	131072	The User or Group has permission to read the permissions of the object.
adRightReference	8192	The User or Group has permission to reference the object.
adRightUpdate	1073741824	The User or Group has permission to update the object.
adRightWithGrant	4096	The User or Group has permission to grant permissions to other users or groups.
adRightWriteDesign	2048	The User or Group has permission to change the design of the object.
adRightWriteOwner	524288	The User or Group has permission to change the owner of the object.
adRightWritePermissions	262144	The User or Group has permission to change the permissions of the object.

RuleEnum

Constant Name	Value	Description
adRICascade	1	Updates and deletes are cascaded.
adRINone	0	Updates and deletes are not cascaded.
adRISetDefault	3	Set the foreign key to its default value for updates and deletes.
adRISetNull	2	Set the foreign key to Null for updates and deletes.

SortOrderEnum

Constant Name	Value	Description
adSortAscending	1	The key column is in ascending order.
adSortDescending	2	The key column is in descending order.

DBPROPVAL_NC

Constant Name	Value	Description
DBPROPVAL_NC_END	1	Null values are collated at the end of the list, irrespective of the collation order.
DBPROPVAL_NC_HIGH	2	Null values are collated at the high end of the list.
DBPROPVAL_NC_LOW	4	Null values are collated at the low end of the list.
DBPROPVAL_NC_START	8	Null values are collated at the start of the list, irrespective of the collation order.

DBPROPVAL_IN

Constant Name	Value	Description
DBPROPVAL_IN_DISALLOWNULL	1	Keys containing NULL values are not allowed. Generate an error if an attempt is made to insert a key that contains NULL.
DBPROPVAL_IN_IGNORENULL	2	Keys containing NULL values are allowed, but are ignored and not added to the index. No error is generated.
DBPROPVAL_IN_IGNOREANYNULL	4	Keys consisting of multi-columns will allow a NULL in any column, but the key is ignored and not added to the index. No error is generated.

ADOX Constants

DBPROPVAL_IT

Constant Name	Value	Description
DBPROPVAL_IT_BTREE	1	The index is a B-tree.
DBPROPVAL_IT_CONTENT	3	The index is a content index.
DBPROPVAL_IT_HASH	2	The index is a hash file using linear or extensible hashing.
DBPROPVAL_IT_OTHER	4	The index is some other type of index.

G

ADOX Dynamic Properties

Property Support

The following table shows a list of all OLE DB dynamic properties for ADOX, and indicates which of them Microsoft Access and Microsoft SQL Server support. Since this list contains dynamic properties, not every property may show up under all circumstances. Other providers may also implement properties not listed in this table.

A tick indicates the property is supported, and a blank space indicates it is not supported.

Property Name	Object	Jet	SQL
Auto-Update	Index	✓	
Autoincrement	Column	✓	✓
Clustered	Index	✓	✓
Default	Column	✓	✓
Description	Column	✓	
Fill Factor	Index	✓	✓
Fixed Length	Column	✓	✓
Increment	Column	✓	
Index Type	Index	✓	
Initial Size	Index	✓	
Jet OLEDB:Allow Zero Length	Column	✓	
Jet OLEDB:AutoGenerate	Column	✓	

Property Name	Object	Jet	SQL
Jet OLEDB:Cache Link Name/Password	Table	✓	
Jet OLEDB:Column Validation Rule	Column	✓	
Jet OLEDB:Column Validation Text	Column	✓	
Jet OLEDB:Compressed UNICODE Strings	Column	✓	
Jet OLEDB:Create Link	Table	✓	
Jet OLEDB:Exclusive Link	Table	✓	
Jet OLEDB:Hyperlink	Column	✓	
Jet OLEDB:IISAM Not Last Column	Column	✓	
Jet OLEDB:Link Datasource	Table	✓	
Jet OLEDB:Link Provider String	Table	✓	
Jet OLEDB:One BLOB per Page	Column	✓	
Jet OLEDB:Remote Table Name	Table	✓	
Jet OLEDB:Table Hidden In Access	Table	✓	
Jet OLEDB:Table Validation Rule	Table	✓	
Jet OLEDB:Table Validation Text	Table	✓	
NULL Collation	Index	✓	
NULL Keys	Index	✓	
Nullable	Column	✓	✓
Primary Key	Column		✓
Primary Key	Index	✓	✓
Seed	Column	✓	
Sort Bookmarks	Index	✓	
Temporary Index	Index	✓	
Temporary Table	Table	✓	✓
Unique	Column		✓
Unique	Index	✓	✓

Column Object

Name	Description	DataType
Autoincrement	Indicates whether or not the column is autoincrementing.	Boolean
Default	Specifies the default value for the column, to be used if no explicit value is supplied.	Variant
Description	The column description.	String
Fixed Length	Indicates whether or not the column holds fixed length data.	Boolean
Increment	The value by which auto-increment columns are increased.	Long
Jet OLEDB: Allow Zero Length	Indicates whether or not zero length strings can be inserted into the field.	Boolean
Jet OLEDB:Autogenerate	Indicates whether or not, for a GUID data type, a GUID should be automatically created.	Boolean
Jet OLEDB:Column Validation Rule	The validation rule to apply to column values before allowing the column to be set.	String
Jet OLEDB:Column Validation Text	Errors string to display if changes to a row do not meet the column validation rule.	String
Jet OLEDB:Compressed UNICODE Strings	Indicates whether or not Jet should compress UNICODE strings. Only applicable to Jet 4.0 databases.	Boolean
Jet OLEDB:Hyperlink	Indicates whether or not the column is a hyperlink.	Boolean
Jet OLEDB:IISAM Not Last Column	When creating columns (or a table) for installable IISAMS, this indicates whether or nor this is the last column.	Boolean
Jet OLEDB:One BLOB Per Page	Indicates whether or not BLOB columns can share data pages.	Boolean
Nullable	Indicates whether or not the column can contain NULL values.	Boolean

Name	Description	DataType
Primary Key	Indicates whether or not the column is part of the primary key.	Boolean
Seed	The initial seed value of an auto-increment column.	Long
Unique	Indicates whether or not the column allows unique values.	Boolean

Index Object

Property Name	Description	DataType
Auto-Update	Indicates whether or not the index is maintained automatically when changes are made to rows.	Boolean
Clustered	Indicates whether or not the index is clustered.	Boolean
Fill Factor	Identifies the fill-factor of the index. This is the storage use of page-nodes during index creation. It is always 100 for the Jet provider.	Long
Index Type	The type of the index.	DBPROPVAL_IT
Initial Size	The total number of bytes allocated to the index when it is first created.	Long
NULL Collation	Specifies how NULL values are collated in the index.	DBPROPVAL_NC
NULL Keys	Specifies whether key values containing NULLs are allowed.	DBPROPVAL_IN
Primary Key	Indicates whether or not the index represents the primary key on the table.	Boolean
Sort Bookmarks	Indicates whether or not repeated keys are sorted by bookmarks.	Boolean
Temporary Index	Indicates whether or not the index is temporary.	Boolean
Unique	Indicates whether or not index keys must be unique.	Boolean

Table Object

Property Name	Description	DataType
Jet OLEDB:Cache Link Name/Password	Indicates whether or not the authentication information for a linked table should be cached locally in the Jet database.	Boolean
Jet OLEDB:Create Link	Indicates whether or not a link is created to a remote data source when creating a new table.	Boolean
Jet OLEDB:Exclusive Link	Indicates whether or not the remote data source is opened exclusively when creating a link.	Boolean
Jet OLEDB:Link Datasource	The name of the remote data source to link to.	String
Jet OLEDB:Link Provider String	The connection string to the remote provider.	String
Jet OLEDB:Remote Table Name	The name of the remote table in a link.	String
Jet OLEDB:Table Hidden In Access	Indicates whether or not the table is shown in the Access user interface.	Boolean
Jet OLEDB:Table Validation Rule	The validation rule to apply to row values before committing changes to the row.	String
Jet OLEDB:Table Validation Text	Errors string to display if changes to a row do not meet the table validation rule.	String
Temporary Table	Indicates whether or not the table is a temporary table.	Boolean

ADOX Dynamic Properties

ADOMD Constants

MemberTypeEnum

Name	Value	Description
adMemberAll	2	The member is the All member, at the top of the members hierachy.
adMemberFormula	4	The member identifies a formula.
adMemberMeasure	3	The member identifies a Measure.
adMemberRegular	1	The member identifies a regular member.
adMemberUnknown	0	The type of member is unknown.

MDMEASURE_AGGR

Name	Value	Description
MDMEASURE_AGGR_SUM	1	The aggregate function is SUM.
MDMEASURE_AGGR_COUNT	2	The aggregate function is COUNT.
MDMEASURE_AGGR_MIN	3	The aggregate function is MIN.
MDMEASURE_AGGR_MAX	4	The aggregate function is MAX.
MDMEASURE_AGGR_AVG	5	The aggregate function is AVG.
MDMEASURE_AGGR_VAR	6	The aggregate function is VAR.
MDMEASURE_AGGR_STD	7	The aggregate function is one of SUM, COUNT, MIN, MAX, AVG, VAR, STDEV.

Name	Value	Description
MDMEASURE_AGGR_CALCULATED	127	The aggregate function is derived from formula that is not a standard one.
MDMEASURE_AGGR_UNKNOWN	0	The aggregate function is not known.

MDLEVEL_TYPE

Name	Value	Description
MDLEVEL_TYPE_REGULAR	0	The level is a regular level.
MDLEVEL_TYPE_ALL	1	The level identifies the top of the hierarchy, or All levels.
MDLEVEL_TYPE_CALCULATED	2	The level is a calculated level.
MDLEVEL_TYPE_TIME	4	The level is a time level.
MDLEVEL_TYPE_TIME_YEARS	20	The level is a time level, based on years.
MDLEVEL_TYPE_TIME_HALF_YEAR	36	The level is a time level, based on half-years.
MDLEVEL_TYPE_TIME_QUARTERS	68	The level is a time level, based on quarters.
MDLEVEL_TYPE_TIME_MONTHS	132	The level is a time level, based on months.
MDLEVEL_TYPE_TIME_WEEKS	260	The level is a time level, based on weeks.
MDLEVEL_TYPE_TIME_DAYS	516	The level is a time level, based on days.
MDLEVEL_TYPE_TIME_HOURS	772	The level is a time level, based on hours.
MDLEVEL_TYPE_TIME_MINUTES	1028	The level is a time level, based on minutes.
MDLEVEL_TYPE_TIME_SECONDS	2052	The level is a time level, based on seconds.
MDLEVEL_TYPE_TIME_UNDEFINED	4100	The level type is not defined.
MDLEVEL_TYPE_UNKNOWN	0	The level type is unknown.

MDTREEOP

Name	Value	Description
MDTREEOP_ANCESTORS	32	Show only members that are ancestors of the selected member.
MDTREEOP_CHILDREN	1	Show only members that are children of the selected member.
MDTREEOP_SIBLINGS	2	Show only members that are siblings of the selected member.
MDTREEOP_PARENT	4	Show only members that are parents of the selected member.
MDTREEOP_SELF	8	Show the selected member in the list.
MDTREEOP_DESCENDANTS	16	Show only members that are descendants of the selected member.

MDPROPVAL_AU

Name	Value	Description
MDPROPVAL_AU_UNSUPPORTED	0	Updating of aggregated cells is not supported.
MDPROPVAL_AU_UNCHANGED	1	Aggregated cells can be changed, but the cells that make up the aggregation remain unchanged.
MDPROPVAL_AU_UNKNOWN	2	Aggregated cells can be changed, but the cells that make up the aggregation remains undefined.

MDPROPVAL_FS

Name	Value	Description
MDPROPVAL_FS_FULL_SUPPORT	1	The provider supports flattening.
MDPROPVAL_FS_GENERATED_COLUMN	2	The provider supports flattening by using dummy names.
MDPROPVAL_FS_GENERATED_DIMENSION	3	The provider supports flattening by generating one column per dimension.

ADOMD Constants

1193

Name	Value	Description
MDPROPVAL_FS_NO_SUPPORT	4	The provider does not support flattening.

MDPROPVAL_MC

Name	Value	Description
MDPROPVAL_MC_SINGLECASE	1	The provider supports simple case statements.
MDPROPVAL_MC_SEARCHEDCASE	2	The provider supports searched case statements.

MDPROPVAL_MD

Name	Value	Description
MDPROPVAL_MD_BEFORE	2	The BEFORE flag is supported.
MDPROPVAL_MD_AFTER	4	The AFTER flag is supported.
MDPROPVAL_MD_SELF	1	The SELF flag is supported.

MDPROPVAL_MF

Name	Value	Description
MDPROPVAL_MF_WITH_CALCMEMBERS	1	Calculated members are supported by use of the WITH clause.
MDPROPVAL_MF_WITH_NAMEDSETS	2	Named sets are supported by use of the WITH clause.
MDPROPVAL_MF_CREATE_CALCMEMBERS	4	Named calculated members are supported by use of the CREATE clause.
MDPROPVAL_MF_CREATE_NAMEDSETS	8	Named sets are supported by use of the CREATE clause.
MDPROPVAL_MF_SCOPE_SESSION	16	The scope value of SESSION is supported during the creation of named sets and calculated members.

Name	Value	Description
MDPROPVAL_MF_SCOPE_GLOBAL	32	The scope value of GLOBAL is supported during the creation of named sets and calculated members.

MDPROPVAL_MJC

Name	Value	Description
MDPROPVAL_MJC_IMPLICITCUBE	4	An empty FROM clause is supported, and the cube is implictly resolved.
MDPROPVAL_MJC_SINGLECUBE	1	Only one cube is supported in the FROM clause.
MDPROPVAL_MJC_MULTICUBES	2	More than one cube is supported in the FROM clause.

MDPROPVAL_MMF

Name	Value	Description
MDPROPVAL_MMF_COUSIN	1	The COUSIN function is supported.
MDPROPVAL_MMF_PARALLELPERIOD	2	The PARALLELPERIOD function is supported.
MDPROPVAL_MMF_OPENINGPERIOD	4	The OPENINGPERIOD function is supported.
MDPROPVAL_MMF_CLOSINGPERIOD	8	The CLOSINGPERIOD function is supported.

MDPROPVAL_MNF

Name	Value	Description
MDPROPVAL_MNF_MEDIAN	1	The MEDIAN function is supoprted.
MDPROPVAL_MNF_VAR	2	The VAR function is supported.
MDPROPVAL_MNF_STDDEV	4	The STDDEV function is supported.
MDPROPVAL_MNF_RANK	8	The RANK function is supported.

Name	Value	Description
MDPROPVAL_MNF_AGGREGATE	16	The AGGREGATE function is supported.
MDPROPVAL_MNF_COVARIANCE	32	The COVARIANCE function is supported.
MDPROPVAL_MNF_CORRELATION	64	The CORRELATION function is supported.
MDPROPVAL_MNF_LINREGSLOPE	128	The LINREGSLOPE function is supported.
MDPROPVAL_MNF_LINREGVARIANCE	256	The LINREGVARIANCE function is supported.
MDPROPVAL_MNF_LINREGR2	512	The LINREGR2 function is supported.
MDPROPVAL_MNF_LINREGPOINT	1024	The LINREGPOINT function is supported.
MDPROPVAL_MNF_DRILLDOWNLEVEL	2048	The DRILLDOWNLEVEL function is supported.
MDPROPVAL_MNF_ DRILLDOWNMEMBERTOP	4096	The DRILLDOWNMEMBERTOP function is supported.
MDPROPVAL_MNF_ DRILLDOWNMEMBERBOTTOM	8192	The DRILLDOWNMEMBERBOTTOM function is supported.
MDPROPVAL_MNF_ DRILLDOWNLEVELTOP	16384	The DRILLDOWNLEVELTOP function is supported.
MDPROPVAL_MNF_ DRILLDOWNLEVELBOTTOM	32768	The DRILLDOWNLEVELBOTTOM function is supported.
MDPROPVAL_MNF_DRILLUPMEMBER	65536	The DRILLUPMEMBER function is supported.
MDPROPVAL_MNF_DRILLUPLEVEL	131072	The DRILLUPLEVEL function is supported.

MDPROPVAL_MO

Name	Value	Description
MDPROPVAL_MO_TUPLE		The tuple.[VALUE] clause can be qualified by a cube name as an argument.

MDPROPVAL_MOQ

Name	Value	Description
MDPROPVAL_MOQ_DATASOURCE_CUBE	1	Cubes can be qualified by the data source name.
MDPROPVAL_MOQ_CATALOG_CUBE	2	Cubes can be qualified by the catalog name.
MDPROPVAL_MOQ_SCHEMA_CUBE	4	Cubes can be qualified by the schema name.
MDPROPVAL_MOQ_CUBE_DIM	8	Dimensions can be qualified by the cube name.
MDPROPVAL_MOQ_DIM_HIER	16	Hierarchies can be qualified by the dimension name.
MDPROPVAL_MOQ_DIMHIER_LEVEL	32	Levels can be qualified by the schema name, and/or the hierarchy name.
MDPROPVAL_MOQ_LEVEL_MEMBER	64	Members can be qualified by a level name.
MDPROPVAL_MOQ_MEMBER_MEMBER	128	Members can be qualified by their ancestor names.

MDPROPVAL_MS

Name	Value	Description
MDPROPVAL_MS_SINGLETUPLE	2	Only one tuple is supported in the WHERE clause.
MDPROPVAL_MS_MULTIPLETUPLES	1	Multiple tuples are supported in the WHERE clause.

MDPROPVAL_MSC

Name	Value	Description
MDPROPVAL_MSC_LESSTHAN	1	The provider supports the less than operator.
MDPROPVAL_MSC_GREATERTHAN	2	The provider supports the greater than operator.

ADOMD Constants

Name	Value	Description
MDPROPVAL_MSC_LESSTHANEQUAL	4	The provider supports the less than or equal to operator.
MDPROPVAL_MSC_GREATERTHANEQUAL	8	The provider supports the greater than or equal to operator.

MDPROPVAL_MSF

Name	Value	Description
MDPROPVAL_MSF_TOPPERCENT	1	The TOPPERCENT function is supported.
MDPROPVAL_MSF_BOTTOMPERCENT	2	The BOTTOMPERCENT function is supported.
MDPROPVAL_MSF_TOPSUM	4	The TOPSUM function is supported.
MDPROPVAL_MSF_BOTTOMSUM	8	The BOTTOMSUM function is supported.
MDPROPVAL_MSF_DRILLDOWNLEVEL	2048	The DRILLDOWNLEVEL function is supported.
MDPROPVAL_MSF_DRILLDOWNMEMBER	1024	The DRILLDOWNMEMBER function is supported.
MDPROPVAL_MSF_DRILLDOWNMEMBERTOP	4096	The DRILLDOWNMEMBERTOP function is supported.
MDPROPVAL_MSF_DRILLDOWNMEMBERBOTTOM	8192	The DRILLDOWNMEMBERBOTTOM function is supported.
MDPROPVAL_MSF_DRILLDOWNLEVELTOP	16384	The DRILLDOWNLEVELTOP function is supported.
MDPROPVAL_MSF_DRILLDOWNLEVELBOTTOM	32768	The DRILLDOWNLEVELBOTTOM function is supported.
MDPROPVAL_MSF_DRILLUPMEMBER	65536	The DRILLUPMEMBER function is supported.
MDPROPVAL_MSF_DRILLUPLEVEL	131072	The DRILLUPLEVEL function is supported.
MDPROPVAL_MSF_PERIODSTODATE	16	The PERIODSTODATE function is supported.

Name	Value	Description
MDPROPVAL_MSF_LASTPERIODS	32	The LASTPERIODS function is supported.
MDPROPVAL_MSF_YTD	64	The YTD function is supported.
MDPROPVAL_MSF_QTD	128	The QTD function is supported.
MDPROPVAL_MSF_MTD	256	The MTD function is supported.
MDPROPVAL_MSF_WTD	512	The WTD function is supported.
MDPROPVAL_MSF_TOGGLEDRILL STATE	262144	The provider supports toggling of the drilled down state.

ADOMD Constants

MDPROPVAL_NL

Name	Value	Description
MDPROPVAL_NL_NAMEDLEVELS	1	The provider supports named levels.
MDPROPVAL_NL_NUMBEREDLEVELS	2	The provider supports numbered levels.
MDPROPVAL_NL_SCHEMAONLY	4	The provider supports 'dummy' levels, for display only.

MDPROPVAL_RR

Name	Value	Description
MDPROPVAL_RR_NORANGEROWSET	1	The provider does not support range rowsets.
MDPROPVAL_RR_READONLY	2	The provider supports read-only range rowsets.
MDPROPVAL_RR_UPDATE	4	The provider supports updatable range rowsets.

MD_DIMTYPE

Name	Value	Description
MD_DIMTYPE_UNKNOWN	0	The dimension type is unknown.
MD_DIMTYPE_TIME	1	The dimension is a time dimension.
MD_DIMTYPE_MEASURE	2	The dimension is a measure dimension.
MD_DIMTYPE_OTHER	3	The dimension is neither a time nor a measure dimenstion.

ADOMD Dynamic Properties

The following table shows a list of all OLE DB properties for the Microsoft OLAP
Provider.

Cell Object

Name	Description	Type
CELL_ORDINAL	The ordinal number of the cell.	Long
FORMATTED_VALUE	The formatted value of the cell.	String
VALUE	The unformatted value of the cell.	String

Connection Object

Name	Description	Type
Active Sessions	The maximum number of sessions allowable. Zero indicates no limit.	Long
Asynchable Abort	Whether transactions can be aborted asynchronously. Read-only.	Boolean
Asynchable Commit	Whether transactions can be committed asynchronously. Read-only.	Boolean
Asynchronous Initialization	Indicates the asynchronous initialization setting. This can only be DBPROPVAL_ASYNCH_INITIALIZE from the ADO constants.	Long

Name	Description	Type
Auto Synch Period	Identifies the time (in milliseconds) of the synchronization between the client and the server. The default value is 10,000 (10 seconds).	Long
Autocommit Isolation Levels	Indicates the transaction isolation level when in auto-commit mode. Can be one of the DBPROPVAL_TI constants from ADO.	Long
Cache Policy	Reserved for future use.	Long
Catalog Location	The position of the catalog name in a table name in a text command. The value can be one of the DBPROPVAL_CL constants from ADO.	Long
Catalog Term	The name the data source uses for a catalog, e.g., 'catalog' or 'database'. Read/Write.	String
Catalog Usage	Specifies how catalog names can be used in text commands. Can be zero or more of DBPROPVAL_CU constants from ADO.	Long
Client Cache Size	The amount of memory used by the cache on the client. A value of 0 means there is no limit on the client memory that can be used. A value of 1-99 indicates the percentage of virtual memory to use for the cache. A value above 100 indicates the amount in Kb that can be used by the cache.	Long
Column Definition	Defines the valid clauses for the definition of a column. Can be one of the DBPROPVAL_CD constants from ADO.	Long
CompareCaseNot SensitiveString Flags	Identifies the type of comparison to perform for case-insensitive strings.	Long
CompareCase SensitiveString Flags	Identifies the type of comparison to perform for case-sensitive strings.	Long

Name	Description	Type
Connect Timeout	The amount of time, in seconds, to wait for the initialization to complete. Read/Write.	Long
Connection Status	The status of the current connection. Can be one of the DBPROPVAL_CS constants from ADO.	Long
CREATECUBE	The statement used to create a cube.	String
Current Catalog	The name of the current catalog.	String
Data Source	The name of the data source to connect to.	String
Data Source Name	The name of the data source.	String
Data Source Object Threading Model	Specifies the threading models supported by the data source object.	Long
Data Source Type	The type of data source.	Long
DBMS Name	The name of the product accessed by the provider.	String
DBMS Version	The version of the product accessed by the provider.	String
Default Isolation Mode	Identifies whether the isolation mode is 'isolated', or the mode requested by the rowset properties. Isolated mode will be used if this value starts with Y, T or a number other than 0.	String
Execution Location	Identifies whether the query is resolved. Values can be: 0, for automatic selection. This is the default. 1, for automatic selection. 2, to execute the query on the client 3, to execute the query on he server.	Long
Extended Properties	Contains provider specific, extended connection information.	String

Name	Description	Type
Flattening Support	Indicates the level of support by the provider for flattening.	MDPROPVAL_FS
GROUP BY Support	The relationship between the columns in a GROUP BY clause and the non-aggregated columns in the select list. Can be one of the DBPROPVAL_GB constants from ADO.	Long
Heterogeneous Table Support	Specifies whether the provider can join tables from different catalogs or providers. Can be one of the DBPROPVAL_HT constants from ADO.	Long
Identifier Case Sensitivity	How identifiers treat case sensitivity. Can be one of the DBPROPVAL_IC constants from ADO	Long
Initial Catalog	The name of the initial, or default, catalog to use when connecting to the data source. If the provider supports changing the catalog for an initialized data source, a different catalog name can be specified in the Current Catalog property.	String
INSERTINTO	The statement used for inserting data into a local cube.	String
Integrated Security	Contains the name of the authentication service used by the server to identify the user.	String
Isolation Levels	Identifies the supported transaction isolation levels. Can be one of the DBPROPVAL_TI constants from ADO.	Long
Isolation Retention	Identifies the supported transaction isolation retention levels. Can be one of the DBPROPVAL_TR constants from ADO.	Long

Name	Description	Type
Large Level Threshold	Defines the number of levels a Dimension can have before it is deemed to be a 'large' dimension. A large level Dimension will have the levels sent from the server in increments, rather than all at once.	Long
Locale Identifier	The locale ID of preference for the consumer.	Long
Location	The location of the data source to connect to. Typically this will be the server name.	String
Maximum Index Size	The maximum number of bytes allowed in the combined columns of an index. This is 0 if there is no specified limit or the limit is unknown.	Long
Maximum Row Size	The maximum length of a single row in a table. This is 0 if there is no specified limit or the limit is unknown.	Long
Maximum Row Size Includes BLOB	Identifies whether Maximum Row Size includes the length for BLOB data.	Boolean
Maximum Tables in SELECT	The maximum number of tables allowed in the FROM clause of a SELECT statement. This is 0 if there is no specified limit or the limit is unknown.	Long
MDX DDL Extensions	Defines any DDL extensions supported by the provider.	Long
MDX USE Extensions	Defines the USE extensions supported by the provider, allowing creation of user defined functions.	Long
Mode	Specifies the access permissions. Can be one of the DB_MODE constants from ADO.	Long
Multiple Results	Identifies whether the provider supports multiple results objects and what restrictions it places on those objects.	Long

OMD Dynamic Properties

Name	Description	Type
Multiple Storage Objects	Identifies whether the provider supports multiple, open storage objects at the same time.	Boolean
Multi-Table Update	Identifies whether the provider can update rowsets derived from multiple tables.	Boolean
NULL Collation Order	Identifies where NULLs are sorted in a list.	Long
NULL Concatenation Behavior	How the data source handles concatenation of NULL-valued character data type columns with non-NULL valued character data type columns.	Long
Number of axes in the dataset	Maximum number of axes that the provider supports.	Long
OLE DB Services	Specifies the OLE DB services to enable.	Long
OLE DB Version	Specifies the version of OLE DB supported by the provider.	String
OLE Object Support	Specifies the way in which the provider supports access to BLOBs and OLE objects stored in columns.	Long
ORDER BY Columns in Select List	Identifies whether columns in an ORDER BY clause must be in the SELECT list.	Boolean
Output Parameter Availability	Identifies the time at which output parameter values become available. Can be one of the DBPROPVAL_AO constants in ADO.	Long
Pass By Ref Accessors	Whether the provider supports the DBACCESSOR_PASSBYREF flag.	Boolean
Password	The password to be used to connect to the data source.	String
Persist Security Info	Whether or not the consumer requires that the data source object persist sensitive authentication information, such as a password, in encrypted form.	Boolean

Name	Description	Type
Persistent ID Type	Specifies the type of DBID that the provider uses when persisting DBIDs for tables, indexes and columns. Can be one of the DBPROPVAL_PT constants in ADO.	Long
Prepare Abort Behavior	Identifies how aborting a transaction affects prepared commands. Can be one of the DBPROPVAL_CB constants in ADO.	Long
Prepare Commit Behavior	Identifies how committing a transaction affects prepared commands. Can be one of the DBPROPVAL_CB constants in ADO.	Long
Procedure Term	Specifies the data source provider's name for a procedure, e.g., 'database procedure', 'stored procedure'.	String
Prompt	Specifies whether to prompt the user during initialization.	Integer
Provider Friendly Name	The friendly name of the provider.	String
Provider Name	The filename of the provider.	String
Provider Version	The version of the provider.	String
Provider's ability to qualify a cube name	Identifies how object names in a schema can be qualified in an MDX expression.	MDPROPVAL_MOQ
Quoted Identifier Sensitivity	Identifies how quoted identifiers treat case. Can be one of the DBPROPVAL_IC constants from ADO.	Long
Read Only Session	Reserved for future use.	String
Read-Only Data Source	Whether or not the data source is read-only.	Boolean
Reset Datasource	Specifies the data source state to reset. Can be one of the DBPROPVAL_RD constants from ADO.	Long

ADOMD Dynamic Properties

Name	Description	Type
Rowset Conversions on Command	Identifies whether callers can enquire on a command and about conversions supported by the command.	Boolean
Schema Usage	Identifies how schema names can be used in commands. Can be one of the DBPROPVAL_SU constants from ADO.	Long
Server Name	The name of the server.	String
SOURCE_DSN	The connection string for the source data store.	String
SOURCE_DSN_SUFFIX	The suffix to append to the SOURCE_DSN property for a local cube.	String
SQL Support	Identifies the level of support for SQL. Can be one of the DBPROPVAL_SQL constants from ADO.	Long
Structured Storage	Identifies what interfaces the rowset supports on storage objects. Can be one of the DBPROPVAL_SS constants from ADO.	Long
Subquery Support	Identifies the predicates in text commands that support sub-queries. Can be one of the DBPROPVAL_SQ constants from ADO.	Long
Support for cell updates	Indicates whether the provider supports updating of the cells.	MDPROPVAL _PR
Support for creation of named sets and calculated members	Indicates the level of support for named sets and calculated members.	MDPROPVAL _MF
Support for MDX case statements	The level of support for case statements.	MDPROPVAL _MC
Support for named levels	The level of support for named and/or numbered levels.	MDPROPVAL _NL
Support for outer reference in an MDX statement	The level of support for outer references.	MDPROPVAL _MO

Name	Description	Type
Support for query joining multiple cubes	The level of support for joining multiple cubes.	MDPROPVAL _MJC
Support for querying by property values in an MDX statement	Indicates whether or not the provider supports the query of property statements.	Boolean
Support for string comparison operators other than equals and not-equals operators	The level of support for complex string comparison operators.	MDPROPVAL _MSC
Support for updating aggregated cells	The level of support for updating aggregated cells.	MDPROPVAL _AU
Support for various <desc_flag> values in the DESCENDANTS function	The level of support for flags when describing descendants.	MDPROPVAL _MD
Support for various member functions	The level of support for functions that act on members.	MDPROPVAL _MMF
Support for various numeric functions	The level of support for numeric functions.	MDPROPVAL _MNF
Support for various set functions	The level of support for set functions.	MDPROPVAL _MSF
Table Term	The name the data source uses for a table, e.g., 'table' or 'file'.	String
The capabilities of the WHERE clause of an MDX statement	The WHERE clause support for tuples.	MDPROPVAL _MS
Transaction DDL	Indicates whether Data Definition Language (DDL) statements are supported in transactions. Can be one of the DBPROPVAL_TC constants from ADO.	Long

ADOMD Dynamic Properties

Name	Description	Type
USEEXISTINGFILE	When using CREATE CUBE or INSERT INTO, indicates whether an existing local cube file is overwritten. If the value starts with Y, T or a number other than 0, the existing file is used. If the value starts with any other character the existing cube file is overwritten.	String
User ID	The User ID to be used when connecting to the data source.	String
User Name	The User Name used in a particular database.	String
Window Handle	The window handle to be used if the data source object needs to prompt for additional information.	Long
Writeback Timeout	The maximum amount of time (in seconds) to wait whilst committing changes back to the server.	Long

CubeDef Object

Name	Description	Type
CATALOG_NAME	The name of the catalog to which the cube belongs.	String
CREATED_ON	The date the cube was created.	Date/Time
CUBE_GUID	The GUID of the cube.	GUID
CUBE_NAME	The cube name.	String
CUBE_TYPE	Will be CUBE for a standard cube and VIRTUAL CUBE for a virtual cube.	String
DATA_UPDATED_BY	The ID of the person who last update data in the cube.	String
DESCRIPTION	The cube description.	String
LAST_DATA_UPDATE	The date the cube data was last updated.	Date/Time

Name	Description	Type
LAST_SCHEMA_UPDATE	The date the cube schema was last updated.	Date/Time
SCHEMA_NAME	The name of the schema to which this cube belongs.	String
SCHEMA_UPDATED_BY	The ID of the person who last updated the schema.	String

Dimension Object

Name	Description	Type
CATALOG_NAME	The name of the Catalog to which this Dimension belongs.	String
CUBE_NAME	The name of the Cube to which this Dimension belongs.	String
DEFAULT_HIERARCHY	The unique name of the default Hierarchy for this Dimension.	String
DESCRIPTION	The description of the Dimension.	String
DIMENSION_CAPTION	The caption of the Dimension.	String
DIMENSION_CARDINALITY	The number of members in the Dimension. This figure is not guaranteed to be accurate.	Long
DIMENSION_GUID	The GUID of the Dimension, or Null if no GUID exists.	GUID
DIMENSION_NAME	The name of the Dimension.	String
DIMENSION_ORDINAL	The number or the ordinal of the Dimension. This is zero-based.	Long
DIMENSION_TYPE	The type of the Dimension.	MD_DIMTYPE
DIMENSION_UNIQUE_NAME	The unique name of the Dimension.	String
IS_VIRTUAL	Indicates whether or not the Dimension is a virtual dimension.	Boolean

Name	Description	Type
SCHEMA_NAME	The schema name to which this Dimension belongs.	String

Hierarchy Object

Name	Description	Type
ALL_MEMBER	The name of the default member if the first level is All, or Null if the first level is not All.	String
CATALOG_NAME	Catalog name in which the table is defined or Null if the provider does not support catalogs.	String
CUBE_NAME	The name of the Cube to which this Hierarchy belongs.	String
DEFAULT_MEMBER	The default Level for this Hierarchy, or Null if no default exists.	String
DESCRIPTION	The description of the hierarchy.	String
DIMENSION_TYPE	The type of the dimension.	MD_DIMTYPE
DIMENSION_UNIQUE_NAME	The fully qualified name of the Dimension to which this Hierarchy belongs.	String
HIERARCHY_CAPTION	The caption of the Hierarchy.	String
HIERARCHY_CARDINALITY	The number of members in the Hierarchy. This figure is not guaranteed to be accurate.	Long
HIERARCHY_GUID	The GUID of the Hierarchy, or Null if no GUID exists.	GUID
HIERARCHY_NAME	The name of the Hierarchy.	String
HIERARCHY_UNIQUE_NAME	The fully qualified name of the Hierarchy.	String

Name	Description	Type
SCHEMA_NAME	Schema name in which the table is defined or Null if the provider does not support schemas.	String

Level Object

Name	Description	Type
CATALOG_NAME	Catalog name, or Null if the provider does not support catalogs.	String
CUBE_NAME	The Cube name to which the level belongs.	String
DESCRIPTION	The description of the level.	String
DIMENSION_UNIQUE_NAME	The unique name of the Dimension to which the level belongs.	String
HIERARCHY_UNIQUE_NAME	The unique name of the Hierarchy to which the level belongs.	String
LEVEL_CAPTION	The Caption of the level.	String
LEVEL_CARDINALITY	The number of members in the level. This figure is not guaranteed to be accurate.	Long
LEVEL_GUID	The GUID of the level, or Null if no GUID exists.	GUID
LEVEL_NAME	The level name.	String
LEVEL_NUMBER	The index number of the level.	Long
LEVEL_TYPE	The Type of the level.	MDLEVEL_TYPE
LEVEL_UNIQUE_NAME	The unique level name.	String
SCHEMA_NAME	Schema name, or Null if the provider does not support schemas.	String

Member Object

Name	Description	Type
EXPRESSION	The expression which underlies a calculated measure.	String
column	A column for each member.	String

MSMQ Constants

MQACCESS

Name	Value	Description
MQ_PEEK_ACCESS	32	Messages can only be looked at, and cannot be removed from the queue.
MQ_RECEIVE_ACCESS	1	Messages can be retrieved from the queue or peeked at.
MQ_SEND_ACCESS	2	Messages can only be sent to the queue.

MQAUTHENTICATE

Name	Value	Description
MQ_AUTHENTICATE	1	The queue only accepts authenticated messages.
MQ_AUTHENTICATE_NONE	0	The default. The queue accepts authenticated and non-authenticated messages.

MQCALG

Name	Value	Description
MQMSG_CALG_DES	26113	Hashing algorithm used when authenticating messages.
MQMSG_CALG_DSS_SIGN	8704	Hashing algorithm used when authenticating messages.

Name	Value	Description
MQMSG_CALG_MAC	32773	Hashing algorithm used when authenticating messages.
MQMSG_CALG_MD2	32769	Hashing algorithm used when authenticating messages.
MQMSG_CALG_MD4	32770	Hashing algorithm used when authenticating messages.
MQMSG_CALG_MD5	32771	The Default. Hashing algorithm used when authenticating messages.
MQMSG_CALG_RC2	26114	Hashing algorithm used when authenticating messages.
MQMSG_CALG_RC4	26625	Hashing algorithm used when authenticating messages.
MQMSG_CALG_RSA_KEYX	41984	Hashing algorithm used when authenticating messages.
MQMSG_CALG_RSA_SIGN	9216	Hashing algorithm used when authenticating messages.
MQMSG_CALG_SEAL	26626	Hashing algorithm used when authenticating messages.
MQMSG_CALG_SHA	32772	Hashing algorithm used when authenticating messages.

MQCERT_REGISTER

Name	Value	Description
MQCERT_REGISTER_ ALWAYS	1	Enumerate the flags when registering a certificate whether or not the certificate already exists.
MQCERT_REGISTER_IF_ NOT_EXIST	2	Enumerate the flags when registering a certificate if certificate does not already exist.

MQDEFAULT

Name	Value	Description
DEFAULT_M_ACKNOWLEDGE	0	Default value for the Acknowledgement property of a Message.
DEFAULT_M_APPSPECIFIC	0	Default value for the AppSpecific property of a Message.

Name	Value	Description
DEFAULT_M_AUTH_LEVEL	0	Default value for the AuthLevel property of a Message.
DEFAULT_M_DELIVERY	0	Default value for the Delivery property of a Message.
DEFAULT_M_JOURNAL	0	Default value for the Journal property of a Message.
DEFAULT_M_PRIORITY	3	Default value for the Priority property of a Message.
DEFAULT_M_PRIV_LEVEL	0	Default value for the PrivLevel property of a Message.
DEFAULT_M_SENDERID_TYPE	1	Default value for the SenderId property of a Message.
DEFAULT_Q_AUTHENTICATE	0	Default value for the Authenticate property of a Queue.
DEFAULT_Q_BASEPRIORITY	0	Default value for the BasePriority property of a Queue.
DEFAULT_Q_JOURNAL	0	Default value for the Journal property of a Queue.
DEFAULT_Q_JOURNAL_QUOTA	-1	Default value for the JournalQuota property of a Queue.
DEFAULT_Q_PRIV_LEVEL	1	Default value for the PrivLevel property of a Queue.
DEFAULT_Q_QUOTA	-1	Default value for the Quota property of a Queue.
DEFAULT_Q_TRANSACTION	0	Default value for the Transaction property of a Queue.

MSMQ Constants

MQERROR

Name	Value	Description
MQ_ERROR	-1072824319	Generic error code.
MQ_ERROR_ACCESS_DENIED	-1072824283	Access to the specified queue or computer is denied.
MQ_ERROR_BAD_SECURITY_CONTEXT	-1072824267	Security context specified by PROPID_M_SECURITY_CONTEXT is corrupted.

Name	Value	Description
MQ_ERROR_BUFFER_OVERFLOW	-1072824294	Supplied message body buffer is too small. A partial copy of the message body is copied to the buffer, but the message is not removed from the queue.
MQ_ERROR_CANNOT_IMPERSONATE_CLIENT	-1072824284	MSMQ information store server cannot impersonate the client application. Security credentials could not be verified.
MQ_ERROR_COMPUTER_DOES_NOT_SUPPORT_ENCRYPTION	-1072824269	Encryption failed. Computer (source or destination) does not support encryption operations.
MQ_ERROR_CORRUPTED_INTERNAL_CERTIFICATE	-1072824275	MSMQ-supplied internal certificate is corrupted.
MQ_ERROR_CORRUPTED_PERSONAL_CERT_STORE	-1072824271	Microsoft® Internet Explorer personal certificate store is corrupted.
MQ_ERROR_CORRUPTED_SECURITY_DATA	-1072824272	Cryptographic function (CryptoAPI) has failed.
MQ_ERROR_COULD_NOT_GET_ACCOUNT_INFO	-1072824265	MSMQ could not get account information for the user.
MQ_ERROR_COULD_NOT_GET_USER_SID	-1072824266	MSMQ could not get the specified sender identifier.
MQ_ERROR_DELETE_CN_IN_USE	-1072824248	Specified connected network (CN) cannot be deleted because it is defined in at least one computer. Remove the CN from all CN lists and try again.
MQ_ERROR_DS_ERROR	-1072824253	Internal error with MQIS.
MQ_ERROR_DS_IS_FULL	-1072824254	MSMQ information store is full.
MQ_ERROR_DTC_CONNECT	-1072824244	MSMQ cannot connect to the Microsoft® Distributed Transaction Coordinator (MS DTC).

Name	Value	Description
MQ_ERROR_FORMATNAME_ BUFFER_TOO_SMALL	-1072824289	Specified format name buffer is too small to contain the queue's format name.
MQ_ERROR_ILLEGAL_CONTEXT	-1072824229	The lpwcsContext parameter of MQLocateBegin is not NULL.
MQ_ERROR_ILLEGAL_CURSOR_ ACTION	-1072824292	An attempt was made to peek at the next message in the queue when cursor was at the end of the queue.
MQ_ERROR_ILLEGAL_ FORMATNAME	-1072824290	Format name specified is not valid.
MQ_ERROR_ILLEGAL_ MQCOLUMNS	-1072824264	Indicates that pColumns is NULL.
MQ_ERROR_ILLEGAL_ MQQMPROPS	-1072824255	No properties are specified by the MQQMPROPS structure, or it is set to NULL.
MQ_ERROR_ILLEGAL_ MQQUEUEPROPS	-1072824259	No properties are specified by the MQQUEUEPROPS structure, or it is set to NULL.
MQ_ERROR_ILLEGAL_ OPERATION	-1072824220	The operation is not supported on this specific platform.
MQ_ERROR_ILLEGAL_ PROPERTY_SIZE	-1072824261	The specified buffer for the message identifier or correlation identifier is not the correct size.
MQ_ERROR_ILLEGAL_ PROPERTY_VALUE	-1072824296	Property value specified in the PROPVARIANT array is illegal.
MQ_ERROR_ILLEGAL_ PROPERTY_VT	-1072824295	VARTYPE specified in the VT field of the PROPVARIANT array is not valid.
MQ_ERROR_ILLEGAL_PROPID	-1072824263	Property identifier in the property identifier array is not valid.
MQ_ERROR_ILLEGAL_QUEUE_ PATHNAME	-1072824300	MSMQ pathname specified for the queue is not valid.

MSMQ Constants

Name	Value	Description
MQ_ERROR_ILLEGAL_ RELATION	-1072824262	Relationship parameter is not valid.
MQ_ERROR_ILLEGAL_ RESTRICTION_PROPID	-1072824260	Property identifier specified in MQRESTRICTION is invalid.
MQ_ERROR_ILLEGAL_ SECURITY_DESCRIPTOR	-1072824287	Specified security descriptor is not valid.
MQ_ERROR_ILLEGAL_SORT	-1072824304	Illegal sort specified.
MQ_ERROR_ILLEGAL_SORT_ PROPID	-1072824228	Property identifier specified in MQSORTSET is not valid.
MQ_ERROR_ILLEGAL_USER	-1072824303	User is not legal.
MQ_ERROR_INSUFFICIENT_ PROPERTIES	-1072824257	Not all properties required for the operation were specified.
MQ_ERROR_INSUFFICIENT_ RESOURCES	-1072824281	Insufficient resources to complete operation (for example, not enough memory). Operation failed.
MQ_ERROR_INTERNAL_USER_ CERT_EXIST	-1072824274	Internal user certificate exists.
MQ_ERROR_INVALID_ CERTIFICATE	-1072824276	Security certificate specified by PROPID_M_SENDER_CERT is invalid, or the certificate is not correctly placed in the Microsoft® Internet Explorer personal certificate store.
MQ_ERROR_INVALID_HANDLE	-1072824313	Specified queue handle is not valid.
MQ_ERROR_INVALID_OWNER	-1072824252	Object owner is not valid. Owner was not found when trying to create object.
MQ_ERROR_INVALID_ PARAMETER	-1072824314	One of the IN parameters supplied by the operation is not valid.
MQ_ERROR_IO_TIMEOUT	-1072824293	MQReceiveMessage I/O timeout has expired.
MQ_ERROR_LABEL_BUFFER_ TOO_SMALL	-1072824226	Message label buffer is too small for received label.

Name	Value	Description
MQ_ERROR_LABEL_TOO_LONG	-1072824227	Message label is too long. It should be equal to or less than 250 unicode characters incliding EOS.
MQ_ERROR_MACHINE_EXISTS	-1072824256	Machine with the specified name already exists.
MQ_ERROR_MACHINE_NOT_FOUND	-1072824307	Specified machine could not be found in MQIS.
MQ_ERROR_MESSAGE_ALREADY_RECEIVED	-1072824291	Message pointed at by the cursor has already been removed from the queue.
MQ_ERROR_MESSAGE_STORAGE_FAILED	-1072824278	Recoverable message could not be stored on the local computer.
MQ_ERROR_MISSING_CONNECTOR_TYPE	-1072824235	Specified a property typically generated by MSMQ but did not specify PROPID_M_CONNECTOR_TYPE.
MQ_ERROR_MQIS_READONLY_MODE	-1072824224	MQIS database is in read-only mode.
MQ_ERROR_MQIS_SERVER_EMPTY	-1072824225	The list of MSMQ information store servers (in registry) is empty.
MQ_ERROR_NO_DS	-1072824301	No connection with the Site Controller server. Cannot access the MQIS.
MQ_ERROR_NO_INTERNAL_USER_CERT	-1072824273	No internal certificate available for this user.
MQ_ERROR_NO_RESPONSE_FROM_OBJECT_SERVER	-1072824247	No response from MQIS server. Operation status is unknown.
MQ_ERROR_OBJECT_SERVER_NOT_AVAILABLE	-1072824246	Object's MSMQ information store server is not available. Operation failed.
MQ_ERROR_OPERATION_CANCELLED	-1072824312	Operation was cancelled before it could be started.
MQ_ERROR_PRIVILEGE_NOT_HELD	-1072824282	Application does not have the required privileges to perform the operation.

MSMQ Constants

Name	Value	Description
MQ_ERROR_PROPERTY	-1072824318	One or more of the specified properties caused an error.
MQ_ERROR_PROPERTY_ NOTALLOWED	-1072824258	Specified property is not valid for the operation (for example, specifying PROPID_Q_INSTANCE when setting queue properties).
MQ_ERROR_PROV_NAME_ BUFFER_TOO_SMALL	-1072824221	The provider name buffer for cryptographic service provider is too small.
MQ_ERROR_QUEUE_DELETED	-1072824230	Queue was deleted before the message could be read. The specified queue handle is no longer valid and the queue must be closed.
MQ_ERROR_QUEUE_EXISTS	-1072824315	Queue (public or private) with identical MSMQ pathname is registered. Public queues are registered in MQIS. Private queues are registered in the local computer.
MQ_ERROR_QUEUE_NOT_ AVAILABLE	-1072824245	Error while reading from queue residing on a remote computer.
MQ_ERROR_QUEUE_NOT_ FOUND	-1072824317	Public queue is not registered in MQIS. This error does not apply to private queues.
MQ_ERROR_RESULT_BUFFER_ TOO_SMALL	-1072824250	Supplied result buffer is too small. MQLocateNext could not return at least one complete query result.
MQ_ERROR_SECURITY_ DESCRIPTOR_TOO_SMALL	-1072824285	Supplied security buffer is too small.
MQ_ERROR_SENDER_CERT_ BUFFER_TOO_SMALL	-1072824277	Supplied sender certificate buffer is too small.
MQ_ERROR_SENDERID_ BUFFER_TOO_SMALL	-1072824286	Supplied sender identification buffer is too small to hold sender identification.

Name	Value	Description
MQ_ERROR_SERVICE_NOT_AVAILABLE	-1072824309	Application was unable to connect to the Queue Manager.
MQ_ERROR_SHARING_VIOLATION	-1072824311	Sharing violation when opening queue. The application is trying to open an already opened queue that has exclusive read rights.
MQ_ERROR_SIGNATURE_BUFFER_TOO_SMALL	-1072824222	The signature buffer is too small.
MQ_ERROR_STALE_HANDLE	-1072824234	Specified handle was obtained in a previous session of the Queue Manager service.
MQ_ERROR_SYMM_KEY_BUFFER_TOO_SMALL	-1072824223	The symmetric key buffer is too small.
MQ_ERROR_TRANSACTION_ENLIST	-1072824232	Cannot enlist transaction.
MQ_ERROR_TRANSACTION_IMPORT	-1072824242	MSMQ could not import the specified transaction.
MQ_ERROR_TRANSACTION_SEQUENCE	-1072824239	Transaction operation sequence is incorrect.
MQ_ERROR_TRANSACTION_USAGE	-1072824240	Either the queue or the message is not transactional. Transaction messages can only be sent to a transaction queue, and transaction queues can only receive transaction messages.
MQ_ERROR_UNSUPPORTED_ACCESS_MODE	-1072824251	Specified access mode is not supported. Supported access modes include MQ_PEEK_MESSAGE, MQ_SEND_MESSAGE, and MQ_RECEIVE_MESSAGE.
MQ_ERROR_UNSUPPORTED_DBMS	-1072824302	Current version of Database Management System is not supported.

MSMQ Constants

Name	Value	Description
MQ_ERROR_UNSUPPORTED_ FORMATNAME_OPERATION	-1072824288	Requested operation is not supported for the specified format name (for example, trying to open a queue to receive messages using a direct format name).
MQ_ERROR_USER_BUFFER_ TOO_SMALL	-1072824280	Supplied buffer for user is too small to hold the returned information.
MQ_ERROR_WRITE_NOT_ ALLOWED	-1072824219	Write operations to MQIS are not allowed while an MSMQ information store server is being installed.

MQJOURNAL

Name	Value	Description
MQ_JOURNAL	1	When a message is removed from the queue it is stored in the queue journal.
MQ_JOURNAL_NONE	0	The default. Messages are not stored in a journal when they are removed from the queue.

MQMAX

Name	Value	Description
MQ_MAX_Q_LABEL_LEN	124	The maximum length of the queue label.
MQ_MAX_Q_NAME_LEN	124	The maximum length of the queue name.

MQMSGACKNOWLEDGEMENT

Name	Value	Description
MQMSG_ACKNOWLEDGMENT_FULL_ REACH_QUEUE	5	Posts positive and negative acknowledgements, depending upon whether or not the message reached the queue. This can happen when the time-to-reach-queue timer expires, or when a message cannot be authenticated.
MQMSG_ACKNOWLEDGMENT_FULL_ RECEIVE	14	Post a positive or negative acknowledgement depending on whether or not the message is retrieved from the queue before its time-to-be-received timer expires.
MQMSG_ACKNOWLEDGMENT_NACK_ REACH_QUEUE	4	Posts a negative acknowledgement when the message cannot reach the queue. This can happen when the time-to-reach-queue timer expires, or a message can not be authenticated.
MQMSG_ACKNOWLEDGMENT_NACK_ RECEIVE	12	Posts a negative acknowledgement when an error occurs and the message cannot be retrieved from the queue before its time-to-be-received timer expires.
MQMSG_ACKNOWLEDGMENT_NEG_ ARRIVAL	4	Indicates a negative message arrival.
MQMSG_ACKNOWLEDGMENT_NEG_ RECEIVE	8	Indicates a negative message receive.
MQMSG_ACKNOWLEDGMENT_NONE	0	The default. No acknowledgement messages are posted.
MQMSG_ACKNOWLEDGMENT_POS_ ARRIVAL	1	Indicates a positive message arrival.
MQMSG_ACKNOWLEDGMENT_POS_ RECEIVE	2	Indicates a positive message receive.

MSMQ Constants

1229

MQMSGAUTHLEVEL

Name	Value	Description
MQMSG_AUTH_LEVEL_ALWAYS	1	The message must be authenticated when it arrives at the destination queue.
MQMSG_AUTH_LEVEL_NONE	0	The default. The message does not have to be authenticated when it arrives at the destination queue.

MQMSGCLASS

Name	Value	Description
MQMSG_CLASS_ACK_REACH_QUEUE	2	The original message reached its destination queue.
MQMSG_CLASS_ACK_RECEIVE	16384	The original message was retrieved by the receiving application.
MQMSG_CLASS_NACK_ACCESS_ DENIED	32772	The sending application does not have access rights to the destination queue.
MQMSG_CLASS_NACK_BAD_DST_Q	32768	The destination queue is not available to the sending application.
MQMSG_CLASS_NACK_BAD_ ENCRYPTION	32775	The destination Queue Manager could not decrypt a private (encrypted) message.
MQMSG_CLASS_NACK_BAD_ SIGNATURE	32774	MSMQ could not authenticate the original message. The original message's digital signature is not valid.
MQMSG_CLASS_NACK_COULD_NOT_ ENCRYPT	32776	The source Queue Manager could not encrypt a private message.
MQMSG_CLASS_NACK_HOP_COUNT_ EXCEEDED	32773	The original message's hop count is exceeded.
MQMSG_CLASS_NACK_NOT_ TRANSACTIONAL_MSG	32778	A non-transaction message was sent to a transactional queue.

Name	Value	Description
MQMSG_CLASS_NACK_NOT_TRANSACTIONAL_Q	32777	A transaction message was sent to a non-transactional queue.
MQMSG_CLASS_NACK_PURGED	32769	The message was purged before reaching the destination queue.
MQMSG_CLASS_NACK_Q_DELETED	49152	The queue was deleted before the message could be read from the queue.
MQMSG_CLASS_NACK_Q_EXCEED_QUOTA	32771	The original message's destination queue is full.
MQMSG_CLASS_NACK_Q_PURGED	49153	The queue was purged and the message no longer exists.
MQMSG_CLASS_NACK_REACH_QUEUE_TIMEOUT	32770	Either the time-to-reach-queue or time-to-be-received timer expired before the original message could reach the destination queue.
MQMSG_CLASS_NACK_RECEIVE_TIMEOUT	49154	The original message was not removed from the queue before its time-to-be-received timer expired.
MQMSG_CLASS_NORMAL	0	Indicates a normal MSMQ message.
MQMSG_CLASS_REPORT	1	Indicates a report message.

MSMQ Constants

MQMSGCURSOR

Name	Value	Description
MQMSG_CURRENT	1	Notification starts when a message is at the current cursor location.
MQMSG_FIRST	0	The default. Notification starts when a message is in the queue.
MQMSG_NEXT	2	The cursor is moved, then notification starts when a message is at the new cursor location.

MQMSGDELIVERY

Name	Value	Description
MQMSG_DELIVERY_EXPRESS	0	The default. The message stays in memory until it can be delivered.
MQMSG_DELIVERY_RECOVERABLE	1	In every hop along its route, the message is forwarded to the next hop or stored locally in a backup file until delivered, thus guaranteeing delivery even in the case of a machine crash.

MQMSGIDSIZE

Name	Value	Description
MQMSG_CORRELATIONID_SIZE	20	Size of CorrelationID byte array.
MQMSG_XACTID_SIZE	20	Size if the TransactionID byte array.
MQMSG_MSGID_SIZE	20	Size of MessageID byte array.

MQMSGJOURNAL

Name	Value	Description
MQMSG_DEADLETTER	1	If the message time-to-be-received or time-to-reach-queue setting expires, keep the message in the dead letter queue on the machine where time expired.
MQMSG_JOURNAL	2	If the message is transmitted (from the originating machine to the next hop), keep it in the machine journal on the originating machine.
MQMSG_JOURNAL_NONE	0	The default. The message is not kept in the originating machine's journal.

MQMSGMAX

Name	Value	Description
MQ_MAX_MSG_LABEL_LEN	249	Maximum length of the message Label property.

MQMSGPRIVLEVEL

Name	Value	Description
MQMSG_PRIV_LEVEL_ BODY	1	The message is a private (encrypted) message.
MQMSG_PRIV_LEVEL_ BODY_BASE	1	The message is a private (encrypted) message with 40 bit encryption.
MQMSG_PRIV_LEVEL_ BODY_ENHANCED	3	The message is a private (encrypted) message with 128 bit encryption.
MQMSG_PRIV_LEVEL_ NONE	0	The default. The message is a non-private (clear) message.

MQMSGSENDERIDTYPE

Name	Value	Description
MQMSG_SENDERID_TYPE_ NONE	0	**SenderID** is not attached to the message.
MQMSG_SENDERID_TYPE_ SID	1	The default. The **SenderID** property contains a SID for the user sending the message.

MQMSGTRACE

Name	Value	Description
MQMSG_SEND_ROUTE_TO_ REPORT_QUEUE	1	Each hop made by the original message generates a report that is recorded in a report message, which is send to the report queue specified by the source Queue Manager.
MQMSG_TRACE_NONE	0	The default. No tracing for this message.

MSMQ Constants

MQPRIORITY

Name	Value	Description
MQ_MAX_PRIORITY	7	Maximum queue priority.
MQ_MIN_PRIORITY	0	Minimum queue priority.

MQPRIVLEVEL

Name	Value	Description
MQ_PRIV_LEVEL_BODY	2	The queue accepts only private (encrypted) messages.
MQ_PRIV_LEVEL_NONE	0	The queue accepts only non-private (clear) messages.
MQ_PRIV_LEVEL_ OPTIONAL	1	The default. The queue does not force privacy, and accepts both clear and encrypted messages.

MQSHARE

Name	Value	Description
MQ_DENY_NONE	0	The queue is available to everyone for sending, peeking, or retrieving messages.
MQ_DENY_RECEIVE_SHARE	1	Messages can only be retrieved by this process.

MQTRANSACTION

Name	Value	Description
MQ_MTS_TRANSACTION	1	Specifies that the call is part of the current MTS transaction.
MQ_NO_TRANSACTION	0	Specifies the call is not part of a transaction.
MQ_SINGLE_MESSAGE	3	Sends a single message as a transaction.
MQ_XA_TRANSACTION	2	Specifies that the call is part of an externally coordinated, XA compliant, transaction.

MQTRANSACTIONAL

Name	Value	Description
MQ_TRANSACTIONAL	1	All messages sent to the queue must be done through an MSMQ transaction.
MQ_TRANSACTIONAL_NONE	0	Default. No transaction operations can be performed on the queue.

MQWARNING

Name	Value	Description
MQ_INFORMATION_DUPLICATE_PROPERTY	1074659333	Property already specified with same value. When duplicate settings are found, the first entry is used and subsequent settings are ignored.
MQ_INFORMATION_FORMATNAME_BUFFER_TOO_SMALL	1074659337	Supplied format name buffer is too small. Queue was still created.
MQ_INFORMATION_ILLEGAL_PROPERTY	1074659330	Specified identifier in property identifier array aPropID is not valid.
MQ_INFORMATION_OPERATION_PENDING	1074659334	Asynchronous operation is pending.
MQ_INFORMATION_PROPERTY	1074659329	One or more of the specified properties resulted in a warning. Operation completed anyway.
MQ_INFORMATION_PROPERTY_IGNORED	1074659331	Specified property is not valid for this operation (for example, PROPID_M_SENDERID is not valid; it is set by MSMQ when sending messages).
MQ_INFORMATION_UNSUPPORTED_PROPERTY	1074659332	Specified property is not supported by this operation. This property is ignored.

MSMQ Constants

RELOPS

Name	Value	Description
REL_EQ	1	The default. Queue searching operator. Find only items that are Equal to the search string.
REL_GE	6	Queue searching operator. Find only items that are Greater than or Equal to the search string.
REL_GT	4	Queue searching operator. Find only items that are Greater Than the search string.
REL_LE	5	Queue searching operator. Find only items that are Less than or Equal to the search string.
REL_LT	3	Queue searching operator. Find only items that are Less Than to the search string.
REL_NEQ	2	Queue searching operator. Find only items that are Not Equal to the search string.
REL_NOP	0	Queue searching operator.

MSMQ Constants

K

CDO Windows 2000 Constants

The following constants are predefined in CDO for Windows 2000. To include them in ASP code, set a reference to the type library with a METADATA tag:

```
<!--METADATA TYPE="typelib"
              UUID="CD000000-8B95-11D1-82DB-00C04FB1625D"
              NAME="CDO for Windows 2000 Library" -->
```

You can include this METADATA tag in individual pages or in the global.asa page.

CdoConfigSource

The CdoConfigSource enumeration is used with the IConfiguration.Load method to specify the set of values that the object loads.

Name	Value	Description
cdoDefaults	-1	Loads all applicable default values from Outlook Express and Internet Information Services.
cdoIIS	1	Loads configuration default values from the local Internet Information Service.

Name	Value	Description
cdoOutlookExpress	2	Loads configuration values from the default identity of th e default Outlook Express account.

CdoDSNOptions

The CdoDSNOptions enumeration is used with the IMessage.DSNOptions property to set delivery status notification flags for the message.

Name	Value	Description
cdoDSNDefault	0	No DSN commands are issued.
cdoDSNNever	1	No DSNs are issued.
cdoDSNFailure	2	Return a DSN if delivery fails.
cdoDSNSuccess	4	Returns a DSN if delivery succeeds.
cdoDSNDelay	8	Return a DSN if delivery is delayed.
cdoDSNSuccessFailOrDelay	14	Return a DSN is delivery succeeds, fails or is delayed.

CdoEventStatus

The CdoEventStatus enumeration is used when implementing a transport event sink using Microsoft Collaboration Data Objects (CDO). The second argument to the various event interface methods, such as ISMTPOnArrival.OnArrival, INNTPOnPostEarly.OnPostEarly, and INNTPOnPost.OnPost, are set to this enumeration type. Event sinks signal to the event source whether to continue running subsequent sinks, or to skip all remaining sinks and return.

Name	Value	Description
cdoRunNextSink	0	Proceed to run the next sink.
cdoSkipRemainingSinks	1	Do not notify (skip) any remaining sinks for the event (in other words, this sink has consumed the event).

CdoImportanceValues

The CdoImportanceValues enumeration is used to set the urn:schemas:httpmail:importance field for a Message object.

Name	Value	Description
cdoLow	0	Imporance of message low.
cdoNormal	1	Importance of message normal.
cdoHigh	2	Importance of message high.

CdoMessageStat

The CdoMessageStat enumeration is used within transport event sinks to set the http://schemas.microsoft.com/cdo/smtpenvelope/messagestatus field value.

Name	Value	Description
cdoStatSuccess	0	Proceed to deliver message, success.
cdoStatAbortDelivery	2	Discard message and do not deliver.
cdoStatBadMail	3	Do no deliver message and plave in bad mail location.

CdoMHTMLFlags

The CdoMHTMLFlags enumeration is used to set an argument when calling the IMessage.CreateMHTMLBody method. These values can be combined with the logical or (|) operator as desired.

Name	Value	Description
CdoSuppressNone	0	Download all resources referred to in elements within the resource at the specified Uniform Resource Identifier (URI) (not recursive).
CdoSuppressImages	1	Do not download resources referred to in IMG elements.
CdoSuppressBGSounds	2	Do not download resources referred to in BGSOUND elements.
CdoSuppressFrames	4	Do not download resources referred to in FRAME elements.
CdoSuppressObjects	8	Do not download resources referred to in OBJECT elements.
CdoSuppressStyleSheets	16	Do not download resources referred to in LINK elements.
CdoSuppressAll	31	Do not download any resources referred to from within the page.

CdoNNTPProcessingField

The CdoNNTPProcessingField enumeration is used from within Network News Transfer Protocol (NNTP) OnPost and OnPostEarly event sinks to set or update the value of the http://schemas.microsoft.com/cdo/nntpenvelope/nntpprocessing field.

Name	Value	Description
CdoPostMessage	1	Post the message.
CdoProcessControl	2	Send the message through control process.
CdoProcessModerator	4	Send the message to moderator.

CdoPostUsing

The CdoPostUsing enumeration is used when setting the http://schemas.microsoft.com/cdo/configuration/postusing field to specify how a message should be posted. Posting can occur through the network using the Network News Transfer Protocol (NNTP) protocol, or by writing the message to the local NNTP service drop directory (if available). The postusing field listed above defaults to cdoPostUsingPickup if there is an NNTP service installed on the local computer.

Name	Value	Description
cdoPostUsingPickup	1	Post the message using the local NNTP service pickup directory.
cdoPostUsingPort	2	Post the message using NNTP over the network.

CdoPriorityValues

The CdoPriorityValues enumeration is used to set the urn:schemas:httpmail:priority field for a Message object.

Name	Value	Description
cdoPriorityNonUrgent	-1	Not urgent.
cdoPriorityNormal	0	Normal priority.
cdoPriorityUrgent	1	Urgent.

CdoProtocolsAuthentication

The CdoProtocolsAuthentication enumeration is used to specify the mechanism used when authenticating to a Simple Mail Transfer Protocol (SMTP) service over the network.

Name	Value	Description
cdoAnonymous	0	Do not authenticate.
cdoBasic	1	Use basic (clear-text) authentication. The configuration sendusername/sendpassword or postusername/postpassword fields are used to specify credentials.
cdoNTLM	2	Use NTLM authentication (Secure Password Authentication in Microsoft® Outlook® Express). The current process security context is used to authenticate with the service.

CdoReferenceType

The CdoReferenceType enumeration is used when calling the IMessage.AddRelatedBodyPart method. Using this enumeration, you can specify how a related Multipurpose Internet Mail Extensions (MIME) entity, such as an included image, is to be referenced within messages that are formatted in MIME Encapsulation of Aggregate HTML Documents (MHTML) using a Content-ID or Content-Location header.

Name	Value	Description
cdoRefTypeId	0	The *Reference* parameter contains a value for the Content-ID header. The Hypertext Markup Language (HTML) body refers to the resource using this Content-ID header.
cdoRefTypeLocation	1	The *Reference* parameter contains a value for the Content-Location MIME header. The HTML body refers to the resource using this message-relative Uniform Resource Locator (URL).

CdoSendUsing

The CdoSendUsing enumeration is used to set the http://schemas.microsoft.com/cdo/configuration/sendusing field when configuring the Message object. This field listed above defaults to the value cdoSendUsingPickup if there is a local Simple Mail Transfer Protocol (SMTP) service available on the computer.

Name	Value	Description
cdoSendUsingPickup	1	Send message using the local SMTP service pickup directory.
cdoSendUsingPort	2	Send the message using the network (SMTP over the network).

Table Continued on Following Page

CdoSensitivityValues

The CdoSensitivityValues enumeration is used to set the
http://schemas.microsoft.com/exchange/sensitivity field for a Message object.

Name	Value	Description
cdoSensitivityNone	0	Not specified.
cdoPersonal	1	Personal.
cdoPrivate	2	Private.
cdoCompanyConfidential	3	Confidential.

CdoTimeZoneId

The CdoTimeZoneId enumeration is used to set the urn:schemas:calendar:timezoneid
field for a Message object.

Name	Value	Description
cdoUTC	0	Universal Coordinated Time (UTC).
cdoGMT	1	Greenwich Mean Time (GMT); Dublin, Edinburgh, London
cdoLisbon	2	Lisbon, Warsaw (GMT+01:00).
cdoParis	3	Paris, Madrid (GMT+01:00).
cdoBerlin	4	Berlin, Stockholm, Rome, Bern, Brussels, Vienna (GMT+01:00).
cdoEasternEurope	5	Eastern Europe (GMT+02:00).
cdoPrague	6	Prague (GMT+01:00).
cdoAthens	7	Athens, Helsinki, Istanbul (GMT+02:00).
cdoBrasilia	8	Brasilia (GMT-03:00).
cdoAtlanticCanada	9	Atlantic Time (Canada) (GMT-04:00).
cdoEastern	10	Eastern Time (US & Canada) (GMT-05:00).
cdoCentral	11	Central Time (US & Canada) (GMT-06:00).
cdoMountain	12	Mountain Time (US & Canada) (GMT-07:00).
cdoPacific	13	Pacific Time (US & Canada); Tijuana (GMT-08:00).

Name	Value	Description
cdoAlaska	14	Alaska (GMT-09:00).
cdoHawaii	15	Hawaii (GMT-10:00).
cdoMidwayIsland	16	Midway Island, Samoa (GMT-11:00).
cdoWellington	17	Wellington, Auckland (GMT+12:00).
cdoBrisbane	18	Brisbane, Melbourne, Sydney (GMT+10:00).
cdoAdelaide	19	Adelaide (GMT+09:30).
cdoTokyo	20	Tokyo, Osaka, Sapporo, Seoul, Yakutsk (GMT+09:00).
cdoHongKong	21	Hong Kong, Perth, Singapore, Taipei (GMT+08:00).
cdoBangkok	22	Bangkok, Jakarta, Hanoi (GMT+07:00).
cdoBombay	23	Bombay, Calcutta, Madras, New Delhi, Colombo (GMT+05:30).
cdoAbuDhabi	24	Abu Dhabi, Muscat, Tbilisi, Kazan, Volgograd (GMT+04:00).
cdoTehran	25	Tehran (GMT+03:30).
cdoBaghdad	26	Baghdad, Kuwait, Nairobi, Riyadh (GMT+03:00).
cdoIsrael	27	Israel (GMT+02:00).
cdoNewfoundland	28	Newfoundland (GMT-03:30).
cdoAzores	29	Azores, Cape Verde Island (GMT-01:00).
cdoMidAtlantic	30	Mid-Atlantic (GMT-02:00).
cdoMonrovia	31	Monrovia, Casablanca (GMT).
cdoBuenosAires	32	Buenos Aires, Georgetown (GMT-03:00).
cdoCaracas	33	Caracas, La Paz (GMT-04:00).
cdoIndiana	34	Indiana (East) (GMT-05:00).
cdoBogota	35	Bogota, Lima (GMT-05:00).
cdoSaskatchewan	36	Saskatchewan (GMT-06:00).
cdoMexicoCity	37	Mexico City, Tegucigalpa (GMT-06:00).
cdoArizona	38	Arizona (GMT-07:00).

Name	Value	Description
cdoEniwetok	39	Eniwetok, Kwajalein (GMT-12:00).
cdoFiji	40	Fiji, Kamchatka, Marshall Islands (GMT+12:00).
cdoMagadan	41	Magadan, Solomon Islands, New Caledonia (GMT+11:00).
cdoHobart	42	Hobart (GMT+10:00).
cdoGuam	43	Guam, Port Moresby, Vladivostok (GMT+10:00).
cdoDarwin	44	Darwin (GMT+09:30).
cdoBeijing	45	Beijing, Chongqing, Urumqi (GMT+08:00).
cdoAlmaty	46	Almaty, Dhaka (GMT+06:00).
cdoIslamabad	47	Islamabad, Karachi, Sverdlovsk, Tashkent (GMT+05:00).
cdoKabul	48	Kabul (GMT+04:30).
cdoCairo	49	Cairo (GMT+02:00).
cdoHarare	50	Harare, Pretoria (GMT+02:00).
cdoMoscow	51	Moscow, St. Petersburg (GMT+03:00).
cdoInvalidTimZone	52	Invalid time zone identifier.
cdoUTC	0	Universal Coordinated Time (UTC).
cdoGMT	1	Greenwich Mean Time (GMT); Dublin, Edinburgh, London.
cdoLisbon	2	Lisbon, Warsaw (GMT+01:00).
cdoParis	3	Paris, Madrid (GMT+01:00).
cdoBerlin	4	Berlin, Stockholm, Rome, Bern, Brussels, Vienna (GMT+01:00).
cdoEasternEurope	5	Eastern Europe (GMT+02:00).
cdoPrague	6	Prague (GMT+01:00).
cdoAthens	7	Athens, Helsinki, Istanbul (GMT+02:00).
cdoBrasilia	8	Brasilia (GMT-03:00).
cdoAtlanticCanada	9	Atlantic Time (Canada) (GMT-04:00).
cdoEastern	10	Eastern Time (US & Canada) (GMT-05:00).

Name	Value	Description
cdoCentral	11	Central Time (US & Canada) (GMT-06:00).
cdoMountain	12	Mountain Time (US & Canada) (GMT-07:00).
cdoPacific	13	Pacific Time (US & Canada); Tijuana (GMT-08:00).
cdoAlaska	14	Alaska (GMT-09:00).
cdoHawaii	15	Hawaii (GMT-10:00).
cdoMidwayIsland	16	Midway Island, Samoa (GMT-11:00).
cdoWellington	17	Wellington, Auckland (GMT+12:00).
cdoBrisbane	18	Brisbane, Melbourne, Sydney (GMT+10:00).
cdoAdelaide	19	Adelaide (GMT+09:30).
cdoTokyo	20	Tokyo, Osaka, Sapporo, Seoul, Yakutsk (GMT+09:00).
cdoHongKong	21	Hong Kong, Perth, Singapore, Taipei (GMT+08:00).
cdoBangkok	22	Bangkok, Jakarta, Hanoi (GMT+07:00).
cdoBombay	23	Bombay, Calcutta, Madras, New Delhi, Colombo (GMT+05:30).
cdoAbuDhabi	24	Abu Dhabi, Muscat, Tbilisi, Kazan, Volgograd (GMT+04:00).
cdoTehran	25	Tehran (GMT+03:30).
cdoBaghdad	26	Baghdad, Kuwait, Nairobi, Riyadh (GMT+03:00).
cdoIsrael	27	Israel (GMT+02:00).
cdoNewfoundland	28	Newfoundland (GMT-03:30).
cdoAzores	29	Azores, Cape Verde Island (GMT-01:00).
cdoMidAtlantic	30	Mid-Atlantic (GMT-02:00).
cdoMonrovia	31	Monrovia, Casablanca (GMT).
cdoBuenosAires	32	Buenos Aires, Georgetown (GMT-03:00).
cdoCaracas	33	Caracas, La Paz (GMT-04:00).
cdoIndiana	34	Indiana (East) (GMT-05:00).

CDO for Windows 2000 Constants

Name	Value	Description
cdoBogota	35	Bogota, Lima (GMT-05:00).
cdoSaskatchewan	36	Saskatchewan (GMT-06:00).
cdoMexicoCity	37	Mexico City, Tegucigalpa (GMT-06:00).
cdoArizona	38	Arizona (GMT-07:00).
cdoEniwetok	39	Eniwetok, Kwajalein (GMT-12:00).
cdoFiji	40	Fiji, Kamchatka, Marshall Islands (GMT+12:00).
cdoMagadan	41	Magadan, Solomon Islands, New Caledonia (GMT+11:00).
cdoHobart	42	Hobart (GMT+10:00).
cdoGuam	43	Guam, Port Moresby, Vladivostok (GMT+10:00).
cdoDarwin	44	Darwin (GMT+09:30).
cdoBeijing	45	Beijing, Chongqing, Urumqi (GMT+08:00).
cdoAlmaty	46	Almaty, Dhaka (GMT+06:00).
cdoIslamabad	47	Islamabad, Karachi, Sverdlovsk, Tashkent (GMT+05:00).
cdoKabul	48	Kabul (GMT+04:30).
cdoCairo	49	Cairo (GMT+02:00).
cdoHarare	50	Harare, Pretoria (GMT+02:00).
cdoMoscow	51	Moscow, St. Petersburg (GMT+03:00).
cdoInvalidTimZone	52	Invalid time zone identifier.

CDO for NTS Constants

The following constants are predefined in CDO 1.21. To include them in ASP code, set a reference to the type library with a METADATA tag:

```
<!-- METADATA TYPE="typelib" uuid="{0E064ADD-9D99-11D0-ABE5-00AA0064D470}" -->
```

You can include this METADATA tag in individual pages or in the global.asa page. For Visual Basic these constants are included automatically when you reference the CDONTS library.

CdoAttachmentTypes

Specifies the type of an attachment.

Name	Value	Description
CdoEmbeddedMessage	4	Message contains an embedded message.
CdoFileData	1	Message has embedded file.

CdoBodyFormats

Shows how the body of the text is formatted.

Name	Value	Description
CdoBodyFormatHTML	0	Specifies body is HTML formatted.
CdoBodyFormatText	1	Specifies body is Text formatted.

CdoEncodingMethod

Specifies the encoding type of a message.

Name	Value	Description
CdoEncodingBase64	1	File is Base64 encoded.
CdoEncodingUUencode	0	File is UUencoded.

CdoFolderTypes

Constants for accessing the Inbox and Outbox folders.

Name	Value	Description
CdoDefaultFolderInbox	1	Inbox folder.
CdoDefaultFolderOutbox	2	Outbox folder.

CdoImportance

Specifies the importance of a message: low, medium, or high.

Name	Value	Description
CdoHigh	2	High importance.
CdoLow	0	Low importance.
CdoNormal	1	Normal importance.

CdoMailFormats

Specifies the encoding format for the current mail.

Name	Value	Description
CdoMailFormatMime	0	Format with MIME.
CdoMailFormatText	1	Format with RFC 822 and UUEncode.

CdoMessageFormats

Specifies the encoding format for mails in the current session.

Name	Value	Description
CdoMime	0	Format with MIME.
CdoText	1	Format with RFC 822 and UUEncode.

CdoMessageFormats

Specifies the encoding format for mails in the current session.

Name	Value	Description
CdoMime	0	Format with MIME.
CdoText	1	Format with RFC 822 and UUEncode.

CdoRecipientTypes

Specifies the type of recipient: To, CC, or BCC.

Name	Value	Description
CdoBcc	3	BCC to recipient.
CdoCc	2	CC to recipient.
CdoTo	1	Primary recipient.

XML DOM Errors

Parse Error Messages

The following errors are obtained from the XMLDOMParseError object's errorCode property:

Name	Description
MSG_E_FORMATINDEX_BADINDEX	The value passed in to formatIndex needs to be greater than zero.
MSG_E_FORMATINDEX_BADFORMAT	Invalid format string.
MSG_E_SYSTEM_ERROR	System error: %1.
MSG_E_MISSINGEQUALS	Missing equals sign between attribute and attribute value.
MSG_E_EXPECTED_TOKEN	Expected token %1 found %2.
MSG_E_UNEXPECTED_TOKEN	Unexpected token %1.
MSG_E_MISSINGQUOTE	A string literal was expected, but no opening quote character was found.
MSG_E_COMMENTSYNTAX	Incorrect syntax was used in a comment.
MSG_E_BADSTARTNAMECHAR	A name was started with an invalid character.
MSG_E_BADNAMECHAR	A name contained an invalid character.
MSG_E_BADCHARINSTRING	The character '<' cannot be used in an attribute value.

Name	Description
MSG_E_XMLDECLSYNTAX	Invalid syntax for an xml declaration.
MSG_E_BADCHARDATA	An Invalid character was found in text content.
MSG_E_MISSINGWHITESPACE	Required white space was missing.
MSG_E_EXPECTINGTAGEND	The character '>' was expected.
MSG_E_BADCHARINDTD	Invalid character found in DTD.
MSG_E_BADCHARINDECL	An invalid character was found inside a DTD declaration.
MSG_E_MISSINGSEMICOLON	A semi colon character was expected.
MSG_E_BADCHARINENTREF	An invalid character was found inside an entity reference.
MSG_E_UNBALANCEDPAREN	Unbalanced parentheses.
MSG_E_EXPECTINGOPENBRACKET	An opening '[' character was expected.
MSG_E_BADENDCONDSECT	Invalid syntax in a conditional section.
MSG_E_INTERNALERROR	Internal error.
MSG_E_UNEXPECTED_WHITESPACE	Whitespace is not allowed at this location.
MSG_E_INCOMPLETE_ENCODING	End of file reached in invalid state for current encoding.
MSG_E_BADCHARINMIXEDMODEL	Mixed content model cannot contain this character.
MSG_E_MISSING_STAR	Mixed content model must be defined as zero or more('*').
MSG_E_BADCHARINMODEL	Invalid character in content model.
MSG_E_MISSING_PAREN	Missing parenthesis.
MSG_E_BADCHARINENUMERATION	Invalid character found in ATTLIST enumeration.
MSG_E_PIDECLSYNTAX	Invalid syntax in PI declaration.
MSG_E_EXPECTINGCLOSEQUOTE	A single or double closing quote character (\' or \") is missing.
MSG_E_MULTIPLE_COLONS	Multiple colons are not allowed in a name.
MSG_E_INVALID_DECIMAL	Invalid character for decimal digit.
MSG_E_INVALID_HEXIDECIMAL	Invalid character for hexidecimal digit.

Name	Description
MSG_E_INVALID_UNICODE	Invalid unicode character value for this platform.
MSG_E_WHITESPACEORQUESTIONMARK	Expecting whitespace or '?'.
MSG_E_SUSPENDED	The parser is suspended.
MSG_E_STOPPED	The parser is stopped.
MSG_E_UNEXPECTEDENDTAG	End tag was not expected at this location.
MSG_E_UNCLOSEDTAG	The following tags were not closed: %1.
MSG_E_DUPLICATEATTRIBUTE	Duplicate attribute.
MSG_E_MULTIPLEROOTS	Only one top-level element is allowed in an XML document.
MSG_E_INVALIDATROOTLEVEL	Invalid at the top level of the document.
MSG_E_BADXMLDECL	Invalid xml declaration.
MSG_E_MISSINGROOT	XML document must have a top level element.
MSG_E_UNEXPECTEDEOF	Unexpected end of file.
MSG_E_BADPEREFINSUBSET	Parameter entities cannot be used inside markup declarations in an internal subset.
MSG_E_PE_NESTING	The replacement text for a parameter entity must be properly nested with parenthesized groups.
MSG_E_INVALID_CDATACLOSINGTAG	The literal string ']]>' is not allowed in element content.
MSG_E_UNCLOSEDPI	Processing instruction was not closed.
MSG_E_UNCLOSEDSTARTTAG	Element was not closed.
MSG_E_UNCLOSEDENDTAG	End element was missing the character '>'.
MSG_E_UNCLOSEDSTRING	A string literal was not closed.
MSG_E_UNCLOSEDCOMMENT	A comment was not closed.
MSG_E_UNCLOSEDDECL	A declaration was not closed.
MSG_E_UNCLOSEDMARKUPDECL	A markup declaration was not closed.
MSG_E_UNCLOSEDCDATA	A CDATA section was not closed.
MSG_E_BADDECLNAME	Declaration has an invalid name.

XML DOM Errors

Name	Description
MSG_E_BADEXTERNALID	External ID is invalid.
MSG_E_BADELEMENTINDTD	An XML element is not allowed inside a DTD.
MSG_E_RESERVEDNAMESPACE	The namespace prefix is not allowed to start with the reserved string "xml".
MSG_E_EXPECTING_VERSION	The 'version' attribute is required at this location.
MSG_E_EXPECTING_ENCODING	The 'encoding' attribute is required at this location.
MSG_E_EXPECTING_NAME	At least one name is required at this location.
MSG_E_UNEXPECTED_ATTRIBUTE	The specified attribute was not expected at this location. The attribute may be case sensitive.
MSG_E_ENDTAGMISMATCH	End tag '%2' does not match the start tag '%1'.
MSG_E_INVALIDENCODING	System does not support the specified encoding.
MSG_E_INVALIDSWITCH	Switch from current encoding to specified encoding not supported.
MSG_E_EXPECTING_NDATA	NDATA keyword is missing.
MSG_E_INVALID_MODEL	Content model is invalid.
MSG_E_INVALID_TYPE	Invalid type defined in ATTLIST.
MSG_E_INVALIDXMLSPACE	XML space attribute has invalid value. Must specify 'default' or 'preserve'.
MSG_E_MULTI_ATTR_VALUE	Multiple names found in attribute value when only one was expected.
MSG_E_INVALID_PRESENCE	Invalid ATTDEF declaration. Expected #REQUIRED, #IMPLIED or #FIXED.
MSG_E_BADXMLCASE	The name 'xml' is reserved and must be lower case.
MSG_E_CONDSECTINSUBSET	Conditional sections are not allowed in an internal subset.
MSG_E_CDATAINVALID	CDATA is not allowed in a DTD.

Name	Description
MSG_E_INVALID_STANDALONE	The standalone attribute must have the value 'yes' or 'no'.
MSG_E_UNEXPECTED_STANDALONE	The standalone attribute cannot be used in external entities.
MSG_E_DOCTYPE_IN_DTD	Cannot have a DOCTYPE declaration in a DTD.
MSG_E_MISSING_ENTITY	Reference to undefined entity.
MSG_E_ENTITYREF_INNAME	Entity reference is resolved to an invalid name character.
MSG_E_DOCTYPE_OUTSIDE_PROLOG	Cannot have a DOCTYPE declaration outside of a prolog.
MSG_E_INVALID_VERSION	Invalid version number.
MSG_E_DTDELEMENT_OUTSIDE_DTD	Cannot have a DTD declaration outside of a DTD.
MSG_E_DUPLICATEDOCTYPE	Cannot have multiple DOCTYPE declarations.
MSG_E_RESOURCE	Error processing resource '%1'.
XML_IOERROR	Error opening input file: '%1'.
XML_ENTITY_UNDEFINED	Reference to undefined entity '%1'.
XML_INFINITE_ENTITY_LOOP	Entity '%1' contains an infinite entity reference loop.
XML_NDATA_INVALID_PE	Cannot use the NDATA keyword in a parameter entity declaration.
XML_REQUIRED_NDATA	Cannot use a general parsed entity '%1' as the value for attribute '%2'.
XML_NDATA_INVALID_REF	Cannot use unparsed entity '%1' in an entity reference.
XML_EXTENT_IN_ATTR	Cannot reference an external general parsed entity '%1' in an attribute value.
XML_STOPPED_BY_USER	XML parser stopped by user.
XML_PARSING_ENTITY	Error while parsing entity '%1'. %2
XML_E_MISSING_PE_ENTITY	Parameter entity must be defined before it is used.

XML DOM Errors

Name	Description
XML_E_MIXEDCONTENT_DUP_NAME	The same name must not appear more than once in a single mixed-content declaration: '%1'.
XML_NAME_COLON	Entity, EntityRef, PI, Notation names, or NMToken cannot contain a colon.
XML_ELEMENT_UNDECLARED	The element '%1' is used but not declared in the DTD/Schema.
XML_ELEMENT_ID_NOT_FOUND	The attribute '%1' references the ID '%2' which is not defined anywhere in the document.
XML_DEFAULT_ATTRIBUTE	Error in default attribute value defined in DTD/Schema.
XML_XMLNS_RESERVED	Reserved namespace '%1' can not be redeclared.
XML_EMPTY_NOT_ALLOWED	Element cannot be empty according to the DTD/Schema.
XML_ELEMENT_NOT_COMPLETE	Element content is incomplete according to the DTD/Schema.
XML_ROOT_NAME_MISMATCH	The name of the top most element must match the name of the DOCTYPE declaration.
XML_INVALID_CONTENT	Element content is invalid according to the DTD/Schema.
XML_ATTRIBUTE_NOT_DEFINED	The attribute '%1' on this element is not defined in the DTD/Schema.
XML_ATTRIBUTE_FIXED	Attribute '%1' has a value which does not match the fixed value defined in the DTD/Schema.
XML_ATTRIBUTE_VALUE	Attribute '%1' has an invalid value according to the DTD/Schema.
XML_ILLEGAL_TEXT	Text is not allowed in this element according to DTD/Schema.
XML_MULTI_FIXED_VALUES	An attribute declaration cannot contain multiple fixed values: '%1'.
XML_NOTATION_DEFINED	The notation '%1' is already declared.
XML_ELEMENT_DEFINED	The element '%1' is already declared.

Name	Description
XML_ELEMENT_UNDEFINED	Reference to undeclared element: '%1'.
XML_XMLNS_UNDEFINED	Reference to undeclared namespace prefix: '%1'.
XML_XMLNS_FIXED	Attribute '%1' must be a #FIXED attribute.
XML_E_UNKNOWNERROR	Unknown error: %1.
XML_REQUIRED_ATTRIBUTE_MISSING	Required attribute '%1' is missing.
XML_MISSING_NOTATION	Declaration '%1' contains reference to undefined notation '%2'.
XML_ATTLIST_DUPLICATED_ID	Cannot define multiple ID attributes on the same element.
XML_ATTLIST_ID_PRESENCE	An attribute of type ID must have a declared default of #IMPLIED or #REQUIRED.
XML_XMLLANG_INVALIDID	The language ID "%1" is invalid.
XML_PUBLICID_INVALID	The public ID "%1" is invalid.
XML_DTD_EXPECTING	Expecting: %1.
XML_NAMESPACE_URI_EMPTY	Only a default namespace can have an empty URI.
XML_LOAD_EXTERNALENTITY	Could not load '%1'.
XML_BAD_ENCODING	Unable to save character to '%1' encoding.
SCHEMA_ATTRIBUTEVALUE_NOSUPPORT	A namespace was found but not supported at current location.
SCHEMA_SCHEMAROOT_EXPECTED	Incorrect definition for the root element in schema.
SCHEMA_ELEMENT_NOSUPPORT	Element "%1" is not allowed in this context.
SCHEMA_ETNAME_MISSING	An ElementType declaration must contain a "name" attribute.
SCHEMA_ETYPE_MISSING	An element declaration must contain a "type" attribute.
SCHEMA_ETORDER_UNKNOWN	Schema only supports order type "seq", "one" and "many".

DOM Errors

1261

Name	Description
SCHEMA_ ELEMENTDT_NOSUPPORT	Content must be "textOnly" when using datatype on an Element Type.
SCHEMA_ETORDER_DISABLED	Order must be "many" when content is "mixed".
SCHEMA_ETCONTENT_UNKNOWN	Content must be of type "empty","eltOnly","textOnly" or "mixed".
SCHEMA_ETMODEL_UNKNOWN	The value of model must be either "open" or "closed".
SCHEMA_ELEMENT_DISABLED	Cannot contain child elements because content is set to "textOnly".
SCHEMA_ELEMENT_MISSING	Must provide at least one "element" in a group.
SCHEMA_ ATTRIBUTE_NOTSUPPORT	The attribute "%1" on an %2 is not supported.
SCHEMA_ATNAME_MISSING	AttributeType declaration must contain a "name" attribute.
SCHEMA_ATNAME_DUPLICATED	Duplicated attribute declaration.
SCHEMA_ATREQUIRED_INVALID	Invalid value for "required" attribute.
SCHEMA_DTTYPE_UNKNOWN	Unknown Attribute datatype.
SCHEMA_DTTYPE_DUPLICATED	Duplicated datatype declaration.
SCHEMA_ ENUMERATION_MISSING	An element with a "values" attribute must contain a type attribute of the value "enumeration".
SCHEMA_DTVALUES_MISSING	Must provide a "values" attribute on an element that contains a type attribute of the value "enumeration".
SCHEMA_ATYPE_MISSING	Attribute declaration must contain a "type" attribute.
SCHEMA_ATYPE_UNDECLARED	The specified attribute must first be declared using an AttributeType declaration.
SCHEMA_GROUP_DISABLED	A "group" is not allowed within an ElementType that has a "textOnly" content model.
SCHEMA_ GMATTRIBUTE_NOTSUPPORT	The attribute "%1" on a group is not supported.

Name	Description
SCHEMA_DTVALUES_VALUES_MISSING	The values for enumeration type are missing.
SCHEMA_ATTRIBUTE_DEFAULTVALUE	The default value "%1" is invalid.
SCHEMA_DTTYPE_DISABLED	Datatype is not allowed when content model is not "textOnly".
SCHEMA_ELEMENT_EMPTY	Child element is not allowed when content model is "empty".
SCHEMA_ELEMENT_DATATYPE	Child element is not allowed when datatype is set.
SCHEMA_DTTYPE_MISSING	Type is missing on the datatype element.
SCHEMA_MINOCCURS_INVALIDVALUE	The value of attribute "minOccurs" should be "0" or "1".
SCHEMA_MAXOCCURS_INVALIDVALUE	The value of attribute "maxOccurs" should be "1" or "*".
SCHEMA_MAXOCCURS_MUSTBESTAR	The value of attribute "maxOccurs" must be "*" when attribute "order" is set to "many".
SCHEMA_ELEMENTDT_EMPTY	The value of data type attribute can not be empty.
SCHEMA_DOCTYPE_INVALID	DOCTYPE is not allowed in Schema.

XML DOM Errors

DOM Error Messages

The following errors are returned by the various methods in the XML DOM:

Name	Description
XMLOM_DUPLICATE_ID	The ID '%1' is duplicated.
XMLOM_DATATYPE_PARSE_ERROR	Error parsing '%1' as %2 datatype.
XMLOM_NAMESPACE_CONFLICT	There was a Namespace conflict for the '%1' Namespace.
XMLOM_OBJECT_EXPAND_NOTIMPL	Unable to expand an attribute with Object value.
XMLOM_DTDT_DUP	Can not have 2 datatype attributes on one element.
XMLOM_INSERTPOS_NOTFOUND	Insert position node not found.

Name	Description
XMLOM_NODE_NOTFOUND	Node not found.
XMLOM_INVALIDTYPE	This operation can not be performed with a Node of type %1.
XMLOM_INVALID_XMLDECL_ATTR	'%1' is not a valid attribute on the XML Declaration. Only 'version', 'encoding', or 'standalone' attributes are allowed.
XMLOM_INVALID_INSERT_PARENT	Inserting a Node or its ancestor under itself is not allowed.
XMLOM_INVALID_INSERT_POS	Insert position Node must be a Child of the Node to insert under.
XMLOM_NO_ATTRIBUTES	Attributes are not allowed on Nodes of type '%1'.
XMLOM_NOTCHILD	The parameter Node is not a child of this Node.
XMLOM_CREATENODE_NEEDNAME	createNode requires a name for given NodeType.
XMLOM_UNEXPECTED_NS	Unexpected NameSpace parameter.
XMLOM_MISSING_PARAM	Required parameter is missing (or null/empty).
XMLOM_INVALID_NAMESPACENODE	NameSpace Node is invalid.
XMLOM_READONLY	Attempt to modify a read-only node.
XMLOM_ACCESSDENIED	Access Denied.
XMLOM_ATTRMOVE	Attributes must be removed before adding them to a different node.
XMLOM_BADVALUE	Invalid data for a node of type '%1'.
XMLOM_USERABORT	Operation aborted by caller.
XMLOM_NEXTNODEABORT	Unable to recover node list iterator position.
XMLOM_INVALID_INDEX	The offset must be 0 or a positive number that is not greater than the number of characters in the data.
XMLOM_INVALID_ATTR	The provided node is not a specified attribute on this node.

Name	Description
XMLOM_INVALID_ONDOCTYPE	This operation can not be performed on DOCTYPE node.
XMLOM_INVALID_MODEL	Cannot mix different threading models in document.
XMLOM_INVALID_DATATYPE	Datatype '%1' is not supported.

XML DOM Errors

Index

Index

Index